Advanced Corporate Finance

Policies and Strategies

Joseph P. Ogden
University at Buffalo, State University of New York

Frank C. Jen
University at Buffalo, State University of New York

Philip F. O'Connor
Southern Utah University

Upper Saddle River, New Jersey 07458

To Vonda, Sara, and Laura.—JPO
To Daisy.—FCJ

Library of Congress Cataloging-in-Publication Data

Ogden, Joseph P.
    Advanced corporate finance : policies and strategies / Joseph P. Ogden,   Frank
C. Jen, Philip F. O'Connor.
        p. cm
    Includes bibliographical references and index.
    ISBN 0-13-091568-8
        1. Corporations--Finance. I. Jen, Frank C. II. O'Connor, Philip F., 1966- III. Title.

HG4026 .O334 2002
658.15--dc21
                                                                        2002027090

Executive Editor: Mickey Cox
Editor-in-Chief: P. J. Boardman
Managing Editor (Editorial): Gladys Soto
Assistant Editor: Beth Romph
Editorial Assistant: Kevin Hancock
Executive Marketing Manager: Beth Toland
Managing Editor (Production): John Roberts
Production Editor: Renata Butera
Production Assistant: Joe DeProspero
Permissions Coordinator: Suzanne Grappi
Associate Director, Manufacturing: Vincent Scelta
Production Manager: Arnold Vila
Manufacturing Buyer: Michelle Klein
Cover Design: Bruce Kenselaar
Composition: UG / GGS Information Services, Inc.
Full-Service Project Management: UG / GGS Information Services, Inc.
Printer/Binder: VonHoffman

Credits and acknowledgments borrowed from other sources and reproduced, with permission, in this textbook appear on appropriate page within text.

Pearson Education LTD.
Pearson Education Australia PTY, Limited
Pearson Education Singapore, Pte. Ltd
Pearson Education North Asia Ltd
Pearson Education, Canada, Ltd
Pearson Educación de Mexico, S.A. de C.V.
Pearson Education—Japan
Pearson Education Malaysia, Pte. Ltd

10 9 8 7 6 5 4 3 2 1

ISBN 0-13-091568-8

Brief Contents

Contents

PART III: MANAGING EQUITY AND DEBT   357

PART IV: THE MARKETS FOR CORPORATE CONTROL   545

PART V: ORGANIZATIONAL ARCHITECTURE, RISK MANAGEMENT, AND SECURITY DESIGN   653

Preface

This textbook provides an advanced, organized, and comprehensive discussion of theoretical and empirical literature on corporate financial policies and strategies, particularly those of U.S. nonfinancial firms. The textbook is written for use in an advanced MBA or advanced undergraduate course in corporate finance. The text is essentially the first to address, on an organized, comprehensive, and focused basis, the needs of students to acquire a thorough understanding of corporate financial policies and strategies.

We define corporate financial policies and strategies broadly to include not only managerial decisions regarding the issuance and retirement of debt and equity securities and the firm's overall *capital structure*, but also decisions regarding issues such as (a) the firm's governance and ownership structures; (b) contracting between a firm and its management, creditors, and other *stakeholders*; (c) dividends and stock repurchases; (d) mergers, acquisitions, takeovers, buyouts, equity carve-outs, and spin-offs; (e) financial distress and its resolution; and (f) risk management and the design of securities. The text focuses early and often on theories that have been developed to explain a firm's corporate financial policies and strategies in rational, economic terms. We also discuss a plethora of empirical studies that have been conducted to test these theories. We occasionally illustrate theory by referring to financial decisions made by a specific firm.

From an introductory corporate finance textbook such as *Corporate Financial Management* (Emery and Finnerty; Prentice Hall, 1997), *Principles of Corporate Finance* (Brealey and Myers, 6th ed.; McGraw-Hill, 2000), or *Corporate Finance* (Ross, Westerfield, and Jaffe; McGraw-Hill, 2002), students come to understand that in the modern theory of corporate finance, shareholders' dictum to the firm's management is to maximize the market value of the firm's equity. Students also learn that management must undertake two principal tasks to achieve this objective:

(a) Develop and monitor profitable capital investment projects.
(b) Secure and manage the capital necessary to pursue these projects.

However, the dictum to maximize value leads to a large number of fundamental questions, including, but not limited to, the following: Will the firm's management adhere to this dictum, or will they engage in self-serving, value-reducing behavior? (Alternatively stated, how can shareholders induce management to adhere to this dictum, and at what cost?) If we assume that management is willing to adhere to the dictum, specifically *how* do they accomplish the task of maximizing the market value of the firm's equity? Are there important interactions between a firm's capital investment decisions and its financing decisions, and if so, what are these interactions and how do firms deal with them?

The treatment of such issues in an introductory corporate finance text tends to be broad, rather than deep, for several reasons: (a) An introductory text must *introduce* basic aspects of both investment and financing decisions in some detail; (b) students also must become familiar with numerous ancillary topics related to financial markets, basic capital budgeting decisions, the basic roles of financial institutions, and working capital management; (c) breadth, rather than depth, often must be emphasized for the sake of nonfinance students, because the introductory course may be the only finance course they take; and (d) corporate finance theory, as it relates to both capital investment and financing decisions, has developed such depth and breadth that it cannot be fully addressed in an introductory course.

For example, in an introductory corporate finance course, a student learns that an important decision for a firm is the determination of its *optimal capital structure* (i.e., the proportions of debt and equity that should be used to finance the firm's assets). The student may learn that taxes and costs of financial distress may influence the capital structure decision. However, the typical student is unlikely to develop an understanding of other factors that affect this decision, such as agency costs of debt, agency costs of managerial discretion, and information asymmetry.

The student may also only begin to understand that a firm's financial policies are likely to interact with other aspects of the firm, such as the industry in which it operates and the nature of its assets. Moreover, an introductory course generally offers a student only a glimpse of the complex financial structures that are characteristic of large firms, as well as the complexity of executive compensation contracts and corporate debt contracts, and the firm's need to manage risk.

For these reasons, most major business schools include advanced courses in corporate finance in their MBA or undergraduate finance curricula. These advanced courses often focus separately on capital investment and financing decisions. Unfortunately, at this point the availability of textbooks breaks down. Indeed, only recently has an advanced textbook been written to address capital investment decisions, *Valuation: Measuring and Managing the Value of Companies* (Copeland, Koller, and Murrin, 3rd ed.; John Wiley & Sons, 2000), and no advanced textbook presently exists that focuses exclusively on corporate financial policies and strategies at an advanced level.[1] Among the most recent textbooks, *Financial Markets and Corporate Strategy* (Grinblatt and Titman; McGraw-Hill, 1997) claims to have goals similar to those of this text. As the authors state, their text "provides an in-depth analysis of financial theory, empirical work, and practice. It is primarily designed as a text for a second course in corporate finance for MBAs and advanced undergraduates" (p. viii). However, most of the chapters in their text are devoted to reviewing and perhaps slightly expanding or refocusing material covered in an introductory text, so they ultimately fall short in providing a truly advanced and comprehensive treatment of corporate financial policies and strategies. Indeed, the bulk of their text resembles an introductory text, as the authors admit: "we also envision this as a textbook for a first course in finance for highly motivated students with some previous finance background" (p. viii).

Due to the dearth of textbooks designed exclusively for an advanced course on corporate financial policies and strategies, professors often use an introductory corporate finance text as a reference text, from which they can at least promote a discussion of many specific advanced issues. They then typically supplement this discussion with class notes, journal articles, or perhaps books such as *The Revolution in Corporate Finance* (Stern and Chew, 3rd ed.; Blackwell, 1998), *Takeovers, Restructuring, and*

---

[1]The dearth of textbooks in advanced corporate finance is in sharp contrast to the plethora of excellent advanced textbooks in investment management (e.g., *Investments* by Sharpe, Alexander, and Bailey [Prentice Hall], and *Investments* by Bodie, Kane, and Marcus [Irwin/McGraw-Hill], to name only two), derivatives (e.g., *Options, Futures, and Other Derivatives* by Hull [Prentice Hall]), or international financial management (e.g., *Foundations of Multinational Finance* by Shapiro [Prentice Hall]).

Corporate Governance (Weston, Chung and Siu, 3rd ed.; Prentice Hall, 2001), *The Modern Theory of Corporate Finance* (Smith, 2nd ed.; McGraw-Hill, 1990), or *The New Corporate Finance* (Chew, 2nd ed.; McGraw-Hill, 1999).

Indeed, the authors of this textbook have developed extensive class notes for our advanced course on corporate financial policies and strategies over several years, and have now organized and expanded these notes into a textbook. The advantage of having a full textbook to address advanced issues in corporate finance is that it provides the student with an *organized, comprehensive, and understandable treatment* of the issues, as opposed to the fragmented treatment that results from cobbling together notes, articles, or readings on individual topics.

In addition, our survey of advanced corporate finance courses taught at major universities indicates that in many cases the course is often narrow in scope (e.g., focusing only on mergers and acquisitions). This may be acceptable if the finance program includes several courses that each focus on a narrow topic, but most programs have only one or two advanced corporate finance courses. Under these circumstances, we believe that students will be better served with the more comprehensive treatment of the issues that this text provides.

TOPICAL COVERAGE

As noted above, this text is unique in terms of its organized, advanced, and comprehensive focus on corporate financial policies and strategies. It is designed explicitly for an advanced course in corporate finance, so we dispense with lengthy introductory expositions of basic finance theory, focusing instead on advanced theory and how it can be used to explain corporate financial decisions.

In Part I, comprising the first six chapters, we provide a thorough review of corporate finance theory as well as supporting empirical evidence. Chapter 1 provides an initial empirical perspective on issues covered throughout the text. Both cross-sectional and time series composite values of numerous financial variables are shown and discussed, including assets, liabilities, book and market equity, leverage ratios, market-to-book equity ratios, sources and uses of cash, equity ownership distribution, return on equity, price-earnings ratios, dividend payout ratios, and dividend yields.

Chapter 2 provides a review of theory on the effects of corporate financial decisions under *ideal*, or *perfect*, market conditions. The chapter reiterates the famous Modigliani–Miller (M&M) proofs of the irrelevance of capital structure and the effects of leverage on the cost of debt and equity capital under ideal conditions. We also introduce both the Capital Asset Pricing Model (CAPM) and the Black–Scholes Option Pricing Model (BSOPM). We introduce these important models at an early stage of the text because they provide important insights into the analysis of corporate financial decisions throughout the remainder of the text. We also show that these three models can be jointly reconciled.

In Chapters 3 through 6, we analyze the principal *real-world factors* (otherwise known as *market imperfections*) that affect a firm's financial policies. Chapter 3 discusses the importance of the separation of ownership and control in the modern corporation, and then focuses on the effects of various *principal–agent conflicts* among the *stakeholders* on the firm's financial policies. The two conflicts of interest that we are most concerned with are between (a) a firm's management and its shareholders; and (b) the firm's shareholders and its creditors. Chapter 4 discusses the problem of *information asymmetry* between the management of a publicly traded firm and outside investors. According to established theory, a firm's management has better information about the true value of the firm than do either shareholders or creditors. This asymmetry can have profound effects on a firm's financial policies. Chapter 5 analyzes the roles of government, securities markets, financial institutions, ownership structure, board oversight, and contracting devices in mitigating deadweight costs that are otherwise associated with these real-world problems. In Chapter 6 we analyze the effects of various real-world factors on a firm's leverage.

In Part II, comprising Chapters 7 through 10, we develop more comprehensive perspectives on a firm's financial policies and strategies, and also introduce techniques and models for the valuation of a firm's equity and debt securities. In Chapter 7 we discuss the effects of a firm's *industry* on its financial policies and strategies. Chapter 8 follows with a comprehensive view of the firm, including its business environment, external and internal governance structures, business strategy, operational and financial structures, risks, performance, and contingencies. In Chapter 9, we discuss the Efficient Market Hypothesis and the valuation of equity. Finally, Chapter 10 deals with the valuation of corporate bonds.

In Part III, comprising Chapters 11 through 15, we delve deeper into issues related to the management of a firm's equity and debt. These analyses focus on private equity and the acquisition of *venture capital* (Chapter 11), the initial public offering of stock (Chapter 12), managing internal equity and the offering of seasoned equity (Chapter 13), dividend and stock repurchase policies (Chapter 14), and strategic decisions related to corporate debt (Chapter 15).

Part IV, comprising Chapters 16 through 18, analyzes the implications of decisions related to the markets for corporate control. In Chapter 16, we focus on mergers, acquisitions, takeovers, and buyouts. Chapter 17 features extensive analyses of decisions made by firms under financial distress, including operational restructuring, equity carve-outs, and spin-offs. Chapter 18 deals with decisions associated with severe financial distress, including debt restructuring, bankruptcy, reorganization, and liquidation.

Finally, in Part V, which comprises Chapter 19, we attempt to synthesize the material covered in the previous chapters by presenting the concept of a firm's *organizational architecture*. The chapter also deals with the burgeoning areas of *risk management* (which includes, but is not limited to, the use of *derivatives* to hedge risk) and *security design*.

In sum, the analyses in this text show that developing a firm's financial policies and strategies is a complex task involving numerous factors, many of which are only partially under management's control. As such, management must (a) have a thorough understanding of the firm's circumstances with respect to these factors, (b) determine the extent to which the firm's circumstances can be altered or "optimized," and (c) establish appropriate financial policies and strategies.

We conclude this topical discussion with a caveat about two important topics that we *do not* cover in the textbook. First, we do not focus extensively on international corporate finance issues (e.g., the international activities of U.S. firms, the financial policies and strategies of firms in countries other than the U.S., or the overall financial systems in other countries). Second, we do not directly cover issues associated with *capital budgeting* and *value creation*; instead, we address these issues only indirectly as they relate to the firm's financial policies and strategies. We exclude these two topics primarily to avoid information overload, and secondarily because these topics are adequately covered in other textbooks.

PEDAGOGICAL FEATURES

Ultimately, corporate finance theory simply attempts to explain rational human behavior, particularly the behavior of corporate managers as they deal with other rational individuals, including shareholders, creditors, customers, and competitors. Nevertheless, the study of advanced corporate finance theory can be a daunting task for any student. For this reason, we have incorporated a number of features into the text to facilitate students' understanding of the material:

- We try to avoid theoretical and mathematical derivations for three reasons: (a) They tend to be tedious for the reader; (b) points can be made quite adequately without them; and (c) we provide references to literature where such derivations can be found.
- The text is replete with figures and tables that illustrate both concepts and empirical evidence related to the theories and hypotheses being discussed.
- To illustrate the practical application of theory, we include short articles from the financial press and other practical literature, in a series that we dub "Real-World Focus."
- We frequently illustrate the practical application of theory by examining financial decisions made by an individual firm, in recurring sections titled "A Case in Point."
- Although we refer extensively to theoretical and empirical studies in the academic literature, we attempt to boil them down their essential content. Still, the relevant literature is vast, and we cannot cover all topics in full detail. Therefore, we have attempted to be exhaustive in our lists of references, because each paper provides a unique viewpoint, whether theoretical or empirical, on a particular issue. References for each chapter can be found at **http://www.prenhall.com/ogden**. We encourage readers to pursue these papers for more information.
- At the end of each chapter, we provide a concise summary of the learning objectives covered in the chapter, as well as an extensive list of end-of-chapter questions and problems, arranged in three tiers. The first tier includes basic "Review Questions and Problems." The second tier, called "Creative Thinking Issues," raises questions for which no ready answer exists. The third tier, called "Projects and Analyses," challenges students to develop their analytical, research, and financial decision-making skills by analyzing data statistically, developing a model, or analyzing financial decisions, policies, or strategies of a specific firm.

ACKNOWLEDGMENTS

We gratefully acknowledge valuable reviews of drafts of this textbook conducted by the following individuals: Thomas H. Noe (Tulane University), Steven J. Shapiro (University of New Haven), Wenyuh Tsay (California State University, San Marcos), Hal Heaton (Brigham Young University), and Abdel-hameed Bashir (Grambling State University). We are especially grateful to Dosoung Choi (Seoul National University) for extensive work on notes that helped to spawn the idea for the text. We also thank Jon Bell (University at Buffalo) for valuable comments.

About the Authors

Joseph P. Ogden is presently an associate professor of finance at the University at Buffalo, SUNY. He has published articles in a number of professional journals, including *Journal of Finance*, *Review of Financial Studies*, *Journal of Financial and Quantitative Analysis*, *Journal of Corporate Finance*, *Financial Management*, and *Review of Quantitative Finance and Accounting*. He was chairman of the Department of Finance and Managerial Economics in SUNY–Buffalo's School of Management from 1994 to 1999. He is also involved in financial consulting. Dr. Ogden received his Ph.D. in finance from Purdue University, his MBA from Oklahoma State University, and his B.S. in psychology from the University of South Dakota.

Frank C. Jen is M&T Chair Professor in Banking (emeritus) at the University at Buffalo, SUNY. He has published articles in numerous academic and professional journals, including *Journal of Finance*, *American Economic Review*, *Journal of Business*, *Journal of Financial and Quantitative Analysis*, *Journal of Applied Corporate Finance*, *Journal of Commercial Lending*, and *Review of Quantitative Finance and Accounting*.

Dr. Jen is extensively involved in international activities, including designing and teaching international executive education programs, doing research on global issues, and coordinating and presenting papers at international conferences. He was Co-Director and Director of the University at Buffalo's China MBA Program from 1984 to 1991, and he helped found the National Center for Industrial Science and Technology Management Development in Dalian, China in 1980. He served as Visiting Professor and Associate Dean, American Faculty from 1980 to 1991. He is now cooperating with many different groups on executive education in China. His Advanced Commercial Lending program designed principally for U.S. bankers has attracted participants from Korea, Thailand, Indonesia, Malaysia, Taiwan, and the United Arab Emirates. Dr. Jen received his Ph.D. and MBA in finance from the University of Wisconsin, and his B.S. from North Central College.

Philip F. O'Connor has been assistant professor of finance at the University at Buffalo, SUNY, at the University of Wyoming, and is currently a finance professor at Southern Utah University. He has conducted research on corporate finance issues such as the resolution of financial distress and the firm's claim structure, and determinants of the firm's debt structure. Dr. O'Connor received his Ph.D. from the University of Maryland, his MBA from the University of Wisconsin, and his B.M.S. from the University of Waikato, New Zealand.

PART

Corporate Finance

I

To reach the goal of an advanced understanding of corporate financial policies and strategies, one must initially gain general perspectives on both empirical evidence and theory. The six chapters in Part I are designed to provide these perspectives.

We begin in Chapter 1 with an overview of empirical evidence that reflects the financial policies of publicly traded U.S. nonfinancial firms over the past 20 years. We examine these firms' tendencies to finance growth using internal versus external capital, cross-sectional and time-series variations in leverage, dividend payout ratios, market-to-book equity ratios, price/earnings ratios, and so on.

Chapters 2 to 6 provide a thorough, yet readable, overview of modern corporate finance theory. Chapter 2 provides a review of the effects of corporate financing decisions on value and risk under theoretically ideal conditions. The chapter reiterates the famous "Modigliani–Miller" proofs of the irrelevance of capital structure and the effects of leverage on the risk and cost of debt and equity capital. We also introduce the Capital Asset Pricing Model (CAPM), the Binomial Pricing Model (BPM), and the Black–Scholes Option Pricing Model (BSOPM). We introduce these important models at an early stage of the text because their implications are crucial to all of our analyses of financial decisions throughout the remainder of the text.

In Chapters 3 to 5 we introduce the principal *real-world factors* (also called *market imperfections*) that may affect a firm's financial policies and strategies. Chapter 3 focuses on the effects of various *principal–agent relationships* among the *stakeholders* of the firm on the firm's financial policies, risk, and value. Chapter 4 discusses the effects of *information asymmetry* (between a firm's management and outside investors) on a firm's financial policies, risk, and value. Chapter 5 discusses the roles of government regulations, security markets, financial institutions, ownership structures, and contracting devices to mitigate deadweight costs that are otherwise associated with these factors.

Finally, in Chapter 6 we focus exclusively on the leverage decision. We analyze, both theoretically and empirically, the effects of taxes, costs of financial distress, agency and information asymmetry problems, and other factors on management's decision regarding the relative amounts of equity and debt to have in the firm's capital structure. This material is necessary as background for deeper and more refined studies of leverage effects in later chapters.

CHAPTER

Empirical Perspectives on the Financial Characteristics of Publicly Traded U.S. Nonfinancial Firms

1.1   INTRODUCTION

The purpose of this chapter is to provide empirical perspectives on the financial characteristics of publicly traded, nonfinancial firms incorporated in the United States. It is important to gain a broad perspective on firms' actual financial practices before delving into the many hypotheses that have been proffered to explain these practices. Thus, in this chapter we deliberately avoid discussions of theories and hypotheses. Instead, the analyses serve to illustrate many of the key factors that affect firms' financial policies and strategies (which will be elaborated on in the remainder of the text). Simply put, this chapter shows the way things *are*, while subsequent chapters explain *why* they are this way. Consequently, we warn the reader that this chapter raises more questions than it answers.

The chapter is organized as follows. In Section 1.2, we examine the evolution of the numbers of publicly traded U.S. nonfinancial firms in recent history. In Sections 1.3 and 1.4, we analyze composite balance sheets, both cross-sectionally and over time. Section 1.5 provides an analysis of composite cash flows. In Sections 1.6 and 1.7, we examine distributions of leverage and ownership structures, respectively. In Section 1.8, we examine composite return on equity, price-earnings ratios, dividend payout ratios, and dividend yields over time. Finally, Section 1.9 summarizes the chapter's learning objectives.

In this and later chapters, we report the results of various types of statistical analyses on samples of firms. At the end of this chapter, we provide two appendices to facilitate the reader's interpretation of these analyses. Appendix A illustrates the screening process that we used to develop samples of firms. Appendix B reviews basic statistics and regression analysis.

1.2   THE EVOLUTION OF FIRMS OVER TIME

We begin our analysis with a perspective on the *numbers* of U.S.-incorporated nonfinancial firms whose equity traded publicly at years-end 1980–2000. Figure 1-1 shows (a) the number of firms that *existed* at the end of each year; (b) the number of firms that *entered* each year, each via an *initial public offering* (IPO) of their stock;[1] and

----
[1] We discuss IPOs in Chapter 12.

FIGURE 1-1   Number of Publicly Traded U.S. Nonfinancial Firms and Determinants of Annual Changes, 1980–2000

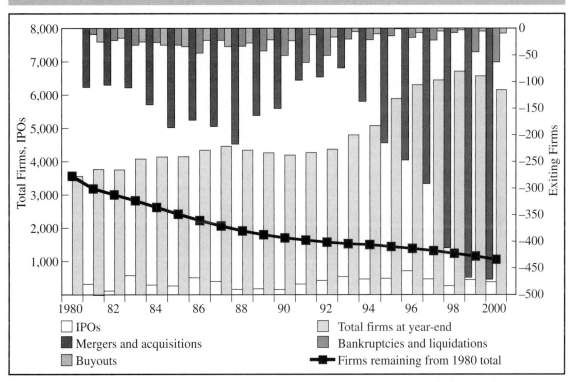

Source: Raw data from Standard & Poor's *Research Insight* database, 2001.

(c) the number of firms that *exited* each year for any of several reasons. Over this period, the number of firms nearly doubled, from 3,561 at year-end 1980 to 6,146 at year-end 2000.

Turnover may be the best word to describe the results in Figure 1-1. Of the 3,561 firms that existed at year-end 1980, only about one-third (1,048 firms) still existed at year-end 2000, an annual attrition rate of 5.9 percent. Meanwhile, a total of 7,355 new firms entered via IPOs during this period. Thus, a total of 10,916 (= 3,561 + 7,355) publicly traded U.S. nonfinancial firms existed during part or all of this period.

So what happened to the 4,770 firms (= 10,916 − 6,146) that exited over this period? The answer is found by examining the bars in the upper portion of Figure 1-1, which use the right side (negative) axis. Each of these bars shows the number of firms in a given year that were deleted from the sample for each of the following reasons (with the total number of firms eliminated for each reason over the entire sample period provided in brackets): (1) mergers and acquisitions [3,796]; (2) bankruptcy or liquidation [639]; (3) the firm reverted to private equity ownership via a *buyout* [335].[2]

---

[2]We discuss mergers, acquisitions, buyouts, and takeovers in Chapter 16, and bankruptcies and liquidations in Chapter 18.

These are aggregate figures, so they tend to reflect changes in macroeconomic conditions in the United States over time. For instance, the influence of the 1990–1991 recession is evident in terms of: (a) an increase in bankruptcies, (b) a decrease in IPOs, and (c) a decrease in mergers and acquisitions activity.

1.3   COMPOSITE BALANCE SHEETS FOR PUBLICLY TRADED U.S. NONFINANCIAL FIRMS

Next, we examine the composite assets, liabilities, and shareholders' equity of publicly traded U.S. nonfinancial firms at year-end 2000, expressed in the form of a *composite balance sheet*. A composite balance sheet is generated by summing each of the balance sheet items for a sample of firms at a given point in time, and then displaying these items in balance sheet form.

Table 1-1 shows composite balance sheets for all 6,146 firms in our year-end 2000 sample, as well as several subsamples of these firms. (See Appendix A for details of these subsamples.) The subsamples are defined in terms of indexes developed by Standard & Poor's Corporation (henceforth S&P). The subsamples consist of firms included in the S&P Industrials index, the S&P Transportations index, the S&P Utilities index, the S&P MidCaps index, the S&P SmallCaps index, and all other firms not included in any of these indexes. The last of these subsamples, called Non-S&Ps, generally consists of the smallest firms in the U.S. markets.

1.3.1   Composite Assets

At year-end 2000, the firms in the full sample collectively reported total assets (henceforth TA) of $9,360 billion. Current assets account for approximately one-third of composite TA (33.4 percent), whereas noncurrent assets account for the remaining two-thirds (66.6 percent). Current assets consist of cash and equivalents (6.8 percent of TA), receivables (15.5 percent), inventories (7.2 percent), and other current assets (4.0 percent). Noncurrent assets primarily consist of net property, plant, and equipment (henceforth PP&E; 32.5 percent of TA), but also include various investments (7.9 percent of TA, including investments at equity [2.9 percent] and other investments [5.0 percent]), intangibles [13.6 percent], and other assets [12.6 percent].

Composite TA are greater, of course, for large firms. As we scan the composite TA of the various subsamples of firms in the table, the most impressive observation is that the 357 firms in the S&P Industrials, though they account for only 5.8 percent of all firms, account for well over half (57.5 percent) of the composite TA of all firms. Obviously, the S&P Industrials includes many of the largest firms in the United States. In contrast, the 4,863 firms that are not included in any of the S&P indexes account for 79.1 percent of all firms, and yet these firms collectively account for only 19.7 percent of the composite TA of all firms. These results highlight an important characteristic of the distribution of firms in the United States: there are a few hundred extremely large firms and thousands of relatively small firms.

Perusing the various subsamples, we find that, for the S&P Industrials, S&P MidCaps, S&P SmallCaps, and Non-S&P firms, the proportions of current and noncurrent assets are fairly homogeneous, in the ranges of 30.4 to 44.7 percent and 55.3 to 69.6 percent, respectively. In sharp contrast, for the S&P Transports and Utilities, the

TABLE 1-1 Composite Balance Sheets and Market Equity Values

Publicly Traded U.S. Nonfinancial Firms and Indicated Subsamples, Year-End 2000

[Number of Firms]	All Firms [6,146] $ billions	% of TA	S&P Industrials [357] $ billions	% of TA	S&P Transports [10] $ billions	% of TA	S&P Utilities [40] $ billions	% of TA	S&P MidCaps [339] $ billions	% of TA	S&P SmallCaps [537] $ billions	% of TA	Non-S&P [4,863] $ billions	% of TA
Current Assets	*3,129*	*33.4%*	*1,918*	*35.6%*	*21*	*12.2%*	*223*	*24.9%*	*253*	*35.1%*	*153*	*44.7%*	*561*	*30.4%*
Cash & equivalents	633	6.8%	322	6.0%	7	3.8%	21	2.4%	53	7.4%	26	7.7%	204	11.1%
Receivables	1,446	15.5%	1022	19.0%	7	4.2%	81	9.0%	104	14.4%	51	15.1%	181	9.8%
Inventories	673	7.2%	406	7.5%	2	1.3%	15	1.7%	67	9.3%	55	16.0%	128	7.0%
Other Current Assets	376	4.0%	168	3.1%	5	2.8%	106	11.9%	29	4.0%	20	5.9%	48	2.6%
Noncurrent Assets	*6,231*	*66.6%*	*3,467*	*64.4%*	*154*	*87.8%*	*674*	*75.1%*	*468*	*64.9%*	*189*	*55.3%*	*1,281*	*69.6%*
Plant, Property & Equipment	3,039	32.5%	1549	28.8%	129	73.7%	423	47.2%	257	35.7%	116	34.1%	563	30.6%
Investments at Equity	267	2.9%	178	3.3%	12	6.9%	19	2.1%	12	1.6%	3	0.8%	43	2.4%
Other Investments	467	5.0%	299	5.5%	1	0.5%	64	7.2%	30	4.2%	8	2.4%	65	3.5%
Intangibles	1,277	13.6%	699	13.0%	4	2.2%	45	5.0%	96	13.4%	38	11.1%	395	21.5%
Other Noncurrent Assets	1,182	12.6%	742	13.8%	8	4.6%	123	13.7%	72	10.0%	23	6.8%	214	11.6%
TOTAL ASSETS (TA)	**9,360**	**100.0%**	**5,385**	**100.0%**	**175**	**100.0%**	**897**	**100.0%**	**720**	**100.0%**	**341**	**100.0%**	**1,841**	**100.0%**
Current Liabilities	*2,550*	*27.2%*	*1,632*	*30.3%*	*31*	*17.9%*	*274*	*30.6%*	*178*	*24.8%*	*86*	*25.1%*	*349*	*19.0%*
Debt in Current Liabilities	773	8.3%	551	10.2%	4	2.0%	84	9.4%	39	5.4%	13	3.7%	82	4.4%
Accounts Payable	817	8.7%	519	9.6%	9	5.1%	71	7.9%	67	9.3%	33	9.7%	118	6.4%
Taxes Payable	85	0.9%	65	1.2%	1	0.5%	5	0.6%	7	0.9%	2	0.7%	6	0.3%
Other Current Liabilities	875	9.4%	498	9.2%	18	10.2%	113	12.6%	65	9.1%	38	11.1%	143	7.8%
Noncurrent Liabilities	*3,609*	*38.6%*	*1,923*	*35.7%*	*95*	*54.0%*	*440*	*49.1%*	*284*	*39.4%*	*112*	*32.9%*	*756*	*41.0%*
Deferred Taxes & ITC	468	5.0%	239	4.4%	26	14.6%	88	9.8%	37	5.1%	10	3.1%	68	3.7%
Other Liabilities	775	8.3%	485	9.0%	21	12.2%	80	8.9%	50	7.0%	14	4.2%	123	6.7%
Long-Term Debt	2,243	24.0%	1121	20.8%	48	27.1%	258	28.8%	192	26.7%	85	25.1%	538	29.2%
Minority Interest	124	1.3%	77	1.4%	0	0.0%	14	1.5%	5	0.7%	2	0.6%	27	1.5%
Stockholders' Equity	*3,201*	*34.2%*	*1,831*	*34.0%*	*49*	*28.2%*	*183*	*20.4%*	*258*	*35.8%*	*143*	*41.9%*	*736*	*40.0%*
Preferred Stock	69	0.7%	12	0.2%	0	0.1%	8	0.9%	2	0.3%	1	0.3%	46	2.5%
Common Equity	3,132	33.5%	1820	33.8%	49	28.0%	175	19.5%	256	35.5%	142	41.7%	690	37.5%
LIABILITIES & STOCK EQUITY	**9,360**	**100.0%**	**5,385**	**100.0%**	**175**	**100.0%**	**897**	**100.0%**	**720**	**100.0%**	**341**	**100.0%**	**1,841**	**100.0%**
Market Equity Value	*11,700*		*8,572*		*78*		*455*		*707*		*294*		*1,593*	
Market-to-Book Equity Ratio	*3.7*		*4.7*		*1.6*		*2.6*		*2.8*		*2.1*		*2.3*	

Source: Raw data from Standard & Poors *Research Insight* database, 2001.

5

composite proportions of current assets are only 12.2 percent and 21.9 percent, respectively, and of noncurrent assets are 87.8 percent and 75.1 percent, respectively. By examining the asset components more closely, we find that the Transports and Utilities have much lower proportions of receivables and inventories, and much higher proportions of PP&E, than other firms. These differences are observed because transportation and utility firms are inherently more capital-intensive (i.e., they must invest heavily in airplanes, trains, electric power plants, etc.) than the typical industrial or retail firm.

1.3.2 Composite Liabilities and Equities

On the other side of the ledger, composite liabilities, various in kind, together finance $6,160 billion, or approximately two-thirds (65.8 percent) of the composite TA of all firms. This total includes $2,550 billion in current liabilities (27.2 percent of TA) and $3,609 billion of noncurrent liabilities (38.6 percent of TA). Among the noncurrent liabilities, the single most important category is long-term debt, which is used to finance about one-quarter of composite TA ($2,243 billion, or 24.0 percent of TA). Long-term debt includes both publicly issued bonds and debt that is privately placed with banks, finance companies, and insurance companies. If we add the current portion of long-term debt (i.e., debt in current liabilities, 8.3 percent of TA) to this total, debt actually finances approximately one-third (32.2 percent) of composite TA.

Equities, predominantly common stock, finance $3,201 billion, or the remaining one-third of composite TA (34.2 percent). Among the equities, common stock finances 33.5 percent of composite TA, whereas preferred stock finances less than 1 percent (0.7 percent). As we will see in a time series analysis later, preferred stock appears to be a dying security in the capital structures of U.S. nonfinancial firms.

1.3.3 Composite Market Equity Values and Market-to-Book Equity Ratios

The final two rows of Table 1-1 show (a) composite market values of common equity and (b) the ratio of composite market equity to composite book equity, which we call the *market-to-book equity ratio*. For all firms, composite market equity value was $11,700 billion, whereas composite book equity value was $3,132 billion. Thus, the composite market-to-book equity ratio was 3.7. Among the subsamples, the S&P Industrials had the highest composite market-to-book equity ratio at 4.7, and the S&P Transports had the lowest ratio at 1.6.

What do these results mean? Literally, the results indicate that the market equity values of the sampled firms, in general, far exceed their book equity values. According to prevailing finance theory, the ratios indicate that these firms in general are expected to produce future earnings that, in present value terms, far outstrip the book value of the assets used to generate them. In other words, firms are expected to be very efficient in *creating value* for shareholders. As such, these results reflect a very positive image of the current financial health of U.S. firms. In addition, the results may have important implications for these firms' financial policies. In later chapters we devote a good deal of attention to the valuation of corporate equities and their implications for corporate financial policies. Meanwhile, owing to the potential importance of the market-to-book equity ratio, we provide a historical perspective on composite values of this ratio in the next section.

1.4 TIME SERIES BEHAVIOR OF COMPOSITE VARIABLES

In the previous section, we examined composite accounting variables and market values for year-end 2000. At any point in time, such data provide important information about firms with respect to both their financial condition and market assessments of value. However, it is also important to have a historical perspective on these data. In this section, we provide this perspective by examining the values of composite variables over time.

1.4.1 Proportions of Composite Assets, Liabilities, and Equities over Time

Here we analyze composite values of assets, liabilities, and equities over time. Figures 1-2a and 1-2b show trends in the proportions of composite assets and liabilities/equities, respectively, for all publicly traded U.S. nonfinancial firms that existed at the end of years 1980–2000.

Focusing initially on Figure 1-2a, over this period composite TA increased more than fivefold, from $1,778 billion in 1980 to $9,360 billion in 2000. Throughout the period, PP&E constituted the largest single component of composite TA. However, the proportion of TA accounted for by PP&E decreased fairly steadily over this

FIGURE 1-2A Composite Total Assets and Percentage Components of Publicly Traded U.S. Nonfinancial Firms, Years-End 1980–2000

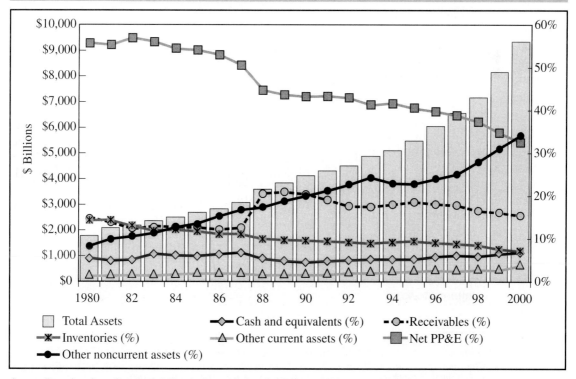

Source: Raw data from Standard & Poor's *Research Insight* database, 2001.

FIGURE 1-2B   Percentage Distributions of Composite Liabilities and Shareholders' Equity of Publicly Traded U.S. Nonfinancial Firms, Years-End 1980–2000

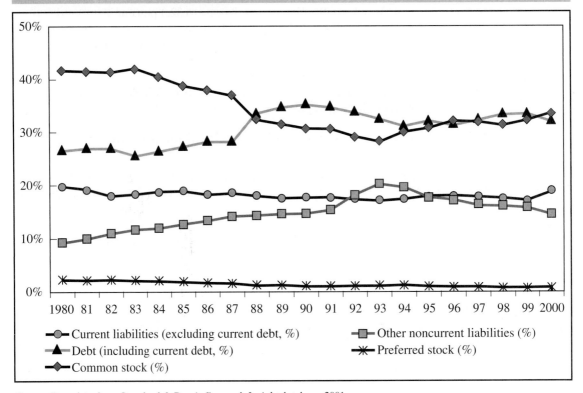

Source: Raw data from Standard & Poor's *Research Insight* database, 2001.

period, from 55.7 percent in 1980 to only 32.5 percent in 2000. Inventories also decreased proportionately over this period, from 14.3 percent in 1980 to 7.2 percent in 2000. In contrast, the aggregate proportion of *all other noncurrent assets* increased tremendously, from only 8.3 percent in 1980 to 34.2 percent in 2000. These assets include investments at equity,[3] other investments and advances,[4] intangibles,[5] and so on. The proportionate increases in these assets attest to the increasing complexity of U.S. firms over time.

Turning to the results in Figure 1-2b, we initially note that common stock and debt account for the largest proportions of total asset financing throughout the 21-year period. Both common and preferred stock have decreased in proportion over time. Common stock fell in proportion from 41.7 percent in 1980 to a low of 28.4 percent in

---

[3]This item represents long-term investments and advances to unconsolidated subsidiaries and affiliates in which the parent company has significant control, as stated in the consolidated financial statements.
[4]This item represents long-term receivables and other investments and advances, including investments in unconsolidated companies in which the firm does not have a controlling interest.
[5]Intangibles include brand names, customer lists, licensing agreements, patented technology, and so on.

1993, before rebounding to 33.5 percent in 2000. Preferred stock fell from 2.3 percent in 1980 to only 0.7 percent in 2000.

Meanwhile, both debt and other noncurrent liabilities have increased in proportion over time. Debt increased from 26.8 percent in 1980 to 32.3 percent in 2000, while other noncurrent liabilities increased from 9.4 percent in 1980 to 14.6 percent in 2000. Regarding the latter, for most firms the predominant item in this liability category is long-term employee compensation and benefit accruals. The proportional increase in this liability attests to the growing importance of pension and compensation liabilities, and highlights the importance of the *stakeholder* theory of the firm (which we discuss in Chapter 3). Overall, the results in Figure 1-2b indicate that leverage has increased over time.

1.4.2   Time Series Behavior of Composite Book and Market Equity Values and Market-to-Book Equity Ratios

The results in Table 1-1 indicate that market-to-book ratios varied substantially across firms at year-end 2000. This is an important observation because, as we discuss in later chapters, a firm's market-to-book equity ratio is both a reflection of, and may influence, its financial policies and strategies. For this reason, we also examine the time series behavior of composite market and book equity values, as well as the composite market-to-book equity ratio. These are displayed in Figure 1-3.

FIGURE 1-3   Composite Book and Market Values of Common Equity (BEQ and MEQ), and Composite Market-to-Book Equity Ratios of Publicly Traded U.S. Nonfinancial Firms, Years-end 1980–2000

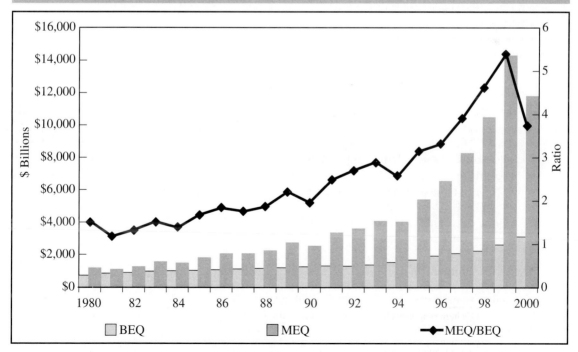

Source: Raw data from Standard & Poor's *Research Insight* database, 2001.

Composite book equity increased over fourfold, from $741 billion at year-end 1980 to $3,134 billion at year-end 2000. However, composite market equity increased almost 11-fold, from $1,114 billion at year-end 1980 to $11,700 billion at year-end 2000! As a result of the greater rate of increase in market equity values, the composite market-to-book equity ratio increased fairly steadily from 1.5 at year-end 1980 to 5.4 at year-end 1999, before falling sharply back to 3.7 at year-end 2000. As we indicated earlier, a standard interpretation of the market-to-book equity ratio is that it is a measure of the market's expectation of a firm's ability to create value from its assets and operations. If this is correct, it appears that over time managers of U.S. nonfinancial firms have dramatically increased their ability to create value.

1.5   ANALYSES OF COMPOSITE CASH FLOWS

We gain another perspective on firms in the aggregate by examining their composite cash inflows and outflows over time—that is, by examining composite *sources and uses of funds* statements. Here we examine composite sources and uses figures for the S&P Industrials for 1988–2000.

FIGURE 1-4A   Composite Sources of Funds for Firms in the S&P Industrials, 1988–2000

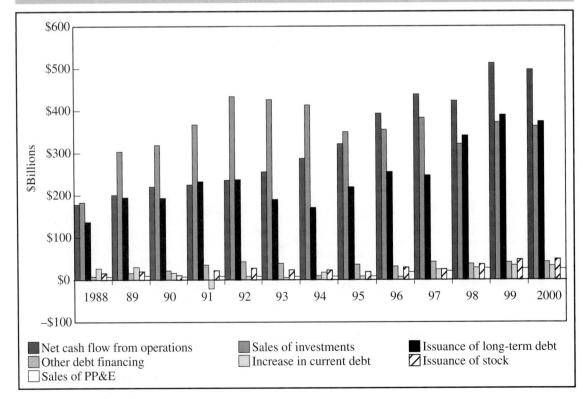

Source: Raw data from Standard & Poor's *Research Insight* database, 2001.

Sources of funds, listed in roughly descending order of their usual composite size, include (a) net cash flow from operations, (b) sales of investments, (c) proceeds from the issuance of long-term debt, (d) other debt financing, (e) increases in current debt, (f) proceeds from the issuance of stock, and (g) sales of PP&E. Annual composite values of each of these sources of funds are displayed in Figure 1-4a. Uses of funds, also listed roughly in descending order of their usual composite size, include (a) increases in investments; (b) capital expenditures; (c) reductions in long-term debt; (d) acquisitions; (e) cash dividends; and (f) repurchases of stock.[6] Annual composite uses of funds are displayed in Figure 1-4b.

The most important conclusion to be drawn from the results in Figures 1-4a and 1-4b is that the greatest *net* source of funds for the S&P Industrials is net cash flow from operations (also called *internally generated funds*). This is so in part because annual debt issuances, as a source of funds, are largely offset (in composite) by annual reductions in debt, as a use of funds. Similarly, annual sales of investments, as a source of funds, were largely offset by annual increases in investments, as a use of funds. For the entire period, operations contributed net cash of $4,186 billion.

FIGURE 1-4B   Composite Uses of Funds for Firms in the S&P Industrials, 1988–2000

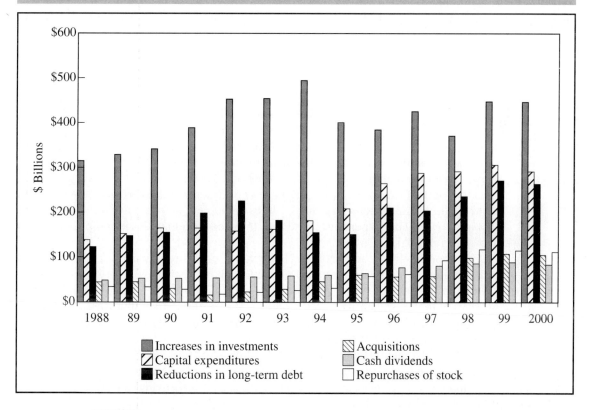

Meanwhile, debt issuances ($3,177 billion), taken net of cumulative debt reductions ($2,522 billion), contributed only $656 billion, whereas sales of investments ($4,589 billion), taken net of increases in investments ($5,252 billion), actually *absorbed* $663 billion.

Two additional points regarding the sources and uses evidence are noteworthy. First, the S&P Industrials tend to engage in a great deal of purchases and sales of investments, as well as debt issuance and debt retirements. Second, although both composite dividends and stock repurchases generally increased over time, the growth of composite stock repurchases far outpaced the growth in dividends. Consequently, for each year beginning in 1997, the composite value of stock repurchases actually exceeded the composite value of cash dividends.

1.6   LEVERAGE DISTRIBUTIONS FOR INDIVIDUAL FIRMS

The decision of a firm's management regarding the mix of debt and equity securities that it uses to finance its assets—that is, its *leverage decision*—is an important financial decision. We discuss the leverage decision extensively throughout the text, devoting the entirety of Chapter 6 to this decision. Table 1-1 and Figure 1-2b show *composite* leverage figures for firms in various categories cross-sectionally and over time, respectively.

In this section, we provide two depictions of leverage for *individual firms*. In the first, we examine the *debt ratios* of individual firms, measured as D/TA, where D and TA are the book values of the firm's debt and total assets, respectively. We calculated the distributions of debt ratios, in 5 percent increments, across firms in each of the S&P index categories defined earlier, as of year-end 2000. These distributions are displayed in Figure 1-5.

In general, book debt ratios vary substantially across firms in each category, though for all categories relatively few firms have book debt ratios exceeding 50 percent. For the S&P Industrials, MidCaps, SmallCaps, and Non-S&P firms, book debt ratios are broadly distributed, with firms included in every debt ratio range shown. However, for each of the firm categories the book debt ratios tend to be fairly low; well over half of the firms in each category have debt ratios that are less than 30 percent. In contrast, for the S&P Transports and Utilities, 78 percent of firms have book debt ratios that are *greater than* 30 percent. These results are consistent with the composite figures shown in Table 1-1.

The book debt ratios of Non-S&P firms, although broadly distributed, are oddly concentrated at both extremes; 36.0 percent of these firms have debt ratios of either zero or in the range of zero to 5 percent, while 17.0 percent have book debt ratios greater than 50 percent. Low leverage is the norm for small firms. Those with extremely high leverage ratios generally are firms that are under financial distress. That is, they have sustained losses that (a) have eroded their equity base and (b) likely have prevented them from paying down debt incurred in the past.

Our second examination of leverage is motivated by results shown in both Table 1-1 and Figure 1-3. These results indicated that the *market value* of the typical firm's equity generally far exceeds its *book value*. Thus, if market value, rather than book value, is a better measure of a firm's equity, then the debt ratios shown in Figure 1-5 are generally and substantially upward-biased measures of leverage.

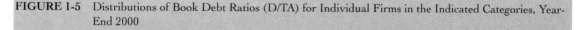

FIGURE 1-5   Distributions of Book Debt Ratios (D/TA) for Individual Firms in the Indicated Categories, Year-End 2000

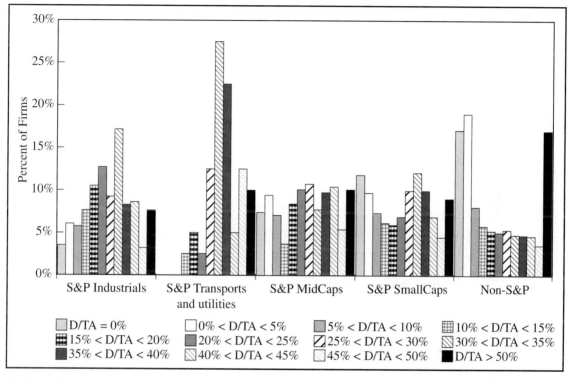

Medians: Industrials (26.5%); Transports/Utilities (35.4%); MidCaps (27.6%); SmallCaps (26.5%); Non-S&P (15.1%).
Source: Raw data from Standard & Poor's *Research Insight* database, 2001.

To correct this bias (if indeed it is a bias), we calculated year-end 2000 leverage ratios for individual firms using an alternative measure of leverage based on market values. For each firm, we (a) restated total capitalization as the sum of the *book values* of liabilities and preferred stock plus the *market value* of equity, denoting this alternative measure of total assets as TA_{mkt}; and (b) calculated leverage as the ratio of the firm's debt, D, to TA_{mkt}, or D/TA_{mkt}. The results are displayed in Figure 1-6.

As expected, the leverage distributions shown in Figure 1-6 differ substantially from the corresponding distributions shown in Figure 1-5. For the S&P Industrials, MidCaps, SmallCaps, and the Non-S&P firms, the market debt ratios shown in Figure 1-6 tend to be much lower than the corresponding book debt ratios shown in Figure 1-5. However, the difference is much less dramatic for the S&P Transports and Utilities; for instance, the median market debt ratio is only slightly lower than the median book debt ratio (35.4 percent versus 30.2 percent). The change is less dramatic for the Transports and Utilities for two reasons: (a) market-to-book equity ratios tend to be lower for the Transports and Utilities than for other firms (see Table 1-1), and (b) the capital structures of these firms tend to consist of smaller proportions of equity than other firms (see Table 1-1).

FIGURE 1-6   Distributions of Market Debt Ratios for Individual Firms in the Indicated Categories, Year-End 2000

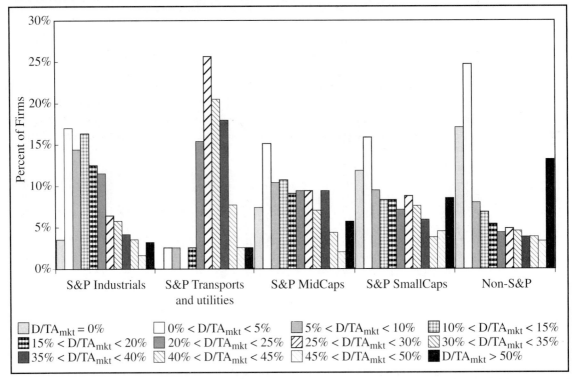

Medians: Industrials (14.7%); Transports/Utilities (30.2%); MidCaps (17.7%); SmallCaps (18.0%); Non-S&P (10.1%).
Source: Raw data from Standard & Poor's *Research Insight* database, 2001.

1.7   OWNERSHIP STRUCTURES

The distribution of a firm's shares among classes of investors is called its *ownership structure.* We explain in Chapters 3 and 4 that a firm's ownership structure is an integral part of its financial policies and strategies. A primary determinant of a firm's ownership structure is whether the firm's equity is privately held or trades publicly on an exchange. Most of our attention in this text is focused on publicly traded firms, so here we examine distributions of equity ownership for publicly traded firms.[7]

For the typical publicly traded firm, major classes of shareholders include (a) the firm's managers and board directors, who are called *insiders*, (b) financial institutions, especially mutual funds and pension funds, (c) individual investors at large, and (d) other firms. Owners in categories (b), (c), and (d) are called *outsiders*. If insiders hold a large proportion of a firm's equity shares, it is said that the firm is *closely held.* Conversely, if numerous outsiders dominate the ownership of a firm's shares, the firm's ownership is *diffuse.*

---

[7]In Chapter 12 we discuss the decision of a private firm to either remain private or to go public via an IPO, and in Chapter 16 we discuss the decision of some public firms to revert to private ownership via a *buyout.*

Here we briefly examine the ownership structures of publicly traded U.S. nonfinancial firms at year-end 1999, sorted into five categories. These categories include (a) the 50 largest firms in the sample (based on market equity value), (b) all nonfinancial firms in the S&P 500 index, (c) firms in the S&P MidCap index, (d) firms in the S&P SmallCap index, and (e) Non-S&P firms.

For each category of firms, we calculated the average proportions of shares held by (a) insiders, (b) mutual funds, (c) pension funds and other institutions, and (d) outside individuals and firms. The results are displayed in Figure 1-7.

The average proportion of shares owned by insiders is strongly inversely related to firm size. The proportion of insider ownership ranges from 11.8 percent for the 50 largest firms to 48.2 percent for the Non-S&P firms. According to these results, the ownership of larger firms is relatively diffuse, whereas small firms are relatively closely held. Institutional ownership also varies considerably by firm size, ranging from only 21.9 percent for the Non-S&P firms (9.8 percent for mutual funds and 12.1 percent for pension funds) to 63.4 percent for S&P 500 firms.[8]

FIGURE 1-7   Ownership Structures for Publicly Traded U.S. Nonfinancial Firms: Average Percentages of Shares Owned by Investors in Indicated Classes for Indicated Categories of Firms, Year-End 1999

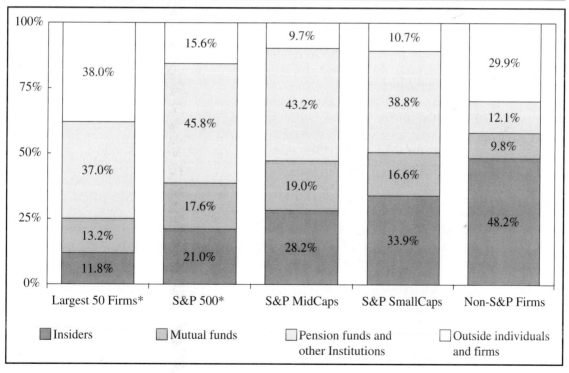

*Excluding financial firms.
Source: 10(k) reports.

---

[8]One reason for the relatively high institutional ownership of S&P 500 firms is that the return on S&P 500 index has become a standard benchmark against which institutions' portfolio performances are judged. Hence, institutional portfolio managers are especially interested in holding stocks that are included in the S&P 500 index.

1.8   COMPOSITE ROE, P/E RATIOS, DIVIDEND PAYOUT RATIOS, AND DIVIDEND YIELDS OVER TIME

To round out our empirical analyses of publicly traded U.S. nonfinancial firms, we calculated composite values of return on equity (ROE), price-earnings (P/E) ratios, dividend payout ratios, and dividend yields. We calculated these composite variables for all firms, as well as several subsamples of firms, for each year from 1980–2000. The composite ROE and P/E ratio values are displayed in Table 1-2, and the composite dividend payout ratio and dividend yield values are displayed in Table 1-3.

1.8.1   Composite ROE over Time

For all firms, composite ROE varied considerably over time, though it was positive in every year. The median composite ROE for all firms was 13.5 percent. Composite ROE was clearly negatively affected by the 1990–1991 recession, as the three lowest annual composite ROE figures occurred in 1991, 1992, and 1993.

Among the three categories of S&P firms for which data was available for all years, median composite ROE was highest for the firms in the S&P Industrials (16.4 percent), followed by the S&P Utilities (11.8 percent) and finally the S&P Transports (10.5 percent). The table also reports the standard deviations of the composite ROE for these categories, which we can use as a crude measure of risk. The S&P Utilities were the least risky category of firms with a composite ROE standard deviation of 2.0 percent, followed by the S&P Industrials at 5.1 percent and finally the S&P Transports at 6.1 percent. The S&P Utilities were less risky in large part because they were a government-regulated industry throughout this period. At the other extreme, the S&P Transports emerge as more risky by this measure in part because they collectively sustained the worst performance around the 1990–1991 recession, actually sustaining losses in both 1991 and 1992. (The U.S. transportation industry was largely deregulated in 1980.)

Regarding the S&P MidCaps and SmallCaps, we initially note that these indexes existed only for the years 1991 to 2000 and 1994 to 2000, respectively. Nevertheless, it is interesting to note that both categories of firms exhibited positive composite ROE values for every year in which they are measured. The median composite ROE was higher for the S&P MidCaps, at 11.4 percent, than for the SmallCaps, at 8.4 percent.

Finally, the median composite ROE for the Non-S&P firms over the 21-year period is 8.3 percent. These firms, too, were adversely affected by the 1990–1991 recession, as their composite ROE fell to 1.4 percent and 5.1 percent in 1991 and 1992, respectively. Surprisingly, however, they also sustained losses in 1998, 1999, and 2000 (−0.2, −7.5, and −12.3 percent, respectively), years when the firms in all other categories generated substantial profits. We suspect that these results reflect, at least in part, the tremendous influx of high-tech firms (e.g., *dot-coms*), which emerged and sustained substantial losses in these years.

1.8.2   Composite P/E Ratios over Time

Composite price-earnings (P/E) ratios are also displayed in Table 1-2. The P/E ratio for an individual firm is typically calculated as the ratio of the firm's stock price to its latest annual earnings. Correspondingly, our annual composite P/E ratios are calculated each year as the ratio of the year-end composite market equity values of a sample of firms to their composite earnings for the year.

TABLE 1-2 Annual Values of Composite ROE and P/E Ratios Publicly Traded U.S. Nonfinancial Firms and Indicated Subsamples, Years-End 1980–2000

Year-End	All Firms ROE	All Firms P/E Ratio	S&P Industrials ROE	S&P Industrials P/E Ratio	S&P Transports ROE	S&P Transports P/E Ratio	S&P Utilities ROE	S&P Utilities P/E Ratio	S&P MidCaps ROE	S&P MidCaps P/E Ratio	S&P SmallCaps ROE	S&P SmallCaps P/E Ratio	Non-S&P ROE	Non-S&P P/E Ratio
1980	17.2%	10.3	17.3%	10.0	10.5%	12.3	12.5%	15.5					17.8%	11.9
1981	16.4%	8.4	16.8%	8.1	11.6%	9.5	9.1%	21.0					16.1%	9.7
1982	11.7%	11.7	11.8%	11.8	7.0%	16.9	7.4%	22.7					10.6%	13.5
1983	12.0%	13.8	11.8%	13.6	11.4%	12.6	11.5%	12.8					11.2%	17.7
1984	13.5%	10.5	13.4%	10.4	12.0%	9.0	10.3%	31.9					11.0%	13.6
1985	11.0%	15.7	11.5%	15.6	9.9%	13.6	11.4%	15.2					8.3%	21.4
1986	10.1%	18.9	11.3%	17.7	0.3%	471.4	8.2%	23.8					6.5%	30.2
1987	12.9%	14.4	14.7%	13.8	8.7%	15.7	9.7%	19.0					9.2%	19.9
1988	14.7%	13.0	17.9%	11.6	11.0%	10.2	10.1%	17.9					8.9%	21.7
1989	14.3%	15.9	16.4%	14.6	10.0%	14.1	11.8%	13.9					10.1%	22.5
1990	12.0%	16.9	13.7%	15.8	4.7%	23.7	12.9%	14.1					8.6%	23.3
1991	7.6%	34.1	8.4%	32.2	-5.5%	*	11.8%	10.6	10.9%	26.3			1.4%	123.1
1992	3.6%	74.5	1.2%	222.5	-5.8%	*	12.6%	9.6	9.3%	29.5			5.1%	59.4
1993	9.2%	33.1	9.8%	32.5	4.0%	62.1	13.1%	10.4	9.9%	28.7			7.7%	44.5
1994	15.1%	19.0	19.0%	17.2	8.9%	21.2	12.4%	9.2	12.5%	21.0	8.3%	28.6	4.1%	33.6
1995	14.8%	23.4	19.4%	19.8	13.4%	18.7	13.7%	6.9	12.8%	22.1	8.1%	36.0	9.7%	49.3
1996	16.3%	23.4	22.1%	20.6	15.8%	15.0	9.1%	6.4	12.5%	24.4	9.4%	31.7	6.2%	65.7
1997	14.2%	29.6	19.1%	25.9	16.2%	14.6	13.5%	6.2	11.4%	30.1	9.7%	32.3	3.1%	118.3
1998	14.0%	35.5	20.3%	31.3	13.4%	16.1	13.6%	5.5	10.2%	35.2	6.4%	40.9	-0.2%	*
1999	13.6%	46.3	21.4%	35.8	13.1%	12.8	12.4%	6.1	11.3%	28.7	8.4%	34.1	-7.5%	*
2000	9.6%	42.8	20.2%	28.0	12.0%	14.8	8.1%	34.8	14.5%	21.8	9.9%	23.1	-12.3%	*
Median	**13.5%**	**18.9**	**16.4%**	**17.2**	**10.5%**	**14.8**	**11.8%**	**13.9**	**11.4%**	**27.5**	**8.4%**	**32.3**	**8.3%**	**22.9**
Std. Dev.	**3.3%**		**5.1%**		**6.1%**		**2.0%**		**1.6%**		**1.2%**		**6.9%**	

*Composite earnings were negative in this case.

Source: Raw data from Standard & Poor's *Research Insight* database, 2001.

TABLE 1-3   Composite Dividend Payout Ratios and Dividend Yields

Publicly Traded U.S. Nonfinancial Firms and Indicated Subsamples, Years-End 1980–2000

Year-End	All Firms		S&P Industrials		S&P Transports		S&P Utilities		S&P MidCaps		S&P SmallCaps		Non-S&P	
	Payout Ratio	Dividend Yield	Payout Ratio	Dividend Yield	Payout Ratio	Dividend Yield	Payout Ratio	Dividend Yield	Payout Ratio	Dividend Yield	Payout Ratio	Dividend Yield	Payout Ratio	Dividend Yield
1980	39.8%	3.9%	40.6%	4.1%	33.2%	2.7%	66.9%	4.3%					33.3%	2.8%
1981	41.1%	4.9%	41.8%	5.1%	31.3%	3.3%	79.5%	3.8%					35.8%	3.7%
1982	52.1%	4.4%	53.0%	4.5%	53.8%	3.2%	97.9%	4.3%					47.4%	3.5%
1983	52.6%	3.8%	53.6%	4.0%	33.2%	2.6%	65.1%	5.1%					50.1%	2.8%
1984	44.7%	4.2%	42.0%	4.1%	28.4%	3.2%	145.2%	4.6%					47.0%	3.4%
1985	55.9%	3.6%	52.7%	3.4%	34.2%	2.5%	89.7%	5.9%					61.6%	2.9%
1986	67.3%	3.6%	59.8%	3.4%	1133.6%	2.4%	119.0%	5.0%					93.7%	3.1%
1987	54.2%	3.8%	47.3%	3.4%	40.6%	2.6%	100.1%	5.3%					69.5%	3.5%
1988	51.6%	4.0%	42.1%	3.6%	127.3%	12.5%	95.5%	5.3%					67.0%	3.1%
1989	50.6%	3.2%	43.9%	3.0%	30.8%	2.2%	78.3%	5.6%					64.1%	2.8%
1990	57.9%	3.4%	50.8%	3.2%	66.7%	2.8%	71.8%	5.1%					69.9%	3.0%
1991	88.0%	2.6%	79.7%	2.5%	—*	1.9%	72.1%	6.8%	50.0%	1.9%			237.5%	1.9%
1992	189.3%	2.5%	547.9%	2.5%	—*	1.9%	69.7%	7.3%	55.4%	1.9%			110.3%	1.9%
1993	76.5%	2.3%	76.4%	2.4%	101.5%	1.6%	64.9%	6.2%	51.8%	1.8%			59.3%	1.3%
1994	45.4%	2.4%	40.3%	2.3%	45.1%	2.1%	65.8%	7.2%	41.1%	2.0%	24.9%	0.9%	53.3%	1.6%
1995	49.0%	2.1%	41.9%	2.1%	30.5%	1.6%	57.4%	8.3%	35.6%	1.6%	27.1%	0.8%	64.6%	1.3%
1996	40.6%	1.7%	37.2%	1.8%	23.6%	1.6%	56.5%	8.9%	38.7%	1.6%	26.3%	0.8%	72.3%	1.1%
1997	40.8%	1.4%	38.1%	1.5%	18.5%	1.3%	56.7%	9.2%	34.7%	1.2%	20.4%	0.6%	79.7%	0.7%
1998	41.5%	1.2%	35.6%	1.1%	18.1%	1.1%	55.8%	10.1%	35.8%	1.0%	27.2%	0.7%	—*	1.0%
1999	38.8%	0.8%	32.0%	0.9%	17.5%	1.4%	59.2%	9.6%	30.0%	1.0%	21.2%	0.6%	—*	0.3%
2000	43.4%	1.0%	29.6%	1.1%	15.5%	1.0%	87.1%	2.5%	20.2%	0.9%	15.5%	0.7%	—*	0.4%
Median	*50.6%*	*3.2%*	*42.1%*	*3.0%*	*33.2%*	*2.2%*	*71.8%*	*5.6%*	*37.3%*	*1.6%*	*24.9%*	*0.7%*	*64.4%*	*2.8%*

*Composite earnings were negative in this case.

Source: Raw data from Standard & Poor's *Research Insight* database, 2001.

An individual firm's P/E ratio tends to be very volatile, in part because of a mismatch between numerator and denominator. According to valuation theory, a firm's stock price reflects investors' assessments of the firms' expected *future earnings*, as well as their willingness to pay for these expected future earnings, whereas the denominator in the ratio is simply the firm's earnings over the *past year*. A similar mismatch occurs with composite P/E ratios, though its effect on P/E volatility tends to be less dramatic. Nevertheless, P/E ratios, whether for individual firms or in composite, must be interpreted with considerable caution. (We discuss P/E ratios in greater detail within the context of our discussion of equity valuation in Chapter 9.)

With this caveat in mind, we examine the evidence. For all firms, the median composite P/E ratio was 18.9. However, this ratio exhibited a sharp upward trend over time. The composite P/E ratio ranged around a value of 10 during the early 1980s; in contrast, the values were 46.3 and 42.8 in 1999 and 2000, respectively. These results indicate that investors were willing to pay three to four times as much for the representative firm's per share earnings in recent years as compared to the early 1980s. These results are consistent with those discussed earlier indicating that aggregate market-to-book equity ratios have increased dramatically over the same period. Thus, a similar interpretation of the composite P/E trend is apropos: over time, the market has attributed to U.S. firms an increasing potential for creating value for shareholders, as reflected in market equity values relative to either book equity or earnings.

Among the three categories of firms for which data is available for all years, the S&P Industrials had the highest median composite P/E ratio at 17.2, followed by the S&P Transports at 14.8 and the S&P Utilities at 13.9. At year-end 2000, the composite P/E ratios for the S&P Industrials, Transports, and Utilities were 28.0, 14.8, and 34.8, respectively.

1.8.3   Composite Dividend Payout Ratios over Time

We devote a considerable amount of attention in this textbook to a firm's financial decisions and their effects on the market value of the firm's equity. Included among these financial decisions is, of course, the firm's dividend decision. For our final analysis in this chapter, we present evidence on firms' tendencies, in composite, to pay dividends.

Our first measure of this tendency is the *payout ratio*. For an individual firm, the payout ratio is the fraction of the firm's earnings in a given year that are paid out as cash dividends in that year. In composite, the payout ratio is the ratio of the sum of the dividends paid by a sample of firms in a given year to the sum of these firms' earnings for that year. Composite payout ratios for each year from 1980 to 2000 are shown in Table 1-3, for all firms as well as the usual subsamples.

For all firms, composite payout ratios varied considerably over time, ranging from 38.8 percent in 1999 to 189.3 percent in 1992. Clearly, the results for 1991 to 1993 were affected by the 1990–1991 recession. (In these years, payout ratios were very high because composite earnings were relatively low while composite dividends remained relatively stable.) The median payout ratio was 50.6 percent. Thus, firms have tended to distribute about half of their earnings in dividends. However, the composite payout ratio has trended downward over the years. For 1980 to 1986, the median composite payout ratio was 52.1 percent, whereas for 1995 to 2000, the median composite payout ratio was only 41.2 percent.

For the S&P Industrials, Transports, and Utilities, median composite payout ratios were 42.1, 33.2, and 71.8 percent, respectively. Traditionally, utilities have paid out a much larger fraction of their annual earnings in dividends. For each of these groups, composite payout ratios were affected by the 1990–1991 recession.

For the S&P MidCaps and SmallCaps, composite payout ratios were calculable only for recent years. For these years, the median composite payout ratios were 37.3 percent and 24.9 percent, respectively. These firms tend to pay a smaller fraction of their earnings in dividends.

For the Non-S&P firms, the median payout ratio was very high at 64.4 percent, suggesting that these firms generally pay a large fraction of their earnings in dividends. However, these results are somewhat deceptive because of the aberrant effects of the 1990–1991 recession and the fact that these firms sustained composite losses in 1998, 1999, and 2000.

1.8.4   Composite Dividend Yields over Time

An individual firm's *dividend yield* is the ratio of the firm's latest quarterly dividend payment, at an annual rate, to the firm's current stock price. We calculate a composite dividend yield as the ratio of the sum of the dividends paid by all firms in a given sample and year divided by the sum of their year-end market equity values. Table 1-3 displays composite dividend yields for years-end 1980–2000.

For all firms, the median composite dividend yield was 3.2 percent. However, composite dividend yields varied considerably over time, ranging from 4.9 percent in 1981 to 0.8 percent in 1999. Moreover, composite dividend yields have clearly trended downward over time. For 1980 to 1986, the median value was 3.9 percent, whereas for 1995 to 2000 the median value was only 1.3 percent. This downward trend in dividend yields is partially explained by the downward trend in composite dividend payout ratios discussed above. However, the decrease in composite dividend payout ratios can explain only a small portion of the decrease in composite dividend yields. For instance, if in 1999 firms had paid out 50 percent of their earnings in dividends, rather than the actual 38.8 percent (i.e., dividends would have been about 30 percent higher than they actually were), the composite dividend yield for 1999 would have been 1.0 percent rather than 0.8 percent, which is still less than one-third the median value for 1980 to 1986.

So how can we explain the bulk of the decline in composite dividend yields? It must be explained by greater growth in the *denominator* of the dividend yield ratio, market equity values, relative to the *numerator*, composite dividends. Indeed, while composite dividends increased at an annual rate of 5.2 percent from 1980 to 2000 (i.e., from $43 billion in 1980 to $119 billion in 2000), composite market equity values increased at an annual rate of 12.5 percent from 1980 to 2000 (i.e., from $1,114 billion at year-end 1980 to $11,700 billion at year-end 2000).

For the S&P Industrials, Transports, and Utilities, median composite dividend yields were 3.0, 2.2, and 5.6 percent, respectively. Dividend yields were substantially higher for the Utilities than for the other two groups in large part because utility firms tend to pay out a higher proportion of their earnings in dividends, as noted earlier. However, composite dividend yields decreased for *all three* of these major firm groups over time, and most precipitously for the S&P Industrials, whose median composite dividend yield fell from 4.1 percent for 1980 to 1986 to only 1.3 percent for 1995 to 2000.

1.9   S

number of important financial characteris-
nonfinancial firms, both cross-sectionally
of this evidence.

such firms nearly doubled, from 3,561 at year-
firms that existed at year-end 1980, only about
nd 2000, an annual attrition rate of 5.9 percent.
three reasons: (a) they were merged into or
hey underwent bankruptcy or liquidation [639
equity ownership via a buyout [335 firms].
ia IPOs over this period.

one-third current assets and two-thirds non-
E (especially for transportation and utility
eir assets using roughly equal proportions of
owever, transportation and utility firms use
ir capital structures.

equity ratios generally far exceeded the par-
ustrials, 4.7, (c) S&P Transports, 1.6, (d) S&P
allCaps, 2.1, and (g) Non-S&P firms, 2.3. This
nt of the extent to which these firms will be
posite market-to-book equity ratios have
ear-end 1980 to 3.7 at year-end 2000.

s, the predominant composite *net* source of
rom operations, while the major composite
dition, firms recently have increased their
market relative to dividends; in each of the
repurchases exceeded the composite value

5. A closer statistical analysis of year-end 2000 debt ratios of individual firms indicates that both book debt ratios (D/TA) and market debt ratios (D/TA$_{mkt}$) vary substantially, both within and across firm categories, though relatively few firms had book debt ratios exceeding 50 percent. Market debt ratios are generally much lower than book debt ratios because market equity values generally far exceed book equity values, as noted above.

6. Our ownership structure analysis focused on the relative shareholdings of various classes of investors for each of several categories of firms. Four major classes of owners were identified: insiders, mutual funds, pension funds and other institutions, and individuals and firms. A strong negative relationship exists between firm size and the proportion of shares held by insiders (e.g., 11.8 percent for the 50 largest firms versus 48.2 percent for Non-S&P firms). Institutional ownership proportions are higher for firms included in the various S&P indexes.

7. Over the years 1980 to 2000, composite ROE for all firms was positive in every year, and the median value was 13.5 percent. Among the S&P Industrials, Transports, and Utilities, the Transports had the lowest median composite ROE, the highest volatility of composite ROE, and were the only category to sustain composite losses related to the 1990–1991 recession.

8. Over the years 1980 to 2000, we observed the following results with respect to composite P/E ratios. For all firms, the median composite P/E ratio was 18.9, though a substantial upward trend was observed, as the value rose from 10.3 at year-end 1980 to 42.8 at year-end 2000.

9. Over the years 1980 to 2000, the median composite dividend payout ratio for all firms was 50.6 percent. Composite payout ratios generally fell over time; the values for 1999 and 2000 were only 38.8 percent and 43.4 percent, respectively.

10. Over the years 1980 to 2000, the median composite dividend yield for all firms was 3.2 percent. Composite dividend yields fell steadily and dramatically, from values of approximately 4 percent in the early 1980s to approximately 1 percent in the late 1990s and 2000. The primary reason for this trend was that composite market equity values grew at a much faster average annual rate (12.5 percent) than composite dividends (5.2 percent).

Review Questions and Problems

1. Over the years 1981 to 2000, 4,770 U.S. nonfinancial firms exited the U.S. markets for publicly traded equity. Given the numbers provided in the text, calculate the percentage of firms that exited for each of the following reasons:
   a. Merger or acquisition
   b. Bankruptcy or liquidation
   c. Buyout

2. Referring to the results in Table 1-1, discuss differences in composite asset components across firm categories.

3. Referring to the results in Table 1-1, discuss differences in composite liability and equity components across firm categories.

4. Referring to results in Table 1-1 and Figure 1-3, respectively, discuss differences in composite market-to-book equity ratios both across firm categories and over time.

5. Over the years 1980 to 2000, how have the proportional components of the composite assets of publicly traded U.S. nonfinancial firms changed? Include quantitative evidence in your answer.

6. Over the years 1980 to 2000, how have the proportional components of composite liabilities and equity changed for publicly traded U.S. nonfinancial firms? Support your answer with evidence.

7. Shown in Table 1-4 are values of six variables for selected individual firms as of year-end 2000: total assets (TA), PP&E, debt (D), book and market equity values (BEQ and MEQ), and the sum of net income for 1998 to 2000 (NI, 3 years). Select several of these firms, compute each of the following ratios for each firm, and for each ratio briefly comment on differences across firms:
   a. PP&E/TA (capital intensity of assets)
   b. D/TA (book debt ratio)
   c. D/TA_{mkt} (market debt ratio)
   d. MEQ/BEQ (market-to-book equity ratio)
   e. MEQ/[NI (3 years)/3] (P/E ratio based on average earnings over 3 years)

8. Summarize and discuss the evidence in Figure 1-7 on ownership structure distributions for various categories of firms.

9. Summarize and discuss the evidence in Table 1-2 on composite ROE and P/E ratios, both across firm categories and over time.

10. Summarize and discuss the evidence in Table 1-3 on composite dividend payout ratios and dividend yields, both across firm categories and over time.

TABLE 1-4   Financial Variables for Selected Firms as of Year-End 2000

Company	Ticker	TA	PP&E	D	BEQ	MEQ	NI (3 years)
S&P Industrials ($ billion)							
General Electric	GE	437.0	40.0	201.3	50.5	475.0	32.7
Exxon Mobil	XOM	149.0	89.8	13.4	70.8	302.2	32.0
Pfizer	PFE	33.5	9.4	5.4	16.1	290.2	10.3
Cisco Systems	CSCO	32.9	1.4	0.0	26.5	268.7	6.1
Wal-Mart	WMT	70.3	36.0	22.1	25.8	237.3	13.3
Microsoft	MSFT	52.2	1.9	0.0	41.4	231.3	21.7
Merck & Co.	MRK	39.9	11.5	6.9	14.8	215.9	18.0
Intel	INTC	47.9	15.0	1.1	37.3	202.3	23.9
Oracle	ORCL	13.1	0.9	0.3	6.5	162.7	8.4
SBC Communications	SBC	98.7	47.2	27.0	30.5	161.6	20.1
Coca-Cola	KO	20.8	4.2	5.7	9.3	151.1	8.1
Intl Business Machines	IBM	88.3	16.7	28.6	20.4	149.1	22.1
S&P Transports ($ billion)							
Southwest Airlines	LUV	6.7	5.8	0.9	3.5	16.8	1.5
Union Pacific	UNP	30.5	28.2	9.9	8.7	12.6	1.0
FedEx	FDX	11.5	7.1	1.8	4.8	11.4	1.8
Brlngtn Nthrn Santa Fe	BNI	24.4	22.4	6.8	7.5	11.2	3.3
Delta Air Lines	DAL	21.9	14.8	6.0	5.3	6.2	2.9
AMR	AMR	26.2	18.6	6.3	7.2	5.9	3.1
CSX	CSX	20.5	12.6	6.7	6.0	5.6	1.1
Norfolk Southern	NSC	19.0	11.1	7.6	5.8	5.1	1.1
US Airways Group	U	9.1	5.0	3.0	−0.4	2.7	0.5
Ryder System	R	5.5	3.6	2.0	1.3	1.0	0.7
S&P Utilities ($ billion)							
Enron	ENE	65.5	11.7	10.2	10.3	61.4	2.6
Duke Energy	DUK	58.2	24.5	14.7	10.1	31.4	4.5
AES	AES	31.0	17.8	19.4	4.8	25.3	1.2
Exelon	EXC	34.6	12.9	15.7	7.2	22.4	1.7
Southern	SO	31.4	21.6	11.8	10.7	21.6	3.6
Williams Co.'s	WMB	40.2	19.7	14.1	5.9	17.6	0.9
El Paso	EPG	27.4	11.7	9.0	3.6	16.8	0.7
Dominion Resources	D	29.3	14.8	14.1	7.0	15.9	1.3
S&P MidCaps ($ billion)							
Health Management Assc	HMA	1.77	1.07	0.53	1.03	5.04	0.45
Washington Post	WPO	3.20	0.93	0.92	1.48	4.76	0.78
3Com	COMS	6.49	0.71	0.03	4.04	2.98	1.11
Murphy Oil	MUR	3.13	2.18	0.56	1.26	2.72	0.40
Microchip Technology	MCHP	0.81	0.44	0.01	0.62	2.60	0.22
National Fuel Gas	NFG	3.24	2.68	1.58	0.99	2.47	0.27
Georgia-Pacific Timber	TGP	1.62	1.24	0.64	0.15	2.39	0.74
Outback Steakhouse	OSI	1.02	0.69	0.02	0.81	2.02	0.36
Amern Eagle Outfitters	AEOS	0.35	0.08	0.00	0.26	1.95	0.16
Clayton Homes	CMH	1.51	0.31	0.10	1.04	1.58	0.44
Tyson Foods	TSN	4.85	2.14	1.54	2.18	1.55	0.41
Pennzoil-Quaker State	PZL	2.77	0.48	1.28	0.82	1.01	−0.45
Federal Signal	FSS	0.99	0.11	0.46	0.36	0.89	0.17
Papa Johns Int'l	PZZA	0.40	0.25	0.15	0.17	0.54	0.11
Airborne	ABF	1.75	1.31	0.32	0.86	0.47	0.26

Creative Thinking Issues

1. Can you think of reasons why both IPO and mergers and acquisitions activity fell around the 1990–1991 recession?
2. Why has PP&E declined in proportion to TA in recent years?
3. Can you think of a reason why preferred stock has declined in importance in the capital structures of U.S. firms over time?
4. Can you think of some factors, in addition to those mentioned in the text, that may cause a specific firm to employ more or less leverage in its capital structure than other firms, or perhaps than the firm has employed in the past?
5. Can you think of reasons why public firms largely avoid issuing additional shares of common stock?
6. Why are purchases and sales of investments so large in the composite sources-and-uses figures shown in Figures 1-4a and 1-4b?
7. Why have firms chosen to favor stock repurchases over dividends in recent years?
8. Can you think of some reasons why small firms tend to be more closely held than large firms?
9. Can you think of reasons why market-to-book equity ratios and P/E ratios have increased so dramatically over the past 20 years?

Projects and Analyses

1. Aggregate data roughly similar to that which we used to generate some of the empirical evidence presented in this chapter can be easily obtained from the *statistical releases* Web site of the Federal Reserve Board (www.federalreserve.gov/releases; click on *Flow of Funds Accounts of the United States: Historical Data*). Gather the necessary historical data, and replicate some of the empirical evidence presented in figures and tables throughout the chapter.
2. Choose a single publicly traded U.S. nonfinancial firm in which you have an interest, and gather recent balance sheet, income statement, and market data on the firm. Use it to compare your firm's financial characteristics to evidence presented in figures and tables in the chapter. Discuss similarities and differences.

A p p e n d i x   A

Developing Samples of Publicly Traded U.S. Nonfinancial Firms

For the analyses in this chapter, we restricted our attention to publicly traded nonfinancial firms that are incorporated in the United States. Our source for accounting and market data for these firms is Standard & Poor's (S&P) *Research Insight* database (August 2001 version). This database includes accounting and market data on over 20,000 firms, including firms that were active in August 2001 as well as inactive or *historical* firms that filed reports with the Securities and Exchange Commission (SEC) at any time during the (approximate) 20-year period ending in this month.

Using this database, we developed 21 main samples, one for each of the years 1980 to 2000. Each sample includes firms that were active at the end of the year. To illustrate the development and characteristics of these samples, the results of the screening process used to develop the year-end 2000 sample are shown in Panel A of Table 1.A-1. Starting with the universe of 21,327 active and inactive firms on the database, the first screen eliminated 12,071 firms that were not publicly traded at year-end 2000. The second screen eliminated an additional 1,045 firms that were not incorporated in the United States. The third and final screen eliminated an additional 2,065 financial institutions. Thus, the final sample for year-end 2000 included 6,146 firms.

Panel B shows a breakdown of the firms in the 2000 sample with respect to (a) the exchanges on which their equities trade, (b) their statuses regarding inclusion in an S&P index, and (c) their average and median TA. Focusing initially on the totals shown in the last row, a total of 4,328 firms in the 2000 sample, or approximately two-thirds of the total sample, traded on the National Association of Securities Dealer's Automated Quotation (NASDAQ) market. A total of 1,364 firms traded on the New York Stock Exchange (NYSE), and 454 firms traded on the American Stock Exchange (AMEX).

For all firms, the average and median TA were $1,529 million and $108 million, respectively. However, an examination of these statistics across firm categories reveals that most of the largest U.S. firms trade on the NYSE, whereas most of the smallest firms trade on the NASDAQ or AMEX.

Next we focus on firms in the various S&P indexes. The S&P 500 index includes 500 of the largest firms in various industries. Among the 500 firms in this index at year-end 2000, 407 met all of the sample criteria discussed above.[9] Of these 407 firms, S&P classifies 357 of them as *Industrials*, which includes major manufacturers (such as General Motors Corp.) as well as major retailers (such as Sears, Roebuck & Co.). A total of 10 firms are placed in the *Transportation* index, including airlines such as Delta Air Lines

---

[9]This total implies that 93 firms from the original 500 were excluded. Of these, 14 were incorporated outside the United States and 79 were financial institutions.

TABLE 1.A-1   Characteristics of Samples of Firms Used in Various Analyses

Panel A: Screening Process Used to Develop Sample of Firms for Year-End 2000

Sequential screening criteria	No. Firms Screened Out	No. Firms Remaining
Universe of active and nonactive firms	—	21,327
Less:		
Firms not exchange-traded at Year-End 2000*	−12,071	9,256
Firms incorporated outside U.S.	−1,045	8,211
Financial institutions	−2,065	6,146

Panel B: Subsamples of Firms for Year-End 2000

		Exchange			Average TA ($ millions)	Median TA ($ millions)
		NYSE	AMEX	NASDAQ		
S&P 500 firms	407	344	2	61	15,887	6,832
Industrials	357	294	2	61	15,143	5,267
Transports	10	10	0	0	17,710	19,734
Utilities	40	40	0	0	22,356	18,602
S&P MidCap firms	339	239	5	95	2,140	1,458
S&P SmallCap firms	537	276	9	252	636	436
Non-S&P firms	4,863	505	438	3,920	381	62
All firms	6,146	1,364	454	4,328	1,529	108

*Firms that traded on regional exchanges or on the NASDAQ's pink sheets were excluded.
Source: Raw data from Standard & Poor's Research Insight database, 2001.

and railroad firms such as Norfolk Southern. Finally, 40 firms are *Utilities* (such as Duke Energy and Southern Co.). Note that most of these firms traded on the NYSE, and are generally very large, based on their average and median TA.

Among the 400 firms that comprised the S&P *MidCap* index at year-end 2000, 339 met all screening criteria. Most of these firms traded on the NYSE, although representation on the NASDAQ is relatively more substantial for this index than for the S&P 500 index. Among the 600 firms that comprise the S&P *SmallCap* index at year-end 2000, 537 met all screening criteria. For the SmallCap index, representation is approximately evenly divided between the NYSE and NASDAQ markets, with a few AMEX firms included as well. Finally, 4,863 firms that are not included in any of the S&P indexes met all screening criteria. Almost 81 percent of these firms (3,920 firms) traded on the NASDAQ market, and 505 and 438 firms traded on the NYSE and AMEX, respectively.

For the Non-S&P firms, average and median values of TA were $381 million and $62 million, respectively. The disparity between the average and median values is due to *skewness* in the distribution of TA among these firms, which include a few large firms such as AT&T Wireless, and thousands of smaller firms.

A Review of Basic Statistics and Regression Analysis

BASIC STATISTICS

Statistics provide a variety of means to summarize data and to make inferences about the characteristics of a sample of observations of a random variable. For instance, given a sample of N observations of a random variable X, the average value, or *sample mean*, denoted as $\overline{X}$, is calculated as

$$Sample\ Mean = \overline{X} = \frac{1}{N}\sum_{i=1}^{N} X_i.$$

Other statistics measure the *dispersion* of the observations of a random variable. One such measure is the *sample variance*, denoted as $\hat{\sigma}_x^2$, which is calculated as

$$Sample\ Variance = \hat{\sigma}_x^2 = \frac{1}{N-1}\sum_{i=1}^{N}(X_i - \overline{X})^2.$$

The sample variance is the (adjusted) average value of the *squared deviations* of the individual observations from the sample mean. Thus, the units involved in the sample mean are squared values, and as such the sample variance measure is difficult to interpret in comparison to the sample mean. However, an alternative measure of dispersion, the *sample standard deviation*, is defined in the same units as the original sample observations. The sample standard deviation, denoted as $\hat{\sigma}_x$, is simply the square root of the sample variance:

$$Sample\ Standard\ Deviation = \hat{\sigma}_x = \sqrt{\hat{\sigma}_x^2}.$$

Together, the sample mean and sample standard deviation can be used to make inferences about the population from which the sample was drawn. For instance, we can perform a statistical test about the true mean of the population, which we will denote as μ_x. Specifically, we can perform a test to determine the likelihood that μ_x is reliable different from some specified value, denoted as μ_x^*. For such a test, the relevant *test statistic* is the "t" statistic, which is calculated as

$$t\ statistic = t = \frac{\overline{X} - \mu_x^*}{\hat{\sigma}_x/\sqrt{N}}.$$

If we assume that the underlying distribution of X is "normal," we can use the t statistic for inference. In a t-test, the *null hypothesis* is that $\mu_x = \mu_x^*$. (Often, the null hypothesis is that $\mu_x^* = 0$.) In general, if the absolute value of the t statistic is small, the null hypothesis is accepted; if it is large, the null is rejected in favor of an alternative hypothesis that $\mu_x > \mu_x^*$ or $\mu_x < \mu_x^*$. The magnitude of t required to reject the null hypothesis depends on both N and the "cutoff" probability established by the researcher. For instance, if N is relatively large and the researcher's cutoff probability is 5 percent, the researcher will reject the null hypothesis if $|t| > 2.0$.

SIMPLE REGRESSION STATISTICS

Simple regression analysis is used to determine whether a linear relationship exists between a dependent variable, Y, and an independent variable, X (also called an explanatory variable). The proposed linear relationship is modeled as

$$Y = a + bX + e,$$

where a is the intercept and b is the slope of the linear relationship, and e is an error term which allows for random deviations about the proposed linear relationship. Given corresponding sets of N observations on both Y and X, the standard method used to estimate a linear relationship between them is called *ordinary least squares* (OLS) regression, which provides best linear unbiased estimators (BLUE) of the coefficients a and b. That is, the OLS method "fits" values for a and b such that the sum of the squared values of the error terms e is minimized. As an automatic consequence of the OLS technique, once the equation is fitted, the average value of the errors e is zero, or $E(e) = 0$. Thus, the estimated value of a, which we will denote as $\hat{a}$, can be interpreted as the conditional "prediction" of Y given that $X = 0$. The estimated slope of the regression equation, denoted as $\hat{b}$, is the sensitivity of Y to a unit change in X.

A number of additional statistics provide information on the quality of the fit of the estimated linear relationship. A standard measure of the overall fit of the regression equation is given by the R^2 *statistic*. Defining the variances of Y and X as σ_Y^2 and σ_X^2, respectively, the R^2 statistic is calculated as[10]

$$R^2 \text{ } statistic = R^2 = \frac{\hat{b}^2 \sigma_x^2}{\sigma_Y^2}.$$

As such, the R^2 statistic can be interpreted as the fraction of the variance of the dependent variable that is "explained" by slope-adjusted variations in the independent variable. By this measure, a perfectly fitted equation is one in which $R^2 = 1.0$. At the other extreme, if X has no influence on Y whatsoever, then $R^2 = 0$ (and, of course, $\hat{b} = 0$ as well). In most cases, of course, $0 < R^2 < 1.0$.

Other assessments of the goodness of fit of the regression equation can be made by examining the *standard errors* of the estimated coefficients $\hat{a}$ and $\hat{b}$, denoted as se_a and se_b. Given that we have estimated the coefficients using only a sample of observations drawn from a population, the estimated coefficients are subject to error relative to the corresponding true values of the coefficients as they could be determined if the entire population was used in the analysis. In this sense, the coefficient estimates are subject to estimation error. The standard error of a regression coefficient is a measure of the range of possible values, around the estimated value, that the coefficient is likely to have in the true population. The formulas for se_a and se_b are

$$\text{se}_a = \sqrt{\frac{\left(\sum_{i=1}^{N} X_i^2 \right) \left[\frac{\sum_{i=1}^{N}(Y_i - \hat{b}X_i)^2}{N-1} \right]}{N \sum_{i=1}^{N}(X_i - \overline{X})^2}},$$

and

$$\text{se}_b = \sqrt{\frac{\left[\frac{\sum_{i=1}^{N}(Y_i - \hat{b}X_i)^2}{N-1} \right]}{\sum_{i=1}^{N}(X_i - \overline{X})^2}}.$$

If we also assume that the estimated coefficients are normally distributed, we can calculate

---

[10]In the case of simple linear regression, the R^2 statistic is also the square of the correlation between Y and X, ρ_{XY}, where $\rho_{XY} = \sigma_{XY}/[\sigma_X \sigma_Y]$. In this equation, σ_X and σ_Y are the standard deviations of X and Y, respectively, and σ_{XY} is the covariance of X and Y, calculated as

$$\sigma_{XY} = \frac{\sum_{i=1}^{N}(X_i - \overline{X})(Y_i - \overline{Y})}{N-2}.$$

a *t statistic* for each of the coefficients to test its significance:

$$t_a = \hat{a}/se_a$$

and

$$t_b = \hat{b}/se_b.$$

Multiple Regression Statistics

In *multiple regression analysis*, two or more independent variables are proposed to explain variations in the dependent variable, Y. The proposed model with k independent variables is

$$Y = a + b_1 X_1 + b_2 X_2 + \ldots + b_k X_k + e,$$

where a is the intercept, the $b_i (i = 1, 2, \ldots, k)$ are the slope coefficients, and e is the error term. Diagnostics analogous to those discussed above for the simple regression analysis apply here, with one notable exception regarding the R^2 statistic. Defining the variance of the errors e as σ_e^2,

in a multiple regression the R^2 *statistic* is calculated as

$$R^2 \ statistic = R^2 = 1 - \left[\frac{\sigma_e^2}{\sigma_Y^2} \right].$$

The R^2 statistic tends to increase with each additional independent variable that is added to the equation, even if the next independent variable has no incremental power to explain variations in Y. This is because, given a fixed number of observations (N) in the regression, each additional independent variable reduces by 1 the *degrees of freedom* for the dependent variable. Thus, the R^2 statistic should be adjusted for the number of independent variables in the regression. By adjusting the R^2 statistic, the resulting statistic, which is called the Adjusted R^2, provides a better measure of the true explanatory power of the collective independent variables. The Adjusted R^2 statistic is calculated as

$$Adjusted \ R^2 = \left[\frac{N-1}{N-k-1} \right] R^2 - \left[\frac{k}{N-k-1} \right].$$

CHAPTER

Valuation and Financing Decisions in an Ideal Capital Market

2.1 INTRODUCTION

Using the Nobel Prize as the measure of quality, we find that some of the most important contributions to financial economics are models of the valuation of securities and their implications for corporate financing decisions, developed under assumptions that characterize an *ideal capital market* (also called a *perfect capital market*). In this chapter, we discuss several theoretical models of the valuation of financial assets developed under such conditions. Researchers who developed these models have won the Nobel Prize in economics for these and other contributions to financial economics.[1] Each model has distinct characteristics based on distinct approaches to the problem of valuation, yet all have been developed under ideal capital market assumptions. Remarkably, all of the models we discuss are jointly reconcilable.

We introduce these valuation models early in the text because, collectively, they have two important implications for corporate finance: (a) they provide explicit valuation models for a firm and its debt and equity securities; and (b) they specify the effects of the firm's choice of *capital structure* (i.e., mix of debt and equity financing) on the risk and required expected returns of its securities.

The first and third models that we discuss, the Modigliani–Miller (1958) capital structure irrelevance theorems and the Black–Scholes (1973) Option Pricing Model, yield conditional specifications of the values, risk, and required expected returns on corporate securities based on *arbitrage* arguments. The second model, the Capital Asset Pricing Model (Sharpe 1964; Lintner 1965; Mossin 1966), provides *general equilibrium* specifications of the values, risk, and expected returns on assets based on *Modern Portfolio Theory* (Markowitz 1952, 1959). We also show that these models are jointly reconcilable; that is, under specified conditions, the three models yield the same results with respect to the values, risk, and expected returns on a levered firm's debt and equity securities. The reconcilability of these theoretical models constitutes an important unification of finance theory as it relates to both valuation and corporate financing decisions under ideal market conditions.

2.2 DEFINING AN IDEAL CAPITAL MARKET

An *ideal capital market* is defined by a set of five assumptions.

- *Assumption 1: Capital markets are frictionless.*
  Market participants face no transaction costs or taxes. Investors face no brokerage com-

---

[1]The Laureates include Harry Markowitz, Robert Merton, Merton Miller, William Sharpe, and Myron Scholes.

missions or fees on trades, and short selling is unrestricted. Firms face no transaction costs in issuing or retiring securities, and there are no costs associated with bankruptcy.

- *Assumption 2: All market participants share homogeneous expectations.*
  Value-relevant information is costlessly available to all market participants, and all participants rationally process such information to determine the value of any security. Thus, all participants share common expectations about the prospects of investments.
- *Assumption 3: All market participants are atomistic.*
  No single market participant can affect the market price of a security via trades.
- *Assumption 4: The firm's investment program is fixed and known.*
  The firm's capital investment program, and therefore its assets, operations, and strategies, are fixed and known to all investors.
- *Assumption 5: The firm's financing is fixed.*
  Once chosen, the firm's capital structure is fixed.

The first three assumptions establish the setting within which securities trade. The last two assumptions restrict the scope of a firm's investment and financing decisions. Overall, the assumptions allow certain activities by either a firm or investors, but disallow other activities.

In establishing these assumptions, we recognize that they may conflict with activities actually observed in the *real world* (i.e., in actual capital markets). The purpose of studying theory under ideal conditions is twofold. First, we gain insights into the effects of a firm's decisions on the values and risk of its securities (i.e., such decisions may yet have the predicted effects even if real-world conditions only approximate the ideal). Second, armed with an understanding of the effects of corporate financial decisions under ideal conditions, we are in a better position to understand the *incremental effects* (where the increments may be large) of certain real-world factors (which constitute violations of one or more of the ideal capital market assumptions) on both these decisions and their effects. We discuss the most important of these factors in Chapters 3 through 6.[2]

2.3   MODIGLIANI AND MILLER'S PROPOSITIONS ON THE IRRELEVANCE OF CAPITAL STRUCTURE

In 1958, Franco Modigliani and Merton Miller (henceforth, M&M) published a landmark paper in the *American Economic Review*: "The Cost of Capital, Corporation Finance and the Theory of Investment." In this paper they defined the assumptions of an ideal capital market, and developed two important (and controversial) propositions concerning the effects of corporate financing decisions on the values and risk of a firm's debt and equity securities.

> M&M Proposition I: The market value of a firm is constant regardless of the amount of leverage (i.e., debt relative to equity) that the firm uses to finance its assets.

---

[2]Early in Chapter 3, we discuss consequences of violations of the assumptions of the ideal capital market. This discussion sets the stage for the introduction of other theories of corporate financial policies and strategies in Chapters 3 through 6, which in turn form the basis for more focused analyses throughout the remainder of the text.

Proposition I implies that a firm's management cannot change the market value of the firm merely by altering its capital structure. This proposition is also referred to as the *Leverage Irrelevance Theorem* or the *Capital Structure Irrelevance Theorem*.

> M&M Proposition II: The expected return on a firm's equity is an increasing function of the firm's leverage.

As we will see, Proposition II follows directly from Proposition I. It is important because it shows that leverage does have effects—specifically, on the risk and expected return of a firm's equity—despite the conclusion from Proposition I that leverage has no effect on the overall value of the firm.

2.3.1   Analysis of M&M Proposition I

Defining the Market Value of a Firm

Before we proceed to an analysis of M&M Proposition I, we must *define* the market value of a firm so that the definition is clearly distinguished from M&M Proposition I itself, which provides an important statement about the effect of a *change* in leverage on the firm's market value. The market value of a firm is, *by definition*, equal to the sum of the market values of all claims on its cash flows (i.e., all of the firm's outstanding securities). Consequently, the market value of an unlevered firm is *defined* as the total market value of the firm's equity shares, whereas the market value of a levered firm is *defined* as the sum of the total market values of its debt and equity securities. In addition, because investors can derive value from holding the firm's securities only because the firm holds assets that have value and produce income, against which the securityholders have a claim, we can interchangeably refer to the value of the *firm* or the value of the *firm's assets*. Thus, we can state Equations 2.1 and 2.2 in definition form:

$$\text{For an unlevered firm: } V_U \equiv E_U, \tag{2.1}$$

and

$$\text{For a levered firm: } V_L \equiv D + E_L. \tag{2.2}$$

In Equation 2.1, V_U denotes the market value of (the assets of) an unlevered firm and E_U denotes the total market value of its equity shares. In Equation 2.2, V_L denotes the market value of (the assets of) a levered firm, and D and E_L denote the total market values of its debt and equity securities, respectively.

Proof of M&M Proposition I via Arbitrage Arguments

Given definitional Equations 2.1 and 2.2, M&M Proposition I states that the market value of a firm (defined by a *fixed* set of assets) is constant regardless of the amount of leverage it employs. Proposition I is expressed in Equation 2.3, which holds that, for all possible levels of leverage,

$$V_U = V_L. \tag{2.3}$$

Arbitrage is the basis for M&M Proposition I. To explain the arbitrage involved, consider two scenarios in which Equation 2.3 does not hold. In the first scenario, a firm's assets are currently financed entirely with equity that has a total market value of $E_U \equiv V_U$. But suppose the firm's assets could instead be financed with specified proportions of both debt and equity, and that the resulting market value of the *levered* version of the firm is $V_L \equiv D + E_L$, where $V_L > V_U$. Under these circumstances, any investor, acting as an *arbitrageur*, could simply (a) purchase the fraction α of the existing firm's equity at a cost of αV_U, (b) place these equity shares in a trust, and then (c) sell securities that represent debt and equity claims against the shares in the trust. The total proceeds that the investor would receive for these debt and equity claims would be $\alpha(D + E_L)$, or equivalently, αV_L. Given the inequality specified above, the investor would realize an instant arbitrage profit of $\alpha(V_L - V_U)$.

In the second scenario, the firm's assets are currently financed with specific proportions of both debt and equity such that the market value of the firm is $V_L \equiv D + E_L$. However, let us assume that $V_L < V_U$, where $V_U \equiv E_U$ is the market value of the firm if it were instead financed entirely with equity. Under these circumstances, an arbitrageur could simply (a) purchase equal proportions, α, of both the debt and equity of the firm at a cost of $\alpha V_L = \alpha(D + E_L)$; (b) place these securities in a trust; and then (c) sell shares of a new security that represents equity ownership of the securities in the trust. The arbitrageur can sell these shares at a total price of $\alpha V_U > \alpha V_L$, and thereby realize an instant arbitrage profit of $\alpha(V_U - V_L)$.

Note that, in either of these scenarios, *all* investors would attempt to perform the indicated arbitrage, and their collective trading activity would alter market values until any such arbitrage is eliminated. Thus, in equilibrium $V_U = V_L$; a firm must have the same value regardless of its capital structure. In other words, Proposition I must hold via arbitrage.[3]

2.3.2   Analysis of M&M Proposition II

Modigliani and Miller's Proposition II, which relies on the result of Proposition I, states that the expected return on a firm's equity increases with the firm's leverage. To explain Proposition II, we begin by defining a firm's *weighted average cost of capital*, or WACC. A firm's WACC is a value-weighted average of the required expected returns on, or *costs of*, the firm's debt and equity, denoted as r_D and r_{LE}, respectively. The formula for WACC is given in Equation 2.4:

$$\text{WACC} = r_D \left[\frac{D}{D + E_L} \right] + r_{LE} \left[\frac{E_L}{D + E_L} \right]. \qquad (2.4)$$

A firm's WACC can be interpreted as the implicit discount rate used by the market on the firm's future cash flows to determine the value of the firm's assets under a specified capital structure. As such, we can alternatively denote a firm's WACC as r_A, the required expected return on the firm's assets under a specified capital structure. Therefore, we can substitute r_A for WACC in Equation 2.4, yielding Equation 2.5:

$$r_A = r_D \left[\frac{D}{D + E_L} \right] + r_{LE} \left[\frac{E_L}{D + E_L} \right]. \qquad (2.5)$$

---

[3]Modigliani and Miller's original proof of Proposition I is provided in Appendix A.

However, via Proposition I the value of the firm's assets does not vary with changes in the firm's capital structure. Therefore, Proposition I implies that r_A must also be constant regardless of the firm's leverage. This is an important *corollary* to Proposition I. It is important because it implies that the expected return on the firm's assets depends entirely on the nature of the firm's assets (specifically the riskiness of the assets) and not on the firm's capital structure. By extension, it implies that a firm's *capital budgeting decisions* (i.e., the firm's choice of projects to pursue) should be made by discounting the expected future cash flows of any proposed project (using a discount rate based on the riskiness of the project, regardless of how it will be financed), and then comparing the present value of the expected future cash flows to the initial cost of the project.

With this background, we can now express Proposition II in equation form. Solving Equation 2.5 for r_{LE} yields Equation 2.6:

$$r_{LE} = r_A + \left[\frac{D}{E_L}\right](r_A - r_D). \tag{2.6}$$

That is, the required expected return on a firm's equity is equal to the required expected return on the firm's assets, r_A, plus an adjustment that is the product of a measure of the firm's leverage (D/E_L) and the difference between the required expected returns on the firm's assets and the firm's debt $(r_A - r_D)$.

So does Equation 2.6 automatically imply that Proposition II is true? Two considerations can be combined to suggest that Proposition II is indeed correct. First, we know from Proposition I that r_A is constant regardless of D/E_L. Second, assuming that the firm's assets are risky and that investors require a premium on the expected returns on risky assets (including securities), then r_A will be greater than r_D, and thus $(r_A - r_D) > 0$ will hold. This will be so because the firm's debtholders have a *priority claim* on the firm's earnings (i.e., they get paid *first*), and thus the risk they face is generally less than the risk of the firm's overall earnings. Therefore, if r_A is constant and $(r_A - r_D) > 0$, it appears that r_{LE} will increase with D/E_L.

However, to address this question properly we must examine the behavior of the terms on the right side of Equation 2.6 more closely. We can do this best by taking the derivative of r_{LE} in Equation 2.6 with respect to D/E_L, recalling in doing so that r_A is constant via Proposition I. The result is given in Equation 2.7:

$$\left[\frac{\partial r_{LE}}{\partial (D/E_L)}\right] = (r_A - r_D) - \left[\frac{D}{E_L}\right]\left[\frac{\partial r_D}{\partial (D/E_L)}\right]. \tag{2.7}$$

In essence, Proposition II states that the derivative in Equation 2.7 will be positive for all levels of leverage. However, whether r_{LE} increases with D/E_L depends critically on the values of the two expressions on the right side of Equation 2.7. To assess the possible values of these expressions, we need more information about how the market determines the required expected returns on the firm's assets and its securities. Specifically, we need more information on r_A and r_D.

Suppose initially that investors are *neutral* with respect to the risk of the firm's assets—that is, they do not demand a premium for risk of the firm's assets. Then $r_A = r_f$, where r_f is the return on a risk-free security such as a U.S. Treasury bill. Furthermore, the risks of both the firm's debt and equity are strictly functions of the risk of the firm's assets, so investors will also necessarily be neutral to the risk of the firm's debt and equity securities; therefore, $r_{LE} = r_D = r_f$ will hold as well, regardless of the firm's leverage. Note that, in this case, the values of r_A, r_{LE}, and r_D are consistent with Equation 2.6. However, the results are inconsistent with Proposition II because r_{LE} does not vary with D/E_L.

A more realistic assumption is that r_A contains a *risk premium*. In this case, the expected return on the firm's equity will also contain a risk premium, as will the firm's debt, if the debt is risky. But, for the moment, we will assume that the firm's debt is risk free for all possible values of D/E_L. In this case r_D will be equal to r_f, the derivative on the right side of Equation 2.7 will be equal to zero, and r_{LE} will be an increasing, linear function of D/E_L, with a slope coefficient of $(r_A - r_D) = (r_A - r_f)$, as can be seen from either Equation 2.6 or 2.7.

However, although debt may be virtually default-free for a few firms, this is not the case in general. A more general scenario is specified with Assumptions A and B:

Assumption A: Investors demand a premium for the risk of a firm's securities.
Assumption B: The firm's debt is risky and its risk increases with the firm's leverage.

It follows that (a) r_D must also increase with leverage; (b) the derivative term in brackets in the right side of Equation 2.7 is positive; and thus (c) the entire expression $(D/E_L)[\partial r_D/\partial(D/E_L)]$ is positive. Therefore, it is not clear from inspection of Equation 2.7 that $\partial r_{LE}/\partial(D/E_L)$ is positive, as Proposition II asserts, because the right side of Equation 2.7 is the *difference* of two expressions, both of which are positive, and we cannot determine the size of either of these expressions for any given level of leverage.

In the end, the present model structure is insufficient to *prove* that Proposition II is true. We can only argue that Proposition II has merit because equityholders, who have only a residual claim to the firm's assets, bear more risk than debtholders, who have a priority claim: therefore, r_E should be greater than r_D for any given level of leverage. Moreover, it seems likely that, when leverage increases marginally from any given level, equityholders realize greater increase in risk per dollar of investment than do debtholders, in which case r_{LE} must increase at a faster rate with D/E_L than does r_D, in which case Proposition II will be true. However, to address the issue formally, we require greater specification of the nature of the firm's risk and that of its debt and equity securities, as well as the market's required compensation for risk in the form of an expected return premium. Fortunately, as we will see, the Capital Asset Pricing Model and the Black–Scholes Option Pricing Model combine to provide such specifications (although they, too, are only models).

As a final comment on the M&M model structure, note that the firm's assets are fixed, so the total amount of firm risk is constant and must be borne in its entirety by the firm's claimants—debtholders and equityholders—for any level of leverage. By extension, a change in the firm's leverage simply involves a *redistribution* of the firm's total risk among the claimants. If we also assume that the market provides compensation (in the form of expected return premium) that is *linearly* related to the risk borne by a given claimant, we gain additional insight into the behavior of r_{LE} and r_D as specified in Equations 2.6 and 2.7.

For instance, when we assumed that $r_A > r_f$ and that the firm's debt is risk free for all levels of leverage (which implies that debtholders bear none of the firm's risk while equityholders bear all of the firm's risk), we found that the expected return on the equity increases linearly with leverage—specifically, at the rate of $r_A - r_f$ per unit change in D/E_L. However, when we allow the risk of the firm's debt to be positive and to increase with leverage, the required expected return on the debt also increases with leverage (i.e., $\partial r_D / \partial (D/E_L) > 0$ in Equation 2.7); we then find that the required expected return on the firm's equity increases at a slower rate with leverage: $(r_A - r_D) - (D/E_L)[\partial r_D / \partial (D/E_L)] < (r_A - r_D)$. This is logical because debtholders are bearing an increasing share of the firm's risk as leverage increases.

2.4   MILLER AND MODIGLIANI ON THE IRRELEVANCE OF DIVIDEND POLICY

In another paper, Miller and Modigliani (1961) show that, under ideal market conditions, the firm's dividend decision is also irrelevant to the value of a firm's equity. We will postpone a formal proof of this assertion until Chapter 14. However, the basic argument is quite intuitive. If the firm's capital investment and debt policy are fixed, then as the firm increases its dividend, it will eventually have to finance such payments by issuing additional shares. However, we can view a dividend as simply a partial liquidation of the original shareholders' interest in the firm. Hence, we can view the payment of a dividend and the simultaneous issuance of new shares (at a fair market price) as a forced sale of a portion of the original shareholders' claim on the firm to new shareholders. But this sale occurs at a fair market price; so it is a matter of indifference to all parties, including the original shareholders who can, if they wish, use their dividend cash to restore their proportional claim on the firm by purchasing some of the issued shares.

2.5   THE CAPITAL ASSET PRICING MODEL

In this section, we provide an abridged review of Modern Portfolio Theory (Markowitz 1952, 1959) and the Capital Asset Pricing Model (CAPM) (Sharpe 1964; Lintner 1965; Mossin 1966), which is based on Modern Portfolio Theory.[4] The CAPM provides *equilibrium* specifications of the risk and corresponding required expected returns on all assets and securities, including a firm's assets, debt, and equity.

2.5.1   Portfolio Diversification and Modern Portfolio Theory

Modern Portfolio Theory involves two basic constructs. The first concerns the statistical effects of diversification on the expected return and risk of a portfolio. The second concerns the attitudes of investors toward risk; specifically, it is assumed that investors are *averse* to risk, but are sufficiently *tolerant* of risk to bear it if sufficient compensa-

---

[4]Most recent investment textbooks provide a more complete development of portfolio theory and the CAPM, as well as alternative equilibrium pricing models such as the Arbitrage Pricing Theory of Ross (1976).

tion, in the form of higher expected return, is provided. Furthermore, it is assumed that investors are concerned only with the expected return and standard deviation of their overall portfolio. Modern Portfolio Theory addresses the task of identifying the portfolio that maximizes an investor's *expected utility,* given the investor's willingness to trade off risk and expected return.

Statistics for a Portfolio of Two Securities

To begin our brief review of the statistical effects of diversification on a portfolio's expected return and risk, consider two securities, A and B. The expected returns on these securities are denoted as r_A and r_B, respectively, and their return standard deviations are denoted as σ_A and σ_B, respectively. The correlation between the returns on securities A and B is denoted as ρ_{AB}, where of course, $-1 \leq \rho_{AB} \leq 1$.

The expected return on a portfolio of securities A and B, denoted as r_p, is

$$r_p = w_A r_A + w_B r_B, \tag{2.8}$$

where w_A and w_B are the *portfolio weights,* the proportions of the investor's wealth invested in securities A and B, respectively. (As a budget constraint, $w_A + w_B = 1$ must hold.) Note that r_p is a simple weighted average of r_A and r_B.

The standard deviation of the portfolio, denoted as σ_p, is

$$\sigma_p = [w_A^2 \sigma_A^2 + w_B^2 \sigma_B^2 + 2w_A w_B \sigma_A \sigma_B \rho_{AB}]^{1/2}. \tag{2.9}$$

Note that σ_p^2, the term inside the brackets of Equation 2.9, is not a simple weighted average of the variances of securities A and B except, as can be shown, for the case in which $\rho_{AB} = 1$. In the general case in which $\rho_{AB} < 1$, σ_p^2 will be *smaller* than a weighted average of σ_A^2 and σ_B^2, and thus σ_p will be smaller than a weighted average of σ_A and σ_B. In this sense, we can say that an investor can reduce the risk of her portfolio by diversifying across securities that are not perfectly correlated; the lower the correlation between the two securities' returns, the greater will be the risk-reducing benefit of diversification.

A Numerical Example   Suppose $r_A = 10$ percent, $r_B = 10$ percent, $\sigma_A = 40$ percent, $\sigma_B = 40$ percent, and $\rho_{AB} = 0.25$. If an investor places all of her investable wealth in only one of these stocks, the expected return and risk of her portfolio will be $r_p = 10$ percent and $\sigma_p = 40$ percent. However, if she divided her money equally across the two stocks (i.e., $w_A = w_B = 0.5$), the expected return and risk of her portfolio would be

$$r_p = 0.5(10\%) + 0.5(10\%) = 10\%$$

and

$$\sigma_p = [0.5^2(40)^2 + 0.5^2(40)^2 + 2(0.5)(0.5)(40)(40)(0.25)]^{1/2}$$
$$= 31.6\%.$$

That is, by diversifying, the investor can obtain the same expected return as she could by investing in either of the individual securities, but she faces less risk.

Statistics for an N-Security Portfolio

For the general case in which the investor's portfolio contains N securities, r_p and σ_p are calculated using Equations 2.10 and 2.11, respectively:

$$r_p = \sum_{i=1}^{N} w_i r_i \tag{2.10}$$

and

$$\sigma_p = \left[\sum_{i=1}^{N} \sum_{j=1}^{N} w_i w_j \sigma_{ij} \right]^{1/2}, \tag{2.11}$$

where $\sigma_{ij} = \sigma_i \sigma_j \rho_{ij}$ if $i \neq j$, and $\sigma_{ij} = \sigma_i^2$ if $i = j$. That is, if $i \neq j$, σ_{ij} is the *covariance* between returns on securities i and j, whereas if $i = j$, we have security i's *variance*.

In the special case in which the investor places equal amounts of money into each of N securities (i.e., the investor develops an *equally weighted* portfolio of N securities), Equations 2.10 and 2.11 reduce to Equations 2.12 and 2.13:

$$r_p = \frac{1}{N} \sum_{i=1}^{N} r_i \tag{2.12}$$

and

$$\sigma_p = \left[\frac{1}{N} \times (\overline{\sigma_i^2}) + \left(1 - \frac{1}{N} \right) \times (\overline{\sigma_{ij}}) \right]^{1/2}, \tag{2.13}$$

where $\overline{\sigma_i^2}$ is the average *variance* of the individual securities in the portfolio, and $\overline{\sigma_{ij}}$ is the average of all pairwise *covariances*. Note that as $N \to \infty$, the first term in brackets in Equation 2.13 approaches zero, while the second term converges to $\overline{\sigma_{ij}}$. It is in this sense that the variance of a well-diversified portfolio is determined entirely by *covariances* and not at all by the *variances* of the individual securities.

The average covariance of a diversified portfolio is somewhat difficult to interpret, so we offer the following alternative formula. In most practical circumstances, $\overline{\sigma_{ij}}$ can be approximated by the product of the average of all pairwise *correlations* among the securities, denoted as $\overline{\rho_{ij}}$, and $\overline{\sigma_i^2}$; that is, $\overline{\sigma_{ij}} \approx \overline{\rho_{ij}} \overline{\sigma_i^2}$. Therefore, as $N \to \infty$,

$$\sigma_p \approx [\overline{\rho_{ij}} \overline{\sigma_i^2}]^{1/2}. \tag{2.13a}$$

Numerical Examples   We now illustrate the effect of diversification on the risk of an investor's portfolio. Suppose that for a set of N securities, or for any subset of the N securities, $\overline{\sigma_i^2} = 40^2 = 1{,}600$, and $\overline{\rho_{ij}} = 0.25$. Using Equation 2.13, we calculated the standard deviation of the investor's equally weighted portfolio for various values of N.

The results are displayed in Figure 2-1. The figure shows that portfolio risk decreases, but at a decreasing rate, as N increases; as $N \to \infty$, it reaches an asymptote of $[\overline{\rho_{ij}} \overline{\sigma_i^2}]^{1/2} = [0.25(1{,}600)]^{1/2} = 0.20 = 20$ percent. The figure also shows portfolio standard deviations for two additional values of $\overline{\rho_{ij}}$, 0.50 and 0.10. Note that as the average

FIGURE 2-1   Annual Return Standard Deviation, σ_p, for an Equally Weighted Portfolio as a Function of the Number of Risky Securities in the Portfolio, N, for Alternative Values of the Average Pairwise correlation (ρ) between the Securities' Returns

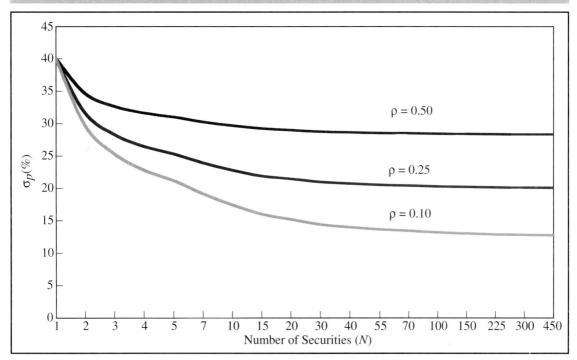

correlation between the securities decreases, portfolio risk also decreases, emphasizing the critical role of correlation in determining the benefits of diversification.

Risk Aversion and the Investor's Optimal Portfolio in the Absence of a Risk-free Security

As we observed in Chapter 1, thousands of securities are available in the U.S. financial markets today (and many more are available in non-U.S. markets) with varying expected returns, standard deviations, and correlations with other securities. Moreover, a virtually infinite number of portfolios can be developed by varying the number of securities in the portfolio, the specific securities included, and the portfolio weights applied to each security.

The question now is which portfolio should a risk-averse investor choose? We initially address this issue assuming that no risk-free security exists. Among all portfolios of risky securities, the choices can be narrowed considerably by eliminating all portfolios that are *dominated*. A portfolio is dominated if another portfolio provides both a higher expected return and lower risk (i.e., lower return standard deviation). In other words, a dominated security or portfolio is relatively *inefficient* in terms of providing compensation for risk.

FIGURE 2-2   Efficient Frontier and Individuals' Optimal Portfolios Without a Risk-free Security

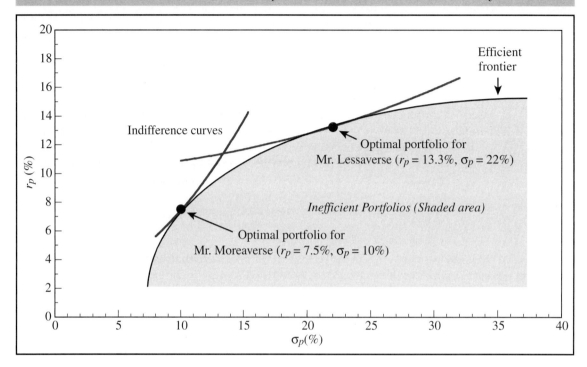

After eliminating all dominated portfolios, we are left with only *efficient portfolios*, which necessarily form a continuous, concave curve in r_p–σ_p space known as the *efficient frontier*. Figure 2-2 provides an illustration of the efficient frontier. The figure also shows *indifference curves*[5] and optimal portfolios for two investors, Mr. Moreaverse and Mr. Lessaverse, whose respective tolerances for risk are indicated by their names. The expected return and standard deviation of Mr. Moreaverse's optimal portfolio are r_p = 7.5 percent and σ_p = 10 percent. The corresponding figures for Mr. Lessaverse are r_p = 13.3 percent and σ_p = 22 percent.

Optimal Portfolios with Risky and Risk-free Securities: The Portfolio Separation Theorem

Next, we consider the effect of adding a *risk-free security* to the set of securities available to investors. By suitably modifying Equations 2.8 and 2.9, and noting that the variance of the risk-free security is zero, the formulas for the expected return and standard deviation of a two-asset "complete" portfolio, C, consisting of the risk-free security and any risky portfolio p, are

$$r_C = w_f r_f + w_p r_p \qquad\qquad \textbf{(2.14)}$$

---

[5]An indifference curve is a plotting of points in r_p–σ_p space that yield a specific level of expected utility for a given investor, reflecting his or her risk aversion.

and

$$\sigma_C = w_p \sigma_p. \qquad (2.15)$$

Note that σ_C increases linearly with w_p, the proportion invested in the risky portfolio. In addition, assuming that $r_p > r_f$, r_C also increases linearly with w_p. As a result, for a portfolio that combines investments in the risk-free security and any risky portfolio, the available combinations of risk and expected return available to the investor can be described graphically as a ray in r_C–σ_C space that emanates from the point representing the risk-free security and passes through the point representing a given risky portfolio, p.

Which risky portfolio should an investor choose for his or her complete portfolio? We have already established via the dominance argument that all risk-averse investors will rationally select from among the risky portfolios on the efficient frontier. However, each of the risky portfolios on the efficient frontier, when used in combination with the risk-free security, yields a different set of investment opportunities that specify a linear trade-off between expected return and risk. Therefore, some of these linear investment opportunity sets dominate others that have a lower *slope* in r–σ space (i.e., they provide a greater expected return premium per unit of risk).

Ultimately, only one risky portfolio, used in combination with the risk-free security, provides a set of investment opportunities, each of which is not dominated by any other portfolio. This portfolio is identified graphically by the point on a ray emanating from the risk-free security and is tangent to the (original) efficient frontier. This portfolio is therefore called the *tangency portfolio*, and we denote it as portfolio T. For any given level of risk, there exists a point on the r_f–T ray that dominates any given portfolio on the (original) efficient frontier. Therefore, we invoke the dominance argument again; all investors will choose an optimal portfolio that is among those in the r_f–T set. A particular investor will choose from among the portfolios in this set according to his or her risk tolerance by varying proportional investments in the risk-free security and portfolio T. However, to the extent that any investor puts money at risk, he or she will optimally choose risky portfolio T. Consequently, in the presence of a risk-free security, the choice of the optimal portfolio of risky assets is separated from the investor's risk tolerance, a result known as the *Portfolio Separation Theorem.*

An Illustration of the Portfolio Separation Theorem

The Portfolio Separation Theorem is illustrated in Figure 2-3, which extends the results shown in Figure 2-2 by adding the risk-free security. Both Mr. Moreaverse and Mr. Lessaverse will optimally choose to hold a complete portfolio that consists of weighted investments in the risk-free security and the tangency portfolio T. Note that the original efficient frontier is now obsolete and replaced by a new efficient frontier defined by a ray emanating from the risk-free security and passing through tangency portfolio T. In the example, the expected return and standard deviation of portfolio T are $r_T = 12$ percent and $\sigma_T = 18$ percent.

Both investors are now able to construct new optimal portfolios that have higher utility than the optimal portfolios they chose in the absence of the risk-free security. Mr. Moreaverse now chooses a complete portfolio that has lower risk and a lower expected return ($r_C = 6.5$ percent and $\sigma_C = 3.9$ percent versus $r_p = 7.5$ percent

FIGURE 2-3   The Tangency Portfolio and Individuals' New Optimal Portfolios with a Risk-free Security

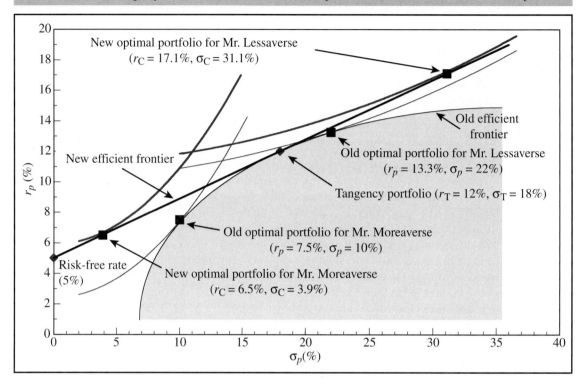

and σ_p = 10 percent), while Mr. Lessaverse now chooses a portfolio that has higher risk and a higher expected return (r_C = 17.1 percent and σ_C = 31.1 percent versus r_p = 13.3 percent and σ_p = 22 percent). Given each investor's choices of r_C and σ_C, we can use either Equation 2.14 or Equation 2.15 to determine the portfolio weights that each investor places in the risk-free security and tangency portfolio T (where portfolio T replaces portfolio p in these equations), w_f and w_T = (1 − w_f), respectively. Using Equation 2.15, we find that Mr. Moreaverse invests $w_T = \sigma_C/\sigma_T$ = 3.9/18 = 0.2167, or 21.67 percent, of his money in portfolio T and the remainder, w_f = 0.7833, or 78.33 percent, in the risk-free security. Mr. Lessaverse actually places 172.8 percent of his money in portfolio T ($w_T = \sigma_C/\sigma_T$ = 31.1/18 = 1.728), which he can do by taking a *short position* (i.e., holding a *negative* portfolio weighting position) in the risk-free security (which is equivalent to *borrowing* at the risk-free rate); that is, w_f = −0.728.

2.5.2   Market Equilibrium: The Capital Market Line (CML)

In the equilibrium derived in the Capital Asset Pricing Model, investors collectively hold all risky securities, and all individual investors hold the same portfolio of risky securities. In this *market portfolio*, denoted as M, the portfolio weight for each risky security is equal to the ratio of the total market value of the security to the total market value of all risky securities. As in the (nonequilibrium) depiction of portfolio choice shown in Figure 2-3, each and every investor chooses a complete portfolio, C, consisting of weighted investments in the risk-free security and the market portfolio that is consistent with their risk tolerance. Therefore, the choices available to investors create a line in r–σ space that is formed by the points representing the risk-free security and M. This line is called the *capital market line*, or *CML*:

$$r_C = r_f + \left[\frac{\sigma_C}{\sigma_M}\right](r_M - r_f). \tag{2.16}$$

Numerical Examples Using the CML

Suppose the risk-free rate is $r_f = 5$ percent and the expected return and standard deviation of the market portfolio are $r_M = 12$ percent and $\sigma_M = 18$ percent, respectively. Sally decides to place 20 percent of her funds in the risk-free security and the remaining 80 percent in the market portfolio. Applying Equations 2.14 and 2.15 to this case, her complete portfolio has an expected return of $r_C = 10.6$ percent and standard deviation of $\sigma_C = 14.4$ percent. By plugging these numbers into Equation 2.16, the reader can verify that they reconcile.

The CML has practical use in either of two situations, both of which require knowledge of the values of r_f, r_M and σ_M. First, suppose an investor's objective is to achieve a specified target expected return of r_C on her portfolio. The specified value of r_C can be plugged into Equation 2.16 and the equation can then be solved for σ_C, the amount of risk she must bear to achieve r_C. For example, using the values of r_f, r_M, and σ_M stated above, if the investor wishes to achieve an expected return of $r_C = 8$ percent, she must bear risk of $\sigma_C = 7.714$ percent. Furthermore, the resulting value of the ratio σ_C/σ_M is equal to the proportion of her complete portfolio that must be invested in the market portfolio to achieve this objective; that is, $w_M = (\sigma_C/\sigma_M) = 7.714/18 = 0.4286$, or 42.86 percent, with the remainder, 57.14 percent, invested in the risk-free security.

Second, suppose an investor declares that he can bear only a limited amount of risk in his portfolio, expressed as $\sigma_C = 11$ percent. This value of σ_C can be plugged into Equation 2.16, whereupon we can solve for r_C, the expected return that the investor can achieve by bearing this amount of risk. In this case, $r_C = 9.28$ percent. Again, the value of the ratio σ_C/σ_M is the proportion of the investor's wealth that is invested in the market portfolio. In this case, $w_M = 11/18 = 0.611$, or 61.1 percent, and the remainder, $1 - 0.611 = 0.389 = 38.9$ percent, is invested in the risk-free security.

2.5.3   The Security Market Line (SML)

The CAPM also specifies the equilibrium expected return on any individual security as a function of its relative contribution to the risk of the market portfolio. For any security i, r_i is a function of the security's *beta*, denoted as β_i and defined in Equation 2.17:

$$\beta_i = \frac{\sigma_{iM}}{\sigma_M^2}, \tag{2.17}$$

where σ_{iM} is the covariance of returns on security i and the market portfolio, and σ_M^2 is the variance of returns on the market portfolio.

Although the risk measure β_i is derived formally in the CAPM, it also has a simple, intuitive interpretation. Recalling our earlier conclusion that the variance of a well-diversified portfolio is determined entirely by the covariances among the securities, it stands to reason that the contribution of a given security to the risk of the market portfolio (which is a well-diversified portfolio indeed) can be measured by the covariance of the security's returns with the returns on the market portfolio. And indeed, this is the numerator of β_i in Equation 2.17. Furthermore, note that the denominator of the right side of Equation 2.17 is the variance of the market portfolio; because the market portfolio is a well-diversified portfolio, this variance is equal to the *average* of the pairwise covariances of all securities in the market (though, in this case, σ_M^2 is a *value-weighted* average of covariances).

Therefore, β_i can be interpreted as the ratio of the covariance of stock i with the market portfolio to the (value-weighted) average of all of the pairwise covariances of the stocks in the market portfolio. As such, beta is a measure of the *relative* size of the risk contribution of a given security. It is not surprising then that the average value of the betas of all securities, and thus of the market portfolio itself, is 1.0. Securities with betas greater than 1.0 are more risky, and thus will have higher expected returns in equilibrium, whereas securities with betas less than 1.0 are relatively less risky and will have lower expected returns in equilibrium.

Formally, the relationship between the equilibrium expected return on any asset i, r_i, and β_i is given in Equation 2.18:

$$r_i = r_f + \beta_i(r_M - r_f). \tag{2.18}$$

Note that the relationship between r_i and β_i is linear. This linear relationship is known as the *security market line*, or *SML*. For example, if the risk-free rate is 5 percent and the expected return on the market portfolio is 12 percent, the equilibrium expected return on a security with a beta of 0.85 is

$$r_i = 5\% + 0.85[12\% - 5\%] = 10.95\%.$$

2.6   THE BINOMIAL PRICING MODEL

In this section we introduce a simple model to value corporate securities, called the Binomial Pricing Model. We use this model both to provide an alternative proof of M&M Proposition I and to explore firm-specific risk–return relationships that depend on the firm's capital structure.

2.6.1   Assumptions

The assumptions required for the Binomial Pricing Model include all of those associated with the ideal capital market, plus an additional assumption about the distribution of the future value of a firm's assets. With this additional assumption, discussed next, the model uses arbitrage arguments to determine the values of a levered firm's debt and equity securities.

2.6.2   The Distribution of a Firm's Future Value in the Binomial Pricing Model

The *binomial distribution* provides the simplest model of risk. Applied to a firm's assets, values of the assets are modeled over a single period, which extends from date 0, the current date, to date T, a future date. The future value of the assets can take on only two possible values, which are defined relative to the assets' current value. Denoting the current value of the firm's assets as V, the future value of the firm's assets can take on only one of two possible values, V_T^u or V_T^d, where $V_T^u > V$ and $V_T^d < V$. That is, over the single period involved, the value of the firm's assets can either rise to V_T^u or fall to V_T^d.

Our choices of values of V_T^u and V_T^d define the riskiness of the firm's assets. Appropriate values for V_T^u and V_T^d depend on three factors: (a) the value of V, (b) the actual riskiness of the value of the firm's assets that we are attempting to model, and (c) the span of time involved in the model's single period. To address (a), it is generally assumed that V_T^u and V_T^d represent proportional "up" and "down" *jumps* relative to V. The *up* jump is denoted as u, where $u > 1$, and the *down* jump is denoted as d, where $d = 1/u < 1$. Thus,

$$V_T^u = uV \tag{2.19}$$

and

$$V_T^d = dV. \tag{2.20}$$

Regarding factors (b) and (c), we generally wish to model risk as a function of time, where risk increases with the length of the period. To do so, we must address factors (b) and (c) simultaneously. For instance, to model the riskiness of the assets of a particular firm, if the length of the period is a year, we would choose a particular value of the risk parameter u, whereas if the period is five years, another, larger value of u should be specified. Cox, Ross, and Rubinstein (1979) provided a formula for the parameter u that produces an approximation for the riskiness of the firm in terms of the per-annum return standard deviation, as if the returns were normally distributed. The formula is

$$u = e^{\sigma\sqrt{T}}, \tag{2.21}$$

where σ is the per-annum return standard deviation of the firm's assets, and T is the length of the model's period in years. This formula allows us to specify reasonable values of u.

A Numerical Example
Suppose the current value of a firm is $V = 100$, and the annual standard deviation of returns on the firm's assets is $\sigma = 20$ percent. If $T = 1$ year, then

$$u = e^{\sigma\sqrt{T}} = e^{0.20\sqrt{1}} = 1.2214,$$

and thus, $d = 1/u = 0.8187$. Given these values, the future values of the firm in the up and down states are

$$V_1^u = uV = 1.2214(100) = 122.14$$

and

$$V_1^d = dV = 0.8187(100) = 81.87.$$

That is, the one-year return on the firm's assets is either +22.14 percent or –18.13 percent.

The Expected Return on the Firm's Assets

To complete the specification of the binomial distribution of a firm's assets, we must specify the probabilities of the up and down jumps. We denote the probability of an up jump as p, so the probability of a down jump is $(1 - p)$. Consequently, the expected value of the firm's assets at date T, $E(V_T)$, is

$$E(V_T) = pV_T^u + (1 - p)V_T^d, \tag{2.22}$$

and the expected return on the firm's assets is

$$r_A = p\left[\frac{V_T^u - V}{V}\right] + (1 - p)\left[\frac{V_T^d - V}{V}\right]. \tag{2.23}$$

Continuing with the numerical example developed above, if we set $p = 0.7$, the expected future value of the firm's assets is

$$E(V_1) = 0.7(122.14) + 0.3(81.87) = 110.06,$$

and the expected return on the firm's assets is

$$r_A = 0.7\left[\frac{122.14 - 100}{100}\right] + 0.3\left[\frac{81.87 - 100}{100}\right] = 0.7[0.2214]$$
$$+ 0.3[-0.1813] = 0.1006, \text{ or } 10.06\%.$$

Finally, if the firm has no debt, the value of the firm's equity is equal to the value of its assets. In this case, Equations 2.19 through 2.23 apply equivalently to the value of the firm's equity. However, our primary interests in the binomial model are (a) to value a levered firm's debt and equity, and (b) to further illustrate M&M Proposition I. We now turn to these tasks.

2.6.3   The Binomial Pricing Model and the Valuation of the Debt and Equity of a Levered Firm

If the future value of a levered firm's assets follows the binomial distribution, we can determine the values of the firm's debt and equity. We assume that the firm has pure-discount debt consisting of a promise to pay debtholders the amount X at date T.

Case 1: Default-Free Debt

First, we analyze a simple case in which the firm's pure-discount debt is riskless, or *default free*. If $X < V_T^d$, the debt is devoid of default risk, so the debt can (and must) be valued using the risk-free interest rate, r_f:

$$D = \frac{X}{(1 + r_f)^T} \quad \text{if} \quad X < V_T^d, \tag{2.24}$$

and the value of the firm's levered equity is, as before,

$$E_L \equiv V_L - D. \qquad \qquad \textbf{(2.25)}$$

To illustrate Equations 2.24 and 2.25, we extend the earlier numerical example by assuming that the firm has debt with $X = 50$. Note that $X = 50 < V_1^d = 81.87$, so the debt is default free. The risk-free rate is $r_f = 0.05 = 5$ percent. Thus, the value of the firm's debt is

$$D = \frac{X}{(1 + r_f)^T} = \frac{50}{(1 + 0.05)^1} = 47.62,$$

and the value of the firm's levered equity is

$$E_L \equiv V_L - D = 100 - 47.62 = 52.38.$$

The Payoffs on Levered Equity   The actual payoff on levered equity at date T depends on the value of the firm's assets at date T. Denoting the equity payoffs in the up and down states as E_T^u and E_T^d,

$$E_T^u = V_T^u - X$$

and

$$E_T^d = V_T^d - X.$$

For the current numerical example,

$$E_1^u = V_1^u - X = 122.14 - 50 = 72.14$$

and

$$E_1^d = V_1^d - X = 81.87 - 50 = 31.87.$$

The Expected Return on Levered Equity   The formula for the expected return on the firm's levered equity, r_{LE}, is

$$r_{LE} = p \left[\frac{E_T^u - E_L}{E_L} \right] + (1 - p) \left[\frac{E_T^d - E_L}{E_L} \right]. \qquad \qquad \textbf{(2.26)}$$

For the current numerical example,

$$r_{LE} = 0.7 \left[\frac{72.14 - 52.38}{52.38} \right] + 0.3 \left[\frac{31.87 - 52.38}{52.38} \right]$$

$$= 0.1460, \text{ or } 14.66\%.$$

The Levered Firm's WACC   Given the computed values of, and expected returns on, the levered firm's debt and equity for this example, we can also verify that the firm's

WACC is equal to the previously calculated expected return on the firm's assets (10.06 percent):

$$\text{WACC} \equiv r_D \left[\frac{D}{D + E_L} \right] + r_{LE} \left[\frac{E}{D + E_L} \right]$$

$$= 5\% \left[\frac{47.62}{100} \right] + 14.66\% \left[\frac{52.38}{100} \right]$$

$$= 10.06\%. \ \checkmark$$

Case 2: Default-Risky Debt

If the firm's debt is default-risky (i.e., $V_T^u > X > V_T^d$), we have a more complex, but still tractable, valuation problem. In the up state, bondholders will receive the promised amount of X, so $D_T^u = X$, and equityholders will receive $E_{LT}^u = V_T^u - X$. In the down state, the firm defaults; bondholders receive $D_T^d = V_T^d < X$, and equityholders receive nothing ($E_{LT}^d = 0$).

We initially value the firm's levered equity. We can do so by creating a risk-free *hedge portfolio* with a long position in the levered firm's assets and a short position in δ units of the firm's levered equity.[6] The value of the hedge ratio, δ, must be chosen to create a risk-free portfolio. The portfolio is risk free if the payoff on the portfolio at date T is the same in both the up and down states; that is, if

$$[V_T^u - \delta E_{LT}^u] = [V_T^d - \delta E_{LT}^d]. \tag{2.27}$$

Solving for δ yields

$$\delta = \frac{V_T^u - V_T^d}{E_{LT}^u - E_{LT}^d}. \tag{2.28}$$

The cost of this portfolio is $V - \delta E_L$, where E_L is the unknown that we wish to determine. The portfolio is riskless, so its present value, or cost, must be equal to the discounted value of the date T payoff, discounting at the risk-free rate. The expressions on both the left side and the right side of Equation 2.27 represent the common date T payoff on the portfolio, so we can choose either. We arbitrarily select the left side expression; the cost of the portfolio must be equal to the present value of this expression:

$$V - \delta E_L = \frac{V_T^u - \delta E_{LT}^u}{(1 + r_f)^T}. \tag{2.29}$$

Solving Equation 2.29 for E_L yields

$$E_L = V \left[\frac{1}{\delta} \right] - \left[V_T^u \left(\frac{1}{\delta} \right) - E_{LT}^u \right] \bigg/ (1 + r_f)^T. \tag{2.30}$$

---

[6] A position in the firm's assets can be created by purchasing both the debt and equity of the firm.

An alternative form of the model can be obtained by recognizing that $E_{LT}^u = V_T^u - X$. Making this substitution in Equation 2.30 and rearranging yields

$$E_L = V\left[\frac{1}{\delta}\right] - \left[X + V_T^u\left\{\frac{1}{\delta} - 1\right\}\right]\bigg/(1 + r_f)^T. \qquad (2.31)$$

Finally, given the value of E_L from either Equation 2.30 or 2.31, the value of the debt is simply

$$D \equiv V - E_L. \qquad (2.32)$$

A Numerical Example   We continue with the current numerical example except that $X = 90$, so the debt is default-risky (i.e., $X = 90 > V_1^d = 81.87$). We initially solve for δ in Equation 2.28:

$$\delta = \frac{V_1^u - V_1^d}{E_{L1}^u - E_{L1}^d} = \frac{122.14 - 81.87}{(122.14 - 90) - 0} = 1.253.$$

Then we use Equation 2.31 to find the value of the firm's levered equity:

$$E_L = V\left[\frac{1}{\delta}\right] - \left[X + V_1^u\left\{\frac{1}{\delta} - 1\right\}\right]\bigg/(1 + r_f)^T$$

$$= 100\left[\frac{1}{1.253}\right] - \left[90 + 122.14\left\{\frac{1}{1.253} - 1\right\}\right]\bigg/(1.05)^1$$

$$= 17.58.$$

The value of the debt is $D = 100 - 17.58 = 82.42$. Note that the value of the debt is less than the value of a default-free bond with the same promised payment and maturity $[X/(1 + r_f) = 90/(1.05) = 85.71]$. This is because in the down state the payoff on the debt will be only 81.87, rather than 90.

2.6.4   A Proof of M&M Proposition I Based on the Binomial Pricing Model

The Binomial Pricing Model can be used to provide a model-specific proof of M&M Proposition I, as follows. Suppose that a firm is initially financed entirely with equity so that the market value of its assets at date 0 is equal to the market value of its unlevered equity, or $V_U \equiv E_U$. At date T, the firm's assets will provide a payoff of either $V_T^u = uV$ or $V_T^d = dV$ in the up and down states, respectively.

Now suppose the firm issues default-free debt that consists of a promise to pay the amount $X < V_T^d$ at date T, and uses the proceeds to retire equity. Following this *recapitalization*, the firm's remaining (levered) equity will receive a payoff of either $E_{LT}^u = V_T^u - X$ or $E_{LT}^d = V_T^d - X$ in the up and down states, respectively, at date T. The debt is riskless, so it is correctly priced using the risk-free discount rate; thus, $D = X/(1 + r_f)^T$. According to M&M Proposition I, the value of the firm's levered equity should be $E_L = V_U - D$, where we note again that V_U is the value of the firm as an unlevered entity.

But suppose that $E_L < V_U - D$; that is, the firm's levered equity is *undervalued*. Under these circumstances, an arbitrageur has the following risk-free arbitrage opportunity. The arbitrageur can purchase the fraction α of both the firm's levered equity and debt. The total cost of these purchases is $\alpha E_L + \alpha D = \alpha(E_L + D)$. The payoffs on this portfolio at date T will be $[\alpha(V_T^u - X) + \alpha X] = \alpha V_T^u$ and $[\alpha(V_T^d - X) + \alpha X] = \alpha V_T^d$ in the up and down states, respectively. The arbitrageur can then place these securities in a trust and sell the entire trust in the market in the form of equity claims against the trust. As the date T payoff on the trust is strictly proportional (with a proportionality factor of α) to the payoff on the equity of the original unlevered firm, the arbitrageur's proceeds from selling the trust will be αV_U. However, $E_L < V_U - D$, so $V_U > E_L + D$, and thus $\alpha V_U > \alpha(E_L + D)$. That is, the proceeds from selling the portfolio are greater than the cost of purchasing it, so the arbitrageur yields an immediate profit of $\alpha V_U - \alpha(E_L + D) = \alpha[V_U - (E_L + D)]$. This arbitrage opportunity would be available to any and all investors in an ideal market, so their collective trading—specifically, their pursuit of the levered firm's shares—will drive up the price of the shares until the arbitrage opportunity vanishes; that is, until $E_L = V_U - D$.

Analogous proofs can be constructed for the case in which $E_L > V_U - D$, as well as the circumstance in which the firm's debt is default-risky. These proofs are left as an exercise for the reader.

2.7   THE VALUATION OF OPTIONS AND THE PRICING OF CORPORATE DEBT AND EQUITY SECURITIES

2.7.1   Introduction

Corporate assets and liabilities, certain equity-related contracts, and management contracts are replete with implicit or explicit *options*, as we will see in later chapters. Moreover, as we show in this section, the equity of a levered firm can be seen as a *call option* on the firm's assets. In addition, options are one of a class of *derivative securities* (which also include forward contracts, futures contracts, and swap contracts) that are important tools that firms use to manage risk, as we discuss in Chapter 19. As you can see, an understanding of options is an essential prerequisite to an understanding of many of the more intricate aspects of corporate financial policies and strategies.

2.7.2   Definitions and Basic Payoff Structures of Call and Put Options

Basic options are of two types, call and put, defined as follows:

Call Option: A call option gives the holder the right (but not an obligation) to *purchase* a specified asset, known as the *underlying asset*, from another party, referred to as the *writer* or *seller* of the option, at a specified price, called the *exercise price* or *strike price*, until a specified future date, known as the *expiration date*. In exchange for this privilege, the holder pays a price to the writer in advance, called the *premium*, though we will refer to it as simply the option's price.

Put Option: A put option gives the holder the right (but not an obligation) to *sell* the underlying asset to the writer at a specified strike price, until the expiration date. In exchange for this privilege, the holder pays a price (or premium) to the writer in advance.

If an option (call or put) can be exercised only on the expiration date, it is called a *European style* option, whereas if the option can be exercised on any day prior to expiration, it is called an *American style* option. In all of the analyses to follow, we focus on European style options. However, the analyses are generally applicable to American options as well, because under most circumstances it is not optimal for the option holder to exercise an American option prior to expiration.

On the expiration date T, the holder of a call option will rationally choose to exercise the option if and only if the price of the underlying asset is greater than the exercise price. Denoting as V_T the price of the underlying asset on the expiration date, and the option's exercise price as X, the holder's rational decision can be expressed as *exercise if and only if $V_T > X$*. Therefore, the payoff on the call option at expiration can be expressed as $Max(V_T - X, 0)$. Further, if we define as C the initial price paid by the option holder, the holder's ex-post profit on an investment in a call option can be expressed as $Max(V_T - X, 0) - C$. For a put option, the corresponding decision is *exercise if and only if $X > V_T$*, so the payoff and profit on the put option are $Max(X - V_T, 0)$ and $Max(X - V_T, 0) - P$, respectively, where P is the initial price of the put.

2.7.3   The Put-Call Parity Theorem

In 1969, Hans Stoll published a seminal paper in the *Journal of Finance* that revealed a fundamental relationship that must hold between the prices of European call and put options written on the same underlying asset (which is assumed to provide no cash flows such as dividends) and that have the same exercise price and expiration date. This relationship is called the *put–call parity equation*, and is based on a risk-free arbitrage argument under the ideal market conditions. The relationship is given in Equation 2.33:

$$V + P = C + \frac{X}{(1 + r_f)^T}, \qquad\qquad \textbf{(2.33)}$$

where V is the current value of the underlying asset.

The Arbitrage Argument That Yields the Put–Call Parity Equation
   The arbitrage argument that leads to Equation 2.33 is quite simple, yet insightful. The left side of the equation is the current cost of a portfolio consisting of the underlying asset and a put option on the underlying asset; the right side is the current cost of a portfolio consisting of a call option on the underlying asset and a risk-free pure-discount bond that provides a payoff of X at date T. So why should the cost of these two portfolios be equal? It is because these two portfolios provide identical payoffs at date T no matter what is the price of the underlying asset on that date. To see this, note that, for both portfolios, the amount of the payoff at date T depends only on V_T, and in

particular whether, at time T, $V_T > X$ or $V \leq X$. The date T payoffs on each portfolio under these two conditions are shown to be equal:

Initial portfolio (cost)	Time T payoff if $V_T > X$	Time T payoff if $V_T \leq X$
$V + P$	$V_T + 0 = V_T$	$V_T + (X - V_T) = X$
$C + X/(1 + r_f)^T$	$(V_T - X) + X = V_T$	$0 + X = X$

Applying the Put–Call Parity Equation to the Values of the
Pure-Discount Debt and Equity of a Levered Firm

The put–call parity relation can be applied directly to specify a relationship that must hold, by arbitrage, between the values of a levered firm's pure-discount debt and its equity. The key insight that yields this result is the recognition of the *limited liability* of equityholders to repay the debt. Specifically, when the debt matures at date T, equityholders will pay off debtholders if and only if the value of the firm, V_T, is greater than the promised payment to debtholders, X; that is, if $V_T > X$. If $V_T < X$, equityholders default, receiving no payoff themselves, and debtholders will take ownership of the firm, thereby receiving a payoff of only V_T instead of the promised payment of X. As such, the firm's equity can be seen as a call option on the firm's assets, with an exercise price of X and time to expiration of T years. Therefore, we can replace C in Equation 2.33 with E_L, and interpret the equation as applying to a firm with underlying assets that have a value of V and pure-discount debt with a promised payment and maturity of X and T, respectively. After doing so and rearranging, we have the following formula for the value of the equity of the levered firm:

$$E_L = V - \left[\frac{X}{(1 + r_f)^T} - P \right].$$ (2.34)

To interpret Equation 2.34, note initially that E_L must also obey the definitional equation $E_L \equiv V - D$. Together, these two equations imply that the value of the firm's debt must be:

$$D = \frac{X}{(1 + r_f)^T} - P.$$ (2.35)

The expression for D in Equation 2.35 provides an interesting interpretation of the value of the debt of a levered firm as equal to the value of a risk-free *counterpart* bond less the value of a put option. In this interpretation, instead of viewing that the debtholders own the firm and have sold a call option on the firm's assets to the equityholders, we take the alternative, though equivalent, view that the equityholders own the firm's assets, have sold a risk-free bond to the debtholders, and simultaneously have purchased a put option from the debtholders that allows the equityholders to sell the firm's assets to the debtholders at a price of X if $V_T < X$. (The put option is, in effect, an insurance policy.) As such, if the firm's debt is default-risky, or equivalently if $P > 0$, the value of the firm's debt is less than the value of a risk-free pure-discount bond with the same promised payment and maturity (i.e., $D < X/(1 + r_f)^T$ if the debt is risky, and the difference is equal to P).

We now illustrate this application of the put–call parity equation using the numbers from the two cases developed earlier for the Binomial Pricing Model. As you recall, for both cases we assumed that $V = 100$, $r_f = 5$ percent, and the firm's debt matures in $T = 1$ year. In the first case, the debt had a promised payment of $X = 50$ and was risk free, so its value is $D = X/(1 + r_f)^T = 50(1.05)^{-1} = 47.62$. Consequently, the value of the levered equity is $E_L = 100 - 47.62 = 52.38$. In other words, the value of the put option, P, in either Equation 2.34 or 2.35 is zero in this case. However, in the second case, $X = 90$ and the debt is risky, with a value of $D = 82.42$, which is less than the value of a risk-free counterpart, $X/(1 + r_f)^T = 90/(1.05) = 85.71$. The difference, $X/(1 + r_f)^T - D = 85.71 - 82.42 = 3.29$, is the value of the put option in Equations 2.34 and 2.35; that is, $P = 3.29$.

2.7.4 The Black–Scholes Option Pricing Model (BSOPM)

In their famous paper published in the *Journal of Political Economy* in 1973, Fisher Black and Myron Scholes developed a formula to value European options written on non–dividend-paying stocks. This model, which is now known as the Black–Scholes Option Pricing Model (BSOPM), was instrumental in the development of the U.S. options markets, which began trading in the same year in Chicago.

Their model can be applied to the pricing of (a) the debt and equity of a levered firm, (b) various options embedded in stock-related securities such as warrants, (c) options embedded in corporate bonds such as call and put provisions, (d) the conversion option in convertible bonds, and (e) stock option grants in executive compensation contracts. We discuss these applications throughout the text. Here, we introduce the model and illustrate its application to the pricing of the debt and equity of a levered firm.

As with the other models we have already discussed, the BSOPM is developed under the assumptions of an ideal capital market. Black and Scholes also assumed that (a) the risk-free interest rate is constant, and (b) the future value of the underlying asset against which the option is written is *log-normally distributed*, or equivalently, the instantaneous *returns* on the underlying asset are *normally distributed* with a constant mean (μ) and variance (σ^2). One question that has been addressed extensively in the finance literature is whether stock returns are normally distributed. Though we do not discuss this literature here, we provide an illustration of the distribution of returns for one stock, IBM. Figure 2-4 shows the distribution of IBM's monthly returns for the years 1980 to 2000. IBM's mean monthly return over this period was 1.21 percent, and its standard deviation was 7.56 percent. Superimposed on this distribution is the probability density associated with a normal distribution that has the same mean and standard deviation.

The derivation of the BSOPM model involves the construction of a risk-free *hedge portfolio* involving the underlying asset and the option, as was the case for the Binomial Pricing Model. For their model, however, Black and Scholes must assume that this risk-free portfolio will be continuously rebalanced. Nevertheless, a risk-free portfolio can be constructed at each instant of time because, instantaneously, the returns on the asset and the option are perfectly correlated. By continually rebalancing the hedge portfolio so that it remains risk free, Black and Scholes were able to derive a *closed form solution* for the price of the option using *continuous-time mathematics*. The BSOPM equation for the price, C, of a European call option is given in Equation 2.36:

$$C = V[N(d)] - e^{-r_f T}X[N(d - \sigma\sqrt{T})], \qquad (2.36)$$

FIGURE 2-4   The Distribution of IBM's Monthly Stock Returns, 1980–2000

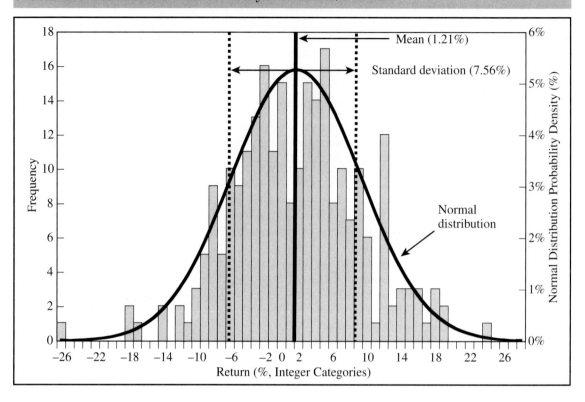

where

$$d = \frac{\ln\left(\dfrac{V}{X}\right) + [r_f + (\sigma^2/2)]T}{\sigma\sqrt{T}},$$

V is the current value of the underlying asset, X is the exercise price of the option, σ is the annual standard deviation of returns on the underlying asset, T is the time to expiration of the option in years, r_f is the annual risk-free rate, $N(d)$ is the cumulative standard normal probability density function evaluated at d, and $\ln(x)$ is the natural log function. A table of values of $N(d)$ for various values of d is provided in Appendix B. Analytically, it can be shown that the value of the call option is an increasing function of V, r, σ and T, and is a decreasing function of X.

It can also be shown that the BSOPM is consistent with the put–call parity Equation 2.33. Therefore, the value of a put option can also be calculated using Equation 2.36 by initially calculating the value of the corresponding call option (i.e., a call option on the same underlying asset with the same exercise price and expiration date as the put option), and then using the put–call parity Equation 2.33 to solve for P. Analytically, the value of the put option is an increasing function of X, σ, and T and a decreasing function of V and r_f.

In the remainder of this section, we illustrate the use of the BSOPM to determine the values, risk, and expected returns on the debt and equity of a levered firm. In later chapters, we provide examples of the use of the BSOPM to price other options and to address other valuation and financing issues.

2.7.5   Using the BSOPM to Determine the Values of the Debt and Equity of a Levered Firm

To use the BSOPM to determine the values of the debt and equity of a levered firm, we follow the same approach that we employed with the Binomial Pricing Model and the put–call parity equation, so we will not repeat all of these details. In short, the idea is to use Equation 2.36 to value the firm's levered equity (i.e., as a call option), and then simply use the value identity of $D \equiv V - E_L$ to value the firm's pure-discount debt. Of course, to do so we require input values for V, r_f, X, σ, and T, noting that in this application σ is the annual standard deviation of returns on the firm's *assets*.

A Numerical Example

To illustrate, we consider the two cases developed in the section on the Binomial Pricing Model and also used to illustrate the put–call parity equation. In the first case, $V = 100, r_f = 5$ percent, $X = 50, \sigma = 20$ percent, and $T = 1$ year. For these values, the BSOPM values of the firm's debt and levered equity are $E_L = 52.44$ and $D = 47.56$, respectively. These values differ only slightly from the values obtained using the Binomial Pricing Model using essentially the same inputs (i.e., we found $E_L = 52.38$ and $D = 47.62$).

In the second case, the values of all parameters are the same except that $X = 90$. For this case, the BSOPM values of the firm's debt and levered equity are $D = 83.30$ and $E_L = 16.70$, respectively. Again, these values differ only slightly from those obtained using the Binomial Pricing Model (i.e., we found $D = 82.42$ and $E_L = 17.58$).

2.7.6   Using the BSOPM to Assess the Risk of the Debt and Equity of a Levered Firm

The BSOPM also can be used to develop formulas for the risk of both the debt and equity of the levered firm (see Galai and Masulis 1976 for details). The formulas are based in part on the fact that, instantaneously, returns on both the debt and equity of the levered firm are perfectly correlated with the returns on the firm's assets, though with different sensitivities. For the simple levered firm described above, it can be shown that the instantaneous annual standard deviations of the returns on a levered firm's debt and equity, σ_D and σ_{LE}, respectively, are

$$\sigma_D = [1 - N(d)]\left(\frac{V}{D}\right)\sigma \tag{2.37}$$

and

$$\sigma_{LE} = [N(d)]\left(\frac{V}{E_L}\right)\sigma. \tag{2.38}$$

The Weighted-Average Risk of Capital via the BSOPM

The firm is a portfolio of its debt and equity, so the standard deviations of the returns on the firm's assets, debt, and equity must adhere to the two-asset portfolio standard deviation Equation (2.9). Furthermore, as noted earlier, returns on both the firm's debt and equity are instantaneously perfectly correlated with returns on the firm's assets, so their returns are also instantaneously perfectly correlated. Therefore, the reduced-form formula for the relationship between σ, σ_D, and σ_{LE} is

$$\sigma = \sigma_D \left[\frac{D}{V} \right] + \sigma_{LE} \left[\frac{E_L}{V} \right]. \tag{2.39}$$

Numerical Examples   To illustrate, in the first of the two cases discussed earlier (where $V = 100$, $r_f = 5$ percent, $X = 50$, $\sigma = 20$ percent, and $T = 1$ year), the BSOPM values for the debt and equity were found to be $D = 47.56$ and $E_L = 52.44$. Using Equations 2.37 and 2.38, we find that $\sigma_D = 0.00004$, or 0.004 percent per annum, and $\sigma_{EL} = 0.3814$, or 38.14 percent per annum, which is nearly twice the standard deviation of the firm's assets. Finally, we can use Equation 2.39 to check these results:

$$\sigma = \sigma_D \left[\frac{D}{V} \right] + \sigma_{LE} \left[\frac{E_L}{V} \right]$$

$$0.20 = 0.00004(0.4756) + 0.3814(0.5244)$$
$$0.20 = 0.0000 + 0.2000$$
$$0.20 = 0.20. \qquad\qquad ✓$$

In the second case, all of the parameters are the same except that $X = 90$. The BSOPM values for the debt and equity were found to be $D = 83.30$ and $E_L = 16.70$, respectively. The security standard deviations are $\sigma_D = 0.0457$, or 4.57 percent per annum, and $\sigma_{EL} = 0.9697$, or 96.97 percent per annum. The results of the check using Equation 2.39 are

$$\sigma = \sigma_D \left[\frac{D}{V} \right] + \sigma_{LE} \left[\frac{E_L}{V} \right]$$

$$0.20 = 0.0457(0.8330) + 0.9697(0.1670)$$
$$0.20 = 0.0381 + 0.1619$$
$$0.20 = 0.20. \qquad\qquad ✓$$

Two Broader Perspectives on the Risk of the Securities of a Levered Firm via the BSOPM

Figures 2-5 and 2-6 provide broader perspectives on the relationships illustrated in the numerical examples above. In both figures, we use the following parameter values as a basis: $V = 100$, $\sigma = 0.20$, $r_f = 5$ percent, and $T = 1$ year. Figure 2-5 shows σ_{LE}, σ_D, and the market leverage ratio D/V, all as functions of X. The values of all three variables increase with X. At extremely high leverage levels, σ_{LE} exceeds 100 percent per annum, and σ_D approaches σ.

Figure 2-6 displays combinations of σ and D/V that yield values of σ_D of 1, 5, 10, and 20 percent. Figure 2-6 can be used in a variety of ways. For instance, if we take the risk of a firm's assets, σ, as given, then the firm's choice of leverage determines the risk

FIGURE 2-5   Annual Return Standard Deviations for the Equity (σ_{EL}) and Debt (σ_D) of a Levered Firm, and Market Debt Ratio, *D/V*, All as Functions of the Promised Payment, *X*, on 5-Year Pure-Discount Debt

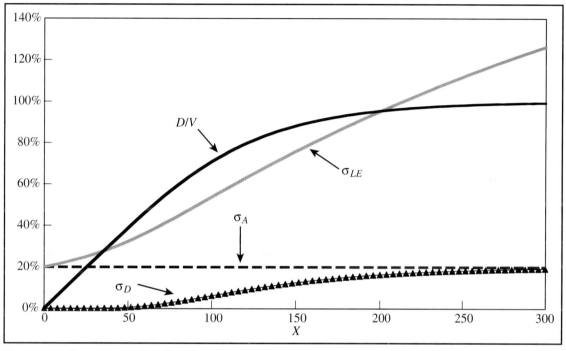

V = 100 throughout. Values are based on the BSOPM.

of the firm's debt. Alternatively, if the firm desires to restrict the risk of the debt that it issues, it must restrict its leverage accordingly.

2.7.7   Using the BSOPM to Determine the Expected Returns on a Levered Firm's Debt and Equity

Given the expected return on the firm's assets, r_A, as well as V, σ, X, T, and r_f, the expected returns on the firm's debt and equity, r_D and r_{EL}, respectively, can be determined using the BSOPM structure. The relevant equations are 2.40 and 2.41:

$$r_D = r_f + \left[(1 - N(d)) \frac{V}{D} \right] (r_A - r_f) \tag{2.40}$$

and

$$r_{LE} = r_f + \left[N(d) \left(\frac{V}{E_L} \right) \right] (r_A - r_f). \tag{2.41}$$

Moreover, these equations yield values for r_D and r_{LE} that, along with the corresponding values of D and E_L, are consistent with the requirement that their weighted average (i.e., the WACC) is equal to r_A, as specified in Equation 2.5.

FIGURE 2-6   Combinations of Leverage (D/V) and Asset Standard Deviation (σ) Yielding Standard Deviations of 1, 5, 10, and 20 percent for the Firm's 5-Year Pure Discount Debt

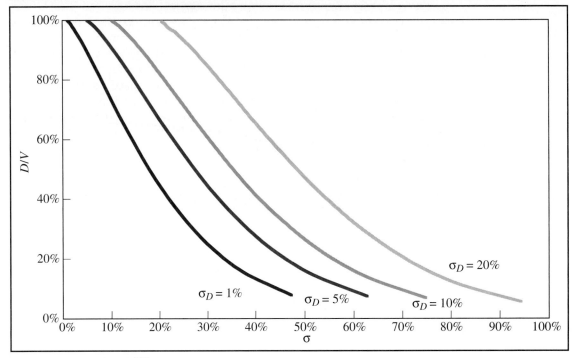

Values are based on the BSOPM.

To illustrate, we continue with the two cases developed earlier. In addition, we assume that $r_A = 10$ percent. In the first case, $X = 50$. Using Equations 2.40 and 2.41, the expected returns on the firm's debt and equity are $r_D = 5.001$ percent, and $r_{LE} = 14.534$ percent. Using Equation 2.5 as a check, we find

$$r_A = r_D \left[\frac{D}{V} \right] + r_{LE} \left[\frac{E_L}{V} \right]$$

$10\% = 5.001\%(0.4756) + 14.534\%(0.5244)$
$10\% = 2.3785\% + 7.6216\%$
$10\% = 10\%.$ ✓

In the second case, $X = 90$, and expected returns on the firm's debt and equity are $r_D = 6.142$ percent and $r_{LE} = 29.243$ percent. Again using Equation 2.5 as a check, we find

$$r_A = r_D \left[\frac{D}{V} \right] + r_{LE} \left[\frac{E_L}{V} \right]$$

$10\% = 6.142\%(0.8330) + 29.243\%(0.1670)$
$10\% = 5.116\% + 4.884\%$
$10\% = 10\%.$ ✓

2.7.8   A Firm-Specific Security Market Line Based on the BSOPM

Working with the two-asset portfolio formulas, Equations 2.8 and 2.9, it is a simple matter to verify that when two (or more) risky assets are perfectly positively correlated, their plotted points in r–σ space must be collinear, and the line must also pass through the point representing the return on the risk-free security, as a no-arbitrage condition. As we have noted, in the setting of the BSOPM the returns on the assets, equity, and debt of a levered firm are all (instantaneously) perfectly correlated, so Equations 2.37, 2.38, 2.40, and 2.41 must yield points in r–σ space that are collinear with the points representing the levered firm's assets and the risk-free security.

Figure 2-7 shows that this is indeed the case for the examples that we have been analyzing. The points representing the risk-free security, the levered firm's assets, as well as its debt and equity, are all collinear. Indeed, we might refer to this line as a *firm-specific security market line*.

2.8   RECONCILING THE M&M PROPOSITIONS, THE CAPM, AND THE BSOPM

For our final analysis, we show how the M&M propositions, the CAPM, and the BSOPM can be reconciled with respect to various aspects of the pricing of the assets, debt, and equity of a levered firm. Although a formal proof of this reconciliation can be

FIGURE 2-7   An Illustration of a Firm-Specific Security Market Line

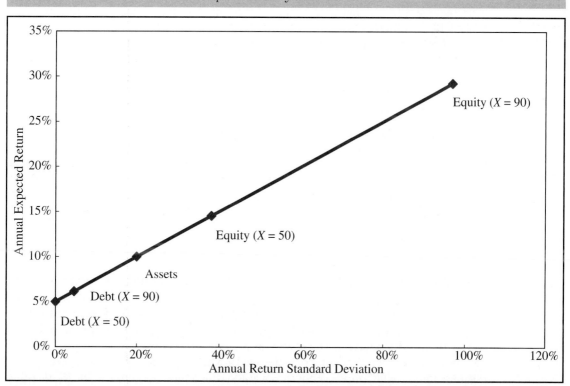

Parameter values are V = 100, r$_f$ = 5%, σ = 20%, T = 1 year, and X = 50 or X = 90 as indicated. Values are based on the BSOPM.

constructed, here we simply illustrate it by reconciling a numerical example that we have been presenting throughout the chapter.

We begin by invoking the CAPM. We assume that $r_f = 5$ percent and $r_M = 12$ percent, and that the beta of the focal firm's assets is $\beta_A = 0.7143$. Thus, the security market line (SML) equation (2.18) can be used to determine the equilibrium expected return on the firm's assets, r_A:

$$r_A = 0.05 + 0.7143[0.12 - 0.05] = 0.10, \text{ or } 10\%.$$

Next, for completeness we assume that the value of the firm's assets, $V = 100$, has been determined in the market by discounting the expected value of the firm's assets after 1 year, $E(V_1) = 110.00$, at the equilibrium discount rate of $r_A = 10$ percent:

$$V = \frac{E(V_1)}{(1 + r_A)^T} = \frac{110}{(1.10)^1} = 100.$$

Thus, the value of the firm's assets is consistent with the CAPM.

Next, we invoke the BSOPM to value the firm's pure-discount debt and levered equity, using parameter values of $V = 100$, $\sigma = 20$ percent, $r_f = 5$ percent, $X = 90$, and $T = 1$ year. Our work in the previous section yielded the following values: $D = 83.30$ and $E_L = 16.70$. Note that the sum of the values of the firm's debt and equity obtained from the BSOPM is equal to the value of the firm, $V = 100$, so the BSOPM results are consistent with M&M Proposition I.

However, the assigned values of β_A, applicable to the CAPM, and σ, applicable to the BSOPM, must be reconciled with each other. This can be accomplished by assuming that the return on the assets over any period t, denoted as R_{At}, can be described by Equation 2.42 below, which is known as the *market model*:

$$R_{At} = \alpha_A + \beta_A R_{Mt} + \epsilon_{At}, \tag{2.42}$$

where $\beta_A R_{Mt}$ and ϵ_{At} are the *systematic* (or *market-related*) and *firm-specific* components of R_{At}, respectively, and are assumed to be independent. The market model allows us to decompose the variance of the asset's returns into the two components shown in Equation 2.43:

$$\sigma^2 = \beta_A^2 \sigma_M^2 + \sigma_{\epsilon A}^2, \tag{2.43}$$

where $\beta_A^2 \sigma_M^2$ and $\sigma_{\epsilon A}^2$ are the firm's *market risk* and *firm-specific risk*, respectively. The CAPM is consistent with, though not dependent upon, the market model. Equation 2.43 is useful because it provides a relationship between σ, which is relevant for the BSOPM, and β_A, which is relevant for the CAPM. Of course, we have specified the values of these parameters as $\sigma = 0.20$ and $\beta_A = 0.7143$. However, Equation 2.43 also includes the parameters σ_M and $\sigma_{\epsilon A}$, neither of which has been specified. Therefore, we must assume a value for one of these variables, which then forces the value of the other and completes the reconciliation. We assume that $\sigma_M = 0.18$ (or 18 percent), which implies that $\sigma_{\epsilon A} = 0.1532$:

$$\sigma^2 = \beta_A^2 \sigma_M^2 + \sigma_{\epsilon A}^2$$
$$0.20^2 = 0.7143^2(0.18)^2 + 0.1532^2$$
$$0.04 = 0.01653 + 0.02347$$
$$0.04 = 0.04. \qquad\qquad ✓$$

Next, we reconcile expected returns on the firm's debt and levered equity, which can be calculated using either the BSOPM or the CAPM. In the previous section, we used the BSOPM to calculate the expected returns on the debt and equity for this example, and found $r_D = 6.142$ percent and $r_{LE} = 29.243$ percent. These expected returns should reconcile with numbers that can be obtained from the CAPM's SML Equation 2.18. However, to perform this reconciliation, we must know the betas of the debt and equity, β_D and β_{LE}, respectively. These betas can be calculated using Equations 2.44 and 2.45, which are based on the BSOPM:

$$\beta_D = \left[(1 - N(d)) \frac{V}{D} \right] \beta_A \qquad\qquad \textbf{(2.44)}$$

and

$$\beta_{LE} = \left[(N(d)) \frac{V}{E_L} \right] \beta_A. \qquad\qquad \textbf{(2.45)}$$

The resulting values are $\beta_D = 0.1632$ and $\beta_{LE} = 3.463$. Therefore, via the CAPM, the expected returns on the debt and equity are

$$r_D = 0.05 + 0.1632(0.12 - 0.05) = 0.06142, \text{ or } 6.142\%,$$

and

$$r_{LE} = 0.05 + 3.463(0.12 - 0.05) = 0.29243, \text{ or } 29.243\%,$$

both of which coincide precisely with the values obtained earlier.

Of course, the values and expected returns on the firm's assets, debt, and levered equity also should be consistent with the WACC equation (2.5). A check reveals that this is the case:

$$r_A = r_D \left[\frac{D}{D + E_L} \right] + r_{LE} \left[\frac{E_L}{D + E_L} \right]$$
$$0.10 = 0.06142 \left[\frac{83.30}{100} \right] + 0.29243 \left[\frac{16.70}{100} \right]$$
$$0.10 = 0.10. \ ✓$$

This completes our reconciliation of the three models.

2.9   Summary of Learning Objectives

After studying this chapter, the reader should have a fairly thorough understanding of the setting that we refer to as an *ideal capital market*, as well as four asset pricing models we analyzed within this setting: *Modigliani and Miller's (M&M) Propositions I and II*; the *Capital Asset Pricing Model (CAPM)*; the *Binomial Pricing Model*; and the *Black-Scholes Option Pricing Model (BSOPM)*. One overriding point regarding these models is that the M&M Propositions, the Binomial Pricing Model, and the BSOPM are based on the concept of *arbitrage*, whereas the CAPM is a *general equilibrium* pricing model based on *Modern Portfolio Theory*.

Regarding the M&M model, Proposition I asserts that the value of a firm with defined assets is independent of its *capital structure*. An important corollary to Proposition I is that the expected return on a firm's assets, r_A, must be constant regardless of the firm's leverage, because r_A is the discount rate implicitly used by the market to discount the firm's future cash flows and therefore to determine the market value of the firm's assets. This implies that the firm's *weighted average cost of capital* (WACC), the value-weighted average of the expected returns on the firm's debt and equity, must be constant for all levels of leverage, and equal to r_A. That is, $r_A = r_D(D/V) + r_{LE}(E_L/V)$. This relationship is used to suggest M&M Proposition II: the expected return on a firm's equity is an increasing function of a measure of the firm's leverage, D/E_L. By solving the previous equation for r_E, we obtain $r_{LE} = r_A + (D/E_L)(r_A - r_f)$. However, Proposition II cannot be proved within the structure of the M&M model, primarily because we cannot specify the behavior of r_D as leverage changes. Fortunately, the CAPM and BSOPM combine to provide the additional structure required to prove Proposition II, at least under the structure imposed by these models.

The CAPM provides a general equilibrium pricing equation for all assets, including the debt and equity of a firm. The CAPM's *security market line* (SML) equation is $r_i = r_f + \beta_i(r_M - r_f)$, where r_i is the expected return on security i, r_f is the risk-free interest rate, β_i (or *beta*) is the relevant measure of security i's risk, and r_M is the expected return on the *market portfolio*, a well-diversified portfolio that includes all risky assets and is held by all investors in equilibrium. The SML provides critical input for the analysis in the chapter, as it specifies the equilibrium value of r_A, given r_f, r_M and β_A. The SML also imposes restrictions on r_D and r_E such that, given r_f and r_M, r_D and r_{LE} are determined by their respective betas, β_D and β_{LE}. However, the CAPM does not specify the values of β_D and β_{LE}, even if β_A, and therefore r_A, are known.

The final piece of the puzzle is provided by the BSOPM. The BSOPM determines the no-arbitrage value of the firm's levered equity, E_L, as the value of a *call option* on the firm's assets. Specifically, for a firm that has equity and one issue of pure-discount debt in its capital structure, the firm's equity can be seen as a call option on the firm's assets, with an *exercise price* of X and *time to expiration* of T, where X and T are the promised payoff and time to maturity of the firm's pure-discount debt. Given V, X, T, r_f, and σ, the BSOPM can be used to determine the values of the firm's levered equity and debt, E_L and D. Moreover, equations associated with the BSOPM can be used to determine r_D and r_{LE} directly, given r_A; or they can be determined indirectly by specifying the values of β_D and β_{LE} (given β_A) and using the CAPM's SML equation.

Review Questions and Problems

1. List and briefly explain the five assumptions of an ideal capital market.

2. Suppose a firm is financed entirely with equity, and the current market value of its assets and equity is $V_U = E_U = 100$. As an arbitrageur, you know that if the firm was capitalized with 50 percent equity and 50 percent debt, the market values of the debt and equity of this levered version of the firm would be $E_L = 60$ and $D_L = 50$, respectively. What would you do?

3. Suppose a firm is financed with 50 percent equity and 50 percent debt, and the current market value of the firm is $V_L = 100$, with $E_L = 50$ and $D = 50$. As an arbitrageur, you know that if the firm was financed entirely with equity, the market value of its assets and equity would be $V_U = E_U = 125$. What would you do?

4. The expected returns on the equity and debt of a levered firm are $r_E = 15$ percent and $r_D = 7$ percent, and the current market value of the equity and debt are $E = 66$ and $D = 44$, respectively. What is the firm's weighted average cost of capital (WACC)?

5. Firm XYZ is currently financed entirely with equity. The market value of the firm's assets and equity is $V_U = E_U = 500$, and the expected return on the firm's assets and equity is $r_A = r_E = 12.5$ percent. Suppose the firm issues debt with a value of $D = 200$, and uses the proceeds to retire equity. The market value of the firm remains the same, $V_L = E_L + D = 500$. If the expected return on the debt is $r_D = 7$ percent, what is the expected return on the firm's levered equity?

6. The expected returns and standard deviations for stocks A and B are $r_A = 14$ percent and $r_B = 19$ percent, respectively, and $\sigma_A = 23$ percent and $\sigma_B = 34$ percent, respectively. The correlation of the returns on the two stocks is $\rho_{AB} = 0.3$. What is the expected return, r_P, and standard deviation, σ_P, of a portfolio with weights of $w_A = 0.60$ and $w_B = 0.40$ in stocks A and B, respectively?

7. Suppose you develop a mutual fund that includes 500 NASDAQ stocks. all with equal weights in the fund's portfolio. The average return standard deviation of the stocks is 44 percent, and the average pairwise correlation among the stocks is 0.30. What is your estimate of the standard deviation of the fund's portfolio?

8. For your retirement fund, you have decided to place 40 percent of your contributions into a risk-free asset that pays 4 percent interest per annum, and the remaining 60 percent in an available stock mutual fund that approximates the holdings of the mythical *market portfolio*. You expect this fund to provide an average return of $r_P = 9$ percent, but will expose you to risk, measured in terms of an estimated standard deviation of $\sigma_P = 20$ percent. What are your estimates of the expected return and standard deviation of your complete portfolio, r_C and σ_C, respectively?

9. Suppose the beta of the stock of Microsoft, Inc., is $\beta_{msft} = 1.45$. If $r_f = 4$ percent and $r_M = 9$ percent, what is the equilibrium expected return on Microsoft stock, r_{msft}, according to the CAPM? As an analyst of the firms in the high-technology industry, you expect Microsoft to provide a return of 10 percent over the next year. Comparing your estimate with the equilibrium expected return on Microsoft that you just calculated, would you recommend to your investors that they buy Microsoft stock?

10. A firm is currently financed with equity, with a market value of $E_L = 250$, and one issue of pure-discount debt with a promised payment of $X = 150$ in $T = 5$ years,

which has a market value of $D = 100$. The risk-free interest rate is $r_f = 4$ percent. Using the put–call parity equation, calculate the value of the equityholders' implicit put option to default on the debt.

11. Using the Binomial Pricing Model, find the values of, and expected returns on, a firm's pure-discount debt and equity given the following parameter values: $V = 500$, $u = 1.5$, $p = 0.7$, $r_f = 5$ percent, $X = 250$, and $T = 3$. Repeat the analysis using $X = 400$.

The following information applies to problems 12 to 15: For a firm financed with equity and a single issue of pure-discount debt, assume that $V = 4,000$, $\sigma = 0.30$, $X = 5,000$, $T = 10$ years, and $r_f = 4$ percent.

12. Verify that the fair value of the firm's equity, according to the BSOPM, is $E_L = 1,686.40$.

13. Calculate the return standard deviations of the firm's debt and equity, σ_D and σ_{LE}, respectively.

14. Calculate the expected returns on the firm's debt and equity, r_D and r_{LE}, respectively, given $r_A = 8$ percent.

15. Calculate the expected returns on the firm's debt and equity, r_D and r_{LE}, respectively, using the CAPM and the BSOPM, given $\beta_A = 0.8$ and $r_M = 9$ percent.

Creative Thinking Issues

1. Without peeking ahead to the remaining chapters of the text, can you think of any implications of violations of one or more of the assumptions that characterize an ideal capital market?

2. How could a commercial bank or investment bank use the analysis in this chapter to evaluate the pending loan or bond issue of a firm?

3. Generate the proof suggested in Section 2.6—that is, a proof of M&M Proposition I within the context of the Binomial Pricing Model where the firm's debt is default-risky.

Projects and Analyses

1. Based on the analysis in this chapter, it is reasonable to hypothesize that the standard deviation of a firm's equity is positively related to the firm's leverage. Obtain the monthly, quarterly, or annual returns on a number of stocks, and calculate the standard deviation of the returns on each stock. Then obtain estimates of the firm's leverage (from the firm's annual report or another source) and regress the estimated standard deviations on the estimated leverage values. The relationship should be positive. (However, the relationship may not hold because, as empirical evidence indicates, riskier firms tend to have lower leverage, a confounding effect.)

2. Find estimates of the betas of a number of stocks using a source such as *Standard and Poors Stock Guide*. From another source, obtain the returns (monthly, quarterly, or annual) on these stocks for the past five years. Regress the average returns on these stocks against their estimated betas as a crude test of the CAPM.

The slope of the regression, which is an estimate of the slope of the SML, should be positive.

3. Check a business newspaper such as the *Wall Street Journal* for quotations on the prices of a pair of call and put options that trade on a given (non–dividend-paying) stock and that have the same exercise price and expiration date. Then obtain an estimate of the risk-free rate by examining the yields on U.S. Treasury securities. Use this data to determine whether the prices of the options are consistent with the put–call parity equation.

4. The BSOPM can be used to calculate the *implied volatility* of a firm's equity, using the following procedure. Find a price quote for a specific call option on a specific (non–dividend-paying) stock, noting also the corresponding price of the stock and exercise price and time to expiration of the option. Estimate the current risk-free rate by examining the yields on U.S. Treasury securities. Then use the BSOPM, in a trial-and-error manner, to determine the value of σ that yields a model price equal to the actual price of the option.

5. For a more challenging project that involves *implied volatility*, estimate the implied volatilities of the stocks of a number of firms by using the procedure described in the previous problem. Then obtain estimates of the leverage of each of these firms, which can be obtained from a variety of sources such as each firm's annual report. Regress the implied volatility estimates on the leverage estimates. According to the analysis in this chapter, the relationship should be positive. (The relationship may not hold, however, because empirical evidence indicates that riskier firms tend to have lower leverage, a confounding effect.)

6. Using the BSOPM and associated equations, investigate the effect of debt maturity on the values, risk, and expected returns on the debt and equity of a levered firm. This can be done using either of two approaches. For both approaches, fix values for V, σ, r_A, and r_f. In the first approach, fix a value of X and vary T, calculating $E_L, D, r_{LE}, r_D, \sigma_{LE}$, and σ_D for each value of T. In the second approach, fix a value for the debt, D, and for each of several values of T, find the value of X that produces the selected value of D, and calculate $E_L, D, r_E, r_D, \sigma_{LE}$, and σ_D for each value of T.

A p p e n d i x   A

Original Proof of M&M Proposition I

The original arbitrage proof of Proposition I provided by Modigliani and Miller is basically as follows. Suppose an unlevered firm exists that generates expected annual earnings of *EARN* and has a current market value of $V_U \equiv E_U$. The firm pays out all of its earnings as dividends. An investor, Mr. Baldy, is considering the purchase of the fraction α of this firm's equity. The initial outlay for this investment, which we will refer to as *Investment 1*, is αV_U, or equivalently, αE_U, and the investment is expected to provide an annual dollar return of $\alpha EARN$:

Investment 1

Initial Outlay
$$\alpha V_U = \alpha E_U$$

Expected Annual Dollar Return
$$\alpha EARN$$

Suppose instead that Mr. Baldy could engage *Investment 2*, the purchase of the fraction α of the equity of a levered firm that generates the same expected yearly earnings, *EARN*, as the unlevered firm above, and has identical risk. The market value of this firm is, of course, $V_L \equiv E_L + D_L$. This firm must pay annual interest on its debt in the amount *INT*, and then pay the residual earnings to equityholders in the form of dividends. Thus, the expected annual dividend to equityholders is *EARN – INT*. The initial outlay and expected annual dollar return from this investment are

---
Investment 2

Initial Outlay
$$\alpha E_L$$

Expected Annual Dollar Return
$$\alpha(EARN - INT)$$

If Mr. Baldy can borrow on the same terms as the levered firm above, he has yet a third investment opportunity. He can borrow the amount αD_L on personal account and use this money plus his own contribution, as necessary, to purchase the fraction α of the stock of the unlevered firm. *Investment 3* therefore requires a net outlay of $\alpha V_U - \alpha D_L$. His yearly net dollar return will be equal to his share of the dividends of the unlevered firm less the yearly interest payments on the money he borrowed:

Investment 3

Initial Outlay (Net)
$$\alpha V_U - \alpha D_L$$

Expected Annual Dollar Return (Net)
$$\alpha(EARN - INT)$$

Notice that the expected annual dollar returns on Investments 2 and 3 are identical. If the initial *costs* of these two investments were not also equal, a risk-free arbitrage opportunity would exist in which an investor could short-sell or *offer* the more expensive investment and undertake or *purchase* the less expensive investment. Thus, as a no-arbitrage condition, Investments 2 and 3 must have the same value:

$$\alpha E_L = \alpha V_U - \alpha D_L$$

or

$$E_L = V_U - D_L$$

or

$$E_L + D_L = V_U.$$

That is, V_L, the value of the levered firm, must be equal to V_U, the value of the unlevered firm. This proves that, in an ideal capital market, the value of a levered firm is equal to the value of an otherwise identical unlevered firm. In other words, capital structure decisions do not affect the value of a firm.

We can use the three investments described above to generate an alternative proof of Proposition I. Suppose that Mr. Baldy wishes to *replicate* Investment 1 using the securities that have been issued by the otherwise-identical levered firm described above. He can do so by purchasing the fraction α of both the debt and equity of the levered firm. His initial outlay will be αD_L for the debt securities and αE_L for the equity securities, or $\alpha(D_L + E_L) \equiv \alpha(V_L)$ in total. The expected dollar returns from his debt and equity investments will be αINT and $\alpha(EARN - INT)$, respectively, or $\alpha[INT + \{EARN - INT\}] = \alpha[EARN]$ in total. Note that the expected dollar return on this investment is identical to that provided by purchasing the fraction α of the unlevered firm (see Investment 1). Therefore, the two investments must have the same value. That is, $\alpha(V_L) = \alpha V_U$, or $V_L = V_U$.

Appendix B

Values of the Cumulative Normal Distribution Function, N(∂), for Various Values of ∂

d	N(d)	d	N(d)	d	N(d)	d	N(d)	d	N(d)	d	N(d)
−3.00	0.0013	−1.60	0.0548	−0.80	0.2119	0.00	0.5000	0.80	0.7881	1.60	0.9452
−2.95	0.0016	−1.58	0.0571	−0.78	0.2177	0.02	0.5080	0.82	0.7939	1.62	0.9474
−2.90	0.0019	−1.56	0.0594	−0.76	0.2236	0.04	0.5160	0.84	0.7995	1.64	0.9495
−2.85	0.0022	−1.54	0.0618	−0.74	0.2296	0.06	0.5239	0.86	0.8051	1.66	0.9515
−2.80	0.0026	−1.52	0.0643	−0.72	0.2358	0.08	0.5319	0.88	0.8106	1.68	0.9535
−2.75	0.0030	−1.50	0.0668	−0.70	0.2420	0.10	0.5398	0.90	0.8159	1.70	0.9554
−2.70	0.0035	−1.48	0.0694	−0.68	0.2483	0.12	0.5478	0.92	0.8212	1.72	0.9573
−2.65	0.0040	−1.46	0.0721	−0.66	0.2546	0.14	0.5557	0.94	0.8264	1.74	0.9591
−2.60	0.0047	−1.44	0.0749	−0.64	0.2611	0.16	0.5636	0.96	0.8315	1.76	0.9608
−2.55	0.0054	−1.42	0.0778	−0.62	0.2676	0.18	0.5714	0.98	0.8365	1.78	0.9625
−2.50	0.0062	−1.40	0.0808	−0.60	0.2743	0.20	0.5793	1.00	0.8413	1.80	0.9641
−2.45	0.0071	−1.38	0.0838	−0.58	0.2810	0.22	0.5871	1.02	0.8461	1.82	0.9656
−2.40	0.0082	−1.36	0.0869	−0.56	0.2877	0.24	0.5948	1.04	0.8508	1.84	0.9671
−2.35	0.0094	−1.34	0.0901	−0.54	0.2946	0.26	0.6026	1.06	0.8554	1.86	0.9686
−2.30	0.0107	−1.32	0.0934	−0.52	0.3015	0.28	0.6103	1.08	0.8599	1.88	0.9699
−2.25	0.0122	−1.30	0.0968	−0.50	0.3085	0.30	0.6179	1.10	0.8643	1.90	0.9713
−2.20	0.0139	−1.28	0.1003	−0.48	0.3156	0.32	0.6255	1.12	0.8686	1.92	0.9726
−2.15	0.0158	−1.26	0.1038	−0.46	0.3228	0.34	0.6331	1.14	0.8729	1.94	0.9738
−2.10	0.0179	−1.24	0.1075	−0.44	0.3300	0.36	0.6406	1.16	0.8770	1.96	0.9750
−2.05	0.0202	−1.22	0.1112	−0.42	0.3372	0.38	0.6480	1.18	0.8810	1.98	0.9761
−2.00	0.0228	−1.20	0.1151	−0.40	0.3446	0.40	0.6554	1.20	0.8849	2.00	0.9772
−1.98	0.0239	−1.18	0.1190	−0.38	0.3520	0.42	0.6628	1.22	0.8888	2.05	0.9798
−1.96	0.0250	−1.16	0.1230	−0.36	0.3594	0.44	0.6700	1.24	0.8925	2.10	0.9821
−1.94	0.0262	−1.14	0.1271	−0.34	0.3669	0.46	0.6772	1.26	0.8962	2.15	0.9842
−1.92	0.0274	−1.12	0.1314	−0.32	0.3745	0.48	0.6844	1.28	0.8997	2.20	0.9861
−1.90	0.0287	−1.10	0.1357	−0.30	0.3821	0.50	0.6915	1.30	0.9032	2.25	0.9878
−1.88	0.0301	−1.08	0.1401	−0.28	0.3897	0.52	0.6985	1.32	0.9066	2.30	0.9893
−1.86	0.0314	−1.06	0.1446	−0.26	0.3974	0.54	0.7054	1.34	0.9099	2.35	0.9906
−1.84	0.0329	−1.04	0.1492	−0.24	0.4052	0.56	0.7123	1.36	0.9131	2.40	0.9918
−1.82	0.0344	−1.02	0.1539	−0.22	0.4129	0.58	0.7190	1.38	0.9162	2.45	0.9929
−1.80	0.0359	−1.00	0.1587	−0.20	0.4207	0.60	0.7257	1.40	0.9192	2.50	0.9938
−1.78	0.0375	−0.98	0.1635	−0.18	0.4286	0.62	0.7324	1.42	0.9222	2.55	0.9946
−1.76	0.0392	−0.96	0.1685	−0.16	0.4364	0.64	0.7389	1.44	0.9251	2.60	0.9953
−1.74	0.0409	−0.94	0.1736	−0.14	0.4443	0.66	0.7454	1.46	0.9279	2.65	0.9960

(continued)

d	$N(d)$	d	$N(d)$	d	$N(d)$	d	$N(d)$	d	$N(d)$	d	$N(d)$
−1.72	0.0427	−0.92	0.1788	−0.12	0.4522	0.68	0.7517	1.48	0.9306	2.70	0.9965
−1.70	0.0446	−0.90	0.1841	−0.10	0.4602	0.70	0.7580	1.50	0.9332	2.75	0.9970
−1.68	0.0465	−0.88	0.1894	−0.08	0.4681	0.72	0.7642	1.52	0.9357	2.80	0.9974
−1.66	0.0485	−0.86	0.1949	−0.06	0.4761	0.74	0.7704	1.54	0.9382	2.85	0.9978
−1.64	0.0505	−0.84	0.2005	−0.04	0.4840	0.76	0.7764	1.56	0.9406	2.90	0.9981
−1.62	0.0526	−0.82	0.2061	−0.02	0.4920	0.78	0.7823	1.58	0.9429	2.95	0.9984

CHAPTER

Separation of Ownership and Control, Principal–Agent Conflicts, and Financial Policies

3.1 INTRODUCTION

This chapter begins our transition from analyses of corporate financial decisions made under ideal capital market conditions (Chapter 2) to a focus on how these decisions are made under real-world conditions. In Chapters 3 through 6, we examine theories of corporate financial decisions that describe several fundamental *real-world factors*, which represent *violations* of the assumptions of the ideal capital market, and explain how firms deal with them. In turn, these theories lay the foundation for topics covered in later chapters.

The overarching consequences of the relaxation of these assumptions are that a firm's *ownership structure*, *management*, and *contracting devices* all emerge to play visible, dynamic, and indeed critical, roles in determining the firm's capital investment policy, financial policies and strategies, and overall value. This is in sharp contrast to the virtual absence of a visible role for ownership structure, management, or contracting devices in the setting of an ideal capital market, where the firm's assets are fixed and known, and the firm engages a simple, irrelevant, once-and-for-all financing decision. In the ideal capital market setting, it is not surprising that a firm's financing decision is independent of its capital investment decision, because the investment decision has already been made! As Modigliani–Miller (M&M) Proposition I illustrates, given the firm's assets, the firm's once-and-for-all financing choice simply determines the distribution of the firm's (known) risk and value among debt and equity claimants.

Of course, even outside the setting of an ideal capital market, the question of how the market determines the values of a firm's assets, debt, and equity is fundamental, and the valuation models discussed in Chapter 2 remain relevant. However, when we relax the assumptions of the ideal capital market, many equally fundamental questions emerge. What should be management's overall objective? What is the firm's optimal size and ownership structure? How does management choose the firm's assets and operating strategy? How does management choose the firm's capital structure? Should the firm pay dividends to shareholders? Do interactions exist between the firm's capital investment and financing choices? How do shareholders select, compensate, and monitor the firm's management? To address these questions effectively, we must understand the roles of ownership structure, management, and contracting devices in a firm.

We begin this chapter by explaining how the theories discussed in Chapter 3 through 6 relate to violations of the assumptions of the ideal capital market. We follow with discussions of (a) the importance of *limited liability* and the *separation of ownership and control* in the corporation, and (b) the directive that a firm's management should follow. These discussions provide necessary background for the main topic of the chapter: Agency Theory and the effects of two important *principal–agent conflicts* on corporate financial policies. The conflicts are between (a) shareholders and management and (b) shareholders and creditors.

3.2   REAL-WORLD FACTORS: VIOLATIONS OF IDEAL CAPITAL MARKET ASSUMPTIONS

In this section, we briefly discuss several real-world factors and their potential effects on a firm's financial policies. These factors are cast in terms of violations of one or more of the assumptions that define the ideal capital market.

3.2.1   Violations of Assumption 1: Frictionless Markets

The first assumption of the ideal capital market is that capital markets are frictionless; that is, they are devoid of transaction costs and taxes. There are at least five potentially important consequences of violations of this assumption.

First, transaction costs and personal taxes may affect investors' ability to undertake arbitrage, which is critical to the development of the M&M Propositions, the Capital Asset Pricing Model (CAPM), the Binomial Pricing Model, and the Black--Scholes Option Pricing Model (BSOPM).

Second, variation in personal tax rates and transaction costs across both investors and securities may differentially affect the values of corporate securities (e.g., debt versus equity), and ultimately a firm's preference for issuing one type of security versus another.

Third, if the firm's earnings are taxed, and interest payments are deductible while dividends are not (as the U.S. corporate tax code specifies), a firm's preference for debt versus equity financing may be determined in part by the effects of taxes on the market value of the firm.

Fourth, if a firm faces substantial transaction costs in issuing securities, such frictions may inhibit its ability to undertake otherwise profitable investment opportunities, and may also affect its choice of debt versus equity financing. Suppose the cost of issuing either debt or equity is substantial, and the cost of issuing equity is substantially higher than the cost of issuing debt. The firm may find it optimal to issue debt rather than equity, which would lead to high leverage. Alternatively, the firm may find that the lowest-cost financing is *internal equity financing* (i.e., funding projects via retained earnings). This policy would impart a bias toward equity financing, and therefore low leverage, and may also require the firm to reduce or eliminate dividends to shareholders.

Fifth, costs of financial distress and bankruptcy, which are basically *transaction costs* associated with the presence of debt in a firm's capital structure, may inhibit the firm's issuance of debt securities. (We discuss these costs in Chapter 6.)

3.2.2   Violations of Assumption 2: All Market Participants Share Homogeneous Expectations

Assumption 2 states that all market participants have the same information regarding value-relevant information concerning a firm. This assumption disallows several real-world problems that may affect a firm's financial decisions and, more fundamentally, the quality of the market for the firm's securities. Chief among these is *information asymmetry* between investors and the firm's management. Owing to their position as *insiders*, a firm's management has more information about the value of the firm than investors. As we will see, this circumstance can affect a firm's financial decisions and market value. (The information asymmetry problem is also relevant to assumption 4.)

3.2.3   Violations of Assumption 3: Atomistic Competition

Assumption 3 states that all investors are *atomistic;* that is, their wealth, or at least the wealth that they are willing to bring to bear to purchase a given firm's securities, is small relative to the total value of a given firm's securities. Here, two real-world factors that constitute violations of this assumption are important. *First*, if an individual investor has either sufficient wealth or sufficient borrowing capacity to purchase or sell a substantial proportion of an individual firm's securities, the investor's trades may affect the market value of these securities. Consequently, the value of the firm's securities, and thus the firm's financial decisions, may reflect the personal preferences and value assessments of such a dominant investor. *Second*, the firm itself can issue substantial quantities of securities, and may have sufficient cash to engage in substantial *repurchases* of outstanding securities. Transactions of either type may affect the market value of the firm's securities.

The Shareholder–Management Principal–Agent Problem

On the other hand, the *satisfaction* of assumption 3 also can be problematic. Closely related to the concept of atomistic competition is the stipulation that the ownership of a firm's securities is *diffuse*. The problem here is that, if no single investor has a substantial portion of his or her wealth invested in a given firm, no investor has an incentive to *monitor* the firm's management to ensure that they are acting in the shareholders' interest.

Under these circumstances, it is difficult to imagine that management would make decisions that are strictly in the shareholders' interest (i.e., in the absence of an effective *incentive device*). Instead, managers will tend to manage the firm in a manner that maximizes their own *utility* rather than shareholders' wealth. We describe this situation as a principal–agent conflict, where the shareholders are the *principals* and managers are the shareholders' *agents*.

In the classic contracting paradigm, an agent is hired by a principal to perform duties that serve the principal's interests. (For example, you are the principal when you hire a taxicab driver, the agent, to take you to the airport.) The problem is that the agent also has an incentive to serve his or her *own* interests, which may conflict with the interests of the principal. In Section 3.7 we discuss theory regarding conflicts of interest between shareholders and management.

In Chapter 5, we discuss several contracting devices that can be used to mitigate conflicts of interest between shareholders and managers. One such device is the requirement that managers hold the firm's equity shares (or options on the firm's shares) in their personal portfolios. Devices such as this, though imperfect, serve to *align* the interests of shareholders and management. However, such devices are often costly. In the present case, depending on the size of managers' holdings of their firm's shares relative to the aggregate number of shares outstanding, the above requirement may result in the firm's shares being closely held by the firm's managers. If so, the requirement results in a substantial violation of the assumption of atomistic competition. Moreover, the *liquidity* of the firm's shares may be compromised. (We discuss the importance of liquidity later in the chapter.) In any event, it is ironic that an assumption of the ideal capital market must be violated to mitigate the adverse effects of a particular real-world problem!

3.2.4   Violations of Assumption 4: The Firm's Capital Investment Program Is Fixed and Known

Relaxing the assumption that the firm's capital investment program is *fixed* engenders a number of possible interactions between the firm's investment and financing decisions. For example, suppose a firm initially engages a capital investment program that is financed with both debt and equity. As we will show in this chapter, if the debt is default-risky, the firm's management, acting in the shareholders' interest, has an incentive to change the capital investment program in a manner that results in an *expropriation* of wealth from the debtholders to the equityholders.

Violation of the assumption that all market participants *know* the details of the firm's capital investment program also presents problems. Theory posits that a firm's management must keep strategic information regarding its operations private (i.e., known confidentially by insiders only). As such, we have the information asymmetry problem noted earlier. As we discuss in Chapter 4, information asymmetry can have a deleterious effect on the quality of the market for a firm's securities. Briefly, one resolution to this problem is for management to *signal* the firm's value via their willingness to invest a substantial portion of their personal wealth in the firm's shares. By doing so, however, the firm's managers may own a substantial proportion of the firm's shares, and therefore would not be atomistic competitors. So again, we have the ironic situation that an assumption of the ideal capital market must be violated to resolve a particular real-world problem.

3.2.5   Violations of Assumption 5: Once Chosen, the Firm's Financing Is Fixed

Suppose a firm initially finances its assets with specified proportions of debt and equity, and then later issues additional debt, using the proceeds to pay a dividend to shareholders. If the new debt has the same priority as the original debt, the value of the original debt will probably fall, an effect called *claim dilution*. Moreover, the firm's shareholders have an incentive to take such an action, because shareholders' wealth likely increases by the amount of the original debtholders' loss (i.e., the sum of the dividend and the market value of the remaining equity will be greater than the total value of the equity prior to the issuance of the new debt). The shareholders will have thereby *expropriated wealth* from the original debtholders.

This is an example of the second of the two principal–agent conflicts that we discuss. In this case, the principals are debtholders and the agents are shareholders. The possibility that management would take expropriatory actions against debtholders on shareholders' behalf has potentially serious consequences for the firm's ability to raise funds by issuing debt securities (i.e., debt versus equity financing of a firm may no longer be a matter of indifference).

3.2.6   Summary and Perspective

This section impresses the point that much of what is interesting, important, and challenging about corporate financial policies and strategies relates to *real-world factors*, which represent violations of the assumptions of an ideal capital market. The discussion also motivates our analyses later in this chapter and in Chapters 4 through 6, where we examine these factors and how firms deal with them on a formal, theoretical basis. However, as we delve into real-world problems, there are three reasons we should not abandon the lessons learned from the valuation models presented in Chapter 2.

First, even if one or more of the ideal capital market assumptions is violated, the fundamental conclusions drawn from these theoretical models may yet hold, at least in approximation. To the extent that this is so, they provide insights of the first order with respect to the effects of corporate financial decisions on both risk and value.

Second, a variety of legal structures (e.g., corporate law and the U.S. Securities and Exchange Commission), institutions (e.g., commercial banks, investment banks, and securities exchanges), and contracting devices (e.g., provisions in bond contracts and executive compensation contracts) exist that serve, at least in part, to mitigate either the extent of the violations themselves or their adverse effects. As such, they serve to establish capital markets that, as closely as practicable, approximate the ideal. We discuss these structures, institutions, and contracting devices throughout the remainder of the text, giving special attention to them in Chapter 5.

Third, as we will see, analyses of the effects of these real-world factors often rely on predictions that emerge from the valuation models presented in Chapter 2, at least as a backdrop.

3.3   LIMITED LIABILITY AND THE SEPARATION OF OWNERSHIP AND CONTROL

The *corporation* is a distinct legal entity, tethered to its owners with equity shares. Two of the most important features of the corporate form of business organization are *limited liability* and the *separation of ownership and control*.

3.3.1   Limited Liability

Under the limited liability provision, shareholders' financial responsibility for any and all liabilities that the corporation incurs is limited to the assets of the corporation, and does not extend to shareholders' personal assets (whether the shareholder is an individual, a financial institution, another corporation, or any other entity). If the corporation defaults on its liabilities, creditors may force the firm into *bankruptcy proceedings*, but their claims are limited to corporate assets. Alternatively, if the firm's liabilities become onerous, the firm can *voluntarily* enter bankruptcy proceedings as a means of protecting shareholders' financial interest in the firm. (We discuss corporate bankruptcy proceedings in detail in Chapter 18.)

3.3.2   Separation of Ownership and Control

In an influential book, Berle and Means (1932) were first to formally discuss issues associated with the separation of ownership and control in the modern corporation. In most large firms, *ownership* is vested in one group, the shareholders, whereas *control* of the firm's operations is vested in a separate group, management, who are hired by the shareholders,[1] though we hasten to note the important and common circumstance in which management holds some of the firm's shares, or conversely, some shareholders are part of the management team.

To a certain extent, the separation of ownership and control simply reflects a common dichotomy in virtually any economy. Some individuals have *capital*, but lack the time and/or expertise to undertake profitable real investments; other individuals have the *expertise* to undertake profitable real investments, but lack capital. The corporation brings together these two factors of production, capital and labor, under a formal, efficient structure.

3.3.3 Both Limited Liability and Separation Reflect Investors' Risk Aversion

Both limited liability and the separation of ownership and control reflect investors' *risk aversion*. Regarding limited liability, each shareholder is concerned about the preservation, as well as the growth, of his or her personal wealth. The limited liability feature of the corporation allows an investor to make an equity investment in a firm without risking his or her personal wealth beyond the amount invested in the firm. This is particularly important because shareholders relinquish control of the corporation, and therefore their equity investment, to management. Moreover, as Jensen and Meckling (1976) point out, if shareholders' liability were unlimited, individual shareholders would wish to monitor each other's wealth so as to estimate their own liability, which would be very costly if shares were widely held.

The separation of ownership and control also allows shareholders to reduce the risk of their private portfolios by diversifying their equity investments across firms. This would be difficult if they also had to exercise control over each firm's operations. Indeed, the value to shareholders of diversification is so great that the separation of ownership and control is a virtual necessity for the successful financing of large corporations. The separation is necessary in part because diversification generally implies that none of the equityholders of a given corporation will have a sufficient proportional stake in the firm, nor will they have a sufficient portion of their personal wealth invested in a single firm, to warrant the effort required to actively manage, or perhaps even to *monitor*, the firm's operations. Consequently, shareholders must hire managers and delegate control of each firm's operations to them.

3.3.4 Reaping the Benefits of Diversification

Diversification not only reduces the risk of investors' personal portfolios, but also indirectly increases the *liquidity* of their equity investments. The *liquidity* of a security is defined in terms of an investor's ability to buy or sell the security quickly, at a low transaction cost, and at a price that reflects its fair market value. Liquidity is important to investors because the ultimate purpose of investment is to provide for future consumption, which the investor may desire either sooner or later.

---

[1]More precisely, shareholders elect a board of directors, who then hire the firm's top management, who in turn hire the next level of management, and so on.

Diversification increases the liquidity of equity shares via the following sequence of events. *First*, *en masse* diversification among shareholders leads to a wide dispersion of each firm's shares among investors. *Second*, ownership diffusion fosters the development of a *secondary market* for a firm's shares, wherein investors can buy or sell a security according to their need for an investment versus liquidity. *Third*, as a positive feedback effect, the development of liquid secondary markets for the shares of many

FIGURE 3-1   Diversification's Positive Feedback Loop

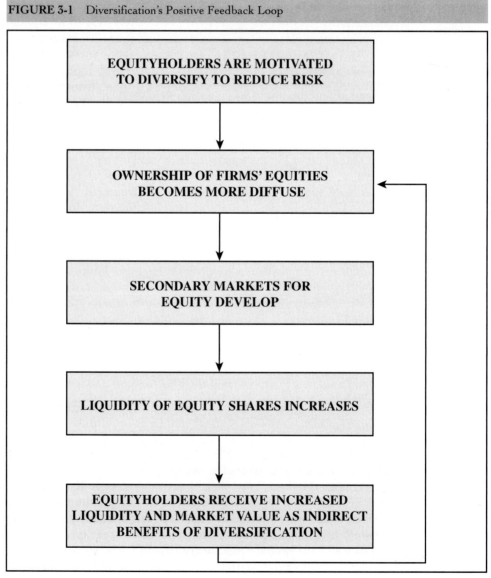

Equityholders' Motivation to Diversify Leads to Diffuse Ownership, Increased Value, and Enhanced Liquidity

firms further facilitates investors' ability to diversify. This chain of developments is illustrated in Figure 3.1.

Moreover, ownership diffusion and attendant diversification have at least three positive effects on the value of a firm's shares. *First*, based on our analysis of portfolio theory and the CAPM in Chapter 2, well-diversified investors demand an expected return premium only for the *systematic risk* of a firm's shares, because *firm-specific risk* is eliminated through diversification. If instead investors were not diversified, they may well demand compensation for the firm's *total risk*, and as a result the value of each firm's shares would likely be lower (and their cost of equity capital would be higher, which would limit capital investment).

Second, the value of any security is positively related to its liquidity, and the natural development of secondary markets among diversified investors increases the liquidity of each firm's securities. *Third*, both shareholders' diversification and the existence of a liquid secondary market for a firm's shares improves the firm's ability to generate new equity funds to pursue profitable capital investment projects over time, whether these funds are generated internally via retained earnings or externally though the issuance of stock.

Regarding internal equity, if shareholders were not diversified and/or a liquid secondary market did not exist for a firm's equity, shareholders would likely require the firm to pay higher dividends (which constitute a periodic, partial liquidation of the firm's assets) as a substitute for the illiquidity of the firm's shares. Dividends reduce the pool of internally generated funds available to the firm to pursue profitable investment projects. (We discuss dividend policy in depth in Chapter 14.) Regarding new external equity, the firm is in a better position to attract new equity funds if shareholders are diversified and a liquid secondary market for the firm's shares exists. (We discuss a firm's *initial public offering* [IPO] of stock in Chapter 12, and *seasoned equity offerings* [SEOs] in Chapter 13.)

3.4   THE CRITICAL ROLE OF MANAGEMENT IN A FIRM WITH DIFFUSE OWNERSHIP

For shareholders to realize the numerous benefits of diffuse ownership and diversification detailed above, managers must be hired to develop and manage each firm's capital investment projects. Shareholders, as principals, must hire managers, as agents, for the obvious reason, noted above, that in a firm with diffuse ownership no individual shareholder has a sufficient stake in the firm to warrant spending their time controlling, or perhaps even monitoring, the firm's operations. Therefore, *management is hired to act in the shareholders' interest*.

But this arrangement raises a number of questions. Is there a single common interest among a diffuse group of shareholders? If so, can shareholders devise a contract with management that will ensure that management will act strictly in accordance with the shareholders' interest? What operational and financial policies and strategies should management follow to act in the shareholders' interest? Are the firm's financial policies and strategies affected by the nature of management's contract with shareholders? We begin to address these questions in this chapter, and pursue them at length in later chapters.

3.5   THE CLASSIC DIRECTIVE TO MANAGEMENT: MAXIMIZE THE FIRM'S MARKET VALUE

Traditionally, the assumed common interest of a firm's shareholders has been expressed in the following directive to the firm's management, which we call the *classic directive to management:*

Classic Directive: *Maximize the Market Value of the Firm (V).*

As we ponder this directive, two basic questions emerge immediately. *First*, is this the appropriate dictum to management? *Second*, if it is the appropriate dictum, will management adhere to it? These are important questions fraught with complex issues, so we address them in a series of discussions that encompass the remainder of the chapter.

3.5.1   Maximizing V for an All-Equity Firm with a Perfect Contract with Management

Initially, we invoke two assumptions (which are relaxed later) that allow us to limit the breadth of the issues involved. *First*, we assume that the firm is financed entirely with equity shares that (a) are owned by a diffuse group of shareholders and (b) trade publicly in a liquid secondary market. *Second*, we assume that shareholders have a perfect contract with management. That is, shareholders have been able to devise a contract that ensures that management will act strictly in the shareholders' interest. With these assumptions, maximizing the market value of the firm, V, is equivalent to maximizing the market value of the firm's equity, E_U. Moreover, the classic directive is appropriate, for reasons discussed next.

3.5.2   Market Value as the Best Criterion According to the Efficient Market Hypothesis

The market value of a firm's shares emerges from trading among investors. If investors (at least collectively) are rational, the market value of the firm's shares will be equal to their *true value*, defined simply as the (appropriately discounted) present value of future expected cash flows. This argument is the essence of the well-known *Efficient Market Hypothesis* (Fama 1970). We formally discuss the Efficient Market Hypothesis in Chapter 9. For now, we briefly explain the implications of this hypothesis for management decisions regarding both capital investments and financing.

Regarding capital investment decisions, as introductory corporate finance textbooks show, management should undertake any and all projects that increase the firm's stock price—that is, all projects that have a positive *net present value* (*NPV*). However, management can correctly determine a project's *NPV* only if they know how the market will value the project's future cash flows. Therefore, it is incumbent upon management to have knowledge of the market's pricing process. For instance, the CAPM may or may not accurately reflect the market's pricing of risky assets. If it does, management should employ it to value projects and decide on their adoption. If it does not, management should be aware of whatever process the market uses to price the firm's projects, and use that process in deciding whether to adopt a given project.

The Efficient Market Hypothesis is not dependent on the correctness of any specific pricing model. At the same time, however, the Efficient Market Hypothesis makes only a *qualitative* statement about market prices in that it does not specify the market's pricing process—only that it is rational. The hypothesis simply states that investors rationally and continuously impound all information about a project or an entire firm (including rationally determined expectations about its future cash flows and their riskiness) in determining the value of a project or a firm.

Regarding financing decisions, the Efficient Market Hypothesis applies both under ideal capital market conditions and in the presence of real-world factors. As you recall, under ideal capital market assumptions the firm's financing decisions are a matter of indifference; that is, they do not affect the market value of the firm. Thus, if the market is ideal, the value of a firm, determined rationally in the market, is unrelated to the firms' financing decisions.

However, a critical point brought out by the Efficient Market Hypothesis is that financing decisions are a matter of indifference *only if* they convey no new information to the market about the value of the firm's future cash flows. In an ideal market, financing decisions are *forced* to be value-irrelevant, because we assume that the firm's assets are fixed and known, and therefore the subsequent financing decision conveys no new information. However, as we will see, under real-world conditions financing decisions may convey new information to the market about the value of the firm or a specific project.

The Bottom Line

In the case of an all-equity firm, two arguments can be used to justify the classic directive to management to maximize the market value of the firm. *First*, if the market is efficient, the market value of the firm is equal to the firm's true value. That is, the market value of the firm rationally impounds a great deal of information about the firm's risk and profit potential, and management can use it as a guide for better financial decisions. *Second*, it can be argued that the ultimate goal of the firm's shareholders, to maximize their future utility of consumption, is achieved by maximizing their personal wealth, measured in terms of market values.

3.5.3   Basic Decision Rules for Management

To illustrate the basic decision rules for management under the classic directive, suppose the stock of firm XYZ is owned by a diffuse group of shareholders, and trades publicly in a liquid and efficient secondary market. The shareholders have just hired new management. Assume that shareholders have been able to devise a contract with management that ensures that management will act strictly in the interest of shareholders.

Two radical possibilities that management should consider immediately are (a) the firm should be entirely liquidated, and the proceeds paid to shareholders as a liquidating dividend, at which point the firm ceases to exist, or (b) the firm (as a going concern) should be sold. If management is unable to identify or continue strategic plans that yield greater wealth for shareholders than *both* of these alternatives, the firm should be liquidated or sold, whichever provides a higher cash return to shareholders. In either case, management is maximizing shareholders' market wealth, even though shareholders do not retain their shares but instead receive cash.

At first, these alternatives appear to constitute a dereliction of management's duty to do their job. In fact, they are legitimate alternatives that management should consider not only when they are initially hired, but also on a regular basis. Moreover, part of the expertise that management should bring to a firm is an awareness of other firms in the industry and their potential willingness to purchase the focal firm, either as a whole or piecemeal, at a high price.

However, if management has strategic plans that they expect to yield greater market value than can be realized by liquidating or selling the firm, management should pursue them. For most firms, the most important strategic plans involve capital investment projects that management devises to compete in the product or service markets in which the firm is, or could be, engaged. This text does not directly address these types of strategic plans. Rather, we deal with issues associated with the firm's financial policies and strategies. However, as we will see, the firm's financial policies and strategies often interact with the firm's capital investment strategies. Moreover, whether or not such an interaction exists, the firm may be able to engage in certain financial strategies that create value for the firm's shareholders.

3.6   EXTENDED STAKEHOLDERS, CONFLICTS OF INTEREST, CONTRACTS, AND A REVISED DIRECTIVE: MAXIMIZE THE MARKET VALUE OF EQUITY

Some researchers, managers, and social scientists have argued that, in making decisions, managers should consider the interests of other parties (i.e., in addition to the firm's shareholders) who have direct or indirect interests, or *stakes*, in the firm. Such *extended stakeholders* include (a) governments, which may impose taxes on the firm's profits and constraints on the firm's operations (such as operational and product safety regulations); (b) creditors, who have a claim on the firm's future cash flows and its assets; (c) the firm's general employees, who depend on the firm for their personal income, and medical and retirement benefits; (d) the firm's suppliers, whose operations and profits are tied to those of the firm; (e) the firm's customers, who purchase and use the products and services that the firm provides; (f) society at large, which may either benefit from, or be harmed by, various activities of the firm; and finally, (g) managers themselves, who ultimately are interested in maximizing their own personal utility.

How should the firm's management deal with the interests of these extended stakeholders? We provide a two-part answer to this question.

3.6.1   The Firm as a Nexus of Contracts

Management must appreciate the critical role that each extended stakeholder plays in the firm's operations or financing, as the case may be. However, as all of the extended stakeholders are ultimately pursuing their own interests, conflicts of interest are bound to occur frequently. Dealing effectively with these conflicts of interest is one of the most important challenges that managers face. *Contracts* are the primary means by which management deals with these conflicts. Indeed, a firm may be described as a *nexus of contracts* between the firm and each of its stakeholders (Jensen and Meckling 1976). Each contract is partially under management's control and simultaneously constrains management. Moreover, each contract affects the firm's risk and profitability, and thus the market value of the firm's equity. After all, equityholders have a residual claim to the firm's future cash flows, where *residual* means *after contracts with all other stakeholders have been settled.*

REAL-WORLD FOCUS

Peter Drucker on the Importance of Customers

Below are excerpts from an interview of famous management consultant Peter Drucker.

Corporate America and Dr. Peter Ferdinand Drucker have fallen out of favor with each other. Drucker still has his disciples, but at the bleeding edge of business, the old master's lifework is commonly seen as simplistic, portentous, off the mark, idealistic, out of date. Not for 20 years have the corporate world's heavy hitters hung on his every word. For his part, The Man Who Invented Corporate Society (a biographer's apt label) disdains a corporate order that is in thrall to stock prices and that rewards its chief executives as though they were power forwards. "Earnings per share" does not exist in Peter Drucker's vocabulary. The religion of shareholder supremacy has him shaking his head. "That's right, I am not very happy with the unbalanced emphasis on stock price and market cap and short-term earnings. . . . The most critical management job is to balance short term and long term. In the long term, today's one-sided emphasis is deleterious and dangerous." (The saving grace, he added, is that many companies pay lip service to short-term shareholder interests. "Actually, they are much better managed," he said.)

To his thinking, two personages, the customer and the highly skilled employee, are at least as precious as the investor. Increasingly, as pension beneficiaries, owners of stock options, or mutual fund investors, they are one and the same person . . . Some 45 years ago Drucker declared a celebrated premise. "There is only one valid definition of business purpose: to create a customer." Does that premise still pertain? "What else?" he asked. "Who else pays the bills?" From that conviction has come his creed: Value and service first, profit later. Maximizing profit, perhaps never . . .

His latest reflections . . . take aim at the Internet . . . He writes that only now, with the explosive emergence of e-commerce as a sales channel for goods and services, is "the truly revolutionary impact of the Information Revolution beginning to be felt." Like the railroad at the industrial dawn, e-commerce is "totally new, totally unprecedented, totally unexpected." In its day, the railroad drastically altered the conception of distance that people carried in their heads. "In the mental geography of e-commerce, distance has been eliminated," Drucker writes. "There is only one economy and only one market." That's a game effort, but "portentous" may be the right word: "full of unspecifiable significance; exciting wonder and awe."

. . . This is a man who absorbed management across the desk from Alfred P. Sloan, the General Motors patriarch, who invented the modern corporation. Drucker's widely influential work, *The Practice of Management*, was published during Eisenhower's first term. His opus, *Management: Tasks, Responsibilities, Practices*, became a best seller three decades ago . . .

Drucker taught that a manager's success lay in an acute grasp of what the business was really all about, usually a grasp of its contribution to the public good. . . . Results are obtained by exploiting opportunities, not by solving problems. What advice could be hoarier than that? Yet how many established companies have embraced the opportunity of the Internet, rather than feared the threat? Any leadership position is transitory and likely to be short-lived . . . What exists is getting old. Drucker was already preaching that a successful company must cannibalize its own products, before the competition does. The apostles of our New Economy were yet unborn.

The pertinent question for managers, he wrote, "is not how to do things right but how to

(*continued*)

find the right things to do." It is pure Drucker: Effectiveness always trumps efficiency. And this was (and is) close to his heart: "The one truly effective way to cut costs is to cut out an activity altogether. There is little point in trying to do cheaply what should not be done at all."

Drucker has kept abreast (or ahead) of the changing tides in business. In 1985, he published *Innovation and Entrepreneurship*, an entirely respectable treatment that by today's IPO standards seems impossibly conservative . . . "This is the discipline of innovation . . . It means having a clear mission. It means defining what you mean by results. It means the ability and willingness to abandon where you don't get results. And then when you find the real opportunity, the unique opportunity where you can make the greatest difference, zone in on it, and reassess and reassess and reassess."

Source: Excerpts from "Peter Drucker Still Preaches Customers over Profits," F. Andrews, *The New York Times*, November 17, 1999. Copyright © 1999 The New York Times Company. Reprinted by permission.

3.6.2   A Revised Directive: Maximize *E*

In the light of the stakeholder view of the corporation, we might rephrase our question as, Should shareholders adopt the classic directive, or adopt an alternative directive? The short answer is that management should be given the following revised directive.

Revised Directive: *Maximize the Market Value of the Firm's Equity* (*E*).

Management should adhere to this directive even if at times their decisions do not simultaneously maximize the market value of the firm, and even though it does not result in the maximization of other stakeholders' utilities (even their own). In other words, this revised directive is a mandate to management to resolve conflicts with other stakeholders (through contracting) in a manner that is consistent with shareholders' interest, as expressed. After all, shareholders are the *principals* in their relationship with management, while managers are the shareholders' *agents*.

Given this revised directive, all extended stakeholders must realize that management will tend to *minimize* the value of their claims in order to *maximize* the market value of the firm's equity, *E*. For instance, the firm's employees should understand that management would tend to provide the lowest possible wages and salaries, subject to the dictates of a competitive labor market. Likewise, the firm's suppliers and customers should understand that the firm is continuously attempting to maximize profits in its dealings with them, subject to the competitive dictates of these respective markets.

3.6.3   Three Important Extended Stakeholders

Working under the revised directive, the firm's dealings with three particular groups of extended stakeholders occupy a disproportionate amount of our attention in the corporate finance literature. The first group includes governments. According to the revised directive, management should take full advantage of all legal means to minimize the present value of government tax claims against the firm. One such legal means is to simply take advantage of the deductibility of interest payments on debt by employing more debt in the firm's capital structure. We analyze the effects of interest deductibility on the value of the firm's equity and on the firm's leverage decision in Chapter 6. In addition, management can choose, or switch to, a depreciation schedule that is more tax favored.

Creditors constitute a second important group of extended stakeholders. If the firm has debt outstanding, management, acting in the shareholders' interest, has a derived incentive to take actions to reduce the market value of the debt, if such actions serve simultaneously to increase the market value of the firm's equity. Management would thereby be *expropriating* wealth from the creditors to the shareholders. We provide examples of such expropriation later in this chapter.

Creditors protect their interest in the firm by three primary means. *First*, promised payments to creditors have a priority status within the law. If the firm fails to make timely payments of interest and/or principal, creditors can force the firm into bankruptcy proceedings, wherein they have a priority claim. (We discuss bankruptcy proceedings in detail in Chapter 18.) *Second*, creditors generally place various *restrictive covenants* and other *provisions* in the debt contract that serve to protect their interests. *Third*, creditors can *monitor* the firm's activities for compliance with stipulations in the debt contract. (We discuss debt covenants and provisions, as well as creditor monitoring, briefly in Chapter 5 and extensively in Chapter 15.)

The third group of extended stakeholders consists of managers themselves. Managers have a personal interest in controlling the firm in a manner that serves to maximize their utility rather than shareholders' wealth. Such *self-serving* behavior is obviously costly to shareholders, and these costs are referred as *agency costs of managerial discretion.* In the next section, we discuss examples of such self-serving behavior. In Chapters 5 and 8, we discuss various mechanisms that shareholders can employ to minimize these costs, including (a) the design of *incentive-compatible* executive compensation contracts and (b) monitoring compliance with the revised directive.

3.7   MANAGERS AS EXTENDED STAKEHOLDERS: AGENCY COSTS OF MANAGERIAL DISCRETION

In this section, we consider the effects of managerial self-interest on the value of the firm and its financial policies. We discuss the incentives of managers to maximize their own wealth (or, more precisely, their utility of wealth), which we assume is derived primarily from their compensation as managers, rather than to maximize the market value of the firm's equity. In the first subsection, we discuss opportunities for management to increase their compensation at the expense of shareholders. In the second subsection, we discuss opportunities for management to reduce the firm's risk at the shareholders' expense.

3.7.1   Opportunities for Management to Increase Their Compensation

Managers may employ any of several schemes to increase their compensation from the firm, including those discussed below.

Excessive Consumption of Perquisites

Managers have an incentive to take additional compensation in the form of *perquisites.* That is, they can use the firm's money to make expenditures that provide

Management and "Empire Building"

One of the most common, and costly, agency problems of management is *empire building*—self-serving actions taken by managers to maximize the size of the firm, rather than the market value of the firm's equity. The following is an excerpt from comments made by the renowned investor Warren Buffet, taken from the 1984 annual report of Berkshire Hathaway:

Many corporations that consistently show good returns both on equity and on overall incremental capital have, indeed, employed a large portion of their retained earnings on an economically unattractive, even disastrous, basis. Their marvelous core businesses, however, whose earnings grow year after year, camouflage repeated failures in capital allocation elsewhere (usually involving high-priced acquisitions of businesses that have inherently mediocre economics). The managers at fault periodically report on the lessons they have learned from the latest disappointment. They then usually seek out future lessons. (Failure seems to go to their heads.)

In such cases, shareholders would be far better off if earnings were retained only to expand the high-return business, with the balance paid in dividends or used to repurchase stock (an action that increases the owners' interest in the exceptional business while sparing them participation in subpar businesses).

Managers of high-return businesses who consistently employ much of the cash thrown off by those businesses in other ventures with low returns should be held to account for those allocation decisions, regardless of how profitable the overall enterprise is.

Nothing in this discussion is intended to argue for dividends that bounce around from quarter to quarter with each wiggle in earnings or in investment opportunities. Shareholders of public corporations understandably prefer that dividends be consistent and predictable. Payments, therefore, should reflect long-term expectations for both earnings and returns on incremental capital. Since the long-term corporate outlook changes only infrequently, dividend patterns should change no more often. But over time distributable earnings that have been withheld by managers should earn their keep. If earnings have been unwisely retained, it is likely that managers, too, have been unwisely retained.

Source: Excerpts from the 1984 Annual Report of Berkshire Hathaway, Inc. Copyright © 1984 Berkshire Hathaway, Inc. Reprinted by permission.

them with personal benefits. For instance, the manager may purchase a Learjet to make his overseas trips more pleasant, or hold meetings in exotic resorts doubling as vacation spots.

Manipulating Earnings and Dividends

Suppose management's annual bonuses are based on the firm's performance for the year, where performance is measured by return on common equity (ROE). Management then has an incentive to distort earnings upward to receive a larger bonus. Alternatively, management may lower (or fail to increase) dividends over time as a means of retaining more cash within the firm, which they can use to draw additional compensation.

Enron's End-Runs

Houston-based Enron Corp. (NYSE: ticker ENE) provides products and services related to natural gas, electricity, and communications to wholesale and retail customers. The firm also makes markets in electricity and natural gas, delivers energy and other physical commodities, and provides financial and risk management services. With annual revenue of more than $150 billion and assets of more than $60 billion, the firm handles transactions representing approximately one-quarter of the traded electricity and natural-gas volumes in the United States.

Enron was riding high at year-end 2000. Its stock price had doubled in 2000 to $82.50, as the firm benefited from rising energy prices and the California energy crisis. However, by November 28, 2001, Enron's stock price had plummeted 99 percent to $0.61, negotiations to be acquired by Dynegy Inc. fell apart, and the firm was on the brink of bankruptcy. With 744 million shares outstanding, the stock-price plunge wiped out nearly $61 billion in market equity value.

WHAT HAPPENED?

Some of the loss was attributed ill-timed investments in broadband telecommunications, retail energy services, and a water company.

However, considerable attention by the financial press, and of late the SEC, has focused on Enron's controversial dealings with two limited partnerships that were set up and run by its chief financial officer, Andrew Fastow, who was replaced on October 25, 2001. The two partnerships were involved in billions of dollars of transactions with Enron, and internal partnerships indicate that Mr. Fastow and associates made millions of dollars from the part-

nerships. Meanwhile, in October the firm announced a $618 million third-quarter loss and disclosed a $1.2 billion charge to shareholder equity related to transactions it had carried out with the partnerships. Enron has received sharp criticism from analysts and major shareholders concerning the apparent conflict of interest.

OTHER STAKEHOLDERS HURT, TOO

Other stakeholders also have been adversely affected by Enron's troubles.

- *Creditors*, including bondholders and banks, stand to lose as the credit rating on Enron's debt fell to "junk" status in the wake of the collapse.

- *Insurers* may absorb total losses of more than $3 billion, from a combination of exposures in contract-related *surety bonds*, directors-and-officers liability, and other areas.

- Many of Enron's *customers* may also suffer losses, including hotels, manufacturers, retailers, and technology firms that had long-term contracts with Enron to supply various commodities.

- Fellow *energy traders* such as Duke Energy Corp. and Aquila (80 percent owned by Utilicorp) also have reported substantial exposure to the Enron debacle.

- *Employees* who participated in Enron's 401(k) employee-retirement plan, which was 60 percent invested in Enron stock, also sustained heavy losses. Some members of the plan are suing Enron for failing to warn participants about the risk of investing in Enron stock, and because Enron "locked down" the plan's assets from October 17 to November 19, 2001, during which time participants were prevented from selling Enron shares.

(continued)

Sources: "Duke Says Has $100 Million in Exposure to Enron," *Reuters*, 29 November 2001.

"Enron Shares Fall Anew," *Reuters*, 29 November 2001.

Francis, T., and E. Schultz. "Enron Is Sued by 401(k) Members Amid Firm's Plunging Stock Price," *Wall Street Journal Online*, 23 November 2001.

"A Legion of Corporations and Individuals Stand to Suffer Losses in Enron Collapse," *Buffalo (New York) News*, 2 December 2001.

Smith, R., and J. R. Emshwiller. "Enron Replaces Fastow as Finance Chief; Move Follows Concerns over Partnerships," *Wall Street Journal Online*, 25 October 2001.

———. "Enron Says Its Links to a Partnership Led to $1.2 Billion Equity Reduction," *Wall Street Journal Online*, 18 October 2001.

———. "SEC Seeks Information on Enron Dealings with Partnerships Recently Run by Fastow," *Wall Street Journal Online*, 21 October 2001.

Smith, R., and G. Zuckerman. "Dynegy Terminates Deal to Buy Enron, after Enron's Debt Is Cut to Junk Status," *Wall Street Journal Online*, 28 November 2001.

Maximizing the Size of the Firm, Rather Than Its Value

In the (labor) market for corporate managers, compensation is highly correlated with the size of the firm. Thus, left unchecked, management has an incentive to maximize the size of the firm, rather than the market value of the firm's equity. They can do this through excessive internal expansion, acquisitions, or reducing dividends, even if these actions are not in the shareholders' interest. This is known as the *overinvestment problem* (to be distinguished from the *underinvestment problem* that we discuss later in the chapter). Managers who overinvest are said to be engaging in *empire building*.

Siphoning Corporate Assets

A particularly brazen example of managerial self-interest involves siphoning corporate assets. For example, a firm's executives may establish a separate "shell" firm, which they own, and then direct cash flow from the focal firm to the shell. This could be done under the guise of (very favorable) payments for goods or services that the shell firm provides to the focal firm.

3.7.2 Opportunities for Management to Decrease the Riskiness of Their Employment Income

It is important to recognize that managers and shareholders are likely to have very different views of the riskiness of the firm. Assuming that shareholders are diversified, their risk with respect to the firm is limited to the stock's *systematic risk*. In contrast, assuming that the bulk of a manager's wealth consists of compensation from the firm that he or she manages, the manager is exposed to the firm's *total risk*. Therefore, management may tend to take actions to reduce the firm's total risk even if such actions may not be in the shareholders' interest. Management may use any of the following schemes to decrease the firm's risk, and thus the risk of their personal portfolios.

Excessive Diversification

Management may pursue *pure conglomerate mergers*, which add no value to shareholders, not only to increase the size of the firm but also to reduce firm-specific risk (e.g., by diversifying the firm's operations across industries, which is of no value to already diversified shareholders). Reducing the probability of the firm's failure reduces the probability that the manager would be out of a job.

Bias toward Investments with Near-Term Payoffs

If management compensation is tied to the firm's earnings, management has an incentive to bias their selection of capital investment projects toward investments that pay off well in a short period of time, even if these investments may not maximize shareholder value in the long run. This bias may be particularly severe if top managers have only a short period of time before they retire.

Underemployment of Debt

Suppose there is a particular *optimal* (i.e., *E* maximizing) amount of leverage that a firm should employ. Management may choose a lower level of leverage than is optimal in this sense, because the probability of bankruptcy, and thus the loss of their jobs, increases with leverage.

Management Entrenchment

A firm's CEO will naturally tend to steer the firm toward investments that reflect his or her unique talents. Over time, this policy will make it difficult for the shareholders to remove the CEO even if he is not performing adequately. That is, a CEO has become *entrenched*. An alternative ploy is the inclusion of *poison pills* in the firm's charter, in an executive compensation contract, or in a bond contract. For instance, a *poison put* provision in a bond contract makes the firm's debt due immediately if the firm is the target of a successful hostile takeover, after which the firm's incumbent management is fired. The poison pill increases the cash cost, and thus reduces the probability of a takeover.

Yet another tactic management may use to keep their jobs involves the payment of *greenmail*. Suppose an arbitrageur who has substantial capital believes that the management of a given firm is failing to maximize the market value of the firm's equity, perhaps because management is relatively incompetent or is making self-serving decisions. In the arbitrageur's opinion, the firm's shares are undervalued relative to their potential under better management. The arbitrageur has an incentive to purchase the undervalued shares until their accumulated shares, perhaps in combination with those of other shareholders who have been persuaded by the arbitrageur's argument, is sufficient to vote out incumbent management. As this process is unfolding, the firm's current management realizes the threat to their positions and may offer to purchase the arbitrageur's shares, using company funds, at a substantial premium to the current market price if the arbitrageur promises to *cease and desist*. Such a payment is called *greenmail*.

In a similar vein, a firm's management can reduce the risk of losing their positions by thwarting the attempts of *activist investors* to purchase the firm's shares. Activist investors purchase the shares of underperforming firms and then attempt to either oust the firm's incumbent management or force reform.

Management can limit the number of activist investors by systematically limiting activists' access to the firm's shares. They can do this by any of several means. *First*, they could include stock options in their compensation contracts that allow themselves to purchase a substantial number of the firm's shares over time. *Second*, they could encourage individual investors with relatively little wealth (who may be more passive than a wealthy investor, a mutual fund, or a pension fund) to purchase shares. Many firms have *dividend reinvestment plans* that allow eligible individual investors to automatically reinvest their dividends into shares of the firm. Generally, the firm purchases the requisite shares in the secondary market, but gives the participating shareholder a discount to the price actually paid, and also waives commission costs. *Third*, management could use the firm's cash to *repurchase* shares. (We discuss stock repurchases in Chapter 14.)

Packing the Board
Management may be able to garner the appointment of individuals to the firm's board of directors who have a favorable bias toward management. This ploy is referred to as *packing the board*.

3.8   CONFLICTS OF INTEREST BETWEEN SHAREHOLDERS AND CREDITORS: AGENCY COSTS OF DEBT

The relationship between a firm's shareholders and its creditors also engenders conflicts of interest. They are principal–agent conflicts because the creditors, as principals, have lent money to the firm with the expectation that the firm, as the agent, will act in the interest of the creditors, at least so far as to repay the loan with interest. However, we know that the firm's management, who control the firm's operations, is instructed to act in the *shareholders'* interest, and no person can serve two masters. Consequently, if and when conflicts of interest arise between the firm's shareholders and its creditors, management's duty is to resolve such conflicts in a manner that serves the shareholders' interest to maximize the market value of the firm's *equity*. Therefore, creditors must realize that the firm's management will have a derived incentive to take actions to *reduce* the value of their claim if such actions serve to increase shareholders' wealth. Such actions are *expropriations* of creditors' wealth by shareholders.

3.8.1   Maximize *E* by Minimizing *D*

Here we provide three examples of actions that the management of a levered firm could take to expropriate wealth from existing debtholders. The first example involves a leverage-increasing *recapitalization*, or *recap*. The second example involves increasing the riskiness of the firm's assets. In the third example, a levered firm pays an immediate dividend to shareholders. In all three examples, we utilize the Binomial Pricing Model (introduced in Chapter 2) to compute security values, and thus to gauge the effects of each action on both debtholders' and stockholders' wealth. For reference, the calculations for all three examples are summarized in Table 3.1.

Example 1 of Expropriation: A Leverage-Increasing Recap
In this example, the firm's market value is $V = 100$. Using the setting of the binomial model, assume that this value obtains because, in five years (i.e., at date $T = 5$), the value of the firm will be either $V_5^u = 200$ with probability $p = 0.7$, or $V_5^d = 50$ with probability $(1 - p) = 0.3$, so that the expected value of the firm in five years is $E(V_5) = 155$. Thus, the market's discount rate, applied to this expected value to yield the current firm value of $V = 100$, is $r_A = 9.16$ percent. The firm currently has one issue of pure-discount debt outstanding. We refer to this issue as the firm's *original* debt, and denote

---

TABLE 3-1 Expropriation of Creditors: Summaries of Three Examples

Example 1: A Leverage-Increasing Recapitalization

Before Recap			*Recap Details*	*After Recap*		
ASSETS	LIABILITIES AND EQUITY		Firm issues new equal-priority debt with a value of D(new) = 24.62, paying proceeds to shareholders as a dividend.	ASSETS	LIABILITIES AND EQUITY	
100	Debt (original)	39.18		100	Debt (original)	30.78
	Equity	60.82			Debt (new)	24.62
					Equity	44.60

Effect on Orig. Debtholders: **−8.40**
Effect on Equityholders: **8.40**

Example 2: Increasing the Riskiness of the Firm's Assets

Before Risk Increase			*Details of Risk Increase*	*After Risk Increase*		
ASSETS	LIABILITIES AND EQUITY		Management alters operations so that the range of payoffs in up and down states is greater. Debt was default-free, but is now default-risky.	ASSETS	LIABILITIES AND EQUITY	
100	Debt	39.18		100	Debt	30.74
	Equity	60.82			Equity	69.26

Effect on Debtholders: **−8.44**
Effect on Equityholders: **8.44**

Example 3: Paying a Dividend to Shareholders

Case 1: Dividend Paid out of Idle Cash

Before Dividend Payment			*Details of Dividend Payment*	*After Dividend Payment*		
ASSETS	LIABILITIES AND EQUITY		A dividend of 25 is paid to shareholders out of idle cash. As a result, the value of the firm falls from 100 to 75.	ASSETS	LIABILITIES AND EQUITY	
100	Debt	39.18		75	Debt	27.11
	Equity	60.82			Equity	47.89

Effect on Debtholders: **−12.06**
*Effect on Equityholders:** **12.06**

Case 2: Dividend Paid from Proceeds of Asset Sale

Before Dividend Payment			*Details of Dividend Payment*	*After Dividend Payment*		
ASSETS	LIABILITIES AND EQUITY		A dividend of 25 is paid to shareholders via proceeds from a sale of 25% of the firm's assets at fair value.	ASSETS	LIABILITIES AND EQUITY	
100	Debt	39.18		75	Debt	34.45
	Equity	60.82			Equity	40.55

Effect on Debtholders: **−4.73**
*Effect on Equityholders:** **4.73**

*Reflects revised value of equity plus dividend.

its value as $D(\text{original})$. The original debt consists of a promise to pay $X(\text{original}) = 50$ at date $T = 5$. Note that $X(\text{original}) = V_5^d = 50$, so the debt is default-free. Assuming a risk-free rate of 5 percent, then $D(\text{original}) = X(\text{original})/(1 + r_f)^T = 50/(1.05)^5 = 39.18$. Therefore, the value of the firm's levered equity, $E_L(\text{original})$, is $E_L(\text{original}) = V - D(\text{original}) = 100 - 39.18 = 60.82$.

Now suppose the firm sells an additional issue of pure-discount debt, which we call *new* debt. The new debt consists of a promise to pay $X(\text{new}) = 40$ in five years. Further, we assume that (a) the new debt has the same priority status as the original debt, and (b) the firm immediately distributes the proceeds of the new debt issue as a dividend to shareholders.

The new debt has the same priority and maturity as the original debt, so for valuation purposes the promised payments on the two debt issues can be pooled to determine the overall value of the firm's debt. Thus, the firm now has debt outstanding with a total promised payment of $X(\text{pooled}) = X(\text{original}) + X(\text{new}) = 50 + 40 = 90$, all due in five years. However, note that now *all* of the firm's debt is default risky, because $X(\text{pooled}) = 90 > V_5^d = 50$.

Meanwhile, the proceeds of the new debt offering is paid out as a dividend, so the firm's assets remain unchanged and, from M&M Proposition I, the value of the firm remains unchanged at $V = 100$. Therefore, to value the firm's pooled debt and equity after the recap, denoted as $D(\text{pooled})$ and $E_L(\text{new})$, respectively, we must calculate values of the parameters of the Binomial Pricing Model:

$$\delta = \frac{V_5^u - V_5^d}{E_{L5}^u(\text{new}) - E_{L5}^d(\text{new})} \tag{3.1}$$

$$= \frac{200 - 50}{110 - 0} = 1.3636,$$

and therefore

$$E_L(\text{new}) = V\left[\frac{1}{\delta}\right] - \left[X(\text{pooled}) + V_5^u\left\{\frac{1}{\delta} - 1\right\}\right]\Big/(1 + r_f)^T \tag{3.2}$$

$$= 100\left[\frac{1}{1.3636}\right] - \left[90 + 200\left\{\frac{1}{1.3636} - 1\right\}\right]\Big/(1.05)^5$$

$$= 44.60.$$

Therefore, $D(\text{pooled}) = V - E_L(\text{new}) = 100 - 44.60 = 55.40$.

As an implication of the equal-priority assumption (a) above, the value of the original debt is equal to the fraction 5/9 of the pooled value of all debt, or $D(\text{original}) = (5/9)D(\text{pooled}) = (5/9)55.40 = 30.78$, whereas the value of the new debt, and thus the amount that new creditors will pay for the new debt, is equal to the fraction 4/9 of the pooled value of all debt, or $D(\text{new}) = (4/9)D(\text{pooled}) = (4/9)55.40 = 24.62$. Note that, as a consequence of the recap, the value of the original debt has fallen by 8.40, from 39.18 to 30.78. Meanwhile, shareholders' wealth has increased by the same amount of 8.40, from 60.82 in stock value before the recap to 44.60 in stock value plus 24.62 in cash (i.e., the proceeds of the net debt issue, paid as a dividend), or 69.22 in total, after the recap. The original debtholders' loss is indeed shareholders' gain.

Example 2 of Expropriation: Increasing the Riskiness of the Firm's Assets

Another means by which management can expropriate wealth from existing debtholders is to increase the riskiness of the firm's assets. To illustrate, we start with the original data for example 1 (i.e., $V = 100$, $X = 50$, $T = 5$, $V_5^u = 200$, $V_5^d = 50$, $p = 0.7$, $E(V_5) = 155$, $r_A = 9.16$ percent, $r_f = 5$ percent, $D = 39.18$, and $E_L = 60.82$).

Now suppose the firm's management changes its operational strategy in a manner that increases the firm's risk. Under the new operational strategy, $V_5^u(\text{new}) = 300$ and $V_5^d(\text{new}) = 33.33$, while the probability of the upstate remains at $p = 0.7$. Our first task is to determine the value of the firm. The expected value of the firm at $T = 5$ is $E(V_5) = 0.7(300) + 0.3(33.33) = 220$, which is substantially higher than under the original operating strategy. However, the risk is also higher, so the applicable market discount rate is likely to be higher than the value of 9.16 percent that we found for the original firm. Arbitrarily, we assume that the new discount rate is 17.08 percent so that the value of the firm remains at $V = 100$ [$= 220/(1.1708)^5$]. We can now value the firm's debt and equity, denoted as $D(\text{new})$ and $E_L(\text{new})$, respectively, under the new operating strategy:

$$\delta = \frac{V_5^u(\text{new}) - V_5^d(\text{new})}{E_{L5}^u(\text{new}) - E_{L5}^d(\text{new})}$$

$$= \frac{300 - 33.33}{250 - 0} = 1.0667,$$

and therefore

$$E_L(\text{new}) = V\left[\frac{1}{\delta}\right] - \left[X + V_5^u(\text{new})\left\{\frac{1}{\delta} - 1\right\}\right]\Big/(1 + r_f)^T$$

$$= 100\left[\frac{1}{1.0667}\right] - \left[50 + 300\left\{\frac{1}{1.0667} - 1\right\}\right]\Big/(1.05)^5$$

$$= 69.26.$$

Therefore, $D(\text{new}) = V - E_L(\text{new}) = 100 - 69.26 = 30.74$. As a result of management's switch to a higher-risk operational strategy, the value of the firm's debt decreases by 8.44, from 39.18 to 30.74, and the value of the firm's equity increases by the same amount, 8.44, from 60.82 to 69.26.

Example 3 of Expropriation: Paying an Immediate Dividend to Stockholders

In our third example, management expropriates wealth from a firm's existing debtholders by paying a dividend to shareholders. Again, we will start with the following original data: $V = 100$, $X = 50$, $T = 5$, $V_5^u = 200$, $V_5^d = 50$, $p = 0.7$, $E(V_5) = 155$, $r_A = 9.16$ percent, $r_f = 5$ percent, $D = 39.18$, and $E_L = 60.82$. In each of the two cases described below, the firm's management has decided to pay a dividend of $Q = 25$ immediately to shareholders. In the first case, we assume that the dividend is paid out of *idle cash*—that is, cash that the firm does not need to pursue its current operational strategy, and that would have earned interest at the risk-free rate of 5 percent for the next five years. (Note that the payoff on this riskless investment would have been available, as necessary, to pay debtholders at date $T = 5$.) In the second case, the firm obtains the funds required for the dividend by selling 25 percent of the firm's assets, which we assume yields fair-value proceeds of 25.

Case 1: Paying a Dividend out of Idle Cash   In this case, a dividend of $Q = 25$ is paid out of the firm's idle cash. After the dividend is paid, the value of the firm decreases to $V(new) = 75$, and the possible payoffs at time $T = 5$ are reduced to $V_5^u(new) = 168.09$ $[= 200 - 25(1.05)^5]$ and $V_5^d(new) = 18.09$ $[= 50 - 25(1.05)^5]$. With these post-dividend values, we can compute new values for the firm's debt and equity, $D(new)$ and $E_L(new)$, respectively:

$$\delta = \frac{V_5^u(new) - V_5^d(new)}{E_{L5}^u(new) - E_{L5}^d(new)}$$

$$= \frac{168.09 - 18.09}{118.09 - 0} = 1.2702,$$

so

$$E_L(new) = V(new)\left[\frac{1}{\delta}\right] - \left[X + V_5^u(new)\left\{\frac{1}{\delta} - 1\right\}\right]\bigg/(1 + r_f)^T$$

$$= 75\left[\frac{1}{1.2702}\right] - \left[50 + 168.09\left\{\frac{1}{1.2702} - 1\right\}\right]\bigg/(1.05)^5$$

$$= 47.89.$$

Therefore, $D(new) = V(new) - E_L(new) = 75 - 47.89 = 27.11$. As a result of the payment of the dividend out of idle cash, the value of the firm's debt decreases by 12.06, from 39.18 to 27.11, and shareholders' wealth increases by the same amount, 12.06, from 60.82 in stock value to 47.89 in stock value plus 25 in cash, or 72.89 in total.

Case 2: Paying a Dividend Using Proceeds from a Sale of Assets   In the second case, the firm pays a dividend of $Q = 25$, obtaining funds to do so from a sale of 25 percent of the firm's general assets. After the asset sale and dividend payment, the value of the firm decreases to $V(new) = 75$, and the payoffs at date $T = 5$ are reduced to $V_5^u(new) = 150$ $[= 0.75(200)]$ and $V_5^d(new) = 37.50$ $[= 0.75(50)]$. With these post-dividend values, the values of $D(new)$ and $E_L(new)$ can be calculated:

$$\delta = \frac{V_5^u(new) - V_5^d(new)}{E_{L5}^u(new) - E_{L5}^d(new)}$$

$$= \frac{150 - 37.50}{100 - 0} = 1.125,$$

so

$$E_L(new) = V(new)\left[\frac{1}{\delta}\right] - \left[X + V_5^u(new)\left\{\frac{1}{\delta} - 1\right\}\right]\bigg/(1 + r_f)^T$$

$$= 75\left[\frac{1}{1.125}\right] - \left[50 + 150\left\{\frac{1}{1.125} - 1\right\}\right]\bigg/(1.05)^5$$

$$= 40.55.$$

Therefore, $D(\text{new}) = V(\text{new}) - E_L(\text{new}) = 75 - 40.55 = 34.45$. As a result of the payment of the dividend using funds obtained from a sale of assets, the value of the firm's debt decreases by 4.73, from 39.18 to 34.45, and shareholders' wealth increases by the same amount, 4.73, from 60.82 in stock to 40.55 in stock plus 25 in cash, or 65.55 in total. Interestingly, even though in both cases shareholders receive a dividend of 25, the expropriation of debtholders is substantially greater if idle cash is used to pay the dividend (12.06) than if the cash for the dividend is generated by a sale of assets (4.73). This difference is due primarily to the fact that the firm's date $T = 5$ "down-state" value, $V_5^d(\text{new})$, is lower in the former case (18.09) than in the latter case (37.50).

So What Is a Creditor to Do?

The three examples above illustrate the conflicts of interest that can and do arise between shareholders and creditors. They also emphasize how important it is for debtholders to protect their interest via *covenants* in the debt contract. For instance, in the three examples above, respectively, the following (hypothetical) covenants could be included in the debt contract to protect debtholders: (a) The firm can issue no new debt unless it is subordinated to the firm's original debt; (b) if the firm makes substantial changes in its operating strategy, the firm's debt will be immediately due and payable; and (c) the firm cannot pay dividends while the debt is outstanding.

3.8.2 Deadweight Costs of Debt: The Underinvestment Problem

Our final numerical examples illustrate the *underinvestment problem*, also known as the *debt overhang* problem. Myers (1977) showed that a firm could incur *deadweight costs* when it has default-risky debt outstanding and a profitable investment opportunity, which, if it is to be undertaken, must be financed with equity funds. Under such circumstances, a portion of the *NPV* of the new project will transfer to the firm's debtholders, and, depending on the circumstances, the residual benefits to stockholders may be lower than the project's cost, in which case management, acting in the shareholders' interest, will not adopt the project (even though it is profitable per se).

To illustrate the underinvestment problem, we analyze two similar cases. In the first case, the project would be financed with internal equity (i.e., idle cash), which would otherwise be used to pay an immediate dividend to shareholders. In the second case, the firm's shareholders must contribute equity capital. In both cases, we use the Binomial Pricing Model. We assume that management follows the revised directive in making their decisions, to maximize shareholder wealth. Specifically, in each case management evaluates the effect of the project on shareholders' wealth, and chooses the alternative that maximizes shareholder wealth. For reference, calculations for these cases are summarized in Table 3.2.

Case 1: Idle Cash Is Used to Either Pay an Immediate Dividend or Fund a Project

In this case, a levered firm is defined by the following parameter values, structured in terms of the Binomial Pricing Model: $V = 100$, $X = 99$, $T = 5$, $V_5^u = 150$, $V_5^d = 66.67$, $p = 0.8$, $r_f = 5$ percent, and thus $D = 70.77$ and $E_L = 29.23$. Included among the firm's assets is a total of $Q = 25$ in idle cash, which is currently invested in the risk-free security. The firm's date $T = 5$ payoffs given above include the payoff on this investment, which is 31.91 $[= 25(1.05)^5]$ in both states.

TABLE 3-2   The Underinvestment Problem: Summaries of Cases

Case 1, Alternative 1: Pay an Immediate Dividend of 25

Before Dividend		*Dividend Details*	*After Dividend*		
ASSETS	LIABILITIES AND EQUITY	Firm pays a dividend of 25, rather than pursuing a profitable investment opportunity.	ASSETS	LIABILITIES AND EQUITY	
100	Debt 70.77		100	Debt	64.06
	Equity 29.23			Equity	35.94

Effect on Orig. Debtholders: **–6.71**
Effect on Equityholders: *   **6.71**

Case 1, Alternative 2: Pursue a Profitable Project via Idle Funds

Before Project Is Adopted		*Details of Project*	*After Project Adoption*		
ASSETS	LIABILITIES AND EQUITY	Project requires an outlay of 25, which is taken from idle cash. The project provides a riskless payoff of 40 in 5 years.	ASSETS	LIABILITIES AND EQUITY	
100	Debt 70.77		106.34	Debt	72.47
	Equity 29.23			Equity	33.87

Effect on Debtholders: **1.70**
Effect on Equityholders: **4.64**

Case 2: Pursue a Profitable Project via External Equity

Before Project Is Adopted		*Details of Project*	*After Project Adoption*		
ASSETS	LIABILITIES AND EQUITY	Project requires an outlay of 25, which is raised through cash infusion from existing shareholders. The project provides a riskless payoff of 40 in 5 years.	ASSETS	LIABILITIES AND EQUITY	
100	Debt 70.77		31.34	Debt	77.57
	Equity 29.23			Equity	53.77

Effect on Debtholders: **6.80**
Effect on Equity: ** **–0.46**

---

*Reflects revised value of equity plus dividend.

**Net of increase in equity value of 24.54 (= 53.77 – 29.23) less external cash infusion of 25.

Of course, management can choose to simply maintain the status quo. We assume, however, that management has the following two alternative courses of action as well: (a) liquidate the investment in the risk-free security and pay a dividend of $Q = 25$ immediately to shareholders, or (b) invest in the profitable project described below.

Alternative 1: Use the Idle Cash to Pay a Dividend   If a dividend of 25 is paid, shareholders' wealth will consist of 25 in cash plus the updated value of their shares. Regarding the latter, the relevant updated values are $V(\text{new}) = 75$, $V_5^u(\text{new}) = 118.09$, $V_5^d(\text{new}) = 34.76$, and thus $D(\text{new}) = 64.06$ and $E_L(\text{new}) = 10.94$. As such, the shareholders' wealth would now be $10.94 + 25 = 35.94$, which exceeds their initial wealth by 6.71 (= 35.94 – 29.23). Once again, the shareholders' gain is equal to the debtholders' loss, because $D(\text{new}) - D = 64.06 - 70.77 = -6.71$.

Alternative 2: Invest the Idle Cash in a Profitable Project   Alternatively, management could use idle cash to invest in a profitable project. The project requires the entire amount currently invested in the riskless security, 25, as an initial outlay. The project is actually riskless, providing a payoff of 40 at date $T = 5$ in both up and down states; that is, $P_5^u = P_5^d = 40$. The project is clearly profitable, because its date $T = 5$ payoff is greater than the payoff that would be realized on the riskless security, 31.91 [= $25(1.05)^5$]. The present value of the payoff on the project is 31.34 [= $40/(1.05)^5$], so its *NPV* is $31.34 - 25 = 6.34 > 0$. Therefore, if management converts the idle cash into the project, the value of the firm increases to $V(\text{new}) = 106.34$. In addition, both the up-state and down-state values increase to $V_5^u(\text{new}) = 158.09$ and $V_5^d(\text{new}) = 74.76$, respectively. As a result, the new values of the firm's debt and equity are $D(\text{new}) = 72.47$ and $E_L(\text{new}) = 33.87$.

Pursuing the profitable project via idle cash benefits both the firm's debtholders, by 1.70 [= $D(\text{new}) - D = 72.47 - 70.77$], and the firm's shareholders, by 4.64 [= $E_L(\text{new}) - E_L = 33.87 - 29.23$]. Also note that the sum of the increases in the values of the firm's debt and equity, 6.34 (= 1.70 + 4.64) is equal to the project's *NPV*.

If management has only the choice between keeping the cash idly invested in the risk-free security or investing in the profitable project, they should choose to invest in the project, because doing so increases shareholders' wealth. However, if management has the additional alternative of paying an immediate dividend to shareholders, then they should pay the dividend, because this choice yields the *highest* wealth for shareholders, 35.94 versus 33.87. Thus, as a direct result of the presence of risky debt in the firm's capital structure, the firm forgoes a profitable project, and the result is a dead-weight wealth loss of 6.34.

Case 2: Shareholders Must Contribute External Equity Funds to Undertake the Project
In the second case, shareholders must contribute 25 from their own pockets to undertake the same project as described in case 1. If the project is not undertaken, the firm's parameter values remain as $V = 100$, $X = 99$, $T = 5$, $V_5^u = 150$, $V_5^d = 66.67$, $p = 0.8$, $r_f = 5$ percent, and thus $D = 70.77$ and $E_L = 29.23$. If management decides to adopt the project, and thus shareholders contribute 25 for its undertaking, the value of the firm will increase to $V(\text{new}) = 131.34$, and the firm's date $T = 5$ payoffs will rise to $V_5^u(\text{new}) = 190$ and $V_5^d(\text{new}) = 106.67$. Note that $V_5^d(\text{new}) > X$, so the firm's debt is now riskless, and therefore its value rises to $D(\text{new}) = 99/(1.05)^5 = 77.57$. Consequently, the value of the firm's equity will be $E_L(\text{new}) = V(\text{new}) - D(\text{new}) = 131.34 - 77.57 = 53.77$.

The value of the firm's equity rises by only 24.54 (= 53.77 – 29.23), which is insufficient to compensate shareholders for their investment of 25. Therefore, if the only alternatives available to management are to do nothing or to raise external equity from shareholders and adopt the project, management, acting in the interest of the firm's shareholders, should do nothing, even though the project has a positive *NPV*! The reason is that, upon adoption of the project with new equity funds, the value of the firm's debt increases by an amount, 6.80 (= 77.57 – 70.77), that exceeds the *NPV* of the project, leaving shareholders to actually lose 0.46 (= 24.54 – 25) in wealth.

3.9 REVISITING THE ISSUE OF SEPARATION OF OWNERSHIP AND CONTROL

At this point you may be wondering (a) whether agency costs of managerial discretion are sufficiently large as to exceed the cited benefits of separation of ownership and control, and (b) whether a firm should ever use debt in its capital structure, given that (1) debt engenders an additional principal–agent conflict between shareholders and debtholders and (2) debt can cause distortions in the firm's capital investment program. These are important issues that we will address in detail in later chapters. Here we will make only some preliminary comments on both issues.

3.9.1 A Trade-off between Agency Costs of Managerial Discretion and Benefits of the Separation of Ownership and Control

In practice, it is difficult to quantify the benefits of separation of ownership and control or the agency costs of managerial discretion, so it is difficult to know whether the benefits exceed the costs. However, it seems likely that, for some firms, agency costs of managerial discretion can be quite large relative to the benefits of separation. For instance, in some firms it may be difficult to monitor (a) management's consumption of perquisites, (b) management's possible manipulation of earnings and/or dividends to their own advantage, and (c) the efficacy of management's capital investment program. For such firms, separation of ownership and control may lead to excessive agency costs of managerial discretion, and the firm can be viable only if the firm's managers are also its owners, at least to some extent. This may explain why hundreds of successful firms are privately and/or closely held.

On the other hand, as we saw in Chapter 1, presently there are thousands of public firms in the United States, most of them with diffuse ownership. This evidence suggests that the benefits of separation generally exceed agency costs of managerial discretion.

3.9.2 Should a Firm with Diffuse Ownership Have Debt in Its Capital Structure?

If debt engenders additional principal–agent conflicts and causes distortions in the firm's capital investment program, why should a firm ever have debt in its capital structure? One possible reason is that debt serves a positive role in *disciplining* management so that they will be more likely to act in the shareholders' interest. We discuss this issue in Chapter 5. Another possible explanation is that the effective cost of debt to the firm may be relatively low because interest payments are tax deductible whereas dividends are not. We discuss this issue in Chapter 6. Finally, despite aggregate statistics showing a substantial use of corporate debt (see Chapter 1), hundreds of firms have virtually no debt in their capital structure. For such firms, the deadweight costs of debt may be so large that debt is not a viable financing instrument.

3.10 Summary of Learning Objectives

In this chapter, we discussed several *real-world factors* that may affect corporate financial decisions and values. Essentially, these real-world factors constitute violations of one or more of the assumptions of an ideal capital market. The real-world factors that are the focus of this chapter include the effects of ownership structure and various *principal–agent conflicts* within the firm, which are inherent in the nature of the corporate form of business organization, especially the features of *limited liability* and the *separation of ownership and control.*

In most large corporations, ownership is vested in one group, the shareholders, while control of the firm's operations is vested in a separate group, management. The separation is necessary because, in order to enjoy the vital risk-reducing benefits of diversification, individual shareholders of a given firm generally will hold only a small proportion of the firm's shares, and will have only a relatively small proportion of their personal portfolio invested in any single firm. Consequently, no shareholder will find it in his or her financial interest to expend the effort required to manage, or even to monitor, the firm's operations. Instead, shareholders hire managers to control the firm's operations.

What instructions should shareholders give to management? The *classic directive* to management is to maximize the current market value of the firm. However, large corporations are complex entities, constituting a *nexus of contracts* with many *extended stakeholders* (including governments, creditors, employees, suppliers, customers, and managers themselves), all of whom are ultimately interested in maximizing their personal utility. Given these conflicting interests, shareholders must adopt a *revised directive* to management: maximize the market value of the firm's *equity*, even if at times management's actions do not simultaneously maximize the market value of the *firm.*

However, as stakeholders themselves, management is tempted to make *self-serving decisions* that are costly to shareholders. These costs are called *agency costs of managerial discretion.* Two types of managerial self-serving behavior are recognized: (a) actions that increase management's compensation (including excessive consumption of perquisites, manipulation of earnings and dividends, maximizing the size of the firm, rather than the market value of equity, and siphoning corporate assets), and (b) actions that reduce the riskiness of management's compensation (including excessive diversification, a bias toward investments with near-term payoffs, underemployment of debt, management entrenchment, attracting passive investors, and "packing the board").

Additional conflicts of interest arise between shareholders and debtholders; costs associated with these conflicts are called *agency costs of debt.* The conflict arises because management, acting in the interests of shareholders, may take actions that expropriate wealth from debtholders to shareholders. Debt may also cause distortions in the firm's capital investment program—in particular, the *underinvestment problem.*

For many firms, separation of ownership and control may lead to excessive agency costs of managerial discretion, and the firm can be viable only if the firm's managers are also its owners. This may explain why hundreds of successful firms are privately owned or at least closely held. Many firms also have no debt in their capital structures, suggesting that for these firms the debt security is not a viable financing instrument due to deadweight costs. On the other hand, thousands of firms in the United States are publicly traded, and most of these firms have debt in their capital structures. This evidence suggests that for many, if not most, firms the benefits of separation of ownership and control, as well as the benefits of debt financing, exceed their respective costs.

Review Questions and Problems

1. Briefly discuss the effects of violations of each of the assumptions of the ideal capital market listed below:
   a. Assumption 1: Frictionless markets.
   b. Assumption 2: All market participants share homogeneous expectations.
   c. Assumption 3: Atomistic competition.
   d. Assumption 4: The firm's capital investment program is fixed and known.
   e. Assumption 5: Once chosen, the firm's financing is fixed.

2. How are the basic factors of production (labor and capital) related to the separation of ownership and control in the modern corporation?

3. How do limited liability and the separation of ownership and control reflect risk aversion on the part of the owners of (equity) capital?

4. Why is the separation of ownership and control a virtual necessity for the successful financing of large corporations?

5. Explain the two major benefits to shareholders of the separation of ownership and control.

6. What are the three positive effects of shareholders' diversification across firms on the market value of an individual firm's shares?

7. Define the *classic directive*, and describe a set of circumstances in which it is the appropriate directive for management to follow in order to act in the shareholders' interest.

8. How does the stakeholder theory of the firm influence our understanding of the proper directive for a firm's management to follow? What is an alternative directive under these circumstances?

9. List and briefly discuss four self-serving actions that management may take to increase their compensation.

10. List and briefly discuss five self-serving actions that management may take to decrease the risk of their personal portfolios.

11. What is *empire building*? Why is it a compelling goal for managers?

12. List and briefly discuss three actions that a firm's management can take to expropriate wealth from the firm's debtholders to the firm's shareholders.

13. Explain the *underinvestment problem* facing a firm that has risky debt outstanding.

14. (This problem involves calculations using the Binomial Pricing Model.) Suppose a firm's initial parameter values are $V = 500$, $X = 400$, $T = 3$, $V_3^u = 750$, and $V_3^d = 333$, $p = 0.7$, and $r_f = 5$ percent.
   a. Compute the current values of the firm's levered equity, E_L, and debt, D(original).
   b. Compute updated parameter values after the following actions by the firm's management. Management issues additional pure-discount debt that has a promised payment of 688.5 at time $T = 3$ and has the same priority as the firm's original debt. This new debt is sold at its fair value. Management uses the proceeds to double the firm's operations (i.e., V, V_3^u, and V_3^d all double in value). Compute the effect of this expansion on the values of the original debtholders' and shareholders' securities.

15. (This problem involves calculations using the Binomial Pricing Model.) Suppose a firm's initial parameter values are $V = 500$, $X = 400$, $T = 3$, $V_3^u = 750$, $V_3^d = 333$, $p =$

0.7, and r_f = 5 percent. V, V_3^u, and V_3^d include the firm's current investment of 161 of idle cash in the risk-free security.

a. Compute the current values of the firm's debt and levered equity, D and E_L, respectively.

b. Compute updated parameter values after management uses idle cash to retire *half* of the firm's debt at a price of 161. How did the firm's debtholders and shareholders fare with this decision?

16. (This problem involves calculations using the Binomial Pricing Model.) Suppose a firm's initial parameter values are $V = 500$, $X = 400$, $T = 3$, $V_3^u = 750$, $V_3^d = 333$, $p = 0.7$, and $r_f = 5$ percent.

a. Calculate the current values of the firm's debt and levered equity, D and E_L, respectively.

b. Calculate the value of the firm's debt and levered equity, D(new) and E_L(new), after the following actions by the firm's management. The firm's management, fearing that they will lose their jobs if the firm goes bankrupt, immediately sell all of the firm's assets for a fair price of 500, and invest the proceeds in the riskless security. How did debtholders and shareholders fare with this decision?

17. (This problem involves calculations using the Binomial Pricing Model.) Suppose a firm's initial parameter values are $V = 500$, $X = 400$, $T = 3$, $V_3^u = 750$, $V_3^d = 333$, $p = 0.7$, and $r_f = 5$ percent.

a. Compute the current values of the firm's debt and levered equity, D and E_L, respectively.

b. Compute updated parameter values after the following actions by the firm's management. Management has identified a project that requires an initial outlay of 150 and will provide time $T = 3$ payoffs of either $P_3^u = 300$ or $P_3^d = 0$. Management has determined that the present value of the project's payoffs is 207, so its *NPV* is 57. The project can be undertaken only if shareholders contribute the required capital of 150 out of their own pockets. Should management recommend that shareholders contribute the funds?

Creative Thinking Issues

1. From the perspective of the benefits of the separation of ownership and control, how might the economic growth of a (closed) economy be affected by the size and industrial diversity of the economy?

2. Given current accounting regulations imposed on publicly traded companies by the Securities and Exchange Commission (SEC) and the Financial Accounting Standards Board (FASB), what opportunities do managers have to manipulate the firm's earnings for their private benefit?

3. In discussing principal–agent conflicts between management and shareholders, we generally focus on the firm's senior management. However, principal-agent conflicts exist at all levels of management in a large firm. Thus, principal-agent conflicts may exist between the firm's senior managers and its middle managers. That is, senior management want middle managers to act in the interest of the firm's shareholders (even if senior managers themselves stray from this directive), while middle managers may wish to act in their own interest. Discuss this secondary agency conflict, and think of some mechanisms that senior management may use to resolve the conflict.

4. How would you adjust any of the valuation models developed under ideal conditions for any one of the real-world factors discussed in this chapter?

Project and Analyses

1. Choose a firm and identify its major stakeholders. (SEC filings are useful for this task.)
2. Identify two firms, one of which appears to have a substantial number of profitable investment opportunities, while the other does not. Examine their capital structures and, if possible, the specifics of senior management's compensation contracts. Do the differences in the firms' capital structures and/or senior management's compensation contracts appear to reflect the difference in their investment opportunities?
3. Identify a firm whose management, in your opinion, has been engaging in *empire building*. Provide specific evidence of their activities in this regard, and evaluate the firm's recent earnings and stock-price performances.
4. Review the empirical evidence presented in Chapter 1, and develop a list relating specific evidence to one or more of the real-world factors presented in this chapter.

CHAPTER

Information Asymmetry and the Markets for Corporate Securities

4

4.1 INTRODUCTION

In this chapter, we formally introduce the problem of *information asymmetry* in the markets for corporate securities, and its implications for a firm's debt and equity markets, ownership structure, capital structure, and dividend policy. In brief, the problem is as follows. A firm's management generally has better information about the value of the firm than its (actual or potential) shareholders and creditors. This is so because the firm's management must refrain from releasing information about the firm's strategic plans to either the firm's shareholders or its creditors, lest this information be leaked to the firm's competitors, which would cripple the firm's ability to compete and therefore reduce the firm's value. Therefore, the firm faces a dilemma: without funds, it cannot pursue profitable investment projects, and yet it is difficult or impossible to sell securities to ill-informed public investors.[1]

4.2 ECONOMIC THEORIES OF THE EFFECTS OF INFORMATION ASYMMETRY

Theories of the effects of information asymmetry on the market for a publicly traded asset were first formulated in the economics literature, though the importance of their application to financial markets was quickly recognized. Therefore, we begin by discussing two of the pioneering theoretical analyses of information asymmetry in the economics literature, those of Akerlof (1970) and Spence (1973). A review of these classic articles serves not only to provide alternative contexts in which issues related to information asymmetry can be viewed, but also to introduce many of the basic concepts and terminology that are employed later in the finance literature.

4.2.1 Akerlof: Information Asymmetry and the Market for *Lemons*

Akerlof (1970) provided the first theoretical analysis of the implications of information asymmetry for the market for an asset trading in a public market. To illustrate his arguments, Akerlof referred to the market for used automobiles. Below we provide a synopsis of his analysis.

Suppose a large number of units of a particular model of automobile are manufactured and sold in a given year, and the quality of these units ultimately varies from excellent to *lemon*. (For the uninformed, an automobile that displays frequent or

---

[1]Like Chapter 2, this chapter features the works of several recent Nobel laureates. The winners of the 2001 Nobel Prize in Economics were George Akerlof, Michael Spence, and Joseph Stiglitz.

chronic mechanical problems is called a *lemon*.) Later, the owners of many of these units wish to sell their unit for reasons that are not known to (or not believed by) prospective buyers.

Moral Hazard

Some of the units in the secondary market are lemons and some are not. Sellers who have a lemon, of course, know they have lemon. However, they have an incentive to exaggerate the quality of their unit, because telling the truth about the condition of their unit will limit the proceeds from the sale and will make it difficult to sell the unit. Instead, for the short selling period involved, the seller of a lemon (who, it is assumed, lacks moral scruples) can put his or her unit in a condition that *mimics* the condition of better quality units, and then claim that the unit is of good quality.

Consequently, prospective buyers of this model will be unable to distinguish the lemons from the non-lemons among all the units that are for sale in the secondary market. All prospective buyers face the *hazard* that they will unwittingly purchase a lemon rather than a good-quality unit. In subsequent literature, this problem is called *moral hazard*.

Pooling Equilibrium

If the sellers of lemons are successful in the *mimicking* strategy, the (temporary) equilibrium price will be the same for all units. This common price will reflect the average quality of all units in the market, which all prospective buyers are assumed to know. In the finance literature, this type of equilibrium is called a *pooling equilibrium*, because all units in the market are combined, or pooled, to determine the common price.

However, this equilibrium is not sustainable. Sellers who know that they have a high quality unit know that the value of their unit is higher than the current market price. Thus, many owners of non-lemon units (particularly those who own excellent units) will withdraw their units from the market, causing the average quality of the units remaining in the market to fall. If we continue with the assumption that prospective buyers always know the average quality of the units available in the market, a subsequent pooling equilibrium price will emerge that is *lower* than the initial price (i.e., the price prior to the exit of the owners of high quality units). This process, involving the exit of owners of higher quality units and a subsequent reduction in the average quality and market price of the remaining units, might continue until only the lowest quality units, the lemons, remain in the market. Essentially, the market for used units of this model collapses.

Adverse Selection

Akerlof provides additional illustrations of the lemons problem, and also discusses mechanisms that are used to mitigate the problem. This discussion presages the development of analogous theories and models in corporate finance. For instance, Akerlof discusses the problem of *adverse selection* in the health insurance market. In general, health insurers attempt to estimate, for each individual insurance applicant, the probability that he or she will file an insurance claim, and insurance premiums are priced accordingly. However, this is a costly and imperfect process, in large part because each individual knows the status of his or her own health better than the insurer; hence, we have a case of information asymmetry. Ultimately, an insurer must offer a common premium to a specified group of individuals that reflects the average health of the individuals in the group, even though the individuals in the group differ in terms of their health, and thus the probability of a claim. The inevitable result is that those members of the group who are less healthy (and thus more likely to file a claim) will be more likely to purchase an insurance policy. Thus, a policy originally priced to reflect the average health of an identified group will be inadequate to compensate the insurer for the *ex post* subgroup of individuals that actually purchase a policy.

Screening

As Akerlof notes, health insurers attempt to attenuate this adverse selection problem by more effectively *screening* potential customers to create a more homogeneous group to which a specific insurance policy and premium can successfully apply. He illustrates screening by referring to the case of group insurance, in which all employees of a given organization, such as a large firm, are offered a common insurance policy and premium. Although the individual employees undoubtedly vary in terms of their health, and thus the probability of a claim, the identification of an employment group represents an effective screening from the population at large, because all of the employees are at least healthy enough to hold a job. The insurer also benefits from economies of scale in screening costs per individual relative to the costs of screening all individual applicants in a population.

Certification, Costly Signaling, and the Separating Equilibrium

Akerlof also introduces the concept of *certification* as a means of mitigating the lemons problem. Here Akerlof focuses on the job market, considering the role of education as a means by which prospective employees can certify their qualifications, and thereby separate themselves from other prospective employees who are less qualified.

Although Akerlof does not use such terms, education is a means by which high-quality prospective employees can force a *separating equilibrium* (as opposed to a pooling equilibrium as described above) by using a *costly signal* (i.e., bearing the cost and effort of obtaining a particular degree) of their quality. However, to be effective in creating such a separating equilibrium, the educational signal also must be *credible*—a poor education may be indistinguishable from no education in the eyes of prospective employers.

Reputation

Akerlof also stresses the importance of *reputation* as a means of mitigating the lemons problem. Here Akerlof uses the credit markets to illustrate his points. He argues that potential borrowers sometimes can be effectively screened by examining their past repayment records, or reputations.

Contract Enforcement

In addition, lenders can take actions *ex post* to attempt to enforce repayment from a defaulting borrower (i.e., a borrower revealed *ex post* to be a lemon). Of course, the effectiveness of the contract enforcement mechanism depends largely on (a) specifications in the loan contract that would allow the lender to take enforcement actions (such as seizing collateralized property in the event of default) (b) the ability of the lender to monitor the borrower's behavior, particularly with respect to the use of the borrowed funds, and (c) the effectiveness of the legal system to which the lender appeals to enforce repayment in the event of default.

Guarantees

Finally, Akerlof discusses the important role of *guarantees* in mitigating the lemons problem. He refers to a market for merchandise that is potentially fraught with variations in quality that are unobservable to consumers. Firms that produce a high-quality version of a particular product have an incentive to provide a costly signal of the quality of their product that is difficult or impossible for the producers of low-quality versions of the product to mimic. Depending on the product, a money-back guarantee can be an effective signal. The cost of mimicking will be higher for the producers of the low-quality version of the product (i.e., more frequent refunds on returned merchandise).

4.2.2 Spence: Job Market Signaling

Spence (1973) extends Akerlof's theoretical analysis of the information asymmetry problem by introducing the concepts of *information transfer mechanisms*, which lead to *information equilibria*. (See Alchian and Demsetz 1972, Riley 1979, Rothschild and Stiglitz 1976, and Wilson 1977 for additional theoretical analyses.) Although the subject of Spence's paper is the job market, he argues that his paradigm applies to other markets as well, including the credit markets.

We summarize Spence's labor market model as follows. Suppose that, in evaluating a job applicant, an employer has access to two types of observable attributes: unalterable attributes or *indices*, such as age, race and sex; and *signals*, which are subject to manipulation by the applicant. The effectiveness, or *power*, of a signal depends critically on two closely related conditions: (a) the signal must be correlated with, or effectively *reveal*, the applicant's inherent productive capability, and (b) a signal that is proffered by a (truly) more productive applicant cannot be easily *mimicked* by less productive applicants. Condition (a) suggests that the power of a signal is directly related to the cost of obtaining it.

An example of a *costly signal* in the job market is education. Using the example of education as a signal, Spence describes what will come to be known as a *separating equilibrium*: "An equilibrium is defined in the context of a feedback loop, in which employer expectations lead to offered wages to various levels of education, which in turn lead to investment in education by individuals" (p. 368). Spence's "feedback loop" equilibrium structure includes feedback that the employer receives after hiring employees over time: "After hiring, the discovery of the actual relationships between education and productivity in the sample leads to revised expectations or beliefs. Here the cycle starts again. An equilibrium is best thought of as a set of beliefs that are confirmed or at least not contradicted by the new data at the end of the loop just described. Such beliefs will tend to persist over time as new entrants into the market flow through" (p. 368).

4.3 THE BASIC CAUSE OF INFORMATION ASYMMETRY IN THE MARKETS FOR CORPORATE SECURITIES

Product market competition and the separation of ownership and control in a firm conspire to create an asymmetry between the firm's management and the financial markets regarding value-relevant information about the firm. To explain, assume that the common interest of the shareholders of a publicly traded firm is to maximize the market value of the firm's equity, and that shareholders can devise a perfect contract with management to ensure that management will act strictly in this interest. (That is, we ignore the shareholder–management principal–agent problem for now.)

To create value for their shareholders, management must develop strategic plans and operations that will yield profits as it operates in its product or service market, which is assumed to be competitive. Of course, by their very nature strategic plans and operations must not be divulged to the firm's competitors. Consequently, management cannot divulge the firm's strategic plans and operations even to the firm's shareholders. Why? Because if they had a policy of doing so, then the firm's competitors could simply purchase some of the firm's shares in the secondary market, thereby becoming shareholders, thereby gaining access to this strategic information! By extension, management would be reluctant to divulge strategic information to the firm's creditors, at least to the extent that the debt is publicly traded.

For these reasons, management generally, and necessarily, has better information about the state of the firm's operations—and thus the true value of the firm's shares—than do the firm's shareholders, creditors, and the market as a whole. This problem has a number of important implications for our analyses throughout the text because it (a) further emphasizes the critical role of management in a firm with diffuse ownership, (b) raises questions about the informativeness of the market values of the firm's securities, (c) may affect the firm's optimal ownership structure and governance, (d) poses problems in terms of devising an optimal contract with management, and (e) can effect several aspects of the firm's financial policies and strategies. We discuss these implications throughout the remainder of the chapter.

4.4 THE VALUATION OF PUBLICLY TRADED EQUITY UNDER ASYMMETRIC INFORMATION: AN ILLUSTRATION

The discussions thus far suggest that the market value of a publicly traded firm may not reflect its true value because it may not reflect information known only to the firm's insiders. Instead, market values may tend to reflect pooling equilibria. Indeed, only if a firm can successfully signal its *true value* will its market value reflect its true value. As such, there are a number of possible outcomes with regard to the relationships between the market values of firms and their true values. In Table 4-1 we illustrate several possible outcomes for a set of hypothetical firms labeled A, B, C, D, and E.

The first column of numbers in the table contains the true values of each firm, which range in descending order from 500 for firm A to 100 for firm E. The average true value is 300. But if the market is unable whatsoever to distinguish the values of these five firms, the market values of all five will reflect a pooling equilibrium; that is, the market values of all five firms will be equal to their average true value, or 300, as indicated in the second column of numbers in the table. This pooling equilibrium results in the mispricing of four of the five firms, ranging from gross undervaluation (500 true value versus 300 market value) to gross overvaluation (100 true value versus 300 market value).

Alternatively, consider the scenario in which the market is partially able to separate these firms into two groups. The first group includes firms A, B, and C, which are known to have higher true values than the firms in the second group, D and E. As indicated in the column of numbers labeled *Partially Separating Equilibrium*, the market values of firms A, B, and C will reflect the average of their true values, or 400, whereas

TABLE 4-1 Theoretical Consequences of Information Asymmetry
True Values versus Market Values of Firms in a Pooling Equilibrium,
a Partially Separating Equilibrium, and a Fully Separating Equilibrium

| | | Market Values | | |
Firm	True Value	Pooling Equilibrium	Partially Separating Equilibrium	Fully Separating Equilibrium
A	500	300	400*	500
B	400	300	400*	400
C	300	300	400*	300
D	200	300	150**	200
E	100	300	150**	100
Average	*300*	*300*	*300*	*300*

*Market value reflects average of true values of firms A, B, and C.
**Market value reflects average of true values of firms D and E.

the market values of firms D and E will reflect the average of their true values, or 150. A partially separating equilibrium such as this may occur if firms A, B, and C are able to send a (common) powerful signal to the market regarding their true value that firms D and E are unable to mimic. In this scenario, mispricing is reduced relative to the case of a pooling equilibrium, though it is not eliminated.

Finally, we consider the possibility of a fully separating equilibrium. As indicated in the last column of numbers in the table, under a fully separating equilibrium the market value of each and every firm reflects its true value. A fully separating equilibrium such as this can be obtained only if each firm can send a unique and powerful signal of its true value to the market, a signal that the other firms (i.e., firms with lower true values) cannot mimic.

4.5 INFORMATION ASYMMETRY AND THE QUALITY OF THE MARKET FOR A FIRM'S EQUITY

The discussions in the previous sections suggest that information asymmetry can affect the *quality* of the market for a firm's securities. The quality of the market for a stock is closely related to its information efficiency—that is, the extent to which a stock's current price incorporates all available information, and therefore is an accurate reflection of its true value. If all information is freely available to all investors (as in an ideal market), the market for corporate securities should be highly efficient in this regard. However, under conditions of information asymmetry, obtaining a high level of information efficiency is problematic.

The crux of the problem is that some traders may have access to private information that is not available to other traders. If the market price at a given point in time does not reflect such private information, these *informed traders* can profit from their trades with the relatively *uninformed traders*. If such circumstances are chronic, the relatively uninformed traders may find it impossible to earn even normal (risk-adjusted) returns on corporate securities, and therefore will not participate in the markets for corporate securities. In extreme cases, the market for a corporate security will fail.

Actions Speak Louder Than Words

Below we summarize Healy and Palepu's (1995) analysis of the struggle of CUC International's management to convince the market of the firm's value. It serves as a case study in information asymmetry and signaling.

Healy and Palepu provide the following description of CUC's business:

> CUC International is a membership-based consumer services company which markets its membership programs to credit card holders of major financial, retailing, and oil companies, including Chase Manhattan, Citibank, Sears, J.C. Penney, and Amoco . . . CUC's most popular product is *Shoppers Advantage*. Consumers pay an annual membership fee for this service, which entitles them to call the company's operators on a toll-free line or to use on-line computer access seven days a week to inquire about and/or buy brand-name products . . . Purchase orders are executed through independent vendors who directly ship the merchandise to the customers, enabling the company to carry no inventory . . . (pp. 114–115)

Over the period of 1984 to 1987, CUC reported impressive growth in operating cash flows. This growth continued in 1988 to 1989 when it introduced three new products: *Travelers Advantage*, *AutoVantage*, and *Premier Dining*. However, its stock price began to falter after analysts expressed concern about the profitability of the new products. Attention focused on burgeoning marketing costs, which the firm capitalized and expensed over three years.

> [B]etween late October 1988 and March 1989 the firm's stock price declined by 35% relative to the market . . . CUC's managers were puzzled by the substantial stock price drop . . . Based on internal data, management's forecasts of the pay-offs from new products would more than justify the increased marketing outlays . . . (p. 118)

Given their information about the potential of the firm's new products, CUC's management believed that the company's stock was significantly undervalued. They viewed this as a serious problem, because in early 1989 they were considering the stock acquisition of Entertainment Publications, a company engaged in publishing merchandise coupon books. Management also was concerned that the undervaluation would increase the threat of a hostile takeover by an informed investor (p. 121).

The authors analyzed data from analyst reports, press releases, management reports, and interviews with management and key analysts. This data led them to develop two potential explanations for the divergence in managers' and investors' valuations of CUC.

> The first explanation . . . is that the two groups had a divergence in beliefs about the value of marketing outlays for new products . . . Given their knowledge of the firm's marketing plans and the types of customers they were attracting, management believed that capitalizing marketing costs and then expensing them over several years, rather than writing off the entire amount immediately, provided investors with a more accurate picture of the future cash flow benefits of marketing outlays . . .
>
> Financial analysts, however, argued that CUC's accounting was aggressive. They viewed the value of the firm's marketing outlays as highly uncertain because future membership renewal rates for new products are difficult to forecast . . . (pp. 121–122)
>
> In responding to analysts' concerns . . . management pointed out that the time and resources spent in developing and implementing effective marketing strategies produced information that is not generally available to investors, including data on the success rates of prior marketing efforts, the types of potential customers that are most likely to respond to future marketing campaigns, the types of customers that renew their subscriptions, and the sensitivity of renewal and sign-up rates to changes in economic conditions. Management argued that based on this information the additional membership acquisition outlays required as start-up for the new products being introduced were profitable investments for stockholders . . . (pp. 122–123)

(continued)

A second explanation ... is that investors believed that managers were not acting in the interest of stockholders in managing assets in place or making new investments. We refer to this explanation as an agency explanation. For CUC, the divergence in interest could be manifested in inefficient operating management or overinvestment in new membership acquisition ... (p. 123)

Healy and Palepu point out that some of the evidence is consistent with both explanations: "it is difficult to determine whether investors' initial skepticism about the firm's future performance arose from a concern about management's motives in increasing marketing outlays or from a genuine difference in opinion about the value of these investments" (p. 125).

The authors then document a series of actions taken by CUC's management to convince investors that management believed the firm's stock was undervalued.

In early 1989 CUC's management abandoned its efforts to communicate the value of marketing outlays through financial reporting. It decided not to provide internal market research data that justified its view of the value of marketing outlays for new products to dispersed outside stockholders and analysts because the disclosure of such proprietary data would enable other companies to replicate CUC's innovative business concept and strategy. Instead, CUC's managers changed the firm's accounting policy and adopted a series of financial policy measures between March 1989 and February 1990 with a view to signaling their optimism about the value of marketing for new products. First, they paid a large special dividend financed by debt and announced plans to increase management's ownership stake in the company. They subsequently used the firm's excess cash flow to accelerate debt repayments and to repurchase stock, underscoring the firm's strong cash flow position ... (pp. 125–126)

These actions had their intended effect: "in the 12 months from the day prior to the recapitalization to the day after the repurchase announcements, CUC's stock price increased by 43% relative to the market, offsetting the prior decline" (p. 132). Moreover, the firm's stock continued to outperform the market for several years: "From the day after the repurchase to December 31, 1993, CUC's stock price increased by a further 520% relative to the market" (p. 132).

Source: Reprinted from *Journal of Financial Economics* 38, no. 2, P. M. Healey and K. G. Palepu, "The Challenges of Investor Communication: The Case of CUC International, Inc.," pp. 111–40, Copyright 1995, with permission of Elsevier Science.

In this section, we discuss three common measures of the *quality* of the secondary market for a firm's stock. In Chapter 5, we discuss the role of *disclosure regulations* imposed by the U.S. Securities and Exchange Commission (SEC) in limiting the scope of information asymmetry in the U.S. markets for publicly traded securities.

4.5.1 Measures of the Quality of Trading in a Stock

Ultimately, the quality of trading in a stock depends on many factors, of which information asymmetry is only one (albeit an important one). Here we briefly discuss three common measures of quality: (a) *float*, (b) *turnover*, and (c) *bid-ask spread*. In the next subsection, we provide values of these three measures for a sample of stocks.

Float

A stock's *float* is the number of shares that are, at least potentially, actively traded. Float is generally measured as the number of shares outstanding less the total number of shares held by insiders and other investors who own at least 5 percent of the outstanding shares. A stock's float is important because it measures the potential for a typical investor to purchase the firm's shares, and by extension the potential interest of the investing public in the firm's shares. Moreover, if insiders or other well-informed investors hold a substantial proportion of a given firm's shares, investors may perceive that they face a substantial information disadvantage in trading the firm's shares (despite the prohibition on insider trading).

Turnover

A stock's turnover is defined as the ratio of the number of shares traded over a specified period of time (such as a year) to the total number of shares outstanding. Thus, turnover is a measure of the investing public's actual, or *ex post*, trading interest. Based on the discussions above, information asymmetry may dampen trading interest in a firm's shares. In addition, a stock's turnover is positively related to the natural volatility of the value of a firm's shares, which in turn depends on the overall flow of value-relevant information concerning the firm.

Bid-Ask Spread

We can also gain valuable insight into the quality of the market for a given firm's shares by examining its typical bid-ask spread. To explain this measure, we must first explain some details of trading in U.S. equity markets. In each of the U.S. stock markets (NYSE, AMEX, and NASDAQ), *dealers* continuously provide bid and ask quotes for each of its listed stocks during trading hours.[2] The *bid price* is the price at which the dealer is willing to *purchase* a specified number of the firm's shares, while the *ask price* is the price at which the dealer is willing to *sell* a specified number of shares. By offering to purchase or sell a firm's shares at any time, it is said that a dealer *makes a market* for the stock; thus, dealers are called *market makers*.

Of course, a dealer always sets his or her ask price slightly higher than the bid price. The difference between a dealer's ask and bid prices is known as the *bid-ask spread*. Generally, we express the bid-ask spread as a percentage of the stock price. Specifically, the percentage spread is the ratio of the difference between the ask and bid prices to the average of the bid and ask prices, as shown in Equation 4.1:

$$\text{Bid} - \text{Ask Spread }(\%) = \left[\frac{\text{Ask} - \text{Bid}}{(\text{Ask} + \text{Bid})/2} \right] \times 100. \qquad \textbf{(4.1)}$$

How does a stock's bid-ask spread relate to the quality of the market for the stock? We provide a two-part answer to this question. First, the spread is one of three recognized components of the overall cost of trading a stock. The other two are *brokerage commissions* and *price impact*. Price impact refers to the tendency for an investor's trade to affect the price of the stock—specifically, for a purchase to raise the price and a sale to lower the price. Spread is clearly costly to an investor if the investor must

---

[2]On the NYSE and AMEX, a *specialist* is designated as the exclusive dealer for a given stock. In contrast, on the NASDAQ many dealers compete for trading business in any given stock. Also, on the NYSE and AMEX traders (working through their brokers) can meet on the floor of the exchange to negotiate a price, while on the NASDAQ all trades in any given stock involve a dealer as one of the trading parties.

purchase a given stock at the dealer's ask price and later sell it at the dealer's bid price. Overall trading costs tend to inhibit trading in a stock, and can ultimately affect the informational efficiency of the market for the stock. This is so because, as a practical matter, trading must occur in order for new information to be incorporated into the price of a stock.

Second, according to theory (e.g., Stoll 1989), the bid-ask spread contains three components, all of which represent costs that the dealer incurs, and are passed on to traders via the spread. These three costs are (a) *adverse selection costs*, (b) *inventory costs*, and (c) *order processing costs*. Of these, adverse selection costs are most pertinent to our discussion in this chapter, and are briefly explained as follows.

As a dealer establishes a particular set of bid and ask prices, he or she stands ready to trade at these prices with any trader. In theoretical models, two distinct types of investors are relevant: (a) *liquidity traders*, who buy or sell only to adjust the composition of their portfolios (and explicitly *not* on the basis of any private information), and (b) *informed traders*, who trade on the basis of private information that they possess and which, it is assumed, is not reflected in the current market price. Unfortunately, the dealer cannot distinguish between the liquidity and informed traders. Therefore, the dealer must set the spread so that expected profits from trades with liquidity traders at least offset expected losses from trades with informed traders. As such, the spread depends critically on the relative proportions of liquidity versus informed traders who are present in the market for a stock, which in turn depend on the extent to which the market for the stock is beset by information asymmetry.

A serious problem arises if informed trading is relatively frequent. In this case, the dealer must set a relatively wide spread. However, because the spread is a cost of trading for liquidity traders, these traders will tend to reduce their trading in the stock, which then exacerbates the problem. In the extreme, a dealer may not be able to set a spread that yields an expected profit overall, in which case the market for the stock fails.

4.5.2   Float, Turnover, and Bid-Ask Spreads for a Sample of Stocks

In Table 4-2 we provide values of each of the above measures of market quality for a sample of stocks. The sample consists of the stocks of selected firms in each Standard & Poor's (S&P) index as of year-end 1999. For each of these firms, (a) float is measured as the ratio of free-floating shares to total shares outstanding, based on trading data for November 2000 and expressed in percent; (b) turnover is measured as the ratio of the volume of trading in the stock during three months, September–November 2000, to total shares outstanding, expressed as a percentage annual rate; and (c) the bid-ask spread is measured using bid and ask quotes obtained on November 27, 2000.

Float varies considerably across the sampled firms, ranging from 36.2 percent for Titan International Corp. (a SmallCap firm) to 99.0 percent for seven firms, six of which are included among the S&P Industrials and the other among the S&P Utilities. Based on the median float percentages shown for each S&P index sample, float percentage tends to be directly related to firm size (90.8 percent for the Industrials, 71.0 percent for the MidCaps, and 65.1 percent for the SmallCaps).

Turnover varies tremendously across the sampled stocks, ranging from 24.2 percent for Titan International to 677.0 percent for Mercury Interactive, both of which

TABLE 4-2   Bid-Ask Spreads, Float, and Annual Turnover

Selected Stocks in the Indicated S&P Indexes, December 31, 1999

Company	Stock Exchange	Ticker	Float[1]	Annual Turnover[2]	Bid-Ask Spread[3]
S&P Industrials					
AT&T	nyse	T	99.0%	139.6%	0.32%
Cisco Systems	nasdaq	CSCO	98.0%	206.0%	0.12%
Exxon Mobil Corp	nyse	XOM	99.0%	44.0%	0.07%
General Electric	nyse	GE	99.0%	38.2%	0.37%
General Motors	nyse	GM	87.0%	122.5%	0.25%
IBM	nyse	IBM	99.0%	108.5%	0.19%
Intel	nasdaq	INTC	93.0%	226.3%	0.14%
MERCK	nyse	MRK	99.0%	63.6%	0.14%
Microsoft	nasdaq	MSFT	81.0%	206.2%	0.09%
Procter & Gamble	nyse	PG	99.0%	78.7%	0.09%
YAHOO!	nasdaq	YHOO	46.0%	592.4%	0.15%
MEDIAN:			**90.8%**	**166.0%**	**0.17%**
S&P Transports					
Brlngtn Nthrn Santa Fe	nyse	BNI	87.0%	77.8%	0.23%
Delta Air Lines	nyse	DAL	72.0%	143.8%	0.38%
FEDEX	nyse	FDX	79.0%	86.4%	0.02%
Union Pacific	nyse	UNP	82.0%	82.4%	0.13%
US AIRWAYS	nyse	U	62.1%	81.8%	0.16%
MEDIAN:			**79.0%**	**82.4%**	**0.16%**
S&P Utilities					
Duke Energy	nyse	DUK	97.0%	123.3%	0.29%
Enron	nyse	ENE	88.0%	80.4%	0.24%
Southern Co.	nyse	SO	99.0%	79.8%	0.21%
MEDIAN:			**97.0%**	**80.4%**	**0.24%**
S&P MidCaps					
Airborne Freight	nyse	ABF	78.1%	200.1%	1.34%
Alaska Air Gp	nyse	ALK	83.9%	210.4%	0.22%
Burlington Inds	nyse	BUR	65.5%	122.9%	4.44%
Clayton Homes	nyse	CMH	71.0%	43.0%	1.82%
Federal Signal	nyse	FSS	96.0%	57.8%	0.57%
Harley-Davidson	nyse	HDI	85.0%	69.0%	0.41%
Mark IV Industries	nyse	IV	*	*	*
Microchip Tech	nasdaq	MCHP	65.0%	406.8%	0.96%
Millennium Pharm.	nasdaq	MLNM	52.0%	352.3%	0.21%
Murphy Oil	nyse	MUR	59.0%	113.3%	0.10%
Officemax	nyse	OMX	82.0%	163.1%	2.35%
Ogden Corp.	nyse	OG	69.1%	81.6%	0.84%
Pennzoil-Quaker St.	nyse	PZL	71.0%	77.4%	0.97%
Starbucks	nasdaq	SBUX	93.0%	268.4%	0.14%
Storage Tech	nyse	STK	52.0%	118.5%	0.61%
Tyson Foods	nyse	TSN	39.7%	36.0%	0.48%
MEDIAN:			**71.0%**	**118.5%**	**0.61%**

TABLE 4-2 (continued)

Company	Stock Exchange	Ticker	Float[1]	Annual Turnover[2]	Bid-Ask Spread[3]
		S&P SmallCaps			
Brown Shoe	nyse	BWS	81.0%	89.8%	0.53%
Diagnostic Products	nyse	DP	62.8%	108.0%	0.81%
Fedders	nyse	FJC	75.6%	34.3%	3.73%
Huffy	nyse	HUF	62.8%	432.3%	1.75%
Mercury Interactive	nasdaq	MERQ	77.0%	677.0%	0.30%
Nashua	nyse	NSH	38.6%	58.1%	7.79%
Photronics	nasdaq	PLAB	77.9%	372.7%	0.31%
Primark	nyse	PMK	*	*	*
Project Softw. & Dev.	nasdaq	PSDI	60.0%	194.1%	0.59%
Titan International	nyse	TWI	36.2%	24.2%	3.45%
Toro	nyse	TTC	85.0%	78.5%	0.72%
Vertex Pharm.	nasdaq	VRTX	65.1%	590.6%	0.44%
MEDIAN:			**65.1%**	**108.0%**	**0.72%**

Correlation Matrix

	Float	*Turnover*	*Spread*
Float	1.00		
Turnover	−0.20	1.00	
Spread	−0.46	−0.17	1.00

[1]Floating Shares Percentage = (Floating Shares)/(Total Shares Outstanding): Floating shares exclude shares held by insiders and 5% owners.
[2]Annual Turnover = (Shares traded in most recent three months)/(Total Shares Outstanding), at an annual rate.
[3]Bid-Ask Spread = (Ask Price – Bid Price)/([(Ask Price + Bid Price)/2]. Ask and bid prices were obtained during trading day of November 27, 2000.
*Firm was acquired in 2000.

are S&P SmallCap stocks. Turnover does not appear to be closely related to firm size, though the highest median turnover is observed for the S&P Industrials (166.0 percent).

Bid-ask spreads also vary substantially across the sampled firms, ranging from 0.02 percent for FEDEX (a firm in the S&P Transports) to 7.79 percent for Nashua (a SmallCap firm). Based on the median values shown, bid-ask spreads are strongly inversely related to firm size, as the median spreads are 0.17, 0.16, and 0.24 percent for the S&P Industrials, Transports, and Utilities, respectively, and 0.61 percent and 0.72 percent for the S&P MidCaps and SmallCaps, respectively.

Finally, Table 4-2 also shows a matrix of the correlations of the values of these measures for the sampled stocks. The results indicate that float is weakly negatively related to turnover and somewhat more strongly negatively related to bid-ask spread, whereas turnover and bid-ask spread are weakly negatively correlated.

4.6   OPTIMAL OWNERSHIP STRUCTURE UNDER ASYMMETRIC INFORMATION: LELAND AND PYLE

In this section, we review the seminal theoretical model of Leland and Pyle (1977), who analyzed the effects of information asymmetry on a firm's value and ownership structure.

4.6.1   Statement of the Problem

Leland and Pyle begin with a discussion of the problem of information asymmetry in financial markets:

> In financial markets, informational asymmetries are particularly pronounced. Borrowers typically know their collateral, industriousness, and moral rectitude better than do lenders; entrepreneurs possess "inside" information about their own projects for which they seek financing.
>
> Lenders would benefit from knowing the true characteristics of borrowers. But moral hazard hampers the direct transfer of information between market participants. Borrowers cannot be expected to be entirely straightforward about their characteristics, nor entrepreneurs about their projects, since there may be substantial rewards for exaggerating positive qualities. And verification of true characteristics by outside parties may be costly or impossible. Without information transfer, markets may perform poorly . . . (p. 371)

4.6.2   Summary and an Illustration of the Model

Although the mathematical details of Leland and Pyle's model are too complex to present here, their model can be summarized as follows. An entrepreneur seeks financing for a project whose true value is known only to him. A direct transfer of information about the true value of the project from the entrepreneur to outside investors is impossible. However, information may be transferred by a credible signal. Here, the signal is the entrepreneur's willingness to invest in his own project, as measured by α, the fraction of the equity in the project that the entrepreneur retains. The entrepreneur invests the remainder of his personal wealth in the market portfolio.

The entrepreneur's signal is *powerful* because it imposes two types of costs on the entrepreneur. First, the entrepreneur is investing a portion of his personal wealth into the project, so if the true value of the project is low, he will lose a substantial portion of his personal wealth. Second, as the entrepreneur invests more of his personal wealth in the project, less remains for him to invest in the market portfolio—that is, the entrepreneur loses benefits of diversification, and correspondingly is more exposed to the risk of the project. Consequently, the power of the signal increases with α, so the market value of the project increases with α.

The entrepreneur's overall expected utility changes with α as a result of a trade-off. As α increases, (a) the market value of the project increases, and therefore the expected utility of the entrepreneur's fractional investment in the project, but (b) the entrepreneur loses utility as a result of becoming less diversified. Ultimately, the entrepreneur chooses the level of α, denoted as α^*, which maximizes his expected utility.

We illustrate this trade-off in Figure 4-1. Shown are the market value of the project, and the entrepreneur's overall expected utility of wealth, both as functions of

FIGURE 4-1 The Market Value of an Entrepreneur's Project and the Entrepreneur's Overall Expected Utility, Both as Functions of α, the Fraction of the Project Retained by the Entrepreneur.

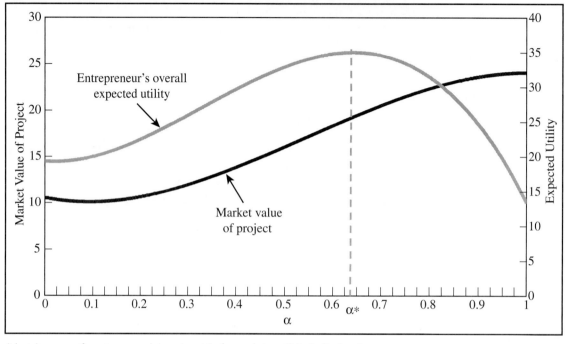

*As α increases, the entrepreneur's investment in the market portfolio is displaced.

α. In this example, the resulting optimal fraction of the project retained by the entrepreneur is α* = 0.64, or 64 percent.

4.6.3 Explaining Observed Variations in Ownership Structure as a Consequence of Information Asymmetry

The basic implication of Leland and Pyle's model is that information asymmetry is a fundamental problem that limits the *optimal* extent to which the ownership of a firm's shares can become diffuse, and thereby limits the associated benefits of diversification, both for the individual entrepreneur and perhaps the general investing public as well. Alternatively stated, Leland and Pyle's model suggests that *insiders* must own a substantial proportion of the firm's shares, which necessarily limits ownership diffusion and its attendant benefits.

Their argument may help to explain the following empirical observations about ownership structures, some of which we discussed in Chapter 1 (review Figure 1-7), and some of which we discuss later: (a) many firms, even some that are very large, are privately owned[3]; (b) Many firms are wholly owned subsidiaries of other firms, so they have but one owner; and (c) many publicly traded firms are *closely held*.

---

[3]An example of such a firm is Delaware North, Inc., a privately held firm that is included in the Fortune 500 list of the largest firms in the United States.

Information Asymmetry and the Initial Public Offering

The problem outlined by Leland and Pyle may be particularly severe in the case of a heretofore-private firm that is seeking to go public via an initial public offering (IPO) of its stock. (We discuss IPOs in detail in Chapter 12.) Their model provides a prediction that is qualitatively consistent with observations on IPOs. Generally, in an IPO only a fraction of the firm's shares (approximately a third) are offered to the public, while the firm's managers and initial financiers retain substantial ownership. Presumably, such ownership retention is a necessary signal of insiders' assessment of value.

Information Asymmetry and Ownership Structure in General

The information asymmetry problem also applies to other firms because, as we have argued, information asymmetry naturally emerges between the management and diffuse shareholders of any firm operating in a competitive product market. So the question arises, why do we observe large, publicly traded and diffusely owned firms at all? One answer to this question is that the benefits of separation of ownership and control generally outstrip costs of information asymmetry that attend the separation.

An alternative answer emerges from a less extreme interpretation of Leland and Pyle's arguments. Interpreted more narrowly, their arguments suggest the managers of a firm can send a credible signal of the firm's true value by tying a substantial portion of *their personal wealth* to the firm, rather than by necessarily owning a substantial fraction of the firm's shares. For many, if not most, managers, this is likely to be the case by default, because their current wealth is insufficient to purchase a substantial portion of the firm's shares. Moreover, the dependence of a manager's wealth on the value of his firm can be brought even closer by (a) tying the manager's salary to the firm's performance through earnings-based bonuses or (b) including stock options in the manager's contract, which will pay off only if the firm's stock price rises. (We discuss performance-based provisions in executive compensation contracts in more detail in Chapters 5 and 8.)

4.7 INFORMATION ASYMMETRY AND EXTERNAL FINANCING

In this section we briefly review several theoretical analyses of the effects of information asymmetry on a firm's optimal policies regarding leverage, terms in its debt contracts, and external financing in general. These brief discussions presage more extensive discussions on these topics in later chapters.

4.7.1 Firm Risk and Optimal Leverage

Researchers have argued that a firm's leverage may be a powerful signal of true value under conditions of information asymmetry. An example is provided by Ross (1977). In Ross's model, managers have private information regarding future cash flows. Management can distinguish its firm as a higher quality firm by issuing debt. By committing the firm to make future payments of interest and principal, management signals its confidence in the sustainability of the firm's future cash flows. Ross's model yields an interior optimum capital structure; that is, the firm employs a positive, but limited, amount of debt relative to equity.

4.7.2   Information Asymmetry and the Role of Collateral in Loans

Besanko and Thakor (1987) argue that *collateral* can act as an effective screening mechanism to mitigate the information asymmetry problem in the corporate debt market. Riskier borrowers have greater default risk, and as such they face a higher probability of losing their collateral, so they choose an unsecured loan contract with a higher interest rate. Borrowers who are less risky choose a secured loan contract with a lower interest rate. Thus, their theory suggests that collateral can serve as a powerful signal of value.

4.7.3   The *Pecking Order Hypothesis* of Corporate Financing

In his presidential address to the American Finance Association in 1983, Stewart Myers (1984) provided a description of observed corporate financing behavior called the *Pecking Order Hypothesis*.[4] He pointed out three aspects of corporate financial behavior that managers appear to exhibit nearly universally.

First, managers tend to maintain stable dividends even in the face of fluctuations over time in earnings, stock price, or investment opportunities.

Second, managers appear to prefer *internal financing* (i.e., equity financing via retained earnings) to *external financing* (i.e., funds raised via the issuance of debt or equity).

Third, if the firm is compelled to procure funds externally, managers prefer to issue the least risky security that is feasible under the circumstances. Securities that could be issued, listed in increasing order of riskiness, are straight debt, convertible debt, preferred stock, and finally, common stock. The pecking order of corporate financing ranges from internal equity/retained earnings (at the top) to common stock (at the bottom). Myers then conjectured that managers' preference rankings for these sources of financing must in some way reflect their differential costs.

In a subsequent path-breaking article, Myers and Majluf (1984) formulated Myers's observations and conjecture into a theoretical model that explains these aspects of observed corporate financing behavior as consequences of information asymmetry. They argue that the market is chronically underinformed about the relative values of various projects that firms (potentially) bring to the market, so the market tends to undervalue these projects, and thus tends to undervalue the securities issued to finance them. Basically, a pooling equilibrium forms such that, on average, uninformed investors break even on the securities they purchase. Consequently, managers (who are assumed to act in the interests of the firm's shareholders) find that the effective *cost* of external financing is generally higher than it should be, because the firm tends to surrender a substantial portion of a project's *NPV* to investors who purchase the issued securities.

This surrender of value to new investors is particularly severe if the firm issues equity, because the difference between management's valuation of the project versus the market's valuation is fully reflected in the price that the market is willing to pay for the issued security (i.e., equity). In the worst case, a manager may actually reject a profitable project if it must be financed with external equity, because the surrender cost exceeds the project's *NPV*.

---

[4]The phrase *pecking order* is borrowed from naturalists' observations of a feeding hierarchy among groups of fowl such as chickens, wherein the group's leaders get to peck at a food source first, followed by those who are lower in the hierarchy.

Issuing risky debt is also problematic. However, debt enjoys a priority status, so differences in management's and the market's valuation of a debt security should be smaller. Therefore, if external financing must be considered, debt is preferred to (i.e., is less costly than) equity.

Of course, the best way to avoid the surrender of value to the markets is to avoid external financing altogether—that is, by using internal financing. Therefore, firms tend to maintain *financial slack* at all times to be able to pursue a profitable project at any time without resorting to external financing, particularly external equity financing. Narrowly defined, financial slack includes cash and marketable securities. Broadly defined, it also includes so-called *unused debt capacity*.

An important exception to the above is the case in which management, based on their inside information, believes that their firm is *overvalued* in the market. In this case, management is motivated to issue equity. However, the market is aware of this *adverse selection* problem; consequently, a firm's announcement of their intention to issue equity conveys management's inside information to the market, and the firm's stock price falls. (We discuss evidence of, and explanations for, the generally negative market reaction to seasoned equity offering announcements in Chapter 13.)

4.8 INFORMATION ASYMMETRY AND DIVIDEND POLICY

In this section, we discuss several models in which a firm's dividend policy serves as a signal of value to a market that is at an information disadvantage relative to the firm's management.

4.8.1 Bhattacharya: Signaling with Dividends

Bhattacharya (1979) developed one of the first models that employs dividends as a signal of management's private information about the firm's future cash flows. The basic intuition behind Bhattacharya's model is as follows. Two kinds of firms exist, "good" and "bad," where expected net cash flow is higher for a good firm than for a bad firm. Managers know the expected net cash flow of their own firm (i.e., whether their firm is good or bad), but the market cannot distinguish a good firm from a bad firm. Further, it is assumed that (a) external financing is costlier than internal financing, (b) firms will always pay promised dividends in full, and (c) each manager's wealth is positively related to the firm's stock price.

Under these conditions, Bhattacharya shows that (a) only the manager of a good firm will promise to pay a dividend and (b) the amount of the dividend will be just sufficient to make the manager of the bad firm refrain from paying a *mimicking* dividend. The key aspect of the model is that, while the benefit of paying a dividend is the same for each firm, the *cost* of doing so is higher for the bad firm. That is, the bad firm has a higher probability of not having enough cash to pay the promised amount and hence a higher probability of needing costlier external financing to cover this shortfall. As a result, the bad firm is reluctant to promise a dividend. Thus, the market is able to discern a firm's true value from its dividend policy, so we have a separating equilibrium.

4.8.2 Miller and Rock: The Signaling Power of Cash Payouts

Miller and Rock (1985) developed an ingenious signaling model in which cash payouts by a firm, including dividends, share repurchases, or debt retirements, serve similar roles as powerful signals of the firm's earnings capacity, and thus its value. Any such cash payout reveals that the firm has been generating, and is expected to continue to generate, high net cash flows. In contrast, the issuance of securities, particular equity securities, reveals negative information about the firm's ability to generate earnings. Miller and Rock's model is consistent with empirical evidence (which we discuss in Chapters 13 and 14) that the firm's stock price generally rises when a firm announces a dividend increase and generally falls when the firm announces either a dividend cut or an intention to issue stock.

4.9   THE COMPOUND PROBLEM: PRINCIPAL–AGENT CONFLICTS AND INFORMATION ASYMMETRY

To this point, our discussions in Chapters 3 and 4 have treated principal–agent conflicts (i.e., either management–shareholder or shareholder–creditor conflicts) and information asymmetry as separate problems. Indeed, many of the early theoretical analyses address one or the other of these problems, but not both simultaneously. This is understandable, because each of these problems already involves complex issues, and so addressing them simultaneously would be an even more arduous task. Nevertheless, these problems generally are not separable.

To illustrate, consider again one of the most important issues identified in Chapter 3, namely the problem of getting a firm's management to adhere to the *revised directive* to maximize the market value of the firm's equity given that they have a private incentive to maximize their own personal welfare. This problem is surely exacerbated under conditions of information asymmetry, because the market value of the firm does not reflect private information known only to the firm's management. Consequently, shareholders may often be unable to determine accurately whether management is abiding by the revised directive.

In another context, under conditions of asymmetric information the firm's management has both an opportunity and incentives to exaggerate the quality of the projects that they develop over time. Regarding incentives, managers may exaggerate the quality of their new projects for at least two reasons. First, in an attempt to adhere to the revised directive, managers may exaggerate the quality of a new project to ratchet up the price of the firm's stock, which is the object of their efforts. Second, if a manager's compensation is a function of the price performance of the firm's stock, he or she has a self-serving incentive to hype up the firm's stock price, especially in the short term. (Incidentally, for either of these reasons the financial markets will question management's credibility as a source of unbiased information about the firm's value.)

In the remainder of this section, we briefly discuss three theoretical papers that, in different contexts, attempt to address agency conflicts and the information asymmetry problem simultaneously.

4.9.1   Asymmetric Information, Managerial Self-Interest, and a Firm's Financing and Dividend Policies

Noe and Rebello (1996) developed a theoretical model that simultaneously examines the effects of asymmetric information and managerial self-interest on a firm's financing and dividend policies. The setting is a firm that seeks funding for an investment opportunity, the details of which are known only to the firm's manager and a large inside shareholder. The firm's budget constraint dictates that, as more dividends are paid, more external financing is required. Thus, two questions arise. (a) Should the firm pay low or high dividends? And (b) when external financing is required, should the firm issue debt or equity?

In Chapter 3, we argued that shareholders could limit management's ability to pursue their self-interest by limiting the *free cash flow* available to them. Thus, dividends reduce agency costs of managerial discretion by disgorging excess cash. In addition, dividends may be necessary as a signal of value in an asymmetric-information world. On the other hand, higher dividends tend to increase the firm's need for external financing, which is costly given the adverse-selection problem. Noe and Rebello argue that the firm's dividend policy is determined by the relative importance of these problems. Regarding external financing, the manager generally wishes to minimize debt financing because of the discipline it imposes. However, "the costs of adverse selection associated with equity financing may force increased reliance on debt financing" (p. 639).

4.9.2 Agency Costs of Debt, Information Asymmetry, and Optimal Capital Structure

Harris and Raviv (1990) developed a theoretical model of optimal capital structure in which debt serves simultaneously (a) as a means to provide investors with information about the firm and (b) as a disciplining device to limit management's engagement in self-serving activities. In their model, the informativeness of debt is twofold:

> First, the mere ability of the firm to make its contractual payments to debtholders provides information. Second, in default management must placate creditors to avoid liquidation, either through informal negotiations or through formal bankruptcy proceedings. This process, although costly, disseminates considerable information to investors . . . This suggests that, if investors are uncertain about the quality of management and the efficacy of business strategy, they can use debt to generate information about these aspects. (pp. 321–322)

In other words, debt disciplines management via the stringent alternatives of either making timely payments of interest and principal or facing the exposure to bankruptcy proceedings, and it simultaneously provides information useful for this purpose. We discuss Harris and Raviv's theory, and other theories of optimal capital structure, in Chapter 6.

4.9.3 Adverse Incentives, Information Asymmetry, and Credit Rationing

Many firms obtain private debt financing from commercial banks (as well as other financial institutions such as insurance companies and finance companies). In dealing with a given corporate borrower, a bank will often restrict the amount of debt financing that they will provide, rather than, say, offering a schedule that involves higher interest rates as the amount borrowed increases. From an economic standpoint, it has been puzzling why banks ration credit instead of simply raising interest rates in this manner.

Stiglitz and Weiss (1981) developed a theory that attempts to solve this puzzle. They suggest that banks ration credit among their pool of borrowers instead of varying interest rates because the latter policy is fraught with two problems:

[T]he interest rate a bank charges may itself affect the riskiness of the pool of loans by either: 1) sorting potential borrowers (the adverse selection effect); or 2) affecting the actions of borrowers (the incentive effect). Both effects derive directly from the residual imperfect information which is present in loan markets after banks have evaluated loan applications. (p. 393)

4.10   Summary of Learning Objectives

In the first part of this chapter, we reviewed two seminal articles in the economics literature that broke ground on an issue that has since been recognized as important to our understanding of corporate finance: *information asymmetry*. Our review of these articles served to (a) describe the problems associated with a situation in which the seller of an asset has better information about its quality, and therefore its value, than potential buyers; (b) emphasize the seriousness of the problem, because in a worst-case scenario the market for an asset may collapse; and (c) introduce standard terminology used in discussing the problem, such as *moral hazard, adverse selection,* and *pooling versus separating equilibria.* The articles also served to introduce various mechanisms that are used in markets to mitigate the problem of information asymmetry, all of which focus on the creation of *separating equilibria.* These mechanisms include the use of (a) *screening devices*, (b) *costly signals* that are difficult or impossible to *mimic*, (c) the seller's establishment of a *reputation*, (d) *ex post contract enforcement*, and (e) *guarantees*.

The remainder of the chapter focuses on the implications of information asymmetry for (a) the ownership structure of the firm, (b) the firm's capital structure, and (c) the firm's dividend policy. Regarding ownership structure, we reviewed an important article by Leland and Pyle (1977). Their theoretical analysis shows that the willingness of an entrepreneur to invest in his or her own project is a powerful, if costly, signal of the value of the firm.

Regarding capital structure choice under information asymmetry, Ross (1977) argues that managers can distinguish their firm as a higher quality firm by issuing debt. Regarding internal versus external financing in general, Myers and Majluf (1984) argue that when there is information asymmetry between the market and managers, external financing will be costlier than internal financing. Furthermore, there is a *pecking order*, or preference structure, regarding financing choices. When in need of financing, firms prefer first to use retained earnings, then debt, and lastly external equity.

Besanko and Thakor (1987) argued that *collateral* can act as an effective screening device. Riskier borrowers have higher default risk, and thus face a higher probability of losing their collateral, so they choose an unsecured loan contract with a high interest rate. In contrast, low-risk borrowers choose secured debt with a low interest rate.

Regarding dividends, Bhattacharya (1979) developed a model in which dividends represent a costly signal of management's private information about future cash flows. Miller and Rock (1985) argued that various types of payoffs, including dividends, share repurchases, and debt retirements, can serve as effective signals of the firm's value.

Finally, we emphasized the importance of recognizing that problems associated with agency conflicts (Chapter 3) and information asymmetry (Chapter 4) are generally not separable, but instead may often be simultaneous and confounding. Harris and Raviv (1990) developed a theory of optimal capital structure in which debt serves simultaneously to provide information to investors and to discipline management. Stiglitz and Weiss (1981) provided an explanation for the common practice of banks rationing credit to a given firm, rather than simply increasing the interest rate on marginal borrowings. Banks ration because of a basic flaw in the interest-rate adjustment mechanism: if they raise the interest rate with the amount of borrowing, the bank gives the borrower an incentive to switch to a riskier project.

Review Questions and Problems

1. Regarding Akerlof's *lemons problem*,
   a. Explain the problem and its implications.
   b. Discuss possible resolutions to the problem.
2. In economic models focusing on information asymmetry, how do we describe
   a. A *pooling equilibrium*?
   b. A *separating equilibrium*?
3. Describe the problem of *moral hazard* in the market for an asset fraught with information asymmetry.
4. Describe the problem of *adverse selection* in the insurance market.
5. Briefly explain the usefulness of each of the following means of mitigating the effects of information asymmetry in the credit markets:
   a. Screening
   b. Certification
   c. Costly signaling
   d. Reputation
6. List and briefly explain the three conditions that must hold in order for *ex post* contract enforcement to be an effective means of mitigating the asymmetric information problem in credit markets.
7. Discuss the basic cause of information asymmetry in the market for corporate securities.
8. Define and discuss the three measures of the quality of the market for a stock that were mentioned in the chapter.
9. In Leland and Pyle's model of the effects of information asymmetry on ownership structure,
   a. What is the *costly signal* employed by the entrepreneur?
   b. Identify the two costs associated with the entrepreneur's signal.
10. Discuss the possible effects of information asymmetry on a firm's optimal leverage.
11. Discuss the *Pecking Order Hypothesis* of corporate financing.
12. Discuss the signaling role of collateral in a bank loan.
13. Briefly explain Bhattacharya's model in which dividends serve as a costly signal of firm value.
14. Discuss Miller and Rock's explanation of the signaling power of cash payouts.
15. Explain how principal–agent problems can be exacerbated under conditions of information asymmetry.

16. Explain the effects of asymmetric information and managerial opportunism on a firm's financing and payout policies as explained by Noe and Rebello (1996).
17. Discuss Harris and Raviv's theory of optimal capital structure.
18. Why do firms *ration* credit to borrowers rather than simply adjusting the interest rate for additional borrowings?

Creative Thinking Issues

1. Models of information asymmetry in finance focus on the situation in which management has a strict information advantage over other market participants, including the firm's current shareholders. Develop a scenario in which a firm's management is *less* informed than outside investors (at least collectively). What are the implications for a firm's financial policies?
2. Do you think information asymmetry is the primary reason for the prohibition on insider trading, or are there other reasons? In your opinion, what would be the likely effect of the removal of this prohibition on the quality of the market for a firm's stock?
3. Can you think of any means by which a firm, facing potentially adverse effects of information asymmetry as it attempts to issue new stock, can offer a *guarantee* of the value of the stock as a means of mitigating these effects?
4. Suppose you are on the board of directors of a firm whose management regularly possesses strategic information that is vital to the firm's value. What would you recommend regarding the firm's financial policies to deal with the resulting information asymmetry?

Projects and Analyses

1. Review the empirical evidence presented in Chapter 1 and develop a list relating specific evidence to one or more of the theories presented in this chapter.
2. Choose a firm and conduct an analysis of whether any of the following financial aspects of the firm appear to reflect information asymmetry:
   a. the market value of the firm
   b. the firm's ownership structure
   c. the firm's capital structure
   d. the firm's dividend policy

C H A P T E R

The Roles of Government, Securities Markets, Financial Institutions, Ownership Structure, Board Oversight, and Contract Devices

5.1 INTRODUCTION

In Chapters 3 and 4, we discussed two important classes of real-world problems that a publicly owned firm faces in developing its financial policies: principal–agent conflicts and information asymmetry problems. In this chapter, we focus on the roles of the following mechanisms in resolving, or at least mitigating, these problems: (a) government laws and regulations, (b) securities markets, (c) financial institutions, (d) board oversight, (e) ownership structure, and (f) contracting devices. Although we briefly discussed the roles of some of these mechanisms in this regard in Chapters 3 and 4, it is important to gain a perspective on how all of these mechanisms work *in tandem* to mitigate these problems.

Our discussions of these mechanisms are ordered in a progression from broad to narrow. First, we analyze the overarching restrictions imposed on the activities of all publicly traded firms by governments and security markets. Second, we discuss the roles of various participants in the securities markets, such as analysts, speculators, and arbitrageurs. Third, we focus on the relationship between ownership structure and financial policies. Fourth, we analyze the oversight role of a firm's board of directors. Fifth, we discuss the roles of various financial institutions, acting as underwriters, creditors, or equity investors. Sixth and finally, we discuss the critical role of contracts, especially between the firm and (a) its management; and (b) creditors.

Figure 5.1 provides a visual depiction of the moderating influences of these mechanisms. In the figure, mechanisms are divided between those that involve external versus internal parties.

5.2 GOVERNMENT LAWS AND REGULATIONS

Governments employ several mechanisms to alleviate both principal–agent conflicts and information asymmetry problems. These mechanisms include (a) contract law, enforcement, and regulations, and (b) general intervention in security markets.[1]

---

[1]Much of the material in this section is available at the SEC's website, www.sec.gov.

FIGURE 5-1 External and Internal Moderating Influences on a Firm

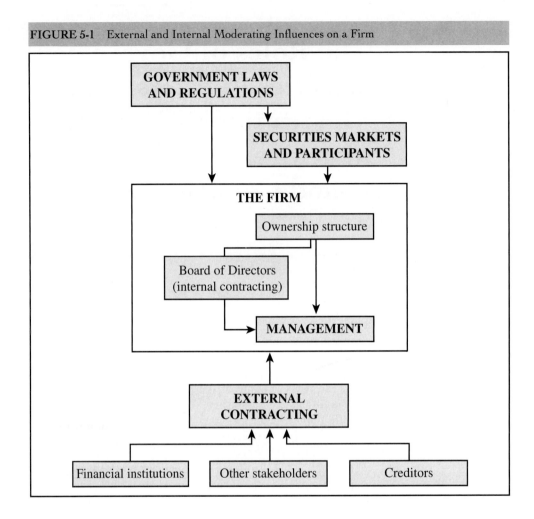

5.2.1 Contract Law, Enforcement, and Regulations

Federal, state, and local governments in the United States all play dual roles in providing the firm with services and protection on one hand, and imposing taxes, regulations, and restrictions on the other hand. The most fundamental services that governments provide are the *establishment of property rights* through legislation and the *enforcement of legal contracts* (and therefore the *protection* of property rights) through the judicial system. In addition, governments, presumably acting in the interests of constituent individuals who need employment, often provide firms with valuable financial incentives to locate in a particular geographic location such as a state or county.

Governments also impose regulations and restrictions on a firm's activities. For example, pharmaceutical companies expend substantial funds developing new drugs, but inevitably take a risk as to when and whether the federal Food and Drug Administration (FDA) will approve them for sale to the public. In addition, *changes* in regulations represent a risk factor. For example, deregulation of the U.S. transportation industry in the late 1970s (as well as the U.S. public utility industry presently) caused tremendous turmoil, but also created new opportunities for firms in the industry.

5.2.2   Government Intervention in the Securities Markets

Following the stock market crash of 1929, the U.S. Congress was under pressure to rectify observed abuses in the issuance and trading of securities in public markets. Congress' response consisted of two historic acts: the Securities Act of 1933 and the Securities Exchange Act of 1934.

The Securities Act of 1933

The Securities Act of 1933 has two basic objectives: (a) to require that investors are provided with material information concerning securities offered for public sale, and (b) to prevent misrepresentation, deceit, and other fraud in the sale of securities. The primary means of accomplishing these objectives is to require public issuers to disclose financial information through the process of *registration.* Registration is intended to provide adequate and accurate disclosure of material facts concerning the company and the securities it proposes to sell to the public so that investors can make a realistic appraisal of the merits and risks of the securities and exercise *informed* judgment in determining whether to purchase them.

The Securities Exchange Act of 1934 and the SEC

With the passage of the Securities Exchange Act of 1934, Congress created the Securities and Exchange Commission (SEC), the principal federal government regulatory body for securities markets in the United States. The SEC is an independent, nonpartisan, quasi judicial regulatory agency. The SEC's mission is to administer federal securities laws and issue rules and regulations to provide protection for investors and to ensure that the securities markets are fair and honest. This is accomplished primarily by promoting adequate and timely disclosure of information to the investing public. (The SEC also serves as adviser to federal courts in corporate reorganization proceedings under Chapter 11 of the Bankruptcy Reform Act of 1978.)

One of the most important functions of the SEC is to provide the means by which firms can comply with the registration requirement of the Securities Act of 1933. Registration statements filed with the SEC are available to the public, and require (a) a description of the company's properties and business, (b) a description of the security to be offered for sale and its relationship to the company's other capital securities, (c) information about the company's management, and (d) financial statements certified by independent public accountants. In addition, firms that wish to have their securities traded on an exchange must file annual and other periodic reports to update information contained in the original filing. In addition, issuers must send certain reports to requesting shareholders.

Voting Rights

Another provision of the Securities Act of 1934 governs soliciting proxies (votes) from holders of registered securities for the election of directors and/or for approval of other corporate action. Solicitations, whether by management or shareholder groups, must disclose all material facts concerning matters on which holders are asked to vote.

The Wild and Wooly Securities Markets before Regulation . . . And Now?

Here we present ruminations on the history of the U.S. stock market by *New York Times'* writer Floyd Norris.

The stock market was a wild and largely unregulated place when the century began. In 1901, much of the nation watched in befuddlement as the price of Northern Pacific soared without apparent reason, then plunged. The rail line had been the subject of an unannounced takeover war, in which two powerful groups—one led by J. P. Morgan and the other by Edward Harriman—tried to secure control by buying shares in the open market. When the battle was over, speculators were ruined as losses on Northern Pacific shares forced the liquidation of other stocks, causing the entire stock market to plunge. "Disaster and Ruin in Falling Market," read the headline in *The Times.* "Panic without a Parallel in Wall Street."

In those days, companies were free to give investors as much, or as little, information as they wished. There were no generally accepted accounting principles, so the profit figures that were issued were of questionable quality. Dividends—real cash payments to shareholders—were the principal measure of a company's soundness.

That began to change in the late 1920s, as individual investors poured into stocks for the first time, and the lure of capital gains began to take hold. There was still relatively little regulation, and there were plenty of reports of "pools" that manipulated stock prices. Many investors concluded that they wanted to make money by trading with the pools, and reports that a pool was involved became a sure way to get a stock moving.

The 1929 crash ended that public infatuation with stocks. "Wall Street was a street of vanished hopes, of curiously silent apprehension and of a sort of paralyzed hypnosis yester-

day," *The Times* reported on October 30, 1929, after the worst day of the crash. "Men and women crowded the brokerage offices, even those who have been long since wiped out, and followed the figures on the tape. Little groups gathered here and there to discuss the falling prices in hushed and awed tones. They were participating in the making of financial history. It was the consensus of bankers and brokers alike that no such scenes will ever again be witnessed by this generation. To most of those who have been in the market it is all the more awe-inspiring because their financial history is limited to bull markets."

In an editorial, *The Times* was harshly critical of the "orgy of speculation" in stocks that preceded the crash and sneered at "those newly invented conceptions of finance" that had been used to justify such high stock prices. But it was otherwise sanguine, forecasting that the Federal Reserve would keep the economy on an even keel. It was wrong.

During and after the Great Depression that followed, the stock market became an object of scorn. The Securities and Exchange Commission was established with a mandate to prevent market manipulation, and the Fed was given the power to keep investors from borrowing too much money to buy stocks. Not, of course, that anyone wanted to do so. It became accepted wisdom that companies should pay far higher dividends on their stocks than they paid in interest on their bonds. After all, the shareholder needed to be compensated for the risk of another crash.

But stocks did gradually recover, and by the 1950s the public was showing a renewed interest. In 1954 the Dow rose above its 1929 high, and around the same time the dividend yield on stocks fell below the bond interest rate. Congress mounted an investigation, and the Senate Banking Committee called for more regulation in a report that saw signs of dangerous speculation. "When preoccupation with the stock market results in widespread distortion of perspective, the stock market may become a potential threat to the stability of the economy," warned the committee majority.

In fact, there was no such threat on the horizon. By 1966, the Dow was flirting with 1,000—although it could not quite manage a close above that level. (That came in 1972.) But even as the Dow churned in the late 1960s, investors flocked to initial public offerings, many of which doubled during the first day of trading. In a report dated January 1969, Merrill Lynch warned, rightly as it turned out, that there was "considerable risk" in buying such issues.

One measure of how that boom differed from the current one was reflected in that report, in which Merrill Lynch laid out its requirements for underwriting new issues: "We require that a company have substantial earnings, that its growth record extend over several years, that the company be important to its industry, and that the price to be paid for the shares be reasonable in relation to actual and projected earnings."

The final gasp of that love affair with stocks came in the early 1970s, with the "one-decision stocks," companies that institutional investors loaded up on because they were growing rapidly. It was held that such stocks need never be sold, because they would keep growing.

Then came the brutal bear market of 1973–74, in which the Dow fell 45 percent and many other stocks did worse. Inflation and interest rates were on the rise, and stocks seemed hopeless. "The Death of Equities" was proclaimed on the cover of *Business Week* in 1978. By 1982, the Dow was lower than it had been in 1966.

But by then, inflation was coming down and the descent of interest rates from record highs was starting. The stock market began to rise in August 1982, starting a bull market that continues to this day. The 1987 crash, which seemed epochal at the time, is now remembered as a great buying opportunity.

In the final year of the century, an initial public offering boom eclipsed anything that had been seen before. The best performers tended to be Internet companies with little in the way of operating history, and a lot in the way of hopes. The best performer of the group was the Internet Capital Group, which invests in other Internet companies and has shown little in the way of revenue, and no profits, in its four-year history. Its shares ended the year at $170, or 28 times the price at which they were sold to investors in August. Merrill Lynch was the lead underwriter.

The Internet boom was a principal reason that the Nasdaq index rose 85.6 percent in 1999, by far the best annual performance ever for a major American index. For the decade, the Nasdaq was up 795 percent, more than twice as much as the Dow. With capital gains so bountiful, few investors are concerned about dividends.

As stock prices rose during the last 17 years, a new investment gospel gradually spread, holding that stocks are always the best long-term investment. If the previous stock market boom produced "one-decision stocks," this one has produced the "one-decision market," in which no long-term investor should ever get out of stocks.

The studies supporting that thesis tended to concentrate on American prices—ignoring the much worse results in some other countries—and they implicitly assumed that the American economy would continue to grow and prosper as it has in the past. In 1999, books appeared with forecasts that the Dow would soar to 36,000 or higher within a few years.

Peter L. Bernstein, a financial historian and author of *Against the Gods*, a book exploring how investors and others have dealt with risk through the centuries, dismisses such projections. "They tell us that we know more about portfolio values 20 or 30 years from now than we know about what values will be tomorrow or next year," he said in a recent article. To him, that is ridiculous. To many investors today, it is a sure thing.

Source: "Toward Dow 3,000,000 and Other Ruminations," F. Norris, *The New York Times,* January 1, 2000. © 2000 The *New York Times* Company. Reprinted by permission.

Holders also must be given an opportunity to vote "yes" or "no" on each matter. Where a contest for control of corporate management is involved, the holders are enabled to vote intelligently on corporate actions requiring their approval. The SEC's rules require the advance filing of proposed proxy material for examination by the SEC for compliance with the disclosure requirements. In addition, the rules permit shareholders to submit proposals for a vote at annual meetings.

The Prohibition on Insider Trading

A firm's *insiders,* including management and members of the board of directors, are privy to private information about the true value of their stock, because (a) they receive information on the success (or lack thereof) of their current operations on a virtually continuous basis, and (b) they actually *devise* the firm's strategic plans, and, as we discussed in Chapter 4, generally must keep the details of such plans confidential. Thus, corporate insiders have a substantial information advantage over other investors, and could make considerable personal profit (at the expense of less informed investors) by trading in the firm's securities on the basis of such private information.

For this reason, the SEC prohibits *insider trading.* This does not mean that insiders cannot own shares of their firm. It also does not mean that insiders cannot occasionally buy or sell their firm's shares. Instead, the rule prohibits an insider from engaging in short-term trading in the firm's stock for the purpose of generating a personal profit or avoiding personal losses. If an insider realizes a short-term profit on his or her short-term trading in the firm's stock, he or she must surrender the gains to the firm, and may be subject to other penalties. Insiders are also prohibited from (a) informing (i.e., *tipping*) others of material inside information which they could use to buy or sell securities before such information is available to the public, and (b) making short sales of their company's equity securities. (See Meulbroek [1992] for more information on insider trading laws, as well as an empirical analysis of the effects of illegal insider trading on stock prices.)

Ownership and Trading Disclosures

Section 16 of the 1934 Act requires that all officers of a company and beneficial owners of more than 10 percent of its registered equity securities must file an initial report with the SEC, and with the exchange on which the stock is listed, showing their holdings of each of the company's equity securities. Thereafter, they must file reports for any month during which there was any change in those holdings.

The Securities Exchange Act also requires disclosure of important information by anyone seeking to acquire more than 5 percent of a company's securities by direct purchase or tender offer. Such an offer often is extended in an effort to gain control of the company. As with the proxy rules, this allows shareholders to make informed decisions on these critical corporate events.

Curbing the Advantages of Professional Analysts/Traders

Another type of informed trader is the *professional analyst.* Analysts, it is argued, generate valuable private information about the true value of a firm's shares via (a) their analytical expertise and (b) their superior access to information gathering and processing technologies.

SEC Regulation FD: Ending Selective Disclosure

Here we provide excerpts of a new SEC regulation regarding insider disclosure, which took effect on October 23, 2000. This SEC action underscores the importance of information asymmetry and of the SEC's role in mitigating its adverse effects on security markets.

Regulation FD (Fair Disclosure) is a new issuer disclosure rule that addresses selective disclosure. The regulation provides that when an issuer, or person acting on its behalf, discloses material nonpublic information to certain enumerated persons (in general, securities market professionals and holders of the issuer's securities who may well trade on the basis of the information), it must make public disclosure of that information. The timing of the required public disclosure depends on whether the selective disclosure was intentional or non-intentional; for an intentional selective disclosure, the issuer must make public disclosure simultaneously; for a non-intentional disclosure, the issuer must make public disclosure promptly. Under the regulation, the required public disclosure may be made by filing or furnishing a Form 8-K, or by another method or combination of methods that is reasonably designed to effect broad, non-exclusionary distribution of the information to the public.

SELECTIVE DISCLOSURE: REGULATION FD

As discussed in the Proposing Release, we have become increasingly concerned about the selective disclosure of material information by issuers. As reflected in recent publicized reports, many issuers are disclosing important nonpublic information, such as advance warnings of earnings results, to securities analysts or selected institutional investors or both, before making full disclosure of the same information to the general public. Where this has happened, those who were privy to the information beforehand were able to make a profit or avoid a loss at the expense of those kept in the dark. We believe that the practice of selective disclosure leads to a loss of investor confidence in the integrity of our capital markets. Investors who see a security's price change dramatically and only later are given access to the information responsible for that move rightly question whether they are on a level playing field with market insiders. Issuer selective disclosure bears a close resemblance in this regard to ordinary "tipping" and insider trading. In both cases, a privileged few gain an informational edge—and the ability to use that edge to profit—from their superior access to corporate insiders, rather than from their skill, acumen, or diligence. Likewise, selective disclosure has an adverse impact on market integrity that is similar to the adverse impact from illegal insider trading: Investors lose confidence in the fairness of the markets when they know that other participants may exploit "unerodable informational advantages" derived not from hard work or insights, but from their access to corporate insiders. The economic effects of the two practices are essentially the same. Yet, as a result of judicial interpretations, tipping and insider trading can be severely punished under the antifraud provisions of the federal securities laws, whereas the status of issuer selective disclosure has been considerably less clear.

Regulation FD is also designed to address another threat to the integrity of our markets: the potential for corporate management to treat material information as a commodity to be used to gain or maintain favor with particular analysts or investors. As noted in the Proposing Release, in the absence of a prohibition on selective disclosure, analysts may feel pressured to report favorably about a company

(*continued*)

or otherwise slant their analysis in order to have continued access to selectively disclosed information. We are concerned, in this regard, with reports that analysts who publish negative views of an issuer are sometimes excluded by that issuer from calls and meetings to which other analysts are invited.

Finally, as we also observed in the Proposing Release, technological developments have made it much easier for issuers to disseminate information broadly. Whereas issuers once may have had to rely on analysts to serve as information intermediaries, issuers now can use a variety of methods to communicate directly with the market. In addition to press releases, these methods include, among others, Internet webcasting and teleconferencing. Accordingly, technological limitations no longer provide an excuse for abiding the threats to market integrity that selective disclosure represents. To address the problem of selective disclosure, we proposed Regulation FD. It targets the practice by establishing new requirements for full and fair disclosure by public companies.

COST-BENEFIT ANALYSIS

Regulation FD requires that when an issuer intentionally discloses material nonpublic information to securities market professionals or holders of the issuer's securities who are reasonably likely to trade on the basis of the information, it must simultaneously make public disclosure. When the issuer's selective disclosure of material nonpublic information is not intentional, the issuer must make public disclosure promptly.

BENEFITS

Regulation FD will provide several important benefits to investors and the securities markets as a whole. First, current practices of selective disclosure damage investor confidence in the fairness and integrity of the markets. When selective disclosure leads to trading by the recipients of the disclosure or trading by those whom these recipients advise, the practice bears

a close resemblance to ordinary "tipping" and insider trading. The economic effects of the two practices are essentially the same; in both cases, a few persons gain an informational edge—and use that edge to profit at the expense of the uninformed—from superior access to corporate insiders, not through skill or diligence. Thus, investors in many instances equate the practice of selective disclosure with insider trading.

The Chicago Board Options Exchange also commented that selective disclosure is extremely detrimental to the markets, in that the unusual trading and increased volatility that result from selective disclosure can cause market makers substantial losses and potentially lead to wider and less liquid options markets. This argument can be extended to the primary markets for the securities as well. Economic theory and empirical studies have shown that stock market transaction costs increase when certain traders may be aware of material, undisclosed information. A reduction in these costs should make investors more willing to commit their capital.

Second, the regulation likely also will provide benefits to those seeking unbiased analysis. This regulation will place all analysts on equal footing with respect to competition for access to material information. Thus, it will allow analysts to express their honest opinions without fear of being denied access to valuable corporate information being provided to their competitors. Analysts will continue to be able to use and benefit from superior diligence or acumen, without facing the prospect that other analysts will have a competitive edge solely because they say more favorable things about issuers.

COSTS

The regulation will impose some costs on issuers. First, issuers will incur some additional costs in making the public disclosures of material nonpublic information required by the regulation. Regulation FD gives issuers two options for making public disclosure. The issuer can: (1) file or furnish a Form 8-K; or (2) disseminate the information through another method or combination of methods of disclosure that is reasonably designed to provide broad, non-exclusionary distribution of the information to the public (press release, tele-conference, or web-conference).

Because the regulation does not require issuers to disclose material information (just to make any disclosure on a non-selective basis), we cannot predict with certainty how many issuers will actually make disclosures under this regulation. For purposes of the Paperwork Reduction Act, however, we base our estimate of the paperwork burden of the regulation on our belief that issuers will make on average five public disclosures under Regulation FD per year. Since there are approximately 13,000 issuers affected by this regulation, we estimate that the total number of disclosures under Regulation FD per year will be 65,000.

While it is possible that issuers may incur some cost in connection with the implementation of corporate policy relating to disclosure, as well as decisions not to make disclosure under the regulation, we believe that any additional costs would not be substantial.

The regulation may also lead to some increased costs for issuers resulting from new or enhanced systems and procedures for disclosure practices. As indicated by some commenters, we believe that many, if not most, issuers already have internal procedures for communicating with the public; for many issuers, therefore, new procedures to prevent selective disclosures will not be needed. There might be a cost to these issuers, however, for enhancing and strengthening existing procedures to safeguard against selective disclosures that are not intentional to ensure prompt public release when such disclosures do occur.

One potential cost of the regulation that we have identified is the risk that the regulation might "chill" corporate disclosures to analysts, investors, and the media. We recognized the concern that issuers may speak less often out of fear of liability based on a post hoc assessment

that disclosed information was material, and that if such a chilling effect resulted from Regulation FD, there would be a cost to overall market efficiency and capital formation.

A number of commenters also raised the concern about a chilling effect as a significant potential cost of Regulation FD, and several of these suggested that we were underestimating this effect. A common theme among these commenters was that the regulation would result in the flow of less information to the marketplace, rather than more, and that the cost of this effect would be greater surprise and volatility. However, these commenters were unable to quantify these costs. Moreover, other commenters, including issuers who would be subject to the regulation, did not necessarily agree that their communications would be significantly chilled.

In response to the concerns about a diminished flow of information, as discussed elsewhere in this Release, we have made several significant modifications that we believe reduce the likelihood of a chilling effect. These modifications include narrowing the scope of the regulation so that it does not apply to all communications with persons outside the issuer, narrowing the types of issuer personnel covered by the regulation to senior officials and those who would normally be expected to communicate with securities market professionals or security holders, and clarifying that where the regulation requires "knowing or reckless" conduct, liability will attach only when an issuer's personnel know or are reckless in not knowing that the information selectively disclosed is both material and nonpublic. Additionally, we have added an express provision in the regulation's text designed to remove any doubt that private liability will not result from a Regulation FD violation.

In addition, there are numerous practices that issuers may employ to continue to communicate freely with analysts and investors, while becoming more careful in how they disclose information. Moreover, the regulation only covers the selective disclosure of material

(*continued*)

nonpublic information; the level of non-material information available to the market need not decrease.

We believe issuers will have strong reasons to continue releasing information given the market demand for information and a company's desire to promote its products and services. One economic study has found that more public disclosure is associated with factors that have been shown to reduce the cost of capital.

CONSIDERATION OF IMPACT ON THE ECONOMY, BURDEN ON COMPETITION, AND PROMOTION OF EFFICIENCY, COMPETITION, AND CAPITAL FORMATION

As discussed above, we believe that Regulation FD . . . will bolster investor confidence in the integrity of the markets and the fairness of the disclosure process. By enhancing investor confidence and participation in the markets, Rule FD should increase liquidity and help to reduce the costs of capital. Accordingly, the proposals should promote capital formation and market efficiency.

Several commenters suggested that Regulation FD might have some effects on competition. One commenter suggested that the regulation would have a negative effect on competition because analysts operating independently of, and in competition with, each other can more effectively pursue an independent line of inquiry and ferret out negative information that management would rather not disclose. According to this commenter, "[l]eveling the playing field for analysts, as among themselves and vis-a-vis the general public, will undermine the great advantages of the current system." We disagree. We believe, to the contrary, that the regulation will encourage competition because it places all analysts on equal competitive footing with respect to access to material information. Analysts will continue to be able to use and benefit from superior diligence or acumen, without facing the prospect that other analysts will have a competitive edge simply because they have been favored with selective disclosure. Additionally, analysts will be able to express their honest opinions without fear of being denied access to material corporate information.

Source: www.sec.gov/rules/final/33–7881.htm. "Proposing Release" refers to Exchange Act Release No. 42259 (Dec. 20, 1999) [64 FR 72590].

In the past, professional analysts have enjoyed two additional advantages over the typical investor. *First,* they have had a superior ability to trade quickly on the basis of either emerging public information or their own self-generated private information.

Second, until recently, professional analysts have actually been able to converse privately with a firm's insiders to obtain private information about such issues as management's earnings forecasts. However, the SEC has recently taken action to eliminate the unfairness of this practice by imposing *Regulation FD,* where FD stands for *Fair Disclosure.* Under this regulation, if a firm's insider discloses nonpublic information to an analyst, the insider must immediately disclose this information to the public.

More on the Issue of Disclosure
The Securities Acts and the establishment of the SEC were important for the development of the markets for corporate securities for a number of reasons. Perhaps the most important reason, and certainly the most obvious, is that they require a flow of credible, substantive, and timely information from firms to investors, thereby reducing information asymmetry between the firm's management and its securityholders. As

we know from our analysis of the information asymmetry problem in Chapter 4, markets in which investors have inadequate information regarding the characteristics of a security can fail.

Limitations on Disclosure

The SEC's disclosure rules do not entirely eliminate information asymmetry nor do they necessarily even render the problem insignificant. As we stated in Chapter 4, this is primarily because firms must be able to keep certain critical information regarding their competitive strategies confidential (i.e., within the confines of the firm's top management) or else such information will be *leaked* to the firm's competitors and its value may be lost. Depending on the competitiveness of the industry in which a firm operates, a substantial portion of the firm's market value may depend on the ability of the firm's management to compete strategically. Recognizing this problem, SEC disclosure rules stop short of requiring a firm to divulge its most strategic information to the public. Thus, although investors know the firm's general business lines, properties, and operations, and know that management is continuously developing competitive strategies, they may not be told much about the *how* and *when* of management's strategies.

It is important to recognize the potentially substantial implications of such *residual* information asymmetry for the firm's financial policies. For instance, a firm would generally prefer to finance strategy-based expansion using retained earnings, or *internal equity,* to avoid the scrutiny that accompanies external debt or equity financing via the issuance (and registration) of new securities. In particular, firms in highly competitive industries may wish to avoid public debt financing not only because of the disclosure required with their registration, but also because of (a) constraints imposed in a bond contract and (b) creditors' monitoring of the firm's activities. Furthermore, limitations on disclosure may require the use of other mechanisms, such as contracting, to mitigate agency costs of managerial discretion, as we discuss later. In extreme cases, a firm may prefer to remain private rather than face disclosure rules.

Voluntary Disclosure, Liquidity, and the Cost of Capital

Despite competitive pressures, it may not always be the case that firms provide only the minimum disclosure required by law. *Voluntary disclosure* may often be required to mitigate costs associated with information asymmetry. For instance, management may realize that the firm's *reputation* with investors is valuable, and can be sustained only if certain information is provided on both periodic and timely bases. Indeed, some critics have argued that government imposition of disclosure rules is unnecessary, because firms will find it in their interest to disclose adequate information to the market.

Diamond and Verrecchia (1991) developed a theoretical model that focuses on a firm's decision whether to voluntarily disclose private information. They show that "revealing public information to reduce information asymmetry can reduce a firm's cost of capital by attracting increased demand from large investors due to increased liquidity of its securities" (p. 1325). They argue that voluntary disclosure is particularly important for large firms, because the liquidity of their shares—and simultaneously a lower cost of capital—will result only if institutional investors are willing to take large positions in the firm's stock.

Similarly, Fishman and Hagerty (1989) provide a theoretical analysis of the effect of a firm's disclosure policy on its market value and capital investment decisions. They argue that firms have an incentive to engage in *voluntary disclosure* because doing so leads to a more efficient price for their equity, which in turn can lead to more efficient capital investment decisions. However, their model suggests that firms actually have an incentive to produce *too much* information, in the sense that the benefits do not justify the costs. Moreover, mandatory disclosure rules may actually exacerbate this problem.

On the other hand, the firm's management may be prone to provide misleading information, either for the benefit of the shareholders or for their personal benefit. For instance, a CEO may wish to report relatively favorable earnings numbers for a given quarter or year if his or her bonus is tied to the firm's earnings performance. Although firms undoubtedly have some leeway in manipulating earnings (at least in the short run), their discretion is limited by the legal requirement that independent auditors certify their financial statements.

Regulation of Corporate Control Transfers
Federal and state laws regulate the *markets for corporate control*. This phrase refers to deals, including mergers, acquisitions, takeovers, and buyouts, in which the ownership of an entire firm changes hands in a single transaction. For instance, federal antitrust laws may be invoked to disallow a merger or acquisition. We discuss the markets for corporate control in detail in Chapter 16.

5.3 SECURITIES MARKETS

Securities markets also provide mechanisms to mitigate principal–agent conflicts and information asymmetry problems. This section briefly discusses two such mechanisms.

5.3.1 Securities Markets and Information Generation

Securities markets, particularly the secondary markets, provide important information to management about the values of their securities, the firm's current cost of debt and equity capital, and the Net Present Value (NPV) of potential capital investment projects. The financial press also provides valuable information, as well as opinions, about a firm's performance, prospects, and management. Moreover, the corps of analysts that follow the typical public firm provide information about the performance of the firm and the efficacy of its management. Indeed, analysts (as well as the financial press) play oversight roles for investors that the investors may find impossible to perform for themselves, especially if each investor has only a relatively small stake in any single firm because he or she is diversified.

Of course, analysts must receive compensation for their efforts in gathering and processing information about firms. If an analyst operates independently of a securities firm, he or she must receive compensation in the form of fees that investors pay to gain access to the analyst's information. If a securities brokerage firm employs the analyst, the securities firm pays the analyst, and is itself compensated via commissions and fees that trading customers pay in part to have (semiprivate) access to the securities firm's proprietary information.

Chung and Jo (1996) argue that analysts' monitoring of a firm provides additional benefits that serve to enhance the market value of the firm's equity: "We postulate that security analysts' monitoring of corporate performance helps motivate managers, thus reducing the agency costs associated with the separation of ownership and control. We also argue that the information intermediary function provided by security analysts helps expand the breadth of investor cognizance" (p. 493). They also document evidence consistent with these arguments.

5.3.2   Security Market Mechanisms That Discipline Management

Several market mechanisms also exist to discipline a firm's management, and thus to mitigate agency costs of managerial discretion. The most obvious disciplining mechanism is that the market determines the price of the firm's stock. If management is managing the firm poorly, a low stock price will result, and shareholders will, sooner or later, pressure management to *shape up or ship out*. Another powerful threat is a hostile takeover of the firm, after which management is fired. (We discuss takeovers in Chapter 16.)

5.4   OWNERSHIP STRUCTURE

In this section, we briefly discuss two aspects of a firm's ownership structure that can serve to restrain self-interested managerial behavior: (a) shareholder activism and (b) the interaction between a firm's ownership structure and its capital structure.

5.4.1   Shareholder Activism

Shareholders can promote their interest directly by (a) voting on major proposals presented by management, (b) submitting their own proposals for a vote, and (c) monitoring management's decisions. Shareholders who actively pursue such activities are called *activists*.

Unfortunately, shareholder activism is problematic in several respects. Shareholder activism is time consuming and expensive, and the typical individual investor, who owns only a small fraction of a given firm's shares, will receive only a small benefit from his or her investment in activism; other, passive investors get a *free ride* on such efforts[2]. The per-share cost of activism can be reduced if shareholders form a group. However, group members must regularly communicate with each other (as well as with the firm's other, more transient, shareholders), must bear costs associated with administration, publicity, and legal matters, and, perhaps most importantly, must agree on any reforms that they propose.

On the other hand, investors who have large shareholdings receive a large share of the benefits of monitoring management, and these investors are more likely to pursue actions that force management to act in the shareholders' interest. Many large institutional investors, including mutual funds and pension funds, have the capital necessary to bear the cost of activism. It may also be in the interest of these organizations to protect their large investment. Indeed, it may be argued that mutual funds provide a

---

[2]*Free riders* are shareholders who freely gain the benefits of time and money expended by other shareholders to increase the value of the firm's equity. The essence of the free rider problem is that shareholders may know that an expenditure could be made to increase firm value, but refrain from making the expenditure because their private benefit, which is solely in the form of an increase in the value of *their* shares, is insufficient to warrant the expenditure, even if the benefit to *all* shareholders exceeds the amount of the expenditure.

critical means by which individual investors can *"have their cake and eat it too"*, as the saying goes. A mutual fund or pension fund allows individual investors to automatically invest in a well-diversified portfolio, and at the same time the pooled funds may be sufficiently large to allow the fund's manager to wield considerable influence on the managements of the firms in which the fund invests. One of the most active pension funds in the United States in recent years is the California Public Employees Retirement System (CalPERS).

Wealthy individual investors may also devote themselves to promoting the interest of a firm's shareholders, while also privately profiting from their efforts. Examples are Warren Buffet and Robert Monk. In 1992, Monk led a shareholder fight against Sears Roebuck & Co. to protest management's waste of corporate assets. His campaign included an advertisement in the *Wall Street Journal* that severely admonished Sears' board of directors for its failure to make management accountable to shareholders. His campaign included five proposals: (1) make shareholder votes confidential, (2) separate the positions of Chairman of the Board and CEO/President, (3) study whether the firm should divest of certain operations, (4) end staggered board terms, and (5) require directors to own a minimum number of shares. (We provide additional discussion of shareholder activism in Chapter 8.)

5.4.2 Ownership Structure, Capital Structure, and Restraints on Management

As we argued in Chapter 3, management is likely to lose their stake in the firm if the firm goes bankrupt, so they may desire to use less leverage in the firm's capital structure than is optimal from shareholders' viewpoint (if indeed such an optimal amount of debt exists; see Chapter 6). The firm's board, acting in the shareholders' interest, could *impose* the higher, optimal level of leverage. However, a firm's board may be ineffectual in this regard if it is *packed* with management's cronies. If this is the case, two other mechanisms may emerge to resolve the problem. First, if the firm's managers themselves are major shareholders (or are otherwise given incentives to act in the shareholders' interest), they are self interested in maximizing the market value of the firm's shares. If so, either (a) they would be willing to have higher leverage, or (b) if higher leverage is optimal primarily because of the discipline it imposes on management, such discipline, and thus higher leverage, may be unnecessary if management is already incented to maximize the market value of the firm's shares. Second, the firm's shareholders may include *major nonmanagerial shareholders,* who would have an incentive to bring pressure on management to increase the firm's leverage.

Empirical Evidence

Friend and Lang (1988) tested the assertions about management and leverage empirically. They classified firms in their sample into four groups, sorting on the bases of the following two criteria. First, they sorted firms into two groups according to whether a firm is *closely held* versus *publicly held.* They predicted that firms whose management has a greater equity stake in the firm would have higher debt ratios. Second, they sorted each firm in a group into two subgroups according to whether the firm has major nonmanagerial shareholders, which, as argued above, should be associated with higher debt ratios. Their basic empirical results, summarized in Table 5.1, are consistent with these predictions.

TABLE 5-1   Debt Ratios and Ownership Structure

Mean Debt Ratios of Firms in Four Groups Defined by Ownership Structure

	Closely Held Firms		Publicly Held Firms	
	No Major Non-managerial Shareholders	*Major Non-managerial Shareholders*	*No Major Non-managerial Shareholders*	*Major Non-managerial Shareholders*
Mean	0.227	0.264	0.220	0.249
Standard Deviation	0.148	0.142	0.120	0.132

Source: Friend and Lang (1988).

We mention this study for two reasons. First, it emphasizes the complexity of a firm in terms of the interactive effects of ownership structure and capital structure. Second, it emphasizes that alternative mechanisms can be brought to bear (or used in tandem) to mitigate agency costs of managerial discretion.

5.4.3   Ownership Structure and Corporate Value: Some Empirical Evidence

Our discussions in Chapters 3 and 4, as well in this chapter, raise an interesting question: Is there a relationship between the market value of a firm and its ownership structure? Alternatively stated, is there an *optimal* (i.e., value maximizing) ownership structure? This question is complex because, from a theoretical standpoint, a firm's ownership structure affects, and is affected by, other variables, and these variables also influence the firm's market value. Included among the other variables are levels of principal–agent conflicts and information asymmetry, and their effects on still other variables such as the firm's operating strategy, capital structure, and dividend policy. This complexity suggests that if an optimal ownership structure exists, it is largely firm specific, though some cross-sectional tendencies may be identifiable.

Despite the complexity of the issue, researchers have attempted to determine whether a relationship generally exists between a firm's ownership structure and its market value. One widely cited empirical study of this issue is by McConnell and Servaes (1990). The authors collected two large samples of nonfinancial firms, one from 1976 (1,173 firms), and the other from 1986 (1,093 firms). For each sample, they examined the relationship between the fraction of a firm's shares owned by insiders and the firm's market value. They measured the market value of the firm via Tobin's Q ratio for the firm, defined as "the market value of the common stock plus the estimated market value of debt and preferred stock divided by the replacement value of assets" (p. 600). (Note that Tobin's Q ratio is closely related to the market-to-book equity ratio.)

The authors then conducted a regression analysis to test for a relationship between Tobin's Q ratio, as the dependent variable, and the fraction of outstanding shares owned by insiders, denoted as INSOWN, as the independent variable. However, because they suspected that the relationship might be nonlinear, they added an additional independent variable to the regression, the square of insider ownership fraction, or $(INSOWN_i)^2$. Thus, the form of their regression was:

$$(\text{Tobin's } Q)_i = a + b_1\ INSOWN_i + b_2\ (INSOWN_i)^2 + e_i. \tag{5.1}$$

For both samples, the authors found that all of the coefficients in regression Equation 5.1 were significant. For 1976 and 1986, respectively, the estimated values of the coefficients were as follows: a, 0.9302 and 1.2413; b_1, 1.2145 and 3.0644; and b_2 −1.2304 and −4.0740. For both samples, the coefficient of $INSOWN_i$ was positive, while the coefficient of $(INSOWN_i)^2$ was negative. These results indicate that the relationship between Tobin's Q and insider ownership fraction is concave.

Figure 5.2 provides a graphical depiction of McConnell and Servaes's results. For the 1976 sample, Tobin's Q reaches a maximum when the insider ownership fraction is equal to 0.494, or 49.4 percent. For the 1986 sample, Tobin's Q reaches a maximum when the insider ownership fraction is equal to 0.376, or 37.6 percent.

McConnell and Servaes recognized that the relationship between Tobin's Q and insider ownership is complex:

> As in all empirical work, a number of caveats should be noted. Perhaps the most important is the question of causality between insider ownership and Q. It can be argued that managers and founders are more inclined to retain a large fraction of successful firms. It may also be that the managers of success-

FIGURE 5-2 The Relationship between Tobin's Q and the Fraction of Shares Owned by Insiders Estimates for 1976 and 1986

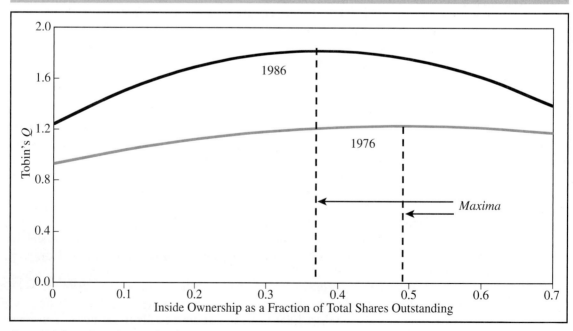

Source: McConnell and Servaes (1990).

ful firms are more likely to be rewarded with additional forms of stock ownership. These firms also are more likely to be firms with high Q ratios. Such a scenario could explain a positive relation between Q and insider ownership, in which the line of causality runs from Q to insider ownership rather than the other way around. However, this line of reasoning cannot explain the observed negative relation between ownership and Q that occurs as ownership becomes highly concentrated in the hands of insiders . . . (p. 611)

5.5 BOARD OVERSIGHT

The existence of a board of directors in every corporation is probably the most visible indication that the interests of largely passive investors must be protected from managerial self-interest. The board generally has a variety of tools at its disposal to control management's activities, including, but not limited to, the following:

1. ***Requiring board approval of major capital expenditures, acquisitions, divestitures, and security offerings.*** Generally, the board of directors must approve all mergers and acquisitions. Management may also be required to get board approval for major capital expenditures, major sales of assets, divestiture of certain lines of business, or sales of securities.

2. ***Controlling the firm's capital structure:*** By requiring a higher level of debt in the capital structure, the board can: (a) put management's *feet to the fire,* inducing them to avoid decisions that may benefit them personally but are detrimental to shareholder value; and (b) engage the monitoring or covenant restrictions of debt contracts that can further discipline management.

3. ***Hiring outside consultants to scrutinize major projects.*** Boards often hire independent consultants to scrutinize management's overall performance and the profit estimates of a proposed project.

4. ***Firing the CEO.*** If the firm is failing to add value for shareholders, and the failure can be traced to management incompetence or self-interest, the board should fire management and find competent replacements.

Principal–agent conflicts occur between shareholders and managers if and when managers have different incentives than shareholders. The managers want personal benefits, including a higher and more secure income, benefits, perks, social status, and power. Shareholders want the market value of their shares to rise. It is incumbent upon the firm's board of directors to mitigate such conflicts of interest by monitoring management's decisions. However, in Chapter 3 we noted a problem in some firms in which management is able to *pack the board* with individuals who are likely to be friendly to management and therefore serve only to *rubber stamp* management's decisions. For this reason, it is important that (a) the board includes *independent* individuals (e.g., individuals from outside the firm), and (b) they have real power to control management's self-serving behavior.

Vafeas (1999) studied the frequencies of board meetings for 307 public firms for the years 1990 to 1994. His empirical results support the efficacy of board oversight, especially when a firm is faltering: "The annual number of board meetings is inversely related to firm value. This result is driven by increases in board activity following share price declines. I further find that the operating performance improves following years of abnormal board activity. These improvements are most pronounced for firms with poor prior performance . . ." (We provide additional discussion of the oversight role of a firm's board of directors in Chapter 8.)

5.6   FINANCIAL INSTITUTIONS

A rich variety of financial institutions exist in the United States, including commercial banks, insurance companies, finance companies, venture capital firms, and security underwriters. Historically, these firms have provided specialized and segmented services to firms (as well as individuals). However, in recent years financial institutions have attempted to broaden the scope of their business to include services historically provided by other types of institutions. As a result, the distinctions among the various financial institutions have become blurred, particularly as the long-standing Glass-Steagall Act[3] is gradually being repealed.

In any event, all financial institutions have a common generic service, that of being a *financial intermediary.* In this section, we briefly discuss several theoretical articles that explain the intermediary services that financial institutions provide for firms, and the importance of these services in resolving principal–agent conflicts and information asymmetry problems. We also discuss the role of financial institutions in generating, disseminating, and analyzing data on a wide variety of economic and financial variables that are important to firms.

5.6.1   Financial Intermediaries and the Resolution of Information Asymmetry Problems

In Chapter 4, we discussed part of an important paper by Leland and Pyle (1977). In that portion of the paper, the authors discuss the *signaling* role of equity ownership by an entrepreneur in establishing the fair market value for a firm in the presence of information asymmetry between the entrepreneur and potential outside shareholders.

In the latter portion of that paper, Leland and Pyle suggest that information asymmetry also explains the existence of financial intermediaries. The setting of this latter argument is as follows. Firms are essentially in the business of expending resources to obtain proprietary information on production or service technologies, and then selling this information by issuing securities that represent claims against the profits from these technologies.

However, a firm faces a dilemma as it tries to sell their proprietary information. *On one hand,* any buyer could purchase only some of the firm's securities, thereby gaining access to the proprietary information, and then share or resell it to other buyers (i.e., they sell the proprietary information, not the securities) for a private gain. *On the other hand,* if the firm attempts to resolve this problem by not revealing the proprietary

---

[3]The Glass-Steagall Act, passed by Congress in 1933 in the wake of the Great Depression, prohibited a single financial institution from being involved in both commercial banking and investment banking (i.e., the underwriting of securities) simultaneously. Proponents of the Act argued that commercial banks were too prone to speculating in stocks using depositor's money.

information to buyers, the buyers have no means of assessing the value of the information they are asked to purchase, and the market for corporate securities could fail.

According to the authors, this dilemma can be resolved if the firm employs a financial intermediary. Sellers of highly valuable proprietary information would deal with an intermediary that is in a position to *verify* the quality of the information and yet will keep such information *confidential.*

We can illustrate Leland and Pyle's arguments by referring to the activities of any of several types of financial institutions. For instance, commercial banks are regularly privy to confidential information regarding the strategic plans of their borrowing business clients. Insurance companies are also important lenders to midsized and large companies through the *private placement* bond market, and they are privy to confidential information about the issuing firm.

Securities underwriters also are regularly privy to confidential information about a firm that wishes to offer debt or equity securities to the public, and they also have valuation expertise. Booth and Smith (1986) developed a theory of the role of underwriters, as intermediaries, in reducing information asymmetry problems associated with the issuance of risky corporate securities. They argue that the underwriter (a) is privy to the issuer's private information, (b) prices the issue to incorporate this information, and (c) is *believed* by investors because the underwriter has its long-term reputation (and with it, future business) at stake. In this sense, underwriters *certify* the quality of securities that they underwrite.

Several researchers have expanded on Leland and Pyle's arguments, emphasizing the dual roles of banks as lenders and *confidants.* For instance, Sharpe (1990) argues,

> Customer relationships arise between banks and firms because, in the process of lending, a bank learns more than others about its own customers. This information asymmetry allows lenders to capture some of the rents generated by their older customers; competition thus drives banks to lend to new firms at interest rates that initially generate expected losses. As a result, the allocation of capital is shifted toward lower quality and inexperienced firms. This inefficiency is eliminated if complete contingent contracts are written or, when this is costly, if banks can make nonbinding commitments that, in equilibrium, are backed by reputation. (p. 1069)

Campbell and Kracaw (1980) take an even broader view, arguing that financial intermediaries (e.g., banks) exist to mitigate a number of real-world problems simultaneously and efficiently: "Our hypothesis is that intermediaries emerge as information producers because the production of information, the protection of confidentiality, the provision of transactions services, as well as other intermediary services, are naturally complimentary activities" (p. 864).

5.6.2 Financial Intermediaries Produce Valuable Economic, Business, and Financial Information

Financial intermediaries also specialize in the production and analysis of global, national, regional, local, and industry-specific economic, business, and financial information. For instance, a commercial bank sells such information to business clients, either directly through consulting relationships or indirectly by providing it as a part of a profitable loan. A bank also can use such information to screen potential borrowers more effectively and thus to develop a more profitable loan portfolio. Securities firms also sell such information directly via consultancy or indirectly through underwriting fees. In both cases, the financial intermediary can spread the cost of gathering such information across a large number of clients, so they enjoy economies of scale in the production and sale of information. Meanwhile, individual firms benefit from the information generated by financial institutions because it helps them to (a) make better capital investment decisions, and (b) decide on the timing and form (e.g., debt versus equity) of a pending security offering. (See Ramakrishnan and Thakor [1984] for discussion of these issues.)

5.7 CONTRACTING DEVICES

In this section, we discuss the critical role of *contracting* to mitigate principal–agent conflicts and information asymmetry problems. In the first subsection, we discuss the essential features of typical executive compensation contracts, and in the second subsection we discuss the importance of *terms* in debt contracts.

5.7.1 Executive Compensation Contracts

A firm hires its senior management from the pool of available and qualified individuals in the competitive labor market. Thus, as a starting point, an executive's compensation will be commensurate with his or her talents and the difficulty of the management task. For instance, statistics indicate that executive compensation is strongly positively related to the size of the firm.

The typical executive's personal wealth and income is predominantly dependent on the firm's performance. As such, an executive's portfolio is not well diversified, in contrast to most of the firm's shareholders. (Using portfolio terminology, executives generally bear not only the firm's *systematic* risk, but also its *firm-specific* risk.) Consequently, equilibrium executive compensation would likely include compensation for the added risk they bear because, in effect, they are forced to hold a relatively undiversified personal portfolio. Equilibrium managerial compensation will also reflect the risk that, even if executives do a good job, they could lose their position in the event of a merger, acquisition, takeover, buyout, or bankruptcy.

Developing Incentive-Compatible Executive Compensation Contracts

In Chapter 3, we discussed a critical problem facing a firm with diffuse ownership: to devise a contract with management that ensures that they act strictly in the shareholders' interest. This is a problem because executives have a private incentive to maximize their own utility *after* they are hired. Such private incentives may conflict with shareholders' interest, resulting in decisions that are costly to shareholders.

To mitigate costly conflicts of interest, firms often include provisions for performance-based contingency pay in executive compensation contracts. The intent of these provisions is to *align* the interests of executives with those of the firm's shareholders, namely, to maximize the firm's stock price. Thus, a substantial proportion of a typical executive's annual total compensation consists of incentive compensation such as (a) a bonus that is contingent on the firm's accounting earnings, or (b) grants of stock or stock options, the value of which depends on the firm's stock price performance.

Such incentives ultimately may serve this purpose reasonably well. However, they may cause other distortions in management's handling of the firm's capital investment program and financial policies, which can be costly to shareholders. To see this, we emphasize again that, even with an incentive-based compensation contract, a substantial portion of a manager's wealth is likely to be tied to the single firm that he or she manages. As a result, the manager may be motivated to (suboptimally) reduce the firm's operating risk, and to underemploy debt, as means of reducing the riskiness of his or her personal portfolio. This problem is only exacerbated if the manager's compensation is rendered *hypersensitive* to the performance of the firm via either earnings-based bonuses or stock-related grants.

This discussion has two important implications. *First,* it suggests that the best managers may be those who already possess a substantial amount of wealth independent of the firm so that their wealth is relatively less dependent on the compensation from the firm that they manage. *Second,* it suggests that contracts intended to mitigate a particular problem may actually backfire and exacerbate the problem. (We discuss executive compensation contracts in greater detail in Chapter 8.)

5.7.2 Restrictive Covenants and Provisions in Debt Contracts

Corporate debt contracts are generally complex, as we discuss in Chapter 15. Here we briefly discuss some terms in corporate debt contracts that serve to mitigate principal–agent conflicts and information asymmetry problems. Of course, the most important provision in a corporate debt contract is the *default clause,* which specifies that if the firm fails to make any scheduled payment, the firm is technically in default and the creditors can seize ownership and control of the firm, subject to bankruptcy proceedings. Therefore, the threat of bankruptcy is a powerful tool to discipline the firm's management, whether management is acting in the interests of the shareholders or in their self-interest.

Of course, creditors prefer to avoid default, because they are likely to realize losses as well. Thus, payment provisions and restrictive covenants are included in a debt contract, designed in large part to reduce the probability of default. Among these, the provision for *periodic* payments of interest and (in many cases) principal is the most important. This provision not only serves to provide cash returns to the creditors over a shorter time horizon (i.e., presumably before the firm can experience serious financial distress), but also (a) serves to discipline management to generate sufficient cash flow to service the debt, and (b) failure to make timely interim payments serves as an *early warning* to creditors that the firm is under financial distress.

Restrictive covenants also protect the interests of creditors in the face of conflicts of interest with either shareholders or management. For instance, in some debt contracts specific assets such as property, plant, or equipment are *mortgaged* or *collateralized.* Collateralization allows the creditors to have an explicit claim on the collateralized property in the event of bankruptcy, and also prohibits the sale of such property without either the expressed approval of secured creditors or the simultaneous retirement of the debt. Moreover, Rajan and Winton (1995) argue that covenants and collateral serve as incentives to a lender, particularly a bank, to *monitor* the borrower's activities.

Debt contracts also generally either prohibit the payment of dividends to shareholders outright, or allow dividend payments only if the firm is generating sufficient earnings. Such restrictions on dividends protect creditors from shareholders' incentive to systematically siphon off the value of the firm to themselves.

Debt can also serve the interests of the borrowing firm's shareholders by restricting management's self-serving behavior. This is particularly true of privately placed debt, wherein financial intermediaries provide valuable monitoring services for a firm's (passive and uninformed) shareholders, which can mitigate agency conflicts between the shareholders and the firm's management. For instance, a bank *line of credit* agreement generally must be renewed periodically. At the time of each renewal, the firm must pass the bank's scrutiny or lose their ability to continue to borrow (at least from that particular bank). Failure to pass periodic scrutiny tests can serve as an *early warning* signal that the firm is failing. (We discuss bank lending practices in greater detail in Chapter 15.)

5.8 Summary of Learning Objectives

This chapter provides an overview of the major mechanisms by which corporate financing problems, especially principal–agent conflicts and information asymmetry problems, are mitigated in the United States. Information asymmetry problems are mitigated primarily via (a) government requirements for firms to provide adequate, accurate, and timely disclosure of value-relevant information; (b) the scrutiny of various participants in the security markets, including analysts; and (c) confidentiality agreements between a firm and a financial institution. Principal–agent conflicts are mitigated primarily via (a) oversight by the firm's board of directors, (b) shareholder activism, (c) a requirement that insiders hold their firm's shares in their personal portfolios, (d) other incentives in an executive's compensation contract, (e) the disciplining role of debt in a firm's capital structure; and (f) payment provisions and restrictive covenants in corporate debt contracts.

Review Questions and Problems

1. Discuss the roles of governments in mitigating principal–agent conflicts and information asymmetry problems in corporate finance.
2. Discuss the content of the Securities Act of 1933 and the Securities Exchange Act of 1934, and their roles in mitigating both principal–agent conflicts and information asymmetry problems in corporate finance.
3. Define the prohibition on insider trading and discuss the rationale for this regulation.
4. Discuss each of the following aspects of corporate disclosure.
   a. mandatory disclosure rules
   b. necessary limitations on disclosure
   c. voluntary disclosure
5. Explain the purpose of the SEC's recently imposed Regulation FD.
6. Discuss the roles of analysts and the financial press in mitigating both principal–agent conflicts and information asymmetry problems.
7. Discuss the importance and limitations of shareholder activism.
8. How does a firm's ownership structure influence its capital structure?

9. Discuss the empirical evidence presented in the text about the relationship between the fraction of a firm's shares owned by insiders and the firm's market value.
10. Describe the tools available to a firm's board of directors to discipline management to act in the shareholders' interest. What may undermine their effectiveness in this regard?
11. Explain the roles of financial institutions as *financial intermediaries.*
12. How does an underwriter mitigate the information asymmetry problem facing a firm that is attempting to raise debt or equity capital?
13. Explain why it is important for a financial institution to specialize in the production and analysis of economic, business, and financial information.
14. Explain the rationale for performance incentives in executive compensation contracts. How might they backfire?
15. List several provisions and restrictive covenants in corporate debt contracts, and explain how each serves to protect creditors' interest. Which of these might also serve shareholders' interest?

Creative Thinking Issues

1. Do you believe unregulated securities markets could be successful?
2. Develop an argument for the elimination of the prohibition on insider trading.
3. From the perspective of the roles played by financial institutions as discussed in this chapter, can you think of some good reasons for the repeal of the Glass-Steagall Act? For its retention?
4. What specifications would you place in a corporation's charter with respect to
   a. the composition of the board of directors?
   b. explicit powers of the board?
5. How would you design a compensation contract for the CEO of a young and growing company that is highly risky?
6. As an underwriter, explain the provisions and restrictive covenants you would recommend for inclusion in a firm's bond contract. Which would you exclude, and why?

Projects and Analyses

1. Do research on one of the following:
   a. The political milieu that surrounded the development of the Securities Acts of 1933 and 1934.
   b. The gradual expansion of the SEC's regulatory roles since 1934.
   c. The present structure of the SEC.
   d. The current challenges facing the SEC as it attempts to oversee such developing markets as derivatives, trading and issuance of securities over the Internet, and trading in foreign securities.
2. Choose a publicly traded firm, and examine it carefully for evidence of mechanisms in place to mitigate principal–agent or information asymmetry problems.
3. Gather the necessary data on a sample of firms, and test the relationship between Tobin's Q ratio and insider ownership fraction (or alternatively, the fraction of shares held by institutions). Consider estimating this relationship using regression Equation 5.1.

CHAPTER

6

The Leverage Decision

6.1 INTRODUCTION

This chapter addresses one of the firm's most important financial decisions—how much leverage to maintain in its capital structure. Our analyses thus far suggest that this decision is complex. *First*, the evidence presented in Chapter 1 indicates that corporate leverage varies substantially both over time (Figure 1-2b) and cross-sectionally (Figures 1-5 and 1-6).

Second, our review of corporate finance theories in Chapters 2 through 5 revealed the following important aspects of leverage: (a) For a given firm, the riskiness of both debt and equity increase with leverage (Chapter 2); (b) principal–agent conflicts (both between shareholders and management and between shareholders and creditors) both affect, and are affected by, leverage (Chapter 3); (c) information asymmetry problems may also affect the firms' optimal leverage (Chapter 4); and (d) the extent to which principal–agent conflicts and information asymmetry problems are, or are not, mitigated via various mechanisms may also influence a firm's leverage (Chapter 5). And if these factors aren't sufficient, in this chapter we add two additional factors—taxes and costs of financial distress and bankruptcy—to the mix!

Despite the complexity of the leverage issue, we attempt to draw together the implications of these various factors to reach some overall conclusions about a firm's leverage. We discuss and present empirical evidence to solidify our conclusions. In the end, we come to the tentative conclusion that all of the factors noted above affect a firm's leverage decision; that is, a firm's leverage probably does involve complex trade-offs among many factors. Because of the importance and complexity of the leverage decision, we continue to discuss this issue from several additional perspectives in later chapters. The material in this chapter prepares us for these discussions.

6.2 THE IRS CODES: CORPORATE AND PERSONAL TAXATION

In this section, we discuss the basics of the taxation of U.S. corporations and individuals according to U.S. Internal Revenue Service (IRS) codes. The purpose of this discussion is to introduce the issue of taxation. In subsequent sections, we address the issue of whether taxes affect a firm's leverage decision.

6.2.1 Corporate Taxation

The corporation is a distinct legal entity. Hence, according to the IRS code, the earnings of the corporation itself are subject to federal taxation.[1] The tax rate schedule for corporations is *progressive*; that is, the tax rate increases in stages with the firm's taxable income. The corporate tax rate schedule in effect for January 1998 is shown in the upper panel of Table 6-1.

For this chapter, one feature of the IRS corporate tax code is particularly important: interest payments to creditors are deductible from a firm's taxable income, while dividend payments to shareholders are not deductible. As such, the IRS code appears to impart an important tax advantage to corporate debt relative to equity, and therefore an incentive for firms to have more debt in their capital structures. However, the truth may not be this simple, as we discuss later.

Taxes on corporate earnings are a burden that ultimately limits (a) the profitability of any project that a firm undertakes, (b) returns that the firm can provide to shareholders, and thus (c) the value of the firm. Immediately following World War II, the tax rate on corporate income was very high (far in excess of 50 percent for the highest income range). More recently, corporate tax rates have been reduced. One of the most significant recent reductions came about with the Tax Reform Act of 1986, which reduced corporate tax rates across all income ranges (e.g., the highest tax rate was reduced from 45 percent to 38 percent).

TABLE 6-1   Recent Federal Tax Rate Schedules for Corporations and Individuals

Federal Corporate Income Tax Rate Schedule, January 1998

Taxable Income Range	Marginal Tax Rate for Range	Average Tax Rate at Top of Range
Up to $50,000	15%	15.0%
$50,000–$75,000	25%	18.3%
$75,000–$100,000	34%	22.3%
$100,000–$335,000	39%	34.0%
$335,000–$10,000,000	34%	34.0%
$10,000,000–$15,000,000	35%	34.3%
$15,000,000–$18,333,333	38%	35.0%
Over 18,333,333	35%	35.0%

Federal Individual Ordinary Income Tax Rate Schedule for 1997

Taxable Income Range	Marginal Tax Rate for Range	Average Tax Rate at Top of Range
Up to $41,200	15%	15.0%
$41,200–$99,600	28%	22.6%
$99,600–$151,750	31%	25.5%
$151,750–$271,050	36%	30.1%
Over $271,050	39.6%	—

Source: Internal Revenue Service, U.S. Treasury Department.

---

[1]Corporations may also be subject to state and local taxes. For simplicity, we focus only on federal taxation.

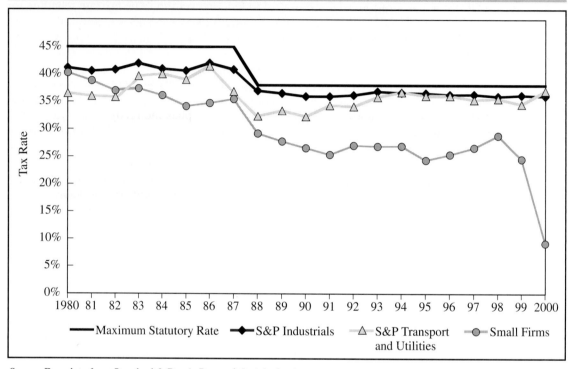

FIGURE 6-1 Statutory Maximum Corporate Income Tax Rates and Median Average Corporate Tax Rates for Indicated Categories of Firms, 1980–2000

Source: Raw data from Standard & Poor's *Research Insight* database.

A firm's dollar earnings tend to be positively related to the firm's size. Thus, given a progressive tax rate schedule, large firms generally pay taxes at a higher average rate than small firms. Statistics shown in Figure 6-1 are consistent with this point. The figure shows median average corporate tax rates for several classes of firms from 1980 to 2000, along with the highest statutory rate for each year. The firm classes include the S&P Industrials, the S&P Transports and Utilities (together), and other, generally smaller, firms. For most years, firms in the S&P Industrials had the highest median average tax rate, and this rate was consistently close to the maximum statutory rate. The S&P Transports and Utilities, which also tend to be very large firms, generally had the second-highest median average tax rates. Finally, the smaller firms consistently had the lowest tax rates, generally 5 percent to 10 percent lower than the S&P Industrials.

6.2.2 Taxation of Individuals

Individuals are also subject to federal income taxation (and possibly state and local income taxation, as well). As with firms, the federal income tax rate schedule for individuals is progressive, but rates have generally fallen from their peak (90 percent for the highest income range) in the years after World War II.[2] The federal individual ordinary income tax rate schedule for 1997 is shown in the lower panel of Table 6-1.

In the aggregate, the bulk of individuals' income derives from employment wages and salaries. However, individuals also derive income from other sources, including four sources that are important in this chapter: dividends, realized capital gains, taxable interest, and tax-exempt interest.

Dividends are taxed as ordinary income. Dividends are also not deductible for the paying firm, so dividends are subject to *double taxation*, once at the corporate level and again at the personal level. Double taxation also applies indirectly to an individual's realized capital gains on a stock. However, historically the tax rate has been lower on realized capital gains than on ordinary income. In addition, capital gains are taxed only when they are *realized* upon the sale of an asset at a profit. Therefore, by holding a stock for a longer period, an investor can *defer* his or her realization of capital gains, and thus reduce the effective tax rate on such gains. As for bonds, interest income from U.S. government bonds and corporate bonds is taxed as ordinary income, whereas interest income from municipal bonds (i.e., bonds issued by state and local municipalities) is exempt from federal taxation.

Figure 6-2 shows, for 1998, the aggregate income that U.S. individual taxpayers reported to the IRS from each of the four sources listed above. Individuals reported $88.6 billion in dividends, $360.7 billion in realized capital gains, $103.2 billion in taxable interest, and $48.5 billion in tax-exempt interest.

The figure also shows the distributions of income from each of these sources for groups of individuals sorted by their adjusted gross income (AGI), and the average tax rate for each group. Regarding the income distributions, the percentages increase with AGI for every income source. Individuals in the highest income range (AGI > $200,000) received the highest proportion from every income source. This is expected, because individuals in this group are among the wealthiest individuals in the United States, and are disproportionately likely to invest in securities.

However, these individuals also have the highest average tax rates. Thus, they have a greater incentive to hold tax-favored securities. Results in the figure are consistent with this incentive. The high-income individuals' shares of income from taxable interest and dividends are relatively lower, while their shares of income from realized capital gains and tax-exempt interest are relatively higher.

The results in Figure 6-2 provide some indication of the tax status of investors who hold corporate securities, and their propensity to pay taxes on income from these holdings. However, other major investor groups, as well as other investment vehicles available to individuals, are not directly represented in these figures. For instance, historically insurance companies and pension funds have held the bulk of publicly issued corporate bonds, whereas commercial banks have held the bulk of privately placed corporate debt. In addition, thousands of mutual funds collectively hold trillions of dollars of corporate bonds and equities. (However, a mutual fund must *pass through* virtu-

[2]A large reduction in personal tax rates occurred after Ronald Reagan's election with the passage in 1981 of the Kemp-Roth tax bill, which sharply lowered individual income tax rates, cutting the top rate from 70 percent to 50 percent.

FIGURE 6-2 Aggregate Reported Income of U.S. Individuals from Indicated Sources, and Percent of Source Income Received by, and Average Tax Rate for, Individuals in Indicated Ranges of Adjusted Gross Income (AGI), 1998

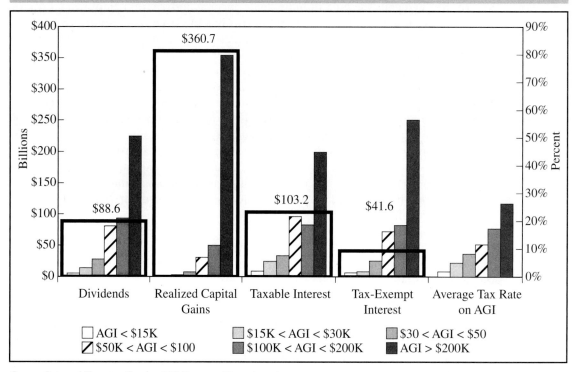

Source: Internal Revenue Service, U.S. Treasury Department.

ally all dividends, realized capital gains, and interest it receives to the individual investors who hold the fund's shares.)

Finally, the results also do not reflect the reinvested dividends and interest that individual investors earn on tax-deferred pension plans such as IRAs, 401(k) plans, and Keogh plans. Investors do not immediately pay taxes on either dividend or interest paid into such plans, so their effective tax rate on investment income in these plans may be quite low.

6.3 MODIFYING THE ORIGINAL M&M PROPOSITIONS TO ACCOUNT FOR CORPORATE TAXES

We begin our analysis of the effects of taxation on leverage by reviewing Modigliani and Miller's (1963) modification of their original propositions (discussed in Chapter 2) to allow for corporate taxes. Their modified model adjusts for the deductibility of interest on corporate debt.

6.3.1 A Numerical Example of the Effect of Interest Deductibility on Firm Value

To illustrate the modification, consider the case of Jones Company, which earns $1,000,000 annually before interest and taxes, and pays out all after-tax earnings in dividends. The firm is subject to a 34 percent tax rate. We calculated the total after-tax cash flow to all of the firm's securityholders under two alternative capital structures. In the first, the firm is financed entirely with equity, while in the second the firm has $3 million of debt. The interest cost of the debt is 10 percent per annum, or $300,000 annually. The resulting cash flows under each capital structure are shown in Table 6-2.

Total annual cash flow to securityholders is greater if a firm has debt in its capital structure than if it is financed entirely with equity. The difference is $102,000 ($762,600 – $660,000). The extra return to securityholders is due to the deductibility of interest expense in the levered version of the firm, which reduces taxes by the same amount, $102,000 (from $340,000 to $238,000).

This numerical example highlights two important effects of corporate taxation. *First*, the government emerges as a *stakeholder*, with a claim on the firm's earnings. *Second*, management can reduce cash flow to the government, and thereby increase cash flow to debtholders and shareholders collectively, by increasing the amount of debt in the firm's capital structure.

6.3.2 The Present Value of the Tax Shield of Interest

Miller and Modigliani provide a general specification the effect of interest deductibility on the value of a firm by (a) using variables to represent the various parameters involved, and (b) making two simplifying assumptions. The first assumption is that the firm's debt consists of a single issue of perpetual debt, which provides an annual cash coupon at a rate of $c = r_D$, where r_D is the required return. The value of the debt is denoted as D. The second assumption is that the corporate tax rate, τ_c, and the deductibility of interest, are fixed into perpetuity.

Using the above notation, a firm's annual *tax shield* (i.e., the annual reduction in taxes due to interest deductibility) can be expressed as the product of the tax rate and the annual coupon interest, or

$$\text{Annual tax shield} = \tau_c c D. \qquad \qquad \textbf{(6.1)}$$

TABLE 6-2 **The Jones Company: Corporate Taxes and Cash Flow to Stockholders and Bondholders under Alternative Capital Structures**

	All-Equity	Levered	Differences
Earnings before interest and taxes	$1,000,000	$1,000,000	
Less: Interest expense	$0	$300,000	
Earnings before taxes	$1,000,000	$700,000	
Less: Taxes at 34%	$340,000	$238,000	($102,000)
Earnings after taxes (paid as dividends)	$660,000	$462,000	
Total cash flow to stockholders and bondholders	$660,000	$762,000	$102,000

We have assumed that both the debt and the tax shield carry into perpetuity, so we can calculate the present value (*PV*) of the tax shield using the constant perpetuity formula, with r_D as the discount rate:

$$PV \text{ (tax shield)} = \frac{\tau_c c D}{r_D} = \frac{\tau_c r_D D}{r_D} = \tau_c D. \tag{6.2}$$

That is, as the firm substitutes an additional dollar of debt for a dollar of equity in the firm's capital structure, the value of the firm increases by τ_c.

6.3.3   The Levered Firms Value Adjusted for Interest Deductibility

As a consequence of this tax effect, M&Ms original Proposition I must be modified. Specifically, the *tax-adjusted* value of a levered firm, denoted as V_L^*, is equal to the value of an unlevered version of the firm, V_U, plus the present value of the tax shield:

$$V_L^* = V_U + PV(\text{tax shield}) = V_U + \tau_c D. \tag{6.3}$$

Equation 6.3 illustrates the point that, when we modify M&M Proposition I for corporate taxes, the value of a firm is no longer constant across leverage, but instead *increases monotonically* with leverage. Thus, we have the seemingly absurd result that, for management to maximize the market value of the firm, the firm should be virtually 100 percent debt financed! Needless to say, this result has spawned a controversy about a firm's optimal leverage that continues to this day. We address this issue later.

A Numerical Example
To illustrate our equations, we return to the numerical example of Jones Company. In the levered version of the firm, $c = 0.10$, and $D = \$3$ million, and thus the annual tax shield is $0.34(0.10)(\$3$ million$) = \$102,000$. Assuming that $r_D = 0.10$, the present value of the firm's tax shield is

$$PV(\text{tax shield}) = 0.34(\$3 \text{ million}) = \$1.02 \text{ million.}$$

Thus, the value of the levered version of the firm, V_L^*, exceeds its unlevered value, V_U, by $1.02 million.

Taxes, Arbitrage, and a Firm's Market Value under Alternative Capital Structures
Although our analyses fairly reflect the effect of interest deductibility on a firm's *true value*, it can be argued that a firm's *market value* will likely reflect the tax advantage of debt even if the firm is currently financed entirely with equity. To see this, consider the following scenario. Jones Company is currently a private, all-equity firm owned by Mr. Jones. However, Mr. Jones wishes to liquidate his investment in the firm by selling it to public investors. His objective is simply to maximize the proceeds he receives from selling the firm, where proceeds equal the sum of the market values of the securities sold.

Our previous calculations suggest that Mr. Jones would receive greater total proceeds if he sells both debt and equity claims against the firm (i.e., if he packages it as a levered firm by issuing both equity and debt claims) than if he sells it as an all-equity firm, because the total annual cash flow to securityholders is greater in the former case. In other words, it appears that Mr. Jones can maximize the *market value* of the firm, and thus his proceeds from selling it, by minimizing the value of the government's claim.

However, if instead Mr. Jones issues only equity claims against the firm, investors who compete for the firm's equity shares realize that, after they purchase the shares, they can immediately (and, we assume, costlessly) *recapitalize* the firm by issuing debt and using the proceeds to pay themselves a dividend.[3] After the recap, the total value of the firm's debt and equity securities should be the same as it would have been if Mr. Jones had issued debt and equity claims in the first place. Thus, if shareholders can initially purchase the firm's (unlevered) equity shares at a total price that is less than the total value of the debt and equity *after* the recap, they would realize an immediate riskless arbitrage profit. Such arbitrage profit opportunities should be eliminated in a competitive market, so Mr. Jones should reap the same total proceeds whether he sells his interest in the firm by issuing equity shares or any combination of debt and equity, and these proceeds should be equal to the *maximum market value* that can be realized across all possible capital structures, regardless of the capital structure that Mr. Jones presents to the market. This is simply an invocation of the M&M arbitrage argument presented in Chapter 2, except that (a) corporate earnings are taxed, and (b) the true value of the firm increases with leverage due to interest deductibility.

6.3.4 The Levered Firm's Tax-Adjusted WACC

Next, we specify a firm's *tax-adjusted* weighted average cost of capital (WACC). We show how M&M Proposition II must be modified to account for corporate taxation and interest deductibility.

Jones Company's Unlevered Value

We illustrate the effect of taxes on a firm's WACC by continuing our example of Jones Company, developing general formulas in the process. The calculations shown in Table 6-2 indicate that, as an all-equity firm, Jones Company is expected to generate annual after-tax dividends of $660,000. Suppose Jones Company's unlevered cost of capital, or equivalently, its unlevered cost of equity capital, is $r_A = r_E = 15$ percent. Dividends are expected to carry into perpetuity, so the total value of Jones Company's assets, V_U, or equivalently, the value of the firm's unlevered equity, E_U, is

$$V_U = E_U = \frac{\$660{,}000}{0.15} = \$4.4 \text{ million.}$$

Jones Company's Levered Value and Cost of Capital: Ignoring Interest Deductibility

In the levered version of the firm, Jones Company has 10 percent perpetual riskless debt with a value of $D = \$3$ million. Initially we *ignore* the benefit of interest deductibility in order to calculate values that can be contrasted to those obtained later when we *recognize* the benefit of interest deductibility. The original M&M Proposition

---

[3]Note that we are currently ignoring taxes at the personal level, whether they would apply to dividend income, capital gains, or interest income.

I implies that the value of Jones Company's levered equity is E_L = $1.4 million (= $4.4 million – $3.0 million), and according to the original M&M Proposition II, the cost of the firm's levered equity, r_{LE}, can be calculated using the original WACC equation, repeated in Equation 6.4:

$$r_A = r_D \left(\frac{D}{D + E} \right) + r_{LE} \left(\frac{E}{D + E} \right). \qquad (6.4)$$

Thus, for this example,

$$15\% = 10\% \left(\frac{\$3.0 \text{ million}}{\$4.4 \text{ million}} \right) + r_{LE} \left(\frac{\$1.4 \text{ million}}{\$4.4 \text{ million}} \right),$$

or

$$r_{LE} = 25.713\%.$$

Jones Company's Levered Value and Cost of Capital: Recognizing Interest Deductibility
Now we recognize the benefit of interest deductibility by applying Equation 6.3, giving us the following tax-adjusted value of Jones Company as a levered firm:

$$\begin{aligned} V_L^* &= V_U + PV(\text{tax shield}) = V_U + \tau_c D \\ &= \$4.4 \text{ million} + 0.34(\$3 \text{ million}) \\ &= \$5.42 \text{ million.} \end{aligned}$$

Using this result, we can calculate the tax-adjusted value of Jones Company's levered equity, E_L^*:

$$\begin{aligned} E_L^* &= V_L^* - D \\ &= \$5.42 \text{ million} - \$3.0 \text{ million} \\ &= \$2.42 \text{ million.} \end{aligned}$$

Note that the value of Jones Company's levered equity has increased by $1.02 million (from $1.4 million to $2.42 million), and that this increase reflects the (now-recognized) present value of the tax shield.

Next, we define a firm's after-tax WACC, denoted as r_A^*, as the discount rate that renders the present value of the perpetual expected after-tax cash flows (*ATCF*) to all securityholders, annual values of which are denoted as $ATCF_t$, equal to V_L^*:

$$V_L^* = \frac{ATCF_t}{r_A^*}. \qquad (6.5)$$

For Jones Company, we find from Table 6-2 that $ATCF_t$ = $762,000, so

$$V_L^* = \$5.42 \text{ million} = \frac{\$762,000}{r_A^*},$$

or

$$r_A^* = 14.059\%.$$

Next, we can use Equation 6-6 below to solve for the firm's tax-adjusted cost of levered equity, r_{LE}^*:

$$r_A^* = r_D \left(\frac{D}{D + E_L^*} \right) + r_{LE}^* \left(\frac{E_L^*}{D + E_L^*} \right), \tag{6.6}$$

or

$$14.059\% = 10\% \left(\frac{\$3.0 \text{ million}}{\$5.42 \text{ million}} \right) + r_{LE}^* \left(\frac{\$2.42 \text{ million}}{\$5.42 \text{ million}} \right),$$

or

$$r_{LE}^* = 19.091\%.$$

Finally, we can apply this value of r_{LE}^* as a discount rate for the annual expected after-tax cash flow to shareholders, \$462,000 (from Table 6-2), to verify the value of Jones Company's levered equity:

$$E_L^* = \left(\frac{\$462,000}{0.19091} \right) = \$2,419,988 \approx \$2.42 \text{ million.}$$

6.3.5 Two Important Issues Concerning the Effects of Interest Deductibility on a Firm's WACC

Our analyses raise two important issues. *First*, why do we use the *pre-tax* cost of debt, rather than the *after-tax* cost of debt, in Equation 6.6 to calculate a firm's tax-adjusted WACC? *Second*, for the levered version of Jones Company, why is the cost of equity capital *lower* when the tax advantage of debt is recognized than when it is not recognized (i.e., 19.091 percent versus 25.713 percent)? We address both issues now.

Why Use the Pretax Cost of Debt in the Tax-Adjusted WACC Formula?
The first issue alludes to an alternative formula for a firm's tax-adjusted WACC that is found in most corporate finance textbooks. Denoting these alternative specifications of the firm's tax-adjusted WACC and cost of equity as r_A° and r_{LE}°, respectively, the alternative formula is given in Equation 6.7:

$$r_A^\circ = r_D(1 - \tau_c) \left(\frac{D}{D + E_L^*} \right) + r_{LE}^\circ \left(\frac{E_L^*}{D + E_L^*} \right). \tag{6.7}$$

Equation 6.7 seems reasonable, because it attaches the benefit of interest deductibility to the debt itself, reducing its effective cost from r_D to $r_D(1 - \tau_c)$. So let us try to apply Equation 6.7 to the Jones Company example. Note that $V_L = \$5.42$ million and $E_L^* = \$2.42$ million must hold via the tax-adjusted version of Proposition I. Also, for consistency, $r_A^{\circ} = 14.059$ percent must hold as calculated earlier. Thus, we have values for all parameters in Equation (6.7) except r_{LE}°, so we can solve for r_{LE}°:

$$14.059\% = 10\%(1-0.34)\left(\frac{\$3 \text{ million}}{\$5.42 \text{ million}}\right) + r_{LE}^{\circ}\left(\frac{\$2.42 \text{ million}}{\$5.42 \text{ million}}\right),$$

or

$$r_{LE}^{\circ} = 23.306\%.$$

Note that this value is different from the value for r_{LE}^*, 19.091 percent, obtained earlier. Using this value of r_{LE}° to calculate the value of Jones Company's levered equity, denoted as E_L°:

$$E_L^{\circ} = \left(\frac{\$462,000}{0.23306}\right) = \$1,982,322,$$

which is clearly not the correct value of the firm's levered equity according to the tax-adjusted version of M&M Proposition I, $2.42 million.

So what is wrong with Equation 6.7? The problem is that the equation fails to recognize that it is the *equityholders* who benefit from interest deductibility, and this benefit not only affects the value of the firm's levered equity, but also its risk and its cost. To correctly account for the effect of interest deductibility, we must recognize that equityholders now have a claim to two distinct income streams. The first income stream is that to which they have a claim in the absence of interest deductibility, which in this case is an income stream with an expected annual payment of $360,000 [= (1 – 0.34) $1,000,000 – $300,000].

The second stream is equal to the reduction in income taxes owing to interest deductibility, which is $102,000 per year in this case. Therefore, the overall cost of levered equity is a value-weighted average of the costs of these two income streams. The value of the first stream is $1.4 million, and the cost is $r_E = 25.713$ percent, as we computed before we recognized interest deductibility. The value of the second stream is $\tau_c D$, or in this case, 0.34($3 million) = $1.02 million, and the cost is r_D, or in this example, 10 percent. Thus, the tax-adjusted cost of levered equity is

$$r_{LE}^* = r_{LE}\left(\frac{E_L}{E_L + \tau_c D}\right) + r_D\left(\frac{\tau_c D}{E_L + \tau_c D}\right), \tag{6.8}$$

where r_{LE} and E_L are the *unadjusted* cost and value of the levered firms equity. For Jones Company,

$$r_{LE}^* = 25.713\%\left(\frac{\$1.4 \text{ million}}{\$2.42 \text{ million}}\right) + 10\%\left(\frac{\$1.02 \text{ million}}{\$2.42 \text{ million}}\right),$$

or

$$r_{LE}^* = 19.091\%,$$

which reconciles with the value of r_{LE}^* obtained earlier via Equation 6.6.

Why Does the Cost of Levered Equity Fall When Interest Deductibility Is Recognized?

Regarding the second issue, Equation 6.8 suggests why a levered firm's tax-adjusted cost of equity is lower than its unadjusted cost. That is, interest deductibility bestows not only a value to shareholders but also reduces the risk of the levered equity, because equityholders now receive a second, lower-risk, cash flow stream. Furthermore, though we do not show this explicitly, the reduction in risk to shareholders is actually due to the fact that the government, as a stakeholder, holds a quasi equity claim on the firm's earnings. This is so because the government receives a fixed fraction of the firm's earnings after interest.

6.3.6   Section Summary: A Fundamental Question

The analyses in this section can be summarized succinctly: When we incorporate the effect one important real-world factor, corporate taxation coupled with interest deductibility, we obtain the seemingly absurd result that the value of a firm increases monotonically with leverage. But this implies that, to maximize the market value of the firm, management should have virtually 100 percent debt in its capital structure! As we saw in Chapter 1, no firms in the United States have such extreme leverage. Indeed, many firms have no debt.

Thus, at this point we have a fundamental question:

> Why do firms fail to take greater advantage of the deductibility of corporate interest to increase the value of their equity?

The corporate finance literature provides several competing answers to this question, which we discuss in the next three sections.

6.4   INTEREST DEDUCTIBILITY VERSUS COSTS OF FINANCIAL DISTRESS AND BANKRUPTCY: THE TRADITIONAL TRADE-OFF THEORY

The *Traditional Trade-off Theory* provides one answer to the question raised at the end of the previous section. According to this theory, as a firm increases debt relative to equity in its capital structure, *expected costs of future financial distress and bankruptcy* (defined later) also rise, eventually enough to fully offset the benefit of the tax shield, at the margin. At this point, firm value is maximized, and beyond this point firm value actually falls.

Thus, the Traditional Trade-off Theory suggests (a) for a given firm there exists a unique optimal capital structure that consists of a *finite* level of leverage, and (b) the optimal amount of leverage varies across firms, for two reasons: (1) Corporate tax rates vary across firms, and (2) the rate at which expected costs of future financial distress and bankruptcy increase with leverage also varies across firms.

To explain the Traditional Trade-off Theory, we address four questions sequentially: (a) How can we quantify more precisely the effect of interest deductibility on the value of a firm's equity? (b) What circumstances lead a firm into financial distress? (c) What are the costs of financial distress? (d) What are the implications of future financial distress for the firm's capital structure policy?

6.4.1   A Closer Look at the Effects of Leverage on Equity Value Accounting Only for Interest Deductibility

In the previous section, we showed that, accounting only for interest deductibility, the market value of a firm increases with leverage, and the added value accrues to the firm's shareholders. In this subsection, we show how a firm's market-to-book equity ratio is affected.

Suppose a new firm, Jones Company, is being proposed that consists of assets that will be purchased to pursue a project. The project is expected to generate earnings into perpetuity. However, the project generates only ordinary earnings after taxes—which is to say that the firm, as a project, has a *NPV* of zero.

This firm does not appear to create value for the firm's shareholders, so we would question why it should be developed at all. However, Jones Company's developers intend to partially finance the firm with perpetual debt, using interest deductibility to create value for shareholders. In the previous section we showed that, if the firm employs the amount D of perpetual debt in its capital structure, the value of the firm increases by $\tau_c D$, and shareholders gain this amount of $\tau_c D$ as added value. In addition, as leverage increases, the amount of equity that the firm employs simultaneously decreases. As a result, as leverage increases, an ever-larger tax benefit of debt is concentrated on an ever-smaller equity base. Therefore, the developers use leverage not only to take advantage of interest deductibility per se, but also because it creates value for shareholders on an ever-more-concentrated basis as leverage increases.

By our assumption, if Jones Company were financed entirely with equity, the market value of the equity would be equal to the book value of its assets. Thus, the firm's market-to-book equity ratio would be 1.0. However, as the firm adds leverage, the tax benefit of debt should increase this ratio. From this viewpoint, a particularly revealing analysis involves charting the effect of interest deductibility on a firm's market-to-book equity ratio as a function of both τ_c and leverage, where, as explained above, the book value of a firm's equity represents the value of the equity in the absence of (or ignoring) the tax benefit of debt. For the chart, we (a) use four alternative values of τ_c, 10, 20, 30, and 40 percent, and (b) calculate the firm's market-to-book equity ratio as a function of the firm's debt ratio for each value of τ_c. The resulting chart is shown in Figure 6-3.

As expected, the firm's market-to-book equity ratio increases with both τ_c and leverage. Also, for all tax rates the effect of leverage on the market-to-book equity ratio is highly convex, increasing at a fairly slow rate at lower levels of leverage, and then accelerating at more extreme leverage ratios. For the highest tax rate considered, 40 percent, the market-to-book equity ratio does not exceed 1.5 until leverage reaches a fairly high level of 45 percent. However, the ratio then reaches 2.0 with a further small increase in leverage to 55.5 percent, 3.0 as leverage increases to 62.5 percent, and 10.0 at a leverage ratio of 69 percent.

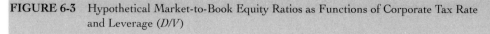

FIGURE 6-3 Hypothetical Market-to-Book Equity Ratios as Functions of Corporate Tax Rate and Leverage (*D/V*)

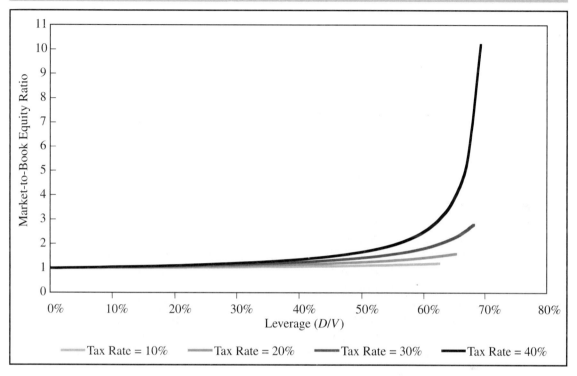

6.4.2 Circumstances That Lead to Financial Distress and Bankruptcy

What are the circumstances that lead a firm into financial distress and bankruptcy? To illustrate, suppose Jones Company has established its business plan and is about to purchase the assets required to execute the plan, which could be financed by various means ranging from all-equity to high leverage. Through subsequent operations over time, either (a) the business plan proves successful, in which case all requisite payments of interest and principal (if any) are made on a timely basis, and shareholders receive returns on their investment; or (b) the business plan proves unsuccessful, and cash outflow chronically exceeds cash inflow. Our primary focus is on the latter case.

Financial Distress

Clearly, if Jones Company is experiencing chronic net cash outflow it cannot continue in that state forever. At some point, the firm will face *financial distress*, a situation in which available cash is insufficient to pay suppliers, employees, and, if the firm has debt, creditors. Signs of *first-stage financial distress* include negative net cash flow and earnings, and a falling market equity value. If the hemorrhaging continues, management must take actions to rectify the situation. Signs of *second-stage financial distress* include management's attempts to reduce costs, such as employee layoffs and temporary plant closings.

If the situation persists, the firm enters *third-stage financial distress*, characterized by late payments to suppliers, employees, and creditors, and possibly more drastic actions such as (a) issuing new debt or equity securities, if indeed this would be possible, (b) selling assets, (c) merging with a more successful firm in the industry, or (d) negotiating with creditors to reschedule debt payments. If none of these actions resolves the problem, the firm will enter *end-stage financial distress:* bankruptcy.

The U.S. Bankruptcy Code: Liquidation or Reorganization

The U.S. bankruptcy code provides for two types of corporate filings: *liquidation*, which is a filing under *Chapter 7* of the bankruptcy code; and *reorganization*, which is a filing under *Chapter 11* of the code.

Under Chapter 7, a trustee is appointed to oversee the liquidation of the firm's assets and the distribution of the proceeds to claimants. The trustee distributes proceeds in strict order of priority:

1. Claims for administrative expenses and claims for expenses incurred in preserving and collecting the estate.
2. Claims of tradespeople who extended unsecured credit after an involuntary case has begun but before a trustee is appointed.
3. Wages due workers if earned within the 90 days preceding the earlier of the filing of the petition or the cessation of business. The amount of wages is limited to $4,000 per person.
4. Claims for unpaid contributions to employee benefit plans that were to have been paid within 180 days prior to filing. However, these claims, plus wages, are not to exceed the $4,000 per employee limit.
5. Unsecured claims for customer deposits, not to exceed $1,800 per individual.
6. Taxes due to federal, state, and any other governmental agency.
7. Unfunded pension plan liabilities. These claims are superior to those of general creditors for an amount up to 30 percent of the common and preferred equity; any remaining unfunded pension claims rank with those of the general creditors.
8. Claims of general or unsecured creditors.
9. Claims of preferred shareholders, who may receive an amount up to the par value of the issue.
10. Claims of common shareholders.

The second, and more commonly used, bankruptcy alternative is Chapter 11 reorganization. Here the firm's assets, liabilities, and equity are restructured with the objective of providing the business with a chance to survive. The firm must file a reorganization plan within 120 days of receiving the court's order for relief. The plan must address creditors' claims within general classes. The reorganization plan is subject to the approval of creditors and court confirmation, and all administrative expenses must be paid. Though the process involves mandated deadlines, firms often request extensions that result in years of litigation.

6.4.3   Costs of Financial Distress and Bankruptcy

Costs of Financial Distress

A firm incurs several deadweight costs when its financial position weakens, even if the firm does not declare bankruptcy. These are called *costs of financial distress*. Bankruptcy involves additional deadweight costs. When a firm considers adding debt to its capital structure, both the borrowing firm and its creditors must be concerned that the firm might incur such costs in the future.

As a general definition, any loss of value that can be attributed to a firm's deteriorating financial strength is a cost of financial distress. Most such costs fall into one of three categories: (a) loss of competitiveness in a product/service market, (b) concessions to stakeholders to compensate them for the risk of doing business with a distressed firm, and (c) loss of the value of the interest tax shield (as well as the value of *depreciation* as a tax shield).

Perhaps the greatest cost of financial distress for a firm is a loss of competitiveness, which may occur for several reasons. *First*, the firm may be forced to pass up valuable projects because it lacks internal financing and has little or no access to the external capital markets. *Second*, the distressed firm may be forced to sell valuable assets, subsidiaries, or divisions to shore up its liquidity. *Third*, its competitors may push new products or lower prices in an effort to financially *squeeze* the distressed firm out of business. (See Opler and Titman [1994] for discussion and empirical evidence.)

A distressed firm may also be forced to renegotiate contracts with its suppliers, employees, customers, and creditors. *Suppliers* want prompt payment and continuing business. They generally are willing to provide trade credit, but only to financially secure buyers. In an industry with few suppliers, a distressed firm may be forced to pay higher prices to its suppliers to compensate for risk, and may be denied trade credit. *Employees* may demand greater wages or salaries to compensate for the heightened risk that they will lose their jobs. If the distressed firm cannot comply, it may lose many of its best employees, and thereby incur additional losses in terms of lost workforce talent and experience.

A firm's *customers* generally demand warranties and after-sales service, and their long-term availability is in question for a distressed firm. Therefore, buyers may either demand compensation in the form of lower prices, or take their business elsewhere. A distressed firm may also lose valuable relationships with its *creditors*. For instance, a bank that has heretofore provided a line of credit to the firm may rescind the line in the face of the firm's financial distress. Alternatively, the firm may be forced to accept onerous terms in debt renegotiations.

Finally, a distressed firm also may lose the value of the interest deductibility on its debt. The tax advantage of debt can be realized only if a company generates earnings (though the IRS allows limited tax-loss carryforwards). As earlier calculations suggest, the value of the interest tax shield is large and increases with leverage. Symmetrically, the opportunity cost of losing the usefulness of the interest tax shield is large and increases with leverage.

Bankruptcy Costs

Bankruptcy costs include legal, administrative, and accounting costs associated with the bankruptcy process. Additional costs are associated with a subsequent private debt *workout*, or with the liquidation of some or all of the firm's assets, often at low, *fire sale* prices.

6.4.4 Implications of Financial Distress for a Firm's Value and Capital Structure

What are the implications of potential future financial distress for a firm's leverage decision? To address this question, we develop a simple model to represent the overall cost of financial distress and its relationship to leverage. We assume that the expected cost of future financial distress, denoted as $E(CFFD)$, can be expressed as the product of the probability of future financial distress, Prob(FFD), times the cost of future financial distress should it actually occur, $CFFD$:

$$E(CFFD) = [\text{Prob}(FFD)]CFFD. \tag{6.9}$$

We are interested in the effects of financial distress on the *current* market value of the firm, so we are particularly interested in the *present value* of the expected costs of future financial distress, denoted as $PV[E(CFFD)]$. The $PV[E(CFFD)]$, in turn, can be expressed mathematically if we make the further simplifying assumptions that financial distress, if it does occur, will occur in year T, and that the appropriate discount rate to apply to $E(CFFD)$ is r_{cfd}. These assumptions yield Equation 6.10:

$$PV[E(CFFD)] = \frac{E(CFFD)}{(1 + r_{cfd})^T}. \tag{6.10}$$

Of course, a firm can experience financial distress even if the firm has no debt in its capital structure. That is, even if the firm has no debt, it can experience chronic losses that deplete its financial resources, eventually affecting relationships with suppliers, customers, and employees, and ultimately its competitive position. However, $PV[E(CFFD)]$ is likely to increase with leverage for two reasons. *First*, debt obligates the firm to make periodic fixed payments, which the firm may not be able to meet if it experiences chronic losses. *Second*, referring to Equation 6.10, the periodic payments required on debt securities are an ongoing burden, which may shorten the amount of time, T, until financial distress occurs.

To gauge the effect of leverage on $PV[E(CFFD)]$, and thus the value of the firm, we must recognize that it is an *incremental* effect. That is, to the extent that $PV[E(CFFD)]$ increases with leverage, each marginal increase is attributable to the associated marginal increase in debt. Consequently, the effect of adding a specified amount of debt to the firm's capital structure on $PV[E(CFFD)]$, and thus the value of the firm, is the accumulation of the associated marginal increases in $PV[E(CFFD)]$. We denote that portion of the overall value of $PV[E(CFFD)]$ that is due to a specific amount of debt as $PV[E(CFFD_{debt})]$.[4]

With this specification, we can now provide an equation for the value of a levered firm that accounts for both the positive and negative effects of debt—namely, the value

---

[4]Andrade and Kaplan (1998) emphasize the need to distinguish costs associated with *economic distress* (i.e., operating losses) from costs that are purely associated with leverage and are therefore properly termed costs of *financial distress*.

of the tax shield and the effect of leverage on the present value of expected costs of future financial distress:

$$V_L = V_U + \tau_c D - PV[E(CFFD_{debt})]. \qquad \textbf{(6.11)}$$

According to the Traditional Trade-off Theory, for low levels of leverage the marginal value of $\tau_c D$ exceeds the marginal value of $PV[E(CFFD_{debt})]$, and therefore firm value increases with leverage. However, at high levels of leverage, marginal increases in $PV[E(CFFD_{debt})]$ are greater than τ_c (which is the marginal value of the tax shield), so firm value decreases with leverage. Consequently, the optimal, or firm value-maximizing, amount of leverage is finite.

As we noted earlier, an additional implication of the Traditional Trade-off Theory is that the optimal amount of leverage differs across firms, because firms differ in terms of their tax rate and the rate of increase in $PV[E(CFFD_{debt})]$ as leverage increases. Figure 6-4 illustrates how the values of two hypothetical firms, A and B, change with leverage according to this theory. For both firms, unlevered firm value is 100, and the present value of the tax shield is computed using $\tau_c = 0.34$. For firm A, $PV[E(CFFD_{debt})]$ tends to increase at a slower rate with leverage, and as a result its

FIGURE 6-4   An Illustration of the Traditional Trade-off Theory: Optimal Leverage for Firms A and B Differ Because for the Latter the *PV* of Expected Costs of Financial Distress Increases with Leverage at a Faster Rate

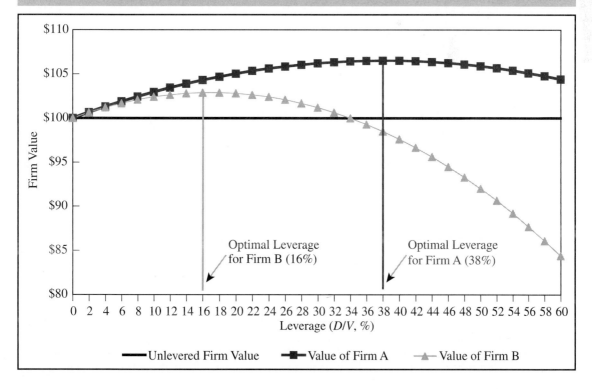

optimal debt ratio is relatively high at 38 percent. In contrast, for firm B, $PV[E(CFFD_{\text{debt}})]$ increases at a relatively faster rate with leverage, so its optimal leverage is relatively low at 16 percent.

6.5 EMPIRICAL EVIDENCE ON THE TRADITIONAL TRADE-OFF THEORY

Many empirical studies of the Traditional Trade-off Theory have been published in the finance literature. In this section, we briefly discuss several of these studies, taking note of key variables that researchers have used in their tests. We then conduct our own empirical tests of the theory.

6.5.1 Previous Empirical Studies of the Traditional Trade-off Theory

Empirical studies of the Traditional Trade-off Theory involve either time series or cross-sectional tests, all focusing on basic predictions of the theory. Time series tests are generally based on two aspects of changes in a firm's leverage over time. *First*, each firm's leverage should be fairly stable over time. This must be so if the notion of an *optimal* amount of leverage is to be meaningful. *Second*, a firm's operations and financing activities over time are likely to cause a firm's leverage to change, and thus to temporarily deviate from the optimal. (For instance, if the firm has recently realized unusually high earnings, and the firm has a policy of retaining earnings, then the firm's current leverage may be temporarily lower than the optimal. Alternatively, the firm may borrow all of the money required for a given project, causing its leverage to be temporarily higher than the optimal.)

If we assume that it is rational for a firm's management to take actions only *gradually* to restore the firm's leverage to its optimal, then the firm's leverage will exhibit a *mean-reverting* tendency over time. That is, if a firm's leverage is currently higher than its historical average, we should observe that the firm subsequently reduces its leverage, and vice versa. Several researchers have conducted time series tests of the Traditional Trade-off Theory, including Taggart (1977), Marsh (1982), Jalilvand and Harris (1984), Auerbach (1985), and Opler and Titman (1994). All of these studies find evidence of mean reversion.

In cross-sectional tests, researchers have focused on both sides of the trade-off. Regarding the tax benefit of debt, researchers have tried to identify factors that would affect the firm's tax status. Here, the firm's profits (implicitly juxtaposed against the tax rate schedule) are a measure of a firm's ability to take advantage of interest deductibility. Consistent with this argument, Mackie-Mason (1990) documents evidence that firms with *tax-loss carryforwards* are less likely to issue debt.

Regarding the offsetting costs of debt, researchers have focused on variables that should be related to (a) the probability that the firm will face financial distress or bankruptcy in the future, and (b) costs that would be incurred if financial distress or bankruptcy occurs. Some researchers refer to the *Collateral Hypothesis*. According to this hypothesis, a firm's *debt capacity* (i.e., its ability to borrow in the credit markets) is limited to the value of its collateralizable assets—basically, its property, plant, and equipment (PP&E). Other assets, notably intangible assets, are not collateralizable, and therefore cannot be financed with debt.[5]

The Collateral Hypothesis relates to the Traditional Trade-off Theory in that collateralizable assets are more likely to maintain their value in bankruptcy or liquidation if the firm itself fails, and therefore creditors' losses will be smaller in the event that the firm fails. Thus, a firm's debt ratio should be positively related to its *capital intensity* (e.g., the ratio of PP&E to total assets). Schwartz and Aronson (1967) document evidence that debt ratios vary substantially across industries, and tend to be higher in industries in which a large proportion of the constituent firms' assets consist of PP&E. At the other extreme, Long and Malitz (1985) provide evidence that leverage is negatively related to capitalized research and development (R&D) expenditures, a proxy for intangible assets.

6.5.2 Our Tests of the Traditional Trade-off Theory

In this subsection, we conduct several empirical tests of the Traditional Trade-off Theory. Before we proceed to these tests, however, we point out that we have already provided some evidence consistent with this theory. In Chapter 1, we found that firms in the S&P Transports and Utilities indexes have relatively high capital intensity (see Table 1-1), and also have relatively high debt ratios (see Figure 1-5). In addition, we found that larger firms tend to be exposed to higher average tax rates (see Figure 6-1), and also tend to have higher debt ratios (see Figure 1-5).

For all of the tests conducted below, the sample includes all publicly traded U.S. nonfinancial firms that (a) were included in one of the various S&P indexes at year-end 1996, and (b) also survived to year-end 1999 as a publicly traded firm. A total of 1,025 firms met these criteria.[6]

Regressing Market-to-Book Equity Ratios Against Debt Ratios

Our first test, a cross-sectional test, is based on our earlier simulation analysis of the combined effects of interest deductibility and leverage on a firm's market-to-book equity ratio (see Figure 6-3). This analysis suggests that, across firms, market-to-book ratios should be positively related to leverage due to the benefit of interest deductibility and the concentration of this benefit on a smaller equity base as leverage increases. Of course, this analysis ignores the offsetting costs of financial distress and bankruptcy. Nevertheless, according to the theory the relationship should still hold because each firm presumably increases its leverage until the *cumulative* tax benefit of debt (net of the creeping offsetting costs) is exhausted. Therefore, a firm that exhausts this net benefit at a lower level of leverage would have realized a smaller cumulative tax benefit, and thus should have a relatively low market-to-book equity ratio, whereas a firm that can optimally extend its leverage to a higher level should have realized a larger cumulative benefit, and thus should have a higher market-to-book equity ratio.

---

[5]Of course, one of the never-ending debates in the banking industry is whether a bank should depend on a borrower's collateralizable assets or on its ability to generate earnings to ensure payment of debt obligations.
[6]A total of 1,276 publicly traded U.S. nonfinancial firms in the S&P Industrials, Transports, Utilities, MidCap, and SmallCap indexes were available at year-end 1996. Of these, 232 firms did not survive to year-end 1999 because they were acquired, and 1 because it filed for bankruptcy. Another 18 firms were deleted because they had extreme or missing values for one or more of the variables used in the tests.

We test this prediction by regressing year-end 1999 market-to-book equity ratios against corresponding year-end 1999 debt ratios for the sampled firms. The results of this regression are displayed in Figure 6-5. Surprisingly, there is actually a reliable *negative* relationship between market-to-book equity ratio and leverage, based on the value of the slope coefficient (–0.053; *t*-value of –4.28). However, the adjusted R^2 statistic is quite small at 1.7 percent, suggesting that the relationship is not a close one. Overall, these results are inconsistent with the Traditional Trade-off Theory.

Or are they? Other researchers have also documented a lack of an empirical relationship between market-to-book equity ratio and leverage. The following is a possible explanation that actually reconciles the evidence with the Traditional Trade-off Theory. A firm's market-to-book equity ratio is determined not only by the (net) tax benefits of debt, but also, and perhaps more importantly, by the market's assessment of the value of its future profitable investment opportunities. Thus, a firm that is recognized to have substantial future profitable investment opportunities will tend to have a high market-to-book equity ratio. However, these future opportunities would be considered to be an intangible asset, and therefore cannot be financed with debt. Consequently, and as a separate argument, firms with substantial future investment opportunities will tend to have higher market-to-book equity ratios and *lower*

FIGURE 6-5   Year-End 1999 Market-to-Book Equity Ratios Regressed against Year-End 1999 Leverage (*D*/TA, %): 1,025 Firms in the Various S&P Indexes at Year-End 1996

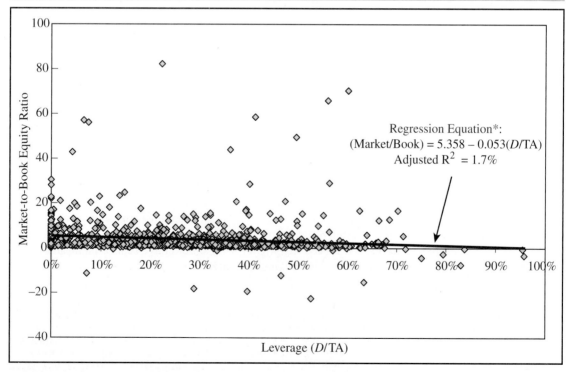

t-Statistics for the intercept and slope coefficients are 13.51 and –4.28, respectively.

debt ratios. (See Shyam-Sunder and Myers [1999] for further discussion of this argument.) Based on the evidence in Figure 6-5, these opposing predictions basically cancel out.

Regressing Current Debt Ratios against Past Debt Ratios
Our second test, a simple time series test, involves the dual predictions that firms' debt ratios are relatively stable but have a mean-reverting tendency. We test these predictions by regressing the debt ratios of firms at year-end 1999 against their debt ratios at year-end 1996. If debt ratios are stable over time (but vary cross-sectionally), we should find a strong positive relationship between firms' debt ratios at these two points in time. On the other hand, if debt ratios vary randomly across both firms and time, the relationship should be negligible.

If firms' debt ratios are subject to mean reversion, the coefficient of this regression should be somewhat smaller than 1.0. This should be so because, according to the argument, a firm that has a relatively low debt ratio in 1996 is likely to have adjusted its debt ratio *upward* by 1999, whereas a firm with a relatively high debt ratio in 1996 is likely to have adjusted its debt ratio *downward* by 1999.

The results of this regression are shown in Figure 6-6. The relationship between debt ratios at these two dates is positive and strong, based on the values of the slope

FIGURE 6-6   Results of a Regression of Debt Ratios at Year-End 1999 against Debt Ratios at Year-End 1996: 1,025 Firms in Various S&P Indexes at Year-End 1996

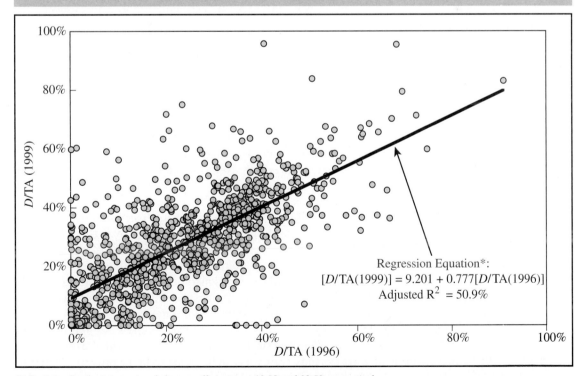

t-Statistics for the intercept and slope coefficients are 13.88 and 32.59, respectively.

coefficient (0.777; t-value of 32.59) and the adjusted R^2 statistic, 50.9 percent. The value of the slope coefficient is smaller than 1.0, indicating that debt ratios are mean reverting. Thus, the results are consistent with the Traditional Trade-off Theory.

A Multiple Regression Test of the Traditional Trade-off Theory

Our third and final test of the Traditional Trade-off Theory, also a cross-sectional test, involves multiple regression analysis. (See Appendix B in Chapter 1 for a brief review of multiple regression statistics.) The dependent variable in the regression consists of the year-end 1999 debt ratios of the firms in the sample. Thirteen independent variables are included in the regression, all of which relate to the theory. These variables are divided into two groups. We refer to the first six variables as *firm characteristic variables*, and the other seven as *policy and decision variables*. We now define the independent variables in each group, and provide a brief rationale for including them in the regression.

Firm Characteristic Variables   The first firm characteristic variable is the natural log of the firm's total assets at year-end 1999, denoted as $\ln(TA_{1999})$. We expect larger firms generally to have higher debt ratios. Evidence presented in Chapter 7 indicates that large firms are generally more profitable and their earnings are generally less volatile, suggesting that large firms can support higher debt ratios without substantially increasing the probability of financial distress. In addition, larger firms generally are exposed to higher tax rates (see Figure 6-1), which further motivates them to increase leverage.

The second firm characteristic variable is capital intensity, measured by PP&E at year-end 1999 as a percentage of TA at year-end 1999, and denoted as $PP\&E_{1999}/TA_{1999}$. If a firm can more readily finance tangible assets with debt, debt ratios should be positively related to $PP\&E_{1999}/TA_{1999}$.

The third firm characteristic variable is a firm's R&D expenditures over the 1997–1999 period as a percentage of TA_{1999}, denoted as $R\&D_{1997-99}/TA_{1999}$. As discussed earlier, capitalized R&D expenditures are an intangible asset that, according to theory, cannot be financed with debt. Thus, we expect debt ratios to be negatively related to $R\&D_{1997-99}/TA_{1999}$.

The fourth firm characteristic variable is a firm's tax-loss carryforward at year-end 1999 as a percentage of TA_{1999}, denoted as $(\text{Tax-Loss Carryforward}_{1999})/TA_{1999}$. A firm that has a large amount of tax-loss carryforward has less incentive to have debt in its capital structure, because the carryforward already acts as a tax shield. This is particularly the case if the carryforward is expected to reduce the firm's effective tax rate. Thus, we expect debt ratios to be negatively related to tax-loss carryforward.

The fifth firm characteristic variable is a firm's net income over the 1997–1999 period as a percentage of TA_{1999}, denoted as $NI_{1997-99}/TA_{1999}$. Most firms retain the bulk of their earnings, so a firm's equity base tends to increase with earnings. Thus, to the extent that a firm has generated (and retained) income, the firm's debt ratio will be lower. Moreover, a highly profitable firm that retains its earnings may be less likely to issue additional debt, because it can simply finance additional capital expenditures via retained earnings. On the other hand, losses reduce a firm's equity base, and therefore increase the firm's debt ratio unless the firm also reduces its debt, which is unlikely if the firm is experiencing losses. Thus, we expect debt ratios to be negatively related to $NI_{1997-99}/TA_{1999}$.

The sixth and final firm characteristic variable is the firm's market-to-book equity ratio at year-end 1999, denoted as MEQ_{1999}/BEQ_{1999}. Based on our earlier discussion and results, it is unclear whether leverage is related to market-to-book equity ratio, because there are conflicting influences.

Policy and Decision Variables   We refer to the remaining seven independent variables in the regression as *policy and decision variables* because, at least to some extent, these variables are under the control of the firm's management. The first variable is the net change in the firm's debt from 1996 to 1999 as a percentage of TA_{1999}, denoted as $(\text{Change in Debt})_{1997-99}/TA_{1999}$. It may seem obvious that a firm's debt ratio in 1999 will be higher (or lower) to the extent that it increases (or decreases) its debt over the previous three years, and therefore that the coefficient of this variable will be positive.

However, this may not necessarily be the case. For instance, if firms generally change the amount of debt in their capital structures *in tandem* with changes in equity so as to maintain stable leverage over time, then $(\text{Change in Debt})_{1997-99}/TA_{1999}$ will be unrelated to 1999 debt ratios. On the other hand, firms issue debt relatively infrequently and in relatively large amounts. As a result, the debt ratio of an individual firm tends to be *lumpy* over time, being relatively high immediately after a given debt issue and relatively low when a substantial amount of time has passed since the firm's last debt issuance. Thus, we expect the coefficient of $(\text{Change in Debt})_{1997-99}/TA_{1999}$ to be positive.

The second variable is the sum of dividends over the 1997–1999 period as a percentage of TA_{1999}, denoted as $DIV_{1997-99}/TA_{1999}$. To the extent that a levered firm pays dividends, the firm's debt ratio will be higher. Therefore, we expect the coefficient of this variable to be positive. However, it should be noted that debt contracts often restrict dividends, particularly for firms with high leverage. To the extent that such restrictions are more binding on highly levered firms, the coefficient of this variable will be smaller, or perhaps even negative.

The third variable is the sum of the firm's sales of common stock over the 1997–1999 period as a percentage of TA_{1999}, denoted as $(\text{Sales of Common Stock}_{1997-99})/TA_{1999}$. Stock sales increase a firm's equity base, and thus decrease the firm's debt ratio, so we expect the coefficient of this variable to be negative.

The fourth variable is the sum of a firm's stock repurchases over the 1997–1999 period as a percentage of TA_{1999}, denoted as $(\text{Repurchases}_{1997-99})/TA_{1999}$. Stock repurchases decrease the firm's equity base, and thus increase the firm's debt ratio, so we expect the coefficient of this variable to be positive.

The fifth variable is the net change in the firm's non-debt current liabilities over the 1997–1999 period as a percentage of TA_{1999}, denoted as $(\text{Change in Non-Debt Current Liabilities}_{1997-99})/TA_{1999}$. For several reasons, a firm may increase or decrease its reliance on current liabilities relative to debt financing. For instance, a distressed firm may be effectively barred from the debt market, and therefore may be forced to rely on current liabilities to finance operations, at least temporarily. In any event, if current liabilities are at least a partial substitute for long-term debt financing, a proportional change in current liabilities should induce an opposing change in the firm's debt ratio, so we expect the coefficient of this variable to be negative.

The sixth policy and decision variable is a zero-one variable, or *dummy variable*, that isolates firms that had no debt in their capital structure at year-end 1996. This variable is denoted as DUMMY1, where DUMMY1 = 1 if $D/TA_{1996} = 0$ and DUMMY1 = 0 otherwise. A total of 68 firms in the sample (6.6 percent) had no debt at year-end 1996. The absence of debt in a firm's capital structure may relate to one or more of the firm's characteristics (e.g., the firm is small or has negligible tangible assets), or it may be due to management's explicit policy to avoid debt financing. If the firm's characteristics alone dictate that it has no debt, and these characteristics are adequately controlled using the other variables in the regression, then the coefficient of DUMMY1 will be zero. On the other hand, if the coefficient of DUMMY1 is negative, the result suggests that the isolated firms avoid debt financing as a matter of policy.

The seventh and final policy and decision variable is a dummy variable that isolates firms that had high debt ratios at year-end 1996. This variable is denoted as DUMMY2, where DUMMY2 = 1 if $D/TA_{1996} > 50$ percent and DUMMY2 = 0 otherwise. A total of 46 firms in the sample (4.5 percent) had such high debt ratios at year-end 1996. Mean-reverting tendencies and firm characteristics notwithstanding, a firm that had an extremely high debt ratio at year-end 1996 is likely to have a high debt ratio at year-end 1999 for two reasons. *First*, the high debt ratio may be a matter of management's (aggressive) financial policies and strategies. *Second*, if the firm had an extremely high debt ratio in 1996 because of substantial losses that have eroded its equity base, it may take a long time for the firm to recover its equity base and therefore reduce its leverage. Thus, we expect the coefficient of DUMMY2 to be positive.

Results of the Multiple Regression Analysis   The results of the multiple regression analysis are displayed in Table 6-3. Note initially that the coefficients of most of the independent variables are highly significant (based on the *t*-values), and most have the anticipated sign based on our discussion. Moreover, these variables collectively explain two-thirds of the cross-sectional variation in debt ratios, based on the adjusted R^2 statistic (66.3 percent).

Next, we briefly discuss the coefficients of the independent variables, focusing initially on the firm characteristic variables. The value of the coefficient of $\ln(TA_{1999})$ is 1.73, indicating that larger firms tend to have higher debt ratios. To interpret the value of this coefficient, consider two hypothetical firms, one with TA of $13,416 million and the other with TA of $567 million. These values correspond to the average TA of the firms in the S&P Industrials and S&P SmallCap indexes, respectively, in 1999. The natural logs of these values are 9.50 and 6.34, respectively. According to the regression results, the predicted difference in the debt ratios of these two firms is 1.73(9.50 – 6.34) = 5.47 percent. That is, the hypothetical large firm would have a debt ratio that is approximately 5 percentage points higher than the hypothetical small firm.

The coefficient of $PP\&E_{1999}/TA_{1999}$ is positive and significant, indicating that debt ratios are positively related to capital intensity. (However, the value of the coefficient is quite small at 0.06, indicating that as PP&E/TA increases by 1 percent, the typical firm's debt ratio increases by only 0.06 percentage points.) In addition, the coefficient of the R&D variable is negative, as expected, and is highly significant. Thus, these two results are consistent with the Collateral Hypothesis.

Surprisingly, the coefficient of the tax-loss carryforward variable is positive (and moderately significant), rather than negative as expected. However, this result may reflect a spurious positive relationship between the debt ratio and tax-loss carryforward variable that is induced by their common relationship to the firm's recent earnings,

TABLE 6-3   Results of a Regression of Leverage (D/TA, %) at Year-End 1999 against Firm Characteristics and Managerial Decision Variables

1,025 Firms in Various S&P Indexes at Year-End 1996

	Coefficient	Standard Error	*t*-Statistic	*P* Value
Intercept	12.62	1.79	7.06	0.00
Firm Characteristic Variables				
Firm Size [$\ln(TA_{1999})$]	1.73	0.22	7.73	0.00
$PP\&E_{1999}/TA_{1999}$, %	0.06	0.02	4.08	0.00
$R\&D_{1997-99}/TA_{1999}$, %	−0.22	0.02	−9.08	0.00
(Tax-Loss Carryforward$_{1999}$)/TA_{1999}, %	0.03	0.02	1.95	0.05
$NI_{1997-99}/TA_{1999}$, %	−0.24	0.02	−13.71	0.00
MEQ_{1999}/BEQ_{1999}	0.01	0.05	0.15	0.88
Policy & Decision Variables				
(Change in Debt$_{1997-99}$)/TA_{1999}, %	0.52	0.02	25.56	0.00
$DIV_{1997-99}/TA_{1999}$, %	0.10	0.05	1.96	0.05
(Sales of Common Stock$_{1997-99}$)/TA_{1999}, %	−0.19	0.04	−4.60	0.00
(Repurchases$_{1997-99}$)/TA_{1999}, %	0.10	0.03	3.52	0.00
(Change in Non-Debt Current Liabilities$_{1997-99}$)/TA_{1999}, %	−0.37	0.04	−9.32	0.00
DUMMY1(= 1 if D/TA_{1996} = 0; = 0 otherwise)	−10.42	1.35	−7.74	0.00
DUMMY2(= 1 if D/TA_{1996} > 50%; = 0 otherwise)	25.74	1.53	16.84	0.00
Summary Statistics				
Adjusted R^2 = 66.3%				
Average Value of Dependent Variable: 27.0%				

Source: Raw data from Standard & Poor's *Research Insight* database.

$NI_{1997-99}/TA_{1999}$. For instance, if a firm has experienced losses, its debt ratio is likely to be higher, and it is likely to have a substantial tax-loss carryforward. (Indeed, the correlation between $NI_{1997-99}/TA_{1999}$ and the tax-loss carryforward variable is −0.50.)

The coefficient of $NI_{1997-99}/TA_{1999}$ is negative, as expected, consistent with the argument that earnings increase a firm's equity base and thus drive down its debt ratio. Finally, the coefficient of MEQ_{1999}/BEQ_{1999} is small and insignificant, suggesting that there is no (net) relationship between leverage and market-to-book equity ratio, even after controlling for other factors.

Regarding the policy and decision variables, the coefficient of (Change in Debt)$_{1997-99}/TA_{1999}$ is positive, highly significant, and substantial in size at 0.52. This result suggests that a 1 percent increase in the typical firm's outstanding debt increases its debt ratio by about 0.52 percent. The coefficient of $DIV_{1997-99}/TA_{1999}$ is also positive, though relatively small at 0.11. This result indicates that, to the extent that a firm pays dividends to stockholders, its debt ratio will tend to be higher.

The coefficient of (Sales of Common Stock$_{1997-99}$)/TA_{1999} is negative and highly significant. This result indicates that a firm that has recently increased its equity base via sales of stock will tend to have a lower debt ratio as a result. In direct contrast, the coefficient of (Repurchases$_{1997-99}$)/TA_{1999} is positive and fairly substantial in size at 0.10, indicating that a firm that has recently *reduced* its equity base by repurchasing shares tends to have a higher debt ratio as a result.

The coefficient of [Change (Non-Debt Current Liabilities$_{1997-99}$)]/TA$_{1999}$ is –0.37. This result suggests that non-debt current liabilities partially substitute for debt in many firms' capital structures.

The value of the coefficient of the *no debt* variable, DUMMY1, is –10.42 and is highly significant. This result indicates that firms that had no debt in 1996 continue to have relatively low debt ratios in 1999—approximately 10 percentage points lower, on average. This result indicates that the firms isolated with this dummy variable have a debt policy that is distinct from other firms' debt policies. Finally, the value of the coefficient of the *high debt ratio* variable, DUMMY2, is 25.74, indicating that, even after controlling for other factors, firms that had extremely high debt ratios in 1996 continue to have higher debt ratios in 1999—approximately 26 percentage points higher on average.

6.5.3   Critiquing the Traditional Trade-off Theory

The empirical results discussed above are basically consistent with the Traditional Trade-off Theory. Nevertheless, the theory is not without its detractors. Researchers have criticized the theory in terms of both the *benefit* and *cost* factors involved in the trade-off. In this subsection, we briefly discuss an argument brought against the *cost* aspect of the trade-off. In the next section, we discuss a theory developed by Miller (1977) that debunks the purported *benefit* of interest deductibility.

Haugen and Senbet (1978) argue that costs attributed to bankruptcy are more appropriately attributed to *liquidation*, and liquidation is a capital budgeting decision that is independent of the event of bankruptcy. Furthermore, they argue that if bankruptcy costs were substantial, a competitive capital market would provide the firm with lower-cost alternatives. For instance, a distressed firm could issue new equity shares (at a fair price) to generate sufficient funds to repurchase some or all of the firm's debt. If a firm otherwise has profitable business operations but is currently bound down by debt, it is conceivable that another, financially stronger firm in the industry would find the firm to be a good acquisition, which would thereby avert many of the cited costs of financial distress.

6.6   PERSONAL TAXES AND THE MILLER EQUILIBRIUM

Miller (1977) provided an alternative *offsetting factor* to explain why firms do not adopt extremely high leverage ratios to take full advantage of interest deductibility. The offsetting factor in Miller's model is *personal taxes*. Miller argues that, although debt is a tax-advantaged security at the corporate level, it is a tax-*dis*advantaged security at the personal level. Moreover, Miller's model yields an equilibrium in terms of the aggregate amount of corporate debt that should exist in the economy as a function of corporate and personal tax rates. This equilibrium is called the *Miller Equilibrium*.

6.6.1   Personal Tax Clienteles

Miller's argument is based on the observation that investors differ with respect to the tax rates that they face on ordinary income (such as dividends and interest) versus capital gains. In particular, Miller assumes that most investors face a relatively high tax rate on ordinary income, but a relatively low effective tax rate on capital gains. The effective tax rate on capital gains is low for two reasons. *First*, though in some recent years realized capital gains have been taxed at the same rate as ordinary income, currently, and for the most part historically, the tax rate on realized capital gains has been lower than on ordinary income. *Second*, capital gains are subject to taxation only upon their *realization*—that is, when an investor sells an asset such as a stock at a profit. Thus, an investor who holds a purchased stock for a long time *defers* the realization of any gains on the stock, and thereby lowers the effective tax rate on such gains. Historically, the bulk (perhaps three-quarters) of an investor's total return on a typical stock is from tax-favored capital gains, with the remainder accounted for by dividends that are taxed as ordinary income. In contrast, historically the bulk of investors' returns on corporate bonds is from interest income, which is taxed as ordinary income. Therefore, at the level of the individual investor who faces taxation, corporate equity may well be tax-favored relative to corporate debt.

Of course, other individuals may face low effective tax rates on both ordinary income and capital gains. We noted earlier that many investors hold their securities in tax-sheltered vehicles such as a pension fund, a 401(k) plan, or an insurance-company variable annuity. Other investors, such as nonprofit institutions, face no taxes on investment income or capital gains because they are tax exempt.

What are the implications of different personal tax rates among investors for their preferences for corporate securities and a firm's choice of debt versus equity financing? At the level of the individual investor, one likely implication is that each investor would rationally invest in those securities that, for that investor, provide the highest (risk-adjusted) *after-tax* return, all other factors ignored. For instance, high-income investors may rationally tend to avoid high-dividend–paying stocks as well as corporate bonds, purchasing instead non–dividend-paying stocks and tax-exempt municipal bonds. On the other hand, depending on their need for current income, a tax-exempt individual or nonprofit institution would prefer high-yielding stocks or corporate bonds. Consequently, a given corporate security may attract a particular *clientele* of investors for whom that security carries a relative tax advantage.

A Numerical Example

To illustrate the notion of tax clienteles, we provide a numerical example that uses the following notation for various tax rates:

τ_p = an investor's personal tax rate on ordinary income from dividends or interest,

τ_{cg} = an investor's effective tax rate on realized capital gains, adjusted for deferral,

τ_{pe} = an investor's effective personal tax rate on the overall income from a given equity investment, which depends on τ_p, τ_{cg}, and the issuing firms policy of providing returns in the form of dividends versus capital gains, and

τ_c = a firm's corporate income tax rate.

Suppose Jones Company is considering how to finance a new capital expenditure. The company is considering three alternatives: (a) issue equity, and elect to pay an annual dividend that represents half of the project's annual earnings; (b) issue equity, but do not pay dividends at all, in which case the investor's entire return would be in

the form of capital gains; or (c) issue debt. Regardless of the financing, the project produces earnings before interest and taxes of $100 million annually. As such, the only two
consequences of the choice are (a) the exposure of the project's annual earnings to corporate taxes; and (b) the form of the return to investors and the associated personal tax
effects. Management examines the preferences of each of four classes of investors for
each alternative security.

> ***Investor Class A: Nonprofit Institutions.*** These investors are tax-exempt,
> so $\tau_p = 0$, $\tau_{cg} = 0$, and $\tau_{pe} = 0$.
> ***Investor Class B: Retirement Fund Investors.*** For these investors, securities
> are placed in a tax-deferred retirement account. They are subject to an effec-
> tive ordinary income tax rate of $\tau_p = 30$ percent, and an effective capital gains
> rate of $\tau_{cg} = 15$ percent.
> ***Investor Class C: Wealthy Long-Term Investors.*** These investors are not eli-
> gible for tax-deferred investments. These investors are subject to a tax rate of
> $\tau_p = 40$ percent on ordinary income. However, they are long-term investors, so
> $\tau_{cg} = 0$. Thus, if they purchase the firm's equity, the effective value of τ_{pe} is
> highly sensitive to the firm's dividend policy.
> ***Investor Class D: Wealthy Short-Term Investors.*** These investors are not
> eligible for tax-deferred investments. These investors face a tax rate of $\tau_p = 40$
> percent on ordinary income; because they are short-term investors, $\tau_{cg} = 40$
> percent as well, so $\tau_{pe} = 40$ percent regardless of the firm's dividend policy.

The results of management's analysis of the financing alternatives and the preferences of the alternative investor classes are displayed in Table 6-4. For each
investor class and security combination, the upper portion of the table displays calculations of both corporate and individual taxes, and the resulting after-tax income
to the investor. The lower portion of the table indicates the security that provides
the highest after-tax income for each class of investor, as well as the firm's ranking
of combinations of investor class and security in terms of after-tax returns to
investors.

The results indicate that investors in classes A, B, and D receive their highest
after-tax income if the firm issues bonds, whereas investors in class C receive their
highest after-tax income if the firm issues non–dividend-paying equity. For none of
the investor classes is after-tax income maximized if the firm chooses to issue dividend-paying equity. Regarding the firm's ultimate choice of security to issue, it is
reasonable to suppose that they would choose that combination of security and
investor class for which the security provides the highest after-tax annual returns.
Thus, as revealed by the rankings, Jones Company's first choice would be to issue
bonds to investor class A, for which after-tax annual returns are equal to the full
$100 million. However, if no class A investors are available, the firm's second choice
is to issue bonds to investors in class B, for which after-tax annual returns are $70
million. If no investors are available in classes A or B, the firm's third choice is to
issue non–dividend-paying equity to investor class C, for which after-tax annual
returns are $66 million. If no investors are available in classes A, B, or C, the firm's
final choice is to sell bonds to investors in class D, for which after-tax annual returns
are $50 million.

TABLE 6-4 After-Tax Annual Income to Various Classes of Investors on Alternative Jones Company Securities, and Resulting (1) Investor-Class Preference for Security and (2) Firm Rankings for Investor Class and Security Combination

Investor Class	BONDS A	B	C	D	DIVIDEND-PAYING EQUITY A	B	C	D	NON-DIVIDEND-PAYING EQUITY A	B	C	D
τ_p	0	30%	40%	40%	0	30%	40%	40%	0	30%	40%	40%
τ_{cg}	0	15%	0%	40%	0	15%	0%	40%	0	15%	0%	40%
Security Alternative												
Corporate-Level Calculations												
Pretax annual corporate income	$100.00	$100.00	$100.00	$100.00	$100.00	$100.00	$100.00	$100.00	$100.00	$100.00	$100.00	$100.00
Corporate tax ($\tau_c = 34\%$)	$0.00	$0.00	$0.00	$0.00	$34.00	$34.00	$34.00	$34.00	$34.00	$34.00	$34.00	$34.00
After-tax annual corporate income	$100.00	$100.00	$100.00	$100.00	$66.00	$66.00	$66.00	$66.00	$66.00	$66.00	$66.00	$66.00
Investor-Level Calculations												
Annual income received from firm	$100.00	$100.00	$100.00	$100.00	$66.00	$66.00	$66.00	$66.00	$66.00	$66.00	$66.00	$66.00
Less: Ordinary income tax	$0.00	$30.00	$50.00	$50.00	$0.00	$9.90	$13.20	$13.20	$0.00	$0.00	$0.00	$0.00
Less: Capital gains tax	$0.00	$0.00	$0.00	$0.00	$0.00	$4.95	$0.00	$13.20	$0.00	$9.90	$0.00	$26.40
After-Tax Income to Investors	$100.00	$70.00	$50.00	$50.00	$66.00	$51.15	$52.80	$39.60	$66.00	$56.10	$66.00	$39.60
Investor class's security preference												
A	*											
B		*										
C											*	
D								*				
Firm's overall ranking of investor class and security combination	1	2	9	9	3	8	7	11	3	6	3	11

175

6.6.2 The Miller Equilibrium

Miller considered personal tax clienteles such as those in our example. However, to simplify the analysis, Miller makes the (controversial) assumption that all investors have an effective overall tax rate on equity income equal to zero; that is, he assumes that $\tau_{pe} = 0$. Thus, investors differ only with regard to their personal tax rates on interest income. Specifically, on a cross-sectional basis investors exhibit a continuum of tax rates on interest income ranging from $\tau_p = 0$ to some maximum value denoted as τ_p^{max}. Miller also assumes that all firms face the same corporate tax rate, τ_c, where $\tau_c < \tau_p^{max}$ must hold if equilibrium is to be obtained, as we will see.

Under Miller's construction, corporate bonds offer a higher after-tax return to all investors who are subject to the tax relationship in Equation 6.13:

$$(1 - \tau_p) > (1 - \tau_c), \tag{6.12}$$

or equivalently, $\tau_p < \tau_c$. In contrast, stocks provide a higher after-tax return to all investors who are subject to the tax relationship in Equation 6.14:

$$(1 - \tau_p) < (1 - \tau_c), \tag{6.13}$$

or equivalently, $\tau_p > \tau_c$.

To generate Miller's equilibrium, suppose initially that all firms are entirely financed with equity. Although this condition satisfies the clientele of investors for whom tax relationship 6.13 holds, it is not optimal for investors for whom tax relationship 6.12 holds. At this point, then, firms will have an incentive to issue bonds to appeal to the clientele of investors for whom 6.12 holds. Firms should be able to do this profitably, because bonds provide higher after-tax returns than equity for the unsatisfied clientele. Suppose firms begin to appeal to this clientele by offering debt-for-equity swaps to them. The first firms to offer such a swap would rationally appeal to investors who have the lowest tax rate, $\tau_p = 0$, because profits from the swap should be greatest for this group.

However, eventually the savings available from this group of investors will be exhausted, so additional firms offering debt-for-equity swaps must appeal to investors in higher tax brackets. Eventually, the aggregate amount of corporate debt outstanding will be sufficient to satisfy all investors in the clientele for which tax relationship 6.12 holds, and we will have reached equilibrium in the market for corporate securities. Miller's equilibrium is illustrated in Figure 6-7. In the figure, the equilibrium aggregate amount of corporate debt outstanding is denoted as D_{Agg}^*.

Miller's equilibrium has three important implications. *First*, there exists an optimal amount of corporate debt *in the aggregate*. *Second*, once this equilibrium is reached, no individual firm can affect its market value by changing its capital structure. This is so because, at equilibrium, each individual firm faces marginal investors for whom $\tau_p = \tau_c$, and as such the firm will provide the same after-tax return to these marginal investors whether the firm chooses equity (in which case taxes are paid at the corporate level) or debt (in which case the same amount of taxes are paid at the individual level). *Third*, the optimal aggregate level of corporate debt changes if the personal ordinary income tax rate schedule changes relative to the corporate tax rate, or vice versa. Figure 6-7 also illustrates this effect.

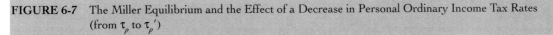

FIGURE 6-7 The Miller Equilibrium and the Effect of a Decrease in Personal Ordinary Income Tax Rates (from τ_p to τ_p')

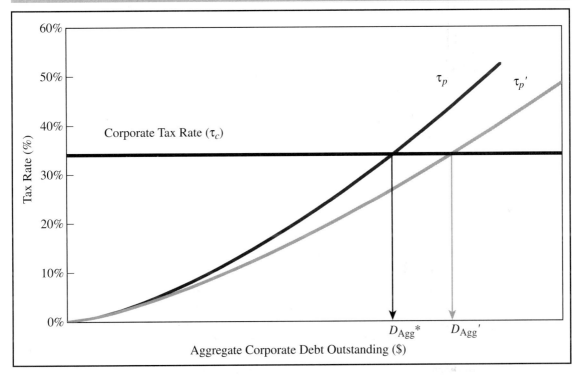

6.6.3 Firm-Specific Optimal Leverage Based on Tax Considerations Alone

In a subsequent theoretical paper that relates to, but is somewhat at odds with, both the Traditional Trade-off Theory and the Miller Equilibrium, DeAngelo and Masulis (1980) show that a finite, firm-specific optimal leverage ratio can be conceived by considering corporate and personal tax considerations alone. At the corporate level, the incremental value of the tax shield diminishes as leverage increases because the firm eventually falls into a lower marginal tax rate.

Moreover, this point of diminishing returns to additional debt occurs at a lower level of leverage if the firm has other tax shields, such as accounting depreciation, depletion allowances, investment tax credits, and loss carryforwards, which of course vary across firms as well as over time for a given firm. Meanwhile, at the personal level, they assume that debt is tax-disadvantaged relative to equity, as in Miller's model. However, the model focuses on an individual firm, so the relative disadvantage of debt versus equity at the personal level is assumed to be constant. Therefore, a firm should increase its leverage until the marginal tax benefit of debt at the corporate level, which decreases as leverage increases, is equal to the marginal tax disadvantage of debt at the level of the marginal investor.

6.7 AGENCY THEORY AND THE LEVERAGE DECISION

In Chapter 3, we discussed several principal–agent conflicts that have potential implications for the firm's leverage decision. Such conflicts may affect the leverage decision despite the availability of mechanisms, discussed in Chapter 5, to mitigate these conflicts. In this section, we provide several theoretical perspectives on this issue. In the first subsection, we briefly review theory suggesting that leverage has a negative effect on the value of a firm. In the second subsection, we discuss the possible value-enhancing effect of leverage from an agency-theoretic perspective. In the third subsection, we discuss an alternative trade-off theory of optimal capital structure that is based on these two offsetting effects of debt on the value of a firm. In the fourth subsection, we briefly discuss theory that relates the capital structure decision to broader issues of *corporate governance* and *security design*.

6.7.1 Negative Effects of Debt: Agency Costs of Debt

In Chapter 3, we found that conflicts of interest can bedevil the relationship between a firm's shareholders and creditors. In most discussions of this type of principal-agent conflict, it is assumed that the firm's management, who are responsible for the operations of the firm, acts in the *shareholders'* interest. Consequently, if and when conflicts of interest arise between the firm's shareholders and creditors, management's duty is to resolve such conflicts in a manner that serves the shareholders' interest to maximize the market value of the firm's equity.

Thus, creditors realize that a borrowing firm's management has a derived incentive to *reduce* the value of their claim on the firm. As you recall, such actions are called *expropriations* of creditors' wealth by shareholders. The primary means by which a firm's management can expropriate creditors' wealth include (a) increasing the risk of the firm's assets, (b) issuing additional debt, and (c) siphoning off the value of the firm's assets to shareholders by paying large dividends or repurchasing shares.

In addition, we discussed the underinvestment (or debt overhang) problem, in which the benefits of a new investment project tend to be shared between the firm's shareholders and its creditors, assuming that the debt is risky. Creditors benefit because they gain a claim on the future payoff on the project, which thereby reduces default risk. Creditors benefit even more if equity funds are used to make the initial investment, whether equity funds are obtained by selling new equity shares or by retaining earnings that would otherwise have been used to pay dividends. Because a portion of the benefits of a new project are transferred to the firm's creditors, the critical question is whether the *net benefit* of the project to shareholders is positive. If not, the firm's management (acting in the shareholders' interest) will not invest in the project, even though it is profitable per se. As a result, firms with risky debt outstanding may chronically underinvest.

Of course, if the firm's debt is free of default risk, no such incentives exist, because management cannot take actions that will affect the value of the debt. Therefore, any discussion of expropriation is restricted to cases in which the firm's debt is default risky. Moreover, management's derived incentive to expropriate is directly related to default risk, because greater default risk implies that the value of a creditor's claim is more susceptible to changes as a result of management's actions. Of course, in anticipation of such *ex post* expropriations, creditors will require *ex ante* compensation in the form of a higher interest cost on the debt. Thus, shareholders ultimately bear the cost of the conflict of interest.

6.7.2 A Positive Role for Debt: Disciplining Management

Leverage may have a positive affect on the value of a firm by mitigating costs stemming from conflicts of interest between the firm's shareholders and management. Management, acting in a self-serving manner, may choose a smaller level of leverage than is optimal for the firm for at least three reasons: (a) The probability of bankruptcy, and thus management's loss of income, increases with leverage; (b) creditors, acting in their own interest, will tend to restrict management's actions (including self-serving actions) by a combination of monitoring and covenants in the bond contract; and (c) the fixed, periodic, mandatory payments required in a debt contract limit the amount of *free cash flow* that management has available to engage in self-serving behavior, including empire building and the excessive consumption of perks. Thus, to the extent that the firm's board of directors can impose a higher level of debt for the firm, shareholder value may be enhanced.

Hanka (1998) provides empirical evidence consistent with the disciplinary role of debt. Hanka's focus is on firms' stakeholders, particularly employees and creditors. He tests the proposition that firms with more debt are less generous to employees because more of the firm's surplus has been contractually promised to creditors. In other words, for firms with debt, employees' wages tend to be compressed to competitive levels. Using data for the period of 1973 to 1993, Hanka finds evidence consistent with this proposition, as he explains: "For the last two decades, firms with higher debt have reduced their employment more often, used more part time and seasonal employees, paid lower wages, and funded pension plans less generously. These effects are economically significant and cannot be explained by variation in performance. Thus debt seems to discipline the employment relationship" (p. 245).

6.7.3 Optimal Leverage via Agency Theory: A Second Trade-off Theory

Jung, Kim, and Stulz (1996) develop a model of optimal capital structure that focuses on the two offsetting effects of debt on the value of the firm, as we have discussed. Their model also incorporates the effect of a firm's investment opportunities on this trade-off. Their model is illustrated in Figure 6-8.

To understand the figure, focus initially on curves M and D, which represent marginal agency costs of managerial discretion and marginal agency costs of debt, respectively, for a firm that has a particular amount of investment opportunities. Note that the former is a *decreasing* function of leverage and the latter is an *increasing* function of leverage. In this case the firm's optimal leverage, labeled as L in the figure, is the point at which these two marginal costs equate.

So what happens if the firm's investment opportunities improve? Such an improvement *decreases* the marginal agency cost of managerial discretion across the board, from schedule M to schedule M′ in the figure. This is so because, as the authors state, "the objectives of management and shareholders become more congruent when investment opportunities become better." However, the marginal agency cost of debt

FIGURE 6-8 Optimal Leverage (L, L′) as Determined by Agency Costs of Debt (D, D′), Agency Costs of Managerial Discretion (M, M′), and Investment Opportunities (IO)

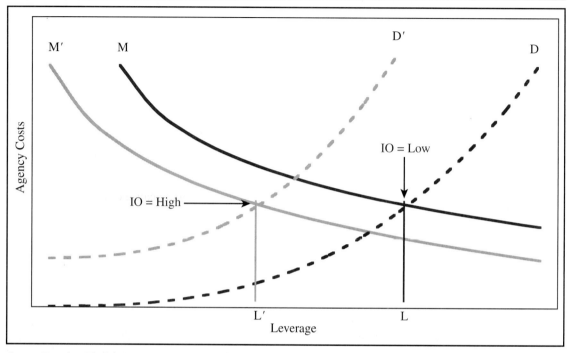

Source: Based on Fig. 1 in Jung, Kim and Stulz (1996).

increases across the board, from schedule D to schedule D′ in the figure. This is so "because the firm has more to lose from financial distress" (p. 163). The net result is that the firm's optimal leverage decreases from L to L′.

6.7.4 Capital Structure, Governance, and Security Design: The Incomplete Contracting Paradigm

Aghion and Bolton (1992) developed a theory of capital structure that is based on the allocation of control rights within a firm. In their model, a firm consists of a manager who needs funding for a project, and a wealthy investor. The manager is concerned with both ordinary managerial compensation and perks, while the investor is concerned only with monetary returns. A *complete* contract between the manager and the investor, which would fully specify future investment and operating decisions, is impossible to devise because it is impossible to imagine all possible future circumstances and decisions *ex ante*.

Under these circumstances, a question arises: What type of security, debt or equity, should be sold to the investor? The answer depends critically on the optimal allocation of control rights. If (voting) equity is issued, the investor gains control rights immediately. If debt is issued, the investor obtains only *contingent* control rights (i.e., the investor gains control rights only if the firm performs poorly—it goes "bankrupt").

Aghion and Bolton's analysis suggests that a firm's optimal mix of equity and debt (i.e., its optimal capital structure) may reflect an optimal *distribution* of control rights among a firm's manager, its shareholders, and its creditors. Their analysis also relates to our discussions of corporate governance in Chapter 8 and optimal security design in Chapter 19.

6.8 ASYMMETRIC INFORMATION AND LEVERAGE

Theories that focus on the information asymmetry problem suggest that leverage can affect the value of a firm. For instance, Leland and Pyle (1977) and others argue that debt financing, whether it is placed directly with a financial institution or issued to the public through an underwriter, can alleviate the information asymmetry problem. In either case, the financial institution involved is in a position to examine the firm's private, strategic information to determine the fair value of the debt, yet the firm does not risk the revelation of this information to its competitors because of the confidentiality bond that it has with the institution. In addition, debt is the second-best financing alternative in the *pecking-order* hierarchy (Myers 1984, Myers and Majluf 1984), behind internal financing and ahead of external equity. If the firm has a positive *NPV* project but requires external funds, debt will be more fairly valued (i.e., involves a smaller surrender of value) than outside equity.

Can the Pecking-Order Model Explain Capital Structure Variations?
In a recent paper, Shyam-Sunder and Myers (1999) conduct empirical tests that pit the Traditional Trade-off Theory against the Pecking-Order Model of capital structure. As a preface to these tests, they provide an interesting insight into the implications of the Pecking-Order Model for a firm's capital structure:

> In the pecking order theory, there is no well-defined optimal debt ratio. The attraction of interest tax shields and the threat of financial distress are assumed second-order. Debt ratios change when there is an imbalance of internal cash flow, net of dividends, and real investment opportunities. Highly profitable firms with limited investment opportunities work down to low debt ratios. Firms whose investment opportunities outrun internally generated funds borrow more and more. Changes in debt ratios are driven by the need for external funds, not by any attempt to reach an optimal capital structure. (pp. 220–221)

Based on these arguments, the authors' empirical tests focused on measuring a firm's current cash flow *deficit* or *surplus*, and the power of this variable to forecast the firm's subsequent financing decisions, including and especially changes in the firm's debt. This model is pitted against a forecasting variable based on the Traditional Trade-off Theory, namely the deviation between the firm's current debt ratio and its historical average debt ratio (i.e., the mean-reverting tendency). The results of their empirical tests strongly favor the Pecking-Order Model over the Traditional Trade-off Theory. They find that when a firm has a cash flow deficit it tends to issue debt, rather than equity, to bridge the gap (see also Frank and Goyal 2002). However, Chirinko and Singha (2000) criticized the structure of the empirical model used by Shyam-Sunder and Myers, arguing that the model cannot adequately distinguish between the two hypotheses.

Fama and French (2002) tested predictions of both the Traditional Trade-off Theory and the Pecking-Order Model about both dividends and leverage. They employed data on U.S. nonfinancial, non-utility firms over the years 1965 to 1999. They summarize their results as follows:

> Confirming predictions shared by the trade-off and pecking order models, more profitable firms and firms with fewer investments have higher dividend payouts. Confirming the pecking order model but contradicting the trade-off model, more profitable firms are less levered. Firms with more investments have less market leverage, which is consistent with the trade-off model and a complex pecking order model. Firms with more investments have lower long-term dividend payouts, but dividends do not vary to accommodate short-term variation in investment. As the pecking order model predicts, short-term variation in investment and earnings is mostly absorbed by debt. (p. 1)

6.9   YET A THIRD TRADE-OFF MODEL: BALANCING AGENCY COSTS GIVEN INFORMATION ASYMMETRY

Stulz (1990) developed a theory of optimal capital structure that incorporates both principal–agent and information asymmetry problems. The setting of his model is as follows. The information asymmetry problem is manifest because shareholders can observe neither the firm's true cash flows nor management's investment decisions, whereas management, of course, observes both. The principal–agent problem is also present because management derives private benefits from any corporate investment, so they have an incentive to overinvest. Consequently, management always claims that current cash flow is insufficient to fund all profitable investment opportunities, whereas shareholders, who *are* aware of management's incentive, find management's claims to lack credibility and therefore refuse to provide funds, even when cash flows are truly insufficient to pursue all profitable investments.

Without a resolution to this problem, management tends to invest too much when cash flow is truly higher than necessary to fund all profitable investments, and too little when cash flow is truly insufficient to fund all profitable investments. In the first case, the agency cost is shareholders' losses from inefficient (excess) investment; in the second case, the agency cost is the opportunity cost of lost profits from foregone profitable investments.

Stulz argues that if the firm's capital structure consists of a judicious mix of debt and equity, both the underinvestment and overinvestment problems can be mitigated:

> A debt issue that requires management to pay out funds when cash flows accrue reduces the overinvestment cost but exacerbates the underinvestment cost. An equity issue that increases resources under management's control reduces the underinvestment cost but worsens the overinvestment cost. Since debt and equity issues decrease one cost of managerial discretion and increase the other, there is a unique solution for the firm's capital structure. (p. 23)

6.10   Summary of Learning Objectives

In this chapter we formally addressed one of the most important financial decisions for a firm: the amount of leverage to maintain in its capital structure. Theories about the relevance of this decision focus on one or more real-world factors. These factors include some that we introduced in previous chapters (principal–agent conflicts and information asymmetry) as well as factors that we introduced in this chapter (taxes and costs of financial distress). The potential affects of these factors on a firm's optimal leverage has been well articulated in the literature. However, considerable controversy remains because empirical evidence supports the arguments of each of several competing theories.

The IRS Codes. Features of the U.S. IRS tax code that may affect a firm's leverage decision include the following: (a) Both personal and corporate tax rates are progressive; (b) at the corporate level, interest payments on debt are a deductible expense, but dividends are not deductible; and (c) at the personal level, interest income and dividends are taxed as ordinary income, but capital gains are generally tax-favored—a lower tax rate generally applies, and taxes are due only upon their realization.

Modifying the M&M Propositions for Corporate Taxes. We showed how the original M&M propositions must be modified to account for the deductibility of corporate interest expense. This analysis provided two important results. First, we came to the seemingly absurd conclusion that firms should be financed with virtually 100 percent debt in their capital structures in order to maximize the firm value. Second, the government emerges as a stakeholder in each firm, holding a quasi equity claim.

The Traditional Trade-off Theory. The Traditional Trade-off Theory was developed to explain why firms do not generally have high leverage as implied by the tax-adjusted M&M model. The theory posits that, as a firm increases its leverage, the tax advantage of debt is increasingly, and eventually completely, offset by expected future costs of financial distress and bankruptcy. This theory also can explain why a firm's leverage tends to be mean reverting over time, and why leverage varies cross-sectionally.

The Miller Equilibrium. In Miller's model, the tax advantage of debt at the corporate level is offset by a corresponding tax *disadvantage* of debt at the level of the individual investor. Equilibrium in the capital markets is characterized by an optimal amount of corporate debt in the aggregate. However, each individual firm is indifferent between financing with debt or equity because the tax advantage of debt at the corporate level is offset by a tax disadvantage at the personal level.

A Second Trade-off Theory: Offsetting Agency Costs. Agency theory suggests that debt can have both negative and positive effects on firm value. The negative effect of debt is due to incentives for the firm's management, acting in the shareholders' interest, to take actions to *expropriate* wealth from the firm's creditors. In anticipation of such actions, creditors require a higher *ex ante* yield on the firm's debt, and in this way the agency cost of debt is ultimately borne by shareholders. In addition, leverage induces *underinvestment*, particularly if creditors capture part of the benefit of a new project. On the positive side, agency theory suggests that debt can be used as a *disciplinary device* against management's tendency to engage in various self-serving, value-destroying activities. The trade-offs between the agency-related benefits and costs of debt may yield an optimal level of leverage.

Corporate Leverage and the Pecking-Order Model. The Pecking-Order Model also appears to hold promise for explaining observed cross-sectional variations in leverage. In this hypothesis, a firm has no optimal leverage per se. Instead, at each point in time in which a firm needs to fund a project, it chooses the best alternative from among internal equity, external debt, or external equity. The key determinant of this choice is whether the firm is currently running a cash flow deficit (in which case external financing is required, and debt is preferred) or surplus (in which case internal equity is used).

Information Asymmetry and Leverage. Debt serves to mitigate the information asymmetry problem, particularly if the debt is either held by, or negotiated through, a financial intermediary. This is so because the financial institution involved is in a position to examine the firm's private, strategic information to determine the fair value of the debt, yet the firm does not risk the revelation of this information to its competitors because of the confidentiality bond that it has with the institution.

A Third Trade-off Theory: Balancing Agency Costs under Conditions of Information Asymmetry. A firm's leverage decision may be influenced by a specific trade-off between agency costs of managerial discretion and costs associated with information asymmetry. The agency problem is that managers have a private incentive to overinvest. Due to information asymmetry, shareholders cannot view the firm's true cash flows, but they *are* aware of management's incentive to overinvest. As a result, shareholders' find management's claims that they have profitable investment opportunities to lack credibility and therefore limit the availability of equity funds to management, even when cash flows are truly insufficient to pursue all profitable investments. The cash flow requirements of debt mitigate the overinvestment problem, but debt also introduces the underinvestment problem. Thus, if the firm's capital structure consists of a judicious mix of debt and equity, both the underinvestment and overinvestment problems can be mitigated.

Review Questions and Problems

1. Describe the basic features of the IRS tax code as it applies to both corporations and individuals.
2. In a world with corporate taxes, explain how the government becomes a stakeholder in each firm. How risky is the government's claim on a firm's earnings?
3. Firm XYZ is currently a privately held, all-equity firm. The firm's shareholders are about to sell all of the firm's shares to the public in an initial public offering (IPO). Assume that an optimal capital structure exists that involves a finite proportion of debt. Present the arbitrage argument that, even though the current shareholders present an all-equity firm to the public, the proceeds that the current shareholders receive will be equal to the value of the firm at its optimal capital structure.
4. Compute the present value of the tax shield generated when Smith Company issues $100 million of 8 percent perpetual debt. The corporate tax rate is 34 percent.
5. Discuss the stages of financial distress, and the deadweight costs associated with financial distress.
6. Firm XYZ is currently financed entirely with equity that has a total market value of $100 million. Management is considering a debt-for-equity swap to add leverage

to the firm's capital structure. Management recognizes two factors that would affect the value of the firm as leverage is added. First, the addition of permanent debt in the amount of D would provide a tax shield that has a value of $\tau_c D$, where for firm XYZ, $\tau_c = 0.34$. The second, and offsetting, factor is the present value of expected costs of future financial distress associated with debt, $PV[E(CFFD_{debt})]$, which increases at an accelerating rate with leverage. Management decides that the relationship of $PV[E(CFFD_{debt})]$ to leverage can be approximated with the following equation: $PV[E(CFFD_{debt})] = \alpha D^2$, where $\alpha = 0.005$. Given these specifications, find the value of debt, D^*, that maximizes the value of the firm. What is the firm's debt ratio, and what is the market value of the firm if it has the optimal amount of debt?

7. Repeat the previous problem, but assume that $\alpha = 0.01$.
8. Describe the underinvestment, or debt-overhang, problem, and describe how it can affect a firm's use of debt financing.
9. List and briefly explain the real-world factors that
   a. induce a *positive* relationship between firm value and leverage.
   b. induce a *negative* relationship between firm value and leverage.
10. Below is the list of firm characteristic and policy-and-decision variables that were used as independent variables in our cross-sectional regression of year-end 1999 firm debt ratios.
    a. Beside each variable, indicate the sign of the relationship found in the regression.
    b. For each variable, briefly explain *why* the sign was positive or negative.

Independent Variable	Sign of Coefficient (+ or −)?
ln(TA)	_____
PP&E/TA	_____
R&D/TA	_____
(Tax-Loss Carryforward)/TA	_____
NI/TA	_____
MEQ/BEQ	_____
(Change in Debt)/TA	_____
DIV/TA	_____
(Sales of Common Stock)/TA	_____
(Repurchases)/TA	_____
(Change in Non-Debt Current Liabilities)/TA	_____
DUMMY1 (no debt in 1996)	_____
DUMMY2 (high debt ratio in 1996)	_____

11. Working with the Miller Equilibrium model, sketch the effect of a cut in the corporate tax rate on the equilibrium aggregate amount of corporate debt.
12. Discuss the effects of principal–agent conflicts on a firm's leverage decision.
13. Discuss the effects of information asymmetry on a firm's leverage decision.
14. Explain how a judicious mix of equity and debt can optimally mitigate both the underinvestment and overinvestment problems.

Creative Thinking Issues

1. Can you think of reasons why the U.S. government allows a deduction for corporate interest but not for dividends? (You may want to consult a textbook on corporate tax law.)
2. Debt ratios vary tremendously across individual firms, but for each firm the debt ratio tends to be fairly stable over time. Moreover, leverage ratios over time exhibit mean reversion. This evidence seems to strongly support the Traditional Trade-off Theory. How might the evidence instead be interpreted as supporting the Pecking-Order Model?
3. In Chapter 1, we found that over the past 20 years U.S. nonfinancial firms generally have increased their leverage (as measured by book debt ratio; see Figure 1-2b) and decreased their dividend payout (see Table 1-3). In Chapters 5 and 6, we discussed theoretical arguments that dividends and debt, respectively, can be used to discipline management by soaking up free cash flow. Based on the evidence mentioned, do you think that we are witnessing the substitution of debt for dividends as a disciplinary device? Explain your answer.

Projects and Analyses

1. Review the empirical evidence presented both in Chapter 1 and in this chapter. Then try to explain the evidence in terms of the capital structure theories presented in this chapter.
2. Gather time series data on a given firm's debt ratio. Conduct a test to determine whether the firm's debt ratio exhibits mean reversion. Also, for each period determine whether the firm appears to be running a cash surplus or deficit, and determine whether the extent of the surplus or deficit forecasts either (a) the firm's propensity to issue or retire debt or equity, or (b) changes in the firm's leverage.

PART

Analysis of the Firm and the Valuation of Equity and Debt

As the analyses in Part I show, developing a firm's financial policies and strategies is a complex task, involving numerous factors, many of which are at best only partially under management's control. To address these factors effectively, management must (a) have a thorough understanding of the firm's status with respect to these factors, (b) determine the extent to which the firm's status can be altered if this is desirable, and (c) establish financial policies and strategies that are consistent with the firm's status.

Part II, comprising Chapters 7 to 10, provides a number of tools that a manager can use to address the problem of designing the firm's financial policies and strategies. In Chapter 7, we provide a structured set of discussions and empirical analyses focusing on interactions between industry factors and a firm's financial policies and strategies. In Chapter 8, we provide the first of two comprehensive perspectives on a firm's financial policies and strategies (the second is provided in Chapter 19). We adopt a structural approach for this purpose. The structures include (a) the firm's business environment, (b) internal governance and business strategy, (c) operational and financial structures, and (d) determinants of risk, performance, and contingencies.

In Chapters 9 and 10, we discuss the valuation of equity and debt securities, respectively. Chapter 9 introduces the concepts of market efficiency and event study methodology, and also treats the issues of the cost of equity capital and the valuation of equity. Chapter 10 is the first of two chapters that focus on corporate debt contracts (the second is Chapter 15); we discuss terms often included in publicly issued corporate bond contracts, the process by which corporate bonds are issued, and the valuation of bonds.

CHAPTER 7

Industry Analysis and Financial Policies and Strategies

7.1 INTRODUCTION

Many aspects of the industry in which a firm operates affect the firm's operating strategy, profitability, and risk, and therefore its financial policies and strategies. In this chapter, we provide a structured set of analyses that focus on interactions between industry factors and a firm's financial decisions. These analyses give us a strong impression that the financial decisions of an individual firm are not made in isolation; instead, they reflect the characteristics and dynamics of the industry in which the firm competes, and the firm's status within its industry.

The chapter is organized as follows. In Sections 7.2 to 7.5, we discuss theoretical and empirical research on the relationships between industry factors and a firm's management, performance, and financial policies and strategies. In Section 7.2, we discuss research on principal–agent conflicts and financial decisions in an industry context. In Section 7.3, we discuss research that relates optimal leverage to industry dynamics. In Section 7.4, we discuss research on financial strategies for a firm operating in a competitive industry. In Section 7.5, we discuss research on two specific cooperative relationships in which firms often engage: the *joint venture* and the *strategic alliance*.

In Sections 7.6 to 7.9, we present and discuss empirical evidence on the financial policies of publicly traded U.S. nonfinancial firms from an industry perspective. Section 7.6 provides recent figures on the numbers of publicly traded U.S. nonfinancial firms sorted by industry, and their composite market equity values. Section 7.7 focuses on the diversity of the activities of firms in eight of the largest U.S. industries, and Section 7.8 provides more detailed analyses of the firms in these industries. In Section 7.9, we provide historical analyses of the composite growth, profitability, financing, market values, and entry and exit of firms in two major U.S. industries, *Business Services* and *Chemicals and Allied Products*. Finally, Section 7.10 summarizes the chapter's learning objectives.

7.2 PRINCIPAL–AGENT CONFLICTS IN AN INDUSTRY SETTING

In this section, we review two theoretical studies that address, from an industry perspective, one or the other of the two major principal–agent conflicts that we have been studying—the shareholder–management conflict and the shareholder–creditor conflict.

7.2.1 Financial and Industrial Structure with Principal–Agent Conflicts

Williams (1995) develops a model of industry equilibrium that incorporates agency costs due to both shareholder–management and shareholder–creditor conflicts. The author motivates his analysis by explaining the limitations of traditional agency theory vis-à-vis its focus on individual firms in isolation:

> The literature on corporate agency has produced some now familiar predictions: if a manager maximizes his personal welfare, then, depending on his firm's capital structure, he may pick excessively risky projects, forego profitable projects, and consume dissipative perks. With few exceptions these standard results have been derived for a single firm in isolation, rather than an industry in equilibrium. As shown by the exceptions, the equilibrium may have very different properties if firms within an industry compete in a product market. This suggests that the standard predictions may have only limited empirical content. More importantly, the theoretical literature on corporate agency has yet to explain the limited empirical evidence on financial and industrial structure. This evidence includes the observed correlations between a firm's profitability, its physical capital, and the book value of its debt. (pp. 433–34)

Williams argued that equilibrium in an industry will reflect the effects of agency costs of managerial discretion (specifically, the consumption of perks) on capital investment. Some firms will be able to raise external capital to pursue profitable capital investments. Others, however, will be unable to do so because "they cannot credibly commit to avoid dissipative perks" (p. 464). The resulting industry equilibrium is characterized by the following dichotomy: (a) a few large, capital-intensive, highly profitable, levered firms; and (b) many smaller, labor-intensive, relatively unprofitable firms with little or no leverage. He explains his model and its implications as follows:

> In this model each firm within an industry can produce a homogeneous good using one of two technologies: one labor-intensive and the other capital-intensive. The labor-intensive technology requires no initial investment but has a higher variable cost of production. To finance the investment required for capital-intensive production, a firm can sell a bond and stock in a perfectly competitive capital market. Given plausible values of two critical parameters, some firms are forced in the resulting equilibrium to forego investments with positive net present values (NPVs). More managers would like their firms to invest, but they cannot raise the required capital from outside investors. Because the foregone investments have positive NPVs, capital-intensive firms earn positive profits in equilibrium, while labor-intensive firms can have negative NPVs after the cost of entry. This foregone investment is a consequence of competition within an industry and thus is unrelated to previous explanations of optimal investments for isolated firms. Capital-intensive firms are typically less risky and always much larger in size than are labor-intensive firms. Also, at least some debt is optimal for capital-intensive firms, but the optimal debt is not unique. In short, the industry has a core of large, profitable, secure, capital-intensive firms, each with at least some external debt, and a competitive fringe of small, marginally profitable or unprofitable, risky, labor-intensive firms. Even as the cost of entry converges to zero, a few capital-intensive firms can

continue to earn extraordinary profits, while all labor-intensive firms can fail and thereby effectively exit the industry. In this sense, industries can be concentrated even with vanishingly small costs of entry because access to capital is effectively another barrier to entry, given costly agency. (pp. 433–34)

Later, we test Williams' assertions using data on firms in U.S. industries.

7.2.2   The Asset Substitution Problem in an Industry Context

Maksimovic and Zechner (1991) show that a particular agency cost of debt, the asset substitution problem (aka the risk-shifting problem, discussed in Chapter 3), must be addressed in an industry framework. This is because, in industry equilibrium, "the riskiness of a project's cash flows is determined endogenously and depends on the investment decisions of all firms" (pp. 1633–34). Initially, individual firms in an industry are indifferent between alternative capital structures. However, if the tax advantage of debt is added, "individual firms are no longer indifferent between all alternative financial structures . . . large amounts of debt create incentives to subsequently invest in . . . [riskier projects] . . . As a result, some firms find it optimal to limit their debt issues and thus commit to invest in [less risky projects] . . . In equilibrium the cash flow from the low risk project compensates firms for the foregone tax shields. Individual firms are indifferent between issuing the maximum amount of debt consistent with the subsequent choice of [less risky projects] . . . and becoming highly levered and choosing the riskier project" (p. 1634). As such, their results are somewhat analogous to Miller's (1977) tax equilibrium (discussed in Chapter 6).

Maksimovic and Zechner's analysis has several interesting empirical implications, as they explain:

[First] even when the financial structure affects the equityholders' incentives to invest, firms in the same industry are indifferent between alternative financial structures. This is consistent with empirical findings indicating that apparently similar firms in the same industry exhibit diverse financial structures.

Second . . . the riskiness of an investment project depends on the decisions of all firms in the industry. A firm adopting a technology chosen by most of its competitors is partly hedged against shocks in its production costs since they will be reflected in the price of the goods sold. This natural hedge is not available for deviant firms. Thus, the cash flows of firms adopting a technology which is chosen by a minority of firms should be more volatile.

Third . . . changes in the corporate tax rate can have a surprising effect on firms' optimal debt level because the value of tax shields influences the equilibrium distribution of projects in the industry. Increasing the corporate tax rate makes the project with the higher debt capacity more attractive and, consequently, more firms choose it. This tends to lower the highest cash flows generated by this project and thus decreases the debt capacity of firms choosing this project. Thus, firms that choose the risky project decrease their debt levels as the corporate tax rate increases. By contrast . . . firms choosing the low risk project are able to increase their debt level as a response to an increase in the tax rate.

Fourth, the model suggests a link between technology choice and financial structure. Within an industry, firms that adopt the technology chosen by the majority of firms generate higher expected earnings before interest and taxes and are less levered than firms that deviate and adopt a technology which is only chosen by a few firms. (pp. 1634–35)

7.3 THE DYNAMICS OF ASSET LIQUIDITY AND OPTIMAL LEVERAGE IN AN INDUSTRY

In their theoretical paper, Shleifer and Vishny (1992) focus on the problem of liquidating the assets of a distressed or bankrupt firm, given that distress and failure are likely to occur when the firm's *entire industry* is depressed. Their analysis relates closely to the Traditional Trade-off Theory (see Chapter 6), but from an industry perspective:

> [We] explore the determinants of liquidation values of assets, particularly focusing on the potential buyers of assets. When a firm in financial distress needs to sell assets, its industry peers are likely to be experiencing problems themselves, leading to asset sales at prices below value in best use. Such illiquidity makes assets cheap in bad times, and so ex ante is a significant private cost of leverage. We use this focus on asset buyers to explain variation in debt capacity across industries and over the business cycle, as well as the rise in U.S. corporate leverage in the 1980s. (p. 1343)

Asset liquidity is an important determinant of the costs of financial distress. This paper has focused on economy- and industry-wide determinants of asset liquidity. Our main conclusions are as follows:

(1) Asset liquidation—through an auction or other sale—does not necessarily allocate assets to the highest value users. As a result, assets with no alternative uses can fetch prices below value in best use when sold during an industry- or an economy-wide recession or when industry buyers are prevented from bidding by regulation. Such fire sales can have substantial private and social costs.

(2) Optimal debt levels are limited by asset illiquidity. For example, even holding cash flow volatility constant, cyclical and growth assets have a lower optimal level of debt finance. Similarly, conglomerates and multi-division firms have a higher optimal debt level at the same level of cash flow volatility.

(3) The optimal leverage of a firm depends on the leverage of other firms in its industry. An industry might have an optimal debt capacity even when its individual firms do not.

(4) Asset liquidity and therefore optimal debt levels change over time. High markets tend to be liquid markets. Beliefs in high liquidity of assets can be self-fulfilling.

(5) Well-documented increases in leverage in the 1980s, both by firms involved in corporate control transactions and by other firms, were attributable at least in part to the liquid market for corporate divisions. This liquid market for divisions was in turn the result of exogenous factors such as relaxed antitrust enforcement and the influx of foreign buyers as well

as of an important self-reinforcing component. The widespread expectation of future liquidity and debt capacity created current liquidity and debt capacity. (pp. 1364–65)

7.4 INDUSTRY COMPETITION AND FINANCIAL STRATEGIES

In this section, we review several theoretical and empirical studies that view a firm's financial decisions as an integral part of the firm's overall competitive strategy.

7.4.1 Leverage Aggressiveness Versus Having a *Long Purse*

Recent theoretical research on capital structure focuses on the influence of product market competition on a firm's capital structure. This work has thus far yielded two principal hypotheses. The first is the *Leverage Aggressiveness* (or *Strategic Commitment*) *Hypothesis*, developed by Brander and Lewis (1986) and Maksimovic (1988). This hypothesis posits that leverage helps boost a firm's sales growth relative to that of its industry rivals because the firm, via its leverage, commits to aggressive competition in the product markets, which leads less aggressive competitors to yield part of their market share. The second is the *Long Purse Hypothesis* (Tesler 1966), which posits that a firm might deliberately choose low leverage so as to be able to pursue predatory market strategies to *squeeze* a highly levered rival, perhaps to the point of bankruptcy.

Campello (2002) provides empirical evidence consistent with both of these hypotheses. On one hand, a firm's sales growth is positively related to leverage, consistent with the Leverage Aggressiveness Hypothesis. On the other hand, this relationship holds only in industries in which leverage varies widely across firms. Moreover, Campello finds that the relationship between leverage and sales growth is *reversed* in recessions, suggesting that in hard times the highly levered firm may be vulnerable to the predatory market strategies of less-levered rivals (i.e., rivals with long purses).

7.4.2 Balancing Managerial Agency Costs Against the Cost of Competitors' Aggressiveness

In their theoretical model of industry equilibrium, Bolton and Scharfstein (1990) argue that an individual firm operating in a competitive industry should tailor its financial policies to its desired competitive position in the product market. Regarding the firm's capital structure decision, the authors initially remind us of Jensen's (1986) *free cash flow* argument that a firm's board should force the issuance of debt in order to soak up free cash flow and thereby thwart management's incentive to overinvest. However, within the context of a competitive industry, an increase in leverage makes a firm more vulnerable to aggressive product market strategies by its competitors that increase the focal firm's risk of failure. Thus, a firm should increase leverage until the marginal benefit of reducing managerial agency costs balances marginal costs of competitors' aggressiveness.

7.4.3 Retaining the Option to Increase Leverage

Fries, Miller, and Perraudin (1997) developed a model of equilibrium in a competitive industry that has implications for a firm's optimal capital structure. Their model allows firms to enter into and exit from the industry; however, each firm's initial capital investment is irreversible. They also assume that the (net) tax advantage of debt exceeds bankruptcy costs so that debt has a net advantage over equity. However, due to the *free rider problem*, firms cannot *decrease* the amount of debt in their capital structure over time, though they can *increase* it. Their model provides several interesting implications for the capital structures of firms in an industry. Most importantly, they show that the optimal *initial* capital structure for a firm depends crucially on the demand elasticity for industry output, and may generally be relatively low. However, firms maintain valuable *options* to increase leverage opportunistically.

In a similar vein, Maksimovic (1990) discusses the importance of the type of loan contract that a firm receives from a bank, given that the firm is operating in a competitive industry. As we discuss in Chapter 15, commercial loan contracts are of two basic types: (a) a simple loan, with no commitments on the part of the bank to lend additional amounts to the firm in the future, and (b) a commitment contract (such as a *line of credit*), wherein the firm can borrow immediately and has the option to borrow additional amounts in the future at a predetermined interest rate (which may be a function of a short-term interest rate benchmark). The commitment contract imparts a valuable option to the firm. Thus, typically a firm must pay a substantial fee to a bank to secure a loan commitment. Given that a fee is involved in a loan commitment, a question arises: Why would a firm pay this fee rather than engage in sequential simple loans with the bank (or with any bank) over time if and when the firm requires funds?

Maksimovic argues that a firm can use a loan commitment as a strategic device to compete more effectively against industry rivals. To see why, consider the case of firm A, which is competing with rivals in an industry in which the future market demand for the industry's output is uncertain. Suppose all firms in the industry establish their initial composite output capacity according to current market demand. However, later market demand may rise or fall unexpectedly. If market demand rises, those firms that are in a position to expand their output quickly (e.g., by tapping funds via a loan commitment) will gain market share, while other firms stand to lose. On the other hand, if market demand falls, any firm that has overcommitted in terms of output capacity (e.g., because they borrowed a large amount via a simple loan) will suffer substantial losses and may fail. In other words, a loan commitment provides a firm with valuable *financial flexibility*, allowing it to compete strategically in a competitive and uncertain product market.

7.4.4   Using Debt to Deter Entry

As Jensen (1993) has argued from a theoretical standpoint, and Kaplan (1989) and Jarrell, Brickley, and Netter (1988) have shown empirically, leveraged takeovers and buyouts result in increased profitability. (We discuss takeovers and buyouts in Chapter 16.) However, McAndrews and Nakamura's (1992) theoretical analysis suggests that an increase in leverage can per se improve profitability: "leverage itself can improve the competitive position of firms at the expense . . . of business rivals, and that leverage aggressiveness, rather than increased efficiency, may be responsible for the increased profitability of buyouts." (p. 98). Their model yields this result even though they do not include a tax incentive for debt: "debt can serve to commit a firm to more aggressive behavior in the . . . market" (p. 99). Thus, an incumbent firm can deter entry into its industry by increasing its leverage.

7.4.5 Associations Between Financial Decisions and Production and Product Market Decisions

Several researchers have pointed out that a firm's production and product market decisions interact with its financial decisions. For instance, researchers have argued that the firm's product quality, warranties, and pricing depend on the firm's risk of bankruptcy. If a firm has a substantial risk of bankruptcy due to high leverage, it may choose to cut costs by compromising product quality, and its product warranties may be of little value to purchasing consumers. From another viewpoint, a firm may deliberately increase its leverage, and thus its bankruptcy risk, as a means of securing concessions from its employees, suppliers, or customers (see Titman 1984).

Empirical research has also shown that, for firms in a given industry, financial decisions can affect production and product market decisions. Phillips (1995) studied production and pricing decisions in four industries in which firms had recently and substantially increased their financial leverage. In three of the four industries, Phillips found that industry output was *negatively* associated with the average industry debt ratio. In addition, Phillips found that, following these leverage-increasing recaps, managers' incentives to maximize shareholders' wealth increased substantially. Firms generally increased their profit margins and decreased output, suggesting that the leverage increase decreased agency costs and inefficient investment. Furthermore, firms within each of these industries increased leverage roughly simultaneously, so it may be argued that rival firms in a given industry must respond in concert to financial decisions, by one or more of its rivals, that lead to greater efficiency.

7.4.6 Designing Executive Compensation as a Competitive Strategy

In Chapter 3, we briefly discussed the importance of incentives in an executive's compensation contract as a means of aligning the executive's interest with that of the firm's shareholders. Generally, executive compensation contracts include incentive devices that induce management to increase either the firm's earnings or its share price. (We discuss these devices in detail in Chapter 8.) However, several authors have argued that, in designing incentives in a CEO's compensation contract, a firm's board should consider the effects of such incentives on the CEO's competitive strategy.

In Reitman's (1993) model, the optimal compensation contract includes not only the more traditional sales and profit incentives and grants of stock, but also *stock options*. Stock options play a unique role in curbing management's overly aggressive behavior, which otherwise emerges naturally from "the tendency for firms to try to induce lower output in the future from their competitors by competing hard now" (p. 513).

> The crucial aspect of a stock option that makes this restraint of aggressive behavior possible is its inherent nonlinearity: the stock option is worthless when the stock price falls below the strike price. Intuitively, a manager's stock option will only be "in the money" if the rival firm refrains from producing too much. This allows owners to commit their managers to playing less aggressively if the rival firm does likewise, but to retaliate with sales maximization if confronted with the overly aggressive behavior (p. 514).

In other words, if the managers of two competing firms are both given stock options, there is at least the possibility that both will choose to compete less aggressively, rather than inexorably engaging in mutually destructive excess competition.

Aggarwal and Samwick (1999) initially raise, and then answer, the following question: Why do compensation contracts more often tie a manager's compensation to the firm's *absolute performance* rather than to its performance *relative to* its industry rivals? After all, why should the manager of a firm in a high-profit industry enjoy substantial performance bonuses (even if the firm's earnings are below that of its rivals), while the manager of a firm in a low-profit industry suffers lower performance bonuses even if the firm outperforms its rivals?

Their answer is that relative performance incentives affect the firm's competitive strategy in a way that reduces returns to shareholders: "[s]trategic interactions among firms can explain the lack of relative performance-based incentives in which compensation decreases with rival firm performance. The need to soften product market competition generates an optimal compensation contract that places a positive weight on both own and rival performance. Firms in more competitive industries place greater weight on rival firm performance relative to own firm performance." They examined actual executive compensation contracts, and found evidence consistent with their argument.[1]

7.5   JOINT VENTURES AND STRATEGIC ALLIANCES

To round out our discussion of the literature on financial policies and strategies in an industry context, we briefly discuss two types of cooperative relationships that have frequently been observed among pairs of firms in a given industry: the *joint venture* and the *strategic alliance*. Both relationships (a) involve a temporary sharing of some of the resources of both participating firms; (b) are formed so that both firms can compete more effectively in their common industry, solve inter-firm contracting problems, reduce trading risk at key stages of the industry, or develop, market, or distribute a new product or service; and (c) represent only a partial and temporary combination of corporate resources, to be distinguished from a merger or acquisition, which involves a complete and permanent combination of two firms. The relationships differ in that the joint venture is a more formal arrangement involving the creation of a jointly owned private firm, whereas in a strategic alliance the two firms simply agree to pool specific resources.

McConnell and Nantell (1985) studied 136 joint ventures involving U.S. companies over the years 1972 to 1979, paring their sample from the "Joint Venture Roster" listings in various issues of the trade journal *Mergers and Acquisitions*. They conducted an *event study*[2] of the market's reaction to the announcements of these joint

---

[1]In related literature, Hart (1983), Scharfstein (1988), Hermalin (1982), and Schmidt (1997) examined whether product market competition induces management to increase their efforts, while Vickers (1985), Fershtman and Judd (1987), and Sklivas (1987) discuss how *precommitments* in managerial contracts can alter strategic competition. See also Fumas (1992) for additional analysis of relative performance contracts.
[2]We formally introduce event study methodology in Chapter 9. The procedure basically involves calculating raw returns on each firm's stock around the date of a specific newsworthy event (such as the announcement of a joint venture), subtracting some measure of the stock's expected return to create *abnormal returns*, and averaging the abnormal returns across all firms in the sample. The idea is to gauge the effect of new information on a firm's market equity value.

ventures, and found average two-day abnormal returns of +0.73 percent for the participating firms. They concluded that "U.S. domestic joint ventures are wealth-creating intercorporate transactions for the shareholders of the participating companies" (p. 534).

Chan, Kensinger, Keown, and Martin (1997) conducted an event study of 345 strategic alliances undertaken over the years 1983 to 1992. They also found that the market generally reacts favorably to the announcement of a strategic alliance. The stocks of the participating firms realized event-period abnormal returns of +0.64 percent, on average. In addition, they found that announcements of *horizontal* alliances were particularly well received by the market: "Horizontal alliances that involve the transfer or pooling of technical knowledge tend to produce larger wealth effects than marketing alliances. These results suggest that alliances add the most value by allowing firms to maintain the focus of their business while making use of the complementary technical skills of partner firms" (p. 217).

7.6   AN EMPIRICAL PERSPECTIVE ON FIRMS IN MAJOR U.S. INDUSTRIES

In the remaining sections of the chapter, we provide empirical analyses of various financial aspects of publicly traded U.S. nonfinancial firms from an industry perspective. We begin in this section with two broad perspectives. The first focuses on the distributions of firms across major U.S. industries, and the second on the distribution of composite market equity values across industries.

7.6.1   A Preliminary Note on SIC Codes

To sort firms into industries, we use the official industry classification system developed and maintained by the federal government's Office of Management and Budget, called the Standard Industry Classification (SIC) code system. The SIC is a four-digit system in which virtually any firm can be classified according to its business activity. The first two digits are used to sort firms into major industries, while the last two digits sort firms within each major industry into narrower categories, or subindustries, according to the specific products or services they provide within the industry. Associated with each two-digit or four-digit code is a brief description of the associated business activity. For instance, Merck & Co., a major manufacturer of pharmaceuticals, is assigned to the four-digit SIC code value of 2834: The first two digits, 28, define the broad industry classification of *Chemicals and Allied Products*, and the second two digits, 34, define the narrower business activity of *Pharmaceutical Preparations*.

Many firms within a major industry have activities that span several of the categories identified by the last two SIC code digits, and some firms' activities even cross several categories defined by the first two digits. Therefore, a firm is assigned a *Primary SIC Code* value that is consistent with its largest business segment, and, as applicable, one or more *Secondary SIC Code* values for each of its other business activities. As such, a great number of subindustries and samples of firms can be developed using four-digit SIC codes or primary and secondary SIC codes. Due to space limitations, most of our analysis involves firms sorted only by the first two digits of a firm's Primary SIC Code.

Alliance, Joint Venture, or M&A?

Shown below are excerpts from a research article on alliances and joint ventures in *McKinsey Quarterly*.

Rarely does a day pass when the front pages of the world's financial publications don't trumpet the latest corporate alliance. Over the past decade, corporations have transformed themselves from 100 percent owners of their own assets into fuzzy-walled organizations linked with dozens of partners in strategic alliances such as joint ventures, cross-selling agreements, and patent-licensing deals. Alliances are particularly crucial to . . . businesses that need to mitigate risk while pursuing growth options.

Our earlier research indicated that alliances have a long-term success rate of about 50 percent, measured in strategic and financial terms. Since the long-term success factors for alliances are well known, smart managers can improve the odds. Nonetheless, the stakes have risen for companies entering into alliances. Besides focusing more and more on short-term performance, investors and analysts are closely watching alliance announcements. Managers should therefore be asking new questions: Do alliance announcements affect share prices? Are these effects correlated with ultimate success? Most important, how can you tell when to use alliances instead of acquisitions and when to use certain deal structures and not others?

To answer these questions, we examined the effect of alliance announcements on the share prices of more than 2,100 companies. This research sample spanned most major countries, all industries, and a variety of alliance structures, including equity joint ventures, contractual alliances, and minority equity stakes accompanied by one or more contractual alliances. Our analysis separated out the abnormal return in the days surrounding each alliance announcement—that is, the change in share price that was not explained by overall market trends.

The results of our analysis, combined with insights gleaned from our wide experience, indicate that it is unwise for managers to proceed with an alliance without thinking through its implications for share prices. First of all, large alliances do move market capitalization. That alone should get managers' attention. Additionally, we found that alliances are better received than mergers and acquisitions in fast-moving, highly uncertain industries such as electronics, mass media, and software. They are also the preferred choice for companies trying to build new businesses, enter new geographies, or access new distribution channels. Contractual alliances, simple and flexible, are better received by the market than more complicated equity joint ventures. And, finally, when it comes to alliances, it turns out that polygamy pays: Multipartner alliances and consortia tend to be quite well received.

THINK CAREFULLY ABOUT YOUR ANNOUNCEMENT

For large alliances at least, the evidence is unequivocal: They do create shareholder value. Just over half (52 percent) of large alliances caused the share price of the parent to rise or fall by more than one standard deviation of its normal movement, and of these, 70 percent of the price reactions were increases—a "win rate" that is substantially higher than the percentage for acquirers in M&A transactions . . . Among alliances as a whole, share prices moved by a comparable extent for only 29 percent of the participants at the time of the alliance announcement, and just half of those were price increases. Since alliances provide a highly tailored way to access capabilities such as specific products or technologies, many deals are small

(continued)

relative to the parents' overall business and may not provoke much movement in share prices.

Why do big alliances have such impressive success rates? For one thing, big deals attract more scrutiny from the market. They also tend to make companies more likely to invest significant management resources in thinking through the strategy, choosing the partner, developing an appropriate deal structure, and communicating the purpose of the deal to the market. And managers involved in big alliances tend to follow the lessons identified in this article more often than do managers involved in small ones.

The effects of alliance announcements appear to be a good indicator of longer-term success. Our sample included 25 companies involved in alliances that were extensively covered by reporters and analysts roughly one year later. Analysts and reporters felt that 16 of the partners had fulfilled their strategic and financial objectives in the alliances they had entered; of these, 14 were rewarded with share price increases of more than one standard deviation after the alliance was announced. Commentators regarded the alliances of 9 companies as long-term failures, and 8 of these 9 alliance announcements were associated with a significant decline in share price.

Since the market does respond to alliances and is often right about which of them will create value in the long run, it makes sense to understand how the market arrives at its response. Specifically, when does the market reward alliances over M&A structures? Our evidence suggests that investors and analysts favor alliances for reducing risk and building businesses in turbulent environments as well as for uniting multiple partners. The market also views alliances more favorably when they are simple.

ALLIANCES FOR CHANGE

In fast-moving, highly uncertain industries, the market tends to prefer alliances to M&A . . . It rewarded alliances much more richly in elec-

tronics, media, and software, for example: Nearly three-fourths of the media and entertainment alliance announcements were winners (that is, they raised the announcing company's stock price by more than one standard deviation), compared with just 53 percent of the acquiring companies in M&A transactions. (In this article, when we discuss returns to M&A deals, we are always talking about returns to the acquirer. The vast majority of alliances are either win-win or lose-lose. By contrast, in many acquisitions the seller gains, while the acquirer often overpays and thus loses share value.)

As technology rapidly transforms the way media companies can reach an increasingly global audience, alliances allow them to leverage their content, enter new geographies, and place several bets rapidly. Why pay an acquisition premium and endure the rigors of post-merger integration when you can get most of the upside by using alliances to leverage intangibles such as content, cartoon characters, and customer relationships? In June 1998, for instance, the U.S. television network NBC announced that it would enter the Internet age through a joint venture with CNET Net-works (an Internet media company) to operate the Snap.com portal. Analysts expressed approval, and investors pushed up the stock price of the parent company, General Electric, by more than 4 percent.

Of our sample's 75 electronics and software companies that made significant alliance announcements, 64 percent were winners, compared with just 33 percent of acquirers involved in M&A transactions in this industry sector. When Displaytech and Hewlett-Packard, for instance, announced an alliance to develop and manufacture display systems for consumer electronics products, HP's stock climbed by nearly 6 percent and Displaytech's by more than 17 percent, creating close to $4 billion in value. Likewise, Sony had an abnormal return of 15 percent on a market cap of $33 billion when it announced that it had taken a 5 percent stake in Next Level Communications, a maker of advanced digital-TV set-top devices . . .

ALLIANCES FOR GROWTH

Most of the value created in the U.S. economy in the past decade stemmed from building new businesses rather than squeezing benefits from incumbency in core ones. Alliances for growth can involve new capabilities, new channels, and new geographies.

New Capabilities

Building new businesses means assembling a host of new capabilities: products, customer relationships, technologies, and so on. Few organizations, especially those launching e-businesses, can develop these capabilities internally with sufficient speed. Alliances give companies a way to leverage their existing skills while they quickly and flexibly access the capabilities of others. In addition, alliances often involve less capital commitment and risk than do acquisitions—a big advantage in areas in which a company's management capabilities are unproved.

As a result, alliances are generally a preferred vehicle for building a new business. Of the 236 companies that used alliances to do so, 54 percent were rated successes by the market, compared with only 40 percent for acquirers in comparable M&A transactions . . .

The market's reaction makes sense. When both partners in an alliance are creating a new business, the alliance permits them to share the risk. Nippon Television, Time Warner, and Toshiba, for example, joined forces in a joint venture to produce and distribute digital-TV software on a global basis. The joint-venture announcement was well received by the market.

New Channels

Alliances should also be the vehicle of choice for companies seeking to expand sales through new distribution channels. Of the 54 sampled companies that allied in hopes of expanding in this way, 60 percent were deemed successful by the market. When the British bank Abbey National, for instance, teamed up with the grocer Safeway to offer Safeway shoppers in-store financial services, investors responded positively, creating nearly $660 million in value for Abbey National shareholders, or abnormal returns of 4.2 percent. Especially in mature businesses, customer acquisition costs can be much lower for alliances than for go-it-alone strategies.

New Geographies

Previous work shows that many companies have used alliances successfully to enter new geographies.

Corning, for instance, has used alliances very effectively to enter new geographic markets and achieve a range of other objectives. When the company teamed up with Asahi Glass and Samsung in December 1996 to build a Mexican factory that manufactures glass funnels and panels for color-TV tubes, the announcement was accompanied by a significant share price increase for Corning, which owns 40 percent of the venture.

NETWORKS AND CONSORTIA

Although lessons about alliances often use marriage as an analogy, the metaphor is flawed: Companies are not people, and an alliance that comes to an end is no tragedy. Equally important, companies may benefit from forming multiple or multipartner alliances to meet various needs—not necessarily to the disadvantage of any of the parties.

In particular, multipartner alliances can give their participants targeted access to specific assets of the partners. By contrast, M&A can be highly impractical when three or more partners wish to combine some of their assets; if a two-way merger is costly and disruptive, a three-way merger is more so. And even if the expected benefits of the merger or acquisition are very large, they may pale in comparison with the transaction costs of the deal itself.

Multipartner alliances are particularly attractive for setting standards. The small U.K.-based software company Psion, for instance, developed an operating system for mobile handheld devices. Psion needed to have its sys-

(continued)

tem adopted by industry leaders many times its size. They knew that a standard operating system would stimulate the market for their hardware. So in June 1998, Psion joined forces with Ericsson, Motorola, and Nokia to create Symbian, a joint venture to support the adoption of Psion's operating system—to the benefit of all parties. The announcement of the joint venture created a combined abnormal return of $10 billion.

Many of the most successful business builders also use alliances to position themselves at the center of a network in which they can leverage intangible capital without owning many expensive assets. Nokia's market capitalization, for example, has grown by $253 billion over the past five years. The company has leveraged a broad range of alliances to access manufacturing capacity, to conduct joint R&D, and to make products available to large numbers of customers rapidly. Nokia has joint ventures with Capitel Group in China and Gradiente in Brazil, participates in technology alliances such as Bluetooth and Symbian, and reaches customers through strategic supply arrangements with AT&T, NTT DoCoMo, and Sprint.

SIMPLER IS BETTER

Although most of the results of our alliance study addressed situations in which alliances might be preferred to M&A, the study also yielded an interesting bit of wisdom about the types of alliances most favored by the market. After all, a manager's work doesn't end with the decision to "do an alliance"; it is also necessary to choose among a variety of structures.

The details of how to structure an alliance are, of course, case specific. Nonetheless, in general the market does seem to prefer simpler and more flexible deal structures. Looking at the alliance announcements that we could classify as winners or losers (that is, ones that were

associated with an expected change in the share price greater than one standard deviation), stock prices increased for 68 percent of the companies announcing the sale or purchase of an equity stake and for 56 percent of those forming a contractual alliance involving no equity. But among the joint ventures only 50 percent were winners.

Joint ventures are less well received for several reasons. First, they usually take longer to get going than do contractual alliances. A joint venture is a completely new company, separate from either of the partners and often owning assets contributed by them. It thus requires complex governance structures and a significant commitment of senior management's time. Furthermore, joint ventures don't last forever: They have a median life span of seven years, and the arrangements needed to unwind them at the end don't always go smoothly. So while a joint venture might be the right answer in certain cases, companies considering one should first explore simpler deal structures that capture most of the value at lower cost and with less complexity. Another strike against joint ventures is that analysts often are skeptical of any deal that may complicate the parent company's future strategic options, and many joint ventures fit this description. After all, a joint venture can compromise the ability to sell a company at a fair acquisition price, and many joint ventures are in fact steps toward a sale to one of the partners. Therefore, if management wants to proceed with a joint venture—or with a similarly frowned-upon alliance, such as a merger in a fast-moving industry—the announcement should articulate with absolute clarity how the deal fits into the company's overall strategy. It should also spell out the benefits for the company and its partners, the effects on current partners, and the options that management expects the alliance to create in the future . . .

As is the case throughout the text, the principal source of our data is Standard & Poor's (S&P's) *Research Insight* database. In this database product, S&P provides the following explanation for their assignment of a Primary SIC Code value to each firm according to the SIC code system: "Individual companies are assigned a four-digit Primary SIC Code by analyzing the product line breakdown provided in each 10-K. Additional sources such as stock reports and Annual Reports are used when necessary. The product line accounting for the largest percent of sales will determine the Primary SIC Code. The assigned classification is reviewed each year when the company is updated."[3]

7.6.2   The Numbers of Firms in Major U.S. Industries

For our initial perspective on U.S. industries, we sorted each of the 6,146 publicly traded U.S. nonfinancial firms in our year-end 2000 sample into a major industry category according to the first two digits of its Primary SIC Code. (See Appendix A of Chapter 1 for details of this sample.) Then we tallied the number of firms in each industry, and ranked the industries in descending order of number of firms. The results are displayed in Figure 7-1.

The 6,146 firms in the sample sort into a total of 66 industries. For each industry, Figure 7-1 displays its brief descriptive *name*, its two-digit SIC code (in brackets), and the tally of firms. By a fair margin, the *Business Services* industry [73] has the largest tally, 1,120 firms, followed by *Chemicals and Allied Products* [28] (522 firms), *Electronic and Other Electric Equipment* [36] (516 firms), *Measurement Instruments, Photographic Goods, Watches* [38] (435 firms), *Industrial Machinery, Computer Equipment* [35] (414 firms), and so on.

7.6.3   Composite Market Equity Values of Firms
in Major U.S. Industries

An alternative perspective on the sizes of U.S. industries is obtained by examining composite market equity values for each industry. For each industry, we calculated the composite market equity value as the sum of the year-end 2000 market equity values of the firms in the industry. The results are displayed in Figure 7-2. For comparison purposes, we retain the same ordering of industries as shown in Figure 7-1; that is, the major industries remain sorted in descending order of number of firms.

Not surprisingly, as a general tendency, composite market equity values are directly related to the number firms in the industry. For example, the *Business Services* industry is largest in terms of number of firms (1,120 firms) and second largest in composite market value at $1,328 billion. However, there are important exceptions to this tendency. For instance, the *Chemicals and Allied Products* industry has approximately half as many firms as the *Business Services* industry (522 firms versus 1,120 firms), but its composite market equity value is much greater ($1,963 billion versus $1,328 billion.). The *Communications* industry ranks sixth in terms of number of firms (229 firms), but third in terms of composite market equity value at $1,172 billion. On the other hand, while the *Measurement Instruments, Photographic Goods, and Watches* industry ranks fourth in terms of number of firms (435 firms), it ranks only eleventh in terms of composite market equity value at $353 billion.

---

[3]10-K and 10-Q are codes for the main annual and quarterly reports, respectively, that publicly traded firms file with the SEC. These and other filed reports are available for each filing firm in the SEC's *EDGAR* database at the SEC's Web site, www.sec.gov.

FIGURE 7-1   Numbers of U.S. Firms by Industry

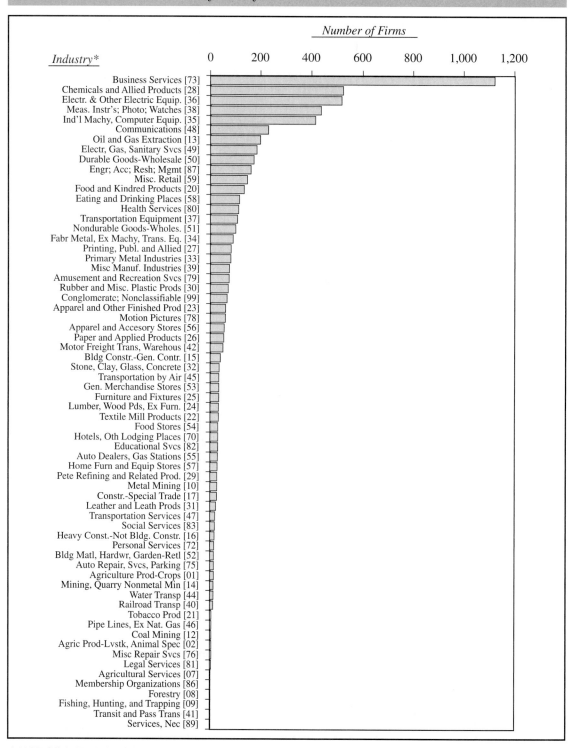

Number of Firms

Industry*

6,146 Publicly Traded U.S. Nonfinancial Firms, Year-End 2000

*Number in brackets are two-digit SIC codes.

Source: Raw data from Standard & Poor's *Research Insight* database, 2001.

FIGURE 7-2 Composite Market Equity Values by Industry

6,146 Publicly Traded U.S. Nonfinancial Firms, Year-End 2000

Numbers in brackets are two-digit SIC codes.
Source: Raw data from Standard & Poor's *Compustat* database, 2000.

In the next two sections, we focus on eight U.S. industries that are among the largest in terms of composite market equity value. The firms in these eight industries collectively accounted for approximately two-thirds of the composite market equity values of all publicly traded U.S. nonfinancial firms at year-end 2000 ($8,006 billion out of $11,700 billion). The eight industries are listed here in alphabetical order, along with the number of firms and composite market equity value (MEQ) for each, as of year-end 2000.

Industry	Number of Firms	Composite MEQ ($ billion)
Business Services	1,120	1,328
Chemicals and Allied Products	522	1,963
Communications	229	1,172
Electric, Gas, and Sanitary Services	184	527
Electronic and Other Electric Equipment	516	1,059
Food and Kindred Products	139	483
Industrial Machinery, Computer Equipment	414	1,018
Petroleum Refining and Related Products	27	457

7.7   THE DIVERSITY OF ACTIVITIES OF FIRMS IN U.S. INDUSTRIES

Although the primary two-digit SIC code is useful in sorting firms on a broad-brush basis, its usefulness is limited in two respects. *First*, the two-digit codes often combine firms into the same class even though their business activities differ substantially. *Second*, the primary two-digit codes obscure the fact that many firms are involved in multiple activities.

In this section, we examine the activities of firms based on *four-digit* SIC codes. The four-digit SIC code defines a unique *business segment*, and therefore provides a more precise description of a firm's main line of business. In the first analysis, we use four-digit codes to identify the primary business segment of each firm in the *Business Services* industry. In the second analysis, we examine the firms in each of the eight major U.S. industries identified in the previous section to determine the distribution of the number of business segments in which individual firms are involved.

7.7.1   Primary Business Segments of Firms in the *Business Services* Industry

To illustrate the diversity of the activities of firms in a major industry, we focus on the firms in the *Business Services* industry. As we documented above, this industry is the largest in terms of number of firms and second largest in composite market equity value. We sorted the 1,120 firms in this industry into categories according to their primary business segment, calculated the composite market equity values of the firms in each business segment, and identified the two largest firms in each business segment in terms of year-end 2000 market equity value. The results are displayed in Table 7-1.

The firms in the *Business Services* industry sort into a total of 21 primary business segments. These segments define such diverse activities as *Advertising* and *Photofinishing*, though the bulk of firms are clustered into three business segments: *Prepackaged Software* (439 firms), *Computer Programming and Data Processing* (247

TABLE 7-1 Market Equity Values (MEQ) for Segments of the Business Services Industry Composite MEQ, and MEQ of Two Largest Firms in Each Segment, Year-End 2000

Business Segment	Four-Digit SIC Code	Number of Firms	Composite MEQ ($ billion)	Composite Book Debt Ratio	Composite Market/Book Equity Ratio	Largest Firm Firm Name	Largest Firm MEQ ($ billion)	Second-Largest Firm Firm Name	Second-Largest Firm MEQ ($ billion)
Advertising	7310	23	10.0	39.9	3.0	Lamar Advertising	3.08	Catalina Marketing	2.16
Advertising Agencies	7311	8	35.7	14.2	6.6	Omnicom Group	14.67	Interpublic Group	13.10
Credit Reporting Agencies	7320	7	7.0	33.9	9.0	Equifax	4.05	Dun & Bradstreet	2.10
Mailing, Reproduction, Commercial Art Services	7330	9	1.7	29.2	1.7	Getty Images	1.62	Applied Graphics Tech	0.03
Direct Mail Advertising Services	7331	9	3.1	10.5	1.7	Harte Hanks	1.60	Advo	0.89
Services to Dwellings, Other Buildings	7340	4	1.4	11.6	2.6	ABM Industries	0.70	Rollins	0.60
Misc. Equipment Rental and Leasing	7350	6	1.2	60.9	0.5	United Rentals	0.94	Nationsrent	0.09
Equipment Rental and Leasing, Not elsewhere classified	7359	22	12.0	46.1	2.3	Crown Castle Intl	5.37	Hanover Compressor	2.95
Employment Agencies	7361	6	1.7	4.5	3.2	Heidrick & Struggles	0.81	Korn Ferry Intl	0.80
Help Supply Services	7363	38	13.5	20.9	1.8	Robert Half Intl	4.74	Manpower	2.88
Computer Programming, Data Processing	7370	247	271.5	23.5	3.3	Intl Business Mach	149.12	Electronic Data Sys	26.94
Computer Programming Services	7371	22	5.8	12.0	3.4	Wind River Systems	2.46	Speechworks Intl	1.48
Prepackaged Software	7372	439	783.8	6.1	5.2	Microsoft	231.29	Oracle	162.68
Computer Integrated System Design	7373	157	54.2	11.2	2.6	Redback Networks	6.27	Sabre Hldgs	5.58
Computer Processing, Data Preparation Services	7374	23	91.9	9.6	6.0	Automatic Data Proc	39.96	First Data	20.81
Computer Rental and Leasing	7377	5	2.0	69.0	1.4	Comdisco	1.74	First Natl Bancorp	0.12
Misc. Business Services	7380	8	0.2	32.2	0.2	Protection One	0.11	Comtex News Network	0.03
Detection, Guard, Armor Car Services	7381	4	0.3	13.7	1.0	Wackenhut	0.15	Kroll O Gara	0.13
Photofinishing Laboratories	7384	2	0.0	10.0	0.7	Photoworks	0.01	Walker Intl Inds	0.00
Telephone Interconnection Systems	7385	4	0.3	20.6	0.2	Digital Island	0.28	Norstan	0.02
Business Services, Not elsewhere classified	7389	77	30.4	17.8	3.9	Convergys	6.99	Total System Services	4.36
Totals (or Composite)		**1,120**	**1,327.6**	**17.1**	**4.2**		**475.98**		**247.74**
Percent of All Industry Firms			**100.0%**				**35.9%**		**18.7%**

Source: Standard & Poor's *Research Insight* database, 2001.

205

firms), and *Computer Integrated Systems Design* (157 firms). At year-end 2000, the firms in these categories had composite market equity values of $784 billion, $272 billion, and $54 billion, respectively, together accounting for 84 percent of the industry's composite market equity value of $1,328 billion.

The remainder of Table 7-1 shows the largest and second-largest firms in each primary business segment, and their market equity values. For instance, the *Prepackaged Software* category is dominated by Microsoft Corporation, which had a market equity value of $231 billion at year-end 2000. Meanwhile, the *Computer Programming and Data Processing* category is dominated by International Business Machines Corporation (IBM), with a market equity value of $149 billion.

Together, the largest firms in these categories (i.e., only 21 firms out of 1,120) had a composite market equity value of $476 billion, accounting for 35.9 percent of the industry's composite market equity value. The second-largest firms in each category collectively accounted for an additional $248 billion, or 18.7 percent of the industry's composite market equity value. Thus, in the *Business Services* industry, composite market equity value is concentrated in a relatively few, huge firms, with respect to both the industry as a whole and within each business segment. As we will see in the next section, concentration of value is a hallmark of all major U.S. industries.

7.7.2   Business Segments of Firms in Eight Major U.S. Industries

In the previous subsection, we focused on the *primary* business segment of individual firms in the *Business Services* industry. In this subsection, we examine the *numbers* of business segments in which each of the firms in a given industry is involved. This analysis provides a perspective on the extent to which individual firms are involved in a variety of distinct business activities versus having a narrow *focus* on a single business activity. For this purpose, we focus on the previously identified eight U.S. industries.

Larger firms are likely to have more business segments than smaller firms for at least two reasons. *First*, larger firms generally are more mature firms, and therefore have had more time, as well as more financial and managerial resources, to pursue profitable opportunities in ancillary business segments, via horizontal integration, vertical integration, and so on. *Second*, due in part to the greater ownership diffusion of larger firms (see Figure 1-7 in Chapter 1), the management of a larger firm may be more prone to engage in self-serving (and unprofitable) *empire building* by pursuing activities in non-core business segments.

The evidence is presented in Table 7-2. To develop this table, we initially sorted the firms in each industry into two groups: (1) large firms, defined as those with total assets at year-end 2000 in excess of $1 billion, and (2) all other firms. We then calculated the proportions of the firms in each industry size group that are involved in only one business segment, two business segments, and so on.

The resulting proportions indicate that, for every industry, most of the large firms have multiple business segments (as many as 10). In contrast, for six of the eight industries, the majority of the smaller firms in the industry have only a single business segment. These results indicate that larger firms generally are more diverse in their business activities. The question remains, though, whether greater diversity translates into greater profitability and market value. We provide evidence apropos this question in the next section.

TABLE 7-2   Distributions of Industry Firms by Number of Business Segments

Firms in Eight Major U.S. Industries, Sorted into Groups by Size, Year-End 2000

Industry Classification/Firm Size*	Number of Firms	Percent of Firms with Indicated Number of Business Segments					
		1	2	3	4	5	6–10
Business Services							
Large Firms	90	44.4	7.8	15.6	20.0	4.4	7.8
All Other Firms	937	69.9	10.5	9.3	6.0	2.7	1.7
Chemicals and Allied Products							
Large Firms	75	26.7	6.7	22.7	20.0	12.0	12.0
All Other Firms	416	79.8	6.7	8.2	4.1	0.7	0.5
Communications							
Large Firms	81	51.9	6.2	11.1	12.3	9.9	8.6
All Other Firms	133	63.2	11.3	12.0	8.3	2.3	3.0
Electric, Gas, and Sanitary Services							
Large Firms	82	9.8	11.0	20.7	14.6	22.0	22.0
All Other Firms	63	49.2	6.3	17.5	19.0	4.8	3.2
Electronic and Other Electric Equipment							
Large Firms	68	44.1	10.3	17.6	20.6	4.4	2.9
All Other Firms	427	63.9	10.1	15.7	6.8	2.3	1.2
Food and Kindred Products							
Large Firms	37	40.5	5.4	16.2	13.5	10.8	13.5
All Other Firms	88	71.6	8.0	10.2	5.7	3.4	1.1
Industrial Machinery, Computer Equipment							
Large Firms	56	26.8	5.4	19.6	23.2	14.3	10.7
All Other Firms	326	60.4	8.6	16.0	10.1	4.0	0.9
Petroleum Refining and Related Products							
Large Firms	14	7.1	0.0	28.6	14.3	7.1	42.9
All Other Firms	11	45.5	9.1	18.2	27.3	0.0	0.0
All Eight Industries							
Large Firms	**503**	**34.0**	**7.6**	**17.9**	**17.7**	**10.9**	**11.9**
All Other Firms	**2,401**	**68.3**	**9.3**	**11.6**	**6.9**	**2.5**	**1.4**

*Large firms are defined as those with $TA_{2000} > \$1$ billion.
Source: Raw data from Standard and Poor's *Research Insight* database, 2001.

7.8   ANALYSES OF FIRMS IN EIGHT MAJOR U.S. INDUSTRIES

In this section, we expand our analysis of the firms in each of the eight focal industries. These analyses include: (a) a market value concentration analysis, (b) analyses of recent and historical profitability, leverage, and valuation ratios, and (c) for large firms, analyses of the relationships between the number of business segments that a firm has and both its profitability and market value.

7.8.1   Market Equity Value Concentrations

Here we examine the concentration of market equity values among the firms in each of the eight focal industries. For each industry, we sorted firms in increasing order of their year-end 2000 market equity values, and plotted cumulative industry market values against the corresponding cumulative number of firms arranged in this order. The results for all eight industries are displayed in Figure 7-3.

Each of the curves in the figure is highly convex. These results indicate that, for every industry, composite market equity value is concentrated among a small percentage of firms. Indeed, for each of the eight industries, the largest 10 percent (or fewer) of firms account for 50 percent of the industry's composite market equity value. By this measure, the least concentrated industry is the *Electric, Gas, and Sanitary Services* industry, where the largest 16 out of 184 firms (8.7 percent) are required to account for the majority (51.6 percent) of the industry's composite market equity value. In contrast, the *Electronic and Other Electric Equipment* and *Business Services* industries are the most concentrated. For the former, only 8 of the 516 firms (1.6 percent) account for 50.3 percent of the industry's composite market equity value, and for the latter, only 7 of the 1,120 firms (0.6 percent) account for 50.8 percent of the industry's composite market equity value.

FIGURE 7-3   Cumulative Market Equity Values by Industry

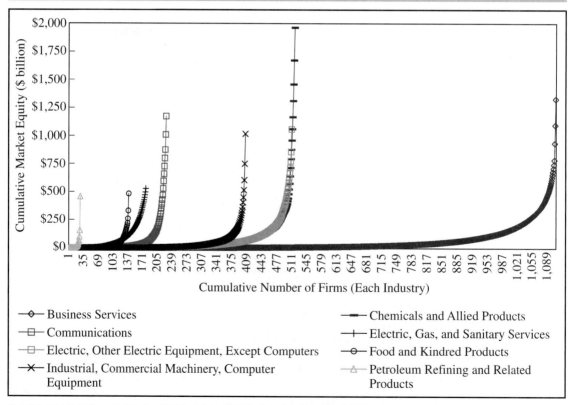

Publicly Traded Firms in Each of Eight Major U.S. Industries, Year-End 2000

Note: Firms in each industry are sorted by market equity value.

Source: Raw data from Standard & Poor's *Research Insight* database, 2001.

7.8.2   Composite PP&E/TA, ROE, Debt Ratio, and Market-to-Book Equity Ratio by Industry and Firm Size

Next, we examine composite values of four financial variables for groups of firms in each of the eight focal industries: the ratios of property, plant, and equipment (PP&E)/total assets (TA), return on common equity, (ROE), debt ratio, and market-to-book equity ratio. We are interested in examining each of these variables from an industry viewpoint for several reasons. For instance, by examining variations in PP&E/TA both across industries and across firms within an industry, we can determine which types of firms are more capital intensive versus labor intensive. In the theoretical article that we discussed earlier, Williams (1995) posits that industries will typically consist of a few large, capital-intensive firms and many more smaller, labor-intensive firms. Williams also suggests that larger firms in the industry (a) will have higher debt ratios and (b) will be more profitable. In addition, we have the opportunity to retest the *Collateral Hypothesis*, which we discussed and tested in Chapter 6. As you recall, according to this hypothesis a firm can finance its capital assets with long-term debt, whereas nontangible assets must be financed with equity.

The analysis is structured by sorting the firms in each industry into groups according to their TA at year-end 1999: TA < $10 million; $10 million < TA < $100 million; $100 million < TA < $1 billion; $1 billion < TA < $10 billion; and TA > $10 billion. Then for each size group, the composite value of each of the four financial variables is calculated. The results are displayed in Table 7-3, with separate panels for each variable. The values in the first column of a panel are composite values for all firms in each industry, with the last value applying to all firms in all eight industries. The remaining values in each panel are composite values for each industry and size group, with the exception of the last row, which shows composite values for all firms in each size group.

Capital Intensity and Debt Ratios across Industries and Firm Size Groups

The first panel of the table shows year-end 1999 composite values of PP&E/TA, in percent. The overall composite value of PP&E/TA is 36.1 percent. However, composite values of PP&E/TA vary substantially across industries, ranging from 14.6 percent and 16.8 percent for the *Business Services* and *Industrial Machinery, Computer Equipment* industries, respectively, to 57.3 percent and 63.2 percent for the *Electric, Gas, and Sanitary Services* and *Petroleum Refining and Related Products* industries, respectively. PP&E/TA also tends to vary substantially and directly with firm size, ranging from 15.6 for firms with TA < $10 million to 37.7 percent for firms with TA of $10 billion and above. Moreover, the observed positive relationship of composite PP&E/TA and firm size holds, to a greater or lesser extent, for each of the eight industries examined. As such, these results are consistent with Williams's prediction that larger firms will be more capital intensive.

The second panel shows year-end 1999 composite debt ratios. The overall composite debt ratio is 30.4 percent. However, composite debt ratios vary substantially across industries, ranging from 18.1 percent for the *Electronic and Other Electric Equipment* industry to 44.0 percent for the *Electric, Gas, and Sanitary Services* industry. It also appears that composite debt ratios are positively related to firm size, though the relationship is far from perfect, either for all industries combined or for each industry separately. The positive relationships observed between firm size and both composite

TABLE 7-3 Year-End 1999 Composite Capital Intensity and Debt Ratio, 2000 Composite ROE, and Year-End 2000 Composite Market-to-Book Equity Ratio

Publicly Traded Firms in Eight Major U.S. Industries, Sorted by TA at Year-End 1999

Industry	All Firms	Firm Size Range (TA$_{1999}$)				
		<$10 million	$10 million to $100 million	$100 million to $1 billion	$1 billion to $10 billion	>$10 billion
YEAR-END 1999 COMPOSITE CAPITAL INTENSITY (PP&E/TA, %)						
Business Services	14.6	13.3	10.6	13.4	16.0	14.5
Chemicals and Allied Products	31.4	15.5	20.2	28.5	36.4	29.1
Communications	32.7	19.4	32.6	30.7	30.2	33.3
Electric, Gas, and Sanitary Services	57.3	24.6	45.0	64.9	61.0	55.1
Electronic and Other Electric Equipment	24.8	16.2	17.3	23.9	27.6	23.4
Food and Kindred Products	32.7	28.9	37.6	40.4	35.5	30.1
Industrial Machinery, Computer Equipment	16.8	15.7	17.0	21.0	19.4	13.0
Petroleum Refining and Related Products	63.2	25.0	77.0	54.3	56.9	64.1
All Eight Industries	**36.1**	**15.6**	**16.9**	**25.2**	**36.3**	**37.7**
YEAR-END 1999 COMPOSITE DEBT RATIO (%)						
Business Services	19.7	24.5	11.3	17.5	20.7	21.2
Chemicals and Allied Products	27.5	21.6	19.9	32.0	32.7	24.2
Communications	32.4	21.2	36.1	51.0	48.4	28.9
Electric, Gas, and Sanitary Services	44.0	30.8	30.8	41.3	42.1	45.2
Electronic and Other Electric Equipment	18.1	26.5	18.5	24.6	22.2	12.8
Food and Kindred Products	35.4	23.7	26.7	31.0	39.1	33.6
Industrial Machinery, Computer Equipment	24.8	34.6	18.0	25.0	21.3	28.6
Petroleum Refining and Related Products	19.8	17.8	34.0	34.4	27.6	18.6
All Eight Industries	**30.4**	**25.5**	**16.8**	**27.9**	**33.2**	**29.7**
2000 COMPOSITE RETURN ON EQUITY (%)						
Business Services	–8.8	–104.3	–60.3	–28.8	–3.4	30.9
Chemicals and Allied Products	18.9	–119.1	–47.5	–0.9	18.9	27.1
Communications	3.5	–143.2	–83.8	–21.3	–31.0	8.0
Electric, Gas, and Sanitary Services	8.5	*	5.0	4.9	11.5	6.6
Electronic and Other Electric Equipment	13.4	–100.4	–13.0	1.4	15.3	20.2
Food and Kindred Products	21.9	–31.2	4.9	11.9	25.7	21.5
Industrial Machinery, Computer Equipment	13.6	–135.7	–22.7	9.3	18.6	12.9
Petroleum Refining and Related Products	24.4	*	–9.6	16.3	24.2	24.6
All Eight Industries	**8.6**	**–110.7**	**–44.2**	**–11.8**	**8.6**	**15.0**
YEAR-END 2000 COMPOSITE MARKET-TO-BOOK EQUITY RATIO						
Business Services	4.2	5.4	2.6	3.0	4.9	6.1
Chemicals and Allied Products	8.4	6.4	5.4	6.8	6.1	10.0
Communications	2.0	3.1	2.0	1.7	2.9	1.9
Electric, Gas, and Sanitary Services	2.3	*	1.7	2.0	2.0	2.5
Electronic and Other Electric Equipment	4.1	6.4	3.4	5.0	3.9	4.0
Food and Kindred Products	7.3	2.7	1.5	1.8	5.8	9.7
Industrial Machinery, Computer Equipment	5.6	6.4	4.0	5.6	5.6	5.8
Petroleum Refining and Related Products	3.4	*	0.6	1.7	1.6	3.6
All Eight Industries	**4.0**	**5.8**	**3.3**	**3.9**	**4.2**	**4.0**

*Composite book equity was negative.
Source: Raw data from Standard & Poor's *Research Insight* database, 2001.

PP&E/TA and composite debt ratios further corroborate Williams's theory. Indeed, using the composite data across firm size for all industries (i.e., the last rows in each panel), the correlation between composite PP&E/TA and composite debt ratio is 0.79.

The Collateral Hypothesis does not fare quite as well. Using composite figures for each industry (i.e., first-column figures), the correlation between composite PP&E/TA and composite debt ratio is only 0.38. This relationship is rendered particularly weak because of the results for the *Petroleum Refining and Related Products* industry, which has the highest composite PP&E/TA at 63.2 percent but one of the lowest composite debt ratios, 19.8 percent! Perhaps PP&E associated with oil refining and processing cannot easily be used as collateral in debt contracts. If we exclude this industry, the correlation between composite PP&E/TA and composite debt ratio improves dramatically to 0.89.

Profitability and Market Values across Industries and Firm Size
The third panel of Table 7-3 shows composite ROE by industry and firm size. For 2000, composite ROE varied substantially across industries, ranging from –8.8 percent for the *Business Services* industry to 24.4 percent for the *Petroleum Refining and Related Products* industry. In addition, a clear and substantial positive relationship exists between firm size and composite ROE for each and every industry. Firms in the smallest two size categories generally sustained substantial losses in 2000. In sharp contrast, the largest firms (TA > $10 billion) all had positive composite earnings in 2000. However, large-firm composite ROE varied substantially across industries, from 6.6 percent for the *Electric, Gas, and Sanitary Services* industry to 30.9 percent for the *Business Services* industry. Of course, one year's results provide only a limited perspective on an industry's profitability. In the next section, we provide time series evidence on composite ROE for two industries.

The figures in the final panel show that year-end 2000 composite market-to-book equity ratios also varied substantially across both industries and firm size. For industries as a whole, the *Chemicals and Allied Products* industry garnered the highest ratio, 8.4, while the *Communications* industry had the lowest ratio, 2.0. For the largest firms, the correlation between composite market-to-book equity ratio and composite ROE is 0.60, indicating that large firms in more profitable industries garnered correspondingly higher market-to-book equity ratios, as we would expect.

7.8.3   Determinants of ROE Differentials across Industries and Firm Size: DuPont Analysis

In this subsection, we scrutinize the variation in composite ROE across both industries and firm size that we observed in Table 7-3. We do this by employing the well-known *DuPont ROE breakdown analysis*. This analysis begins with the definition of ROE over a period extending from date $t-1$ to date t, given in Equation 7.1:

$$\text{ROE}_t = \frac{\text{NI}_t}{\text{BEQ}_{t-1}}, \tag{7.1}$$

where NI_t is the firm's net income over the period and BEQ_{t-1} is the firm's book equity at date $t-1$.

A DuPont analysis involves breaking down a firm's ROE into components that can reveal the extent to which each of several aspects of a firm's operations contributes to the firm's bottom line. Two such breakdowns are given in Equations 7.2 and 7.3:

$$\text{ROE}_t = \left(\frac{\text{NI}_t}{\text{TA}_{t-1}}\right)\left(\frac{\text{TA}_{t-1}}{\text{BEQ}_{t-1}}\right), \tag{7.2}$$

and

$$\text{ROE}_{t-1,t} = \left(\frac{\text{NI}_t}{\text{SALES}_t}\right)\left(\frac{\text{SALES}_t}{\text{TA}_{t-1}}\right)\left(\frac{\text{TA}_{t-1}}{\text{BEQ}_{t-1}}\right), \tag{7.3}$$

where TA_{t-1} is the firm's total assets at date $t-1$ and SALES_t is the firm's sales over the period. The first right side term in Equation 7.2 indicates the firm's ability to generate net income from its assets; the second right term is directly related to the firm's leverage, and thus indicates the extent to which the mapping of the firm's ROA onto its ROE is *magnified* via leverage.

In this subsection, we use breakdown Equation 7.3. The first right term is the firm's *profit margin*, and indicates the ability of a firm to generate net income from sales. The second right term indicates the firm's ability to generate sales from TA (known as the *total asset turnover* ratio). The third right term, as before, indicates the extent to which the mapping of the firm's ROA onto its ROE is *magnified* via leverage.

Though the DuPont analysis is generally used for individual firms, we apply it to the *composite* ROE of a given sample of firms. Specifically, for each of the eight focal industries, we sorted firms into two groups, small and large, according to whether their year-end 1999 TA was less than or greater than \$1 billion, and then applied Equation 7.3 to the composite figures for each group, as well as to all firms in the industry. The results are displayed in Table 7-4.

Note initially that for all eight industries, composite ROE is greater for the large firms than for the small firms. By examining the three breakdown ratios that determine ROE, we can determine the source of the ROE differentials between the small and large firms. For all eight industries, the ratio that appears most important in explaining the observed ROE differentials is $\text{NI}_t/\text{SALES}_t$. The large firms' consistent ability to convert sales into net income makes them more profitable than small firms. In turn, this difference is likely due to the greater economies of scale that large firms generally enjoy. In contrast, for none of the eight cases does $\text{SALES}_t/\text{TA}_{t-1}$ performance vary enough to explain the observed variations in ROE differentials between small and large firms. Indeed, small firms are generally more efficient in terms of total asset turnover. Finally, in six of the eight industries large firms have greater leverage as measured by $\text{TA}_{t-1}/\text{BEQ}_{t-1}$, which serves to magnify the ROE differential between small and large firms.

7.8.4 Number of Business Segments, Profitability, and Market Equity Value

For our final analysis of this section, we focus again on the numbers of business segments in which firms are engaged in order to provide a cursory test of the competing hypotheses mentioned earlier. As you recall, theory suggests that the typical multiseg-

TABLE 7-4   Composite DuPont Analyses of Eight Major U.S. Industries, 2000

$$ROE_t = (NI_t/BEQ_{t-1}) = (NI_t/Sales_t)(Sales_t/TA_{t-1}) (TA_{t-1}/BEQ_{t-1})$$

Industry	Firm Size*	ROE	(NI/Sales)	(Sales/TA)	(TA/BEQ)
				Decimal Values	
Business Services	Small	−0.3730	−0.6802	0.5002	1.0964
	Large	0.1113	0.0623	0.8208	2.1760
	All Firms	−0.0883	−0.0571	0.8934	1.7311
Chemicals and Allied Products	Small	−0.1712	−0.1402	0.7966	1.5331
	Large	0.2438	0.1079	0.9048	2.4970
	All Firms	0.1888	0.0890	0.8956	2.3693
Communications	Small	−0.2760	−0.2611	0.4568	2.3140
	Large	0.0452	0.0494	0.4363	2.0961
	All Firms	0.0351	0.0381	0.4370	2.1030
Electric, Gas, and Sanitary Services	Small	0.0496	0.0221	0.7517	2.9836
	Large	0.0862	0.0348	0.6164	4.0216
	All Firms	0.0851	0.0344	0.6195	3.9892
Electronic and Other Electric Equipment	Small	−0.0317	−0.0189	1.2795	1.3107
	Large	0.1794	0.1086	1.0489	1.5758
	All Firms	0.1344	0.0811	1.0913	1.5193
Food and Kindred Products	Small	0.1095	0.0359	1.4395	2.1215
	Large	0.2317	0.0573	1.1281	3.5852
	All Firms	0.2193	0.0556	1.1477	3.4359
Industrial Machinery, Computer Equipment	Small	0.0326	0.0152	1.2689	1.6858
	Large	0.1592	0.0586	1.1896	2.2824
	All Firms	0.1356	0.0520	1.2011	2.1716
Petroleum Refining and Related Products	Small	0.0958	0.0153	1.8262	3.4346
	Large	0.2453	0.0653	1.6116	2.3325
	All Firms	0.2444	0.0647	1.6136	2.3394
All Eight Industries	**Small**	**−0.1993**	**−0.1323**	**1.0492**	**1.4353**
	Large	**0.1308**	**0.0657**	**0.8078**	**2.4650**
	All Firms	**0.08585**	**0.0446**	**0.8281**	**2.3247**

*Large firms are those with $TA_{1999} > $1 billion.
Source: Raw data from Standard & Poor's *Research Insight* database, 2001.

ment firm may be more or less profitable than the typical single-segment firm, depending on whether in the former the firm's management pursued expansion into additional business segments to (a) take advantage of profitable investment opportunities versus (b) engage in self-serving empire building. If hypothesis (a) is generally true, then multisegment firms should be observed to be *more profitable* and to have *higher market equity values*; if hypothesis (b) is generally true, multisegments firms should be observed to be *less profitable* and to have *lower market equity values*.

For this test, we use data for only the largest firms in the eight focal industries; specifically, those with TA at year-end 1997 in excess of $1 billion. Each firm is sorted into one of six groups according to number of business segments at year-end 1997: 1, 2, 3, 4, 5, or 6–10. For each group, we calculated average composite values of ROE and market-to-book equity ratio for 1998–2000. We then plotted these values against number of business segments. These plots are displayed in Figure 7-4. The figure also dis-

FIGURE 7-4 Values of Financial Variables by Number of Business Segments

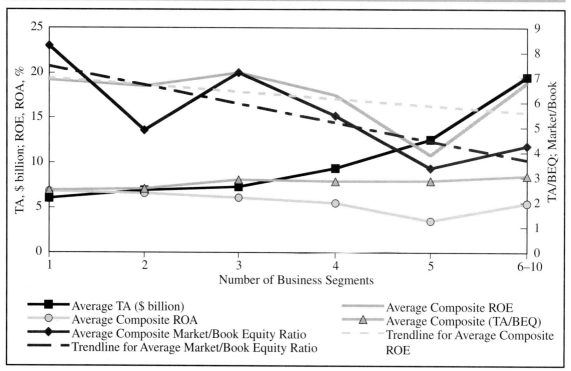

Composite Values (except TA) for Large Firms in Eight U.S. Industries, Sorted by Number of Business Segments
Note: Averages for 1998–2000. Large firms have TA$_{1997}$ > $1 billion.
Source: Raw data from Standard & Poor's *Research Insight* database, 2001.

plays (a) average TA of the firms in each group, (b) regression-based trendlines for both ROE and market-to-book equity ratio, and (c) DuPont ROE breakdown variables for Equation 7.2 (i.e., ROA and TA/BEQ).

Note initially that average TA tends to increase with number of business segments. This result is consistent with results shown in Table 7-2, where we found that number of business segments is positively related to firm size. Here, though, we are finding that even among *large firms* firm size and number of business segments are positively related. Certainly larger firms are larger because they have been successful in the past, and also in many cases because they have had more time to develop, apparently often into other business segments. Nevertheless, the query remains whether the managements of these multisegment firms have consistently pursued *profitable* expansion into other business segments.

Number of Business Segments and Profitability

The ROE evidence indicates that larger, multisegment firms were generally *less* profitable than smaller, single-segment firms in 1998 to 2000, as the trendline imposed on the ROE values is *downward* sloping. An inspection of the values of the DuPont breakdown variables reveals that ROA is *negatively* related to number of business segments, whereas TA/BEQ is slightly *positively* related to number of business segments. However, the lower ROAs for the larger, multisegment firms are obviously not fully off-set by their higher leverage because, as noted, ROE is negatively related to number of business segments. Thus, the evidence is consistent with the hypothesis that the managements of larger, multisegment firms have been engaging in inefficient empire building (i.e., rather than pursuing highly profitable investments in non-core business segments).

Number of Business Segments and Market-to-Book Equity Ratio

How do the profitability results discussed above translate into market values? We address this question by referring to the market-to-book equity ratios shown in the figure. These ratios vary substantially across the groups, but, as the trendline indicates, market-to-book equity ratio is strongly *negatively* related to number of business segments. The average composite market-to-book equity ratio ranges from 8.3 for the single-segment firms to 3.4 and 4.3 for the firms with 5 and 6–10 business segments, respectively.

As such, these results are qualitatively consistent with the profitability results, and therefore also suggest that the managements of larger, multisegment firms engage in empire building. These results are also qualitatively consistent with the results of more rigorous empirical tests conducted by Lang and Stulz (1994), Berger and Ofek (1995), Servaes (1996), and Denis, Denis, and Sarin (1997), all of whom document evidence of the so-called *diversification discount*—the tendency for diversified firms to have lower market equity values.

7.9   HISTORICAL ANALYSES OF TWO U.S. INDUSTRIES

In the previous three sections, we analyzed various aspects of the *current* status of firms in major U.S. industries. However, as any historian would argue, we can fully understand our current situation only by reference to the past. Therefore, in this section we provide several detailed analyses of the historical development of two major U.S. industries, *Business Services* and *Chemicals and Allied Products*. In our main historical analysis, we examine the composite growth, performance, financial policies, and valuation of each industry over the years 1980 to 2000.

So that the reader can better appreciate the possible interactions among these variables, we display them *together* in time series. We do this by means of a *montage* that combines all composite variables for a given industry in a single, albeit complex, figure. The montage for the *Business Services* industry is shown in Figure 7-5, and the montage for the *Chemicals and Allied Products* industry is shown in Figure 7-6. In the first subsection we discuss the montage for the *Business Services* industry, and in the second subsection we discuss the montage for the *Chemicals and Allied Products* industry. In the third subsection, we provide a historical perspective on the entry and exit of firms in both industries.

7.9.1   The *Business Services* Industry: Historical Composite Growth, Profitability, Financial Policies, and Market Equity Values

Growth of the Business Services *Industry*

Figure 7-5 features three aspects of growth in the *Business Services* industry over time. *First*, the number of firms increased almost sixfold, from 181 firms in 1980 to 1,120 firms in 2000. *Second*, composite TA increased almost 13-fold, from $46 billion in

FIGURE 7-5 Industry Montage: Business Services

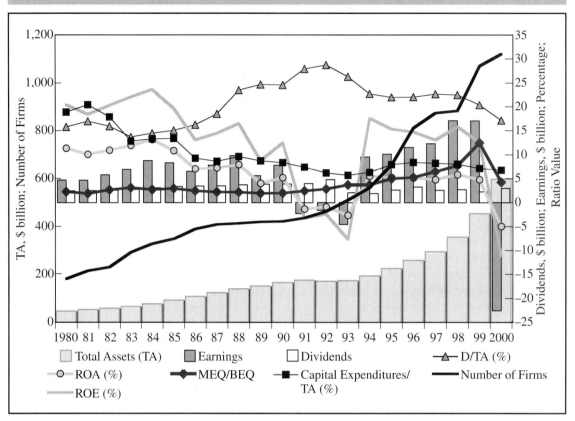

Composite Values for Publicly Traded U.S. Firms in the Industry, 1980–2000
Source: Raw data from Standard & Poor's *Research Insight* database, 2001.

1980 to $597 billion in 2000. *Third*, annual composite capital expenditures as a percentage of composite TA was high for the period as a whole, averaging 10.2 percent. However, this percentage has decreased rather dramatically over time, from 17 percent annually for 1980 to 1984 to less than 8 percent annually for 1996 to 2000. These figures indicate that the *Business Services* industry has been a high-growth industry over the overall period, but that growth is declining.

Profitability of the Business Services *Industry*

Business Services clearly has been a profitable industry over the period as a whole, sporting an average ROE of 12.1 percent. However, its profitability has been declining. The industry's composite earnings increased at a much slower rate than its composite TA, increasing less than fourfold from $4.7 billion in 1980 to $17.1 billion in 1999, compared to the tenfold increase in composite TA over the same period. Worse, the industry sustained a record loss of $22.6 billion in 2000. Average composite ROA decreased from 11.5 percent annually for 1980 to 1984 to only 3.1 percent annually for 1996 to 2000. Average composite ROE also decreased over time, from 21.0 percent annually for 1980 to 1984 to 9.0 percent for 1996 to 2000. The statistic for the latter period includes a jolting ROE result of –11.2 percent in 2000, which eclipsed the previous worst-year result of –7.7 percent in 1993.

Financial Policies in the Business Services *Industry over Time*

Composite leverage in the *Business Services* industry varied irregularly over the years. The composite debt ratio was 15.8 percent in 1980, increased steadily to 28.8 percent in 1992, and then fell to 17.1 percent in 2000. The leverage increase appears to have been due at least in part to industry losses in 1991 to 1993, which eroded the equity of firms in the industry. The subsequent leverage decrease appears to be due to both a 57 percent reduction in composite dividends in 1993 and the industry's return to profitability in 1994.

The Evolution of Composite Market-to-Book Equity Ratios in the Business Services *Industry*

Figure 7-5 also shows year-end composite market-to-book equity ratios for the industry. This ratio increased almost sixfold, from 2.3 at year-end 1980 to an amazing value of 12.5 at year-end 1999, before falling sharply with the 2000 crash in the prices of technology stocks to a final value of 4.2 at year-end 2000. The tremendous rise in this ratio through 1999 is puzzling in light of two of the results discussed earlier: (a) composite capital expenditures relative to TA has generally *decreased* over time, suggesting that profitable growth opportunities have decreased; and (b) the industry's composite ROE also has been *decreasing* over time. We provide a formal analysis of market valuation in Chapter 9. For now, we offer the following additional perspectives.

The states of both the U.S. economy and the U.S. financial markets changed dramatically over the years 1980 to 2000. Regarding the economy, in 1980 interest rates and inflation were high and volatile. Consequently, the overall discount rate that the market applied to determine the prices of all U.S. stocks was probably very high, and thus market values were relatively low, in 1980. Since 1980, both interest rates and inflation have abated substantially, and thus market discount rates probably decreased commensurately. These developments alone may explain a substantial portion of the general rise in market-to-book equity ratios through 1999. In addition, tax rates were relatively high in 1980, and investors had relatively few options to defer the taxation of security income (such as 401(k) plans, IRAs, etc.) in 1980. Consequently, the effective tax rate on investment income was relatively high in 1980, which probably also contributed to relatively low market valuations. Since 1980, tax rates declined and opportunities to defer taxation of security income proliferated, which probably also contributed to the general rise in market valuations.

Figure 7-5 facilitates interpretation of the changes in the *Business Services* industry that may have affected market valuations. The sample period can be divided into four fairly distinct subperiods, 1980 to 1988, 1989 to 1993, 1994 to 1999, and 2000. Each subperiod exhibited unique characteristics on each of six dimensions. For the first subperiod, the industry exhibited the following characteristics: (a) tremendous growth in both the number of firms and the composite TA of the firms in the industry, (b) high, though steadily declining, capital expenditures relative to TA, (c) relatively high and steady composite ROE, (d) a slight increase in composite leverage, (e) steady and substantial increases in composite dividends, and (f) steady composite market-to-book equity ratios, ranging only between 1.9 and 3.1.

The years 1989 to 1993 were tumultuous for the industry, characterized by (a) negligible growth in both the number of firms and the composite TA of the firms in the industry, (b) continuing decreases in capital expenditures relative to TA, (c) sharply falling, and ultimately negative, composite ROE, (d) a sharp increase in composite leverage, (e) a dramatic *decrease* in composite dividends, from $3.7 billion in 1988 to only $2.1 billion in 1993, and (f) a sharp increase in the composite market-to-book equity ratio, from 2.2 at year-end 1988 to 3.7 at year-end 1993.

The industry's troubles in 1989 to 1993 were undoubtedly related to the economic recession of 1990–1991. However, the recession probably cannot explain the bulk of the industry's decline during this period, because the recession was relatively brief and mild by historical standards, and the economy was expanding for at least a year prior to the industry's *bottoming out* in 1993. Instead, the industry itself was undergoing a fundamental restructuring during this period, highlighted by the decline in the preeminence of IBM and the rise of Microsoft. (We discuss IBM's restructuring during this period in Chapter 17.)

The market apparently reacted positively to the industry's restructuring during this period, because the composite market-to-book equity ratio nearly doubled during this period, after languishing throughout the more profitable period of 1980–1988. That is, although the industry experienced some very painful restructuring during the period of 1988 to 1993, the market's opinion was that this restructuring was constructive, and that afterward the industry would reemerge as a profitable, growing industry—which indeed it did. The *en masse* decisions by firms in the industry to slash dividends in 1993 allowed firms to retain more of their earnings, which served as a source of *internal funds* for new investment, as well as to reverse the industry's potentially dangerous trend toward higher leverage.

The subperiod of 1994 to 1999 was characterized by (a) a return to tremendous growth in both the number of firms and the composite TA of the firms in the industry, (b) modestly rising capital expenditures relative to TA, (c) a return to relatively high and steady composite ROE, (d) a slight *decrease* in composite leverage, (e) generally increasing composite dividends, and (f) a continuation of the sharp increase in the composite market-to-book equity ratio, from 3.7 at year-end 1993 to 12.5 at year-end 1999.

Finally, 2000 was an unmitigated disaster for the *Business Services* industry. As mentioned earlier, composite ROE was –11.2. Even more devastating was the loss of 47 percent of composite market equity value, falling from $2,514 billion at year-end 1999 to $1,328 billion at year-end 2000. Market equity shrank not only for the many smaller "dot-coms" that suffered or failed in 2000, but also for large firms in the industry: IBM and Microsoft lost 23.3 percent and 61.6 percent of their market equity values, respectively.

7.9.2 The *Chemicals and Allied Products* Industry: Historical Composite Growth, Profitability, Financial Policies, and Market Equity Values

Growth of the Chemicals and Allied Products *Industry*

Figure 7-6 features several aspects of growth in the *Chemicals and Allied Products* industry over the years 1980 to 2000. Both the number of firms and composite TA increased fairly steadily, with no substantial stagnant period as was the case for the *Business Services* industry. Over the entire period, the number of firms and composite TA increased over threefold and fourfold, respectively, from 169 firms and TA of $133

FIGURE 7-6   Industry Montage: Chemicals and Allied Products

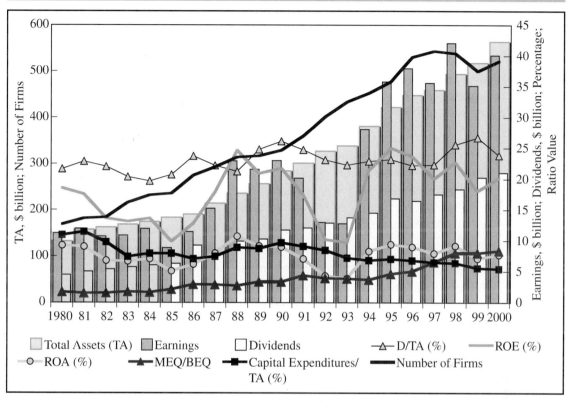

Composite Values for Publicly Traded U.S. Firms in the Industry, 1980–2000
Source: Raw data from Standard & Poor's *Research Insight* database, 2001.

billion in 1980, to 522 firms and TA of $565 billion in 2000. In addition, annual composite capital expenditures as a percentage of composite TA was high for the period as a whole, averaging 8.0 percent, though this percentage has trended slightly downward over time. These figures indicate that *Chemicals and Allied Products* has been a high-growth industry over the period as a whole. However, note that all of the growth values cited here are smaller than the corresponding values for the *Business Services* industry.

Profitability of the Chemicals and Allied Products *Industry*
The industry's annual composite ROE has been volatile, but strictly positive, over the sample period. The industry experienced composite ROE troughs of 9.7 percent and 9.9 percent in 1993 and 1985, respectively, and peaks of 24.7 percent and 25.1 percent in 1988 and 1995, respectively. Thus, this industry suffered no periods of losses as we had observed for the *Business Services* industry. The industry's average composite ROE was 17.8 percent. Thus, by this measure the industry has generally been more profitable than the *Business Services* industry (which had an average composite ROE of 12.1 percent). Moreover, composite ROE increased at a modest rate over this period, rather than decreasing as was the case for the *Business Services* industry.

Financial Policies in the Chemicals and Allied Products *Industry*

Regarding financial policies, the industry's composite debt ratio remained fairly steady, increasing only slightly over the period as a whole from 21.7 percent in 1980 to 23.8 percent in 2000. Meanwhile, the industry's composite dividends increased fairly steadily (with one substantial interruption in 1987) from $4.5 billion in 1980 to $21.0 billion in 2000. As such, firms in the *Chemicals and Allied Products* industry collectively maintained steadily growing composite dividends over time, in contrast to *Business Services* industry.

*The Evolution of Composite Market-to-Book Equity Values
in the* Chemicals and Allied Products *Industry*

From years-end 1980 to 2000, the industry's composite market-to-book equity ratio increased from 1.7 to 8.4. This was a less dramatic increase than we observed for the *Business Services* industry. It is difficult to reconcile this difference, because the *Chemicals and Allied Products* industry had posted higher average composite ROE over this period, and composite ROE had been trending upward, rather than downward, over the period.

7.9.3 Entry and Exit of Firms in the Two Industries

For our final empirical analysis of the *Business Services* and *Chemicals and Allied Products* industries, we examine the annual entry and exit of firms in each industry for 1980 to 2000. An *entry* in an industry refers to a firm that has gone public via an initial public offering (IPO), and an *exit* refers to the cessation of trading in a firm's stock because the firm was acquired, went bankrupt or was liquidated, or was taken private via a buyout. The entry and exit of firms provides important insights into the dynamics of an industry. For instance, IPOs indicate both the ease of entry into the industry and the potential for growth; exits, depending on the reason, suggest the ease of exit and the contracting or consolidating of the industry.

For each industry and year, we calculated both the number of firms that entered the industry via IPOs and the number of firms that exited the market. These numbers were then converted to percentages by dividing by the total number of firms in the industry at the end of the previous year. The results for both industries are displayed in Figure 7-7.

Several results in Figure 7-7 are interesting. *First*, both entry and exit percentages are generally greater for the *Business Services* industry than for the *Chemicals and Allied Products* industry. On average, the *Business Services* industry experienced a 15.4 percent annual entry rate, and a 5.9 percent annual exit rate. The corresponding averages for the *Chemicals and Allied Products* industry were 9.2 percent and 3.8 percent, respectively. The differences suggest that entry and exit barriers are greater in the *Chemicals and Allied Products* industry. This conclusion seems reasonable, because (a) firms in this industry (particularly pharmaceutical firms) must incur substantial research and development (R&D) expenditures and delays before they can bring products to market, and (b) firms in the *Chemicals and Allied Products* industry must have nearly twice as much PP&E (as a percent of TA) as firms in the *Business Services* industry, based on figures shown in Table 7-3.

Second, the entry percentages for both industries appear to be directly related to the business cycle, because both industries experienced relatively few entrants just prior to and during the recession of 1990 to 1991. Thus, not surprisingly, the correlation between the entry percentages for the two industries is positive at 0.42. In contrast, the pro-cyclical tendency of exit percentages for both industries may be driven by mergers

FIGURE 7-7 Entry and Exit for *Business Services* and *Chemicals and Allied Products* Industries

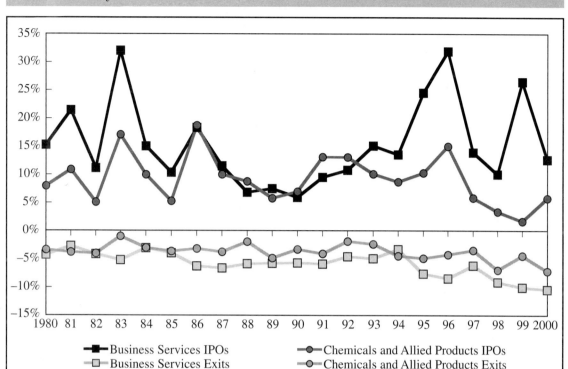

Entry (via IPO) and Exit (Merger/Acquisition, Bankruptcy/Liquidation, or Buyout) Values Are Percent of Total Industry Firms at End of Previous Year, 1980–2000

Note: Exits are represented as negative percentages.
Source: Raw data from Standard & Poor's *Research Insight* database, 2001.

and acquisitions (M&A) activity. In any event, the exit percentages for the two industries are also positively correlated at 0.59.

Third and finally, it is interesting to ponder whether entry and exit percentages over time for a given industry would positively or negatively correlated. On one hand, we might suppose that contemporaneous influences of the *business cycle* would induce a *negative correlation* between entry and exit percentages for the simple reason that, when business conditions are good, more firms enter and fewer firms exit (at least because of failure), and vice versa when business conditions are bad. On the other hand, suppose that both entry and exit percentages reflect the *dynamics* of an industry, where dynamics refers to changes in technology, growth opportunities, and competition. To the extent that this is true, then if an industry exhibits greater dynamics during some periods and less during others, entry and exit percentages over time might be *positively correlated*.

To test these opposing predictions, we calculated the correlation of entry and exit percentages for each of the two focal industries. For the *Business Services* industry, the correlation was modestly positive at 0.22. In contrast, for the *Chemicals and Allied Products* industry, the correlation was *negative* and more substantial at –0.51. Thus, we should perhaps conclude with a conservative statement that the entry and exit dynamics for a given industry are complex.

7.10 Summary of Learning Objectives

In this chapter, we reviewed theory and evidence relating firms' financial policies and strategies to the industry in which they operate. Here we summarize the theory and empirical sections of the chapter.

Summary of Theory

1. Agency theory suggests that a dichotomy will develop among the firms in an industry. A few firms will be large, capital-intensive, levered, and highly profitable, while the rest will be small, labor-intensive, less levered, and less profitable.

2. As a consequence of the asset substitution problem associated with debt, the firms in a given industry will tend to segregate; some will be highly levered and will pursue more risky projects, and the rest will have low leverage and will pursue less risky projects.

3. An industry may have an optimal debt capacity even though individual firms within the industry do not. This occurs because bankruptcies and liquidations within the industry will tend to cluster at times when the industry is depressed, so assets must be sold at *fire sale* prices. *Ex ante*, this increases the expected future cost of financial distress and bankruptcy, therefore limiting composite debt capacity in the industry.

4. A firm's leverage should be set to optimally balance managerial agency costs (which decrease with the firm's leverage) against costs associated with competitors' *aggressiveness* in terms of product market strategy (which increase with the firm's leverage).

5. Depending on the level of competition in an industry, executive compensation contracts should reflect the firm's industry-relative performance as well as absolute performance.

6. A firm operating in a competitive industry should maintain excess debt capacity as a competitive strategy. A bank loan commitment can help in this regard. In essence, the firm purchases a valuable option to tap additional debt capacity as necessary.

7. Leverage commits a firm to an aggressive product market strategy, and thus can be used to deter the entry of rivals into the industry.

8. Cooperative relationships among firms, including *joint ventures* and *strategic alliances*, are becoming important means by which firms can compete effectively in an industry.

Summary of Empirical Evidence

1. At year-end 2000, 6,146 publicly traded U.S. nonfinancial firms existed. They sort into 66 industries, though the firms in eight major industries account for two-thirds of the composite market equity value of $11,700 billion. These industries are *Business Services* (1,120 firms; $1,328 billion); *Chemicals and Allied Products* (522 firms; $1,963 billion); *Communications* (229 firms; $1,172 billion); *Electric, Gas, and Sanitary Services* (184 firms; $527 billion), *Electronic and Other Electric Equipment* (516 firms; $1,059 billion); *Food and Kindred Products* (139 firms; $483 billion), *Industrial Machinery, Computer Equipment* (431 firms; $1,338 billion), and *Petroleum Refining and Related Products* (27 firms; $457 billion).

2. Larger firms tend to be diversified, with investments in multiple business segments, whereas most small firms are involved in only a single business segment. However, evidence indicates that large, multisegment firms are subject to the *diversification discount*; that is, they tend to have lower market-to-book equity ratios. This evidence is consistent with the *Empire Building Hypothesis*.

3. Capital intensity (PP&E/TA), profitability (ROE), and leverage (debt ratio) all vary substantially across industries, and all are positively related to *firm size*. Market-to-book equity ratios also vary substantially across industries; however, they are not closely related to firm size.

4. A detailed historical analysis of the *Business Services* and *Chemicals and Allied Products* industries over the years 1980 to 2000 indicates that (a) both have been high-growth industries, though growth has slowed for both over time, (b) the *Chemicals and Allied Products* industry was generally the more profitable of the two industries, and (c) entry and exit has been easier in the *Business Services* industry.

Review Questions and Problems

1. Explain how the asset substitution problem can create a *leverage dichotomy* among the firms in a given industry in which some firms adopt leverage and pursue riskier projects, and other firms are less levered and pursue less risky projects.
2. Explain how the dynamics of asset liquidity in an industry create the circumstance in which the optimal leverage of an individual firm depends on the leverage of other firms in its industry.
3. Theorists have argued that a firm's leverage decision can be used as a competitive tool. Regarding this issue,
   a. explain the Leverage Aggressiveness Hypothesis.
   b. explain the Long Purse Hypothesis.
4. Explain how a firm's optimal leverage may be determined by a trade-off between managerial agency costs and costs of rivals' product-market aggressiveness.
5. From the perspective of industry competition, explain the value to a firm of retaining debt capacity (i.e., retaining the option to increase leverage at any time).
6. How can an incumbent firm in a given industry use leverage to deter entry?
7. Discuss the possible interactions between a firm's production and product-market decisions and its financing decisions.
8. Explain how provisions in a CEO's compensation contract can affect the firm's competitive strategy.
9. Compare and contrast *joint ventures* and *strategic alliances* as means by which a firm can compete more effectively in its industry.
10. Based on the year-end 2000 figures presented in the chapter, what are the three largest U.S. industries in terms of
    a. number of firms?
    b. composite market equity value?
11. From a theoretical perspective, how would you explain the empirical evidence presented in Table 7-3 indicating that industries tend to be characterized by (a) a few large, capital-intensive, highly profitable, levered firms, and (b) many smaller, labor-intensive, relatively unprofitable firms with less leverage.
12. Empirical evidence presented in Table 7-3 indicates that firms in the *Petroleum Refining and Related Products* industry are highly capital intensive and yet have relatively low leverage. Is this evidence inconsistent with the Collateral Hypothesis? Explain.
13. Briefly describe the two reasons cited in the text regarding why a firm would become involved in activities in multiple business segments. Which of these reasons is better supported by the empirical evidence presented in the text?
14. What do you conclude from our eight-industry analysis of the relationships between capital intensity and debt ratios? (Discuss relationships across both industries and firm size.)
15. What do you conclude from our eight-industry analysis of profitability and market values? (Discuss relationships across both industries and firm size.)

The next four problems require the values ($ billion) for large firms in two industries shown in Table 7-5.

16. Choose one of the two industries and calculate, for each firm and the composite, the following ratios: capital intensity (PP&E/TA); debt (D/TA); return on equity (NI_t/BEQ_{t-1}; and market-to-book equity (MEQ_t/BEQ_t). Examine these ratios for any cross-sectional relationships.

17. Choose one of the two industries, and conduct a DuPont ROE breakdown analysis on each firm. Which of the breakdown ratios appears to be most important in explaining ROE differentials across the firms?

18. Using the *composite figures* for each industry, conduct a DuPont ROE breakdown analysis of each industry. Which of the breakdown ratios appears to be most important in explaining the composite ROE differential across these two industries?

19. Select one of the two industries, and compute the ROE and market-to-book equity ratio for each firm. Is the anticipated positive relationship between these two variables apparent? Are the market-to-book equity ratios negatively related to the number of business segments as predicted by the diversification discount hypothesis?

TABLE 7-5   Values of Financial Variables for Large Firms in Two Industries

Industry Firm	Number of Business Segments	Values ($ billion) at Year-End 1999				2000 Values ($ billion)		Values ($ billion) at Year-End 2000	
		PP&E	TA	Debt	BEQ	Sales	NI	BEQ	MEQ
Business Services									
Microsoft	4	1.6	37.2	0.0	27.5	23.0	9.4	41.4	231.3
Oracle	n/a	1.0	7.3	0.3	3.7	10.1	6.3	6.5	162.7
IBM	7	17.6	87.5	28.4	20.3	88.4	8.1	20.4	149.1
Automatic Data Proc	4	0.6	5.8	0.2	4.0	5.9	0.8	4.6	40.0
Veritas Software	1	0.1	4.2	0.5	3.4	1.2	− 0.6	3.0	35.8
Siebel Systems	1	0.1	1.2	0.3	0.7	1.8	0.2	1.3	29.0
Electronic Data Sys	4	2.5	12.5	2.7	4.5	19.2	1.1	5.1	26.9
BEA Systems	1	0.0	0.4	0.3	0.1	0.5	0.0	0.4	25.6
I2 Technologies	1	0.1	0.9	0.4	0.3	1.1	− 1.8	8.5	21.8
First Data	6	0.7	17.0	1.6	3.9	5.7	0.9	3.7	20.8
YAHOO	1	0.1	1.5	0.0	1.3	1.1	0.1	1.9	16.5
Composite		*24.2*	*175.5*	*34.5*	*69.6*	*158.1*	*24.6*	*96.7*	*759.5*
Chemicals and Allied Products									
Pfizer	3	5.3	20.6	5.5	8.9	29.6	3.7	16.1	290.2
Merck & Co	3	9.7	35.6	6.0	13.2	40.4	6.8	14.8	215.9
Johnson & Johnson	4	6.7	29.2	4.3	16.2	29.1	4.8	18.8	146.1
Bristol Myers Squibb	1	4.6	17.1	1.8	8.6	18.2	4.1	9.2	144.6
Lilly (Eli) & Co	1	4.0	12.8	3.1	5.0	10.9	3.1	6.0	105.1
Proctor & Gamble	6	12.6	32.1	9.4	11.8	40.0	3.5	12.0	102.3
American Home Products	3	4.6	23.9	5.6	6.2	13.3	− 0.9	2.8	83.3
Schering Plough	1	2.9	9.4	0.7	5.2	9.8	2.4	6.1	83.0
Pharmacia	5	3.3	16.5	6.7	5.3	18.1	1.0	11.7	78.6
Abbott Laboratories	6	4.8	14.5	2.2	7.4	13.7	2.8	8.6	74.9
Composite		*58.6*	*211.7*	*45.2*	*88.0*	*223.1*	*31.3*	*106.1*	*1,323.9*

Creative Thinking Issues

1. Have any of the relevant theoretical analyses discussed in this chapter added to your understanding of the determinants of a firm's financial leverage? If so, which ones and how?

2. What financial variables would you examine to determine which of two rivals in an industry has been winning? What variables would you examine to determine which of these two rivals is more likely to dominate in the future?

3. Assume that you are on the board of directors of a firm that has a strong rival in its industry. Develop recommendations to the board regarding the firm's capital structure policy and the details of the CEO's compensation contract. (Make any assumptions necessary to further define the situation.)

4. Porter (1980) identifies five *forces* that determine competition in an industry: (a) *Entry/Exit Barriers*, (b) *Bargaining Power of Suppliers*, (c) *Bargaining Power of Buyers*, (d) *Threat of Substitute Products*, and (e) *Rivalry among Competing Firms*. Choose a firm in a particular industry and discuss the likely influence of each of these forces on the firm's financial policies and strategies.

Projects and Analyses

1. Perform an analysis of the capital structures of a sample of firms in a particular industry. Are the observed variations in leverage across these firms consistent with any of the theoretical models discussed in this chapter?

2. This project involves the calculation of the *diversification discount*. Identify a specific multisegment firm, and identify the segments in which it operates. Then identify single-segment firms in the same industry as each of the segments of the multisegment firm, and calculate the *fair value* of the equity of the multisegment firm using corresponding market-to-book equity ratios (or price-to-sales ratios) calculated for the single-segment firms. Compare your estimate of fair value to the actual market equity value of the focal firm and compute the diversification discount (or premium) as the ratio of actual market value to fair value.

CHAPTER

The Firm's Environment, Governance, Strategy, Operations, and Financial Structure

8

8.1   INTRODUCTION

In this chapter, we develop a comprehensive perspective on a firm that is centered on its *financial structure*. We do this by taking a structural approach to the analysis of a firm, where the structures include the firm's (a) *business environment*, (b) *internal governance* and *business strategy*, and (c) *operational* and *financial* structures. A fourth component of the analysis involves determinants of a firm's risk, performance, and contingencies. We reexamine the previously discussed effects of principal–agent conflicts and information asymmetry on all aspects of the firm. The analysis also provides the proper perspective for, and a preview of, the narrower and deeper analyses of specific financial decisions that we pursue in Chapters 9 through 18. In Chapter 19, we provide a second comprehensive perspective on a firm's financial policies and strategies, which incorporates material discussed in these later chapters.

Figure 8-1 illustrates the perspective that we develop in this chapter, and also serves to highlight the organization of the chapter. The top panel depicts the components of a firm's *business environment and external governance*, including (a) the state of the economy (current and projected gross domestic product, taxes, regulations, interest rates, inflation, productivity growth), (b) *resources* available to the firm (real estate; property, plant, and equipment; labor and management talent; technology; product and service providers), (c) *financial markets* (equity markets, debt markets, derivatives markets), and (d) *external governance groups* (governments, stock exchanges, creditors, external auditors, business media, analysts).

The second panel identifies the firm's two overarching internal constructs: its *internal governance structure* and its *business strategy*. The internal governance structure includes three elements: (a) the voting rights of shareholders and *shareholder activism*, (b) oversight by the firm's *board of directors*, and (c) the firm's *management hierarchy* and *internal capital market*. The three elements of business strategy are (a) the firm's targeted product and service market(s), (b) management's long-term goals with respect to market share and profitability, and (c) the firm's competitive strategy for meeting these goals.

The firm's internal governance structure and business strategy determine the firm's *operational* and *financial structures*, depicted in the third panel. Operational structure is defined in terms of the firm's (a) overall size, (b) production function, especially its capital/labor mix, (c) capital budgeting procedures, and (d) internal auditing system, and quality and cost controls. Financial structure includes (a) equity ownership

FIGURE 8-1 The Firm's Environment, Governance, Structures, and Dynamics

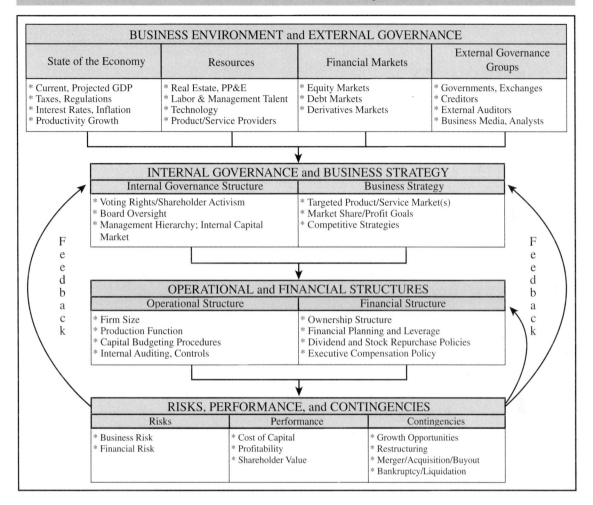

structure, (b) financial planning and leverage, (c) dividend and stock repurchase policies, and (d) executive compensation policy.

Together the firm's business environment, external governance, internal governance, business strategy, and operational and financial structures determine the firm's (a) risks (business, financial), (b) performance (cost of capital, profitability, shareholder value), and (c) contingencies (growth opportunities, restructuring, merger, acquisition, buyout, bankruptcy, liquidation). These are depicted in the fourth and final panel.

The factors in the final panel can be viewed from either an *ex ante* (i.e., expectations) or *ex post* (i.e., realized) perspective. From an *ex ante* viewpoint, a firm's management *anticipates* the factors, given the firm's environment, strategy, and operational and financial structures. From an *ex post* viewpoint, the factors represent *realizations* that stem from the firm's business strategy and operational and financial structures, as well as how the firm's strategy and structures played out in the business environment.

Ex post realizations also provide valuable information *inputs* for senior management, who will use this information to modify either their operational and financial structures, or, perhaps more fundamentally, their business strategy. The feedback arrows on the right side of the figure signify the feedback role of realizations to management. Realizations also provide input for those involved in the firm's internal governance—that is, voting shareholders and board directors. For instance, if the firm's realizations are negative and the blame can be placed on the firm's senior management team, the board may fire the management team and hire a replacement team who will be expected to improve results by altering the firm's business strategy and its operational or financial structures. The arrow on the left side of the figure signifies this separate feedback role of realizations.

8.2   THE FIRM'S BUSINESS ENVIRONMENT

In this section, we briefly address each element of a firm's business environment, and how it influences the firm's internal structures and operations.

8.2.1   The State of the Economy

The current and projected state of the economy can have a profound effect on a firm's business strategy, its operational and financial structures, and its risks, performance, and contingencies. We address these issues via a brief historical perspective on the U.S. business environment since World War II.

From the end of World War II through the early 1980s, firms faced not only high taxes, but also substantial, and actually increasing, government intervention in the form of regulations, antitrust restrictions on mergers and acquisitions, and so on. To these burdens was added, from 1974 to 1982, (a) high inflation and high and volatile interest rates and (b) two atrocious economic recessions. A recession is always a wrenching event for businesses and individuals, but long periods of chronic sub-par economic performance are even more devastating. The years 1974 to 1982 were such a period. By comparison, the economic environment of the period 1983 to 2000 was far superior. Interest rates, inflation, and regulations all abated, technological advancements proliferated, and both external and internal corporate governance structures strengthened.

Macroeconomic Variables and Aggregate Corporate Performance: 1960–2000
In Table 8-1, we compare several macroeconomic variables and aggregate corporate performance measures for three distinct periods over the years 1960–2000: 1960–1973, 1974–1982, and 1983–2000. Macroeconomic variables include gross domestic product (GDP) growth, inflation (measured by the consumer price index [CPI]), the yield on one-year U.S. Treasury bills, taxes, and labor productivity growth. Corporate performance measures include aggregate values of ROE, earnings growth, stock returns, and market-to-book equity ratios.

Regarding the macroeconomic variables, for the years 1974 to 1982 real GDP growth was much lower, and inflation and interest rates were much higher, than in the prior and subsequent periods. The growth of labor productivity was also lower in this period. Aggregate corporate performance followed suit. Average ROE was actually highest in 1974 to 1982, but was lowest after adjusting for inflation (i.e., in *real* terms). Average growth of aggregate corporate earnings was also lowest in this period, which was particularly disappointing given the high inflation of the period.

TABLE 8-1   Values of Macroeconomic Variables and Aggregate Corporate Performance Measures 1960–1973, 1974–1982, and 1983–2000

Period	Macroeconomic Variables					Aggregate Corporate Performance Measures			
	Average Real Growth of GDP	*Average Annual Inflation Rate (CPI)*	*Average 1-Year T-Bill Rate*	*Average Corporate Tax Rate*	*Average Annual Growth of Labor Productivity*	*Average Annual ROE*	*Average Annual Growth of Corporate Earnings*	*Average Annual Stock Market Return*	*Period-End Market/ Book Equity Ratio*
1960–1973	4.2%	3.3%	4.9%	44.3%	2.8%	10.4%	8.7%	6.4%	1.7
1974–1982	2.0%	8.7%	9.6%	36.5%	1.2%	13.1%	5.1%	10.3%	1.1
1983–2000	3.6%	3.2%	6.6%	37.1%	2.1%	10.4%	8.5%	14.7%	3.3

Source: U.S. Government statistics (various), and Standard & Poor's *Research Insight* database.

Average aggregate returns on stocks were actually lowest in 1960 to 1973 at 6.4 percent, compared with 10.3 percent in 1974 to 1982 and 14.7 percent in 1983 to 2000. However, the average annual *real* return, measured here as simply the difference between the average annual *nominal* return and the average inflation rate, was actually lowest in 1974 to 1982 at 1.6 percent (= 10.3 percent – 8.7 percent), compared to 3.1 percent for 1960 to 1973 and an astounding 11.5 percent for 1983 to 2000. Two of the factors that likely contributed to higher stock returns in 1983 to 2000 were (a) falling inflation and interest rates and (b) higher average growth of corporate earnings (8.5 percent versus only 5.1 percent in 1974 to 1982). Thus, it is not surprising that period-end aggregate market-to-book equity ratios suggest that investors had the dimmest view of corporate value creation at year-end 1982, when the ratio was only 1.1, and the brightest view at year-end 2000, when the ratio was 3.3.

Stock Returns Versus the Cost of Equity Capital
Do the observed average aggregate returns on stocks in each of these three periods correspond to the market's *ex ante* expected return? For managers, this is an important issue because the market's *ex ante required expected return on equity* corresponds to a firm's *cost of equity capital*. Thus, if observed average returns coincided with expected returns, the results suggest that expected returns on stocks, and thus the cost of equity capital, vary substantially over time, and perhaps with the state of the economy.

In conclusion, for two reasons it is important for any manager to keep abreast of the state of the macroeconomy, and, to the extent possible, to forecast future economic conditions: (a) Economic conditions appear to affect the profitability of capital investment projects, and *unexpected changes* in economic conditions may constitute a major risk factor; and (b) the state of the economy affects a firm's overall weighted average cost of capital (WACC) by affecting the costs of both debt and equity capital.

8.2.2   Resources Available to the Firm

A firm's ability to compete in its chosen product and service market(s) may depend as much on its ability to secure resources equitably as on its business strategy per se. Such resources include real estate and property, plant, and equipment (PP&E), talented labor and management personnel, cost-effective technologies, and low-cost product and service providers. Generally, a firm must constantly search for resources at lower cost to secure and maintain a competitive advantage. Technological advances allow a firm's earnings to grow over time because they increase the productivity of both labor and capital. In the long run, changes in technology impact both the emergence of new firms and the demise of old firms that fail to adapt to emerging technologies.

A firm must obtain a wide variety of products and services from product and service providers, including labor, electricity, transportation, distribution services, and legal services. In securing these resources, economies of scale are an important determinant of success. Overall, a firm's management must effectively negotiate a vast *nexus of contracts* with a variety of *stakeholders*. Stakeholders include not only those mentioned, but also several in the financial markets, to which we now turn.

8.2.3 Financial Markets

Three financial markets are important to a typical firm: equity markets, debt markets, and derivatives markets. As we have discussed previously, it is important for a firm to have a liquid public market for its equity because it (a) enhances the value of shares and (b) provides better access to external equity and debt financing. At the same time, however, the separation of ownership and control that attends public status engenders both of the fundamental problems that we have been addressing—principal–agent conflicts and information asymmetry. Structures, contracts, and operations of a public firm are designed, at least in part, to mitigate these problems and their costs while retaining the benefits of public equity.

Equity investors determine the ultimate measure of management performance: the firm's stock price. By investors we mean not only those who currently own a firm's shares, but also (a) *potential investors* who continuously monitor the prices of firms' stocks and compare them to their corresponding assessments of true value; (b) investors who might take a short position in a stock that they believe is overpriced; and (c) other firms, as well as major investors in the market, who regularly scrutinize the efficacy of a firm's management and stand ready to take control of the firm if its management performs poorly. Management must also be cognizant of investors' risk tolerance and preferences for dividends.

Debt markets are important because public firms generally rely on the debt markets for the bulk of their externally generated funds (review Figures 1-4a and 1-4b). As we discussed in Chapter 6, various characteristics of a firm determine the relative amount of debt funds in its capital structure (i.e., its leverage). Moreover, in Chapter 7 we discussed arguments that the leverage decision can be integrated into a firm's overall competitive strategy. In Chapter 15, we show that several factors determine both the specific source from which a firm obtains debt funds (i.e., public versus private lenders) and the terms in a given debt contract.

Derivative instruments, including forward contracts, options, and swaps, are playing an increasingly important role in firms' financial policies and strategies, particularly in terms of hedging business risk, interest rate risk, or currency risk. We discuss the corporate use of derivatives in Chapter 19.

8.2.4 External Governance Groups

As we discussed in Chapter 5, federal, state, and local governments all play dual roles in providing services and protection to firms on one hand, and imposing taxes, regulations, and restrictions on the other hand. The most fundamental services that governments provide to firms are the *establishment of property rights* through legislation and the *enforcement of legal contracts* (and therefore the *protection* of property rights) through the judicial system. Governments also impose taxes, regulations, and restrictions on corporate activity. As such, governments constitute an *external governance group*, where we define such a group as outsiders who exert some control over, or impose constraints on, a firm's activities.

Creditors constitute a second external governance group because, via both covenants in debt contracts and monitoring, creditors constrain a firm's activities. The primary rationale for both of these creditor governance mechanisms is to resolve conflicts of interest between the firm and its creditors, as we discussed in Chapter 3. We discuss these issues in greater detail in Chapter 15.

The business media, as well as various professional business analysts and commentators, constitute a third external governance group. The television and newspaper press are constantly on the beat for new information about firms' activities, and are quick to communicate such information to the interested investing and consuming public. In addition, a cadre of financial analysts regularly scrutinizes the strategies and operations of virtually all publicly traded firms (especially large firms), and judges their investment value. As such, the light that shines on a firm's activities emanates not only from the periodic financial reports that a public firm submits to the Securities and Exchange Commision (SEC), but also, and perhaps more importantly, from the business media and analysts.

Scrutiny by the media and analysts has at least two important implications for a firm. *First*, the information they generate reduces information asymmetry between the firm and investors. Of course, this is a two-edged sword. The positive edge is that the market for a firm's stock will be more efficient and liquid if information asymmetry is reduced. The negative edge is that it may be more difficult for a firm to keep valuable strategic information private. Confidentiality is often critical if a firm is to maintain a competitive advantage over its rivals—and thus to create value for its shareholders.

Second, analysts and financial commentators indirectly provide *oversight* of the firm's management, which serves shareholders' interest. Analysts and commentators are quick to critique decisions and to point out management that appears to be engaging in excessive consumption of perquisites, shirking their duties, or engaging in self-serving empire building. As such, this external governance group plays an indirect role in mitigating agency costs of managerial discretion.

8.3 INTERNAL GOVERNANCE AND BUSINESS STRATEGY

In this section, we discuss elements of a firm's *internal governance structure* and *business strategy*. In Figure 8-1, we placed these two constructs at the same level. It could be argued that the firm's governance structure supersedes the firm's business strategy, and therefore should be placed *above* the firm's business strategy. However, for most firms the original entrepreneurs have already fixed the firm's targeted product or service market(s), perhaps long ago. Moreover, a firm's business strategy may largely determine the composition of, as well as the nature of the oversight role played by, the firm's board of directors. On the other hand, senior management, working with the board of directors, determines the firm's business strategy, as well as its operational and financial structures, on an ongoing basis. For these reasons, we place the firm's governance structure and business strategy on equal footing.

8.3.1   Internal Governance

A public firm's internal governance structure consists of shareholders, the board of directors, and the firm's managerial hierarchy and internal capital market.

Voting Rights and Shareholder Activism

In Figure 1-7 of Chapter 1, we identified four major classes of shareholders in publicly traded U.S. nonfinancial firms in 1999: (a) insiders, (b) mutual funds, (c) pension funds and other institutions, and (d) *outside* individuals and other firms. The figure also shows that the distribution of share ownership across these classes varies substantially by firm size. Insiders dominate in small firms, whereas institutions (classes *b* and *c*) collectively dominate in large firms.

Common stockholders generally, though not always, have voting rights at a rate of one vote per share. But on what issues do they vote? In the regular course of corporate affairs, shareholders vote periodically in elections for the firm's board directors, and vote on major actions such as a merger, acquisition, or a sale of assets. In addition, *shareholder activism* occurs fairly frequently, and may actually be on the rise. We discuss two types of shareholder activism: the *proxy contest* and the *shareholder-initiated proposal*.

Proxy Contests

One example of shareholder activism is the *proxy contest*. A typical proxy contest involves a campaign among competing groups for the right to cast shareholders' votes on their behalf, or by *proxy*, in elections for a firm's board directors. The contest pits *incumbents*, who are individuals who currently hold the board seats and either are among the firm's senior management or support them, against *dissidents*, or *insurgents*—outsiders who wish to oust the incumbents in order to affect change.

Pound (1991) provided an historical perspective on the SEC's proxy regulations, and conducted an empirical analysis to determine the effects of these regulations on shareholder initiatives:

> [P]roxy rules began in 1935 as a minimal series of disclosure requirements and a prohibition against fraud. By 1956, they imposed extensive and wide-ranging disclosure requirements on anyone wishing to communicate about voting issues and required that all such communications be cleared in advance—in essence, censored—by the SEC. I present evidence that, since that time, the rules have significantly increased the costs of communication and coordinated action among shareholders. They have thus deterred shareholder initiatives and inhibited the development of a private market for information about voting issues. (p. 241)

REAL-WORLD FOCUS

Shareholder Activism circa 2001

It doesn't take a scientific survey to know there are lots of unhappy stockholders in America this spring—plunging share prices tell you that. Now, with the annual-meeting season getting underway, shareholders will have a chance to complain to management face-to-face. Voting on proxies, they can even try to change directors and alter corporate policies.

These days, however, shareholders don't have to wait for the annual meeting to vent their frustrations. Many, especially the big institutional shareholders like pension funds, are working year-round to get companies to adopt better business strategies.

But is shareholder activism really an effective way to boost stock performance?

There is no foolproof formula shareholders can use to ensure better returns, of course. But shareholder pressures on management have paid off frequently enough to encourage more and more attempts not only to boost profits but to press social, environmental, and other non-monetary agendas.

"If this power of investors is used effectively, it is without question good for the companies, good for the employees and good for investors," says Wharton management professor Michael Useem, director of the Center for Leadership and Change Management and author of a 1996 book entitled *Investor Capitalism: How Money Managers Are Changing the Face of Corporate America.*

Some shareholders have always sought to influence the management of public companies—shareholders are, after all, the owners. But activism became more intense in the 1980s and 1990s, and many who have studied it believe corporate managers have been forced to become more responsive to shareholder pressures, not just in well-publicized showdowns at annual meetings but in quiet negotiations behind the scenes.

Useem said shareholder groups rarely succeed with so-called gadfly motions focusing on things like pollution clean-up, improved union relations, canceling business with undesirable nations, or granting benefits to same-sex partners. But he says shareholder groups have had some success on corporate governance matters like eliminating staggered terms for directors—the "classified boards" these groups see as devices for protecting poor-performing managers.

Annual studies by the Investor Responsibility Research Center have shown gradual progress on some issues shareholder groups hold dear. Outside directors rather than company executives now dominate boards of directors and the key committees that set executives' pay. And there has been a steady rise in the use of stock options to compensate executives and directors, linking their interests to the interests of shareholders.

While activists rarely get majority votes on such issues at annual meetings, companies often agree to changes to avoid the embarrassment of public challenges that win substantial blocks of votes, Useem said. Even a 5 percent to 7 percent vote for a measure opposed by management may be seen as a public humiliation.

While activism in the first part of the 20th century was primarily aimed at improving shareholder returns, a 1970 ruling by the U.S. Court of Appeals in the District of Columbia opened the door for activists to demand that social issues be put to shareholder votes. That ruling arose from an effort to get Dow Chemical to limit napalm sales.

Activists became more influential after a 1993 SEC ruling that made it much easier for shareholders to act in unison, a change sought by major shareholder groups. Previously, shareholders faced regulatory hurdles, including the need for SEC approval to work in concert.

(continued)

Another key factor in the rise of activism is the growing role of professional money managers. In 1980, only about 25 percent of U.S. stock was controlled by pensions, insurance companies, mutual funds, and other "institutions." Today the figure is around 60 percent, largely because of the rise of mutual funds. Professional money managers know how to exert pressure, and they control enough votes to get companies' attention.

"With that kind of concentration of economic resources, these guys are looking out there and seeing some big under-performers and saying to themselves, I bought this stock high and now it's low. I can sell and lick my wounds or I can call the board and say, 'Get that manager out of there!' " Useem said.

"Given their increasing dominance in the equity markets, it is perhaps not surprising that institutions have become more active in their role as shareholders," writes Stuart L. Gillan of the SEC's Office of Economic Analysis, and Laura T. Starks, finance professor at the University of Texas.

In their 1998 study, *A Survey of Shareholder Activism: Motivation and Empirical Evidence*, they trace the current style of institutional activism to January 1985 when California State Treasurer Jesse Unruh founded the Council of Institutional Investors. The organization was formed to lobby for investor rights after a greenmailing case in which Texaco paid the Bass brothers of Texas $137 million. In the following years, the CII and its members, together and individually, started submitting proxy proposals aimed at changing the way targeted companies were governed.

Today CII is the most prominent shareholder group, representing 110 pension funds controlling about $1 trillion in assets. The organization still focuses on governance issues, opposing companies' "poison pill" anti-takeover measures, pressuring to have all of a company's directors face election at the same time, and demanding that boards and their executive compensation and nominating committees be dominated by outsiders rather than company executives.

Also influential are the California Public Employees' Retirement System, the State of Wisconsin Investment Board, and the Teamster Affiliates Pension Plan. Some other organizations take less direct approaches. The Investor Responsibility Research Center, for instance, provides surveys and other services to money managers and other shareholders but does not take positions on specific issues.

Big mutual fund companies such as Vanguard and Fidelity exert powerful pressures on under-performing companies, but do it very quietly, Useem said. "The most active movers and shakers have been the public pension funds. They put out their lists of bottom dwellers," he added, referring to companies with disappointing stocks.

Each year the CII publicizes a "Focus List" of 20 to 30 companies whose returns have most seriously fallen behind their industry averages. Landing on the list earns a company special attention from CII and its members—proxy initiatives to change corporate practices, votes for competing slates of directors, public embarrassment, demands that top executives be removed.

"These lists are not good to be on," said Useem. "CII and other groups are using pressure by mortification. You seek to embarrass, to humiliate the company for being a bottom dweller."

In the 1990s, CII has put less emphasis on presenting issues for shareholder votes and more emphasis on negotiating with a company's executives and directors—an approach sometimes called "relationship investing." Of course, harsher measures wait in reserve, giving executives good reason to compromise.

Does this work?

Yes, according to a 1995 study done for CII by Tim C. Opler of the Max M. Fisher College of Business at Ohio State University and Jonathan Sokobin of the Edwin L. Cox School of Business at Southern Methodist University. The study looked at 96 companies on CII focus lists from 1991 through 1993. It found that in the year after being placed on the list the average company's share price rose 21 percent, compared to 9.5 percent for the market benchmark, the Standard & Poor's 500. The study concluded that this market-beating return earned investors $39.7 billion more than they would have made by investing in the S&P 500.

To make sure this superior performance was caused by CII pressures rather than other factors, Opler and Sokobin also looked at several control groups. This included similar companies that had performed about the same as the focus-list group before the targeted companies were put on the list. These comparable groups did not rebound to the extent the targeted companies did, reinforcing the conclusion that shareholder activism had indeed pushed through change at the targeted companies.

Tallying the types of management moves the 96 companies made to improve performance, the researchers found that 29 instituted layoffs, 29 sold parts of the business, 24 cut costs and 20 made acquisitions. In addition, eight changed chief executive officers and 14 made other top management changes.

"The results are broadly consistent with the view that coordinated institutional governance activism is effective," the researchers conclude. Many firms on the focus list, they note, were subject to CII lobbying and negotiation rather than proxy battles. "It might very well be that management teams are most responsive to activism efforts which are private and done in the context of a long-term relationship," they write.

There is no way to be certain that the results were not due to some other influence, such as a fairly common rebound after a slump. Indeed, value investing is based on historical evidence this happens.

But Useem believes landing on a focus list does spur a company to change. "There's a prima face case that to be targeted by these big guys really does put some starch into everybody's shirt."

Source: "When Shareholder Groups Complain, Management Would Do Well to Listen," Knowledge @ Wharton, May 1, 2001. Copyright @ 2001 The Wharton School of the University of Pennsylvania, http://knowledge.wharton.upenn.edu. Reprinted by permission.

Dodd and Warner (1983) studied 96 proxy contests for board seats in NYSE and AMEX firms over the years 1962 to 1978. They found that, while the market generally responds favorably to a proxy contest announcement, dissidents generally failed to obtain a majority of board seats (though they generally won some seats). Ikenberry and Lakonishok (1993) explain the daunting task that dissenters face:

> The task faced by dissidents is difficult, and the costs of preparing and executing a proxy fight are substantial and borne directly by dissident shareholders who might expect reimbursement only if they are successful. Regulatory constraints, as well as obstructions raised by management during the process, not only add to the cost but are generally viewed as reducing dissidents' chances of winning. Historically, institutional investors, for a variety of reasons, have also been reluctant to support dissidents. Finally, aside from these barriers, the dissident slate in many cases represents a relatively unproven alternative in comparison to the incumbent board. For dissidents with less than a majority ownership in the firm, the success of the contest depends on the collaboration of the existing shareholder base. We expect rational shareholders to favor the slate of nominees they perceive most likely to enhance the value of their equity. Thus, we would expect shareholders at large to be less likely to empathize with dissidents unless there exists evidence of suboptimal performance by the incumbent management of targeted firms. (p. 406)

The authors analyzed the precontest and postcontest performance of 97 firms involved in proxy contests concerning the election of board directors over the years 1968 to 1987. Not surprisingly, the firms in their sample, on average, posted poor performance with respect to both stock price (–34.4 percent) and operating income growth (–39.3 percent) relative to benchmarks in the five years prior to the commencement of the contest.

However, postcontest performance was surprising: "[I]n proxy contests where dissidents obtain one or more seats, abnormal returns following resolution of the contest are significantly negative. Two years following the contest, the cumulative abnormal return has declined by more than 20 percent. The operating performance of the same firms during the postcontest period is also generally consistent with the pattern observed using stock returns. Our findings suggest that the poor operating performance subsequent to a dissident victory is both unexpected and disappointing to the market" (p. 407).

Mulherin and Poulsen (1998) provide an explanation for Ikenberry and Lakonishok's surprising postcontest results. They argue that Ikenberry and Lakonishok's sample contains a type of *survivorship bias*. That is, in order to enter their sample, a firm had to survive as a publicly traded firm for five years after the contest. Mulherin and Pousen show that many firms involved in a proxy contest *are acquired during the contest*, and the shareholders of these firms enjoy substantial wealth gains. In addition, "for firms that are not acquired, the occurrence of management turnover has a significant, positive effect on shareholder wealth because firms replacing management are more likely to restructure following the contest" (p. 279).

Shareholder-Initiated Proposals

Another example of shareholder activism is the *shareholder-initiated proposal*. A proposal generally involves changing some aspect a focal firm's internal governance, such as the structure or composition of the firm's board of directors (e.g., increasing the required number of *outsiders* among board members). Shareholder-initiated proposals became popular in the 1990s, following the decline of takeover activity in the 1980s. The purpose of these proposals is to improve the focal firm's performance, and thus its market value. Thus, they are visited upon firms that have been performing poorly.

Gordon and Pound (1993) analyzed 266 shareholder-sponsored proposals to change some aspect of the firms' governance structure during the 1990 proxy season. Many proposals were successful. However, as possible indications of conflicts of interest between shareholders and management, the authors found (a) a negative relationship between the percentage of votes cast in favor of proposals and the percentage of stock held by both corporate insiders and large non-management blockholders who sit on the board, and (b) a positive relationship between votes for proposals and the percentage of shares held by outside blockholders. Karpoff, Malatesta, and Walkling (1996) also studied shareholder-initiated corporate governance proposals. They argue that such proposals can increase the firm's market value for at least two reasons: (a) Even if the proposal is unsuccessful, management may get the message that shareholders are unhappy with their performance; and (b) "Shareholder proposals also can increase values if they complement broader efforts to gain control of a corporation or to exert pressure for specific policy changes. For example, shareholder proposals have been introduced at several companies, including Avon Products, Inc., Gillette Co., Lockheed Corporation, and USX, Inc., to facilitate hostile takeover bids" (p. 369).

On the other hand, shareholder proposals may destroy value:

> Another view holds that shareholder activism tends to impair firm man-
> agement, degrade performance, and decrease firm value. Wohlstetter (1993),
> for example, claims that most shareholder activists and pension fund man-
> agers have neither the skills nor the experience to improve on managers'
> decisions. Activists' attempts to influence corporate decisions therefore tend
> to disrupt the firm's operation . . . Reflecting yet another view, Romano
> (1993) and Saxton (1994) observe that public institutional investors ulti-
> mately are subject to political control and sometimes pursue objectives other
> than value maximization. It is possible that public institutions use corporate
> governance proposals to gain influence over the target firms' decisions, and
> to induce the firms to pursue politically motivated, value-decreasing invest-
> ments. If this view is correct, corporate governance proposals sponsored
> specifically by *public* institutions will tend to decrease firm values and operat-
> ing performance. (pp. 369–370)

The authors tested these hypotheses empirically, using a sample of 522 proposals
during the years 1986 to 1990. The issue addressed in most of these proposals can be
classified into one of three categories: (a) external corporate control issues (e.g., to
opt out of a state antitakeover law or to lower the requirement of a supermajority of
votes to approve a merger); (b) internal corporate governance issues (e.g., to eliminate a *classified board*,[1] or to require one share, one vote rules); and (c) compensa-
tion-related issues (e.g., granting restricted stock or stock options to senior managers). They examined whether these proposals had a consistent effect on the
sampled firms' share values, operating performance, or financial policies. They summarize their evidence succinctly as follows: "There is no persuasive evidence that
these proposals increase firm values, improve operating performance, or influence
firm policies" (p. 393).

Finally, Gillan and Starks (2000) studied 2,042 shareholder-sponsored governance
proposals over the years 1987 to 1994, focusing on the effects of both the type of sponsor and the type of proposal on both the outcome of the vote and the market's reaction. They summarize their results as follows:

> Our evidence suggests that shareholder voting and stock market reaction
> depend on the issues addressed by the proposals as well as the identity of the
> proposal sponsor. Proposals sponsored by the so-called gadflys (active indi-
> vidual investors) garner fewer votes and are associated with a slight positive
> impact on stock prices. In contrast, proposals sponsored by institutional
> investors (i.e., public pension funds) or coordinated groups of investors
> receive significantly more votes and appear to have some small but measur-
> able negative impact on stock prices. In general, we find that noncoordinated
> activism has been relatively ineffective when measured by voting outcomes.
> We find slightly more success in the activism of institutional investors and

---

[1]A board is classified if directors' elections are staggered over several years. In a *declassified* board, elections are held annually for all directors.

coordinated groups. The voting outcomes indicate that, while the percentage of votes cast in favor of the proposals averaged less than a majority, the percentage nonetheless increased over the sample period. Moreover, with the average level of voting support for such votes proposals approaching 35%, these activists have a stronger basis when negotiating with corporate management. (p. 303)

Board Oversight and Consultancy

Corporate boards generally have 6 to 12 members. The four principal functions of the board are (a) hiring, compensating, and, if necessary, firing senior management; (b) voting on major management proposals, including capital expenditures, acquisitions, and divestures; (c) voting on the issuance of stock and bonds, the payment of dividends, the adoption of a stock repurchase program, and other major financial activities; and (d) serving senior management as a source of strategic information and advice. The firm's CEO is generally the chairman of the board, and as such he or she largely controls the board's agenda.

An important aspect of a board's composition is the proportion of *outsiders* versus *insiders*. A board member is considered to be an insider if he or she (a) has been a long-term employee of the firm, having risen within the firm's management hierarchy, or (b) was appointed by virtue of some relationship with senior management (such as a family relationship, especially in firms that are closely held). Outsiders have not been employed by the firm and have had no long-term relationship with the CEO.

It is often argued that insiders on a board are less effective in their oversight role. The argument is that, because they have had a long-term relationship with, and therefore are beholden to, the CEO, they are little more than *rubber stamps* for the CEO's decisions. By extension, a firm's board is considered to be weak if the majority of board members are insiders, and strong if the majority are outsiders.

Ultimately, the optimal board structure would probably include both insiders and outsiders, due to the unique experiences that both types of members bring to the board. Insiders bring a wealth of experience, perspective, and insight gained from their long-term employment within the firm, while outsiders bring an alternative set of experiences from their employment with other firms in the industry or in other industries, or from their general knowledge of business strategies. In addition, apropos the point made earlier, outsiders are more likely to have an independent voice, and presumably would be more willing to challenge the CEO if and when they believe the CEO is advocating a bad or self-serving decision.

However, one class of outsiders may be of dubious value on a board: bankers. Kroszner and Strahan (2001) investigate "the trade-off between the benefits of bank monitoring when a banker is represented on a firm's board and costs from two sources: conflicts of interests between lenders and shareholders and U.S. legal doctrines that generate lender liability for bankers on boards of firms in financial distress" (p. 415). Empirically, they find that "consistent with high costs of active involvement, bankers are on boards of large, stable firms with high proportions of collateralizable assets and low reliance on short-term financing. While permitting banks to own equity could mitigate conflicts, the protection of shareholder versus creditor rights could continue to reduce U.S. banks' role in corporate governance" (p. 415).

Battle of the Board

Here is an article on the history of board governance in the United States and the challenge of building a good board.

Trustees and staff of the California Public Employees' Retirement System are developing guidelines to grade companies in Calpers' portfolio according to the independence of their boards. Calpers cannot be ignored: Its $80 billion in equities makes it one of the nation's largest shareholders and a force to be reckoned with in the governance arena.

A study conducted with Diane Del Guercio at the University of Oregon shows that Calpers has the power to provoke significant changes, such as takeover attempts, shifts in turnover, restructurings, and asset sales. CEOs would be wise to embrace the idea of strongly independent boards. For if investors can't get boards to work well, they may resort to other measures: sitting on boards themselves, lobbying for direct government regulation, or supporting a return of corporate raiders.

THE BATTLE FOR GOVERNANCE

The growing power and independence of boards in the United States represents a reversal of a trend that dates back to the early years of this century. A seminal event occurred in 1914, when representatives of J. P. Morgan resigned from 30 company boards in a single day. They and other institutional investors had held sway in boardrooms for more than two decades, leaving CEOs with little real decision-making power. But as they came under critical public and political scrutiny, these investors beat a hasty retreat. Meanwhile, family owners were also losing influence as company founders aged and ownership tilted toward outsiders. So a new group of professional CEOs, bred in new management schools, took the reins of corporate America.

Their grip loosened in the 1950s, when an economic boom drove a wave of investors into stocks. Increased individual ownership raised expectations and fed a belief in shareholder democracy. New regulations requiring the disclosure of senior management pay, along with the rise of the corporate raider, spurred a growing number of contested elections for boards, known as proxy contests. Following a concerted lobbying and publicity effort on governance issues by the Business Roundtable, new regulations introduced in 1956 clamped down on proxy battles, and CEOs prevailed at the end of the decade.

Today, institutional investment is booming again. After falling as low as 15 percent in the 1940s, institutional ownership returned to turn-of-the-century levels of 50 percent and higher in the mid-1980s. Takeovers flourished in the 1980s environment of few regulatory restrictions and easy financing via junk bonds. Then public opinion turned against raiders, state regulations and court decisions made takeovers more difficult, junk bonds dried up, and management created innovative defences against takeovers. Many CEOs believed they had won the governance battle.

However, institutional investors sought other ways to prod CEOs. In 1992, the Securities and Exchange Commission (SEC) made it easier for investors to coordinate on governance issues. Shareholders issued "hit lists" of underperforming companies, announced their own proposals, and communicated directly with management. But it didn't make sense for . . . institutions to intervene in each of the thousands of companies whose stock they held. They turned instead to boards—shareholders' elected representatives—as management watchdogs.

STOCKS AT A PREMIUM

What do these investors want? The bottom line is long-term returns . . . Institutional investors rely on strong, independent boards to create

(continued)

shareholder value. They believe strong boards will help companies correct mistakes, recover from crises, and find, support, and reward outstanding CEOs . . .

Recent research conducted by McKinsey in conjunction with *Institutional Investor* found that many large private money managers—especially those looking for long-term value—are willing to pay a higher stock price for companies with good, independent board governance. We surveyed 50 money managers representing about $850 billion in assets and found they were willing to pay a premium of 11 percent on average for good governance.

BUILDING THE BEST BOARD

CEOs can benefit personally from strong, independent boards. As major stockholders themselves, they should pursue strategies that increase the stock price. Harmonious relations with investors free CEOs to focus their time and energy on substantive business issues. CEOs will find, too, that investors are much more patient and understanding in bad times if they trust the board. And while a weak board may rubber-stamp the CEO's decisions when times are good, often its first response to a crisis is to fire the CEO—whereas a strong board with substantive knowledge of strategy and company performance will tend to support management . . .

After all, the best boards aren't built by outsiders. Only the CEO has the knowledge and the position to build the optimal board for his or her company. Rather than fight the tides, CEOs should take the lead by tailoring strong boards for their companies, thereby shaping the next era of corporate governance to their—and their shareholders'—benefit.

Source: "Why Investors Push for Strong Corporate Boards," by J. A. Hawkins, *The Wall Street Journal*, June 30, 1997. © 1997 Dow Jones & Company, Inc. Reprinted by permission.

Will a Board Fire a CEO for Poor Performance?

If a firm's board observes chronic poor performance, the CEO probably should be fired. However, evidence indicates that the likelihood that the CEO will be dismissed for poor performance depends on (a) the relative balance of power between the CEO and the board, (b) whether other top managers in the firm's hierarchy can pressure a poorly performing CEO to step down, and (c) whether activist shareholders exist. Regarding (a), if outsiders dominate the board, the probability of CEO dismissal should be strongly negatively related to a firm's performance. On the other hand, if the firm's board is *packed* with the CEO's cronies, it is less likely that the CEO will be fired even for very poor performance.

Several authors have tested these predictions empirically. Warner, Watts, and Wruck (1988) studied the correlation between a firm's stock performance and top management turnover. They found an inverse relationship between the probability of a change in top management and a firm's past stock price performance. They note that the relationship could be due to either monitoring by the board or pressure from other top managers or major shareholders. Weisback (1988) used both prior stock price performance and prior earnings as predictors of CEO dismissal. He finds that, in general, CEO dismissal is negatively related to both past stock price performance and past earnings. However, he finds that these negative relationships are *stronger* for firms with outsider-dominated boards than for firms with insider-dominated boards. Weisback's results emphasize the importance of having an independent board.

An empirical study by Borokhovich, Parrino, and Trapani (1996) also emphasizes the importance of having outside board members. They examined 969 CEO successions at 588 large public firms between 1970 and 1988 to determine the relationship between board composition and the probability that a new CEO is appointed from outside the firm. Their empirical results indicate "a strong positive relation between the percentage of outside directors and the frequency of outside CEO succession. The likelihood that an executive from outside the firm is appointed CEO increases monotonically with the percentage of outside directors. This monotonic relation is observed for both voluntary and forced departures. Evidence from stock returns around succession announcements indicates that, on average, shareholders benefit from outside appointments, but are harmed when an insider replaces a fired CEO" (p. 337).

Liability Protection for Board Members

Shareholders have sued board directors for losses arising from alleged mismanagement. Brook and Rao (1994) explain that, over the years 1984 to 1987, a *director liability crisis* emerged because of accelerating litigation against corporate directors. The threat of litigation severely decreased the supply of qualified outside directors nationwide. In response to this crisis, many states have passed *liability limitation* statutes, which allow firms to adopt new *liability limitation provisions* (LLPs) that protect directors from shareholder suits. Heron and Lewellen (1998) documented evidence that some firms have actually changed the state of their incorporation to one that provides better protection for directors.

Many corporate executives purchase liability insurance, known as *directors' and officers'* (D&O) insurance. Holderness (1990) argued that liability insurers have an incentive to monitor corporate performance. Chalmers, Dann, and Harford (2002) examined 72 firms that went public in the years 1992 to 1996. They find a negative relationship between post-IPO stock price performance and the amount of insurance coverage purchased by a manager.

Management Hierarchy and Internal Capital Markets

The management hierarchy in a typical firm starts at the top with the firm's president, board chairman, and CEO. Separate individuals may hold each of these positions, or a single person may hold two or all three positions. Some of the typical duties of the president are analogous to those of an ambassador, speaking for the firm's positions in discussions and negotiations with external parties.

The CEO generally has the ultimate responsibility for the firm's (a) major capital budgeting decisions, including strategic and logistical planning of capital investments and divestitures, and (b) financial structure, including financial planning, debt issuances and retirements, equity issuances and repurchase programs, dividend policy, and compensation policies. For task (a), many CEOs obtain assistance from the firm's COO (Chief Operating Officer). For task (b), a CEO obtains assistance from the CFO (Chief Financial Officer). In addition, given the increasing importance of gathering and processing information pertinent to both tasks, many firms also have a CIO (Chief Information Officer). Each of these officers has a staff of assistants.

Large firms have extensive management hierarchies. For instance, large manufacturing and retail firms have regional or divisional managers who are responsible for the firm's operations within their sphere, and for executing senior management's operational dictums. (Ah, the joys of middle management!)

The balance of responsibility for operations between senior and regional or divisional management defines the *steepness* of the firm's management hierarchy. A firm has a relatively *steep* hierarchy if the balance of responsibility is in the hands of senior management; a firm's hierarchy is relatively *flat* if middle managers make most of the decisions. Aspects of a firm's industry and operational structure probably largely dictate the steepness or flatness of the firm's hierarchy, but the CEO's philosophy and strategy also influence the firm's hierarchical structure.

Several strands of literature address determinants of a firm's hierarchical structure and its effect on the firm's efficiency, profitability, and financial policies. *First*, the literature on the economics of organizations is replete with theories of a firm's optimal hierarchy. Relevant papers include those by Aghion and Tirole (1997), Fumas (1993), Milgrom and Roberts (1990), Monks and Minow (1995), Radner (1992), Stiglitz (1975), Thakor (1990), and Williamson (1970, 1975, 1988, 1992, 1994). Recurring themes in this literature concern the effects of incentives and information costs on the optimal hierarchical structure.

Second, a substantial literature has developed recently to address important issues associated with capital budgeting decisions in a multidivisional firm. We refer to this literature collectively as *internal capital market theory*. We discuss this literature in detail in Chapter 13. Briefly, the senior management of a multidivisional firm generally faces a limit on available internal cash for pursuing corporatewide capital investments. Senior management generally instructs division managers to submit capital investment proposals. If the sum of the divisional managers' proposed spending exceeds the available cash, senior management must *ration* the cash by accepting only some proposed projects. Thus, division managers compete for cash allocations from headquarters. Theory on this subject addresses issues such as how this rationing is done and whether it results in an efficient allocation of the firm's internal capital. (Later, we discuss issues of managerial compensation in a multidivisional firm.)

8.3.2   Business Strategy

A firm's business strategy has three essential elements: (a) targeting specific product or service markets, (b) establishing goals in terms of market share and profits and (c) developing an effective competitive strategy against rivals in the industry. Most of our discussion of these issues, particularly as they relate to the firm's financial policies and strategies, was taken up in Chapter 7. Thus, here we simply reiterate that a firm's business strategy and size will largely determine both its operational and financial structures. For instance, we recall Williams's (1995) argument that the typical industry will consist of a few large, capital-intensive, highly profitable firms that have at least some debt in their capital structures, and many smaller, labor-intensive, less profitable firms that have little or no debt. In addition, a firm may adopt either (a) high leverage as a signal of their intent to compete aggressively (and to deter entry) or (b) a low-leverage strategy that allows it to squeeze out highly levered firms (i.e., the Long Purse Hypothesis.)

8.4   OPERATIONAL STRUCTURE

In this section, we discuss pertinent aspects of a firm's operational structure.

8.4.1   The Capital Budgeting Process

Capital investment decisions are arguably the most important decisions that a firm's management makes, because they determine the activities in which the firm engages to create value for shareholders. In an introductory finance course, we teach the *NPV* rule for capital budgeting decisions: *A firm should adopt any and all positive-NPV projects, where NPV is determined by discounting the project's expected cash flows at the firm's WACC.*

In an ideal market (Chapter 2), how a firm obtains the funds required to pursue positive-*NPV* projects (i.e., issuing equity or debt, or using retained earnings) is a matter of indifference, because all securities are sold at a fair price, and all capital structures yield the same WACC. Thus, capital budgeting and financing decisions are *separable*. In this setting, corporate governance focuses exclusively on monitoring management's ability to identify positive *NPV* projects, because financing decisions are perfunctory.

However, as we discussed in Chapters 3 through 7, costs associated with principal–agent conflicts and information asymmetry can adversely affect a firm's capital investment and financing decisions. For instance, (a) a self-serving manager may adopt negative *NPV* projects in the process of building his or her empire, (b) a firm with risky debt outstanding has an incentive to increase the riskiness of the firm's operations as a means of expropriating wealth from creditors, or (c) a firm with risky debt outstanding may forego a positive *NPV* project if only the firm's creditors benefit.

In Chapter 13, we discuss the problem of *delegation* in a multidivisional firm. Briefly, the problem is that a divisional manager may have better information about the profitability of a proposed project for the division than does the firm's senior management. If the divisional manager also has a self-serving incentive to build his or her own divisional empire, he or she may exaggerate the quality of a proposed project in order to secure greater capital funds from headquarters. Thus, senior managers must design incentive-compatible contracts with divisional managers that mitigate these problems.

8.4.2   The Advantages of Being Large

A recurring theme of the evidence presented in previous chapters is that large firms are generally more profitable and less risky. Unfortunately, we cannot provide a definitive answer to the question of why some firms become large and profitable and others do not.

However, most large firms have followed a similar path to success. *First*, these firms had innovative, strategy-wise founders, who were accompanied or succeeded by equally competent CEOs. *Second*, virtually all of the largest industrial firms provide products or services for which a national (or global) market exists, and each of these firms was among the first to enter the market for these products or services, at least on a national scale. By being a *first mover*, they had the opportunity to capture quasi monopoly profits (at least temporarily), and were able to exploit these opportunities effectively following an IPO, which gave them greater access to debt and equity markets for additional capital.

Third, to a certain extent *success breeds success* in that these firms exploit economies of scale (and, less often, of scope) to produce their products and services at a lower cost, which in turn allows them to realize greater profits and to squeeze out competitors. *Fourth* and finally, regarding financial policies and strategies, for the most part firms fund expansion using internal equity (i.e., retained earnings; review Figures 1-4a and 1-4b). According to the Pecking Order Hypothesis, this is the preferred method of financing growth under conditions of asymmetric information, which renders external capital, particularly external equity capital, costly. As such, a profitable firm has an inherent advantage in financing growth.

8.4.3   The Firm's Production Function

A firm's balance between capital and labor intensity depends on the industry in which it operates and its size (review Table 1-1 and Table 7-3). Firms in the transportation and utilities industries tend to be large and are by far the most capital-intensive firms in the U.S. market. Large industrial and manufacturing firms such as General Motors are also highly capital intensive by necessity. For such firms, economies of scale, and thus profitability, are closely related to capital intensity. At the other extreme, firms in service industries (e.g., Microsoft) tend to be more labor intensive. In Section 8.7, we examine variation in capital intensity within the context of our analyses of business and financial risk.

8.4.4   Internal Auditing: Quality and Cost Controls

The odyssey of a capital investment project only begins when the board approves expenditures. The process of building the necessary PP&E and developing details of marketing strategies requires on-going adjustments. In many firms, an internal auditing committee oversees the entire product development process. The internal auditing team provides valuable services in terms of ensuring that (a) all parties involved in a project are working on coordinated and timely bases; (b) original plans and specifications are followed, or alternatively that necessary changes are approved by senior management; (c) effective product quality and cost controls are instituted at every stage of the process; and (d) reports on all activities are accurate. Internal auditing and cost-control procedures are vital aspects of any firm's operations, especially a firm operating in a highly competitive product or service market.

8.5   FINANCIAL STRUCTURE

Next, we discuss the four elements of a firm's financial structure: (a) ownership structure, (b) financial planning and leverage, (c) dividend and stock repurchase policies; and (iv) executive compensation. Our discussion of executive compensation is the most extensive, so we devote a separate section to it.

8.5.1   Ownership Structure

From an agency-theoretic perspective, the crux of the ownership structure issue is a trade-off between the advantages of diffuse ownership (diversification, liquidity, and access to external capital) versus costs of managerial discretion. Thus, optimal (i.e., equity-value maximizing) ownership structures may vary across firms due to factors that affect this trade-off. For instance, the extent to which conflicts between shareholders and management can or cannot be resolved via combinations of monitoring (e.g., by the board of directors) and mechanisms to align managements' interests with shareholders' interests (e.g., incentives in the CEO's compensation contract) may vary substantially across firms, and these variations may induce variation in ownership structures across firms. Optimal ownership structure may also depend on the firm's industry and its size. Here we briefly discuss two studies on these issues.

One way to examine the trade-off noted above is to study the effect of incentive-alignment devices on a firm's market value. To the extent that managerial agency conflicts can be resolved via such devices, more of the benefits of ownership diffusion can be realized. Several researchers have focused on one such device, executive stock ownership. Specifically, they studied the relationship between the fraction of a firm's shares held by executives and the firm's market value. Studies by Morck, Shleifer, and Vishny (1988), and McConnell and Servaes (1990) found that as executive stock ownership increases from zero to about 3 percent to 5 percent, firm value (measured by Tobin's Q ratio) increases, as expected. However, as ownership increases beyond these levels, both studies find that firm value no longer increases. Perhaps at higher levels of insider ownership, the stock becomes less liquid, or management begins to distort the firm's investment policy.[2]

Another way to explore the trade-off is to determine whether the likelihood of top executive turnover is related to the firm's ownership structure. Denis, Denis, and Sarin (1997) examined this issue. They summarize their findings as follows: "Controlling for stock price performance, the probability of top executive turnover is negatively related to the ownership stake of officers and directors and positively related to the presence of an outside blockholder" (p. 193). In other words, top executives may be able to *entrench* themselves despite poor performance if they own a substantial number of the firm's shares. However, they are less able to do so if individual outside investors hold a substantial fraction of the firm's shares. The authors' first result may at least partially explain the lack of a positive relationship between insider share ownership and firm performance when such ownership becomes substantial, because at some point insiders can actually use their shares to leverage their entrenched position. The second result hints at a secondary trade-off: If outside blockholders are required to mitigate the negative value effects of management entrenchment, it is at the cost of less diffuse ownership and its attendant benefits.

8.5.2   Financial Planning and Leverage

We provided an in-depth discussion of the leverage decision in Chapter 6, so here we briefly discuss several additional factors that influence a firm's leverage.

Financial Planning
Financial planning addresses two issues: (a) the timing and amounts of future capital expenditures on projects, and the earnings they will produce, and (b) how a firm will finance its capital expenditures, debt payments, dividends, and stock repurchases

---

[2]We discussed McConnell and Servaes' analysis in detail in Chapter 5.

over time. Financial planning analysis reveals the firm's expected future needs (if any) for external debt or equity funds. In other words, the purpose of financial planning is to balance both the amounts and the timing of future outflows against net cash inflow from operations and proceeds from a debt or equity issue, where the last is the *plug figure* required for the balance. Thus, for example, a firm's leverage may vary over time depending on whether the firm has recently secured debt funds for capital investments because it lacked sufficient internal cash.

Leverage, Investment, and Firm Growth

Several studies have provided evidence that, across firms, there is a negative relationship between leverage and growth.[3] Lang, Ofek, and Stulz (1996) provided important insights into this relationship. They tested two competing arguments about the relationship. On one hand, a negative relationship between growth and leverage may be expected for either of two reasons: (a) based on Myers's underinvestment hypothesis (Chapter 3), debt financing can be costly for a firm with substantial future growth opportunities, and (b) a firm with profitable growth opportunities may have such opportunities because it possesses valuable private, strategic information, and thus information asymmetry prevents the firm from obtaining external financing, including debt financing, at a fair price. On the other hand, it seems odd that a firm that is expected to be highly profitable would have trouble obtaining debt financing if and when its current capital expenditures exceed its available internal funds.

To examine these issues, the authors conducted tests to determine whether the relationship between growth and leverage *differs* for firms that have high versus low Tobin's Q ratios, where a firm's Q ratio measures the extent to which the market recognizes future profitability of the firm's investments. The key to understanding their tests is in realizing that two firms can be observed to be growing at the same rate (measured by capital expenditures, sales growth, or employee hiring), and yet they may differ in terms of their Q ratio because one firm's management is pursuing highly profitable investments while the other firm's management is pursuing marginal or unprofitable investments (i.e., empire building).

The authors found a negative relationship between growth and leverage only for firms with low Q ratios. No such relationship is found for firms with high Q ratios. For the low Q ratio firms, the negative relationship suggests that for some of these firms, but not others, leverage is used as a *brake* on management's tendency to grow purposelessly. For the high Q ratio firms, the lack of a relationship suggests that such firms are free to choose their leverage without regard to problems (a) and (b)—that is, firms with highly profitable investment opportunities can freely tap the debt market for external financing that they might require over time.

All-Equity Firms

Lang, Ofek, and Stulz's analysis may explain the all-equity capital structures of some profitable, high-growth firms such as Microsoft. For many years Microsoft has been one of the most profitable firms in the *Business Services* industry, and certainly has exploited many profitable investment opportunities. Moreover, based on Microsoft's

---

[3]For example, Opler and Titman (1994) provide evidence that sales growth is lower for firms with high leverage, especially for firms in distressed industries.

consistently high market-to-book equity ratio (which is similar to the *Q* ratio), the market has clearly recognized its substantial potential for future profitable investments. Yet Microsoft consistently has had little or no debt in its capital structure. Of course, it is possible that Microsoft's no-debt policy simply reflects the personal preferences of its founder, CEO, and largest shareholder, William H. Gates. However, Microsoft's free cash flow has consistently exceeded its capital expenditures, suggesting that the firm simply has rarely needed to tap the debt markets for expansion.[4]

Why do other firms have no debt? Agrawal and Nagarajan (1990) explore this question by comparing the characteristics of publicly traded all-equity firms against a control sample of similar-size firms with leverage. They find that all-equity firms tend to be small firms, and differ in several respects from their levered counterparts: (a) All-equity firms tend to have fewer shareholders; (b) Managers of all-equity firms have larger stockholdings; (c) There is a greater family involvement in operations in all-equity firms; (d) Managerial ownership in all-equity firms is positively related to the extent of family involvement; and (e) All-equity firms have greater liquidity positions (i.e., they hold relatively more liquid assets such as cash and marketable securities). They interpret their findings as follows: "Overall, the evidence is consistent with the view that managerial choice of an all-equity capital structure is aimed at reducing the risk associated with large undiversifiable investments of personal wealth and family human capital in these firms" (pp. 1330–31).

This study highlights three important points with respect to closely held firms. *First*, ownership structure affects the use of leverage, in part because the owner or manager's risk tolerance is brought directly to bear on the firm's leverage decision. *Second*, in a closely held firm debt is not needed as a disciplining device to wield against a self-serving manager. *Third*, closely held, all-equity firms may be less valuable because their shares are less liquid, and perhaps also because they do not take advantage of the tax benefits (if any) of debt.

8.5.3   Dividend and Stock Repurchase Policies

We provide a detailed discussion of dividend and stock repurchase policies in Chapter 14. Hence, our discussion here consists only of a brief synopsis of the material covered there.

Dividend Policy

In an ideal capital market, it can be shown that a firm's dividend policy has no effect on the firm's market value. This is so because it does not affect the firm's ability to follow the basic *NPV* rule discussed earlier; the firm can at any time raise funds to pursue profitable projects by issuing debt or equity securities, as necessary, at a fair price. Thus, a traditional rule of thumb regarding dividend policy, that after all profitable projects are undertaken management should pay out all excess funds to shareholders as dividends, is rendered irrelevant in an ideal capital market (assuming that the firm at least invests idle cash in a fairly valued security such as the risk-free asset).

---

[4]In addition, Microsoft's capital intensity generally has been very low, indicating that it has a relatively small amount of collateralizable assets. In the years 1996 to 2000, the firm's ratio of PP&E/TA was 13.1 percent, 10.2 percent, 6.7 percent, 4.3 percent, and 1.6 percent, sequentially.

However, several real-world factors may affect a firm's dividend policy. For instance, dividends are not tax-deductible at the corporate level, and are fully taxable for recipient investors, so the firm's value-maximizing strategy may be to pay no dividends. In addition, in a world in which the issuance of debt or equity is costly (because of transaction costs or costs associated with principal–agent conflicts and information asymmetry), firms whose capital expenditures equal or exceed their income (or, more precisely, their *free cash flow*) may find that paying dividends is a costly endeavor, because it causes the firm to enter the external capital markets more frequently.

On the other hand, dividends can serve to mitigate principal–agent and information asymmetry problems. For instance, dividends discipline the firm's management, who may otherwise tend to use idle cash to engage in excessive consumption of perquisites or in empire building. Alternatively, with information asymmetry, dividends may serve as an effective *signal* of the firm's ability to generate earnings in the future. Finally, if the firm has debt outstanding, retaining idle cash essentially serves the creditors' interests, rather than shareholders' interest, by reducing the firm's default risk. Therefore, levered firms have an incentive to pay dividends as a means of expropriating creditors' wealth. Of course, this is why debt contracts generally restrict the borrowing firm's ability to pay dividends.

Stock Repurchase Plans

Stock repurchases are becoming more common among U.S. nonfinancial firms, and indeed have recently eclipsed dividends in terms of composite cash flow (review Figure 1-4b). When a firm's management decides to repurchase its own shares, it generally adopts a formal plan to do so, announces this plan to the public, and proceeds to repurchase shares over an extended period of time.

Firms adopt stock repurchase plans for several reasons. For instance, management may believe that the firm's shares are underpriced in the market, and that the shareholders' interest is served by purchasing shares, at least with available idle cash, both as an investment and perhaps to drive the stock price up. In addition, stock repurchases are a more flexible means (i.e., than dividends or debt payments) of disgorging excess cash and thereby reducing management's opportunities to engage in self-serving empire building. The flexibility of a stock repurchase plan also allows management to fine-tune its leverage over time, or to thwart a takeover attempt.

8.6 EXECUTIVE COMPENSATION, FINANCIAL POLICIES, AND FIRM PERFORMANCE

In Chapters 3 and 5, we briefly discussed the role of incentive devices in executive compensation contracts as a means of aligning managers' and shareholders' interests. Incentives generally include (a) a requirement that management own some of the firm's shares, (b) annual bonuses that are tied to the firm's earnings, and (c) grants of restricted stock or stock options that, by design, provide compensation that is strictly a function of future stock price performance.[5]

[5]Incentives are also often given to rank-and-file employees. Perhaps the most popular incentive device for employees at large is the Employee Stock Ownership Plan (ESOP). The following papers discuss ESOPs: Beatty (1995), Chang (1990), Chang and Mayers (1992), Chaplinsky and Niehaus (1990), Gordon and Pound (1990), Shackelford (1991), and Scholes and Wolfson (1990).

In this section, we (a) discuss problems with standard incentive devices in executive compensation contracts; (b) discuss the recent development of an alternative incentive device, the long-term performance plan; (c) discuss additional empirical evidence on the relationship between provisions in an executive's compensation contract and a firm's financial policies and performance; and (d) present details of the 1999 compensation of a sample of CEOs.

8.6.1   Problems with Incentive Devices

No performance incentive device is perfect. A basic problem is that the bulk of a typical executive's wealth is already tied to his or her compensation from the firm over time, even without a performance incentive. As such, an executive's personal portfolio is not well diversified. Thus, the executive's personal portfolio is heavily exposed to the firm's *total risk*, in sharp contrast to the typical diversified shareholder, who bears only the firm's *systematic risk*. Consequently, a risk-averse executive is personally motivated to reduce the firm's (a) *business risk*, by suboptimally reducing operating leverage or taking on only low-risk projects, and (b) *financial risk*, by reducing the firm's leverage below its optimal level, if such exists. (See Haubrich (1994) for discussion and analysis of this issue.)

In addition, the potential exists for performance incentives to *backfire* by inducing the executive to engage in other value-destroying activities, as Shleifer and Vishny (1997) explain:

> The more serious problem with high powered incentive contracts is that they create enormous opportunities for self-dealing for the managers, especially if these contracts are negotiated with poorly motivated boards of directors rather than with large investors. Managers may negotiate for themselves such contracts when they know that earnings or stock price are likely to rise, or even manipulate accounting numbers and investment policy to increase their pay. For example, Yermack (1997) finds that managers receive stock option grants shortly before good news announcements and delay such grants until after bad news announcements. His results suggest that options are often not so much an incentive device as a somewhat covert mechanism of self-dealing. (p. 745)

Nevertheless, the ubiquity of incentive devices in executive compensation contracts attests to their importance, and presumably their positive net worth. At the same time, however, both the observed cross-sectional variation in incentive devices and their complexity suggest that it is difficult to reconcile the interests of senior management and shareholders via terms in a compensation contract.

Earnings-Based Bonuses Versus Stock-Related Grants: ex post
Reward Versus ex ante *Motivation*

There is considerable debate over whether shareholders' interest can be better served by focusing management's attention on (a) earnings, by including an earning-based bonus provision in the CEO's compensation contract or (b) stock price performance, by granting stock or stock options. An earnings-based bonus plan may be better because it rewards the CEO for *realized* performance. On the other hand, stock and stock option grants focus directly on the shareholders' interest—to increase the market value of the firm's equity. As it turns out, both of these incentive devices are problematic.

An Incentive to Lie

Here we reprint an article by Michael C. Jensen, managing director of organizational strategy practice at the Monitor Group and a professor emeritus at Harvard Business School. He is also the founding editor of the *Journal of Financial Economics*. References to his academic work are replete throughout this text.

The end of the year brings out the creativity in managers as they seek to meet revenue targets and assure their bonuses. I once watched the management of a manufacturing company struggle to reach their year-end targets. In late fall, they announced a price increase of 10 percent effective January 2. Now it may be that a price increase was needed, but it was not in line with the competition, nor was it likely that January 2, of all dates, was the best time for the increase. A price increase on January 2 would, however, cause customers to order before year-end and thereby help managers reach their targets.

Sound familiar? Such budget-gaming is rife. Missing your target is a costly mistake for a manager and, as this example shows, managers will go to great lengths to avoid it. In quest of their targets, many managers take actions that benefit themselves at the cost of their companies.

Consider this: Managers at a heavy equipment manufacturer were so set on making their targets that they shipped unfinished industrial products from their plant in England to the Netherlands. At great cost and inconvenience, they finished assembling their product in a warehouse close to their customer. By doing so, they booked the sale in the necessary quarter, assured their bonus, and lowered their company's profit.

Budget systems are based on the premise that managers should be rewarded for achieving targets and punished for missing them. Tell a manager that he will get a bonus when targets are realized and two things will happen. First,

managers will attempt to set easy targets, and, second, once these are set, they will do their best to see that they are met even if it damages the company. The result: Almost every company uses a budget system that rewards people for lying and punishes them for telling the truth. Indeed, in some cases the more managers lie, the more money they make.

Managers, therefore, both game the realization of targets and conspire in the setting of targets. Here's how:

- **Gaming the realization of targets.** A manager who is in danger of just missing his target will accelerate shipments and revenues from next year into this year and move expenses from this year to next even though by doing so overall profits are reduced *two* years running. Similarly, managers have been known to load the distribution channel with more product than it can handle because shipping the product allows them to recognize revenues this year, rather than next. Managers do this even though they expect the product will be returned and even though they know that makes it harder to hit next year's target.

This can become fraudulent. In one case managers shipped fruit baskets that weighed exactly the same amount as their product and booked them as sales. In another, Informix, an Internet software company, and its auditor paid $142 million to settle lawsuits resulting from SEC charges that they fraudulently increased earnings by $295 million in the 1994–97 period. The SEC charged, among other things, that managers attempting "to meet or exceed the Company's internal revenue and earnings goals" moved revenues from one quarter to the previous quarter by backdating sales agreements.

Similarly Sabratek, a maker of health care equipment, has been sued for a series of alleged revenue enhancing frauds. Among the allegations are claims that the company delivered products to entities that had not ordered them, parked inventory, and stuffed the distribution channel.

- **Gaming the setting of targets.** Managers have information that is important in setting budget targets. However, once a reward system is tied to budgeting practices, managers have no interest in seeing such information accurately portrayed. Indeed it is in their best interest to underestimate what they can accomplish.

Such gaming starts a vicious cycle. If subordinates have an incentive to lie about what they cannot do, superiors are then led to lie about how much their subordinates can do. Now no one in the system can accurately estimate what truly can be done. The budget process has been corrupted and critical information has been hidden, destroyed or polluted.

Budgets play an important coordination role in companies. Once we establish a budget-targeting process that hides and destroys information, this coordinating role is severely hampered. Uncoordinated, chaotic actions that lead to high costs, low quality, missed opportunities, and dissatisfied customers are the result.

Almost no one in this system believes he is lying, and few would actually say they are doing wrong. Indeed, in most corporate cultures much of this is expected, even praised. Stopping it will not be easy.

To restore integrity to the process, we must begin not by telling managers to stop lying, although that would be laudable. Instead we must begin by eliminating the use of budget targets in compensation formulas. Only then can we be sure that we are paying people to perform, not to lie.

Source: "Why Pay People to Lie?" *The Wall Street Journal*, Jan. 8, 2001, p. A32. © 2001 Dow Jones & Company, Inc. Reprinted by permission.

Regarding annual earnings-based bonuses, the problem arises that the manager becomes fixated on the firm's short-term accounting earnings, potentially to the detriment of the firm's long-term profitability, on which the firm's share value ultimately depends. Another problem is that management can manipulate earnings, at least in the short run. Management has considerable discretion regarding reported earnings, such as switching depreciation methods, or recognizing or delaying revenues and write-downs. (Of course, their ability to manipulate earnings is limited because calculations must abide by generally accepted accounting principles [GAAP], and must pass the scrutiny of an independent auditor.)

A problem with stock-related grants is that the firm's stock price depends not only on the firm's performance, but also other factors that are beyond a manager's control, including marketwide factors that affect stock prices in general. In addition, if we recognize that, due to information asymmetry, the market's valuation of the firm's stock is partially dependent on information coming directly from the firm's management, then the potential exists for management to manipulate the firm's stock price (at least in the short run) by, for example, exaggerating the profit potential of existing or pending projects, or manipulating earnings to affect a change in the market price of the firm's shares.

8.6.2 Long-Term Performance Plans

Due to the cited problems associated with both annual earnings-based bonus plans and stock-related grants, alternative incentive devices have developed recently. Some involve a variation on one of these two incentive mechanisms, or a fairly complex *pack-*

age that includes several incentives. In addition, many firms have scrapped annual earnings-based bonuses and stock-related grants in favor of a *long-term performance plan*, which rewards executives according to the firm's earnings or stock-price performance over three to five years, rather than annually as is the case with the earnings-based bonus.

A positive effect of a long-term performance plan is that a manager may be more willing to jettison poorly performing assets even if doing so would adversely affect the firm's short-term earnings because of the write-down. Tehranian, Travlos, and Waegelein (1987) investigated this issue. They found that the market's reaction to an asset sale announcement is more favorable if the firm's management has a long-term performance plan than if it doesn't, and conclude that "long-term performance plans serve as an effective mechanism to motivate managers to make better decisions" (p. 933).

Kumar and Sopariwala (1992) investigated both the market's response to the announcement of the adoption of a long-term performance plan and subsequent changes in the adopting firm's performance. They summarize their results as follows: "This study reports significant positive excess returns around the announcement of performance plan adoption, which is consistent with the view that such plans would reduce the agency problem. In addition, this study finds an association between the adoption of long-term performance plans and subsequent growth in profitability, suggesting that long-term performance plans may have been successful in motivating an enhancement in the accounting measures of profitability used to reward managers under the plan. Finally, the excess returns around the announcement of performance plan adoption are found to be positively correlated with subsequent change in growth of earnings per share, the most commonly used accounting performance measure" (p. 561).

8.6.3 Relationships Between Executive Compensation and the Firm's Governance, Leverage, Investment Opportunities, and Performance

Relationships between a firm's executive compensation and its financial policies are complex. Contingencies involved in the executive compensation contract may both affect, and be affected by, other financial variables. As such, it is not easy to discern these relationships either theoretically or empirically. Nevertheless, researchers have been able to identify some regularities in contracts that are consistent with theory. Attention has focused on relationships between executive compensation and (a) internal governance structure, (b) leverage, (c) investment opportunities, (d) dividend policy, and (e) performance. Below we summarize several of these studies.

Executive Compensation, Board and Ownership Structures, and Performance
Core, Holthausen, and Larcker (1999) conducted an empirical analysis of the interactions among executive compensation, internal governance, and performance. Their sample included 495 observations of executive compensation for 205 U.S. firms in the early 1980s. One hypothesis they test is that, for firms with weak boards, executive compensation will be higher and firm performance lower, both because the boards of these firms have not resolved the agency problem of managerial discretion:

We find that measures of board . . . structure explain a significant amount of cross-sectional variation in CEO compensation . . . Moreover, the signs of the coefficients on the board . . . structure variables suggest that CEOs earn greater compensation when governance structures are less effective. We also find that the predicted component of compensation arising from these characteristics of board . . . structure has a statistically significant negative relation with subsequent firm operating and stock return performance. Overall, our results suggest that firms with weaker governance structures have greater agency problems; that CEOs at firms with greater agency problems receive greater compensation; and that firms with greater agency problems perform worse. (p. 371)

Mehran (1995) examined relationships between executive compensation and executive stock ownership, the percentage of board members that are outsiders, the percentage of shares held by insiders and outside blockholders, and firm performance:

An examination of the executive compensation structure of 153 randomly-selected manufacturing firms in 1979–1980 provides evidence supporting advocates of incentive compensation, and also suggests that the form rather than the level of compensation is what motivates managers to increase firm value. Firm performance is positively related to the percentage of equity held by managers and to the percentage of their compensation that is equity-based. Moreover, equity-based compensation is used more extensively in firms with more outside directors. Finally, firms in which a higher percentage of the shares are held by insiders or outside blockholders use less equity-based compensation. (p. 163)

The Form of Executive Compensation and Managerial Risk-Taking

Agrawal and Mandelker (1987) studied the effects of provisions in executive compensation contracts on a firm's financial policies. Their premise was that managers generally have a self-serving incentive to decrease the volatility of the firm. However, they hypothesize that managers who either hold shares in their firm or have stock options on the firm's equity are less likely to engage in risk-reducing activities because their compensation contract better aligns their interest with that of the firm's shareholders. In other words, we should observe that managers who hold shares or stock options are more willing to take actions that increase risk (assuming that such actions are in the shareholders' interest), while managers who do not hold shares or stock options bias toward risk-reducing actions.

To test this hypothesis, the authors identified firms that had taken one of two types of actions that could change the firm's volatility—a capital investment or a change in leverage. Then, for each firm that announced a capital investment, they examined the subsequent change in the variance of returns on the firm's stock, and divided the firms into two groups: those that subsequently experienced an *increase* in variance and those that subsequently experienced a *decrease* in variance. Similarly, they divided the leverage-changing firms into two groups: those firms that increased leverage and those that decreased leverage. Finally, they calculated the common stock and options holdings of managers in each group.

The authors summarize their empirical findings as follows:

> [First] we find that the common stock and options holdings of managers of firms for which the return variance increases upon an investment announcement are larger than for firms for which it decreases . . . Second, we find that the security holdings of managers of firms with a debt-equity ratio that increases are larger than those for whi ch this ratio decreases. . . Overall, our findings are consistent with the hypothesis that executive holdings of common stock and options in the firm have a role in reducing managerial incentive problems. (p. 836)

Executive Compensation, Ownership and Governance Structures, and Leverage

Mehran (1992) examined 170 U.S. manufacturing firms over 1973 to 1983 to test hypotheses from agency theory about the relationship between a firm's leverage and (a) executive incentive plans, (b) managerial equity investment, and (c) monitoring by the board and major shareholders. Consistent with theory, he found "a positive relationship between the firm's leverage ratio and 1) percentage of executives' total compensation in incentive plans, 2) percentage of equity owned by managers, 3) percentage of investment bankers on the board of directors, and 4) percentage of equity owned by large individual investors" (p. 539).

Investment Opportunities, Financial Policies, and Executive Compensation

Smith and Watts (1992) developed several hypotheses about relationships among a firm's investment opportunities, financial policies, and executive compensation:

1. [W]e predict that firms with more growth options . . . use stock options more frequently because management is more difficult to monitor in such firms (p. 269).
2. [T]he marginal product of investment decision makers is greater than the marginal product of supervisors and good decision makers are less numerous than good supervisors. Therefore, the larger the proportion of firm value represented by growth options, the greater the manager's compensation (p. 274).
3. Regulation restricts the manager's investment discretion and reduces the marginal product of the decision maker, so regulation should reduce the level of compensation (p. 274).
4. We suggest that managers' actions are less readily observable if the firm has more investment opportunities. It is difficult for shareholders or outside board members who do not have the manager's specific knowledge to observe all the investments from which the manager chooses. In general, the larger the proportion of firm value represented by growth options, the more likely that thc firm ties compensation to the effect of the manager's actions on firm value . . . Hence the larger the proportion of firm value represented by intangible investment opportunities, the more likely the firm is to have a formal incentive compensation plan . . . (pp. 275–76)
5. More growth options are likely to make accounting numbers poorer measures of performance . . . The impact of managers' actions on those opportunities is not accurately measured by accounting numbers. This effect should reduce the use of accounting-based incentive plans . . . (p. 276)

The authors examined industry-level data from 1965 to 1985. They document evidence consistent with the above hypotheses: "[F]irms with more growth options . . . have lower dividend yields . . . higher executive compensation, and greater use of stock-option plans. We also find that regulated firms have higher leverage, higher dividend yields, lower executive compensation, and less frequent use of both stock-option and bonus plans. Finally, we find that larger firms have higher dividend yields and higher levels of executive compensation . . . These relations imply associations among the corporate policies themselves" (p. 264).

Baber, Janakiraman, and Kang (1996) extended Smith and Watts's arguments to predict "stronger associations between compensation and performance for firms with greater investment opportunities. We also predict greater use of market-based, rather than accounting-based, performance indicators as a basis for incentive payments when investment opportunities are substantial components of firm value" (p. 297). Using data on 1,249 U.S. firms for 1992 to 1993, they find evidence consistent with these predictions.

Evidence on the Pay-Performance Relationship

Jensen and Murphy (1990) analyzed the sensitivity of CEO compensation (including pay, options, and stockholdings) and firm performance. They estimate that, on average, CEO wealth changes by only $3.25 for every $1,000 change in shareholder wealth. These results are very surprising, suggesting that CEOs have very little personal incentive to increase shareholder wealth. These results draw into question the basic rationale behind compensation plans, that they should contain performance incentives that align managers' and shareholders' interests. The authors suggest that the argument may fail because executives are risk averse and may therefore generally refuse to accept the risk attendant to such incentives.

Jensen and Murphy's results may have been affected by the fact that they used data on *ex post* compensation, rather than the more complex *ex ante* terms in executive compensation contracts. Kole (1997) addressed this issue by examining shareholder-authorized compensation arrangements, which provide the critical *ex ante* perspective. He emphasizes the flexibility that a firm's board (or compensation committee) has in negotiating a contract with senior management: "For example, when an executive receives an option to purchase 100 shares of his employer's common stock, that right has many facets, including the exercise price, the terms of the option's exercise schedule, and the award of associated appreciation rights or restrictions on the disposition of the underlying stock" (p. 80).

8.6.4 Empirical Evidence on 1999 Compensation of Industrial-Firm CEOs

For a practical perspective on CEO compensation, we present and briefly analyze data on the compensation of CEOs at 88 large U.S. industrial firms for their fiscal year 1999. All 88 firms were included among the S&P Industrials. We obtained 1999 CEO compensation data for each firm from SEC filings, which report, among other details, four categories of CEO compensation: (a) *salary*, (b) *bonus*, (c) *long-term compensation*, and (d) grants of restricted stock and stock options, denoted as *S/O grants*.

The details are displayed in Table 8-2. For each firm in the sample we show (a) the firm's name, (b) its TA, debt ratio, and market-to-book equity ratio at fiscal year-end 1998,

TABLE 8-2 CEO Compensation for 88 Firms in the S&P Industrials Index, Fiscal Year 1999

| Company | 1998 Values | | | 1999 Performance (%) | | CEO | Compensation Items ($ million) | | | | |
| | | | | | | | Direct Compensation | | | S/O Grants* | Total Compensation |
	TA ($ billion)	D/TA	MEQ/BEQ	ROE	Stock Return		Salary	Bonus	Long Term		
Air Prod. & Chem.	7.5	36.0	2.4	15.2	0.3	Wagner	0.90	0.47	0.00	2.55	3.92
Alberto-Culver	1.1	16.4	2.5	15.2	-0.1	Bernick	1.35	0.63	0.00	0.00	1.98
Alcoa	17.5	20.0	2.3	16.8	125.9	O'Neill	0.95	2.00	0.01	32.12	35.08
Amerada Hess	7.9	33.6	1.7	14.4	15.3	Hess	1.00	1.15	0.00	0.00	2.15
Anheuser-Busch	12.5	37.8	7.4	35.8	9.7	Busch III	1.13	2.25	0.02	10.74	14.14
Applied Materials	4.9	12.7	4.1	16.7	158.9	Morgan	0.78	1.27	0.00	0.00	2.05
ADM	13.8	31.9	1.7	4.5	-15.3	Andreas	2.44	0.00	0.00	0.60	3.04
Ashland	6.1	26.8	1.6	13.2	-25.4	Chellgren	0.83	0.76	0.03	3.60	5.23
AT&T	59.6	11.3	5.2	4.3	2.4	Armstrong	1.40	2.26	0.68	0.00	4.34
Atlantic Richfield	25.2	28.3	2.8	15.5	37.3	Bowlin	0.98	1.56	1.25	0.00	3.79
Auto. Data Proc.	5.2	8.4	6.5	17.4	21.6	Weinbach	0.66	0.49	0.00	1.81	2.96
Avon	2.4	10.5	40.7	-74.5	-24.1	Jung	0.67	0.51	1.17	0.00	2.35
Baker Hughes	7.8	35.5	1.8	1.7	21.7	Lukens	0.83	0.00	0.00	0.00	0.83
BellSouth	39.4	30.9	6.0	23.3	-4.6	Ackerman	1.10	2.40	1.34	8.95	13.79
Bestfoods	6.4	41.3	16.6	83.0	0.8	Shoemate	0.98	2.20	4.97	3.21	11.36
Boeing	36.7	19.0	2.5	20.1	28.8	Condit	1.09	1.90	0.00	1.43	4.43
Burlington Res.	5.9	32.8	2.1	0.0	-6.3	Shackouls	0.83	0.62	0.11	0.00	1.55
Campbell Soup	5.6	45.6	27.7	308.1	-16.9	Morrison	0.88	0.00	0.00	9.22	10.10
Caterpillar	25.1	49.6	3.2	17.3	4.7	Barton	0.94	0.44	0.50	3.12	4.99
Chevron	36.5	20.7	3.2	11.7	7.5	Derr	1.35	1.97	1.27	0.00	4.58
Cisco Systems	8.9	0.0	14.0	17.9	94.6	Chambers	0.31	0.64	4.01	120.76	121.70
Clorox	3.0	35.9	9.1	15.7	13.1	Sullivan	0.88	1.19	4.01	0.00	6.07
Coca-Cola Co.	19.1	26.9	19.7	25.6	-12.1	Ivester	1.35	0.00	0.00	0.00	1.35
Colgate-Palmolive	7.7	35.9	13.2	50.5	41.6	Mark	1.27	2.93	0.00	5.54	9.74
Compaq Computer	23.1	0.0	6.2	3.8	-35.4	Capellas	0.85	1.00	4.99	0.00	6.84
ConAgra	12.1	28.0	4.4	13.9	-8.3	Rohde	0.95	0.92	1.66	0.00	3.54
Corning	5.0	24.1	6.9	20.7	189.5	Ackerman	0.82	1.46	0.08	0.00	2.35
Crane	1.5	28.2	3.2	17.8	-30.5	Evans	0.73	0.55	0.00	0.00	1.27
Cummins Engine	4.5	27.0	1.1	11.2	39.4	Henderson	0.91	0.84	0.09	1.89	3.74
Deere	18.0	45.1	2.0	5.8	4.2	Becherer	1.03	0.00	0.00	2.68	3.71
Donnelley (R.R.)	3.8	28.0	4.5	27.4	-41.8	Davis	0.81	0.86	0.00	0.00	1.68
Dover	3.6	28.8	4.2	19.9	25.3	Reece	0.85	1.10	0.43	0.00	2.38
Dow Chemical	23.8	24.7	2.7	15.9	51.5	Stavropoulos	0.99	1.56	0.06	3.73	6.34
DuPont	38.5	28.9	4.4	1.7	27.1	Holliday Jr.	1.00	1.80	0.00	0.00	2.80
Eaton	5.7	26.9	2.5	23.5	5.0	Hardis	0.95	1.35	0.00	1.14	3.43
Fluor	5.0	14.6	1.9	6.6	5.0	Carroll Jr.	0.90	1.00	0.03	1.31	3.24
FMC	4.2	35.6	2.5	29.0	2.3	Burt	0.88	0.37	1.19	0.00	2.45
Fort James	7.8	49.9	8.4	31.0	-30.2	Marsh	0.99	0.70	0.13	4.76	6.58
Freeport-McMoRan	4.2	58.6	-7.0	-65.8	102.4	Moffett	1.00	2.75	0.91	0.00	4.66
General Dynamics	4.6	6.8	3.4	27.8	-8.1	Chabraja	0.84	1.55	2.89	0.00	5.28
General Electric	355.9	49.2	8.6	25.2	53.5	Welch Jr.	3.33	10.00	31.33	24.83	69.48
General Mills	4.1	56.0	74.4	-212.7	1.7	Sanger	0.69	1.05	0.00	0.86	2.60
Gillette	11.9	27.3	11.8	42.2	-12.8	Hawley	0.98	0.48	0.00	0.00	1.45
Goodrich. (B.F.)	4.2	30.2	1.7	13.1	-20.7	Burner	0.82	1.03	0.32	0.00	2.17
Harnischfeger	2.8	40.2	0.6	34.4	-88.0	Hanson	0.65	0.00	0.00	0.00	0.65
Hershey Foods	3.4	37.7	8.5	41.9	-22.3	Wolfe	0.78	0.00	0.09	0.00	0.87

Hewlett-Packard	33.7	9.8	3.6	17.0	24.1	Fiorina	0.29	0.37	0.00	0.00	0.65
Honeywell Intl.	15.6	22.4	4.7	17.9	31.8	Bonsignore	1.09	2.00	25.35	0.00	28.43
Ikon Office Solutions	5.7	51.4	0.9	2.3	50.7	Forese	0.75	0.75	0.00	2.58	4.08
Ingersoll-Rand	8.3	34.7	2.9	17.7	17.9	Henkel	0.58	1.00	0.00	3.65	5.23
IBM	86.1	34.2	8.8	38.0	17.5	Gerstner Jr.	2.00	7.20	5.25	0.00	14.45
ITT Industries	5.0	15.2	2.9	21.2	−14.5	Engen	1.04	1.49	0.00	0.51	3.04
Kellogg	5.1	44.3	15.5	41.6	−7.2	Gutierrez	0.64	0.46	0.00	0.96	2.06
Kimberly-Clark	11.7	23.1	7.3	32.8	22.4	Sanders	0.95	1.90	0.00	6.44	9.29
Lockheed Martin	28.7	37.9	2.7	11.6	−46.9	Coffman	1.26	0.00	0.10	2.84	4.19
Lucent Technologies	26.7	17.4	16.5	25.5	87.6	McGinn	1.10	3.40	3.90	0.00	8.40
Micron Technology	4.7	22.0	1.8	−1.7	229.1	Appleton	0.61	3.04	0.00	0.00	3.64
Microsoft	22.4	0.0	17.1	28.3	66.4	Gates	0.40	0.22	0.00	0.00	0.62
Minn. Min. & Mfg.	14.2	21.9	4.8	28.0	41.2	DeSimone	1.05	1.72	1.34	0.00	4.11
Motorola	28.7	19.3	3.0	5.0	142.4	Galvin	1.28	1.90	13.15	0.00	16.33
Nabisco Group	28.9	36.2	1.2	7.8	−41.3	Kilts	0.90	1.14	7.29	0.00	9.33
Navistar Intl.	6.2	34.3	1.8	42.3	101.2	Horne	0.83	1.70	0.00	1.22	3.76
Occidental Petroleum	15.3	44.8	1.9	15.9	34.4	Irani	1.20	1.62	2.06	0.00	4.88
Paccar Petroleum	6.8	43.8	1.8	27.7	13.5	Pigott	0.94	0.83	0.24	1.10	3.11
Parker Hannifin	3.5	22.1	2.5	16.7	22.2	Collins	0.99	0.70	1.93	0.88	4.50
Philip Morris	59.9	24.5	8.0	50.1	−54.4	Bible	1.63	4.40	0.29	13.26	19.58
Pitney Bowes	7.7	38.9	10.9	40.6	−25.6	Critelli	0.85	0.93	1.19	0.00	2.96
PPG Industries	7.4	23.3	3.5	18.3	10.4	LeBoeuf	0.80	0.90	0.01	4.50	6.21
Praxair	8.1	40.4	2.4	19.3	44.5	Lichtenberger	0.89	0.80	2.18	0.00	3.87
Procter & Gamble	31.0	26.0	10.1	30.9	−0.7	Jager	1.32	0.82	0.57	0.00	2.70
Ralston Purina	5.6	46.9	8.0	40.0	−3.4	McGinnis	0.65	0.83	0.69	2.14	4.31
Rockwell Intl.	7.2	14.8	2.1	22.1	128.3	Davis Jr.	0.78	1.75	0.03	3.61	6.16
Safeway	11.4	43.7	9.7	23.8	−41.3	Burd	0.75	1.01	0.00	0.00	1.76
Sara Lee	11.0	28.0	14.2	93.1	−17.3	Bryan	0.96	1.46	0.29	17.87	20.59
SBC Comm.	45.1	31.4	8.2	24.6	−7.5	Whitacare Jr.	1.43	6.00	4.15	7.12	18.70
Stanley Works	1.9	29.3	3.7	20.4	11.9	Trani	0.93	1.40	1.68	0.00	4.01
Sun Microsystems	5.7	0.8	4.7	21.4	217.1	McNealy	0.12	3.62	0.00	0.00	3.74
Sunoco	4.8	20.9	2.2	6.4	−32.6	Campbell	0.84	0.13	0.00	1.26	2.23
Sysco	3.8	27.1	6.3	25.4	18.1	Lindig	0.80	0.90	0.00	0.82	2.52
Temple-Inland	16.0	31.4	1.7	9.9	13.5	Grum	0.70	0.70	0.00	0.00	1.40
Texaco	28.6	25.5	2.5	9.8	5.7	Bijur	0.95	1.02	2.17	0.00	4.13
Texas Instruments	11.3	11.5	5.1	15.2	126.3	Engibous	0.74	2.20	0.00	0.00	2.94
Textron	13.7	43.2	3.9	14.3	2.7	Campbell	1.00	1.40	2.18	19.73	24.31
Union Carbide	7.3	30.5	2.3	11.9	59.8	Joyce	0.97	0.94	0.02	4.43	6.36
Unisys	5.6	20.8	91.1	24.9	−7.3	Weinbach	1.30	1.32	0.00	0.00	2.62
United Technologies	18.4	11.9	5.6	11.4	21.0	David	1.20	2.20	0.00	0.00	3.40
USX	14.5	25.1	2.2	13.6	−15.4	Usher	1.24	1.40	0.29	0.00	2.93
Weyerhaeuser	12.8	37.1	2.2	8.6	45.1	Rogel	0.99	1.50	0.00	2.24	4.73

*S/O Grants are grants of restricted stock and stock options; values are estimates.
Source of Compensation Data: SEC filings of each firm.

(c) its ROE and stock return for fiscal 1999, (d) the CEO's name, and (e) the CEO's salary, bonus, long-term compensation, S/O grants, and total compensation for fiscal 1999.

A total of 14 CEOs had total compensation exceeding $10 million, led by Cisco Systems's John T. Chambers ($121.7 million), GE's John F. Welch Jr. ($69.5 million), and Alcoa's Paul H. O'Neill ($35.1 million). In terms of TA, Cisco Systems was relatively small among the firms in the sample (TA = $8.9 billion), GE was the largest (TA = $335.9 billion), and Alcoa was about average in size (TA = $17.5 billion). However, all of these firms reported good ROE results in fiscal 1999 (17.9, 25.2, and 16.8 percent, respectively), and all three firms realized high stock returns in fiscal 1999 (94.6, 53.5, and 125.9 percent, respectively).

At the other extreme, five CEOs had total compensation of less than $1 million each, including the CEOs of Hershey Foods, Baker Hughes, Hewlett-Packard, Harnischfeger, and Microsoft. Of these firms, only Microsoft realized high values of both ROE (28.3 percent) and stock return (66.4 percent) in fiscal 1999. Apparently Microsoft's CEO, William H. Gates, already the wealthiest person in the world, didn't need the money.

In Table 8-3, we provide several statistical analyses of the compensation figures and related items for the firms listed in Table 8-2. The first row of statistics applies to all 88 firms. On the whole it was a good year for these firms, as the average values of ROE and stock return were 19.9 percent and 22.5 percent, respectively. Consequently, it was a very good year for the CEOs, as the average values of salary, bonus, long-term compensation, S/O grants, and total compensation were $0.98 million, $1.44 million, $1.54 million, $3.89 million, and $7.86 million, respectively. Interestingly, the average value of S/O grants accounts for almost half (49.5 percent) of average total compensation. This result not only reflects the general good performance of these firms in fiscal 1999, but also attests to the relative importance S/O grants.

A cursory analysis of the figures for individual firms in Table 8-2 indicates that the sampled firms vary substantially in size, based on TA. In addition, and as we would expect, compensation tends to be positively related to firm size. Thus, for Table 8-3 we adjust for the relationship between firm size and compensation by calculating compensation items for each firm as a percent of the firm's TA, and reporting the averages of these percentages in the final five columns of the table. We also sorted firms into two groups according to firm size and show results for each group. The TA-adjusted figures in the first row show that executive compensation is generally a tiny percentage of a firm's TA. The averages are 0.013 percent for salary, 0.016 percent for bonus, 0.011 percent for long-term compensation, 0.036 percent for S/O grants, and 0.076 percent for total compensation.

The second set of rows in the table reflects our sorting of firms by TA. All 88 firms are included in the S&P Industrials, and all are large relative to the many smaller firms in the U.S. market—indeed, all 88 firms had TA at the end of fiscal year 1998 in excess of $1 billion. With this caveat, we designated a firm as *large* if its fiscal year-end 1998 TA exceeded $10 billion, and as *small* otherwise. As expected, the dollar values of the individual components of compensation are directly related to firm size; average total compensation figures are $6.24 million and $9.79 million for the small and large firms, respectively.

Two additional points emerge from the sort. *First*, average S/O compensation as a percentage of total compensation was greater for the small firms (61.5 percent) than for the large firms (40.2 percent). Of course, our sample is relatively small and covers only one year, so we cannot draw firm conclusions. Nevertheless, these differences suggest

TABLE 8-3 Average Values for Fiscal 1999 CEO Compensation and Related Items for 88 Industrial Firms Listed in Table 8-2

	Number of Firms	1988 Values			1999 Performance (%)		Compensation Items ($ million)					Percent of 1998 TA				
		TA ($ billion)	D/TA	MEQ/BEQ	ROE	Stock Return	Salary	Bonus	Long Term	S/O Grants*	Total	Salary	Bonus	Long Term	S/O Grants*	Total
All Firms	88	18.3	28.5	7.6	19.9	22.5	0.98	1.44	1.54	3.89	7.86	0.013	0.016	0.011	0.036	0.076
Sort by Firm Size																
Small (TA < $10 billion)	48	5.3	29.7	8.9	19.6	26.2	0.83	1.06	0.51	3.84	6.24	0.020	0.023	0.013	0.049	0.105
Large (TA > $10 billion)	40	33.9	27.1	6.0	20.4	18.0	1.16	1.90	2.79	3.94	9.79	0.005	0.007	0.009	0.019	0.041
Sort by Debt Ratio																
D/TA < 20%	20	16.4	11.0	7.5	12.0	58.4	0.84	1.52	1.34	8.08	11.78	0.015	0.019	0.010	0.083	0.126
20% < D/TA < 40%	51	15.3	29.3	6.6	21.7	13.4	1.03	1.41	1.25	2.06	5.75	0.013	0.015	0.012	0.018	0.058
D/TA > 40%	17	29.5	46.7	10.5	24.2	7.4	1.02	1.46	2.66	4.42	9.56	0.012	0.013	0.011	0.035	0.071
Sort by Market-to-Book Equity Ratio																
(MEQ/BEQ) < 4.0	46	12.3	30.0	2.1	13.1	23.1	0.95	1.06	0.91	2.23	5.17	0.016	0.016	0.009	0.021	0.062
(MEQ/BEQ) > 4.0	42	24.8	26.9	13.6	27.4	21.8	1.01	1.86	2.24	5.70	10.80	0.011	0.015	0.013	0.053	0.091
Sort by ROE																
ROE < 10%	19	16.5	29.9	7.8	-14.5	26.1	0.98	1.11	1.61	0.61	4.31	0.011	0.014	0.009	0.008	0.042
ROE > 10%	69	18.8	28.1	7.5	29.4	21.5	0.98	1.53	1.53	4.79	8.83	0.014	0.016	0.012	0.043	0.085
Sort by Stock Return																
R < 10%	45	14.7	30.7	10.4	23.2	-14.8	1.02	1.09	0.90	2.63	5.64	0.015	0.013	0.008	0.023	0.059
R > 10%	43	22.1	26.3	4.6	16.6	61.5	0.94	1.81	2.22	5.20	10.17	0.011	0.019	0.014	0.050	0.094

*S/O Grants are grants of restricted stock and stock options; values are estimates.

that the CEOs of the smaller firms either (a) desire relatively more risky, stock-related compensation or (b) are *required* by their boards to accept incentive compensation.

Second, total compensation as a percent of TA was more than twice as high for small firms (0.105 percent) as for large firms (0.041 percent). This differential may reflect several factors, including (a) economies of scale in CEO compensation, (b) greater bargaining power of the CEOs of smaller firms, (c) the responsibilities of CEOs at smaller firms are relatively greater, or (d) the job of CEO is more risky in smaller firms.

The third set of rows in the table display the results of our sorting of each firm into one of three groups according to its fiscal year-end 1998 debt ratio: D/TA < 20 percent (20 firms); 20 percent < D/TA < 40 perent (51 firms); and D/TA > 40 percent (17 firms). ROE is directly related to leverage, but stock returns are inversely related to leverage. Meanwhile, the CEOs of the low-leverage firms had the highest average total compensation, whether this is measured in dollars or as a percent of TA. This result is driven entirely by the higher average value of S/O grants that the CEOs of the low-leverage firms received, which in turn may be due, at least in part, to the higher stock returns that these firms realized on average.

The fourth set of rows in the table display the results of a market-to-book equity sort. Here we sorted each firm into one of two groups according to whether the fiscal year-end 1998 value of this ratio was less than or greater than 4.0. Firms with higher market-to-book equity ratios were twice as large as those with lower ratios, and their average ROE was also twice as high. However, the high-ratio firms had slightly lower stock returns, on average. In any event, average total compensation of the CEOs of the high-ratio firms ($10.80 million) was about twice as high as that for the low-ratio firms ($5.17 million), with S/O grants accounting for most of the difference. As a percentage of TA, these differences are somewhat smaller, but still indicate that the CEOs of the high-ratio firms garnered higher compensation.

Next, we gauged the effect of firm performance on CEO compensation via two separate sorts. We sorted each firm into one of two groups according to its ROE: ROE > 10 percent or ROE < 10 percent. We also sorted firms according to whether their stock return was less than or greater than 10 percent. The results of these sorts are displayed in the final two sets of rows in the table.

Regarding the ROE sort, the ROE of 69 of the 88 firms exceeded the 10 percent cutoff value. However, the average stock return for the high-ROE firms, 21.5 percent, was actually slightly *lower* than that for the low-ROE firms, 26.1 percent. Again, we cannot make strong conclusions from such a limited sample. However, the results suggest a complex relationship exists between contemporaneous accounting returns and stock returns. For instance, even though ROE was low for the low-ROE group, results may have exceeded the market's *expectations*. Alternatively, market expectations may have been met, on average, for both groups, and yet the higher average return for the low-ROE group may simply reflect that the market *priced* the stocks of this group to provide a higher expected return, perhaps because the low-ROE stocks were riskier *ex ante*. In any case, such phenomena are important because CEO compensation is generally a function of accounting earnings or stock price performance.

The average total compensation for the CEOs of the high-ROE group was roughly twice that for the low-ROE group, whether measured in dollars ($8.83 million versus $4.31 million) or as a percentage of TA (0.085 percent versus 0.042 percent). Similarly, the average total compensation for the CEOs of the high-stock return group was roughly twice that of the low-stock return group, whether measured in dollars ($10.17 million versus $5.64 million) or as a percent of TA (0.094 percent versus 0.059 percent). These results indicate that, in determining CEO compensation, firm performance did indeed matter for this sample of firms in fiscal year 1999.

8.7 RISKS, PERFORMANCE, AND CONTINGENCIES

In this section, we discuss items in the final level of Figure 8-1: risks, performance, and contingencies.

8.7.1 Business Risk and Financial Risk as Determinants of Equity Risk

Business Risk

Once management decides on its business strategy and operational structure, the riskiness of the firm's operating earnings, that is, its *business risk*, is well defined. An important aspect of a firm's business strategy that determines its business risk is the industry in which the firm has chosen to operate. Two aspects of a firm's operational structure influence its business risk: size and capital intensity. Regarding firm size, a large firm has two advantages that reduce its business risk. *First*, a large firm is generally more diversified geographically (in terms of its customer base, alternative suppliers, employees, plants, etc.). *Second*, a large firm generally enjoys a quasi monopoly status within its industry by virtue of economies of scale. Although this status will not insulate the firm from a decline in aggregate demand for the industry's products, it does blunt competition from smaller, less efficient industry rivals.

Regarding capital intensity, a traditional argument is that a firm's business risk is positively related to its capital intensity, or *operating leverage*. The argument is that a capital-intensive firm is laden with substantial fixed costs, and therefore its operating earnings are more sensitive to changes in revenues. In contrast, a labor-intensive firm has lower business risk because it is able to adjust its work force on a relatively short-term basis in response to changes in revenues. However, the relationship between capital intensity and business risk may be difficult to discern empirically, because the typical capital-intensive firm is larger, and therefore will enjoy the business risk-reducing effects of large size discussed above. Thus, the question arises as to which effects dominate (i.e., firm size versus capital intensity) in determining a firm's business risk. In the next section, we present empirical evidence on this issue.

Business Risk, Financial Risk, Leverage, and Equity Risk

The riskiness of the firm's *equity* depends not only on the firm's business risk, but also on the firm's financial leverage, because financial leverage works to *concentrate* the firm's business risk on a smaller equity base. The term *financial risk* is used to refer either to a firm's risk of bankruptcy or to the effects of leverage on earnings and stock-price volatility. For a given set of risky assets and operations, a firm's financial risk, under either definition, increases with its financial leverage.

A firm's business risk and financial leverage work *in tandem* to determine the risk of the firm's equity. Therefore, if management is focused on the interest of the firm's equityholders, and the riskiness of the firm's equity is an important aspect of their interest, we would expect that management's leverage decision would depend at least in part on the firm's business risk. Specifically, it is reasonable to suppose that firms that have higher business risk will tend to have lower leverage. Consider the scenario in which a firm's management initially decides on its optimal business strategy and operational structure, which defines its business risk, and then considers its leverage. If management wishes to limit the firm's equity risk to some tolerable level, management must employ less financial leverage when its business risk is higher. The empirical analysis in the next section also addresses this issue.

8.7.2 Cost of Capital, Profitability, and Share Value

In the traditional capital budgeting paradigm, a firm's management identifies projects whose expected internal rate of return (IRR) exceeds the firm's WACC. Except for odd cases, this criterion is equivalent to the criterion that a project must have a positive *NPV*. Only such projects are truly *profitable* because they increase share value. Next, we briefly discuss some problems with this paradigm. (We discuss other problems in Chapter 13.)

Determining the IRR of a project is not a simple matter. Although the initial capital expenditure required for a project may be relatively easy to estimate, it is often more difficult to estimate a project's expected future cash inflows, in terms of both amounts and timing. Estimating future cash flows is rendered even more complex by the ever-present issue of future *contingencies*. For instance, if initial feedback on the project's profitability is favorable, additional capital expenditures may be warranted. On the other hand, if cash flows are disappointing, the project may be abandoned and the assets liquidated or redeployed.

Estimating the firm's WACC is also problematic. It is likely that a firm's WACC depends on its business risk and quite possibly on its capital structure (though we might reasonably assume that the firm is aware of the capital structure that yields its minimum WACC, if such exists). In addition, a firm's WACC at any point in time depends on the state of the economy, as we noted earlier.

A basic question emerges from this discussion: Do firms generally adopt projects whose IRRs exceed their respective WACCs, and if so, by how much? In a recent paper, Fama and French (1999) addressed this question. They examined composite data on the investments and returns on U.S. nonfinancial firms over the years 1950 to 1996, treating the entire nonfinancial corporate sector as a single investment project. Their estimate of the average real aggregate WACC over this period is 5.95 percent, and the average real IRR on aggregate investment, 7.38 percent. Thus, according to their estimates, firms had generally invested in projects whose IRRs exceeded their WACC by (a mere?) 1.43 percent.

8.7.3 Contingencies

Managers regularly encounter *contingencies* as a result of past performance, whether the performance has been good or disappointing. In the final panel of Figure 8-1, we identify four classes of contingencies: (a) *growth opportunities* (expansion in existing product or service markets; opportunities to invest in other product or service markets); (b) *restructuring* (e.g., scaling back or abandoning existing product or service lines); (c) *merger, acquisition,* or *buyout*; and (d) *bankruptcy* or *liquidation*.

Ultimately, decisions related to these contingencies, rather than the profitability of the firm's original projects, are likely to determine the bulk of the firm's future profitability and shareholder value. For this reason, it is critical that management's and shareholders' interests are aligned. If they are not, decisions related to these contingencies will be suboptimal. For instance, as we noted above, many firms may be observed to be growing, but only some of these firms are pursuing *profitable* growth opportunities, while in others management is engaged in self-serving empire building.

Two hallmarks of the development of U.S. firms in the 1980s and 1990s have been improvements in (a) internal corporate governance and (b) the alignment of management's and shareholders' interests via incentive devices in executive compensation contracts. This has led not only to more disciplined pursuit of profitable growth opportunities per se, but more specifically an increase in *focus*, defined loosely as the pursuit of core competencies instead of empire building. This increase in focus is manifest in the recent proliferation of spin-offs, equity carve-outs, and related transactions, which we discuss in Chapter 17.

Mergers and acquisitions are important contingencies for both acquiring firms and targets. For an acquiring firm, an acquisition may allow it to gain critical economies of scale in its existing product market or to pursue a profitable opportunity in a complementary product market. For a target, being acquired generally results in handsome gains to shareholders relative to the status quo, whether the firm has been profitable or is in financial distress. Alternatively, a public firm's management (or other parties), generally with the help of a lender, may consider buying all of the firm's equity and taking the firm private. (We discuss mergers, acquisitions, and buyouts in Chapter 16.)

Finally, bankruptcy and liquidation are generally contingencies of last resort for a company that is in financial distress. By declaring bankruptcy, the firm gets protection from its creditors and an opportunity to reemerge after reorganizing its assets and financial structure. In liquidation, the firm's assets are sold, the proceeds distributed to the firm's claimants on a priority basis, and the firm ceases to exist. (We discuss financial distress, bankruptcy, reorganization, and liquidation in Chapters 17 and 18.)

8.8 EMPIRICAL ANALYSES OF RISK

In this section, we empirically examine determinants of a firm's risk. Our examination is guided by the flow of decisions and consequences shown in Figure 8-1. The data for this year-end 1999 analysis includes subsets of the firms in the eight major U.S. industries identified in Chapter 7. Here, the number of firms in each industry is smaller because we required that each firm in the sample existed as a publicly traded firm throughout the 1990s; that is, that they are *seasoned* firms.

We explored determinants of and relationships among (a) business risk, which we measure by the annualized standard deviation of a firm's quarterly return on assets, $\sigma(ROA)$; (b) capital intensity, measured by PP&E/TA; (c) leverage, calculated as D/TA; and (d) equity risk, measured as the annualized standard deviations of a firm's quarterly ROE or stock returns, denoted as $\sigma(ROE)$ and $\sigma(R)$, respectively. For each firm, we calculated values of these variables using quarterly data for 1993 to 1999.

In structuring the analysis, we assume that a firm's most fundamental strategic decisions involve (a) the industry in which it operates and (b) its size. Therefore, we sorted firms into groups by industry and size. We examine the extent to which cross-sectional variation in firms' capital intensities is explained by these two factors by calculating and comparing the median capital intensity of firms in each of the industry and size groups. Next, we examine the extent to which industry, size, and capital intensity are related to variation in business risk and leverage, and how equity risk is related to all of these variables.

Empirical Results

The results of our calculations are displayed in Table 8-4. The table contains five panels, with each panel showing the cross-sectional median value of the indicated variable for the firms in an industry and firm size group, as well as for all firms in an industry and all firms in a specified size range.

Not surprisingly, the results for capital intensity, shown in the first panel, are similar to those we reported in Chapter 7 (review Table 7-3). Capital intensity varies considerably across industries, and tends to vary directly with firm size for most, though not all, industries. Firms in the *Business Services* and *Industrial Machinery, Computer Equipment* industries exhibit the lowest median capital intensity (13.0 percent and 18.8 percent, respectively) whereas firms in the *Electric, Gas, and Sanitary Services* and *Petroleum Refining and Related Products* industries exhibit the highest median capital intensity (69.2 percent and 65.2 percent, respectively).

Median values of our business risk measure, $\sigma(ROA)$, are shown in the second panel. Business risk varies substantially across industries, from 1.5 percent for the *Electric, Gas and Sanitary Services* industry to 11.0 percent for the *Business Services* industry. Moreover, perhaps the most striking result in the panel is the strong *inverse* relationship between median $\sigma(ROA)$ and firm size, which holds for every industry. For all industries combined, the median $\sigma(ROA)$ is *five times* higher for the smallest firms (19.4 percent) than for the largest firms (3.8 percent)! Clearly, industry and firm size are important determinants of business risk.

Using these results, we can test the relationship between capital intensity and business risk. Based on the strong inverse relationship observed between firm size and business risk, it is clear that to test this relationship we must control for firm size. We can take advantage of variation in median PP&E/TA across industries for each firm size group, testing whether median values of PP&E/TA across industries for a given size group are correlated with corresponding median values of $\sigma(ROA)$, shown in the second panel. The resulting *column correlations* are shown in the last row of the second panel. Surprisingly, the column correlations are strongly *negative*, rather than positive. These results, combined with those indicating that capital intensity tends to increase with firm size while business risk strongly decreases with firm size, suggest that, if there is any credence whatsoever to the argument that capital intensity increases business risk, it is overwhelmed by other aspects of the firm, notably its industry and size.

The third panel displays the distributions of median leverage across industries and firm size. (These results are similar to those shown in Chapter 7, Table 7-3.) Median leverage varies considerably across industries, ranging from 11.0 percent for the *Business Services* industry to 37.6 percent for the *Electric, Gas, and Sanitary Services* industry. In addition, there is a general tendency for leverage to increase with firm size. By comparing these values with corresponding values for business risk, we can test the hypothesis that leverage and business risk are inversely related. The column correlations between leverage and business risk are shown in the second-to-last row of the

TABLE 8-4   Median Values of Key Financial Variables

834 Firms in Eight Major Industries, Sorted by Total Assets (TA) at Year-End 1999*

Industry	All Firms	<$100 million	$100 million to $1 billion	$1 billion to $10 billion	>$10 billion
			Firm Size Range (TA)		
MEDIAN CAPITAL INTENSITY (PP&E/TA, %)					
Business Services	13.0	12.0	13.5	13.0	21.4
Chemicals and Allied Products	27.2	19.9	29.1	31.1	31.9
Communications	41.8	—	41.4	40.5	43.0
Electric, Gas, and Sanitary Services	69.2	24.2	76.0	70.3	67.0
Electronic and Other Electric Equipment	23.4	21.4	24.5	25.1	35.2
Food and Kindred Products	37.6	32.2	44.3	37.2	26.7
Industrial Machinery, Computer Equipment	18.8	17.0	19.9	19.6	14.0
Petroleum Refining and Related Products	65.2	87.3	46.3	65.3	65.2
All Eight Industries	**26.7**	**19.1**	**25.2**	**39.6**	**41.8**
MEDIAN STANDARD DEVIATION OF RETURN ON ASSETS (σ(ROA), %)					
Business Services	11.0	29.7	9.4	4.1	5.0
Chemicals and Allied Products	9.1	25.7	6.5	5.3	5.8
Communications	4.0	—	6.0	5.8	3.9
Electric, Gas, and Sanitary Services	1.5	9.0	1.5	1.5	1.5
Electronic and Other Electric Equipment	10.3	17.6	8.1	4.6	5.4
Food and Kindred Products	4.8	8.7	5.7	3.9	3.7
Industrial Machinery, Computer Equipment	10.4	21.2	7.2	7.7	3.9
Petroleum Refining and Related Products	7.1	8.5	7.7	7.0	4.8
All Eight Industries	**6.8**	**19.4**	**6.7**	**3.5**	**3.8**
Column Correlation with (PP&E/TA)	*− 0.81*	*− 0.61*	*− 0.89*	*− 0.28*	*− 0.41*
MEDIAN LEVERAGE (D/TA, %)					
Business Services	11.0	12.4	10.1	10.2	16.4
Chemicals and Allied Products	18.0	10.1	19.8	26.9	22.6
Communications	33.5	—	39.5	30.4	31.6
Electric, Gas, and Sanitary Services	37.6	18.7	36.9	38.0	37.8
Electronic and Other Electric Equipment	15.3	14.7	15.2	17.1	14.8
Food and Kindred Products	26.4	8.2	25.4	34.7	27.0
Industrial Machinery, Computer Equipment	17.0	14.1	20.0	16.8	40.2
Petroleum Refining and Related Products	25.4	36.2	20.6	32.8	26.6
All Eight Industries	**21.5**	**13.2**	**20.1**	**30.8**	**30.1**
Column Correlation with (σ(ROA))	*− 0.98*	*− 0.47*	*− 0.81*	*− 0.30*	*− 0.75*
Column Correlation with (PP&E/TA)	*0.84*	*0.88*	*0.77*	*0.87*	*0.20*
MEDIAN STANDARD DEVIATION OF RETURN ON EQUITY (σ(ROE), %)					
Business Services	24.9	51.2	16.4	12.5	8.8
Chemicals and Allied Products	19.0	48.7	13.4	13.7	14.7
Communications	14.3	—	24.5	7.4	15.2
Electric, Gas, and Sanitary Services	4.5	15.6	4.4	3.9	5.5
Electronic and Other Electric Equipment	17.6	32.5	14.5	10.4	7.9
Food and Kindred Products	12.3	13.6	11.8	13.2	11.4
Industrial Machinery, Computer Equipment	21.5	32.6	14.6	14.7	17.9
Petroleum Refining and Related Products	16.2	16.2	28.2	16.6	13.1
All Eight Industries	**14.9**	**34.0**	**12.7**	**9.2**	**11.3**
Column Correlation with (D/TA)	*− 0.90*	*− 0.43*	*− 0.08*	*− 0.32*	*0.35*

(continued)

TABLE 8-4   Median Values of Key Financial Variables (*continued*)

834 Firms in Eight Major Industries, Sorted by Total Assets (TA) at Year-End 1999*

Industry	All Firms	<$100 million	$100 million to $1 billion	$1 billion to $10 billion	>$10 billion
			Firm Size Range (TA)		
MEDIAN STANDARD DEVIATION OF STOCK RETURN ($\sigma(R)$, %)					
Business Services	56.5	86.1	49.9	31.2	30.7
Chemicals and Allied Products	41.0	57.3	38.7	29.9	22.1
Communications	29.8	—	39.1	33.1	23.1
Electric, Gas, and Sanitary Services	19.9	35.0	21.5	18.9	18.9
Electronic and Other Electric Equipment	55.9	67.7	54.5	42.6	36.5
Food and Kindred Products	30.0	48.1	32.7	25.6	24.7
Industrial Machinery, Computer Equipment	47.0	65.1	40.1	43.6	35.2
Petroleum Refining and Related Products	25.5	88.3	37.8	26.1	15.8
All Eight Industries	**40.3**	**65.5**	**40.2**	**27.1**	**21.7**
Column Correlation with (σ(ROE))	*0.83*	*0.39*	*0.38*	*0.30*	*0.05*
Column Correlation with (D/TA)	*−0.92*	*0.45*	*−0.73*	*−0.74*	*−0.26*

*Figures for individual firms are annualized averages based on quarterly values for 1993–1999.

leverage panel. For each and every column (i.e., firm size group), the correlation between leverage and business risk is negative, as expected. These results indicate that firms tend to choose lower leverage the higher their business risk. The results are consistent with the view that firms tend to limit equity risk (and bankruptcy risk) by offsetting higher business risk with lower leverage.

The results also afford a test of the relationship between capital intensity and leverage. The column correlations between PP&E/TA and D/TA are shown in the last row of the leverage panel. For each firm size category, the correlation between capital intensity and leverage is *positive*. There are at least two explanations for these results. *First*, by definition capital-intensive firms have more collateralizable assets to support debt. *Second*, referring again to Williams' theoretical argument (see Chapter 7), capital-intensive firms may be inherently more profitable and less risky, and are therefore better able to garner debt financing by virtue of their superior ability to make future interest and principal payments.

The fourth panel shows median values of equity risk measured by σ(ROE). Median σ(ROE) varies considerably across industries, ranging from 4.5 percent for the *Electric, Gas, and Sanitary Services* industry to 24.9 percent for the *Business Services* industry. In addition, median σ(ROE) is strongly negatively related to firm size for every industry. Indeed, the median value of σ(ROE) for the smallest firms, 34.0 percent, is three times as high as the median value for the largest firms, 11.3 percent. The inverse relationship between equity risk and firm size is primarily due to the inverse relationship between business risk and firm size (second panel), and occurs despite the fact that leverage is positively related to firm size (third panel). Thus, across firms leverage differences *only partially* counterbalance the effects of business risk on equity risk.

The last row of the fourth panel displays column correlations between median values of σ(ROE) and leverage. *A priori*, it is difficult to predict what this relationship would be. On one hand, we expect a positive relationship because leverage increases equity risk, *ceteris paribus*. On the other hand, firms that would have high equity risk because they have high business risk may choose lower leverage, which augers for a negative relationship. Using all firms in each of the industries for the computation of the medians, we find a strong negative correlation of –0.90, indicating that the latter argument holds sway. However, when we separate the firms by size, the column correlations are much smaller, and in the case of the largest firms, the correlation is actually slightly positive.

We find similar results using our alternative measure of equity risk, σ(R), as displayed in the fifth and final panel. Median values of σ(R) vary considerably across industries, ranging from 19.9 percent for the *Electric, Gas, and Sanitary Services* industry to 56.5 percent for the *Business Services* industry. In addition, median values of σ(R) are strongly negatively related to firm size for every industry; median σ(R) is three times higher for the smallest firms than the largest firms, 65.5 percent versus 21.7 percent. Meanwhile, the column correlations shown in the second-to-last row of this panel show that σ(R) and σ(ROE) are positively related, as expected. Finally, the column correlations between σ(R) and leverage, shown in the last row of the panel, are generally negative, indicating that the second of the two arguments discussed above dominates.

8.9   Summary of Learning Objectives

In this chapter, we presented a comprehensive perspective on a firm's environment, governance, business strategy, operational and financial structures, risks, performance, and contingencies.

Business Environment. The state of the economy (current and projected GDP, taxes, interest rates, inflation, productivity growth) affects a firm's cost of capital, risk, and profitability. A firm requires a host of resources to operate successfully, including real estate, PP&E, labor and management talent, access to cost-effective technology, and products and services secured from other firms. Also, three financial markets are important to a firm: equity markets, debt markets, and derivatives markets.

External Governance. External governance groups, entities that constrain a firm's activities, include governments, stock exchanges, creditors, external auditors, business media, and analysts. Governments provide services and protection and impose taxes, regulations, and restrictions. Government regulations impose costs and risk on a firm's operations, but also create opportunities. Creditors restrict a firm's activities via both covenants in the debt contract and monitoring. The business media and analysts provide value-relevant information and scrutinize managers' actions.

Internal Governance. A firm's internal governance structure includes (a) the voting rights of shareholders and *shareholder activism*, (b) oversight by the firm's *board of directors*, and (c) the firm's *management hierarchy*. As owners, common stockholders have voting rights on various matters. Examples of shareholder activism are proxy contests and shareholder-initiated proposals. The four most important functions of a firm's board of directors are hiring, compensating, and, as necessary, firing the firm's senior management; voting on management proposals; voting on the issuance of stock and bonds, the payment of dividends, and other major financing activities; and providing information and advice. Insiders on a board may be less effective in their oversight role because they are beholden to the CEO, so outsiders should be included in the optimal board. The typical management hierarchy in a corporation starts at the top with the firm's president and CEO, who are occasionally the same person. Many firms also have a COO (Chief Operating Officer), a CFO (Chief Financial Officer), and a CIO (Chief Information Officer). In addition, large corporations have extensive management hierarchies, including regional and divisional managers. The balance of responsibility for operations (and perhaps financing) between senior, regional, and divisional management defines the *steepness* of the firm's hierarchy.

Business Strategy. The basic elements of a firm's business strategy include the firm's targeted product or service market(s), management's long-term goals with respect to market share and profitability within the industry, and the firm's competitive strategy for meeting these goals. A firm's business strategy and size will largely determine both its operational and financial structures.

Operational Structure. The elements of a firm's operational structure include (a) the overall size of the firm, (b) the firm's production function, especially the capital/labor mix, (c) the firm's capital budgeting procedures, and (d) the firm's internal auditing system, and quality and cost control mechanisms. Regarding size, economies of scale are almost universally important, particularly as the associated increase in capital intensity decreases costs. Capital intensity is generally positively related to size, leverage, and profitability, and negatively related to risk. Principal–agent conflicts and information asymmetry can adversely affect the firm's capital investment decisions.

Financial Structure. The main elements of a firm's financial structure are equity ownership structure, leverage, dividend policy, and executive compensation policy. From an agency viewpoint, the crux of the ownership structure issue is a trade-off between the advantages of diffuse ownership versus costs of managerial discretion. Leverage may be advantageous from a tax viewpoint, and also it serves to discipline management. However, it increases the firm's equity risk. Dividend policy is problematic because dividends are not deductible at the corporate level, and are fully taxable for recipient investors. In addition, for firms whose capital expenditures equal or exceed their free cash flow, paying dividends is costly because it causes the firm to enter the external capital markets more frequently. On the other hand, dividends can serve to mitigate costs associated with managerial discretion and information asymmetry. Performance incentives in executive compensation contracts are a means of aligning management's and shareholders' interests, and include (a) a requirement that management own some of the firm's shares, (b) annual bonuses tied to the firm's accounting earnings, (c) grants of restricted stock and stock options, or (d) a long-term performance plan.

Risks. The two broad classes of risk that a firm faces are business risk and financial risk. Once a firm's management decides on its business strategy and operational structure, the firm's business risk is well defined, determined in large part as a function of the firm's size and capital intensity. The riskiness of the firm's equity depends on both the firm's business risk and its financial leverage.

Contingencies. Managers regularly face contingencies, including (a) expanding in existing product and service markets, (b) considering new investment opportunities in other products and services, (c) disinvesting if a project shows no promise for future profits, (d) participating in a merger or acquisition, and (e) undergoing bankruptcy or liquidation. On an on-going basis, decisions related to contingencies are likely to determine the bulk of the firm's future profitability and shareholder value. For instance, many firms may be observed to be growing, but only some of these firms are pursuing profitable opportunities.

Review Questions and Problems

1. Discuss the elements of each of the following components of a firm's business environment.
   a. The state of the economy
   b. Resources
   c. Financial markets
   d. External governance groups
2. List several *external governance groups*, and explain the oversight role played by each.
3. List and briefly discuss the three elements of a firm's internal governance structure.
4. List and briefly discuss the three elements of a firm's business strategy.
5. List and briefly discuss the four elements of a firm's operational structure.
6. List and briefly discuss the four elements of a firm's financial structure.
7. Explain how the current and expected future states of the economy may affect a firm's capital investment and financing decisions by affecting its (a) expected profits, (b) risk, and (c) WACC.
8. Explain how a firm's risks, profitability, and contingencies can be viewed from either an *ex ante* or an *ex post* viewpoint.
9. Define and discuss each of the following examples of shareholder activism.
   a. The proxy contest
   b. The shareholder-initiated proposal
10. Discuss the oversight role of a firm's board of directors, and the factors that make it weak or strong.
11. Define and discuss the notion of the *steepness* of a firm's managerial hierarchy, and how it relates to a firm's capital budgeting decisions.
12. Explain some of the real-world problems associated with a firm's capital budgeting process.
13. How does a firm's internal governance structure interact with its business strategy?
14. What factors determine a firm's ownership structure?
15. Discuss the various advantages of being a large firm.
16. Several studies have examined the relationship between the percentage of a firm's shares held by executives and the firm's financial policies and performance. Summarize their findings.
17. Discuss empirical evidence on the relationship between a firm's ownership structure and the likelihood of top executive turnover given poor performance.
18. Lang, Ofek, and Stulz (1996) tested two competing hypotheses about the relationship between leverage and growth. List these hypotheses and summarize the results of their empirical tests.
19. Why do many small firms have no debt in their capital structures?
20. Discuss real-world trade-offs involved in a firm's dividend and share repurchase policies.
21. Discuss the pros and cons of using incentive devices in managerial compensation contracts.

22. Discuss the efficacy of the following incentive devices in an executive compensation contract: (a) an annual earnings-based bonus, (b) grants of restricted stock, (c) grants of stock options, and (d) long-term performance pay.
23. Discuss the relationships between executive compensation and a firm's governance, leverage, investment opportunities, and performance.
24. Define *business risk* and *financial risk*. What is the relationship between them?
25. Discuss the effects of each of the following on a firm's business risk: (a) the firm's chosen industry, (b) the firm's size, (c) the firm's capital intensity.
26. Suppose that at the end of year 1 a firm has TA = $100 million, and it is financed with debt with a book value of $30 million and equity with a book value of $70 million. The firm must pay 10 percent interest annually on its debt. In year 2, the firm realizes dollar returns of $12 million on assets. Ignore taxes.
    a. Compute the firm's ROA.
    b. Compute the firm's ROE.
27. Why is the standard deviation of a firm's stock return, $\sigma(R)$, generally much greater than the standard deviation of its ROE, $\sigma(ROE)$?

Creative Thinking Issues

1. Can you think of an alternative explanation for the various column correlations shown in Table 8-4?
2. Suppose you are asked to design separate incentive-compatible contracts for the CEOs of two firms in the pharmaceutical industry. The first firm is large, highly profitable, has relatively low business risk and high leverage, and its ownership is relatively diffuse. The second firm is small, only marginally profitable, has high business risk and no leverage, and its shares are closely held. How would the contracts differ? (Add other assumptions as necessary.)
3. We have discussed several mechanisms to mitigate agency costs of managerial discretion. Which of these is most important? Does the most effective mechanism depend on characteristics of the firm?

Projects and Analyses

1. Select a firm, and identify its (a) external and internal governance structures, (b) business strategy, (c) operational and financial structures, and (d) risk, performance, and contingencies.
2. Examine and discuss the details of the compensation contracts for the CEOs of several firms.
3. Construct a valuation model for a firm in which the firm's capital intensity varies directly with its size. As capital intensity and size increase, so do the firm's expected profits, while its business risk decreases. The firm's WACC initially decreases with capital intensity and size, but then increases. Model trade-offs, provide numerical examples of firm-value maximizing capital intensity and size.
4. Identify a firm whose CEO has received stock options. (Table 8-2 can be helpful in this effort.) Find the details of the stock options from the firm's filings on the SEC's *EDGAR* website. Value the options using the Black–Scholes Option Pricing Model (Chapter 2), stating all necessary assumptions.

CHAPTER

Market Efficiency, Event Studies, Cost of Equity Capital, and Equity Valuation

9.1 INTRODUCTION

In Chapter 3, we argued that a firm's shareholders would direct management to maximize the *market value* of the firm's equity. Therefore, it is important for a manager to understand the factors that determine the market values of securities. This chapter focuses on determinants of market value and a closely related issue, the cost of equity capital.

In Section 9.2, we introduce the *Efficient Market Hypothesis* and discuss its implications for security pricing. In Section 9.3, we briefly discuss security analysis and some practical limitations on market efficiency. In Section 9.4, we introduce an important tool, *event study methodology*, which is widely used to gauge the impact on the value of the firm's equity of value-relevant *events*, such as a firm's announcement of new capital investment or a security offering. Section 9.5 discusses the results of several classic event studies. In Section 9.6, we discuss determinants of a firm's cost of equity. In Section 9.7, we present and analyze several popular equity valuation models. In Sections 9.8, 9.9, and 9.10 we use these models to explore the market's pricing of stocks in the S&P Industrials, both cross-sectionally and over time. Finally, Section 9.11 summarizes the chapter's learning objectives.

9.2 THE EFFICIENT MARKET HYPOTHESIS

The *Efficient Market Hypothesis* (henceforth *EMH*; see Fama 1970, 1991) addresses, in general terms, the effects of competition in the financial markets on the market prices of securities. The EMH is one of the most important and pervasive, as well as controversial, concepts in the theory of finance.

9.2.1 A Brief Description of the EMH

The EMH emerges from the same set of assumptions that define the ideal capital market (Chapter 2). The EMH asserts that, at all times, a security's market price fully reflects the true, *rational value* of the security; in other words, the security is *fairly priced*. For this to occur, the security's market price must rationally reflect all available value-relevant *information*. Rational investors use all available information useful in determining (a) the security's expected future cash flows, (b) the riskiness of these cash flows, and (c) the appropriate discount rate to apply to the security's expected cash flows.

In his 1970 paper, Fama specified three forms of the EMH. In the *weak form*, a security's price reflects all information that may be contained in the security's *historical prices* (i.e., past price patterns). In the *semistrong form*, a security's price reflects *all publicly available information*. Finally, the market is *strong form* efficient if a security's price reflects *all information*, both public information and information held privately (e.g., by insiders or analysts).

9.2.2   A Mathematical Depiction of the EMH

The EMH can be expressed in mathematical terms. Suppose the price of a given stock is being determined in the market now, at date t. For simplicity, we assume that the firm that has issued the stock will liquidate all of its assets one period hence, at date $t + 1$, and the proceeds from this liquidation constitute the only return that investors will receive on the stock. To determine the security's price now, investors focus on determining the expected liquidation price at date $t + 1$, denoted as $E(P_{t+1})$.

According to the EMH, the market price of this security at date t, denoted as P_t, fully reflects a specified set of information available at date t, denoted as I_t. In other words, P_t is equal to a *rational expectation* of the date $t + 1$ price of the security based on I_t, $E[P_{t+1} | I_t]$, discounted via a rational discount rate that is also based on I_t, $r(I_t)$:

$$P_t = \frac{E[P_{t+1} | I_t]}{1 + r(I_t)}. \tag{9.1}$$

$E[P_{t+1} | I_t]$ is a *rational expectation* if the market's assessment of the probability distribution of $(P_{t+1} | I_t)$ is in fact the *true* probability distribution of $[P_{t+1} | I_t]$. If P_t is not efficiently priced in this sense, the actual expected return on the security will not be equal to $r(I_t)$, and in effect the security is *mispriced*.

A Numerical Example

Suppose the rational expectation of the price of a security at date $t + 1$ is $E[P_{t+1} | I_t] = \$100$, and the rational discount rate (or expected return) for the security is $r_t(I_t) = 10$ percent. Then the efficient price of the security at date t is $P_t = \$100/1.1 = \$90.91$. But suppose the current market price is $80. Then the security's *actual* expected return is 25 percent (= [$100/$80] − 1, in percent) rather than 10 percent, and the security is *underpriced*.

Note that this underpricing may be due to investors' incorrect assessment of the security's expected price at date $t + 1$ or to an incorrect assessment of the rational discount rate. In either case, competitive pressures should force the security's price to rise quickly to the efficient price of $90.91. Of course, the EMH posits that securities are efficiently priced *at all times*, so the price of this security should not have deviated from the efficient price in the first place.

For a manager to adhere to shareholders' interest to maximize market equity value, the manager must understand the process by which the market determines the price of the firm's shares. The EMH provides some critical *qualitative* insights into this process. However, to generate *quantitative* assessments of value, we must appeal to specific pricing models such as those presented later in the chapter.

9.3 INFORMATION ASYMMETRY, SECURITY ANALYSIS, AND LIMITATIONS ON MARKET EFFICIENCY

As we discussed in Chapter 4, an information asymmetry is likely to exist between a firm's management and outside investors, where the latter are at an information disadvantage as they attempt to determine the true value of a firm. How can the market be efficient under such conditions? We provide a multifaceted response to this important question.

Clearly, it is important that the scope of the information asymmetry problem is limited. After all, if investors have no reliable information about a firm, they cannot determine a rational value for its securities. The mandatory disclosure rules of the Securities and Exchange Commission (SEC) serve to mitigate information asymmetry in U.S. security markets (Chapter 5). Disclosure increases the information available to investors, allowing the market price of a firm's securities to be efficient, at least with respect to the disclosed information.

The set of information available to investors about a firm is limited by, but generally not limited to, information disclosed by the firm's management. Investors can augment their information by engaging in *security analysis*. Indeed, the price for any security will be efficient only if investors gather information, process it rationally, and subsequently impound it into the price of the security through trades.

However, gathering and processing information about a security is a costly endeavor. Trading is also costly. Meanwhile, the only *benefit* an investor receives from security analysis is from realizing superior returns on his or her portfolio by identifying mispriced securities. But if the market is already efficient with respect to the information gathered, the investor can realize no such benefit, and thus no investor will engage in costly security analysis. On the other hand, how can the market be efficient if no one gathers such information? This is the *paradox of market efficiency* (Grossman and Stiglitz 1980).

A resolution to the paradox comes by realizing that the market cannot be utterly efficient. Instead, the prices of securities will tend to deviate from their true values. Such deviations motivate analysts to bear the cost of analysis and trading, and their efforts keep the security prices close to their true values. Thus, we should judge the efficiency of the market for a security on a *scale* (i.e., small versus large deviations) rather than as an *absolute*. Moreover, analysts must realize that the security analysis industry itself is competitive. Price-value deviations will tend to be small, and only superior analysts will realize profits.

The efficiency of the market for a security ultimately depends on several factors: (a) characteristics of the security and the issuer, (b) characteristics of the market in which the security trades, and (c) the efficiency of technology available to analysts to gather and process information, and to trade. Economies of scale in the production and processing of information, as well as in trading, dictate that the market will be more efficient for the shares of large firms than small firms. Efficiency also depends on trading costs, including commissions and bid-ask spread. Finally, to identify and act on small and fleeting deviations of price from value, a trader must possess efficient technologies for both information processing and trading.

9.4 *EVENT STUDIES*: GAUGING THE VALUE OF NEW INFORMATION

Even before his landmark paper establishing the Efficient Market Hypothesis appeared in the *Journal of Finance* in 1970, Eugene Fama was working with colleagues on its implications. One result of his efforts was the milestone work of Fama, Fisher, Jensen, and Roll (1969). This paper, which is based on the EMH (specifically, semi-strong efficiency), established a technique for gauging the effect of new information on the market value of a security. Researchers have since used this technique, called *event-study methodology*, to conduct hundreds of empirical studies. This section explains this methodology.

9.4.1   Background

According to the semistrong form of the EMH, the current price of a firm's stock accurately reflects a vast amount of public information about the firm, including new value-relevant information that has just been made public. If this hypothesis is correct, then as new information about a firm arrives, the market price of the firm's stock should *immediately* and *unbiasedly* change to reflect this information.

New information may take the form of a government press release about some aspect of the economy (e.g., the latest figures on gross domestic product growth, inflation, or labor productivity). Alternatively, an individual firm might announce (a) its earnings for the most recent quarter, (b) plans to pursue a new project or to abandon an existing line of business, (c) a plan to acquire or merge with another firm, (d) plans for new debt or equity financing, or (e) a change in dividends or stock repurchase policy.

By studying the market's reactions to management's announcements, a firm's shareholders can judge the efficacy of management's capital investment program, financing policies, and strategies. At the same time, by studying the market's reactions to their announced decisions and performance, managers can better understand the process by which the market determines the price of the firm's equity, and thereby will be in a better position to manage the firm in a manner that maximizes market price.

9.4.2   Event Study Methodology

It is not a simple matter to gauge the valuation effect of a specific announcement. Two fundamental problems bedevil the effort. *First*, we can never be certain whether, or to what extent, the market has already impounded the information contained in an announcement. For instance, the market may have fully anticipated the information, or insiders may have leaked the information to some investors. What if we assume that our focal information is *new* information, but in fact it is *old news? Second*, we must recognize that the market receives new, value-relevant information about each and every firm on a continuous basis, including marketwide information, industry-specific information, and firm-specific information. How can we isolate the market's reaction to a specific piece of new information when other information is arriving simultaneously?

The Problem of Market Anticipation

Suppose we find that there is no apparent market reaction to a given announcement by a firm. We cannot easily distinguish whether (a) the information is new, but has no effect on value or (b) the information has an effect on value, but the market became aware of, and impounded, the information before the announcement. The study of the valuation effects of announcements is generally plagued by the question of the market's anticipation of the focal information.

To deal with this issue, researchers have two main tools at their disposal. *First*, the researcher can examine the *run-up* (or *run-down*, as the case may be) of the stock's price in the days or weeks prior to the announcement to determine whether the market anticipated the information pertinent to the announcement. *Second*, the researcher can estimate the market's *ex ante* expectations about the content of the information, and then focus on the magnitude of the *surprise*—that is, the deviation (if any) of realizations from expectations. We refer to two examples to illustrate the second tool.

Consider a firm that pays a regular quarterly dividend. Evidence indicates that firms generally pay the same quarterly dividend in a given quarter as they paid in the previous quarter. As such, any *change* in the firm's dividend is an unusual event. Therefore, at the time that a firm announces its next quarterly dividend, we may generally assume that the market expects it to be the same amount as the firm paid in the previous quarter. Thus, *any* change in the firm's dividend is likely to be a surprise to the market.

A firm's earnings are an even more fundamental determinant of its value. Consequently, analysts for all publicly traded firms monitor macroeconomic, industry, and firm-specific information to update their earnings forecasts. Therefore, at the time of a firm's earnings announcement, the price of the firm's stock likely reflects a *consensus* of analysts' earnings forecasts. Thus, the change in the price of the firm's stock upon the firm's earnings announcement should be proportional to the *difference* between the firm's actual announced earnings and the consensus estimate. Expressed in percentage terms, this difference is called *earnings surprise*.

The Problem of Simultaneous Information: Event Study Methodology

Regarding the second problem, researchers use a two-step procedure to adjust for the valuation effects of other contemporaneous information to isolate the valuation effect of a specific event. These adjustments combine to form what is known as *event study methodology*, the standard means by which researchers gauge the impact of an announcement, called an *event*, on the value of a firm's stock.

Step 1: Adjusting for the Contemporaneous Return on the Market Portfolio

In the first step, the researcher typically adjusts the event-period *raw return* on a focal firm's stock for contemporaneous returns on the stock market, yielding the stock's event-period *abnormal return*. This adjustment eliminates that portion of the stock's return that is due to the effects of contemporaneous information that affected the entire stock market.

A Case in Point On February 13, 1984, Sears, Roebuck & Co. announced an increase in its quarterly dividend from $0.38 per share to $0.44 per share, an increase of 15.8 percent. Generally, we would expect a substantial positive market reaction to a firm's announcement of a substantial dividend increase. However, Sears' stock price increased by only 0.35 percent on that day. One explanation for the small price increase is that the market experienced a loss of –0.85 percent on that day, as measured by the return on the Standard and Poor's (S&P) 500 index. Relative to the market, Sears' stock price rose by a more substantial 1.20 percent [= 0.35% – (–0.85%)].

Using the Market Model to Adjust for Contemporaneous Market Returns   Researchers generally make a more sensitive adjustment for contemporaneous market returns by using the *market model* (Chapter 2). The market model involves a regression of returns on the focal firm's stock against contemporaneous returns on a proxy for the market portfolio:

$$R_{i,t} = \alpha_i + \beta_i R_{m,t} + \varepsilon_{i,t}, \tag{9.2}$$

where $R_{i,t}$ and $R_{m,t}$ are the day t returns on stock i and the market portfolio, respectively, α_i and β_i are the intercept and slope coefficients of the regression for stock i, respectively, and $\varepsilon_{i,t}$ is the *regression residual.* The market model provides a more sensitive adjustment of the return on a stock for contemporaneous market returns for two reasons. *First*, the intercept of the regression, α_i, captures the average return on stock i given that the market return is zero. *Second*, the term $\beta_i R_{m,t}$ captures the *sensitivity* of returns on stock i to contemporaneous market returns.

The regression residual, $\varepsilon_{i,t}$, captures the deviation of the return on stock i on day t from its normal relationship to the market, and is therefore called stock *i's abnormal return* on day t. In an event study, we focus on the abnormal return on a stock because, according to theory, it captures the effect of new firm-specific information on the stock's price.

To estimate regression Equation 9.2, researchers typically use daily returns on the stock and the market over a period of time that excludes the focal event period, obtaining estimates of the intercept and slope coefficients, denoted as $\hat{\alpha}_i$ and $\hat{\beta}_i$. With these estimates, the researcher then calculates the abnormal return on stock i on the event date, designated as *day 0*. The event-day abnormal return, denoted as $\varepsilon_{i,0}$, is calculated using Equation 9.3:

$$\varepsilon_{i,0} = R_{i,0} - (\hat{\alpha}_i + \hat{\beta}_i R_{m,0}). \tag{9.3}$$

Pursuing again the case of Sears' 1984 dividend announcement, we estimated regression Equation 9.2 using percentage daily returns on Sears' stock and the S&P 500 index for two calendar years prior to the announcement (i.e., 1982 to 1983). The results were:

$$R_{\text{Sears},t} = 0.12\% + 1.46 R_{\text{S\&P},t} + \varepsilon_{\text{Sears},t}$$

The t-statistics for the intercept and slope coefficients were 1.91 and 23.73, respectively, and the adjusted R^2 was 52.7 percent. We then inserted the estimates of the values for the intercept and slope coefficients into Equation 9.3 to obtain Sears' abnormal return on the dividend announcement date:

$$\varepsilon_{\text{Sears},0} = 0.35\% - [0.12\% + 1.46(-0.85\%)] = 1.47\%.$$

Step 2: Washing Out the Effects of Other Information Released Simultaneously
The purpose of the second step in event study methodology is to *wash out* the valuation effects of other firm-specific factors that may have affected a stock's price on the event day to isolate the valuation effect of the focal event more precisely. This is

done by (a) collecting a sample of firms, all of which have made a similar type of announcement (though on different *calendar* dates), (b) calculating the event-day abnormal return on each firm's stock, and (c) calculating the average:

$$\bar{\varepsilon}_0 = \frac{1}{N} \sum_{i=1}^{N} \varepsilon_{i,0}, \tag{9.4}$$

where N is the number of events in the sample. The need to average abnormal returns across similar events exposes another limitation of event study methodology: The methodology cannot be used to accurately gauge the valuation effect of a single event for a single firm.

Using a Two-Day Event-Period Window   Researchers generally use an event-period *window* of two days, rather than one day, to calculate abnormal returns. These two days include the announcement day and the following trading day. This is done in part because many announcements are made after the close of trading on the announcement day, so it is necessary to include the stock's abnormal return on the following trading day, denoted as day +1, to adequately capture the market's reaction to the new information. We denote the two-day abnormal return for firm i as $\varepsilon_{i,(0,+1)}$. For an individual firm, $\varepsilon_{i,(0,+1)}$ is calculated using Equation 9.5:

$$\varepsilon_{i,(0,+1)} = R_{i,(0,+1)} - [2\hat{\alpha}_i + \hat{\beta}_i R_{m,(0,+1)}]. \tag{9.5}$$

Returning to Sears' dividend announcement, the returns on Sears' stock and the S&P 500 index on day +1 (i.e., February 14, 1984) were 4.23 percent and 1.07 percent, respectively. Hence, the (compounded) two-day returns were 4.59 percent and 0.20 percent, respectively. To calculate Sears' market-model based abnormal return over two days, we must double the intercept of the estimated market model regression, because we are working with two-day returns rather than one-day returns. That is, the intercept must be 0.24 percent rather than 0.12 percent. With this adjustment, the two-day abnormal return on Sears' stock is

$$\varepsilon_{\text{Sears},(0,+1)} = 4.59\% - [0.24\% + 1.46(0.20\%)] = 4.06\%.$$

Finally, we can calculate the average two-day abnormal return across a sample of firms (or events) using Equation 9.6:

$$\bar{\varepsilon}_{(0,+1)} = \frac{1}{N} \sum_{i=1}^{N} \varepsilon_{i(0,+1)}. \tag{9.6}$$

9.4.3   Good/Bad *News* versus Good/Bad *Management*

The market's positive or negative reaction to a given announcement by a firm does not necessarily represent a corresponding adjustment of the market's opinion of the efficacy of the firm's management. Of course, an unexpected increase in earnings or dividends generally does reflect well on the firm's management, whereas an unexpected decrease in earnings or dividends generally reflects badly. However, even bad managers occasionally beat market expectations, and good managers occasionally fall short of market expectations. In another context, a manager may announce a dividend cut that disappoints the market, but it still may be the correct decision under the circumstances.

9.5   RESULTS OF SELECTED EVENT STUDIES

In this section, we discuss the results of six classic event studies. These studies focused on individual firms' announcements of (a) capital expenditure plans, (b) earnings, (c) a change in leverage, (d) a seasoned equity offering, (e) a change in quarterly dividends, and (f) a merger. The results of these event studies are summarized in Table 9-1.

9.5.1   Announcements of Capital Expenditure Plans

McConnell and Muscarella (1985) analyzed the valuation effects of firms' announcements of revisions in their capital expenditure plans. The authors predicted that (a) a firm announcing an *increase* in capital expenditures is revealing that it has relatively more profitable investment opportunities, and hence the firm's stock price is expected to *rise* upon the announcement, whereas, (b) a firm announcing a *decrease* in capital expenditures is revealing that its supply of profitable investment opportunities is dwindling, and hence its stock price is expected to *fall* upon the announcement.

Playing devil's advocate, we offer the following competing hypothesis of the possible effects of these announcements. If managers tend to engage in unprofitable capital expenditures that serve to build their empire, an announcement of an increase in capital expenditures is bad news (i.e., management's spending is out of control) and a decrease is good news (i.e., management's excess spending is being curtailed).

McConnell and Muscarella examined capital expenditure announcements made by two types of firms, industrials and public utilities. Their industrials sample included 547 announcements made by 285 different firms; their public utility sample included 111 announcements made by 72 different firms.

The empirical results appear to be consistent with the authors' predictions. On average, industrial firms announcing an increase in capital expenditures realized a positive event-period abnormal return of 1.12 percent, while those announcing a decrease realized a negative abnormal return of –1.93 percent. The corresponding results for the public utility firms were weaker (0.03 percent and –1.06 percent, respectively). The authors explain the weaker results for public utility firms by pointing out that utility firms are regulated to the extent that they cannot earn a rate of return on capital investments that exceeds their cost of capital. Consequently, a utility firm's capital budgeting decisions should have a smaller impact on its share price.

However, even for the industrial firms the magnitudes of the reported average abnormal returns seem rather small given the importance of capital expenditure decisions. The alternative hypothesis noted above provides a potential explanation. For *some* firms that announced an *increase* in capital expenditures, the market may have reacted negatively because the information implies that management intends to intensify its self-serving empire building. Conversely, for *some* firms that announced a *reduction* in capital expenditures, the market may have reacted positively because the information implied that some mechanism (e.g., the emergence of a stronger board)

TABLE 9-1   Results of Event Studies of Six Types of Announcements

Announcement Type		Average Abnormal Return (%)
Capital Expenditure Plans (McConnell and Muscarella 1985)		
FIRM TYPE	TYPE OF CHANGE	
Industrial	Increase	1.12*
Industrial	Decrease	–1.93*
Public utility	Increase	0.03
Public utility	Decrease	–1.06*
Earnings Changes (Joy, et al. 1977)		
ACTUAL EARNINGS RELATIVE TO EXPECTATIONS:		
Positive surprise		6.71*
No surprise		–0.45
Negative surprise		–8.16*
Capital Structure Changes (Masulis 1980)		
Leverage decrease		–5.37*
Leverage increase		7.63*
Seasoned Equity Offerings (Masulis and Korwar 1986)		
Industrial firms		–3.25*
Public utilities		–0.68*
Dividend Changes (Pettit 1972)		
Increase > 10%		1.48*
Increase of 1%–10%		0.88
Cut or elimination		–4.23*
Mergers (Dodd 1980)		
Bidding firm		–1.16*
Target firm		13.04*

Statistic is significantly different from zero.

has been brought to bear to discipline management's tendency to engage in empire building. An alternative explanation is that the market may have anticipated many of these announcements.

9.5.2 Earnings Announcements

Joy, Litzenberger, and McEnally (1977) focused on firms' announcements of their quarterly earnings. As we discussed in the previous section, for such a study it is important to have some idea of what the market *expected* a firm's earnings to be in order to sort firms by the deviation of their *actual* earnings from the market's *expected* earnings. The authors of this study developed several alternative models of earnings expectations, including a *naïve no-change* model and a model that forecasts earnings by extrapolating past earnings trends. They then sorted firms into three categories according to whether their actual earnings constituted a positive surprise, no surprise, or a negative surprise.

The results shown in Table 9-1 are associated with the authors' naïve no-change model (though results for other models are similar). On average, (a) firms with positive earnings surprises realized a substantial positive abnormal return of 6.71 percent; (b) firms providing earnings close to expectations (no surprise) realized a trivial negative abnormal return of −0.45 percent, and (c) firms with negative earnings surprises realized a substantial negative abnormal return of −8.16 percent. These results indicate that earnings announcements convey considerable information to the market. Consequently, it is not surprising that earnings expectations and announcements garner considerable attention in the financial press.

9.5.3 Exchange Offer Announcements

Masulis (1980) studied the market's reaction to a firm's announcement of a change in its capital structure. He focused on two opposing capital structure changes. The first is an exchange of equity for debt, which results in a *decrease* in leverage. The second is an exchange of debt for equity, which results in a leverage *increase*. His evidence indicates that announcements of a leverage *decreasing* exchange generally generated a negative abnormal return, −5.37 percent on average. In contrast, announcements of a leverage *increasing* exchange generally yielded a positive abnormal return, 7.63 percent on average.

Masulis discussed several explanations for these results, but much of his discussion focused on two explanations. *First*, a leverage increase increases the firm's tax shield, and therefore increases the value of the firm's equity, whereas a leverage decrease accomplishes the opposite (and therefore appears to be at odds with shareholders' interest). *Second*, an increase in the firm's debt via an exchange induces an expropriation of wealth from existing creditors, while extinguishing debt accomplishes the opposite.

9.5.4 Announcement of a Seasoned Equity Offering

Masulis and Korwar (1986) examined the valuation effect of a publicly traded firm's announcement of an equity offering, known as a *seasoned equity offering*, or SEO. For industrial firms, they found a substantial *negative* average abnormal return of −3.25 percent. For public utility firms, the average abnormal return, while also negative, was smaller in magnitude at −0.68 percent.

These results are consistent with those of many other subsequent studies that have found a negative market reaction to a SEO announcement. Researchers have offered several explanations for this effect, which we discuss in detail in Chapter 13. In brief, one explanation is as follows. With information asymmetry, a firm's management has better information than the market about the true value of the firm. Thus, it would often be the case that the market price of a firm's stock deviates substantially from management's assessment of its value. If we also assume that the firm's management acts in the interest of the firm's *current* shareholders, management will tend to issue new shares when the market price exceeds management's assessment of its true value. Of course, the market becomes aware that firms tend to offer new shares when their management believes that their shares are overpriced. As a result, the market generally reacts negatively to a SEO announcement. (See Myers and Majluf 1984.)

9.5.5   Dividend Announcements

Pettit (1972) focused on firms' announcements of changes in dividends. The hypothesis he pursued is as follows: "Firms [tend] to increase dividends only when there [is] a high probability that cash flows in the future would be sufficient to support the higher rate of payment, and dividends [are] decreased only when management [believes] that cash flows [are] insufficient to support the present dividend rate . . . [It] follows that changes in dividend payments supply the market with information regarding management's assessment of the level of the firm's long run cash flows" (p. 994).

The author's sample included 52 firms that announced a dividend increase of more than 10 percent, 39 firms that announced a dividend increase of from 1 percent to 10 percent, and 44 firms that announced a cut or elimination of their dividend. Pettit found that, on average, (a) firms that announced a substantial increase in their dividend realized a substantial positive abnormal return of 1.48 percent, (b) firms that announced a minor increase in their dividend realized a somewhat smaller positive abnormal return of 0.88 percent, and (c) firms that announced a cut or elimination of their dividend experienced a substantial negative abnormal return of –4.23 percent. These results are consistent with the author's hypothesis, and indicate that decisions to change dividends convey considerable information to the market. (We discuss dividend policy in greater detail in Chapter 14.)

9.5.6   Merger Announcements

Finally, Dodd (1980) studied the valuation effects of a merger announcement on the prices of the stocks of both the *bidding* firm and the *target* firm. Dodd found that, at the announcement of a merger, the bidding firm experienced a slight *negative* abnormal return, –1.16 percent on average, while the target firm experienced a substantial *positive* abnormal return, 13.04 percent on average. In Chapter 16, we discuss motives for merger, additional empirical analyses of the effects of merger-related announcements, postmerger stock price performance, and other topics related to transfers of corporate control.

9.6   THE COST OF EQUITY CAPITAL

A firm's cost of equity is the expected return that shareholders demand on their equity. The cost of equity undoubtedly varies across firms, as well as over time for any given firm, depending on several factors. In this section, we discuss (a) two models for a firm's cost of equity and (b) factors that can affect a firm's cost of equity that are not directly addressed in these models.

9.6.1   Using the Capital Asset Pricing Model to Determine a Firm's Cost of Equity

As we discussed in Chapter 2, the Capital Asset Pricing Model (CAPM) provides a specification of the equilibrium expected return on a firm's equity. This specification is given by the security market line (SML) relationship, which we repeat in Equation 9.7:

$$r_{i,t} = r_{f,t} + \beta_{i,t}(r_{m,t} - r_{f,t}),$$ **(9.7)**

where $r_{i,t}$ is the equilibrium expected return on firm i's equity, $r_{f,t}$ is the return on the risk-free security, $r_{m,t}$ is the expected return on the market portfolio, and $\beta_{i,t}$ is the stock's *systematic risk*. Note that we included time subscripts for all of the variables in Equation 9.7. We do so to emphasize that the expected return on a security can change over time with changes in (a) the risk-free rate, (b) the security's beta, or (c) the expected return on the market portfolio.

The SML specification is appealing for at least three reasons. *First*, given that a risk-free security is always available (e.g., certificates of deposit and Treasury bills), it is reasonable to suppose that a firm's cost of equity should be some amount in excess of the riskless rate. *Second*, it reflects the assumption that a firm's investors are well diversified, and therefore demand a premium only for *systematic risk*. The ownership structures of most publicly traded firms are very diffuse (review Figure 1-5), so this assumption seems reasonable. *Third*, although technically the CAPM is a single-period model, our expression for the risk premium on the market, $r_{mt} - r_{ft}$, suggests that this premium may vary over time, depending on the aggregate risk aversion of investors or on business conditions, as we emphasized in Chapter 7.

9.6.2   The Fama and French Three-Factor Model

Since its appearance in 1964, the validity and testability of the CAPM has been the subject of intense debate in the academic literature. Early empirical tests provided basic support for the model in terms of the critical prediction that the expected return on a security is positively related to its beta. (See Sharpe and Cooper 1972; Black, Jensen, and Scholes 1972; or Fama and MacBeth 1974.) However, Roll (1977) argued that the market portfolio cannot be observed, so the CAPM cannot be tested. (Researchers have always used *proxies* for the market portfolio, such as a value-weighted portfolio of all stocks on the New York Stock Exchange.) Thus, no empirical test can be devised to prove (or disprove) the model's validity. Fama and French (1992) found that, after accounting for other variables, specifically *firm size* and *book-to-market equity ratio*, beta has no power to explain the cross-sectional dispersion in average returns on stocks.

Based on the evidence in their 1992 paper, Fama and French (1993) developed an alternative model for expected returns on stocks. They suggested a *Three-Factor Model* of the expected return *premium* required on a risky security. The three factors are (a) the expected premium on the market portfolio at date t, $(r_{mt} - r_{ft})$, (b) the difference between the expected returns on portfolios of stocks of small and large firms, denoted as SMB_t, and (c) the difference between the expected returns on portfolios of stocks that exhibit high and low book-to-market equity ratios, denoted as HML_t.[1] The expected return premium for exposure to each factor is positive.

According to the *FF Three-Factor Model*, as it is known, the expected return on security i is

$$r_{it} = r_{ft} + b_{it}(r_{mt} - r_{ft}) + s_{it}SMB_t + h_{it}HML_t, \tag{9.8}$$

where $b_{it}, s_{it},$ and h_{it} are the *sensitivities* of returns on stock i to returns on separate portfolios constructed to represent each factor. That is, investors demand a premium on

[1]Note that Fama and French use the *inverse* of the market-to-book equity ratio that we have emphasized.

TABLE 9-2	Average Monthly Returns on Portfolios Sorted into Book-to-Market Equity Ratio Quintiles and Firm Size Quintiles, 1963–1993				
Firm Size Quintile	**Book-to-Market Equity Ratio Quintiles**				
	Low	*2*	*3*	*4*	*High*
Small	0.31%	0.70%	0.82%	0.95%	1.08%
2	0.48%	0.71%	0.91%	0.93%	1.09%
3	0.44%	0.68%	0.75%	0.86%	1.05%
4	0.51%	0.39%	0.64%	0.80%	1.04%
Big	0.37%	0.39%	0.36%	0.58%	0.71%

Source: Fama and French (1996).

stock *i*, over and above the riskless rate, to the extent that the stock (a) is sensitive to general market movements, (b) behaves like a small-firm stock (versus a large-firm stock), and (c) behaves like a high book-to-market stock (versus a low book-to-market stock). Note again that we included time subscripts for all of the variables in Equation 9.8 to emphasize that the value of each variable may change over time.

In a subsequent paper, Fama and French (1996) provide empirical estimates that give us an idea of the premiums associated with the latter two factors. Using data for the years 1963 to 1994, they report the average monthly returns on portfolios of U.S. stocks cross-sorted into book-to-market equity ratio quintiles and firm size quintiles. These average monthly returns are reproduced in Table 9-2. The results are indeed impressive. For each book-to-market quintile, average returns are generally inversely related to firm size, and for each firm size quintile, average returns are directly related to book-to-market equity ratio.

Critics argue that the Fama and French model is ad hoc, without theoretical foundation. In defense, the authors have argued that both the book-to-market factor and the firm size factor are *risk proxies*. To see why this might be so, consider why some firms would have higher book-to-market ratios than others. The risk interpretation is that a firm with a high book-to-market equity ratio (i.e., a relatively low market equity value) is likely to be a *distressed* firm. Such a firm may have sustained losses recently, and consequently has a substantial risk of bankruptcy (and perhaps higher leverage as well). Likewise, the typical small firm is chronically in a much more precarious position with respect to failure than the typical large firm. Regarding the latter argument, evidence presented in Chapters 7 and 8 is clearly supportive.

9.6.3 Additional Factors That Affect a Firm's Cost of Equity

Although the models presented above address the primary determinants of the typical firm's cost of equity, other factors may have at least minor effects. Here we briefly discuss four such factors: (a) ownership structure and agency costs of managerial discretion, (b) the costs of internal versus external equity, (c) the premium for *illiquidity*, and (d) leverage.

Ownership Structure and Agency Costs of Managerial Discretion
The CAPM assumes that a firm's equity ownership is diffuse, and therefore only systematic risk is relevant in determining the cost of equity. However, to the extent

that a firm's equity is held closely, this assumption may not hold. If a particular investor holds a substantial proportion of a given firm's shares, and this investor is not diversified, he or she might seek to influence the firm's management to incorporate an additional premium into the firm's cost of equity that compensates this investor for *firm-specific* risk. This may be the case whether the substantial owner is an insider or an outsider.

Internal versus External Equity: Signaling and Flotation Costs

The *Pecking-Order Hypothesis* (Chapter 4) suggests that information asymmetry can affect a firm's cost of equity. With information asymmetry, a firm would prefer to finance expenditures with internal equity rather than external financing, and if external financing is required, debt is preferred to equity. Internal equity is less costly simply because the firm avoids an ill-informed market that may underprice any security that the firm offers.

External equity is especially costly because either (a) the market will underprice an issue of equity, failing to incorporate the profitability of the projects that the firm will pursue with the proceeds, or (b) the firm must bear considerable costs to signal its true value to the market. External equity is also costly in terms of fees paid to underwriters who assist the firm in selling, or *floating*, the issue. Ultimately, a firm's management should consider calculating their overall cost of equity as a weighted average of equity funds obtained internally and externally.

A Premium for Illiquidity

Financial consultants generally observe that investors demand a very substantial premium for the illiquidity of some firms' shares, particularly those of small, thinly traded stocks. Depending on the state of the market for such stocks, this premium may be as high as 30 percent to 40 percent.

Leverage

Our analyses of ideal capital market models in Chapter 2 show that the expected return on a firm's equity increases with leverage on a risk basis alone. Using the Black–Scholes Option Pricing Model (BSOPM), we showed that a firm's equity beta increases with leverage, and its expected return follows suit. In later chapters, we argued that several real-world costs, including agency costs of debt and costs of financial distress, are closely related to leverage. These costs induce an *additional* relationship between a firm's leverage and its cost of equity.

Bhandari (1988) examined this issue empirically. He examined data on hundreds of firms over the years 1948 to 1981 to determine whether a firm's stock return is related to leverage after controlling for *both* equity beta and firm size. He found that, even after controlling for beta and size, a stock's return was positively related to leverage.

9.7   BASIC EQUITY VALUATION MODELS

In this section, we review five well-known models for the valuation of a firm's equity. These include the Dividend Growth Model, the Constant Dividend Model, the Two-Stage Dividend Growth Model, the Sustainable Growth Model, and the Investment Opportunities Model. To illustrate these models, we focus again on Sears, Roebuck & Co.

9.7.1   A Case in Point: Sears, Roebuck & Co.

Figures 9-1 and 9-2 show time series values of several variables pertinent to the valuation of Sears' stock over the years 1979 to 2000. Figure 9-1 shows Sears' quarterly earnings per share (*EPS*), quarterly dividends per share (*DPS*), and quarter-end price per share (*PPS*). Figure 9-2 shows the firm's annual return on common equity (ROE), dividend yield, payout ratio, and estimated equity beta.

Sears' Earnings History

Two aspects of the time series behavior of Sears' EPS are interesting. *First*, quarterly EPS tends to increase through the quarters of the calendar year. This seasonality in Sears' earnings is due in large part to a substantial concentration of retail sales and profits during the *holiday season* (i.e., the fourth quarter of the calendar year). *Second*, Sears sustained losses in only two quarters, the consecutive quarters ending in September and December of 1992. However, these losses were very large.

Following these losses, Sears' management commenced a major restructuring of operations in 1993. This restructuring included (a) spinning off their Dean Witter subsidiary, (b) selling 20 percent of their Allstate insurance subsidiary, and (c) selling two

FIGURE 9-1   Sears, Roebuck & Co.

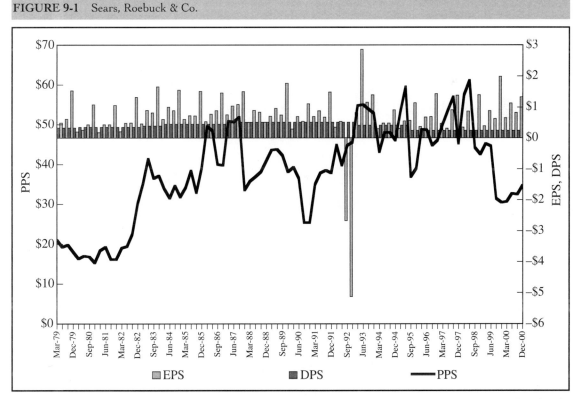

Quarterly Earnings per Share (EPS), Quarterly Dividends per Share (DPS), and Quarter-End Price per Share (PPS), 1979–2000

Source: Raw data from Standard & Poor's *Research Insight* database, 2001.

subsidiaries: Coldwell Banker Residential Services and Sears Mortgage Banking Group. The 1993 spin-off of Dean Witter resulted in a nontaxable distribution of shares of Dean Witter that was worth $14.39 per Sears' share. In 1995, the firm spun off their remaining interest in Allstate, resulting in another stock dividend worth $30.24 per Sears' share. (We discuss restructuring, including spin-offs, in Chapter 17.)

Sears' Dividend History

Sears' paid a quarterly dividend of $0.32 per share in 1979. The dividend increased to $0.34 in 1980, $0.38 in 1983, $0.44 in 1984, and $0.50 in 1987. The dividend was then reduced to $0.40 in the restructuring year of 1993, and then to $0.23 in 1995 following the Allstate spin-off.

Sears' Stock Price History

Sears' stock price rose by only 65.5 percent from year-end 1979 ($18/share) to year-end 2000 ($34.75/share), while the value of the S&P 500 index rose by 1,123 percent over this period. However, Sears' price increase does not reflect the value of the Dean Witter and Allstate share distributions noted above. Assuming that these distributions, as well as quarterly dividends, were reinvested in Sears' stock, the cumulative return on Sears' stock over this period was 1,034 percent, or 11.7 percent per year.

FIGURE 9-2   Sears, Roebuck & Co.

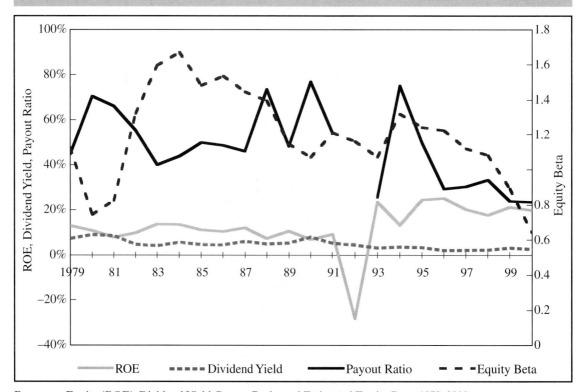

Return on Equity (ROE), Dividend Yield, Payout Ratio, and Estimated Equity Beta, 1979–2000

These figures compare somewhat more favorably to the corresponding returns on the S&P 500 index, 2,794 percent cumulatively, or 16.5 percent per year.

Sears' ROE, Dividend Yields, Payout Ratios, and Beta over Time

Figure 9-2 shows annual values of Sears' ROE, dividend yield, payout ratio, and estimated equity beta for the years 1979 to 2000. Dividend yields were computed as the ratio of calendar year *DPS* to year-end *PPS*. Payout ratio was calculated as *DPS/EPS*. (The payout ratio for 1992 is omitted because Sears sustained a loss in this year.) Annual beta estimates were calculated using daily returns on Sears' stock and the S&P 500 index for the previous two years.

The firm's ROE varied considerably over the period, but its history can be divided into two distinct subperiods. For the years 1979 to 1991, Sears' average ROE was 10.5 percent. Skipping the loss year of 1992, the firm's average ROE improved dramatically to 20.7 percent over 1993 to 2000. Meanwhile, average dividend yield and payout ratio were much lower in the second subperiod (2.7 percent and 36.4 percent, respectively) than in the first subperiod (5.9 percent and 55.2 percent, respectively). Finally, beta estimates varied substantially over time, ranging from 0.64 in 2000 to 1.67 in 1984; the average value was 1.20.

9.7.2   The Dividend Growth Model

The Dividend Growth Model is based on two assumptions: (a) The value of a stock is equal to the present value of its expected future dividends, and (b) the expected growth rate of dividends is constant into perpetuity. The formula for the Dividend Growth Model is given in Equation 9.9:

$$V_E = \sum_{t=1}^{\infty} \frac{DPS(1+g)^{t-1}}{(1+r_E)^t} = \frac{DPS}{(r_E - g)}, \tag{9.9}$$

where V_E is the current value of the firm's equity, *DPS* is the expected dividend at date $t = 1$, g is the expected annual growth rate of dividends, and r_E is the discount rate (i.e., the cost of equity).

Let's use the Dividend Growth Model to value Sears' stock at year-end 2000. We expect Sears to pay dividends of *DPS* = $0.98 in 2001, a 6.5 percent increase over the 2000 amount of $0.92. We assume that dividends will continue growing at an annual rate of g = 6.5 percent forever. We use the SML (Equation 9.7) to estimate the discount rate, with r_f = 5.4 percent (the year-end 200 yield on 1-year Treasury bills), r_m = 12 percent, and β_{Sears} = 0.64 (the estimated value at year-end 2000). Hence,

$$r_E = 5.4\% + 0.64(12\% - 5.4\%) = 9.6\%.$$

Applying these values in Equation 9.9, our estimate of the value of Sears' stock is

$$V_E = \frac{\$0.98}{(0.096 - 0.065)} = \$31.61.$$

The actual market price of Sears' stock at year-end 2000 was $34.75. Hence, if we are confident in our estimate, we conclude that Sears' stock was slightly *overpriced* at year-end 2000.

9.7.3   The Constant Dividend Model

Although the Dividend Growth Model captures important aspects of the value of a firm's equity, it is also problematic. The assumption that dividends are expected to grow at a constant rate into perpetuity may be unrealistic for many, if not most, firms. For this reason, several variants of the Dividend Growth Model have been developed, which may be more realistic for some firms. In this subsection and the next, we discuss two such variants: the *Constant Dividend Model* and the *Two-Stage Dividend Growth Model*.

If we assume that a particular firm is expected to pay a *constant* annual per-share dividend of *DPS* into perpetuity, Equation 9.9 reduces to the simpler form of Equation 9.10, which is the Constant Dividend Model:

$$V_E = \frac{DPS}{r_E}. \tag{9.10}$$

Suppose we expect Sears' annual dividend to remain constant at $0.92 forever, and that the appropriate discount rate is $r_E = 9.6$ percent as calculated above. Our estimate of the value of Sears' stock is then

$$V_E = \frac{\$0.92}{0.096} = \$9.58.$$

This value is less than one-third of the value we obtained by assuming that Sears' dividends will grow at 6.5 percent forever. The difference highlights the sensitivity of a stock's value to one's estimate of dividend growth. The results also explain why stock prices are so volatile: Changes in either the market's assessment of a firm's growth or the discount rate have a magnified effect on stock value.

9.7.4   The Two-Stage Dividend Growth Model

The Two-Stage Dividend Growth Model is also a variant of the Dividend Growth Model. Here, dividends are expected to grow initially at a temporary rate of g_S for T years, after which dividend growth reverts to a normal rate of g_N. The formula for this model is given in Equation 9.11:

$$V_E = \sum_{t=1}^{T} \frac{DPS(1 + g_S)^{t-1}}{(1 + r_E)^t} + \left[\frac{DPS(1 + g_S)^T}{r_E - g_N} \right] \left(\frac{1}{(1 + r_E)} \right)^T. \tag{9.11}$$

Again we attempt to value Sears' stock at year-end 2000, this time assuming that dividends will grow at an annual rate of $g_S = 3$ percent for the next five years, after which dividends will grow at an annual rate of $g_N = 6.5$ percent into perpetuity. Our estimate of the 2001 annual dividend is $DPS = \$0.95$ ($\approx \$0.92[1.03]$), and we again assume that $r_E = 9.6$ percent. The resulting value of Sears' stock is

$$V_E = \sum_{t=1}^{5} \frac{0.95(1.03)^{t-1}}{(1.096)^t} + \left[\frac{0.95(1.03)^5}{0.096 - 0.065} \right] \left(\frac{1}{(1.096)} \right)^5 = \$26.31.$$

9.7.5   The Sustainable Growth Model

The numerical examples emphasize that our estimate of the value of a firm's equity depends critically on our estimate of the annual expected dividend growth rate, *g*. In this subsection, we provide a formal method of estimating *g*. This method involves the concept of *sustainable growth*.

Estimating Sustainable Growth
The concept of *sustainable growth* is based on three assumptions:

Assumption 1: The firm's future capital investments will be funded with fixed proportions of debt and equity, and equity funds will be obtained exclusively from retained earnings. As such, the firm's earnings growth depends in part on management's propensity to reinvest at least a portion of the firm's earnings into new capital investments over time, rather than paying out all earnings in dividends.
Assumption 2: All future capital investments carry into perpetuity, and all are expected to provide a ROE equal to *k*, where *k* > 0 and presumably, *k* > r_E.
Assumption 3: Management retains a constant fraction, *b*, of the firm's earnings to fund investments. The remainder is paid out as dividends. The fraction *b* is the firm's *earnings retention*, or *plowback*, ratio. Hence, $(1 - b)$ is the firm's *payout* ratio. A consequence of this assumption is that the growth rates of dividends and earnings are equal.

Under these assumptions, the expected growth rate of the firm's dividends is simply

$$g = bk. \tag{9.12}$$

When *g* is calculated using Equation 9.12, it is known as the firm's *sustainable growth rate*, because firm's dividends can be expected to grow only to the extent that (a) the firm tends to plow back earnings into future capital investments and (b) these future investments generate a positive return (i.e., *k* > 0).

To estimate Sears' sustainable growth rate using Equation 9.12, we need estimates of *b* and *k*. For *b*, we use Sears' average plowback ratio for 1979 to 2000, which was 0.52, or 52 percent. For *k*, we use the average of Sears' ROE over this period, 12.4 percent. Thus, our estimate of Sears' sustainable growth rate is

$$g = bk = (0.52)(0.124) = 0.064 = 6.4\%.$$

The Sustainable Growth Model
By combining the Dividend Growth Model (Equation 9.9) with the expression for *g* given in Equation 9.12, we can create a new valuation model for a firm's equity. We call this new model the *Sustainable Growth Model*. This model develops from the Dividend Growth Model and the sustainable growth formula by (a) substituting $(1 - b)EPS$ for *DPS*, in Equation 9.9 and (b) substituting *bk* for *g* in Equation 9.9. Making

these substitutions and dividing through by $(1 - b)$ yields Equation 9.13, the Sustainable Growth Model:

$$V_E = \frac{EPS}{r_E - \left\{\dfrac{b}{1-b}\right\}(k - r_E)}. \tag{9.13}$$

Note that even though the firm's management should accept only those projects for which $k > r_E$, this is not a requirement of the model.

To use Equation 9.13 to value Sears' stock at year-end 2000, we need an estimate of EPS, which in this case is Sears' EPS for 2001. We obtained our estimate by adjusting Sears' 2000 EPS, 3.91, for the estimated sustainable growth rate of 6.4 percent: $E_1 = \$3.91(1.064) = \$4.16$. Using this estimate and previous estimates of the other parameters, our estimate of Sears' stock value is

$$V_E = \frac{\$4.16}{0.096 - \left\{\dfrac{0.52}{1-0.52}\right\}(0.124 - 0.096)} = \$63.35.$$

Issues Regarding the Sustainable Growth Model With the Sustainable Growth Model, a pertinent question arises: If a firm has profitable investment opportunities (i.e., $k - r_E > 0$), why would management pay any dividends at all? The basic answer is that a firm's supply of profitable investments must be limited, and the firm's management sets its earnings retention rate to allow funding of all such investments.

To see this, consider two extreme cases. In the first case, a firm has sufficient profitable investment opportunities such that it should pay no dividends at all. Then $b = 1$, and the value of the expression on the right of Equation 9.13 is undefined. This occurs because we are assuming that the firm can forever invest all earnings in projects that provide an expected return that exceeds its cost of equity—in which case the firm has an infinite value.

In the second case, the firm has no profitable investments whatsoever. In this case, the firm should pay out all earnings as dividends (i.e., $b = 0$), earnings will be constant into perpetuity, and Equation 9.13 reduces to the Constant Dividend Model.

9.7.6 The Investment Opportunities Model

Our final equity valuation model represents an attempt to isolate the present value of a firm's *profitable future investment opportunities*. Hence, we call it the *Investment Opportunities Model*. For this model, we assume that the value of a firm's equity can be divided into two components. The first component is the present value of a constant perpetuity of earnings that the firm can generate from its current *assets in place*, EPS/r_E. The second component is the present value of the firm's profitable future investment opportunities, denoted as *PVPFIO*. The equation for the Investment Opportunities Model is

$$V_E = \frac{EPS}{r_E} + PVPFIO. \tag{9.14}$$

One important application of the Investment Opportunities Model involves estimating the *market's* assessment of a firm's *PVPFIO*. This is done by setting V_E equal to the stock's current market price, evaluating EPS/r_E, and solving Equation 9.14 for *PVPFIO*.

We follow this approach to estimate *PVPFIO* for Sears' stock at year-end 2000. The price of Sears' stock at year-end 2000 was $34.75. We evaluate EPS/r_E as the ratio of Sears' 2000 *EPS*, $3.91, to the estimated discount rate, $r_E = 0.096$, which yields $40.73. Thus, our estimate of Sears' *PVPFIO* is –$5.98. This result suggests that, at year-end 2000, the market did not credit Sears with having profitable future investment opportunities.

Value-Earnings Ratios

Equation 9.14 also can be used to interpret a stock's price-earnings ratio (P/E). If we divide Equation 9.14 through by *EPS*, we obtain the following equation for a stock's *value-earnings ratio*:

$$\frac{V_E}{EPS} = \frac{1}{r_E} + \frac{PVPFIO}{EPS}. \tag{9.15}$$

Consider two firms that have the same cost of equity. The first firm has profitable future investment opportunities, the second does not. According to Equation 9.15, the first firm should have a higher P/E ratio.

9.7.7 Perpetuities and the 60 Percent Rule

In stock valuation models such as Equations 9.10 or 9.14, dividends or earnings are assumed to be constant into perpetuity. Although this assumption is reasonable in that a common stock has an indefinite life, it is also troublesome in that it is difficult to conceive of values in the distant future.

To interpret values from such models, it is useful to determine the fraction of the overall value of a stock represented by the present value of expected future dividends or earnings over a more reasonable, finite period of time. In addition, it is important to ascertain the effect of changes in the discount rate on the relative contributions of near-term versus distant future cash flows to the value of a stock.

To facilitate both of these needs, we offer Figure 9-3. The figure shows, for various values of the discount rate, r, the percentage of the overall value of a constant perpetuity that is accounted for by the cumulative present value of expected payments in years 1, 2, 3, and so on, out to 30 years into the future.

For any given future year, the cumulative percentage of the overall value of the stock is directly related to r. For instance, if $r = 5$ percent, only 18 percent of the overall present value of the stock is accounted for by the present value of cash flows through year 5. If $r = 20$ percent, the proportion is approximately 60 percent.

We also point out a curious relationship that we have discovered and have dubbed the *60 Percent Rule*. This relationship uses the inverse of the discount rate, or $1/r$. (If we are valuing future dividends, $1/r$ is called the *dividend multiple*, and if we are valuing future earnings, $1/r$ is called the *earnings multiple*.) For the eight discount rates shown in Figure 9-3, 4, 5, 6.67, 10, 12.5, 16.67, 20, and 25 percent, the corresponding multiples are 25, 20, 15, 10, 8, 6, 5, and 4, respectively. Upon inspection of

FIGURE 9-3   The 60 Percent Rule

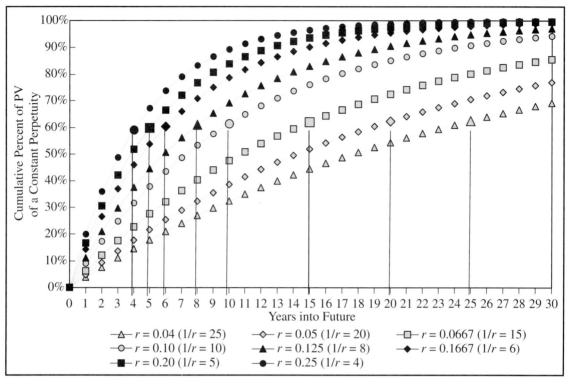

For a Given Discount Rate, r, Approximately 60 Percent of the Total Present Value of a Constant Perpetuity Is Accounted for by the Cash Flows in the First $(1/r)$ Years

the cumulative value percentages for the various discount rates, we find that, for any given discount rate, approximately 60 percent of the overall value of the stock is accounted for by the cumulative present values of the cash flows for the number of years equal to the corresponding multiple (i.e., $1/r$). This result is highlighted in the figure.

9.8   EMPIRICAL ANALYSES OF THE PRICING OF STOCKS IN THE S&P INDUSTRIALS

In this section, we conduct several empirical analyses of the market's pricing of stocks in the S&P Industrials at the end of each year from 1979 to 2000. We assume that the firms in the S&P Industrials are sufficiently homogeneous with respect to the discount rate on their earnings that they can be *pooled*. This is a questionable assumption, but it allows us to analyze the market's general pricing of these stocks both cross-sectionally and over time, and thereby to gain insights into pricing dynamics.

Realizing Profitable Growth Opportunities

Here are excerpts from an article in *The McKinsey Quarterly* on the practical problem of realizing profitable growth.

Why do so many growth strategies fail to realize their aspirations, yielding either far less growth than expected or growth that generates no profits? And how can senior managers mobilize their organizations to create growth that is both sustainable and profitable? Our research and work with a range of companies highlights two requirements for profitable growth. Each is challenging in itself. To attain both together is rare, but highly lucrative.

1. BUILD AN ENGINE OF GROWTH— AN INTEGRATED, MUTUALLY REINFORCING SET OF GROWTH STRATEGIES DESIGNED TO DELIVER CONTINUOUSLY ESCALATING LEVELS OF PERFORMANCE.

To do so, management must focus on questions like "How do we get better and better over time?" and "How do we translate every improvement into still higher targets, stronger capabilities, and superior sources of customer value?" This is a dynamic view of growth, and forging a great growth engine takes strong management; "satisficers" need not apply.

2. PROACTIVELY IDENTIFY AND MANAGE THE FRICTIONAL FORCES THAT RESTRICT PROFITABLE GROWTH.

This means eliminating, or at least minimizing, growth-induced bottlenecks, of which there are two kinds: imbalances across processes (between product development and order fulfillment, say), and bottlenecks within processes (such as overloaded testing resources in product development). Close attention to controlling frictional forces is vital for at least two reasons: First, a growth engine that revs faster usually creates more friction; second, multiple performance-limiting frictional forces call for an integrated plan of attack.

Combining both of these strategic elements lays the foundation for achieving turbocharged profitable growth. Going aggressively down either path in isolation—focusing either on the engine or on the sources of friction—is likely to produce disappointing results. Without lubrication, a fast-revving engine will soon tighten up and seize, yielding unsustainable growth or even "boom-bust" behavior. Conversely, simply to remove friction releases little growth because the engine is too weak to power real improvements. Friction-focused approaches are also liable to shift a reigning bottleneck from one process to another rather than eliminate it entirely.

Fortunately, real-life success stories of turbocharged profitable growth do exist. Take Intel, which has built up an 80 percent market share in microprocessors for PCs over the past 15 years. One commentator even predicted that it could become the most profitable company in the world. With 35 percent annual compound growth in after-tax profits, the company's growth is certainly turbocharged. So what did Intel do?

First, it paid attention to three crucial processes in establishing its engine of growth:

- Devising top-performing delivery mechanisms.

Intel invested heavily in microprocessor R&D and wafer fab capacity to cut commercialization cycle times for powerful new products such as Pentium. It achieved 12- to 18-month time-to-market advantages over its closest competitor. What made this an engine of growth was Intel's premium pricing early in the product life cycle, coupled with its high market share and aggressive improvement targets. The result: ample revenues to reinvest in doing it all over again.

- Proactively shaping industry structure.

After Intel has introduced a new-generation product, it drops prices on the old generation by 50

(continued)

percent or more at the point when competitors are ready to launch their new products. In this way, it quickly relegates its rivals' new products to old goods that command low prices. And the resulting modest profits limit competitors' ability to invest in R&D and manufacturing capacity, allowing Intel to sustain its lead.

- Stimulating new market demand.

Aware that producing ever mightier microprocessors can outstrip consumers' need for computing power, Intel has built into its mandate multiple efforts to stimulate demand for greater microprocessor capacity. It has helped produce many of the Application Program Interfaces (API) that link computers to telephones and faxes; devised new standards for more powerful communications busses; and proposed standards to accelerate multimedia software programs.

Second, Intel has been equally assiduous in anticipating and removing friction. When the Pentium microprocessor came out, for example, the company soon noticed that many PC hardware OEMs had difficulty in designing around its more complex architecture. Market acceptance was thus inhibited by assimilation capacity—a clear threat to a growth engine that depended on rapid product introduction and ramp-up.

In response, Intel began supplying enabling components (chipsets and motherboards) to help PC OEMs accommodate the Pentium. Not only was a potential problem averted, but a source of friction was arguably converted into a new advantage. As more OEMs grew to depend on Intel solutions, the company's role as a de facto industry standard setter expanded.

Intel has been far more focused than most companies on managing both engine and friction elements. Two further cases show the pitfalls of overemphasizing one or the other:

- Strong growth engine but weak lubrication of frictional forces = unsustainable growth.

One specialty chemical producer had an ambitious aim: to become the world industry leader from its solid position at number 3. It set clear growth targets and aligned managers' incentives. First-year sales and profits rocketed; in the second year, however, they began to tail off. After three years, jubilation at reaching number 1 was subdued by the realization that profits had plummeted to a net loss, despite large gains in volume and market share.

What had happened? A set of frictional forces had taken over. First, in a technology- and service-intensive business, commitments to new customer programs outstripped the capacity of existing information systems to track and understand customer profitability. As a result, the quality of pricing and customer targeting decisions deteriorated.

Second, in their zeal to build position, the company's marketing and technology organizations in the United States, Europe, and Asia Pacific committed separately to new product grades that made their product slates progressively more individual. Product extensions stretched technological resources, and worldwide technology platforms gradually eroded. This fragmentation reinforced the trend toward unique regional products and manufacturing processes, setting a downward spiral in motion.

Third, sophisticated customers became adept at playing off hungry suppliers in price negotiations. Ultimately, the company's neglect of these emerging frictional forces stopped a dynamic growth engine dead in its tracks, and a painful boom-bust period ensued.

- Weak growth engine with regular lubrication of frictional forces = constrained growth.

A telecommunications company facing deregulation saw that it needed to cut costs and grow revenues. After slashing staff numbers, it became the darling of Wall Street. It ran regular sales campaigns to boost revenues for new services such as voicemail and second line installation. Profits rose briefly, but then, despite strenuous efforts, refused to budge.

With hindsight, several lessons became clear to management. First, it had cut costs at the expense of training and by providing incentives for the most mobile, productive employees to take early retirement. Skill levels had fallen, limiting the company's scope for revenue capture.

Second, sales campaigns were making system bottlenecks worse. The evidence was plain: declining accessibility to customer calls, high error rates in the face of expanding workloads, and an increase in missed appointments. As multiple sources of friction took over, the company's growth engine stalled.

What message can we draw from these case histories? Put simply, that senior managers seeking profitable growth need to develop cohesive strategies to build their growth engine and understand and manage frictional forces.

Not either; both. This process must be rooted in powerful insights into the drivers of customer satisfaction and a thorough understanding of competitive and industry dynamics. It must be regarded as a continuous effort, not a one-off planning event. Early success in building the growth engine will inevitably reveal new opportunities; equally, each step will expose and trigger new sources of friction.

The concepts of the growth engine and frictional forces are not only powerful, but easy to understand and communicate. They provide a basis for aligning an entire organization around the design of a profitable growth strategy. Companies embarking on such a strategy will find that the promise of economic gains and the sense of organizational excitement are palpable, reinforcing the prospects of still greater success. Winners will move boldly on both fronts. Losers will try narrow, cautious strategies that risk delivering neither growth nor profitability.

Source: This article is excerpted from: "Keys to Profitable Growth," J. Avila, N. Mass, M. Turchan, *The McKinsey Quarterly*, no. 1, 1996, pp. 202–206. © 1996 McKinsey & Co. The article can be found on the publication's Web site, www.mckinseyquarterly.com. Used by permission.

9.8.1 Interpreting a Cross-Sectional Regression of Stock Prices on Earnings

Consider the following cross-sectional regression of the contemporaneous prices of a sample of firms at date t against their respective *EPS*:

$$PPS_{it} = \theta_{0t} + \theta_{1t} EPS_{it} + \varepsilon_{it}. \tag{9.16}$$

Firms with higher *EPS* should have higher *PPS*, so we expect the slope coefficient, θ_{1t}, to be positive.

The coefficients of regression Equation 9.16 take on greater meaning within the context of the Investment Opportunities Model, Equation 9.14. Comparing the two equations, we see that the intercept, θ_{0t}, represents the average per-share value of *PVPFIO*, and the slope coefficient, θ_{1t}, represents the inverse of the common discount rate—that is, $\theta_{1t} = 1/r_{Et}$.

To estimate regression Equation 9.16, we use stocks in the S&P Industrials at the end of each year from 1979 to 2000.[2] However, while these stocks may be reasonably homogeneous with respect to the discount rate applied to their earnings, they are likely to vary substantially in terms of the per-share value of *PVPFIO*. Therefore, we ignored the estimated value of the intercept. Instead, we used Equation 9.14 to calculate separate per-share values of *PVPFIO* for *each stock* by setting V_E equal to PPS_{it}, applying the estimated common discount rate, $\hat{\theta}_{1t}$, to EPS_{it}, and solving for the estimate, denoted as $PV\hat{P}FIO_{it}$:

$$PV\hat{P}FIO_{it} = PPS_{it} - \left(\frac{1}{\hat{\theta}_{1t}}\right) EPS_{it}. \tag{9.17}$$

[2]For each year, we initially estimated the regression using all stocks in the S&P Industrials. We then excluded firms that plotted as extreme *outliers* (i.e., deviations from the regression line). This procedure generally excluded less than 4 percent of the stocks. Finally, we reestimated the regression using the remaining firms to obtain final results.

Results of a Regression of PPS *against* EPS *for S&P Industrials, Year-End 1995*

Figure 9-4 displays the results of regression Equation 9.16 applied to stocks in the S&P industrials at year-end 1995. As expected, the relationship between PPS_{it} and EPS_{it} is positive and quite strong, based on the adjusted R^2, 45.4 percent. The estimated value of the slope coefficient, $\hat{\theta}_{1t} = 7.30$, indicates that the market discounted the earnings of these firms at an average rate of $r_E = 13.7$ percent ($= 1/7.30$, in percent). This value seems reasonable, particularly relative to the riskless rate at the time, 5.24 percent, measured by the yield on one-year Treasury bills at year-end 1995.

Results of Regressing (PPS – BVPS) *against* PVPFIO *for S&P Industrials' Stocks*

We also test the efficacy of our valuation approach by calculating values of $PV\hat{P}FIO_{it}$ for individual stocks using Equation 9.17, and comparing them to corresponding values of an alternative measure of the present value of future investment opportunities. This alternative measure is the difference between a stock's price per share (PPS_{it}) and its book value per share ($BVPS_{it}$), or ($PPS_{it} - BVPS_{it}$). The ($PPS_{it} - BVPS_{it}$) should be a reasonable alternative measure of the per-share value of a firm's profitable future investments, much as the market-to-book equity *ratio* is a measure of a firm's ability to create value from its assets.

FIGURE 9-4   Regression of Price per Share (PPS) against Earnings per Share (EPS)

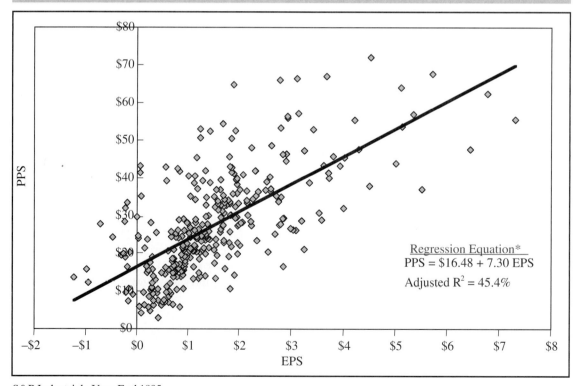

S&P Industrials, Year-End 1995

t values of intercept and slope coefficients: 18.9 and 16.4.
Source: Raw data from Standard & Poor's *Research Insight* database, 2001.

FIGURE 9-5   Regression of the Difference of Price per Share and Book Value per Share (PPS – BVPS) against Estimated PV of Profitable Future Investment Opportunities (PVPFIO)

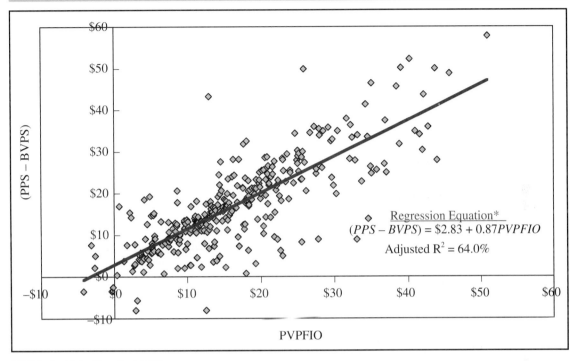

S&P Industrials, Year-End 1995

t values of intercept and slope coefficients: 4.0 and 23.9.
Source: Raw data from Standard & Poor's *Research Insight* database, 2001.

To test the relationship between these two measures, we regressed (PPS_{it} – $BVPS_{it}$) on $PV\hat{P}FIO_{it}$. This regression is given in Equation 9.18:

$$(PPS_{it} - BVPS_{it}) = \lambda_{0t} + \lambda_{1t}PV\hat{P}FIO_{it} + e_{it}. \tag{9.18}$$

Figure 9-5 displays the results of this regression for 1995 data on the S&P Industrials. The results indicate that these two measures of the values of firms' profitable future investment opportunities are indeed closely related, based on the adjusted R^2, 64.0 percent. Moreover, the value of the slope coefficient, $\hat{\lambda}_{1t} = 0.87$, is reasonably close to 1.0, suggesting that there is a nearly one-to-one relationship between these two measures. These results suggest that our valuation approach is reasonable.

9.8.2   An Overview of the Valuation of the S&P Industrials, 1979–2000

Next, we use the approach we have outlined to provide an overview of the valuation of stocks in the S&P Industrials for years-end 1979 to 2000. For each year, we calculated the average values of (a) PPS_{it}, (b) (PPS_{it} – $BVPS_{it}$), and (c) $PV\hat{P}FIO_{it}$. We also calcu-

FIGURE 9-6 Market Prices and Price Components

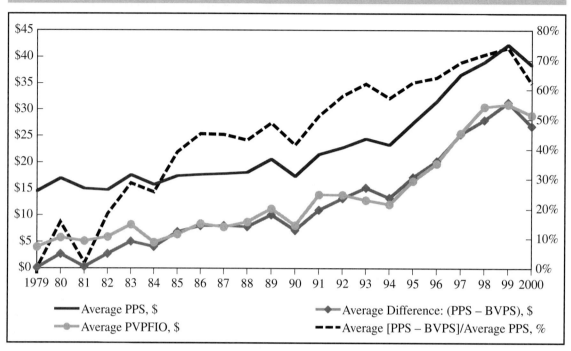

Price per Share (PPS), Difference of PPS and Book Value per Share (BVPS), Estimates of PVPFIO, and (PPS – BVPS) as a Percentage of PPS

Averages for S&P Industrials, Years-End 1979–2000
Source: Raw data from Standard & Poor's *Research Insight* database, 2001.

lated the ratio of the average value of ($PPS_{it} - BVPS_{it}$) to average PPS_{it} for each year. The results are displayed in Figure 9-6.

Average *PPS* generally increased throughout the period, and at an accelerated pace after 1990. The alternative estimates of the average per-share value of future investment opportunities, (*PPS – BVPS*) and *PVPFIO*, increased in concert, and were very close to each other over the years, indicating that they are similar measures of the values of profitable future investment opportunities.

The average value of (*PPS – BVPS*) as a proportion of average *PPS* also increased over time. This proportion was near zero at years-end 1979 and 1981, gradually rose to 74.2 percent at year-end 1999, and then fell back to 62.1 percent in 2000. Virtually all of the increase in average *PPS* over the years is accounted for by the increase in the average value of profitable future investment opportunities.

9.9 AN EMPIRICAL ANALYSIS OF COMPOSITE EARNINGS YIELDS

In this section, we provide an alternative perspective on the pricing of stocks in the S&P Industrials by analyzing the behavior of *composite earnings yields* over the years 1979 to 2000. We begin with a preliminary discussion of the earnings yield of an individual stock.

9.9.1   The Earnings Yield of an Individual Stock

The earnings yield of an individual stock is the ratio of *EPS* to *PPS*. A stock's earnings yield is also the reciprocal of the P/E ratio, which appears daily in the financial sections of newspapers for virtually all publicly traded firms. Both earnings yield and price-earnings ratio are measures of the market's willingness to pay for the stock in relation to the firm's current earnings.

However, a typical firm's quarterly or annual earnings are quite volatile over time, and investors (presumably) judge the value of the firm's stock on the basis of their assessments of the firm's long-term potential for *future* earnings. In this sense the components of either ratio are mismatched, so interpreting their values is problematic. In addition, as noted earlier, two firms that have the same current earnings may have different prices and thus different earnings yields and P/E ratios, because they differ in their potential for profitable growth.

9.9.2   Composite Earnings Yields

A composite earnings yield is defined as the ratio of the sum of the current earnings of a sample of firms to the sum of these firms' current market equity values. The composite earnings yield is likely to be more informative of the market's general pricing of the stocks in the sample, though it necessarily provides less information about the pricing of individual stocks in the sample. This is so because much of the earnings volatility of individual firms is washed out in the composite. Indeed, as we discover in the remainder of this section, composite earnings yields reveal a great deal about the general pricing of stocks over time.

9.9.3   Developing Formulas for Composite Earnings Yield

To facilitate the empirical analysis to follow, we develop a formula for composite earnings yield. This formula is developed by converting the Sustainable Growth Model (Equation 9.13), which applies to an individual firm, to the context of a *composite firm*.

Reinterpreting the Parameters of the Sustainable Growth Model

The first step in converting the Sustainable Growth Model to a formula for composite earnings yield is to reinterpret the parameters. To do so, we treat the firms included in the composite as one large firm, denoted as *composite firm j*. Denoting the date *t composite* earnings, *composite* market equity value, composite plowback ratio, composite expected return on investment, and common discount rate as $EARN_{jt}$, V_{Ejt}, b_{jt}, k_{jt}, and r_{jt}, respectively, the resulting modified Sustainable Growth Model is

$$V_{Ejt} = \frac{EARN_{jt}}{r_{Ej} - \left\{\dfrac{b_{jt}}{1 - b_{jt}}\right\}(k_{jt} - r_{Ejt})}. \tag{9.19}$$

It is important to emphasize the time dimension here. Even though for a given application of the model the values of the relevant parameters (i.e., r_{Ejt}, b_{jt}, and k_{jt}) are assumed to be constant into perpetuity, the market's *assessment* of the values of these parameters may change over time. Indeed, the main purpose of our analysis is to develop estimates of the values of these parameters over time.

A General Composite Earnings Yield Formula

We can now create a general *composite earnings yield formula* by dividing Equation 9.19 through by $EARN_{jt}$ and then taking the reciprocal of both sides, yielding Equation 9.20:

$$\frac{EARN_{jt}}{V_{Ejt}} = r_{Ejt} - \left(\frac{b_{jt}}{1 - b_{jt}}\right)(k_{jt} - r_{Ejt}). \tag{9.20}$$

The composite earnings yield contains two terms: (a) the required expected return on the composite stocks, r_{Ejt}, and (b) an adjustment for the propensity of composite firm j to pursue profitable investments. The adjustment factor is the product of a term related to the composite earnings retention ratio, b_{jt}, and the difference between the composite expected return on investments and the discount rate.

Note that if either $b_{jt} = 0$ (i.e., composite firm j retains no earnings) or $(k_{jt} - r_{Ejt}) = 0$ (i.e., composite firm j has no profitable future investments), then the composite earnings yield is simply equal to the discount rate, r_{Ejt}. Otherwise, if $b_{jt} > 0$ and $k_{jt} > r_{Ejt}$, the composite earnings yield will be *less than* r_{Ejt}.

A Specific Composite Earnings Yield Formula Based on the CAPM

We can generate a more specific composite earnings yield formula by injecting the CAPM's SML formula into Equation 9.20. The SML specifies that the required expected return on the equity of composite firm j is

$$r_{Ejt} = r_{ft} + \beta_{jt}(r_{mt} - r_{ft}), \tag{9.21}$$

where r_{ft} is the date t riskless rate, r_{mt} is the date t expected return on the market portfolio, and β_{jt} is the equity beta of composite firm j.

Substituting the expression for r_{Ejt} in Equation 9.21 into Equation 9.20 yields our alternative composite earnings yield formula:

$$\frac{E_{jt}}{V_{Ejt}} = r_{ft} + \beta_{jt}(r_{mt} - r_{ft}) - \left(\frac{b_{jt}}{1 - b_{jt}}\right)\{k_{jt} - [r_{ft} + \beta_{jt}(r_{mt} - r_{ft})]\}. \tag{9.22}$$

Although Equation 9.22 may seem a bit intimidating, note that the right side of the equation has three basic terms: (a) the current riskless rate, (b) the current risk premium on composite firm j's equity, and (c) an adjustment for the propensity of composite firm j to pursue profitable investments.

9.9.4 Composite Earnings Yields and Components: S&P Industrials, 1979–2000

We tested three predicted relationships based on Equation 9.22. Composite earnings yields should be (a) directly related to the riskless rate, (b) directly related to the market risk premium, and (c) inversely related to the difference between the expected return on capital investments and the discount rate.

To operationalize this test, we calculated composite earnings yields on the stocks in the S&P Industrials for years-end 1979 to 2000. Then we compared these values to (a) yields on one-year Treasury bills, (b) estimated market risk premiums (measured annually as the difference between the estimated common discount rate and the one-year Treasury bill yield), and (c) the difference between the composite firms' ROE and the estimated common discount rate. The time series values of these variables are displayed in Figure 9-7.

Composite earnings yields generally fell over the years, ranging from a high of 13.5 percent at year-end 1979 to a low value of 2.6 percent at year-end 1998. The yield on one-year Treasury bills also generally fell over the years. The estimated discount rate exhibits a U-shape over time. Finally, composite ROE and the estimated market risk premium generally *increased* over time.

To examine relationships among these variables, we generated the correlation matrix shown in Table 9-3. The highest correlation in the matrix is between composite earnings yields and Treasury bill yields, 0.90. This result is consistent with the first prediction from Equation 9.22.

In contrast, the correlation between composite earnings yields and estimated market risk premiums is strongly negative, –0.64. This result is *inconsistent* with the second prediction. Finally, the correlation between composite earnings yield and the difference between composite ROE and the common discount rate is strongly negative at –0.61. This result is consistent with the third prediction.

FIGURE 9-7   Composite Earnings Yields, Yields on 1-Year U.S. Treasury Bills, Estimated Common Discount Rate, Composite ROE, Estimated Risk Premium, and Difference between Composite ROE and Estimated Common Discount Rate

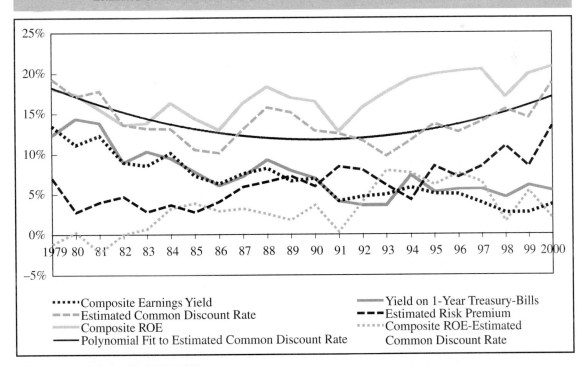

S&P Industrials, Years-End 1979–2000
Source: Standard & Poor's *Research Insight* database, 2001.

TABLE 9-3 Correlation Matrix of Composite Earnings Yield, Yield on 1-Year Treasury Bills, Estimated Risk Premium, and Difference between Composite ROE and Estimated Common Discount Rate

S&P Industrials, Years-End 1979–2000

	Composite Earnings Yield	Yield on 1-Year T-Bills	Estimated Risk Premium	Composite ROE–Estimated Common Discount Rate
Composite earnings yield	1.00			
Yield on 1-year T-bills	0.90	1.00		
Estimated risk premium	–0.64	–0.59	1.00	
Composite ROE – Estimated common discount rate	–0.61	–0.63	0.13	1.00

9.10 REAL OPTIONS AND THE MARKET'S PRICING OF R&D EXPENDITURES

9.10.1 Real Options

The valuation models discussed in previous sections place great emphasis on a firm's profitable future investments. Recently, we have come to understand that many of these future investments can be interpreted as call options. We refer to them as *real options*. A real option is a future investment opportunity that a firm implicitly owns now and that could be exercised (by engaging in a capital expenditure) if, at the time it expires, it is *in the money* (i.e., it has a positive net present value).

The literature is now fairly replete with examples of real options in corporate finance.[3] Perhaps the most famous and general of these is the *growth option*. A firm obtains a growth option when it commits to a specific product market. For instance, it may later choose to expand its production capacity or to venture into tangentially related products in the future, if such actions prove profitable at some future date. The focus example emphasizes that most of the contribution of real options valuation techniques is in capturing the value of *flexibility* in project decision-making.

9.10.2 Do R&D Expenditures Create Valuable Real Options?

A firm's research and development (R&D) expenditures indicate the ability and willingness of a firm's management to develop profitable future investment opportunities. The question is, does the market recognize the value of a firm's R&D expenditures by imparting a higher price to the firm's stock? Lev and Sougiannis (1996) addressed this question empirically. They estimated the R&D capital of a large sample of public firms, and tested whether a firm's R&D capital is related to either the market value of its equity or subsequent stock returns. They found that both market equity values and subsequent stock returns are positively related to estimated R&D capital.[4]

---

[3]See Sick (1989), Triantis and Hodder (1990), Quigg (1993), Trigeorgis (1993), or Childs, Ott, and Triantis (1998).

[4]Additional studies of the valuation of R&D expenditures include Bublitz and Ettredge (1989), Chan, Martin, and Kensinger (1990), Cockburn and Griliches (1988), Cohen and Levinthal (1989), Hall (1993), and Pakes (1985).

Get Real!

This article provides several practical insights into valuation via *real options*.

Have you ever been involved in a capital investment decision where the net present value calculations proved negative, but the management team decided to go ahead anyway? Or been confronted with a positive NPV project where your intuition warned you not to proceed? Often, it is not your intuition that is wrong, but your time-honored NPV decision-making tools.

But there is another way. Managers can use a different tool: real option value. When a situation involves great uncertainty and managers need flexibility to respond, ROV comes into its own. If the decision you face involves low uncertainty, or you have no scope to change course when you acquire new information later on, then NPV works fine. If not, you will want to know more about what real options are and how to value them.

Below, we compare the main decision-making tools and show why traditional techniques such as NPV, economic profit (EP), and decision trees are incomplete, often misleading, and sometimes dead wrong. We also look at how real options have been used in several practical situations, drawing on simple examples for illustrative purposes rather than going into the mechanics of valuing complicated real options.

Real options began to be properly understood in 1973, when Fischer Black, Myron Scholes, and Robert Merton devised rigorous "arbitrage-free" solutions to value them. Applications have proliferated, particularly in securities markets, where the theory held up remarkably well when tested against actual prices . . .

As yet, option pricing has not been much used in the evaluation of corporate investments, for three reasons: The idea is relatively new, the mathematics are complex, making the results hard to grasp intuitively, and the original techniques required the source of uncertainty to be a traded world commodity such as oil, natural gas, or gold . . .

WHAT ARE REAL OPTIONS?

[A]n option is the right, but not the obligation, to buy (or sell) an asset at some point within a predetermined period of time for a predetermined price . . .

If the market price is higher than the exercise price, the call option is said to be "in the money" . . . [If] . . . the market price is lower than the exercise price, then the call is "out of the money," and would not be exercised.

The value of the option also increases with the level of uncertainty of the underlying variable. The logic is straightforward . . . The greater the uncertainty, the higher the probability that the option will finish in the money, and the more valuable the option.

So far we have mentioned three of the five variables that affect the value of the option. It increases with the value of the underlying variable and with its uncertainty, and it decreases as the exercise price goes up. The fourth variable is the time to maturity of the option . . . [U]ncertainty increases with time . . . [so] the longer the time to maturity, the more valuable an option is.

Finally, the value of the option increases with the time value of money, the risk-free rate of interest. This is because the present value of the exercise cost falls as interest rates rise.

REAL OPTIONS CAN BE EASY TO OVERLOOK

One of the problems in learning how to use real options is that we often don't know how to recognize them in real-life managerial settings . . .

[This example] . . . concerns a manufacturer of jet engines. In this highly competitive indus-

(continued)

try, the secret is to get your engines onto the wings of aircraft; that done, you have locked up the profits from a 30-year stream of spare parts. What the manufacturer's financial officers did was to buy aircraft and lease them, with their own engines on the wings, to airlines. They also extended lease cancellation options that gave the airlines the right to cancel delivery of the aircraft at any time before delivery and a year after, for only a small penalty payment.

The financial officers wondered how much these cancellation options were worth. Analysis revealed that they were worth on average 83 percent of the value of the engine on narrow-body aircraft, and 19 percent on wide-body aircraft . . . The financial officers were horrified. What should they do?

Their new understanding of real options showed them that the cancellation option was most valuable to airlines that experienced high variability in demand. They stopped offering lease cancellation options to these airlines. A year or so later, passenger revenue miles fell steeply throughout the industry. Thanks to its change of policy, the company saved tens of millions of dollars . . .

HOW REAL OPTIONS CAPTURE THE VALUE OF FLEXIBILITY

Real options capture the value of managerial flexibility in a way that net present value analysis does not . . .

Suppose there is a 50 percent chance that after investing $100 million in [a] new factory, management will be rewarded with strong sales for many years. Revenues exceed costs, and the factory produces an operating income stream with a present value of $150 million.

On the other hand, suppose there is a 50 percent chance that demand is poor and the present value of the operating income stream is only $10 million.

A traditional NPV analysis of this bet would put the expected present value of the future operations of the factory at $80 million (the average of $150 million and $10 million).

This is not enough to offset the upfront investment of $100 million, and the project has an NPV of minus $20 million. It will almost certainly be thrown out.

But rather than invest the whole $100 million up front, what if management elects to buy the option to expand, at the price of $10 million for the pilot?

There is a 50 percent chance that the pilot succeeds; management responds by building the factory (for $110 million) and reaping profits of $150 million, as before. However, both building the factory and obtaining the profits are delayed a year because of the pilot, so we discount them both back one year at 10 percent to a $100 million investment and a $135 million profit, or a net $35 million gain.

There is also a 50 percent chance that the pilot fails, in which case management halts the project with no further outlay.

The overall value of the project (ignoring for simplicity's sake subtle points about investor risk sensitivity and the degree of correlation between the project and the market) is thus $7.5 million (the average of $35 million and zero, minus the upfront $10 million). Management should indeed proceed with the pilot . . .

HORSES FOR COURSES

Real option valuation is most important in situations of high uncertainty where management can respond flexibly to new information, and where the project value without flexibility is near breakeven. (If the NPV is very high, the project will go full steam ahead, and flexibility is unlikely to be exercised. And if the NPV is strongly negative, no amount of flexibility will help.) Optionality is of greatest value for the tough decisions—the close calls where the traditional NPV is close to zero . . .

Consider two investments: a new brewery and a pharmaceutical R&D program. The brewery is a one-off investment in a fairly stable environment in which demand can be forecast reasonably confidently. If the brewery's operating margins are high, its NPV will be high. The only alternative to going ahead is deferral, which is unlikely since there is little uncertainty about when new capacity will be needed or what the operating margins will be. DCF methods will work well in this setting because their implicit assumptions are valid.

The pharmaceutical R&D program is another matter. Investment is needed at several stages, with substantial outlays on basic research, developmental testing, clinical testing, and product rollout. At each stage, management can choose to abandon the project, defer it, go ahead as planned, or spend more to accelerate it. Flexibility is high, as is uncertainty, and the value of the project without flexibility may be marginal. In this setting, most of the assumptions of DCF do not hold. Option valuation will give much better results . . .

CLASSIFYING REAL OPTIONS

Individual real options can be classified into growth options (scaling up, switching up, or scoping up a project), deferral/learning options, and abandonment options (scaling down, switching down, or scoping down a project) . . .

The seven basic real options can also occur in combinations, as compound options. A company that invests in an R&D project, say, may be buying both the option to commercialize the resulting product and the option to engage in subsequent R&D projects to develop future generations of related products. These subsequent R&D projects themselves contain options for commercialization and further development, leading to a type of compound option called a growth staircase.

Real options can also depend on more than one source of uncertainty. The value of an option to commercialize an R&D project, for instance, depends on at least two: technological uncertainty (will the scientists succeed in inventing the new product?), and market uncertainty (what will the demand for this new product be?). Options that depend on multiple sources of uncertainty are often called rainbow options.

A DEFERRAL OPTION (NATURAL RESOURCE DEVELOPMENT)

Real options played an important role in a decision made by one coal-mining company. It needed to work out how much to bid for the lease of a plot of land that could be developed into a coal mine. Using the current price of coal and extrapolating its growth into the future, and forecasting extraction costs, taxes, and the estimated quantity of coal in the mine, the company calculated the NPV of the cashflows involved in developing the mine and selling the coal, and concluded that the lease was worth $59 million—not very much.

However, the company knew that the price of coal could fluctuate substantially. As its current price was close to the project's breakeven point, the revenue projections were highly sensitive to future price changes.

The company realized that acquiring the lease would give it an option: to defer opening the mine until such time as the price of coal rose far enough to make the project's economics reasonable. This option turned out to be worth $57 million—almost as much as opening the mine immediately. When the value of the option was factored in, the lease was actually worth $116 million.

The company successfully bid $72 million, waited until the price of coal rose, and made a tidy profit from the mine.

LEARNING OPTIONS (NATURAL RESOURCE DEVELOPMENT AND R&D)

Learning options arise when a company is able both to spend money to speed up its acquisition of important information (for example, to reduce technological uncertainty in R&D or to learn more about the quantity of resources in the ground in exploration and development projects) and to use what it has learned about the market demand for the project output to modify future investment decisions. It must balance the value of the option to act on the information learned against the cost of acquiring that information.

(continued)

Take the company considering a site for a mine. It must weigh the value of deferring development of the mine against the value of the information it could gain about the quantity of ore in the mine as a result of full or partial development. This is an example of a rainbow option. The sources of uncertainty are the price of coal and the quantity of coal in the mine.

Deferral is valuable because of the uncertainty surrounding the price of the coal the mine will eventually sell. If the economics are presently near breakeven, waiting gives management the chance to react to price shifts. However, partial development is also valuable because it reduces uncertainty about the quantity of coal in the mine, while preserving management's ability to adjust future investment according to what is learned. Partial development thus represents a learning option that is in conflict with the deferral option; the company cannot exercise both.

Multi-stage R&D projects generally contain a series of embedded options based on technological and market uncertainty. They too are learning options. Undertaking an R&D project gives management the right, but not the obligation, to commercialize a product if and when the R&D effort is successful and the economics of producing and marketing the product are attractive. Although an R&D project viewed in isolation may have a negative NPV, the option to commercialize the result is often extremely valuable—enough to determine that the project be undertaken anyway.

Making irreversible investment decisions in the face of uncertainty is risky. Being able to change a decision as new information becomes available helps reduce the risk. Traditional decision-making tools such as NPV, EVA, and earnings per share neglect the value of such flexibility. Real options, on the other hand, provide a theoretically sound tool for valuing management's strategic scope. Recent advances in theory have made ROV techniques applicable to a multitude of real-world situations. At the same time, advances in technology have enabled option pricing capability to move out of Wall Street and into mainstream corporations.

Source: This article is excerpted from: "How Much is Flexibility Worth?" T. E. Copeland, P. T. Keenan, *The McKinsey Quarterly*, no. 2, 1998, pp. 38–49. © 1998 McKinsey & Co. The article can be found on the publication's Web site, www.mckinseyquarterly.com. Used by permission.

We now conduct a test of the market's pricing of the R&D expenditures of firms in the S&P Industrials from 1979 to 2000. Our test employs the methodology developed in the previous sections, and is structured as follows. For each year, we obtain each firm's total R&D expenditures. Then, for each year and firm, we divide the firm's total R&D expenditures by the number of common shares outstanding at the end of that year to obtain a per-share figure for R&D expenditures, denoted as $(R\&D/Share)_{it}$. To determine whether the market values R&D expenditures, we test the relationship between $(R\&D/Share)_{it}$ and $(PPS - BVPS)_{it}$, where the latter is our measure of the market's assessment of the per-share value of a firm's profitable future investments. The regression equation is

$$(PPS_{it} - BVPS_{it}) = \varphi_{0t} + \varphi_{1t}(R\&D/Share)_{it} + \gamma_{it} \qquad (9.23)$$

If the market generally prices a given firm's stock in proportion to the firm's R&D expenditures, the slope coefficient of this regression, φ_{1t}, should be positive. In addition, the size of φ_{1t} reflects the market's general assessment of the potential for firms' R&D expenditures to generate future profits.

9.10.3 Evidence on the Market Value of R&D Expenditures

We estimated Equation 9.23 using data on firms in the S&P Industrials annually for 1979 to 2000, and retained the estimated slope coefficient, φ_{1t}, for each year. This coefficient can be interpreted as the average market value of $1 of R&D expenditures per share. These coefficient estimates are displayed in Figure 9-8. The figure also shows annual values of the ratio of composite R&D expenditures to composite book equity. This is a measure of the sampled firms' propensity to make R&D expenditures.

Our estimates of the per-share market value of R&D expenditures vary considerably over time. The average value of these estimates is $1.03. This result suggests that, for the period as a whole, R&D expenditures barely *broke even* in terms of creating value.[5] However, the estimated per-share market value of R&D expenditures generally increased over the years, peaking at $3.91 in 1999 before falling back to $1.54 in 2000. Interestingly, the estimated values are relatively low or negative around the recessions of 1980 to 1981 and 1990 to 1991.

FIGURE 9-8 Annual Estimates of the Market Value per $1 of R&D Expenditures per Share, and Ratio of Composite R&D Expenditures to Composite Book Equity

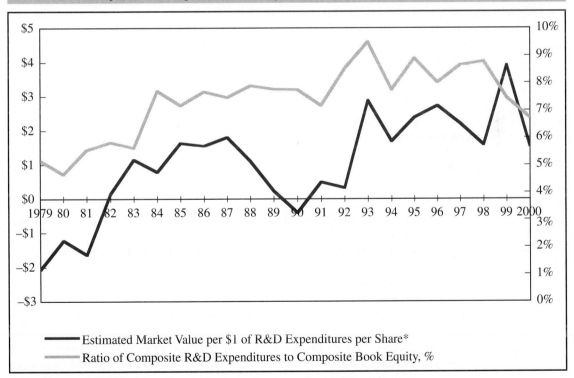

S&P Industrials, 1979–2000

Estimates are based on yearly regressions of (PPS – BVPS) against corresponding per share R&D expenditures. The correlation between the two series is 0.68.

---

[5] For each year, R&D expenditures are made throughout the year, but our measurement of their effect on a stock's market value is assessed at the end of the year. Also note that accounting rules dictate that R&D expenditures are to be expensed, rather than capitalized.

Finally, we test a hypothesis that managers tend to invest more in R&D when it is priced more highly in the market. If managers are rational with respect to R&D expenditures, we expect this to be the case. We test this hypothesis by examining the correlation between relative R&D expenditures and the estimated per-share market value of R&D contemporaneously. The correlation is 0.68. As expected, the two are positively related.

9.11   Summary of Learning Objectives

This chapter addresses three concepts that are important for the manager of a publicly traded firm. *First*, we define and discuss the Efficient Market Hypothesis. The key insight of this hypothesis is that, at any time, the market price of a firm's equity is equal to its true value. Researchers have made effective use of this hypothesis by conducting *event studies* of the effect of new information on a firm's market value. We examined the results of event studies focusing on the market's reactions to individual firms' announcements of (a) a revised capital expenditure plan, (b) earnings, (c) a capital structure change, (d) a seasoned equity offering, (e) a change in dividends, and (f) a merger.

Second, we discussed determinants of a firm's cost of equity capital. Both the CAPM and the Fama and French Three-Factor Model appear to have merit in providing estimates of a firm's cost of equity. However, other factors that are not directly accounted for in these models also affect a firm's cost of equity, such as transaction and signaling costs, principal–agent conflicts, and an illiquidity premium.

Third, we presented several models for the valuation of a firm's equity. Two key requirements for these valuation models are (a) the firm's current dividends or earnings, (b) an estimate of either the growth in dividends or earnings or, alternatively, the present value of the firm's profitable future investments, and (c) the discount rate.

In sum, this chapter provides several tools that a firm's management can use to improve their ability to discern how the market values the firm's equity, and thus to succeed in the directive of maximizing the same.

Review Questions and Problems

1. Describe the Efficient Market Hypothesis (EMH): (a) in words and (b) in mathematical terms.
2. Explain the paradox of market efficiency. Then explain how the paradox can be resolved.
3. List and briefly define the three forms of market efficiency.
4. Describe event study methodology in detail.
5. Over the weekend prior to April 3, 2000, a U.S. District Court ruled that Microsoft was a monopoly. On Monday, April 3, Microsoft's stock return was –14.471 percent, while the return on the S&P 500 (the "market") was 0.493 percent. For the two years leading up to this date, the "market model" relationship between Microsoft's daily returns and the market's daily returns was as follows:

$$R_{MSFT,t} = 0.19\% + 0.60(R_{m,t}) + \varepsilon_{MSFT,t}.$$

Using this result, compute the abnormal return on Microsoft's stock on April 3, 2000.

6. Summarize and discuss the results of each of the six classic event studies discussed in the chapter.
7. Using the CAPM, determine Microsoft's cost of equity given: $r_f = 5$ percent, $r_m = 12$ percent, and $\beta_{Msft} = 1.81$.
8. Critique the Fama and French Three-Factor Model for the cost of equity.
9. Discuss the potential effect of each of the following factors on a firm's cost of equity:
    a. Ownership structure and agency costs of management
    b. Signaling and flotation costs
    c. Illiquidity
    d. Leverage
10. IBM paid cash dividends totaling $0.51 per share in 2000. Over the previous three years, IBM's dividends grew at an annual rate of 9.59 percent. Assume that this dividend growth rate will continue into perpetuity, and that the proper discount rate for IBM's equity is $r_E = 10.5$ percent.
    a. Compute the value of IBM's stock at year-end 2000.
    b. The actual price of IBM stock at year-end 2000 was $85. Comparing this price to your calculation of IBM's value in (a), was IBM overpriced or underpriced at year-end 2000?
11. General Electric Corp. (GE) paid cash dividends totaling $0.57 per share in 2000. Over the previous three years, GE's dividends grew at an annual rate of 15.4 percent. Assume that this growth rate will continue for five more years, after which dividend growth will revert to a normal annual rate of 8 percent into perpetuity. Also assume that the appropriate discount rate for GE is 11 percent.
    a. Compute the value of GE's stock at year-end 2000.
    b. The actual price of GE stock at year-end 2000 was $47.9375. Comparing this price to your calculation of GE's value in (a), was GE overpriced or underpriced at year-end 2000?
12. Merck & Co. paid cash dividends totaling $1.21 per share in 2000, while its earnings per share was $2.90 per share. Over the five-year period of 1996 to 2000, Merck's average ROE was 41.5 percent, and its overall dividend payout ratio was 0.445. Assume that (a) the ROE figure is a fair estimate of the expected return on Merck's future investments, (b) the historical payout ratio will persist into perpetuity, and (c) Merck's discount rate is 25 percent.
    a. Compute the value of Merck's stock at year-end 2000.
    b. The actual price of Merck's stock at year-end 2000 was $93.925. Comparing this price to your calculation of Merck's value in (a), was Merck overpriced or underpriced at year-end 2000?
    c. Can you identify some aspect of the numbers in this problem that seems wrong?
13. The price of Merck & Co.'s stock at year-end 2000 was $93.925. The company earned $2.90 per share in 2000. If Merck's discount rate is 25 percent, what is the value of *PVPFIO*?

Creative Thinking Issues

1. Do you believe that the market is efficient in any of the following forms? Why or why not?
    a. Weak form
    b. Semistrong form
    c. Strong form

2. Two widely known competing investment philosophies state that an investor should choose, for his or her portfolio, stocks of (a) firms whose earnings have been growing at a faster rate than other firms (the *growth* philosophy) versus (b) firms that are currently underpriced (the *value* philosophy). If at a given time all stocks in the market were sorted by P/E, which stocks would those that adhere to the growth philosophy choose? Which would the value philosophy adherents choose? What is the basic assumption of each philosophy regarding the market's valuation of firms' future investments?

3. As investors entered the period of 1995 to 1999 (i.e., at the end of 1994), do you think they *priced* U.S. stocks (represented by the S&P 500 index) to provide an average annual return of 28.7 percent, or were the actual returns, which averaged 28.7 percent *ex post, higher* than expected? Support your opinion with evidence, analysis, and arguments.

4. Do you believe that stocks in the U.S. market are currently overpriced, fairly priced, or underpriced? Support your opinion with evidence, analysis, and arguments.

Projects and Analyses

1. Identify a sample of firms, all of which have announced their latest quarterly earnings on the same trading day. For each firm, collect data on the firm's reported earnings per share (*EPS*) and the return on the firm's stock on the day of the earnings announcement. Sort these firms in ascending order according to (a) *EPS* or (b) if possible, some measure of *earnings surprise* (e.g., the difference between the firm's actual reported *EPS* and analysts' consensus forecasts of *EPS* prior to the announcement). Plot a graph of the stock returns against the sorting variable, and determine whether the expected positive relationship occurs.

2. Select a firm, and generate several formal estimates of its cost of equity.

3. Generate your own numerical examples of the valuation of the stock of a (hypothetical or actual) firm using each of the following models: (a) the Dividend Growth Model, (b) the Constant Dividend Model, (c) the Two-Stage Dividend Growth Model, (d) the Sustainable Growth Model, and (e) the Investment Opportunities Model.

4. Collect data on the current *PPS* and *EPS* for a sample of firms. Regress *PPS* against *EPS*, and interpret the resulting values of the intercept and slope coefficients.

CHAPTER

Corporate Bonds: Terms, Issuance, and Valuation

10

10.1 INTRODUCTION

In Chapter 1, we found that debt is the principal source of long-term external financing for U.S. nonfinancial firms (review Figure 1-4a). For large firms, long-term debt generally takes the form of publicly issued corporate bonds, while smaller firms are more likely to borrow via private debt contracts with banks or other financial institutions. As an integral part of its financial policies and strategies, a firm's management must decide not only the amount of debt to have in the firm's capital structure, but also the portfolio of bonds and other debt contracts, and the terms to include in each contract. These decisions turn on the firm's strategies in dealing with risk, taxes, principal–agent conflicts, and information asymmetry.

More than a simple *fixed income* security, the typical corporate bond is a complex financial instrument. Its value and risk reflects (a) conditions in the economy and the financial markets, (b) characteristics of the issuer, and (c) terms in the bond contract. Given the complexity of corporate debt contracts and their strategic usage, we divide our analysis of corporate debt into two chapters. In this chapter, we discuss the terms in publicly issued corporate bond contracts, the process by which they are issued, and their valuation.[1] In Chapter 15, we follow up with analyses of a firm's strategic selections of debt funding sources and terms. (We also discuss innovations in the corporate bond market in Chapter 19.)

This chapter is organized as follows. In Section 10.2, we describe the basic structure of the corporate bond contract, or *indenture*, focusing on various terms, covenants, and provisions that are often included. In Section 10.3, we discuss the process by which a firm issues a bond in the U.S. public bond market. In Sections 10.4 and 10.5, we discuss determinants of a bond's risk. In Section 10.6, we discuss determinants of the yield and expected return on a corporate bond. In Section 10.7, we present a popular approach to estimating the fair yield to maturity on a corporate bond, the *bond yield spread matrix*. Section 10.8 is devoted to a detailed analysis of the valuation of a particularly complex security, the *convertible bond*. Finally, Section 10.9 summarizes the chapter's learning objectives, as usual.

10.2 TERMS IN CORPORATE BOND CONTRACTS

In this section, we discuss terms that are generally included in a corporate bond contract. The *basic terms* of the contract specify (a) the amount and timing of future coupon interest and principal promised by the borrowing firm to bondholders, (b) the

---

[1]To focus on the many issues specific to corporate bonds, we do not discuss the general pricing of bonds. For reference purposes, we provide two appendixes. Appendix A discusses a bond's *yield to maturity* and *duration*. Appendix B discusses theories of the *term structure of interest rates*.

security and priority status of the issue, and (c) the trustee that has been appointed to protect the interests of bondholders. Additional terms include *restrictive covenants* and *alternative retirement provisions*. A restrictive covenant is any specification in the contract that restricts the borrowing firm's activities. An alternative retirement provision allows either the borrowing firm or bondholders to alter the timing or form of the promised principal payments under specified conditions.

10.2.1   Basic Terms of a Bond Contract

Promised Payments

The most fundamental terms in a bond contract specify the amount and timing of future cash payments promised by the borrowing firm to bondholders. In exchange for these promised future cash payments, the firm receives cash from the initial purchasers of the bonds. In a traditional *fixed-income* bond, the borrower promises to make fixed periodic (usually semiannual) interest, or *coupon,* payments at a specified rate relative to the amount borrowed, the *principal*, and to repay the principal on a specified *maturity date*.

Some corporate bonds provide coupon interest at a variable or *floating* rate. Coupon interest may float with (a) the yield on U.S. Treasury securities, (b) the London Interbank Offered Rate (LIBOR), or (c) the firm's credit rating. Still other bonds are pure-discount (that is, *zero-coupon*) bonds, which provide no coupon interest whatsoever; or *deferred-coupon* bonds, which commence paying interest after a deferment period of several years.

Appointment of a Trustee

In Chapter 3, we discussed conflicts of interest between a borrowing firm and its creditors. This problem is exacerbated in the case of a public bond, because the ownership of public bonds is generally dispersed among many bondholders. For these reasons, the interests of the investors in a public corporate bond are protected in part by the appointment of a *trustee* (usually a bank), who is charged with monitoring the firm's compliance with the various terms, covenants, and provisions in the contract. If the firm fails to make any promised payment in a timely manner (usually allowing for a 30-day grace period), the trustee declares the firm to be in *default* and bondholders can force the firm into bankruptcy. The firm is also technically in default if it fails to comply with a covenant or provision.

Security and Priority Status of a Bond

The corporate bond indenture also specifies the *security* and *priority status* (or *seniority*) of the issue. These terms are particularly important in the event that the firm defaults and bondholders must seek relief in bankruptcy court. A bond that is secured with real estate such as a building or warehouse is called a *mortgage* bond. Holders of mortgage bonds not only enjoy the pledge of real estate as collateral, but also generally garner the highest seniority among all debt claims against the firm. A bond secured with equipment (generally purchased with the proceeds of the offering) is called an *equipment certificate* or *chattel mortgage*. If the issuing firm does not pledge specific assets as collateral, the bond is called a *debenture*. If a debenture has the highest priority among all of the firm's debentures, it is called a *senior debenture*. A debenture that explicitly has the lowest priority is called a *subordinated debenture*.

10.2.2 Restrictive Covenants

Restrictive covenants are designed to protect the interests of the bondholders, and as such provide a clear indication of conflicts of interest between shareholders and bondholders. A covenant may be included to restrict the borrower's (a) use of the proceeds of the bond offering, (b) future operations (e.g., an asset sale), (c) future debt financing, or (d) freedom to pay dividends to shareholders.

Restrictions on the Use of Proceeds

In many, though not all, corporate bond contracts, the borrower must use most or all of the proceeds for a purpose or purposes stated in the contract. From our discussions in Chapter 3 of incentives for a firm to expropriate wealth from bondholders, it is clear why such a restriction may be required. Suppose a firm states that it wishes to use the proceeds of a bond offering to retire a like amount of bank debt, and investors value the bond with the assumption that the preexisting bank debt will be retired immediately. If the firm then fails to retire the bank debt, the value of the bonds will likely fall, because the firm is maintaining higher leverage than the bond investors anticipated. (This loss will be greater if the bank debt has a higher priority.)

Restrictions on Future Operations

As we also demonstrated in Chapter 3, after issuing debt the firm's management, acting in the interest of its shareholders, has an incentive to increase the riskiness of the firm's activities and thereby expropriate wealth from the bondholders. This can be accomplished in a number of ways, including making investments in relatively risky projects, changing the firm's production methods or marketing strategies, and selling certain critical assets such as plant and equipment.

The bondholders' interest can be protected if a covenant prohibits such means of expropriation. A common example of such a restriction is the *mortgage*, in which real assets are pledged as security. The firm cannot sell the pledged assets as long as the mortgage bonds are outstanding, and the bondholders have a priority claim on the pledged assets in the event of bankruptcy.

However, restricting a firm's operations is problematic because (a) it requires foresight with regard to the type of expropriative activities in which the firm might engage, (b) it may interfere with management's ability to operate the firm profitably, and (c) enforcement requires costly monitoring by the bondholders and the trustee. Therefore, whether the bond contract includes covenants that explicitly preclude expropriative activities depends on the balance of a trade-off between the value of the protection that such a restriction provides to bondholders and the dual costs of restricting the firm's pursuit of profitable investment opportunities and monitoring compliance.

Restrictions on Future Financing Activities

Another means by which management may expropriate wealth from bondholders is to issue additional debt. If the new debt has the same or higher priority as previously issued debt, the value of the old bondholders' claim against the firm is *diluted*. Thus, some bond contracts restrict the firm's ability to issue additional debt. Again, however, such restrictions may inhibit management's ability to (a) pursue future profitable investment opportunities that require debt financing, and (b) adjust the firm's capital structure over time. Thus, restrictions on additional financing can be costly.

A lesser restriction (if any) is more commonly included, which requires any new debt to be *subordinated* to the bonds currently being offered. This lesser restriction allows the firm to maintain access to the debt markets in the future, and at the same time protects the interest of the existing bondholders. Indeed, the subsequent issuance of subordinated debt may *enhance* the value of the existing bonds, because it results in the infusion of cash into the firm, which presumably will be used to generate additional earnings, against which the original bondholders have a priority claim.

Restrictions on Dividends

Yet another means by which management can expropriate wealth from the firm's bondholders is to increase dividends. In the extreme, dividend payments can be used to *siphon off* the value of the firm to the shareholders, leaving the bondholders with a claim against a firm that is little more than an empty shell. In rare cases, a bond contract will include an absolute prohibition on the payment of dividends. More commonly, dividends are only *limited* under normal circumstances, and are *prohibited* only if the firm fails to generate a minimum level of earnings or to maintain a minimum net worth.

10.2.3   Alternative Retirement Provisions

Next, we describe several common alternative retirement provisions, including (a) the *call provision*, (b) the *sinking fund provision*, (c) the *put provision*, and (d) the *conversion provision*. Later, we discuss the effects of these provisions on a bond's value and risk.

The Call Provision

Long-term corporate bonds often include a call provision. The call provision allows the firm to repurchase (i.e., retire or *call*) some or all of the bonds prior to their scheduled maturity by paying a prespecified *call price*. Some bonds are callable at par value. For others, a schedule of call prices is established, which begins in the first year at par value plus one year's coupon interest (the latter representing the *call premium* or *call penalty*), and declines linearly to par value near maturity. Most call provisions also specify an initial *deferment period* during which time the firm cannot call the bonds. A less restrictive deferment allows the firm to call the bonds for purposes other than to refinance the debt at a lower interest cost.

The call provision imparts a valuable option to the borrowing firm, which management will use to the advantage of the shareholders, and thus to the disadvantage of the bondholders. Bondholders are compensated *ex ante* for the call provision in terms of a *yield premium*. Later, we provide estimates of the effect of a call provision on a bond's yield.

The Sinking Fund Provision

The *sinking fund provision* requires the firm to retire a specified percentage of the bonds each year, following a specified deferment period. The sinking fund provision reduces the effective maturity of a corporate bond, and thus reduces default risk.

However, the typical sinking fund provision also imparts a valuable option to the firm in terms of *how* it satisfies the obligation. The firm can either (a) call the bonds by lottery (according to the individual bond's serial numbers), typically at their par value, or (b) purchase the requisite number of bonds in the open market. Of course, management will choose the option that is less costly. Therefore, if the market price of the bonds is higher than its par value, the firm will choose to call the requisite number of bonds via the lottery mechanism. On the other hand, if the market price is lower than par value, the firm will engage in open market purchases of the requisite number of bonds, and present them to the trustee to satisfy the sinking fund requirement. This option will be used to the disadvantage of bondholders, so bond investors will demand a yield premium for this option. Thus, the overall effect of the sinking fund provision on a bond's yield is ambiguous. (See Kidwell, Marr, and Ogden [1989] for discussion and empirical analyses.)

The Put Provision

Some corporate bonds include a put provision, which provides bondholders with a put option; that is, the right to redeem their bonds at any time, usually after a deferment period of three to five years, and usually at the bond's par value. Bondholders will use the put option to their advantage, so the inclusion of a put provision should lower the required yield on the bond.

With the general put provision, the bondholder may find it optimal to redeem the bond if its value, as an outstanding issue, is less than the put price. This circumstance may arise either because the general level of interest rates has risen since the bond was issued, or the firm's default risk has increased. However, in the latter case if the firm reaches the point of bankruptcy very suddenly, the firm may declare bankruptcy before the bonds can be redeemed, rendering the put option worthless, even though it is obviously deeply *in the money*. (See Chatfield and Moyer [1986] for discussion and empirical analyses.)

The Conversion Provision

Historically, about 10 percent of long-term corporate bonds issued in the United States have included a *conversion provision*. The conversion provision allows bondholders to exchange their bonds for shares of the firm's equity at a specified *conversion ratio*, expressed in terms of the number of shares received for each bond. Essentially, the convertible bond is a portfolio of an otherwise equivalent nonconvertible bond and a call option on the firm's stock. We discuss other details of the conversion provision, and the valuation of convertibles, in Section 10.8.

10.3   THE CORPORATE BOND ISSUANCE PROCESS

Issuing a corporate bond in the U.S. public bond market is a seven-step process. *First*, the issuing firm selects an *underwriter*—that is, an investment bank that assists the firm in virtually every subsequent step in the process. *Second*, the issuer decides the amount of the offering. *Third*, the firm decides on the terms, covenants, and provisions that will be included in the contract. *Fourth*, the issue is registered with the Securities and Exchange Commission (SEC). *Fifth*, the firm may seek to have the bond *rated* by one or more credit rating agencies such as Moody's or Standard & Poor's. *Sixth*, the underwriter generates a tentative price for the issue. *Seventh*, the issue is marketed and sold to public investors. We now discuss each of these steps, and follow with an overview of corporate bonds issued by U.S. nonfinancial firms from 1979 to 1999.

10.3.1   Selecting an Underwriter

To float a bond in the U.S. public bond market, a firm must obtain the services of an investment-banking firm such as Merrill Lynch or Goldman Sachs. Generally, investment banks form a temporary alliance, called a *syndicate*, to underwrite a bond issue. One of the investment banks serves as the lead underwriter. The lead underwriter undertakes the bulk of the *due diligence* required to investigate the firm, to get the issue registered with the SEC, and to obtain a credit rating for the issue. In return, the lead underwriter receives the lion's share of the fees charged to the firm for the underwriting. The main task of other syndicate members is to assist in marketing the issue. For their services, the firm pays the underwriters a fee that is commonly expressed as a percentage of the proceeds of the offering, and this percentage is called the *underwriter spread*.

Negotiated Underwriting versus Competitive Bidding

An issuer can choose an underwriter by either of two methods. In a *negotiated underwriting*, the firm negotiates with a single investment bank. In *competitive bidding*, the firm solicits bids from among several investment banks for the job of underwriting the issue. The optimal method of selecting an underwriter has been a matter of considerable debate in the corporate finance literature. A traditional argument is that an issuing firm should opt for competitive bidding, because it will result in a lower underwriter spread.

However, Logue and Tinic (1999) essentially argue that *you get what you pay for*. If a firm obtains the services of an underwriter at a low cost through competitive bidding, the underwriter is likely to make only the minimum effort in conducting due diligence and attracting investors for the offering. In the end, this may be costly because the firm's bonds may sell at a lower price (i.e., a higher yield) as a result.

10.3.2   Deciding the Amount of the Offering

By the time a firm selects an underwriter for a bond offering, its management probably has a good idea of how much it wants to borrow. However, in many cases the underwriter may influence the size of the offering. The underwriter may evaluate the firm's financial condition and funding needs, as well as the condition of the credit markets, and suggest a larger or smaller offering. Once the issue is registered with the SEC, however, a complete withdrawal of an offering is a fairly rare occurrence. From 1979 to 1999, we found 12,751 bond issues that were placed in the U.S. public bond market by U.S. nonfinancial firms. (We discuss these offerings later.) In contrast, we found only 252 pending issues that were withdrawn.

10.3.3   Deciding Terms, Covenants, and Provisions

Deciding on the basic terms, covenants, and provisions to include in a bond contract is a delicate and complex task. Here the lead underwriter may earn the bulk of its fees, particularly in the case of a high-risk offering. The underwriter acts as an intermediary between the firm, which may have definite preferences, and potential bond purchasers, who have their own preferences. (We discuss these issues in Chapter 15.)

10.3.4   Registering the Offering with the SEC

As we discussed in Chapter 5, the SEC requires the registration of all securities offered to the public. The SEC currently provides two alternative methods of registering a public bond issue. In the *traditional method*, the firm files the necessary documents and must issue the registered bonds within 180 days. For many years, issuers complained that this time constraint was too restrictive, not allowing the issuer the flexibility to either time the issue date or to issue the bonds on a piecemeal basis.

In response to these complaints (as well as competition from the less restrictive Eurobond market), in 1982 the SEC adopted Rule 415, also known as the *shelf registration* rule. It allows qualifying firms to register a bond offering and then sell it either as a whole or piecemeal at any time over several years. Rule 415 provides firms greater flexibility in tapping the bond market over time.

10.3.5   Obtaining a Bond Rating

An important part of the issuance process is obtaining a rating for a bond issue from an independent credit rating agency. The two most notable credit rating agencies in the U.S. are Moody's Investor Service and Standard & Poor's. Two additional rating agencies are Duff & Phelps Credit Rating Co. and Fitch, Inc. These agencies provide an independent assessment of the issuer's creditworthiness (or, conversely, the issuer's default risk), assigning a rating that corresponds to this assessment. Rating agencies charge a fee for this service. The issue's rating is then made public, generally before the issue is sold to the public.

A credit rating provides important information to potential investors—specifically, an independent assessment of default risk. Obtaining a rating can also help the issuer. Researchers have argued that the rating process serves a *certification* function in terms of mitigating the information asymmetry problem. (The underwriter serves this function as well. We discussed certification in Chapters 4 and 5.)

10.3.6   Pricing the Issue

We discuss the *nitty gritty* of corporate bond pricing later in the chapter. Here we discuss some of the basic mechanics of the pricing process in practice. The pricing process commences after (a) the amount of the offering has been determined, (b) all of the terms (sans the coupon rate), covenants, and provisions have been fixed, (c) the issue has been registered with the SEC, (d) if possible, a tentative rating for the issue has been secured, and (e) the issuer, in consultation with the underwriter, has set the issue date.

The underwriter then examines the offering and estimates the coupon rate that will be required to render the bond's market price equal to its *par value* (or *face value*).[2] The required coupon rate depends not only on issuer characteristics and contract terms, but also on market factors. The most important market factor is the yield on a default-free U.S. Treasury security that has (approximately) the same maturity as the pending issue. The yield on the focal Treasury security changes on a daily basis, so the underwriter typically delays setting the coupon rate on a pending corporate bond until the issue date.

On the issue date, the underwriter checks the yield on the focal Treasury security, and then fixes the coupon rate on the new issue equal to the Treasury yield plus a *yield premium* that the underwriter estimates will be required to render the market price of

---

[2]Obviously, this is not the case for pure-discount bonds. However, for the vast majority of new corporate bonds, the objective is to set terms, especially the coupon rate, such that the bond's initial price is equal to par value.

the bond equal to its par value. Generally, the underwriter can accurately estimate the required yield premium well in advance, based on current yield premiums on outstanding corporate bonds that have similar characteristics.

10.3.7   Marketing and Selling the Issue

Although the marketing and selling of a new corporate bond issue is last in our list, it is certainly not of least importance. Nor does it necessarily commence only after all of the other steps have been taken. The underwriting syndicate spends days or weeks lining up potential buyers for a new issue.

The bulk of corporate bonds issued in the United States are held by financial institutions, including life and casualty insurance companies, commercial banks, mutual funds, and pension funds. Underwriters have regular contacts with such institutions and keep abreast of their demand for corporate bonds in general, and corporate bonds with certain characteristics in particular (e.g., bonds with an investment-grade rating). Underwriters that are also brokerage firms (e.g., Merrill Lynch) may put out the word to individual clients that a new corporate bond is available. In addition, the syndicate generally places nonsolicitation advertisements in the *Wall Street Journal* or other important newspapers notifying the public of the availability of the issue. These are called *tombstone* ads.

10.3.8   A Case in Point

On May 26, 1998, Phillips Petroleum Co. filed a universal shelf registration statement with the SEC for $700 million of various types of debt and equity securities. Combined with $300 million remaining under earlier shelf registrations, the firm could issue a total of $1 billion of securities. Pursuant to the registration, Phillips hired Merrill Lynch, on a negotiated basis, to be the lead underwriter for an offering of $200 million of 7 percent, 30-year debentures. The company stated that the proceeds were to be used for "general corporate purposes." The bonds were callable at any time (i.e., without a deferment).[3] The contract did not include a sinking fund, and the bonds were not convertible. The debentures garnered a rating of "A–" from Standard & Poor's. (We discuss S&P ratings later.) The total underwriter fee was $1.75 million, so the underwriter spread was 0.875 percent.

Presumably, the coupon rate on the debentures was set to render the market value of the debentures equal to their par value. The issue-date yield on 30-year U.S. Treasury bonds was 5.66 percent, so if the price of the debentures had been 100 percent of par value, their yield, 7 percent, would have represented a 134 basis-point *spread over Treasuries*. However, the bonds sold at a price of $99.293 per $100 of par value. As a result, the issue-date yield on the debentures was 7.06 percent, representing a 140 basis-point spread over Treasuries.

10.3.9   Initial Analyses of Corporate Bonds Issued Publicly in the United States, 1979–1999

We conclude this section with two discussions of statistics associated with 12,751 corporate bonds issued by U.S. nonfinancial firms in the U.S. public bond market from 1979 to 1999.

---

[3]The call provision in the Phillips was an innovative type known as a *make whole* call provision. We discuss this and other innovations in corporate bond contracting in Chapter 19.

An Overview of Corporate Bond Issues: 1979–1999

Our first depiction is provided in Figure 10-1. The figure shows the following aspects of corporate bonds issued each year from 1979 to 1999: (a) number of issues, (b) aggregate proceeds, (c) median years to maturity, (d) percent of bonds with a speculative-grade rating, (e) percent of bonds that have a floating coupon rate (as opposed to fixed), (f) percent of bonds that are callable, (g) percent of bonds with a sinking fund, and (h) percent of bonds that are convertible.

Based on both the number of issues and aggregate proceeds, the U.S. market for corporate bonds has grown substantially from 1979 (230 issues, aggregate proceeds of $16.6 billion) to 1999 (725 issues, $153.9 billion). In terms of aggregate volume, new issues increased over ninefold from 1979 to 1999.

Other Publicly Issued Corporate Bonds Not Reflected in the Figures

The figures cited above actually *understate* the growth of public bonds issued by U.S. nonfinancial firms over this period. This is so because during this period two additional public markets for corporate bonds emerged that are not reflected in the figures. The first is the *Eurobond market*, which developed in the 1960s and became an important source of debt funds for U.S. firms in the 1980s. The Eurobond market is a global market for corporate bonds issued by firms from many different countries. This market has been attractive to U.S. firms, particularly large firms, because it is less regulated.

FIGURE 10-1 Aggregate Statistics on Corporate Notes and Bonds Issued Publicly in the United States

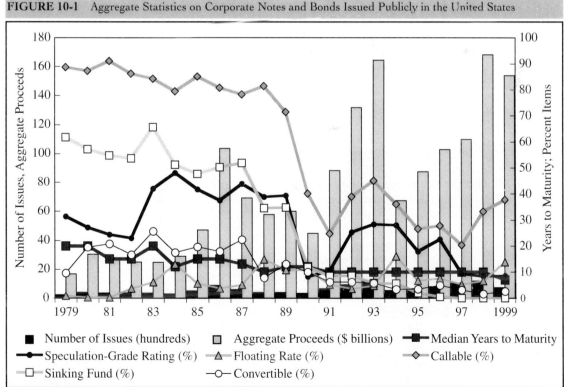

U.S. Nonfinancial Firms, 1979–1999
Source: Raw data from Securities Data Corporation new-issue database.

The second is the market for *144A issues*. In response to competition from the Eurobond market, the SEC adopted Rule 144A in 1990. This rule allows U.S. firms to issue bonds in the U.S. market with minimal regulatory *red tape* as long as they are sold only to *qualified investors* (e.g., financial institutions). As such, Rule 144A bonds are sold and traded in a *quasi-public* bond market.

Speculative-Grade Bonds

The public market for new speculative-grade bonds, also known as high-yield or *junk* bonds, was created virtually single-handedly by Michael Milken and his firm, Drexel Burnham Lambert, in the late 1970s. Prior to that time, the only corporate bonds that carried a speculative-grade rating were so-called *fallen angels*. These are bonds that initially garnered an investment-grade rating, but later the issuer experienced financial distress so that their rating fell into the speculative-grade category.

As Figure 10-1 shows, the proportion of new corporate bonds that carried a speculative-grade rating was quite substantial throughout the 1980s, peaking at 48 percent in 1984. However, the market for high-yield bonds collapsed in 1990 due to a confluence of events. The recession of 1990 to 1991 caused many of the previously issued high-yield bonds to default, shaking investor confidence. In addition, Milken was prosecuted and later convicted for securities law violations, and Drexel Burnham Lambert was forced to cease operations. The high-yield bond market revived in the 1990s, but it has yet to reestablish the prominence it had in the 1980s.

The Shortening of Maturities

One of the most important phenomena highlighted in Figure 10-1 is the steady shortening of the maturities of corporate bonds over the covered period. In 1979, the median maturity was 20 years; in 1989, 12 years; and in 1999, only 7 years. As bond maturities shortened, the prevalence of call provisions and sinking fund provisions also decreased. In 1979, the percentages of bonds with call provisions and sinking funds were 88.7 percent and 62.7 percent, respectively. By 1989, these percentages had decreased to 71.4 percent and 34.8 percent, respectively, and by 1999 the percentages were 37.8 percent and zero, respectively. Indeed, the sinking fund provision may be obsolete; it was not included in any corporate bonds issued from 1997 to 1999.

A principal factor that led to the shortening of corporate bond maturities was the occurrence of high and volatile interest rates in the late 1970s and early 1980s. Prior to this time, the standard corporate bond was a 30-year, fixed-coupon, callable bond. (We discuss this development in Chapter 15.)

Convertible Bonds

Finally, convertible bonds became relatively less prevalent over the covered period. In the 1980s, convertibles steadily represented roughly 20 percent of all new public corporate bonds. By the late 1990s, less than 5 percent of new public corporate bonds were convertible.

10.3.10   Additional Statistics on Corporate Bond Issues

Table 10-1 provides several summary statistics on the corporate bonds in our sample. The table is divided into two main sections, one for *nonconvertible bonds* (also known as *straight* bonds), and the other for *convertible bonds*. We separate the bonds because

TABLE 10-1 Issuance Details of 12,751 Corporate Bonds Issued Publicly by U.S. Nonfinancial Firms, 1979–1999

Bond Classification	Number of Bonds/ Percent	Security and Priority Status					Primary Use of Proceeds (%)					Debt Cost Measures	
		Negotiated/ Bidding	Shelf Registration	Secured	Debentures		Acquisition/ Buyout	Capital Investment	General Corporate Purposes	Refinance Debt	All Other Purposes	Average Underwriter Spread (%)	Average Yield Spread* (basis points)
					NOT SUBORDI-NATED	SUBORDI-NATED							
Nonconvertible	**11,562**	90.5%	65.5%	23.2%	66.4%	10.4%	3.6%	0.5%	28.2%	35.4%	32.4%	1.17	158
Rating Grade and Maturity Category													
Investment Grade	*81.5%*	*88.4%*	*75.7%*	*26.2%*	*73.1%*	*0.7%*	*1.4%*	*0.5%*	*30.8%*	*30.9%*	*36.5%*	*0.75*	*104*
Maturity ≤ 10 years	57.1%	92.4%	79.5%	16.9%	82.6%	0.6%	1.0%	0.5%	30.1%	28.3%	40.1%	0.62	91
Maturity > 10 years	42.9%	83.0%	70.6%	38.7%	60.4%	0.8%	1.9%	0.5%	31.6%	34.3%	31.7%	0.90	121
Speculative Grade	*18.5%*	*99.7%*	*20.5%*	*9.9%*	*37.1%*	*52.9%*	*13.3%*	*0.4%*	*17.0%*	*55.1%*	*14.1%*	*2.72*	*385*
Maturity ≤ 10 years	69.8%	99.7%	21.3%	9.9%	42.7%	47.4%	12.3%	0.5%	17.8%	59.0%	10.4%	2.64	392
Maturity > 10 years	30.2%	99.7%	18.7%	10.1%	24.1%	65.8%	15.6%	0.3%	15.0%	46.3%	22.8%	2.88	369
Convertible	**1,189**	100.0%	7.7%	0.3%	10.8%	88.9%	3.2%	0.2%	29.5%	29.8%	37.3%	3.10	-127
Rating Grade and Maturity Category													
Investment Grade	*19.3%*	*100.0%*	*17.9%*	*0.0%*	*30.1%*	*69.9%*	*3.1%*	*0.0%*	*28.8%*	*31.4%*	*36.7%*	*1.68*	*-220*
Maturity ≤ 10 years	24.5%	100.0%	46.4%	0.0%	50.0%	50.0%	3.6%	0.0%	51.8%	37.5%	7.1%	1.78	102
Maturity > 10 years	75.5%	100.0%	8.7%	0.0%	23.7%	76.3%	2.9%	0.0%	21.4%	29.5%	46.2%	1.65	-241
Speculative Grade	*80.7%*	*100.0%*	*5.3%*	*0.3%*	*6.3%*	*93.4%*	*3.2%*	*0.2%*	*29.7%*	*29.4%*	*37.5%*	*3.43*	*-108*
Maturity ≤ 10 years	26.8%	100.0%	11.3%	0.0%	5.8%	94.2%	3.5%	0.8%	42.4%	36.2%	17.1%	4.14	122
Maturity > 10 years	73.2%	100.0%	3.1%	0.4%	6.4%	93.2%	3.1%	0.0%	25.0%	26.9%	45.0%	3.17	-130

*Issue-date difference between bond's yield to maturity and yield on a U.S. Treasury security with comparable maturity.
Source: Raw data from Securities Data Corporation (SDC) new-issues database.

the conversion provision profoundly affects the character of a bond, as we will see here and in later analyses. Only 9.3 percent of the bonds issued during this period were convertible.

Underwriting and Registration Methods Employed

For 90.5 percent of the nonconvertible bonds, and for *all* of the convertible bonds, the issuing firm opted for the negotiated underwriting method (rather than competitive bidding) to secure underwriting services. Approximately two-thirds (65.5 percent) of the issuers of nonconvertible bonds employed shelf registration (versus traditional registration); only 7.7 percent of convertible bond issuers availed themselves of this alternative.

Security and Priority Status

We also examined the security and priority status of the bonds in the sample. We defined an issue as secured if it was backed by a pledge of either real estate or equipment. All other bonds were defined as either nonsubordinated debentures (e.g., senior debentures) or subordinated debentures. Among the nonconvertible bonds, 23.2 percent were secured, 66.4 percent were nonsubordinated debentures, and 10.4 percent were subordinated debentures. For the convertible bonds, the corresponding proportions were 0.3, 10.8, and 88.9 percent, respectively. Thus, convertible bonds generally are weaker in terms of security and priority.

Primary Use of Proceeds

We also sorted each class of bonds into five categories according to the issuer's stated primary use of the proceeds of the offering. These purposes are (a) acquisition or buyout, (b) capital investment, (c) general corporate purposes, (d) refinancing existing debt, and (e) all other purposes or unstated. Among both nonconvertible and convertible bonds, relatively few firms stated that the primary purpose of the issue was for acquisition/buyout or capital investment. Rather, stated purposes were fairly evenly divided among general corporate purposes, refinancing debt, and other purposes/unstated.

These results may be partially explained in terms of the information asymmetry paradigm. When a firm issues debt, it may very well plan to use the proceeds for expenditures that advance their strategic plans. However, it may be problematic for them to state precisely the use of the proceeds. Consequently, it is not surprising that so many firms select the fairly vague category of *general corporate purposes* or even refuse to state the purpose of the offering in public documents. On the other hand, if the primary purpose is truly to simply refinance debt, this is not likely to reveal strategic plans, and so this purpose may be readily stated.

Debt Cost Measures

The final two columns of Table 10-1 show average values of two debt cost measures: average underwriter spread and average yield spread over Treasuries. The average underwriter spread for nonconvertible bonds was 1.17 percent, and for convertible bonds was 3.10 percent. These results indicate that convertible bonds are more costly to underwrite, in part because greater due-diligence and selling efforts are required for such issues.

The average yield spreads for nonconvertible and convertible bonds were 158 basis points and –127 basis points, respectively. For nonconvertible bonds, yield spreads have a reasonably straightforward interpretation in terms of premiums required for default risk, callability, and maturity, as we explain later. In contrast, yield spreads on convertible bonds are more difficult to interpret because the conversion option essentially allows the firm to have a lower coupon rate, and thus a lower yield, as we explain in Section 10.8.

Differences by Rating Grade

We created subsamples of the nonconvertible and convertible issues by dividing them into two groups by their rating grade: investment grade versus speculative grade. The vast majority of nonconvertible bonds (81.5 percent) had an investment-grade rating, and the vast majority of convertible bonds (80.7 percent) had a speculative-grade rating. For nonconvertible bonds, interesting differences across the rating dimension are (a) investment-grade bonds are more likely to be either secured or at least not subordinated, whereas most speculative-grade bonds are subordinated debentures; (b) issuers of speculative-grade debt are relatively more likely to be refinancing existing debt; and (c) both the average underwriter spread and average yield spread are several times higher for speculative-grade bonds than for investment-grade bonds.

Differences by Maturity

We also sorted each of the previously defined subsamples into two categories according to maturity: bonds that mature in 10 years or less, and bonds that mature in more than 10 years. Among the interesting differences across maturity are the following. *First,* most nonconvertible bonds sort into the shorter-term category, and most convertible bonds have longer terms to maturity. *Second,* for nonconvertible investment-grade bonds, security is more common among longer-term issues (38.7 percent) than for shorter-term issues (16.9 percent). *Third,* among nonconvertible speculative-grade bonds, subordination is more common among longer-term issues (65.8 percent) than among shorter-term issues (47.4 percent).

10.3.11   Determinants of Underwriter Spreads

In this subsection, we examine underwriter spreads on the corporate bonds in our sample more closely, for three reasons. *First,* they often constitute a significant portion of the overall cost of obtaining debt funds. *Second,* the evidence shown in Table 10-1 indicates that underwriter spreads vary substantially across issues.

Third, and most importantly, we wish to examine the argument that underwriter spreads reflect substantial fixed costs. This argument is well established in the finance literature (e.g., see Smith 1986). The basic argument is that, for any bond issue, the underwriter must expend a similar amount of effort to (a) conduct due diligence, (b) file the necessary documents with the SEC, or (c) contact potential investors who may be willing to purchase the bonds. If this is true, we should observe that underwriter spread is inversely related to the size of the offering, reflecting economies of scale in the issuance process. However, an underwriter's efforts also depend on the characteristics of the issuer and the bond.

As before, we separated our sample of bonds into nonconvertible and convertible classifications. The bonds in each classification were then sorted into rating grades, and these were further subdivided into two groups according to maturity. Finally, to test for economies of scale in the issuance process, we sorted the bonds in each group into subgroups according to the size of the offering: (a) $0 million to $9.99 million; (b) $10 million to $49.9 million; (c) $50 million to $99.9 million; (d) $100 million to $499.9 million; and (e) $500 million or more. We then calculated average underwriter spreads for each subgroup. The results are displayed in Table 10-2.

For all nonconvertible bonds, underwriter spreads are somewhat inversely related to offer size, but the differences are not dramatic. The average spread ranges from 1.01 percent for offerings in the $50 million to $99.9 million range, to 2.08 percent for the smallest issues. In sharp contrast, for all convertible bonds underwriter spreads are clearly and substantially inversely related to offer size. Average underwriter spreads range from 2.04 percent for the largest issues to 7.53 percent for the smallest issues.

Our conclusions are modified somewhat when, for each bond classification, we separate the bonds by rating grade. For the nonconvertible bonds, a negative relationship between underwriter spread and issue size clearly emerges for bonds in both rating grades. However, for the convertible bonds, this negative relationship is strong only for the speculative-grade issues.

Perhaps the clearest evidence of economies of scale in the issuance process emerges when we further sort bonds by maturity. For almost every maturity-related row in the table, a negative relationship between underwriting spread and issue size is clearly evident.

Overall, the evidence in Table 10-2 is consistent with substantial economies of scale in the issuance process. In Chapter 15, we discuss the implications of these economies of scale for a firm's choice of debt funding source, particularly the choice between public and private debt issues.

TABLE 10-2 Average Underwriter Spreads as a Percent of Offering Proceeds

For Indicated Classifications of Corporate Bonds, and Sorted by Issue Size Based on 12,751 Bonds Issued Publicly by U.S. Nonfinancial Firms, 1979–1999

Bond Classification	All Bonds	Issue Size ($ million)				
		0–9.99	10–49.9	50–99.9	100–499.9	500+
Nonconvertible	**1.17**	**2.08**	**1.23**	**1.01**	**1.13**	**1.29**
Rating Grade and Maturity Category						
Investment Grade	*0.75*	*1.80*	*0.78*	*0.65*	*0.68*	*0.72*
Maturity ≤ 10 years	0.62	1.43	0.60	0.55	0.55	0.56
Maturity > 10 years	0.90	2.57	1.01	0.75	0.81	0.91
Speculative Grade	*2.72*	*5.16*	*3.33*	*2.74*	*2.48*	*2.42*
Maturity ≤ 10 years	2.64	4.80	3.21	2.76	2.48	2.15
Maturity > 10 years	2.88	5.80	3.43	2.71	2.48	2.83
Convertible	**3.10**	**7.53**	**3.52**	**2.39**	**2.07**	**2.04**
Rating Grade and Maturity Category						
Investment Grade	*1.68*	*0.78*	*2.09*	*1.65*	*1.64*	*1.79*
Maturity ≤ 10 years	1.78	0.78	*n/a*	1.61	1.92	1.59
Maturity > 10 years	1.65	*n/a*	2.09	1.66	1.54	2.16
Speculative Grade	*3.43*	*7.69*	*3.59*	*2.54*	*2.36*	*2.62*
Maturity ≤ 10 years	4.14	8.94	5.06	2.86	2.49	2.11
Maturity > 10 years	3.17	6.74	3.34	2.41	2.26	2.87

Source: Raw data from Securities Data Corporation (SDC) new-issues database.

10.4 BOND RISK: MATURITY AND LEVERAGE EFFECTS

In this section, we model the effects of maturity and leverage on the risk of a corporate bond. First, we model these relationships using the Black–Scholes Option Pricing Model (BSOPM). In Chapter 2, we established that the equity of a levered firm can be viewed as a call option on the firm's assets. We also showed that the BSOPM can be used to determine the instantaneous annual standard deviation of returns on either the (pure-discount) debt or the (non–dividend-paying) equity of a levered firm. Here we wish to use the model to ascertain the riskiness of a levered firm's debt as a function of debt maturity.

The formula for the instantaneous annual standard deviation of returns on a corporate bond, σ_D, is:

$$\sigma_D = [1 - N(d)]\left(\frac{V}{D}\right)\sigma,\tag{10.1}$$

where $N(d)$ is the cumulative normal distribution function, V and D are the values of the firm's assets and debt, respectively, and σ is the instantaneous annual standard deviation of returns on the firm's assets.

FIGURE 10-2 Debt Risk as a Function of Maturity

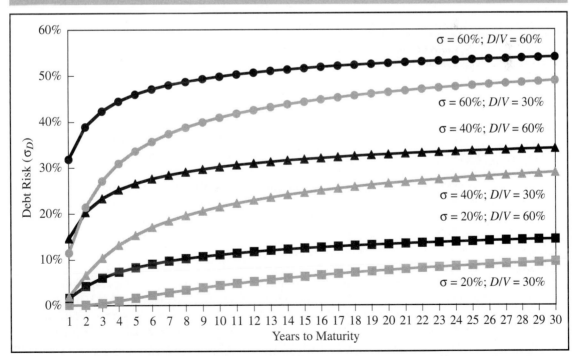

Instantaneous Annual Standard Deviation of Pure-Discount Debt (σ_D) as a Function of Maturity for Combinations of Firm Risk (σ) and Leverage (D/V), Based on the Black–Scholes Option Pricing Model

We wish to examine the relationship between debt risk and maturity by calculating values of σ_D using Equation 10.1 for debt maturities ranging from 1 to 30 years. To do so, however, we must deal with the following problem. It is clear that debt risk is also a function of the firm's leverage and the risk of the firm's assets. Therefore, we select several combinations of leverage and firm risk, and calculate debt risk by maturity for each of these combinations. We use two alternative values of firm leverage, $D/V = 30$ percent and $D/V = 60$ percent, as well as three alternative values of firm risk, $\sigma = 20$ percent, $\sigma = 40$ percent, and $\sigma = 60$ percent. For each value of maturity and σ, leverage is held constant by altering the promised maturity payment on the debt, X.

The results of the calculations are displayed in Figure 10-2. Each curve in the figure is labeled to indicate the combination of leverage and firm risk used in the calculations. For all combinations of D/V and σ, debt risk increases with maturity, and in most cases debt risk increases at a *decreasing rate* with maturity. In addition, by comparing across values of σ for a given level of leverage, we see that debt risk increases with σ for each and every value of debt maturity. Likewise, by comparing across values of D/V for a given level of σ, we see that debt risk increases with leverage for each maturity. These results provide at least a rough indication of the relative impacts of asset risk, leverage, and maturity on debt risk.

10.5   DEFAULT RISK AND CORPORATE BOND RATINGS

As noted earlier, the two most prominent credit rating agencies in the United States are Moody's and Standard & Poor's (S&P). Their ratings on corporate bonds are designed to measure, at least on an ordinal scale, the probability that the issuing firm will default on its promised payments. In this section, we discuss the S&P rating system for corporate bonds, and conduct several empirical analyses of determinants of S&P ratings.

10.5.1   S&P's Corporate Bond Ratings

The ratings that S&P assigns to corporate bonds are shown in Table 10-3, along with a brief description of the financial status of the typical issuer that garners a given rating. S&P ratings are grouped into two major categories, *investment grade* and *speculative grade*.

Among the investment-grade ratings, the AAA rating is given only to those firms that have an extremely strong financial capacity to meet interest and principal obligations on a timely basis. As we will see shortly, very few firms in the United States are financially sound enough to warrant this rating. Bonds rated AA, A, and BBB are also included in the investment-grade category.

Speculative-grade bonds are those rated BB, B, CCC, CC, or C, where BB bonds are the least speculative and those rated C the most speculative. The issuers of bonds in this group are currently financially solvent, and may even be profitable, but face one or more major risk factors—such as vulnerability to competitive pressures, a downturn in the economy, or lessening demand for its products—and they may have high leverage. For grades AA through CC, S&P adds "+" or "−" modifiers to indicate a relatively strong or weak issuer, respectively, within the grade. Finally, S&P assigns a rating of D to the bond of a firm that is in default.

TABLE 10-3 Standard & Poor's Definitions of Its Ratings for Long-Term Corporate Bonds

Rating	Definition
	Investment-Grade Ratings
AAA	An obligation rated AAA has the highest rating assigned by Standard & Poor's. The obligor's capacity to meet its financial commitment on the obligation is extremely strong.
AA	An obligation rated AA differs from the highest rated obligations only in small degree. The obligor's capacity to meet its financial commitment on the obligation is very strong.
A	An obligation rated A is somewhat more susceptible to the adverse effects of changes in circumstances and economic conditions than obligations in higher rated categories. However, the obligor's capacity to meet its financial commitment on the obligation is still strong.
BBB	An obligation rated BBB exhibits adequate protection parameters. However, adverse economic conditions or changing circumstances are more likely to lead to a weakened capacity of the obligor to meet its financial commitment on the obligation.
	Speculative-Grade Ratings
BB	An obligation rated BB is less vulnerable to nonpayment than other speculative issues. However, it faces major ongoing uncertainties or exposure to adverse business, financial, or economic conditions which could lead to the obligor's inadequate capacity to meet its financial commitment on the obligation.
B	An obligation rated B is more vulnerable to nonpayment than obligations rated BB, but the obligor currently has the capacity to meet its financial commitment on the obligation. Adverse business, financial, or economic conditions will likely impair the obligor's capacity or willingness to meet its financial commitment on the obligation.
CCC	An obligation rated CCC is currently vulnerable to nonpayment, and is dependent upon favorable business, financial, and economic conditions for the obligor to meet its financial commitment on the obligation. In the event of adverse business, financial, or economic conditions, the obligor is not likely to have the capacity to meet its financial commitment on the obligation.
CC	An obligation rated CC is currently highly vulnerable to nonpayment.
C	A subordinated debt or preferred stock obligation rated C is CURRENTLY HIGHLY VULNERABLE to nonpayment. The C rating may be used to cover a situation where a bankruptcy petition has been filed or similar action taken, but payments on this obligation are being continued. A C also will be assigned to a preferred stock issue in arrears on dividends or sinking fund payments, but that is currently paying.
D	An obligation rated D is in payment default. The D rating category is used when payments on an obligation are not made on the date due even if the applicable grace period has not expired, unless Standard and Poor's believes that such payments will be made during such grace period. The D rating also will be used upon the filing of a bankruptcy petition or the taking of a similar action if payments on an obligation are jeopardized.
Plus (+) or minus (–)	The ratings from AA to CCC may be modified by the addition of a plus or minus sign to show relative standing within the major rating categories.
r	This symbol is attached to the ratings of instruments with significant noncredit risks. It highlights risks to principal or volatility of expected returns which are not addressed in the credit rating.
N.R.	This indicates that no rating has been requested, that there is insufficient information on which to base a rating, or that Standard and Poor's does not rate a particular obligation as a matter of policy.

Source: Standard & Poor's Web site. Reprinted by permission.

The S&P Analytical Framework

The analytical framework that S&P uses to rate corporate bonds includes all of the following factors: (a) industry risk and potential, (b) business analysis, (c) the issuer's financial policies, (d) the firm's capital structure and bond provisions, (e) cash flow analysis, (f) financial flexibility analysis, and (g) measurements of net cash inflows and cash needs. The method by which S&P combines these factors is highly proprietary. However, ratings can be largely explained via observable measures of the financial status of the issuing firm, as we show next.

10.5.2   Empirical Analyses of the Determinants of S&P Ratings

In this subsection, we provide five empirical analyses of S&P bond ratings and their determinants.

The Typical Financial Characteristics of a Firm with a Given S&P Rating

For our first analysis of S&P ratings, we use a sample of 840 U.S. nonfinancial firms that were rated by S&P at year-end 1999. These firms were sorted into groups according to S&P rating, and average values of several financial variables were calculated for firms in each rating group. These variables include (a) market-to-book equity ratio (MEQ/BEQ), (b) median fixed-charge-coverage ratio (FCC) over the previous three years, (c) the standard deviation of the firm's return on assets (ROA) over five years ending in 1999, as a measure of business risk, (d) book debt ratio, as a measure of leverage, (e) the natural log of the firm's total assets, as a measure of firm size [ln(TA)], (f) capital intensity, measured as property, plant, and equipment to TA(PP&E/TA), (g) the firm's equity beta, and (h) the firm's current dividend yield.

The results are displayed in Table 10-4. As expected, higher-rated firms tend to have higher average values of MEQ/BEQ, FCC, ln(TA), and PP&E/TA, and lower values of σ(ROA), D/TA, and β. One surprise in the results is that dividend yields tend to be higher for higher-rated firms. Of course, dividends tend to *increase* default risk. A possible explanation for this result is that firms that are more financially sound are more likely to be able to pay dividends. That is, for stronger firms any dividend constraint that may be included in a bond contract is less likely to be binding.

Regression Analysis of S&P Ratings

Next, we examine the extent to which financial variables can explain rating variation in a multiple regression setting. The dependent variable in the regression is S&P bond ratings, converted to numerical values as shown in Table 10-4. The independent variables include all of the variables shown in Table 10-4. The results of the regression analysis are displayed in Table 10-5. The independent variables collectively explain the bulk of the variation in S&P numerical ratings, based on the adjusted R^2, 67.5 percent. In addition, the coefficients of all independent variables (save, perhaps, dividend yield) have the expected sign, and all are highly significant.

Testing the Stability of S&P Ratings

Our third empirical analysis focuses on the stability of the S&P ratings of individual firms over time. For this purpose we collected a sample of 1,209 U.S. nonfinancial firms that were rated by S&P at year-end 1996, and sorted them by rating

TABLE 10-4 Average Values of Variables That Influence Corporate Bond Rating

840 U.S. Nonfinancial Firms Sorted by S&P Bond Rating, 1999

Rating Alphabetical	Rating Numerical	Number of Firms	Market-to-Book Equity Ratio	Median Fixed-Charge Coverage	Standard Deviation of ROA	Book Debt Ratio (%)	Firm Size [ln(TA)]	Capital Intensity (PP&E/TA) (%)	Equity Beta (β)	Dividend Yield (%)
AAA	2	6	8.4	17.9	0.6	26.4	10.9	35.6	0.81	1.6
AA+	4	1	4.0	13.7	0.3	24.0	9.5	23.2	0.68	2.3
AA	5	13	8.7	8.5	1.1	31.7	9.2	48.9	0.62	2.9
AA–	6	20	7.7	9.0	1.4	28.5	8.9	42.7	0.63	3.0
A+	7	43	5.7	8.2	1.0	31.9	8.8	40.4	0.61	3.0
A	8	90	3.3	6.7	1.0	30.8	8.6	42.0	0.69	3.0
A–	9	57	3.5	5.9	1.5	34.1	8.4	47.9	0.80	2.5
BBB+	10	95	2.9	5.3	1.4	33.9	8.2	48.9	0.81	2.6
BBB	11	92	2.5	5.2	1.6	33.0	8.2	36.7	0.85	1.9
BBB–	12	72	1.8	4.4	1.4	34.5	8.0	38.6	0.90	1.5
BB+	13	56	2.9	3.2	2.3	41.8	7.7	40.9	0.87	1.2
BB	14	67	1.4	3.3	2.2	43.8	7.2	40.2	1.01	1.2
BB–	15	88	3.6	3.1	3.0	45.3	6.8	33.4	0.93	0.6
B+	16	79	1.7	2.5	3.1	49.3	6.5	36.7	0.99	0.5
B	17	40	1.3	0.9	5.3	57.8	6.4	29.4	1.27	0.0
B–	18	9	0.0	–0.5	5.1	70.1	6.3	30.6	1.39	0.0
CCC+	19	7	–1.5	0.7	7.1	59.0	5.9	53.9	0.71	0.0
CCC	20	3	–0.2	1.8	3.6	50.6	7.4	23.6	0.37	1.0
CCC–	21	1	0.2	4.0	2.7	62.2	6.2	77.5	1.26	0.0
CC	23	1	–0.6	0.2	4.4	84.8	5.8	91.4	–0.17	0.0

Source: Raw data from Standard & Poor's *Research Insight* database.

TABLE 10-5   Determinants of Corporate Bond Ratings

**Multiple Regression of S&P *Numerical* Bond Ratings against
Indicated Explanatory Variables
840 U.S. Nonfinancial Firms, 1999**

Dependent Variable: S&P Numerical Bond Rating*

Independent Variable	Slope Coefficient	t Value	Probability
Intercept	19.729	35.9	<0.001
Market-to-book equity ratio	−0.069	−5.9	<0.001
Median fixed-charge-coverage	−0.241	−13.1	<0.001
Standard Deviation of ROA (%)	0.134	4.6	<0.001
Book debt ratio [D/TA, (%)]	0.036	7.5	<0.001
Firm size [ln(TA)]	−1.016	−18.7	<0.001
Capital intensity [PP&E/TA (%)]	−0.014	−4.7	<0.001
Equity beta [β]	0.816	5.2	<0.001
Dividend yield (%)	−0.323	−9.5	<0.001
Adjusted R^2 67.5%			

*Numerical Ratings are as follows: AAA = 2, AA+ = 4, AA = 5, AA− = 6, A+ = 7, A = 8, A− = 9, BBB+ = 10, BBB = 11, BBB− = 12, BB+ = 13, BB = 14, BB− = 15, B+ = 16, B = 17, B− = 18, CCC+ = 19, CCC = 20, CCC− = 21, CC = 23.
Source: Raw data from Standard & Poor's *Research Insight* database.

grade. We then calculated the numbers of firms in each rating grade that (a) had the same rating at year-end 1999, (b) sustained a rating *downgrade* by year-end 1999, (c) experienced a rating *upgrade* by year-end 1999, and (d) had no rating at year-end 1999.

The results are shown in Table 10-6. Approximately one-third of the firms (405 firms) had the same rating at year-end 1999 as they had at year-end 1996. Of the firms whose rating changed, slightly more were downgraded (238) than were upgraded (209). Finally, 357 of the firms had no rating at year-end 1999. These results indicate that ratings change fairly frequently.

Rating Changes and Changes in Financial Variables

A change in a firm's bond rating is an important event, because it reflects a substantial change in the firm's financial strength. What causes a firm's rating to change? We addressed this question by examining more closely the firms identified in the previous analysis as having realized a rating change between 1996 and 1999. We sorted these firms into groups according to the numerical change in their rating and calculated, for each group, the average sales growth, the average change in debt ratio, and average change in market equity value, from year-end 1996 to year-end 1999. The results are displayed in Table 10-7.

As expected, those firms that experienced a rating upgrade generally experienced higher sales growth, a reduction in their debt ratio, and a substantial increase in their market equity value. In contrast, those firms that sustained a rating downgrade generally had weaker sales growth, increased their debt ratio, and sustained a substantial fall in market equity value.

TABLE 10-6   Changes in S&P Ratings From Year-End 1996 to Year-End 1999

1,209 U.S. Nonfinancial Firms Rated at Year-End 1996

Rating Distribution, 1996		Number of Firms with Same Rating in 1999	Number of Firms Downgraded by 1999	Number of Firms Upgraded by 1999	Number of Firms Not Rated in 1999
Rating	*No. Firms*				
2 (AAA)	23	16	3	n/a	4
4 (AA+)	11	3	6	1	1
5 (AA)	27	17	9	1	0
6 (AA–)	43	23	15	2	3
7 (A+)	61	26	20	5	10
8 (A)	111	59	23	9	20
9 (A–)	82	26	29	12	15
10 (BBB+)	91	40	22	16	13
11 (BBB)	109	43	19	25	22
12 (BBB–)	89	24	19	24	22
13 (BB+)	62	14	8	21	19
14 (BB)	95	28	10	27	30
15 (BB–)	125	27	22	14	62
16 (B+)	155	39	21	27	68
17 (B)	76	17	8	12	39
18 (B–)	32	1	3	9	19
19 (CCC+)	11	0	1	3	7
20 (CCC)	5	2	0	0	3
21 (CCC–)	1	0	0	1	0
Totals:	**1,209**	**405**	**238**	**209**	**357**

Source: Raw data from Standard & Poor's *Research Insight* database.

TABLE 10-7   Rating Changes and Changes in Firm Fundamentals

Average Changes in Sales, Debt Ratio, and Market Value of Equity for 852 Firms Sorted by Change in S&P Numerical Rating from Year-End 1996 to Year-End 1999

Change in S&P Numerical Rating	Number of Firms	Average Change		
		Sales	*Debt Ratio*	*Market Equity Value*
<–3	12	119.3%	–1.7%	147.7%
–3	12	163.0%	–4.6%	447.6%
–2	47	83.7%	–3.8%	215.4%
–1	138	71.8%	2.3%	125.5%
0	405	110.8%	2.3%	65.6%
+1	129	27.5%	7.9%	8.9%
+2	46	43.9%	9.7%	5.9%
+3	24	33.8%	14.9%	–13.4%
>+3	39	15.3%	19.2%	–53.0%

Source: Raw data from Standard & Poor's *Research Insight* database.

FIGURE 10-3   Average Change in S&P Numerical Bond Ratings of U.S. Nonfinancial Firms, 1986–1999, and Annual U.S. GDP Growth, 1985–1999*

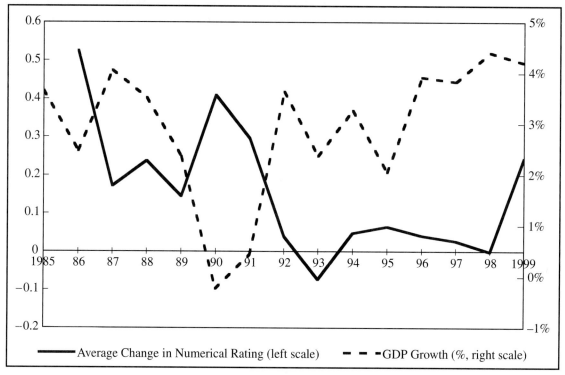

The correlation between these two series is –0.49.
Sources: Standard & Poor's *Research Insight* database; U.S. Department of Commerce.

Macroeconomic Effects on Aggregate Average Corporate Bond Ratings

Finally, we examined the effect of macroeconomic conditions on corporate bond ratings by calculating annual average changes in the numerical ratings over the years 1986 to 1999, and comparing these changes to gross domestic product (GDP) growth over the years 1985 to 1999. The results are displayed in Figure 10-3. The results indicate a strong inverse relationship, as we would expect. The contemporaneous correlation between these series is –0.49. The most notable feature in the figure is a substantial increase in average numerical bond rating during the recession of 1990 to 1991, and a substantial decrease thereafter.

10.6   MODELING YIELDS AND EXPECTED RETURNS ON CORPORATE BONDS

In this section, we provide several models of the yield and expected return on a corporate bond. We focus on the effects of three characteristics of a bond on its yield: default risk, maturity, and callability.

10.6.1   The Effect of Default Risk on a Bond's Yield and Expected Return

First, we present two alternative models of the effect of default risk on the yield to maturity and expected return on a corporate bond. For simplicity, we work only with simple pure-discount bonds.

Determining the Promised Yield on a Bond

We define a pure-discount corporate bond as a promise to pay the amount X in T years. Given the current market price of the bond, denoted as P, the bond's yield to maturity, denoted as y, can be calculated by solving for y in Equation 10.2, or more directly by using Equation 10.3:

$$P = \left(\frac{X}{(1 + y)^T} \right) \qquad (10.2)$$

$$y = \left(\frac{X}{P} \right)^{1/T} - 1. \qquad (10.3)$$

For a default-risky corporate bond, y is called the bond's *promised yield to maturity*, because the formulas implicitly assume that the issuer will make the promised payment of X with certainty.

A Case in Point

Consider the pure-discount bond issued in 1995 by Cellular Communications, Inc., detailed below:

> On August 17, 1995, **Cellular Communications, Inc.** issued 5-year, non-callable, zero-coupon senior notes with a total principal of $281.6 million. The lead underwriter for the issue was Donaldson Lufkin & Jenrette, who was hired on a negotiated basis. The issue was registered via the traditional registration method. The notes were rated CCC+ by S&P. The firm received proceeds of 148.6 million, or $52.783 per $100 of par value. Thus, the promised yield to maturity on this issue was 13.63% (= $(100/52.783)^{1/5} - 1$, in percent). This yield represented a spread of 726 basis points over the issue-date yield on 5-year U.S. Treasuries (6.37%). The underwriter spread was 7.1% of the offering proceeds. [*Source*: Securities Data Corp.]

Expected Return versus Promised Yield on a Default-Risky Bond

There is a positive probability that Cellular Communications will default on the bond detailed above. Consequently, as we will show, y is an *upward-biased* measure of the bond's *expected return to maturity*, r_D. The expected return on a bond, not its promised yield, is more relevant to both the bondholder and the firm. For the bondholder, r_D is the expected return on the bond, and for the firm, r_D is the true cost of debt.

We denote the expected payoff at maturity on a T-year default-risky pure-discount corporate bond as $E(X)$. It must be the case that $E(X) < X$ because the investor cannot receive more than the promised amount X at maturity (and will receive that amount only if the firm does not default), and the investor will receive a smaller amount if the firm defaults.

Given $E(X)$, we can calculate r_D using Equation 10.4:

$$r_D = \left(\frac{E(X)}{P}\right)^{1/T} - 1. \tag{10.4}$$

Suppose, for simplicity, we model the payoff on a default-risky pure-discount bond as a binomial process. With probability p the firm will pay the promised amount of X at maturity, and with probability $1 - p$ the firm will default, paying only the amount X', where $X' < X$. Then the expected payoff is

$$E(X) = p(X) + (1 - p)(X'). \tag{10.5}$$

For example, suppose we believe that the probability is $p = 0.9$ that Cellular Communications will pay the full face value of $X = \$100$ when the bond matures, and that with probability $(1 - p) = 0.1$ the firm will default, in which case the payment will be only $X' = \$40$. The expected payoff at maturity is then

$$E(X) = 0.9(\$100) + 0.1(\$40) = \$94,$$

and the bond's expected return to maturity is

$$r_D = \left(\frac{\$94}{52.783}\right)^{1/5} - 1 = 0.1223, \text{ or } 12.23\%.$$

Note that $E(X) < X$, so $r_D < y$ (i.e., $12.23\% < 13.63\%$).

The Invisibility of the Expected Return Premium on a Default-Risky Bond
In our example, we calculated the expected payoff at maturity on the Cellular Communications bond by arbitrarily assigning a probability of default and a payment in the default state. In reality, a bond investor cannot observe the market's expectation of the payoff on a bond. Therefore, even though the promised yield exceeds the yield on a default-free Treasury bond, the investor cannot be assured that the bond's *expected return* exceeds the yield on the riskless bond (i.e., that the promised yield embeds a default-risk premium).

To see this, suppose we change the probability of successful payment to $p = 0.53$. Then the expected payoff at maturity on the Cellular Communications bond changes to

$$E(X) = 0.53(\$100) + 0.47(\$40) = \$71.80,$$

and the bond's expected return to maturity changes to

$$r_D = \left(\frac{\$71.80}{52.783}\right)^{1/5} - 1 = 0.0635, \text{ or } 6.35\%.$$

Thus, the expected return is actually 2 basis points *lower* than the yield on the corresponding Treasury, 6.37 percent.

Calculating the Yield and Expected Return on a Corporate Bond Using the BSOPM

In Chapter 2, we provided the following formula for the instantaneous annual expected return, r_D, on the default-risky debt of a levered firm based on the Black–Scholes Option Pricing Model (BSOPM):

$$r_D = r_f + \left[\{1 - N(d)\} \left(\frac{V}{D}\right) \right] (r_V - r_f), \tag{10.6}$$

where again $N(d)$ is the cumulative normal distribution function, V is the value of the firm, D is the value of the debt, and r_V is the instantaneous annual expected return on the firm's assets.

To illustrate Equation 10.6, consider a firm whose assets have a value of $V = \$100$. The firm's management wishes to finance half of the assets with a pure-discount bond, so $D = \$50$. The expected return and standard deviation of the firm's assets are $r_V = 10$ percent and $\sigma = 30$ percent, respectively, and $r_f = 5$ percent. Management wishes to gauge the effect of varying the bond's maturity on its yield and expected return.

We can use the BSOPM to determine, for each maturity under consideration, the promised payment, X, required to render the value of the bonds equal to the required financing of $D = \$50$. We can then calculate, for each maturity, the bond's promised yield via Equation 10.3, and expected return via Equation 10.6.

We performed these calculations for debt maturities of 1 to 20 years. The results are displayed in Figure 10-4. The results reveal three important relationships: (a) Both promised yield and expected return increase at a decreasing rate with maturity; (b) expected return is always less than promised yield; and (c) the difference between the promised yield and expected return increases at a decreasing rate with maturity.

10.6.2   The Effect of a Call Provision on a Bond's Required Yield to Maturity

In this subsection, we develop a simple model to illustrate the effect of a call provision on a bond's required, or *fair*, yield to maturity. The required yield on a new bond is the coupon rate that renders the bond's market price equal to its face value.

Determinants of the Effect of a Call Provision on a Bond's Yield

The effect of a call provision on a bond's yield depends on a several factors. To model the effects of these factors, it is useful to recognize that the call provision is essentially a *call option* held by the issuing firm to purchase (i.e., retire) the bond at a specified price in the future. We assume that the issuing firm's management will exercise this option if and when it is in the *shareholders'* interest to do so. As with any call option, the value of the call provision is a function of the volatility of the value of the underlying asset (in this case, the bond as an uncalled security), time to expiration, and the call price (the exercise price).

The value of the call provision to the issuer, and thus its affect on a bond's yield, ultimately depends on the probability that the call will be exercised. In turn, this probability is related to the probability that the bond's future yield will fall sufficiently below its level at issuance to warrant a call. The probability that the yield will fall is important because the market price of any bond is inversely related to its yield; thus, if a bond's yield falls, its price rises and the firm is more likely to find it optimal to exercise the call.

FIGURE 10-4   Promised Yield versus Expected Return on Risky Debt by Maturity

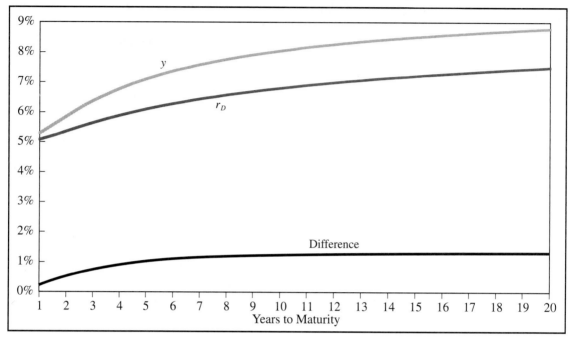

Promised Yield (y) and Expected Return (r_D) on Pure-Discount Corporate Debt, Both as Functions of Debt Maturity
BSOPM: $D/V = 0.5$; $\sigma = 30\%$, $r_f = 5\%$; $r_V = 10\%$

The probability of a call is also inversely related to the duration of the *deferment period*. As the duration of the deferment period approaches the bond's maturity, the value of the call provision approaches zero. The probability of a call is also inversely related to the call price. As the call price rises, the probability that the bond's uncalled value would be higher than the call price diminishes. Finally, the probability of a call is *directly* related to the volatility of the bond's yield (and thus the volatility of the bond's price). In turn, the volatility of a bond's yield is a function of both the volatility of the general level of interest rates and the volatility of the bond's default-risk premium.

A Simple Model of the Effect of the Call Provision on a Bond's Yield
We now develop a simple model to illustrate the effects discussed above. Assume that a firm has issued a callable bond with T years to maturity. The firm has only one opportunity to call the bond, at time T^*, at a call price of CP. The coupon rate on the bond will be set to render the bond's offering price equal to its par value of $100, encompassing the effect of the call provision. That is, the bond's coupon rate is set equal to the initial required yield at date 0, denoted as y_0.

To model the key factor of future yield volatility, we assume that at time T^* the yield on the bond (as an uncalled security) will have either risen to $y_{high} = y_0 + \varepsilon$, or fallen to $y_{low} = y_0 - \varepsilon$, with equal probability. Thus, ε is our yield-volatility parameter; as we increase the value of ε, yield volatility increases. Under these circumstances, the firm will rationally call the bond only if the lower value of future yield obtains, and then only if the uncalled value of the bond exceeds the call price.

The desired output of the model is the value of the yield premium required for adding a call provision on the new bond. Thus, after specifying values of all parameters, we solve for the coupon rates required to render the values of both the callable and noncallable versions of the bond equal to par value. The yield premium is then the difference between these required coupon rates.

We estimated yield premiums for a total of 16 cases, where each case involves a unique combination of T, T^*, CP, and ε. For T, we used alternative values of 10 and 20 years. For T^*, we used alternative values of 3 and 6 years. For CP, we alternately assumed that the bond can be called at a price of par ($100) plus a full-year of coupon interest (C), or at par value. Finally, we chose two alternative values of the yield volatility parameter ε, 2 percent and 4 percent. For all cases, the initial yield required on the noncallable bond is 8 percent.

The resulting estimated yield premiums, expressed in basis points, are displayed in Table 10-8. The estimated yield premiums range from (a) 0 basis points for the case in which $T = 10$ years, $T^* = 6$ years, $CP = 100 + C$, and $\varepsilon = 2$ percent; to (b) 289 basis points for the case in which $T = 20$ years, $T^* = 3$ years, $CP = 100$; and $\varepsilon = 4$ percent. As expected, the required yield premium is directly related to interest rate volatility and bond maturity, and inversely related to the length of the call deferment period and the call price.

TABLE 10-8   Results of Simulation Model of Yield Premium for a Call Provision

Yield Premium (in Basis Points) Required for Adding a Call Provision to a Bond Contract under Indicated Circumstances

	Original Maturity = 10 years				
	Call Deferment Period				
	6 YEARS CALL PRICE*			3 YEARS CALL PRICE*	
Interest Volatility**	100 + C	100		100 + C	100
Low	0	44		22	94
High	56	159		119	199

	Original Maturity = 20 years				
	Call Deferment Period				
	6 YEARS CALL PRICE*			3 YEARS CALL PRICE*	
Interest Volatility**	100 + C	100		100 + C	100
Low	49	87		72	131
High	163	205		2209	289

Bond principal is 100; C = annual dollar coupon.
**Interest rate volatility is modeled with a binomial distribution of the bond's (noncalled) yield at the date that all deferment expires. Initial yield is 8%. For low volatility, the future yield is either 6 percent or 10 percent with equal probability. For high volatility, the future yield is either 4 percent or 12 percent with equal probability.*

10.7 ESTIMATING THE FAIR YIELD ON A CORPORATE BOND: THE *BOND YIELD SPREAD MATRIX* APPROACH

At this point, we understand that determining the *fair* yield on a corporate bond is a complex task. The yield depends on the base level of interest rates, as well as the bond's maturity, callability, and default risk. In this section, we present an approach to estimating the fair yield on a corporate bond that is widely used by professional bond analysts and traders.

Suppose we need to establish the fair yield to maturity on a corporate bond that a firm is about to issue. Of course, the yields on all bonds are determined in large part by the general level of interest rates as expressed in the yields on U.S. Treasury securities of various maturities. Thus, a logical place to begin is to examine the current yield to maturity on a U.S. Treasury security that has a similar maturity (and coupon rate, if possible). Of course, the bond in question is likely to have a higher yield than this *corresponding Treasury*, but our task has already been reduced to determining the *yield spread* required on the focal bond over the yield on the corresponding Treasury.

The focal bond's fair yield spread depends in part on the bond's default risk. The task of estimating the part of the spread that is required for default risk is made easier if the focal bond has been rated by a credit rating agency such as Moody's or S&P. In such a case we can estimate the default-risk component of the overall yield spread on the focal bond by examining the yield spreads on other corporate bonds that have the same rating. Otherwise, if we have the values of the relevant parameters, we can use the regression results displayed in Table 10-5 to generate a *pseudorating* for the focal bond.

If the focal bond is callable, we must also estimate the call component of the spread. As we discussed, the yield premium required for the call provision depends on many factors. We could attempt to locate bonds that have a similar call provision and examine the yield premiums on these bonds. However, it would be important to select bonds that also have similar default risk and maturity. At this point, the number of comparable bonds may be small, and our estimate may be subject to substantial sampling error.

In the end, we see that the many characteristics of a corporate bond present a complex *mosaic* from which it is difficult to estimate a fair yield spread. Although some professional bond analysts may adopt the piecemeal approach described above, many others use an alternative approach that may result in more accurate estimates of the fair yield spread for a particular bond. This alternative approach involves the development of a *bond yield spread matrix*.

The Bond Yield Spread Matrix

A bond yield spread matrix is developed by sorting many corporate bonds into separate groups according to characteristics such as their credit rating, maturity, and callability. Then the yield spreads on all bonds in a given group are averaged. The average yield spreads are then displayed in a matrix-style table.

Table 10-9 is an illustration of a bond yield spread matrix. The values in this matrix are based on the yield spreads on 8,880 newly issued nonconvertible bonds issued by U.S. nonfinancial firms over the years 1979 to 1999. The bond characteristics that we chose for the matrix are S&P rating (sans the modifiers), maturity (10 years or less versus greater than 10 years), and callability.

TABLE 10-9   Illustration of a Bond Yield Spread Matrix

Yield Spreads (Over Maturity-Matched U.S. Treasury Securities, in Basis Points)
Based on 8,880 New Nonconvertible Corporate Bonds Issued by U.S. Nonfinancial Firms, 1979–1999

	S&P Rating							Regression
	AAA	**AA**	**A**	**BBB**	**BB**	**B**	**CCC**	**Adjusted R^2**
All bonds with indicated rating	76	79	94	133	279	447	534	73.8%
Sorted by Maturity:								75.2%
Maturity ≤ 10 years	42	59	78	120	280	453	536	
Maturity > 10 years	95	96	115	151	274	431	530	
Sorted by Callability								76.1%
Noncallable	42	59	76	113	236	408	687	
Callable	99	96	121	159	300	449	530	
Sorted by Maturity and Callability								76.8%
Maturity ≤ 10 years; Noncallable	34	52	69	107	236	415	687	
Maturity ≤ 10 years; Callable	58	72	102	150	304	456	530	
Maturity > 10 years; Noncallable	53	72	92	129	236	233	n/a	
Maturity > 10 years; Callable	110	106	131	166	290	433	530	

Source: Raw data from Securities Data Corp. new-issues database.

The behavior of the spreads in the table generally meet well with our expectations. Specifically, (a) yield spreads increase monotonically with default risk, (b) controlling for default risk, yield spreads generally increase with maturity, and (c) controlling for both default risk and maturity, yield spreads are higher for callable bonds than for non-callable bonds.

A good measure of the accuracy of a bond yield spread matrix is the adjusted R^2 from a regression that includes each of the groups as a dummy independent variable. The last column in Table 10-9 reports the adjusted R^2 for several such regressions. The first regression includes dummy variables only for the various S&P ratings, and results in an adjusted R^2 of 73.8 percent. For the second regression, dummy variables are included for every rating and maturity combination. The addition of maturity results in a marginal improvement in the adjusted R^2 to 75.2 percent. When credit ratings are crossed against callability rather than maturity, the resulting adjusted R^2 is 76.1 percent. Finally, when dummy variables are used to represent all combinations of rating, maturity, and callability, the adjusted R^2 rises to 76.8 percent.

Overall, the results indicate that simple dummy variables representing three important bond characteristics (rating, maturity, and callability) can explain the bulk of the variability of yield spreads on newly issued noncallable corporate bonds. Clearly, though, rating is the most important variable.

10.8   A FOCUS ON CONVERTIBLES

In this section, we describe the contract structure of a typical convertible bond, and provide several theoretical and empirical analyses of the pricing of convertible bonds. We analyze convertible bonds separately because the conversion provision has a profound impact on a bond's value and risk.

10.8.1   The Basic Contract Structure of a Convertible Bond

The convertible bond differs fundamentally from other corporate bonds because the conversion provision allows the bondholders to exchange their bonds for shares of the focal firm's stock. This exchange is made at a specified *conversion ratio*, expressed in terms of the number of shares received for each bond. To a close approximation, the convertible bond is a portfolio consisting of an otherwise equivalent nonconvertible bond plus a call option on the firm's stock.

At the time that a convertible bond is issued, the conversion option is typically *out of the money* in option terms. That is, denoting the stock price and exercise price as S and X, respectively, $S < X$. However, the time to expiration of the conversion option generally is very long, so the option's value on the issue date is substantial. Thus, if at issuance a convertible bond carried a coupon rate that would render its initial market price equal to par value if it were not convertible, then *with* the conversion provision the bond's initial market price would be substantially in excess of its par value.

Instead, the coupon rate on a convertible bond is much lower. For a newly issued convertible bond, the coupon is set at a rate that is just sufficient to render the bond's initial market price equal to its par value *after* accounting for the value of the conversion option. Alternatively, if the coupon rate is already fixed, the exercise price of the conversion option can be altered to render the bond's price equal to par value. This discussion points up an important trade-off between the coupon rate and the moneyness of the conversion option, which we explore later.

Convertible bonds invariably also include a call provision. Thus, if the firm's call privilege *superseded* the bondholders' conversion privilege, the firm would tend to exercise the call provision if and when the uncalled value of the bonds exceeds the call price, which in the case of the convertible bond would likely be at a time when the conversion option had a high value (i.e., is deeply in the money). If this were the case, the value of the conversion provision would be severely limited.

Instead, if the firm attempts to call a convertible bond, the bondholders have the *preemptory right* to convert the bonds into stock. Nevertheless, the call provision in a convertible bond is valuable to the firm for two reasons: (a) the firm can *force* the conversion of an in-the-money convertible bond by attempting to call the bond, whereas the bonds may be more valuable if the conversion option remained unexercised; and (b) the forced conversion mechanism gives the firm flexibility to change its capital structure (specifically, to decrease leverage) should management deem this necessary or desirable.

10.8.2   A Basic Approach to Valuing a Convertible Bond

To a close approximation, the value of a typical convertible bond is equal to the value of a portfolio that consists of an otherwise equivalent nonconvertible bond plus a call option on the firm's stock. Denoting the values of the convertible bond, a nonconvertible equivalent bond, and the conversion option as P^{cvb}, P^{ncvb}, and P^{cvo}, respectively, then

$$P^{\text{cvb}} = P^{\text{ncvb}} + P^{\text{cvo}}. \tag{10.7}$$

The conversion option portion of the convertible bond renders the value of the convertible bond especially sensitive to the price of the firm's stock. Furthermore, the value of the convertible bond is directly related to the option's time to expiration and the volatility of the firm's stock, and is inversely related to the conversion price, which is determined by the conversion ratio.

The Riskiness of Convertible Bonds versus Callable and Noncallable Bonds

Figure 10-5 provides an illustration of the relationship between the value of a convertible bond and the value of the issuing firm. For comparative purposes, the figure also shows the corresponding relationship for a nonconvertible callable bond and a nonconvertible noncallable bond. The callable bond exhibits the lowest sensitivity to changes in the value of the firm, and therefore is the least risky; the convertible bond exhibits the highest sensitivity to changes in the value of the firm, and therefore is the most risky.

10.8.3 The Trade-off Between *S/X* and Yield Spread for Convertible Bonds

As noted earlier, an important trade-off exists between the coupon rate on a convertible bond and the moneyness of the conversion provision. Here we explore the nature of this trade-off in simulation by calculating alternative combinations of *S/X* and coupon rate that render the value of a hypothetical 25-year convertible bond equal to its par value.

FIGURE 10-5   Values of Noncallable, Callable, and Convertible Bonds as Functions of Firm Value

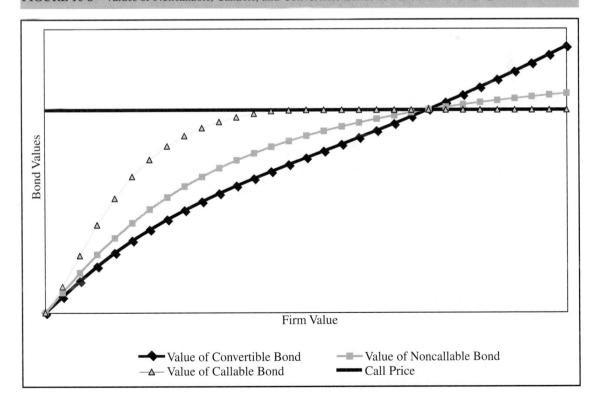

To make the simulations somewhat realistic, we use empirical data on the yield spreads on long-term callable bonds by credit rating shown in Table 10-9. Specifically, we establish six hypothetical bonds with ratings of AA, A, BBB, BB, B, and CCC, and assume that these bonds would require yield spreads of 106, 131, 166, 290, 433, and 530 basis points, respectively, if they were not convertible. These yield spreads, added to the assumed risk-free rate of 8 percent, provide the yields, or discount rates, we need to calculate the value of each bond as a nonconvertible bond (i.e., P^{ncvb} in Equation 10.7).

We also need to calculate the value the conversion option for each bond. For all bonds, we assume that the conversion option expires in eight years. For bonds rated AA, A, BBB, BB, B, and CCC, we assume that the annual standard deviations of the firm's stock returns are 25.0, 27.5, 30.0, 32.5, 35.0, and 37.5 percent, respectively. Finally, after fixing a value for S/X, we compute the value of the conversion option using the BSOPM. Of course, the intention is to identify combinations S/X (which determines the value of P^{cvo} in Equation 10-7) and coupon rate (which determines P^{ncvb}) that render the overall value of the convertible bond equal to its par value (i.e., P^{cvb} = $100).

The results of these calculations are displayed in Table 10-10. For bonds with each of the hypothetical ratings, we show various combinations of yield spread and S/X that render the value of the convertible bond equal to its par value. We also show the percentage contribution of the conversion option to the overall value of the bond for each combination.

Note initially that, with two minor exceptions, the required yield spreads are negative. This result attests to the substantial value of the conversion option. The numbers also reveal the following relationships: (a) For any given rating, yield spread is inversely related to S/X; (b) The percentage contribution of the conversion option to the bond's value is directly related to S/X; (c) For any given value of S/X, the required yield spread is positively related to (our assessment of) default risk; and (d) The percentage contribution of the conversion option to the bond's value is directly related to default risk.

10.8.4   Empirical Evidence on the Pricing of New Convertible Bonds

Finally, we empirically test relationship (c) above; that is, the prediction of a positive relationship between the required yield spread on a convertible bond and the bond's default risk. The data used for this test consists of 500 convertible bonds newly issued by U.S. nonfinancial firms from 1979 to 1999 that were rated by S&P. The distribution of S&P ratings on these bonds are as follows, with the number of bonds shown in brackets: AA– [4], A+ [6], A [12], A– [22], BBB+ [26], BBB [26], BBB– [27], BB+ [28], BB [11], BB– [41], B+ [56], B [91], B– [112], CCC+ [12], CCC [22], CCC– [1], and CC [3].

One problem with the proposed test is that, according to the simulation analysis, the required yield spread is also a function of S/X. Thus, variations in S/X may obscure the relationship that we expect to find between yield spread and default risk. To determine how much of a problem this might be (and as a matter of curiosity), we chart distributions of S/X by rating. The results are displayed in Figure 10-6.

TABLE 10-10 Simulations of Trade-off between *S/X* Ratio and Yield Spread for Convertible Bonds

Hypothetical Yield Spreads (Relative to a Riskless Rate of 8 Percent, in Basis Points) Required to Render the Price of a New Convertible Bond Equal to Par Value

Bond Rating Simulated	Nonconvertible Yield Spread (basis points)	Equity Standard Deviation		Ratio of Stock Price to Exercise Price (*S/X*)							
				0.70	0.73	0.76	0.79	0.82	0.85	0.88	0.91
AA	106	25.0%	Required yield spread (basis points)	−168	−190	−215	−240	−265	−291	−317	−343
			Contribution of convertible provision	26.9%	29.2%	31.6%	34.1%	36.6%	39.1%	41.6%	44.2%
A	131	27.5%	Required yield spread (basis points)	−164	−186	−211	−236	−264	−290	−316	−342
			Contribution of convertible provision	28.4%	30.5%	32.9%	35.4%	38.1%	40.6%	43.1%	45.6%
BBB	166	30.0%	Required yield spread (basis points)	−175	−200	−225	−256	−281	−310	−341	−370
			Contribution of convertible provision	29.9%	32.1%	34.3%	37.1%	39.3%	41.8%	44.5%	47.1%
BB	290	32.5%	Required yield spread (basis points)	−95	−130	−155	−190	−215	−250	−275	−310
			Contribution of convertible provision	31.3%	33.7%	36.1%	38.5%	41.0%	43.5%	46.0%	48.5%
B	433	35.0%	Required yield spread (basis points)	−12	−44	−77	−107	−145	−180	−212	−245
			Contribution of convertible provision	32.8%	35.1%	37.5%	40.0%	42.4%	44.9%	47.5%	50.0%
CCC	530	37.5%	Required yield spread (basis points)	37	3	−32	−68	−103	−139	−175	−211
			Contribution of convertible provision	34.2%	36.6%	39.0%	41.5%	43.9%	46.4%	49.0%	51.5%

Note: The required yield spread is a function of (a) the yield spread required on a nonconvertible equivalent bond, (b) the return standard deviation of the firm's equity, and (c) the ratio of the issuer's stock price to the exercise price (*S/X*). The percentage contribution of the value of the conversion provision to the overall value of the bond is also shown. All bonds have 25 years to maturity. The conversion option, assumed to expire in 8 years, is valued using the BSOPM.

FIGURE 10-6 Distributions of Ratio of Stock Price to Exercise Price (*S/X*) for Convertible Bonds Sorted by S&P Rating and Then by *S/X*

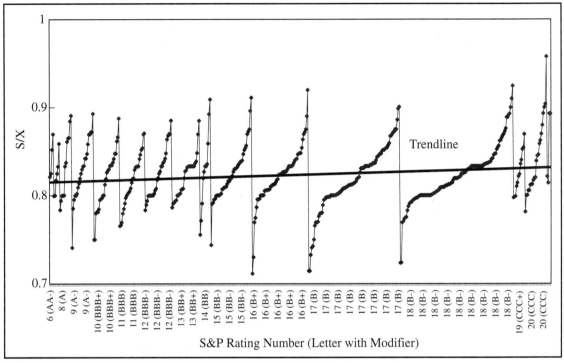

500 New Convertible Bonds Issued in the U.S. by U.S. Nonfinancial Firms, 1979–1999
Source: Raw data from Securities Data Corporation new-issues database.

Note initially that all of the *S/X* ratios are less than 1.0. This result confirms our earlier statement that the conversion options on new convertible bonds are generally out of the money. Indeed, the vast majority of *S/X* ratios (428 bonds, or 85.6 percent) fall in a narrow range of 0.80 to 0.90. The average value of the *S/X* ratio for this sample of bonds is 0.823, and there is a very slight tendency for the *S/X* ratio to be higher for lower-rated bonds (see the trendline). In any event, variation in *S/X* is not likely to pose a problem for our main test, to which we now turn.

We test the relationship between yield spreads and default risk by simply charting yield spreads against S&P ratings. The results are displayed in Figure 10-7.

Note initially that yield spreads vary considerably across the bonds within a given rating category. However, as the trendline indicates, there is a clear and substantial positive relationship between yield spreads and default risk. Based on the trendline, the predicted fair yield spread for a convertible bond rated AA– is –320 basis points, and for a CC-rated bond is –46 basis points.

FIGURE 10-7 Distributions of Yield Spreads on Convertible Bonds Sorted by S&P Rating and Then Yield Spread

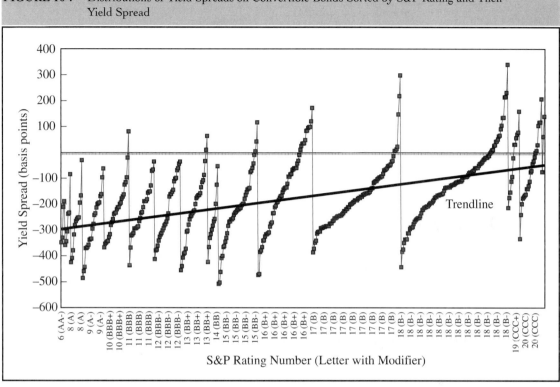

500 New Convertible Bonds Issued in the U.S. by U.S. Nonfinancial Firms, 1979–1999
Source: Raw data from Securities Data Corporation new-issues database.

10.9 Summary of Learning Objectives

In this chapter, we discussed and analyzed basic terms, covenants, and provisions that are often included in corporate bond contracts. We also discussed the issuance process and the valuation of corporate bonds.

Covenants and Provisions

Restrictive covenants are included to protect the interests of bondholders. Restrictions may be placed on the firm's (a) investment activities, (b) future debt financing, or (c) dividend policy.

Common *alternative retirement provisions* include (a) the call provision (an option held by the issuer allowing it to retire the bonds prior to their stated maturity), (b) the put provision (an option held by bondholders allowing them to present the bond to the firm for repayment of principal prior to the stated maturity), (c) the sinking fund (a requirement of the issuer to retire a small portion of the issue each year), and (d) the conversion provision (an option held by bondholders allowing them to present the bonds to the firm in exchange for shares of the firm's stock).

The Issuance Process

The process of issuing a corporate bond in the U.S. public bond market involves seven steps. *First*, the issuing firm selects an *underwriter*; that is, an investment bank that assists the firm in virtually every subsequent step in the issuance process. *Second*, the issuer decides the amount of the offering. *Third*, the firm decides on the terms, covenants, and provisions that will be included in the contract. *Fourth*, the issue is registered with the SEC. *Fifth*, the firm may seek to have the bond *rated* by one or more credit rating agencies such as Moody's and Standard and Poor's. *Sixth*, the underwriter generates a tentative price for the issue. *Seventh*, the issue is marketed and sold to public investors.

Default Risk, Bond Ratings, Yields, and Expected Returns

In our detailed analysis of default risk, we listed and described the alphabetic rating grades of one major credit rating agency, Standard & Poor's, which are qualitative measures of default risk. We also conducted several empirical analyses of the ratings of U.S. nonfinancial firms. These analyses indicated that the following variables collectively explained the bulk of the variation in bond ratings: (a) market-to-book equity ratio, (b) fixed charge coverage ratio, (c) the standard deviation of ROA, (d) debt ratio, (e) firm size, (f) capital intensity (PP&E/TA), (g) equity beta, and (h) dividend yield.

We also examined the effects of default risk on a bond's yield and expected return, showing that (a) the yield on a default-risky bond is an upward-biased estimate of the bond's expected return, and (b) the risk, yield, and expected return on a default-risky bond all increase with maturity.

Yield Premium for Callability

We also examined the effects of callability on the yield on a corporate bond. The yield premium for callability is directly related to bond maturity and expected yield volatility, and inversely related to call price and the length of the call deferment period.

The Bond Yield Spread Matrix

Given the complexity of the typical corporate bond, we advocate the development of a bond yield spread matrix for pricing purposes. The yield spread matrix that we developed sorts a large sample of new nonconvertible bonds into categories by rating, maturity, and callability. Collectively, these variables explained about 77 percent of the variation in yield spreads.

Convertible Bonds

Historically, convertible bonds have accounted for about 10 percent of all publicly issued corporate bonds, though in recent years this percentage has been less than five. We conducted both theoretical and empirical analyses of convertible bonds. The conversion option generally represents a substantial proportion of overall value of a convertible bond. Thus, the coupon rate and yield to maturity on a newly issued convertible bond are generally less than the yield on corresponding U.S. Treasuries. A critical aspect of the pricing of new convertible bonds is a trade-off between the moneyness of the conversion option (S/X) and the required yield spread.

Review Questions and Problems

1. List and briefly discuss the basic terms in a corporate bond contract.
2. List the restrictive covenants that are often included in a corporate bond contract, and briefly explain why each is included.
3. Explain the trade-off involved in deciding whether to include a restrictive covenant in a bond contract.
4. Describe the call provision and discuss its effect on a bond's value and yield.
5. Describe the sinking fund provision and discuss its effect on a bond's value and yield.
6. Describe the put provision and discuss its effect on a bond's value and yield.
7. Describe the conversion provision and discuss its effect on a bond's value and yield.
8. List and briefly discuss the seven steps in the issuance process for a corporate bond.
9. Discuss the determinants of underwriter spreads on new corporate bond issues.
10. Discuss the evolution of terms and provisions in corporate bond contracts over the years 1979 to 1999.
11. Discuss the relationships between a corporate bond's maturity and its risk, yield, and expected return.
12. List the S&P rating grades for corporate bonds, and describe the financial status of firms that garner each rating.
13. The Cellular Communications bond discussed in the chapter had an S&P rating of CCC+, corresponding to a numerical rating of 19. Federal Express Corporation issued a noncallable 20.4-year bond on the same day (August 17, 1995) that garnered an S&P rating of BBB+, corresponding to a numerical rating of 10.
    a. Using the figures for these firms given below, and the regression coefficients provided in Table 10-5, calculate your own estimates of the numerical rating for each bond.
    b. Which variables are most important in explaining the difference between the actual numerical ratings of these bonds and your corresponding estimates?

Independent Variable	Cellular Communications	Federal Express
Market-to-book equity ratio	2.53	1.86
Median fixed charge coverage	2.23	3.08
Standard deviation of ROA (%)	3.72	2.54
Debt/TA (%)	54.63	24.56
ln(TA)	6.48	8.77
PP&E/TA (%)	0.3	57.75
Equity beta	1.99	0.82
Dividend yield (%)	0	0

14. A six-year pure-discount corporate bond has a current price of $44 per $100 of par value. The probability is $p = 0.8$ that the issuer will repay the principal of $100 at maturity, and $(1 - p) = 0.2$ that the issuer will default, in which case bondholders will receive only $30. The yield on the corresponding Treasury is 8.45 percent. Calculate the bond's
    a. yield spread.
    b. expected return premium.

15. The capital structure of firm XYZ consists of a noncallable pure-discount bond with total market value of $145 million, and stock with a total market value of $156 million. The bond matures in five years, and the promised payment is $247 million. The annual expected return and standard deviation of the firm's assets are $r_V = 15$ percent and $\sigma = 44$ percent, respectively. The risk-less rate is 5 percent.
    a. Calculate the bond's promised yield to maturity.
    b. Using the BSOPM, calculate the bond's instantaneous annual return standard deviation.
    c. Using the BSOPM, calculate the bond's instantaneous annual expected return.
16. Regarding the Federal Express bond referred to earlier (20.4 years to maturity; S&P rating of BBB+; noncallable), the yield on the corresponding Treasury bond was 6.96 percent. Taking the appropriate spread value from the bond yield spread matrix shown in Table 10-9, estimate the fair yield spread on this bond. The actual issue-date yield was 8.06 percent. Provide an explanation for the difference, if any, between your yield spread estimate and the actual yield spread.
17. On March 4, 1996, Unisys Corporation issued a 10-year convertible bond rated B– by S&P. The issue sold at its par value of $100, so both its yield to maturity and coupon rate were 8.25 percent. The issue-date value of shares into which a Unisys bond could be converted was $80 per $100 of bond value. The issue-date yield on 10-year Treasuries was 5.94 percent, so the Unisys bond's spread to Treasuries was 231 basis points. The average spread to Treasuries on 10-year *nonconvertible* bonds rated B– is 500 basis points.
    a. Estimate the fair value of the nonconvertible component of the Unisys bond's value.
    b. Estimate the fair value of the conversion option component of the Unisys bond using the BSOPM. Assume (a) the conversion option will effectively expire in three years (when the bond's call deferment expires), and (b) the annual return standard deviation on Unisys stock is 44 percent.

TABLE 10-11   Pricing Details for a Sample of Newly Issued Convertible Bonds

Issuer	Issue Date	Principle Amount ($ million)	Years to Maturity	Coupon Rate and Yield (%)	S&P Rating Alphabetical	Numerical	S/X	Spread to Treasury (basis points)
Cessna Aircraft Co.	06/23/83	100	25	8.000	BBB	11	0.87	–288
Wendy's International	12/10/85	50	25	7.250	BBB+	10	0.78	–270
Carnival Cruise Lines	06/29/92	100	5	4.500	BBB	11	0.82	–183
Hilton Hotels Corp.	05/09/96	500	10	5.000	BBB	11	0.79	–182
Hospital Corp. of America	04/07/83	50	15	9.000	A–	9	0.74	–169
Church & Dwight Co.	03/26/86	40	25	6.500	B	17	0.81	–152
UtiliCorp United Inc	07/17/86	50	25	6.625	BBB–	12	0.80	–99
General Host Corp.	06/26/86	100	10	6.500	B	17	0.85	–93
General Cinema Corp.	03/29/83	100	25	10.000	BBB	11	0.83	–67
Northwest Natural Gas	01/22/87	15	25	7.250	A	8	0.84	–30
InterNorth Inc.	05/26/83	240	25	10.500	BBB+	10	0.75	–20
Swift Energy Co.	11/19/96	100	10	6.250	B+	16	0.81	10
Hexcel Corp.	07/18/96	100	7	7.000	B–	18	0.81	28
Centronics Data Comp.	06/03/85	40	5	10.000	CCC	20	0.85	29
Tenet Healthcare Corp.	01/05/96	320	10	6.000	B+	16	0.83	35
WorldCorp Inc.	05/18/92	65	12	7.000	B+	16	0.85	48
Unisys Corp.	03/04/96	260	10	8.250	B–	18	0.80	231

c. Compute the fair value of the convertible bond as the sum of your estimates in (a) and (b).

18. Table 10-11 shows pricing details for a number of newly issued convertible bonds, all of which sold at their par value. Analyze the pricing of these bonds, focusing on the trade-off between S/X and spread to Treasury, and the effects of rating and maturity.

Creative Thinking Issues

1. As a firm confers with its underwriter about whether to include any specific restrictive covenant or provision in a pending corporate bond contract, do you think that management's preferences or the market's preferences are paramount in the decision? Explain how your answer depends on (a) the characteristics of the issuer, and (b) the state of the corporate bond market.

2. How might the quickening pace of technological change have affected firms' decisions to shorten the maturities of new corporate bonds?

3. Given their tremendous knowledge bases, why are the two major rating firms, S&P and Moody's, not more directly involved in the underwriting of corporate bonds? Alternatively, given the substantial knowledge bases of underwriters such as Merrill Lynch, why do they not rate corporate bonds?

4. Bond ratings provide important information to the financial markets. To be useful, however, a rating must be updated to reflect the current financial status of the issuer. In the past, S&P simply announced a change in a firm's bond rating if and when the conditions warranted. However, several years ago S&P developed their *Credit Watch* procedure, whereby the agency announces that the rating on a given issuer's debt is under review for a possible upgrade or downgrade, as the case may be. Subsequently, the agency announces either that the extant rating is confirmed or that the rating has been changed. Why would S&P adopt this early-warning procedure, rather than simply announcing a rating change when it is warranted?

Projects and Analyses

1. Collect a sample of firms that have rated corporate bonds. For each firm, gather values for any financial variables that you think would be strong determinants of the firms' bond ratings. Convert the ratings to numerical values, and regress the numerical ratings against the determinant variables that you selected. Interpret the results.

2. Use the BSOPM to conduct alternative analyses of the effects of debt maturity on a bond's risk and expected return.

3. Using a search vehicle such as the Internet or the *Wall Street Journal Index*, identify a sample of firms whose S&P or Moody's bond ratings have been upgraded, and a corresponding sample of firms whose ratings have been downgraded. Collect summaries of the reasons cited in the financial press for the rating change, and compare these stated reasons with macroeconomic, industry, or firm-specific financial data.

Appendix A

Yield to Maturity and Duration

YIELD TO MATURITY

The promised yield to maturity on a coupon bond is determined by solving for y in Equation A10.1:

$$P = \sum_{t=1}^{T} \frac{C_t}{(1+y)^t}, \qquad \textbf{(A10.1)}$$

where C_t is the promised cash payment (either coupon interest or principal) in year t, and the bond matures in T years. For a traditional fixed-coupon bond, the coupon payments form an annuity, so

$$P = C(PVAF_{y,T}) + \frac{X_T}{(1+y)^T}, \qquad \textbf{(A10.2)}$$

where C is the (constant) annual coupon payment, $PVAF_{y,T}$ is the present-value annuity factor, and X_T is the principal payment at maturity.

A Case in Point

In March 1999, Lucent Technologies issued a 30-year bond with a fixed coupon rate of 6.45 percent, or $6.45 per year per $100 of par value. The offering price was $99.461. Thus, its yield to maturity was 6.491 percent. When the bond was offered, it garnered an S&P rating of A. However, two years later, in March of 2001, Lucent's financial condition had deteriorated, and the rating on this bond was lowered to BBB–. As a result, the bond's price fell, trading at a price of $73.438 on March 16, 2001. At this price (and with a remaining maturity of 28 years), the bond's yield to maturity rose to 9.081 percent.

DURATION

The example of the Lucent Technologies bond highlights the sensitivity of a bond's price to a change in its yield. Macaulay (1938) provided a formal measure of the sensitivity of a bond's price to a change in its yield. This measure is called *duration*. A bond's duration is the negative of the bond's price elasticity with respect to the discount factor, $(1 + y)$. Developing the duration formula involves a three-step process. First, we take the derivative of the bond's price, as calculated using Equation A10.1, with respect to $(1 + y)$:

$$\frac{dP}{d(1+y)} = \sum_{t=1}^{T} -tC_t(1+y)^{-t-1}$$

$$= \frac{\sum_{t=1}^{T} -tC_t(1+y)^{-t}}{(1+y)}. \qquad \textbf{(A10.3)}$$

Second, we multiply Equation A10.3 through by $(1 + y)/P$, obtaining the bond's price elasticity:

$$\frac{dP/P}{d(1+y)/(1+y)} = \sum_{t=1}^{T} -tC_t(1+y)^{-t}/P.$$

$$\textbf{(A10.3)}$$

Finally, we drop the negative sign inside the summation expression on the right side of Equation A10.3 to obtain a positive number for the result, which is the bond's duration, D:

$$D = \sum_{t=1}^{T} tC_t(1+y)^{-t}/P. \qquad \textbf{(A10.4)}$$

Thus, a bond's duration is the absolute value of the percentage change in a bond's price for a given percentage change in the bond's discount factor, $(1 + y)$. However, the formula is based on derivative calculus, so it is accurate only for a small change in $(1 + y)$. An inaccuracy arises for large changes in $(1 + y)$ because a bond's price is a strongly convex function of $(1 + y)$ over large ranges of y.

We can obtain insight into the duration formula by initially referring to the case of a pure-discount bond. In this case the summation in brackets in Equation A10.4 has only one term, and this term is $TC_T(1 + y)^{-T}$. But $C_T(1 + y)^{-T}$ is simply the price of the bond, so the duration of a pure-discount bond, denoted as D_{pdb} is simply T:

$$D_{pdb} = T[P]/P = T. \qquad \text{(A10.5)}$$

For this reason, we can interpret the value of a bond's duration in terms of *years*. For instance, the duration of a 30-year pure-discount bond is equal to 30. This means that the price of a pure-discount bond will change by 30 percent per 1 percent change in its discount factor (in the opposite direction, of course).

By extension, we can view a coupon-bearing bond as a portfolio of pure-discount bonds, one for each of its payments. Thus, the duration of a coupon bond is a value-weighted average of the durations of its component pure-discount bonds. For the same reason as indicated above, the duration of a coupon bond can be interpreted in terms of years, though it is clear that the duration of any coupon bond, measured in years, will be less than the bond's maturity, in years.

Examples

For our first example, suppose we have a pure-discount bond that promises $100 in 30 years. Currently its yield to maturity is 8 percent, so its price is $P = \$100/(1.08)^{30} = \$9.938$. Now suppose the bond's yield decreases to 7.8 percent. The bond's duration is 30 years, so the percentage change in its price, $\Delta P/P$, should be equal to 5.56 percent [$= -30(0.2\%)/(1.08)$]. The actual new price of the bond is $P' = \$100/(1.078)^{30} = \$10.506$, and the actual percentage change in the bond's price is $(10.506 - 9.938)/9.938 = 0.0572$, or 5.72 percent. The small discrepancy between the actual change in the bond's price and the predicted change is due to the convexity problem.

For our second example, we again focus on the Lucent Technologies bond referred to earlier. At the time the bond was issued it had a duration of $D = 14.01$ years. We can use this value to predict the percentage change in the bond's price if the bond's yield changed from its issue-date yield of 6.491 percent to the yield two years later, 9.081 percent, or an increase of 2.59 percent. The predicted percentage price change is $\Delta P/P = [-14.01(2.59 \text{ percent})/(1.06491)] = -37.04$ percent. The actual percentage in the bond's price was $(73.438 - 99.461)/99.461 = -26.16$ percent. Here the discrepancy between the predicted and actual percentage price changes is quite large, and is due to two factors. *First*, we again have the convexity problem, which is more severe in this case because the change in the bond's yield was very large. *Second*, we ignored the change in the bond's maturity, which decreased by two years from 30 years to 28 years.

Appendix B

Theories of the Term Structure of Interest Rates

The *term structure of interest rates* refers to the relationship between the interest rate on a default-free bond and its maturity. A graphical depiction of this structure is called a *yield curve*. Yield curves for U.S. Treasury securities are presented daily in the *Wall Street Journal* and other business publications. The yields on default-free bonds are important because they form the base for yields on all other bonds, including corporate bonds. Moreover, as we explain below, the term structure of interest rates contains important information about the state of the macroeconomy.

SPOT INTEREST RATES

The yield on a default-free pure-discount bond, such as a U.S. Treasury bill or a *strip*, for a given maturity is known as the *spot interest rate* for that maturity. We denote the spot interest rate now, at time 0, on a default-free pure-discount bond that matures in t years, as $s_{0,t}$. The formula for $s_{0,t}$ is

$$s_t = \left(\frac{X_t}{P}\right)^{1/t} - 1, \qquad \textbf{(B10.1)}$$

where P is the current price of the bond and X_t is the cash payment, or par value, at maturity.

On December 31, 1999, the prices of U.S. Treasury strips with one and two years to maturity were \$94.295 and \$88.581, respectively, per \$100 of par value. Thus, the one-year and two-year spot interest rates were $s_{0,1}$ = 6.05 percent and $s_{0,2}$ = 6.25 percent.

HYPOTHESES ABOUT THE TERM STRUCTURE OF INTEREST RATES

Three hypotheses have been developed in the literature to explain the term structure of interest rates. These are the Pure Expectations Hypothesis, the Liquidity Preference Hypothesis, and the Market Segmentation Hypothesis. We discuss each of these briefly below. But first, we review two factors that affect the general level of interest rates: the real rate and inflation.

FACTORS AFFECTING THE GENERAL LEVEL OF INTEREST RATES

Irving Fisher (1930) developed what has become known as the classic theory of interest. Fisher argued that, in equilibrium, the current spot rate will provide investors with compensation for the *real rate of interest* plus full compensation for the current rate of *price inflation* in the economy. According to Fisher's theory, the spot interest rate, $s_{0,t}$, is determined by the following equation:

$$s_{0,t} = (1 + R_{0,t})(1 + i_{0,t}) - 1, \qquad \textbf{(B10.2)}$$

where $R_{0,t}$ is the current real rate and $i_{0,t}$ is the current rate of inflation. For reasonably small values of $R_{0,t}$ and $i_{0,t}$, the relationship can be approximated as

$$s_{0,t} \approx R_{0,t} + i_{0,t}. \qquad \textbf{(B10.3)}$$

The real interest rate is the interest rate that would prevail in the absence of inflation.

Since Fisher developed this relationship, researchers have refined it considerably. Two refinements are particularly important for the corporate financial manager. First, according to Rational Expectations Theory, the inflation term in the equation should be equal to the market's expectation of inflation over the term of the spot bond. Thus, $i_{0,t}$ in Equation B10.2 (or Equation B10.3) would be replaced with $E(i_{t,0})$.

Fisher's equation, and its extension via Rational Expectations Theory, has three important implications for the managers of borrowing firms. *First*, as a borrower the firm cannot expect to derive an advantage by borrowing at a time when inflation is high, expecting to pay back the loan with *cheaper dollars*. *Second*, the current level and term structure of interest rates provides management with an indication of expected inflation over any investment horizon. This information should be factored into both capital investment and financing decisions. *Third*, real rates, which represent the real cost of borrowed funds (ignoring default risk), may vary over time. In particular, empirical evidence indicates that real rates vary directly with economic growth. For instance, when the economy is growing at a high rate, many firms at this time have excellent investment opportunities, and thus in the aggregate firms increase their demand for funds, which raises the real rate. The one-year spot interest rate on December 31, 1999, was 6.05 percent. The actual inflation rate for 1999, which we use as a proxy for the market's expectation of inflation in the coming year of 2000, was 2.2 percent, based on the U.S. Consumer Price Index (CPI). Thus, the implied real rate was 3.77 percent (= 1.0605/1.022 – 1, in percent).

THE PURE EXPECTATIONS HYPOTHESIS

The Pure Expectations Hypothesis is based on simple concepts of choice and expectation. Consider an investor who, at date $t = 0$, wishes to invest $10,000 for two years. The investor can simply purchase two-year pure-discount bonds with a total value of $10,000 and realize a total return of $10,000$(1 + s_{0,2})^2$ at the end of year 2. Alternatively, the investor can initially purchase one-year pure-discount bonds with a total value of $10,000, realize a total return of $10,000$(1 + s_{0,1})$ at the end of one year, and then purchase new one-year pure-discount bonds with a total value of $10,000$(1 + s_{0,1})$ and realize a final total return of $10,000$(1 + s_{0,1})(1 + s_{1,2})$ at the end of

the second year, where $s_{1,2}$ is the one-year spot rate in the second year. However, at date 0 the investor does not know the spot rate, $s_{1,2}$, that will prevail in the second year. Thus, the investor's total return on such a *rollover* strategy is uncertain. Nevertheless, at date 0 the investor can develop an expectation of $s_{1,2}$, denoted as $E(s_{1,2})$, so the investor's *expected* total return on the rollover strategy is $10,000$(1 + s_{0,1})[1 + (E(s_{1,2})]$.

According to the Pure Expectations Hypothesis, investors prefer the investment strategy that provides the highest expected total return to a given investment horizon. In the present case, the investor will prefer the two-year bond if $(1 + s_{0,2})^2 > (1 + s_{0,1})[1 + (E(s_{1,2})]$, and will prefer the rollover strategy if $(1 + s_{0,2})^2 < (1 + s_{0,1})[1 + (E(s_{1,2})]$. Because the former case implies an excess demand for two-year bonds, and the latter case implies an excess demand for one-year bonds, equilibrium is reached only when

$$(1 + s_{0,2})^2 = (1 + s_{0,1})[1 + (E(s_{1,2})]. \quad \textbf{(B10.4)}$$

Under this hypothesis, it is a simple matter to extract the market's expected future one-year rate given the observable spot rates $s_{0,1}$ and $s_{0,2}$:

$$E(s_{1,2}) = \frac{(1 + s_{0,2})^2}{(1 + s_{0,1})} - 1. \quad \textbf{(B10.5)}$$

Again using the numbers for year-end 1999, according to the Pure Expectations Hypothesis the expected one-year spot interest rate for 2001 was 6.45 percent (= (1.0625²/1.0605) – 1, in percent).

THE LIQUIDITY PREFERENCE HYPOTHESIS

The liquidity preference hypothesis is based on the assumption that investors generally have a short-term investment horizon, or alternatively, a preference for *liquidity*. As such, given the equality expressed in Equation B10.4, investors would not be neutral to the choice, but would actually prefer to invest in the one-year bond, because the two-year bond imposes a greater loss of liquidity (i.e., their money is tied up for a longer time). Consequently, investors will accept the two-year bond only if

$$(1 + s_{0,2})^2 > (1 + s_{0,1})[1 + (E(s_{1,2})].$$

Consequently, for investors to be indifferent between the one-year and two-year bonds, the two-year bond must include a premium. For reasons explained below, we denote this premium as $_2p_{0,1}$, and the equilibrium relationship among $s_{0,2}$, $s_{0,1}$, $_2p_{0,1}$, and $E(s_{1,2})$ is given in Equation B10.6:

$$(1 + s_{0,2})^2 = (1 + s_{0,1} + {}_2p_{0,1})[1 + (E(s_{1,2})].$$

$$\textbf{(B10.6)}$$

One interpretation of this hypothesis is that a premium is required on multiperiod bonds because investors, who are assumed to be short-term oriented or *myopic*, focus on the expected returns and risk of all investments over a one-period horizon. As such, those investments that are risky over a one-period investment horizon will require a premium. In this case, the one-year bond is riskless, but the two-year bond is risky, because the return on the bond over the first year is determined by the realization of the one-year rate one year hence (i.e., $s_{1,2}$). This in turn will determine the price of the two-year bond after one year, and hence the return on the two-year bond in the first year of investment. This is why the premium term, $_2p_{0,1}$, is associated with the first-year spot rate, $s_{0,1}$, in Equation B10.6.

Another variation on the hypothesis focuses on the effects of uncertain future inflation rates. Suppose investors are generally long-term oriented (e.g., intent on saving for retirement). If an investor invests in a long-term bond, he or she must accept the prevailing spot rate on the long-term bond, which, we assume, reflects expectations of future inflation in all future years associated with the maturity of the bond. In effect, the investor takes a large bet that, on average, the realized

inflation over all these years is equal to the expected inflation rates embedded in the spot rate. If inflation is higher than expected, the real value of the payoff on the bond will be less than the investor expects. Thus the investor faces *inflation risk*. The alternative is to engage in the rollover strategy, investing in one-period bonds each year. The advantage is that the investor can rely on the market to reset the short-term rate each year according to the prevailing inflation rate, and as a result it is more likely that the investor will realize a total return that reflects *ex post* inflation over the multiperiod investment horizon. Thus, even long-term investors will require a premium on long-term bonds.

Returning to our example, suppose investors, at year-end 1999, expected the one-year spot rate at year-end 2000 to be the same as the one-year rate at year-end 1999, 6.05 percent. However, the spot rate on the two-year bond is 6.25 percent, suggesting that investors demand a premium on the two-year bond. The premium is

$$(1.0625)^2 = (1 + 0.0605 + {}_2p_{0,1})[1 + 0.0605],$$

or

$$_2p_{0,1} = 0.0040 = 0.40\%.$$

FORWARD INTEREST RATES

Unfortunately, the liquidity preference hypothesis, as expressed in Equation B10.6, contains two variables that are not directly observable, $E(s_{12})$ and $_2p_{0,1}$. As such, by observing the spot rates $s_{0,1}$ and $s_{0,2}$, we cannot uniquely determine the value of either variable. However, we can extract information on the *sum* of the two variables by solving for the *forward interest rate*, $f_{1,2}$, using Equation B10.7:

$$(1 + s_{0,2})^2 = (1 + s_{01})[1 + f_{1,2}]. \quad \textbf{(B10.7)}$$

Essentially, $f_{1,2}$ is the sum of the two unobservable variables $E(s_{1,2})$ and $_2p_{0,1}$:

$$f_{1,2} = E(s_{1,2}) + {}_2p_{0,1}. \quad \textbf{(B10.8)}$$

In our present example $f_{1,2} = 6.45$ percent ($= 1.0625^2/1.0605 - 1$, in percent). Note that if we adhere to the Pure Expectations Hypothesis, the forward interest rate $f_{1,2}$ is equal to the market's expectation of the one-year rate one year hence. However, under the Liquidity Preference Hypothesis, this forward rate contains two components. Thus, we must assume the value of one of the components in order to solve for the other.

THE MARKET SEGMENTATION HYPOTHESIS

The third hypothesis is the *Market Segmentation Hypothesis*. This theory states that yields on short-term and long-term bonds depend on the supply and demand for bonds of that maturity. Generally, long-term yields are higher than short-term yields. The Segmentation Hypothesis claims that this is because investors generally would have a greater demand for short-term bonds than long-term bonds if their yields are equal. Thus, yields on long-term bonds must generally be higher in equilibrium. However, as supply and demand conditions differentially change in the two segmented markets, the yields on short-term and long-term bonds will change, essentially independently. In other words, according to the Market Segmentation Hypothesis, neither expectations nor risk premiums play an explicit role in determining the yields on bonds of various maturities.

PART

Managing Equity and Debt

III

Part Three is devoted to the many issues associated with managing a firm's equity and debt. We begin at the beginning—that is, we initially discuss the development of a nascent firm, or *venture*. In Chapter 11, we describe the process by which a venture develops, focusing on various means by which a venture's entrepreneurs can obtain capital through the states of its development. In Chapter 12, we discuss (a) the process by which a firm *goes public*, (b) the characteristics of firms that go public, (c) the pricing of initial public offerings (IPOs), and (d) the post-IPO performance of stocks.

In Chapters 13 and 14, we discuss issues that are most pertinent to an established, or *seasoned*, publicly traded firm. Chapter 13 covers three topics. *First*, we provide a fundamental perspective on the management of a firm's equity. *Second*, we discuss the concept of a firm's *internal capital market*, wherein the firm allocates its available internal funds to projects. *Third*, we provide an in-depth analysis of the decision of the management of a publicly traded firm to issue additional equity; that is, to conduct a *seasoned equity offering* (SEO).

In Chapter 14, we focus on a firm's policies regarding cash dividends and stock repurchases, the two principal means by which the firm distributes cash to its shareholders. In Chapter 15, we discuss strategic decisions regarding a firm's liabilities, including the firm's selections of lenders (e.g., borrowing on a private basis versus issuing public debt) and contract terms (e.g., maturity, restrictive covenants, and alternative retirement provisions).

CHAPTER

Private Equity and Venture Capital

11.1 INTRODUCTION

Most of the publicly traded firms in the United States today originated as relatively small, privately owned *start-up* firms, or *ventures*, masterminded by a single individual or a group of individuals. These *entrepreneurs* simultaneously served as the firm's major shareholders, governance body, and management team. By various means, they obtained additional financing for expansion, and eventually sold equity shares to the public via an *initial public offering* (IPO) of equity. (We discuss IPOs in Chapter 12.)

However, for each successful venture there are numerous failures. The frequent failure of ventures is not surprising, because ventures (a) typically attempt to speculate on new frontiers in a particular industry, and consequently face highly uncertain prospects, (b) are generally characterized by relatively inexperienced management and a lack of current earnings, and (c) are especially vulnerable to short-term deterioration in product-market, financial-market, or macroeconomic conditions.

Unless and until a venture's prospects become clearer, raising equity publicly is prohibitively expensive. Moreover, entrepreneurs generally find that they cannot obtain private debt financing (e.g., from a bank) until they have reached a critical stage of development. Consequently, early-stage ventures generally seek funds through the *private venture capital market*. Investors in this market include (a) wealthy individuals who are willing to contribute funds to speculative ventures, (b) governments and universities, and (c) *venture capital firms (VCs)*.

In this chapter, we describe the processes by which a typical venture develops, focusing on how the venture's entrepreneurs obtain capital throughout the *stages* of the venture's development. We find that financing efforts are beset by the fundamental financing problems common to all firms, namely *principal–agent conflicts* (both shareholder–management and shareholder–creditor) and *information asymmetry*. In the case of ventures, these problems can be very severe, and therefore require financial contracting solutions that are unique to the circumstances. Aside from the out-and-out failure of the idea behind the venture, the inadequate resolution of these problems likely accounts for a large proportion of venture failures.

11.2 RUDIMENTS OF VALUING AND FINANCING A VENTURE

As entrepreneurs and potential financiers consider pursuing a venture, the critical question is, *What is the business worth?* In Chapter 9, we showed that we can readily estimate the value of a typical publicly traded firm by examining the firm's past earnings or dividends, forecasting its future earnings or dividends, and then applying a rational discount rate. For a venture, the task of valuation is much more difficult for two reasons. *First*, the typical venture has no history of earnings, and in many cases a market does not yet exist for the proposed venture's product or service! Thus, earnings estimates are often little more than wild guesses. *Second*, the venture may be planning to operate in a new or young industry in which comparable companies are scarce or nonexistent, so establishing a rational discount rate is also highly problematic.

Nevertheless, the value of a venture must be established through some type of rational *valuation process*. One popular, though admittedly ad hoc, approach to valuing a venture that is financed with equity shares involves four steps:

1. Project a future horizon date at which the venture will be a stable, profitable firm, assuming that the firm's long-term business goals are achieved. Forecast the venture's earnings and earnings growth as of that date.
2. Calculate the fair value of the firm as of this horizon date. A normal discount rate, market-to-book equity ratio, or price-earnings ratio (P/E) can be used for this purpose.
3. Calculate the current value of the venture by discounting the calculated horizon-date value of the firm to the present, using an appropriate risk-adjusted discount rate. The annual discount rate for early-stage ventures generally ranges from 50 percent to 70 percent, whereas the annual discount rate for later-stage ventures generally ranges from 30 percent to 40 percent. Adjustments are made for the probability of the venture's success, the length of time to the horizon date, current interest rates, and risk premiums in the market.
4. Finally, use the estimated current value of the venture to partition the venture's shares among the firm's entrepreneurs and investors.

A Numerical Example

Suppose a venture requires $2.5 million in equity financing to move to the next stage of development. The venture's entrepreneurs are negotiating with a private financier for equity financing of this amount. Assuming that the firm's business goals will be achieved, its earnings are projected to be $14 million per year at the horizon date, five years from now, when the firm goes public. The entrepreneurs expect that the horizon-date market value of the firm will be determined by applying a P/E of 9. Thus, the projected horizon-date value of the firm is $126 million [= 9($14 million)]. Given the riskiness of the venture, a discount rate of 50 percent per annum is applied to this value to determine the present value of the venture, yielding a value of $V = \$16.6$ million (= $126 million/$[1.50]^5$). Finally, based on this value and the required contribution of $2.5 million from the financier, the financier should receive 15.1 percent [= $2.5 million/$16.6 million, in percent] of the firm's equity shares.

In reality, valuation and financing issues are more complex than this example illustrates. For a variety of reasons, including and especially information asymmetry and principal–agent conflicts, the entrepreneurs and the financier may disagree on the values of the input parameters. Referring to the stepwise valuation procedure above, they may disagree on (a) the amount of financing required at the current stage of development, (b) the amount of time that will be required to bring the venture to fruition, (c) the future earnings that the firm will realize given that the business plan is successful, and (d) the appropriate discount rate to use in the valuation (especially as this discount rate depends on the probability of the venture's success).

To the extent that they disagree on the current value of the venture, the entrepreneurs and the potential financier will disagree on the appropriate percentage of the venture's equity that the financier should receive. We formally address this issue later. But first, we discuss the *staging process* involved in the development and financing of a venture.

11.3 THE STAGES OF VENTURE DEVELOPMENT AND FINANCING

Any number of environments can become a spawning ground for an entrepreneur's concept for a venture. For instance, a group of employees of a firm in a particular industry may discover that an unmet need exists for a new product or service within that industry. They realize that the production of this new product or service could be highly profitable, and that if they were to work with their current employer to develop that product or service, they would likely realize little of the profits from the innovation. Therefore, they decide to pursue the idea on their own.

The research and development (R&D) centers of many corporations and universities also spawn venture concepts. When a promising concept emerges from such centers, the sponsoring firm or university is generally willing to allow the individuals involved to develop a venture based on the concept, and generally support their efforts financially, as long as the sponsor retains a *piece of the action*.

Developing a venture, however, is no mean task. Typically, development can be divided into eight stages. Given the crucial importance of securing adequate and continuing external capital, these stages are largely *defined* in terms of the unique financing alternatives that must be used.

In this section, we describe each of these eight stages in terms of development activities and financing alternatives. We also discuss the rationale for the stagewise development of a venture. For quick reference, the development activities, financing alternatives, and other details typically associated with each stage are summarized in Table 11-1.

11.3.1 Stage 1: Seed Financing

The seed stage of development is the entrepreneurs' initial effort to formulate a vision of the eventual firm based on the original concept. Entrepreneurs expend a great deal of time, but a relatively small amount of money, to explore the prospect of commercial development of the concept. If the concept involves the development of a product, this stage may involve building a small prototype of the product that would eventually be mass-produced. Alternatively, the entrepreneurs develop a detailed description of the service that would be provided. The entrepreneurs also estimate the market potential for the product or service. The typical duration of the seed stage is 6 months to 1 year.

At this stage, the entrepreneurs may require financing of up to $1 million Financing is required to pay the entrepreneurs at least a modest living wage while they pursue the concept, and to provide office space, equipment, assistants, and so on.

TABLE 11-1 The Stages of a Typical Venture's Development and Financing

	Seed	Start-up	Early Development	Expansion	Profitable/ Cash Poor	Rapid Growth	Bridge/ Mezzanine	Harvest
Development of Venture	Concept development; basic business plan; prototypes; explore market potential	Detail business plan; assemble management team; test prototype; finalize product/ service lines	Secure initial PP&E; initial products sold	Secure additional PP&E; develop marketing strategy; expand production capital; working capital needs emerge	Expand production capacity; working capital needs grow	Marketing strategy refined	Marketing and R&D	Recap; buyout; sell to acquirer; go public
Years Cumulative Capital	0–1 $0–1 million	1–3 $1–5 million	3–5 $5–10 million	3–5 $5–10 million	3–5 $5–10 million	3–5 $5–10 million	5–7 $10+ million	
Sources of Financing	Bootstrap; angels	Angels; VC; corporation; university	Angels; VC; government	VC; government; bank	VC; bank; retained earnings	VC; bank; retained earnings	VC; bank; retained earnings	
Securities Typically Issued	Personal loans; common stock	Notes with warrants; convertible preferred stock; partnership interest; common stock	Guaranteed bonds; notes with warrants; convertible preferred stock; partnership interest; common stock	Guaranteed bonds; secured debt; convertible bonds; convertible preferred stock; common stock	Secured debt; convertible bonds; convertible preferred stock; common stock	Subordinated debt; convertible bonds; convertible preferred stock	Subordinated debt; convertible bonds; convertible preferred stock	

Sources: Based on Plummer (1987) and Sahlman (1990).

Generally, mainstream sources of financing for small businesses (e.g., banks or venture capital firms) are not available for this purpose, so the entrepreneurs must be especially creative in securing seed-stage capital. The two most common sources of seed-stage financing are *bootstrapping* and *angel financiers*.

Bootstrapping

In bootstrapping, the entrepreneurs tap their available personal savings and personal borrowing capacity (e.g., credit card advances and home-equity loans), and may also seek to borrow from family, friends, or business associates. Depending on the product or service to be developed, bootstrap financing may also include customer advances or extended-payment lending from vendors.

Bootstrapping is a widely used and effective means of financing a venture. A recent survey of 100 of *Inc. Magazine*'s 500 fastest growing companies revealed that 80 percent were financed solely via bootstrapping during the seed stage. The survey also revealed that median seed capital was $10,000, an amount that can be readily raised via bootstrapping.

Angel Financiers

An angel financier is a wealthy individual who is very tolerant of risk. Often he or she has some entrepreneurial experience. Angels prefer to invest in small companies that have great growth potential, and they finance these firms in the earliest stages of development. The angel-financing network is very informal. In most cases, an angel becomes aware of a venture through his or her business or personal contacts.

Individually, angels generally invest $500,000 or less in a given venture. They tend to favor straightforward, equity-related securities such as common stock or partnership interests. They generally wish to liquidate their investment by selling their securities at a later stage of development.

Angel financing has existed for a long time. We might consider King Ferdinand and Queen Isabella as angel financiers of Columbus' famous voyages. More recently, Henry Ford launched his auto manufacturing business by securing a total investment of $41,500 from five angels. An angel who invested $100,000 in Amazon.com later sold out for $26 million. (Of course, losses are more common than profits.) Currently, angels in the United States invest an aggregate amount of about $50 billion annually. As such, angels' aggregate investment in ventures is comparable to the amount invested by venture capital firms, or VCs, which we discuss later.

11.3.2   Stage 2: Start-Up

If the results of the seed stage of development are promising, the start-up stage ensues. In this stage, a management team is assembled, and they develop a more detailed business plan. Product or service development takes place, a prototype is tested, and marketing is done to test market potential. The duration of this stage is generally one to two years.

Development at this stage generally requires an additional $1 million to $4 million in committed capital. Fortunately, financing alternatives generally expand commensurately. Angels who committed seed money to the venture are generally prepared to contribute additional funds. VCs may also step in at this stage or, if the entrepreneurs are associated with the venture *incubator* of a corporation or university, these entities are prepared to support development at this stage.

11.3.3 Stage 3: Early Development

If a venture reaches the early development stage, risk has been greatly reduced because the testing of product prototypes, or the test marketing of services, has indicated substantial potential. During this stage, the firm secures its initial property, plant, and equipment (PP&E), and its products are shipped in commercial quantities or its services are provided to customers, as the case may be. However, the firm is not yet profitable at the end of this stage.

Angel financiers involved in earlier stages of development may be willing to contribute additional capital at this stage, but it is more likely that they wish to *cash-out* at this point. A VC may step in to take their place. As PP&E is acquired at this stage, the firm may be able to secure bank financing. Generally, though, bank financing is available only if the issued debt is government guaranteed. If the firm qualifies, it can obtain a government guarantee of its debt either at the federal level through the U.S. Small Business Administration, or through a state's Industrial Development Bond (IDB) program.

11.3.4 Stage 4: Expansion

In this stage, the company has accumulated considerable experience in the marketplace. Even though ultimate success is still highly questionable, major success factors have been identified. On an operational basis, the firm is still losing money throughout this stage, which generally spans about two years. The firm may need additional financing of up to $5 million for the purchase of equipment and inventory, and for increased working capital. Alternative financing sources at this stage include VC firms and banks.

11.3.5 Stage 5: Profitable but Cash Poor

If the expansion stage is successful, the firm generally experiences substantial growth. Operating margins, and perhaps even profit margins, are positive, which eliminates much downside risk. Retained earnings may emerge as a source of financing. However, cash generated through operations is not sufficient to finance fully the required expansion of manufacturing facilities and working capital. If a VC firm is involved, it would continue to be an important source of capital. However, banks may also be willing to lend to the venture, if loans can be secured by real estate, equipment, or receivables.

11.3.6 Stage 6: Rapid Growth toward Liquidity Point

Ventures that reach the rapid growth stage of development are fairly stable and risk has been reduced dramatically. Capital infusions may still be necessary to finance continuing expansion. The likelihood of debt financing is higher in this phase. Debt financing becomes important because the entrepreneurs, as well as other equity investors, are now eager to limit dilution. The *harvest* stage will be in sight, though the precise harvest date and form are as yet undecided.

11.3.7 Stage 7: Bridge Stage (Mezzanine Financing)

The *bridge* or *mezzanine* stage is essentially a final growth-and-preparation stage, required before the firm can harvest the venture. However, the harvest alternative already has been determined, so the firm's growth-and-preparation strategy is generally tailored to this alternative. For instance, if the firm is considering an IPO, it may be shaping its earnings numbers to foster a favorable reception in the market, and may also be waiting for favorable stock market conditions for an offering.

Meanwhile, the firm may still need additional financing for further growth, for financing restructuring, or for a limited cashing-out of early investors. Entrepreneurs remain sensitive to the dilution issue, so common stock financing is generally avoided at this stage. Instead, the firm may issue subordinated debt, convertible bonds, or convertible preferred stock.

11.3.8 Stage 8: Harvest

The final stage of development, harvest, involves the cashing-out and exit of any and all short-term investors. Three main alternatives are available (a) remaining private and replacing short-term investors with long-term investors, (b) being acquired, or (c) going public. Below we briefly discuss each of these alternatives.

Remaining Private, Replacing Short-Term Investors with Long-Term Investors

For a developed firm that chooses to remain private, long-term investors must replace short-term investors. The firm could *recapitalize* by issuing additional private securities to long-term investors and using part or all of the proceeds to cash-out exiting short-term investors. An alternative is a management buyout (MBO). In a MBO, the firm's management raises capital (usually debt capital) to buy out the interests of most or all of the firm's shareholders. (We discuss buyouts, as they apply to publicly traded firms, in Chapter 16.)

Being Acquired

At some point, a developed venture may receive an acquisition bid from a larger, established firm. If the firm agrees to be acquired, all investors receive either cash for the securities that they hold or shares of stock of the acquiring firm. (We discuss acquisitions in Chapter 16, again as they apply to publicly traded firms.)

Going Public

To become a publicly traded firm, a private firm generally obtains the services of an underwriter to register its common shares with the Securities and Exchange Commission (SEC) and sell them to the public in an IPO. In Chapter 12, we discuss the IPO process in detail. Here we simply note that short-term investors can use the IPO to liquidate at least part of their equity positions in the firm by offering them in the *secondary* portion of the IPO. In the *primary* portion of the IPO, the firm issues new common shares to raise cash for the firm. This new cash may be used for any of a variety of purposes, including paying off debt and expanding PP&E.

11.4 VENTURE CAPITAL FIRMS (VCs)

A venture capital firm (VC) is a professional financing organization that provides capital for ventures and generally assists the firm's management with expertise and strategic guidance. Most VCs take the form of a limited liability corporation (LLC), which is actually a type of partnership. Over the past 20 years, VCs have played an increasingly important role in the financing and development of ventures in the United States. In recent years, VCs have contributed private equity capital to approximately half of the U.S. nonfinancial firms that have gone public.[1] Therefore, we devote this section and the next to an extensive discussion of VCs.

11.4.1   The VC as a Financial Intermediary *Extraordinaire*

Like commercial banks and business finance companies, VCs are financial intermediaries—they issue securities to obtain funds from investors, and use these funds to purchase securities issued by firms. However, the similarity ends there. VCs are distinguished from commercial banks and finance companies in five important respects:

1. VCs are partnerships that obtain funds by issuing equity shares on a quasi-private basis. In contrast, most commercial banks and finance companies are public corporations, and they obtain funds by issuing debt (deposits, in the case of banks).
2. VCs specialize in financing very young, high-risk companies, most of which are not yet profitable. In contrast, banks and finance companies generally finance relatively stable, profitable firms.
3. VCs generally accept equity securities, rather than debt securities, in exchange for the capital they provide to a firm.
4. VCs are much more involved in the management of a firm that they support.
5. VCs are less regulated than either commercial banks or finance companies.

Oh, the Risk They Bear!
By the nature of the investments they undertake, VCs take tremendous risk. Examples of the upside and downside results of start-up ventures are Lotus Development Corporation and Ovation Technologies. Regarding Lotus, investors who contributed a total of $4.7 million in two rounds of financing in 1982 saw the market value of their investment increase to almost $130 million by October 1983. Ovation Technologies, on the other hand, raised $6 million in venture capital in 1983, to compete against Lotus. Technical problems forced the company to liquidate, and Ovation Technologies went under in late 1984 without having generated any revenue whatsoever.

High Discount Rates and High Average Returns as Compensation
A venture investment also generally involves a long investment horizon, perhaps five or more years, during which time the investment is extremely illiquid. On an *ex ante* basis, VCs compensate for the risk and illiquidity of venture investments by applying extraordinarily high discount rates in valuing a venture investment, as we illustrated with the example in Section 11.2.

---

[1]These include notable firms in biotechnology (e.g., Biogen, Genentech) and computer-related industries (e.g., Advanced Micro Devices, Apple, Cisco Systems, Compaq, Intel, Lotus Development, Seagate Technologies, and Sun Microsystems).

If VCs' discount rate estimates are rational, they should translate into high average returns *ex post*. Huntsman and Hoban Jr. (1980) analyzed a sample of 110 private equity investments made by VCs in ventures over the years 1960 to 1975. The investments ranged in size from $1,000 to $1.11 million. The average holding period for these investments was approximately five years. They found that the average annualized return on these investments was 19.8 percent. (Over the same period, the average annual return on the S&P 500 index was 6.1 percent).

However, returns varied tremendously, as expected. Figure 11-1 shows the frequency distribution of the annualized returns on the 110 investments in their sample. A total of 18 investments, or 17 percent of the total, resulted in a complete loss. At the other extreme, a total of 17 investments provided annualized returns in excess of 40 percent, including one that provided returns at a rate of 318 percent per annum!

Monitoring and Governance Expertise

VCs have monitoring and governance expertise that is particularly valuable in the venture environment, which is rife with principal–agent conflicts. They have expertise in monitoring the firm's management. As we discussed in Chapter 5, monitoring is an important mechanism to mitigate principal–agent conflicts and their associated costs.

FIGURE 11-1   Frequency Distribution of Annual Rates of Return on Venture Investments

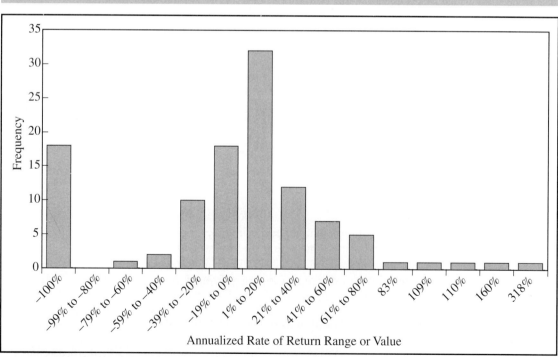

110 Investments, 1960–1975
Source: Huntsman and Hoban Jr. (1980)

The typical VC also is involved with the governance of a backed company. From a perch on the venture's board of directors, a VC can lend their expertise in all of the following areas:

1. VCs provide advice on compensation for key employees, and building customer and supplier relations.
2. VCs aide in the development of tactics, strategies, and legal agreements.
3. VCs provide general advice on how to manage a growing business. Generally, entrepreneurs are well equipped with technical knowledge, but few have experience in managing their own business.
4. VCs provide access to their extensive contacts in the industry.
5. VCs assist a venture in assembling a management team with the right skills and experience.
6. VCs assist the venture in its search for capital.
7. VCs assist the venture in the harvest stage, whether the firm is planning to remain private, engage a buyout, be acquired, or go public.

The importance of the advice and support provided by a VC is demonstrated in the case of NBI, whose lead investor was Burton McMurtry. One of NBI's partners, Tom Kavanagh, stressed the importance of non-monetary contributions of VCs: "It is far more important whose money you get than how much you get or how much you pay for it."

The Role of VCs in Building Human Capital

Hellman and Puri (2002) conducted an empirical analysis of 170 ventures to determine the role of VCs in developing human capital within a supported venture. Their sample included both VC-backed firms and non–VC-backed firms, so by comparison they could ascertain whether VCs actively build human capital.

The authors examined dimensions such as the recruitment process, overall human resource policies, the adoption of stock option plans, and the hiring of a vice president for marketing and sales. Their evidence on each of these dimensions indicates that VC-backed firms develop their human resource capital at a faster pace. They also examined the question of whether VCs get involved with appointments at the top of the firm's hierarchy, specifically, the post of CEO. They found that a firm's founder is more likely to be replaced with an outsider for the CEO position, and that this is likely to happen faster, in VC-backed ventures.

VCs often use their membership on a venture's board to affect necessary changes. Lerner (1995) documents evidence that VC membership on the board increases around the time of a CEO change. Hellman and Puri (2002) provided evidence that, if the firm's founder is acceptable to the VC, the VC will tend to assist in the development of human capital throughout the organization. However, if the VC has trouble with the incumbent CEO, they will concentrate their efforts on replacing the CEO.

11.4.2   Historical Development of the VC Industry

The venture capital industry was born in 1946 with the emergence of two pioneering firms, privately held J. H. Whitney & Co. and publicly traded American Research and Development Corporation (ARD). Whitney & Co. helped develop 350 companies,

Capital Access Partners

Capital Access Partners is a financial services company that focuses on the formation and development of high-tech companies. Below is their description of the services they provide.

CAPITAL FORMATION & INVESTMENT MISSION

Capital Access Partners works in partnership with financial sources to make intelligent, well-informed investments in high technology companies.

We specialize in telecommunications, medical systems, electronics, software, Internet, and high tech service companies.

Capital Access Partners identifies opportunities, investigates candidates, and participates in the entire investment process.

TARGET INVESTMENT OPPORTUNITY

Our primary focus is on growing high technology companies in first and second stage of development. The firm must offer differentiated services and/or products often in focused or niche markets. Most selected opportunities exhibit moderately low risk and yet [are] not suitable for traditional U.S. investment sources [e.g., Venture Groups, NASDAQ].

DUE DILIGENCE

Capital Access Partners has performed due diligence for investors and publicly traded firms in need of an outside confirmation of their potential investments. Our services greatly benefit publicly traded companies wishing to invest in up-and-coming firms in possession of advanced technology. Our investigation highlights the areas of strength and those areas in need of improvement including intellectual property, research practices, market potential, financial practices, quality of management, and sales channels. The final results of our due diligence are a clear understanding of risks, primary benefits, and problem areas that need monitoring. This allows the Chief Executive to have a greater comfort level and confirms or adds to existing examination.

STRATEGIC PARTNERSHIPS

Capital Access Partners has found that strategic partnerships with firms having similar goals is an effective means to growth. These partnerships may involve investment or other mutually beneficial relationships. Capital Access Partners is expert at identifying industry trends so that parties with similar interests can be approached properly and a successful partnership established.

Capital Access Partners can prepare your firm and approach the obvious and not so obvious potential partner in a professional manner.

INVESTOR NEGOTIATION & OVERSIGHT

Capital Access Partners is available to represent investment candidates in negotiations with funding sources. Our principals have experience in all aspects of institutional investment. In this manner, your company receives the highest quality financial, advisory, and structural counsel available to obtain capital on the best possible terms.

ENTREPRENEURIAL SUPPORT SERVICES

Through the course of performing its capital formation services, Capital Access Partners (CAP) has encountered numerous firms which show great promise. Many entrepreneurs have a strong understanding in their own fields but lack knowledge of the capitalization process.

Professional investors seek companies with well-presented strengths [and] the ability to minimize risk. CAP knows how to evaluate risk, understands what professional investors find appealing, and presents the firm in the very best light.

All assignments are performed by senior professionals and are reasonably priced for earlier stage firms. Our results are presented quickly in a non-bureaucratic manner so recommendations may be implemented effectively. Our intent is to create ongoing relationships with firms through demonstrating the value of our output.

BUSINESS PLAN AUTHORING

Capital Access Partners delivers Professional Business Plan Authoring services to fit your budget. We can write a professionally presentable plan directly from your materials or assist in building and modeling the entire business from the ground up. See Business & Market Strategy & Planning for greater detail on the more comprehensive services available.

VENTURE/BUSINESS VALUATION

Capital Access Partners professionals can provide you with services ranging from a quick company financial valuation to formal appraisals and expert witness testimony. The quick valuation supplies the entrepreneur with an independent and unbiased view of what knowledgeable and astute Investors may value the company/startup. Formal appraisals and expert witness engagements entail careful examination and valuation from senior executives experienced in the technology arena.

BUSINESS & MARKET STRATEGY & PLANNING

Capital Access Partners professionals are available for assessing existing plans or assisting startups and companies [to] perform true, comprehensive business and market planning.

Capital Access Partners will review the business plan and meet with the founders/principals on the premises and analyze the status of market, product, and financial plans. This examination provides a written assessment of status and recommendations for improvement from two vantages:

1. Attractiveness to a potential investor and
2. Improving likelihood of operating success.

In-depth planning entails modeling the entire firm's activities for all functional areas (marketing, finance, strategic positioning, intellectual property, staffing, sales, etc.). The plan serves two primary purposes: a formal document that may be presented to potential investors or strategic partners and that provides the firm with a "road map" to success.

STRATEGIC PARTNERING PLANNING/NEGOTIATION

Capital Access Partners offers professional support to plan and negotiate "Strategic Associations" and Joint Ventures both domestic and international. We are able to identify the less obvious potential partners and approach them in a well thought through manner.

Our Technology Negotiator's background includes:

- Domestic and International Experience.
- Representation of major companies such as ITT and with numerous technology venture Startup Companies.
- Experienced in software, VLSI Chips, Systems and in Technology Licensing and Transfer.
- Expert in Win-Win Negotiation.

Source: Capital Access Partners, a Division of Investors Diligence, Inc. Reprinted by permission.

including Minute Maid and Compaq Computer. ARD provided a major innovation by using the research resources of a university, Massachusetts Institute of Technology (MIT), to assist in the development of ventures. This innovation led to the successful development of Digital Equipment Corporation, among other firms. Another important historical development was Arthur Rock's idea to formulate a VC as a *partnership*. Rock also defined the division of responsibilities and returns among the partners.

Key Developments

Despite these pioneering efforts, VCs did not become a major force in the U.S. financial markets until two problems were solved. *First*, VCs had to devise an organizational form that provides an effective legal-liability arrangement for parties who contribute capital to or manage the VC. *Second*, VCs had to find a way to tap large, institutional sources of capital.

The first problem was solved via a combination of state legislation and an Internal Revenue Service (IRS) ruling. Beginning with Wyoming in 1977, many states adopted legislation to create a new legal entity, the *limited liability corporation*, or LLC. The LLC combines aspects of a partnership and a corporation. Unlike a partnership, in which at least one partner must be a general partner who bears personal liability, all members of a LLC are shielded from personal liability to the same extent as corporate shareholders. However, unlike a corporation, the LLC is a *flow-through entity* in the sense that all income and losses are reported directly by its members; that is, the LLC avoids the double-taxation associated with a corporation and its shareholders. In 1988, the IRS issued a ruling to accept the flow-through aspect of a LLC's earnings; that is, the LLC can be treated as a partnership for tax purposes.

The second problem was solved via federal legislation. Three congressional acts adopted in 1979 and 1980 provided VCs access to the large national pool of capital held by pension funds. The *Prudent Man Rule* of the Employee Retirement Income Security Act (ERISA) allowed pension fund managers to invest in venture capital pools and other high-risk investments for the first time. The *Small Business Investment Incentive Act* and the *ERISA Plan Assets Safe Harbor Regulation Act* both (a) simplified the operation of a VC and (b) reduced pension funds' risk exposure by allowing them to participate in a VC as limited partners.

Explosive Growth of VCs in the Past Two Decades

The combination of the pioneering efforts of early VCs and the development of the flow-through LLC led to a virtual explosion of VCs and VC financing over the past two decades. Figure 11-2 displays three relevant annual aggregate statistics for the VC industry from 1980 to 2000: *total capital under management*, *new capital committed*, and *disbursements*. These numbers clearly indicate that the industry has grown tremendously over this period. Aggregate capital under management increased 91-fold from $4 billion at year-end 1980 to $373 billion at year-end 2000.

Growth in the VC industry was severely blunted around the recession of 1990 to 1991. New capital committed decreased by over 70 percent from $5.2 billion in 1989 to only $1.5 billion in 1991. This result highlights the sensitivity of venture development, at least in terms of VC financing, to economic conditions. Growth was particularly phenomenal from 1996 to 2000, though the current economic slowdown of 2000 to 2001 has again put a crimp in the funding of VCs.

FIGURE 11-2   The Growth of VC Financing in the United States

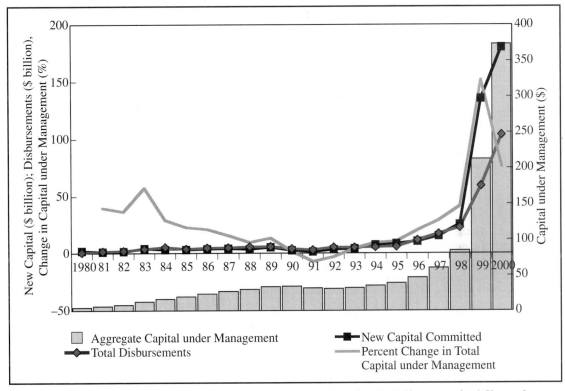

New Capital Committed, Disbursements, and Year-End Aggregate Capital under Management (and Change from Previous Year): 1980–2000
Source: Raw data from Venture Economics/National Venture Capital Association.

11.4.3   The Current State of the VC Industry

As of 2001, the venture capital magazine *Red Herring* listed 668 VCs in the United States, compared with fewer than 100 in 1995. In 2000, VCs raised $180 billion, a 21-fold increase over the $8.4 billion raised in 1995. VCs establish a pool of capital, known as the VC's *fund*, from which they can finance selected ventures. If the VC wishes to expand the capital of an established fund, they must make a formal proposal to do so. More commonly, a VC firm will simply establish a new fund and seek funding for it.

Currently, VCs obtain over 50 percent of their capital from mutual funds and pension funds, with the balance coming from endowments, foundations, insurance companies, banks, trusts, and wealthy individuals. A typical institutional investor allocates 2 percent to 3 percent of their portfolio to *private equity*, including VCs, as part of their overall asset allocation.

Financing VCs and Motivating VC Managers
Gompers and Lerner (1999) provided an extensive empirical analysis of the contract terms in U.S. venture capital partnerships. They documented the following

standard terms in partnership agreements: (a) the initial contract among the partners is for approximately a decade; (b) a percentage of the fund's capital or assets are paid as an annual management fee; (c) a percentage of profits are paid out as investment returns are realized; and (d) to maintain their limited liability status, investors must avoid direct involvement in the fund's activities. Regarding (d), as a practical matter VC investors cannot fire, actively discipline, or even closely monitor the VC's management.

The authors describe the typical compensation contract for a VC manager as follows: "The limited partnership agreement explicitly specifies the terms that govern the venture capitalists' compensation over the entire ten-to-thirteen year life of the fund. It is extremely rare that these terms are renegotiated. The specified compensation has a simple form. The venture capitalist typically receives an annual fixed fee, plus variable compensation that is a specified fraction of the fund's profits. The fixed portion of the specified compensation is usually between 1.5 percent and 3 percent of the committed capital or net asset value, and the variable portion is usually about 20 percent of fund profits" (p. 6). However, they found that compensation in smaller and younger funds is considerably less sensitive to the fund's performance. They also found no relationship between compensation and performance. They suggest that this relationship is lacking because reputational concerns already adequately induce the VC manager to work hard.

Examples of VC Firms

Table 11-2 provides details of 20 VCs that are representative of larger firms in the industry. (The lower panel of the table provides a list of other prominent VCs.) Fifteen of the 20 VCs listed were established within the last 20 years or so, an indication of the industry's youth. Capital under management ranges from $300 million to $25 billion. They tend to locate in areas of the United States known either for high-tech expertise (California) or as financial centers (states surrounding New York City, including New York, New Jersey, Connecticut, and Massachusetts).

VCs tend to finance ventures in high-growth industries, for the obvious reason that the probability that a given venture will be an extraordinary success (and offset losses on failed ventures) is greater in such industries. This argument is supported by the information on the 20 VC's stated industry specialties shown in the table. The most frequently cited specialties are communications, information technology, software, and healthcare. Finally, each VC's preferred investment *stages* are shown in the last column of the table. They vary in their stage preferences, from seed to later stages.

11.4.4   Negotiations Between an Entrepreneur and a VC

The VC's Viewpoint

VC managers are aware that most of the ventures they support will fail. The VC earns a profit overall if a small proportion of the ventures they support provide big payoffs. Given these circumstances, a VC's management must (a) screen out ventures that appear to have poor prospects, (b) assess and work with the managements of selected ventures to maximize the probability of success, and (c) secure a sufficient share of successful ventures' profits for the VC to offset losses on the failures.

TABLE 11-2 Descriptions of 20 Venture Capital Firms, and a List of Other Prominent VCs for 2001

Firm Name	Year Established	Location(s)	Capital under Management ($ million)	Industry Specialties	Investment Stages
Accel Partners	1984	CA	3,000	Communications, Software/Internet	Start-up, various
Austin Ventures	1979	TX	3,100	Communications, Semiconductor, Software and Services	Seed, early stage
Benchmark Capital	1995	CA, Int'l	2,000	Software, Networks, Semiconductor, Consumer and Financial Services	Early stage
Battery Ventures	1983	MA, CA	1,800	Software, Internet/e-Commerce	All stages
Crosspoint Venture Partners	1970	CA	2,000	e-Business, Broadband	Early stage
Domain Associates	1985	CA, NJ	300	Life Sciences/Healthcare	Growth, early stages favored
Enterprise Partners	1985	CA	1,000	Communications, Life Sciences, Internet, e-Commerce, etc.	Early stage, emerging growth
Geocapital Partners	1984	NJ, Int'l	500	Business Marketing, Communications/Networks, e-Commerce, Enterprise	Rapidly growing
Institutional Venture Partners	1980	CA	1,300	Communications, e-Commerce, Digital TV, Wireless, etc.	More developed firms
J.P. Morgan Partners	1984	NY, CA, Int'l	25,000	Various	Early stage, mezzanine, etc.
Mobius Venture Capital	1996	CA, CO	2,500	Technology	Early stage
New Enterprise Associates	1978	MD	5,000	Biotech, Healthcare, Communications, Software	Development stage
Norwest Venture Partners	1961	MA, CA, MN	1,000	Information Technology, Software, Communications Systems, Services	Start-up, expansion
Oak Investment Partners	1978	CA, CT, MN	1,600	Enterprise Software, Communications	Seed through later stage
Olympic Venture Partners	1983	WA, OR	475	Software, Communications, Internet, Biotech	Seed, first round
Sierra Ventures	1982	CA	1,100	Communications, Software, Internet	Early, prepublic
Sprout Group	1969	CA, NY	1,600	Software, Technology, Healthcare, Communications, Retail	Early, growth, mezzanine, buyout
Summit Partners	1984	MA	1,400	Business Services, Communications, Electronics, e-Services, Healthcare, etc.	Early stage
Warburg, Pincus & Co.	1939	CA, NY, Int'l	12,000	Biotech, Business Services, Media, Telecommunications, etc.	Start-up, growth, etc.
J.H. Whitney & Co.	1946	CA, MA, NY, Int'l	5,000	Communications, Financial Services, Information Technology, Healthcare, Industrial	Growth

Other Notable VCs

AT&T Ventures	Draper Fisher Jurvetson	Kleiner, Perkins, Caufield & Byers	Motorola New Enterprises	Tribune Ventures
Atlas Venture	Edison Venture Fund	Matrix Partners	Noro-Moseley Partners	U.S. Venture Partners
BancBoston Ventures	GE Equity	Mayfield Fund	Olympic Venture Partners	Venture Resources
Bessemer Venture Partners	Genesis Group	Mohr, Davidow Ventures	Polaris Venture Partners	Vista Venture Capital
Brentwood Venture Capital	Goldman Sachs	Morgan Stanley Dean Witter	Redpoint Ventures	Weiss, Peck & Greer V.P.
Capital Access Partners	Intel Corp.	Venture Partners	Robertson Stephens	Xerox Technology Ventures
Columbia Capital Corp.	J&W Seligman & Co.		St. Paul Venture Capital	
DLJ Capital			Sequoia Capital	

Sources: Firm Web sites.

The Venture Capital Industry

Venture capital is money provided by professionals who invest alongside management in young, rapidly growing companies that have the potential to develop into significant economic contributors. Venture capital is an important source of equity for start-up companies. Professionally managed venture capital firms generally are private partnerships or closely-held corporations funded by private and public pension funds, endowment funds, foundations, corporations, wealthy individuals, foreign investors, and the venture capitalists themselves.

Venture capitalists generally: Finance new and rapidly growing companies; purchase equity securities; assist in the development of new products or services; add value to the company through active participation; take higher risks with the expectation of higher rewards; have a long-term orientation. When considering an investment, venture capitalists carefully screen the technical and business merits of the proposed company. Venture capitalists only invest in a small percentage of the businesses they review and have a long-term perspective. Going forward, they actively work with the company's management by contributing their experience and business savvy gained from helping other companies with similar growth challenges.

Venture capitalists mitigate the risk of venture investing by developing a portfolio of young companies in a single venture fund. Many times they will co-invest with other professional venture capital firms. In addition, many venture partnerships will manage multiple funds simultaneously. For decades, venture capitalists have nurtured the growth of America's high technology and entrepreneurial communities resulting in significant job creation, economic growth, and international competitiveness. Companies such as Digital Equipment Corporation, Apple, Federal Express, Compaq, Sun Microsystems, Intel, Microsoft, and Genentech are famous examples of companies that received venture capital early in their development.

PRIVATE EQUITY INVESTING

Venture capital investing has grown from a small investment pool in the 1960s and early 1970s to a mainstream asset class that is a viable and significant part of the institutional and corporate investment portfolio. Recently, some investors have been referring to venture investing and buyout investing as "private equity investing." This term can be confusing because some in the investment industry use the term "private equity" to refer only to buyout fund investing. In any case, an institutional investor will allocate 2 percent to 3 percent of their institutional portfolio for investment in alternative assets such as private equity or venture capital as part of their overall asset allocation. Currently, over 50 percent of investments in venture capital/private equity comes from institutional public and private pension funds, with the balance coming from endowments, foundations, insurance companies, banks, individuals, and other entities who seek to diversify their portfolio with this investment class.

WHAT IS A VENTURE CAPITALIST?

The typical person-on-the-street depiction of a venture capitalist is that of a wealthy financier who wants to fund start-up companies. The perception is that a person who develops a brand new change-the-world invention needs capital; thus, if they can't get capital from a bank or from their own pockets, they enlist the help of a venture capitalist. In truth, venture capital and private equity firms are pools of capital, typically organized as a limited partnership, that invests in companies that represent the opportunity for a high rate of return within five to seven years. The venture capitalist may look at several hundred investment opportunities before investing in only a few selected companies with favorable investment opportunities. Far from being simply passive financiers, venture capitalists foster growth in companies through their involvement in the management, strategic marketing, and planning of their investee companies. They are entrepreneurs first and financiers second.

Even individuals may be venture capitalists. In the early days of venture capital investment, in the 1950s and 1960s, individual investors were the archetypal venture investor. While this type of individual investment did not totally disappear, the modern venture firm emerged as the dominant venture investment vehicle. However, in the last few years, individuals have again become a potent and increasingly larger part of the early stage start-up venture life cycle. These "angel investors" will mentor a company and provide needed capital and expertise to help develop companies. Angel investors may either be wealthy people with management expertise or retired business men and women who seek the opportunity for firsthand business development.

INVESTMENT FOCUS

Venture capitalists may be generalist or specialist investors depending on their investment strategy. Venture capitalists can be generalists, investing in various industry sectors, or various geographic locations, or various stages of a company's life. Alternatively, they may be specialists in one or two industry sectors, or may seek to invest in only a localized geographic area.

Not all venture capitalists invest in "start-ups." While venture firms will invest in companies that are in their initial start-up modes, venture capitalists will also invest in companies at various stages of the business life cycle. A venture capitalist may invest before there is a real product or company organized (so called "seed investing"), or may provide capital to start up a

company in its first or second stages of development known as "early stage investing." Also, the venture capitalist may provide needed financing to help a company grow beyond a critical mass to become more successful ("expansion stage financing").

The venture capitalist may invest in a company throughout the company's life cycle and therefore some funds focus on later stage investing by providing financing to help the company grow to a critical mass to attract public financing through a stock offering. Alternatively, the venture capitalist may help the company attract a merger or acquisition with another company by providing liquidity and exit for the company's founders.

At the other end of the spectrum, some venture funds specialize in the acquisition, turnaround, or recapitalization of public and private companies that represent favorable investment opportunities. There are venture funds that will be broadly diversified and will invest in companies in various industry sectors as diverse as semiconductors, software, retailing, and restaurants, and others that may be specialists in only one technology. While high technology investment makes up most of the venture investing in the U.S., and the venture industry gets a lot of attention for its high technology investments, venture capitalists also invest in companies such as construction, industrial products, business services, etc. There are several firms that have specialized in retail company investment and others that have a focus in investing only in "socially responsible" start-up endeavors.

Venture firms come in various sizes from small seed specialist firms of only a few million dollars under management to firms with over a billion dollars in invested capital around the world. The common denominator in all of these types of venture investing is that the venture capitalist is not a passive investor, but has an active and vested interest in guiding, leading, and growing the companies they have invested in. They seek to add value through their experience in investing in tens and hundreds of companies. Some venture firms are successful by

(continued)

creating synergies between the various companies they have invested in; for example, one company that has a great software product, but does not have adequate distribution technology may be paired with another company or its management in the venture portfolio that has better distribution technology.

LENGTH OF INVESTMENT

Venture capitalists will help companies grow, but they eventually seek to exit the investment in three to seven years. An early stage investment may take seven to ten years to mature, while a later stage investment may only take a few years, so the appetite for the investment life cycle must be congruent with the limited partnerships' appetite for liquidity. The venture investment is neither a short-term nor a liquid investment, but an investment that must be made with careful diligence and expertise.

TYPES OF FIRMS

There are several types of venture capital firms, but most mainstream firms invest their capital through funds organized as limited partnerships in which the venture capital firm serves as the general partner. The most common type of venture firm is an independent venture firm that has no affiliations with any other financial institution. These are called "private independent firms." Venture firms may also be affiliates or subsidiaries of a commercial bank, investment bank, or insurance company and make investments on behalf of outside investors or the parent firm's clients. Still other firms may be subsidiaries of nonfinancial, industrial corporations making investments on behalf of the parent itself.

These latter firms are typically called "direct investors" or "corporate venture investors." Other organizations may include government affiliated investment programs that help start up companies either through state, local, or federal programs. One common vehicle is the Small Business Investment Company or SBIC program administered by the Small Business Administration, in which a venture capital firm

may augment its own funds with federal funds and leverage its investment in qualified investee companies.

While the predominant form of organization is the limited partnership, in recent years the tax code has allowed the formation of either Limited Liability Partnerships ("LLPs") or Limited Liability Companies ("LLCs") as alternative forms of organization. However, the limited partnership is still the predominant organizational form. The advantages and disadvantages of each has to do with liability, taxation issues, and management responsibility. The venture capital firm will organize its partnership as a pooled fund; that is, a fund made up of the general partner and the investors or limited partners. These funds are typically organized as fixed-life partnerships, usually having a life of ten years. Each fund is capitalized by commitments of capital from the limited partners. Once the partnership has reached its target size, the partnership is closed to further investment from new investors or even existing investors so the fund has a fixed capital pool from which to make its investments. Like a mutual fund company, a venture capital firm may have more than one fund in existence. A venture firm may raise another fund a few years after closing the first fund in order to continue to invest in companies and to provide more opportunities for existing and new investors. It is not uncommon to see a successful firm raise six or seven funds consecutively over the span of ten to fifteen years. Each fund is managed separately and has its own investors or limited partners and its own general partner. These funds' investment strategy may be similar to other funds in the firm. However, the firm may have one fund with a specific focus and another with a different focus and yet another with a broadly diversified portfolio. This depends on the strategy and focus of the venture firm itself.

CORPORATE VENTURING

One form of investing that was popular in the 1980s and is again very popular is corporate venturing. This is usually called "direct investing" in portfolio companies by venture capital programs or subsidiaries of nonfinancial corporations. These investment vehicles seek to find qualified investment opportunities that are congruent with the parent company's strategic technology or that provide synergy or cost savings. These corporate venturing programs may be loosely organized programs affiliated with existing business development programs or may be self-contained entities with a strategic charter and mission to make investments congruent with the parent's strategic mission. There are some venture firms that specialize in advising, consulting, and managing a corporation's venturing program. The typical distinction between corporate venturing and other types of venture investment vehicles is that corporate venturing is usually performed with corporate strategic objectives in mind while other venture investment vehicles typically have investment return or financial objectives as their primary goal. This may be a generalization as corporate venture programs are not immune to financial considerations, but the distinction can be made. The other distinction of corporate venture programs is that they usually invest their parent's capital while other venture investment vehicles invest outside investors' capital.

COMMITMENTS AND FUND RAISING

The process that venture firms go through in seeking investment commitments from investors is typically called "fund raising." This should not be confused with the actual investment in investee or "portfolio" companies by the venture capital firms, which is also sometimes called "fund raising" in some circles. The commitments of capital are raised from the investors during the formation of the fund. A venture firm will set out prospecting for investors with a target fund size. It will distribute a prospectus to potential investors and may take from several weeks to several months to raise the requisite capital. The fund will seek commitments of capital from institutional investors, endowments, foundations, and indi-

viduals who seek to invest part of their portfolio in opportunities with a higher risk factor and commensurate opportunity for higher returns.

Because of the risk, length of investment, and illiquidity involved in venture investing, and because the minimum commitment requirements are so high, venture capital fund investing is generally out of reach for the average individual. The venture fund will have from a few to almost 100 limited partners depending on the target size of the fund. Once the firm has raised enough commitments, it will start making investments in portfolio companies.

CAPITAL CALLS

Making investments in portfolio companies requires the venture firm to start "calling" its limited partners' commitments. The firm will collect or "call" the needed investment capital from the limited partner in a series of tranches commonly known as "capital calls." These capital calls from the limited partners to the venture fund are sometimes called "takedowns" or "paid-in capital." Some years ago, the venture firm would "call" this capital down in three equal installments over a three year period. More recently, venture firms have synchronized their funding cycles and call their capital on an as-needed basis for investment.

ILLIQUIDITY

Limited partners make these investments in venture funds knowing that the investment will be long-term. It may take several years before the first investments start to return proceeds; in many cases the invested capital may be tied up in an investment for seven to ten years. Limited partners understand that this illiquidity must be factored into their investment decision.

OTHER TYPES OF FUNDS

Since venture firms are private firms, there is typically no way to exit before the partnership totally matures or expires. In recent years, a new form of venture firm has evolved: so-called

(continued)

"secondary" partnerships that specialize in purchasing the portfolios of investee company investments of an existing venture firm. This type of partnership provides some liquidity for the original investors. These secondary partnerships, expecting a large return, invest in what they consider to be undervalued companies.

ADVISORS AND FUND OF FUNDS

Evaluating which funds to invest in is akin to choosing a good stock manager or mutual fund, except the decision to invest is a long-term commitment. This investment decision takes considerable investment knowledge and time on the part of the limited partner investor. The larger institutions have investments in excess of 100 different venture capital and buyout funds and continually invest in new funds as they are formed. Some limited partner investors may have neither the resources nor the expertise to manage and invest in many funds and thus, may seek to delegate this decision to an investment advisor or so-called "gatekeeper." This advisor will pool the assets of its various clients and invest these proceeds as a limited partner into a venture or buyout fund currently raising capital. Alternatively, an investor may invest in a "fund of funds," which is a partnership organized to invest in other partnerships, thus providing the limited partner investor with added diversification and the ability to invest smaller amounts into a variety of funds.

DISBURSEMENTS

The investment by venture funds into investee portfolio companies is called "disbursements." A company will receive capital in one or more rounds of financing. A venture firm may make these disbursements by itself or in many cases will co-invest in a company with other venture firms ("co-investment" or "syndication"). This syndication provides more capital resources for the investee company. Firms co-invest because the company investment is congruent with the investment strategies of various venture firms and each firm will bring some competitive advantage to the investment. The venture firm will provide capital and management expertise and will usually also take a seat on the board of the company to ensure that the investment has the best chance of being successful. A portfolio company may receive one round, or in many cases, several rounds of venture financing in its life as needed. A venture firm may not invest all of its committed capital, but will reserve some capital for later investment in some of its successful companies with additional capital needs.

EXITS

Depending on the investment focus and strategy of the venture firm, it will seek to exit the investment in the portfolio company within three to five years of the initial investment. While the initial public offering may be the most glamourous and heralded type of exit for the venture capitalist and owners of the company, most successful exits of venture investments occur through a merger or acquisition of the company by either the original founders or another company. Again, the expertise of the venture firm in successfully exiting its investment will dictate the success of the exit for themselves and the owner of the company.

IPO

The initial public offering is the most glamourous and visible type of exit for a venture investment. In recent years technology IPOs have been in the limelight during the IPO boom of the last six years. At public offering, the venture firm is considered an insider and will receive stock in the company, but the firm is regulated and restricted in how that stock can be sold or liquidated for several years. Once this stock is freely tradable, usually after about two years, the venture fund will distribute this stock or cash to its limited partner investor who may then manage the public stock as a regular stock holding or may liquidate it upon receipt. Over the last twenty-five years, almost 3,000 companies financed by venture funds have gone public.

MERGERS AND ACQUISITIONS

Mergers and acquisitions represent the most common type of successful exit for venture investments. In the case of a merger or acquisition, the venture firm will receive stock or cash from the acquiring company and the venture investor will distribute the proceeds from the sale to its limited partners.

VALUATIONS

Like a mutual fund, each venture fund has a net asset value, or the value of an investor's holdings in that fund at any given time. However, unlike a mutual fund, this value is not determined through a public market transaction, but through a valuation of the underlying portfolio. Remember, the investment is illiquid and, at any point, the partnership may have both private companies and the stock of public companies in its portfolio. These public stocks are usually subject to restrictions for a holding period and are thus subject to a liquidity discount in the portfolio valuation.

Each company is valued at an agreed-upon value between the venture firms when invested in by the venture fund or funds. In subsequent quarters, the venture investor will usually keep this valuation intact until a material event occurs to change the value. Venture investors try to conservatively value their investments using guidelines or standard industry practices and by terms outlined in the prospectus of the fund. The venture investor is usually conservative in the valuation of companies, but it is common to find that early stage funds may have an even more conservative valuation of their companies due to the long lives of their investments when compared to other funds with shorter investment cycles.

MANAGEMENT FEES

As an investment manager, the general partner will typically charge a management fee to cover the costs of managing the committed capital. The management fee will usually be paid quarterly for the life of the fund or it may be tapered or curtailed in the later stages of a fund's life. This is most often negotiated with investors upon formation of the fund in the terms and conditions of the investment.

CARRIED INTEREST

"Carried interest" is the term used to denote the profit split of proceeds to the general partner. This is the general partners' fee for carrying the management responsibility plus all the liability and for providing the needed expertise to successfully manage the investment. There are as many variations of this profit split both in the size and how it is calculated and accrued as there are firms.

Source: National Venture Capital Association, *The Venture Capital Industry: An Overview*, 2001. Reprinted by permission.

The VC's first task is to select only ventures that show true potential for success. This requires an extraordinary knowledge of the industry in which a venture intends to do business, and a vision of the industry's future. This is why most VCs specialize either in only one industry or in clusters of firms that have some commonality (e.g., advancing technologies).[2] The VC manager must be able to discern that the venture has an idea that at least has the potential to blossom into a major firm in the industry.

Next, the firm must judge the venture's entrepreneurs. Among the questions that the VC manager must address are the following. Do the entrepreneurs exhibit

[2]Some long-standing VCs have shifted their focus over the years, pursuing "hot" sectors of the economy. They do this by establishing new funds over time.

in-depth knowledge, talent, and perseverance? Have they submitted an organized and feasible business plan? Have they committed substantial personal funds to the venture so that they are strongly motivated to succeed? Has management developed compensation contracts for themselves that are heavily laden with incentive pay? Are they prepared to accept advice from the VC on the venture's development? Will they be fair in negotiations?

Regarding the final question, a VC manager must attempt to negotiate terms, at every stage of financing, that are favorable to the VC. This does not mean that the manager can arbitrarily dictate unfair terms. Indeed, if the VC manager does not treat the entrepreneurs fairly, the entrepreneurs will have (a) less incentive to make the venture successful, and (b) greater incentive to take actions that expropriate wealth from the VC. In addition, if the VC becomes *stingy* with capital, the probability of the venture's success will be compromised.

A VC generally accepts common equity shares in exchange for contributed capital. In some cases, the VC may prefer convertible preferred stock. By holding convertible preferred stock, the VC has a priority claim on assets if the venture fails, while the conversion option allows the VC to participate as a shareholder if the venture succeeds.

Finally, VCs must have a critical eye, knowing when to cut losses and fold a failing venture rather than throwing good money after bad.

The Entrepreneur's Viewpoint

Entrepreneurs experience three major problems in negotiating with a VC at various stages. The *first*—and perhaps most difficult—problem is the severe trade-off that the entrepreneur generally faces between obtaining adequate financing for the next stage, on the one hand, and accepting substantial ownership dilution on the other.

A *second* problem has already been noted: A VC may want protection built into the securities they purchase. For instance, a VC may demand convertible preferred stock, which includes a clause that gives the VC a priority claim over the entrepreneurs' equity claims in the event of failure and liquidation.

The *third* problem is that entrepreneurs are often frustrated by (a) the discipline that a VC imposes on them, (b) the VC's periodic demands for information as part of their monitoring effort, and (c) the influence that the VC wishes to have on the development of the venture. These factors engender fear in many entrepreneurs that they are losing control of the venture.

Bradford and Smith (1997) provided the following points of advice for entrepreneurs as they approach VCs:

1. Estimate . . . the break-even return to the private capital investor . . . based on the liquidity-adjusted return of a portfolio of small cap stocks. Any offer of capital below this rate should be worth considering . . .
2. Encourage an auction-like competition among investors for the opportunity of investing in your firm. Take the best deal based on all important considerations, but negotiate with the aim of bringing the investor's overall expected return to as low a level as possible . . .
3. Review alternative financing methods and value enhancements to be sure the private capital investment is the best one possible, after taking the dilution of the entrepreneur's stake into account. (p. 95)

11.4.5 An Illustration of Negotiations Between Entrepreneurs and a VC

We noted in the previous subsection that negotiations between entrepreneurs and a VC can be a delicate matter. On one side of the table, the VC is concerned about getting a fair return for the risk that it is bearing in financing the venture. On the other side, the entrepreneurs are concerned about ownership dilution. Here we provide a hypothetical illustration of the negotiation problem, and how a resolution might be reached. (Note: this illustration does not represent the application of any widely used formula.)

A Numerical Example of Negotiation

Suppose a team of entrepreneurs approaches a VC for common equity financing required for the next stage of a venture's development. Two alternative levels of financing are being considered for this stage: $5 million or $10 million. Both parties recognize that the postfinancing value of the venture depends not only on the amount of capital that the VC provides, but also on the percentage of the equity that the VC retains in exchange for funds provided. Regarding the latter, we assume that, for any given level of funding, the value of the firm is a decreasing function of the VC's ownership percentage. This assumption reflects the adverse effect of dilution on the entrepreneurs' incentives.

Figure 11-3 shows firm values as a function of the VC's ownership percentage for each of the two funding levels. At the $5 million funding level, firm value starts at $8

FIGURE 11-3 Hypothetical Values of a Venture Financed by a VC

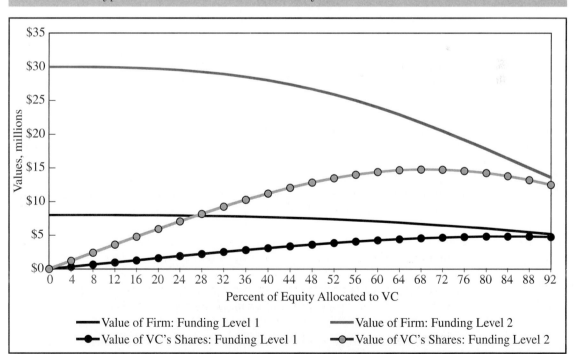

Two Levels of Funding Are Considered: Level 1, $5 million and Level 2, $10 million. Negotiation Involves Funding Level and Percent of Equity Allocated to VC.

million with VC ownership percentage at zero, and decreases to $5.15 million with VC ownership percentage at 92 percent. At the $10 million funding level, firm value starts at $30 million if the VC's ownership percentage is zero, and decreases to $13.58 million with a VC ownership percentage of 92 percent.

The figure also shows the value of the VC's shares as a function of its ownership percentage for both funding levels. At the $5 million funding level, the value of the VC's interest begins at $0 if its ownership percentage is zero, and rises along a concave curve to $4.75 million when its ownership percentage is 92 percent. At this funding level, the value of the VC's ownership interest never rises above $5 million, which is the amount of VC funding that is proposed. Therefore, the VC would reject funding at this level.

With funding at the $10 million level, the value of the VC's shares is above its cost (i.e., $10 million) for all VC-ownership percentages at or above 36 percent. The higher level of funding creates profitable alternatives for the VC, so it is viable.

But one crucial issue remains: What should be the VC's ownership percentage? This is the crux of the negotiations between the entrepreneurs and the VC. We now extend the numerical example to address this issue.

Assuming that the firm will be financed at the $10 million level, the two negotiating parties must determine the percentage of the firm's equity that will be allocated to the VC. Figure 11-4 facilitates our discussion of this issue. The figure shows the values of the interests of both the entrepreneur and the VC as a function of the VC's ownership percentage.

FIGURE 11-4   Negotiations Between an Entrepreneur and a VC

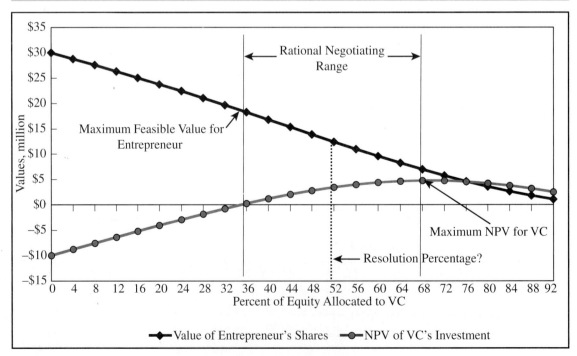

For Hypothetical Situation in Figure 11-3 (Funding Level 2): Value of Entrepreneur's Shares and NPV of VC's Investment as a Function of Percent of Equity Allocated to VC

In the figure, the value of the entrepreneurs' shares decreases monotonically with the VC's ownership percentage, both because the entrepreneur's ownership percentage decreases commensurately and because the value of the *firm* decreases as the VC's ownership percentage increases (due to the adverse dilution effect). As a result, the value of the VC's ownership interest, expressed in terms of net present value (NPV), initially increases with its ownership percentage, peaks at 68 percent, and then declines. This peak occurs because the positive effect of increasing ownership percentage is eventually offset by the ever-decreasing value of the firm.

The scenario reveals that a rational negotiating range for the VC's ownership percentage lies between 36 percent and 68 percent. The lower bound is 36 percent, because below this percentage the VC fails to receive value that is at least commensurate with its contribution of $10 million. The upper bound is 68 percent, because beyond this percentage the values of the interests of both the entrepreneurs and the VC fall with further increases in the VC's ownership percentage. Thus, the two parties would rationally choose a value for the VC's ownership percentage that is between these bounds. The figure shows a tentative resolution to the negotiation in which the VC's ownership percentage is midway between these bounds, or 52 percent.

11.5 THE ROLES OF STAGING AND VC MONITORING IN RESOLVING PRINCIPAL–AGENT CONFLICTS

In this section, we expand our discussion of principal–agent conflicts in venture financing. Several recent papers in the finance literature provide useful insights into both the problem and its resolution.

11.5.1 Principal–Agent Conflicts as a Rationale for Staging

As we noted earlier, principal–agent conflicts often loom large in venture financing. The venture's investors are the principals and the entrepreneurs are agents. If entrepreneurs are allowed to have complete control of the development of their ventures, they may make decisions that are in their personal interest rather than in the interest of outside investors.

Examples of entrepreneurs' self-serving decisions include the following. *First*, the entrepreneur may decide to invest in an unprofitable venture because (a) he or she has an intrinsic passion for the project, or (b) the project will provide personal gratification in the form of recognition from the general public, the scientific community, or others.

Second, outside investors are likely to be wealthy and have diversified portfolios, while the entrepreneur is likely to have a large fraction of his or her limited personal wealth tied up in the venture. Thus, the entrepreneur may not be willing to pursue a rational development of the project if and when it involves a great deal of risk. He or she may tend to pursue the low-risk, low-value path rather than the high-risk, high-value path to development.

Third, the entrepreneur may have strong personal incentives to continue the project even though it is a losing proposition. The entrepreneur may have an irrational psychological fixation to make the project successful, or is simply happy to continue to be paid to develop the venture even though its prospects have diminished. Outside investors obviously prefer to terminate a losing venture rather than to throw good money after bad.

Gompers (1995) provided a theoretical model of the entrepreneur's financial contracting problem from the perspective of principal–agent conflicts. In his model, the main mechanism for mitigating agency costs is the presence of an inside investor who periodically monitors the entrepreneur. However, monitoring is costly. It takes time and resources on both the investor's and the entrepreneur's side to prepare and review the pertinent information. Thus, an optimal balance must be struck between the costs of monitoring, which increase with the frequency and intensity of monitoring, and agency costs, which decrease with the frequency and intensity of monitoring.

Gompers suggested that the end of each stage of development is a *monitoring opportunity*. Optimal monitoring frequency, or equivalently the number of stages in a venture's development, depends on several factors, all of which are related to potential agency costs. Expected agency costs increase as (a) the venture's assets become less tangible, (b) growth options increase, and (c) asset specificity rises. Asset specificity refers to the extent to which the firm's developed real assets are valuable only if the venture succeeds. Asset specificity is a problem because it affects the liquidation value of the venture in the event of its termination.

VCs typically review a venture's management on a monthly basis. The main purpose of such reviews is to determine whether management's decisions are in line with the business plan and investors' interests. They also present an opportunity for the VC to offer strategic advice.

Management must provide a more detailed due-diligence report at the end of each stage of development. Additional financing is tied to the outcome of the report. To make staging effective, the amount of financing provided at the beginning of each stage is just enough to allow the firm to reach the next stage of development. The amount provided depends on the rate at which the venture consumes cash, known as the *burn rate*. Extending the analogy, the date on which the firm's cash resources are exhausted is the *fume date*.

By planning the fume date to coincide with a developmental milestone, the VC can ensure that the next due-diligence report will be generated at the appropriate time. Moreover, by sizing the allocation of capital carefully, the VC can force the entrepreneur to use cash carefully.

11.5.2 The Optimality of Having Both Inside and Outside Investors

Next, we discuss a theoretical paper by Admati and Pfleiderer (1994) that focuses on (a) the role of VCs and (b) the staging of a venture's development in resolving both information asymmetry and principal–agent problems in venture financing. They provide some fundamental and realistic insights into the overall process of financing the development of a venture. In particular, they explain the important role of a VC as both an *insider* and a capital contributor. As an insider, the VC is not only privy to the private information that the entrepreneur possesses about the value of the venture at each stage of development, but also works closely with the firm's management and frequently monitors management's decisions.

Contributions Only from an Outsider: The Overinvestment Problem

To set the stage for their arguments, Admati and Pfleiderer explain a problem that arises when an entrepreneur attempts to contract for funding only with an *outsider*—

that is, an investor who is not privy to the entrepreneur's inside information about the value of the venture. The problem is that the outsider provides funding for the next stage of development, but it is the entrepreneur who makes the continuation or termination decision. In this situation, the entrepreneur has a clear incentive to continue the venture even if it is optimal to terminate it.

This incentive is likely to be strong for three reasons. *First*, the operating budget undoubtedly provides for a salary for the entrepreneur, which would be lost if the venture is terminated. *Second*, by extending the venture's life, the entrepreneur obtains, at no cost, a valuable option on the future value of the firm. Although this option may be currently out of the money, it nevertheless has a positive value if the venture continues, whereas it would be rendered worthless if the venture is terminated. *Third*, the venture is, after all, the entrepreneur's *baby*. That is, the entrepreneur may have a deep psychological attachment to the venture that clouds his or her rational business judgment. For these reasons, a financial contract with an outsider is likely to lead to costly *overinvestment*.

Contributions Only from an Insider: The Underinvestment Problem

Admati and Pfleiderer then consider a second arrangement in which the entrepreneur contracts with an *inside* VC, who provides all funding. In exchange, the VC receives a fractional claim on the venture's future payoffs (i.e., a percentage of the firm's equity shares). However, this arrangement will lead to the classic underinvestment problem of Myers (1977): The VC provides all financing, but receives only a fraction of the future payoffs, so a rational VC will be inclined to underinvest.

Resolution: Have Both an Insider and an Outsider!

The authors then consider a third arrangement, which is typical in practice. In this case, funding at each stage is obtained from both an insider (such as a VC) and an outsider, each receiving a fractional claim to the venture's future payoffs, while the entrepreneurs retain the remaining fraction. By having both inside and outside investors, the overinvestment and underinvestment problems are balanced out, and thus a rational continuation or termination decision would be made at each stage of development.

Bradford and Smith (1997) provide some evidence consistent with Admati and Pfleiderer's arguments. They collected data, from S-1 registration statements, on the number of private capital investors that were associated with each of 41 computer-related firms that went public in 1995. All but seven had more than one private capital investor.

Figure 11-5 depicts a hypothetical contracting arrangement among an entrepreneur, an inside investor (a VC), and an outside investor. Both the inside VC and the outside investor contribute the necessary capital at early stages, expansion stages, and late stages of development. (In this example the VC contributes twice as much as the outsider.) Throughout, each party maintains a fixed fractional claim on future payoffs: in the example, 45 percent for the entrepreneurs, 40 percent for the VC, and 15 percent for the outside investor. Even though the VC contributes only twice as much capital as the outsider at each stage, the VC's percentage claim is more than twice the outsider's claim. This is a likely scenario in part because the VC's critical role as an insider provides it with some bargaining power.

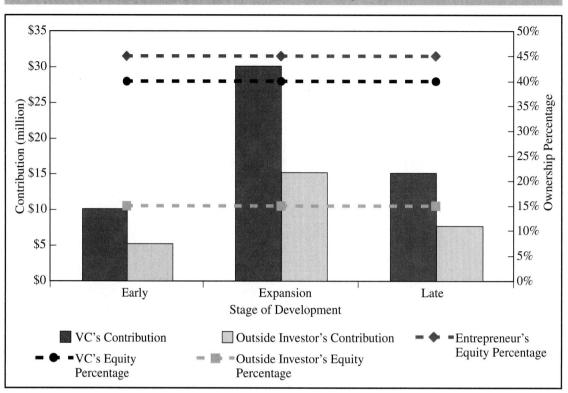

Inside VC and Outside VC Investor Contribute on a 2:1 Ratio; Percent of Equity Owned by Entrepreneur, Inside VC, and Outside Investor are 45, 40, and 15 Percent, Respectively.

11.5.3 Additional Empirical Evidence on VC Stage Preferences

As Table 11-2 illustrated, VCs differ in terms of when they prefer to step in to assist a venture. Some VCs prefer to intervene at the early stages, perhaps even at the seed or start-up stage. By doing so, they can exert more influence over the venture's development. Other VCs prefer to invest in ventures that are at the early development or expansion stages. The reasoning here is that the number of ventures that a VC's management can devote attention to is limited, so they need to focus on ventures that have already proven some promise of success.

Figure 11-6 shows the annual aggregate allocations of VC disbursements by stage from 1980 to 2000. The lion's share of aggregate disbursements goes to ventures that are at the expansion stage of development. Moreover, the trend appears to be away from early stage ventures. In 1980, nearly half (48 percent) of all disbursements went to seed, start-up, and other early stage ventures. By 2000, the aggregate allocation to such ventures was only 23 percent.

FIGURE 11-6 Allocations of VC Disbursements by Stage of Development

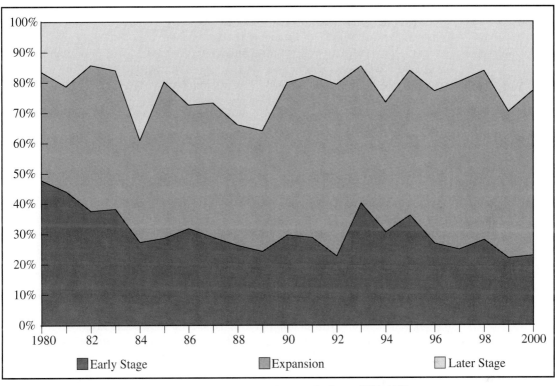

Cumulative Percentages of Aggregate Disbursements to Ventures by Stage, 1980–2000
Source: Raw data from Venture Economics/National Venture Capital Association.

11.6 Summary of Learning Objectives

In this chapter, we provided a detailed discussion of how a venture develops. Development generally occurs in eight stages. In the first stage, called the seed stage, entrepreneurs undertake initial efforts to develop a vision for the eventual firm. Typical financing sources include personal funds *(bootstrapping)* and capital provided by *angels*. In later stages, financing alternatives expand to include capital provided by VCs, banks, or finance companies. The later stages are start-up (stage 2), early development (stage 3), expansion (stage 4), profitable but cash poor (stage 5), rapid growth toward liquidity (stage 6), bridge or mezzanine financing (stage 7), and harvest (stage 8).

We also discussed the important roles of VCs as providers of capital and strategic guidance. The VC industry in the United States has grown tremendously over the past two decades. We provided some analysis of the negotiations among entrepreneurs, VCs as inside equity investors, and outside equity investors. These negotiations largely center on the parties' contributions to the enterprise and determining a commensurate allocation of the venture's shares.

Review Questions and Problems

1. List the eight stages of venture development and financing, and for each stage
   a. discuss the firm's development.
   b. list the typical sources of financing that are available to the firm.
2. Discuss the two forms of early stage financing of a venture: (a) *bootstrapping* and (b) *angel financing*.
3. Discuss some of the problems that entrepreneurs have in negotiating with a VC.
4. Discuss some of the problems that VCs have in negotiating with entrepreneurs.
5. Discuss the historical development of VCs. What factors explain the recent surge in VCs as venture financiers?
6. How does a VC's financing and investments differ from those of other financial institutions?
7. The management of BioFuture, Inc., an up-and-coming venture in the biotech industry, is negotiating with VC Funding, a venture capital partnership, for funding of $55 million, which will be used for expansion. VC Funding is impressed with the venture, and is considering the investment, for which the partnership will receive equity shares. However, VC Funding is concerned that if they demand an equity ownership percentage that is too high, BioFuture's management may be less inclined to work hard to ensure the venture's success. They determine that if they demand a 40 percent equity percentage, the firm will be worth $160 million, but if they demand a 60 percent ownership percentage, the firm's value will be only $90 million. Which equity ownership percentage should they demand?
8. What mechanisms are brought to bear to mitigate principal–agent conflicts and information asymmetry problems in the private equity market? How effective are these mechanisms?
9. Discuss (a) the overinvestment and underinvestment problems as they apply to a venture's development, and (b) how having financing from both an inside investor (e.g., a VC) and a passive outside investor can resolve both problems.
10. Discuss the rationale for *staging* the development of a venture.

Creative Thinking Issues

1. To what extent, if any, do VCs *compete* with banks, finance companies, or other investors to provide capital to ventures?
2. The SEC governs the public equity markets in the United States, but not the private equity market. What are the implications of this circumstance for the efficiency of the private equity market relative to the public equity markets?

Projects and Analyses

1. Develop a manual for entrepreneurs to use in developing a venture. Include details on sources of capital, strategic decisions at various stages, and other matters.
2. Develop a set of criteria for a VC to use to determine whether to support a venture.
3. Develop the terms of a standard contract that a VC would present to a venture's entrepreneurs.
4. Create a model that determines the optimal ownership percentage that a VC should demand in financing a venture.

CHAPTER

Initial Public Offerings of Stock

12

12.1 INTRODUCTION

In Chapter 11, we discussed the stagewise development of a venture. In the eighth and final stage, the *harvest* stage, the firm's entrepreneurs and fellow owners decide whether to be acquired, to agree to a managerial buyout, to remain private, or to go public. This chapter focuses on the latter two alternatives. In Section 12.2, we briefly discuss the issue of remaining private versus going public, and briefly examine some of the largest private firms in the United States.

The rest of the chapter focuses on the process and consequences of going public via an initial public offering (IPO) of stock. In Section 12.3, we discuss the details of the IPO process. In Section 12.4, we examine the characteristics of firms that have gone public in the United States in recent years, and their offerings. In Section 12.5, we discuss post-IPO stock-price performance. In Section 12.6, we discuss a special type of IPO, the *unit IPO*, in which the issuing firm offers a unit consisting of both stock and warrants. Finally, Section 12.7 summarizes the chapter's learning objectives, as usual.

12.2 STAYING PRIVATE VERSUS GOING PUBLIC

In this section, we briefly discuss the benefits and costs of going public versus remaining a private firm.

12.2.1 Benefits of Going Public

In Chapter 3, we discussed several advantages for a firm of having a public market for its equity within the context of our discussion of the separation of ownership and control (review Figure 3-1). Of course, these advantages apply to a firm considering going public in an established securities market. The firm's entrepreneurs can reap the benefits of risk reduction in their personal portfolios by selling at least a portion of their ownership interest to the public and using the proceeds to invest in other securities. Other investors in the firm's heretofore-private equity also benefit in this respect. This is a particularly attractive opportunity if the securities market is replete with alternative, liquid securities. Moreover, en masse diversification among public investors results in a lower cost of capital for the focal firm, thereby increasing the profitability of future capital investment projects.

An additional motive for going public is to reduce debt. Later, we provide evidence that firms that go public generally use a substantial portion of the IPO proceeds to pay off debt obligations. By reducing leverage, the firm's original owners reduce the risk of their private portfolios even if they do not sell their shares in the IPO. Also, by issuing new shares in the IPO, the firm's entrepreneurs and management can dilute the voting power, and thus the influence, of other pre-IPO shareholders.

After the firm's shares are *seasoned* in the listing market, two more advantages of public equity emerge. *First*, the firm can establish stock and stock option plans for its executives and other employees. *Second*, the firm can more readily issue shares (rather than pay cash) to finance an acquisition.

12.2.2   Costs of Going Public

A firm's management and investors must weigh the benefits of going public against several costs, including the following:

1. *Underpricing:* IPOs appear to be substantially *underpriced*, as we show later.
2. *Issuance Costs:* The typical *underwriter spread* for an IPO is 7 percent of the offering proceeds. Other costs include management's time in preparing for the offering.
3. *Loss of control:* New equityholders may press the firm to change its investment, financing, or dividend policies, and may also attempt to replace the firm's management team, including the original entrepreneurs.
4. *Agency Costs of Managerial Discretion:* Separating ownership and control leads to such costs, though they can be mitigated with monitoring and incentive contracting.
5. *Information Asymmetry:* Disclosure requirements may compromise the firm's strategic position in the industry.
6. *Performance Pressures:* Management will face pressure for performance from investors, the financial press, equity research analysts, and bond rating agencies.
7. *Distractions:* Management is often distracted by time-consuming investor-relations tasks, such as press releases and personal visits from or to major shareholders.

12.2.3   At What Stage Should a Firm Go Public?

Chemmanur and Fulghieri (1999) developed a theoretical model of the going public decision. They asked the question, At what stage in its life should a private firm, heretofore financed privately by a venture capital firm (VC), go public? Their model focuses on a trade-off between two costs: (a) The VC can generate information more efficiently (i.e., at a lower cost) than public investors, but (b) the VC commands a higher risk premium on invested capital than would better-diversified (and competitive) public investors. In the early stages of development, the first cost factor dominates and the firm optimally stays private. However, as the firm moves through the stages of development, the overall cost of information production falls. Eventually, the second cost factor dominates, and it is optimal for the firm to go public.

Myers (2000) approaches the issue from a property-rights viewpoint. Suppose the value of the intangible assets that the entrepreneur contributes (i.e., the "idea" behind the venture) must be proved through preliminary expenditures on research and development (R&D), which are funded by a limited number of private outsiders.

Once their value is proved, however, the private outsiders could easily expropriate these assets. "This creates an incentive problem: why should insiders work to establish the assets' value if they have no control over these assets ex post? The problem can be solved by starting up a private, closely held business, and later taking it public to disperse ownership so that ex post exercise of control is costly. Going public reduces outsider investors' bargaining power to preserve incentives for insiders" (p. 1006).

Myers provides the following illustration of his argument:

> Pop quiz: Why have hundreds of biotech companies gone public at early stages of their research programs, while most commercial real estate is still privately held? (Despite the recent popularity of REITs [Real Estate Investment Trusts], only a small fraction of commercial real estate is securitized.) Answer: Success in biotech research means an FDA-approved drug. The value of such a drug no longer depends on the people who created it and can be captured by outside investors. Biotech companies go public to reduce the power of outside equity and preserve incentives for insiders. Developed commercial real estate does not need to be publicly held because value does not depend as much on effort or intangible assets provided by insiders. (p. 1034)

12.2.4   The VC's Desire to Go Public

A VC that has partially financed a successful venture plays several important roles in the IPO process. The VC has not only a substantial financial stake in the firm, but has participated in its development. As such, the VC is in a position to serve a critical *certification* role in mitigating information asymmetry problems as the firm faces the IPO market, even though the firm will also have an underwriter (see Megginson and Weiss 1991). The VC generally participates in negotiations about the offer price and the firm's post-IPO financial and ownership structures.

A VC also has both the incentive and the expertise to optimally time the IPO. Lerner (1994) examined the ability of VCs to time IPOs. He finds evidence consistent with this ability: "Using a sample of 350 privately held venture-backed biotechnology firms between 1978 and 1992, I show that these companies go public when equity valuations are high and employ private financings when values are lower. Seasoned venture capitalists appear to be particularly proficient at taking companies public near market peaks" (p. 293).

At the same time, however, VCs are generally anxious to liquidate their investment. Some analysts have argued that VCs are too aggressive in bringing their firms public quickly, perhaps even *prematurely*. Gompers (1996) argued that smaller, younger VCs often bring their firms public earlier in order to establish a reputation and therefore attract additional capital in the future. He refers to such self-serving behavior on the part of a VC as *grandstanding*. Bradford and Smith (1997) make a different argument: "Some private equity investors—particularly 'short-term' players less concerned about building and preserving a reputation—may be tempted to push owner-managers to go public as soon as IPO markets allow them, even if the companies are not ready for public ownership" (p. 97).

Later we present comparative empirical evidence on the pricing and performance of VC-backed and non–VC-backed IPOs. We examine this evidence to determine whether observed differences suggest that VCs (a) provide valuable negotiating services, or (b) engage in grandstanding.

12.2.5   Staying Private

Many firms prefer to stay private. An example is Delaware North, Inc., a large and profitable firm that specializes in a variety of consumer products and services. It is owned and controlled by the Jacobs family of western New York. Though reasons vary, the manager-owners of firms who choose to stay private have no doubt weighed (and reweighed) the costs and benefits of going public and found that, on balance, the costs outweigh the benefits.

Table 12-1 shows the top 50 firms in *Forbes* 2001 list of the 500 largest privately held firms in the U.S., ranked by 2000 revenue. These are an unusual collection of firms compared to publicly traded firms. They include (a) four of the *Big 5* accounting firms, (b) five supermarket/grocery chains, (c) 10 other firms in the food production or distribution business, (d) three firms related to auto and truck sales, and (e) other firms in disparate industries.

12.3   DETAILS OF THE IPO PROCESS

The typical IPO firm is very young and has often taken a highly speculative position in a nascent industry. IPOs are among the riskiest equity investments in the stock market. The firm generally has only a short earnings history and no history of public valuation. Thus, both principal–agent and information asymmetry problems are likely to be very severe for IPO firms. The challenge put to IPO underwriters is to mitigate costs associated with these problems, though they charge the firm accordingly.

In this section, we discuss the process by which a firm *goes public* with its equity. Though the actual offering of shares to the public generally (though not always) occurs on a single day, the overall process of going public extends for many weeks and entails a variety of costs, both direct and indirect.

12.3.1   Employing an Underwriter

Firms that choose to go public generally hire an investment-banking firm to *underwrite* the offering.[1] The underwriter assists the firm in all legal procedures, and negotiates with potential public investors regarding the offer price. The underwriters mitigate principal–agent problems by structuring the deal (e.g., by imposing temporary *share lockups*, discussed later) and recommending certain financial structures within the firm (e.g., incentive pay for executives, post-IPO ownership structure, and leverage). Also, in its intermediary role an investment bank can be effective in mitigating information asymmetry problems associated with an IPO because (a) it becomes well informed about the operations and prospects of the issuer, and (b) has expertise in, and a reputation for, determining a fair price for the issue.

---

[1]Recently, a few firms have experimented with offering their shares directly to the public, generally via the Internet. To do so, they have revived a small issuer exemption called Regulation A under the Securities Act of 1933. Under Regulation A, a firm can raise up to $5 million in a 12-month period. Two examples of firms that engaged a *direct public offering* via the Internet are Annie's Homegrown, Inc. (natural foods) and Logos Research Systems, Inc. (biblical software).

The underwriter provides most or all of the following services.

1. Providing procedural and financial advice (e.g., suggesting the number of primary and secondary shares to offer).
2. Assisting in the completion and filing of the preliminary prospectus (red herring) and registration statement with the Securities and Exchange Commission (SEC); (form S-1, SB-1, or SB-2) and the state of incorporation.
3. Assisting the firm in responding to questions posed by the SEC, state regulators, and the National Association of Securities Dealers (NASD).
4. Securing a *transfer agent*.
5. Timing the offering to occur under favorable market conditions (to the extent possible).
6. Establishing a fair price for the shares.
7. Either purchasing the entire issue (for resale to the public) or brokering the sale of shares.
8. Providing *aftermarket price support* in early secondary market trading.

In choosing its underwriter, an IPO firm should consider many factors, including the following.

1. *Size*: Underwriters differ in terms of the minimum size of the firm or the offering that they will consider.
2. *Reputation:* Institutional investors, who will likely dominate the purchase of an offering, are sensitive to the manner in which an underwriter has dealt with them in the past.
3. *Specialization:* Underwriters often specialize in particular industries (e.g., biotechnology). A specialized underwriter will be better aware of investors who are interested in the firm's stock, and may have analysts who follow firms in the focal industry.
4. *Aftermarket Support:* Underwriters may vary in terms of their willingness to provide aftermarket support for the firm's stock. This involves both serving as a market maker and bringing the stock to the attention of the market.
5. *Ongoing Commitment:* The underwriter should be willing and able to provide financial advice and service to the firm on an ongoing basis after the offering. This includes underwriting larger issues of equity or debt as the firm grows.
6. *Costs:* Underwriters charge a fee for their services. In the case of an IPO, the standard fee is 7 percent of the offering proceeds. They also generally demand an *overallotment* (or *greenshoe*) option to sell additional shares later. The underwriter may also demand valuable warrants that allow them to purchase shares.

TABLE 12-1 The 50 Largest Private Companies in the United States in 2001

Company	Business	Revenue Rank	Revenue ($ million)	Employees
Cargill	Agriculture and Industrial Commodities	1	49,408	90,000
Koch Industries	Oil, Chemical, Mining, Energy, etc.	2	40,700*	11,500
PricewaterhouseCoopers	Accounting, Auditing, Consulting	3	23,100[2]	160,000
Mars	Candy, Ice cream, Meals, etc.	4	15,500*	30,000
Publix Super Markets	Supermarkets	5	14,575	126,000
Bechtel Group	Engineering, Project Development, Construction	6	14,300	40,000
Deloitte Touche Tohmatsu	Accounting, Auditing, Consulting	7	12,200*	92,000
KPMG International	Accounting, Auditing, Tax Services	8	11,800*	92,800
Fidelity Investments	Mutual Funds, Discount Brokerage, Pension Management	9	11,096	33,186
Ernst & Young	Accounting, Auditing, Tax and Financial Services	10	10,000[2]	80,000
Meijer	General Merchandise, Grocery Stores	11	10,000*	80,000
Andersen	Assurance, Consumer, Accounting, Legal	12	9,340	85,000
HE Butt Grocery	Pantry Food Stores, Food Processing, Photo	13	8,965[2]	60,000
C&S Wholesale Grocers	Wholesale Food	14	8,500	7,000
Huntsman	Chemical, Polymer Manufacturing	15	8,500[1]	15,000
Aramark	Food and Support, Unif; Child Care, Education	16	7,745*	185,000
Premcor	Refine and Market Petro Prods	17	7,312	2,100
JM Family Enterprises	Independent Distributor Toyotas; Insurance and Financial Services	18	7,100	3,400
Marmon Group	Diverse Manufacturing & Service Companies	19	6,786	40,000
Alliant Exchange	Distributor Food to Restaur, Hotels, etc.	20	6,600	12,000
Seagate Technology	Manufacturing Disk Drives, Storage Sol's	21	6,387[1]	48,720
Enterprise Rent-A-Car	Auto Rental, Fleet Services, Car Sales	22	6,300	50,000
Science Applications Int'l	Tech R&D, Systems Integration, Telecomm	23	5,896	41,500
Graybar Electric	Wholesale and Distributor Electrical and Commercial Equipment	24	5,214	10,500
Menard	Home Improvement Centers	25	4,850*	7,600
Levi Strauss & Co	Casual Apparel	26	4,645	17,300

394

Rank	Company	Business		
27	SC Johnson & Son	Household, Personal Care Products, etc.	4,500²	9,500
28	Peter Kiewit Sons'	Heavy Construction, Mining	4,463	11,146
29	Giant Eagle	Supermarkets; Food Whol	4,435	25,600
30	Advance Publications	Newspapers, Mag	4,400*	23,250
31	Hallmark Cards	Greeting Cards; TV; Art Materials	4,233*	24,500
32	ContiGroup Cos	Food Processing	4,000*	14,500
33	InterTech Group	Manufacturing Polymers and Composites	4,000*	18,500
34	Cox Enterprises	Newspapers, TV, etc.	3,925*	52,700
35	Hy-Vee	Supermarkets, Drugstores	3,900²	46,000
36	Milliken & Co	Textiles, Chemical Products	3,900*	20,000
37	Reyes Holding	Distributors Food, Supplies, Beer	3,900	2,800
38	MBM	Distributors Food and Related to Restaurants	3,823	2,500
39	Guardian Industries	Flat Glass; Fiberglass; Auto Glass & Trim	3,800*	17,500
40	Synnex Information Tech.	Manufacturing Electronics Equip; IT distributor	3,700	1,270
41	Alticor	Personal & Household Products (Amway, Quixtar)	3,525*	10,500
42	Southern Wine & Spirits	Distributor Wine, Spirits & Nonalcoholic Beverages	3,500	5,600
43	Hearst	Publish, Broadcasting, Entertainment	3,413*	16,000
44	Eby-Brown	Distributor Candy, Tobacco, etc. to Conv Stores	3,400	2,253
45	McKinsey & Co	International Management Consulting	3,400	13,000
46	Flying J	Truck and Trav Plaza Stops; oil refiners/products/exploration	3,330	10,000
47	Capital Group of Cos	Manages Mutual Funds; Financial Services	3,300*	5,000
48	Gulf States Toyota	Independent Distributor of Toyotas	3,200*	1,650
49	Schneider National	Truckload Carrier	3,089	17,100
50	Core-Mark Int'l	Distributor Tobacco Products, Candy, Food, etc.	3,035	2,582

*Forbes estimates.

[1]Pro forma.

[2]Company provided estimate.

Source: "500 Largest Private Companies," Forbes, November 26, 2001. Selections reproduced by permission.

12.3.2 Costs of Going Public

The IPO firm incurs three categories of costs in the process of going public: (a) compensation paid to the underwriter, (b) additional expenses, and (c) management's efforts to market the offering.

Compensating the Underwriter

For their services, the underwriter charges a fee, called the *underwriter spread*, generally expressed as a percentage of the proceeds of the offering. (We discussed underwriter spreads in the public issuance of corporate bonds in Chapter 10.) As we show later, the typical underwriter spread for an IPO is 7 percent of the offering proceeds. In addition, the underwriter may receive *warrants* to purchase additional shares of the firm's stock. Although warrants are included in only a small proportion of IPO deals, they can add significantly to the issuer's overall cost. Barry, Muscarella, and Vetsuypens (1991) estimate that the typical value of issued warrants is between 45 percent and 80 percent of the underwriter spread.

Other Expenses

The firm also incurs expenses for legal services, printing, and auditing. Ritter (1987) found that these expenses are substantial, ranging from 2 percent to 10 percent of offering proceeds, depending on the size of the offering.

Management's Efforts to Market the Offering

An IPO imposes substantial administrative burdens on the focal firm's management. These include time preparing the registration statement and prospectus, and consulting with legal counsel, accountants, consultants, and underwriters. Another substantial burden involves efforts to market the issue. Generally, the firm's CEO or CFO will engage in weeks or months of travel to *pitch* their pending offering to specific investors or investor groups. Such *road shows* can be extremely costly in terms of both direct travel expenses and the opportunity cost of the executive's time away from the task of running the firm.

12.3.3 Choice of Listing Market

Before 1983, the initial listing requirements on the New York Stock Exchange (NYSE) were very stringent. As a result, very few IPO firms listed on the NYSE. Instead, almost all IPOs were initially listed on the over-the-counter (OTC) market, which evolved into the NASDAQ market in 1970. During this time, the two exchanges had a symbiotic relationship, as some of the more successful firms that originated on the OTC market *graduated* to the NYSE when they met the latter's listing requirements.[2]

However, as the NASDAQ market gained prominence, many successful NASDAQ firms (e.g., Microsoft and Apple Computer) declined to relist on the NYSE when they met the NYSE's listing requirements. Facing the prospect that they would no longer be *fed* successful firms from the NASDAQ, in 1983 the NYSE eased its listing requirements substantially. Subsequently, the NYSE has been the initial listing exchange for a growing number of firms, though the NASDAQ still dominates.

---

[2]The following papers analyze firms that switched their listing from one U.S. market to another: Ying, Lewellen, Schlarbaum, and Lease (1977), Sanger and McConnell (1986), Grammatikos and Papaloannou (1986), Cowan, Carter, Dark, and Singh (1992), and Clyde, Schultz, and Zaman (1997).

Charting Your Course to an Initial Public Offering

This article discusses details of the activities that a firm should undertake as it approaches an IPO.

Although taking your company public may not be in your immediate plans, there are several steps you can take sooner rather than later in the growth of your organization that will lessen the possibility of delay, mitigate the demands on your time, and reduce the cost of a future initial public offering. The most important thing you should know about the IPO process is that timing is everything. Generally speaking, the faster the IPO process moves toward completion, the better the chances of success. The market's receptiveness to IPOs can swing quickly and dramatically. Underwriters speak of a window, which represents the optimum time for a company's stock to hit the market, given market conditions and the anticipated valuation of the company at that time. A lack of preparation for the IPO can cause delay and result in the window closing before the registration statement is declared effective and selling can begin. As a result, the IPO may be pulled or put on ice until the underwriters feel that a new window of opportunity opens, which could take months or, even worse, could never happen at all.

The IPO process, from the first all-hands organizational meeting until the first sale of shares to the public, generally will take from two to four months depending upon the complexity of your company and the extent of corporate clean-up. During this period, you will be focused entirely on the preparation and filing of the registration statement, marketing the IPO on a road show, and responding to comments on the registration statement from the Securities and Exchange Commission. In order to facilitate these monumental tasks and avoid the pitfalls that can arise from a lack of careful preparation, your management team and counsel should resolve virtually all significant matters prior to

this crucial time. Here are some of the most important tips to consider in planning your company's IPO. These issues can be resolved well in advance of the offering and will reduce the possibility of delay which could harm the chances of success of your IPO. To enable you to better visualize and plan for these issues, the outline is organized chronologically according to the time periods preceding the IPO in which each issue should ideally be addressed.

12 MONTHS OR MORE BEFORE THE IPO

- ***Retain Experts***

    When selecting outside legal counsel and accountants to assist in the preparation and filing with the SEC of your company's registration statement covering the stock to be offered to the public, choose firms that have significant experience in public offerings and ongoing public company representation.

- ***Adopt a Stock Option Plan and Issue of Stock Options***

    It is necessary to adopt a stock option plan and begin issuing options as early as possible before the IPO. As it becomes more certain that a company will go public, the value of its stock will begin to rise dramatically. Therefore, it is desirable for management of a company to adopt an option plan well in advance of a prospective IPO and begin granting options to key personnel to establish their relative ownership interests in the company at the earliest possible stage. With a stock issuance and option plan in place, you will avoid the problems which typically arise out of granting stock options at an exercise price below the fair market value which is commonly referred to as cheap stock.

- ***Review Your Company's Contracts***

    Review with your company counsel all contracts with suppliers and corporate partners to make sure that an IPO will not trigger any

(continued)

change of control provisions that would terminate such contracts. Where necessary, amend or replace key contract and agreements that might be jeopardized by the IPO.

- **Review Investor Documents**

Analyze stock purchase agreements and other documents that may provide for the conversion of preferred stock or debt or the acceleration of the exercise periods of warrants upon the occurrence of an IPO. Failing to do so could have a negative effect on the underwriter's ability to sell the IPO or on the price of your company's stock.

- **Review Financial Statements**

The financial statement and accounting requirements imposed on public companies can be significantly more demanding than those you have implemented within your organization. Use a Big Six accounting firm experienced in securities matters to help set up management information systems designed to ease the preparation of financial statements and compliance with public company reporting requirements.

- **Review Loan Documents**

Some loan documents may contain provisions that require you to obtain the consent of your lenders prior to offering a substantial amount of stock. To avoid any last minute holdups, talk to your banker and obtain all necessary consents.

6–12 MONTHS BEFORE THE IPO

- **Corporate Clean-up**

As the IPO approaches, begin to focus on technical issues such as auditing the corporate records with your lawyer to ensure your company is in compliance with all applicable laws (corporate, securities, regulation industry, and the like). You may also consider simplifying the capital and corporate structure of your business so investors see the potential benefits of an investment in your company's stock.

- **Choose Your Underwriters**

Choosing the right underwriter is key to the success of your IPO. Your attorney and

accountant can provide helpful insights and often introductions as to specific investment banks and bankers that have the greatest expertise in your business sector.

- **Analyze Registration Rights**

If your company has granted registration rights to investors or lenders in connection with earlier stage financing transactions, you must open discussions with those parties in order to avoid confusion as to the number of shares available for sale to the public.

- **Clean Up Insider Transactions**

Transactions with insiders involving an amount greater than $60,000 should be reviewed and modified so that they can be disclosed in the prospectus and reported as arms-length transactions.

- **Select Management for Your Public Company**

The administrative and management demands placed upon your company once you are public will be significantly greater and it is likely you will need to add one or more new officers with experience in running public companies.

3–6 MONTHS BEFORE THE IPO

- **Avoid Gun Jumping**

Gun Jumping refers to attempts by a company and the underwriters to publicize a company's plan to go public before a registration statement has been filed. The SEC has the power to delay your offering until it believes the effect of such publicity has been sufficiently mitigated. It is also a good idea to have your lawyer review all promotional literature and press releases to be disseminated during the pre-filing process.

- **Prepare Section 16 Compliance**

Section 16 of the Securities Exchange Act of 1934 provides for a rigid regulatory framework designed to prevent insider trading activities. Discuss the Section 16 compliance program and insider trading policies with your attorney. The reporting requirements of Section 16 are overwhelming and the penalties for violation can be stiff.

- *Review Option Issues*

Review the existing ownership mix of your company to ensure shareholders are satisfied and prepare grants to new employees eligible for options. The importance of the option issues cannot be overemphasized.

- *Prepare for Due Diligence*

Once an IPO commences, underwriters' counsel will want to conduct a due diligence process. They will examine nearly all of your books, records, agreements, securities, and material correspondence to ensure that all disclosures contained in the prospectus are truthful and that no material information required to be included in the prospectus is omitted. To prevent this process from holding up the IPO in any way, you may want to consider pulling together and organizing the documents that the underwriters' counsel is likely to request. Searching for missing documents and creating necessary documentation for matters at the last minute can needlessly delay the IPO and

may create misimpressions about the company's organizational abilities and management controls.

0–3 MONTHS BEFORE THE IPO

Three months before the projected effective date for the registration statement, you will begin drafting the registration statement with your management team and counsel. Shortly thereafter, the first all-hands meeting will be held to organize the many tasks involved in taking your company public. To the extent possible, it is a definite advantage to have anticipated and resolved the significant issues discussed above that are likely to arise in connection with the IPO. From that point forward, your management team and counsel will be completely absorbed in the preparation and filing of the registration statement and applications to list your company's stock on a national exchange or the Nasdaq National Market, not to mention dealing with the last minute issues that always seem to arise.

Source: "Charting Your Course to an Initial Public Offering," B. R. Hallett, *Orange County Business Journal*, v. 19, June 1996. Reprinted by permission.

Corwin and Harris (2001) examined firms that listed on either the NYSE or the NASDAQ from 1991 to 1996 to identify factors that determine a firm's choice of listing market. Their sample included only firms that would have met NYSE listing requirements, even though they may have listed on the NASDAQ. They found that direct issue costs, including underwriter spreads and listing fees, are lower on the NASDAQ than on the NYSE, especially for smaller firms. Their evidence suggests that the listing choice for smaller firms is driven by direct issue costs. They also found that technology firms, firms backed by VCs, and firms that subsequently raise funds through *follow-on* equity offerings are more likely to list on the NASDAQ. Larger and less risky firms are more likely to list on the NYSE.

12.3.4 Projecting the Firm's Initial Asset, Operational, Ownership, Governance, Management, and Capital Structures

Before a firm can make its IPO, the firm must provide *pro forma* projections of the asset, operational, ownership, management, governance, and capital structures that it will exhibit after the offering.

Projected Asset and Operational Structures

The IPO firm's management must provide the market with a vision of the firm's asset and operational structures after the IPO takes place. Many firms go public to raise funds for capital expenditures, acquisitions, or working capital. The market must be made aware of the general parameters of the firm's assets and operations as a matter of regulatory law, but also to mitigate information asymmetry problems. An IPO firm satisfies this requirement by providing *pro forma* balance sheets and income statements that reflect the firm's planned expenditures and operations.

Projected Ownership, Management, Governance, and Capital Structures

An IPO often results in substantial changes in the firm's (a) ownership structure, (b) management, (c) governance structure, and (d) capital structure. For instance, an IPO firm's insiders generally dominate the ownership of the firm's shares just before the offering. However, some insiders (who wish to quit or retire) may wish to take the opportunity afforded by the IPO to cash out some or all of their shares in a *secondary portion* of the IPO. Also IPO firms generally raise funds for the firm in the *primary portion* of the offering, which increases the firm's equity base and therefore reduces leverage. The reduction in leverage is more substantial if the proceeds of the primary portion of the offering are used to pay down debt. Moreover, both the primary and secondary portions of the offering bring in new shareholders.

The post-IPO dispersion of the firm's shares is a delicate issue. On one hand, both the NASDAQ and the NYSE mandate a minimum number of shareholders as a listing requirement. On the other hand, the retention of a substantial proportion of the firm's shares by management and other insiders is a positive signal of the firm's value, and is a means of mitigating agency costs of managerial discretion. An important aspect of insiders' commitment to continuing ownership is the *lockup provision*, whereby insiders agree to hold their shares for a period of time (typically 180 days) after the date of the IPO.

It is also important to assure the market that the firm's post-IPO senior managers are competent and are properly incented, via share ownership or their compensation contracts, to act in the shareholders' interest. Contracts with senior managers may have to be renegotiated. In addition, the firm's governance structure, particularly the firm's board of directors, often must be restructured to meet the new information and consulting needs of a public company. Some incumbent directors may depart or must be forced out and replaced. The firm can take the opportunity of an IPO to bring in new directors.

The underwriter may also advise the firm to *clean up* its capital structure using proceeds from the offering. Securities such as convertible preferred stock and senior or subordinated debt that the firm had issued as a private entity may be retired, via either a cash payment or an exchange for common stock. In any event, the firm's post-IPO capital structure should be consistent with the firm's business risk, financial plans, and incentive structures.

12.3.5 Price Discovery

Once the firm's post-IPO asset, operational, ownership, management, governance, and capital structures have been established, the underwriter is in a position to price the offering. The process by which the underwriter determines the price of an IPO is called *price discovery*, which typically involves two steps. *First*, the underwriter establishes a reasonable range of potential offer prices, taking into account (a) the organizational structures noted earlier, (b) projections reflected in the pro forma balance sheet and income statement, (c) the potential profitability and inherent risk of the firm, and (d) the state of the market.

Second, the underwriter identifies a number of investors who may be interested in purchasing the firm's shares. Bids taken from each investor specify the number of shares that the investor is willing to purchase at each of a range of prices. The underwriter then develops a *demand schedule* for the issue by summing the shares demanded at each price. Finally, the underwriter determines the offer price as the intersection of aggregate demand and offered supply.[3]

12.3.6 Selecting the Offering Method

An IPO firm has a choice of two methods of selling shares. In the *firm commitment* method, the underwriter agrees to purchase all shares offered at a fixed price, and then takes the risk of reselling the shares to the public. In the *best efforts* method, the underwriter makes no guarantee about the price. Instead, the underwriter only agrees to conduct a search for interested buyers, each of whom submit a schedule of the numbers of shares that they are willing to purchase at each of a range of prices, as explained above. Thus, in a firm commitment contract the underwriter acts as a *dealer*, whereas in a best efforts contract the underwriter acts as a *broker*.

Put another way, in the firm commitment method the underwriter assumes price risk, but in the best efforts method the issuing firm assumes price risk. However, in both methods a contract feature serves to mitigate the risk borne by the risk-assuming party. In the firm commitment method, the underwriter generally has an *overallotment* (or *greenshoe*) option, which allows it to sell additional shares if it is profitable to do so. By exercising this option when it is profitable, the underwriter increases its profits on IPOs that turn out to be profitable, which offsets losses on other issues. In the best efforts method, the firm retains options to (a) withdraw the offering if either the offer price or shares committed for sale is below a specified level, or (b) expand the offering if the price is above a specified level.

Bower (1989) studied determinants of an IPO firm's offering method decision. Her theoretical analysis focuses on the effects of information asymmetry on the choice. She found that, to the extent that a firm can separate itself from other firms (i.e., establish a separating equilibrium), it will optimally choose the firm commitment method. Otherwise, if the firm faces a pooling equilibrium, the best efforts method is optimal.

12.4 CHARACTERISTICS OF IPO FIRMS AND THEIR OFFERINGS

In this section, we provide statistics on the characteristics of IPO firms and their offerings. Our sample is restricted to *stock-only IPOs*, the most common IPOs for U.S. nonfinancial firms. In Section 12.5, we follow up with analyses of the post-IPO return performance of these offerings. (We discuss unit IPOs in Section 12.6.)

---

[3]The aggregate supply may be fixed. Alternatively, a supply schedule may emerge if the firm's pre-IPO shareholders may be more or less willing to offer their shares in a secondary offering depending on the price. The quantity of shares supplied may also vary according to the firm's willingness to offer primary shares, again depending on the price. For a more formal analysis of how underwriters determine the offer price and allocation of IPO shares, see Benveniste and Spindt (1989).

12.4.1   The Numbers of IPOs in U.S. Markets, 1970–2000

Over the years 1970 to 2000, a total of 8,010 U.S. nonfinancial firms made their debuts in the U.S. public equity markets. Figure 12-1 displays the total number of IPOs each year. Annual numbers are displayed for all markets combined, as well as separately for each U.S. listing market. We focus initially on the annual totals for all markets.

The annual totals range from only six IPOs in 1975 to a record 660 IPOs in 1996. The general increase in IPOs after 1979 undoubtedly reflects, at least in part, the development of the VC industry. Variation in the numbers of IPOs over time also appears to be related to economic and market conditions. After brisk activity in 1970 to 1972, the IPO market virtually dried up around the recession of 1973 to 1974. Then, after building steadily through 1981, the IPO market slumped in 1982, which was a difficult year for both the economy and the market. Brisk activity quickly returned and was maintained throughout the remainder of the 1980s. Once again, however, IPO numbers reached a temporary nadir in 1990, a recession year, before quickly recovering and remaining as brisk as the economy and the markets through 2000.

FIGURE 12-1   Annual Numbers of IPOs by Issuer's Listing Market*

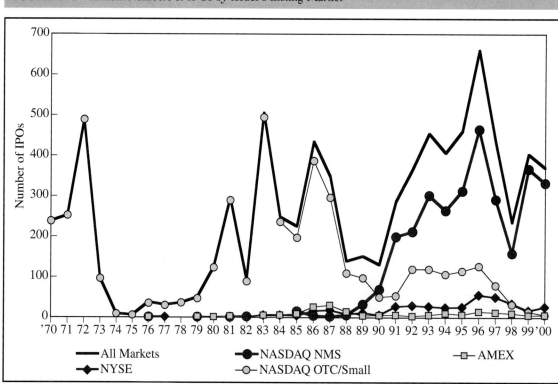

U.S. Nonfinancial Firms, 1970–2000

Excluding 29 IPOs on regional exchanges.
Source: Raw data from Securities Data Corporation's new-issue database.

Through 1988, the NASDAQ's OTC and Small-Issue markets dominated as the listing market for IPOs. The NASDAQ's National Market System (NMS) began to overtake the OTC and Small-Issue markets in 1989, and dominated the new-issue market through 2000.

What about the NYSE, AMEX, and regional exchanges such as the Boston, Midwest, and Pacific exchanges? As we noted earlier, until 1983 the listing requirements on the NYSE and AMEX were very stringent, so very few firms qualified to list on these exchanges. As a result, virtually the only new stocks that appeared on the NYSE or AMEX exchanges were those that originally listed on the NASDAQ or regional markets. However, after 1983 the NYSE had a fairly substantial number of IPOs, and the AMEX also had a few IPOs each year. The regional exchanges, however, have never had substantial IPO activity. Collectively, they listed only 29 firms via IPO in the years 1970 to 2000. (These are not displayed in the figure.)

12.4.2 IPO Dollar Volume over Time and across Exchanges

Figure 12-2 provides a different perspective on IPO volume over the years 1970 to 2000. This figure shows the *total dollar volume* and the *average issue size* of the IPOs for each market and year. Again, the NASDAQ's OTC and Small-Issue markets dom-

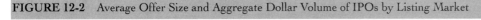

FIGURE 12-2 Average Offer Size and Aggregate Dollar Volume of IPOs by Listing Market

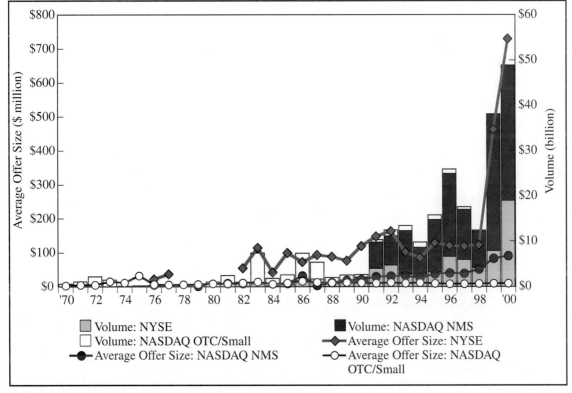

U.S. Nonfinancial Firms, 1970–2000
Source: Raw data from Securities Data Corporation's new-issue database.

inated in terms of total dollar volume through about 1987, after which the NASDAQ's NMS market assumed a dominant position and held sway through 2000. However, the dollar volumes posted by the NYSE from 1990 to 2000 are substantial, and out of proportion to the *numbers* of NYSE-listed IPOs shown in Figure 12-1 for the same years. This is so because NYSE IPOs are generally many times larger than NASDAQ IPOs.

12.4.3   Characteristics of IPO Firms: 1991–2000

In the remainder of this section, we discuss statistics for 3,923 stock-only IPOs completed by U.S. nonfinancial firms during the years 1991 to 2000. We focus on offerings during this period for two reasons. *First*, they are more recent, and therefore reflect recent innovations such as the development of the VC industry. *Second*, more detailed data on these offerings is available from the database that we employ, Securities Data Corporation's new-issues database.

The sample includes 2,141 firms that were not financially supported, or *backed*, by a VC, and 1,782 firms that were backed by a VC. A firm's VC-backing status is a potentially important factor. Therefore, we initially calculate each statistic using all firms in the sample, and then recalculate the statistic after sorting the firms into groups by their VC-backing status. Note that a VC backed nearly half of the IPO firms in the sample. This result attests to the growing presence of VCs as venture financiers in the United States. Indeed, their rise has been accelerating, increasing from 41 percent of all IPOs in 1991 to 1998 to 64 percent of all IPOs in 1999 to 2000.

Our initial set of statistics pertains to characteristics of the issuing firms. The results are displayed in the upper portion of Table 12-2.

Age Statistics

The first statistic is the average age of the IPO firms. Firm age is defined as the number of years between the firm's founding and the IPO date. For all firms, the average age is 7.6 years. This result suggests the average amount of time that a firm (i.e., a venture) requires to pass through the various stages of development (discussed in Chapter 11) before it goes public.

Interestingly, VC-backed firms are, on average, 1.4 years younger than non-VC-backed firms (6.9 years versus 8.3 years). This difference suggests that VCs either (a) are able to develop a firm faster, perhaps because they provide superior access to funds and development expertise during a firm's development; or (b) press a firm to go public prematurely, perhaps because they wish to liquidate their investment, or because they need to establish a reputation for success (i.e., grandstanding).

Firm Size

For all firms, average and median total assets (TA) after the offering are $349 million and $53 million, respectively. Measured by either average or median TA after the offering, VC-backed firms are generally larger than non–VC-backed firms. The discrepancy between the average and median statistics, which holds for all firms as well as both subsamples, reflects skewness in the distribution of the sizes of IPO firms; they consist of relatively few very large firms and numerous small firms.

Leverage

The third set of statistics pertains to the sampled firms' leverage. We measured leverage via a *modified debt ratio*, defined as 1 minus the ratio of book equity to TA, expressed in percent. For all firms, median modified debt ratios before and after the

TABLE 12-2 Firm and Offering Characteristics for IPOs

U.S. Nonfinancial Firms, 1991–2000*

| | | All | VC Backed? | |
	Statistic	Firms	*No*	*Yes*
Number of Firms	Sum	3,923	2,141	1,782
Firm Characteristics				
Firm age: years between firm founding and				
IPO offer date	Average	7.6	8.3	6.9
Total assets after offering ($ million)	Average	$349	$272	$438
	Median	$53	$49	$57
Modified debt ratio [= 1 – (BEQ/TA)]				
Before offering	Median	80%	80%	78%
After offering	Median	29%	32%	27%
EPS before offering				
Last year before	Median	0.06	0.23	–0.36
Two years before	Median	0.03	0.10	–0.13
Three years before	Median	–0.01	0.07	–0.14
Number of firms that intend to pay a dividend	Sum	75	61	14
Offering Characteristics				
Offer price	Average	$12.25	$11.81	$12.78
Market-to-book equity ratio	Median	3.1	2.9	3.5
Price-earnings ratio	Median	10.5	15.7	–3.8
Shares offered as a percent of shares				
Outstanding after offering				
Primary shares	Average	32.2%	33.2%	31.0%
Secondary shares	Average	4.4%	5.3%	3.3%
Proceeds of offering ($ million)	Median	35.0	31.8	37.1
Underwriter spread as a percentage of offering proceeds	Average	7.2%	7.4%	7.1%
	Median	7%	7%	7%
Shares held by insiders as a percentage of total shares				
Before offering	Average	64%	70%	57%
After offering	Average	45%	47%	42%
Days in lockup	Median	180	180	180
Percent of shares subject to lockup	Median	65%	63%	67%
Overallotment option statistics				
Percent of firms with option:	Percent	99.6%	99.6%	99.6%
Shares in option/shares in offering (%)	Median	15%	15%	15%
Overallotment of shares sold/shares in option (%)	Average	93.6%	91.6%	95.7%

*Some values were missing for many variables, so statistics shown reflect only non-missing values.
Source: Raw data from Securities Data Corporation's new-issue database.

offering are 80 percent and 29 percent, respectively. These results, of course, reflect the infusion of equity capital, but also reflect firms' tendencies to use proceeds from the primary portion of the IPO to pay down debt. (We corroborate the latter point with additional evidence later.)

The surprising result here is that these firms were able to establish such highly levered capital structures before they became public firms. Indeed, the typical debt ratio is higher than we observed for seasoned firms in Chapter 1. Non–VC-backed firms tend to have slightly higher median modified debt ratios than VC-backed firms, both before the offering (80 percent versus 78 percent) and after the offering (32 percent versus 27 percent). These results suggest that VCs provide additional equity financing for the firms that they support, while non–VC-backed firms are forced to (or prefer to) rely more heavily on debt financing.

Profitability

Next, we report profitability statistics, consisting of median earnings per share (EPS) for the last year before the offering, two years before, and three years before. For all firms, the medians are positive for the two most recent years, and median EPS increases as the IPO date approaches. This pattern also holds for the non–VC-backed firms. In contrast, the typical VC-backed firm is not profitable in any of these three years, nor does it exhibit a trend toward profitability. These results, in conjunction with the earlier results indicating the VC-backed firms go public at a younger age, suggest that VC firms tend to be aggressive in bringing their firms public, and as a result the typical VC-backed firm has not yet shown a profit.

Dividend Policy

Regarding dividend policy, very few IPO firms expressed an intent to pay a dividend immediately after the offering. Only 75 of the 3,923 firms in the sample (61 non–VC-backed firms and 14 VC-backed firms) expressed such intent. This is not surprising because these generally are firms that are not (yet) highly profitable, and typically need to retain earnings for expansion and to build their equity base.

12.4.4   Offering Characteristics

Next, we examine offering statistics, which are displayed in the lower portion of Table 12-2.

Offer Price

The average offer price for all IPOs is $12.25, though the average is substantially lower for the non–VC-backed firms ($11.81) than for the VC-backed firms ($12.78). The difference (weakly) suggests that VCs may be influential in securing a higher offer price for their firms.

Valuation Statistics

We report two valuation statistics in the table: median market-to-book equity ratio and median price-earnings ratio (P/E). For all firms, the median market-to-book equity ratio is 3.1. VC-backed firms have a slightly higher ratio (3.5) than non–VC-backed firms (2.9), another indication that VCs may be able to secure slightly higher prices for their firms' shares.

The P/E ratio for each firm is the ratio of the offering price to the firm's EPS for the last year prior to the offering. For all firms, the median P/E is 10.5. For the non–VC-backed firms, the median P/E is 15.7. For the VC-backed firms the median is actually negative, –3.8, reflecting the fact that the typical VC-backed firm had negative earnings in the year prior to the offering.

Primary Shares

The average number of primary shares offered as a percent of shares outstanding after the offering is 32.2 percent, and is somewhat higher for non–VC-backed firms (33.2 percent) than for VC-backed firms (31.0 percent). This difference suggests that VC-backed firms may have less need to raise new funds at the IPO, perhaps because they have had better developmental financing from the VC. Of course, VC-backed firms also tend to secure a higher offer price, so they can issue fewer shares to realize a given amount of proceeds.

Secondary Shares

The average number of secondary shares offered as a percent of shares outstanding after the offering is 4.4 percent. The average is higher for non–VC-backed firms (5.3 percent) than for VC-backed firms (3.3 percent). These small percentages indicate that pre-IPO shareholders generally sell very few shares in an IPO, perhaps because of the negative signaling or agency-cost implications.

Offering Proceeds

The median value of proceeds obtained by all firms in the sample was $35.0 million. VC-backed firms received higher median proceeds ($37.1 million) than non–VC-backed firms ($31.8 million). The difference is due in part to the result, discussed earlier, that VC-backed firms generally secure a higher offer price.

Underwriter Spread

The next statistics shown in the table are the average and median underwriter spreads, expressed as a percent of offering proceeds. For all firms, the average spread is 7.2 percent, and the average is slightly higher for non–VC-backed firms (7.4 percent) than for VC-backed firms (7.1 percent). This difference appears to suggest that VCs are able to negotiate lower spreads with the underwriters. Instead, the difference is driven by the fact that the non–VC-backed sample tends to include more very small firms, which are virtually the only firms that must pay a spread higher than the standard 7 percent. The standard 7 percent spread is reflected in the *median* statistics shown in the table. (See Chen and Ritter [2000] and Hansen [2001] for discussions of the 7 percent spread standard.)

Underwriter spreads are substantially higher for IPOs than for either nonconvertible public corporate bond issues (1.17 percent on average; see Table 10-1) or seasoned equity offerings (5.3 percent on average; see Table 13-1). The relative sizes of these spreads reflect the riskiness of the securities offered, with debt as the least risky, followed by seasoned equity and then IPOs. As we have stated, both information asymmetry and principal–agent problems attending an offering tend to be positively related to the riskiness of the security being offered. In turn, underwriter spreads increase with risk because the effort involved in underwriting an offer is positively related to the scope of these problems.

Underwriter spreads in IPOs also appear to reflect economies of scale: The correlation between underwriter spread and the natural log of offering proceeds is –0.75. However, this correlation may be partially spurious because larger firms, which tend to have larger offerings, also tend to be less risky, and as argued above, spread tends to be positively related to the riskiness of the offered security.

Ownership Structure Statistics

Next, we consider ownership structure statistics. We report the average proportion of shares held by insiders before and after the offering. For all firms, the averages are 64 percent and 45 percent, respectively. Thus, insider ownership percentage drops substantially for the typical firm as it goes public, as we would expect given that new shares, held by outsiders, are issued. Insider ownership percentage would also decrease if insiders sell shares in the secondary portion of the offering. However, the relative paucity of secondary shares offered in the typical IPO suggests that this has a smaller effect on insider ownership percentage.

For non–VC-backed and VC-backed firms, the average insider ownership percentages are 70 percent and 57 percent, respectively, before the offering, and 47 percent and 42 percent, respectively, after the offering. The differences across the two groups, both before and after the offering, likely reflect the presence of VCs as noninsider shareholders (i.e., as defined by our source, the SDC database).

Lockup Statistics

Two lockup statistics are also provided in the table. The first is the median number of days that the shares of the affected investors (primarily insiders, but also perhaps VCs, angels, or other major noninsiders) are in lockup. For all firms, as well as the non–VC-backed and VC-backed firms, the median is 180 days, which is obviously the market standard.

The second statistic is the median percentage of outstanding shares (after the offering) that are subject to lockup. The medians are 65, 63, and 67 percent for all firms, non–VC-backed firms, and VC-backed firms, respectively. These proportions substantially exceed the corresponding average proportions of total (postoffering) shares held by insiders, suggesting that the shares of at least some noninsiders are subject to lockup. The results also suggest that in general only about one-third of a firm's outstanding shares are tradeable within the first 180 days after the IPO date.

As we discussed earlier, the lockup provision is a *bonding mechanism* that resolves information asymmetry problems (predominantly) between the insiders and new investors who purchase the firm's shares at or after the offering. Unfortunately, the downside to the lockup provision is that, on average, only a minority of the firm's shares are freely floating in the secondary market in the critical first six months after the offering, which therefore limits the liquidity of the firm's stock (i.e., for investors who are not subject to the lockup).

Overallotment Option Statistics

The final statistics in Table 12-2 pertain to the overallotment option given to the underwriter. For all firms and both subsamples, well over 99 percent of IPO deals include an overallotment option. The median number of shares included in the overallotment option represents 15 percent of all shares in the offering. In addition, underwriters actually sold over 90 percent of the shares allocated in overallotment option, on average.

12.4.5 A Case in Point: Infinium Software, Inc.

We conclude this section by briefly discussing the recent IPO of Infinium Software, Inc. This Massachusetts firm was founded in 1981 in the Cape Cod home of founder Robert A. Pemberton. During its pre-IPO development, the company financed its operations principally through cash flows from operating activities and, to a lesser extent, equipment financing arrangements and a private placement of common stock to VCs in June 1989.

The company is classified in the *Business Services* industry (SIC code 7371, *Computer Programming Services*). The firm provides a range of financial management, human resource management, and materials management software, and also offers a specialized manufacturing system designed to manage process manufacturing operations. The company derives its revenue from two sources: software license fees and services.

On November 17, 1995, the company conducted its IPO on the NASDAQ market under its former name, Software 2000, Inc., adopting the ticker symbol SFWR. (The company changed its name to Infinium Software, Inc., in February 1997, and adopted a new ticker symbol, INFM.) The firm's underwriters were Needham & Co., Robinson-Humphrey, and SoundView Financial. At the time of its IPO, the company had 18 offices, 1,300 customers, $63 million in revenue, and net income of $3.8 million.

In the offering, the company sold 2.3 million shares, including 1.33 million primary shares and 0.97 million secondary shares. The total shares offered represented 21.2 percent of the total shares outstanding after the offering (10.9 million shares). The offer price was $11 per share. Thus, gross proceeds of the offering totaled $25.3 million. The underwriter spread was 7 percent. Insiders held 43.8 percent of the outstanding shares before the offering, and 35.2 percent after the offering. Shares subject to lockup totaled 63.3 percent of post-IPO shares outstanding. The duration of the lockup was 180 days.

Based on the offering price, the firm's market-to-book equity ratio was 6.75, and its P/E was 28.5. The firm had no long-term debt in its capital structure at the time of the offering. However, its current liabilities accounted for 85.7 percent of its TA of $44 million. Thus, its pre-IPO modified debt ratio $[(1 - BEQ)/TA]$ was 89.0 percent. With the help of cash infusions from the IPO and a *follow-up* seasoned equity offering (we discuss SEOs in Chapter 13) in May 1996, the firm was able to pare its modified debt ratio to 52.9 percent as of September 30, 1996.

The firm's SEO occurred on May 9, 1996, or 174 days after the firm's IPO. It included a total of 2.87 million shares, composed of 0.5 million primary shares and 2.37 million secondary shares. The offer price was $14.75. The secondary offering included approximately 400,000 shares sold by founder, board chairman, and CEO Robert A. Pemberton, who thereby reduced his ownership percentage from 32.3 percent to 25.8 percent.

12.5   THE POST-IPO PERFORMANCE OF STOCK-ONLY IPOS

In this section, we analyze the post-IPO return performance of IPO stocks. Paralleling the literature, we devote most of our analysis to return performance on the first day after the offering. We then follow with a shorter analysis of the longer-term return performance of IPO stocks.

12.5.1   First-Day Returns on IPOs: The Underpricing Anomaly

One of the most enduring and widely documented phenomena in the finance literature is the *IPO underpricing anomaly*. Numerous studies have documented evidence of extremely high average returns on IPOs as measured from the offer price to the initial price in the *aftermarket* (i.e., the secondary market). In this subsection, we provide evidence of this anomaly for our sample of stock-only IPOs of U.S. nonfinancial firms over the years 1991 to 2000. In the next subsection, we review literature that provides alternative explanations for this anomaly.

Figure 12-3 shows separate cross-sectional distributions of first-day returns on non–VC-backed IPOs and the VC-backed IPOs. First-day return is defined as the percentage difference between the closing price of the stock on the first day of secondary-market trading and the offer price.

The return distributions of both groups of firms appear to be very similar, as both exhibit tremendous variation. For the VC-backed stocks, first-day returns range from –27.8 percent to 697.5 percent. The corresponding range for the non–VC-backed IPOs is from –67.5 percent to 441.7 percent. These minimums and maximums, as well as the distributions themselves, indicate that first-day returns on IPO stocks are highly skewed to the right (i.e., there are more extreme positive returns than equally extreme negative returns.)

Average, median, and standard deviation statistics for both groups of firms are shown below the figure. The average return on the non–VC-backed IPOs is 18.8 percent, while the average return on the VC-backed IPOs is about twice that, 37.9 percent. These

FIGURE 12-3 Distributions of First-Day Returns on Non–VC-Backed and VC-Backed IPOs

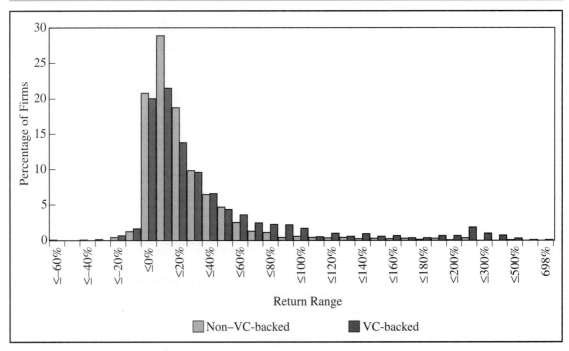

U.S. Nonfinancial Firms, 1991–2000

VC Backed?	Av. %	Med. %	S.D. %
No (1,475)	18.8	10.0	32.4
Yes (1,432)	37.9	14.1	66.9

Source: Raw data from Securities Data Corporation's new-issue database.

are amazing one-day average returns. Due to the skewness of the returns, the median statistics are much lower, though still huge, at 10.0 percent and 14.1 percent, respectively.

As noted earlier, evidence of high first-day returns on IPOs has been amply documented and studied. The general conclusion drawn from these studies is that IPOs are *underpriced* in the offering market, and therefore huge returns are obtained as the price rises from a low offering price to a generally much higher (equilibrium) price in the aftermarket. Next, we summarize the arguments of several authors who have attempted to explain this anomaly.

12.5.2 Why Are IPOs Underpriced?

Researchers have provided a number of explanations for the underpricing of IPOs. Below we list and briefly describe the most popular explanations:

> ***Litigation Risk:*** "[T]he underwriter is an intermediary between the issuer and the capital market and makes pricing decisions that maximize his own welfare. The underwriter sets the issue price knowing that he will be sued in the future if there is evidence that the courts will judge as indicative of overpricing. There is a perfect sequential equilibrium in which some issues are overpriced, some are underpriced, there is underpricing *on average*, and there exists a positive probability of successful litigation against the underwriter" (Hughes and Thakor (1992, p. 710).
>
> ***The Winner's Curse:*** Rock (1986) assumes the existence of both informed and uninformed traders and shows that underpricing emerges to encourage participation by uninformed traders who would otherwise suffer the "winner's curse" in trading with the informed. That is, uninformed investors realize that they tend to be more successful in obtaining shares of overpriced IPOs. To get them to participate, all IPOs must be discounted.[4]
>
> ***Signaling Models:*** Several authors have recently provided an interesting possible reason for underpricing. In these models, the intrinsically higher-valued firms strategically underprice their stock in order to deter mimicking by lower-valued competitors. High-valued firms are underpriced in order to encourage information production by investors that will then be revealed in the secondary market price. These models involve firms dealing directly with investors, rather than through an investment banker. An economic role for the underwriter as an intermediary also emerges in that risk-averse issuing firms may underprice in order to induce some investors to reveal information about market conditions. Under these circumstances, the existence of underwriters improves the economic efficiency of the IPO market. (See Allen and Faulhaber 1989; Benveniste and Spindt 1989; Chemmanur 1993; Grinblatt and Hwang 1989; and Welch 1989.)

---

[4]Underwriters (especially those who are also brokers) often reward valued customers with shares of underpriced IPOs. After receiving their allocation, these customers generally sell them quickly at a (generally) higher price in the secondary market, realizing a quick profit. This activity is called *flipping*. Many critics frown on flipping. However, we must realize that if none of the original purchasers of an IPO flipped, there would be no shares trading in the secondary market! For more information and analyses on flipping, see Aggarwal (2002), Ang and Brau (2002b), Krigman, and Womack, and Shaw (2000).

To these explanations, we add another—compensation for risk. The statistics shown below Figure 12-3 include the cross-sectional standard deviations of first-day returns on the two groups of IPO stocks. These return standard deviations are 32.4 percent and 66.9 percent for the non–VC-backed and VC-backed firms, respectively. These statistics are not annualized; rather, they simply represent the volatility of the return experienced by an investor who repeatedly purchased IPO stocks at their respective offer prices and held them to the end of the trading day. Yet these statistics compare to the return standard deviations typically exhibited by individual seasoned U.S. stocks over an entire year! It is also interesting to note that both the average return and the return standard deviation are roughly twice as high for VC-backed stocks as compared with non–VC-backed stocks. Though it may be argued that much of the risk exhibited in one-day returns on IPO stocks is diversifiable, a risk-return explanation for IPO underpricing cannot be entirely discounted.

12.5.3 Is Underpricing Related to the Firm's Stated Use of the Proceeds of the IPO?

As the statistics shown in Table 12-2 indicated, an IPO predominantly consists of primary shares. Thus, a question arises about the issuing firm's intended use for the proceeds of the primary offering. To address this question, we sorted each firm into one of several groups according to the firm's stated primary use of the proceeds from the primary portion of the IPO, and tallied frequencies. The results are displayed in Table 12-3.

Of the 3,726 firms for which data was available, 2,026 firms, or 54.4 percent of the firms in the sample, stated that the proceeds are to be used for *general corporate purposes*. This is a fairly vague phrase that may suggest that (a) management will use the proceeds for multiple purposes, (b) management has not yet decided precisely how it will use the proceeds, or (c) for competitive reasons, management does not wish to divulge its intentions regarding the proceeds. The second most frequently stated purpose is *debt retirement*, listed as the primary use by 1,261 firms, or 33.8 percent of the firms in the sample. This is not surprising given the evidence shown in Table 12-2 indicating that, prior to the offering, IPO firms tend to have extremely high (modified) debt ratios.

A subsequent question that emerges from these results is whether the degree of underpricing of an IPO is related to the stated use of the proceeds. Suppose underpricing tends to be directly related to the level of information asymmetry that exists between potential IPO investors and the firm's management at the time of the offering. One (though surely not the only) means by which the firm's management could reduce information asymmetry is to commit to a definite stated use for the proceeds. If so, then a concrete stated usage, such as *debt retirement* or *stock repurchase*, would be more effective in reducing information asymmetry—and thus in reducing underpricing—than a relatively vague stated usage such as *general corporate purposes* or *working capital*.

To address this question empirically, we calculated median and average first-day returns on the stocks in each stated primary usage category. These results are also displayed in Table 12-3.

As expected, firms that stated *debt retirement* or *stock repurchase* as their primary usage of proceeds tended to have smaller first-day returns (i.e., were generally subject to less underpricing). The median first-day returns on the stocks of these firms were 6.6 percent and 4.0 percent respectively. On the other hand, firms that stated *general*

TABLE 12-3 Stated Primary Use of Proceeds and First-Day Return Statistics

IPOs of U.S. Nonfinancial Firms, 1991–2000

Stated Primary Use of Proceeds	All Firms				Non–VC-backed				VC-backed			
	Number of Firms	Percent of Firms	Median First-Day Return	Average First-Day Average	Number of Firms	Percent of Firms	Median First-Day Return	Average First-Day Return	Number of Firms	Percent of Firms	Median First-Day Return	Average First-Day Return
Acquisitions	141	3.8%	8.8%	18.2%	103	5.1%	7.1%	14.1%	38	2.2%	12.5%	29.2%
Capital investments[1]	80	2.1%	12.2%	27.5%	43	2.1%	9.1%	126.9%	37	2.2%	13.9%	28.0%
Debt retirement[2]	1,261	33.8%	6.6%	13.0%	820	40.6%	6.9%	12.9%	441	25.8%	6.3%	13.1%
General corporate purposes	2,026	54.4%	12.5%	31.3%	935	46.3%	10.0%	20.9%	1,091	63.9%	17.3%	40.2%
Product development[3]	40	1.1%	21.9%	44.8%	12	0.6%	17.3%	28.3%	28	1.6%	22.4%	51.9%
Stock repurchases[4]	66	1.8%	4.0%	8.9%	55	2.7%	4.7%	9.8%	11	0.6%	3.6%	4.5%
Working capital[5]	112	3.0%	31.6%	66.8%	50	2.5%	16.3%	37.1%	62	3.6%	54.5%	90.7%
All Uses	*3,726*	*100.0%*	*10.0%*	*25.3%*	*2,018*	*100.0%*	*8.6%*	*17.5*	*1,708*	*100.0%*	*13.0%*	*34.5%*

[1]Includes capital expenditures, project finance, and property acquisition categories.
[2]Includes leveraged buyout and recapitalization categories.
[3]Includes marketing and sales, product development, and R&D.
[4]Includes secondary, stock repurchases, and redemptions of Class A shares.
[5]Includes working capital, working funds, operating funds, and cash reserves.
Source: Raw data from Securities Data Corporation's new-issue database.

corporate purposes or *working capital* as their primary usage had much larger first-day returns: medians of 12.5 percent and 31.6 percent, respectively.

The above results pertain to the full sample. We repeated these analyses after separating the firms into two groups according to their VC-backing status. The results for each group of firms are reported in the remaining sections of the table. For both the non–VC-backed and VC-backed firms, the two most frequently stated primary uses of proceeds were *general corporate purposes* and *debt retirement*. Debt retirement was the primary stated purpose for a higher proportion of non–VC-backed firms (40.6 percent) than of VC-backed firms (25.8 percent), perhaps because, according to results reported in Table 12-2, non–VC-backed firms had higher modified debt ratios both before and after the offering.

Regarding underpricing, the evidence indicates that, for both non–VC-backed and VC-backed firms, underpricing was less severe for firms that stated *debt retirement* or *stock repurchase* as their primary use of proceeds, and more severe for firms that stated *general corporate purposes* or *working capital* as their primary use of proceeds.

12.5.4 A Regression Analysis of IPO Underpricing

Following up on both previous literature and some of our own empirical results reported above, we now conduct a closer examination of determinants of IPO underpricing, using multivariate regression analysis. The dependent variable in the regression is the first-day returns, in percent, on IPOs in our 1991 to 2000 sample. The independent variables include six continuous variables and nine zero-one (dummy) variables. The continuous variables are

- Most recent annual EPS
- Underwriter spread in percent, less the 7 percent standard spread
- The natural log of offering proceeds ($ million)
- Primary shares as a percent of total shares outstanding after the offering
- Secondary shares as a percent of total shares outstanding after the offering
- Insiders' shares as a percent of total shares outstanding after the offering

The zero-one variables are

- Listing market is NYSE or AMEX (= 1) versus NASDAQ/OTC (= 0)
- VC backing status (= 1 if the firm was backed by a VC; 0 otherwise)
- Acquisitions as primary use of proceeds
- Capital investments as primary use of proceeds
- Debt retirement as primary use of proceeds
- Product development as primary use of proceeds
- Stock repurchases as primary use of proceeds
- Working capital as primary use of proceeds

Note that we excluded the category *general corporate purposes* as an independent variable. We did this to avoid multicollinearity between the collective use categories and the regression intercept. As a result, the coefficients of the use categories are to be interpreted relative to the excluded category, as well as to each other.

The regression equation was estimated using 1,990 observations, the number of IPOs for which data was available for all variables. The results of the regression are displayed in Table 12-4.

TABLE 12-4   Results of a Regression of First-Day Percent Returns on IPOs against Indicated Explanatory Variables

U.S. Nonfinancial Firms, 1991–2000

Explanatory Variables	Coefficient	t-Statistic
Intercept	–71.73	–9.66
Continuous Variables		
Most recent annual EPS	–1.84	–2.93
Underwriter spread less 7%	15.45	8.63
ln(Proceeds, $ million)	27.19	15.22
Primary shares as % of total shares outstanding after offering	–0.10	–3.99
Secondary shares as % of total shares outstanding after offering	–0.13	–1.58
Insiders' shares as % of total shares outstanding after offering	0.17	2.81
Zero-One (Dummy) Variables		
Listing market is NYSE or AMEX (= 1) vs. NASDAQ/OTC (= 0)	–27.26	–5.55
VC backing status (= 1 if the firm was backed by a VC; else 0)	11.87	4.46
Acquisitions as primary use of proceeds*	–5.99	–0.86
Capital investments as primary use of proceeds*	–7.73	–0.90
Debt retirement as primary use of proceeds*	–17.89	–6.32
Product development as primary use of proceeds*	–4.67	–0.49
Stock repurchases as primary use of proceeds*	–22.02	–1.89
Working capital as primary use of proceeds*	37.19	5.31

Number of Observations = 1,990; Adjusted R^2 = 21.4%;
Mean of Dependent Variable = 32.2%

The primary use category "general corporate purposes" was excluded from the regression, so the coefficients for the other use categories are to be interpreted relative to this excluded category.
Source: Raw data from Securities Data Corporation's new-issue database.

The coefficients of most of the independent variables are statistically significant based on the reported t-statistics, and the adjusted R^2 is fairly substantial at 21.4 percent. Next, we interpret the coefficients of each independent variable.

Coefficients of the Continuous Variables

First, the coefficient of the recent-EPS variable is negative and statistically significant, indicating that firms with lower EPS tend to be subject to greater underpricing. This result suggests that, for the more speculative IPO stocks (e.g., stocks that have not yet shown profits), a greater price concession must be made to investors who purchase at the offering, either as simply a reward for greater risk or perhaps also because these firms are also subject to greater value uncertainty related to information asymmetry.

Second, the coefficient of the underwriter spread variable is positive and statistically significant, indicating that firms that incur higher underwriting fees are more substantially underpriced at the offering. The relationship here is probably indirect. If either principal–agent or information asymmetry problems are more severe for one firm than for another, that firm will probably incur both greater underwriting costs (perhaps in part because the underwriters will have a harder time placing the stock in the market) and a more substantial pricing concession at the offering.

Third, the coefficient of the log of proceeds variable is positive and statistically significant. This result suggests that larger offerings are harder to place in the market, and thus are associated with greater pricing concessions.

Fourth and *fifth*, the coefficients of both the primary and secondary shares variables are negative and the former is statistically significant. The coefficients are similar in magnitude. These results suggest that firms that offer lower proportions of their total (postoffering) shares to the market are subject to greater underpricing. These results are puzzling, and seem at odds with the results for the proceeds variable, which bears a positive coefficient. However, the results are more sensible if we consider reversing the direction of causality. Suppose a firm comes to realize in advance that its shares will be severely underpriced at the offering. It is likely to respond (to the extent that it can respond shortly before the offering date) by offering fewer primary shares to the market, perhaps hoping to issue more shares later at a more favorable price. Likewise, existing shareholders may offer fewer shares in the secondary portion of the offering to the extent that the shares will be subject to substantial underpricing.

Sixth, the coefficient of the insiders' shares variable is positive and statistically significant. To the extent that a firm's insiders will be holding a greater proportion of the firm's total shares after the offering, the firm's stock tends to be more underpriced. This result seems to be inconsistent with arguments based on both agency and information asymmetry theories, which suggest that the value of a firm's shares should be positively related to the proportion of shares held by insiders. On the other hand, the results are consistent with an argument that, if fewer shares of a firm's stock are free-floating in the aftermarket (i.e., because insiders are holding them), the shares will be less liquid, and therefore may be subject to greater underpricing.

Coefficients of the Zero-One Variables

The coefficient of the first zero-one variable, listing market, is negative and significant. Its value, –27.26, can be interpreted directly as indicating that, after controlling for all of the other independent variables in the regression, if the firm is listing on either the NYSE or AMEX (as opposed to the NASDAQ or OTC markets), its first-day return will be 27.26 percent *lower*; that is, it is subject to much less underpricing.

We know from the results shown in Figure 12-2 that firms listing on the NYSE or AMEX are much larger than those listing on the NASDAQ/OTC markets; that is, NYSE/AMEX IPOs tend to be larger, and thus probably less risky. As a result, they are probably less exposed to the cited factors that lead to underpricing This interpretation is consistent with our earlier evidence indicating that NYSE and AMEX IPOs also enjoy lower underwriter spreads. Alternatively, the relationship may be a consequence of differences in the underwriting procedures associated with listing on one market versus another, or other differences in the characteristics of firms who choose to list on the major exchanges versus the NASDAQ/OTC.

The coefficient of the second zero-one variable, the firm's VC-backing status, is positive and significant. Its value, 11.87, indicates that if the firm was backed by a VC, its underpricing will be 11.87 percent *greater*, on average. (These results are consistent with those shown in Figure 12-3.) This result is not consistent with the argument that VCs can more successfully *negotiate* a higher price for the firm's stock at the offering. Nor is the result consistent with the argument that VCs can successfully *certify* a new issue in order to avoid underpricing related to information asymmetry. Instead, the result is consistent with the argument that VCs are aggressive in pushing a backed venture toward IPO status, and are perhaps more willing than insiders and other investors in non–VC-backed firms to accept a substantial price concession at the offering.

The remaining zero-one variables represent firms' stated primary use of proceeds. Only the coefficients of *debt retirement*, *stock repurchases*, and *working capital* are statistically significant. The negative coefficients for the first two variables are consistent with results in Table 12-3 indicating that firms that state either of these purposes are subject to less underpricing. The positive coefficient for the working capital variable suggests that stating this purpose does not serve well to mitigate the information asymmetry problem.

12.5.5   Returns in the Aftermarket: The Post-IPO Underperformance Anomaly

Another well-documented anomaly associated with IPOs is evidence that IPOs *underperform* other stocks in the aftermarket for up to three years. In this subsection, we document evidence of this anomaly using our 1991 to 2000 sample. In the next subsection, we review literature that attempts to explain this anomaly.

Figure 12-4 shows the cross-sectional distribution of *first-year returns*, excluding first-day returns, on the IPOs in our non–VC-backed and VC-backed subsamples. In many respects, these results parallel the results for first-day returns shown in Figure

FIGURE 12-4   Distributions of First-Year Returns on IPOs Excluding First-Day Return

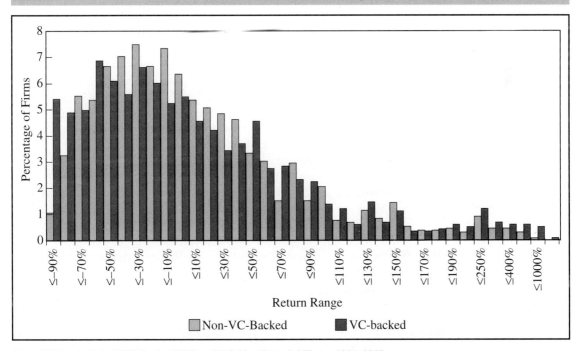

Non–VC-Backed and VC-Backed IPOs of U.S. Nonfinancial Firms, 1991–2000

VC Backed?	Av. %	Med. %	S.D. %
No (1,323)	6.0	–10.9	77.1
Yes (1,167)	9.3	–14.0	105.9

Source: Raw data from Securities Data Corporations' new-issue database.

12-3. The distributions exhibit tremendous variation and skewness. First-year returns on non–VC-backed stocks range from –98.2 percent to 823.5 percent, while the corresponding range for the VC-backed stocks is from –99.2 percent to 1,271.3 percent. The VC-backed stocks have a slightly higher average first-year return, 9.3 percent versus 6.0 percent for the non–VC-backed firms. Again, due to skewness the median first-year returns are much lower, –14.0 percent and –10.9 percent, respectively. And again, the VC-backed stocks appear to be more risky, exhibiting a return standard deviation of 105.9 percent, versus 77.1 percent for the non–VC-backed stocks.

Detailed Return Histories

Next, we extend the results shown in Figures 12-3 and 12-4 by providing detailed histories of the realized returns on IPOs through the first year. We computed both average and median returns on IPOs for various investment horizons relative to the offering date, including the first day as well as one week, one month, six months, and one year after the offering. Further, we work with both raw returns and returns in excess of the contemporaneous returns on the NASDAQ composite index, which we view as an appropriate benchmark index because it is more representative of small firms than, say, the S&P 500 index. Return statistics are computed for all firms, as well as separately for non–VC-backed and VC-backed firms. Finally, cumulative returns are calculated both *including* and *excluding* the first-day return. The results of these calculations are displayed in Table 12-5. The upper panel of the table shows cumulative returns that include the first day; the lower panel shows cumulative returns that exclude the first day.

Average first-day raw returns are 25.3, 17.5, and 34.5 percent for all firms, non–VC-backed firms, and VC-backed firms, respectively. After the first day, average cumulative returns tend to rise with the return horizon, ultimately resulting in average one-year average cumulative returns of 31.2, 22.3, and 42.2 percent for all firms, non–VC-backed firms, and VC-backed firms, respectively. The gap between the average returns on the non–VC-backed and VC-backed stocks, 17.0 percent (= 34.5 percent – 17.5 percent) after the first day, increases only slightly to 19.9 percent (= 42.2 percent – 22.3 percent) at the one-year horizon.

The median raw return statistics, shown in the next three rows of the upper panel, differ markedly, and in two respects, from the corresponding average returns. *First*, median first-day returns are lower: 10.0, 8.6, and 13.0 percent for all firms, non–VC-backed firms, and VC-backed firms, respectively. As we discussed earlier, median returns are much lower than average returns because of the tremendous skewness of the cross-sectional distributions of first-day IPO returns.

Second, for both subsamples as well as all firms, median cumulative returns do not rise uniformly with the return horizon. For all groups of firms, median one-year cumulative returns are actually *lower* than the median first-day returns! These results (vaguely) suggest that the typical IPO firm actually provides *negative returns* for the year after the first day!

The third and fourth sections of the upper panel display corresponding results in terms of NASDAQ index-adjusted returns. The adjustment has little effect on the average and median first-day returns, because the average one-day return on the NASDAQ index is very small (about 10 basis points). However, adjusting for the NASDAQ index return has a larger and larger impact on the performances of the sampled firms

TABLE 12-5   Cumulative Return Statistics on IPOs, Sorted by VC-Backing Status

U.S. Nonfinancial Firms, 1991–2000

VC Backed?*	Return Type, %	Statistic	Return Horizon				
			1 day	1 week	1 month	6 months	1 year
RETURNS *INCLUDE* FIRST-DAY RETURN							
All	Raw Return	Average	25.3	25.6	32.2	36.5	31.2
No	Raw Return	Average	17.5	17.5	20.6	25.3	22.3
Yes	Raw Return	Average	34.5	35.2	46.0	50.1	42.2
All	Raw Return	Median	10.0	9.4	14.3	13.0	3.1
No	Raw Return	Median	8.6	8.0	10.7	10.7	3.1
Yes	Raw Return	Median	13.0	12.5	20.8	16.8	3.5
All	Raw Return – Return on NASDAQ	Average	25.6	25.3	30.9	27.7	13.9
No	Raw Return – Return on NASDAQ	Average	16.9	17.2	19.3	16.1	2.2
Yes	Raw Return – Return on NASDAQ	Average	35.9	34.9	44.6	41.6	28.1
All	Raw Return – Return on NASDAQ	Median	9.9	9.1	13.5	6.8	−11.8
No	Raw Return – Return on NASDAQ	Median	8.4	7.3	10.1	3.4	−14.2
Yes	Raw Return – Return on NASDAQ	Median	13.3	12.9	19.4	12.3	−8.2
RETURNS *EXCLUDE* FIRST-DAY RETURN							
All	Raw Return	Average	—	0.1	4.7	9.6	7.4
No	Raw Return	Average	—	−0.1	2.3	7.2	6.0
Yes	Raw Return	Average	—	0.2	7.6	12.5	9.2
All	Raw Return	Median	—	0.0	0.7	−2.1	9.8
No	Raw Return	Median	—	0.0	0.0	−1.2	−7.9
Yes	Raw Return	Median	—	−0.5	2.2	−3.7	−12.3
All	Raw Return – Return on NASDAQ	Average	—	−0.1	3.3	1.5	−8.7
No	Raw Return – Return on NASDAQ	Average	—	−0.2	1.2	−1.0	−12.6
Yes	Raw Return – Return on NASDAQ	Average	—	0.1	6.0	4.5	−3.9
All	Raw Return – Return on NASDAQ	Median	—	−0.9	0.4	−8.9	−24.6
No	Raw Return – Return on NASDAQ	Median	—	−0.9	−0.2	−8.7	−24.7
Yes	Raw Return – Return on NASDAQ	Median	—	−1.0	1.5	−9.0	−23.9

Non–VC-Backed and VC-backed samples include 2,018 and 1,708 observations, respectively, for a total of 3,726 IPOs. However, not all IPO firms survived for one year, due to acquisition, bankruptcy, etc.

Source: Raw data from Securities Data Corporation's new-issue database.

as the investment horizon increases. As a result, average one-year adjusted returns are 13.9, 2.2, and 28.1 percent for all firms, non–VC-backed firms, and VC-backed firms, respectively, while the corresponding median one-year adjusted returns are −11.8, −14.2, and −8.2 percent, respectively.

In summary, assuming that an investor could purchase an IPO stock at its offering price, the *average* return exceeds the return on the NASDAQ index, especially for VC-backed firms. However, judging from the *median* statistics, the typical experience of such an investor would be that an IPO tends to underperform relative to the NASDAQ index, especially for non–VC-backed firms.

What would an investor's returns be if he or she could not obtain the stock at its offer price, and instead purchased it as it began trading in the secondary market? The statistics displayed in the lower panel of the table address this question. Shown are cumulative raw and NASDAQ index-adjusted returns for up to one year, but excluding the first-day return. The numbers are consistently and substantially lower than the corresponding values shown in the upper panel. For instance, the *average* one-year index-adjusted returns are –8.7, –12.6, and –3.9 percent for all firms, non–VC-backed firms, and VC-backed firms, respectively, while the corresponding *median* one-year index-adjusted returns are –24.6, –24.7, and –23.9 percent, respectively!

12.5.6 Explanations for Poor Post-IPO Performance

Various studies have provided evidence that the post-IPO performance of firms is quite poor for as long as three to five years. These studies show that over this time period average returns have been only 3 percent to 5 percent per year. (See Ritter 1991, and Loughran and Ritter 1995.)

Recently, Brav and Gompers (1997) explored this anomaly empirically. They found that the longer-term underperformance of IPO firms is not related to their IPO status, but to their status as *small firms*:

> [T]he long-run underperformance of recent initial public offering (IPO) firms in a sample of 934 venture-backed IPOs from 1972 to 1992 and 3,407 non–VC-backed IPOs from 1975 to 1992 . . . [shows] that venture-backed IPOs outperform non–VC-backed IPOs using equal weighted returns. Value weighting significantly reduces performance differences and substantially reduces underperformance for non–VC-backed IPOs. In tests using several comparable benchmarks and the Fama-French (1993) three-factor asset pricing model, venture-backed companies do not significantly underperform, while the smallest non–VC-backed firms do. Underperformance, however, is not an IPO effect. Similar size and book-to-market firms that have not issued equity perform as poorly as IPOs. (p. 1791)

12.6 UNIT IPOS

In this section, we focus on firms that go public via a *unit IPO*. The unit consists of a share of stock and one or more warrants that give the investor the right to purchase additional shares at a later date at a specified price. Shortly after the offering, the shares and warrants begin trading as separate securities.

In the first subsection, we discuss two rationales for some firms' use of unit IPOs. In the second subsection, we contrast the characteristics of firms that employ a unit in their IPO with those of firms that go public via shares only. In the third subsection, we briefly discuss details of the warrant portion of a unit IPO and associated statistics.

12.6.1 Two Rationales for Going Public via Units

Schultz (1993) argued that unit IPOs are a form of staged financing that can mitigate a particular *principal–agent problem*. If the firm receives more funds at the IPO than it needs to pursue all profitable investments, the firm's management will tend to squander the excess. But with a unit IPO, management receives only as much as it needs immediately, with the promise that they can raise new funds later, via the warrants.

Chemmanur and Fulghieri (1997) argued that the unit IPO package is an effective signal of the firm's value under conditions of severe information asymmetry. Their argument has the added feature that it explains why only high-risk firms offer units, while lower-risk firms go public with stock only. Consider two firms, G and B, which are indistinguishable to investors. In truth, though, firm G is a high-risk firm that also has high expected cash flows, and firm B is a low-risk firm with low expected cash flows. It is assumed that the insiders of both firms are risk averse.

If both firms issue warrants, the warrants of firm G will have a higher *true* value, both because firm G has higher expected cash flows and because the variance of firm G's underlying assets, against which the warrants are written, is higher. It would seem unwise for firm G to issue warrants because they receive the same proceeds from their issuance and yet they have a greater (true) dollar value in the market. However, because of their risk aversion, the two firms' insiders' may assign very different *private valuations* to the warrants. Specifically, firm G's insiders may assign a lower private value to the warrants precisely because they are attached to a more risky underlying asset. If the difference in private value dominates the difference in market value, the warrants will be less costly for the insiders of firm G than for the insiders of firm B. Thus, firm G's issuance of warrants is an effective signal.

12.6.2 Characteristics of Firms That Offer Unit IPOs

To illustrate the types of firms that offer units in their IPO, we compared the characteristics of 438 U.S. nonfinancial firms that completed unit IPOs in the years 1991 to 2000 with 3,923 firms that completed stock-only IPOs during the same period. The results are displayed in Table 12-6.

Here, we highlight the indicated differences for unit IPO firms.

1. They are younger, smaller firms, raising much less capital in the IPO.
2. They are less likely to list on the NYSE or AMEX.
3. They are much less likely to be VC-backed.
4. They generally pay an underwriter spread of 10 percent rather than the standard 7 percent.
5. They are associated with a longer lockup period, though a smaller percentage of shares are subject to lockup.
6. They are more highly levered and less profitable prior to the offering.
7. They are less likely to state *debt retirement* as the primary use of proceeds (despite the fact that they tend to have higher leverage); instead, they are more likely to cite *general corporate purposes*.

12.6.3 Warrant Details

Finally, we examine various features of the units in the 438 unit IPOs completed in the period 1991 to 2000. The results are displayed in Table 12-7. The upper panel of the table documents statistics on the numbers of shares and warrants offered in the units, and the lower panel documents details of the terms associated with the warrants.

As for the number of shares that are offered in each unit, in almost three-fourths of the cases a single share is included, though about one in five units includes two

TABLE 12-6   Comparing the Features of 438 Unit IPOs with 3,923 Stock-Only IPOs

U.S. Nonfinancial Firms, 1991–2000

Firm and Offering Statistics	Units	Stock Only
Firm age: average years between firm founding and IPO offer date	5.3	7.6
Median total assets after offering ($ million)	$7.2	$52.8
Average offer price	$5.4	$12.2
Median proceeds of offering ($ million)	$6	$35
Percentage of firms listing on NYSE or AMEX	3.9%	13.2%
Percentage of firms that are VC-backed	14.2%	45.4%
Median underwriter spread, %	10.0%	7.0%
Average primary shares as a percentage of total shares offered	98.9%	89.7%
Average primary shares as a percentage of total shares outstanding after offering	40.1%	32.2%
Average secondary shares as a percentage of total shares outstanding after offering	44.5%	4.4%
Average ratio of shares held by insiders to total shares outstanding *before* offering	64.3%	64.0%
Average ratio of shares held by insiders to total shares outstanding *after* offering	40.0%	44.9%
Median % of shares subject to lockup	48.9%	59.6%
Median days in lockup	390	180
Percentage of deals with overallotment option	97.9%	99.6%
Financial Statistics		
Median modified debt ratio *before* offering	94.6%	79.5%
Median modified debt ratio *after* offering	21.3%	29.5%
Median EPS before offering		
Last year before	–0.285	0.06
2 years before	–0.2	0.03
3 years before	–0.11	–0.01
Median market-to-book equity ratio	3.1	3.1
Median P/E	–3.6	10.5
Primary Use of Proceeds (% of Firms)		
Acquisitions	2.3%	3.7%
Capital expenditures	1.8%	2.2%
Debt retirement	19.9%	33.9%
General corporate purposes	73.5%	54.4%
Product development	1.4%	1.1%
Stock repurchases	0.2%	1.7%
Working capital	0.9%	3.0%
Sum of Primary Use Percentages	100.0%	100.0%

Source: Raw data from Securities Data Corporation's new-issue database.

shares and 1 in 20 include three or more shares. Among those that include a single share, the unit also typically includes a single warrant, though in some cases either a half-warrant (i.e., two such half-warrants are required to purchase an additional share of stock) or two warrants are included. For those that include two or more shares, the number of warrants included also tends to increase, though not proportionately with the increase in shares.

TABLE 12-7 Statistics on Shares and Warrants Offered in 438 Unit IPOs

U.S. Nonfinancial Firms, 1991–2000

			Number of Warrants Offered		
Shares and Warrants Offered in Unit					
	Number of Firms	**% of Firms**	AVERAGE	MINIMUM	MAXIMUM
Units offering 1 share	320	73.1%	1.0	0.5	2.0
Units offering 2 shares	96	21.9%	1.3	1.0	2.0
Units offering 3 or more shares	22	5.0%	1.9	1.0	4.0

Warrant Details

	AVERAGE	MINIMUM	MAXIMUM
Warrant exercise price: percent excess over per-share unit price	16.0	0.0	200.3
Deferment paid before warrants can be exercised (years)	0.5	0.0	5.3
Years until warrants can be detached	0.2	0.0	2.0
Years until warrants are callable by issuing firm	1.0	0.1	5.0
Years to expiration of warrant	4.2	1.0	7.0

Source: Raw data from Securities Data Corporation's new-issue database.

As for the warrants, several details are relevant. *First*, the typical warrant is substantially out-of-the-money. On average, the exercise price is 16 percent higher than the per-share unit price. *Second*, a deferment period is included in some, though not most, warrant contracts, which specifies a period (on average, six months) before the warrants can be exercised. *Third*, some, though again not most, warrant contracts specify a delay period before which the investor can detach, and separately sell, the attached warrant(s). *Fourth*, most warrants are also *callable* by the firm. That is, the firm can call the warrants, at which time the investor must either exercise the warrant or, generally, receive a nominal cash payment. *Fifth*, on average warrants expire after 4.2 years, though the range is one to seven years.

12.7 Summary of Learning Objectives

In the first portion of this chapter, we briefly discussed the costs and benefits of going public. We also briefly discussed the characteristics of large firms in the United States that have chosen to remain private. The bulk of the chapter, however, focused on IPOs. We provided a detailed analysis of the process by which a firm goes public via an IPO. We also discussed the pricing of IPO stocks and their short-term and longer-term return performance. First-day returns are very high, on average, but also extremely volatile. Longer-term returns are also extremely volatile, but are poor, on average. Finally, we discussed the *unit IPO*, in which the issuing firm offers a unit consisting of both stock and warrants. Units are generally offered by very small, high-risk firms.

Review Questions and Problems

1. Discuss the benefits and costs of going public.
2. Discuss the details of the IPO process, including various decisions that are involved.

3. What are the advantages and disadvantages for a firm's management and investors of going public versus staying private?
4. Nutrition, Inc., a vitamin supplement manufacturer, is financed entirely with equity that is currently privately owned by its managers. The firm is expected to generate earnings of $5 million per year into perpetuity, and all earnings are paid out in dividends. The owner-managers receive no additional compensation. For all owner-managers, shares of the firm's equity accounts for the bulk of their personal wealth. As a result, in determining their personal valuation of the firm they apply a high discount rate of 33 percent to their future expected dividends, and therefore they value the firm at $15.15 million (= $5 million/0.33). The firm's management team has recently consulted with an investment-banking firm about selling all of the firm's equity publicly; that is, about *going public* with the firm's shares. Assuming that the current management will continue to operate the firm, the investment banking firm estimates that the market will value the firm's equity by applying a 25 percent discount rate to expected future dividends. However, expected dividends to public shareholders will be only $4 million, because managers will now be paid a total of $1 million per year in salaries. Ignoring taxes and transaction costs,
   a. what will be the market value of the firm's public shares?
   b. accounting for both the present value of management's salaries and the proceeds from the public sale of shares, what is your estimate of management's wealth gain from going public?
5. Why is it necessary, and perhaps even desirable, to underprice an IPO?
6. What is the principal factor that determines whether a firm will choose the *best efforts* method versus the *firm commitment* method to market its IPO?
7. Discuss the theories that have been suggested to explain empirical evidence that IPOs are initially underpriced. Are these arguments persuasive?
8. According to evidence discussed in the text, what factors appear to affect the degree of underpricing of an IPO?
9. Explain the rationale for share lockups following an IPO.
10. Define a unit IPO, and discuss two rationales for their use.

Creative Thinking Issues

1. Why do so many large and profitable U.S. firms remain private?
2. Do you think that direct IPOs via the Internet will be a viable means by which firms can go public?
3. Critique the following alternative explanation for the underpricing of IPOs. The owners of the IPO firm tend to be the firm's original entrepreneurs as well as its managers. The bulk of their personal wealth is tied up in the single, illiquid investment that is their firm, so the value they place on the firm's shares is much lower than the market value of the firm. Consequently, they are simply willing to accept a relatively low price for the firm's shares.

Projects and Analyses

1. Calculate and analyze the first-day returns and longer-term returns on a sample of recent IPOs.
2. Generate a detailed report on the experience of a firm that recently conducted an IPO.

CHAPTER

Managing Internal Equity and Seasoned Equity Offerings

13

13.1 INTRODUCTION

In this chapter and the next, we focus on decisions that relate most directly to the management of the firm's *equity*. This chapter covers three such topics. *First*, we provide a basic theoretical perspective on the management of a firm's internal equity. *Second*, we discuss the concept of the firm's *internal capital market*, wherein the firm allocates its available internal funds to projects. *Third*, we discuss the decision of the management of a publicly traded firm to issue additional equity. In Chapter 14, we discuss the closely related topics of a firm's dividend and stock repurchase policies.

This chapter is organized as follows. In Section 13.2, we provide a perspective that is useful for the analysis of a firm's financial decisions—we call it the *equity management perspective*. In Section 13.3, we introduce and discuss the theory of an internal capital market. In Sections 13.4 to 13.7, we discuss the process by which a firm issues seasoned equity, its affects on the firm's value, and related issues. Section 13.8 summarizes the chapter's learning objectives.

13.2 THE EQUITY MANAGEMENT PERSPECTIVE

Ultimately, a firm's financial policies and strategies revolve around the management of the firm's *equity*. Therefore, a useful approach to studying corporate financial policies and strategies overall is to focus on managerial decisions that directly affect the firm's equity. In this *equity management* approach, management seeks to control both the firm's book and market equity values, considering the effects of various operating and financing decisions on the levels of both over time. (Even though the management's prime directive is to maximize the *market value* of the firm's equity, for practical reasons management must devote considerable time and effort into managing the firm's *book equity*.)

13.2.1 An Equity Management Model

Figure 13-1 displays a basic equity management model for a publicly traded firm. This model is based on Myers (2000). In this depiction, the firm is formed of two basic inputs: accumulated equity, which is shareholders' input, and operational skills, management's input. These inputs are the respective party's *property*, and each expects a return on the property that they contribute to the firm. Overall returns each period consist of the firm's generated net cash flow, which is net of all expenses including *normal* salaries for the firm's managers. Note that this model ignores external financing, whether from a seasoned equity offering (SEO) or a sale of debt securities. This is a reasonable approximation to reality because, as we found in Chapter 1, firms generally finance their expenditures over time with retained earnings (review Figures 1-4a and 1-4b).

FIGURE 13-1   An Equity Management Model for a Public Firm

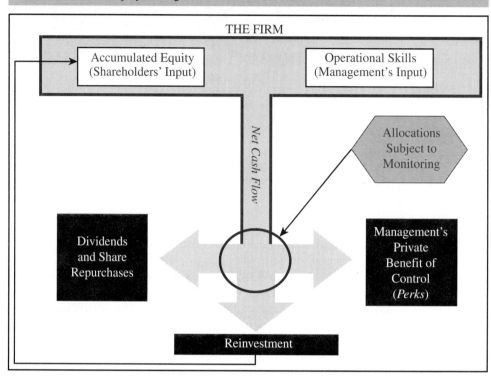

Source: Based on Myers (2000).

In the model, the firm's net cash flow is allocated in three directions: (a) dividends and stock repurchases, (b) reinvestment, and (c) management's *private benefits of control* (i.e., perks). Dividends and stock repurchases are cash returns to the firm's continuing and exiting shareholders, respectively. Reinvestment refers to retained cash flow that is *genuinely* reinvested in new projects. Reinvested funds become the property of continuing shareholders, as indicated by the feedback arrow. Finally, managers may be able to direct a portion of the firm's cash flow to themselves, thereby extracting private benefits.

13.2.2   The Contracting Problem

In this model, the basic contracting problem derives from that fact that the firm's shareholders are a diffuse group, so their exercise of control is costly. Thus, the firm's managers have some slack that allows them to extract private benefits. Mechanisms must be put in place to limit managers' ability to extract such rents, or else the firm's shareholders will eventually withdraw their equity contribution (i.e., they will fire management). Three such mechanisms are prevalent, though all of them are imperfect: (a) requiring the regular payment of dividends (or perhaps requiring stock repurchases), (b) monitoring the firm's allocation of net cash flow, and (c) incentive-aligning provisions in managers' compensation contracts. We discuss each of these mechanisms in turn.

13.2.3 Imperfect Solution 1: Dividends

Shareholders can demand that the firm's management pay dividends on a regular basis. Jensen (1986) suggested this solution within the context of his *Free Cash Flow Hypothesis*. Dividend payouts reduce the amount of cash that managers can use to provide themselves private benefits. More recently, Zwiebel (1996), Warther (1997), and Myers (2000) argue that management will pay dividends that are just sufficient to ward off intervention by outside investors. The optimal dividend in this respect depends on (a) the value added by the firm's management, (b) costs to outsiders of organizing to take control of the firm, and (c) the fraction of shares held by insiders.

Dividends are costly if the firm's shareholders are subject to taxation, because dividends are taxed as ordinary income. Some researchers have argued that *stock repurchases* can serve the same purpose as dividends in terms of disgorging excess cash. Stock repurchases can be less expensive if exiting shareholders face a lower tax rate on realized capital gains than continuing shareholders face on dividends. We discuss a firm's dividend and stock repurchase policies in more detail in Chapter 14.

13.2.4 Imperfect Solution 2: Monitoring

Regardless of whether the firm pays dividends, outside shareholders must *monitor* the disposition of the firm's net cash flow. One means by which monitoring is accomplished in a diffusely held public firm is management's (legally required) disclosure via periodic financial statements that are independently audited for accuracy. The Federal Accounting Standards Board (FASB) is the leading promulgator of accounting standards and procedures in the United States. These standards and procedures limit, but do not eliminate, management's ability to divert cash flow to their private benefit, at least without the firm's shareholders knowing about it.

However, monitoring via disclosure is also an imperfect solution to the contracting problem, as Myers (2000) explains.

> The first purpose of monitoring is . . . to confirm whether and when investments are made. Absent monitoring, positive-NPV investments are passed by. If monitoring can confirm investment, thereby ruling out excess consumption by insiders and allowing most (of the cost of a new investment) to be financed by dividends foregone, then all positive-NPV investments will be made . . .
>
> When ownership is dispersed and costs of collective action are important, monitoring should occur each period without triggering costs of collective action. So insiders and outside equity would agree at startup to operate a delegated monitoring system. Monitoring cannot be done by insiders, and dispersed outside investors cannot monitor efficiently on their own. For example, accountants can be hired and given rules for distinguishing the purchase and sale of assets from operating costs and revenues.
>
> Once established, such monitoring procedures inevitably lead to agency costs. There are two reasons. First, monitoring of investment cannot be perfect, because the monitor needs to know the purpose of expenditure. (For example, is the retention of well-paid managers with allegedly special skills an investment for "long-run competitive strength" or private benefits to

insiders? Does absorption of operating losses from a struggling division amount to investment to retain a valuable call option on revenues from the division's markets, or just protection for the division's workers and managers?) Wherever there is a fuzzy line between expenditure to create value for outsiders and outlays captured by insiders, the insiders have a strong incentive not to invest but consume. But they have to find ways to consume that are not obvious. Thus they seek private benefits of control, such as perks or overemployment.

Second, once procedures to monitor investment are set up, they can also be used *at relatively low marginal cost* to reduce insiders' capture of operating cash flow. In other words, monitoring may be used not only to confirm new investment, but also to prevent insiders from taking their "fair share" of cash flows generated by assets in place. Again, insiders will try to limit the value reachable by outsiders or to hide cash they would rather consume in private benefits of control.

Thus traditional agency costs seem unavoidable. Because the act of investment is frequently non-verifiable, monitoring is necessarily imperfect, but also indispensable if the firm's growth opportunities are valuable. But monitoring cannot be designed or operated to protect assets-in-place only. It has to watch how cash flows are used. In many cases the purposes of expenditure will not be obvious: Apparent investments may actually benefit insiders, and operating costs may actually be investments. . . . (pp. 1031–1032)

To the two reasons cited by Myers for the development of agency costs of monitoring, we add a third: *bribing the monitor*. Management has an incentive to bribe a monitor to overlook managements' self-serving activities, because a successful bribe allows management to retain private benefits of control (net of the amount of the bribe). In the wake of the recent Enron Corp. scandal that has embroiled the Big 5 accounting firm Arthur Andersen LLP, the Securities and Exchange Commission (SEC) is presently considering a proposal to prohibit an auditor from receiving consulting fees from a firm that they audit. Critics equate such consulting fees to bribes.

13.2.5 Imperfect Solution 3: Incentive Compensation

We discussed the evolution of executive compensation contracts in Chapter 8. Critical terms in executive compensation contracts—namely earnings-based bonuses, stock and stock-option grants, and long-term performance incentives—are designed to solve the contracting problem between managers and outside equity-holders. But this solution is imperfect as well, as Myers (2000) explains: "Ideally these would give managers the correct fraction of cash flows from assets in place. Then monitoring which prevented insiders from taking additional cash or private benefits would also assure the right investment decisions. But such schemes can't work perfectly. For example, the cash given in each period to insiders should depend on the net present values (*NPV*s) of that period's investment opportunities, because insiders coinvest in new assets by cutting back their capture of cash flow. But the *NPV*s are not verifiable, and usually not knowable by outside investors or monitors" (p. 1033).

13.3   INTERNAL CAPITAL MARKET THEORY

In this section, we explain the theory that many firms essentially operate an *internal capital market*. To some extent, the theory is an enrichment, via modern finance theory, of a more traditional paradigm—*capital budgeting*.

13.3.1   The Traditional Capital Budgeting Paradigm

The traditional capital budgeting paradigm has two elements. The first element consists of the rule or rules by which a firm's management determines whether an individual proposed project is profitable. For instance, the firm may define any project that has a positive *NPV* as profitable.

The second element consists of the method by which management chooses from among alternative profitable projects if circumstances are such that some profitable projects cannot be pursued due to the firm's limited internal capital. For instance, management might select that feasible set of projects which has the highest total *NPV*. Note that this element rests on the assumption that the firm's capital budget is limited to its available internal funds—external financing is not an option. If in a given year the firm's budget is insufficient to fund all profitable projects, management must engage in *capital rationing*.

13.3.2   Limitations of the Traditional Capital Budgeting Paradigm

The traditional capital budgeting paradigm is empirically supported in two respects. *First*, virtually all major firms practice the first element of the paradigm (the financial evaluation of proposed projects) and, as necessary, the second element (capital rationing). *Second*, from the composite sources and uses figures presented in Chapter 1 (review Figures 1-4a and 1-4b), we know that U.S. nonfinancial firms generally obtain the bulk of their funds for expansion from internal equity (retained earnings). External debt and equity financing are at best minor net sources of funds for the typical nonfinancial firm.

At the same time, the traditional capital budgeting paradigm leaves several important questions unanswered, such as the following.

Why Do Some Firms Have Multiple Activities?
The very existence of a multiple-activity firm is open to question. The question raises bedrock issues, pitting the *raison d'être* of a firm against the *raison d'être* of external capital markets. For instance, why do some firms operate in only a single business segment, while others have multiple segments? Under what conditions would it be optimal for a firm to pursue an activity internally versus outsourcing the activity to an independent firm?

Why Is the Capital Budget Limited?
Why would a firm not simply pursue any and all positive-*NPV* projects, even if at times the firm must raise external debt or equity capital, or suspend dividends, to do so? The traditional paradigm provides no formal answer to this question, save perhaps that (a) external financing is *costly*, or (b) management tends to have more optimistic views about projects than shareholders, and a limited budget is a way to discipline management into accepting only the highest NPV projects.

How Is Information about a Proposed Project Obtained?

Regarding the details of the capital budgeting process, basic corporate finance textbooks generally provide at least a cursory treatment of methods of estimating the cash flows and discount rate for a proposed project, and computing its *NPV*. However, little is said about who in the organization ultimately generates these estimates. As we discuss later, this is a problem if the person estimating a project's profitability stands to gain personally by exaggerating its profitability.

What Are the Roles of Headquarters and Division Managers?

The traditional capital budgeting paradigm does not suggest if, when, why, or how senior managers at the firm's headquarters or the division managers are involved in the process. In some multidivisional firms, senior management makes all final decisions regarding the allocation of the firm's capital budget, while in others these decisions are delegated to division managers. If a specific, objective criterion such as *NPV* is established for accepting or rejecting a project, this criterion could be communicated to all managers who have proposed projects, and presumably they can decide for themselves whether a project should be funded, assuming that funds are available. Should senior managers intervene only when capital rationing is involved?

13.3.3 Internal Capital Market Theory: Underpinnings

An internal capital market is defined as a system that a firm's senior management uses to determine the allocation of the firm's limited available internal equity capital among competing projects developed by managers within the firm's hierarchy. The theory of the internal capital market has developed in recent years to address the questions we have raised, as well as others. The theory helps us to better understand both (a) the existence of multisegment firms and (b) their capital budgeting practices. In several respects, the theory is well rooted in both agency and information asymmetry theories, as we explain next.

An Internal Capital Market May Dominate the External Capital Market

As a backdrop to the theory, we recognize that both agency and information asymmetry theories explain why a firm, in pursuing capital investments, is generally constrained to its internally generated cash (review discussions in Chapters 3 and 4). For instance, external *debt* financing is problematic because a conflict of interest arises between the borrowing firm and its creditors. External *equity* financing is problematic because of the information asymmetry problem.

Gertner, Scharfstein and Stein (1994) provide two additional reasons why an internal capital market, managed by a firm's headquarters, may be superior to external financing (e.g., from a bank).

> ***Increased monitoring incentives.*** Even if internal and external providers of capital have the same ability to monitor, internal providers will choose to monitor more intensely. This is because they have residual control over the assets, and therefore get more of the gains from monitoring . . .
> ***Better asset redeployability.*** When corporate headquarters owns multiple related business units, there is an added advantage of an internal capital market. If one unit performs poorly, its assets can be redeployed efficiently:

They can be directly combined with the other assets controlled by corporate headquarters. In contrast, an external provider would have to sell the assets to another user and may not get paid their full value. (pp. 1212–1213)

The Allocation of Internal Funds Is Not Perfunctory

If capital markets are imperfect, internal capital markets will tend to exist, and where a firm has an internal capital market, it often must ration capital. Moreover, the internal allocation of capital is not perfunctory. Two fundamental problems of capital budgeting within a multidivisional firm involve *decentralized information* and *incentive problems*.

13.3.4   Decentralized Information and Incentive Problems

Harris and Raviv (1996) focus on two related aspects of the internal capital allocation process: *decentralized information* and *incentive problems*. They provide two motivations for their theoretical analysis. *First*, they cite the allegations of others (Porter 1992; Poterba and Summers 1992) that "U.S. firms invest too little and tend to overemphasize short-term results . . . [using] hurdle rates to evaluate investment projects that are higher than their estimated costs of capital" (p. 1139).

Second, they point out a gap in modern finance theory regarding the details of the internal capital allocation process: The traditional *NPV rule* is devoid of any treatment of important details about the process, and thus fails to address problems that may lead to faulty capital investment decisions. For either a multilevel or multidivisional firm, much of the critical information on capital investment opportunities that is generated within the firm is taken in by managers at various levels, rather than by senior management. Thus, any such firm must decide the extent to which managers at these levels are (a) given autonomy to make capital budgeting decisions based on information that they generate, versus (b) instructed to share such information with senior managers, who then determine the allocations of available internal capital. In other words, the capital budgeting process that the firm adopts "governs the way in which managers at various levels produce and share information about proposed investments and determines which decisions are delegated, to whom, and under what constraints" (p. 1140).

In practice, a typical balance between extremes (a) and (b) above is struck by requiring individual managers to periodically submit capital investment proposals to senior management (and thereby to share the information that they have acquired), who then use the information contained in these proposals to allocate the firm's available internal capital. However, this practice engenders an information asymmetry-induced principal–agent conflict. Individual managers have a private incentive to pursue empire building by exaggerating the profit potential of the projects they propose. Meanwhile, senior management is chronically at an information disadvantage as they attempt to ascertain the true profitability of such proposals. Suppose senior management cannot effectively distinguish between proposals from managers A and B, both of which require substantial capital. Manager A's proposal is based fairly on his or her private information that the funds would be invested profitably, whereas manager B's request is based on a private empire-building motive. If this problem were not addressed, the overall firm would tend to overinvest.

Senior management has at least two means to control this problem. They can monitor a manager over time to determine *ex post* the extent to which he or she engages in inefficient empire building (e.g., their division is observed to be less profitable). Unfortunately, *ex post* audits are akin to closing the fence gate after the horse has escaped. Alternatively, senior management can order an *ex ante* audit of a specific manager's proposal. Unfortunately, such audits are costly. Harris and Raviv suggest an alternative scheme in which individual managers are always *threatened* with the possibility of an *ex ante* audit. The probability of an audit increases with the relative size of the capital request; if an audit is conducted and reveals that the proposal is unprofitable, no capital will be allocated to the manager's project.

Gertner, Scharfstein, and Stein (1994) point out another drawback of the internal capital market—*decreased entrepreneurial incentives*: "Giving control rights to capital providers through an internal capital allocation process is costly, however, in that it diminishes managerial incentives. Because the manager does not have control, he is more vulnerable to opportunistic behavior by corporate headquarters. Thus, the manager may not get all of the rents from his efforts, which reduces his incentives" (pp. 1212–1213).

13.3.5 The Role of Corporate Headquarters in a Firm's Internal Capital Market

Stein (1997) also addressed the problem of allocating a fixed amount of internal capital among competing proposals. He asked two fundamental questions: "First . . . under what circumstances can it make sense to combine several technologically distinct projects under one roof, and have them seek funding from corporate headquarters, as opposed to setting them up as stand-alone companies that each raise external financing on their own? Second, given this rationale, what is the optimal size and scope of an internal capital market? Should headquarters be involved in funding a large number of projects, or just a few? And should these projects be unrelated to one another, or in similar lines of business?" (p. 111).

Stein's response to the first question is that an internal capital market can engender efficient competition among divisions for scarce funds. Unlike the external capital market, "headquarters has control rights that enable it to pursue 'winner-picking'—the practice of actively shifting funds from one project to another. . . . For example, the cash flow generated by one division's activities may be taken and spent on investment in another division. Simply put, individual projects must compete for the scarce funds, and headquarters' job is to pick the winners and losers in this competition."

Stein's analysis also suggests that the competitive aspect of the internal capital market structure can mitigate the empire-building problem with respect to project managers: "[F]or a given amount of available funding, headquarters may—in the pursuit of its own self-interests—do a reasonable job of reallocating resources across projects. Thus a partial solution to the agency problem of empire-building project managers is to take control from them and give it to an empire-building supervisor, who is no more noble but who has less parochial interests" (p. 131). Moreover, while senior management may have private empire-building motives, in dealing with division managers they would nevertheless prefer to manage a more valuable firm than a less valuable firm, and thus would impose some value-creation discipline on division managers, which in the end serves the interests of the firm's shareholders.

Regarding the second question, Stein suggests that an internal capital market is most efficient when headquarters oversees a limited number of projects that are narrowly focused. Having too many projects suggests empire building (or at least an unwieldy enterprise), but having too few projects does not allow the resource-reallocation mechanism to operate effectively. How many projects are too few, or too many? It depends in part on the capabilities of senior management.

13.3.6 Divisional Rent-Seeking and Inefficient Investment in Internal Capital Markets

Scharfstein and Stein (2000) also expounded on the incentive problems associated with the allocation of internal capital. They raised the question of "how spreading or concentrating the power to make resource-allocation decisions affects efficiency" (p. 2559). With their agency-theoretic model, they show "how rent-seeking behavior on the part of division managers can subvert the workings of an internal capital market. By rent-seeking, division managers can raise their bargaining power and extract greater overall compensation from the CEO" (p. 2537).

13.3.7 The Delegation Issue

One of the crucial issues concerning an internal equity market is the extent to which a firm's headquarters delegates capital budgeting decisions to division managers. Harris and Raviv (1998) developed a theoretical model to analyze the critical parameters of this issue. They argued that delegation is valuable in that it saves on the costly investigation of proposed projects. Therefore, delegation should be more extensive when the costs of such investigations are larger. Again, headquarters limits the capital requests of division managers by threatening to audit proposals.

13.3.8 The Cross-Subsidization Problem

Scharfstein and Stein's (2000) model also suggests that multidivisional firms often engage in inefficient *socialism* in allocating internal capital, where stronger divisions subsidize weaker ones. This is called the *cross-subsidization problem*.

Two recent empirical studies document evidence of this problem. Shin and Stulz (1998) examined the cash flows of each of the business segments of individual multi-segment firms, comparing these to each other and to corresponding cash flows of single-segment firms. Their data consisted of a large number of firms of each type. They found two pieces of evidence consistent with the hypothesis. *First*, capital investment by a given segment of a diversified firm is sensitive to the cash flow of the firm's *other* segments. *Second*, investment by a segment of a diversified firm is *less sensitive* to its own cash flow than is the investment of a comparable single-segment firm.

Lamont (1997) examined oil companies that have non-oil units, and their response to the precipitous fall in the price of oil price in 1986, which severely constricted these firms' internal capital. He found that these firms reduced their investment in non-oil units, relative to the relevant industry norm, regardless of the profitability of these units. The results indicate that multiunit firms may be overly dependent on fluctuations in internal capital flows over time, and therefore often are inefficient in terms of pursuing profitable investment opportunities in their various units.[1]

---

[1]Schnure (1997) challenges Lamont's results. He shows that many of these companies were cash rich in 1986.

Value-based Management

This article excerpt discusses problems with capital budgeting, and advocates a *value-based management* approach.

- *When a budgeting process—at any level—is not continuously focused on using capital efficiently, potential sources of value remain hidden.*

Most capital budgeting processes are out of control. On the big decisions—the major investments—disciplined analyses of expected returns do, of course, get done. But on the countless smaller capital requests that flow up the decision-making channels of most organizations, such discipline is usually lacking. What's missing, however, is not a top-down commitment to using net present value techniques. The problem is not methodological. What's missing is a consistent management focus at the grassroots level on identifying all opportunities to generate and capture value by using capital more efficiently . . .

MANAGING VALUE

Finance textbooks wax eloquent about capital budgeting methodologies as if the use of theoretically correct techniques inevitably results in an optimal allocation of capital. From time to time, academic surveys of CFOs look to see how many of their companies regularly use DCF, IRR, or NPV when evaluating significant investment decisions. But using proper analytic methods does not, and cannot, by itself ensure real capital efficiency—the greatest possible enhancement of free cash flows by making sensible reductions in the need for working and/or physical capital . . .

- *Capital efficiency starts with a managerial understanding of the ways in which capital-dependent projects get defined and implemented at the front lines.*

The potential impact of improved capital efficiency is enormous. Companies can often cut their capital expenditures by between 10 and 25 percent without any change in revenues or in the quality of services provided to their customers. At the same time, they can often reduce maintenance costs and implementation times (as projects get simplified) and improve interfunctional cooperation (as the new approach gets embedded in general managerial practice). One company, for example, reduced its working capital by $500 million in one year. This dramatic improvement had nothing to do with budgeting methodology, but everything to do with developing a value-based approach to capital management throughout the organization . . .

Today, capital efficiency represents such a huge and largely untapped source of value because only limited attention is usually paid to it. And what attention does get paid usually comes from far too high up the chain of command.

WHY DOES IT MATTER?

The advantages of improved capital efficiency . . . are obvious. Those that can do more with less are rewarded by the capital markets. If the same operating cash flows can be achieved by using less working capital or less physical capital, a company's free cash flow increases, which is reflected in a higher market price for its shares. A company that generates a dollar of earnings by spending twenty cents of capital will enjoy a higher share price than a competitor that generates a dollar of earnings by spending fifty cents of capital.

THE SEVEN SYMPTOMS OF CAPITAL INEFFICIENCY

Capital budgeting problems often reveal themselves in subtle ways. The presence of one or more of these symptoms should act as a warning that there are capital inefficiencies at work:

- ***Blanket spending.*** A large portion of the capital budget is spent "automatically" by operating personnel or field engineers via guidelines or procedures that do not require economic justification.

- ***Unintegrated approach.*** Company budgeting and planning processes treat operating and maintenance spending and capital expenditure as separate rather than integrated uses of company resources.

- ***Myopic planning.*** It is either "feast or famine" with capital spending, depending on current earnings or cash flow. Alternatively, budgets are set on an annual, incremental basis rather than as part of a multi-year investment program.

- ***"Entitled" spending.*** An approach to setting annual capital budgets based on expenditure levels in previous years, this is often accompanied by significant year-end spending sprees to "make budgets."

- ***Missed budget targets.*** There is a skewed bell-shaped curve of project spending results, with many projects over but few under initial spending projections, particularly after adjustments for the scope of work accomplished.

- ***Badly aligned incentives.*** A de facto performance management system admonishes field personnel and engineers for breakdowns and capacity constraints without placing adequate emphasis on prudent risk management or economic efficiency.

- ***No post-audit procedure.*** There is limited follow-up to assess the magnitude or timing of benefits generated by capital programs.

LOCATING INEFFICIENCIES

In general, improvements in capital efficiency result from eliminating non-value-based drivers of demand for capital, promoting creative exploration of lower-cost options, and intensifying attention to day-to-day project execution. Although most CFOs and line managers would agree that additional effort along each of these dimensions will produce incremental benefits, few anticipate the magnitude of savings that can actually be captured. When realization finally dawns, their first reaction—after the initial shock—is to question the motives or intelligence of field personnel. Surely they must have been aware of these inefficiencies?

[M]ost inefficiencies are grounded in "legitimate" past practices, hidden constraints, or misaligned incentives. Left undetected, these subtle influences will continue to deprive companies of significant capital improvement opportunities for years to come.

Focus on Value

Eliminating non-value-based drivers of capital spending requires careful analysis of the root causes and assumptions that lead to capital requests in the first place. Deferral or elimination of projects is often the greatest source of savings . . .

Focus on Costs

Promoting creative exploration of lower-cost options involves examining opportunities for improvement on a "total system," rather than a component, basis, and undertaking a value-based review of projects on a line-item basis. Taking a total system view of projects can help identify, upstream or downstream of the proposed fix, lower-cost alternatives that are capable of delivering equal or greater impact.

For example, a company might be about to invest in a project for removing impurities from the downstream phase of a process. By reviewing total system costs, it might discover that there are cheaper options that prevent impurities from entering the system in the first place, perhaps through investment in better maintenance of equipment upstream. Such lower-cost options are, however, often overlooked when individual operating units seek ways to reduce annual operating budgets. But if the distinction between operating and capital funds is relaxed, creative ways to reduce total costs are more likely to be uncovered.

Conducting a value-based review of a project's line-item features is analogous to the "line-item veto" privilege often sought by heads

(continued)

of government in dealings with their respective legislatures. In business, however, the challenge is less to master the politics of the situation than to get the necessary expertise in place to review projects effectively on a disaggregated basis. As one steel company discovered, the payoff for doing so can be significant: Involving field personnel in generating, evaluating, and selecting ideas for project simplification led to a 27 percent reduction in the capital required to complete 20 projects . . .

Focus on Execution

Intensifying day-to-day attention to project execution can be a source of improvement for most companies. Frequently, the opportunity manifests itself in the form of chronic budget overruns. These are always a problem, of course, but we have found that overruns in blanket spending are more frequent and add up to a larger overall figure . . .

VALUE-BASED MANAGEMENT

Disciplined efforts to achieve capital efficiency must, therefore, start with a management commitment to value creation and a managerial process for getting all levels of an organization, particularly the front line, to act in ways consistent with that commitment. Such an orientation is especially important for companies that need to take a long-term view of their business and have relatively high capital intensity. For large projects, the analysis of investment decisions should follow traditional textbook NPV methodology. But for the thousands of smaller decisions that arise from the design of property, plant, and equipment, or from blanket spending, there is need for a consistent but less cumbersome way of thinking. We call this process value-based management.

Detailed net present value calculations do not work here. The scale is all wrong. Value drivers do. Value drivers are the specific, easily tracked metrics—cost per foot of installed cable or pipeline, peak-load transformer utilization, or time to completion of a project—that link micro-level decisions to capital efficiency . . .

Nurturing and leveraging grass-roots awareness of such drivers of value are, thus, essential parts of any process genuinely focused on value creation. At one company, for example, engineers hoarded vital equipment, in violation of policy, as protection against a breakdown in operations. The resulting excess inventory of components amounted to virtually a year's supply. Only when the engineers, together with procurement and stores personnel, were able to establish a guaranteed 24-hour delivery time for replacement parts could this wasteful practice be corrected—and capital efficiency improved . . .

The value-based management process starts with a diagnosis. Does the company exhibit any of the tell-tale symptoms of inefficient capital management . . . ? How much potential is there for capital efficiency improvements? How valid are the existing performance metrics, such as capacity utilization? How accurate a database is there for reviewing levels of blanket spending? How do decision makers at grass-roots levels actually make blanket spending decisions? What incentives do they have to improve capital efficiency?

Having gained a better understanding of how decisions are actually made, an organization can move to the second step: developing a new process that focuses on grass-roots activity, but with good support from the top as well as across functions on such tasks as developing benchmarks. Bottom-up activities include careful identification of value drivers that can be monitored for continuous improvement, coupled with revised reporting requirements to focus on them. At the top, there must be a review process that centers on a two-way dialogue about both blanket spending and major projects. Its purpose is to make all levels of management smarter about where—and how—value gets created. Senior management needs better to understand the design of projects and the reasoning behind blanket spending; grass-roots managers, the importance of efficient capital spending.

Perhaps the most important part of the VBM process is the third step—changing the mindset of the organization. Workshops should be conducted at the grass-roots level to identify value drivers and brainstorm new capital efficiency ideas. Step 4 then reinforces the change in mindset by revising guidelines and incentives. Incentives are always a thorny issue. It is important, for example, to understand trade-offs between customer needs and potential equipment failures, then to work toward agreement on guidelines that concentrate on capital efficiency and indemnify field engineers against sporadic equipment breakdowns.

There is always a tendency to slip back into bad habits after an initial capital efficiency program has achieved its first success. The final step, therefore, is follow through. The goal is to have ongoing advances in value-driver performance via continuous improvement programs. Post-audit reviews of major projects enable learning about what went wrong and how to do things better next time. Boosting capital efficiency is a "piano tuner" problem. The task is never finished. But the benefits are clearly worth the continuous application of energy and attention. Value-based management pays.

Source: This article is excerpted from "The Hidden Value of Capital Efficiency," T. E. Copeland, K. J. Ostrowski, *The McKinsey Quarterly*, 1993, no. 2, pp. 45–58. Copyright © 1993 McKinsey & Company, Inc. The article can be found on the publication's Web site, www.mckinseyquarterly.com. Used by permission.

13.3.9   Implications for Conglomerates

The theory of internal capital markets also has implications for the issue of firm diversification versus focus—that is, for mergers and acquisitions (discussed in Chapter 16) as well as their opposites—divestiture activities such as asset sales, equity carve-outs, and spin-offs (discussed in Chapter 17).

Stein's (1997) theoretical model suggests that the optimal diversification of a firm depends on the developmental status of the external capital market. If the external capital market is not well developed, such that the allocation of capital to projects via external financing mechanisms is relatively inefficient, relatively more capital will be allocated via internal capital markets, and firms will tend to be more diversified. On the other hand, if the external market is efficient, individual firms should be more narrowly focused. Thus, for an economy with an external capital market that is in transition toward greater efficiency, we should observe heretofore-diversified firms, such as conglomerates, converting to a narrower focus via divestiture.

Researchers have pointed to the decades of the 1960s and 1970s as a period when internal capital markets may have been superior to external capital markets in the United States. Hubbard and Palia (1999) examined 392 bidding firms involved in mergers in the 1960s. Those bidders that realized the highest returns from mergers were cases in which the bidding firm was financially *unconstrained* while the target firm was financially *constrained*. They also found that bidder firms generally retained the target firm's management, "suggesting that management may have provided company-specific operational information, while the bidder provided capital-budgeting expertise" (p. 1131).

Conversely, it has been suggested that external capital markets in the United States developed sufficiently in the decades of the 1980s and 1990s to warrant en masse divestiture, especially among conglomerates. We discuss this side of the story in Chapter 17.

13.3.10   Internal Capital Markets and the Exit Decision

According to internal capital market theory, single-segment (or *focused*) firms and diversified firms with an efficient internal capital market would react differently to financial distress. Diversified firms should react more swiftly to deteriorating profits in a given business line because they have the flexibility of redeployment.

Khanna and Tice (2001) examined the capital expenditure decisions of incumbent discount retail firms in response to Wal-Mart's entry into their market. They focused on Wal-Mart because the firm is extremely competitive: "Wherever Wal-Mart entered a new market, it shocked the competitive landscape and incumbent firms responded by changing their investment decisions" (p. 1526). Some of the incumbents focused only on discount retailing (e.g., K-Mart), and others were divisions of diversified firms (e.g., Dayton-Hudson).

The research question was, Would focused incumbents and diversified incumbents react differently to the shock of Wal-Mart's entry? Their evidence is consistent with this prediction: "After Wal-Mart's entry, diversified firms are quicker to either 'exit' the discount business or 'stay and fight.' Also, their capital expenditures are more sensitive to the productivity of their discount business" (p. 1489). Based on this evidence, they conclude: "Internal capital markets function well, as transfers are away from the worsening discount divisions. It appears diversified firms make better investment decisions" (p. 1489).

13.4   THE PROCESS OF ISSUING SEASONED EQUITY

A *seasoned equity offering*, or *SEO*, is the issuance of additional shares by a publicly traded firm. It is distinguished from an initial public offering (IPO) of *unseasoned equity*, which we discussed in Chapter 12. In this section, we discuss the process by which a public firm issues seasoned equity.

13.4.1   How SEOs Relate to Internal Equity Management

Our discussion of internal equity management relates to SEOs in the following sense. We prefaced our discussion with the assumption that a public firm would not seek to raise equity funds in the external capital market because this activity is fraught with principal–agent and information asymmetry problems. A SEO represents an important exception to that dictum.

As we will see, firms state a variety of reasons for undertaking a SEO. One reason constitutes a direct link between the allocation of internal capital and a SEO. Suppose a firm's management has decided to pursue a given level of capital expenditures now and in the near future. The firm has decided on the mix of debt and equity funds that should be used to finance these expenditures. If the amount of *internal* equity funds that will be available is insufficient for the purpose, the firm must either raise the remaining equity funds *externally* via a SEO, or scale back its capital investment program.

The probability that a firm will need to undertake a SEO depends in part on the profitability of existing projects (i.e., the firm's ability to generate internal cash flow to fund additional investments) *relative to* the amount of current and near-term capital expenditures that senior management has decided upon. As a general rule, we should expect the number of investment opportunities that a firm has to be positively related to the profitability of its existing projects. Consequently, as a rule a firm's internal cash flow should be adequate to fund new projects.

Three Types of SEO Candidates

Exceptions to this rule are of three types: (a) a firm that has existing profitable projects but has few profitable investment opportunities (i.e., a so-called *cash cow*), (b) a firm that has existing profitable projects and has profitable investment opportunities, but whose capital outlays exceed available internal funds, and (c) a firm that has no existing profitable projects, but has profitable investment opportunities. The market would not expect firms of type A, the cash cows, to undertake a SEO, because it should have no need to raise external capital. In contrast, the market may expect firms of type B to seek external equity funds occasionally. Indeed, the market may react positively to a SEO announcement from a type B firm to the extent that the information reveals that the firm's future investment opportunities are so profitable as to outstrip the firm's internal cash flow from already profitable projects.

Type C firms are particularly problematic. It would be rational for the management of an unprofitable firm with profitable investment opportunities to undertake a SEO. However, it would face a skeptical market, because the firm's existing projects are unprofitable.

13.4.2   Obtaining Board of Directors Approval

The issuance of additional shares is a decision that must be approved by a firm's board of directors.[2] After all, adding new shares and shareholders has at least three important potential effects: (a) Selling additional equity shares generally brings in new shareholders, and thus alters the ownership structure of the firm; (b) depending on management's intended use of the proceeds of offering, the potential exists for *earnings dilution*, and harm to the value of the firm's existing shares; and (c) the infusion of additional equity into the firm's capital structure reduces the firm's leverage, which may or may not be desirable.

13.4.3   Alternative Methods of Issuing Seasoned Equity

A public company can use any of several methods to issue seasoned equity: (a) a *private placement*, (b) *grants, ESOPS,* or *DRIPS*, (c) a *rights offering,* or (d) a *general public offering.* Below we discuss each of these methods.

Private Placement

In a private sale of equity, the firm sells a block of shares (common or preferred) to a single investor or a small group of investors. The private nature of these transactions, and the fact that they occur more rarely than public offerings of seasoned equity, suggests that they are *special circumstance* financings.

Wruck (1989) examined a sample of 128 private sales of equity by NYSE and AMEX firms over the period July 1979 to December 1985. Common stock and pre-

---

[2]Furthermore, if the issuance requires an increase in the company's *authorized shares,* the decision must also be approved directly by the firm's shareholders.

ferred stock were involved in 101 and 27 sales, respectively. Relatively small firms, on average, made these sales, and the sales were generally consummated at a substantially discounted price. Nevertheless, the market greeted the announcement of a private equity sale with a positive abnormal return of 4.5 percent, on average. This result is in sharp contrast to the negative reaction generally associated with public SEOs, as we discuss later.

Wruck examined the control implications of these sales. On average, a private sale represented a very substantial 19.6 percent of the firm's voting shares. Coupling this with the result of a positive market reaction to the sales, the author concludes that "the decision to sell a block of securities to nonmanagement investors increases shareholder wealth" (p. 4). Wruck suggests that private placement discounts reflect compensation for the expert advice or monitoring services that these private investors provide.

Hertzel and Smith (1993) also examined private sales of equity. They also show that these sales are generally made at substantial discounts from market value, and that the market reacts positively to their announcement. They discuss and test two hypotheses to explain the results: "The market reaction to private sales of equity can reflect resolution of information asymmetries and/or anticipated effects of ownership structure changes. The information hypothesis . . . implies that changes in firm value around private placements can be driven by shifts in the market's assessment of the value of existing firm's assets and investment opportunities. The ownership structure hypothesis, in contrast, implies that market revaluation can be a result of anticipated changes in managerial performance. This dichotomy suggests that firms may turn to equity private placements to finance valuable investment opportunities when financial slack is limited or to improve managerial performance . . . " (pp. 483–484).

Hertzel and Smith documented evidence consistent with both hypotheses. However, the information asymmetry argument may be more relevant for smaller firms: "For the smaller firms that comprise our sample, information effects appear to be relatively more important than ownership effects" (p. 459).

Stock and Stock Option Grants, ESOPs, and DRIPs

Firms employ several other mechanisms to issue equity privately, most notably (a) stock and stock option grants to executives, (b) employee stock ownership plans (ESOPs), and (c) dividend reinvestment plans (DRIPs). We discuss each of these mechanisms briefly below. In all three mechanisms, the firm may issue new shares to the purchasers, or they may reissue shares that are in treasury as a result of prior stock repurchases.

We discussed executive stock and stock option grants in Chapter 8, in the context of our analysis of executive compensation. These grants serve to focus an executive's attention on the interest of the shareholders—to increase the market value of the firm's shares.

In 1974, the U.S. Congress passed legislation establishing ESOPs as retirement plans. An ESOP allows a firm's rank and file employees to purchase the firm's stock, often at a discount to the current market price, and often with matching funds from the firm. They are generally a part of the employee's retirement plan, and thus a part of the employee's overall compensation package.

The finance literature recognizes three motives for a firm's adoption of an ESOP. The *first* motive is the same as for executive stock and stock option plans—employees who own stock in the firm have a stronger incentive to work in the firm's interest, because it is also their interest. Thus, the adoption of an ESOP should *increase the firm's productivity*. *Second*, the U.S. Congress imparted several *tax advantages* for ESOPs that other pension plans do not have (see Shackelford 1991).

Third, the state of Delaware enacted a *freeze-out* law in 1988 that made ESOPs a more effective *takeover defense*, as Beatty (1995) explains: "This law imposes a three-year delay on business combinations not approved by the target company's board of directors unless the bidder can acquire 85 percent of the target's shares that are not controlled by officers and directors. An ESOP can make it impossible for a bidder to obtain the necessary interest if the employees are unwilling to sell their shares" (p. 212). Beatty conducted an event study of firms' adoptions of ESOPs. She posited that the market would react positively to the productivity and tax advantage aspects of an ESOP, but negatively to the extent that the plan had a significant negative impact on the probability of a takeover. She documents evidence consistent with each of these effects.

With a DRIP, a firm's current shareholders can instruct the firm to reinvest dividends into additional shares of the firm's stock. Some firms issue primary shares for this purpose, though most use the cash from the foregone dividend to purchase shares in the open market for the participating shareholders. Most firms pay the associated commission for such purchases, and some firms actually allow shareholders to purchase shares at a slight discount (5 percent to 10 percent) from the market price.

Most DRIPs impose a fairly low maximum on the dollar value of shares that can be purchased by a single participant on any quarterly dividend payment date (e.g., $25,000). For this reason, individual investors are interested in the plans, and institutional investors are not. Indeed, some DRIPs do not allow institutional shareholders to participate in the plan. Such restrictions suggest that a firm's management may adopt a DRIP to attract relatively passive, small individual investors.[3]

Rights Offering

In a rights offering, the firm's current shareholders are issued short-term warrants called *preemptive rights* to purchase new shares on a pro rata basis. The *exercise price* of these warrants is generally set at a deep discount to the current market price of the stock. This is done deliberately to make it prohibitively costly for the holder not to exercise the rights. However, if an incumbent shareholder does not wish to purchase additional shares, he or she can sell the rights in a temporary secondary market established for the rights themselves.

The rights method of offering seasoned equity provides current shareholders an opportunity to prevent a reduction in their proportional ownership of the firm that might otherwise occur when additional shares are offered to the general public. The rights offering method of issuing seasoned equity had been used extensively in the United States in the past, but it is now rarely used.[4]

---

[3]However, even though an individual investor automatically reinvests his or her dividend via a DRIP, the investor remains liable for taxes on the amount of the dividend, as if it was actually paid.

[4]The rights offering method is widely used by firms in other countries (Bohren, Eckbo, and Michalsen 1997).

Hansen (1988) provides an explanation for the demise of the rights issue: "the lack of use of rights offerings in the United States . . . can be explained by transaction-cost conditions. A sample of underwritten rights offerings provides support for the explanation. Firms making underwritten rights offerings paid lower underwriter fees but incurred significantly larger price drops just prior to the offering than did firms making underwritten public offerings. Further analysis reveals that the underwritten-rights-offering price concessions are a form of transaction cost that is not found in underwritten public offerings" (p. 289).

Singh (1997) provides an alternative explanation for firms' preference for a general public offering over a rights offering: "In seasoned equity rights offers, the standby underwriting contract resembles the sale of a put option. In the rights offering period, underwriters reduce their exposure to the standby underwriting by purchasing rights hedged with short sale of the common stock. Consistent with Eckbo and Masulis (1992), offers with large rights sell-offs during the offering period experience significant price decline. The offering period price decline and the nature of constraints confronting underwriters may partially explain the preference for general public offers" (p. 105).

General Public Offering

In a general public offering of seasoned equity, a publicly traded firm sells additional shares of stock to the public. The firm hires investment bankers to underwrite the issue. As we will see later, the general public offering is the most common means by which U.S. nonfinancial firms issue seasoned equity. In the remainder of this section, we discuss details of the general public offering process.

13.4.4   Underwriter Selection via Negotiation or Competitive Bidding

An issuing firm's management can select an underwriter via either *negotiation* or *competitive bidding*. A negotiated underwriting contract results when the firm approaches a single underwriter (e.g., an underwriter with whom the firm has done business in the past) and negotiates the contract and the fee. Alternatively, the firm can advertise that is has a pending security issue, and solicit bids from a number of competing investment banks.

At first blush, it may seem obvious that the firm should opt for competitive bidding, because this would surely result in the lowest underwriting cost. However, the underwriting process can be problematic, particularly if management has strategic, value-relevant private information that it must divulge to the underwriter on a confidential basis to influence the price that the underwriter is willing to attempt to secure for the issue. In such cases, the firm may do better to choose an underwriter that it knows and trusts, even though the cost of the offering in terms of the fee may be higher.

13.4.5   Underwriter Compensation

Underwriter compensation for a SEO can be best understood by recognizing that the overall cost of the offering to the firm consists of three components: (a) *cash compensation* in the form of a spread; (b) implicit costs associated with the adverse selection problem; and, for some offerings, (c) *warrants* awarded to the underwriter.

Underwriter Spread

An underwriter's compensation for a seasoned equity offering virtually always includes a cash component, the amount of which is measured by a *spread*, or percentage of the offering proceeds. As we show later, underwriter spreads are generally smaller for SEOs than for IPOs, and vary more substantially as a function of several variables.

Adverse Selection Costs

The antecedent to the adverse selection problem is, of course, information asymmetry. If the issuing firm's management generally has better information than the market about the value of the firm, the market will assume that the firm is issuing additional shares because its assessment of the true value of the firm is lower than the current market price. Thus, when a firm announces a SEO, the market's interpretation is that the firm's management believes that the firm's shares are overpriced. The market then responds by dropping the market price of the stock.

Booth and Smith (1986) provide a widely regarded hypothesis about the true role of underwriters. They argue that, given the information asymmetry problem, an underwriter's principal job is to minimize the negative effect of a security offering on the firm's stock price (i.e., minimize adverse selection costs). The underwriter can alleviate this problem by receiving (confidentially) value-relevant information from the firm and then vouching for or *certifying* the value of the firm to the market. However, the extent to which the market accepts the underwriter's certification of value depends on the underwriter's *reputation*.

Warrants

In some SEO underwritings, a portion of the underwriter's compensation is in the form of warrants for the purchase of additional shares of the issuing firm's equity. Ng and Smith (1996) argue that warrants may serve as an effective *signal* of the underwriter's valuation of the issue, and therefore as a substitute for underwriter reputation. The warrant allows the holder to purchase the underlying security at a stated price for a specified period. To the holder, the value of the warrant is an increasing function of the holder's perceived value of the underlying security, which in this case is the issuing firm's equity. Thus, if the underwriter (who, we assume, has confidential access to management's strategic value-relevant information) believes that the value of the shares is relatively low, it would value the warrant at a correspondingly low level (relative to both the current market price and the exercise price of the warrants), and therefore would be accepting lower compensation for their services, and would be unlikely to accept this type of compensation. On the other hand, if the underwriter believes that the value of the stock is relatively high, it would be happy to accept warrants as partial compensation. Thus, warrant compensation can be used as an effective signal of value.

Trade-offs among the Cost Components

Trade-offs exist among the components of underwriting costs. For example, an underwriter that has a better reputation for *certifying* the value of an issue deserves higher compensation because its credibility in the marketplace will result in smaller adverse selection costs. On the other hand, underwriting through a smaller, less credible underwriter may result in more severe underpricing, so it should receive less compensation.

13.4.6   Firm Commitment or Best Efforts Pricing?

As is the case with an IPO, a SEO can be sold by either of two methods. In the *firm commitment* method, the underwriter agrees to purchase all of the shares offered at a fixed price, and then takes the risk of reselling the shares to the public. In the *best efforts* method, the underwriter makes no guarantee about the price. Instead, the underwriter only agrees to conduct a search for interested buyers, all of whom submit a schedule of the numbers of shares that they are willing to purchase at each of a range of prices, as we explained previously.

Also as with an IPO, in both selling methods for a SEO, a contract feature serves to mitigate the risk borne by the risk-assuming party. In the firm commitment method, the underwriter often has an *overallotment* (or *greenshoe*) option, which allows it to sell additional shares if it is profitable to do so. By exercising this option when it is profitable, the underwriter increases its profits on SEOs that turn out to be profitable, which offsets losses on other issues. In the best efforts method, the firm retains options to (a) withdraw the offering if either the offer price or shares committed for sale is below a specified level, or (b) expand the offering if the offering price is above a specified level.

Kumar and Tsetsekos (1993) examined all combinations of negotiation versus competitive bidding and firm commitment versus best efforts agreements from the perspective of the Certification Hypothesis. They suggest that the various combinations form a *hierarchy*. They find some empirical support for their argument: "This study posits a hierarchy of investment banking contracts reflecting differential levels of certification. The analysis supporting the existence of this hierarchy is based on the reputational capital paradigm. The firm commitment–negotiated arrangement is perceived to have the highest quality of certification, followed by the firm commitment–competitive, best efforts–negotiated and best efforts–competitive arrangements in that order. The existence of this hierarchy is investigated by measuring market reactions to the announcements of such issues. The empirical results reveal sharp distinctions between firm commitment and best efforts contracts. However, within firm commitment contracts, signaling between negotiated and competitive arrangements is attenuated and the distinction is weak" (p. 117).

13.4.7   Traditional or Shelf Registration?

Prior to 1982, the SEC required firms to issue the securities that it had registered within a few months, after which the registration expired. However, in 1982 the SEC issued Rule 415, which allows qualified firms (generally large firms) up to two years within which to issue securities that were filed under Rule 415. The ruling provides the issuing firm greater flexibility regarding the timing of the issuance. The firm can sell the entire issue at any particular time within the two-year window, or sell portions of the issue on a piecemeal basis throughout this period. For this reason, a Rule 415 registration is referred to as a *shelf registration*, because following registration the firm can place the issue *on the shelf*, taking part or all of it off the shelf at any time to raise equity funds. Supposedly, the flexibility afforded by shelf registration gives the firm a number of advantages:

1. Shares can be issued in short order and on a piecemeal basis (so that they can coincide with the timing and amounts of capital expenditures, acquisitions, or debt retirements).

2. Management can issue shares when market conditions are favorable. For instance, if management generally has private (inside) information about the firm's prospects, they may wish to issue shares when the market price is relatively high in comparison to their private assessment of share value. Alternatively, it may be argued that a firm's cost of equity capital varies over time as, for instance, investors' risk aversion changes over time. If this is the case, and management can accurately assess the firm's equity cost of capital at any time, shares can be issued when the cost of equity capital is relatively low.

3. Shelf registration enhances the firm's ability to take advantage of competition among underwriters. Kidwell, Marr, and Thompson (1984) explain that "once the 415 registration is filed at the SEC, information about the issue becomes public information and is freely available to any investment banker. Firms can contact underwriters directly and ask them to bid on any portion of a shelf issue. Also, investment bankers [may compete by] calling companies and trying to arrange deals for issues on the shelf" (p. 186).

Why SEO Firms Prefer Traditional to Shelf Registration

As we show later (see Table 13-1), few firms employ the shelf registration alternative for a SEO; most use the traditional method. This seems puzzling given (a) the supposed advantages of shelf registration discussed above, and (b) the fact that nearly two-thirds of nonconvertible public debt issues are registered via the shelf registration method (see Table 10-1). However, Rule 415 is quite restrictive in terms of a firm's qualifications for issuing the shelf method of registration.

Denis (1991) provides an additional explanation for the observed preferences: the underwriters of shelf issues tend to perform less due diligence, in part because their compensation is less. Therefore, "the announcement of a shelf offering results in a larger negative impact on the issuing firm's stock price than if the nonshelf procedure had been used. In choosing between the procedures, managers balance this additional cost against the lower direct issuing costs of the shelf procedure. Those firms for which there is more uncertainty about the true value of their securities find the nonshelf procedure less costly" (p. 190). Value uncertainty is a greater concern for equity issues than debt issues, so the costs of shelf registration outweigh the benefits with respect to equity issues, but not necessarily debt issues.

13.4.8 The Mix of Primary and Secondary Shares

A SEO may consist of primary shares exclusively, secondary shares exclusively, or a combination of primary and secondary shares. Primary shares provide funds for the firm itself, which it may use for capital investments, paying off the firm's debt obligations, and so on. Notable sellers of secondary shares in a SEO include the firm's insiders and certain outside blockholders.

Shares held by a firm's insiders generally are *restricted shares*. Restricted shares are defined as any shares that were acquired in unregistered, private sales (or grants) from the firm. According to the SEC's Rule 144A, an insider must hold restricted shares for at least a year, and must file a notice with the SEC before the shares can be sold.

13.4.9 A Stock-Only Offering or Units?

A SEO can consist of either shares only or *units* consisting of shares and warrants for the purchase of additional shares. In Chapter 12, we found that a small proportion of IPOs consist of units, but that only the smallest, most speculative firms offer units. Similarly, only a small proportion of SEOs consist of units, and unit SEOs are made by smaller, younger firms. As we argued in Chapter 12, a unit offering can be considered as a type of staged financing, which may be useful in mitigating the free cash flow problem (see Schultz 1993). This argument may apply as well to unit SEOs as to unit IPOs.

13.4.10 Statistics on SEOs for 1980–2000

We follow the above discussion on the SEO process with two empirical perspectives. In this subsection, we discuss statistics on the SEOs of U.S. nonfinancial firms over the years 1980 to 2000. In the next subsection, we discuss the details of a recent SEO by Kemet Corporation.

Table 13-1 shows statistics for 6,631 SEOs made by U.S. nonfinancial firms over the years 1980 to 2000. The statistics are divided into two categories: characteristics of the offering firms, shown in the upper panel, and offering characteristics, shown in the lower panel.

Firm Characteristics

New York Stock Exchange (NYSE) and American Stock Exchange (AMEX) firms undertook 41 percent of the SEOs in 1980 to 2000, while National Association of Secutities Dealers Automated Quotation and Over-the-Counter (NASDAQ/OTC) firms made the remaining 59 percent. The median number of years between a firm's SEO and its IPO was 2.2 years, and over one-fourth (26.4 percent) of the SEOs were made within one year of the firm's IPO. These *firm age* statistics suggest that a large proportion of SEOs can be classified as *follow-ons* to an IPO. The term "follow-on" has entered the issuance nomenclature not only because firms that have recently gone public are relatively more likely to undertake a SEO per se, but more precisely because such firms are more likely to make a subsequent equity offering for either of two reasons. *First*, the firm needs to raise more equity than they were able to raise in the IPO (i.e., the staged-financing argument). *Second*, many pre-IPO shareholders want to exit but were unable to do so at the IPO.

Based on the median modified debt ratio of 54.2 percent, SEO firms do not have high leverage ratios. They also tend to have fairly typical market-to-book equity ratios and price-earnings ratios (P/E), with median values of 3.5 and 18.2, respectively. On average, insiders' ownership decreases from 33.5 percent to 25.5 percent as a result of a SEO. This change is due to the purchase of offered shares by outsiders at the offering in general and, as applicable, the sale of insiders' shares in the secondary portion of the offering.

Offering Characteristics

Nearly all of the SEOs in the sample (99.6 percent) were general public offerings, indicating that rights offerings (0.4 percent) are indeed rare. Also, (a) in nearly all cases (99.7 percent), the firm secured an underwriter via negotiation rather then competitive bidding (0.3 percent), (b) the great majority of firms registered their offering in the tra-

TABLE 13-1   Descriptive Statistics for Seasoned Equity Offerings

6,631 SEOs of U.S. Nonfinancial Firms, 1980–2000

Firm Characteristics	Statistic	Value
Listed on NYSE or AMEX (versus NASDAQ/OTC)	Percent	41.0%
Firm age:		
Number years since IPO	Median	2.2
Firms public for less than one year	Percent	26.4%
Modified debt ratio before offering	Median	54.2%
Market-to-book equity ratio before offering	Median	3.5
P/E before offering	Median	18.2
Insiders' ownership		
Before offering	Percent	33.5%
After offering	Percent	25.5%
Offering Characteristics	**Statistic**	**Value**
General public offering (versus rights)	Percent	99.6%
Negotiated underwriter (versus competitive)	Percent	99.7%
Traditionally registered (versus shelf)	Percent	93.6%
Stock-only (vs. units)	Percent	96.0%
Ratio of primary shares to total shares offered	Percent	76.4%
Size of offering:		
Proceeds ($ million)	Median	$37
Ratio of proceeds to market equity value before offering (%)	Median	15.7%
Stated primary use of proceeds (% of firms)		
Acquisitions	Percent	4.7%
Capital investments	Percent	1.7%
Debt retirement	Percent	32.2%
General corporate purposes	Percent	46.7%
Product development	Percent	0.2%
Stock repurchases	Percent	14.3%
Working capital	Percent	0.3%
Underwriter spread (% of proceeds)	Average	5.3%

Source: Raw data from SDC new-issues database.

ditional manner (93.6 percent), rather than via a shelf registration (6.4 percent),[5] and (c) the vast majority of SEOs were stock-only offerings (96.0 percent), rather than units (4.0 percent).

The median proceeds from the SEOs in the sample were $37 million, and proceeds represented a median of 15.7 percent of the offering firm's market equity value before the offering. The most common stated primary uses of offering proceeds were *general corporate purposes* (46.7 percent) and *debt retirement* (32.2 percent).

Finally, the average underwriter spread for the SEOs was 5.3 percent. This is substantially lower than the standard 7 percent spread that we found in Chapter 12 for IPOs (see Table 12-2), though it is substantially higher than the 1.17 percent average

---

[5]In Chapter 15, we find that shelf registration is much more popular for public issues of debt.

spread that we found in Chapter 10 for public offerings of nonconvertible debt (see Table 10-1). Underwriter spreads on SEOs also vary substantially on a cross-sectional basis. We analyze the determinants of underwriter spreads on SEOs in the next section.

13.4.11 A Case in Point: Kemet Corporation's 2000 SEO

Kemet Corporation, a NYSE-traded firm (ticker: KEM) based in Greenville, South Carolina, is the largest manufacturer of solid tantalum capacitors and the fourth largest manufacturer of multiplayer ceramic capacitors in the world. Kemet capacitors are used in a wide variety of electronics, including communications systems, data processing equipment, personal computers, and cell phones.

On December 17, 1999, Kemet filed a traditional registration statement with the SEC to sell 5.0 million shares of common stock in a stock-only general public offering. They sold these shares on January 13, 2000, at a price of $46 per share, for gross proceeds of $230 million. The firm negotiated the underwriting of this offering with Merrill Lynch & Co. and Salomon Smith Barney as co-managers of the underwriting syndicate. This SEO came seven years after Kemet's 1992 IPO. The underwriter spread was 4.24 percent. The firm's market-to-book equity ratio before the offering was 10.3. The firm's P/E, based on the offer price and earnings per share for the fiscal year ended March 1998 ($0.63), was 73.0.

The shares offered represented 5.5 percent of Kemet's total shares outstanding before the offering. Half of the shares offered were primary shares, with proceeds to be used to fund capital expenditures and to reduce debt. The remaining shares were secondary shares, offered by Citigroup Foundation, who received these 2.5 million shares in a gift transfer from Citicorp Venture Capital, Ltd. (CVC). In turn, CVC had acquired the shares in 1990 in connection with the acquisition of Kemet Electronics Corporation.

13.5 DETERMINANTS OF UNDERWRITER SPREADS IN SEOs

In this section, we examine determinants of underwriter spreads for 6,631 SEOs completed by U.S. nonfinancial firms over the years 1980 to 2000. Our tests address two questions about the determinants of underwriter spreads. *First*, do underwriter spreads reflect economies of scale in the underwriting process? *Second*, does the variation in spreads reflect other characteristics of the issuing firms or the offerings?

For the observations in our sample, the median underwriter spread was 5.3 percent, though spreads ranged from 0.12 percent to 26.3 percent. The median spread for SEOs is considerably smaller than the standard 7 percent spread for IPOs documented in Chapter 12. This is expected, because the typical IPO is more problematic to underwrite than the typical SEO.

We tested for economies of scale by plotting spreads against offering proceeds, where the latter ranged from $0.4 million to $2,733.7 million. The results are displayed in Figure 13-2.

The results indicate that scale economies are clear and substantial. For the smallest offerings, the underwriter spread is generally greater than 5 percent; for the largest issues, the spread is generally less than 5 percent. The figure also shows the results of fitting a log-linear regression curve to the data. The curve is highly nonlinear, suggest-

FIGURE 13-2   The Relationship Between Underwriter Spread and Offering Proceeds

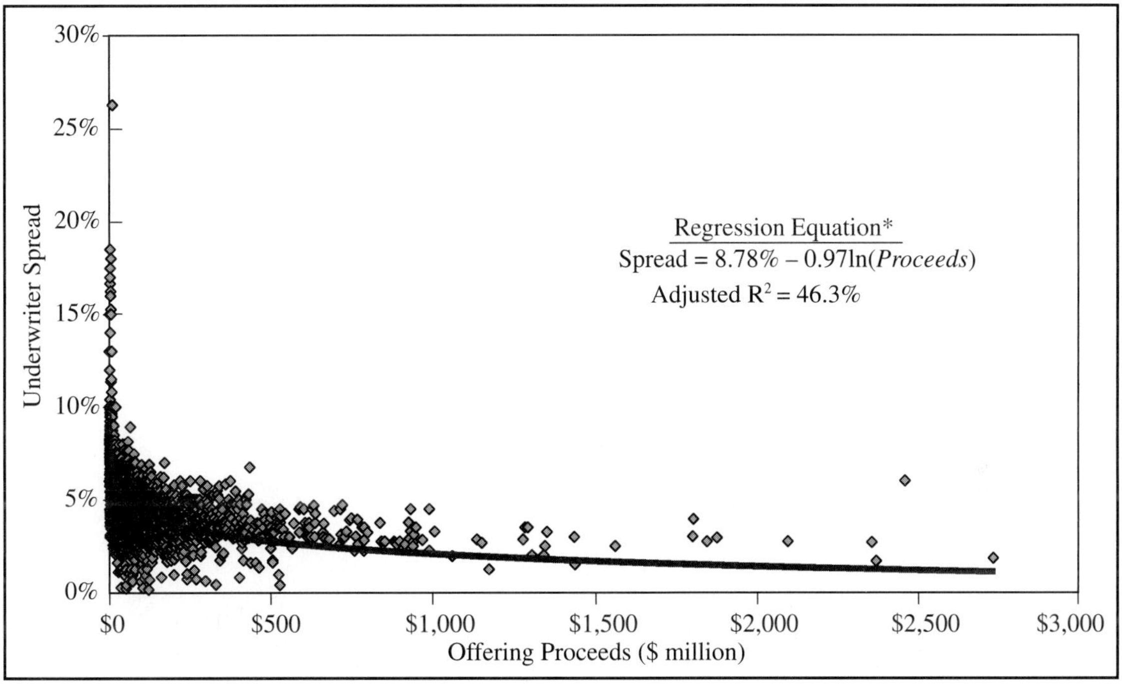

Regression Equation*
Spread = 8.78% − 0.97ln(*Proceeds*)
Adjusted R^2 = 46.3%

6,631 SEOs of U.S. Nonfinancial Firms, 1980–2000
*t *Statistics for intercept and slope coefficients are 181.7 and −75.7, respectively.*
Source: Raw data from SDC new-issues database.

ing that a substantial portion of the underwriting costs passed on to the issuer via the spread is *fixed cost*.[6] The Adjusted R^2 is 46.3 percent, indicating that the log-linear curve explains slightly less than half of the variation in spreads.

We also tested for the influence of other factors on spreads using a multiple regression framework. The dependent variable in the regression is, of course, the spread. The first independent variable is the natural log of offering proceeds, denoted as ln(*Proceeds*). This variable is included to control for the economies of scale documented above.

We also added eight zero-one or dummy independent variables, each of which might affect spread. The first two are dummy variables representing small-sized and medium-sized firms. Smaller firms may be generally more prone to costs associated with both principal–agent conflicts and information asymmetry, and therefore subject to underwriting problems. Consequently, we expect the coefficients of both of these variables to be positive, and the coefficient to be larger for the small-sized firms than for the medium-sized firms. For a similar reason, we added dummy variables representing NYSE/AMEX issuers (as opposed to NASDAQ and OTC/Small-Market issuers) and utility-firm issuers. We expect the coefficients of both variables to be neg-

---

[6]See Altinkilic and Hansen (2000) for a closer empirical analysis of economies of scale in underwriting fees.

TABLE 13-2   Results of a Regression of SEO Underwriter Spread against Indicated Independent Variables

6,631 SEOs of U.S. Nonfinancial Firms, 1980–2000

Dependent Variable: Underwriter Spread (%)

Independent Variable	Slope Coefficient	t-Statistic
Intercept	7.12	121.8
ln(*Proceeds*)	–0.56	–45.5
Small-Sized Firm Dummy	1.61	29.9
Medium-Sized Firm Dummy	0.72	23.9
NYSE/AMEX Dummy	–0.44	–16.6
Utility Firm Dummy	–0.99	–25.3
Competitive Bidding Dummy	–0.65	–2.8
Rights Offering Dummy	–1.62	–8.5
Shelf Registration Dummy	–0.38	–7.8
Units Dummy	2.19	33.8

Mean of dependent variable: 5.32%.
Adjusted R^2 = 70.5%.

ative. We also added dummy variables representing competitive bidding (versus negotiation), rights offerings (versus general public offerings), shelf registration (versus traditional), and units (versus stock-only offerings). The results of the multiple regression are displayed in Table 13-2.

As expected, the coefficient of ln(*Proceeds*) is negative and highly statistically significant, confirming the presence of substantial economies of scale. Also as expected, the coefficients of both firm-size dummy variables are positive and statistically significant. The value of the coefficient of the small-size firm dummy variable, 1.61, is approximately twice as large as that for the medium-sized firm dummy variable, 0.72, indicating that, on average, medium-sized firms pay 0.72 percent higher spreads than large firms, and small firms pay 1.61 percent higher spreads than large firms.

The coefficients of the NYSE/AMEX and utility-firm dummy variables are both negative, also as expected. The coefficients of the competitive bidding, rights, and shelf dummy variables are all negative, while the coefficient of the units dummy variable is positive. Finally, the Adjusted R^2 is 70.5 percent. This statistic indicates that the independent variables collectively explain well over two-thirds of the variation in underwriter spreads in our sample.

13.6   THE VALUATION EFFECT OF A SEO ANNOUNCEMENT: THEORY AND EVIDENCE

Empirical evidence presented in Chapter 1 suggests that firms are very reluctant to issue seasoned equity (review Figure 1-4a). In Chapters 3 and 4, as well as earlier in this chapter, we argued that equity offerings are problematic because of principal–agent conflicts and information asymmetry problems. Thus, it is not surprising that evidence from a large number of event studies consistently indicates that, on average, the market responds negatively to a firm's announcement of an equity offering.[7] The average abnormal return for SEO announcements ranges from –0.75 percent to –3.0 percent, depending on the study and sample. Thus, an equity offering generally conveys bad news to the market. This section reviews the theoretical literature that offers explanations for the market's negative reaction to SEOs.

13.6.1   Do the Issuing Firm's Managers Know That Their Firm's Equity Is Overvalued?

Myers and Majluf (1984) offer an explanation of the negative market reaction to SEOs. They use an argument based on information asymmetry to explain the observed tendency for the market to react negatively to a SEO. Below we summarize their argument, and those of other authors who have based their analyses on this hypothesis.

First, they argue that the market is chronically less informed about the earnings potential of the firm, and therefore examines management's decisions for clues about the firm's earnings. *Second*, they formulate *managerial response criteria* in the face of information asymmetry based on Myers's (1984) *Pecking-Order Hypothesis*. According to this hypothesis, the firm can best avoid the dead-weight costs associated with information asymmetry by simply avoiding issuing securities—that is, by using retained earnings to pursue capital investments over time.

However, if the firm requires external financing, it is better to issue debt securities rather than equity securities. This is so because debt securities, owing to their priority, are less sensitive to the value of the firm, and therefore are less subject to the underpricing problem. External equity is at the bottom of the pecking order, and would (presumably) be offered only if the firm's insiders have private information that the firm's equity is overpriced in the market.

Exceptions to the Myers and Majluf Argument

Cooney and Kalay (1993) develop a model that uncovers potentially important exceptions to the Myers and Majluf prediction that the market reaction to equity issuance will always be negative: "The Myers and Majluf (1984) model predicts a nonpositive price reaction to an announcement of a new issue of equity . . . [T]he Myers and Majluf result is a direct outcome of their assumption that all potential projects facing the firm have a nonnegative net present value. Refining the Myers and Majluf model, by allowing for the realistic possibility of potential projects having negative net present values, leads to different predictions. The refined model predicts positive as well as negative stock price responses, consistent with recent empirical evidence concerning the stock price effects of new stock issues" (p. 149).

Strategic Considerations and the Market's Reaction to Equity Financing

Viswanath (1993) also developed a theoretical model that expands on the Pecking-Order Hypothesis, arguing that the market's reaction to equity issues may not always be negative. One of the predictions of Viswanath's model is that the market's price reaction to a SEO announcement should be *positively* related to the prior *run-up* in the

---

[7]Examples of a large literature on the valuation effects of SEO announcements include Mikkelson and Partch (1986), Asquith and Mullins (1986), Masulis and Korwal (1986), and Denis (1991, 1994).

firm's stock price: "Since one would expect stock prices to rise as the market learns of the existence of NPV > 0 projects, a runup in the stock price could be taken as a proxy of the existence of future NPV > 0 projects" (p. 226). He cites Asquith and Mullins (1986) for evidence that is consistent with this prediction.

13.6.2   Is the Firm Revealing Lower Than Expected Earnings?

Miller and Rock (1985) also developed a theoretical model based on information asymmetry that has implications for the market's reaction to a SEO announcement. In their model, the market estimates a firm's true earnings and values the firm accordingly. However, the market cannot directly observe the true level of a firm's earnings. Therefore, the market must take clues from the firm's investment, dividend, and financing decisions to ascertain the firm's earnings. In general, the market assumes that the firm's earnings are sufficient to fund all profitable investments—that is, that the firm's internal net cash flow is positive. Therefore, an announcement of a SEO generally reveals that the issuing firm has a lower level of earnings than the market expected, and the market price falls.

However, the market's reaction to a SEO depends critically on the market's pre-announcement expectations of optimal investment versus earnings: "The sign and size of the price change following an announcement of new financing will then depend on the relation of optimal investment . . . to the pre-announcement expectation of earnings . . . If the internal net cash flow had been expected to be positive, financing is bad news . . . But if expected earnings had been low relative to (optimal investment), so that some positive financing had been anticipated, the announcement effect might go either way, depending on whether the actual announced financing turned out to be greater or less than expected" (p. 1038).

Their arguments suggest that the market's reaction to a firm's SEO, though generally negative, should be positively related to the firm's pre-announcement market-to-book equity ratio, as a measure of the market's assessment of the issuing firm's investment opportunities relative to its current earnings. Evidence presented in Figure 13-3 is consistent with this prediction.

The figure is generated by (a) sorting 2,960 SEO firms into 12 groups according to their pre-announcement market-to-book equity ratios, and then (b) calculating the average filing-period abnormal return for each group. The following ranges of market-to-book equity ratio are used to form the groups: (a) 0–1, (b) 1–3, (c) 3–5, (d) 5–7, (e) 7–9, (f) 9–11, (g) 11–13, (h) 13–15, (i) 15–17, (j) 17–19, (k) 19–25, and (l) >25. As the trendline indicates, there is positive relationship between abnormal returns and market-to-book equity ratio. Other studies that provide consistent evidence include Barclay and Litzenberger (1988), Dierkens (1991), Pilotte (1992), Denis (1994), and Jung, Kim, and Stulz (1996).

13.6.3   Agency Explanations

It is also possible to generate an explanation for the market's negative reaction to equity issues based on agency theory. One argument is as follows. Management, acting in their own interest rather than that of the shareholders, may desire to underemploy debt in the firm's capital structure, because leverage increases the firm's risk of bankruptcy and the potential for loss of their jobs. Thus, the issuance of equity may reveal

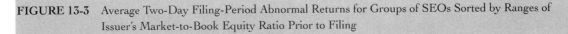

FIGURE 13-3 Average Two-Day Filing-Period Abnormal Returns for Groups of SEOs Sorted by Ranges of Issuer's Market-to-Book Equity Ratio Prior to Filing

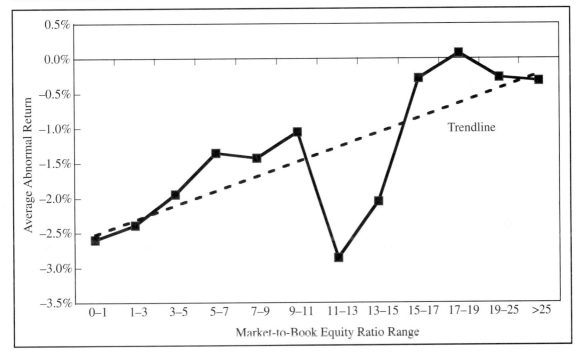

U.S. Nonfinancial, Nonutility Firms, 1980–2000
Sources: Raw data from Standard & Poor's *Research Insight* database and Center for Research in Security Prices (CRSP) database.

that management has succeeded in taking an action that is in their interest rather than in the interest of the firm's shareholders. According to this argument, the market's reaction to a SEO will be most negative if the firm intends to use the proceeds of the offering to reduce outstanding debt.

Jensen's (1986) *Free Cash Flow Hypothesis* provides another agency-based argument in this context. In general, a firm's management has a private incentive to retain cash flow rather than pay a dividend because it can use the cash to make (dubious) investments and thereby increase the size of its *empire*. By extension, a firm's management may undertake a SEO to raise cash for the same purpose. Therefore, the free cash flow argument also predicts a general negative market reaction to a SEO.

However, the market's reaction depends on the market's pre-announcement expectation of the firm's profitable investment opportunities, as Denis (1994) explains: "Jensen (1986) relies on agency arguments in predicting a role for investment opportunities in explaining market reactions to equity offerings . . . [M]anagers have incentives to increase the assets under their control even if doing so causes a reduction in firm value. Thus, the market's reaction to the announcement of an equity offering will depend on its assessment of the likelihood that the funds raised will be invested in positive net present value projects. For those firms with valuable investment opportunities, the market reaction will be positive while for those firms with poor opportunities, the reaction will be negative" (pp. 161–162). Here again, theory suggests that the market's reaction to a SEO should be positively related to the firm's pre-announcement market-to-book equity ratio.

13.7   OTHER ISSUES RELATED TO SEOs

In this section, we briefly focus on several other issues related to SEOs that have been addressed in the literature. These include (a) the pre-offering and post-offering performance of the stocks of firms that have conducted a SEO, (b) evidence of earnings management prior to a SEO filing, (c) insider trading around a SEO, and (d) withdrawn SEOs.

13.7.1   The Pre-offering and Post-offering Stock Returns of SEO Firms

Several empirical studies have documented two interesting aspects of the longer-term pre-offering and post-offering performance of the stocks of firms that conduct a SEO. Regarding pre-offering performance, several empirical studies have found that SEO firms generally realize a large positive *run-up* in their stock prices for one to two years prior to the offering (e.g., Asquith and Mullins 1986; Korajczyk, Lucas, and McDonald 1992). In contrast, other studies have shown that the stocks of issuing firms substantially *underperform* benchmarks for one to five years after the offering (e.g., Loughran and Ritter 1995, Spiess and Affleck-Graves 1995, Teoh, Welch, and Wong 1998, Jegadeesh 2000).

We tested for these two long-horizon behaviors using 3,205 SEOs completed in the years 1980 to 1999. We calculated (a) average cumulative raw returns on the offering firms for a period ranging from one year prior to the SEO filing to one year after the filing, (b) contemporaneous average cumulative returns on the equally weighted index of NYSE, AMEX, and NASDAQ stocks, and (c) the difference. The results are displayed in Figure 13-4.

Consistent with previous studies, the issuing firms in our sample exhibit substantial run-up prior to their SEO filings, on average. The average raw return in the year prior to the offering announcement was 100.0 percent, compared to 40.0 percent for the equally weighted index. However, the issuers underperformed the index in the year after the filing. For the year beginning on day +2 relative to the filing day, the average cumulative return on the issuing firms' stocks is 11.2 percent. This compares unfavorably with the contemporaneous average return of 24.7 percent on the equally weighted index.

13.7.2   Earnings Management and the SEO

In an attempt to explain the run-up phenomenon, researchers have focused on the tendencies of offering firms to *manage* (or, perhaps more accurately, to *manipulate*) their earnings prior to the offering. These studies have consistently found evidence that issuing firms exhibit unusually high earnings prior to the offering, and unusually low earnings after the offering. (e.g., Hansen and Crutchley 1990; McLaughlin, Safieddine, and Vasudevan 1996; Loughran and Ritter 1997; and Teoh, Welch, and Wong 1998). This

FIGURE 13-4 Average Cumulative Raw Returns on Stocks of SEO Firms from One Year before to One Year after Filing Data, Contemporaneous Average Cumulative Returns on Equally Weighted Index of U.S. Stocks, and Differences

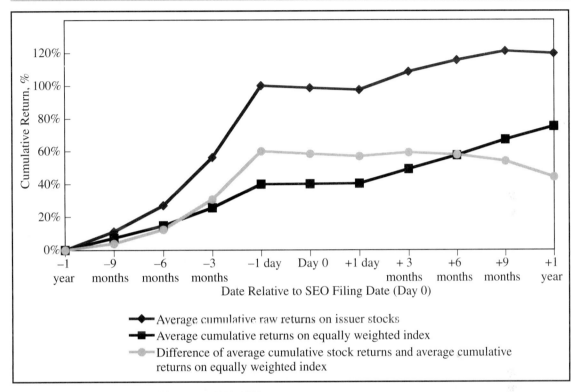

3,205 U.S. Nonfinancial, Nonutility Firms, 1980–1999

evidence suggests that firms that intend to conduct a SEO tend to inflate their earnings in advance to hype up the price of the stock for the offering.

However, for this conjecture to explain both the observed pre-offering and post-offering performance of the stocks of issuing firms, we require additional evidence on two pertinent issues. *First*, it must be shown that the managements of these firms tend to undertake deliberate actions to temporarily inflate their earnings prior to the SEO. *Second*, it must be shown that the market is indeed fooled by the inflated earnings prior to the offering.

Teoh, Welch, and Wong (1998) provided evidence on both issues. *First*, after documenting the basic evidence that issuing firms have high earnings before a SEO and low earnings after, they examined the *components* of these firms' earnings and document evidence that the managements of these firms, to varying degrees, manipulated *discretionary accounting accruals* (i.e., accruals that are, to a certain extent, under their control) in the predicted manner; that is, they temporarily adjusted accruals to report higher earnings prior to the offering, and then reversed these adjustments after the offering, which, of course, resulted in lower post-offering earnings.

Second, they show that there is a strong negative relationship between the extent of such pre-issue earnings manipulations and post-issue stock returns, suggesting that indeed the market was fooled by these earnings manipulations. Rangan (1998) provides analysis and evidence very similar to that provided by Teoh, Welch, and Wong. Loughran and Ritter (1997) also provide important evidence on the matter. They show that, at the time of the offering, the observed earnings multiples of the offering firms' stocks do not suggest that the market expects earnings to deteriorate, again suggesting that investors are fooled by these firms' earnings manipulations.

These results are particularly surprising given the results of an additional study by Brous (1992). Brous shows that analysts tend to *decrease* their earnings forecasts of firms that announce a SEO, and the extent of these decreases is related to the announcement-period abnormal return associated with the offering. These results suggest that the market is aware of the pending post-offering earnings decreases of such firms—at least at the time of the offering announcement, if not before—and yet, based on their poor post-offering performances, the market does not adjust the prices of these stocks to fully reflect this information.

13.7.3 Trading and Stock Price Manipulation around SEOs

Several researchers have investigated various aspects of trading activity around a SEO for clues about possible trading manipulation by informed traders. Safieddine and Wilhelm (1996) summarize their analysis as follows: "We investigate the nature and magnitude of short-selling activity around seasoned equity offerings, the relation between short-selling activity and issue discounts, and the consequences of the Securities and Exchange Commission (SEC's) adoption of Rule 10b-21 in response to concerns about manipulative short-selling practices. Seasoned offerings are characterized by abnormally high levels of short selling and option open interest. Higher levels of such activity are related to lower expected proceeds from the issuance of new shares. Where it could not be circumvented, Rule 10b-21 appears to have curbed short-selling activity and reduced issue discounts" (p. 729).

Lee (1997) examined the relationship between top executives' trading behavior and long-run returns following an SEO, and found that "primary issuers, who sell mostly newly-issued primary shares, significantly underperform their benchmarks, regardless of the top executives' prior trading pattern. However, top executives' trading is reliably associated with the stock returns of secondary issuers, who sell mostly secondary shares previously held by existing shareholders. On average, secondary issuers do not underperform their benchmarks. The results suggest that increased free cash flow problems after issue play an important role in explaining the underperformance of issuing firms" (p. 1439).

13.7.4 Withdrawn Security Offerings

Occasionally, a firm *withdraws* a security offering after it has filed with the SEC. Using Securities Data Corporation's new-issue database, we found 505 withdrawals of SEO filings by U.S. nonfinancial firms over the years 1980 to 2000. This total is small relative to the 6,631 *completed* offerings over this period, indicating that withdrawal is quite unusual. The reasons cited for withdrawal varied widely; some firms merely postponed the offering, while others cited unfavorable market conditions.

Mikkelson and Partch (1988) investigated withdrawn SEOs and withdrawn convertible debt offerings:

> [For] the stock price behavior associated with public offerings of common stock and convertible debt that are withdrawn by the issuing firm, as well as the stock price behavior associated with completed offerings . . . we find that stock returns are negative in the period from the announcement to the withdrawal, and are statistically insignificant from the announcement to the issuance. Stock returns are positive at the withdrawal and negative at the issuance. Furthermore, the average stock returns associated with withdrawals are significantly different from zero only when the reported reason for the withdrawals is unfavorable market conditions. Our evidence suggests that managers' decisions to withdraw equity offerings depend on recent stock price behavior, and that managers' decisions convey information about firm value to market participants. (p. 119)

13.8   Summary of Learning Objectives

This chapter discussed the management of a firm's equity, covering three main topics. *First*, we discussed the basic contracting problem between a firm's shareholders and management. *Second*, we introduced the theory of the internal capital market. *Third*, we related theory to empirical evidence pertaining to seasoned equity offerings (SEOs).

An Equity Management Model

We provided a basic equity management model for a public firm in Figure 13-1. In this depiction, the firm is formed of two basic inputs: accumulated equity, which is shareholders' input, and operational skills, management's input. These inputs yield net cash flows that will be distributed among (a) continuing shareholders (as dividends) and exiting shareholders (as stock repurchases), (b) reinvestment (as retained earnings), and (c) private benefits of control to management (perks).

The basic contracting problem derives from the firm's shareholders being a diffuse group; so their exercise of control is costly. Thus, the firm's managers have some slack that allows them to extract private benefits of control. Mechanisms must be put in place to limit managers' ability to extract such rents, or else the firm's shareholders will eventually withdraw their equity contribution (i.e., they will fire management). Three such mechanisms are prevalent, though all of them are imperfect: (a) requiring the regular payment of dividends (or perhaps requiring stock repurchases), (b) monitoring the firm's allocation of net cash flows, and (c) including incentive devices in managers' compensation contracts.

The Theory of the Internal Capital Market

Theory posits that many firms essentially operate an *internal capital market*. The theory of the internal capital market is an enrichment of the traditional *capital budgeting* paradigm. An internal capital market is defined as a system that a firm's senior management uses to determine the allocation of the firm's limited available internal equity capital among competing projects developed by managers within the firm's hierarchy. The theory of the internal capital market was developed to explain both (a) the existence of multisegment firms. and (b) their capital budgeting practices.

Both agency and information asymmetry theories provide explanations for why a firm's internal capital market may be superior to the external capital market. External debt financing is problematic because a conflict of interest develops between the borrowing firm and its creditor. External equity financing is problematic because of the information asymmetry problem. Moreover, an internal capital market may be better at (a) monitoring investment, (b) redeploying assets (and "winner-picking"), (c) providing entrepreneurial incentives, and (d) instilling competition (e.g., among division managers).

However, internal capital markets are beset by several problems—specifically, problems associated with *decentralized information* and *incentive problems*. For either a multilevel or multidivisional firm, much of the critical information on capital investment opportunities that is generated within the overall firm is taken in by managers at these various levels, rather than by senior management. Thus, any such firm must decide the extent to which managers at these levels are (a) given autonomy to make capital budgeting decisions based on such information versus (b) instructed to share such information with senior management, who then determine the allocations of available internal capital within the firm.

In practice, a typical balance between extremes (a) and (b) is struck by requiring individual managers to submit capital investment proposals periodically to senior management (and thereby to share the information that they have acquired), who then use the information contained in these proposals to allocate the firm's available internal capital. However, this practice engenders an information asymmetry-induced principal–agent conflict: Subordinate managers have a private incentive to pursue empire building by exaggerating the profit potential of the projects that they propose, and senior managers are chronically at an informational disadvantage as they attempt to ascertain the true profitability of such proposals. If this problem is not addressed, the overall firm would tend to overinvest.

Senior management has two imperfect means to control this problem. They can monitor a subordinate manager over time to determine *ex post* the extent to which he or she is engaging in inefficient empire building (e.g., the division is observed to be less profitable). Unfortunately, such monitoring is often a case of too little, too late. Alternatively, senior management can order an *ex ante* audit of a specific manager's proposal. Unfortunately, such audits are costly. A more cost-effective mechanism is simply threatening an *ex ante* audit, where the probability of an *ex ante* audit increases with the size of the proposed budget.

SEOs

We discussed the process by which a firm issues seasoned equity. In the issuance process, the firm faces choices regarding (a) whether to make the issue a private placement, rights offering, or general public offering; (b) how to determine the mix of primary versus secondary shares; (c) whether to provide a stock-only offering or to sell *units* that include warrants; (d) how to choose an underwriter (negotiation versus competitive bidding); (e) whether to secure firm commitment or best-efforts pricing from the underwriter; and (f) whether to employ traditional or *shelf* registration of the issue.

Regarding the valuation effects of SEOs, empirical evidence indicates that the market's reaction to a SEO is generally negative. Both agency theory and information asymmetry theory provide explanations for this result. Both also predict that the market's reaction will be more favorable when the firm's pre-announcement market-to-book equity ratio is higher, a prediction that is supported by empirical evidence. Additional evidence indicates that SEO firms experience a large run-up in their stock prices prior to the offer, and then underperform benchmarks after the offering. Finally, evidence indicates that SEO firms manipulate their earnings prior to the offering to secure a higher price for the offered shares.

Review Questions and Problems

1. Regarding the *equity management model* introduced in this chapter,
   a. describe the structure of the model.
   b. discuss the basic contracting problem in the model.
   c. explain the three prevalent solutions to the contracting problem.
2. What are the two elements of the traditional capital budgeting paradigm?
3. What are the limitations of the traditional capital budgeting paradigm?
4. Discuss the circumstances under which an internal capital market dominates the external capital market.
5. Discuss the dual problems of *decentralized information* and *incentive problems* within the context of allocating internal capital in a multidivisional firm.
6. What mechanisms can senior management use to counteract the incentives of division managers to exaggerate the profitability of projects that they propose?
7. What is the cross-subsidization problem?
8. What are the implications of internal capital market theory for conglomerates?
9. What are the implications of internal capital market theory for a firm's decision to exit a struggling business activity?
10. Describe the various means by which a firm can issue seasoned equity privately.
11. What is a rights offering, and why do firms avoid using this method of issuing seasoned equity?
12. Describe the process by which a public firm issues seasoned equity via a general public offering.
13. Why do SEO firms generally select an underwriter via negotiation rather than competitive bidding?
14. Explain the role of warrants as partial compensation for an underwriter.
15. Regarding shelf registration (i.e., SEC Rule 415),
    a. differentiate shelf registration from traditional registration of a security offering.
    b. explain the advantages of shelf registration.
    c. explain why most SEO firms use traditional registration rather than shelf registration.
16. List and discuss the three components of the overall cost of a seasoned equity issue.
17. Discuss the determinants of underwriter spreads on SEOs.
18. Discuss the prediction of the *Pecking Order Hypothesis*, as developed into a formal model by Myers and Majluf (1984), for the market's reaction to a SEO.
19. Discuss the rationale provided in Miller and Rock's (1985) model for the market's generally negative reaction to a SEO.

20. Discuss agency theory arguments for the market's reaction to a SEO.
21. Summarize the empirical evidence on the market's reaction to a SEO announcement.
22. Why is the market's reaction to a SEO announcement positively related to the issuing firm's market-to-book equity ratio?
23. Discuss the longer-term pre-offering and post-offering stock performance of SEO firms.
24. Discuss the evidence on
    a. SEO firms' earnings management prior to an offering.
    b. informed investors trading activity around a SEO.

Creative Thinking Issues

1. In your opinion, do managers focus more on the book value or the market value of their equity? *Should* they? Why or why not?
2. How might the evidence of the market's negative reaction to SEOs affect the following:
    a. The overall decision of a firm to go public or remain private?
    b. A firm's decision to offer equity privately via a private placement, an ESOP, or other method?
    c. A firm's ownership structure?
    d. A firm's governance structure?
    e. A firm's leverage?
    f. A firm's dividend policy?
3. Does the evidence on the occasional withdrawal of a pending SEO (especially for the frequently cited reason of *unfavorable market conditions*) suggest that the managers of withdrawing firms believe that the market is (a) inefficient, (b) ill informed, or (c) currently imposing a high cost of equity capital? Can you think of other underlying reasons for a withdrawal?

Projects and Analyses

1. Collect annual data on the capital expenditures and net cash flows of a number of firms. Calculate the sensitivity of each firm's capital expenditures to changes in its net cash flow. Attempt to explain differences in this sensitivity across the firms in your sample.
2. Identify a sample of recent SEOs. Then,
    a. calculate and examine abnormal returns on the issuers' stocks around the time of their announcements.
    b. calculate longer-term returns on the offering firms' stocks before and after the offering.
    c. examine the offering firms' earnings performances before and after the offering.

CHAPTER

Dividend Policy and Stock Repurchases

14

14.1 INTRODUCTION

In this chapter we focus on a firm's *payout policies*—that is, policies regarding cash dividends and stock repurchases. Cash dividends and stock repurchases are the two principal means by which a firm pays cash to shareholders. Both are partial liquidations of the firm's assets in the amount of the total payout, though mechanically they differ.

Cash dividends are paid to all shareholders on a pro rata basis. In an ideal market, the result of a dividend payment is that the firm's stock price falls by the per-share amount of the dividend. In a stock repurchase, the firm uses cash to *retire* some outstanding shares, buying shares from any investors who choose to sell. In an ideal market, a firm's stock repurchases reduce its shares outstanding, as well as the firm's assets (i.e., cash), but have no effect on the market price of the shares.

Cash dividends have long been an important component of an investor's return on a stock investment. However, in recent years the dividend component of the returns on U.S. stocks has steadily fallen, both in absolute terms and relative to capital gains. For the years 1950 to 1982, the dividend and capital gains components of average annual returns on New York Stock Exchange (NYSE) stocks in composite were 4.2 percent and 8.0 percent, respectively. Thus, dividends accounted for fully *one third* of average annual returns. In the subsequent years of 1983 to 1999, the corresponding figures were 3.2 percent and 12.8 percent, respectively; hence, the dividend component of total annual average returns was only 20 percent.

In contrast, stock repurchases have increased in importance as a component of firms' payout policies. From 1980 to 2000, the composite market equity values of U.S. nonfinancial firms increased approximately 11-fold, while the dollar value of annual composite stock repurchases increased 27-fold. In recent years, the composite dollar value of stock repurchases has exceeded that of dividends.

Despite decades of debate and research, financial economists, managers, and investors still disagree about whether a firm should pay a dividend, how much the dividend should be, and what the effect is of a dividend on the market equity value of the firm's stock. However, much progress has been made, beginning with Miller and Modigliani's (1961) proof that, in an ideal market, dividend policy is irrelevant as long as the firm's capital investments are fixed. (As we will see, their proof can be extended to show that stock repurchases are also irrelevant in an ideal capital market.)

Both dividend and stock repurchase policies may be rendered *relevant* by any of the real-world factors that we have discussed, including principal–agent conflicts, information asymmetry, taxes, and transaction costs. Moreover, the motivations for a manager's decision to conduct stock repurchases may be very different from those associated with the dividend payment decision.

We begin our analysis of dividends and stock repurchases in Section 14.2 with a discussion of Miller and Modigliani's proof of the irrelevance of dividend policy in an ideal capital market, extending their argument to include stock repurchases. In Section 14.3, we provide several time series and cross-sectional perspectives on the propensities of seasoned, publicly traded U.S. nonfinancial firms to pay dividends and repurchase stock. We then bifurcate most of the rest of the chapter into sections covering dividend policy (Sections 14.4 to 14.9) and stock repurchases (Sections 14.10 to 14.12). Following a brief empirical analysis in Section 14.13, we summarize the chapter's learning objectives in Section 14.14.

14.2 THE IRRELEVANCE OF DIVIDENDS AND STOCK REPURCHASES IN AN IDEAL CAPITAL MARKET

In this section, we briefly reiterate the Miller and Modigliani (1961) proof of dividend irrelevance in an ideal capital market. They argued that, in an ideal capital market, dividend policy is irrelevant as long as the firm's capital investments and debt policy are fixed. Dividend payments are simply financed over time by a combination of excess retained earnings and, as necessary, new equity financing. We extend their argument to show that stock repurchases are also irrelevant in an ideal capital market.

14.2.1 The Basic Argument

Suppose the entrepreneur of a new firm has a profitable single-period capital investment project that requires an initial investment of INV_0 at time 0. The project's expected return is r^*, which is greater than the discount rate applicable to the project's expected future cash flow, r. The present value of the project is

$$PV = \frac{(1 + r^*)INV_0}{(1 + r)},$$ (14.1)

and the project's net present value (NPV) is

$$NPV = -INV_0 + PV > 0.$$ (14.2)

Case 1: No Dividend

We initially assume that, to finance the project, the entrepreneur sells some combination of debt and *outside equity* securities, denoted as $\Delta DEBT_0$ and $\Delta STOCK_0$, respectively:

$$INV_0 = \Delta DEBT_0 + \Delta STOCK_0.$$ (14.3)

In an ideal market, the value of the debt and equity securities sold will be equal to the proceeds received (i.e., the sales themselves are transactions that have NPV of zero). Following the sale of the securities, the entrepreneur retains equity with a value equal to the full amount of the project's NPV. If we denote the value of the entrepreneur's share of the firm's equity as $ENTEQ_0$, then $ENTEQ_0 = NPV$. Modigliani and Miller's (1958) Proposition I, discussed in Chapter 2, applies here.

Case 2: Including a Dividend Payment

Alternatively, the entrepreneur could sell debt and equity securities sufficient not only to finance the project, but also to pay himself an immediate dividend, denoted as DIV_0:

$$INV_0 + DIV_0 = \Delta DEBT_0 + \Delta STOCK_0. \tag{14.4}$$

In this case, the value of the entrepreneur's equity is $ENTEQ'_0 = PV - \Delta DEBT_0 - \Delta STOCK_0 - DIV_0 = NPV - DIV_0$. The entrepreneur also receives the dividend DIV_0, so his wealth is the same as in case 1 (i.e., $ENTEQ'_0 + DIV_0 = ENTEQ_0$).

The constraint on the total value of securities that can be sold is that the sum $\Delta DEBT_0 + \Delta STOCK_0$ cannot exceed the present value (PV) of the project's expected payoff:

$$\Delta DEBT_0 + \Delta STOCK_0 \le PV. \tag{14.5}$$

The dividend is correspondingly constrained:

$$DIV_0 \le PV - INV_0 = NPV. \tag{14.6}$$

Again, an arbitrage proof of the above argument is analogous to the proof of M&M Proposition I.

The above analyses illustrate the two main points that Miller and Modigliani make in their paper. *First*, "the higher the dividend payout in any period the more the new capital that must be raised from external sources to maintain any desired level of investment" (p. 413). *Second*, "the irrelevance of dividend policy, given investment policy, is 'obvious, once you think of it.' It is, after all, merely one more instance of the general principle that there are no 'financial illusions' in a rational and perfect economic environment. Values there are determined solely by 'real' considerations—in this case the earning power of the firm's assets and its investment policy—and not by how the fruits of the earning power are 'packaged' for distribution" (p. 414).

A Numerical Example

Suppose the founder of a new firm has a single-period project that requires an initial investment of $INV_0 = \$10$ million. The project's expected return is $r^* = 30$ percent, and the appropriate discount rate is $r = 12$ percent. The present value of the project's expected payoff is

$$PV = \frac{(1 + r^*)INV_0}{(1 + r)} = \frac{1.3(\$10 \text{ million})}{(1.12)} = \$11.607 \text{ million},$$

and the project's NPV is

$$NPV = -\$10 \text{ million} + \$11.607 \text{ million} = \$1.607 \text{ million}$$

If the entrepreneur sells just enough debt and equity securities to finance the project, say, $\Delta DEBT_0 = \$4$ million and $\Delta STOCK_0 = \$6$ million, then she would retain equity with a value of $ENTEQ_0 = \$1.607$ million (= $\$11.607$ million – $\$10$ million).

If instead the entrepreneur sells debt and equity securities with total values of $\Delta DEBT_0 = \$4$ million and $\Delta STOCK_0 = \$7$ million, she could finance the project, pay herself a dividend of $DIV_0 = \$1$ million, and hold equity with a value of $ENTEQ_0' = \$0.607$ million.

14.2.2   Extending the Argument to Include Stock Repurchases

Miller and Modigliani's dividend irrelevance argument can be readily extended to show the irrelevance of stock repurchases. Consider a seasoned firm that has just received net cash flows from its current operations through date t, denoted as $NCFO_t$. For simplicity, we assume that the firm's assets temporarily consist only of cash in the amount of $NCFO_t$. The firm has decided to make capital investments that require outlays totaling INV_t.

In addition, the firm could issue debt securities in the amount of $\Delta DEBT_t$, issue equity securities in the amount of $\Delta STOCK_t$, repurchase shares in the amount of REP_t, or pay a dividend in the amount of DIV_t. Regarding these choices, the firm must adhere to the following *cash flow constraint* for period t, which is organized to solve for this chapter's focal variables, dividends and stock repurchases:

$$NCFO_t - INV_t + \Delta DEBT_t + \Delta STOCK_t = DIV_t + REP_t. \tag{14.7}$$

As long as the firm does not alter its commitment to capital spending in the amount of INV_t, any combination of values of the other variables that obeys Equation 14.7 results in the same wealth for the firm's shareholders. That is, both dividend and stock repurchase policies are irrelevant.

14.2.3   Examples of the Cash Flow Constraint

In the next section, we examine composite values of the cash-flow items in Equation 14.7. As a prelude, we provide examples of cash flow constraints for eight large U.S. nonfinancial firms for the calendar year 2000. The firms are Coca-Cola, Exxon Mobil, General Electric, General Motors, International Business Machines (IBM), Merck & Co., Sears Roebuck, and Verizon Communications. The cash flows for each firm are displayed in Table 14-1. (These values were taken from each firm's sources and uses statement.)

The following four observations summarize the data in Table 14-1. *First*, the bulk of each firms' *NCFO* in 2000 consisted of the sum of *income before extraordinary items* plus *depreciation and amortization*. *Second*, *NCFO* was generally sufficient to fund investment activities, which in turn consisted primarily of capital expenditures. *Third*, sales of stock generally provided very little cash inflow, whereas net debt issuance (issuance less reduction) generally provided somewhat more substantial cash inflow. *Fourth*, stock repurchases exceeded dividends in 2000 for four of the eight firms.

For our analysis of composite cash flows in the next section, we compress the variables shown in Table 14-1 into six items: net cash flow from operations (*NCFO*), net cash flow from investing activities (*INV*), net change in debt ($\Delta DEBT$ = issuance of

TABLE 14-1   Cash Flow Statements for Indicated Firms, 2000

(Amounts in $ million)	Coca-Cola	Exxon Mobil	General Electric	General Motors	International Business Machines (IBM)	Merck & Co.	Sears Roebuck	Verizon Communications
Operations								
Income before extraordinary items	$2,177	$15,990	$12,735	$4,452	$8,093	$6,822	$1,343	$10,810
Depreciation and amortization	$773	$8,130	$7,736	$13,411	$4,995	$1,277	CF	$12,261
Extraordinary items and Disc. Oper.	$0	–$308	$0	$0	$0	$0	$0	$0
Deferred taxes	$3	$10	$1,153	$0	$29	$0	$0	$3,434
Equity in net loss (earnings)	$380	–$387	CF	CF	CF	CF	CF	–$3,792
Sale of PP&E and Sale of Investments	–$127	$0	$0	$0	–$792	$0	–$19	–$3,793
Funds from operations—other	$1,231	–$576	$239	–$1,342	$0	$612	$2,053	–$1,832
Receivables	–$39	–$4,832	–$537	–$1,351	–$4,720	–$940	–$93	–$2,440
Inventory	–$2	–$297	–$924	–$297	–$55	–$210	–$560	–$530
Accounts payable and accrued liabilities	–$84	CF	$3,297	CF	$2,245	$17	CF	$1,973
Income taxes—accrued	–$96	CF	CF	CF	CF	CF	$0	CF
Other assets and liabilities	–$631	$5,207	–$1,009	$4,877	–$521	$110	–$22	–$264
Net cash flow from operations	*$3,585*	*$22,937*	*$22,690*	*$19,750*	*$9,274*	*$7,687*	*$2,702*	*$15,827*
Investing Activities								
Increases in investments	CF	–$1,648	–$16,076	–$243,950	–$1,079	CF	–$40	–$1,024
Sale of investments	CF	CF	CF	$228,794	$1,393	CF	CF	$0
Change in short-term investments	CF	$41	CF	CF	CF	CF	CF	–$221
Capital expenditures	–$733	–$8,446	–$13,967	–$31,605	–$5,616	–$2,728	–$1,084	–$17,633
Sale of PP&E	$45	CF	$6,767	$15,993	$1,619	$0	CF	CF
Acquisitions	CF	$0	–$2,332	–$6,379	$0	CF	–$1	CF
Other investing activities	–$477	$6,755	–$12,091	$3,374	–$565	–$914	$75	$2,823
Net cash flow from investing activities	*–$1,165*	*–$3,298*	*–$37,699*	*–$33,773*	*–$4,248*	*–$3,641*	*–$1,050*	*–$16,055*
Financing Activities								
Sale of common and preferred stock	$331	$493	$469	$2,792	CF	$2,141	$58	$576
Stock repurchases	$133	$2,352	CF	$1,613	$6,073	$3,545	$1,233	$2,294
Cash dividends	$1,685	$6,123	$5,401	$1,294	$929	$2,798	$322	$4,421
Issuance of long-term debt	$3,671	$238	$47,645	$35,558	$9,604	$442	$824	$8,781
Retirement of long-term debt	$4,256	$901	$32,762	$22,392	$7,561	$443	$2,277	$7,238
Change in current debt	CF	–$5,042	–$8,243	CF	–$1,400	$906	$1,295	$3,515
Other financing activities	$0	–$478	$12,942	$1,069	$0	–$149	$118	$33
Net cash flow from financing activities	*–$2,072*	*–$14,165*	*$14,650*	*$14,120*	*–$6,359*	*–$3,447*	*–$1,537*	*–$1,048*
Other Items								
Exchange rate effect	–$140	–$82	$0	–$255	–$147	–$84	–$2	$0
Change in cash and equivalents	*$208*	*$5,392*	*–$359*	*–$158*	*–$1,480*	*$515*	*$113*	*–$1,276*
Reconciliation	*$0*	*$0*	*$0*	*$0*	*$0*	*$0*	*$0*	*$0*

Note: CF = combined figure (item was combined with another item).
Source: Raw data from Standard & Poor's *Research Insight* database.

long-term debt less retirement of long-term debt, plus change in current debt), sales of stock ($\Delta STOCK$), cash dividends (DIV), and stock repurchases (REP). Thus, we ignore three other cash flow items, which are generally small in magnitude: *other financing activities*, *exchange rate effect*, and *change in cash and equivalents*.

14.3 COMPOSITE CASH FLOWS OVER TIME: A FOCUS ON DIVIDENDS AND STOCK REPURCHASES

In this section, we provide several empirical perspectives on composite cash flows, with emphasis on cash dividends and stock repurchases. These perspectives are gleaned from an examination of annual composite cash flow data for *seasoned*, publicly traded U.S. nonfinancial firms for the years 1980 to 2000. We define a seasoned firm as a firm that has been publicly traded for more than one year. We focus on seasoned firms because they (a) collectively account for the overwhelming bulk of aggregate U.S. market equity value, and (b) are more likely to pay dividends and to conduct stock repurchases.

14.3.1 Composite Cash Flows

Our first perspective is on composite time series values of the six cash flow items defined in the previous section (i.e., $NCFO$, INV, $\Delta DEBT$, $\Delta STOCK$, DIV, and REP). The results are displayed in Figure 14-1.

Three aspects of the various series appear to be consistent with the Pecking-Order Hypothesis (Myers and Majluf 1984), discussed in earlier chapters. *First*, $NCFO$ and INV share a nearly perfect 1:1 relationship over time. It appears that firms do indeed prefer to finance capital investments with internally generated funds. *Second*, the gaps between $NCFO$ and INV over time appear to be closely related to the net change in composite debt, $\Delta DEBT$. This result suggests that debt is the preferred source of external funds to supplement internally generated cash in financing capital investments.

Third, composite proceeds of stock issues ($\Delta STOCK$) are consistently very small, suggesting that seasoned firms generally avoid external equity financing. Notable exceptions to this tendency occurred in 1999 and 2000, when seasoned firms raised $122 billion and $159 billion, respectively, from stock sales. However, underwritten seasoned equity offerings (SEOs) accounted for only part of this total ($32 billion in 1999 and $79 billion in 2000). The remainder is accounted for by (a) cash received in conjunction with a stock-financed acquisition, (b) the exercise of stock options, and (c) spin-offs (discussed in Chapter 16). For example, in July 2000 General Motors sold $2.4 billion of common stock to Fiat SpA.

Of course, dividends and stock repurchases are the focus of this chapter. Composite dividends form the most stable series among those presented. Composite dividends grew at an average annual rate of 4.7 percent over this period, more than doubling from $50 billion in 1980 to $114 billion in 2000. Composite stock repurchases are clearly more volatile than composite dividends, and also exhibited a much higher average growth rate. Repurchases grew at an average annual rate of 17.7 percent, increasing 27-fold from $6.1 billion in 1980 to $160 billion in 2000. As a result of their tremendous growth, composite stock repurchases exceeded composite dividends for

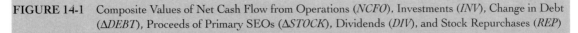

FIGURE 14-1 Composite Values of Net Cash Flow from Operations (*NCFO*), Investments (*INV*), Change in Debt (*ΔDEBT*), Proceeds of Primary SEOs (*ΔSTOCK*), Dividends (*DIV*), and Stock Repurchases (*REP*)

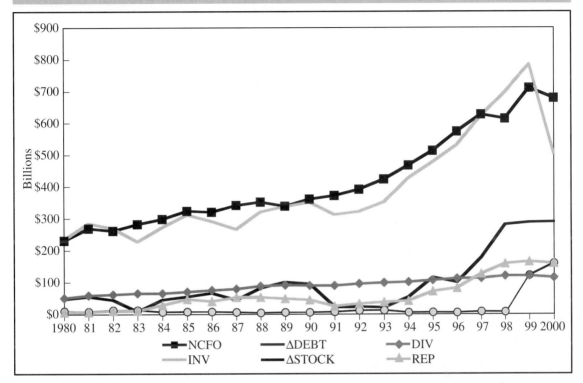

Seasoned Public U.S. Nonfinancial Firms, 1980–2000
Source: Raw data from Standard & Poor's *Compustat.*

the first time in 1997. Composite repurchase value has also grown at a faster rate than *NCFO* over time. In 1980, the ratio of *REP* to *NCFO* was only 2.7 percent; in 2000, the ratio was 23.5 percent.

Correlations among the Composite Cash Flow Items

We provide a closer analysis of relationships among the composite cash flow series shown in Figure 14-1 by calculating correlations of year-to-year *percentage changes* in their dollar values. The resulting correlation matrix is displayed in Table 14-2. The three correlations in the matrix that are statistically significant are highlighted in bold type in the table. These are: (a) $\Delta NCFO$ and ΔINV [correlation of 0.42], (b) ΔINV and $\Delta DEBT$ [0.61], and (c) $\Delta DEBT$ and ΔREP [0.77].

The correlation between $\Delta NCFO$ and ΔINV suggests that firms' capital investments depend heavily on contemporaneous internal cash flow. However, the correlation between ΔINV and $\Delta DEBT$ confirms our earlier conjecture that firms issue debt to *supplement* the financing of capital investments. The correlation between $\Delta DEBT$ and ΔREP is intriguing. Managers may seize the opportunity of favorable economic conditions to increase their leverage via debt-financed stock repurchases. Alternatively, they may repurchase shares using proceeds from debt issuance, and

TABLE 14-2 Correlations of Annual Percentage Changes in Indicated Composite Cash Flows

Seasoned Publicly Traded U.S. Nonfinancial Firms, 1980–2000

Annual Percentage Changes in	ΔNCFO	ΔINV	ΔDEBT	ΔSTOCK	ΔDIV	ΔREP
Net Cash Flow from Operations (ΔNCFO)	1.00					
Investments (ΔINV)	**0.42**	1.00				
Net Change in Debt (ΔDEBT)	0.02	**0.61**	1.00			
Proceeds of Stock Sales (ΔSTOCK)	0.37	0.08	–0.12	1.00		
Dividends (ΔDIV)	0.13	0.19	–0.17	–0.28	1.00	
Stock Repurchases (ΔREP)	0.04	0.36	**0.77**	–0.12	–0.13	1.00

Note: Correlations that are significant at the 10% level are shown in bold type.
Source: Raw data from Standard &Poor's *Research Insight* database.

then distribute the repurchased shares to a target firm (i.e., in an acquisition) that prefers stock to cash (see Allen and Michaely 1995; Fama and French 2001). However, firms may also issue debt to finance stock repurchases even in the absence of a pending stock-financed acquisition. If so, this is an important result because financing stock repurchases with new debt would substantially increase a firm's leverage.

14.3.2 Payout Propensities

Our second perspective on composite dividends and stock repurchases is provided in Figure 14-2. This figure displays, for each year from 1980 to 2000, the percentages of seasoned U.S. nonfinancial firms that paid dividends and that conducted stock repurchases.

The figures provide dramatic evidence of the decreasing propensity of firms to pay dividends. In 1980, 71 percent of seasoned firms paid dividends. This percentage fell steadily throughout the sample period so that in 2000 only 26 percent of seasoned firms paid dividends! The evidence for stock repurchases is in sharp contrast to the evidence for dividends. In 1980, 31 percent of seasoned firms conducted stock repurchases. This percentage waxed and waned, but generally rose over time to 48 percent in 1999 before falling back to 36 percent in 2000.

14.3.3 Payouts Relative to Market and Book Equity

Our third perspective on dividends and stock repurchases focuses on changes over time in their composite dollar values relative to market and book equity values. For each year from 1980 to 2000, we calculated the ratios of composite dividends, composite stock repurchases, and their sum, to both composite market and composite book equity values. The results are displayed in Figure 14-3.

Relative to both equity measures, composite dividends have decreased over the years. The decrease is particularly dramatic in relation to composite market equity values. In 1980, composite dividends represented 4.5 percent of composite market equity value and 6.2 percent of composite book equity value. By 2000, these ratios had fallen to 1.0 percent and 4.7 percent, respectively.

Seasoned Publicly Traded U.S. Nonfinancial Firms, 1980–2000
Source: Raw data from Standard & Poor's *Research Insight* database.

Again, stock repurchases have a different history. In 1980, composite stock repurchases represented only 0.5 percent of composite market equity value and 0.8 percent of composite book equity value. By 2000, the corresponding ratios had risen to 1.4 percent and 6.5 percent, respectively.

The sum of composite dividends and composite stock repurchases represents the total cash payouts by firms to their shareholders (i.e., continuing and exiting shareholders, respectively). In 1980, this sum represented 5.1 percent of composite market equity value and 7.0 percent of composite book equity value. Over the years, the former ratio generally fell, to a final value of 2.4 percent in 2000. However, the latter ratio generally *rose* over the years, peaking at 12.8 percent in 1998 before falling back slightly to end at 11.2 percent in 2000.

14.3.4   Are Dividends Disappearing?

In their paper "Disappearing Dividends," Fama and French (2001) closely analyzed the phenomenon of declining dividends. The authors found that the percentage of firms paying cash dividends fell from 66.5 percent in 1978 to only 20.8 percent in 1999. Their

FIGURE 14-3   Composite Dividends (DIV), Composite Stock Repurchases (REP), and Their Sum Each as a Percent of Composite Market Equity (MEQ) and Composite Book Equity (CEQ)

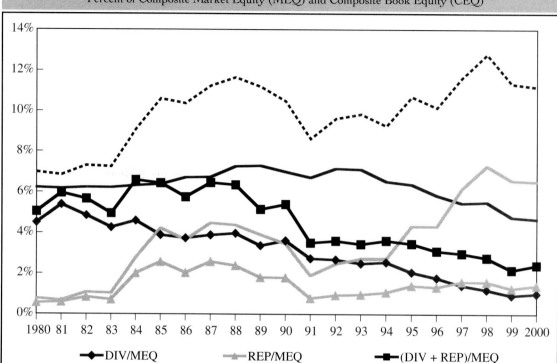

Seasoned Publicly Traded U.S. Nonfinancial Firms, 1980–2000
Source: Raw data from Standard & Poor's *Research Insight* database.

percentages, including and especially the percentage for 1999, tend to be lower than ours (in Figure 14-2) because they include new public firms (i.e., recent IPOs) in their annual samples, whereas we do not.

The authors also attempted to determine whether the phenomenon is due to (a) a change in the characteristics of firms in the market, specifically a shift toward a greater prevalence of firms that have always paid less or no dividends; or (b) an en masse decision of firms either to pay out a smaller proportion of their earnings in dividends or to pay no dividends at all. They documented evidence consistent with *both* explanations, and both are roughly equally important in explaining the phenomenon.

Regarding (a), they found a relative increase over time in the types of firms that traditionally have not paid dividends (i.e., small firms and firms with low profitability or strong growth opportunities). Regarding (b), they documented evidence that even the firms that have been traditional dividend payers (i.e., large, profitable firms) have begun to pay either smaller dividends or no dividends at all. Microsoft is a prime example of the latter.

Dividend Schmividend

Here is an article from *The New York Times* on the decline of dividend payments by U.S. firms.

A growing portion of corporate America appears to be concluding that dividends are no longer needed to attract investors and are therefore an unnecessary cost of doing business. Fewer companies are raising dividends, and more and more major companies do not bother to pay them at all. Dividends used to be a virtual requirement to convince investors that a company was successful and worthy of investment. Some institutional investors were barred from buying stocks that did not pay dividends.

But now, for the first time in recent history—and probably the first time since the Depression—a quarter of the value of the Standard & Poor's index of 500 stocks comes from companies that do not pay dividends. Two decades ago, only 2 percent of the value of the index came from such companies. In those days, a company in the S&P 500 that did not pay a dividend probably had been forced to stop doing so because of financial problems. These days, however, dividends are out of favor, and it is the hottest companies that don't pay them.

"At one time, stocks were considered riskier than other asset classes, so they had to pay dividends," said Arnold Kaufman, the editor of the *Outlook* newsletter published by Standard & Poor's. But now, he said, investors see stocks as less risky, and thus do not demand such protection.

While 402 of the 500 stocks in the index did pay dividends last year, only one of the top 15 performers, and 14 of the top 50, did so. Of the 14 that paid dividends, only one—Morgan Stanley Dean Witter—is paying out at least 1 percent of its share value. Since the company's share price doubled last year, that payout obviously made up a very small portion of the shareholder return. Most of the companies in the S&P 500 that are not paying dividends are successful technology companies that have profits, not hot Internet start-ups. The five largest non-dividend payers in the S&P—Microsoft, Cisco, America Online, Oracle, and MCI WorldCom—are all profitable. As recently as 1997, 90 percent of the value of the index came from companies that paid dividends. But that fell to 85.2 percent in 1998 and to 74.8 percent last year, said Mr. Kaufman.

To some extent, the decline reflects the fact that S&P has been more willing to add technology stocks that do not pay dividends to the index. But it also reflects an investor attitude that puts little pressure on companies to make payouts. While companies can still be penalized for reducing or eliminating dividends, they get little credit for introducing or raising dividends.

To be sure, most companies still pay dividends, and many raise their payouts every year. But the trend is unmistakable. Standard & Poor's reported yesterday that 1,701 dividend increases were reported by American companies last year, or 16.9 percent fewer than in 1998. There were smaller declines in 1997 and 1998 as well. In the past, a sharp decline of 15 percent or more in the number of companies with dividend increases usually came during recessions, when many companies were financially strapped. But the latest downtrend has come as the economy has boomed. The only similar trend occurred in the late 1960s, another time that small technology companies were all the rage and the market for new issues was red hot. Some of the hot issues of that era, such as Electronic Data Systems, became successful companies, but most did not.

A variety of reasons are given for the trend away from dividends, including the tax disadvantages. Dividends are taxable to investors as ordinary income but are not deductible from corporate income, and thus face double taxa-

(continued)

tion. But that has always been true, and the effect presumably should have been greater two decades ago, when tax rates were much higher. Some companies say they instead return money to shareholders by repurchasing shares, allowing the sellers to pay lower capital gains tax rates on the money. But in many cases those purchases only offset the shares being issued to employees who exercise options.

One explanation is that corporate officials are far more likely than in the past to have a large part of their wealth in stock options. Such options become more valuable as the stock price rises, but do not benefit from dividend payments, arguably providing an incentive to companies not to pay dividends. Moreover, if a company runs into a cash squeeze, cutting back on its share repurchases is far less obvious than reducing its dividend.

The most likely explanation, however, would seem to be the most obvious. Investors, after seeing year after year of huge capital gains, no longer see much of a need for dividends as an assured return if the market declines.

The best performing stock in the S&P 500 to pay a dividend last year was Nortel Networks, which ranked fifth in performance with a gain of 304 percent. It last raised its dividend in 1997, when its stock price was one-fifth of today's level. At its current payout rate of 3.75 cents a quarter, Nortel stock yields 0.15 percent a year.

The trend toward lower dividends can be seen in the overall dividend yield on the S&P 500. Once it was a rule of thumb that caution was warranted if stock prices rose so high that the dividend yield fell below 3 percent. At the height in 1987, before that year's crash, the yield had fallen below 2.65 percent, then a record low yield.

But the yield on the S&P 500 last year, based on payouts by the companies during the year and the year-end level of the index, came to just 1.14 percent, down from 1.32 percent in 1998 and 1.6 percent in 1997. The rate has been below 3 percent since 1991, as the stock market recorded its best decade ever.

Source: "Market Place: More Companies Decide Not to Pay Dividends," F. Norris, *The New York Times*, January 4, 2000, © 2000 The New York Times Company. Reprinted by permission.

14.3.5   Are Stock Repurchases Replacing Dividends?

The most obvious question that arises from the empirical evidence in this section is, Are stock repurchases replacing dividends as the preferred payout method? Fama and French (2001) also briefly address this issue empirically: "because repurchases are largely the province of dividend payers, they leave the decline in the percent of payers largely unexplained. Instead, the primary effect of repurchases is to increase the already high earnings payouts of cash dividend payers" (p. 6). We provide evidence on composite dividend and stock repurchase payouts later.

Fama and French also note Bagwell and Shoven's (1989) argument that the increases in repurchases suggest that firms are substituting repurchases for dividends to lower shareholders' taxes. However, empirical tests of this hypothesis have produced mixed results (see DeAngelo, DeAngelo, and Skinner 2000; Grullon and Michaely 2002; Jagannathan, Stephens, and Weisbach 2000).

14.3.6 Have the Benefits of Dividends Declined?

Having documented evidence of the widespread decrease in the propensity of firms to pay dividends, Fama and French conclude their article by suggesting that the benefits of dividends may have declined over time. They mention three such benefits:

First, dividends provide shareholders with periodic cash returns that they can use for consumption. If dividends are not paid, many shareholders would be forced to sell shares periodically to generate cash, and would thereby incur transaction costs. However, if transaction costs for selling stocks have fallen over time, the relative benefit of a dividend is correspondingly reduced.

Second, managers have increased their holdings of stock options that are not protected against the price-reducing effect of a dividend (a point which we discuss later). Thus, they have a private preference not to sanction dividend payments.

Third, dividends may be less essential as a tool of corporate governance because of the advent of alternative mechanisms for controlling agency problems between shareholders and managers (e.g., executive stock options).

14.4 TYPES OF DIVIDENDS AND THE DIVIDEND PAYMENT PROCESS

This section briefly reviews the types of dividends that firms pay and the dividend payment process.

14.4.1 Types of Dividends

Firms pay dividends in the form of cash or additional stock. The most common cash dividend is the regular *quarterly cash dividend*. Occasionally, a firm pays an *extra* or *special* cash dividend, which is expressly *not* intended to be a recurring event.

Some firms pay a *stock dividend*, either in addition to or instead of a cash dividend. Suppose a firm declares a 5 percent stock dividend so that a shareholder receives 1 new share of stock for each 20 shares that he or she owns. This stock dividend actually represents a *dilution* of the market value of each share. In an ideal capital market, after the 5 percent dividend is paid the market value of each share should decrease by 5 percent. However, each shareholder has 5 percent more shares, so the total value of their shares is unchanged.

Stock dividends that involve a larger percentage distribution of additional stock are called *stock splits*. For instance, a firm may declare a 2-for-1 stock split, in which each shareholder receives an additional share for each share he or she owns. In this case, the market value of each share should fall by 50 percent. Henceforth, we focus only on cash dividends.[1]

---

[1]For more information on stock dividends and splits, consult the following references, listed in alphabetical order: Angel (1997), Brennan and Copeland (1988), Conroy, Harris, and Benet (1990), Copeland (1979), Dubofsky (1991), Easley, O'Hara, and Saar (2001), Han (1995), Ikenberry, Rankine, and Stice (1996), Kamara and Koski (2001), Lakonishok and Lev (1987), Lamoreux and Poon (1987), McNichols and Dravid (1990), Mukherji, Kim, and Walker (1997), Nayar and Rozeff (2001), Sheikh (1989), Wiggins (1992), and Woolridge (1983).

14.4.2   The Dividend Payment Process

The dividend payment process begins with a decision by the firm's board of directors to declare a dividend. The date of the board's vote to declare a dividend is called the *declaration date*. In addition to declaring the type and amount of the dividend, the board states the date on which the dividend will be distributed or paid (the *payable date*), and the date on which the firm will examine corporate records to determine the owners of record for the purpose of paying the upcoming dividend (the *record date*). For stocks that trade publicly, an earlier date must then be established on which new purchasers of the stock will no longer have the right to the upcoming dividend; that is, they will not be an owner of record with respect to the upcoming dividend. This date is called the *ex-dividend day*, or *ex-day*.

14.5   DIVIDENDS VERSUS EARNINGS: THE SMOOTHING PHENOMENON

A firm's management must make its decisions on cash dividends within the context of overall equity management. The practical effects of dividends on a firm's equity are (a) dividends reduce the amount of internal equity available for future investments, (b) dividends increase the probability that the firm will have to sell new equity if new investments should be funded with equity, and (c) dividends increase the firm's leverage, if the firm has debt.

These effects suggest that a typical firm would pay a dividend that is highly volatile over time, for three reasons. *First*, the typical firm's profitable investment opportunities (and therefore its need for internal funds) vary considerably over time. *Second*, equity offerings can be expensive and perhaps should be avoided, as we argued in Chapter 13. *Third*, most managers are concerned about their firm's leverage, which will tend to be higher if dividends are paid than if they are not. These points bolster a traditional argument that a firm should adopt a *residual dividend payout policy*—dividends should be paid only if the firm has excess cash after all of these concerns are taken into account.

14.5.1   Lintner's Dividend Smoothing Model

In sharp contrast to the arguments made above, firms that pay dividends appear to go to great pains to *smooth* dividends over time, especially relative to earnings. This smoothing tendency was first modeled and empirically documented by Lintner (1956). Lintner's model of the co-dynamics of a firm's earnings and dividends is given in Equation 14.8:

$$DIV_t - DIV_{t-1} \equiv \Delta DIV_t = \rho(\pi * EARN_t - DIV_{t-1}) \qquad \textbf{(14.8)}$$

where π is the firm's *long-run target payout ratio* and ρ is a *speed of adjustment coefficient*. If $\rho = 1$, dividends are always equal to the fraction π of current earnings. If $\rho < 1$, the firm only *partially* adjusts dividends to deviations of current earnings from the trend.

A Numerical Example

Suppose Firm ABC paid a dividend of $2 per share last year, and this year the firm posted per-share earnings of $5. The firm's target payout ratio is $\pi = 0.50$, and the value of the firm's speed of adjustment coefficient is ρ = 0.2. What is the firm's dividend for this year? The answer is $2.10. Alternatively, if the value of the firm's speed of adjustment variable is ρ = 1.0, its dividend this year would be $2.50.

Lintner's Model in Regression Form
Equation 14.8 can be reexpressed by dividing through by DIV_{t-1} and rearranging, yielding

$$\left[\frac{DIV_t - DIV_{t-1}}{DIV_{t-1}}\right] = -\rho + \rho\left[\frac{\pi^*EARN_t}{DIV_{t-1}}\right]. \tag{14.9}$$

This specification allows us to see that the *percentage change* in a firm's dividend depends on (a) the firm's current earnings relative to the previous dividend, and (b) the parameters ρ and π. For instance, if the firm had no current earnings (i.e., $EARN_t$ = 0), then dividends would fall by the percentage rate of –ρ. Generally, dividends would fall in all instances in which $\pi^*EARN_t < DIV_{t-1}$, would remain unchanged if $\pi^*EARN_t = DIV_{t-1}$, and would rise if $\pi^*EARN_t > DIV_{t-1}$.

Equation 14.9 is also advantageous in that it is in the form of a regression equation (sans an error term). The dependent variable is the percentage change in the firm's dividends, the intercept is –ρ, the independent variable is $[EARN_t / DIV_{t-1}]$, and the slope coefficient is ρ*π. We use this regression form of the model in the empirical analyses that we conduct next.

14.5.2   Empirical Evidence on Dividend Smoothing

Here we provide two empirical perspectives on the tendency of firms to smooth dividends relative to earnings. The first is based on composite numbers, and the second is based on data for individual firms.

Composite Earnings and Dividends over Time
Figure 14-4 shows annual values of composite earnings and composite dividends for seasoned, publicly traded U.S. nonfinancial firms from 1980 to 2000. Also displayed are annual values of the composite *dividend payout ratio*, the ratio of composite dividends to composite earnings.

Composite earnings grew at a faster rate than composite dividends over this period, but composite earnings were also much more volatile. The average percentage changes in composite earnings and composite dividends were 5.4 percent and 3.9 percent, respectively. The standard deviations of percentage changes in composite earnings and composite dividends were 17.8 percent and 3.9 percent, respectively. Clearly, these firms collectively smoothed dividends relative to earnings over this period. Consequently, composite dividend payout ratios are volatile, owing primarily to the volatility of composite earnings. On average, the sampled firms paid out slightly more than half of their earnings in dividends (54 percent). However, the composite payout ratio ranged widely over time, from 40 percent in 1999 to 85 percent in the recession year of 1991.

FIGURE 14-4 Annual Composite Earnings, Dividends, and Dividend Payout Ratios

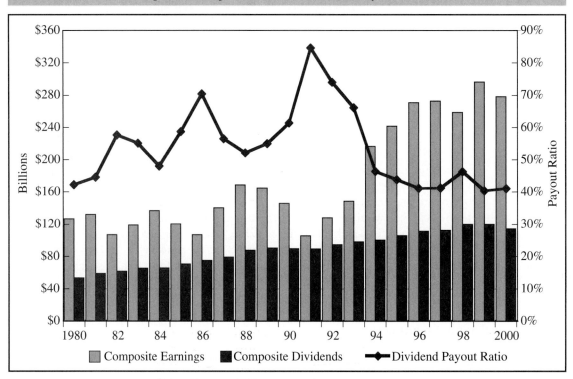

Seasoned Publicly Traded U.S. Nonfinancial Firms, 1980–2000
Source: Raw data from Standard & Poor's *Research Insight* database.

Testing Lintner's Model on Individual Firms

Fama and Babiak (1968) tested Lintner's model using annual data on 392 major industrial firms for the 19-year period of 1946 to 1964. They found average values of 0.317 and 0.521 for ρ and π, respectively.

We also tested Lintner's model using all nonfinancial firms that were included in the Dow Jones Industrial Average (DJIA) at year-end 2000. Of the 30 firms in the index, 27 were nonfinancial firms. For each firm, we estimated the model parameters π and ρ using regression Equation 14.9. We used annual data for the years 1980 to 2000, or a shorter period as the firm's dividend history allowed. The results are displayed in Table 14-3.

For two of the 27 firms, Intel and Microsoft, we lacked sufficient data for estimation. Intel did not commence paying a regular quarterly dividend until 1992, and Microsoft had never paid a dividend through 2000. These cases underscore the point that even large, profitable firms display a declining propensity to pay dividends. For the remaining firms, the median speed of adjustment coefficient, ρ, is only 0.06, though the estimates range widely from −0.16 for Hewlett-Packard to 0.48 for Merck & Co. The median target payout ratio, π, is 0.51, which is close to the median *actual* payout ratios for these firms, 0.44, or 42 percent. However, the estimates of π range very widely, indicating a problem with the specification of the model.

TABLE 14-3   Estimates of Lintner's "Dividend Smoothing" Model

Nonfinancial Stocks Included in the Dow Jones Industrials Index at Year-End 2000

The Model

$$(DPS_t/DPS_{t-1}) = (1 - \rho) + \rho\pi(EPS_t/DPS_{t-1}) + e_t,$$

where ρ = speed of adjustment parameter and π = target long-term payout ratio

Company Name	Years of Data Used to Estimate	Estimates ρ	Estimates π	Actual Payout Ratio: All Years	Adjusted R^2
Alcoa	1980–2000	0.16	0.54	0.37	39.1%
AT&T	1980–2000	0.13	0.45	0.72	5.8%
Boeing	1980–2000	−0.02	−0.36	0.32	−2.2%
Caterpillar	1980–2000	0.12	0.49	0.36	44.5%
Coca-Cola	1980–2000	0.05	1.37	0.45	54.7%
DuPont	1980–2000	0.02	1.81	0.60	25.3%
Eastman Kodak	1980–2000	−0.01	−0.66	0.68	−5.0%
Exxon Mobil	1980–2000	0.05	1.31	0.60	14.5%
General Electric	1980–2000	0.07	1.05	0.42	12.6%
General Motors	1980–2000	0.11	0.53	0.52	40.8%
Hewlett-Packard	1980–2000	−0.16	−0.01	0.17	−5.2%
Home Depot	1980–2000	0.16	0.23	0.11	52.4%
Honeywell International	1980–2000	0.06	0.65	0.38	26.8%
Intel*	n/a	n/a	n/a	n/a	n/a
IBM	1980–2000	0.10	0.28	0.45	29.2%
International Paper	1980–2000	0.02	1.26	0.51	12.4%
Johnson & Johnson	1980–2000	0.01	4.93	0.37	54.0%
McDonald's	1980–2000	0.08	0.36	0.15	5.4%
Merck & Co.	1980–2000	0.48	0.51	0.44	76.3%
Microsoft**	n/a	n/a	n/a	n/a	n/a
Minnesota Mining & Manufacturing	1980–2000	0.16	0.70	0.53	50.2%
Philip Morris	1980–2000	0.03	2.30	0.52	56.8%
Procter & Gamble	1980–2000	−0.01	−2.60	0.45	34.9%
SBC Communications	1985–2000	0.07	1.12	0.58	6.9%
United Technologies	1980–2000	−0.03	−0.43	0.39	21.3%
Wal-Mart Stores	1980–2000	0.22	0.22	0.15	55.0%
Walt Disney	1980–2000	−0.07	−0.16	0.19	11.7%
Medians		*0.06*	*0.51*	*0.44*	*29.2%*

*Intel commenced paying dividends in 1992.
**Through 2000, Microsoft has never paid a dividend.
Source: Raw data from Standard & Poor's *Research Insight* database.

14.6   DIVIDENDS, TAXES, AND TRANSACTION COSTS

In this section, we review theoretical arguments and empirical evidence on the effects of taxes on a firm's dividend policy and the market value of its equity. We (a) explain the basic possible effects of taxes and transaction costs on the dividend decision, (b) introduce the concept of a *dividend clientele*, and (c) discuss two approaches to investigating whether a firm's dividend policy affects its market equity value.

14.6.1   Taxes and Transaction Costs: Corporate and Personal Effects

To illustrate the effects of taxes and transaction costs on a firm's dividend policy, consider ABC Company, which has 1,000,000 shares outstanding. All of the firm's shareholders want to receive regular cash income in the pretax amount of $4 per share per year, for consumption purposes. The market price of ABC stock is $100 per share, and because the stock price has risen recently, all shareholders face taxes on capital gains if they liquidate shares. Each shareholder faces tax rates of τ_p = 39.6 percent on dividend income and τ_{pc} = 28 percent realized capital gains, and transaction costs of tc = 5 percent on any stock sales. Initially we assume that the firm has no positive-NPV investments to pursue this year, and it has the idle cash to pay dividends. If it does not pay dividends, idle cash is invested in zero-NPV investments such as Treasury bills.

Under these circumstances, we will determine whether the shareholders are better off if (a) the firm pays a $4 dividend or (b) each shareholder liquidates 4 percent of their shares. If a dividend is paid, shareholders receive $2.416 after taxes [$2.416 = $4(1 – 0.396)]. If no dividend is paid, shareholders liquidate 4 percent of their shares, receiving $4 in proceeds per share. After paying transaction costs of $0.20 (i.e., 5 percent on each $4 in sales) and capital gains taxes of $1.12 [= $4 * 0.28], they net $2.68. By a slim margin, the shareholders are better off if the firm does not pay a dividend. However, if either (a) shareholders' tax rates on dividend income and capital gains, or (b) the transaction cost for selling shares is altered, shareholders' preference regarding dividends could easily change.

Now suppose ABC has positive-NPV projects this year, which must be funded with equity. If the firm pays dividends totaling $4 million, it must raise this amount by selling new equity. Assuming that issuance costs for new equity are 12 percent of proceeds, issuance costs would be 12 percent of $4 million, or $480,000. Hence, the market value of pre-issuance shares would fall by $0.48 per share to $99.52, reflecting the issuance decision. In effect, shareholders net only $1.936 (= 2.416 – 0.48) from the payment of the dividend, as compared to $2.68 from personal stock sales, as calculated earlier. In this case, shareholders are much better off if the firm refrains from paying a dividend, and so the case illustrates one reason why firms with profitable investment opportunities generally refrain from paying dividends.

14.6.2   Dividend Clienteles

As the example above illustrates, personal taxes, shareholders' liquidity needs, transaction costs (both for shareholders and for the firm), and the firm's investment opportunities all affect investors' preference for dividends. Some individual investors, as well as pension funds, may face low or no taxes and prefer dividends for the income they provide. Other investors face low effective tax rates because they are invested in a tax-deferred retirement plan, and these investors do not need dividends for current income (indeed, would not have access to dividends paid into their plan).[2]

[2]Firms face a very low effective tax rate on the dividends they receive on the stock of other firms that they hold, because 70 percent to 80 percent of dividend income is excluded from taxable income according to the IRS corporate tax code. Thus, a firm that wants a steady inflow of cash from an investment in another firm would want that firm to have a high payout policy.

On the other hand, many high-income investors are in high tax brackets, have long investment horizons, and have no need for additional cash income. Such investors would prefer to hold stocks that pay little or no dividends, and will engage in a buy-and-hold strategy to minimize capital gains taxes. Finally, other investors may be in either low or high tax brackets, but require dividends for cash income.

Such differential preferences for dividends naturally lead to *dividend clienteles*. A dividend clientele is a set of investors who are attracted to the stocks of firms that have the dividend policy they prefer, based on their tax or liquidity circumstances. This suggests that a given firm may be able to increase its market value if it adopts a dividend policy that appeals to investors whose preferences are not satisfied by firms currently in the market.

However, if existing firms collectively satisfy all dividend clienteles, no individual firm can affect the market value of its equity by adopting any particular dividend policy, a condition called *dividend clientele equilibrium*. Nevertheless, managers should monitor the changing desires of investors with respect to dividend policy, because they may be able to identify an unsatisfied clientele, adopt the policy that they desire, and thereby enhance market equity value.

For two reasons, it is important for a manager to know whether the firm's dividend payout policy attracts particular investors via the clientele effect. *First*, we have emphasized the potential importance of a firm's ownership structure on its financial policies and strategies. According to the clientele hypothesis, the firm's dividend policy influences the firm's ownership structure, at least in terms of the type of investors who are attracted to the firm's shares. *Second*, as we discuss later, a firm's dividend policy can affect the equilibrium expected return on the firm's stock, and thus the firm's cost of equity capital.

14.6.3   Taxes and the Ex-Dividend Day Behavior of Stock Prices

One way to examine the effects of taxes on stock prices is to examine the change in the firm's stock price as it *goes ex-dividend*. In an ideal market, the price of a paying firm's stock should decrease by the amount of the dividend per share, denoted as *DPS*, at the moment that the stock goes ex-dividend. However, tax effects may alter this conclusion.

Elton and Gruber (1970) developed a formal expression for the relationship between a paying firm's *DPS* and the difference between the firm's stock prices *before* versus *after* the ex-day, denoted as $(P_B - P_A)$. This relationship is a function of tax rates for the marginal investor in the stock. This relationship is

$$\frac{P_B - P_A}{DPS} = \frac{1 - \tau_p}{1 - \tau_{pc}}. \qquad (14.10)$$

If $\tau_{pc} < \tau_p$ for the marginal investor, the price-change-to-dividend ratio will be less than one. By rearranging Equation 14.10, we can solve for the ex-day price change:

$$P_B - P_A = DPS \left[\frac{1 - \tau_p}{1 - \tau_{pc}}\right]. \qquad (14.11)$$

A Numerical Example

Suppose firm XYZ declares a dividend of *DPS* = $3. The stock is held by investors who share common tax rates of τ_p = 36 percent and τ_{pc} = 18 percent. The ex-day price change should be

$$P_B - P_A = \$3 \left[\frac{1 - 0.36}{1 - 0.18} \right] = \$3[0.78] = \$2.34.$$

That is, the price should fall by 78 percent of the amount of the dividend per share.

Tax Clienteles and Ex-Day Price Changes

Elton and Gruber also argued that investors will cluster into dividend clienteles according to (a) the different dividend yields that stocks offer, and (b) the different tax rates that individual investors face. Investors who face high tax rates on dividends relative to capital gains will tend to hold stocks with low dividend yields, whereas investors with low tax rates on dividends relative to capital gains will tend to hold stocks with high dividend yields. As a result, the ratio of ex-day price change to dividend, which is the implied tax rate differential according to Equation 14.10, should be *inversely* related to dividend yield; it should be low for high dividend yield stocks and high for low dividend yield stocks.

The authors documented evidence consistent with these predictions. They found that the ratio of ex-day price change to dividend is less than 1.0, on average. They also found that firms with low dividend yields have high implied tax rate differentials, while firms with high dividend yields have low implied tax rate differentials. These results are consistent with the clientele hypothesis.

Subsequently, numerous empirical studies have challenged Elton and Gruber's analyses. Two important issues have emerged. *First,* given that stocks are traded at discrete prices that are largely governed by bid and ask prices and minimum "tick" sizes, it is possible that the results first observed by Elton and Gruber could be due at least in part to the fact that a stock price will tend to drop by less than the amount of the dividend due purely to this *price-discreteness effect* (see Bali and Hite 1998).

Second, it may be unreasonable to assume that the marginal trader in a given stock around the ex-day is always one who has a tax preference consistent with the stock's dividend yield. For instance, many arbitrageurs have no preference for dividends versus capital gains. Kalay (1982a), Eades, Hess, and Kim (1985), Boyd and Jagannathan (1994), Lasfer (1995), Bali and Hite (1998), Koski and Scruggs (1998), and Kalay and Michaely (2000) document evidence suggesting that the ex-day behavior of stock prices may not be due to tax effects.

14.6.4   Dividends, Equity Value, and the Cost of Equity Capital

Though the results we have discussed on the ex-dividend day price behavior of stocks casts doubt on the effects of dividend taxation on stock prices, it is still possible that the equilibrium pricing of stocks reflects differences in the taxation of dividends versus capital gains. Equation 14.12, adapted from Brennan (1970) and Litzenberger and Ramaswamy (1979, 1980, 1982), shows how the Capital Asset Pricing Model (CAPM) can be modified to account for the tax-related effect of dividends on a stock's equilibrium expected return:

$$r_i = r_f + \beta_i[r_m - r_f] + \delta[dy_i - r_f],\qquad\qquad\text{(14.12)}$$

where r_i and r_M are the (pretax) expected returns on stock i and the market, respectively, r_f is the risk-free rate, β_i is the stock's systematic risk, dy_i is stock i's dividend yield, and δ is the equilibrium *tax premium* per unit of dividend yield (in excess of the risk-free rate). If investors demand a premium for the tax effect of dividends, then $\delta > 0$ should hold. The value of δ depends on the distribution of tax rates across investors, and also reflects individual investors' optimal holdings as a function of their tax rates (i.e., the tax clientele effect).

Litzenberger and Ramaswamy (1979, 1980, 1982) tested Equation 14.12 using data on U.S. stocks over various periods from 1936 to 1980. They consistently found evidence that the market demands a premium that is positively related to a stock's dividend yield. They also document evidence of the clientele effect, as δ is negatively related to dividend yield. Numerous empirical studies have tested the cross-sectional relationship between dividend yield and stock returns.[3] These studies have generally found that after adjusting for risk, a stock's expected return is positively related to its dividend yield.

However, Chen, Grundy, and Stambaugh (1990) found that dividend yields over time are related to changes in the investment opportunity set (e.g., the state of the economy and the risk aversion of investors). After adjusting for this relationship, they found that the return on a stock is *not* reliably related to dividend yield. Kalay and Michaely (2000) document evidence of a positive relationship between expected returns and dividend yield, but also provided evidence that casts doubt on the tax argument as the correct interpretation of the results.

Fama and French (1998) recently conducted an intriguing empirical study of the effects of dividends on the value of a firm's equity. They analyzed the pricing of U.S. firms over the years 1965 to 1992. Their evidence indicates that dividends have information about value that is missed by earnings, investment, research and development (R&D) expenditures, and debt. The relationship between value and dividends is *positive*, a result that is *inconsistent* with the argument that dividends reduce value due to tax effects.

14.7   DIVIDENDS AND PRINCIPAL–AGENT CONFLICTS

Two principal–agent problems attend a firm's dividend policy. These are the *free cash flow problem* and the incentive of a levered firm to *expropriate wealth from its creditors*. This section briefly reviews literature on the influence of these problems on a firm's dividend policy.

---

[3]References, in alphabetical order, include Ang and Peterson (1985), Bhardwaj and Brooks (1999), Bhattacharya (1979), Black (1976), Black and Scholes (1974), Blume (1980), Bradford and Gordon (1980), Brennan (1970), Brennan and Thakor (1990), Chen, Grundy, and Stambaugh (1990), DeAngelo, DeAngelo and Skinner (1992), Geisler (2000), Goetzmann and Jorion (1995), Gordon (1959), Han (1994), Hubbard and Michaely (1997), Huberman (1990), Kalay and Michaely (2000), Lee (1996), Lewellen, Stanley, Lease, and Schlarbaum (1978), Litzenberger and Ramaswamy (1979, 1980, 1982), Marsh and Merton (1987), Miller (1986), Miller and Scholes (1978), Morgan (1982), Pettit (1977), Poterba and Summers (1984), Rosenberg (1979), and Shefrin and Statman (1984).

14.7.1   Dividends and the Shareholder–Management Conflict

As we discussed in Chapter 3, one of the fundamental principal–agent problems between shareholders and management is the free cash flow problem (Jensen 1986). The problem stems from management's private incentive to increase the size of the firm. Management has this incentive for two reasons. *First*, senior managers' salaries are closely tied to firm size, so if they can succeed in simply making the firm larger (presumably even at the expense of profitability), their salaries will be higher. *Second*, if in the process of making the firm larger the firm becomes very complex, it becomes more difficult for incumbent management to be fired and replaced by new management, thus serving the incumbent management's *entrenchment incentive*.

One way in which management can build a large and complex empire is to refrain from paying dividends; instead, they use excess cash to invest in unprofitable projects and acquisitions. This problem is most severe for highly profitable firms that have relatively few profitable investment opportunities. Management's ability to pursue empire building by refraining from paying dividends is limited by internal and external governance mechanisms. Internally, the firm's board of directors, if they have the gumption, can discipline management by forcing the firm to pay dividends. Externally, the market for corporate control induces managers to pay at least a minimum amount of dividends to prevent outside intervention (see Zwiebel 1996; Warther 1997; Myers 2000). Hence, we have a rationale for dividends despite the possible adverse tax consequences.

The empire-building problem is less severe for firms that are either unprofitable or have profitable investment opportunities whose required expenditures equal or exceed the firm's available internal funds. In either case the firm has no *free cash flow*. For such firms, there is no rationale for dividends based on a management–shareholder principal–agent conflict, so, given the adverse tax effects of dividends, it is optimal to pay little or no dividends.

14.7.2   Dividends and the Shareholder–Creditor Conflict

As we also know from Chapter 3, when a firm has risky debt outstanding, the firm's management, acting in shareholders' interest, has an incentive to take actions to expropriate wealth from the firm's creditors. One means of expropriation is to increase dividends. By increasing dividends, the firm has fewer assets against which creditors have a (priority) claim, and thus the value of a creditors' claim is lower than if the firm did not pay dividends.

Myers's (1977) underinvestment problem also comes into play if the firm is levered. If the firm has both risky debt outstanding and profitable investment opportunities, management, acting in the interests of shareholders, may forgo profitable investments if they provide no benefit to shareholders because they also benefit creditors. Instead, the firm will pay dividends.

These problems lead creditors to demand a contract covenant that restricts the amount of dividends that the borrowing firm can pay. (See Smith and Warner 1979 and Kalay 1982b for empirical evidence on the prevalence of dividend constraints in debt contracts.) Such restrictions can serve both to protect creditors and to mitigate the underinvestment problem.

14.7.3 Dividends and the Interaction of Shareholder–Management and Shareholder–Creditor Conflicts

The two dividend-related principal–agent problems noted above are not independent. Suppose a levered firm's board of directors seeks to increase dividends both to discipline management and to expropriate wealth from creditors. At the same time, creditors, acting in their own interests, seek to decrease dividends. A serious *tug-of-war* may commence among competing stakeholders over the firm's dividend policy. For a profitable, levered firm, the conflict over dividend policy may be particularly severe between the firm's management and the board. This is so because management and creditors both prefer lower dividends and lower leverage (though for very different reasons), while the board presses for higher dividends and higher leverage, both of which are disciplining devices (i.e., both dividends and debt payments soak up free cash flow) (see Jensen, Solberg, and Zorn 1992).

14.7.4 Additional Agency Issues Relating to Dividend Policy

Rozeff (1982) developed a model of a firm that chooses its dividend payout ratio to minimize the sum of agency costs and transaction costs. The former is a decreasing function of insider ownership percentage, while the latter is an increasing function of the dividend payout ratio. His model shows that an increase in insider stock ownership leads to lower agency costs and, thus, to a lower optimal dividend payout ratio.

Rozeff argues that dividend payout and insider stock ownership are substitute mechanisms to control agency costs. Thus, firms with high insider ownership can have low dividend payout, but firms with low insider ownership must have high dividend payout. These predictions appear to be consistent with casual observation, as small firms tend to have high insider ownership and low (or no) dividend payout, while large firms have low insider ownership and (relatively) high dividend payout.

Schooley and Barney Jr. (1994) further develop Rozeff's model. They argue that the substitution between insider ownership and dividend payout works only for lower levels of insider ownership. Beyond a critical insider ownership percentage, management entrenchment starts to occur, which tends to increase agency costs of managerial discretion. Thus, we should observe a nonmonotonic relationship between dividend payout (or dividend yield) and insider ownership. At lower levels of insider ownership, the inverse relationship holds; at higher levels, dividends must increase again to mitigate agency costs of entrenchment. The authors document evidence consistent with this nonmonotonic relationship.

Separately, a generalization of Rozeff's *substitution* argument appears to have power to simultaneously explain two major developments regarding U.S. firms over the last 20 years. *First*, several new mechanisms have emerged to mitigate agency costs of managerial discretion. These include (a) advancements in incentive devices in managers' compensation contracts, (b) an increase in the effectiveness of boards of directors, (c) the emergence of the takeover market, and (d) the increasing institutionalization of stock ownership, which may increase monitoring. *Second*, the propensity of firms to pay dividends has decreased markedly in the past 20 years. Perhaps the new mechanisms have partially supplanted the role of dividends in mitigating agency problems.

Easterbrook (1984) argues that dividends provide two valuable functions in an agency context. The first function is that dividends "keep firms in the capital market, where monitoring of managers is available at lower cost . . . " (p. 658). Keeping the firm's capital investment policy fixed, as dividends increase the firm will have to enter the market more frequently to issue either debt or equity securities to new investors. New investors are better able to monitor the firm's management because "when it issues new securities, the firm's affairs will be reviewed by an investment banker or some similar intermediary acting as a monitor . . . new investors . . . can examine managers' behavior before investing, and they will not buy new stock unless they are offered compensation (in the form of reduced prices) for any remediable agency costs of management" (p. 654). Moreover, if this is the major function of dividends, then dividends would not be closely tied to earnings: "Because the first function of dividends is to keep firms in the capital markets, we would not expect to see a very strong correlation between short-term profits and dividends" (p. 657).

The second function of dividends, according to Easterbrook, is that they "may be useful in adjusting the level of risk taken by managers and the different classes of investors" (p. 658). For this argument, the author assumes that the firm's manager is risk averse and undiversified, and that the firm has debt outstanding. The manager's situation induces him or her to reduce the riskiness of the firm's equity so as to reduce the risk that the firm will go bankrupt and the manager will lose his or her job. One way to reduce risk over time is to refrain from paying dividends (even out of excess cash) because, as equity builds up in the firm, the leverage, and thus the firm's risk of bankruptcy, falls. But such actions benefit creditors at the expense of shareholders. Thus, a judicious amount of dividends can serve to maintain the firm's leverage and thus minimize inadvertent expropriation from shareholders to creditors.

14.8 INFORMATION ASYMMETRY AND SIGNALING WITH DIVIDENDS

As we discussed in Chapter 4, a signaling model is based on the idea that firms with exceptionally high value cannot easily convey that value to the market for two reasons. *First*, they cannot convey value-relevant information directly because such information is generally strategic in nature, and thus communicating it to public shareholders is tantamount to divulging it to the firm's competitors. *Second*, it is difficult to devise a credible signal of the firm's value relative to that of other, weaker firms, because weaker firms have an incentive to mimic any such signal so that their stock too would receive a higher valuation in the market. Thus, a high-value firm must devise a *credible* and *affordable* signal of its higher valuation—one that lower-value firms would find prohibitively expensive to mimic. If the signal is successful, a *separating equilibrium* is obtained.

Several authors have developed theoretical models in which *dividends* are an effective signal of a firm's true value in a market beset by information asymmetry. As in every signaling model, the signal must be costly so as to prevent mimicking. In the models that have been developed, the reason why dividends are a costly signal varies. In Bhattacharya's (1979) model, the cost of the signal is the increased probability of bearing costs of issuing shares in the future. The cost of dividends in Miller and Rock's (1985) model is forgone investment in profitable projects. In John and Williams's (1985) and Bernheim's (1991) models, the cost of the signal is higher taxes on dividends relative to capital gains.

14.9   THE INFORMATION CONTENT OF DIVIDEND CHANGES

Empirical studies have consistently found that, on average, the market reacts positively to dividend increase announcements, and negatively to dividend cuts. Thus, dividend changes appear to convey information to the market. In this section, we review this literature.

14.9.1   Interpreting the Evidence

What information is conveyed by a dividend change? The most straightforward interpretation of the evidence is that a dividend change reveals new information to the market about management's assessment of the firm's long-term earnings prospects. Indeed, the idea behind Lintner's dividend smoothing model is that a firm's management will increase dividends only when they believe that the firm's *permanent* earnings has increased. But this does not imply that dividend policy is relevant, as Miller and Modigliani (1961) argued: "That is, where a firm has adopted a policy of dividend stabilization with a long-established and generally appreciated 'target payout ratio,' investors are likely to (and have good reason to) interpret a change in the dividend rate as a change in management's views of future profit prospects for the firm. The dividend change, in other words, provides the occasion for the price change though not its cause, the price still being solely a reflection of future earnings and growth opportunities" (p. 430).

At least three facets of agency theory explain the basic empirical results. *First*, a dividend increase reveals that the firm's governance mechanisms (e.g., the board) have succeeded in curbing management's penchant for empire building, and a dividend cut reveals the opposite. *Second*, a dividend increase indicates that threats from the external market for corporate control have persuaded management to disgorge free cash flow, and a decrease means the opposite. *Third*, a dividend increase for a levered firm constitutes an expropriation of wealth from the firm's creditors, and a decrease means the opposite.

Theory also suggests that in some cases a dividend increase is bad news, while a dividend decrease is good news. For instance, a firm may decide to cut its dividend because management is planning to increase its capital expenditures in pursuit of profitable investments of which the market was unaware. Conversely, a dividend increase could indicate that a firm's supply of profitable projects has dried up.

Can we interpret dividend changes as signals as indicated by the theoretical models discussed earlier? Perhaps, but as Miller and Rock (1985) state, "one cannot conclude that dividends are serving as signals in the technical sense merely because prices jump on dividend announcements" (p. 1045). In the remainder of this section, we briefly summarize the results of several empirical studies that have attempted to elicit an interpretation of the market's reaction to dividend changes.

14.9.2   Dividend Changes and Future Profitability

Early studies by Watts (1973) and Gonedes (1978) found *no evidence* that dividend changes are related to a firm's future earnings. More recently, Benartzi, Michaely, and Thaler (1997) also find no evidence that dividend-increasing firms have higher earnings going forward. However, they found that these firms experienced significant earnings increases in years –1 and 0 relative to the year of the dividend increase. Moreover, "consistent with Lintner's model on dividend policy, firms that increase dividends are less likely than nonchanging firms to experience a drop in future earnings. Thus, their increase in concurrent earnings can be said to be somewhat 'permanent'" (p. 1007).

Brook, Charlton, and Hendershott (1998) addressed the following basic question: Do firms that increase their dividends subsequently experience an increase in cash flow? They summarize their results as follows:

> We find that firms poised to experience large, permanent cash flow increases after four years of flat cash flow tend to boost their dividends before their cash flow jumps. These firms also have a high frequency of relatively large dividend increases prior to the cash flow shock. Investors appear to interpret the dividend changes as signals about future profitability: Firms that sharply increase their dividends earn large market-adjusted stock returns in the year before their cash flow rises. This direct link between positive cash flow shocks, dividend decisions, and stock returns supports the hypothesis that dividend changes signal positive information about permanent future cash flow levels. However, our results also suggest that signaling plays a relatively minor role in corporate dividend policy. (p. 46)

14.9.3   Dividend Changes and Subsequent Capital Expenditures

Yoon and Starks (1995) attempted to determine the source of the wealth effects surrounding dividend change announcements by pursuing two essentially competing hypothesis. On the one hand, a dividend increase (or vice versa, a decrease) may represent management's signal that the firm's investment opportunity set has improved (or vice versa, deteriorated), and as such the firm will be more (or less) profitable in the future, and therefore will be able to support a higher (or only a lower) dividend. This *Cash Flow Signaling Hypothesis* (originally espoused by Miller and Modigliani in 1961) posits a *positive* relationship between dividend changes and capital expenditure changes.

On the other hand, the *Free Cash Flow Hypothesis* posits that a dividend increase is good news because it means that the firm's management is being disciplined to pay a higher dividend, and therefore in the future will tend to reduce its (largely wasteful) capital expenditures, whereas a dividend decrease is bad news because it suggests that management will have greater flexibility to waste free cash flow on unprofitable investments. As such, the Free Cash Flow Hypothesis posits a *negative* relationship between dividend changes and subsequent capital expenditures.

Because these hypotheses provide opposing predictions about the relationship between dividend changes and subsequent capital expenditures, Yoon and Starks devise an effective test to distinguish between these two hypotheses. They found that dividend changes are *positively* related to subsequent changes in capital expenditures; thus, the results are consistent with the Cash Flow Signaling Hypothesis.

14.9.4   Dividend Changes and Wealth Redistributions

For a levered firm, theory suggests two alternative hypotheses about the market's positive and negative reactions to announcements of a dividend increase and a dividend decrease, respectively. The first is the *Information Content Hypothesis*, which posits that the announcement conveys information about the value of the firm—that it is higher than the market expected in the case of a dividend increase, and lower than expected in the case of a cut. The second is the *Wealth Redistribution Hypothesis*: A dividend increase constitutes an expropriation of wealth from the firm's creditors to the firm's shareholders, while a dividend reduction induces an expropriation of wealth from shareholders to creditors.

Both hypotheses predict that a firm's stock price will move in the same direction as the announced dividend change. However, they represent competing hypotheses about the effect of a dividend change on the price of the announcing firm's *bonds*. The Information Content Hypothesis predicts that bond prices will move in the same direction as the dividend change, because bondholders also benefit from an increase in the overall value of the firm. The Wealth Redistribution Hypothesis predicts that bond prices will move in the opposite direction of the dividend change.

In the end, the effects predicted by these two hypotheses on bond prices probably work in tandem. Even if a dividend change reveals information about the value of the firm in the same direction, the price effect on bonds would be partially muted, for both dividend increases and decreases, relative to the simpler case in which the firm reveals that its value has increased or decreased, respectively (i.e., with no accompanying change in dividends). This is because a dividend increase surely constitutes a strengthening of shareholders' claim on the firm's future cash flows, *ceteris paribus* (all other things equal), while a dividend decrease constitutes a weakening of shareholders' claim.

Moreover, a firm's bondholders *anticipate* expropriation from shareholders via dividends, so they include covenants in the debt contract that restrict dividends in some manner. The general effect of such restrictions is to allow a dividend increase if the firm's value increases (and management, acting in the shareholders' interest, should always take advantage of such a circumstance), and to force a dividend cut if the firm's value decreases. Indeed, this argument supports the Information Content Hypothesis to the extent that, at the time of a dividend announcement, the market was unaware of the altered status of the creditor-imposed restriction on dividends relative to the firm's value.

Handjinicolaou and Kalay (1984) tested these competing hypotheses by examining the effect of dividend change announcements on the prices of bonds for a sample of firms. They summarize their empirical results as follows: "The evidence presented is consistent with the information content hypothesis . . . " (p. 35). "The evidence indicates that there is an asymmetrical reaction of bond prices to unexpected dividend change announcements. Unexpected dividend reductions negatively affect bond prices, while unexpected dividend increases have no significant effect" (p. 51).

14.9.5 Dividend Clienteles and the Information Content of Dividend Changes

Can the Dividend Clientele Hypotheses explain variation in the market's reaction to dividend change announcements? Bajaj and Vijh (1990) investigated this issue. They found that the *magnitude* of abnormal returns (both positive and negative) to dividend change announcements is positively related to the firm's anticipated dividend yield, the firm's size, and the firm's stock price. The authors interpret this evidence as follows. Regarding the dividend yield relationship, dividends are clearly more important to investors who hold high-yield stocks than they are to investors who hold low-yield stocks. Therefore, dividend changes will have a more dramatic effect on the values of high-yield stocks than low-yield stocks. The firm-size and stock-price relationships, they argue, can be explained by recognizing that the flow of value-relevant information is substantially less for small firms, which also tend to be low-priced stocks, than for large firms (or, similarly, high-priced stocks). That is, for information-poor firms, dividends are relatively more important as an indicator of the firm's financial status.

14.9.6   Dividend Initiations and Omissions

A dividend initiation or omission is a radical change in a firm's dividend policy. In this sense, either is a more important, if more unusual, event than a mere change in dividend amount. Below we briefly discuss several event studies of dividend initiations and omissions.

Dividend Initiations

According to evidence from several empirical studies, the market generally welcomes a firm's announcement that it will initiate dividends. All studies have found that the average announcement-period abnormal return is not only positive, but also quite substantial. Asquith and Mullins (1983) identified 168 firms in the period 1964 to 1980 that either began paying dividends for the first time in their history or resumed paying dividends after a hiatus of at least 10 years. The average two-day announcement-period abnormal return on these firms' stocks was +3.7 percent. This figure is several times larger than the average abnormal return associated with dividend increases in general, which is about 1 percent (e.g., Pettit 1972; Aharony and Swary 1980). The authors suggest that the market reaction to dividend initiations is greater because a dividend initiation is more of a surprise than a general dividend increase. They also found that abnormal returns are positively related to the relative size of the initiated dividend.

Venkatesh (1989) found two interesting aspects of the post-announcement price behavior of firms that initiated dividends. *First, stock return volatility* generally decreases after a dividend is initiated. *Second*, the market's reaction to subsequent earnings announcements diminishes after dividend initiation. His interpretation is that, after a dividend initiation, the market focuses more on the firm's dividend policy and less on earnings announcements.

Dyl and Weigand (1998) have a different interpretation of Venkatesh's evidence. They found that *earnings volatility* diminishes after dividend initiation. Thus, they argue, "The decrease in returns volatility and the market's diminished reaction to earnings announcements are also consistent with firms having fewer earnings surprises following the initiation of dividends. If earnings volatility and the number of earnings surprises are reduced in the post-dividend period, we can also expect stock return volatility and the market's reaction to earnings announcements to decrease. . . . This decrease in firm risk is what makes managers willing to initiate cash dividends. Dividend initiation conveys information to the market about the firm's lower risk" (pp. 27–28) (also see Lipson, Maquieira, and Megginson 1998).

Dividend Omissions

Dividend omissions are qualitatively different from dividend cuts because they represent a change in dividend *policy* rather than simply amount. Several empirical studies have found that the market generally reacts very negatively to a dividend omission, including: Ghosh and Woolridge (1988); Healy and Palepu (1988); Christie (1994); and Michaely, Thaler, and Womack (1995). For example, the dividend-omitting firms in Christie's sample were met with abnormal returns of –6.94 percent, on average.

14.10 STOCK REPURCHASES: A BRIEF ON MECHANICS AND EFFECTS

The next three sections of the chapter are devoted to discussions of a firm's decision to repurchase some of its own shares. In this section, we describe the basic mechanics and effects of a stock repurchase. We also compare stock repurchases to regular and special dividends. In subsequent sections, we review a swiftly growing literature on this increasingly important aspect of firms' financial policies and strategies.

14.10.1 Stock Repurchase Mechanics

A firm can use any of three methods to repurchase outstanding shares. *First*, it can adopt and execute an *open-market stock repurchase program*, whereby the firm conducts open-market purchases of its shares, generally on a gradual basis over time. *Second* and *third*, the firm can repurchase shares on a one-time basis, employing either the *Dutch auction self-tender method* or the *fixed-price self-tender method*.

In the Dutch auction method, the firm solicits and collects sell offers from shareholders, after establishing an acceptable range of offer prices. A shareholder can submit an offer to sell a specified number of shares at a specified price within the established price range. If and when the requisite number of shares has been offered, the firm determines the (share-weighted) average price of all offers, applies this price to all tendered shares, and purchases all of them at that price.

In a fixed-price tender offer, the firm also solicits and collects sell offers from shareholders. However, in this case the firm specifies and announces, in advance, both (a) the price at which it will repurchase shares and (b) the total number of shares that it will repurchase, where offers are considered in the temporal order received. Regarding (a), the offer price in a fixed-price tender is invariably substantially in excess of the current market price. Regarding (b), the tendering firm generally retains an option to purchase additional shares in the event that the tender offer is *oversubscribed*.

14.10.2 Treasury Shares and the Potential Effects of Repurchases

By repurchasing its own shares, the firm reduces the number of its outstanding shares. Repurchased shares become *treasury shares*, which can be resold later (e.g., in conjunction with an executive's execution of his or her stock options), or reissued as compensation in an acquisition.

Meanwhile, stock repurchases have at least six potentially important practical effects. *First*, the firm's assets are reduced, because a portion of the firm's cash assets flows out. *Second*, the firm's equity base is reduced. *Third*, if the firm has debt outstanding, leverage increases. *Fourth*, the firm is adding substantially to the demand for its shares in the market, so the market price of the firm's stock may rise. *Fifth*, the firm's active involvement in the secondary market may enhance liquidity, as investors realize that there is a ready buyer if they wish to sell. On the other hand, and *sixth*, repurchases may reduce liquidity by reducing the number of free-floating shares, or by causing dealers in the stock to increase their bid-ask spreads because they face the firm as an ongoing informed trader (i.e., in the case of an open-market repurchase program).

14.10.3 Comparing Stock Repurchases to Dividends

We can compare stock repurchases to the payment of regular or special dividends, because all involve cash flow from a firm to its shareholders, though under different circumstances. Indeed, all are included under the rubric of the firm's *payout policy*. However, as we mentioned earlier, stock repurchases differ from dividends in that cash dividends are paid to all shareholders in equal amounts, and thus the market value of all shares falls by an amount related to the per-share amount of the dividend, whereas in a stock repurchase the firm uses cash to *retire* the outstanding shares of any investors who choose to sell their shares to the firm. In addition, we recall that U.S. tax law treats a regular cash dividend as ordinary income, whereas by selling via a stock repurchase, the investor creates a realized capital gain (or loss), just as if the investor sold his or her shares to another investor in the open market.

From another perspective, we might argue that an open-market stock repurchase program is more closely aligned to a regular dividend, and a Dutch auction or fixed-price tender offer repurchase is more akin to a special dividend. The former pair compare because, like regular dividends, a stock repurchase program generally involves a protracted outflow of cash from the firm to shareholders over time, though in neither case is the firm legally obligated to continue the flow. The latter are comparable because they are strictly one-time events.

14.11 EXPLAINING THE MARKET'S FAVORABLE REACTION TO STOCK REPURCHASE ANNOUNCEMENTS

Many researchers have conducted event studies of the market's reaction to a firm's announcement to repurchase shares. Early studies by Masulis (1980), Dann (1981), and Vermaelen (1981), based on samples from the 1960s and 1970s, found substantial positive average abnormal returns of about 16 percent to 17 percent. Later studies, based on samples from the 1980s, document smaller but still very substantial average abnormal returns of about 8 percent (see Comment and Jarrell 1991; Howe, He, and Kao 1992).

14.11.1 Hypotheses

Researchers have tried to explain these results by (a) appealing to modern corporate finance theory, and (b) generating additional evidence either to test a particular hypothesis or to distinguish among competing hypotheses. Most authors have pursued one or more of the following three hypotheses: (a) the *Signaling Hypothesis* based on information asymmetry theory; (b) the *Free Cash Flow Hypothesis*, based on agency theory; and (c) the *Expropriation Hypothesis*, also based on agency theory.

The *Signaling Hypothesis* posits that a firm's management, who possess private information about the firm's value, will conduct a stock repurchase if and when they believe the firm's stock is underpriced. This can be an effective signal (i.e., not easily mimicked) simply because it is costly in terms of precious corporate cash. Therefore, the stock repurchase decision reveals management's private information about firm value, and specifically about its ability to generate cash in the future. The *Free Cash Flow Hypothesis* applies here because the firm uses internal cash to repurchase shares, cash that is paid directly to (selling) shareholders. Thus, management has less surplus cash flow to pursue inefficient, empire-building, value-destroying investments. The *Expropriation Hypothesis* refers to the incentive of a levered firm with risky debt outstanding to take actions that will shift value from the firm's creditors to its shareholders. In the present context, by reducing the firm's assets and its equity base via stock repurchases, the value of the firm's debt will fall. Absent any other factors, bondholders' losses will be shareholders' gains.

14.11.2 Empirical Evidence

Testing the Expropriation Hypothesis

Dann (1981) tested the Expropriation Hypothesis by examining the effects of a stock repurchase announcement on the values of the repurchasing firm's stock and debt. His sample consisted of 143 cash tender offers made by 122 different companies over the years 1962 to 1976. He found that stockholders benefited substantially from the announcement, gaining approximately 15.8 percent on average in the two-day announcement period. However, the stockholders' gain was apparently not at the expense of the firm's creditors, as the latter's announcement-period returns were negligible.

However, Dann's results do not necessarily imply that stock repurchases do not result in expropriation. Instead, it is likely that the stock repurchase announcement conveyed information that the firm was underpriced. Thus, shareholders unambiguously benefit from the market's upward revaluation of the firm, while creditors' gains for that reason may largely offset losses due to expropriation.

Early Support for the Signaling Hypothesis

Vermaelen (1981), in addition to documenting evidence of positive abnormal returns associated with announcements of fixed-price self-tender offers, provided evidence that supports the Signaling Hypothesis. He found that the announcement-period abnormal return is positively related to (a) the premium of the offer price above the current market price of the stock, (b) the target fraction of the firm's shares solicited in the offer, and (c) the fraction of the firm's shares owned by insiders. These results indicate that the firm uses the information in all of these variables to gauge the extent and credibility of management's signal that the firm's shares are underpriced.

Vermaelen also examined changes in the tendering firm's earnings subsequent to the repurchase announcement. If stock repurchases are a credible signal of management's favorable private information about earnings prospects, these firms should generally realize higher earnings subsequently. Consistent with the hypothesis, he found that, on average, these firms' earnings improved significantly in the announcement year relative to prior years' earnings.

The Relative Signaling Power of Alternative Stock Repurchase Methods

Comment and Jarrell (1991) argued that fixed-price self-tender offers should provide a stronger signal of undervaluation than Dutch auction self-tender offers. Their argument is as follows. As we explained earlier, in a fixed-price self-tender, the firm fixes both (a) the price at which it will repurchase shares, and this price is uniformly at a premium to the current market price, and (b) the total number of shares that it will purchase at this price. Thus, the fixed-price self-tender offer represents a strong commitment on the firm's part, particularly because both the firm and any insiders who own shares face substantial losses if they purchase shares at a price that is too high. In contrast, in a Dutch auction, bidding shareholders determine the premium, and the minimum premium, determined by management, is generally small.

The authors document evidence consistent with their argument: Average abnormal returns are 11 percent surrounding announcements of fixed-price self-tender offers, compared to 8 percent for Dutch auction self-tender offers. Lee, Mikkelson, and Partch (1992) also documented evidence consistent with this argument. They analyzed the personal trades of managers surrounding self-tender offers. For fixed-price self-tender offers, managerial trading activity is consistent with management's belief that the firm's shares are underpriced, but no abnormal managerial trading activity occurs around Dutch auctions.

Casting Doubt on the Signaling Hypothesis

Lie and McConnell (1998) conducted empirical tests that follow up on the work we have discussed. They pose the following research query: If the Signaling Hypothesis is true and fixed-price self-tender offers provide a stronger signal of earnings improvement than do Dutch auction self-tender offers, then subsequent earnings improvements should be greater for the former than for the latter. Their evidence is *not* consistent with the hypothesis:

> [W]e evaluate earnings improvements from before to after the self-tender offers against three different benchmarks . . . With none of these benchmarks do we find any differences in earnings improvement between the two types of self-tender offers. Indeed, with two of the three benchmarks, we find no improvement in earnings for either type of self-tender offer. There is, however, more to the story. According to the data, relative to own-industry benchmarks, both firms that undertake fixed-price self-tender offers and those that undertake Dutch auction self-tender offers have superior earnings performance prior to self-tender offers. On average, over the five years prior to the self-tender offers, the rate of return on assets for these firms exceeds their industry medians by 2 percent to 5 percent per year. Furthermore, this superior performance continues for several years afterward. On this basis, there is no improvement in earnings following self-tender offers. So where is the earnings signal? (p. 162)

Enter the Free Cash Flow Hypothesis

Nohel and Tarhan (1998) conducted empirical tests designed explicitly to differentiate between the Signaling Hypothesis and the Free Cash Flow Hypothesis. Their results are consistent with the *latter*:

> [W]e examine tender offer stock repurchases to differentiate between the information signaling and free cash flow hypotheses. Previous work in this area has focused on announcement period returns. While we also examine announcement returns, our primary emphasis is on operating performance changes surrounding repurchases. We argue that the information contained in changes in operating performance, and its determinants, enables us to differ-

entiate between the two hypotheses. Our primary finding is that operating performance following repurchases improves only in low-growth firms, and that these gains are generated by more efficient utilization of assets, and asset sales, rather than improved growth opportunities. Thus, repurchases do not appear to be pure financial transactions meant to change the firm's capital structure but are part of a restructuring package meant to shrink the assets of the firm. This evidence leads us to conclude that the positive investor reaction to repurchases is best explained by the free cash flow hypothesis. (p. 187)

Are Repurchasing Firms Underpriced?

D'Mello and Shroff (2000) tested the hypothesis that managers repurchase shares when their assessment of the economic value of the firm's stock exceeds the market price. They examined the values of a sample of firms that conducted repurchases via the fixed-price tender offer method. They estimated each firm's pretender economic value using an earnings-based valuation model, and compared this to the firm's pretender market price. They found, "(1) 74 percent of the firms that repurchase shares via fixed-price tender offers are undervalued relative to their preannouncement economic value . . . (2) the tender premium is highly correlated with the magnitude of undervaluation, and (3) the decision to satisfy oversubscription demand is influenced significantly by the magnitude of undervaluation" (p. 2399).

14.12   STOCK REPURCHASES VERSUS DIVIDENDS

Researchers have also compared stock repurchases to dividends as alternative means of executing a firm's payout policy. In this section, we briefly review several such papers.

14.12.1   Underpricing, Management Compensation, and Institutional Ownership

Bartov, Krinsky, and Lee (1998) identified and tested three factors that may determine a firm's choice between dividend increases and stock repurchases as means of distributing cash to shareholders. The *first* is underpricing. A stock repurchase would be a more effective means of taking advantage of, and eventually eliminating, the underpricing of the firm's stock in the market. The *second* factor is management compensation: "Many companies use stock options and stock appreciation rights as part of their compensation packages for key employees. Unlike stock repurchases, which have no direct effect on the value of these options, dividend payments reduce their value. Consequently, managers who own stock options or stock appreciation rights may be more likely to distribute cash to stockholders through an open-market repurchase" (p. 89).

The *third* factor is the extent of holdings by institutional investors: "A number of prominent institutional investors, notably Fidelity, have expressed a preference for stock repurchases over cash dividends. One reason is that, for taxable investors, selling shares, rather than collecting dividends, has a more favorable tax consequence. Therefore, institutional investors—who play an important role in the area of shareholder activism—will pressure firms to consider the income-tax consequences to shareholders of their payout policy" (p. 90).

The authors examined 130 companies announcing the start of open-market repurchase programs between 1986 and 1992, comparing them to other firms from the same industries that did not initiate repurchase programs: "As predicted, our findings suggest that equity undervaluation, extensive use of stock options, and the level of institutional holdings are all important contributors to corporate decisions to use open-market repurchases along with (if not in place of) dividend increases" (p. 90).

14.12.2 Dividends and Repurchases as Alternative Signaling Devices

Several theoretical papers have addressed the issue of the relative usefulness of dividends and stock repurchases as signaling devices. These include the models of Asquith and Mullins Jr. (1986), Ofer and Thakor (1987), and Williams (1988). Here we briefly discuss Ofer and Thakor's model.

Ofer and Thakor's model admits both dividends and (tender-offer) stock repurchases as costly signals in an integrated framework. The authors determine conditions under which a mispriced firm prefers one mechanism to the other. Dividends and stock repurchases are both costly because they may necessitate external financing at a later date. However, stock repurchases are more costly to the firm's manager. This is so because the manager has precommitted to owning a certain number of the firm's shares, so his or her fractional holding of the firm's shares, and thus his or her personal risk exposure, increases more after a repurchase than after a dividend.

Under these conditions, the model provides the following prescription for the choice between dividends and repurchases:

> When the disparity between the true intrinsic worth of an undervalued firm and its market price is relatively low, the firm employs dividend-based signaling because the incentive-compatible dividend is relatively small, implying that the associated signaling cost is lower than that attached to a stock repurchase. However, when the true value of the firm is very high compared with the cross-sectional average, a relatively large dividend is needed for informationally consistent signaling. The attendant cost is "excessive," and the manager now finds repurchase a less costly alternative . . . Consequently, only a firm that perceives a relatively large undervaluation will attempt a stock repurchase. Smaller undervaluations will be rectified through dividend increases. (p. 367)

14.12.3 Repurchase Premiums as a Reason for Dividends

Chowdhry and Nanda (1994) developed a theoretical model that incorporates trade-offs between cash dividends and stock repurchases as alternative means of distributing cash to shareholders. Cash dividends involve a greater cost in terms of taxes; however, the attractiveness of stock repurchases is inversely related to the market price of the stock relative to its true value, the latter of which insiders know better than the market due to information asymmetry.

Their model has several implications that are consistent with empirical evidence. *First*, dividends are smoothed relative to earnings over time because a portion of unexpected earnings is retained for future dividends and repurchases. *Second*, stock repurchases will be sporadic, occurring only when the firm's shares are substantially undervalued in the market. As discussed earlier, repurchase premiums are generally substantial, so the undervaluation must be substantial to justify a tender offer.

14.12.4 Cash Flow Permanence, Financial Flexibility, and the Choice between Dividends and Stock Repurchases

Three closely related empirical papers tested the *Flexibility Hypothesis*—a firm conducts a stock repurchase to the extent that its free cash flow is temporary and uncertain, and pays (or increases) regular dividends to the extent that its free cash flow is more permanent and reliable.

Jagannathan, Stephens, and Weisbach (2000) generated evidence that is consistent with the Flexibility Hypothesis: "Stock repurchases and dividends are used at different times from one another, by different kinds of firms. Stock repurchases are very pro-cyclical, while dividends increase steadily over time. Dividends are paid by firms with higher 'permanent' operating cash flows, while repurchases are used by firms with higher 'temporary,' non-operating cash flows. Repurchasing firms also have much more volatile cash flows and distributions. Finally, firms repurchase stock following poor stock market performance and increase dividends following good performance" (p. 355).

Guay and Harford (2000) examined firms that have either increased their dividends or instigated stock repurchases, focusing on the nature of the commensurate change in their cash flows. They find that firms that increased their dividends have a more permanent increase in their cash flow, while firms that conduct stock repurchases have had a more temporary increase in cash flow. They also find that the price reaction is greater for a dividend increase announcement than for the announcement of a stock repurchase program, which is rational given that the former implies a more permanent increase in cash flows.

Finally, working in an agency framework, Lie (2000) simultaneously tested the Flexibility Hypothesis and the Free Cash Flow Hypothesis by examining samples of firms that either (a) increased their regular quarterly dividend, (b) paid a one-time special dividend, or (c) made a self-tender offer to repurchase shares. He finds that all three types of firms have relatively high levels of excess cash before these events. The excess cash tends to be recurring in the case of the firms that increased regular dividends, but is nonrecurring for both the special dividend and share-repurchasing firms.

14.12.5 Managerial Incentives and Corporate Payout Policy

Fenn and Liang (2000) employ agency theory to formally address linkages among three of the major corporate finance developments of the past 20 years: the proliferations of executive stock options, the relative decline in dividends, and the rise of stock repurchase activity. The authors argue that, although executive stock options appear to have served well to align managers' and shareholders' interests, they engender an unfortunate and partially defeating incentive for managers to reduce dividends. This incentive exists because the value of an executive stock option, like a call option, is negatively affected by the value-leakage effect of dividends.

The incentive is unfortunate and partially defeating because managers already have a self-serving incentive to reduce dividends, as we have argued previously. Stock repurchases, however, do not have this flaw, because they do not result in a fall in the stock price. To the contrary, as we suggested earlier, stock repurchases increase the overall demand for the firm's shares in the secondary market, so they actually might cause the price of the shares to *rise*, a result that is clearly desirable to an executive holding stock options. Thus, stock repurchases are likely to cancel senior management's self-serving desire to minimize the firm's payouts, which is otherwise exacerbated if management holds stock options.

14.12.6 Tax Clienteles and Dividends versus Stock Repurchases

Allen, Bernardo, and Welch (2000) developed a theoretical model to address the question of why some firms prefer to pay dividends rather than to repurchase shares. This seems puzzling given the evidence shown in Figure 14-1 indicating that stock repurchases are becoming more important than dividends as the firms' payout means. However, from a longer historical view, dividends clearly have been the more important payout means. In any event, they develop their model to address this question.

Their model is built on two critical assumptions. *First*, they assume (for simplicity) that two types of investors exist in the market: (a) individuals who face taxation on their investments, and (b) institutions that are untaxed. *Second*, they assume that the untaxed institutions have a greater incentive, and therefore a greater tendency, to become *informed* about a firm's prospects than do the taxed individuals. An important implication under these assumptions is that a firm can attract institutional investors by paying dividends. This will be so simply because, in an equilibrium that spans both types of investors, the prices of dividend-paying stocks will be lower (because the taxed individual investors, who influence the equilibrium price, will demand a higher expected return on dividend-paying stocks due to the adverse tax effects of the dividend), and therefore their expected returns will be higher.

Given these assumptions, the authors argue that a separating equilibrium can develop in which *good firms* pay dividends and *bad firms* do not. That is, good firms pay dividends deliberately to attract the scrutiny of institutional investors, while bad firms do not pay dividends in order to avoid the scrutiny of institutional investors. They also develop an agency model in which "dividends exist to attract informed institutions whose presence ensures that the firms will remain well run" (p. 2501). In both the signaling model and the agency model, dividends must be paid reliably to have the intended effect—hence the practice of smoothing dividends.

14.13 AN EMPIRICAL ANALYSIS OF DIVIDENDS AND REPURCHASES: UTILITIES VERSUS NONUTILITIES

We conclude this chapter by offering an alternative set of depictions of composite dividends, earnings, and stock repurchases for seasoned, publicly traded U.S. nonfinancial firms over time. For each year, we separated these firms into two categories: nonutility firms and utility firms. We then calculated composite earnings, composite dividends, composite stock repurchases, composite dividend payout ratios, and composite repurchase payout ratios for each category of firms and for each year from 1980 to 2000.

We separate utility firms because, as we have discussed previously, their regulated status renders them fundamentally different from other nonfinancial firms. Regulated firms should generally be less risky and less exposed to both principal–agent conflicts and information asymmetry problems. The question we pose is, Do these fundamental differences induce different dividend and repurchase policies? We do not attempt to answer this question on theoretical grounds. Instead, we simply present the evidence and challenge the reader to draw conclusions from it.[4]

---

[4]Hansen, Kumar, and Shome (1994) analyzed the dividend policies of utility firms.

The evidence is presented in Figures 14-5 and 14-6. Figure 14-5, which we discuss first, shows annual values of composite earnings, composite dividends, and composite dividend payout ratios for each category of firms. The composite earnings of the nonutility firms were much more volatile over this period. The average and standard deviation of annual percentage changes in composite earnings were 6.7 percent and 20.6 percent, respectively, for nonutility firms, and 2.6 percent and 12.2 percent, respectively, for utility firms. For both categories, composite dividends are clearly and substantially smoothed relative to earnings. The average and standard deviation of annual percentage changes in composite dividends were 4.8 percent and 5.3 percent, respectively, for nonutility firms, and 2.1 percent and 6.2 percent, respectively, for utility firms. Finally, the correlation of composite dividend payout ratios across the two categories is 0.54.

The average composite dividend payout ratio was higher for utility firms (78 percent) than for nonutility firms (51 percent). Indeed, utility firms had a higher composite dividend payout in *every year*. For utility firms, the composite dividend payout ratio peaked at 101 percent in the recession year of 1991, and then fell to a final value of 70 percent in 2000. For nonutility firms, composite dividend yield also peaked in 1991, at 82 percent, and then fell more dramatically to a final value of 39 percent in 2000.

FIGURE 14-5 Composite Dividends, Composite Earnings, and Dividend Payout Ratios for Nonutility and Utility Firms

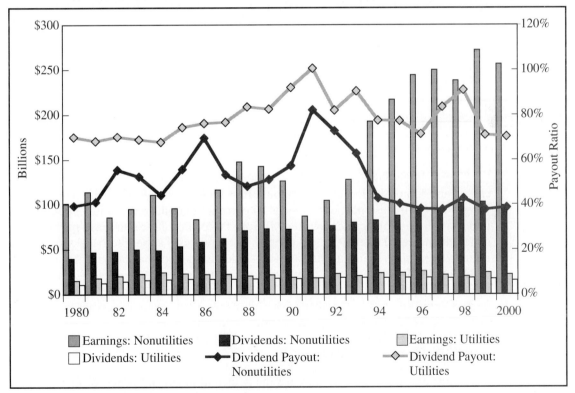

Seasoned Publicly Traded U.S. Nonfinancial Firms, 1980–2000
Source: Raw data from Standard & Poor's *Research Insight* database.

FIGURE 14-6 Composite Earnings, Composite Stock Repurchases, and Repurchase Payout Ratios for Nonutility and Utility Firm

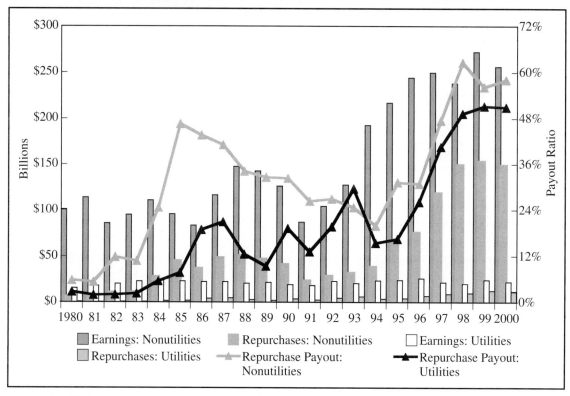

Seasoned Publicly Traded U.S. Nonfinancial Firms, 1980–2000
Source: Raw data from Standard & Poor's *Research Insight* database.

Figure 14-6 shows annual values of composite earnings, composite stock repurchases, and composite repurchase payout ratios for each category of firms. The average composite repurchase payout ratio was 20 percent for utility firms and 32 percent for nonutility firms. For both categories of firms, the composite repurchase payout ratio generally increased over time, and composite repurchases appear to be less smoothed relative to earnings than was the case for dividends. Indeed, the standard deviations of annual percentage changes in composite repurchases were 46 percent for nonutility firms and 57 percent for utility firms. Finally, the correlation of composite repurchase payout ratios across the two categories of firms is 0.82, which is somewhat higher than the corresponding correlation of composite dividend payouts.

14.14 Summary of Learning Objectives

Dividends and stock repurchases are the principal means by which firms distribute cash to shareholders. In this chapter, we reviewed the mechanics of dividend payments and stock repurchases, as well as the theory and empirical evidence pertaining to firms' use of them as part of their financial policies and strategies. We briefly summarize the chapter's major learning objectives as follows:

1. Dividends and stock repurchases are irrelevant in an ideal capital market, as long as the firm's real investments are not disturbed.

2. Aggregate dividends have fallen substantially relative to market equity values over the years 1980 to 2000, but less substantially relative to book equity values or earnings. The proportion of seasoned, publicly traded U.S. nonfinancial firms that pay dividends has decreased dramatically from 71 percent in 1980 to 26 percent in 2000.

3. In sharp contrast, aggregate stock repurchase activity has increased dramatically over the same period. Composite repurchase volume has increased relative to earnings, and the proportion of firms that conduct repurchases has increased.

4. In composite terms over time, firms' capital investment (*INV*) is generally close to, and is highly correlated with, net cash flow from operations (*NCFO*), indicating that firms depend primarily on *NCFO* to fund *INV*. However, *INV* is also highly correlated with net debt issuance (*DEBT*), indicating that firms use debt as a secondary source of financing for *INV*.

5. Dividends are substantially smoothed relative to earnings, based on analyses of both composite and individual-firm data. In contrast, stock repurchases appear to be less smoothed relative to earnings.

6. Hypotheses based on both agency and information asymmetry theories appear capable of explaining cross-sectional variation in firms' dividend and stock repurchase policies.

Review Questions and Problems

1. Explain why dividends and stock repurchases are irrelevant in an ideal capital market.

2. The founder of DEQ Inc. has a single-period project that requires an initial investment of $INV_0 = \$15$ million. The project's expected return is $r^* = 32$ percent, and the appropriate discount rate is $r = 16$ percent. The founder wants to sell enough equity ($\Delta STOCK$) to finance the project and to pay herself a $1 million dividend. Can she do this? If so, what is the value of the equity that she will retain ($ENTEQ'_0$)?

3. Calculate the value of the missing item in Hewlett-Packard's (compressed) cash flow statements.

Hewlett-Packard Co.
Annual Cash Flow Items ($ million)

	1995	1996	1997	1998	1999	2000
NCFO	$1,613	$3,456	$4,321	$5,442	$3,034	$4,425
INV		–$2,175	–$3,012	–$795	–$628	–$1,126
ΔSTOCK	$361		$419	$467	$660	$748
REP	–$686	–$1,089		–$2,424	–$2,643	–$5,570
DIV	–$358	–$450	–$532		–$650	–$638
ΔDEBT	$857	$811	–$285	–$1,091		$165
OTHER*	–$612	–$916	–$187	–$974	–$1,365	
Reconciliation (sum)	$0	$0	$0	$0	$0	$0

OTHER = Other Financing Items + Exchange Rate Effect + Change in Cash & Equivalents

4. Discuss the evidence on composite cash flow items for seasoned, publicly traded U.S. nonfinancial firms from 1980 to 2000 presented in the chapter. This discussion should involve the time series behaviors of *NCFO, INV, ΔSTOCK, REP, DIV*, and *ΔDEBT* individually, and relationships among them.

5. Are dividends disappearing from seasoned U.S. nonfinancial firms? In answering this question, refer to pertinent evidence discussed in the chapter.

6. Describe the process by which a firm pays a cash dividend.

7. Suppose firm XYZ paid a dividend of $1 per share last year, and this year's earnings per share was $3. The firm's target payout ratio is $\pi = 0.50$, and the value of the firm's speed of adjustment variable is $\rho = 0.3$. What is the firm's expected dividend for this year? If instead the value of the firm's speed of adjustment variable was $\rho = 1.0$, what is the firm's expected dividend for this year?

8. Suppose the shares of firm XYZ, which has 2,000,000 shares outstanding, are held by individuals with common tax rates on dividend income and realized capital gains are $\tau_p = 28$ percent and $\tau_{pc} = 14$ percent, respectively. The firm has $2 million in idle cash to either pay the dividend or to repurchase shares. Assume all shareholders face trading costs of 1.5 percent on stock sales. Should the firm (a) pay a $1 dividend per share, or (b) repurchase $2 million of shares? Consider only taxes and transaction costs, and identify the choice that minimizes the sum of these costs across all shareholders.

9. Reconsider the previous problem, assuming instead that the firm has $2 million in cash and $2 million in profitable investment projects that must be funded with equity. If the $2 million is distributed either as a dividend or used to repurchase shares, the firm must raise $2 million from a seasoned equity offering to fund the projects. Transaction costs for the equity issue are $tc = 15$ percent of the proceeds. Adding this cost, what is the net per-share benefit to shareholders of
   a. a dividend.
   b. selling a share to the firm, assuming it chooses to repurchase stock.

10. Suppose firm XYZ's stock is held by investors that share common tax rates of $\tau_p = 28$ percent and $\tau_{pc} = 14$ percent on dividend income and capital gains, respectively. The firm has just declared a per-share quarterly cash dividend of $DPS = \$2$. If the price of the stock both before the ex-dividend day (P_B) and on the ex-dividend day (P_A) is determined by these investors, by how much should the stock price fall on the ex-dividend day?

11. Does the market impose an expected return premium for dividends due to their tax disadvantage? Discuss valuation theory and empirical evidence on this issue.

12. Briefly explain each of the following agency-based arguments about dividend policy:
   a. Dividends and the manager–shareholder conflict.
   b. Dividends and shareholder–creditor conflict.
   c. The substitution of insider ownership and dividends.
   d. Dividends and capital-market monitoring.
   e. Dividends and the allocation of risk among the manager, shareholders, and creditors.

13. For a *signal* to be effective in the context of information asymmetry, it must be costly. List and briefly describe the various costs of dividends that have been used by authors to develop a dividend-signaling model.

14. Discuss criticisms of hypotheses that posit that dividends can serve as a signal of value.

15. Do dividend changes convey information about a firm's future profits? Summarize the evidence.
16. Describe each of the following methods by which a firm can repurchase its stock:
    a. Open-market repurchase program.
    b. Dutch auction.
    c. Fixed-price tender offer.
17. List six possible practical effects of stock repurchases.
18. How do stock repurchases compare to dividends as a payout mechanism?
19. Discuss the arguments and evidence for and against the Signaling Hypothesis as an explanation for the market's positive reaction to a stock-repurchase announcement.
20. Explain how stock repurchases would be superior to dividends as a mechanism to mitigate management's self-serving incentive to minimize payout.

Creative Thinking Issues

1. Most firms announce a specific number of shares that they plan to repurchase in an open-market stock repurchase program. However, most firms only repurchase a fraction of the shares that they specify. Is this a deliberate false signal, or what?
2. You have been hired as an outside consultant for the board of a large firm whose profits declined last year. A board member charges that in recent years management has used free cash flow to make poor capital investments, which are beginning to adversely affect the bottom line. What variables would you examine to test the board member's allegation, and how would the values of these variables affect your recommendations for action to correct the problem?
3. As the CEO of a large, highly profitable manufacturing firm in the electronics industry, you have long believed that the firm's stock is substantially undervalued. You wonder if a signal might boost the stock's price, and you have narrowed the choices to two: a dividend increase or a stock repurchase. What factors would you examine to make the choice?
4. Review empirical evidence on composite dividends and stock-repurchases for nonutility firms and utility firms shown in Figures 14-5 and 14-6. Try to explain the observed differences across these two categories of firms. Include relevant theory or hypotheses in your discussion.

Projects and Analyses

1. Using time series data on one or more *individual* firms, replicate the series shown in Figures 14-1, 14-3, and 14-4.
2. Develop a better dividend-smoothing model (e.g., include past earnings).
3. Analyze the dividend and stock repurchase policies of a specific firm over a number of years. Draw conclusions regarding management's motivations for these activities.
4. Identify several firms that have conducted stock repurchases. What method did each use? Can you identify the reason(s) why each did so?

CHAPTER

Corporate Liabilities: Strategic Selections of Lenders and Contract Terms

15

15.1 INTRODUCTION

Seasoned, publicly traded U.S. nonfinancial firms issue debt as their principal means of raising external capital. This chapter explains the major factors that determine a borrowing firm's decisions regarding (a) the sources (i.e., lenders) from which it obtains debt capital, (b) the terms to include in a debt contract, and (c) the overall structure of the firm's liabilities.

In Section 15.2, we discuss various sources of debt financing, private and public, short-term and long-term, available to firms. In Section 15.3, we present and discuss aggregate data on outstanding corporate liabilities by type and over time. In Section 15.4, we discuss six factors that influence a firm's choice of liability type. In Sections 15.5 and 15.6, we discuss the debt maturity decision and the strategic use of covenants and provisions in a debt contract, respectively. In Sections 15.7 to 15.11, we analyze specific liabilities, including trade credit (Section 15.7), publicly issued and privately placed notes and bonds (Sections 15.8 and 15.9), bank loans (Section 15.10), and lease contracts (Section 15.11). In Section 15.12, we discuss the optimal placement, seniority, and maturity structures of a firm's debt contracts. In Section 15.13, we discuss studies of the market's reaction to debt-related announcements. Finally, Section 15.14 summarizes the chapter's learning objectives, as usual.

At the outset, it is important to place these topics in perspective relative to the material covered in other chapters. *First,* our examination of debt fund sources and contracts reveals some of the most explicit applications of modern finance theory, including contracting devices to mitigate deadweight costs of principal–agent conflicts and information asymmetry, as discussed in Chapters 3, 4, and 5. *Second,* we must remain cognizant of the issue of optimal capital structure, which we covered in Chapter 6. *Third,* management's selections of debt funding sources and contract terms are also related to the resulting values of these contracts, which was the topic of Chapter 10. *Fourth,* in Chapter 19 we discuss recent innovations in corporate debt contracting as part of our discussion of optimal security design.

15.2 ALTERNATIVE DEBT FINANCING SOURCES

In this section, we briefly discuss each of the main sources of short-term and long-term debt financing available to U.S. nonfinancial firms.

15.2.1   Short-Term Debt Financing Alternatives

The main sources of short-term debt financing available to firms include (a) trade credit, (b) factoring, (c) short-term bank loans and lines of credit, and (d) commercial paper.

Trade Credit

When a firm purchases goods from another firm, it is common for the seller to allow the purchaser a number of days to pay for the goods. As such, the purchaser implicitly obtains short-term financing known as *trade credit*. The terms in trade credit are generally quite simple. Suppose the credit terms for a manufacturing firm's purchase of raw materials are 2/10 net 30. The purchaser (a) is allowed a 2 percent discount if payment is made within 10 days of purchase, (b) must pay the full price between 11 and 30 days after purchase, and (c) is delinquent if payment is not made within 30 days. These terms imply an implicit annual interest rate as high as 44.6 percent ($[100/98]^{365/20} - 1 = 0.446$). Trade credit can be very expensive.

Factoring

A firm can liquidate part or all of its accounts receivable balance through *factoring*, whereby the firm sells its accounts receivable to a *factor* such as a finance company or a bank. The factor either (a) purchases the accounts receivable at a discount to their book value, or (b) charges a fee to cover collection costs and to provide a return. A sale of accounts receivable can be either *with* or *without* recourse. In *factoring with recourse*, the factor has the right to collect any defaulted receivables from the selling firm. In *factoring without recourse*, the factor accepts the risk of default on the accounts. In either case, factoring generates cash for the selling firm, which it can use for other purposes. Moreover, collections procedures are left to experts.

Short-Term Bank Loans and Lines of Credit

Banks offer a variety of loan contracts. The simplest is the *promissory note* or *note loan*. These loans are generally unsecured, established simply by the borrower's signing a document promising to repay the borrowed amount, plus interest, by a specified future date. If the maturity date is within one year, the loan is classified as short term, in which case the borrower simply repays the loan, plus interest, at maturity. Longer-term notes generally are repaid in installments. A *commercial loan* is a short-term, renewable loan used to finance a company's immediate working capital needs. For promissory notes and commercial loans, the amount that a bank is willing to lend and the interest rate charged depend in part on the borrower's financial strength. The interest rate usually ranges from the bank's *prime interest rate* to two or three percentage points above the *prime rate*.[1]

Alternatively, the firm could request a *line of credit*. Lines of credit come in two varieties: a *noncommitted line of credit* and a *committed line of credit*. In a *non-committed line of credit*, the borrower taps a limited amount of credit on demand for a fixed period of time. It is an informal arrangement with a bank, requiring little paperwork,

---

[1]The *prime rate* is the interest rate that banks charge on short-term loans to their largest and most credit-worthy customers. The prime rate fluctuates with changes in prevailing market interest rates, especially the *federal funds rate*, which is the rate at which banks trade legal reserves.

and repayment is insured only through a promise and moral suasion. The interest rate is usually equal to the prime lending rate plus several percentage points. The borrowing firm generally must also maintain a *compensating balance* of 2 to 5 percent of the borrowed amount at the bank. A compensating balance is a deposit in a low-interest or noninterest-bearing account, which provides the bank with implicit collateral, and also increases the effective interest rate on the loan.

In a *committed line of credit*, also known as a *revolving credit agreement*, a bank agrees to lend a specified amount to a borrower, and to allow the firm to borrow that amount again after it has been repaid. Generally, the borrower must pay a commitment fee (e.g., 0.25 percent of the loan annually) to establish the credit line, and the bank may also require the firm to maintain a compensating balance.

Banks also provide a number of short-term loan contracts that are *secured*. Typical collateral is the firm's accounts receivables or inventory. A company can pledge its accounts receivables by either of two means: *pledging* or *assignment*. Pledging involves the promise of receivables as collateral. If the borrower defaults, the bank can sell the receivables to recover the amount owed. An assignment is a more formal arrangement, requiring the borrower to sign a promissory note and financing agreement, wherein receivables are formally pledged as collateral.

A firm can also use its inventory to secure a short-term loan. This can be accomplished using a *blanket lien*, a *trust receipt*, or a *field warehousing arrangement*. In a blanket lien, the borrower pledges all of its inventories as collateral. Disadvantages of this agreement are (a) it does permit the bank to sell the inventory in the event of default, and (b) the value of the collateral may fall over the life of the loan. With a trust receipt, inventory is pledged as collateral, and the borrower agrees to hold the inventory in trust. Proceeds of any sale of inventory must be promptly forwarded to the lender. In a field warehousing arrangement, inventory is turned over to a third party, who controls the collateral on behalf of the lender.

Commercial Paper
Commercial paper is a short-term, unsecured, unregistered note that is either sold publicly or placed privately. The commercial paper market involves large issues, and is available to only the largest and most financially sound firms. Commercial paper maturities range from 2 to 270 days. (According to SEC regulations, any security with an original maturity greater than 270 days must be registered.) If necessary, the paper is backed by a bank line of credit. The interest rate is generally only slightly higher than prevailing U.S. Treasury bill rates, so commercial paper issuers enjoy low borrowing costs.

15.2.2   Long-Term Debt Financing Alternatives

A firm can obtain long-term debt funds from several sources (a) commercial banks, (b) finance companies, (c) insurance companies and pension funds, (d) municipalities, and (e) the public market.

Term Loans and Commercial Mortgages from Commercial Banks
Traditionally, small and medium-sized businesses have turned to commercial banks for long-term debt funds, via a *term loan* or a *commercial mortgage*. A term loan generally matures in 15 years or less and is repaid in equal annual payments of interest

and principal. The interest rate (a) may be fixed or variable, (b) is directly related to the borrower's default risk, and (c) is usually higher than the rate on comparable public issue of debt. Floating rates are often tied to the London Interbank Offered Rate (LIBOR), which is the rate on dollar-denominated deposits (*Eurodollars*) traded among banks in London. For instance, a floating-rate loan may require the borrower to pay per-annum interest at LIBOR + 1 percent. Banks often prefer the floating rate because it ties their interest income to their costs of funds over time.

In a commercial mortgage, the borrower pledges real estate as collateral. The maturity of a commercial mortgage is generally 15 years or more, and payments are made in installments.

Loans from Commercial Finance Companies

Commercial finance companies have developed tremendously over the past 20 years. Part of their advance has been at the expense of commercial banks, which have had to face increasing regulatory pressures. Commercial finance companies offer debt-financing alternatives that compare closely with those of commercial banks, including lines of credit and mortgage loans. In addition, they are often willing to lend to high-risk firms that banks may reject. Carey, Post, and Sharpe (1998) argued that legal restrictions on commercial banks limit the level of risk that they can take on loans to firms. They provide evidence that finance companies take higher risk, especially by lending to highly levered firms.

Private Placements of Notes and Bonds

A corporate note or bond that is directly placed with one or more nonbank financial institutions (such as life insurance companies or pension funds) is called a *private placement*. The amounts involved in private placements are generally larger than amounts involved in either bank or finance company loans, though generally smaller than public bond issues.

The critical difference between a public issue of debt and a private placement is that the latter is exempt from Securities and Exchange Commission (SEC) registration. The issuer must abide by three rules to be exempt. *First*, there can be no advertising or soliciting of the issue. *Second*, the issuer must exercise reasonable care to ensure that the purchasers are not underwriters. The purchasers must be buying only for their own investment. *Third*, the SEC must be notified within 15 days of the offering. This exemption results in significant cost savings for the borrowing firm because the firm avoids the administrative, legal, and compliance fees associated with SEC registration. However, lenders charge higher interest on private placements than on public issues in part because private placements are less liquid.

Industrial Development Bonds

Firms can also appeal to state and local governments for low-interest debt capital. Through the *Industrial Development Bond* program, the U.S. federal government allocates a fixed amount of borrowing capacity annually to each state, which it can use to borrow, on a tax-exempt basis, for the expressed purpose of relending these funds to firms. The borrowing firm promises (a) to use the proceeds to pursue a capital investment project within the state and (b) to make the payments on the state's borrowings. Typically, industrial development bonds are a means of financing the construction,

The Finance Company Alternative

Approximately 1.5 million small and medium-size firms in the U.S. have "sub-prime" credit, meaning that they do not qualify for conventional commercial bank financing. How can such a firm raise debt capital when it needs to pursue a profitable growth opportunity? Choosing an appropriate lender is among the most important decisions a borrower can make. A firm is more likely to achieve its long-term goals if it has an effective strategic relationship with a lender.

In an increasing number of cases, sub-prime borrowers are turning to commercial finance companies (CFCs) such as Amresco, CIT Group, CitiCapital, FINOVA, GE Capital, Heller Financial, and over 2,500 others, large and small. According to Federal Reserve Board (FRB) data, in 2001 CFCs owned or managed $527.9 billion in business loans and leases, up 50 percent from $351.7 billion in 1997.

Over the past 10 to 15 years, CFCs have increased their market share of lending to small and medium-size businesses, largely at the expense of commercial banks, which have had to abide by increased risk-based capital requirements that limit the allowed riskiness of their loan portfolios. In addition, in recent years the commercial banking industry has been consolidating through mergers in an attempt to appeal to larger borrowers (via offering larger private loans and by expanding into the business of underwriting public bond issues), thus leaving a large niche for CFCs in the loan market for small and medium-size borrowers.

WHO OWNS CFCS?

CFCs include: (a) the lending arms of domestic and foreign commercial banks; (b) financing subsidiaries of major industrial corporations; (c) independent finance companies (some of which are privately owned, while others are publicly traded); (d) floor plan financing organizations; and (e) factoring organizations.

ARE CFCS REGULATED?

CFCs are regulated with regard to legislation on fair lending practices (e.g., state usury laws). However, CFCs are subject to much less federal and state regulation than are commercial banks, in part because CFCs do not accept deposits, as do commercial banks. Nevertheless, CFCs are governed externally by (a) the money and credit markets, from which they receive the funds that they re-lend to business borrowers; and (b) either public stockholders and analysts or their parent (e.g., General Electric Corporation in the case of GE Capital).

ASSET-BASED LENDING

In the past, small and medium-size firms considered borrowing from a CFC only as a last resort, because CFCs were considered to be little better than *loan sharks*.

Today, CFCs focus almost exclusively on *asset-based lending*, defined as debt financing that is secured with assets whose value can be assessed easily. In recent years the market for asset-based lending has developed tremendously, such that it represents not only a viable, but also a competitive, source of debt finance, especially under tight credit market conditions.

Collateral preferences vary across lenders, and may include any of the following: real estate, equipment, vehicles, accounts receivable, inventory, securities, or other assets.

Asset-based lenders consider a wide variety of stated uses for borrowed funds, including:

- Debt consolidation
- Equipment purchases
- Factoring
- Growth
- Import/export trade
- Inventory financing
- Leasing

- Leveraged buyout financing
- Merger or acquisition
- Project development
- Real estate purchases
- Reorganization in bankruptcy
- Turnaround activities
- Working capital

The FRB divides CFCs' aggregate business lending into three broad categories in terms of collateral: (a) motor vehicles; (b) equipment; and (c) other business receivables. In 2001, the percentages of aggregate lending across these three categories were 12 percent, 65 percent, and 23 percent, respectively. Thus, lending with equipment as collateral dominates. Regarding the equipment category, 27 percent of lending volume involves a loan, whereas the bulk, 73 percent, involves a lease.

Thus, the dominant form of lending from CFCs to firms involves the leasing of equipment. Leasing provides at least six major advantages:

- In the case of a sale-and-leaseback, the lessee sells equipment to the lessor, who immediately leases the asset back to the lessee. A sale-and-leaseback gives the lessee a cash infusion that helps improve its liquidity, which can be used to pursue expansion, acquisitions, etc.

- The lessor may be able to purchase widely used equipment at a bulk discount, whereas an individual firm would not be able to take advantage of such discounts.

- The lessor owns the equipment; so leased equipment is generally excluded from the lessee's balance sheet, which can improve the lessee's debt ratio and thus its overall credit rating.

- Leasing reduces taxes: the lessor is able to take advantage of accelerated tax depreciation, while the lessee cannot.

- Leasing often provides a hedge against equipment obsolescence. For instance, the lessee can often exchange old equipment for new, more advanced, equipment.

- As an advantage for the CFC, in the event of default, the liquidation of the leased asset is rendered much easier if the CFC retains title.

The maturity on an equipment loan or lease generally ranges between one and seven years, depending on the nature of the equipment. Generally, the payment schedule for an equipment loan or lease is set in line with the economic depreciation rate of the secured equipment. Such a schedule reduces the lender's risk of loss upon the sale of the used equipment in the event of default.

In the case of a lease, the lessee generally has three options when the lease expires. *First*, the lessee can simply return the leased asset to the lessor, who then sells it in an established secondary market. *Second*, the lessee may exercise an option to extend the term of the lease for a specified period. *Third*, the lessee can purchase the asset at its stated *residual value*.

INDUSTRY SPECIALIZATION OF CFCs

CFCs generally specialize in lending to firms in particular industries or economic sectors, such as telecommunications, energy, retail, and so on. This is largely because the technical knowledge required to value and re-sell industry-specific assets is costly to obtain, and must be allocated across many loans in order to achieve lending economies of scale.

Moreover, the lender must be familiar with the firms in the borrower's industry so that, in the event of default, the secured assets can be liquidated through a sale to a best-use purchaser. Indeed, by acting as a broker or dealer in the "secondary market" for used equipment, CFCs add to the liquidity, and thus the value, of such equipment.

HOW MUCH WILL A CFC LEND?

CFCs lend to businesses with annual sales of less than $200,000 to more than $1 billion. Amounts financed can range from several thousand dollars to over $1 billion. The amount lent depends on the borrower's business and size, and the quality of their collateral. Regarding collateral, a CFC may lend as little as 40 percent, or up to 80 percent, of the market value of equipment depending in part on the

(continued)

CFC's assessed ability to sell the equipment in the secondary market.

The loan amount frequently exceeds the net worth of the business, suggesting that CFCs are willing to lend up to a fairly high leverage ratio, despite the fact that the typical firm is privately owned, and is therefore relatively illiquid. Indeed, CFCs often step in with asset-based lending to a firm that is experiencing temporary financial distress. Such firms may have sustained losses that (a) triggered immediate debt-retirement covenants on existing bank loans; and (b) denied the firm access to additional bank debt financing, just when it may be most in need. For instance, a CFC may provide a distressed firm with a *bridge loan*, the proceeds from which the borrower can use to pay off bank debt and for liquidity until the firm's financial position improves and bank financing again becomes available.

WHAT ARE THE BENEFITS OF ASSET-BASED FINANCING?

Among the benefits of asset-based financing, loan or lease terms generally involve fewer covenants than is the case for loans from banks or notes and bonds issued in the public credit markets. Thus, CFC borrowers find that they do not need to run their business according to covenants. By contrast, bank loans often have covenants regarding (a) maximum leverage; (b) minimum fixed charge coverage; (c) minimum net worth, etc.

In addition, CFC credit is quite malleable: (a) varying as the borrowing firm grows; and (b) allowing early repayment or additional draw-downs rather than involving fixed amounts and maturity dates and frequent renewal reviews.

WHAT ARE THE COSTS OF ASSET-BASED FINANCING?

The interest cost of a CFC loan depends primarily on: (a) the firm's credit risk; (b) the quality of the collateral posted; and (c) general credit market conditions in the economy. Regarding point (c), loan rates relate to the general level of interest rates as well as current

default-risk premiums in the benchmark corporate bond and commercial paper markets.

Loan interest rates are generally substantially in excess of not only the risk-free rate, but also the yields on even high-yield ("junk") bonds. The interest cost on a typical asset-based loan is approximately 3 percentage points above the prime rate, or alternatively 3 to 5 percentage points higher than the typical bank's commercial loan rate. In addition, some lenders charge loan origination fees and early-retirement penalties.

CFC's reporting requirements represent another indirect cost. Generally, borrowers must submit a monthly or quarterly report to the CFC lender, showing that the firm is solvent and has been adhering to loan requirements, particularly regarding the secured assets. For instance, under a *net lease* contract, the lessee is required to pay for maintenance, repairs, taxes, and insurance, and the lessee must report such payments to the lender. (Under a *full-service* or *maintenance lease*, the lessor makes these payments.)

A BORROWER'S *CREDIT SCORE*

CFCs use credit-scoring devices extensively to assess the creditworthiness of potential borrowers. A potential borrower's credit score generally determines (a) whether the firm will be granted credit; and (b) if the firm is granted credit, under what terms (e.g., covenants in the loan/lease contract and the interest rate).

Key factors in any credit-scoring model include:

- The firm's line of business (e.g., retail).
- The firm's size (e.g., total assets; larger firms are generally less risky).
- The firm's "age" (more mature firms are generally less risky).
- The firm's total liabilities relative to total assets.
- Current liabilities relative to net worth.
- The firm's earnings, especially in relation to interest charges (i.e., the firm's *coverage ratio*).
- The firm's average liquid assets, their seasonality, and their sensitivity to changes in economic conditions.

- Past loan repayment "reputation," particularly the timeliness of past loan payments.
- Evidence of open suits, liens, and judgments.

Many CFCs rely on the credit-scoring expertise of independent agencies such as Dun & Bradstreet (D&B).

ARE CFCS FLEXIBLE?

Like banks, CFCs generally are willing to restructure the debt of a borrowing commercial customer that is struggling financially. However, revised terms will no doubt reflect the firm's deteriorated financial status, and thus can be seen as onerous.

Potential borrowers should also be aware that the availability and cost of CFC loans varies cyclically with the economy. Regarding availability, note that according to FRB data, aggregate CFC loans grew at rates of 11.1 percent, 15.5 percent, and 17.0 percent in the boom years of 1998, 1999, and 2000, respectively, but they grew only 0.6 percent in the recession year of 2001.

STRUCTURED FINANCE

In the present context, the term *structured finance* refers to specialized financing solutions that CFCs provide for select firms under special circumstances (such as financial distress), or as a general means of developing a comprehensive financial structure for the firm. Structured finance transactions are complex, and not all CFCs are prepared to conduct them.

A structured finance solution may involve the customer's issuance of debt- and equity-related securities (such as senior or subordinated debt, large leases, and structured private equity securities), a limited partnership ownership structure, or other comprehensive financial structures.

SECURITIZATION OF ASSET-BASED LOANS AND LEASES

The 1990s witnessed tremendous growth in the *securitization* of the loans of both commercial banks and CFCs. In a securitization deal, a large portfolio of (fairly homogeneous) loans or leases are collected and sold into a portfolio or *pool*, and debt securities are sold against this pool, generally in the public credit markets. Proceeds from the debt sales are remitted to the loan sellers.

Securitization has been an important development for financial institutions, including CFCs, because it allows the financial institution to liquidate the loans/leases that it has originated, thus freeing up precious capital that can be used for additional lending. In 2001, 15.3 percent of aggregate CFC business loans and leases were securitized. Generally, in exchange for a fee the financial institution "manages" (i.e., receives and forwards payments on) the loans or leases that it has sold into a securitization pool.

ADDITIONAL INFORMATION ABOUT COMMERCIAL FINANCE COMPANIES

Additional information about CFCs and the financial products that they provide can be found (a) in trade magazines such as *The Secured Lender*, (b) by directly contacting a specific CFC, or (c) by contacting the trade association Commercial Finance Association (CFA).

purchase, or renovation of commercial real estate. The maturity of the debt can be very long, and the interest rate can be either fixed or floating. Generally, the borrower is responsible for finding a purchaser for the bonds. They are usually either purchased by a bank or placed publicly or privately through an underwriter.

Publicly Issued Notes and Bonds

Each year, hundreds of firms in the United States tap the public credit markets for debt funds by issuing corporate notes or bonds through underwriters. Later, we provide evidence that the largest, least-risky firms dominate the public credit markets, though many smaller, riskier firms also issue notes and bonds publicly.

15.2.3 The Public Issuance of Corporate Notes and Bonds

In Chapter 10, we discussed the process by which a firm issues debt publicly in the United States, so we will not repeat that discussion here. Instead, we briefly discuss three issues associated with the process that we did not discuss in Chapter 10: (a) selecting an underwriter, (b) choosing a registration method, and (c) choosing a placement method. We provided parallel discussions of issues (a) and (b) in the context of seasoned equity offerings (SEOs) in Chapter 13. Issue (c) is unique to the debt market.

Selecting an Underwriter: Competitive Bidding versus Negotiation

In Chapter 13, we discussed the choice for an issuing firm either to put a stock offering up for competitive bidding among underwriters or to negotiate with a single underwriter. This choice is also available for public corporate debt offerings. However, for 99.7 percent of the SEOs examined in Chapter 13, the firm chose negotiation (see Table 13-1). Similarly, in all but 10 of the 1,824 corporate notes and bonds issued publicly from 1999 to 2000, which we discuss later, the firm chose negotiation.

Bhagat and Frost (1986) suggest that managers select negotiation over competitive bidding because with the former managers receive both *pecuniary* and *nonpecuniary* side payments from the underwriter. Smith (1986) suggests that the choice depends on the level of information asymmetry between managers and outside investors: "If the effective monitoring provided through a competitively bid offering is less than that provided through a negotiated underwritten issue, than firms would have incentives to employ negotiated offerings, even though flotation costs are higher" (p. 18).

For issuers with substantial contracting problems, the economics may favor negotiation. In exchange for the higher fees paid in a negotiated underwriting, the firm receives the benefit of greater due diligence by the underwriter, which pays off in a higher offering price than the firm would obtain in a competitive underwriting, where the winning underwriter might perform less due-diligence work.

The preference for negotiation also may be explained in terms of *bonding*. A firm may bond with a single underwriter, who then handles all of the firm's underwriting deals over time, perhaps going back to the firm's initial public offering (IPO). Given the high fixed costs involved in underwriting, especially due-diligence efforts, it may be optimal for a firm, particularly a frequent issuer, to establish a relationship with a single underwriter; in fact, a firm could actually realize lower underwriting fees (at least for follow-up offerings) than they would if they selected a new underwriter to take each issue to market.

Registration Method: Traditional versus Shelf

Also in Chapter 13, we discussed SEC Rule 415, adopted in 1982. This rule created the *shelf* method of registering securities, whereby an eligible firm can register securities that they intend to issue over the next two years, and then issue them on a piecemeal basis over this two-year period. In Chapter 13, we found that very few SEOs are registered via the shelf method. However, as we show later, shelf registration is very popular in the corporate bond market.

For qualified registrants, the shelf registration alternative appears to provide at least two important advantages for bond issuers. *First*, the shelf registration method appears to lower underwriting fees (see Bhagat, Marr, and Thompson 1985; Rogowski and Sorensen 1985; and Fung and Rudd 1986). *Second*, shelf registration provides a firm with potentially valuable flexibility in terms of the timing and amounts of securities to issue at any point of time within the two-year window. Kadapakkam and Kon (1989) document evidence that this timing flexibility is valuable: "the shelf rule enables eligible firms to avoid underpricing to the extent of 0.68 percent on average in the five-day period subsequent to the issue date for bonds with maturity greater than 15 years" (pp. 290–291).

Placement Method: Public versus Rule 144A

SEC Rule 144A, which restricts trading on unregistered securities, was modified in 1990 to allow a new quasi-public market for corporate bonds sold to *qualified institutional buyers* (QIBs). The SEC had a rationale for modifying this rule, as Fenn (2000) explains: "By creating a more liquid class of private placement, the SEC hoped to attract issuers—especially foreign issuers—dissuaded by the illiquidity premiums commanded in the traditional private placement market and the registration requirements of the public market" (p. 384). However, Rule 144A has had an important use that the SEC did not anticipate:

> Rule 144A has been widely adopted by domestic, below-investment-grade firms as a means of quickly issuing securities that are subsequently registered. By issuing high-yield debt as 144A private placements, issuers are able to raise funds as soon as their securities can be marketed to investors. When the bonds are subsequently registered, investors enjoy the benefit of public-market liquidity. The ability to issue debt quickly through the Rule 144A market has revolutionized issuance procedures for junk-rated firms in the same way that Rule 415 shelf registrations did for investment-grade firms. With a shelf registration statement, firms are able to pre-register securities that are issued up to two years in the future. The purpose of pre-registration is to permit rapid issuance as financing needs arise without the delay of waiting for the SEC to approve a registration statement. Yet many junk-rated firms do not meet the SEC's requirements for shelf registration, and even if they do shelf registration is not efficient for firms that cannot accurately predict their future financing requirements . . . The majority of junk-rated firms, therefore, register bonds at issuance, which, until the adoption of Rule 144A, led to potentially costly delays. (p. 384)

To support this argument, Fenn found that nearly all Rule 144A high-yield bonds issued in recent years were subsequently registered. Later, we compare public and Rule 144A bonds issued from 1999 to 2000.

15.3   CORPORATE LIABILITIES: AGGREGATE AMOUNTS BY TYPE AND OVER TIME

In this section, we briefly examine the aggregate amounts and types of corporate liabilities outstanding for U.S. nonfinancial firms at years-end 1980, 1990, and 2000. The data is displayed in Table 15-1. The data for this table was obtained from the Federal Reserve Board's annual *Flow of Funds Accounts*, so the liability types reflect their specifications. They sort firms' liabilities into nine types, which we then place into three groups. These

TABLE 15-1 Components of Aggregate Liabilities over Time						
U.S. Nonfinancial Firms, Years-End 1980, 1990, and 2000.						
	1980		**1990**		**2000**	
	$ billion	*Percent*	*$ billion*	*Percent*	*$ billion*	*Percent*
Short-Term Liabilities						
Trade credit	357	17.7%	626	13.2%	1,286	15.0%
Commercial paper	28	1.4%	117	2.5%	278	3.3%
Taxes payable	44	2.2%	38	0.8%	78	0.9%
Subtotal	*428*	*21.3%*	*782*	*16.5%*	*1,643*	*19.2%*
Long-Term Liabilities						
Bank loans	230	11.5%	546	11.5%	922	10.8%
Commercial mortgages	127	6.3%	248	5.2%	443	5.2%
Industrial development bonds	46	2.3%	115	2.4%	154	1.8%
Corporate bonds	366	18.2%	1,008	21.3%	2,235	26.1%
Subtotal	*769*	*38.2%*	*1,917*	*40.5%*	*3,753*	*43.8%*
Other Liabilities						
Other loans and advances	110	5.4%	473	10.0%	681	8.0%
Miscellaneous liabilities	704	35.0%	1,558	32.9%	2,485	29.0%
Subtotal	*814*	*40.5%*	*2,031*	*43.0%*	*3,166*	*37.0%*
Total	**2,011**	**100.0%**	**4,730**	**100.0%**	**8,562**	**100.0%**

Source: Federal Reserve Board's annual *Flow of Funds Accounts.*

three groups (with their associated liability types shown in parentheses) are Short-Term Liabilities (*trade credit*, *commercial paper*, and *taxes payable*); Long-Term Debt (*bank loans*, *commercial mortgages*, *industrial development bonds*, and *corporate bonds*) and Other Liabilities (*other loans and advances* and *miscellaneous liabilities*).

Among short-term liabilities, trade credit is the most important type, though it has fallen as a percentage of total aggregate liabilities from 17.7 percent in 1980 to 15.0 percent in 2000. Meanwhile, commercial paper gained in importance, rising from 1.4 percent in 1980 to 3.3 percent in 2000.

The corporate bond is the most important type of long-term corporate debt. Corporate bonds have accounted for an increasing proportion of total aggregate liabilities over the years, up from 18.2 percent in 1980 to 26.1 percent in 2000. Bank loans and commercial mortgages—both largely the province of commercial banks—rank second and third, respectively, accounting for roughly 11 percent and 5 percent to 6 percent of total aggregate liabilities over the years. Industrial development bonds bring up the rear, accounting for approximately 2 percent of total aggregate liabilities over the years.

Regarding Other Liabilities, miscellaneous liabilities are more important, accounting for roughly 30 percent of total aggregate liabilities over time. Surprisingly, the nature of these liabilities is not well defined in the Federal Reserve's accounts, though they probably include pension fund liabilities and capitalized leases. Finally, other loans and advances, another ill-defined liability type, appears to be growing in importance over time, rising from 5.4 percent of total aggregate liabilities in 1980 to 10.0 percent and 8.0 percent in 1990 and 2000, respectively. We suspect that this type includes loans from finance companies.

At least two important conclusions can be drawn from Table 15-1. *First*, U.S. nonfinancial firms obtain debt financing from a variety of sources. *Second*, publicly issued debt securities, including both short-term commercial paper and longer-term corporate bonds, have increased in importance over time relative to privately placed liabilities such as trade credit and commercial mortgages.

15.4   SIX PRIMARY DETERMINANTS OF A FIRM'S CHOICE OF LIABILITY TYPE

A borrowing firm chooses the type of liability that it will incur according to the most favorable set of trade-offs involving six basic factors: (a) the length of time that the funds will be needed, (b) interest costs and issuance costs, (c) the lender's need to monitor the firm's operations to minimize principal-agent conflicts, (d) the firm's need to keep *confidential* the strategic information related to the firm's operations, and the associated difficulty that potential lenders have in assessing the borrower's creditworthiness, (e) the firm's need for flexibility, and (f) tax effects. In this section, we discuss each of these factors.

15.4.1   Factor 1: The Length of Time That Funds Will Be Needed

The foremost determinant of the type of liability that a firm will issue is the length of time that the borrowed funds will be needed. Here, form follows function. If a firm needs short-term financing (e.g., to finance inventory), it generally obtains a short-term loan, and if it needs long-term funds (e.g., for property, plant, and equipment), the firm issues long-term debt. This dictum is called the *maturity-matching principle*. This principle is clearly reflected in the aggregate figures in Table 15-1. At the short end of the maturity spectrum, many firms use trade credit, and large firms can issue commercial paper.

Long-term borrowing also tends to follow the maturity-matching principle, but here the situation is more complex. The most straightforward illustration of the maturity-matching principle is the commercial mortgage, where the term of the liability is directly tied to the (long) life of the real estate collateral. In the public debt market, the analogous security is the mortgage bond. However, in both private and public corporate debt markets, secured debt appears to be the exception rather than the rule. As shown in Table 15-1, the aggregate amount of bank loans is more than twice the aggregate amount of commercial mortgages. In Sections 15.8 and 15.9, we find that, among public debt issues, the aggregate volume of *secured* notes and bonds is small compared to that of unsecured notes and bonds. We discuss the maturity-matching principle, and other issues related to maturity, in greater detail in the next section.

15.4.2   Factor 2: Interest Costs and Issuance Costs

A financial manager should be concerned about the *overall* direct costs of debt financing. Direct costs include interest costs and issuance costs. For public debt, issuance costs are called *flotation costs* (or *underwriter spread*). In the private debt market, issuance costs are called *loan origination fees*.

Public issues generally carry the lowest interest cost, followed by private place-ments and finally bank loans. On the other hand, flotation costs, which involve a sub-stantial fixed component, are very high for small issues (often exceeding 5 percent of the issue's proceeds), but become very small for large issues (less than 1 percent of the issue's proceeds). Issuance costs for private placements and bank loans vary less by issue size. Consequently, the choice between raising debt funds publicly versus pri-vately largely involves a trade-off between interest costs and issuance costs. Large bor-rowings, roughly $100 million or more, generally are optimally obtained via a public issue, whereas smaller loans generally are optimally placed privately. (Of course, the other factors we discuss also impinge on the choice.)

Numerical Example 1

Suppose a firm needs to borrow $200 million for five years to fund capital expen-ditures, and is considering the choice of a private placement with several insurance companies, or a public offering underwritten by an investment bank. For simplicity, we assume that in either case the firm will issue pure-discount bonds. The insurance com-panies demand interest at a rate of 9.0 percent, with 2 percent loan origination fee, and the underwriter estimates that the interest rate to be 8.25 percent, and will charge 3 percent flotation cost. What is the effective cost of the loan in each case?

With the private placement, the firm will actually need to borrow $204 million so that, after paying the $4 million loan origination fee, net proceeds will be the required $200 million. At maturity, the firm must pay $313.88 million [= $204 million $\times (1.09)^5$], for an effective interest cost of 9.433 percent [$200 million $\times (1.09433)^5$ = $313.88 million]. With the public issue, the firm will need to borrow $206 million to net $200 million. In this case, at maturity the firm must pay $306.2 million, for an effective interest cost of 8.89 percent [$200 million $\times (1.0889)^5$ = $306.2 million]. Thus, the public offering is cheaper.

Numerical Example 2

Another firm wants to borrow $40 million for five years to fund capital expendi-tures, and is considering the choice of a bank loan or a public issue. As before, the firm will issue pure-discount debt. The bank quotes an interest rate of 11 percent, with a loan origination fee of 2 percent; the underwriter estimates the interest cost to be 10.5 percent and will charge 6 percent flotation cost. With the bank loan, the firm must bor-row $40.8 million to net $40 million, so repayment at maturity is $68.75 million [= $40.8 million $\times (1.11)^5$], for an effective interest cost of 11.44 percent [$40 $\times (1.1144)^5$ = $68.75]. With the public issue, the firm must borrow $42.4 million to net $40 million, so repayment at maturity is $69.85 million [= $42.4 million $\times (1.105)^5$], for an effective interest cost of 11.80 percent. Thus, the bank loan is cheaper.

15.4.3   Factor 3: Agency Costs of Debt

When a firm adds debt to its capital structure, various principal–agent conflicts emerge between the shareholders and creditors (e.g., the risk-shifting incentive). These conflicts, and their attendant deadweight costs, tend to be more severe for riskier firms. The task of mitigating these costs influences the firm's choices of both lender and contract terms.

In public debt contracts, agency costs of debt are dealt with almost entirely via terms in the debt contract. Terms that are adjusted include the bond's maturity, restrictive covenants, and early retirement provisions. (We explain how these adjustments mitigate agency costs of debt in Sections 15.5 and 15.6.) Contract terms are adjusted in private debt contracts as well, to mitigate agency costs of debt. However, in the private debt market lenders have a more powerful tool to mitigate agency costs of debt: *monitoring*.

Monitoring involves the periodic inspection of the firm's business operations and financial policies. Monitoring is feasible for bank and finance company loans and, to a lesser extent, for private placements with insurance companies, because each lender has a sufficient stake in the loan to have an incentive to engage in cost-efficient monitoring. Monitoring is impractical for a public issue because the ownership of the bonds is diffuse, resulting in the classic *free-rider problem*. (Although collectively all debtholders would benefit from monitoring, none of the bondholders individually finds it optimal to bear the entire cost of monitoring. Thus, *ex post* they all suffer losses that ensue from the lack of monitoring.) However, in anticipation of such losses, bondholders charge a higher interest rate up front. In this way, agency costs are borne by the borrowing firm *ex ante*. It is therefore in the interest of the borrowing firm to identify the combination of lender and contract that minimizes agency costs of debt.

15.4.4   Factor 4: Information Asymmetry and the Problem of Assessing Creditworthiness

A critical factor in the choice of lender is the difficulty that the potential lender(s) have in assessing a potential borrower's creditworthiness. Here, the degree of the information asymmetry between borrower and lender is a vital issue. If the potential lender lacks sufficient information, it cannot accurately assess the firm's true creditworthiness, and a contract cannot be consummated.

As we discussed in Chapter 4, the success of a firm that operates in a highly competitive industry depends on its ability to develop strategies that must not be divulged to its competitors. Under these circumstances, it is hazardous for the firm to reveal the very critical information that a lender needs to assess the firm's value and thus the riskiness of the debt. Worse, under such conditions the borrower has an incentive to *exaggerate* its creditworthiness. In extreme cases, information asymmetry may effectively bar a firm from obtaining debt financing at a reasonable cost.

If information asymmetry is severe but not insurmountable, a private lending arrangement may be feasible. The firm can reveal confidential information privately to a small group of lenders with the understanding that this information will be kept strictly confidential. For this reason (and others), small firms and privately held firms generally do not have access to the public debt markets. These firms are generally restricted to the private debt market, where the lender is in a better position to scrutinize the potential borrower *ex ante* and to monitor the firm *ex post*. The information asymmetry problem is generally less severe for large firms whose equity trades publicly. Thus, large firms with public equity should dominate the public corporate debt market. Later, we find this to be the case.

15.4.5   Factor 5: The Firm's Need for Flexibility

Firms that face great uncertainty or fluctuations in the demand for their product or service may require more flexibility in their borrowing terms over time. Such firms may need to (a) retire debt before maturity, (b) increase the amount of their borrowings in short order if, for instance, actual demand for their product or service exceeds initial estimates, or (c) extend the maturity or modify other terms of the loan if they are facing temporary liquidity problems.

Under any of these circumstances, a private lending arrangement with a bank or finance company affords much more flexibility than is possible with a public issue. Private lenders are generally willing to renegotiate the terms and amount of a loan as conditions warrant. Moreover, in cases of severe financial distress, banks often engage in a loan *workout*, working with the firm's management to resolve the crisis on terms that are mutually beneficial. In contrast, if the firm had issued public debt, it may be forced into costly bankruptcy proceedings that may not be optimal for shareholders or creditors. (We discuss financial distress and bankruptcy in Chapters 17 and 18.)

15.4.6 Factor 6: Tax Effects

Generally, taxes do not play an important role in a firm's choice of lender or contract terms. Regardless of the lender or contract, interest is a deductible expense. However, there are at least two circumstances in which taxes can affect a firm's choice of the form of its liability. *First*, we have the aforementioned case of the industrial development bond. If a firm qualifies for a given state's industrial development bond program, it can obtain debt funds at a substantially lower interest cost than it could otherwise obtain. *Second*, as we discuss in Section 15.11, some firms can capture an implicit tax advantage by *leasing* assets rather than purchasing them with borrowed funds.

15.5 THE DEBT MATURITY DECISION

A firm's choice of debt maturity can be as important as the lender decision. In this section, we discuss both traditional arguments and formal theories regarding the debt maturity decision for a borrowing firm.

15.5.1 Traditional Arguments

The Maturity-Matching Principle

A well-regarded traditional approach to selecting the maturity of a given debt contract is the *maturity matching principle*, which we mentioned earlier. In this approach, a firm funds its short-term assets with short-term debt and long-term assets with long-term debt. Intangible assets must be financed with equity. Matching yields three important benefits: (a) The firm's financial flexibility is enhanced, (b) overall financing costs are minimized, and (c) the firm's risk of default is reduced.

Consider a firm that is about to pursue a profitable, long-term capital investment. The project requires substantial up-front capital expenditures for property, plant, and equipment (PP&E). In addition, the firm must be prepared to finance an increase in working capital, including inventory and accounts receivable. Following the maturity-matching principle, management should finance the PP&E with long-term debt that matures as the useful life of the assets expires, and finance the short-term working capital assets with short-term debt.

Regarding PP&E, it would be inappropriate to finance these assets with relatively short-term debt, because the project is unlikely to generate sufficient cash flows to retire the debt when it matures. Moreover, doing so would unnecessarily expose the firm to either (a) the risk of default, (b) the need to sell these relatively illiquid assets at a fire-sale price to pay off the debt, or (c) potentially harsh terms in a debt-refinancing deal. At the same time, it would be inefficient to issue debt with a maturity that substantially *exceeds* the expected useful life of PP&E, for three reasons: (a) The firm would be paying interest on borrowed funds that it no longer needs, (b) the firm would be unnecessarily exposed to default risk by retaining debt even though the project has expired and is no longer generating cash flow to service the debt, and (c) the lenders would be subject to expropriation and self-interested actions by the borrowing firm's management if it has continued access to debt funds after the project is terminated.

Regarding working capital, it is generally unnecessary to finance working capital with long-term debt for two reasons: (a) A project should eventually generate cash to self-finance these assets, and (b) the firm could use trade credit, factoring, or a revolving line of credit, which are more appropriate for the purpose.

Relative Benefits and Costs of Short-Term versus Long-Term Debt

The maturity-matching principle explains much of the observed variation in corporate debt maturities. However, choosing the maturities of a firm's debt obligations also involves complex trade-offs. For example, it may be better for the firm to finance inventory with long-term, fixed-rate debt if the firm expects to finance its rolling inventory on a relatively permanent basis. By doing so, the firm can avoid frequent refinancing costs, the risk of fluctuations in short-term interest rates, and changes in the availability of short-term credit. We discuss related trade-offs below.

Advantages of Short-Term Debt

Short-term debt provides two basic advantages over long-term debt: (a) lower average interest rates, and (b) flexibility regarding the amount borrowed over time. Regarding (a), according to two valuation theories, short-term debt tends to have a lower interest rate. *First*, the Liquidity Preference Hypothesis of the term structure of interest rates posits that yields on bonds tend to increase with maturity for either of two reasons: (1) Lenders demand a premium for loss of liquidity, or (2) longer-term debt securities have more price risk. (See Appendix B in Chapter 10 for a discussion of this hypothesis.) *Second*, our application of the Black–Scholes Option Pricing Model in Chapter 10 showed that the yield and expected return on a default-risky bond tends to increase with maturity (review Figure 10-4). Regarding (b), by using short-term loans, a firm can tailor the amount it borrows to fluctuations in financing needs over time. Such flexibility is important to firms with large seasonal or cyclical working capital requirements.

Drawbacks of Short-Term Debt

Short-term financing also has at least three potential disadvantages. *First*, the firm is likely to incur greater issuance costs over time by rolling over the short-term debt. *Second*, the firm faces the risk that it will be unable to refinance maturing debt. This can occur if the firm encounters financial distress or if overall credit market conditions tighten. *Third*, the firm faces the risk of changing interest rates on its short-term borrowings over time, a risk that it would not face if it had issued long-term, fixed-rate debt.

A Numerical Example

The management of High Growth Company projects that the firm will need $25 million of new debt funds each year for the next three years. The firm needs the funds to pursue its expansion plan, which involves acquiring PP&E and developing a base of working capital. Management also projects that the firm can operate profitably only if and when development funded by all three financing installments is completed. All borrowings can be paid off with accumulated profits in five years.

Management is considering two financing alternatives. The first involves three issues in sequence: $25 million in five-year notes to be issued immediately; $25 million in four-year notes to be issued one year from now; and $25 million in three-year notes to be issued two years from now. The second is to finance the entire amount in a single issue—a $75 million note that matures in five years. Borrowed funds that are temporarily idle will be invested in U.S. Treasury bills until they are needed.

The sequential-note alternative will probably result in lower net interest costs, though interest rates may rise before the second and third notes are issued. However, this alternative will entail higher total issuance costs, because three notes must be issued, rather than one. In addition, with this alternative the firm faces risks that (a) it will be unsuccessful in issuing the second or third notes in the sequence, due to tight market conditions or other factors, or (b) it will be forced to accept unfavorable terms in the second and third issues due to factors that are now unforeseen. Thus, the sequential-note alternative is more risky, and could be more costly. A third alternative, if it is available, may be best. This would involve a *commitment* from a bank or finance company to provide the financing in the required sequence.

15.5.2 Formal Theories

Hopefully, the discussion above has sensitized the reader to the complexity of debt maturity decisions. Theoretical papers have addressed the maturity decision from the perspective of modern corporate finance theory, especially principal–agent conflicts and information asymmetry. Below we review several such papers.

Principal-Agent Conflicts and Debt Maturity

The most widely discussed principal–agent problem that relates to a firm's debt maturity decision is the *underinvestment problem* (also called the *debt overhang problem*; Myers 1977), which we discussed in Chapter 3. As you recall, this problem relates to a firm that has unexercised future profitable investment opportunities. If the firm also has risky debt that matures *after* the time at which a profitable opportunity should be exercised, and internal or external equity funds must be expended to pursue the opportunity, the firm may fail to pursue it because a portion of the project's benefits will accrue to the creditors, which may render the project unprofitable to shareholders. Myers shows that the underinvestment problem can be resolved if the firm issues short-term debt that matures *before* such opportunities would be exercised.

Signaling with Debt Maturity

Flannery (1986) developed a theoretical model that suggests that a firm may be able to use its debt maturity decision to signal its value in an asymmetric information setting. In his model, all firms seek debt funds now for a two-period project. To potential investors at the outset, the projects of all firms appear to have the same profit potential. In truth, however, two types of firms exist, *good firms*, denoted as G, and *bad firms*, denoted as B. The projects of firms G are highly profitable, and the projects of firms B are less profitable. The managers of each firm are aware of their firm's type. However, the market is unable to distinguish the firms until the end of the first period.

If the managements of both firms would voluntarily reveal their type, the market would be able to correctly price the debt issues of each firm. However, the *moral hazard* problem exists: Managers of firms B would not voluntarily identify their firms as bad. Instead, firms B have an incentive to *mimic* the efforts of firms G. If they are successful, a *pooling equilibrium* is obtained in which the debt of all firms would have the same maturity and price, a price that reflects the average quality of the two types of firms. Firms G would sustain a net loss from the market's *underpricing* of their debt, while firms B would enjoy a net benefit from the market's *overpricing* of their debt. In addition, all firms would issue long-term (two-period) debt, rather than short-term (one-period) debt, in order to minimize transaction costs, which must be paid for each issuance of debt, according to the model.

To avoid losses in a pooling equilibrium, firms G have an incentive to provide a costly signal that firms B could not optimally mimic. In Flannery's model, firms G signal their quality by issuing short-term (one-period) debt. The cost of this signal consists of refinancing costs, borne at the start of the second period, that the firm would otherwise rationally avoid by issuing long-term (two-period) debt. If the cost of this signal exceeds the benefit that firms B would obtain by mimicking, they will optimally opt out of the short-term debt market and instead issue long-term (two-period) debt. A separating equilibrium by debt maturity then results in which firms G issue short-term debt while firms B issue long-term debt.

Flannery's model does not encompass all possible circumstances involving information asymmetry in the debt market, nor does it consider other factors associated with the debt maturity decision. However, it does suggest that the debt market may be segmented across borrower quality via debt maturity.

Liquidity Risk and Debt Maturity

Interestingly, both the Myers and Flannery models suggest that profitable firms should issue short-term debt. In contrast, Diamond's (1991a) theoretical model emphasized both the liquidity risk associated with short-term debt and the firm's choice of the source of debt funds. Stohs and Mauer (1996) provided the following interpretation of Diamond's model:

> Given a firm's private information, short-term debt allows for a reduction in borrowing costs when a firm receives good news and the debt is refinanced. However, short-term debt exposes the firm to liquidity risk, that is, loss of unassignable control rents if lenders will not allow refinancing and the firm is liquidated. This trade-off leads to interesting predictions about the type and maturity of debt that firms employ conditional on their credit rating. Very low rated borrowers with high probability of having insufficient cash flows to support long-term debt have no choice but to borrow short-term. They do so via private placements and/or borrowing through intermediaries such as banks. Intermediate credits, who have a choice, tend to issue long-term publicly traded debt because they face a higher liquidity risk than do very high rated borrowers. Finally, very high credits, who face little liquidity risk, are active issuers of short-term directly placed debt such as commercial paper. The empirical prediction is that there is a nonmonotonic relation between debt maturity and bond

rating; firms with high or very low bond ratings use shorter-term debt, although the type of contract will be different for the two groups of borrowers. (pp. 283–284)

Empirical evidence presented later appears to support Diamond's model.

15.5.3 Empirical Evidence on Debt Maturity Decisions

Next, we briefly review several empirical studies that have focused on debt maturity.

The Relationship between Bond Maturity and Bond Rating

Marr and Ogden (1989) examined the relationship between the maturity of a public corporate bond and the issuers' credit rating. They found that high-rated firms tend to issue short-term and long-term debt, but low-rated firms issue medium-term bonds almost exclusively. They suggest that low-risk (highly rated) issuers have greater flexibility with respect to the maturity of their debt, while high-risk (lower rated) issuers are more constrained by principal–agent problems to the medium-term section of the maturity spectrum. For high-risk borrowers, short-term debt is problematic because the firm is more likely to face financial distress, and its attendant costs, as it tries to pay off short-term debt; very long-term debt is problematic because it allows managers more time to take actions that expropriate wealth from bondholders. Guedes and Opler (1996) found similar evidence, and provide a similar explanation. These results are consistent with Diamond's liquidity risk model (see also Sarkar 1999).

Evidence Supporting the Maturity-Matching Principle and the Signaling Hypothesis

Stohs and Mauer (1996) examined the maturity structures of the liabilities of a sample of firms from 1980 to 1989 to determine whether they are consistent with a number of hypothesized factors. Their results support the maturity-matching principle: The average maturity of a firm's liabilities is positively related to the average maturity of its assets. Additional results support Flannery's signaling model: Firms with larger *earnings surprises* (a proxy for information asymmetry) tend to use shorter-term debt.

Why Have Maturities Trended Shorter?

In Chapter 10, we documented a dramatic shortening of the maturities of corporate bonds in recent years (review Figure 10-1). Here we discuss some popular conjectures about this phenomenon.

The traditional long-term, fixed-coupon, callable bond was the mainstay of the corporate bond market for decades prior to the late 1970s. However, in the late 1970s and early 1980s, interest rates became very high and extremely volatile, due in large part to the surge in inflation during this period. Firms issuing the traditional 20-year to 30-year, fixed-coupon, callable bond during this period were faced with extremely high interest rates for two reasons. *First*, the perceived (and actual) volatility of interest rates increased the value of the call provision for the issuer, and therefore the yield premium required in the bond market. *Second*, the market likely had a strong expectation that interest rates would fall in the succeeding years, and therefore a strong expectation that the callable bonds issued during this time would optimally be called by the issuing firms as soon as the deferment period expired.

Regarding the second point, interest rates did indeed fall throughout the 1980s, and a massive number of high-coupon bonds were called in the middle and late 1980s. Reflecting on the opportunity cost realized in holding callable bonds (versus, say, non-callable Treasury bonds) during this period, investors in the bond market continued to demand high yield premiums for the call provision. Corporate borrowers balked at paying such high premiums, and began to issue either variable-rate notes or non-callable bonds. But what of the loss of capital structure flexibility afforded by the call provision? Firms generally resolved this issue by issuing shorter-term notes.

Finally, the quickening pace of technological change (as well as deregulation) may be forcing firms to borrow for shorter terms. Thus, PP&E that in the past was expected to produce income for 20 to 30 years may now be expected to do so reliably for only 5 to 10 years.

15.6 STRATEGIC SELECTIONS OF COVENANTS AND PROVISIONS IN BOND CONTRACTS

In this section, we review the restrictive covenants and alternative retirement provisions that are often included in a corporate bond contract, and explain their role in resolving contracting problems. Briefly, restrictive covenants serve two principal purposes. *First*, they mitigate principal–agent conflicts and information asymmetry problems. *Second*, they provide an early warning of the deterioration of the borrower's financial condition (i.e., they are a type of automatic monitoring device). Early retirement provisions also serve to mitigate agency and information asymmetry problems. Some provisions provide the borrower with valuable flexibility to either (a) alter its capital structure or (b) alter the timing of scheduled payments. Others explicitly protect the lender.

15.6.1 Restrictive Covenants

Restrictive covenants are designed to protect bondholders' interests, and are therefore an explicit recognition of the conflict of interest between shareholders and bondholders. A covenant may be used to restrict the borrower's (a) investment activities, (b) future debt financing, or (c) dividend policy.

Restrictions on Investment Activities

After a firm issues debt, the firm's management, acting in the interest of its shareholders, has an incentive to increase the riskiness of the firm's activities and thereby expropriate wealth from the bondholders. This can be accomplished in a number of ways, including investments in relatively risky projects, changing the firm's production method or marketing strategy, or selling PP&E.

In general, it would be in the bondholders' interest to include covenants that prohibit expropriation. A common example of such a restriction is the *mortgage*, in which real assets are pledged as security. In a mortgage contract, the firm cannot sell the pledged assets as long as the mortgage is outstanding, and the bondholders have a priority claim on the pledged assets in the event of bankruptcy.

In some bond contracts, the firm must maintain a minimum level of business relative to the level existing when the bonds were issued. If this restriction is violated, the bonds become immediately due and payable. For instance, if a borrowing firm's level of sales or accounts receivable falls below 60 percent of its issuance-period level, the bonds become due. This covenant allows the bondholders to be paid before the firm reaches a critical level of financial distress. Moreover, it commits the firm to continue generating cash flow that is at least sufficient to pay interest and principal on the debt.

However, it is clearly problematic to include restrictive covenants because (a) they require foresight with regard to the means by which the borrowing firm would expropriate value from the lenders, (b) they may interfere with management's ability to manage the firm profitably, and (c) enforcement of restrictive covenants requires costly monitoring by creditors. Therefore, whether the bond contract includes provisions that restrict such activities depends on the balance of a trade-off between the direct protection that such restrictions provide to bondholders and the costs to the bondholders (as well as to shareholders) of restricting the firm's pursuit of profitable investments and of engaging in costly monitoring.

Restrictions on Future Financing Activities

Another means by which management could expropriate wealth from bondholders is to issue additional debt. If the new debt has the same or higher priority as existing debt, the value of the existing creditors' claim is *diluted*. Thus, some bond contracts restrict the firm's ability to issue additional debt.

Again, however, such restrictions may severely inhibit management's ability to pursue future profitable investment opportunities that require debt financing as well as adjust its capital structure over time. Thus, restrictions on additional debt are problematic and potentially costly. A lesser restriction that is more commonly included requires any new debt to be *subordinated* to existing debt. This lesser restriction allows the firm to maintain access to the debt markets in the future, and at the same time protects the interest of the existing bondholders. Indeed, the subsequent issuance of subordinated debt may *enhance* the value of the existing bond by infusing additional cash into the firm, which will supposedly be used to generate additional earnings against which the original bondholders have a claim.

Restrictions on Dividend Policy

Yet another means by which management can expropriate wealth from the firm's bondholders is to increase dividends. In the extreme, dividend payments can be used to *siphon off* the value of the firm to the shareholders, leaving the bondholders with a claim against a firm that is little more than an empty shell. In rare cases, a bond contract will include an absolute prohibition on the payment of dividends. More commonly, dividends are merely restricted in amount per se, and prohibited only if the firm fails to generate a certain minimal level of earnings or net worth over time.

15.6.2   Alternative Retirement Provisions

An *alternative retirement provision* provides for the retirement of part or all of a bond issue before its stated maturity. The four main types of alternative retirement provisions are (a) the call provision, (b) the sinking fund, (c) the conversion provision, and (d) the put provision.

Strategic Use of the Call Provision

The call provision allows a firm to retire all or part of a bond issue prior to its scheduled maturity, at a predetermined price. The call provision serves three useful functions.[2] *First*, it allows the firm to adjust its capital structure by eliminating debt at any time that it may be optimal to do so (e.g., the firm may have accumulated profits that it cannot profitably reinvest, in which case retiring debt may be the most profitable use of such funds, especially if the market value of the uncalled debt exceeds the current call price). Although the call provision clearly limits bond investors' capital gains in the event of a call, it may nevertheless be in their interest to provide an incentive for the firm to use idle cash to retire debt rather than overinvest in unprofitable projects, as may be the wont of management.

Second, the call provision provides bondholders a hedge against changes in the value of the bond. This hedged position reduces the ability of management to expropriate value from the bondholders, and thus reduces agency costs of debt. To see this, recall that the callable bond is essentially a portfolio of a *long position* in the noncallable equivalent bond and a *short position* in a call option on that bond. Further, the value of the call option varies directly with the value of the underlying noncallable equivalent bond. But bondholders are short the call, so their position is automatically hedged. Thus, management's incentive to expropriate is reduced, so the principal–agent problem is attenuated.

Third, the call provision can mitigate deadweight costs associated with information asymmetry. The rationale is similar to that provided above concerning the principal–agent conflict. Suppose potential bondholders would undervalue a borrowing firm's *noncallable bond* by the amount δ because they are not privy to management's confidential information about the firm's value (and perhaps particularly about the project that would be pursued with the borrowed funds). Under these circumstances, bondholders would likely undervalue the firm's *callable bond* by a smaller amount. This occurs because the bondholders would also undervalue the call provision by the amount γ, in which they have a short position. (That is, for any given call price, bondholders would ascribe a lower probability to the firm's calling the bonds than would the firm's management.) The net undervaluation would be $\delta - \gamma$.

Strategic Use of the Sinking Fund Provision

The sinking fund provision requires the firm to retire a portion of the debt annually. This tends to reduce the effective maturity of the debt, and so it tends to reduce the default risk of the debt. Agency costs of debt are positively related to the default risk of the debt, so the sinking fund reduces agency costs of debt. Furthermore, assuming that the borrowing firm accumulates profits that cannot be invested profitably, the sinking disciplines the firm's management by forcing management to use excess funds to retire debt rather than engage in unprofitable investments.

Although the sinking fund appears to provide a useful function, evidence presented in Chapter 10 (review Figure 10-1) indicates that it has virtually disappeared as a provision in corporate bond contracts. One reason for the demise of the sinking fund may be that corporate bond maturities have become dramatically shorter, and the sinking fund provision is not as useful or necessary for short-term bonds.

---

[2]For formal arguments, see Bodie and Taggart (1978) or Barnea, Haugen, and Senbet (1980, 1985).

It is also possible that the sinking fund provision disappeared because it had a fatal flaw. To see the flaw, recall that the standard sinking fund allows the firm to retire bonds annually either by (a) purchasing the required number of bonds in the open market, or (b) calling the requisite number of bonds by lottery, typically at or near their par value. If the firm has been profitable, the bonds will likely sell at a premium to par value, and the firm would prefer to retire the bonds via a lottery call. If the firm has not been profitable, the bonds are likely to sell at a discount to their par value, and the firm would prefer to retire bonds via open-market purchases.

However, a problem can arise in the latter case. Due to the nature of the secondary market for corporate bonds, it may be relatively easy for a single arbitrageur (or several arbitrageurs acting in collusion) to *corner the market* for a given sinking fund bond issue. Suppose they are successful cornering the market for a sinking fund bond that has been trading at a substantial discount to par value. At this point, the borrowing firm's option to retire bonds to satisfy the sinking fund requirement via open-market purchases would be eliminated. Instead, the firm would be forced to retire the bonds via the lottery call mechanism, paying the arbitrageurs full par value. Having seen this kind of game played, issuers may have come to balk at including a sinking fund in their bond contracts.[3]

Strategic Use of the Conversion Provision

The conversion provision allows the bondholders to convert the bonds into shares of the firm's common stock at a fixed conversion ratio of shares for bonds valued at par value. The convertible bond can be seen as a portfolio consisting of an equivalent nonconvertible bond plus a call option to purchase the firm's stock. Unlike the nonconvertible bond, the value of the convertible bond is relatively insensitive to changes in the riskiness of the firm (as measured by, say, the standard deviation of returns on the firm's assets) because, although the value of the underlying bond is *inversely* related to changes in the firm's risk, the value of the conversion provision, like a call option, is *directly* related to changes in the firm's risk. As a result, the incentive of the firm's management to pursue risk shifting to expropriate value from the bondholders is reduced, and therefore a major agency cost of debt is mitigated (see Green 1984).

Brennan and Kraus (1987) and Brennan and Schwartz (1988) contend that convertible bonds are useful under conditions in which the market has difficulty estimating the riskiness of the issuing firm. Suppose the market's assessment of the firm's riskiness is higher than management's. As a consequence, the market would value the firm's straight debt *lower* than would management. However, holding equity value constant and appealing to option pricing theory, the market's assessment of the value of the conversion option would be *higher* than management's. The resulting trade-off in value differentials implies that the convertible bond reduces the gap between market and management assessments of value.

In a theoretical model, Stein (1992) developed the idea that a convertible bond is essentially *backdoor equity financing*, referring of course to the possible future conver-

[3]Kalotay (1981), Dunn and Spatt (1984), and Ogden (1988) discuss cornering the market in sinking fund bonds.

sion of the bonds into equity shares. Jen, Choi, and Lee (1997) explain the essence of Stein's model:

> [G]rowth firms with high costs of financial distress find it attractive to issue convertibles to build equity. Such firms would find it difficult to issue equity, as they are subject to adverse selection in the stock market, and thus face negative valuation effects. They cannot afford straight debt financing either, because of the potential for costly financial distress. These firms build equity by using a call provision to force conversion if and when the stock price rises in the future. The market can discern these types of firms easily, because firms with poor growth opportunities would not be able to issue convertibles without exposing themselves to significant costs of financial distress. Thus, convertible bond financing may let these . . . issuers avoid the adverse informational consequences that are typically associated with equity financing. (pp. 8–9)

Mayers (1998) argues that firms issue callable, convertible bonds to lower issue costs attributable to the overinvestment incentive associated with *sequential financing*. To test this hypothesis, he focuses on firms that have called, and thus forced conversion of, their convertible debt. If, when these firms originally issued their convertible bonds, they had intentions consistent with Mayers' hypothesis, those that subsequently force conversion should be observed to engage subsequently in greater capital spending *and* debt financing. He finds evidence of such postcall phenomena: "The evidence shows significant increases in capital expenditures and new long-term debt financing starting in the year of the call" (p. 83).

Variants of the Convertible Bond: Bonds with Attached Warrants, and Exchangeables

Two interesting variants of the convertible bond that are occasionally seen in the corporate debt market are (a) bonds with attached warrants, and (b) exchangeable bonds. Here we briefly discuss each.

Bonds with Attached Warrants   Occasionally a high-risk bond will be issued in a unit that also includes a detachable warrant that allows the investor to purchase a share of the issuing firm's stock. Theoretically, this portfolio of securities may help to resolve the principal–agent problem of risky debt, because bondholders also have a security, the warrant, which increases in value as the firm's equity value rises, thus offsetting losses that the bondholder would incur if management attempts to expropriate wealth from bondholders.

Exchangeable Bonds   An exchangeable bond is distinguished from a convertible bond in that the bonds can be exchanged for shares of a firm other than the issuing firm. For example, the bonds of firm A are exchangeable into shares of target firm B, in which firm A has an ownership interest. The exchangeable bond is issued only in circumstances that correspond to this arrangement. Ghosh, Varma, and Woolridge (1990) argue that an exchangeable bond offering "signifies a potential change in the issuing firm's asset composition through the divestiture of the ownership stake in the target firm" (p. 251). Further, they suggest that such an offering can benefit the firm by enabling it to "(1) eliminate a minority interest in a previously carved-out subsidiary, or (2) implement a change in corporate focus that makes the stake inconsistent with long-run strategy, or (3) relinquish a stake acquired in an aborted attempt to take over the target firm" (p. 252).

Strategic Use of the Put Provision

Some bond indentures include a *put provision*, which allows bondholders to redeem their bonds prior to maturity. Some put provisions may be exercised at any time (or after a deferment period of three to five years). Others may be exercised only if the firm takes an action that may be harmful to bondholders' interest, such as a merger or acquisition. Seemingly, the put provision would provide the ultimate protection for bondholders against the firm's attempt to expropriate. However, the limitations of the put provision can be illustrated by referring to the risk-shifting problem. Suppose that, after issuing a putable bond, a firm shifts to a high-risk operating strategy that will lead to either great success or utter bankruptcy. In the former case, the put provision is not needed; in the latter case, the put provision is worthless, because in bankruptcy the bondholders' claim is the same with or without the put provision.

15.7   CORPORATE USE OF TRADE CREDIT

At first blush, trade credit appears to be an anomaly in the face of modern corporate finance theory, which emphasizes principal–agent conflicts, information asymmetry problems, and the critical roles of financial institutions and contracting devices to deal with them. How can we reconcile theory with the widespread use of trade credit, whereby one (nonfinancial) firm provides financing to another firm using a relatively simple contract? Recent research has shed considerable light on this question. In particular, information asymmetry theory helps explain the existence of trade credit.

15.7.1   Four Theories of Trade Credit

Four theories of trade credit are predominant in the literature. All focus primarily on information asymmetry problems as a motive for trade credit.

Theory 1: The seller or financier may be in a better position than a financial institution to both *evaluate* and to *monitor or control* the buyer or borrower's credit risk. Their evaluations may be superior because (a) the supplier may have a long-standing, close relationship with the buyer or (b) the supplier may have better information about the quality of the product that it is selling to the buyer. Their monitoring and controlling ability may be better because they are in a better position to repossess and resell sold goods if the buyer defaults.

Theory 2: The buyer has a problem accessing the capital markets directly, whereas the seller does not (e.g., because the seller is a larger firm). Because the seller has an implicit equity interest in the buyer's business, the seller is motivated to substitute its own creditworthiness for that of the buyer by borrowing in the capital markets and relending to the seller.

Theory 3: The seller's trade-credit terms serve to indirectly price-discriminate among customers with varying but unobservable creditworthiness, even though direct price discrimination is illegal. The same trade credit terms, such as the 2/10 net 30 terms discussed earlier, are offered to all customers, but the most creditworthy customers are more likely to pay early to avoid the financing costs.

Theory 4: In most trade-credit circumstances, the buyer has access to the purchased products for a brief period before actually paying for them. If this circumstance is also accompanied by a return guarantee from the seller, trade credit serves as a powerful signal of the quality of the seller's product.

The theoretical analysis of Lee and Stowe (1993) is representative. Their model is based on asymmetric information about product quality and risk-sharing motives between the seller and buyer, and explains observed cross-sectional variation in trade-credit terms across firms and industries.

15.7.2   Empirical Evidence on the Use of Trade Credit

Petersen and Rajan (1997) tested the above theories using a unique database compiled by the National Survey of Small Business Finance (NSSBF). The firms in the NSSBF survey are small firms, and therefore are firms that may have difficulty accessing the credit markets. Their empirical results basically support all of these theories. Ng, Smith, and Smith (1999) conducted an extensive empirical investigation of variations in both trade credit policies and trade credit terms across firms and industries in the United States. They found wide variation in trade-credit practices across industries, but little variation across firms within an industry. Their results suggest that trade credit exists as a means of resolving dual information asymmetry problems. Trade credit is more likely to be offered by a seller as product quality uncertainty rises (Theory 4), and trade credit *terms* are adjusted according to the seller's uncertainty about the creditworthiness of buyers (Theories 1 and 3). Their results do not support Theory 2. (Long, Malitz, and Ravid [1993] also provide empirical evidence consistent with Theory 4.)

15.8   ANALYSES OF CORPORATE NOTES AND BONDS ISSUED PUBLICLY, 1999–2000

In this section, we provide statistical analyses of the corporate notes and bonds that were issued publicly in the United States by U.S. nonfinancial firms in 1999 and 2000. We provide statistics for all corporate issuers as well as subsamples of large-firm and small-firm issuers, distinguished by whether they were included in the Fortune 500 list of the largest U.S. firms. The results are displayed in Table 15-2.

A total of 1,824 corporate notes and bonds were issued, generating aggregate proceeds of $982 billion. The average issue size was $539 million, though issue sizes ranged greatly from $0.1 million to $22,100 million. Large firms (as defined) issued 991 notes and bonds, while the more numerous small firms combined to issue 833 notes and bonds. The average issue size was slightly larger for large-firm issues ($575 million) than for small-firm issues ($495 million). As a result, the aggregate dollar volumes of notes and bonds issued by large and small firms were $570 billion and $412 billion, respectively. These results provide our initial indication that the U.S. public corporate debt market is predominantly the purview of large firms.

TABLE 15-2 Details of 1,824 Corporate Notes and Bonds Issued in the U.S. Public Debt Market by U.S. Nonfinancial Firms, 1999–2000

Characteristic	All Issues [$982 billion]		Proceeds ($ million)			Large Issuers [$570 billion]*			Small Issuers [$412 billion]*		
	Number	Percent of All	AVERAGE	MINIMUM	MAXIMUM	Number	Percent of All	Average Proceeds ($ million)	Number	Percent of all	Average Proceeds ($ million)
All Issues	1,824	100%	539	0.1	22,100	991	54%	575	833	46%	495
Issuer's Equity Status											
Publicly traded	1,406	77%	559	0.1	16,988	771	42%	622	635	35%	482
Subsidiary	401	22%	444	1.0	22,100	220	12%	410	181	10%	485
Private	17	1%	1,071	1.0	12,266	0	0%	n/a	17	1%	1,071
Registration Method											
Traditional	74	4%	223	4.0	2,013	37	2%	238	37	2%	208
Shelf (new)	1,146	63%	242	0.1	3,237	703	39%	247	443	24%	234
Shelf (tapped)	604	33%	1,140	1.0	22,100	251	14%	1,544	353	19%	853
Credit Rating											
Investment grade	1,445	79%	501	0.1	22,100	920	50%	541	525	29%	432
Speculative grade	212	12%	694	0.3	5,000	43	2%	877	169	9%	647
Not rated	167	9%	665	1.0	12,266	28	2%	1,232	139	8%	550
Maturity Ranges											
1–5 years	1,223	67%	667	0.1	22,100	655	36%	714	568	31%	612
6–10 years	408	22%	263	0.3	3,237	210	12%	271	198	11%	255
11–15 years	48	3%	181	4.0	2,013	31	2%	203	17	1%	140
16–20 years	35	2%	248	5.0	1,250	23	1%	256	12	1%	233
>20 years	110	6%	385	10.0	2,968	72	4%	458	38	2%	246
Coupon Type											
Fixed	996	55%	243	0.1	3,237	583	32%	257	413	23%	223
Floating/Variable	213	12%	201	3.1	2,500	152	8%	172	61	3%	272
Zero	11	1%	866	100.0	2,027	5	0%	1,333	6	0%	477
Unknown**	604	33%	1,140	1.0	22,100	251	14%	1,544	353	19%	853
Security/Priority											
Secured or guaranteed	137	8%	527	1.0	12,266	77	4%	493	60	3%	571
Senior debenture	192	11%	284	3.0	1,489	90	5%	281	102	6%	286
Debenture	1,439	79%	580	0.1	22,100	812	45%	615	627	34%	535
Subordinated debenture	56	3%	368	5.0	4,000	12	1%	608	44	2%	303
Convertible or Units?											
Convertible	51	3%	546	26.3	2,027	15	1%	820	36	2%	431
Units	4	0%	572	236.4	1,000	1	0%	300	3	0%	662
Neither (straight)	1,769	97%	538	0.1	22,100	975	53%	572	794	44%	497
Callability											
Noncallable	722	40%	186	0.3	2,500	462	25%	178	260	14%	200
Equity (clawback)	18	1%	341	49.8	1,489	3	0%	741	15	1%	260
Make whole	333	18%	355	7.0	2,993	191	10%	416	142	8%	273
Special	23	1%	776	64.7	3,237	14	1%	852	9	0%	657
Traditional	124	7%	140	0.1	1,000	70	4%	95	54	3%	199
Unknown**	604	33%	1140	1.0	22,100	251	14%	1,544	353	19%	853

*Large issuers are firms included in the Fortune 500 index of the largest U.S. firms; all others are classified as small.
**The SDC database does not provide coupon or call provision information for tapped shelf issues.
Source: Raw data from Securities Data Corporations new-issues database.

15.8.1   Results Sorted by Issuer's Equity Status

Three-quarters of the issuers (1,406 issuers, or 77 percent) were publicly traded firms. The remaining issuers were either subsidiaries (401, 22 percent) or private firms (17, 1 percent). Publicly traded firms accounted for 80 percent ($785 billion) of the total volume of publicly issued corporate notes and bonds.

15.8.2   Results Sorted by Registration Method

The overwhelming majority of issues (1,750 issues, 96 percent) were newly registered via the shelf method or represented a *tapping* of a previous shelf registration. The remaining issues were registered via the traditional method. In addition, the average size of the tapped shelf issues, $1,140 million, was about five times larger than either new shelf issues or traditional issues, $242 million and $223 million, respectively. Similar results are obtained after cross-sorting by firm size. Clearly, shelf registration has been a successful innovation in the public corporate debt market. These results contrast sharply with those for SEOs (Chapter 13), where we found that only a few issuers chose shelf registration.

15.8.3   Results Sorted by Credit Rating

Next, we sorted each issue into one of three groups according to its credit rating: investment grade, speculative grade, or unrated. The vast majority of issues, 1,445 in total (79 percent of the total), were investment grade. Only 212 (12 percent) were speculative-grade issues, and 167 issues (9 percent) were unrated. Here the results of the firm-size sorting reveal that 93 percent of the large-firm issues (920 of 991) garnered an investment-grade rating. Only 63 percent small-firm issues (525 of 833) were investment grade.

15.8.4   Results Sorted by Maturity

We also sorted the issues into five categories according to their stated final maturity, as follows: 1 to 5 years, 6 to 10 years, 11 to 15 years, 16 to 20 years, and more than 20 years. The results for all issues, as well as for large-firm and small-firm issues, corroborates the evidence presented in Chapter 10 that corporate debt maturities have trended shorter. Among all issues, 67 percent had maturities of 1 to 5 years, and another 22 percent had maturities of 6 to 10 years. In contrast, only 11 percent of the issues had maturities greater than 20 years.

15.8.5   Results Sorted by Coupon Type

Coupon information for the tapped shelf issues was not available from our source, the SDC database. Of the remaining 1,220 notes and bonds, 996 issues, or 82 percent, bore a fixed-coupon rate, 216 issues, or 17 percent, had a variable or floating coupon, and only 11 issues, or 1 percent, were zero-coupon issues. (In Chapter 19, we discuss floating-rate and zero-coupon bonds, both innovations of the 1980s.)

15.8.6   Results Sorted by Security and Priority

A total of 137 issues, or 8 percent of the total, were either secured by real assets or were guaranteed by another firm (generally by the parent of a subsidiary). The most common issue was the (nonsenior, nonsubordinated) debenture, which accounted for 79 percent of all issues. A total of 192 issues (11 percent) were senior debentures, while only 56 issues, or 3 percent of the total, were subordinated debentures. Of the subordinated issues, a total of 44 were issued by smaller firms. Subordination generally occurs when a firm has preexisting senior debt outstanding, and the senior debt is generally bank debt.

15.8.7 Results Sorted by Convertibility and Unit Status

Historically, about 10 percent of all public issues of corporate bonds have included a conversion provision, though this fraction has varied considerably over time.[4] Relative to the historical norms, convertible issues were scarce in 1999 to 2000, as only 51 issues, or 3 percent of all issues, were convertible. Convertible bonds are generally issued by smaller, riskier firms. Of the 51 convertible bond issues, only 14 had an investment-grade rating, and 22 were unrated. None carried security or a guarantee, and only 15 were issued by Fortune 500 companies. Finally, only 4 of the 1,824 issues were units, consisting of debt and warrants to purchase the issuing firm's stock.

15.8.8 Results Sorted by Callability

Finally, we analyze the occurrence of the call provision. As we noted earlier, before the 1980s the call provision was a standard feature on virtually all corporate bonds. However, the increase in interest rate volatility in the 1980s and other factors forced many changes in the bond market, including an increase in the issuance of shorter-term, noncallable bonds. It is with this background that we examine the "shapshot" activity for 1999 to 2000. Again, details for the call provision are not available for the tapped shelf issues, so we focus on the remaining subtotal of 1,220 issues.

The traditional call provision was included in only 124 issues, or 10 percent of the subtotal, while 722 issues, or 59 percent of the subtotal, were noncallable. A total of 333 issues, or 27 percent of the subtotal, included a new type of call provision called the *make-whole call*. A total of 18 issues, or 1.5 percent of the subtotal, included another new type of call provision, the *equity call provision*, also known as the *clawback provision*. Finally, 23 issues, or 2 percent of the subtotal, included a *special call*, which can be exercised only under conditions specified in the debt contract. We discuss these contract innovations in Chapter 19.

15.9 RULE 144A ISSUES AND PRIVATE PLACEMENTS

In this section, we present statistics on the characteristics of Rule 144A notes and bonds and private-placement notes and bonds that were issued in 1999 and 2000. For perspective, we compare these with the public issues. The statistics for all three markets are displayed in Table 15-3.

The total numbers of public, Rule 144A, and private placement issues were 1,824, 900, and 566, respectively. The total volumes in the three markets were $982 billion, $238 billion, and $34 billion, respectively. The average issue sizes in the three markets

---

[4]Eckbo's sample of straight and convertible bonds issued from 1964 to 1981 includes 723 issues, of which 75, or 10.4 percent, were convertible. According to our analysis in Chapter 10 (review Table 10-1), 9.3 percent of the corporate notes and bonds issued over the period of 1979 to 1999 were convertible (1,189 convertibles out of 12,751 issues).

TABLE 15-3 Public, Rule 144A, and Privately-Placed Corporate Notes and Bonds Issued by U.S. Nonfinancial Firms, 1999–2000

Characteristic	Public ($982 billion)			Rule 144A ($238 billion)			Private ($34 billion)		
	Number	Percent	Average Proceeds ($ million)	Number	Percent	Average Proceeds ($ million)	Number	Percent	Average Proceeds ($ million)
All Issues	1,824	100%	539	900	100%	264	566	100%	60
Issuer's Listing Status									
NYSE/AMEX	1,208	66%	545	283	31%	357	119	21%	95
NASDAQ	165	9%	730	190	21%	287	68	12%	55
OTC/Small Issues	15	1%	253	28	3%	193	19	3%	33
Subsidiary	406	22%	442	253	28%	216	119	21%	64
Private	30	2%	681	146	16%	154	241	43%	46
Credit Rating									
Investment grade	1,445	79%	501	372	41%	304	63	11%	98
Speculative grade	212	12%	694	330	37%	258	9	2%	354
Not rated	167	9%	665	198	22%	202	494	87%	50
Maturity Ranges									
1–5 years	1,223	67%	667	262	29%	297	165	29%	57
6–10 years	408	22%	263	472	52%	263	262	46%	53
11–15 years	48	3%	181	40	4%	146	70	12%	97
16–20 years	35	2%	248	45	5%	301	36	6%	38
>20 years	110	6%	385	81	9%	206	33	6%	85
Coupon Type									
Fixed	996	55%	243	709	79%	260	493	87%	56
Floating/Variable	213	12%	201	156	17%	257	56	10%	100
Zero	11	1%	866	34	4%	400	1	0%	31
Unknown*	604	33%	1,140	1	0%	224	16	3%	54
Security/Priority									
Secured or guaranteed	137	8%	527	197	22%	149	127	22%	89
Senior debenture	192	11%	284	191	21%	319	237	42%	58
Debenture	1,439	79%	580	304	34%	335	133	23%	51
Subordinated debenture	56	3%	368	208	23%	221	69	12%	36
Convertible or Units?									
Convertible	51	3%	546	119	13%	330	21	4%	64
Units	4	0%	572	29	3%	171	6	1%	54
Neither (straight)	1,769	97%	538	752	84%	258	539	95%	60

*The SDC database does not provide coupon information for tapped shelf issues and for some Rule 144A issues and private placements.
Source: Raw data from Securities Data Corporation's new-issues database.

were $539 million, $264 million, and $60 million, respectively. These results indicate that the Rule 144A market is smaller than the public market and the private placement market is even smaller, in terms of both number of issues and average issue size.

15.9.1 Results Sorted by Issuer's Equity Listing Status

Our first sorting was by the listing status of the issuing firm's equity: NYSE/AMEX, NASDAQ, OTC, subsidiary, or private firm. NYSE/AMEX firms accounted for 66 percent of the public issues, 31 percent of the Rule 144A issues, and 21 percent of the private placements. The numerous firms listed on the NASDAQ and OTC markets collectively accounted for 10 percent of public issues, 24 percent of Rule 144A issues, and 15 percent of private placements. Finally, subsidiaries and private firms accounted for 24 percent of the public issues, 4 percent of the Rule 144A issues, and 64 percent of the private placements. These results reinforce the impression gained from Table 15-2 that large, publicly traded firms dominate the public debt market. In contrast, subsidiaries and private firms dominate the Rule 144A and private placement markets. In none of these markets are the numerous firms that are listed on the NASDAQ and OTC markets collectively the dominant players.

These results suggest two additional issuer preferences. *First*, the numerous smaller firms, to the extent that they borrow at all, tend to borrow from private sources such as banks and finance companies rather than in any of these three debt markets. *Second*, subsidiaries and private firms (many of which are large, based on Table 15-2) generally prefer to place notes and bonds more closely with financial institutions, as indicated by their general preference for Rule 144A offerings and private placements.

15.9.2 Results Sorted by Credit Rating

As noted earlier, 79 percent of the public issues bore an investment-grade credit rating. In contrast, only 41 percent and 11 percent of the Rule 144A and private placement issues, respectively, had an investment-grade rating. For the Rule 144A issues, one-third (37 percent) had a speculative-grade rating and one-fifth (22 percent) were unrated. Among the 566 private placements, 494 issues, or 87 percent, were unrated. The unrated issues were relatively small, with an average issue size of only $50 million. These results suggest that the private placement market caters to issuers who prefer to avoid the scrutiny that accompanies the public debt market, in terms of both registration procedures and the credit-rating process. As a result, however, issue size is limited.

15.9.3 Results Sorted by Maturity

All three debt markets share similar distributions by maturity, with strong emphases on shorter-term issues. In all three markets, over two-thirds of the issues had maturities of 10 years or less. However, Rule 144A issues and private placements tend to cluster in the 5 to 10 year maturity range, whereas most public issues have 1 to 5 years to maturity.

15.9.4 Results Sorted by Coupon Type

Regarding coupon type, the vast majority of both Rule 144A issues and private placements bore a fixed-coupon rate (79 percent and 87 percent, respectively), while floating/variable coupon issues accounted for most of the remaining issues in both markets. Zero-coupon issues were rare in these two markets, though they accounted for 4 percent of Rule 144A issues. All of these results compare closely to those for public issues.

15.9.5   Results Sorted by Security and Priority

The proportions of public, Rule 144A, and private debt issues that were secured or guaranteed are 8, 22, and 21 percent, respectively. Thus, security or guarantee status is more common in the latter two markets, though in all markets it is the exception rather than the rule. At the other end of the security/priority spectrum, subordination is more frequent among Rule 144A issues and private placements than public issues, perhaps because these firms also have senior bank debt outstanding.

15.9.6   Results Sorted by Convertibility and Unit Status

The percentages of issues that were convertible were 3, 13, and 4 percent in the public, Rule 144A, and private placement markets, respectively. The corresponding percentages of issues that were units were 0, 3, and 1 percent, respectively. Thus, the percentages of issues that contained an equity component (i.e., either a conversion provision or a warrant) were 3, 16, and 5 percent in the respective markets.

15.10   BANK LOANS AND RELATIONSHIP LENDING

In this section, we focus on the distinctive nature of bank loans.

15.10.1   Relationship Lending and the Distinctiveness of Bank Loans

Perhaps the most salient feature of the private debt markets that distinguishes them from the public debt markets is that in the private debt market, the lender and borrower have a closer relationship with one another. As a result, bank loan contracts are often quite malleable. For this reason, a bank loan is often called an *implicit contract*, deliberately left somewhat open-ended to allow flexibility in the relationship between lender and borrower.

Several features distinguish bank lending: (a) Banks often play the role of business consultant as well as lender,[5] (b) banks generally closely monitor their borrowing customers, and (c) a bank will generally attempt to resolve the financial problems of a troubled borrowing customer (rather than forcing bankruptcy) via an often-arduous process known as a *loan workout*. In addition, as James (1987) argues, a bank will have additional information about a borrowing customer, especially a small or mid-sized firm, because a bank often provides other services to the borrower (e.g., transactions clearing) that are complementary. Thus, bank lending is often called *relationship lending*, and bank loans are called *inside debt*. In sharp contrast, the public debt markets are relatively impersonal, involving contracts that are more formal and rigid, in large part

---

[5]This is especially the case for small firms that operate in the same local or regional market in which the bank operates. In such cases, the bank probably has superior information about the local economy and its likely impact on the firm's prospects, as well as an objective perspective on local competition in the firm's product or service market.

because lenders in the public markets are not in a position to monitor the borrower effectively. Hence, a public debt issue is often called *arm's length debt* or *outside debt*.

Berger and Udell (1995) studied relationship lending in the context of small-firm lines of credit. They appeal to theory to posit that relationship lending is important for small firms because the information asymmetry problem is more severe for them than for large firms. The ongoing relationship that a bank has with a small-firm borrower generates valuable information about the borrower's creditworthiness, which the bank can use to adjust contract terms over time. The authors focus on lines of credit because this type of contract appears to be an ideal example of both relationship lending and a mechanism to resolve severe information asymmetry problems. Their evidence is consistent with the hypothesis: Firms that have had a longer relationship with their bank enjoy easier credit terms (i.e., a lower interest rate and fewer collateral requirements) than firms with a shorter relationship.

15.10.2   The Design of Bank Loan Contracts

Bank loans are designed to reflect the lender–borrower relationship involved. Here we briefly discuss three papers that examine the design of bank loan contracts from this perspective. The first is by Berkovitch and Greenbaum (1991). They examined the *loan commitment* as a form of staged financing. As they see it, the loan commitment resolves a particular type of underinvestment problem:

> The borrower is assumed to have access to a two-stage investment project wherein the investment required in the second stage is not known at the outset. The unknown investment requirement is revealed to the borrower, but not to the bank, at the beginning of the second stage. If the investor borrows at the beginning of the first stage, the realization at the beginning of the second stage might prompt a default in a situation where the project yields positive net present value. The reason is that the borrower does not regard the first-stage investment as a sunk cost. We show that a two-stage contract resembling a loan commitment can solve this under-investment problem. (p. 83)

Dennis, Nandy, and Sharpe (2000) emphasized the importance of setting contract terms in bank revolving credit agreements to resolve contracting problems, including borrowers' incentives to undertake relatively more risky projects or to underinvest. Their empirical analysis of a sample of revolving credit agreements indicates that four contract terms in such agreements are adjusted, as necessary, to resolve such problems: (a) the duration of the contract, (b) the security status (i.e., the extent to which collateral is required), (c) the commitment fee, and (d) the interest rate.

Gorton and Kahn (2000) developed a theoretical model of bank loan contracts that emphasizes the tight link between *renegotiation* and *monitoring*. For instance, a collateral requirement can be understood as a control device that the bank uses to effect a truncation of both the relationship and the bank's losses in the event of default; tight covenant constraints may be included to allow the bank to terminate the loan at any time, at its option, even if the borrower has not defaulted. Further, their model provides some interesting implications for a bank's optimal renegotiating policy, including the following: "[R]enegotiation results in renegotiated interest rates that are not monotone in borrower quality: The healthiest borrowers are left alone, the moderately distressed are granted concessions, while the most distressed are forced to submit to harsher terms" (p. 332).

15.10.3 Should a Firm Have a Financial Relationship with More Than One Bank?

The concept of relationship lending suggests that a firm would develop a close relationship with a *single* bank, for two reasons. *First*, to the extent that information generation and monitoring are costly, it would be inefficient for two or more banks to replicate these activities on behalf of a single borrower. *Second*, the very nature of the relationship between borrower and lender is likely to be upset if several banks must compete for the firm's credit business. One adverse result may be that banks do too little monitoring overall. On the other hand, a borrowing firm has incentives to develop lending relationships with several banks to (a) avoid the constraints of a single bank, in terms of both its control policies and its limitations on available credit, and (b) foster competition that may lead to lower borrowing costs.

Two recent papers have addressed these issues. Detragiache, Garella, and Guiso (2000) initially provide evidence that, for small firms in the United States in 1988, the median number of banking relationships that they had was two, and 55.5 percent of the firms in their sample had a relationship with more than one bank. They then develop a theoretical model to explain (a) why many firms have more than one banking relationship, and (b) determinants of cross-sectional variation in the number of banking relationships. Their model shows that multiple banking relationships ensure a stable supply of credit. They document evidence that supports the predictions of their model.

Relationship lending appears to have a well-founded basis, especially for small and mid-sized firms. However, competition has been putting its viability to the test in recent years. Boot and Thakor (2000) addressed this issue from a theoretical perspective, raising the question of whether relationship lending can survive competition, both from competing banks and from the capital market: "Our key result is that as interbank competition increases, banks make *more* relationship loans, but each has lower added value for borrowers. Capital market competition *reduces* relationship lending (and bank lending shrinks), but each relationship loan has greater added value for borrowers" (p. 679).

15.10.4 Should a Firm Eventually Wean Itself of Bank Debt?

Diamond (1991b) argued that firms with severe information asymmetry problems build reputation by initially taking on costly bank debt. However, once a firm acquires a good reputation, it should move on to arm's length debt to save on monitoring costs. Rajan (1992) argued that there is a fundamental trade-off between bank debt and arm's length debt. Bank debt better mitigates asymmetric information costs for a borrowing firm. However, a bank's control position (a) allows it to extract control benefits, and (b) distorts the firm's investment incentives. He then argued: "borrowing from multiple sources and appropriately setting priority are ways of circumscribing the bank's ability to extract surplus without diminishing its control" (p. 1392).

15.11 THE LEASING ALTERNATIVE

For many U.S. firms, leasing is an important financing vehicle. Sharpe and Nguyen (1995) make this point: "equipment under lease accounts for nearly a third of the total annual new equipment investment in the U.S. in recent years . . . " (p. 293). Grenadier (1995) noted the tremendous growth in leasing in recent U.S. history: "Until the 1950s . . . modern-day leasing was predominantly confined to the rental of real estate. Since then, leasing has burgeoned to include practically any asset imaginable, from copiers to satellites, trucks to airplanes, and power plants to zoo animals" (p. 297).

15.11.1 Lease Terminology

In the typical lease, a firm, the *lessee*, signs a long-term lease with a *lessor*, for an asset such as a piece of equipment. In exchange for the use of the asset for a fixed period of time, the lessee promises to make periodic lease payments. In some cases the lessor is the manufacturer of the leased equipment; in other cases a bank or finance company is the lessor. A dual contract in which a firm sells property to a buyer and immediately leases the property from the buyer is called a *sale and leaseback*.

Leases are classified as either *capital* or *operating*. According to Financial Accounting Standards Board (FASB) Statement 13, a lease is a capital lease if it meets any one of the following criteria:

(a) The lease transfers ownership of the asset to the lessee by the end of the lease term.

(b) The lease contains an option to purchase the leased property at a bargain price.

(c) The lease term is equal to or greater than 75 percent of the asset's estimated economic life.

(d) The present value of the lease payments equals or exceeds 90 percent of the fair value of the leased asset less any investment tax credit retained by the lessor.

If a lease does not meet any of these criteria, it is an operating lease. For accounting purposes, a capitalized lease is treated much like any other owned asset. It must be booked as an asset with a corresponding liability, depreciation is taken over time, and the interest portion of each payment is expensed. Payments on operating leases are expensed as incurred.

15.11.2 Research on Motives for Leasing

Leasing appears to be a close substitute for a dual transaction involving borrowing and purchasing the asset. If this is true, then if a firm has limited debt capacity (see Chapter 6), a lease *displaces* debt in the firm's capital structure. One important difference, however, is that a lease generally includes a potentially valuable option, held by the lessee, to purchase the asset at a specified price, called the *residual*, at the expiration of the contract. Ang and Peterson (1984) empirically tested this *Lease-Debt Substitution Hypothesis*. Surprisingly, they found that leases and debt are not substitutes—firms with leases also tend to have more, not less, debt in their capital structures.

Researchers have argued that tax differentials between the lessor and lessee provide a motivation for leasing by creating a *tax arbitrage*. Graham, Lemmon, and Schallheim (1998) explain that "firms with low marginal tax rates employ relatively more leases than do firms with higher marginal tax rates. The logic behind the leasing prediction is that leases allow for the transfer of tax shields from firms that cannot fully utilize the associated tax deduction (lessees) to firms than can (lessors)" (p. 131).

Ang and Peterson pursued the tax arbitrage argument in an attempt to explain the absence of a substitution effect between leases and debt. They argued that differences in the tax rates of leasing and nonleasing firms might cause the former not only to engage in leasing but also to have more debt. However, they found no difference in the tax rates of leasing and nonleasing firms.

Graham, Lemmon, and Schallheim (1998) argued that many of the previous studies on the relationships among tax rates, leasing, and debt use are contaminated by the fact that both lease payments and interest expense are deductible, and therefore tend reduce a firm's marginal tax rate when this rate is calculated with these deductions in place. They develop an empirical measure of a firm's ex ante, before-financing marginal tax rate, and use this measure in tests on the corporate use of operating leases and debt. They document "a negative relation between operating leases and tax rates, and a positive relation between debt levels and tax rates" (p. 131). Their evidence is consistent with firms' value-maximizing (i.e., tax-minimizing) behavior.

Finally, Sharpe and Nguyen (1995) presented and tested an alternative hypothesis that financial contracting costs may influence a firm's incentive to lease: "We argue that firms facing high costs of external funds can economize on the cost of funding by leasing . . . We find that the share of total annual fixed capital costs attributable to either capital or operating leases is substantially higher at lower-rated, non-dividend-paying, cash-poor firms—those likely to face relatively high premiums for external funds" (p. 271). Some of their empirical results are reproduced in Table 15-4. Consistent with their hypothesis, small firms tend to make much greater use of leases than large firms.[6]

TABLE 15-4   Differences in the Utilization of Leases by Small and Large Firms

Major U.S. Industries, 1986

Industry (number of firms)	Capital Lease Share of PP&E [% of Firms with Capital Lease]		Operating Lease Share of Total Capital Costs		Total Lease Share of Total Capital Costs	
	Small Firms	*Large Firms*	*Small Firms*	*Large Firms*	*Small Firms*	*Large Firms*
Manufacturing (1,167)	10% [58%]	5% [61%]	27%	16%	34%	20%
Transportation (63)	5% [58%]	9% [87%]	32%	16%	36%	23%
Communications (74)	8% [53%]	1% [81%]	17%	4%	23%	5%
Wholesale (135)	13% [45%]	12% [68%]	34%	27%	43%	35%
Retail (254)	25% [81%]	24% [93%]	41%	32%	55%	47%
Services (331)	12% [64%]	7% [65%]	36%	32%	44%	37%

Note: Small firms are those below the industry median in terms of number of employees; large firms are those above the median.
Source: Sharpe and Nguyen (1995).

---

[6]Krishnan and Moyer (1994) also documented evidence that riskier firms are more likely to lease.

15.12 OPTIMAL PLACEMENT, SENIORITY, AND MATURITY STRUCTURES OF A FIRM'S DEBT CONTRACTS

In this section, we discuss the seemingly unrelated issues of debt source and seniority. In practice, we observe that for firms that have multiple debt issues outstanding, one or more issues are senior while other issues are subordinated. Furthermore, bank debt is almost exclusively senior,[7] while public issues may be either senior or junior (i.e., subordinated), but are junior if the firm also has bank debt. Several studies have addressed the dual issue of placement and seniority. Below we discuss several studies of this genre.[8]

15.12.1 The Placement Structure of Corporate Debt

Krishnaswami, Spindt, and Subramaniam (1999) studied the corporate debt placement decision. They examined 297 publicly traded firms over the years 1987 to 1993 that would have had access to either the public or private debt markets (i.e., they excluded very small firms that would not likely have access to the public debt market). They measured a firm's debt placement structure as the fraction of a firm's total long-term debt that is privately placed (i.e., either bank debt or debt issued in the private placement market). Their objective was to study the impact of the following factors on a firm's debt placement structure: (a) flotation costs, (b) principal–agent conflicts, (c) regulation, and (d) information asymmetry.

We have already discussed factors (a), (b), and (d). The authors explain factor (c) as follows: "Smith (1986) argues that regulated firms raise funds more frequently in the capital markets to generate evidence on the firm's cost of capital, which is useful to the firm in the rate setting process. This frequent use of the capital markets disciplines management and limits their discretion in investment and operating decisions. Smith and Watts (1992) also argue that, compared to unregulated firms, regulated firms are less likely to engage in asset substitution and underinvestment because state utility commissions and other regulatory authorities supervise management's decisions. Thus, regulated firms will only find a limited need for the monitoring role of private debt, and would therefore have higher proportions of publicly issued debt" (p. 412).

For the typical firm in their sample, over 60 percent of its long-term debt was privately placed. Variation in this percentage was consistent with the predicted effects of the four factors listed above:

> Flotation costs in public debt issues explain a significant part of the cross-sectional variation in placement structure. Larger firms and firms with larger average issue sizes exploit the scale economies in issuance costs of public debt, and so have lower proportions of private debt. Conditioned on firm size, firms with higher contracting costs due to the moral hazard problems of underinvestment and risk-shifting have higher proportions of private debt. Consistent with Myers (1977), firms with more growth options in their investment oppor-

[7]Carey (1995) examined 18,000 bank loans made over 1986 to 1993; over 99 percent contained a senior priority clause.

[8]See also the following studies on this topic, listed in chronological order; Leeth and Scott (1989), MacKie-Mason (1990a, b), Diamond (1991b), Booth (1993), Chemmanur and Fulghieri (1994), Barclay and Smith (1995b, 1996), Chen, Jen, and Choi (1999), Boot and Thakor (2000), Datta, Iskandar-Datta, and Patel (2000).

tunity set benefit more from the monitoring associated with privately placed debt. This suggests that the greater monitoring and the more restrictive covenants in privately placed debt help mitigate costs that arise due to conflict between bondholders and shareholders. These results are reaffirmed by the evidence that regulated firms have lower proportions of privately placed debt.

Evidence provides only limited support for the view that private debt mitigates the contracting costs associated with adverse selection. Although firms operating under a greater degree of information asymmetry rely more on private debt, we do not find any evidence that firms with favorable private information about their value, i.e., firms that bear the cost of adverse selection, choose more private debt. However, those firms with favorable information about their value that are also subject to a high degree of information asymmetry rely more on private debt. (p. 432)

15.12.2   The Priority Structure of Corporate Liabilities

Barclay and Smith (1995b) examined the liability structures of almost 5,000 firms over the years 1981 to 1991. Their intent was to identify important determinants of the priority structure of a firm's liabilities—that is, to explain cross-sectional variation in the use of claims of different priorities. They test three relevant hypotheses: (a) a contracting cost hypothesis, (b) an information asymmetry hypothesis, and (c) a tax hypothesis. The contracting hypothesis was most strongly supported, so we discuss these results.

The contracting cost hypothesis encompasses both the Myers (1977) underinvestment problem and the asset-substitution (or risk-shifting) problem. The underinvestment problem is, of course, more severe for firms with greater growth opportunities. As we know, shortening debt maturity can mitigate this problem. However, the problem can also be mitigated "if the firm preserves the right to finance new investments with high priority claims, such as secured debt or leases (Stulz and Johnson 1985)" (p. 907). Among the authors' results, firms with more growth opportunities use capitalized leases (which generally have the highest priority among a firm's long-term liabilities) more intensively.

15.12.3   The Seniority of Bank Debt

Welch (1997) developed a theoretical model to address the issue of the seniority of bank debt. He argued, "The expected deadweight lobbying and litigation expenses associated with a fight for preferential treatment (priority or side awards) in financial distress, can be lower if one awards the potentially stronger creditor ex post (the bank) the position with more power ex ante. That is, to maximize the 'deterrence' to avoid a fight between creditors involved in *rent-seeking* activities, it can be efficient to promise the stronger contender priority. Naturally because creditors demand a yield to reflect possible future contest expenses, choosing the optimal priority structure allow firms to raise capital at a lower cost" (pp. 1204).

15.12.4   Optimal Placement, Maturity, and Seniority Structures

Park (2000) presents a model that focuses on monitoring to mitigate the moral hazard problem, and simultaneously depicts the optimal placement, maturity, and seniority structures of a firm's debt contracts. His model is consistent with several features of corporate debt structures commonly observed for firms that have multiple debt issues: (a) Bank debt is senior, (b) senior debt has more restrictive covenants, (c) senior debt has a relatively short maturity, and (d) public debt is junior and subordinated.

To motivate his paper, Park cites evidence that appears to be at odds with theory: "If as has been argued (Fama 1990) junior lenders have stronger incentives than senior lenders to monitor default risks, then we would expect monitoring specialists like banks to be junior, not senior. Moreover, if covenants are used to reduce contracting costs (Smith and Warner 1979), we would expect junior debt contracts to have more restrictive covenants since junior debt is inherently riskier than senior debt because of its lower priority and longer maturity. These observations beg two questions: (a) why is short-term debt further protected by seniority? and (b) why do firms prioritize their debt in the first place?" (pp. 2157–2158).

Park provides a three-part answer to these questions. *First*, the designated monitoring lender has seniority because otherwise this lender must share more of the benefits of its monitoring effort with other lenders. *Second*, holders of senior/monitoring debt should be those lenders who have the lowest monitoring costs (i.e., financial intermediaries). *Third*, senior debt has the most restrictive covenants and shortest maturity to maximize the senior lender's incentive to monitor.

15.13   THE INFORMATION IN DEBT-RELATED EVENTS

In this section, we briefly summarize several event studies of debt-related announcements.

15.13.1   The Market's Reaction to Straight and Convertible Debt Offerings

Dann and Mikkelson (1984) studied announcements of straight and convertible bond offerings. They found that the market's reaction to straight debt offerings was negative but insignificant, while announcements of convertible debt offerings result in significant negative abnormal returns of –2.31 percent, on average. Eckbo (1986) found similar results. He points out that the negative reaction to convertible bonds is analogous to the negative reaction to stock issues (Chapter 13), and is consistent with the asymmetric information theories of Miller and Rock (1985) and Myers and Majluf (1984).

15.13.2   The Market's Reaction to Private Placements of Convertible Debt

Field and Mais (1991) studied the market's reaction to announcements of *private placements* of convertible debt. They found that the market tends to react favorably to such announcements, yielding an average announcement-period abnormal return of +1.80 percent. Thus, the information conveyed by convertible debt issuance announcements appears to be more favorable if the debt is privately placed rather than publicly issued. Among other explanations, they offer this: "A private placement of convertible debt can increase firm value by placing a large block of potential voting rights with outside blockholders who (upon conversion) use their influence to monitor management . . . Further, private placements are negotiated directly with management, creating a relationship which may allow additional monitoring of managerial actions not present when blockholders acquire their securities in the open market" (p. 1926).

15.13.3   The Market's Reaction to Bank Loan Events

James (1987) studied the valuation effect of a firm's announcement of a new bank credit agreement, finding a significant positive average abnormal return of +1.93 percent. In contrast, when a firm issues private or public bonds to *retire* bank debt, the market reacts negatively. This evidence buttresses the argument that banking relationships are unique and valuable.

Lummer and McConnell (1989) examined both new bank loans and renewals. They found that announcements of new bank loans elicit no significant market reaction. However, *loan renewals* are associated with significant abnormal returns—positive if the renewal is on more favorable terms, negative if the renewal is on less favorable terms.

Slovin, Johnson, and Glascock (1992) also examined announcements of bank credit agreements, focusing on the question of whether the market's reaction is related to firm size. They found, "For small firms both renewals and initiations of loan agreements generate significantly positive share price effects. In contrast, for large firms there is little evidence that bank credit announcements convey information to the capital market. Our results are consistent with arguments . . . that it is primarily small, less prestigious firms that receive benefits from screening and monitoring services associated with bank loans" (p. 1057).

15.13.4   The Market's Reaction to Commercial Paper Rating Announcements

Nayar and Rozeff (1994) studied the market's reaction to commercial paper issuances and rating changes: "Highly-rated industrial issues of commercial paper, unaccompanied by bank letters of credit, are associated with significantly positive abnormal returns; lower-rated issues are not. The stock price effects of changes in commercial paper ratings also demonstrate the relevance of ratings to the financing of firms. Rating downgrades, especially those that imply an exit from the commercial paper market, produce significantly negative abnormal returns; upgrades have no effects. Initial commercial paper ratings and subsequent ratings appear to help investors sort firms by their future prospects" (p. 1431).

15.14   Summary of Learning Objectives

This chapter provides a detailed discussion of the rich mosaic of debt funding sources and contract terms available to U.S. firms. We described each of these various sources and contract terms, and explained their purpose in the context of modern corporate finance theory.

A firm can obtain either short-term or long-term debt funds from either private or public sources. In terms of aggregate volume, the most important sources of short-term borrowing are trade credit and commercial paper. The most important instrument for long-term corporate borrowing is the corporate bond, though bank loans and commercial mortgages are also important. We explained the six major factors that influence the decision of the type of debt that a firm should issue: (a) the length of time that funds will be needed, (b) interest costs and issuance costs, (c) agency costs of debt, (d) information asymmetry, (e) the firm's need for flexibility, and (f) taxes.

We discussed the important choice of debt maturity, which depends on the source of debt financing, the nature of the firm's funding needs, and on the financial condition of the firm. We discussed the strategic selections of *restrictive covenants*, such as *security* via a mortgage indenture or restrictions on dividends, and *alternative retirement provisions*, such as the call and conversion provisions.

We also analyzed (a) the rationale for trade credit, (b) the characteristics of notes and bonds issued in the public, Rule 144A, and private placement markets, (c) bank loans, and (d) leasing as an alternative financing vehicle. Following these analyses, we discussed the optimal placement, seniority, and maturity structures of a firm's debt contracts. An important conclusion we drew from these analyses is that the private debt market (led by banks) differs fundamentally from the public debt market. Banks feature *relationship lending*, and bank loans are referred to as *implicit contracts* or *inside debt*. In contrast, public debt is relatively rigid, and is called *arm's length debt* or *outside debt*. The means by which principal–agent conflicts and information asymmetry problems are resolved in the two markets are quite different. Finally, leasing seems to be motivated by tax arbitrage.

Review Questions and Problems

1. Briefly discuss each of the following sources of short-term corporate financing: (a) trade credit, (b) factoring, (c) bank loans and lines of credit, (d) commercial paper.
2. Briefly discuss each of the following alternatives for long-term corporate debt financing: (a) a term loan from a commercial bank, (b) a commercial mortgage, (c) a long-term loan from a finance company, (d) a private placement, (e) an industrial development bond, (f) a public offering.
3. Discuss the trade-offs in choosing an underwriter via competitive bidding versus negotiation.
4. Discuss the advantages to a borrower of shelf registration of a corporate bond offering.
5. Define SEC Rule 144A, and discuss its importance to the U.S. corporate bond market.
6. Based on the categorical aggregate corporate liability data shown in Table 15-1:
   a. Which two categories of aggregate liabilities had the greatest aggregate volume at year-end 2000?
   b. Which categories of aggregate liabilities *grew* in relative size from 1980 to 2000?
   c. Which categories of aggregate liabilities *decreased* in relative size from 1980 to 2000?
7. Discuss each of the following basic factors that influence a firm's choice of liability type: (a) the length of time that funds will be needed, (b) issuance and interest costs, (c) agency costs of debt, (d) information asymmetry, (e) the firm's need for flexibility, and (f) tax effects.

8. Suppose a firm wants to borrow $200 million for 10 years to fund capital expenditures, and is considering the choice of a private placement with several insurance companies or a public issue through an investment banking firm as underwriter. For simplicity, we will assume that in either case the firm will issue pure-discount bonds. The insurance companies demand interest at a rate of 10 percent, with a 3 percent flotation cost, while the underwriter states that the interest cost will be 9.25 percent with 5 percent flotation costs. What is the effective cost of the loan in each case?

9. Explain the *maturity-matching principal* for deciding whether to issue short-term or long-term debt.

10. Discuss traditional arguments about advantages and disadvantages of short-term (versus long-term) debt.

11. Discuss formal theory about the relationship between debt maturity and deadweight costs associated with (a) principal–agent conflicts and (b) information asymmetry.

12. Discuss the reasons given in the text for why corporate debt maturities have shortened in recent years.

13. List and briefly explain the major covenants that are commonly included in bond contracts.

14. Explain the role of the call provision in mitigating deadweight costs associated with (a) principal–agent conflicts and (b) information asymmetry.

15. Explain the role of the sinking fund provision in mitigating deadweight costs associated with (a) principal–agent conflicts and (b) information asymmetry.

16. Explain the role of the conversion provision in mitigating deadweight costs associated with (a) principal–agent conflicts and (b) information asymmetry.

17. List and discuss the four theories of trade credit mentioned in the text.

18. Discuss the economic milieu that surrounded the simultaneous (partial) demise of the traditional 30-year, fixed-coupon, callable corporate bond and the emergence of shorter-term, noncallable notes.

19. Differentiate the public, Rule 144A, and private placements debt markets.

20. Discuss relationship lending and the design of bank loan contracts.

21. Why is bank debt invariably senior?

22. To qualify as a capital lease, a lease contract must meet one of four criteria established by FASB. Otherwise, it is an operating lease. List these criteria.

23. Discuss motives for leasing.

24. Which types of firms are most likely to lease and why?

25. Discuss empirical evidence of the market's reaction to various debt-related announcements.

Creative Thinking Issues

1. Can you think of another reason (besides those mentioned in the text) why corporate debt maturities have shortened in recent years?

2. Which of the covenants or provisions mentioned in the chapter would be *best* to mitigate (a) the underinvestment (or debt overhang) problem? (b) the asset-substitution (or risk shifting) problem? (c) deadweight costs associated with information asymmetry?

3. Why is the shelf registration method more popular for debt issues than for SEOs?

Projects and Analyses

1. Choose a firm that has public bonds outstanding, and examine covenants and provisions in the bond contract. (If the bonds have been issued recently, you may be able to obtain a copy of the offering circular from one of the underwriting firms. Alternatively, summary information on outstanding corporate bonds can be obtained from the appropriate Moody's *Manual*, or from issues of Moody's *Bond Survey*.) Try to determine why each of the covenants and provisions is included in the contract.

2. Ask a loan officer at a local bank for a copy of a standard corporate loan contract or a letter of credit agreement. Analyze it, focusing on the issues addressed in this chapter. Can you improve the contract, and if so, how and for whom (the bank, the borrower, or both)?

3. Examine recent issues of Moody's *Bond Survey* and classify the maturities, ratings, covenants, and provisions associated with all of the corporate bonds that have been issued in recent months.

PART

The Markets for Corporate Control

IV

art Four is devoted to discussions and analyses of the *markets for corporate control*. We interpret this phrase broadly to include (a) transactions in which the ownership of an entire firm changes hands in a single transaction, (b) transactions in which portions of a firm's assets or operations are sold, (c) changes in the terms of a firm's debt contracts in response to financial distress, and (d) bankruptcy and liquidation.

Chapter 16 deals with the transactions of type (a) above. These include mergers, acquisitions, takeovers, and buyouts.

In Chapter 17, we focus on causes and effects of financial distress. We also discuss decisions that firms make in the face of financial distress, many of which involve corporate control transactions of type (a) or (b). For instance, we discuss asset sales, targeted stock, equity carve-outs, and spin-offs. In Chapter 18, we discuss more drastic actions associated with *severe* financial distress, including debt restructuring, being acquired, bankruptcy, reorganization, and liquidation.

CHAPTER

Mergers, Acquisitions, Takeovers, and Buyouts

16

16.1   INTRODUCTION

Mergers, acquisitions, takeovers, and buyouts are the most visible manifestations of the workings of the *markets for corporate control*. They are often dramatic events because in each the ownership of an entire firm changes hands in a single transaction. In this chapter, we define these transactions and discuss theory and evidence pertaining to them. In Section 16.2, we define the focal transactions. In Section 16.3, we discuss motives for each transaction. In Section 16.4, we discuss the legal history of mergers and acquisitions (M&A), provide evidence on the frequency of M&A activity in the United States over time, and discuss event studies and other issues related to M&A. In Sections 16.5 and 16.6, we review research on takeovers and buyouts, respectively. Finally, Section 16.7 summarizes the chapter's learning objectives.

16.2   DEFINING THE TRANSACTIONS

In this section, we define and distinguish the focal transactions—mergers, acquisitions, takeovers, and buyouts. For an initial perspective on the relative importance of these transactions, we offer Table 16-1. This table shows our calculations of the numbers and aggregate market equity values of U.S. nonfinancial firms that were *targets* of the focal transactions over the years 1980 to 2000. Mergers, acquisitions, and takeovers were by far the most important transactions, totaling 4,686 in number and $3,258 billion in aggregate market equity value. Buyouts numbered 485, with an aggregate market equity value of $60 billion. Finally, 337 reverse buyouts, which are IPOs that reverse a previous buyout (and which we discuss later), occurred during this period, with a total market equity value of $65 billion.

16.2.1   Mergers and Acquisitions

In a *merger*, two separate corporations combine to form a single corporate entity. In most cases, the shares of one firm are extinguished and the shares of the other firm remain outstanding. However, in a *consolidation*, both firms cease to exist, and a new corporation is established with a new name, a new board, and a new management team. In the typical merger deal, the shareholders of the defunct firm receive shares of the surviving firm or cash, and the surviving firm acquires the assets (and liabilities) of the defunct firm. For this reason, the term *acquisition* is also used to describe the deal; the surviving firm is the *acquiring firm* or *bidder*, and the defunct firm is the *acquired firm* or *target*. A merger (or acquisition) is formally initiated when the bidding firm's

TABLE 16-1 **Numbers and Aggregate Values of Mergers, Acquisitions, and Takeovers, Buyouts, and Reverse Buyouts**

Publicly Traded U.S. Nonfinancial Firms, 1980–2000

Transaction Type(s)	Total Number	Market Equity Value of Focal/Target Firm ($ billion)
Mergers, acquisitions, and takeovers	4,686	$3,258
Buyouts	485	$60
Reverse buyouts	337	$65

Sources: S&P *Research Insight*, CRSP, and SDC databases.

board of directors approves an offering of stock, cash, or a combination of stock and cash, in exchange for the shares of the target. The deal is consummated if and when the target's board and shareholders vote to accept the offer.

Case in Point

In October 2000, Philadelphia-based Peco Energy Company and Chicago-based Unicom (parent of Commonwealth Edison), two utility companies, completed a *merger of equals*, forming a new firm, Exelon Corporation, which began trading on the New York Stock Exchange (NYSE) on October 23, 2000 (ticker: EXC). Terms of the $8 billion merger gave each Peco stockholder a choice between one share of the new company's stock for each Peco share, or $45 in cash per share. Unicom shareholders chose between 0.95 share in the new company or $42.75 in cash. The merger created the country's fourth-largest power generator, with more than 5 million customers and 14 nuclear reactors. The company stated that the combination will save money by consolidating corporate, administrative, operations, and purchasing functions. Exelon formed its new management team from among executives in Peco Energy and Unicom.

16.2.2 Takeovers

A *takeover* is the purchase of an entire firm by another firm. In some cases, the takeover is consummated on *friendly* terms; that is, the buyer and target firms' management teams negotiate terms amicably. Under these circumstances, the transaction can simply be called an acquisition. The type of takeover that is truly distinct from an acquisition is a *hostile takeover*. In this case, the bidder's intention is to acquire the target and replace the target's incumbent management, who vigorously resist the attempt.

Case in Point

In 1995, IBM Corporation launched a hostile takeover bid for software firm Lotus Development Corporation. However, unlike many of the truly hostile bids of the 1980s (discussed later), IBM's bid turned friendly, and negotiations concluded within a week with IBM's acquisition of Lotus for $10.3 billion. IBM's acquisition of Lotus is an example of a new generation of takeovers—less hostile and more strategic.

16.2.3 Buyouts

A *buyout* occurs when a group of individuals uses cash to purchase the shares of a firm and takes ownership and control of the firm. Generally, the buyers arrange debt or equity financing to facilitate the purchase. The issued debt is an obligation of the purchased firm, and the purchased firm generally has high leverage after the buyout. For this reason, the transaction is often called a *leveraged buyout*, or *LBO*. A *buyout specialist* (an *LBO association*) often assists the buyers in these transactions, both financially and strategically.[1]

If the group of individuals includes members of the target firm's management, the transaction is sometimes called a *management buyout*, or *MBO*. In any event, assuming that the purchased firm had been a publicly traded firm, the buyers take the firm private. For this reason, the transaction is sometimes called a *going private transaction*. Finally, many firms that go private via a buyout reemerge as a publicly traded firm via a subsequent IPO of shares. This transaction is called a *reverse buyout*.

Case in Point

Eckerd Corporation, the drugstore chain, had been trading on the NYSE since 1968 (and on the AMEX before that) when, in 1985, it received a hostile takeover bid. Eckerd's management quickly arranged a MBO and took the company private in 1986. In 1993, the firm conducted a reverse buyout, going public again on the NYSE in 1993. In 1997, Eckerd was acquired by J.C. Penny Company.

16.3 MOTIVES FOR THE TRANSACTIONS

In this section, we discuss typical motives for each of the chapter's focal transactions.

16.3.1 Motives for a Merger or Acquisition

Stated motives for a merger or acquisition include (a) operating synergy, (b) financial synergy and diversification, (c) bankruptcy avoidance, (d) financial slack, (e) hubris, and (f) self-interest of the bidder's management. To facilitate this discussion, we initially define three broad classes of mergers.

Classes of Mergers: Horizontal, Vertical, or Conglomerate

To a certain extent, the motives and benefits of merger depend on the type of merger that is consummated. Mergers are classified into one of three classes, depending on the businesses in which the merging firms are involved. In a *horizontal merger*, two firms that heretofore have been competitors in the same line of business combine. The typical motive for a horizontal merger is to create economies of scale or scope, or to enhance market power. A very visible example of a horizontal merger was the 1998 combination of Chrysler Corporation and Daimler-Benz, to create DaimlerChrysler

---

[1]*Buyout funds* have also emerged and grown substantially in recent years. Most of these funds are offered through major buyout specialist firms, which include KKR; Warburg Pincus Partners; Hicks, Muse, Tate & Furst; Welsh, Carson, Anderson & Stowe; Thomas H. Lee; Blackstone Group; Carlyle Partners; DLJ Merchant Banking; Goldman Sachs Merchant Banking; Apollo Group; CVC European Equity; TPG Partners; Madison Dearborn; Schroder Ventures; and Clayton, Dubilier & Rice.

Corporation. In another horizontal merger, USA Waste Services Inc. acquired Waste Management Inc. for $14.8 billion in 1998.

A *vertical merger* occurs between two firms that had been doing business in different stages of the production process in a given industry. The general economic justification for a vertical merger is that it serves to stabilize (a) the supply of raw materials for a firm that is farther down in the production process, or (b) customer demand for the finished product of the firm that is farther up in the production process. Before its several breakups, AT&T became a vertically integrated company in the communications industry in part via acquisitions. General Motor's acquisition of Fisher Body Company (an auto parts manufacturer) is another example of vertical integration.

A *conglomerate merger* involves the combination of two firms in unrelated industries. This type of merger is the most difficult to justify; the diversification motive, discussed later, is most frequently cited. To many, the conglomerate merger is the prime example of managerial empire building gone amok. An infamous example is the 1974 acquisition of Montgomery Ward & Co. (a retailer) by Mobil Oil Company. ITT became a bloated conglomerate in the 1960s after acquiring more than 150 companies in various industries. Indeed, conglomerate mergers proliferated in the 1960s and 1970s. Many conglomerates proved unwieldy and inefficient, and were unwound in the 1980s and 1990s. (Mobil sold its interest in Montgomery Ward in 1988. In the 1980s, ITT sold many of its former acquisitions.) The unwinding (or *bust-up*) of conglomerates contributed to the rise of various types of *divestitures* in the 1980s and 1990s, which we discuss in Chapter 17.

Operating Synergy

The term *synergy* refers to any source of value-creating efficiency that is brought about by combining the assets, operations, and financial structures of two firms in a merger. Two types of synergy have been recognized in the literature: operating synergy and financial synergy. *Operating synergy* is obtained if the merger results in improvements in any business function, including (a) management, (b) labor costs, (c) production or distribution, (d) resource acquisition and allocation, or (e) market power (see Bradley, Desai, and Kim 1983).

Financial Synergy and Diversification

Financial synergy is obtained in a merger if some aspect of the financial configuration of the merged firm causes its market value to be greater than the sum of the market values of the separate firms. Although financial synergy could be obtained in any merger, discussions of financial synergy have focused primarily on conglomerate mergers because, absent financial synergy, there may be no value-enhancement rationale for a conglomerate merger.

Financial synergy is not possible in an ideal capital market. The argument is in the same spirit as Modigliani and Miller's (1958) proof of the irrelevance of an individual firm's capital structure (Chapter 2). Simply combining two firms cannot create value, even though the cash flow volatility of the merged firm will be smaller than a value-weighted average of the cash flow volatilities of the individual firms, due to the diversification effect. Investors can realize this benefit at the personal level by simply holding both firms in their portfolios.

Should Your Firm Integrate Vertically?

Vertical integration . . . is simply a means of coordinating the different stages of an industry chain when bilateral trading is not beneficial . . . Vertical integration typically reduces some risks and transaction costs, but it requires heavy setup costs, and its coordination effectiveness is often dubious.

There are four reasons to vertically integrate:

- The market is too risky and unreliable—it "fails";
- Companies in adjacent stages of the industry chain have more market power . . . ;
- Integration would create or exploit market power by raising barriers to entry or allowing price discrimination across customer segments; or
- The market is young and the company must forward integrate to develop a market, or the market is declining and independents are pulling out of adjacent stages.

Some of these are better reasons than others. The first reason—vertical market failure—is the most important one.

VERTICAL MARKET FAILURE

A vertical market "fails" when transactions within it are too risky and the contracts designed to overcome these risks are too costly (or impossible) to write and administer. The typical features of a failed vertical market are (1) a small number of buyers and sellers; (2) high asset specificity, durability, and intensity; and (3) frequent transactions. In addition, broader issues that affect all markets—uncertainty, bounded rationality, and opportunism—play a special part in a failed vertical market . . .

Buyers and sellers.   The number of buyers and sellers in a market is the most critical—although the least permanent—variable determining VMF. Problems arise when the market has only one buyer and one seller (bilateral

monopoly) or only a few buyers and a few sellers (bilateral oligopoly) . . . [because] rational supply and demand forces alone do not set transaction prices and volumes deterministically in such markets, as they do in all other vertical market structures. Rather, the terms of transactions, especially price, are determined by the balance of power between buyers and sellers—a balance that is unpredictable and unstable.

Where there is only one buyer and one supplier (especially in long-term relationships that involve frequent transactions), each attempts to leverage its monopoly status. As commercial conditions change unpredictably over time, this leads to a lot of haggling and attempts at exploitation, which are costly and risky.

Bilateral oligopolies have especially complex coordination problems. If, for example, there are three suppliers and three customers, each player sees five other players with whom the collective economic surplus must be shared. If players are not careful, they will collectively compete away all the surplus and pass it along to customers. In order to avoid this, they might try to create monopolies at each stage of the chain, but anti-trust laws prevent them. So players merge vertically, creating, in this case, three players instead of six. When each then sees only two other players seeking slices of the surplus, they have a better chance of behaving rationally . . .

Transaction frequency.   High transaction frequency is another factor that will promote VMF, when it is accompanied by bilateral oligopolies and high asset specificity. Frequent transactions raise costs for the simple reason that haggling and negotiating occur more often and allow for frequent exploitation . . . Even if transaction frequency is high, low asset specificity will mitigate its effects . . . But when assets are specific, durable, and intensive, and transactions are frequent, vertical integration is likely to be warranted. Otherwise, transaction costs and risks will be too high, and complete contracts to eliminate these uncertainties will be difficult to write.

Uncertainty, bounded rationality, and opportunism. Three additional factors have subtle but important implications for vertical strategy. Uncertainties make it difficult for companies to draw up contracts that will guide them as circumstances change . . . Bounded rationality also inhibits companies from writing contracts that fully describe transactions under all future possibilities . . . opportunism [means,] given the chance, people will often cheat and deceive in commercial dealings when they perceive that it is in their long-term interest to do so.

Uncertainty and opportunism can often be seen to drive vertical integration outcomes in the markets for R&D services and the markets for new products and processes generated by R&D. These markets often fail because the end product of R&D is largely information about new products and processes. In a world of uncertainty, the value of new products and processes to a purchaser is not known until it has been observed. But the seller is reluctant to disclose information before payment because a preview could give the product away. The situation is ripe for opportunism . . .

When specific assets are required in the development and application of the new ideas or when the originator cannot protect its property rights through patents, companies will probably benefit from vertical integration. For buyers that would mean developing their own R&D departments; for sellers that would mean forward integrating . . .

DEFENDING AGAINST MARKET POWER

[C]ompanies sometimes integrate because a company in an adjacent stage of the industry chain has more market power. If one stage of an industry chain exerts market power over another and thereby achieves abnormally high returns, it may be attractive for participants in the dominated industry to enter the dominating industry. In other words, the industry is attractive in its own right and might attract prospective entrants from both within the industry chain and outside it . . .

[E]ntry via acquisitions will not create value for the acquirer if it has to hand over the capitalized value of the economic surplus in the form of an inflated acquisition price. Often, the existing players in the less powerful stages of an industry chain pay too much for businesses in the powerful stages . . . While players in weak stages of an industry chain have clear incentives to move into the powerful stages, the key issue is whether they can achieve integration at a cost less than the value of the benefits to be achieved. Unfortunately, in our experience, they often cannot.

Managers often mistakenly believe that, as an existing player in the industry, their entry into a more attractive business within the chain is easier than it is for outsiders. However, the key skills along an industry chain usually differ so substantially that outsiders with analogous skills from other industries are often superior entrants . . .

CREATING AND EXPLOITING MARKET POWER

Vertical integration also makes strategic sense when used to create or exploit market power.

Barriers to entry. When most competitors in an industry are vertically integrated, it can be difficult for nonintegrated players to enter. Potential entrants may have to enter all stages to compete. This increases capital costs and the minimum efficient scale of operations, thus raising barriers to entry . . .

[E]ntry barriers exist in the automobile industry. Auto manufacturers are usually forward-integrated into distribution and franchised dealerships. Those with strong dealer networks tend to have exclusive dealerships. This means that new entrants must establish widespread dealer networks, which is expensive and time consuming. Without their "inherited" dealer networks, manufacturers like General Motors would have lost more market share than they already have to the Japanese . . .

(continued)

Using vertical integration to build entry barriers is often, however, an expensive ploy. Furthermore, success is not guaranteed, as inventive entrants ultimately find chinks in the armor if the economic surplus is large enough . . .

Price discrimination. Forward integration into selected customer segments can allow a company to benefit from price discrimination. Consider a supplier with market power that sells a commodity product to two customer segments with different price sensitivities. The supplier would like to maximize its total profits by charging a high price to the price-insensitive segment and a low price to the price-sensitive segment, but it cannot do so because the low-price customers can resell to the high-price customers and, ultimately, undermine the entire strategy. By forward-integrating into the low price segment, the supplier prevents reselling. There is evidence that the aluminum companies have forward-integrated into fabrication segments with the most price-sensitive demands (such as can stock, cable, and automobile castings) and have resisted integration into segments where the threat of substitution is low.

RESPONDING TO INDUSTRY LIFE CYCLE

When an industry is young, companies sometimes forward-integrate to develop a market. (This is a special case of vertical market failure.) During the early decades of the aluminum industry, producers were forced to forward-integrate into fabricated products and even end-product manufacture to penetrate markets that traditionally used materials such as steel and copper. The early manufacturers of fiberglass and plastic, too, found that forward integration was essential to creating the perception that these products were superior to traditional materials . . .

When an industry is declining, companies sometimes integrate to fill the gaps left by the independents that are pulling out. As an industry declines, weaker independents exit, leaving core players vulnerable to exploitation by increasingly concentrated suppliers or customers . . .

Therefore, financial synergy can be obtained in a merger only if some real-world factor is involved. Here, authors have focused on the Traditional Trade-off Theory of optimal capital structure (see Chapter 6). Suppose firms A and B have limited debt capacity because, for both firms, bankruptcy risk and its associated costs loom large at their respective optimal debt ratios. However, if firms A and B merge, the probability of bankruptcy is reduced, as long as the cash flows of the two firms are not perfectly correlated. As a result, the optimal debt ratio of the merged firm is higher than a value-weighted average of the optimal debt ratios of the separate firms. Along with the increased debt capacity of the merged firm comes an increase in tax benefits from interest deductibility, and thus an increase in overall market value.[2]

Even if value is created in a merger via financial synergy, an important question arises about the *allocation* of the incremental value among the firms' various security-holders. For instance, the original creditors of both firms would benefit from the over-

---

[2]References for these and related arguments about financial synergy include Levy and Sarnat (1970); Lewellen (1971); Higgins and Schall (1975); Lee (1977); Lam and Boudreaux (1984); and Green and Talmor (1985).

all decrease in the probability of bankruptcy that attends the merger, which in turn results from the *co-insurance* associated with creditors now having a claim against a larger combined firm. As a result, the values of the combined firm's debt securities would be higher than their premerger values. This windfall for creditors could easily be greater than the overall value of the financial synergy, in which case the firms' *shareholders* could actually sustain losses upon the merger. Higgins and Schall (1975) suggested that managers could prevent a windfall to creditors, and thus preserve the value of the financial synergy for shareholders, by retiring all existing debt at its premerger market price, and then issuing new debt immediately after the merger. However, this would no doubt entail substantial transaction costs.

Kim and McConnell (1977) suggested a less expensive alternative of simply increasing the leverage of the merged firm "to the point where the post-merger default risk of the previously outstanding debt is increased sufficiently to negate the co-insurance effect and to cancel any wealth-transfers from equity-holders to debt-holders" (p. 352). The authors found that merging firms actually followed this prescription. They identified 39 conglomerate mergers that occurred in 1960 to 1973 in which the merging firm had long-term publicly traded bonds outstanding. They found that (a) the bondholders involved in these mergers realized no abnormal gains (or losses) associated with the merger, on average; and (b) the merged firms generally increased leverage after the merger.

Bankruptcy Avoidance for the Target

Another rationale for merger is the *bankruptcy avoidance* argument. A firm may agree to be acquired because it is close to bankruptcy, and the acquisition averts deadweight costs of bankruptcy (Haugen and Senbet 1978). Evidence suggests that bankruptcy avoidance may be the primary rationale in a substantial proportion of acquisitions. In Chapter 1, we showed that the number of mergers and acquisitions far exceeds the number of bankruptcies and liquidations among U.S. nonfinancial firms over the years 1980 to 2000 (review Figure 1-1). This evidence at least vaguely suggests that troubled firms are more often acquired than go bankrupt. Shrieves and Stevens (1979) document more direct evidence. They found that 15.2 percent of the target firms in their sample of mergers were close to insolvency.

In related research, Clark and Ofek (1994) examined 38 acquisitions of distressed firms over the years 1981 to 1988. They found that the bidder in these acquisitions is more likely to be a firm in the same industry than is the case for acquisitions in general. Thus, acquisitions of distressed firms generally are attempts to restructure the troubled target. However, their evidence indicates that bidders are generally unable to restructure their targets successfully.

Internal Capital Markets, Financial Slack, and Merger

Myers and Majluf's (1984) *Pecking Order Hypothesis* also provides a motive for merger. As you recall, information asymmetry is the key problem in their model, and it leads firms to prefer financing new investments with internal equity rather than to try to raise funds externally by issuing debt or equity. Accordingly, a cash-poor firm with substantial profitable investment opportunities faces the difficult choice of either raising funds in the external markets or passing up profitable investments. However, the firm can resolve this problem if it merges with a cash-rich, investment-poor firm; the merged firm will generally have enough internal cash flow to pursue all profitable investments. Bruner (1988) provides evidence consistent with this motive for merger. (Also, in Chapter 13 we noted Hubbard and Palia's [1999] arguments on this point in the context of internal capital markets.)

The Hubris Hypothesis

Roll (1986) offered the *Hubris Hypothesis* as a motive, or at least an explanation, for an acquisition or takeover. He argued that the bidder's management overvalues the target because they overestimate their ability to create value once they wrest control of the target's assets. The central prediction of this hypothesis is that, at the announcement of an acquisition or takeover, the overall change in the market values of the firms involved should be zero (or slightly negative, because an acquisition is a costly transaction). This is because the market, unlike the bidder's management, realizes that the acquisition provides no synergy.

Roll discussed then-available evidence on the valuation effects of acquisition and takeover announcements to make his case. The evidence consistently shows that target-firm shareholders realize substantial positive abnormal returns. The evidence for bidder-firm shareholders is somewhat mixed, but generally indicates that the effect on bidder-firm shareholders is negligible. Thus, the evidence suggests that value is created in an acquisition or takeover, though target-firm shareholders receive all of the added value. However, a simple summing of the average abnormal returns on the bidder's and target's stocks is an inaccurate measure, because bidders are generally much larger than targets. Instead, we should sum the total (or net) *dollar gains* to both firms to determine the total value created. By this measure, no study has found statistically significant overall gains.

Management Self-Interest: Risk Reduction and Entrenchment

The management of a cash-rich, investment-poor firm has a self-serving incentive to overinvest in unprofitable projects. Merging with a cash-poor, investment-rich firm may mitigate this problem. The balance between cash versus shares as payment for an acquisition may depend in part on the extent to which the bidder has excess cash.

Other agency-related motives for merger also have been proffered. Amihud and Lev (1981) argued that some managers engage in conglomerate mergers to decrease their employment risk. The extent to which managers succumb to such self-serving behavior depends on the extent to which their control over the firm is unfettered by shareholders. Thus, they predict that a firm is more likely to pursue conglomerate merger if the firm's ownership is diffuse than if it is concentrated. They reported evidence consistent with this prediction. Lewellen, Loderer, and Rosenfeld (1989) also test the hypothesis that managers are motivated to merge to reduce the firm's riskiness. However, they find *no* evidence that a conglomerate merger reduces the acquiring firm's riskiness.

Morck, Shleifer, and Vishny (1990) found that bidders generally overpay for their targets, and give two possible reasons for this: "According to Roll (1986), managers of bidding firms are infected by hubris, and so overpay for targets because they overestimate their own ability to run them. Another view of overpayment is that managers of bidding firms pursue personal objectives other than maximization of shareholder value. To the extent that acquisitions serve these objectives, managers of bidding firms are willing to pay more for targets than they are worth to bidding firms' shareholders" (p. 31).

Good Deals

Here we provide excerpts of a study of the determinants of the market's reactions to various M&A deals and related transactions.

No doubt the market is skeptical about M&A, but it is a lot more receptive to some kinds of deals than to others. Inquire before you acquire.

Half or more of the big mergers, acquisitions, and alliances you read about in the newspapers fail to create significant shareholder value, according to most of the research that McKinsey and others have undertaken into the market's reaction to announcements of major deals. For shareholders, the sad conclusion is that an average corporate-control transaction puts the market capitalization of their company at risk and delivers little or no value in return.

Managers could eschew corporate deals altogether. But the right course is to pursue them only when they make sense—in other words, to make sure that all of your deals are above average. Easily said, of course. But what, exactly, does an "above-average" deal look like? We decided to take that question to the stock market.

Our study examined the stock price movements, a few days before and after the announcement of a transaction, of companies involved in corporate deals. Using a multivariate linear regression, we tried to explain those movements in terms of several deal variables, such as deal size, industry, and deal type. Our experience with scores of corporate-control transactions has taught us that mergers, acquisitions, and alliances tend to serve some kinds of strategies better than others. A large part of our study therefore involved identifying the strategic purpose behind each deal we followed and making that purpose one of the variables used to describe it. If the market reacted more enthusiastically to deals that embodied a partic-

ular strategy, our analysis might expose these underlying trends.

Indeed, we found that the market apparently prefers deals that are part of an "expansionist" program, in which a company seeks to boost its market share by consolidating, by moving into new geographic regions, or by adding new distribution channels for existing products and services. The market seems to be less tolerant of "transformative" deals, those that seek to move companies into new lines of business or to remove a chunk of an otherwise healthy business portfolio.

Even within a given type of strategy (whether expansionist or transformative), the market seems to prefer certain kinds of transaction to others. In particular, acquisitions create the most market value overall, despite the well-known "winner's curse," in which buyers pay too high a premium. If a deal is structured as a merger or a sale, it has little clear effect on stock prices.

Choosing to structure deals as joint ventures or alliances, all else being equal, does not create significant value for the participants and may even destroy some value . . . Finally, if a company competes in a growing or fragmented industry, or if the performance of the company has recently lagged behind that of its peers, some signs indicate that the market may reward its transactions more than those of stronger performers. Managers might find it useful to understand these biases as they consider whether or how to proceed with a deal.

One dramatic example of the way the transactions of a company can boost its share price was Heineken's conquest of the European beer market. In the past five years, acquisitions have lifted the company's share price by 12 percent a year, reckoned by the increases that occurred when the deals were announced. In other words, Heineken's acquisition strategy

(continued)

alone generated half of the company's outperformance as compared with the Dutch stock market index for the five-year period.

THE ARCHITECTURE OF A STUDY

We started with a sample of 479 corporate deals announced by 36 companies in the telecommunications, petroleum, and European banking industries over a five-year period. Because we wanted our study to account explicitly for the size of a deal, we excluded all transactions whose monetary value had not been announced publicly. This left us with a core sample of 231 deals: 16 mergers, 151 acquisitions, 18 joint ventures, 18 alliances of other types, and 28 sales of company subsidiaries . . .

The three industries we selected include what we regarded as the most important industry variables: different rates of growth and degrees of consolidation. Such a sample would be fairly representative of the whole universe of companies. But since the companies came from just a few industries, the sample let us add an "industry" variable to our regression and still get meaningful results.

Since we wanted our sample to include companies spanning a range of sizes and degrees of success, we created a graph, for each industry, plotting book value (representing company size) along one axis and market-to-book ratio (representing business success) along the other. We then selected representative companies from each quadrant of the chart.

To compute the excess returns of each company's stock—the stock price movements above or below what you would expect given the movement of broad market indicators—we started with total returns to shareholders during the period. For each company, we then subtracted the cost of equity—that is, the book value of the company's equity multiplied by the cost of equity capital, computed using the capital asset-pricing model and the company's beta. From this number, we subtracted the movement in a broad nationwide stock market index over the five years, adjusting for differences in volatility between the company's share price and the overall stock market.

(Before subtracting the movement in the relevant stock market index, we had reduced that movement by the average cost of equity in the country's stock market, to avoid double-counting the cost of equity.) We undertook this calculation for every company during the five-year period of the study and also during every 11-day period spanning the announcement of a deal: 5 trading days before the announcement, 5 days after it, and the day of the announcement itself.

With these data in hand, we carried out a multivariate regression to assess the correlations between the excess returns created by each deal and various characteristics of that deal. We used a deal size–weighted least-squares multivariate-regression model, in which all dependent and independent variables for each transaction were weighted by the size of that transaction relative to the size of the company undertaking it. In our study, the dependent variable was defined as excess returns relative to the local stock market, corrected for the risk-adjusted cost of capital, during the 11 trading days surrounding the announcement of the deal. The r^2 of the regression was 57 percent . . .

THE STRATEGIC FACTOR

The central results of the study . . . concern a deal's strategic type. Depending on the primary strategic purpose underlying the 231 deals, we assigned each of them to one of five such strategic types. If a deal aimed to consolidate a market by combining two companies in the same industry or to expand a company's geographic bounds ("market consolidation" or "geographic expansion," respectively), all else being equal it earned a 1.1 percent stock market premium in the 11 trading days surrounding its announcement . . . If a transaction sought to gain new distribution channels ("business system extension"), it earned a 4.2 percent premium. All of these deals are broadly expansionist . . .

By contrast, the announcement of a deal whose strategy we classified as transformative—a "portfolio refocus" or a "business diversification"—actually destroyed 5.3 percent of the company's value on average. In a portfolio refocus deal, a company sells off a part of its business portfolio. In a business diversification deal, a company acquires a significant business that takes it outside its core industry.

The market's tendency to favor expansionist over transformative deals makes intuitive sense. The potential synergies from expansionist transactions are usually much greater because they combine similar assets. Even when a transformative deal does promise synergies, they tend to be less predictable than those in expansionist deals and not as easily verified by investors at the time of the announcement. For managers, the lesson is clear: not to shy away from transformative transactions but to ensure that they get closer scrutiny—and pass a higher hurdle—than expansionist ones, and that they actually create tangible value.

WHICH DEAL IS LIKELY TO SUCCEED?

Of course, there is more to a deal than its strategy. After you decide to do an expansionist deal—or decide on a transformative one and manage to convince yourself (and your investors) that it will fare much better than the norm—you still have a good amount to worry about. For further guidance, we consulted the other variables of our regression. We found several interesting results.

FULL DEALS CREATE MORE VALUE

One striking discovery was the difference in the market's reaction to various structural forms a deal might take: an acquisition, a merger, a sale, or a joint venture or alliance.

Mergers and asset sales define the baseline: The market shows no particular reaction to them one way or the other. Acquisitions, by contrast, boost the announcement impact of a deal on the acquirer's stock by 2.7 percent of market cap, all else being equal. This is a strik-

ing result, since acquirers usually pay a hefty acquisition premium. The most likely explanation is that in an acquisition it is always clear which company controls the postmerger integration process. It is therefore much more likely that the full synergies of a deal will be captured in an acquisition than in a merger, in which a lengthy power struggle often ensues between the management teams of the companies involved.

As for joint ventures and alliances, their announcement impact lags behind the average by 3.1 percent of market capitalization. Perhaps the investment community views these deals as incomplete asset combinations that create few immediate synergies but can limit a company's strategic options and sap the attention of managers. There are, of course, a number of outstanding exceptions to the rule, but it does seem to be the case that, all else being equal, "partial" deals are more likely than others to diminish a company's value . . .

Our sample of 231 deals came from three sectors: global telecommunications, global petroleum, and European banking. The very fact that a deal was in the telecom or banking sectors was correlated with a 2.3 percent and 2 percent increase, respectively, in the deal's average impact on a company's stock price. Competing in the petroleum industry, by contrast, actually seems to destroy 4.3 percent of shareholder value relative to the average. The explanation, we suspect, is that opportunities to create synergies and transfer skills through transactions are plentiful in the banking and telecom industries, since both are still growing, and banking is also quite fragmented. Petroleum, by contrast, is relatively stagnant and consolidated.

Second, underperforming companies (with returns below the average of a local stock market index during the five-year period under study) actually appeared to create 1.2 percent more value per deal than did companies that outperformed the norm . . .

This result may sound odd, but there are a few possible explanations for it. Perhaps out-

(continued)

performers already have future "good deals" built into their share price, so the market gives them less credit for good news . . . Or perhaps investors expect underperformers to use their deals to gain access to the skills and knowledge they currently lack, whereas outperformers gain only tangible assets. Finally, there may be a hubris factor at work: Perhaps managers of out-performing companies are less concerned with the market's reaction to deals because those managers can rest on their recently won laurels.

IMPLICATIONS FOR REAL LIFE

Our findings reveal no silver bullet that guarantees success in corporate-control transactions.

As many companies have learned from experience, investors and securities markets can be fickle, and even the most carefully crafted deals can meet with market skepticism when they are announced. But our research does suggest that companies can substantially improve their chances of success by pursuing transactions aimed at expanding the company's current lines of business and not at taking the company into entirely new activities. Also, all else being equal, it is better to acquire than to merge and better to merge than to ally. If you happen to compete in a growing or fragmented industry, expect better deal opportunities than you would get in a more mature or consolidated industry. Finally, if your company is an under-performer and it announces a well-conceived deal, you can look forward to a larger boost to your share price than a top performer would enjoy. Of course, it is possible to create value through corporate-control transactions, such as a string of transformative joint ventures, that the market has often rejected in the past. But managers who attempt this should expect a cool reaction from the stock market. And to minimize the problem, they should put extra effort into identifying and capturing deal synergies and into telling investors why their particular deals hold more promise than apparently similar transactions have in the past.

Source: This article is excerpted from "Deals That Create Value," H. Bieshaar, J. Knight, A. van Wassenaer, *The McKinsey Quarterly*, no. 1, 2001, pp. 64–73. Copyright © 2001 McKinsey & Co. The article can be found on the publication's Web site, www.mckinseyquarterly.com. Used by permission.

16.3.2   Motives for Hostile Takeover

The finance literature discusses four motives for a hostile takeover: (a) failure of the target firm's management, (b) *busting up* an inefficient diversified firm, (c) hubris, and (d) industry shocks.

The Failure of Target Management

Some investment firms, including Berkshire Hathaway (led by Warren Buffet), Mesa Petroleum (led by T. Boone Pickens), Ronald O. Perelman, Carl C. Icahn, and Kohlberg, Kravis, and Roberts, have specialized in taking over firms that have exhibited poor performance. In the 1980s, they were called *corporate raiders*. Martin and McConnell (1991) examined a sample of takeovers to test the hypothesis that takeovers serve to discipline the managements of target firms that are performing poorly. They documented evidence consistent with this hypothesis: (a) prior to the takeover, target firms tend to substantially underperform other firms in their industry, and (b) the turnover rate for target management increases following completion of the takeover.

The central tenet of Jensen's (1986a) Free Cash Flow Hypothesis is that managers tend to overinvest rather than disgorging excess cash by paying dividends. If such firms invest in negative-NPV (net present value) projects, they should exhibit poor performance, and therefore should be well represented among those firms that are the targets of takeovers. However, Servaes (1994) found that takeover targets *do not* overinvest. He examined 700 firms that either were takeover targets or went private over the years 1971 to 1987. He found no evidence that these firms overinvest in capital expenditures prior to the control change.

Bust-up Takeovers

A recurring theme in the finance literature is that managers have self-serving incentives to grow and diversify their firms inefficiently to (a) reduce the risk of the firm's failure, and the loss of their jobs, (b) build an empire that will lead to higher compensation, and (c) build a complex organization that would be difficult for a successor to manage, thereby entrenching themselves. Firms that have grown unwieldy as a result of inefficient diversification are likely to perform poorly, and therefore should be ripe for a *bust-up takeover*. In a bust-up, a diversified firm is taken over and assets or divisions are sold so that the remaining firm is more focused and efficient.

Berger and Ofek (1996) tested this conjecture empirically:

> We examine whether the value loss from diversification affects takeover and breakup probabilities. We estimate diversification's value effect by imputing stand-alone values for individual business segments and find that firms with greater value losses are more likely to be taken over. Moreover, those acquired firms whose losses are greatest are most likely to be bought by LBO associations, which frequently break up their targets. For a subsample of large diversified targets: (1) higher value losses increase the extent of post-takeover bustup; and (2) post-takeover bustup generally results in divested divisions being operated as part of a focused, stand-alone firm. (p. 1175)

See Mitchell and Lehn (1990) for related evidence.

Hubris

Roll's Hubris Hypothesis has an interesting implication for hostile takeovers. Suppose the management of bidding firm B is infected with hubris regarding target firm T. Firm T's management is likely to resist the takeover in part because they (correctly) fail to see how the management of firm B could improve on their performance as managers of firm T's assets.

Industry Shocks

Negative shocks to demand in an industry may spur takeover activity as a means of reducing excess capacity in the industry. Mitchell and Mulherin (1996) examined industry-level patterns in takeover (and restructuring) activity during the 1980s. They found that the rate of such activity tends to be directly related to intra-industry economic shocks. Their evidence indicates that much of the takeover activity observed in the 1980s was driven by broad fundamental factors within industries.

16.3.3 Motives for Buyouts

The literature emphasizes three motives for a buyout: (a) to increase managerial incentives, (b) to avert a takeover, and (c) to realize tax-reduction benefits.

An MBO Increases Management's Incentives

From an agency perspective, it has been argued that managers seek to buy out their own firm's shareholders because they recognize that the firm could be more profitable, but under the current ownership structure they do not have an incentive to pursue the necessary projects. However, they *would* have an incentive if they were the primary owners. But they generally lack the capital to purchase all of the firm's shares on their own. If they can convince lenders, they borrow (against the firm) to buyout other shareholders, and the firm reverts to close private ownership. The firm's high leverage also disciplines the manager-owners, so the firm's profitability should improve. Smith (1990) examined post-buyout changes in operating performance of 58 MBOs completed during 1977 to 1986, and found that buyout firms realize substantial improvements in operating performance subsequent to the buyout relative to the year before.

Averting a Takeover

Managers or employees of a firm may seek a buyout to thwart a hostile takeover attempt, because if the takeover is successful, they might lose their jobs. This appears to be the primary motive for Eckerd's 1996 MBO, discussed earlier.

Tax Benefits

Kaplan (1989b) examined 76 MBOs of publicly held firms completed during 1980 to 1986 for evidence of tax benefits. The two principal sources of potential tax gains are (a) greater interest deductions via higher leverage, and (b) a change in the firm's tax basis, whereby the firm generates higher depreciation deductions after the buyout. They documented evidence of substantial tax benefits, and also found that the premium paid to shareholders in a buyout is directly related to the relative size of tax benefits (see also Marias, Schipper, and Smith 1989).

16.4 MERGERS AND ACQUISITIONS

We begin this section with a brief legal history of mergers and acquisitions. Then we (a) provide evidence on the frequency of M&A activity in the United States over time, (b) discuss determinants of the form of payment in a merger, (c) discuss evidence on the valuation effects of merger announcements, and (d) discuss evidence on the postmerger performance of acquiring firms.

16.4.1 A Brief Legal History of Mergers

The history of legal issues associated with mergers and acquisitions in the United States extends back to the very genesis of large corporations. In the late 1800s, accusations mounted that large firms engage in anticompetitive practices, including and especially the development of *trusts*. A trust is an agreement among the few dominant firms in an industry to coordinate production and, as alleged, to cut prices temporarily in order to drive out or acquire smaller competitors, after which they could raise prices substantially. In 1890, the Sherman Antitrust Act was passed, which both outlawed trusts and prohibited monopolies. The Sherman Act led to the breakup of Standard Oil Company and the American Tobacco Company.

In 1914, Congress passed the Clayton Antitrust Act and legislation that created the Federal Trade Commission to enforce antitrust laws (a function it now shares with the Antitrust Division of the U.S. Department of Justice). The Clayton Act outlawed (a) the practice of creating interlocking boards of directors across two or more firms, (b) fixed-price agreements, (c) agreements to control the supply of a product, and (d) abuse of market power intended to establish or maintain a monopoly.

Antitrust legislation applies to M&A to the extent that they might lead to the types of abuses outlined above. Section 7 of the Clayton Act renders illegal any merger where the effect "may be substantially to lesson competition or to tend to create a monopoly." However, Williamson (1968) argues that the government's case against merger on anticompetitive grounds—specifically that the price of the industry's product will rise—should be balanced against the welfare gains that may come from synergy, which may obviate the need for the merged firm to increase the prices of its products in order to increase profits.

As Stillman (1983) points out, the Celler-Kefauver amendment to the Clayton Act, passed in 1950, substantially extended the reach of the statute, and led to actions against vertical and conglomerate mergers. However, more recently the Justice Department has focused more on horizontal mergers. Stillman discusses trade-offs associated with the government's policy against horizontal mergers:

> An antimerger policy that focuses exclusively on horizontal mergers is consistent in principle with economic efficiency. Mergers between current producers of close substitutes by definition increase industry concentration . . . But while horizontal mergers have the clearest anticompetitive potential, there are also potential efficiency gains from such mergers that the new antimerger policy may sacrifice. In addition to the obvious possibility of complementarities in production and distribution, managers in the same industry may have a comparative advantage at identifying mismanaged firms. By foreclosing these managers from the market for corporate control, an anti-horizontal merger policy may impair efficient allocation of managerial talent and, perhaps more importantly, weaken significantly the incentive of incumbent managers to maximize the value of their firms. (pp. 225–226)

Stillman examined 11 horizontal mergers attempted between 1964 and 1972 that were challenged by antitrust enforcement agencies.[3] He summarized his results as follows: "The paper tests the hypothesis that, but for the government's action, these mergers would have resulted in higher product prices. On balance, the data favor the null hypothesis of no anticompetitive effect" (p. 225).

Finally, Malatesta and Thompson (1993) discuss the Williams Act, passed in 1968, which affects tender offers: "Among other provisions, the Act mandates that bidding

---

[3]The acquiring (acquired) firms in these cases were Chrysler (Mack Trucks), Schenley (Buckingham), Russel Stover (Fanny Farmer), General Dynamics (UEC), Sterling Drug (Lehn and Fink), Bendix (Fram), Cooper Industries (Waukesha Motor), Atlantic Richfield (Sinclair), Gould National (Clevite), Warner Lambert (Parke Davis), and Jim Walter (Panacon).

firms must file reports with the Securities and Exchange Commission describing the acquirer's business plans relating to the target firm and method of financing the acquisition. Furthermore, the Act specifies that tender offers must remain open for a minimum period of 10 days. In addition to regulating the behavior of bidding firms, the Act also contains provisions that increase target management's ability to block or delay tender offers by bringing suit in court" (pp. 364–365). The authors documented evidence indicating that the Williams Act reduced the expected gross present value of acquisition attempts.

16.4.2   Defending Mergers as a Mechanism in the Market for Corporate Control

Manne (1965) provided a perspective on the changing justifications for mergers provided by economists and the U.S. Supreme Court circa the early 1960s. He pointed out that, while rules against vertical mergers were weakening, horizontal mergers remained largely condemned on antitrust grounds. However, he defended horizontal mergers with a *failing-company argument*—that is, a failing firm in an industry can be efficiently absorbed by a healthy firm in the same industry via merger. "[I]f mergers were completely legal, we should anticipate relatively few actual bankruptcy proceedings in any industry which was not itself contracting. The function so wastefully performed by bankruptcies and liquidations would be economically performed by mergers at a much earlier stage of the firm's life" (p. 112).

Manne also argued that mergers perform a useful function in promoting competition in the market for corporate control. A merger is justified if the assets of a poorly managed company are transferred to a company with superior management. Jensen (1993) also defended mergers, acquisitions, and (especially) hostile takeovers on this basis. We discuss Jensen's assertions further in Section 16.5.

16.4.3   Merger Waves and Industry Dynamics

For decades, market analysts have noted that M&A activity in the United States seems to wax and wane gradually over time, much like a sine wave, and have coined the phrase *merger waves* to describe this process. The merger wave of the 1960s is especially touted. In this subsection, we present and discuss time series and cross-industry evidence pertaining to M&A activity, generated using data on 6,109 acquisitions of publicly traded U.S. nonfinancial firms over the years 1960 to 2000. Our initial evidence is displayed in Figure 16-1 and Table 16-2, which we discuss in turn.

Merger Waves

Figure 16-1 shows for each year (a) the number of publicly traded U.S. nonfinancial firms that were acquired, (b) the aggregate value of the acquired firms (i.e., the final total value received by acquired firms' shareholders), (c) the percentage of all publicly traded U.S. nonfinancial firms that were acquired, and, for reference, (d) U.S. gross domestic product (GDP) growth.

The merger wave of the 1960s is clearly evident; the number of acquisitions increased dramatically from only 11 in 1960 to 114 in 1968, then fell steadily to only 29 in 1972. The next wave began to build in the mid-1970s, cresting at 189 acquisitions in 1979 before declining steadily to 132 in 1983. Subsequently, the number of acquisitions

FIGURE 16-1 Annual Number of Publicly Traded U.S. Nonfinancial Firms That Were Acquired, Their Aggregate Final Market Equity Values, Ratio of Acquired Firms to All Publicly Traded U.S. Nonfinancial Firms, and U.S. GDP Growth, 1960–2000

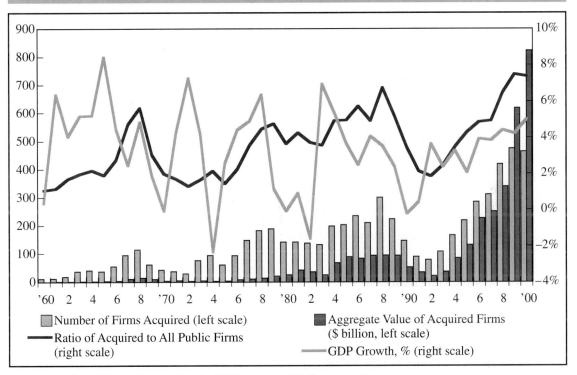

Sources: Standard & Poor's *Research Insight*, CRSP database, U.S. Commerce Department.

rose to a peak of 300 acquisitions in 1988, before falling steadily and sharply to only 78 in 1992. The latest wave of M&A activity began to build only a year later, in 1993, and may have peaked at 474 in 1999.

The number of acquisitions, and their aggregate market equity value, has tended to increase over time with the number and aggregate market equity values of all U.S. firms. Therefore, a better measure of the *relative* intensity of M&A activity over time is the *percentage* of all publicly traded U.S. nonfinancial firms that were acquired in a given year. By this measure, the late 1960s was indeed a major period of M&A activity, as this percentage reached a peak of 5.6 percent in 1968. This proportion was not exceeded until 1988, when 6.9 percent of all publicly traded U.S. nonfinancial firms were acquired. The highest proportion overall occurred during the most recent wave; in 1999, 7.5 percent of all publicly traded U.S. nonfinancial firms were acquired.

The relationship between M&A activity and aggregate economic growth is often debated. On the one hand, we might expect mergers to proliferate when the economy has been growing for some time, because potential acquiring firms likely have greater cash or higher stock prices to facilitate an acquisition. On the other hand, a bidder may find a target to be more attractive in an economic downturn, when a target may be in financial distress. In any event, the contemporaneous correlation between the annual percentage of firms acquired and GDP growth is negligible (0.03).

Acquisitions as a Measure of Industry Vitality

Our earlier discussion suggests that M&A activity may be an important indicator of an industry's *vitality*. For example, a bidder may recognize synergy with a target, or may wish to convert the assets of a poorly performing firm to more efficient uses. Accordingly, the relative frequency of acquisitions in an industry may be a good measure of the industry's vitality, governmental antitrust policies notwithstanding. We used our M&A database for 1960 to 2000 to test this conjecture. We calculated the average annual percentage of public firms that were acquired: (a) in each of the eight major industries analyzed in Chapter 7, (b) among all other U.S. nonfinancial firms as a group, and (c) among all U.S. nonfinancial firms. The results are displayed in Table 16-2.

For all firms, the average annual percentage of firms acquired was 4.1 percent. However, these percentages vary considerably across industries, ranging from only 2.6 percent per year for the *Electric, Gas, and Sanitary Services* (i.e., utilities) industry to 6.5 percent per year for the *Communications* industry. Historically, the firms in the utility industry have been highly regulated and basically assigned to market territories, so low vitality is expected. At the other extreme, the *Communications* industry recently has been revolutionized by both technology and deregulation, so we expect it to score high on our measure of vitality.[4]

TABLE 16-2   A Simple Measure of Industry Vitality: Average Annual Percentage of Publicly Traded Firms That Were Acquired

U.S. Nonfinancial Firms in Selected Industries and Overall, 1960–2000

Industry	Average Annual Percent of Firms Acquired 1960–2000	Total Number of Firms Acquired 1960–2000	Number of Firms at Year-End		
			1960	*1975*	*2000*
Business Services	4.4%	564	5	164	1,107
Chemicals and Allied Products	3.7%	354	74	219	516
Communications	6.5%	217	9	55	225
Electric, Gas, and Sanitary Services (Utilities)	2.6%	187	96	209	178
Electronic and Other Electric Equipment	3.7%	446	60	319	509
Food and Kindred Products	4.5%	225	75	184	133
Industrial Machinery, Computer Equipment	4.1%	457	92	330	405
Petroleum Refining and Related Products	2.7%	39	26	48	27
All Other Industries	4.1%	3,620	611	2,647	3,046
All Firms	4.1%	6,109	1,048	4,175	6,146

Sources: Standard & Poor's *Research Insight*, CRSP databases.

---

[4]Important regulatory developments in the telecommunications industry include the breakup of AT&T in 1984 and the Telecommunications Act of 1996, both of which were intended to increase competition, and therefore vitality. The utility industry's recent deregulation appears to be having a dramatic effect on its vitality. On average from 1960 to 1997, only 1.7 percent of utility firms were acquired. For 1998 to 2000, the average was 12.0 percent.

The Ages and Relative Sizes of Acquired Firms

Next, we examine the ages and relative sizes of acquired firms. Our measure of the age of an acquired firm is the number of years between its initial public offering (IPO) and the date on which it was acquired. Our measure of relative size is the ratio of the market equity value of the target to the market equity value of the bidder. Figure 16-2 displays the distribution of ages, and Figure 16-3 shows the distribution of size ratios.

Acquired firms tend to be relatively young; their median age is only eight years. They also tend to be relatively small; the median ratio of their size to the size of the acquired firm is only 0.21, or 21 percent. Exceptions are not rare, however: almost 10 percent of acquired firms were more than 30 years old, and 8 percent of the acquired firms were *larger* than the acquiring firm.

16.4.4   Determinants of the Form of Payment in a Merger

Historically, mergers were classified into one of two categories according to the form of payment, and the associated accounting and tax treatment, involved. In a *pooling of interest* merger, stock is exchanged between the two firms and one entity survives. This type of merger qualified as a tax-free transaction. However, the Financial Accounting Standards Board (FASB) has recently voted to eliminate pooling of interest accounting for mergers, and henceforth will allow only the purchase method, explained later.

FIGURE 16-2   Age Distribution of Acquired Firms

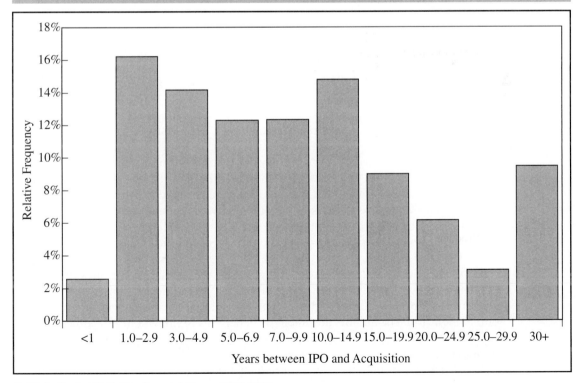

Publicly Traded U.S. Nonfinancial Firms, 1960–2000

Sources: Standard & Poor's *Research Insight*, CRSP database.

FIGURE 16-3 Distribution of Ratio of Market Equity Values of Acquired Firm to Acquiring Firm

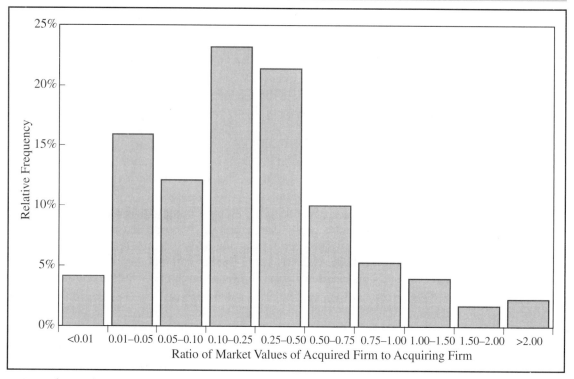

U.S. Nonfinancial Firms, 1960–2000
Sources: Standard & Poor's *Research Insight*, CRSP database.

In a *purchase* merger, the bidder buys the target using cash. This transaction triggers a tax event for the shareholders of the acquired firm. They are taxed on any capital gains they realize upon the surrender of their shares in exchange for cash. For accounting purposes, the acquiring firm treats the acquisition as an investment. The difference between the purchase value and the book value is booked against goodwill, to be charged against future earnings over several years, though these charges are not tax deductible.

Amihud, Lev, and Travlos (1990) argued that the form of compensation in an acquisition, cash or stock, depends in part on concerns of the bidding-firm's management about loss of control: "Corporate insiders who value control will prefer financing [an acquisition] by cash or debt rather than by issuing new stock which dilutes their holdings and increases the risk of losing control" (p. 603). Thus, the probability, and percentage, of cash compensation should increase with bidder management's ownership fraction of their firm. The authors document evidence consistent with this hypothesis.

Martin (1996) asked the question, "How do the characteristics of the acquiring firm, the target firm, and the acquisition itself contribute to the method of financing?" (p. 1227). He found that both the acquirer's and the target's investment opportunities (measured by Tobin's Q ratio) are important determinants of the method of payment—higher investment opportunities are associated with a greater probability of stock financing.

16.4.5 Valuation Effects of Merger Announcements

Event studies have been conducted to determine the valuation effects of M&A announcements on the securityholders of the firms involved. Mandelker (1974), Langetieg (1978), Dodd (1980), and Asquith (1983) all documented evidence indicating that a merger announcement induces a substantial positive abnormal return on the target firm's stock (approximately 20 percent, on average), while the acquiring firm's stockholders are either unaffected or sustain small losses, on average. This evidence is consistent with several of the motives listed earlier (e.g., bidders pay substantial premiums to the target firm's shareholders, perhaps to the point of overpaying for the target). Asquith and Kim (1982) found that the bondholders of neither the bidder nor the target realize significant abnormal returns at announcement, suggesting that other security claimants are unaffected.

However, Asquith, Bruner, and Mullins (1983) found that shareholders of some bidding firms realize significant gains at a merger announcement period, and that gains are positively related to the relative size of the target. Huang and Walkling (1987) found that target shareholders earn higher average abnormal returns if the offer is made in cash (29.3 percent) than if it is made in stock (14.4 percent) or a mixture of cash and stock (23.3 percent).

Eckbo (1983) analyzed horizontal mergers, focusing on the arguments we discussed earlier that they are anticompetitive. He summarizes his analysis and results as follows: "This proposition is tested on a large sample of horizontal mergers in mining and manufacturing industries, including mergers challenged by the government with violating antitrust laws, and a 'control' sample of vertical mergers in the same industries. While we find that the antitrust law enforcement agencies systematically select relatively profitable mergers for prosecution, there is little evidence indicating that the mergers would have had collusive, anticompetitive effects" (p. 241).

Maquieira, Megginson, and Nail (1998) examined wealth changes for holders of all public debt and equity securities of firms involved in 260 stock-for-stock mergers over the years 1963 to 1996: "We find no evidence that conglomerate stock-for-stock mergers create financial synergies or benefit bondholders at stockholders' expense. Instead, we document significant net synergistic gains in nonconglomerate mergers and generally insignificant net gains in conglomerate mergers. Conglomerate bidding-firm stockholders lose; all other securityholders at least break even. Convertible securityholders experience the largest gains, due mostly to their attached option values. Certain bond covenants are value-enhancing while leverage increases are value-reducing" (p. 3).

16.4.6 Postmerger Performance of Acquiring Firms

Several studies have focused on the postmerger performance of acquiring firms. Healy, Palepu, and Ruback (1992) found that merging firms exhibit "significant improvements in asset productivity relative to their industries, leading to higher operating cash flow returns" (p. 135). They also found that the improvement in operating returns is positively related to the abnormal returns at announcement, indicating that the market anticipates differential improvements across merging firms.

In contrast, Agrawal, Jaffe, and Mandelker (1992) found that postacquisition *stock return* performance of acquiring firms is generally poor for a period of five years after a merger. On average, stockholders sustained abnormal losses of −10 percent during this postacquisition period. Rau and Vermaelen (1998) also found that bidding firm stocks underperform benchmarks for long periods after a merger. However, they documented two additional findings. *First*, they found that bidders in tender offers *overperform* on a long-term basis after an acquisition. *Second*, they found that "the long-term underperformance of acquiring firms in mergers is predominantly caused by the poor post-acquisition performance of low book-to-market 'glamour' firms. We interpret this finding as evidence that both the market and the management overextrapolate the bidder's past performance (as reflected in the bidder's book-to-market ratio) when they assess the desirability of an acquisition" (p. 223).

Finally, Loughran and Vijh (1997) documented a dramatic difference in post-merger stock returns across two groups of acquiring firms. They separated 947 acquisitions during 1970 to 1989 into two groups according to method of payment—stock versus cash—and found: "During a five-year period following the acquisition, on average, firms that complete stock mergers earn significantly negative excess returns of –25.0 percent whereas firms that complete cash tender offers earn significantly positive excess returns of 61.7 percent" (p. 1765).

16.5 TAKEOVERS

In this section, we discuss research related to several important aspects of takeovers. *First*, we discuss the characteristics of likely takeover targets. *Second*, we discuss the bidding strategies that a bidder may employ to take over a target firm. *Third*, we discuss defenses that target firm managers employ to resist a takeover. *Fourth*, we discuss antitakeover legislation and the overall decline of the takeover as an external corporate control device.

16.5.1 Characteristics of Bidders and Targets in Takeovers

Here, we discuss evidence on the characteristics of bidder and target firms in takeovers.

Q Ratios and Takeover Gains

Perhaps the best circumstance that would lead to gains for the shareholders of both the bidder and the target in a takeover is when a well-managed firm takes over a poorly managed firm. Tobin's Q ratio is a good measure of the market's assessment of management's ability to create valuable investment opportunities, and therefore a measure of management effectiveness. Therefore, we should see the greatest gains in those takeovers in which the bidder has a high Q ratio (is well managed) and the target has a low Q ratio (is poorly managed). Indeed, Lang, Stulz, and Walking (1989) found that abnormal returns in tender offer announcements are related to the Tobin's Q ratios of both bidders and targets. Shareholders of high Q bidders gain more than the shareholders of low Q bidders, and the shareholders of low Q targets gain more than the shareholders of high Q targets (see also Servaes 1991).

The Target's Free Cash Flow

Jensen's (1986a) *Free Cash Flow Hypothesis* posits that managers tend to overinvest, allocating free cash flow to unprofitable investments rather than paying dividends. If this is a serious problem, we would expect to see many overinvesting firms among takeover targets. However, several studies of completed takeovers have failed to find evidence of overinvestment among targets.[5] Hendershott (1996) provided a possible explanation for these results that is consistent with the Free Cash Flow Hypothesis. He found that many firms use *leveraged restructurings* (which we discuss in Chapter 17) to successfully fend off a takeover attempt. This evidence explains not only why overinvesting firms are not observed among firms that are the targets in *successful* takeovers, but also suggests that the takeover market plays a disciplinary role even in unsuccessful takeover attempts, forcing firms to take disciplinary actions on their own.

16.5.2   Takeover Bids and Strategy

Several studies have focused on the bidder's *strategy* in a takeover, including the bidding process, the accumulation of target shares, and the form of compensation. Below we review several of these studies.

Pre-Tender Offer Share Acquisitions (Toeholds)

The objective for a bidder in a takeover attempt is to minimize the cost of acquiring the target. One strategy is to begin purchasing shares of the target prior to a formal, public tender offer. However, under the Williams Act, the potential bidder is required to make a Schedule 13-D filing with the Securities and Exchange Commission (SEC), disclosing their holdings within 10 days after their ownership reaches 5 percent of the target firm's outstanding shares. With the filing, *the cat is out of the bag*, so a tender offer generally soon follows.

Nevertheless, the bidder generally should take advantage of its temporary anonymity to purchase shares. The bidder generally would be better off acquiring some of the target's shares at a lower price, because doing so reduces the overall cost of the acquisition. Moreover, by gaining such a *toehold*, the bidder may be in a stronger negotiating position in case target firm management decides to resist.

Madden (1981), Holderness and Sheehan (1985), Mikkelson and Ruback (1985), and Choi (1991) all conducted event studies of the effect of an announcement of a toehold filing on the target firm's stock price. All of these studies documented significant positive abnormal returns—about 2 percent on average. The price history of the target firm's stock leading to the filing announcement date is characterized by substantial abnormal losses until about two months before the filing announcement, followed by substantial abnormal gains in the two months immediately preceding the announcement.

The Free Rider Problem

Grossman and Hart (1980b) discuss an important limitation of the tender offer mechanism called the *free rider problem*. The term refers to a situation in which rational behavior by each individual shareholder results in shareholders as a group being worse off. If individual target shareholders (correctly) foresee that the value of their shares will be worth more *after* the takeover than they will receive in the tender offer, they will choose not to tender their shares. If all shareholders choose not to tender, the takeover attempt will fail even when it would have resulted in gains to target shareholders as a group. The authors' proposed solution is to allow the bidder to *dilute* the value of the shares of those who do not tender. The ex ante *threat* of such dilution will induce target shareholders to tender their shares.

---

[5]See Morck, Shleifer, and Vishny (1988a), Bhagat, Shleifer, and Vishny (1990), and Servaes (1994).

Shleifer and Vishny (1986) also address the free rider problem for tender offers in a theoretical model. They consider a setting in which the bidder knows the post-takeover value of the target but the target knows only the *distribution* of possible values. In equilibrium, tender offers succeed and the amount bid for a given firm is the same across bidders. The bid must be equal to the expected post-takeover value of the target (see also Bebchuk 1989).

The Effects of Asymmetric Information on Bidding Strategy and Medium of Exchange
Franks, Harris, and Mayer (1987) found that announcement-period abnormal returns on bidding-firm stocks are higher when the bidder makes a cash offer rather than a stock offer. Brown and Ryngaert (1991) developed a theoretical model of the optimal method of payment in a takeover that incorporates both taxes and asymmetric information. The model serves to explain the Franks, Harris, and Mayer's findings: "In our model, low valuation bidders choose an offer including at least 50 percent stock and high valuation bidders make cash offers. High valuation bidders offer cash to avoid issuing undervalued stock, and low valuation bidders offer stock to avoid the capital gains tax penalty" (p. 666) (see also Eckbo, Giammarino, and Heinkel 1990).

16.5.3 Target Management Resistance and Its Effects

At the center of a takeover battle is the target firm's management. Target management's resistance to the bidder's overtures (or expected resistance to a potential overture) is the key determinant of whether the marriage of bidder and target will be consummated via a friendly acquisition or a hostile takeover, or indeed whether it will be consummated at all.

According to the empirical analysis of Agrawal and Walking (1994), target managers have a good deal to fear from a takeover attempt, and good reason to resist it. They examined the impact of a takeover bid on the careers and compensation of the CEOs of target firms: "We find that acquisition attempts occur more frequently in industries where chief executive officers (CEO) have positive abnormal compensation. Target CEOs are more likely to be replaced when a bid succeeds, than when it fails. CEOs of target firms who lose their jobs generally fail to find another senior executive position in any public corporation within three years after the bid. Consistent with Fama's (1980) notion of 'ex post settling up,' postbid compensation changes of managers retained after an acquisition attempt are negatively related to . . . their prebid abnormal compensation . . . These findings are consistent with the hypothesis that a takeover bid generates additional information that is used by labor markets to discipline managers" (p. 985).

Facing target management resistance, a bidder may be forced to increase its bid for the firm. Thus, target management resistance can be in the target shareholders' interest. Kummer and Hoffmeister (1978) examined separate samples of tender offers that were opposed and unopposed by target management. For the sample of *successful* unopposed tender offers, target-firm shareholders realized average abnormal returns of 16.45 percent, versus 19.80 percent for *successful* opposed tender offers. However, for 15 of the 21 targets in which target management provided opposition, the tender offer failed, and the target shareholders suffered abnormal returns of –11.7 percent, on average.

In their empirical analysis of tender offers, Jennings and Mazzeo (1993) found that (a) a high bid premium tends to lower the likelihood of management resistance, and (b) target management resistance is associated with both an increase in the likelihood of a competing offer arising and a larger increase in target shareholder wealth. As an alternative to either bidding higher or terminating the tender offer process, bidders sometimes offer target management compensation to end its resistance—a so-called *golden parachute* (see Berkovitch and Khanna 1991).

On the other hand, target management may offer to repurchase the bidder's shares at a large premium if the bidder promises to *cease and desist*. The premium payoff is called *greenmail*, and the agreement to cease and desist is called a *standstill agreement* (see Dann and DeAngelo 1983; Eckbo 1990).

A takeover threat may have either positive or negative effects on compensation paid to the target firm's management. Agrawal and Knoeber (1998) identify two opposing effects: a *competition effect* and *a risk effect*. The competition effect refers to the positive association between the probability of a takeover and general competition for a manager's job, which induces a negative correlation between the probability of a takeover and management's compensation. The risk effect refers to the fact that the security of management's job is negatively related to the probability of a takeover, which induces a positive relationship between the probability of takeover and management compensation.

They attempted to separate these opposing effects using a measure of the ex ante probability of a takeover: "Using a sample of about 450 large firms, we find that an increase in the threat of takeover from the first to the third quartile reduces a typical CEO's salary and bonus by $22,800–211,600 due to the competition effect, but raises salary and bonus by $41–255,300 due to the risk effect. The net effect is an increase of $18,700–43,700" (p. 219).

Stock Repurchases as a Takeover Defense

Researchers have recognized an alternative motive for some firms to conduct share repurchases (see Chapter 14): as a defense against a hostile takeover. In a hostile takeover attempt, a well-capitalized bidder generally begins to purchase a substantial portion of the target's shares in the open market. The target's management attempts to counter the bidder's efforts by repurchasing shares. In resisting a takeover, the target firm's management may be driven by either of two motives. *First*, based on their private information, management agrees that the shares are underpriced, but (of course) disagrees that this is due to poor management. Here, management is signaling its private valuation of the firm's shares via repurchases. *Second*, management may have a purely self-serving motive to thwart the bidder's efforts—they recognize that if the bidder succeeds, they will be ousted.

As a practical matter, only a fraction of the typical public firm's total outstanding shares are effectively *in play* in the secondary market at any time, in part because many investors adhere to a buy-and-hold strategy in terms of their equity investments. Therefore, the tug-of-war between the bidder and the firm's management is likely to be waged over a fraction of the firm's outstanding shares. Moreover, as more and more shares are either purchased by the bidder or repurchased by the firm, fewer and fewer floating shares remain available for which either party can vie; at this point the target's stock price may rise substantially. Therefore, for both parties quick action is essential.

The bidder's goal is to purchase a sufficient number of shares before the price rises too much and before the target's management succeeds in repurchasing them. The goal of target management, in opposition, is to repurchase as many shares as possible in a short period of time. For this reason, target management is likely to favor a Dutch auction self-tender offer over either a fixed-price self-tender offer or an open-market repurchase program (see Chapter 14). Management favors the Dutch auction over a fixed-price self-tender because in the former shareholders can choose the price at which they are willing to sell, whereas if management fixes a price via a fixed-price self-tender offer, the bidder may be able to beat that price in the open market.[6]

16.5.4   Antitakeover Legislation and the Decline of Takeovers

We provided evidence in Chapter 1 that takeovers peaked in the late 1980s and there-after declined precipitously. This result is well known. However, it is less clear *why* takeovers declined, and especially why they have not reemerged along with the surge in M&A activity in the 1990s.

Antitakeover Devices and Legislation

Many firms adopted one or more contract devices in the 1980s that were explicitly designed to thwart takeover attempts. These devices are called *poison pills* or *shark repellents*. One type of poison pill is a shareholder rights plan that can be issued as dividends at management's discretion. Another is a put provision in one of the firm's debt contracts that makes the debt due and payable immediately upon the completion of a takeover, which forces the bidder to raise additional cash to pay off the debt (see Linn and McConnell 1983; DeAngelo and Rice 1983; Agrawal and Mandelker 1990; Borokhovich, Brunarski, and Parrino 1997; and Garvey and Hanka 1999).

State legislation designed to thwart takeovers has also been enacted, including (a) *control share laws* and (b) *business combination laws*. Control share laws restrict the voting power of a controlling shareholder, while business combination laws can delay the consummation of business combinations for years (see Szewczyk and Tsetsekos 1992).

Jensen (1993) discusses the unfortunate demise of the takeover as an external corporate control mechanism:

> The era of the control market came to an end, however, in late 1989 and 1990. Intense controversy and opposition from corporate managers, assisted by charges of fraud, the increase in default and bankruptcy rates, and insider trading prosecutions, caused the shutdown of the control market through court decisions, state antitakeover amendments, and regulatory restrictions on the availability of financing . . . In 1991, the total value of transactions fell to $96 billion from $340 billion in 1988. LBOs and management buyouts fell to slightly over $1 billion in 1991 from $80 billion in 1988. The demise of the control market as an effective influence on American corporations has not ended the restructuring, but it has meant that organizations have typically postponed addressing the problems they face until forced to by financial difficulties generated by the product markets. Unfortunately the delay means that some of these organizations will not survive—or will survive as more shadows of their former selves. (p 852)

---

[6]For more information about share repurchases as a takeover defense, see Bagnoli, Gordon, and Lipman (1989), Denis (1990), Bagwell (1991), Sinha (1991), and Persons (1994).

Did Antitakeover Measures Really Kill the Takeover Market?

Was the demise of the takeover market brought about by the proliferation of the contract devices and state statutes discussed above? Comment and Schwert (1997) challenged this view. They examined takeovers over the years 1975 to 1991, which straddles the development of most antitakeover measures. They concluded that these measures "have not systematically deterred takeovers and are unlikely to have caused the demise of the 1980s market for corporate control . . . " (p. 3). However, they did find that these measures increased takeover premiums for target-firm shareholders. It is also possible, though unlikely, that in recent years fewer firms have been so poorly managed that they tempt takeover.

16.6   BUYOUTS

Transactions that affect the ownership and control of a firm take many forms, including not only M&A and takeovers, which we have discussed, but also several types of *buyouts*. A buyout differs from an acquisition or takeover in that a group of individuals, rather than a firm, purchases the target. If the group includes the target firm's management, the transaction is sometimes called a *management buyout*, or *MBO*. If the group includes the target firm's employees in general, the transaction is sometimes called an *employee buyout*, or *EBO*. Buyouts also share the feature that they convert a publicly traded firm to private ownership, and as such they are sometimes called *going private transactions*. If a buyout is facilitated in part by the issuance of debt claims against the focal firm's assets, the transaction is called a *leveraged buyout*, or *LBO*. Finally, in many cases a firm that has gone private via an LBO subsequently reemerges as a publicly traded firm (via another IPO). This transaction is called a Reverse *LBO*.

In this section, we summarize the analyses of several research articles on buyouts. A note of caution is in order: Across authors, the alternative nomenclature noted above is used interchangeably, even though the authors are often referring to very similar transactions.

16.6.1   LBOs

In this subsection, we summarize evidence from several empirical studies of leveraged buyouts.

The Characteristics of LBO Firms

Lehn and Poulsen (1989) tested the Free Cash Flow Hypothesis by examining the source of stockholder gains in a sample of 263 going private transactions over the years 1980 to 1987 against a matching set of firms that did not go private over the same period. They found a significant positive relationship between the amount of a firm's undistributed cash flow and the firm's decision to go private. They also found that the premiums paid to stockholders were significantly related to the size of the undistributed cash flow. Their evidence is consistent with the Free Cash Flow Hypothesis. Opler and Titman (1993) also used the matching-firm technique to examine the characteristics of LBOs. Their results indicate that firms that undertake a LBO generally have "a combination of unfavorable investment opportunities (low Tobin's q) and relatively high cash flow" (p. 1985).

Hostilities Rise Again

UNSOLICITED OFFERS ARE ON THE RISE IN A MARKET RIPE FOR CONSOLIDATION

What's the matter with a little hostility? Nothing at all, if you ask Dimitri J. Boylan, chief executive of online employment service HotJobs.com (HOTJ). Six months after he set plans to merge with TMP Worldwide Inc. (TMPW), parent of rival Monster.com, media giant Yahoo! Inc. (YHOO) on December 12 barged in with an unsolicited offer to buy HotJobs for $436 million in cash and stock. With $81 million more on the table than TMP was willing to pay by late December and stronger growth prospects, it took less than three weeks for Boylan to say yes to Yahoo's hostile bid. "[I was] surprised to get the phone call, but not surprised by the strategy," says Boylan.

HotJobs isn't the only company on the receiving end of such calls these days. As companies ranging from cable-television provider AT&T Broadband to cruise liner P&O Princess Cruises (POC) have discovered, hostile takeovers are back with a vengeance. The combination of a weakened economy, downtrodden stock prices, and new accounting practices sent hostile bids soaring in 2001, with more on the way. "We've clearly seen an uptick," says David M. Baum, co-head of mergers and acquisitions in North America at Goldman, Sachs & Co. "And we're likely to see unsolicited activity accelerate."

Indeed, from just $40 billion in 2000, the value of announced hostile deals more than doubled last year, to $94 billion. That's well above the $81 billion peak hit in the 1988 heyday of the hostile deal, and close to the record set in 1999 as the stock market topped out. That year, the combination of lofty share prices and one outsized deal by Pfizer Inc. (PFE)—which paid $90 billion for Warner-Lambert Co.—led to a record $103 billion in hostile deals.

Not surprisingly, all that predatory deal-making is also spurring more companies to take defensive maneuvers: The adoption of shareholder-rights plans known as poison pills is also back up. And that's not the only way the hostile takeover game has changed since it first burst on the scene in the 1980s. Then, corporate raiders like Carl C. Icahn and Henry R. Kravis scoured the landscape for companies with undervalued assets to restructure and sell. Now, the predators are more likely to be blue-chip industry leaders like Comcast (CMCSA), which is buying AT&T Broadband, and Weyerhaeuser (WY), which is trying to combine with Willamette Industries (WLL) . . .

Why the rise in hostile deals now? The recession is the driving force behind the trend. The weak economy, scarce profits, and rampant overcapacity in many sectors have pushed industry leaders to try to strengthen their positions by forcing consolidation. And for those with the financial muscle, there's little question plenty of assets and businesses can now be gotten on the cheap. With the Standard & Poor's 500-stock index down 13 percent in 2001 alone, shares of weaker companies are at bargain-basement prices.

For mainstream companies, the repercussions of failing at a hostile bid also have lessened. Because failing to pull off a deal used to be considered a major embarrassment on Wall Street, acquirers felt compelled to engage in bidding wars no matter what the cost—so they thought long and hard before moving ahead. Now, even if a takeover fails, investors often reward a predator. "We're seeing more companies make proposals on transactions that are prepared to walk away if the deal does not create value for their shareholders," says Donald Meltzer, head of global M&A at Credit Suisse First Boston.

Regulatory changes are also giving companies greater incentive to fire away. Bankers expect the antitrust environment under President Bush's Administration to be easier, so CEOs are less worried about making aggressive offers to gobble up smaller rivals. "Coming out of the recession, people are less concerned about these issues than getting things rolling again," says James R. Elliott III, head of North American M&A at J. P. Morgan Chase & Co.

Even accounting rules are helping to spur hostile deals. In the past, predators shied away from all deals—hostile and friendly alike—where their own earnings would have been diluted because of the need to amortize goodwill. That's the difference between the amount an acquirer pays for a company and what its assets are on its own balance sheet. But in July, the Financial Accounting Standards Board decided to end the practice of amortizing goodwill. "One of the great defenses against hostile offers has been eliminated," says tax and accounting analyst Robert Willens at Lehman Brothers Inc. The change has been particularly important in industries built on human capital, such as biotech, technology, and financial services, because the difference between companies' asset values and their stock valuations have typically been large.

That's one key reason hostile deals are soaring in the tech sector. Indeed, 62 percent of the hostile bids in 2001 involved failing dot-coms, cash-strapped telecom players, and other tech companies, up from 24 percent of hostile deals just a year earlier. But there's another, more prosaic explanation as well: In the past, acquirers generally avoided hostile deals in tech, since many feared a target's main assets—its engineers, developers, and other valuable employees—would flee. But with the economy in a recession and unemployment rising, unhappy employees have fewer places to move to. "[Tech] takeover targets can't take as much comfort as they have in the past," says Doug W. McNitt, general counsel at webMethods Inc., a Fairfax (Va.) company that specializes in linking computer systems.

That isn't to say companies have been shorn of all defenses. The rise in hostile activity is also spurring another round of poison pills designed to make life tougher for potential acquirers. In 2001, 283 companies adopted poison pills, 74 more than in 2000. And given the plunge in stock valuations they've suffered, it's hardly surprising that tech companies and dot-coms such as BEA Systems Inc. (BEAS) and E*Trade Group Inc. (EGRP) accounted for 31 percent of the poison pills enacted in 2001, up from 24 percent last year. "Many CEOs are actively reviewing their companies' defensive profiles," says Michael J. Boublik, head of East Coast technology M&A at Morgan Stanley Dean Witter & Co.

Some managements are going so far as to hire investment bankers just in case they get hit with a hostile bid. "Over the last 12 months, we have more than doubled our defense retainer business," says CSFB's Meltzer. For now, however, the return of poison pills has left investors relatively sanguine.

The reason? Unlike in the '80s, when such measures were often used to protect entrenched management, today's pills are more geared to prompting unwanted bidders to increase their offers. Bankers now point to a wealth of evidence that they ultimately pay off for investors. J. P. Morgan Securities' research shows that since 1997, U.S. companies worth more than $1 billion with pills in place received a median premium of 35.9 percent, versus 31.9 percent for companies without. "Your typical investor can point to more situations where boards used pills to get higher bids than to boards that used pills to forestall [deals] altogether," says Patrick McGurn, vice-president and director of corporate programs at Institutional Shareholder Services. Considering many of the other earmarks of these hardscrabble times, it's at least a trend that investors can bank on.

Halpern, Kieschnick, and Rotenberg (1999) developed and tested an agency-based hypothesis that LBO firms should fall into two groups, distinguished by their management's motive for pursuing the LBO: "One group consists of firms in which managers own an insignificant fraction of their firm's stock and are vulnerable to a hostile takeover. The other group consists of firms in which managers own a significant fraction of their firm's stock and so face little risk of hostile takeover . . . [but] management faces other problems . . . they do hold large, undiversified portfolios and so have an incentive to take cash out of their firm by taking it private through an LBO. This action further concentrates the residual claims on the post-LBO firm into their hands" (p. 281).

The authors examined 126 LBOs completed over the years 1981 to 1986. Their analysis indicates that LBO firms indeed sort into these two groups. Among many corroborating results, they found "high prior managerial equity LBOs are typically led by management in a voluntary transaction, while low prior managerial equity LBOs are typically led by third parties in the context of a takeover battle" (p. 306).

The Role of the Buyout Specialist

We noted earlier that the purchasers in a buyout often obtain financial and strategic assistance from a *buyout specialist*. Opler (1993) explained the role of a buyout specialist as a *sponsor*:

> These specialists usually finance transactions with equity contributed by a number of investors and debt borrowed from several sources. In essence, many LBO sponsors act as intermediaries between investors and management. There are several ways in which LBO specialists may reduce the costs of financial distress. First, in a financially distressed situation these investor intermediaries have strong incentives to act in the interests of both equity-holders and debtholders . . . Second, LBO specialists work directly on behalf of equityholders and indirectly on behalf of debtholders, given that they negotiate the terms of debt contracts at the beginning of LBOs. As the representative of all classes of liability-holders, they have incentives to encourage management of the LBO target in a way that maximizes the wealth of all parties. Third, LBO sponsors have reputational reasons to protect creditor interests which should minimize agency-related indirect financial distress costs involving asset substitution and underinvestment . . . (pp. 80–81).

Cotter and Peck (2001) examined LBOs completed during 1984 to 1989, comparing various financial aspects of LBOs that involved, versus did not involve, a buyout specialist. Their evidence supports the hypothesis that buyout specialists are *active equity investors*: "We find that when buyout specialists control the majority of the post-LBO equity, the LBO transaction is likely to be financed with less short-term and/or senior debt and less likely to experience financial distress. We also find that buyout specialists have greater board representation on smaller boards, suggesting that they actively monitor managers, and that for these transactions, using debt with tighter terms does not significantly increase the firm's performance. In contrast, in all other transactions using such debt does significantly increase the firm's performance. These findings suggest that active monitoring by a buyout specialist substitutes for tighter debt terms in monitoring and motivating managers of LBOs" (p. 101).

Selling Shareholders Gain in a Buyout

In a buyout, the target's shareholders generally receive a substantial premium above the prebuyout market price of their shares. DeAngelo, DeAngelo, and Rice (1984) and Lehn and Poulsen (1988a) found average abnormal gains to shareholders of 22.3 percent and 13.9 percent, respectively.

The Effects of an LBO on Prebuyout Bondholders' Wealth

A possible consequence of an LBO is expropriation of pre-LBO bondholders' wealth. Two papers investigated this issue, and obtained similar results. Asquith and Wizman (1990) found that "prebuyout bondholders, on average, suffer statistically significant wealth losses in leveraged buyouts. Bonds with strong covenant protection, however, gain value, while those with no protection lose value. The disposition of bonds after buyouts, e.g., remained outstanding, called, tendered, defeased, is also strongly linked to type of covenant protection. We also document that covenant use declines for bonds issued after 1980. Finally, the losses to bondholders are small compared with the gains accruing to shareholders" (p. 195). Warga and Welch (1993) found that "announcements of successful leveraged buyouts (LBOs) during January 1985 to April 1989 caused a significantly negative return on outstanding publicly traded nonconvertible bonds. Yet the average risk-adjusted debt holder losses are less than 7 percent of the average risk-adjusted equity holder gains. Bond losses are related to the pre-LBO rating, but only weakly to equity holder gains" (p. 959).

16.6.2   MBOs

Peck (1996) studied the role of *professional investors* in MBO transactions: "In a sample of 111 MBO offers between 1984 and 1987, almost 30 percent attract new blockholders. These blockholders are primarily professional investors who act to facilitate a takeover by a higher bidder, thus increasing returns to both themselves and other public shareholders. In contrast, I find little evidence that pre-existing blockholders, particularly institutional holders, affect either the offer outcome or actively participate in the buyout contest once it begins. The overall pattern of results suggests that professional investors, particularly equity-holding companies, are 'control specialists' who provide valuable services as brokers in the market for corporate control" (p. 267).

16.6.3   EBOs

Chaplinsky, Niehaus, and Van de Gucht (1998) examined a sample of EBOs to further our understanding of these transactions: "This paper investigates the motivations for and consequences of including a broad group of employees in leveraged buyouts by comparing employee buyouts (EBOs) to transactions where only top level managers participate, or management buyouts (MBOs). We examine the implications of including employees in a buyout from a labor contracting, financing, and management control point of view. A major finding is that employee participation helps to finance the buyout. The EBO allows firms to gain access to pension assets by converting employees' defined benefit pension capital into equity claims, thus freeing the excess assets in the pension plan to help fund the buyout. Also, employee participation substitutes equity claims for cash labor compensation costs and therefore allows the firm to borrow more than otherwise would be possible. There is also evidence consistent with managers including employees to maintain or enhance incumbent management's control" (p. 283).

Return of the LBO

IT MAY NOT BE THE GLORY YEARS, BUT BUYOUT SHOPS ARE BACK, RAISING BILLIONS—AND HEADING INTO UNCHARTED WATERS

A quick glance inside Kohlberg Kravis Roberts & Co.'s New York City headquarters, with its sweeping, panoramic views of Central Park, shows how good the world of leveraged buyouts has been to KKR. And this year, the good times are rolling again. With contributions such as $1 billion from the State of Oregon's pension fund, KKR is well on its way to gathering the capital needed for its newest $6 billion fund, the largest LBO fund ever.

It's the same story at other LBO outfits. The industry is emerging from the shadows into which it was cast in recent years by the sexier and more profitable venture-capital business. LBO funds are set to raise a record $80 billion this year, versus $50 billion in 1999, as pension funds, insurers, university foundations, and superwealthy individuals fall over themselves to pour cash into them in an attempt to beat lackluster stock market returns.

Behind the scenes, however, the LBO industry is in turmoil. The glory days of 1989, chronicled in the movie *Barbarians at the Gate*, when KKR bought food conglomerate RJR Nabisco Inc. for $31 billion, are long gone. Alongside that deal, still the largest LBO ever, today's affairs are modest, not to say puny, in scale: So far in 2000, only five LBOs over $1 billion have been completed, which means large funds looking for big LBO deals are stuck. "For the most part, the day of the large buyout shop is over," says Richard A. Friedman, co-head of merchant banking at Goldman, Sachs & Co.

As pressure to perform builds, many funds are starting to move into uncharted waters.

With the plain-vanilla business of leveraging and reselling Old Economy companies losing much of its appeal, LBO outfits are moving into venture-capital investments, doing buyouts of tech companies—and even taking small, noncontrolling stakes in listed companies. "They have morphed into large, private equity groups that are making investments people wouldn't have considered in the past," says Friedman.

To be sure, the traditional buyout isn't yet dead. Last September, for instance, David A. Stockman, the former White House budget director, announced that he was creating an LBO firm to invest in old industrial companies in the Midwest. To some, the revival of an old idea sounded downright hip: "It's a great shtick," said one of Stockman's competitors. And in one of the biggest deals in years, Donaldson, Lufkin & Jenrette Inc. on October 2 announced that it purchased the largest U.S. meat producer, IBP Inc. (IBP), for $3.7 billion. Just as in an old-fashioned LBO, two-thirds of the deal was financed with debt. IBP's stock had drifted downward from $25 earlier this year to the low teens and had not come close to reaching its all-time high of $33 in five years. "A lot of excellent Old Economy companies have seen their stock prices sink. Only recently have boards of directors begun to consider that it might be time to sell," says Thompson Dean, managing partner of DLJ merchant banking.

But such deals are still few and far between. And many people, including the funds' investors, are miffed at some of the trends, such as a push into venture-capital deals. "One thing I'm concerned about is having LBO funds doing what brought them to the dance, not having them chase the hot new topic," complains Howard J. Bicker, executive director of the Minnesota State Investment Board.

DEBT DEARTH

The hunt for new styles of LBO investing is no big surprise. Today, the major challenge facing the erstwhile Masters of the Universe is simply to find any deal at all. The plethora of industrial conglomerates ripe to buy, break up, and then resell that fed the LBO pipeline in the 1980s has long disappeared, except in Europe, which is why many U.S. firms are now setting up shop there . . . To make matters worse, midsize Old Economy companies in the U.S.—with rare exceptions such as DLJ's deal with IBP—are reluctant to sell to LBO players, mostly preferring to tough it out until stock prices rebound.

Although deals are becoming harder to find, ever more firms are chasing them. Where the likes of Henry R. Kravis of KKR and Theodore J. Forstmann of Forstmann Little & Co.—founders in the 1970s of two of the earliest LBO outfits—once had free rein, they now face 850 competitors. And even leverage, the hallmark of traditional LBOs, isn't what it used to be. For starters, debt, the magic ingredient that boosts returns, is hard to come by since the junk-bond market hit the wall in 1998. In the 1980s, debt accounted for as much as 95 percent of buyout prices. But because of the extra risk of bankruptcies, and low credit ratings, high debt loads over 75 percent are frowned upon by lenders. Having to use two to three times more equity in deals dilutes returns: LBO performances have drifted downward from an annualized return of 35 percent in 1989 to 20 percent in the first quarter of 2000. In the same period, venture-capital returns soared to over 50 percent from 5 percent.

Yet the fall in returns isn't driving investors away. That's because the top 25 percent of LBO funds still regularly beat the returns on the Standard & Poor's 500-stock index . . . Instead, the avalanche of new money is causing an iden-tity crisis in the business. "The changing landscape has left many firms wondering what they want to be when they grow up," says David Rubenstein, founding partner of Carlyle Group, an LBO outfit that manages over $11 billion of funds.

"SCANDALOUS"

Some of the answers they're coming up with are raising eyebrows. By far the most controversial trend is a move to PIPEs, or private investments in public equities. The technique involves taking minority positions in public companies by buying common or convertible preferred stocks. If that sounds just like what mutual funds do, it is—except that investors pay LBO funds a 1 percent management fee and 20 percent of the profits on every deal. "I think it is scandalous," said the head of one LBO firm that hasn't invested in any PIPEs. Brett Fisher, senior vice-president of GIC Special Investments, which manages money on behalf of the government of Singapore, says GIC can make similar investments without the high fees. "We invest in LBO funds to purchase private companies," he adds.

The leading exponent of PIPE investing is Hicks, Muse, Tate & Furst Inc. of Dallas. It invested over $1 billion in local telephone companies only to see the stocks plummet 75 percent or more in value. One of these companies, ICG Communications Inc. (ICGX), a voice and data service provider based in Englewood, Colorado, in which Hicks Muse invested $230 million, has seen its stock tank to 50 cents, from $29 at the time of the deal. Hicks Muse declined to comment.

The Dallas firm wasn't the only one to find its PIPE investments disconnected. Billions of dollars from LBO firms went into PIPEs . . . mostly in telecom. What was the attraction? Simply, telecom equities offered a handy place to park cash and—at the time—the tactic seemed to promise quick returns. The result is a big turn-off. "Most investors in LBO funds hate them because the concept has yet to be

(continued)

proven," says Lawrence M. Schloss, chairman of DLJ's merchant banking. "We shy away from them."

PIPE DREAMS?

All the same, some LBO pros shrug off the embarrassment, blaming the losses on poor timing rather than the structure of the deals or the concept itself. "Those deals were done at the top of the market," says Thomas H. Lee, president of Boston's Thomas H. Lee Co. "The criticism of PIPEs is a canard, a red herring." Lee is a stout defender of PIPEs because his LBO fund invested over $1 billion in them. Lee invested some $700 million in two such deals: Metris Cos. (MXT), a credit-card issuer, and Conseco Inc. (CNC), a financial-services company. Lee rates Metris, which has risen sixfold since the investment, as "one of the best deals we've ever done." Conseco, however, has fallen 57 percent since Lee's investment. In Metris, says Lee, the LBO fund obtained four board seats and in Conseco, one seat, and thus gained influence over strategy.

An unrepentant Lee forecasts that LBO firms will continue to make large investments in public companies in the future. That, of course, remains to be seen. For one thing, PIPE investments have lifted the veil a little on the secretive world of LBO funds. Since their portfolio companies are private, even those performing poorly are normally shielded from the glare of scrutiny by the press. But PIPEs allow investors to track how some of the funds' investments are performing, simply by following the stock prices. "It's like they're airing their dirty laundry day to day," says Marc E. Sacks, executive director of Brinson Partners Inc., which invests in LBOs.

The losses in telecom PIPEs raise an awkward question: As LBO managers start to embrace the New Economy, are they out of their depth? Known for their financial prowess in analyzing cash flows, can they really evolve into tech specialists? The issue is becoming pressing as the trend amplifies. KKR, for instance, has formed a company called Accel-

KKR to build Internet businesses in partnership with large companies like McDonald's Corp. (MCD). The two companies have recently set up a joint venture called eMac Digital to offer a wide array of business services, such as back-office support systems, through the Internet to McDonald's 25,000 franchisees. Meanwhile, T. H. Lee has just raised $1.1 billion for an Internet fund, and Texas Pacific Group (TPL), based in Fort Worth, has a staff of nine specialists for technology turnarounds.

If TPG's experience is any guide, leveraged tech buyouts are here to stay because they have the potential for stratospheric returns. TPG pioneered such deals in 1996 when it bought a loss-making modem maker called AT&T Paradyne Corp. from Lucent Technologies (LU), investing $51 million in equity and $123 million in debt. It was the perfect candidate for a buyout, a small division of a large parent. There were no other buyers, because of the danger of denting their own earnings growth, says David Bonderman, founding partner of TPG. "Large technology companies, which were likely candidates to acquire a company like Paradyne, could hardly afford to take the risk."

But the deal paid off handsomely for TPG, which promptly divided the new company, Paradyne Networks Inc. (PDYN), into three businesses: a leasing unit with a steady but declining cash flow, a broadband technology division, and a high-speed Internet-access division. The two high-tech units, GlobeSpan (GSPN) and Paradyne, went public last year, producing over $1 billion in profits for TPG, which still holds stock in the companies worth over $2 billion. So far, TPG has made back 58 times its original investment. "The market tells you what makes sense. As technology becomes a greater piece of society, it's hard not to do some technologically oriented deals," Bonderman says.

A SPLASH

With returns like that, it was only a matter of time before others began jumping on the tech bandwagon. First, in January, 1999, came Silver

Lake Partners, whose founders include David Roux, James Davidson, and Glenn Hutchins. Silver Lake was followed by Francisco Partners, formed by ex-TPG partner David Stanton, and Sanford R. Robertson, the founder of Robertson Stephens Inc.

Silver Lake made a splash last April with the largest leveraged tech purchase to date: a $2 billion deal to buy Seagate Technology Inc.'s (SEG) disk-drive business. The deal, which is not yet completed, was done in conjunction with Texas Pacific Group. Silver Lake has since made investments in smaller companies: $300 million in research outfit Gartner Group (IT), $200 million in telecom-equipment company Cabletron Systems (CS), and an undisclosed amount in SubmitOrder.com, an e-commerce logistics supplier. But other than Seagate, none of these deals was strictly a tech buyout like Paradyne—in fact, two were PIPEs, which Hutchins defends as being right for the fund. "We are primarily a tech fund, rather than an LBO fund," he says. "We will generate returns in the future not just from leverage but from the operating success of our portfolio companies, regardless of the particular security we buy."

In any event, Hutchins is convinced that specialization, such as Silver Lake's in tech, is the key for LBO firms that want to reproduce the high returns of the past. "We're a one-trick pony, but its a great trick," he says.

If Silver Lake is a one-trick pony, then Carlyle, based in Washington, could be called the cavalry. Considered the Fidelity Investments of the private equity world, its founders, David Rubenstein, William Conway Jr., and Daniel D'Aniello, took their vision in the opposite direction. Not only did Carlyle begin offering an assortment of funds specializing in a slew of private equity products like buyout, high-yield, energy, and venture funds, but it was the first to offer private-equity funds investing in specific regions of Europe and Asia. "We'd like to be the model of the future," says Rubenstein.

Unlike most of its competitors who have just begun setting up abroad, Carlyle has 20 offices around the world. "We're not so smart that we think we can sit in offices on Park Avenue and be Masters of the Universe," says Rubenstein. "It doesn't work that way."

Rubenstein thinks that it's only a matter of time before individual investors are allowed to invest in private equity through their 401(k) retirement plans. That's one reason why Carlyle has created a whole array of investment choices. The risk is that sector funds can be held hostage to the changing fortunes of different industries or countries. While it's too early to see returns internationally so far, Carlyle's returns after fees have been 30 percent over 13 years, putting it squarely in the top quartile of LBO funds.

The race is on to be the biggest, to get the highest returns, to go global. "What you have here is a watershed in which, rather than being a boutique business as it has been for the last 20 years, the LBO industry is now commanding resources at institutional levels," says Charles Frolen, managing director of private equity for General Motors Corp. (GM).

As funds race to differentiate themselves, it appears a change in the pecking order is inevitable. T. H. Lee completed raising a $5.5 billion buyout fund this year, after raising a billion-dollar venture fund this year. That puts Lee in second place for new assets under management, a spot long held by Forstmann Little. Lee is considered to have the best annualized returns in the business at over 40 percent, KKR among the lowest of the top-tier funds at about 20 percent. Behind Lee, others are scrambling to become bigger too, also chipping away at KKR's lead: "Five years ago, KKR was 10 times bigger than the rest of us," said one LBO fund general partner. "But there's no longer a gargantuan lead."

Maybe so. But, if the new trends sprouting up in the business take firm root, the old-style deals will account for a dwindling share of the market. And investors will continue to face more complicated tasks. "It used to be you could say, 'Here's a group that knows how to structure a buyout transaction.' Now you have

(continued)

to ask, 'Do they have the skills to do other things beside a buyout? Do they have technology know-how? Do they have succession plans in place? Are they spread too thin?'" says Mario L. Giannini, president of Philadelphia's Hamilton Lane Advisors Inc.,

which runs a private equity fund of funds and an advisory business.

But who said life was supposed to be easy? If LBO funds can jack up their rates of return to near those of the good old days, a little brain work might have a big payoff.

Source: "Return of the LBO," D. Sparks, *Businessweek Online*, Oct. 16, 2000. Copyright © 2000–2001 The McGraw-Hill Companies Inc. Reprinted by permission.

16.6.4   Postbuyout Performance

Several papers have examined the postbuyout performance and ownership status of firms that have undergone an LBO. The motive for most LBOs is to improve the firm's operating performance, so an *ex post audit* provides important evidence on the efficacy of the transactions. We quote authors' summaries of four such studies in the following paragraphs.

Lichtenberg and Siegel (1990): "We investigate the effects of leveraged buyouts on total factor productivity (TFP) and related variables using a longitudinal database including over 12,000 manufacturing plants. LBOs (particularly MBOs) that occurred during 1983–1986 had a strong positive effect on TFP in the first three post-buyout years: plant productivity increased from 2.0 percent above industry mean in the three pre-buyout years to 8.3 percent above industry mean in the three post-buyout years. However, 1981 and 1982 buyouts had no significant productivity effect. The employment and compensation of white-collar workers decline following buyouts, but those of blue-collar workers are unchanged" (p. 165).

Kaplan (1989a): "This paper presents evidence on changes in operating results for a sample of 76 large management buyouts of public companies completed between 1980 and 1986. In the three years after the buyout, these companies experience increases in operating income (before depreciation), decreases in capital expenditures, and increases in net cash flow. Consistent with the operating changes, the mean and median increases in market value (adjusted for market returns) are 96 percent and 77 percent from two months before the buyout announcement to the post-buyout sale. The evidence suggests that operating changes are due to improved incentives rather than layoffs or managerial exploitation of shareholders through inside information" (p. 217).

Smith (1990): "I investigate changes in operating performance after 58 management buyouts of public companies completed during 1977–1986. Operating returns increase significantly from the year before to the year after buyouts as measured by operating cash flows (before interest and taxes) per employee and per dollar of operating assets. Subsequent changes in operating returns suggest that this increase is sustained. Adjustments in the management of working capital contribute to the increase in operating returns. The increase is not, however, the result of layoffs or reductions in expenditures for advertising, maintenance and repairs, research and development, or property, plant, and equipment" (p. 143).

Kaplan (1991): "This paper documents the organizational status over time of 183 large leveraged buyouts completed between 1979 and 1986. By August 1990, 62 percent of the LBOs are privately owned, 14 percent are independent public companies, and 24 percent are owned by other public companies. The percentage of LBOs returning to public ownership increases over time, with LBOs remaining private for a median time of 6.82 years. The majority of LBOs, therefore, are neither short-lived nor permanent. The moderate fraction of LBO assets owned by other companies implies that asset sales play a role, but are not the primary motivating force in LBO transactions" (p. 287).

16.6.5 Reverse LBOs

Finally, we briefly discuss *reverse leveraged buyouts*. This transaction is essentially a reprise of the firm's initial public offering (IPO), because the firm's equity is again offered to the public. Below we provide authors' summaries of three empirical papers on this topic.

Muscarella and Vetsuypens (1990): "This paper is a report on 72 firms which went public since 1983 but previously underwent a full or divisional LBO. Accounting measures of performance reveal significant improvements in profitability which resulted mainly from these firms' ability to reduce costs. Firms experience dramatic increases in leverage at the LBO, but the leverage ratios are gradually reduced. The evidence is consistent with the hypothesis that the change in the governance structure of these firms towards more concentrated residual claims created a new organizational structure which is more efficient than its predecessor" (p. 1389).

Mian and Rosenfeld (1993): "This paper examines the three-year investment performance of these [reverse buyout] firms after going public, and further explores the high incidence of takeover activity that occurs within this group of firms . . . Over the three-year period beginning one day after the firm goes public . . . 85 reverse LBOs outperform a portfolio of comparable firms matched by industry and firm size . . . We have also attempted to determine what factors were responsible for the positive abnormal performance . . . we find that nearly 80 percent of the acquired firms had an active investor involved in the going-private transaction . . . This result is consistent with [the] contention that a primary motivation for these firms going public is to provide active investors with an opportunity to liquidate their equity stake via a third-party takeover" (pp. 46–47).

Holthausen, and Larcker (1996): "We examine the accounting and market performance of reverse leveraged buyouts (i.e., firms making their first public offering after previously completing a leveraged buyout). On average, the accounting performance of these firms is significantly better than their industries at the time of the initial public offering (IPO) and for at least the following four years, though there is some evidence of a decline in performance. Cross-sectional variation in accounting performance subsequent to the IPO is related to changes in the equity ownership of both operating management and other insiders, and is unrelated to changes in leverage. Finally, there is no evidence of abnormal common stock performance after the reverse leveraged buyout" (pp. 293).

16.7 Summary of Learning Objectives

We studied the four transactions in which the ownership of an entire firm changes: merger, acquisition, takeover, and buyout. For each transaction, we discussed (a) the structure of the transaction itself and the participants, (b) motives, and (c) financial effects, including announcement-period abnormal returns, pre-transaction and post-transaction accounting, and stock-return performance.

In the typical acquisition, a bidder offers cash or shares in exchange for the target firm's shares. Motives for merger include (a) operating synergy, (b) financial synergy, (c) bankruptcy avoidance for the target, (d) matching the financial slack of one firm with the investment opportunities of another firm, (e) hubris, and (f) managerial self-interest in terms of risk reduction and entrenchment. In a typical acquisition announcement, bidding-firm shareholders' gains are negligible, while target-firm shareholders realize substantial gains.

In a hostile takeover, a bidder seeks to take control of a target firm and oust the target's incumbent management. Motives for the bidder include (a) failure of the target firm's management, (b) busting up an inefficient diversified firm, (c) hubris, and (d) industry shocks. Bidders generally begin by establishing a toehold—that is, purchasing a portion of the target's shares in the open market. Thereafter, the bidder generally makes a tender offer for the firm's shares. The bidder may face a *free rider problem* with the target's shareholders, who withhold their shares on the expectation of a better offer later. In addition, target-firm management may resist the takeover attempt by repurchasing shares, thereby keeping them from the bidder. Many firms have embedded antitakeover devices in either their charters or in their debt contracts, and many states have passed antitakeover legislation.

A buyout is conducted by individuals, often the target firm's management, who wish to purchase all of the shares of a public firm and revert to private ownership. Among the motives for a buyout is management's belief that they could make the firm more profitable, but they lack the incentive unless their ownership share is increased. Another motive for buyout is to avoid a hostile takeover. The individuals pursuing the buyout often obtain financial and strategic assistance from a buyout specialist, who also monitors management after the buyout. The high leverage generally adopted by buyout firms also serves to discipline management. Presumably these factors (and the likely circumstance that management owns a substantial portion of the firm's equity after a buyout) explain empirical evidence indicating that a firm's operating performance generally improves after a buyout.

Review Questions and Problems

1. Define, distinguish, and briefly discuss the following transactions: (a) merger, (b) acquisition, (c) takeover, and (d) buyout.
2. Define each of the following types of mergers: (a) horizontal, (b) vertical, and (c) conglomerate.
3. List and briefly explain motives for merger or acquisition.
4. List and briefly explain motives for a (hostile) takeover.
5. List and briefly explain motives for a buyout.
6. Discuss the legal history of mergers and acquisitions.
7. Discuss the arguments that several authors have made in defense of mergers and acquisitions despite public policy concerns.
8. Discuss the determinants of the form of payment in a merger.
9. Briefly summarize the empirical evidence on the valuation effects of merger announcements.
10. Briefly summarize the empirical evidence on the postmerger performance of acquiring firms.

11. Discuss the empirical evidence on the characteristics of bidder and target firms in a takeover.
12. Discuss each of the following issues related to a bidder's strategy in a takeover attempt: (a) pre-tender offer share acquisition (toehold), (b) the free rider problem, and (c) method of compensation.
13. Define a *golden parachute*.
14. Define *greenmail* and the *standstill agreement*.
15. Discuss stock repurchases as a takeover defense.
16. Briefly discuss each of these antitakeover measures: (a) antitakeover devices adopted by firms and (b) antitakeover legislation.
17. Summarize the empirical evidence on the valuation effect of a buyout announcement on the stockholders and bondholders of the target firm.
18. Summarize the empirical evidence on the post-buyout performance of LBO firms.
19. Define a reverse LBO, and summarize evidence on the pre-IPO and post-IPO performance of firms that have conducted a reverse IPO.

Creative Thinking Issues

1. Why do mergers occur in waves over time?
2. Given all that we have discussed on the matter in the text thus far, do you believe internal control mechanisms (e.g., shareholder activism, board oversight) or the external market for corporate control (e.g., acquisitions, takeovers) are more powerful means of controlling agency costs of managerial discretion? In what ways do they make *complementary* contributions to the goal of maximizing shareholder wealth?
3. Are antitakeover devices and legislation justifiable? Why or why not?

Projects and Analyses

1. Identify a recent merger or acquisition (vertical, horizontal, or conglomerate). Analyze motives, payment methods, and financial effects. (A good case is Abbott Laboratories' recent acquisition of Knoll Pharmaceuticals.)
2. Identify a recent hostile takeover (or a current hostile takeover attempt). Analyze motives, payment methods, and resistance. (An interesting recent case is the hostile bid for Willamette Industries Inc. by Weyerhaeuser, Inc.)
3. Identify and analyze a recent buyout. (An interesting case is Donaldson, Lufkin & Jenrette's recent buyout of IBP Inc. for $3.7 billion.)

CHAPTER

Financial Distress and Restructuring

17

17.1   INTRODUCTION

In this chapter, we discuss events, effects, and decisions associated with firms that are in financial distress. After a general discussion about the causes and effects of financial distress, we organize the chapter around the major classes of decisions that are associated with financial distress, including *cost-cutting* and *operational cutbacks*; *asset sales* and *financial restructuring*, and *governance reform* and *top management dismissal*. We defer extensive discussions of more drastic responses to severe financial distress—that is, *private debt restructuring, being acquired,* and *bankruptcy* (with subsequent *reorganization* or *liquidation*)—to Chapter 18, though we mention these issues in this chapter as well.

We address these decisions in the order stated because they (roughly) correspond to the sequence of decisions that a firm may make as it becomes progressively more financially distressed. Facing moderate financial distress, a firm may attempt to cope by cutting costs or paring operations temporarily. If this is insufficient, the firm may need to sell assets or restructure its equity. More serious actions involve governance reform and replacing management. If these efforts fail, and the firm becomes severely distressed, the firm may need to renegotiate debt contracts, be acquired, or file for bankruptcy. Depending on the type of bankruptcy filed, the bankrupt firm is either reorganized or liquidated.

The topics in this chapter relate to topics in other chapters. Specifically, the fundamental problems of principal–agent conflicts and information asymmetry introduced in Chapters 3 through 5 will again come into play. Indeed, these problems tend to be most severe for firms that are financially distressed, and consequently resolutions to these problems tend to be more drastic. In Chapter 6 we delineated the various stages of financial distress, as well as costs of financial distress, within the context of our discussion of a firm's optimal capital structure. Financial distress also may affect a firm's dividend, stock repurchase, and debt policies, as we discussed in Chapters 14 and 15, respectively. Mergers, acquisitions, takeovers, and buyouts are also often related to financial distress, as we discussed in Chapter 16 and discuss again briefly in Chapter 18. Finally, severe financial distress can lead to debt restructuring, being acquired, or bankruptcy, which are the topics of Chapter 18.

This chapter is organized as follows. In Section 17.2, we provide a general discussion of various causes and effects of financial distress. In Sections 17.3 through 17.6, we discuss various responses of firms to financial distress: operational cutbacks (Section 17.3), asset sales (Section 17.4), financial restructuring (Section 17.5), and governance reform and management replacement (Section 17.6). In Section 17.7, we discuss IBM's restructuring decisions in the 1990s. Finally, Section 17.8 summarizes the chapter's learning objectives, as usual.

As you read this chapter, it is useful to view the discussions from two alternative viewpoints. The first is *ex post*. We provide a sequential discussion of events, effects, and decisions that a firm is likely to face when it is actually operating under financial distress. The second viewpoint is *ex ante*. By better understanding financial distress, one can reflect on financial policies and strategies that a firm should adopt *in advance* to avoid or mitigate financial distress and its attendant deadweight costs in the future.

17.2   CAUSES AND EFFECTS OF FINANCIAL DISTRESS

What causes a firm to become financially distressed? What are its effects? It is important to address these questions at the outset, because the answers presage our analysis of decisions that a firm might make in the face of distress. In this section, we address these questions using a *top-down* approach. *First*, we analyze and discuss the influence of macroeconomic growth and government policies and regulations on financial distress rates. *Second*, we examine the avenues by which financial distress is related to industry factors. *Third*, we discuss causes and effects of financial distress from a firm-level perspective.

17.2.1   Macro-Level Factors Affecting Financial Distress

Liquidity, Financial Distress, and Recession

Bernanke (1981) provided some key insights into the relationships among liquidity, economic growth, and financial distress. He argued that, for both firms and individuals, bankruptcy risk plays a role in the propagation of recessions: "Bankruptcy imposes net social costs, so that all agents have an interest in avoiding it. Consumers and firms do this by being careful to retain sufficient liquid assets to meet fixed expenses; banks and other lenders, by being selective in choosing borrowers and limiting the size of loans. The onset of recession strains the system by reducing the flow of income available to meet current obligations and by increasing uncertainty about future liquidity needs. There is a general attempt to insure solvency which leads to a reduced demand for consumer and producer durables—which may in turn generate further income reductions" (p. 155).

Bernanke emphasized the critical relationships among changes in liquidity, financial distress, and recession for both consumers and firms:

> Recessions create financial distress by narrowing the margin between cash
> flow and debt service . . . When the flow constraint is relevant, a principal
> effect of a drop in current income is the reduction of expenditure on illiquid,
> long-lived assets (such as durables). There are two reasons for this. First,
> lower current income increases the short-run probability that the flow con-
> straint will have to be satisfied through costly means, for example, the distress
> sales of assets, borrowing at unfavorable terms, severe reduction in current
> living standard, or, as the last resort, bankruptcy . . . Second, a drop in current
> income typically has ambiguous implications for the consumer's estimates of

future income flows and, hence, for the level of durables holdings consistent with maintenance of solvency in the long run. An asymmetry arises here: Because durables are illiquid, it is more costly to correct (what turns out to be) an overpurchase than an underpurchase. Assuming that waiting for new information will tend to resolve the ambiguity created by the initial income fall (for example, was the drop caused by a permanent demand shift or by temporary cyclical conditions?), even a risk-neutral consumer will be motivated to defer durables purchases until the uncertainty is resolved . . . (p. 156)

With modifications, this story for consumers can be applied to firms. The firm, too, must reconcile long-term spending plans with the necessity of having the cash flow to meet short-term obligations. Low internal liquidity and many fixed expenses increase the risk of financial embarrassment; at least, they raise the cost of new financing. Again, deferral of capital expenditures is an appropriate defense of the balance sheet against a fall in current income. (p. 156)

Bernanke also suggested why bankruptcies occur: "Existing explanations rely on some sort of missing market argument (see Jeremy Bulow and John Shoven [1977] and references therein). We can suggest a solution based on a moral hazard: Lenders cannot observe the objective conditions on which borrowers base their portfolio decisions. If a lender does not develop a reputation for pressing his claims, borrowers have an incentive to become too illiquid in order to force an improvement in terms" (p. 155).

Monetary Policy

Bernanke's focus on liquidity reminds us of the critical role of monetary policy on the nation's overall liquidity. The Federal Reserve Board (the "Fed") affects the level of aggregate liquidity primarily through its *open market operations*. These operations involve the Fed's buying or selling of U.S. Treasury bills (T-bills), out of its considerable inventory, to affect its intended policy to ease or tighten liquidity in the banking system. When it buys bills, an *expansionary* maneuver, it adds legal reserves to the banking industry, which the nation's banks can use to create new loans on a multiplied basis. Selling bills has the opposite, or *contractionary*, effect. Short-term interest rates fall when the Fed is pursuing an expansionary policy, and rise when a contractionary policy is being pursued.

The Fed's principal duty is to protect the purchasing power of the dollar (i.e., to minimize inflation), while also allowing for a sustainable level of real growth in the economy. The Fed operates under the assumption that inflation is positively related to real economic growth. On the one hand, if real economic growth is weak, the Fed can pursue an expansionary policy without much concern about inflation.

On the other hand, when the economy is *overheated* (i.e., the economy has been growing at a high, presumably unsustainable rate), the Fed eventually steps in with contractionary policy to cool the economy and thereby reduce inflation. Of course, a consequence of contractionary monetary policy is a rise in the rates on, and tighter limits on the availability of, short-term loans. These events, combined with the eventual slow-down of the economy itself, increase financial distress for all firms, particularly firms that are financially relatively weak or highly levered.

Revenge of the Credit Cycle

Jerry Jasinowski doesn't need new problems. As president of the National Association of Manufacturers, he already has a surplus. Industrial production has dropped for 12 consecutive months, the longest stretch since late 1944 and 1945. Manufacturing employment is 1.1 million below its recent peak in July 2000. But now comes an added worry. Meeting recently with chief executives, Jasinowski heard that many companies are struggling to get credit. "This credit crunch is now the number one impediment to recovery," he says. Although that may overstate the case, it identifies an emerging and little-noted problem.

It's the revenge of the "credit cycle." In flush times, lenders relax credit standards. They're eager to lend, and exude confidence about repayment. Borrowers brim with optimism. They don't doubt they can repay. Everyone's upbeat. But when economic prospects darken, the process reverses—often with a vengeance. Loan losses obliterate optimism. Lenders tighten credit standards. Borrowers can't get loans or, at any rate, can't get them on terms that seem reasonable and affordable. And sometimes they don't want more, because they're borrowed up to their eyebrows.

The credit cycle applies to both consumer and business lending. But with the cycle now going into its down phase, business lending may suffer most. Consider:

- Banks have toughened approval standards for commercial and industrial (C&I) loans to businesses. Early this year nearly 60 percent of banks surveyed by the Federal Reserve said they were tightening standards for loans to firms with sales exceeding $50 million. In August about two-fifths of banks were still tightening. By contrast, banks consistently loosened credit standards from mid-1993 until late 1998.

- Losses on many business loans are rising. At midyear, banks had $7.8 billion in losses on large syndicated loans (loans of at least $20 million made by a group of three or more lenders), according to a survey by the Fed, the Federal Deposit Insurance Corp., and the Comptroller of the Currency. Losses and loans rated as "doubtful" or "substandard" totaled $117 billion, or about 15 percent of all syndicated loans. Some of these may ultimately go into default. In 2000 the comparable figure was $63 billion, or 9 percent.

- The same thing is happening in bond markets. (Bonds are long-term loans, usually with maturities exceeding 10 years, sold to investors.) So far this year, 185 companies have defaulted on $76 billion of bonds, says Moody's Investors Service. This is 55 percent higher than the $49 billion for all of 2000—and that was a record in dollars, though not as a share of outstanding corporate bonds.

- Companies are devoting a rising share of their cash flow to interest payments on all types of debts (bonds, bank loans, commercial paper—short-term securities of less than a year). In 1996 companies spent about 20 percent of their cash flow for interest payments, says Mark Zandi of Economy.com. By the first half of 2001, that had risen to 28 percent. (Cash flow consists primarily of after-tax profits and depreciation, a noncash expense reflecting the obsolescence of equipment and buildings.)

Some problem loans and defaulted bonds reflect optimistic—often reckless—lending in the late 1990s, when the credit cycle was in its euphoric phase. From 1997 to 1999, companies raised $373 billion by issuing "speculative grade" (aka "junk") bonds, says Diane Vazza of Standard & Poor's. These bonds go to shakier firms, and the volume was almost three times higher than from 1994 to 1996.

Even when issued, a quarter of the bonds were rated B-minus or lower—a sign of high risk. (Standard & Poor's has 26 bond ratings;

(continued)

B-minus is 16th from the top.) But the bonds were snapped up by pension funds and other investors. "These were the go-go years," says Vazza. "It was an elevator ride up, and [everyone] wanted to get on."

The ride down has been bumpy. By Vazza's estimate, three-quarters of this year's defaults involve bonds issued in 1997, 1998, or 1999. About a fifth of those are in telecommunications (companies like 360networks, Winstar, and Teligent). Altogether, their defaulted bonds exceeded $30 billion. But other large defaults involved chemical companies, utilities, paper companies, and retailers.

The harder question is how much the credit cycle will depress the economy. The irony is that, just as the Fed is cutting interest rates, both lenders and borrowers are becoming more skittish. This last occurred in the early 1990s, when repeated cuts in rates only belatedly revived business borrowing. From August 1990 until December 1993, banks' C&I loans continually dropped; the full decline was 9 percent. By most accounts, lenders and borrowers were in much worse shape then than now. Banks faced huge losses on real-estate loans. "Leveraged buyouts" and stock buybacks had left many companies with massive debt loads. Early in 1990 companies were paying almost 40 percent of cash flow for interest, says Zandi.

Still, the same logic applies. As the economy and profits weaken, companies have a harder time paying debts. Lenders worry that good loans will turn bad. Tougher credit standards force companies to concentrate on repaying. This prompts cutbacks in jobs and investment, allowing cash to be diverted to debt service.

One of Jasinowski's members is Behlen MFG Co. of Columbus, Neb. It sells structural steel for construction (office buildings, shopping malls) and livestock pens. Late in 2000 new orders "fell off a cliff," says chief executive Tony Raimondo. The company swung from profit to loss. Its bank instantly put it in a "special workout group." Interest rates were raised, penalties imposed. Behlen restored profitability by laying off 350 of 1,600 workers and cutting new investment. But as yet, the bank hasn't removed the company from its problem-loan list. The company's psychology has changed, and almost everything becomes subordinated to improving the company's credit standing. "You're trying to focus on day-to-day business," says Raimondo, "until the bank gives you the okay."

Source: "Revenge of the Credit Cycle," by R. J. Samuelson, *Washington Post*, Oct. 31, 2001, p. A27, © 2001 The Washington Post Company. Reprinted by permission.

Reversal of Fortune: From Diversification to Focus

Arguably one of the most important corporate phenomena in the United States in the last 40 years is the reversal of the conglomerate diversification trend of the 1960s and 1970s, and, in its place, the rise of corporate *focus* in the 1980s and 1990s. Bhide (1990) and Jensen (1993) argued that this reversal was brought about by economic, technological, and regulatory changes during the 1970s and 1980s. These changes boosted the advantage of external capital markets relative to internal capital markets (Chapter 13).

The effect of this reversal on financial distress rates is many faceted. For instance, if conglomerates were relatively inefficient, and yet were sustainable because they were the norm (i.e., competitors were diversified too), then when the *sea change* to corporate focus began to occur, many inefficient conglomerates, facing keener competition, became distressed. Indeed, many of the transactions that we discuss later (e.g., asset sales, equity carve-outs, and spin-offs) were developed to convert inefficient conglomerates to more focused and efficient enterprises. Comment and Jarrell (1995) explain,

Conventional wisdom holds that economies of scope have been reversed in the 1980s. Managers are now advised to eschew diversification and to shrink the far-flung enterprises that resulted from past diversification strategies. In their public statements, managers are apt to say that they want to concentrate on a core business, and they are likely to rationalize mergers and growth strategies, as well as divestitures and restructuring, as reflecting a strategy of specialization. This view marks a change from the steady increase in diversification since the 1950s and from the several theoretical justifications for diversification that have been advanced, including (a) managerial economies of scale, (b) economies of scope in production and marketing, and (c) financial synergies such as earnings smoothing and the efficiencies that arise with an internal capital market. The new emphasis on specialization is consistent with Jensen (1988), who argues that corporate diversification programs exemplify the theory that managers of firms with unused borrowing power and large free cash flows are more likely to undertake low-benefit or even value-destroying investments. Similarly, Meyer, Milgrom, and Roberts (1992) argue that failing businesses can have too-ready access to cross-subsidies when they are part of a diversified firm. (pp. 67–68)

The authors conducted two distinct analyses of these issues. *First*, they tested whether diversified firms benefited from the purported advantages of diversification (items *a* to *c* [above]): "We show that diversified firms do not take advantage of some of the underlying efficiencies thought to motivate diversification. We consider whether diversification (1) permits a greater use of debt (because the coinsurance of debt reduces default rates), (2) permits a substitution of intersegment cash transfers for arms-length transactions (because transaction costs are lower in internal capital markets than in external capital markets), or (3) increases the likelihood of takeover because (conversely) these intersegment transfers accommodate a waste of free cash flow. We find that debt does not increase systematically with diversification and that diversified firms do not rely any less on external capital market transactions. There is some evidence that diversification does make firms more likely to be takeover targets (p. 68).

Second, the authors found that, throughout the 1980s, firms tended to increase their focus, and that an increase in focus leads to an increase in equity value: "Our findings show a steady trend toward greater focus during the 1980s. We find that 55.7 percent of exchange-listed firms had a single business segment in 1988, compared to 38.1 percent in 1979 . . . Perhaps more important, the trend toward greater focus is associated with greater shareholder wealth. This relation is not trivial in economic magnitude. A change of 0.1 in the absolute value of a revenue-based Herfindahl index of focus is associated with a stock return of about 4 percent, and changes this large occur about one year in ten. Adding or subtracting one business segment is associated with a return of about 5 percent, and changes this large occur about one year in eight" (p. 68).[1]

---

[1]The sales-based Herfindahl index, H, is calculated across n business segments of a firm, and is the sum of the squares of the sales of each segment i, S_i, as a proportion of total sales:

$$H = \sum_{i=1}^{n} \left\{ \frac{S_i}{\sum_{i=1}^{n} S_i} \right\}^2.$$

John and Ofek (1995) studied the effects of increases in focus via asset sales (i.e., divestitures) on corporate performance: "We find that asset sales lead to an improvement in the operating performance of the seller's remaining assets in each of the three years following the asset sale. The improvement in performance occurs primarily in firms that increase their focus; this change in operating performance is positively related to the seller's stock return at the divestiture announcement. The announcement stock returns are also greater for focus-increasing divestitures. Further, we find evidence that some of the seller's gains result from a better fit between the divested asset and the buyer" (p. 105).

17.2.2 Industry-Level Causes of Financial Distress

Three industry-level factors have important effects on the probability that a firm will experience financial distress: competition, industry shocks, and deregulation.

Competition

Porter's (1980) *Five Forces* model of industry competition is useful for identifying possible industry-level causes of financial distress. The five forces include (a) entry/exit barriers, (b) the bargaining power of suppliers, (c) the bargaining power of buyers, (d) the threat of substitute products, and (e) rivalry among competing firms. Each factor is associated with the probability of financial distress for an individual firm in a given industry. Among the possible implications of these factors is that firms in different industries may display different levels of competition as well as different profit sensitivities to changes in macroeconomic and industry conditions over time.

In Chapter 7, we discussed several aspects of industry competition that may affect a firm's financial policies and strategies, and by extension its risk of financial distress. For instance, financial distress is likely to be greater for small firms than for large firms in an industry, based on Williams's (1995) analysis. In addition, theory suggests that highly levered firms commit to riskier projects and aggressive product-market strategies, in part to deter entry (Maksimovic and Zechner 1991; McAndrews and Nakamura 1992).

Industry Shocks

A negative shock to an industry's product demand or costs, especially if it is sustained over time, will eventually force a shakeout of firms in the industry. The weakest firms will be forced into bankruptcy or must consider being acquired by a stronger firm in the industry.

Mitchell and Mulherin (1996) examined industry-level patterns in tender offers, mergers, leveraged buyouts (LBOs), and other restructuring activity over the years 1982 to 1989. They tested the proposition that industry shocks contribute to the frequency of takeover and restructuring activity. Shocks include "deregulation, changes in input costs, and innovations in financing technology that induce or enable alterations in industry structure" (p. 194). The authors summarize their empirical results as follows: "Across 51 industries, we find significant differences in both the rate and time-series clustering of these activities. The interindustry patterns in the rate of takeovers and restructurings are directly related to the economic shocks borne by the sample industries. These results support the argument that much of the takeover activity during the 1980s was driven by broad fundamental factors and have general implications for the stock price spillover effects of takeover announcements, corporate performance following takeovers, and the timing of takeover waves" (p. 193).

Lang and Stulz (1992) investigated the effect of a bankruptcy announcement by one firm on the values of other firms in the industry. They tested for two conflicting effects. On the one hand, there may be a *contagion effect*. The market may lower the values of other firms in the industry because the bankruptcy announcement reveals new, negative information about the status of the industry as a whole. On the other hand, the market may raise the values of other firms in the industry because one of their rivals has failed.

The authors found that the balance of these opposing effects depends on the financial characteristics of firms in the industry: "On average, bankruptcy announcements decrease the value of a value-weighted portfolio of competitors by 1 percent. This negative effect is significantly larger for highly levered industries and industries where the unconditional stock returns of the nonbankrupt and bankrupt firms are highly correlated; the effect is significantly positive for highly concentrated industries with low leverage, suggesting that in such industries competitors benefit from the difficulties of the bankrupt firm" (p. 45).

Industry Deregulation

The deregulation of an industry can induce financial distress in many firms within the industry as the economic structure of the industry changes. Over the past 25 years, the United States has deregulated the transportation industry (airlines, railroads, trucking), the communications industry, and currently the utilities industry. Below we summarize the results of two empirical studies of the financial effects of industry deregulation, one in the communications industry, and the other in the airlines industry.

Chen and Merville (1986) studied the forced breakup of AT&T, which began, by court order, on January 1, 1984, and continued for approximately two years. (AT&T has continued its breakup in recent years on a semivoluntary basis, spinning off firms such as Lucent Technologies and AT&T Wireless.) The authors focused on the issue of whether the breakup induced wealth transfers among AT&T's security claimants and other stakeholders: "The results of our research indicate that economically significant events took place during the deregulation process, which led to transfers of wealth from third parties (consumers and government) to AT&T stockholders and bondholders and from third parties to operating company shareholders . . . However, we could detect no transfers of wealth from bondholders to stockholders during the deregulation process" (p. 1009).

Kole and Lehn (1999) investigated the effects of the Airline Deregulation Act of 1978, and the associated increase in competition, on airline firms' governance structures. They developed several hypotheses about expected effects based on agency theory: "[W]e expect deregulation to increase the concentration of equity ownership . . . By increasing both the importance of the managerial role and the costs of observing managerial performance, deregulation increases the costs of monitoring managers. This change has two reinforcing effects that lead to greater ownership concentration. First, an outside shareholder engages in monitoring only if his private benefits, which are proportional to his equity stake, exceed the costs of monitoring. To make it privately rational for an outside shareholder, or group of shareholders, to incur the higher monitoring costs induced by deregulation, ownership concentration must increase. Second, to internalize the agency problems associated with higher monitoring costs, managers themselves may own larger stakes so that they bear a larger proportion of the wealth consequences associated with their decisions . . . " (pp. 87–89).

The authors also predicted that the level of executive compensation for airline executives should increase, and the form of this compensation should change. Regarding the latter, they argue that before deregulation, executive pay would be relatively more sensitive to the firm's *earnings*, while after deregulation executive pay should be more sensitive to *stock price*. Finally, they predicted that the size of an airline's board of directors would decrease after deregulation. This prediction is based in part on the arguments of Jensen (1993) and evidence in Yermack (1996) that smaller boards are more effective in their monitoring function.

To test these hypotheses, the authors examined changes in the governance structures of airline firms over the 22-year period surrounding the Act. They document evidence consistent with their predictions: "[W]e find that after deregulation (i) equity ownership is more concentrated, (ii) CEO pay increases, (iii) stock option grants to CEOs increase, and (iv) board size decreases. Airline governance structures gravitate toward the system of governance mechanisms used by unregulated firms" (p. 79).

17.2.3   Firm-Level Causes of Financial Distress

Although macroeconomic conditions and industry factors are important determinants of financial distress, firm-specific factors also contribute substantially to a firm's risk of financial distress. Our discussion of business analysis in Chapter 8, as well as our discussion of the valuation of corporate bonds in Chapter 10, suggest several firm-specific factors that can affect the probability of financial distress. These factors include a firm's (a) ownership and governance structures, (b) operating risk, and (c) leverage. For instance, agency costs associated with both managerial discretion and debt, depending on the extent that they are not mitigated through contracting devices, can affect a firm's operational efficiency, leverage, profitability, and risk. However, if a firm is observed to be in financial distress, and even if the cause of the distress can be traced explicitly to bad decisions by management, it may be difficult to distinguish whether the decisions that contributed to distress are due to management's self-serving behavior or to incompetence. (Of course, the difference may be interesting only to academics.)

Financial versus Economic Distress

Andrade and Kaplan (1998) make an important distinction between *financial distress* and *economic distress*. Economic distress occurs when operating income falls or becomes negative, whereas financial distress occurs when the firm cannot meet its legal obligations, particularly with respect to debt payments, whether or not it has an operating profit. The authors examined 31 firms that engaged in highly levered transactions (buyouts and leverage-increasing recapitalizations) during the 1980s and that later became distressed. They found that these firms tended to create value initially; their operating income increased and was actually above industry norms, on average. Thus, they conclude that high leverage was the chief cause of their distress (see also Haugen and Senbet 1978, 1988).

The Dog That Caught the Car

There is a certain glamour to corporate rescue work, to swooping in after disaster strikes, pushing aside the bumblers and, with the dispassionate logic of an outsider, setting things right.

But, as three board members at Waste Management Inc. are finding, there is no glamour the second time around. As newcomers in 1998, the three thought they had fixed the giant trash hauler. They scrubbed its books and merged it into a scrappy competitor with well-regarded management. The stock soared.

Then, this past July, profits fell short of expectations. The stock plunged. The merger, it turned out, was in disarray. The company's books were again a shambles. And top management had to be thrown out. The three board members stepped in again to run things. This time, it was their mess. And they have been struggling to salvage not just a troubled company, but their own reputations.

"We're all embarrassed," says Robert S. "Steve" Miller, whose work at Chrysler Corp. and many high-profile basket cases over two decades has made him one of corporate America's more celebrated Mr. Fix-Its. Adds Roderick M. Hills, a former Securities and Exchange Commission chairman who heads Waste Management's audit committee: "I'm not proud of the fact that, in retrospect, we didn't know what the hell was going on."

This is the humbling account of a high-profile rescue team's second tour of duty not yet finished, at Waste Management: the sensitive matter of succession when the CEO is desperately ill; the surprise delivery of a $40 million corporate jet that they didn't know had been ordered; dubious insider stock sales; the indignity of enduring a lengthy I-told-you-so from the company founder, who opposed the merger—and who now has sued Messrs. Miller and Hills, blaming them for ruining his creation.

The job has been complicated by the three directors' conflicting personalities. Mr. Miller is too easygoing, his cohorts say. Mr. Hills is so tough at times that the others wince. And the third, shareholder activist Ralph V. Whitworth, has had to become a boss instead of a critic. Surprised last July to find himself acting chairman at a company with 68,000 employees, the 44-year-old Mr. Whitworth declares: "I'm the dog that caught the car" . . .

For nearly a decade, people in the garbage business have contended that a smartly run company could defy some basic industrywide problems. A glut of dump capacity that emerged around 1990 depresses disposal prices. And garbage piles up only as fast as the economy moves, so it isn't much of a growth business. Still, the industry has managed to obscure these facts with an unending acquisition binge. The Waste Management directors would be well into their second tour of emergency duty before they fully understood this fact.

Indeed, an acquisition had been the centerpiece of their first run at saving the company. Mr. Miller had stepped in as Waste Management's interim CEO in 1997 at a time when the company was under siege. Massive accounting problems that had overstated profits for years were bubbling to the surface, hammering the company's stock.

An intensive audit overseen for the board by Mr. Hills, who had been named a director in late 1997, led to a $3.54 billion pretax charge in February 1998. Shortly thereafter, USA Waste Services Inc., a smaller but fast-growing trash hauler whose CEO, John E. Drury, was a garbage man's son, agreed to buy Waste Management for $13.43 billion Mr. Drury had once been the No. 2 executive at Waste Management's archrival, Browning-Ferris Industries Inc.; he had been fired in 1990, but had re-emerged as a trash-industry star at USA

(continued)

Waste. And Mr. Drury's top outside adviser on the deal was Mr. Whitworth, whose firm, Relational Investors LLC, specializes in cajoling managements into painful restructurings.

When the merger was announced, Mr. Miller lauded USA Waste for having "the ideal senior management team." Wall Street was enthusiastic. The only notable opposition came from Dean L. Buntrock, Waste Management's founder and former longtime CEO. He wrote a letter trying to dissuade directors from the deal. He argued that USA Waste's various businesses were weak, that its computer system wasn't powerful enough for the merged company, and that Mr. Drury wasn't qualified to run the combined operations. He pleaded with the board to find its own CEO.

But since many of the accounting and other problems that got Waste Management into trouble in the first place occurred on Mr. Buntrock's watch, he had little credibility with his company's board. It approved the merger. The new company adopted the Waste Management name and made Houston, where USA Waste was based, its headquarters. Mr. Miller was to be chairman for one year. Mr. Hills stayed on as audit-committee chief. And Mr. Whitworth joined the board as head of the corporate-governance committee. The heavy lifting was over, or so the three directors thought.

They hadn't attended the USA Waste board meeting on July 15, 1998, the day before the deal closed. Investors had bid up the company's stock about 40 percent since the merger was announced, boosting the deal's value to $19.13 billion.

Soon after the announcement, USA Waste had ordered a Gulfstream IV corporate jet for Mr. Drury at a cost of about $30 million. But at the board meeting, Richard J. Heckmann, a USA Waste director and an airplane enthusiast, took note of Waste Management's substantial international operations and suggested that a Gulfstream V, with its longer range, might now be in order. "It's the only way you're going to go nonstop" from Houston to London, Mr.

Heckmann explains in an interview. G-Vs, as they are known, sell for about $40 million.

There was the matter of the G-IV and the $2 million nonrefundable deposit USA Waste had already made on it. But another USA Waste director, Kosti Shirvanian, had watched the value of his holdings in the company rise to nearly $500 million, up from about $175 million in 1996. "I made a motion to buy a G-V," Mr. Shirvanian recalls. Why? "Because I wanted the G-IV." He bought it for his personal use, and USA Waste ordered a G-V.

Jerome B. York, another USA Waste director who is often a stickler on discretionary expenses, was disgusted, and got up and left the room.

During his years at USA Waste, Mr. Drury had won over Wall Street by seeming to manage a series of ever-larger acquisitions without a hiccup. And in the weeks after the Waste Management deal, he said the combined company would meet its cost-cutting target of $800 million.

But two factors soon emerged that might have prompted Waste Management's board to keep a closer eye on management. In November 1998, Mr. Drury was diagnosed with a brain tumor. After surgery to remove the malignancy, and facing a month of radiation treatments, he nevertheless said he would "resume normal activities" in a week.

His doctors' assessments reassured the directors. And they felt they had a first-rate successor, if needed, in president and chief operating officer, Rodney R. Proto. At a March 1999 board meeting in Phoenix, the CEO was "noticeably weaker—didn't have the cogency," Mr. Whitworth recalls. There were complications in Mr. Drury's condition.

The second factor, Mr. Whitworth says, was that Messrs. Drury and Proto "were arrogant. They really treated the board, and Steve, shoddily." Shortly after the merger, Mr. Whitworth suggested to Mr. Drury, the CEO, that Mr. Drury prepare brief monthly updates of the board on the company's progress. According to Mr. Whitworth, Mr. Drury's response was:

"Bull—. I don't write memos. They either want a lean operation or a bureaucracy." At other times, Mr. Whitworth says, Mr. Drury belittled Mr. Miller behind his back. One director says Mr. Drury had come to regard Mr. Miller as weak-willed. Whatever the cause, "Steve Miller was the chairman, and they ignored him," says Mr. Hills.

[B]ut late on July 6, 1999, the company warned that second-quarter results would fall short of expectations. More ominously, it conceded that it wasn't sure why. Its stock plunged 37 percent the following day.

If the second quarter was so weak, how had Waste Management come within a penny a share of estimates for the first quarter, typically a weaker period? For the board, what had seemed to be a string of unrelated concerns and annoyances was fast coming together to shatter its trust in management.

Mr. Whitworth flew to Houston and grilled Mr. Proto and the company's chief financial officer, Earl D. DeFrates. Had they dressed up the first-quarter earnings with any undisclosed one-time gains? "It sure looked like it to me," Mr. Whitworth says, "but they said no." Mr. DeFrates couldn't be reached for comment; he was fired by the company in July.

INSIDER SELLING

If the first-quarter earnings had included undisclosed gains, some heavy insider selling of Waste Management stock in the weeks before the disastrous second-quarter announcement was going to look very bad. Mr. Proto had sold 300,000 shares for about $16.5 million. A dozen other insiders reported selling, too. Mr. Whitworth says he began asking executives he encountered in the men's room whether they had sold shares. "The first 10 people I asked, I was batting one thousand," he says. "That was disturbing."

. . . Mr. Whitworth also kept badgering the financial people about his suspicions about the first-quarter results. Finally, he says, the company's chief accounting officer, Bruce Snyder, "started belching out everything." (Mr. Snyder won't comment.)

The first quarter results had included a bunch of undisclosed one-time items, and would have to be restated. Now, the insider stock sales definitely looked bad . . .

Source: Abridged from "Star Rescuers Took On Waste Management—And End Up Tarnished," by Jeff Bailey, *The Wall Street Journal*, Feb. 29, 1999. Copyright © 2000 Dow Jones & Co., Inc. Reprinted by permission.

17.2.4   Effects of Financial Distress

Costs associated with all of the real-world factors that we have stressed in previous chapters are exacerbated when a firm is operating under financial distress. Here we briefly discuss how financial distress affects these costs.

Loss of Tax Benefits of Debt and Depreciation

If a levered firm fails to make profits on a chronic basis, it loses the value of the tax shield provided by debt interest and depreciation. Depending on the firm's initial leverage and depreciation base, these losses alone can place the firm at a competitive and strategic disadvantage.

Transaction Costs

The cost of transacting in the financial markets is much higher for firms in financial distress. In some cases, the capital markets may be effectively closed to a firm that is in severe distress, in part because, given the effort required by an investment bank to float the firm's equity or debt securities, the required underwriter spread would be prohibitively high. In addition, transaction costs, or more precisely, restructuring costs, may be high for a distressed firm attempting to restructure its debt, depending on whether the firm attempts to recover via an out-of-court restructuring or in bankruptcy court.

Agency Costs

Agency costs of both managerial discretion and debt are likely to be very high for a firm in financial distress. Regarding the former, the firm's senior management may be reduced to making decisions that keep their pay secure rather than making long-term strategic, value-creating (and risky) decisions on behalf of shareholders. Worse, executives and other key employees may quit, or at least be distracted by a search for alternative employment. Agency costs of debt are also likely to be very severe because the firm likely has very little equity value against a relatively large amount of debt, a situation that is ideal for the expropriation of creditors.

Negative Liquidity Effects

Substantial losses in the market value of a firm's equity can have several cascading negative liquidity effects. *First*, the firm may lose the following of professional analysts, who play a vital role in supporting the flow of information about a stock, which is critical to its liquidity (see Kaen 1990). *Second*, as this occurs, normal trading interest in the stock may fall (e.g., among mutual funds), and the bid-ask spread on the stock may increase. *Third*, depending on the listing requirements of the exchange on which the firm's stock trades, the exchange may *delist* it.[2] At this point, the firm has lost most of its potential to raise equity funds; raising debt funds will be more difficult as well. Moreover, this may come at a time when the firm is most in need of external funds to survive. Lacking effective access to external capital, the firm may be forced into bankruptcy.

A discussion of liquidity at the firm level dovetails with Bernanke's analysis of aggregate liquidity and its effects on financial distress and recession, discussed earlier. Opler, Pinkowitz, Stulz, and Williamson (1999) examined the determinants of variation in individual U.S. firms' cash holdings (including marketable securities) over the period 1971 to 1994: "In time-series and cross-section tests, we find evidence supportive of a static tradeoff model of cash holdings. In particular, firms with strong growth opportunities and riskier cash flows hold relatively high ratios of cash to total non-cash assets. Firms that have the greatest access to the capital markets, such as large firms and those with high credit ratings, tend to hold lower ratios of cash to total non-cash assets. At the same time, however, we find evidence that firms that do well tend to accumulate more cash than predicted by the static tradeoff model where managers maximize shareholder wealth. There is little evidence that excess cash has a large short-run impact on capital expenditures, acquisition spending, and payouts to shareholders. The main reason that firms experience large changes in excess cash is the occurrence of operating losses" (p. 3).

---

[2]A firm's stock may be delisted from an exchange, or trading may be suspended temporarily, if it fails to meet requirements for number of shareholders, minimum stock price, and trading volume. For discussions of delistings and suspensions, see Howe and Schlarbaum (1986) and Sanger and Peterson (1990).

17.2.5 Corporate Performance under Distress

Several studies have examined the performance of firms under financial distress. Here we provide authors' summaries of two such studies. Note that both studies focus on the distressed firm's predistress leverage as a determinant of its performance under distress.

Ofek (1993): "This paper tests the relation between capital structure and a firm's response to short-term financial distress. In a sample of 358 firms that perform poorly for a year, higher predistress leverage increases the probability of operational actions, particularly asset restructuring and employee layoffs. Higher predistress leverage also increases the probability of financial actions such as dividend cuts. These results are consistent with Jensen's (1989) argument that higher predistress leverage increases the speed with which a firm reacts to poor performance. Interestingly, higher managerial holdings reduce the probability of operational actions, especially those that do not generate cash" (p. 3).

Opler and Titman (1994): "This study finds that highly leveraged firms lose substantial market share to their more conservatively financed competitors in industry downturns. Specifically, firms in the top leverage decile in industries that experience output contractions see their sales decline by 26 percent more than do firms in the bottom leverage decile. A similar decline takes place in the market value of equity. These findings are consistent with the view that the indirect costs of financial distress are significant and positive. Consistent with the theory that firms with specialized products are especially vulnerable to financial distress, we find that highly leveraged firms that engage in research and development suffer the most in economically distressed periods. We also find that the adverse consequences of leverage are more pronounced in concentrated industries" (p. 1015).

17.3 OPERATIONAL CUTBACKS: CAUSES AND EFFECTS

Facing substantial operating losses and dropping product demand, a firm's management may decide to cut back on its operations or workforce (i.e., *downsize*), at least temporarily. For a manufacturing firm, this may involve cost cutting, layoffs, or, in more extreme cases, closing a plant. We briefly discuss four empirical papers on cutbacks—two that focus on downsizing, and the other two on plant closings.

17.3.1 Downsizing

Espahbodi, John, and Vasudevan (2000) examined the performance of 118 firms that downsized over the years 1989 to 1993. Not surprisingly, they found that downsizing firms experienced declines in operating performance before a downsizing announcement. The most important evidence pertains to improvements in firm performance after the downsizing announcement, and why they occurred: "Operating performance improves significantly following the downsizing. These firms are able to reduce the cost of sales, labor cost, capital expenditures, and R&D expenditures. We also find that firms that perform poorly in their industries prior to the downsizing and have increases in assets following the downsizing have larger improvements in performance. There is some evidence that the improvements are greater for firms that increase their focus" (p. 107).

A Case in Point: General Dynamics
Dial and Murphy (1995) provided a thorough analysis of a successful downsizing and value creation program at General Dynamics (GD) that began in 1991. The case is interesting because GD, a defense contractor, faced "declining demand in an industry

saddled with current and projected excess capacity . . . " (pp. 261–262) in the post–Cold War era. "While other contractors made defense-related acquisitions or diversified into nondefense areas, GD adopted an objective of creating shareholder value through downsizing, restructuring, and partial liquidation. Facilitating GD's new strategy were a new management team and compensation plans that closely tied executive pay to shareholder wealth creation, including a Gain/Sharing Plan that paid large cash rewards for increases in the stock price" (p. 262).

The authors summarized the implications of GD's experience as follows: "First, the GD case suggests the importance of stock-based compensation in firms characterized by excess capacity: GD downplayed accounting-based bonuses and focused on stock options, restricted stock, and other compensation plans tied to value creation. Second, GD's experience illustrates the large political costs associated with success when success means downsizing and layoffs, and also suggests that these costs can be mitigated by avoiding cash payments, relying instead on gains through ownership. Third, appropriate incentives must be coupled with the appropriate managers . . . Finally, although declining industries with excess capacity offer relatively few opportunities for revenue growth, the GD case suggests that these industries may offer large potential opportunities for value creation" (pp. 305–306).

17.3.2   Plant Closings

Blackwell, Marr, and Spivey (1990) studied the causes and effects of plant-closing events. Regarding causes, they tested competing hypotheses that plant closings are due to (a) declining profitability versus (b) the threat of a takeover. Regarding effects, they examined the effect of a plant-closing announcement on a firm's market equity value, and the subsequent closing on its profitability: "We investigate the underlying causes and the announcement effects of plant closings. The closings in our sample do not appear related to takeover activity. Instead, they appear motivated by declining firm profitability. Firms announcing closings have lower earnings than market or industry medians; earnings typically improve slightly after the announcement. We find a negative stock-market reaction to plant-closing announcements" (p. 277).

Gombola and Tsetsekos (1992) also examined the plant-closing event, focusing on information effects. They also found a negative stock-price reaction to a plant-closing announcement. In addition, they found that plant closings tend to be followed by additional negative news, including "declining profitability and symptoms of retrenchment including cutbacks in employment, asset acquisition, and dividend growth" (p. 31). They also found that variation in announcement-period abnormal returns associated with a plant closing announcement is partially explained by the market's anticipation of these other subsequent events to the extent that they occur.

17.4   DIVESTITURE VIA ASSET SALES

Depending on the economic, industry, operating, and financial circumstances facing a firm in financial distress, the firm may respond by divesting assets or divisions. An asset sale is a private transaction in which the firm receives cash from selling specific assets or divisions to another firm. For example, in its ill-fated struggle to survive in the late 1980s, Eastern Airlines began to sell aircraft. More recently, Xerox Corporation, struggling with losses and debt, sold half of its interest in Fuji Xerox to its Japanese partner, Fuji Photo Film, in 2001. In this section, we discuss research on asset sales.

17.4.1 Theoretical Perspectives on Asset Sales

Shleifer and Vishny (1992) developed a theoretical model that paints a generally negative picture of asset sales by a firm in financial distress. Pulvino (1998) discussed their model:

> Shleifer and Vishny consider the scenario where a firm responds to financial distress by selling assets. Whether the assets are sold to a buyer within the industry or to an outside buyer depends both on buyers' fundamental values and their abilities to pay. Differences in valuations between inside and outside buyers depend largely on characteristics of the assets being sold. If assets are industry specific, an inside buyer is likely to place a higher value on the assets than is an outsider. Oil refineries exemplify industry-specific assets; they generate large cash flows when used to refine oil but significantly smaller cash flows when deployed elsewhere. If assets are generic, then inside buyers and outside buyers are likely to place similar values on the assets. Computers exemplify generic assets; they can be used productively in any number of industries. Even if the inside buyer is a more productive user, and therefore places a higher value on the assets, the selling firm may sell to the industry outsider. This will be particularly true during industry recessions when factors that force the seller to liquidate also create financial constraints for potential inside buyers. In this situation, the inside buyer is unable to offer his fundamental value for the selling firm's assets. If the insider's financial constraints are much more severe than those of the outsider, the outsider will outbid the insider and assets will be redeployed to a lower value use. (p. 942)

In contrast, Hite, Owers, and Rogers (1987) provide theoretical arguments that asset sales promote efficiency by allocating assets to better uses. Lang, Poulson, and Stulz (1995) refer to this argument as the *efficient deployment hypothesis*, and expand on it as follows: "[M]anagers only retain assets for which they have a comparative advantage and sell assets as soon as another party can manage them more efficiently irrespective of their financial situation; stockholders benefit from asset sales equally of whether managers re-invest the proceeds or pay them out" (p. 4).

In addition, Lang, Poulson, and Stulz advanced an alternative hypothesis for asset sales based on agency theory and managerial discretion:

> We take as our starting point that management values firm size and control, so that it is reluctant to sell assets for efficiency reasons alone. For such management, a more compelling motivation to sell assets is that asset sales provide funds when alternative sources of financing are too expensive, possibly because of agency costs of debt or because information asymmetries make equity sales unattractive. With this view, which we call the *financing*

> *hypothesis of asset sales*, the completion of an asset sale is good news about
> the value of the asset because if the value of the asset had turned out to be
> low, the sale would not have taken place. Further, one expects the market to
> discount proceeds of asset sales retained by the firm in the presence of
> agency costs of managerial discretion since shareholders do not capture all of
> the value of the asset sold. (p. 4, italics added)

The results of their empirical analysis, discussed shortly, are consistent with this
hypothesis.

17.4.2 Asset Fire Sales

Pulvino (1998) tested the hypothesis that firms in financial distress often must sell
assets at sharply discounted, or *fire sale*, prices. He focused on the airlines industry and
the sale of aircraft. His evidence indicates that asset sales at discounted prices do
indeed occur, depending on the state of the firm and the industry: "Results indicate
that financially constrained airlines receive lower prices than their unconstrained rivals
when selling used narrow-body aircraft. Capital constrained airlines are also more
likely to sell used aircraft to industry-outsiders, especially during market downturns.
Further evidence that capital constraints affect liquidation prices is provided by airlines' asset acquisition activity. Unconstrained airlines significantly increase buying
activity when aircraft prices are depressed; this pattern is not observed for financially
constrained airlines" (p. 939).

17.4.3 Agency Costs of Managerial Discretion and Asset Sales

As discussed above, Lang, Poulson, and Stulz's (1995) *financing hypothesis of asset
sales* posits that asset sales may not be value enhancing for shareholders. This view contrasts with the *efficient deployment hypothesis*, which suggests that asset sales are
value-enhancing transactions. They tested these competing hypotheses, and documented evidence consistent with the former hypothesis.

> Our main empirical results are consistent with the financing hypothesis
> of asset sales rather than with the efficient deployment hypothesis. First, we
> show that firms selling assets tend to be poor performers and/or have high
> leverage. In particular, for our sample, median net income normalized by
> total assets is insignificantly different from zero in the year before the sale,
> even though we exclude from the sample bankrupt firms and firms in
> default. This result suggests that the typical firm selling assets is motivated
> to do so by its financial situation rather than by the discovery that some
> other firm has a comparative advantage in operating the assets. Second,
> contrary to the efficient deployment hypothesis, we find that the stock-price
> reaction to successful asset sales is strongly related to the use of the pro-
> ceeds. In our sample, the stock-price reaction to asset sales is significantly
> positive for those firms expected to use the proceeds to pay down debt, but
> negative and insignificant for firms which are expected to keep the pro-
> ceeds within the firm. (p. 4)

17.4.4   Who Gains from Asset Sales?

Datta and Iskandar-Datta (1996) investigated the distribution of gains from asset sales among the selling firm's securityholders:

> This study documents that sell-offs, on average, are firm value enhancing, as both stockholders and bondholders gain from such transactions. Further, it reveals that sell-offs can be wealth redistributing, value destroying, or value enhancing depending on the way the sale proceeds are distributed and the motive underlying the sell-off. The wealth effects on stockholders and bondholders are not always symmetrical. Our results suggest that benefits from the sale of assets that do not strategically fit the firm's core business accrue primarily to stockholders, while benefits from distress-related sell-offs accrue to bondholders. Sell-offs result in wealth transfers between securityholders. Restrictive dividend covenants play an important role in protecting bondholders from wealth expropriation. Our analysis suggests that the relative size of the asset sale, the uses of the sale proceeds, and the degree of protection afforded bondholders via a dividend restriction may be relevant in explaining the direction of wealth transfer. (p. 41)

17.5   FINANCIAL RESTRUCTURING

In this section, we discuss two means by which a firm can respond to financial distress through *financial restructuring*, which involves (a) cutting dividends; or (b) equity restructuring in the form of a dual-class recapitalization, targeted stock, an equity carve-out, or a spin-off. (We discuss a third financial restructuring mechanism, debt restructuring, in Chapter 18.)

17.5.1   Dividend Cuts

In Chapter 14, we found that one of the strongest empirical observations regarding dividend policy is that firms *smooth* dividends relative to earnings over time. However, results from papers discussed below indicate that firms with large or chronic losses generally cut dividends quickly and substantially.

DeAngelo and DeAngelo (1990) studied the dividend adjustments of 80 dividend-paying New York Stock Exchange (NYSE) firms as they experienced protracted financial distress over the years 1980 to 1985. (Note that this period was marked by a recession in the United States followed by a choppy recovery.) By year-end 1985, 77 of the 80 firms in the authors' sample were paying lower dividends than they had been paying in 1979. They also found that the typical firm in their sample acted early and aggressively with a dividend reduction in response to financial distress: "For the typical firm, the initial dividend reduction represents a cut of more than 70 percent, made before the firm's first annual loss and immediately after one or two quarterly losses. Almost half the sample made multiple dividend reductions and, for these firms, the initial cut was typically followed quickly by additional severe dividend reductions" (p. 1416).

The authors also found that, although poor earnings appeared to be the primary determinant of dividend reductions, three additional factors also contributed to the decision. *First*, more than half the firms in the sample apparently faced binding debt covenants that forced them to cut their dividends. *Second*, "absent binding covenants, dividends are cut more often than omitted, suggesting that managerial reluctance is to the *omission* and not simply the reduction of dividends. Moreover, managers of firms with long dividend histories apparently view dividend omissions as particularly unattractive, perhaps because they would mark themselves as the first managers in many years whose policies generated insufficient cash to pay dividends" (p. 1415).

Third, for many of the firms in their sample, managers reduced dividends for strategic reasons—for instance, to enhance the firm's bargaining power with labor unions or to bolster its lobbying position with the U.S. Congress. The results of the authors' study underscore the complexity of financial decisions in the face of financial distress, in particular, the extent to which both internal and external stakeholders impinge on financial decisions under distress.

In their paper "Dividends and Losses," DeAngelo, DeAngelo, and Skinner (1992) analyzed 607 dividend-paying NYSE firms over the years 1980 to 1985, focusing on the incidence of dividend reductions. They found that at least one annual loss during this period is a necessary condition for a firm to reduce its dividend: "50.9 percent of the 167 firms with losses during 1980 to 1985 reduced dividends, versus 1.0 percent of 440 firms without losses" (p. 1837). Moreover, they found that among the firms with losses, dividend reductions were more likely if the firm had greater or more protracted losses.

In a subsequent paper, DeAngelo, DeAngelo, and Skinner (1996) examined the *signaling content* of the dividend decisions of 145 NYSE firms whose annual earnings declined after a long history of earnings growth. They summarize their results as follows: "[W]e find virtually no support for the notion that dividend decisions help identify firms with superior future earnings. Dividends tend not to be reliable signals because (i) a behavioral bias (overoptimism) leads managers to overestimate future earnings when growth prospects fade; and (ii) managers make only modest cash commitments when they increase dividends, undermining the reliability of such signals" (p. 341).

Finally, Jensen and Johnson (1995) examined the dynamic relationship between earnings changes and dividend changes, as well as other dynamics of firms that cut their dividends. They found that dividend-cutting firms generally experience (a) negative abnormal returns at the cut announcement, (b) decreased earnings before the cut, and (c) increased earnings after the cut. They also uncovered several interesting tendencies among dividend-cutting firms: "[F]ollowing a dividend drop, firms tend to reduce asset expenditures, external financing activities, employees, and spending on R&D. In addition, firms tend to sell more assets and their sales level remains depressed in the post-dividend-drop period. These post-dividend-drop occurrences may negatively impact a firm's future competitive position and, furthermore, may explain the negative stock price reaction that accompanies the dividend-drop announcement. Overall, our results suggest that a dividend-drop marks the end of a firm's financial decline and the beginning of firm restructuring" (p. 31).

17.5.2 Dual-Class Recaps

In a dual-class recapitalization (or "recap"), a firm creates a second class of common stock that has limited voting rights and generally a preferential claim to the firm's cash flows. This is accomplished by distributing replacement shares to current shareholders, which are designated as *class A shares*. Insiders retain shares that have superior voting rights, designated as *class B shares*. The general purpose of a dual-class recap is to concentrate voting power in the hands of the firm's insiders, and provide compensation to outsiders in the form of a stronger claim to residual cash flows.

Approximately 10 percent of the largest public companies in the United States have a dual-class equity structure. Examples include Ford Motor Co., Charter Communications, Inc., Tyson Foods, Inc., and Dow Jones & Co. The dual structure is controversial. For example, in 2000, the California Public Employees' Retirement System (CALpers) pushed a proposal to Tyson's shareholders to eliminate its dual-class structure, claiming that is was unfair. However, shareholders voted it down.

Moyer, Rao, and Sisneros (1992) provide two possible explanations for dual-class recaps. On the one hand, by dominating voting power, the firm's insiders can better entrench themselves or shirk their duties (i.e., a recap expropriates wealth from outside shareholders to insiders). On the other hand, a dual-class recap can create value for all shareholders if (a) other monitoring and control devices, such as the firm's board of directors, can effectively substitute for the outsiders' loss of voting rights, (b) management's intention with the recap is to make it easier for them to pursue long-term value-enhancing strategies, and (c) insiders are able to extract a higher premium from a bidder in a takeover attempt.

The authors pursued these competing hypotheses by examining 14 firms that had undergone dual-class recaps:

> Our results are inconsistent with the first explanation. The emergence of alternative monitoring mechanisms following dual class recapitalizations offsets, to some extent, the potential for managerial entrenchment and shirking arising from increased voting power. The observed relationship between the increasing potential for managerial entrenchment and increases both in outside board membership and the increased use of debt leverage, actions that are under control of managers, is especially persuasive in this regard. If dual class recapitalizations generally are not undertaken with an objective of transferring wealth from shareholders to managers, then the remaining competing explanation is that they are undertaken with an objective of increasing the efficiency of management and to protect shareholders from undervalued takeover attempts. (p. 45)

Bacon, Cornett, and Davidson III (1997) studied dual-class recap announcements. They tested hypotheses noted above, focusing on changes in the compositions of firms' boards of directors. They examined the extent to which board characteristics determine which of the forces associated with the hypotheses dominates, measuring this by relating market reactions at announcement to board characteristics. Two board characteristics that they found to be important are (a) the number of shares that board members hold (to which the market's reaction is positively related, presumably because share ownership serves to align their interests and shareholders' interests), and (b) board member tenure (to which the market's reaction is negatively related, presumably because it suggests that board members are entrenched). They also found that dual-class recap firms are more insider-controlled than typical publicly traded firms.

17.5.3 Issuing Targeted Stock

Targeted stock, also known as *tracking stock* or *letter stock*, is a class of common stock of a diversified company that is linked to the performance of a particular business unit or division. General Motors (GM) created the first targeted stock. After acquiring Electronic Data Systems (EDS) in 1984, GM issued targeted stock that paid a dividend tied to EDS's earnings. (In 1996, GM spun-off EDS.) The issuance of targeted stock remains a fairly rare event. D'Souza and Jacob (2000) reported: "To date, 14 companies have issued 37 targeted stocks that, at one time or another, have traded in public markets" (p. 460).

D'Souza and Jacob detail the characteristics of targeted stock as follows:

> Targeted stock does not represent direct ownership interest in the targeted business, but rather an ownership interest in the entire company. Holders of a targeted stock are generally entitled to vote on matters pertaining to the entire company. The number of votes that a targeted stockholder is entitled to can either be fixed at the time of issue of the targeted stock or float with the market value of the different targeted stocks.
>
> The issuance of targeted stock does not entail a legal division of the company. The businesses represented by the targeted stocks remain a part of the consolidated entity and share a common board of directors. Although the firm's assets and liabilities are attributed to the various targeted businesses for financial reporting purposes, legal title to the assets and responsibility for the liabilities remain with the consolidated entity.
>
> Financial statements conforming to GAAP [Generally Accepted Accounting Principles] are prepared separately for each targeted business. Holders of targeted stock of a division of a company receive financial statements for that division in addition to the financials for the company as a whole. Earnings per share and dividends are also computed separately for each targeted group. The income reported by the targeted business is the basis for the payment of dividends . . . (p. 463)

Logue, Seward, and Walsh (1996) documented evidence of a positive market reaction to announcements of targeted stock issues (2.9 percent, on average, on the issuing-firm's stock), arguing that it is "likely due to the greater transparency of particular business segments of a broadly diversified firm and to the increased ability to reward division managers for their specific contributions" (p. 43).

D'Souza and Jacob (2000) investigated both the market's reaction to a firm's announcement of the issuance of targeted stock and possible motives for their use: "We analyze market reaction to targeted stock issuances and investigate possible motives for their use. We find a statistically significant abnormal return of 3.61 percent within a three-day window around the announcement of proposed targeted stock issuances, possibly attributable to greater information on targeted stock segments as well as monitoring and motivational advantages. We find lower tax-loss carry forwards among firms that issue targeted stock compared to those that spin off segments, suggesting that tax reasons motivate targeted stock use. The return and cash flows of targeted stocks are affected more by their common corporate affiliation, although industry influences remain strong" (p. 459).

17.5.4   Equity Carve-outs

In an *equity carve-out*, the parent of a multiple-subsidiary firm issues equity claims against a particular subsidiary via a public offering, though the parent retains a majority of the shares, and thus control, of the subsidiary. An example is the Philip Morris carve-out in 2001 of Kraft Foods, Inc., which netted the parent $8.7 billion.

For perspective, Figure 17-1 displays annual aggregate statistics on equity carve-outs from 1980 to 2000. For each year, the figure shows the number of carve-outs conducted by U.S. nonfinancial firms, their aggregate volume (i.e., the sum of parents' proceeds from the offerings), and the average proceeds per issue. Clearly, carve-outs have increased in importance in recent years.

Schipper and Smith (1986) conducted an event study of equity carve-out announcements. They found positive announcement-period average abnormal returns of about 2 percent. Nanda (1991) developed a theoretical model based on the Myers and Majluf's (1984) asymmetric-information framework to explain the market's positive response to an equity carve-out, which contrasts with the negative market reaction to the announcement of a seasoned equity offering (Chapter 13): "We have argued that the choice of financing decision may provide information not just about the subsidiary's assets in place but also about the value of the assets in place of the rest of the corporation. In equilibrium, firms that choose an equity carve-out will typically be those that have been undervalued by the market. The fact that firms have the option of resorting to equity carve-outs, in some cases, allows firms to take on subsidiary projects that might otherwise have been forgone" (p. 1733).

FIGURE 17-1   Equity Carve-outs: Aggregate Proceeds, Number, and Average Proceeds

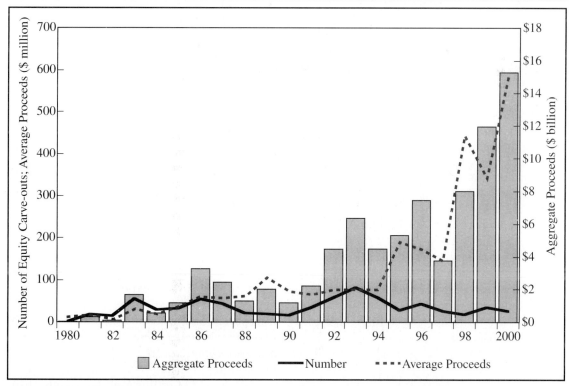

U.S. Nonfinancial Firms, 1980–2000
Source: Securities Data Corp.'s new-issue database.

How to Carve a Turkey

As large corporations learn to handle the flow of capital and information in a more sophisticated way, they are finding it easier to boost shareholder value by restructuring the capital and assets that make up their businesses. In the past decade, hundreds of corporations have used tracking stocks, equity carve-outs, and spin-offs for this purpose. AT&T's 1996 ownership restructuring provides a striking example. Before the company announced that it would spin off Lucent Technologies and NCR, its market value was just $75 billion. Little more than a year later, in January 1998, the separately trading AT&T, Lucent, and NCR had a combined market capitalization of $159 billion.

Tracking stocks, also known as letter or targeted stocks, are a class of parent company stock that tracks the earnings of a division or subsidiary. Typically distributed as a dividend to shareholders in the parent company, these shares can also take the form of an initial public offering (IPO). *Equity carve-outs* are an IPO of a stake in a subsidiary. The parent usually keeps majority ownership. *Spin-offs* occur when the entire ownership of a subsidiary is divested as a dividend to shareholders.

In the case of tracking stocks, control remains in the hands of the parent company's board; in carve-outs and spin-offs, by contrast, management reports to new and separate boards. Similarly, the assets of companies with tracking stocks are not physically separated from those of their corporate parents, though they do have to report earnings separately. In carve-outs and spin-offs, conversely, the subsidiary's assets are transferred to the new company's balance sheet.

Carve-outs have assumed a prominent place in U.S. equity activity. In the past ten years, the U.S. stock market has seen an average of almost 50 carve-outs a year, or about 10 percent of all IPOs. One recent example of a substantial carve-out is DuPont's IPO of Conoco, in October 1998. DuPont raised $4.2 billion for a 30 percent stake in its subsidiary.

The level of spin-off activity has also been high recently: More than 300 spin-offs took place in the United States between January 1988 and September 1998. A notable example of a spin-off was the 1995 breakup of ITT into three businesses—diversified industrial, insurance, and hotels and gaming. By contrast, tracking stocks are few and far between. Since General Motors issued the first of them with its acquisition of EDS in 1984, a total of 23 have been listed in the United States. Several more have been announced and subsequently canceled, and a few others are pending.

CREATING VALUE FOR SHAREHOLDERS

Companies that elect to restructure usually have one goal in mind: creating value for shareholders. Empirical evidence in the form both of price-to-earnings (P/E) multiples and total return to shareholders (TRS)—the combined capital appreciation and dividend yield of an equity—demonstrates that, on average, each form of restructuring creates value.

Gains in stock prices flow from four changes. First, there is an increase in coverage by analysts. This seems to support investment bankers' claims that floating equity in business units not previously exposed to the market makes their operating performance more transparent and raises shareholder returns by revealing hidden value. This transparency, however, comes not from a greater quantity of information provided by the company—it can freely provide more information about business units without restructuring ownership—but from an improvement in the quality of analysts' coverage. Second, the restructured subsidiaries attract new investors. Indeed, there is little overlap between people who invested in a parent company and those who invest in its subsidiaries after a restructuring. Third, the restructuring of ownership usually improves a subsidiary's operating performance through such means as new incentives to management. Finally, restructuring can improve corporate governance and increase strategic flexibility.

IMPROVING COVERAGE BY ANALYSTS

Small divisions or subsidiaries within a large company may find that their growth prospects are not fully appreciated by securities analysts. An analyst specializing in the chemical industry, say, may track as many as 30 companies. This leaves little time to get to know the complexities of a small pharmaceutical subsidiary, whose valuation may suffer as a result. Slight differences in growth expectations can dramatically alter the value analysts place on the subsidiary. When companies launch tracking stocks, equity carve-outs, or spin-offs, they receive more attention from analysts. For all three restructuring options, the combined parent and subsidiary receive 25 percent more coverage in the two years after a transaction. By contrast, the overall number of U.S. equity analysts rose by just 2 percent a year in the 1990s. The increase in attention comes mostly in the form of new coverage of the subsidiary by analysts who specialize in its industry. After the 1996 spin-off from AT&T, Lucent picked up coverage from 24 telecom equipment analysts; previously, only two of them had covered AT&T. The parent, whose remaining analysts can focus on it more closely, benefits as well. Greater coverage from analysts is one reason many high-tech companies undertake carve-outs. Safeguard Scientifics, for instance, confirms that the several carve-outs it has executed have sparked new interest among analysts.

ATTRACTING NEW INVESTORS

In theory, the market values a company as the sum of its parts, analyzing the growth prospects of each of the separate businesses and using the market view of predicted cash flows to determine the price of the stock. In practice, the market consists of many investors with their own individual criteria for making a purchase. The trouble is that investors who find a particular division of a company attractive might reject the stock of the corporate parent because, for example, it competes in a less attractive line of business or has slower growth prospects.

Take US West. In 1995, it was a regional Bell operating company that also owned cable and cellular operations. An investor seeking the comparative stability of a utility stock would also be purchasing the volatility inherent in an emerging growth division. Another investor, wishing to benefit from the capital appreciation potential of the cable and wireless business, would be frustrated by the relatively slow earnings growth of the telecommunications utility. Neither of these investors would be entirely satisfied. Seeking to win over two kinds of investors with different risk and reward profiles, US West therefore created a Media Group tracking stock. While US West's Bell operating company continued to pay stable quarterly dividends, the Media Group offered an opportunity for high capital appreciation but paid no dividends. Just a year after the launch of the Media Group, new investors owned more than 86 percent of its stock.

IMPROVING OPERATING PERFORMANCE

If we examine the operating performance of newly traded subsidiaries during the two years from the time of issue, we see, on average, substantial increases in the return on invested capital (ROIC) both in the tracking stocks and the spin-offs, while the ROIC of carve-outs dips slightly. Carve-outs instead enjoy high revenue growth in the two years after they begin trad-

(continued)

ing, with an average annual gain of 32 percent. The corresponding figure for the S&P 500 from 1990 to 1997 is just 7 percent. Carve-outs thus unleash value through top-line growth rather than cost efficiencies.

Issuing any of these new equities makes it possible for a company to offer managers incentives tied to the market performance of the divisions they run. John England, of the compensation firm Towers Perrin, says, "With carve-outs, companies have a once-in-a-lifetime opportunity to develop a new executive and board compensation program. They can clearly indicate to investors, executives, and other employees that performance, ownership, risk, and reward are bound together."

INCREASING STRATEGIC FLEXIBILITY

The restructuring of ownership permits a company to push management accountability deeper into the organization. For a subsidiary that is newly exposed to the market, greater scrutiny by investors and analysts creates a "second board" to which management must respond. Operating performance generally improves as a result. For management in poorly performing businesses, the new accountability becomes tangible through lower compensation when the stock falters. Both tracking stocks and equity carve-outs increase strategic flexibility by facilitating mergers and acquisitions. In our sample, 22 percent of the tracking stocks were issued for use as acquisition currency. Four carve-outs between 1988 and 1998 were undertaken primarily to raise capital for future acquisitions. Four spin-offs were motivated chiefly by this aim, and an additional five were carried out to eliminate strategic conflicts that prevented the parent or its subsidiary from completing a merger or an acquisition. Spin-offs can increase the strategic flexibility of businesses by allowing a subsidiary to form relationships with companies that do not want competitive information to flow to its parent. After being spun off from AT&T, Lucent was better able

to do business with international telecommunications companies that perceived its parent as a rival.

COMMON CONCERNS

Sometimes a company hesitates to use these restructuring tools, despite their evident advantages, because it is worried about the new entity's stability or fears that costs and complexity will rise.

STABILITY

In the case of tracking stocks and carve-outs, some companies have expressed fears that a subsidiary might be taken over by their rivals or that analysts could exert pressure to spin it off completely. In the case of spin-offs, the corporate parent may doubt the ability of an enterprise to survive independently.

RISING COSTS AND COMPLEXITY

Senior managers at companies contemplating a tracking-stock or carve-out structure must consider the greater complexity brought by new equities. For one thing, the board of directors will have to be responsive to more than one set of shareholders. Moreover, the creation of equities to attract different types of investors places a burden on senior management to communicate effectively and consistently with each group.

The need to share resources within a tracking-stock or carve-out structure adds another layer of complexity: R&D costs, for example, may need to be divided between the income statements of the parent and the subsidiary. Ownership restructuring also creates the potential for conflicts of interest between the two entities. A parent and a subsidiary may, for example, find themselves on opposite sides of a regulatory issue, such as those that bedevil the telecommunications industry. Or a subsidiary that is vertically integrated with its parent might want to pursue business with its parent's competitors. The SABRE Group, for instance, provides reservation systems not only for

American Airlines, its parent, but also for some of American's rivals.

Companies incur transaction and overhead costs, too. The direct transaction costs associated with raising new capital in the market through an equity carve-out can represent 2–5 percent of the transaction's total value; for a spin-off or tracking stock, the figure is around 2 percent. The higher percentage for carve-outs may reflect the fact that their offerings often come in the form of an IPO and not a stock distribution. On top of these transaction costs, companies giving thought to restructuring must take into account the costs of dual governance structures and additional reporting requirements. These expenses, both direct and reckoned in management time and attention, must be weighed against the substantial benefits that ownership restructuring brings to many companies and their shareholders.

WHEN TO RESTRUCTURE . . .

By posing a series of simple questions, senior executives can determine when it might be appropriate to disaggregate by means of a new equity issue, and which option to choose. Those who answer "yes" to most of the following questions should seriously consider an ownership restructuring:

- Do parent and subsidiary operate in different industries?
- Is the subsidiary growing much faster or slower than its parent?
- Do analysts seldom mention the subsidiary's future growth and earnings prospects?
- Are high-performing managers or key technical staffers being lost to smaller competitors, or is there a risk that this might happen?

. . . AND HOW

Once a company has determined that restructuring may be advisable, it must select one of the three options below.

A *spin-off* may make the most sense if the following conditions prevail:

- The parent company is no longer in the best position to create the greatest value from its business through skills, systems, or synergies; in other words, it has ceased to be the natural owner of the business. One reason for the 1996 spin-off of EDS from GM was the desire to free EDS from constraints that prevented it from pursuing certain deals.
- The strategic interests of parent and subsidiary conflict. When US West issued tracking stock for its Media Group in 1995, it expected the telecom services and cable businesses to converge. But when the expected synergy did not materialize, parent and subsidiary found themselves in opposite camps over regulatory issues. The Media Group was spun off as MediaOne in June 1998.

A *majority-owned carve-out* is the most appropriate choice in three circumstances:

- When the parent or the subsidiary needs better access to capital. In general, companies that take the carve-out approach are more highly leveraged than their peers and perform less well, so they are more likely to suffer capital constraints. Carve-outs allow companies to raise capital at a fair price and to fund projects that might otherwise depress earnings.
- When decision-making power in an organization must be devolved to the people who know it best. In companies with centralized capital budgeting, for instance, division managers have an incentive to overstate their investment needs and to waste time lobbying for bigger budgets. Carved-out businesses, by contrast, can gain direct access to capital markets—a key advantage for fast-growing enterprises that might otherwise struggle to win funds. At Thermo Electron, for instance, managers of carve-outs assume primary responsibility for financing and investment decisions.
- When subsidiaries can readily be separated without problems over the price of the transfer. Both boards will have to review contractual agreements, including those establishing transfer prices. Other issues include the sharing of R&D, sales and marketing, and manufacturing resources. If the split can be made without extreme complexity, equity carve-outs are an attractive option.

(continued)

Equity carve-outs may also be preferable to tracking stocks when shareholders are expected to react adversely to a tracking-stock deal. Carve-outs on average have the strongest TRS performance of any restructuring option, while their effect on P/E multiples is roughly comparable to the effect of the other possibilities. In addition, carve-outs are much more common than tracking stocks, so the market understands carve-outs better.

Either an equity carve-out or a tracking stock can create value in the following circumstances:

- When equity is needed for use as an acquisition currency, especially if the acquisition target is not interested in the parent company's shares. GM issued tracking stock when it acquired EDS in 1984. As EDS began trading, its forward-looking P/E was 38, as compared with 5 for GM. When US West issued Media Group tracking-stock shares in 1995, they traded at P/E multiples of 76, as compared with 17 for the parent company, and were used in the following year to acquire Continental Cablevision.

- When a subsidiary could take advantage of its parent company's capital structure to borrow at lower cost. USX and Circuit City both chose tracking stock in part to maintain the ability of the disaggregated entities to borrow at the debt rating of the consolidated company.

- When the margins and growth of a subsidiary are on a par with or better than those of its pure-play peers. If its operating performance lags the industry average, a carve-out or tracking stock probably will not create value and may even destroy it. (By contrast, companies may choose to spin off their poorly performing subsidiaries to improve their performance, even if the subsidiary falters.) Ralston Purina's Continental Baking Group was issued as a tracking stock in 1993 to provide an incentive for management to turn the unit around. By the

time the group was sold in 1995, the stock had sunk to one-third of its original value.

Tracking stocks, in two situations, are likely to be better than either carve-outs or spin-offs, since both require at least some separation of assets:

- If the parent or the subsidiary of a U.S. company has net operating losses that can be used to offset taxable profits. More than 50 percent of the companies that have issued tracking stocks take advantage of the parent's or the subsidiary's net operating losses in this way.[1] Genzyme has used the losses flowing from the high R&D expenses of its Tissue Repair tracking stock to reduce taxes at the corporate level.

- If restructuring seems to be attractive, but the parent and the subsidiary share synergies or use similar business systems. The Delhi Group of USX operated gas-processing plants jointly with Marathon Oil. A spin-off would have required what at that time was an unnatural division of these assets, but the Delhi tracking stock, which began trading in 1992, eliminated the need for a separation.

Companies that restructure their ownership can often improve the performance of business units by exposing them to the market and thus attracting a more focused analyst community and new investors. More important, such companies can improve their operating performance by providing incentives for managers and increasing their strategic flexibility. Used judiciously, spin-offs, equity carve-outs, and tracking stocks are important tools that help corporate management increase value.

---

[1]U.S. tax law also allows consolidation for tax purposes in equity carve-outs whose parent companies maintain more than 80 percent ownership. In these cases, net operating losses in one division can be used to offset taxable profits in another.

Source: This article is excerpted from "Breaking up Is Good to Do: Restructuring through Spin-offs, Equity Carve-outs, and Tracking Stocks Can Create Shareholder Value," P. L. Anslinger, S. J. Klepper, S. Subramaniam, *The McKinsey Quarterly*, no. 1, 1999. Copyright © 1999 McKinsey & Co. The article can be found on the publication's Web site, www.mckinseyquarterly.com. Used by permission.

Allen and McConnell (1998) offered the following hypothesis and supporting evidence to explain equity carve-outs: "This study proposes a managerial discretion hypothesis of equity carve-outs in which managers value control over assets and are reluctant to carve out subsidiaries. Thus, managers undertake carve-outs only when the firm is capital constrained. Consistent with this hypothesis, firms that carve out subsidiaries exhibit poor operating performance and high leverage prior to carve-outs. Also consistent with this hypothesis, in carve-outs wherein funds raised are used to pay down debt, the average excess stock return of +6.63 percent is significantly greater than the average excess stock return of –0.01 percent for carve-outs wherein funds are retained for investment purposes" (p. 163).

Vijh (1999) documented evidence on the long-term performance of equity carve-outs as investments.

Using a sample of 628 carveouts during 1981–1995 . . . the newly issued subsidiary stocks do not underperform appropriate benchmarks over a three-year period following the carveout. This result is in striking contrast with the documented poor performance of initial public offerings and seasoned equity offerings. I conjecture that the superior performance of subsidiary stocks arises because the subsidiary and parent firms can focus on fewer business segments after carveout, and because the parent firms continue to own a monitoring position in the subsidiary firms. I test whether the subsidiary stock performance is related to the number of business segments the parent firm has before carveout. The relationship is not always significant, which suggests another possible explanation, that the market may react efficiently to the likely future performance of carveouts. (p. 273)

A Case in Point: The Equity Carve-outs of Thermo Electron

Allen (1998) investigated the numerous equity carve-outs conducted by Thermo Electron starting in 1983. Prior to that year, Thermo Electron had performed rather poorly since its inception in the late 1950s. In contrast, Allen documents evidence that, from 1983 through year-end 1995, Thermo Electron's stock had substantially outperformed the S&P 500 index, and that "the gains in Thermo Electron stock can largely be attributed to the market performance of the majority-owned carve-outs" (p. 101).

Allen also found "substantial increases in capital investment spending by carve-outs of the company in the first and second years following their separation from the parent" (p. 101). The success of these carve-outs may be attributed in large part to (a) the parent's decentralized governance structure, and (b) market-based compensation contracts given to carve-out managers: "Carve-outs subject units of the company to the scrutiny of the capital markets, allow the compensation contracts of unit managers to be based on market performance, and shift capital acquisition and investment decisions from centralized control to unit managers" (p. 99).

17.5.5   Spin-offs

A spin-off is a pro rata distribution of new equity claims on a subsidiary to the parent's shareholders. Michaely and Shaw (1995) explained the three essential differences between a spin-off and an equity carve-out: "First, shares in a spin-off are distributed to existing shareholders; a carve-out establishes a new set of shareholders. Second, stocks issued through a carve-out generate positive cash flow to the firm; a spin-off does not have immediate cash flow consequences. Third, firms that divest through a carve-out incur significantly greater out-of-pocket expenses and are subject to more stringent disclosure requirements by the SEC" (p. 5). While these statements are generally accurate, transactions involving tracking stock, equity carve-outs, and spin-offs can be complex, as we discuss next.

Doing the Two-Step: Issuing Tracking Stock or Conducting an Equity Carve-out, Followed by Spin-off

Although the issue has not been extensively addressed in the finance literature, it seems logical that, before it spins off a unit, a diversified firm must establish a liquid secondary market for unit's shares, either by issuing tracking stock or by conducting an equity carve-out (see Klein, Rosenfeld, and Beranek 1991). Otherwise, shareholders obtain shares that have no established secondary market.

For example, GM had a long-established secondary market for EDS tracking stock before its 1996 spin-off. Also, AT&T conducted an initial public offering (IPO) of AT&T wireless tracking stock in 2000 before conducting a spin-off in 2001. The AT&T Wireless IPO netted $10.6 billion for AT&T (the largest IPO in U.S. history), even though AT&T retained 82.5 percent of AT&T Wireless shares. In mid-2001, AT&T initially disposed of 438 million shares of AT&T Wireless via an exchange offer for AT&T shares, and then distributed 1.1 billion shares of AT&T Wireless common shares to AT&T shareholders. In December 2001, AT&T sold its remaining 91 million shares of AT&T Wireless in the open market.

An equity carve-out not only allows the parent to raise needed capital via the IPO, but also allows the parent to retain control of the subsidiary before, typically, distributing the remaining shares, which have an established secondary market, via a spin-off at a later date. For example, in May 2001, Reliant Energy conducted an equity carve-out IPO of subsidiary Reliant Resources. Reliant Energy retained approximately 80 percent of Reliant Resource's outstanding shares. However, it announced plans to complete a spin-off of the company within 12 months of the IPO by distributing the remaining shares of Reliant Resources to its shareholders.

Theory and Evidence on the Spin-off Decision

Several studies have found that the market generally responds favorably to a firm's announcement of a spin-off. The average abnormal return surrounding spin-off announcements ranges from 2.4 percent to 4.3 percent, depending on the sample (Hite and Owers 1983; Miles and Rosenfeld 1983; Schipper and Smith 1983; Rosenfeld 1984). In addition, Cusatis, Miles, and Woolridge (1993) documented evidence of longer-term abnormally positive returns on firms involved in a spin-off.

What is it about a spin-off that elicits a favorable market reaction? Researchers have proffered several hypotheses. *First*, a spin-off constitutes an expropriation of wealth from the parent's bondholders to parent's stockholders, because bondholders lose a claim on the spun-off assets. *Second*, a spin-off may relieve regulatory constraints (Schipper and Smith 1983). *Third*, a spin-off may allow restructuring of managerial incentive contracts (Aron, 1991). *Fourth*, a spin-off is generally associated with increased focus and the elimination of negative synergies between the parent and the (former) subsidiary (Hite and Owers 1983; Schipper and Smith 1983;

Daley, Mehrotra, and Sivakumar 1997; Desai and Jain 1999). *Fifth* and finally, a spin-off can create valuable tax advantages (Mauer and Lewellen 1990; Schipper and Smith 1983).

Krishnaswami and Subramaniam (1999) documented evidence consistent with yet a sixth hypothesis about gains from spin-offs. This hypothesis, developed by Nanda and Narayanan (1999), is based on information asymmetry. Krishnaswami and Subramaniam explain Nanda and Narayanan's model as follows: "They assume that the market can observe the aggregate cash flows of the firm but not the individual divisional cash flows, which results in misvaluation of the firm's securities. They develop an equilibrium in which an undervalued firm that requires external capital to finance growth opportunities will resort to raising capital either through a divestiture or after a divestiture, and an overvalued firm will resort to an equity issue without separating its divisions. In the context of spin-offs, since the divestiture does not generate cash inflows to the firm, undervalued firms requiring capital would first engage in a spin-off to attain fair market value for their shares and then issue equity to raise capital" (p. 78).

The authors summarize their empirical results as follows:

> We empirically analyze the information hypothesis that the separation of a firm's divisions into independently traded units through a spin-off enhances value because it mitigates information asymmetry about the firm. Consistent with this hypothesis, we find that firms that engage in spin-offs have higher levels of information asymmetry compared to their industry and size matched counterparts and the information problems decrease significantly after the spin-off. The gains around spin-offs are positively related to the degree of information asymmetry, and this relation is more pronounced for firms with fewer negative synergies between divisions. Finally, firms with higher growth opportunities and firms in need of external capital show a higher propensity to engage in spin-offs. They also raise more capital following a spin-off, which is consistent with the view that these firms mitigate information asymmetry before approaching the capital market for funds. (p. 73)

More discussion is found in McConnell, Ozbilgin, and Wahal (2001) and Allen (2001).

17.5.6   Comparing Equity Carve-outs, Spin-offs, and Asset Sales

Slovin, Sushka, and Ferraro (1995) compared the information about industry rivals that is conveyed by an equity carve-out, a spin-off, and an asset sale (an asset sell-off): "We examine valuation effects on firms in the same industry as entities that are the subject of carve-outs (initial public offerings of subsidiary equity), spin-offs, and asset sell-offs. Share price reactions for rivals are negative in response to equity carve-outs. In comparison, rival stock returns are positive for spin-offs and normal for asset sell-offs, restructuring actions that do not entail a public offering of equity. Our results suggest managers conduct equity carve-outs when outside investors are likely to price the new shares higher than managers' perceived value" (p. 89).

17.6 REFORMING GOVERNANCE OR MANAGEMENT STRUCTURES, OR REPLACING MANAGEMENT

In this section, we discuss three additional mechanisms that a firm might employ to alleviate financial distress: (a) reforming its governance structure, (b) reforming the hierarchical structure of senior management or its compensation contracts, or (c) replacing senior management.

17.6.1 Reforming Governance

To address distress, a firm may consider any of the following four changes in its board structure. *First*, it is often argued that outsiders are better monitors than insiders, so a distressed firm may replace insiders with outsiders (Chapter 8). *Second*, requiring directors to hold equity shares also serves to align their interests with those of the shareholders. *Third*, limiting the tenure of directors, or ending the staggering of board elections, serves both to reduce entrenchment and to bring new ideas into the boardroom on a regular basis. *Fourth*, as Jensen (1989) advocates, a distressed firm should consider reducing the size of its board, as smaller boards may be more effective monitors.

17.6.2 Reforming Management Structure and Contracts

Some firms operate in a top-heavy hierarchical structure, others in a relatively horizontal structure that emphasizes autonomy and individual initiative (Chapter 8). Some firms have abandoned the single-mindedness of a dominant CEO by initiating a *team approach* to senior management.[3] Alternatively, a firm's board might consider revising incentives in senior managers' compensation contracts (Chapter 8).

17.6.3 Replacing Management

Under the most distressed circumstances, a firm's board may be forced to fire the CEO. This action is never taken lightly, because it can cause substantial disruption. Casual empiricism suggests that a CEO is fired when he or she has committed the firm to a course of action that has turned out to be a costly blunder. Under these circumstances, the board, middle managers and other employees, and shareholders have lost faith in the CEO, so he or she simply must depart. Furtado and Karan (1990) provide an excellent review of the literature on the causes and effects of management turnover. They organize their discussion into three major parts, each of which we discuss below.

Factors That Cause Top Management Turnover

A change in top management "can be either disciplinary or the result of planned intervention for future economic growth. Being the guardians of shareholder wealth, it is assumed that boards act in the best interests of the shareholders. Additional monitoring is provided by the other senior managers who also compete for corporate control and by large shareholders. Thus, management turnover in some measure is linked to firm performance, and the hypothesis that has been extensively tested is that weak

---

[3]A recent example is Abbott Laboratories. In 2000, it replaced its president and chief operating officer (COO) with a three-person team.

performance leads to a larger than normal rate of turnover. However, dismissals are either rare or underreported, and their frequency difficult to determine" (p. 61). "[T]wo factors undermine the relationship between performance and turnover . . . when managers also own the firm's stocks, or when boards are dominated by insiders, the relationship between performance and turnover is substantially weakened" (p. 67).

Consequences of Management Change
"The process of management change can be viewed as a strategy to adapt the firm to a changing environment; it is an intervention mechanism that addresses the firm's current and future existence. Researchers even suggest that outside appointments are beneficial to a firm and necessary for a turnaround strategy to be successful" (p. 67). "Two actions seem to occur after management turnover. First, firms may take 'earnings baths' in an attempt to show they subsequently improved performance. Second, there is some connection between a firm's response to the changing environment and characteristics sought in a successor to top posts" (p. 69).

Shareholder Wealth Effects of Turnover
"Market response to change can be viewed either as due to the gain or loss of 'human capital,' or as a response to the 'signal' of the change. For instance, it is believed that managers possess firm-specific or general human capital. When managers with firm-specific capital leave, or when there are few substitutes for the departing manager, turnover should affect firm value. The alternative to firm-specific human capital, general human capital, is costlessly substitutable and occurs when contract costs are zero or when the replacing manager has similar managerial skills. The replacement of a manager who possesses only general human capital should not affect firm value.

A second aspect of the market's reaction to turnover is the signal received. Top managers are insiders, privy to information not publicly available, and thus a change in their ranks can release signals about the firm's current and future status to the outside world. A major problem, however, is the multiplicity of signals that can be given. For example, change may signal redirection in firm policy, reorganization of the firm's assets, change in investment opportunities, an exodus of key managers from poorly performing firms, or all of the above. It is also possible that change, when expected (as in a planned transition for mandatory retirees), may not convey any information. Thus signals can be good, bad, or neutral in their effect in firm value . . . " (p. 69).

Activist Shareholders and CEO Turnover in Distressed Firms
Finally, several empirical studies have documented evidence that (a) activist shareholders often purchase large blocks of shares of poorly performing firms, (b) CEO turnover often results, and (c) the focal firm's shareholders benefit from these actions (Holderness and Sheehan 1985; Barclay and Holderness 1991; Bethel, Liebeskind, and Opler 1998).

17.7   A CASE IN POINT: IBM'S RESTRUCTURING

In this section, we consider the case of International Business Machines (IBM), focusing on its restructuring efforts in the 1990s.

17.7.1   A Synopsis of IBM's Historical Development

IBM was incorporated in the state of New York in 1911 as the Computer-Tabulating-Recording Company, with a product line that included time clocks, scales, and punch card tabulators. Thomas J. Watson became its president in 1915, and would lead the company for over 40 years. In 1924, C-T-R adopted the name International Business Machines Corporation. The firm survived the stock market crash of 1929 and the subsequent Great Depression of the 1930s, even though the U.S. government filed an antitrust suit against IBM in 1932 (and would file additional antitrust suits in 1952 and 1969). In 1956, CEO Thomas J. Watson Jr. reorganized and decentralized the company. In the ensuing years, IBM faced little competition, and thus its earnings grew at substantial double-digit annual rates. The firm marketed its first personal computer (PC) in 1981. More recently, Louis V. Gerstner Jr. took over as CEO from John F. Akers, who resigned in 1993, the year in which IBM posted the worst loss in its history. As of the firm's 2000 proxy statement, Gerstner was CEO and Chairman of the Board.

Prior to the 1990s, IBM had enjoyed a preeminent position in the computer industry for many years, and consistently posted substantial and growing earnings. In 1968, IBM become the most valuable firm in the United States (in terms of market equity value), and basically held that position through 1990 (though it was often nip-and-tuck with AT&T prior to its breakup in 1984, and then with Exxon and General Electric). However, IBM began to falter in 1991, in part because it failed to recognize early the importance of the personal computer. This failure allowed upstart rivals such as Apple Computer, Compaq, and Microsoft to excel. The firm eventually recovered, but only after a bruising restructuring effort.

In the remainder of this section, we examine IBM's activities and financial performance over the years 1980 to 2000. Figure 17-2 facilitates this analysis by showing time series values of various financial variables associated with IBM over this period. Shown are annual values of IBM's net income, cash dividends, and capital expenditures, as well as year-end values of its total assets, debt, other liabilities, book equity, and market equity value. For the purpose of our continuing discussion, we divide our study period into four fairly distinct subperiods: 1980 to 1985, 1986 to 1990, 1991 to 1993, and 1994 to 2000.

17.7.2   IBM Subperiod 1 (1980–1985): *Continued Growth*

From 1980 to 1985, IBM continued to generate substantial and growing earnings, hallmarks of its historical success. The firm's average return on common equity (ROE) was 21.8 percent during these years, and net income nearly doubled from $3.6 billion in 1980 to $6.6 billion in 1985, a compound annual growth rate of 13.0 percent. The market value of IBM's equity nearly tripled from $37.6 billion at year-end 1979 to $95.7 billion at year-end 1985, and investors enjoyed an average annual return of 23.9 percent. Regarding capital structure, IBM continued its historical policy of low leverage throughout this period, with an average debt ratio of only 10.0 percent. The firm also continued its historical pattern of substantial earnings payout and dividend growth, as the average payout ratio was 47.4 percent and dividends grew at a compound annual rate of 6.1 percent.

However, IBM's capital expenditures stagnated during this period, perhaps an ominous sign of things to come. Capital expenditures actually peaked at $6.9 billion in

FIGURE 17-2   Financial details for IBM, 1980–2000

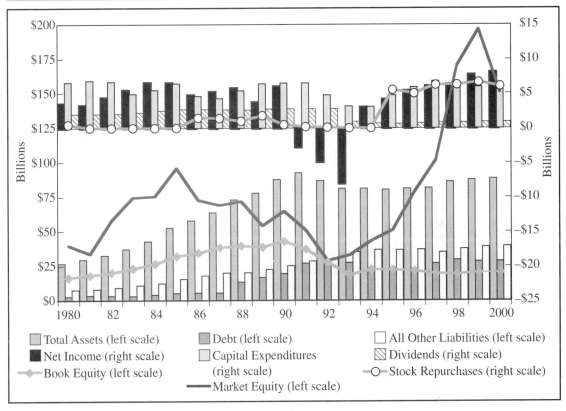

Total Assets (left scale)   Debt (left scale)   All Other Liabilities (left scale)
Net Income (right scale)   Capital Expenditures   Dividends (right scale)
Book Equity (left scale)   (right scale)   Stock Repurchases (right scale)
Market Equity (left scale)

Source: Raw data from Standard & Poor's *Research Insight* database.

1981, a level that would not be exceeded through 2000. Nevertheless, at year-end 1985 IBM's market-to-book equity ratio was 3.0, nearly twice the year-end 1985 composite ratio of 1.7 for all firms in our Chapter 1 sample of U.S. nonfinancial firms (review Figure 1-3). Clearly, the market still respected IBM's ability to create value.

17.7.3   IBM Subperiod 2 (1986–1990): *Stagnation*

In the years 1986 to 1990, IBM stagnated. Its average net income was still substantial at $5.1 billion, but was consistently lower than the $6.6 billion posted in 1985. Average ROE fell to 13.1 percent from 21.8 percent for 1980 to 1985. The market value of the firm's equity plummeted by a third to $64.5 billion at year-end 1990 and the average annual return on IBM stock was –1.1 percent, compared to 13.8 percent for the S&P 500 index. By year-end 1990, the firm's market-to-book equity ratio had fallen to 1.5, compared to 3.0 at year-end 1985 and a composite value of 2.0 for all U.S. nonfinancial firms at year-end 1990.

IBM's management responded to these adverse developments with six initiatives. *First*, annual capital expenditures slipped slightly to an average of $5.4 billion. *Second*, dividend growth slowed to an average annual rate of only 0.5 percent. (Nevertheless, the firm's average dividend payout ratio increased slightly to 54.7 percent.) *Third*, the firm embarked on a substantial stock repurchase program. During the period, IBM repurchased shares of its own stock with a total value of $6.2 billion. *Fourth*, the firm nearly quadrupled its debt, from $5.2 billion at year-end 1985 to $19.5 billion at year-end 1990. As a result, its debt ratio increased from 10.0 percent at year-end 1985 to 22.3 percent at year-end 1990. The increase in debt was obviously required to maintain the firm's capital expenditures and dividends, as well as to finance share repurchases, all in the face of stagnating earnings.

Fifth, in 1985, the company embarked on a series of actions to streamline and reduce resources used in its business. These actions were to expand into full-scale restructuring in the early 1990s, as we discuss below. *Sixth*, in 1989 IBM's board of directors took action to enhance management's incentives to improve performance. This action took the form of a long-term performance plan. This brief description of the plan is taken from documents filed with the Securities and Exchange Commission (SEC):

> The IBM 1989 Long-Term Performance Plan provides for incentive awards to be made to officers and other key employees. The plan is administered by the Executive Compensation and Management Resources Committee of the Board of Directors. The Committee determines the type of award to be granted, which may include stock, a stock option, a Stock Appreciation Right (SAR), cash, or any combination thereof. The number of shares made available for granting in the year was .85 percent of IBM's projected outstanding common stock as of December 31, 1993. Prior to 1989, stock options were issued under the IBM 1986 and predecessor Stock Option Plans.

17.7.4   IBM Subperiod 3 (1991–1993): *Losses and Restructuring*

The years 1991 to 1993 were the worst of times for the company. The firm posted progressive losses of $2.8 billion, $5.0 billion, and $8.1 billion in 1991, 1992, and 1993, respectively. The losses were largely due to charges related to the firm's restructuring activities. The restructuring activities included workforce reductions (which generated charges for employees' *termination incentives*) and related relocations and facility consolidations. The pretax amounts of these restructuring charges were $3.7 billion in 1991, $11.6 billion in 1992, and $8.9 billion in 1993. In addition, capital expenditures plunged 50 percent, from $6.5 billion in 1990 to only $3.2 billion in 1993.

IBM also continued to increase the amount of debt on its books, from $19.5 billion at year-end 1990 to $27.3 billion at year-end 1993. In addition, posted losses in these three years totaling $15.9 billion, and dividends totaling $6.5 billion, contributed to the erosion of the firm's equity base, which decreased from $42.8 billion at year-end 1990 to only $18.6 billion at year-end 1993. As a result of these changes in debt and equity, the firm's debt ratio increased from 22.3 percent at year-end 1990 to 33.7 percent at year-end 1993. Under these deteriorating conditions, management slashed dividends twice in 1993, from $1.21 per share paid in the fourth quarter of 1992 to $0.54 paid in the first quarter of 1993, and then again from $0.54 paid in the second quarter to $0.25 paid in the third quarter.

Regarding valuation, over this period the firm's market equity value decreased by nearly 50 percent, from $64.5 billion at year-end 1990 to $32.7 billion at year-end 1993. (The firm's share repurchases were negligible during this period.) Shareholders sustained average annual returns of –14.0 percent over this three-year period, compared to 16.1 percent for the S&P 500 index. On the bright side, however, the market's assessment of IBM stock actually began to improve in 1993, as (a) market equity value increased from its nadir of $28.7 billion at year-end 1992 to $32.7 billion at year-end 1993, (b) the return on the firm's stock in 1993 was 15.6 percent, compared to 10.1 percent for the S&P 500 index, and (c) the firm's market-to-book equity ratio increased from 1.0 at year-end 1992 to 1.8 at year-end 1993.

17.7.5 IBM Subperiod 4 (1994–2000): *Recovery*

By year-end 1993, IBM had basically completed its restructuring, and was emerging as a more diversified firm in the business services industry. Rather than focusing only on producing mainframe computers, the firm was also a major producer of personal computers, software, and related equipment, and was committed to the burgeoning area of information technology services. Over the years 1994 to 2000, the firm posted growing earnings each year (reaching a record level of $8.1 billion in 2000), and its average ROE, 28.4 percent, actually exceeded that of the first subperiod.

Interestingly, however, the firm chose not to restore dividends, either in terms of dollar amounts (which remained at approximately one-third of their pre-dividend cut level) or payout ratio (which averaged only 13.5 percent over the final subperiod). Nor did the firm pay down its debt, which increased slightly from $27.3 billion at year-end 1993 to $28.6 billion at year-end 2000. The firm's debt ratio decreased only slightly from 33.7 percent at year-end 1993 to 32.3 percent at year-end 2000.

Instead, the firm predominantly retained earnings to fund capital expenditures and to reengage its share-repurchase program. Capital expenditures averaged $5.5 billion annually, and the firm purchased $36 billion of its own stock during this subperiod. Remarkably, despite these substantial stock repurchases (or perhaps, indirectly, *because* of them), IBM's market equity value increased from $32.7 billion at year-end 1993 to $196.6 billion at year-end 1999, before falling back to $150 billion at year-end 2000. Shareholders realized compounded annual returns of 30.4 percent during this subperiod, compared to 18.6 percent for the S&P 500 index.

17.8 Summary of Learning Objectives

In this chapter, we closely examined events, effects, and decisions associated with firms that are in various stages of financial distress. After a general discussion of the causes and effects of financial distress, we organized our discussion around the major classes of decisions that are associated with severe financial distress: *operational cutbacks*, *asset sales* and *financial restructuring*, and *reforming governance* and *management structures*. Many factors can cause a firm to come under financial distress. Factors at the macro-level include a fall in GDP growth or changes in financial markets. Industry-level causes include competition, industry shocks, and deregulation. Firm-level factors include the firm's ownership and governance structures, operating risk, profitability, and leverage. Financial distress can adversely affect (a) the value of tax benefits of debt and depreciation, (b) transaction costs associated with restructuring or issuing securities, (c) agency costs, and (d) the liquidity of the firm's equity.

Responses to financial distress include the following. *Operational cutbacks* involve scaling back operations, layoffs, or plant closings. (The good news here is that a firm's profitability generally improves after such actions are taken.) *Asset sales* may alleviate financial distress by providing badly needed cash. However, assets may have to be sold at *fire-sale* prices, particularly if the sold assets are industry-specific, and the industry itself is distressed. *Financial restructuring* can take any of several forms, including (a) a dividend cut, (b) a dual-class recap, (c) issuing targeted stock against a subsidiary, (d) conducting an equity carve-out of a subsidiary, or (e) completing a spin-off of a subsidiary.

A distressed firm may choose to reform its governance structure by changing the composition or compensation of board members. Alternatively, the firm may alter the hierarchical structure of management or the terms of executive compensation contracts. Finally, the firm's senior management may be replaced. IBM's restructuring effort in the 1990s involved replacing the CEO, replacing insiders with outsiders on the firm's board, and refocusing its product and service mix.

Review Questions and Problems

1. Discuss causes of financial distress at the macroeconomic level.
2. Discuss causes of financial distress at the industry level.
3. Discuss causes of financial distress at the level of an individual firm.
4. Explain how the en masse transformation of U.S. firms from diversification to focus can lead to financial distress for some firms.
5. Distinguish between *financial* and *economic* distress.
6. List and discuss the adverse effects that accompany financial distress.
7. Discuss each of the following firm responses to financial distress (including evidence on its effect on operating performance and shareholder value).
   a. Downsizing (e.g., cost-cutting; layoffs; operational cutbacks)
   b. Plant closings
8. Asset sales can be a response to financial distress.
   a. Describe the efficient deployment hypothesis.
   b. Describe the financing hypothesis of asset sales.
   c. Discuss empirical evidence regarding these two hypotheses.
   d. Discuss the determinants of shareholder gains from asset sales.
   e. Define an asset *fire sale*.
   f. Do asset fire sales exist? Discuss evidence.
   g. Among the selling firm's security claimants, who generally gains from an asset sale?
   h. How do asset sales relate to the concept of *corporate focus*?
9. How do dividend-paying firms alter dividends in response to financial distress, according to evidence?
10. Define and briefly discuss each of the following financial restructuring transactions.
   a. A dual-class recapitalization.
   b. Issuing targeted stock.
   c. An equity carve-out.
   d. A spin-off.

11. Regarding equity carve-outs, discuss (a) motivations, and (b) the market's reaction to their announcement.
12. Researchers have proffered several hypotheses to explain the market's positive reaction to a spin-off announcement. List and briefly describe each.
13. Discuss each of the following means by which a firm could attempt to respond to financial distress (a) reforming the structure of its board, and (b) replacing management.
14. Discuss the actions that IBM took to deal with its faltering performance in the early 1990s.

Creative Thinking Issues

1. Can you think of reasons why firms in different industries may be differentially affected by changes in economic growth? Why might economic growth help some firms in an industry and hurt others?
2. Will the high volumes of equity carve-outs and spin-offs persist in the future, or are they only a temporary phenomenon related to the de-diversification/focus wave?
3. In your opinion, which of IBM's restructuring actions were most effective in restoring its financial strength?

Projects and Analyses

1. Identify a firm that is currently in financial distress. What caused it? What have been the firm's responses to it thus far? Have these responses been well received by the market? Should the firm be considering other alternatives?
2. Analyze the circumstances surrounding each of several targeted stock, equity carve-out, or spin-off events. What patterns emerge? (D'Souza and Jacob [2000] provide a list of targeted-stock issues.)
3. Develop a report on the progress to date of DuPont's corporate restructuring, which was announced on Monday, February 11, 2002. Press reports stated that DuPont would reorganize into five specialized businesses and create a textiles and interiors unit that could later be sold via an equity carve-out. On the announcement day, shares of DuPont (ticker: DD), a component stock in the Dow Jones Industrial Average, rose 4.3 percent.

Debt Restructuring, Being Acquired, Bankruptcy, Reorganization, and Liquidation

18.1 INTRODUCTION

This chapter focuses on firms in severe financial distress, such that they cannot service their debt. Such firms must either (a) negotiate a private restructuring of their debt contracts, (b) be acquired and have their debt retired or assumed by an acquirer, or (c) default and file for bankruptcy. If bankruptcy is the alternative, the firm is either reorganized or liquidated. We begin the chapter with several statistical perspectives on severe financial distress, discussed in Section 18.2. We discuss private debt restructuring in Section 18.3. In Section 18.4, we discuss acquisition, takeover, and buyout transactions as responses to severe financial distress. In Section 18.5, we discuss bankruptcy, the reorganization process, and emergence from bankruptcy. In Section 18.6, we discuss liquidation as an alternative to reorganization. Section 18.7 summarizes the chapter's learning objectives, as usual.

18.2 PERSPECTIVES ON SEVERE FINANCIAL DISTRESS

In this section, we provide five empirical perspectives on severe financial distress.

18.2.1 Perspective I: Severe Distress and Outcomes

Our first perspective is provided in Figure 18-1, which is a composite of statistics from several studies of the dispositions of firms that became severely distressed in the 1970s and 1980s. A firm is initially defined as severely distressed if its three-year stock-price performance was in the bottom 5 percent of all NYSE/AMEX stocks. Of 381 such firms, 49 percent did not default on their debt, nor did they restructure debt. However, the majority, 51 percent, defaulted or restructured debt. Of these firms, 47 percent resolved their default or restructured debt through a private workout, but the majority, 53 percent, filed for bankruptcy under Chapter 11 of the U.S. Bankruptcy Code (discussed later). Of 162 firms that filed under Chapter 11, (a) 60 percent emerged under reorganization plans, (b) 7 percent merged with other companies, (c) 15 percent liquidated under Chapter 7 of the U.S. Bankruptcy Code, and (d) 17 percent had an undetermined fate.

FIGURE 18-1   Statistical Estimates of the Dispositions of Severely Distressed Firms

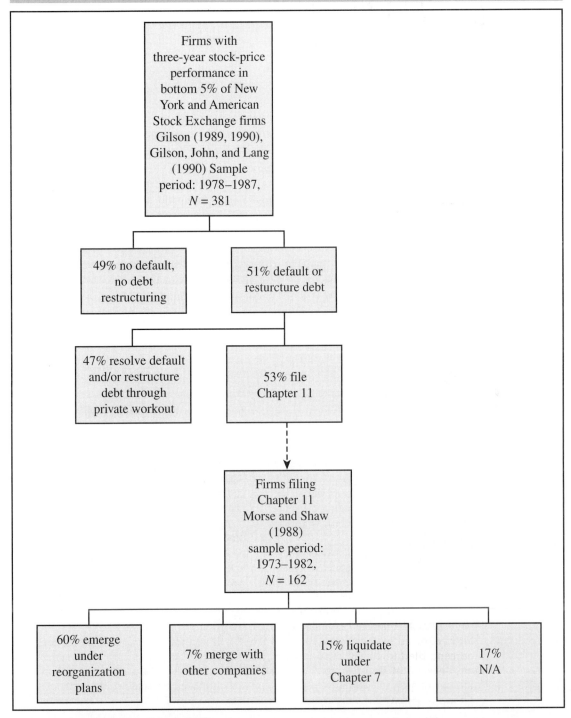

Source: Adapted from Fig. 2 of Wruck (1990).

18.2.2 Perspective II: A Broader View of Severe Distress and Outcomes

For our second perspective, we attempted to broaden the scope of the analysis presented in Figure 18-1. We did this by examining the disposition, as of year-end 2000, of all 5,069 U.S. nonfinancial firms that were publicly traded at year-end 1995. We sorted these firms into five groups: (a) firms that were still publicly traded at year-end 2000, (b) firms that were acquired by year-end 2000, (c) firms that had undergone Chapter 11 reorganization, (d) firms that had undergone Chapter 7 liquidation, and (e) all other firms that were no longer publicly traded at year-end 2000 (including firms that had undergone a buyout, were delisted by their stock exchange, etc.). The firms in each group were then further sorted into two subgroups: firms with positive cumulative earnings over the observation period, and firms with negative cumulative earnings. Our crude measure of financial distress is whether the firm had positive or negative cumulative earnings. Finally, for the firms in each subgroup, we calculated the median percentage change in market equity value (MEQ) from year-end 1995 either to year-end 2000 or until the stock was delisted.

The results of the calculations are displayed in Table 18-1. Note initially that 3,945 of the 5,069 year-end 1995 firms, or 78 percent, were still trading at year-end 2000. However, 1,671 of these firms, or 42 percent, were (by our crude measure) distressed, indicating that financial distress is not uncommon. The median change in MEQ for the distressed firms was –54 percent, compared to 33 percent for firms with positive cumulative earnings.

TABLE 18-1 The Year-End 200 Status of 5,069 U.S. Nonfinancial Firms That Were Publicly Traded at Year-End 1995

	Number of Firms	Percentage of All Year-End 1995 Firms	Median Percentage Change in Market Equity Value
Total Firms at Year-End 1995	**5,069**	**100.0%**	
Firms Still Public at Year-End 2000	**3,945**	**77.8%**	
Firms with positive cumulative earnings	2,274	44.9%	33%
Firms with negative cumulative earnings	1,671	33.0%	–54%
Firms Acquired	**848**	**16.7%**	
Firms with positive cumulative earnings	558	11.0%	72%
Firms with negative cumulative earnings	290	5.7%	–3%
Firms Bankrupt (Chapter 11 Reorganization)	**95**	**1.9%**	
Firms with positive cumulative earnings	3	0.1%	–100%
Firms with negative cumulative earnings	92	1.8%	–100%
Firms Bankrupt (Chapter 7 Liquidation)	**12**	**0.2%**	
Firms with positive cumulative earnings	1	0.0%	–87%
Firms with negative cumulative earnings	11	0.2%	–94%
Firms Bought-Out, Delisted, etc.	**169**	**3.3%**	
Firms with positive cumulative earnings	23	0.5%	–12%
Firms with negative cumulative earnings	146	2.9%	–97%

Sources: Standard & Poor's *Research Insight* database, CRSP database.

A total of 848 firms, or 17 percent of all year-end 1995 firms, were acquired. Of these, nearly two-thirds (558 firms, 66 percent) had positive cumulative earnings, while the other one-third (290 firms, 34 percent) had negative cumulative earnings. Median changes in MEQ were 72 percent and –3 percent, respectively, for these two subgroups. These results suggest that approximately one-third of all acquired firms are distressed.

A total of 95 firms underwent Chapter 11 reorganization, and all but three had negative cumulative earnings. Not surprisingly, the median change in MEQ for these firms was –100 percent. A total of 12 firms underwent Chapter 7 liquidation, and all but one had negative cumulative earnings. For the single firm with positive cumulative earnings, the change in MEQ was –87 percent, while for the 11 firms with negative cumulative earnings, the median change in market equity value was –94 percent. Finally, a total of 169 firms that were not acquired or bankrupt were nevertheless no longer publicly traded at year-end 2000 (e.g., they underwent a buyout). Of these, 146 firms (86 percent) had negative cumulative earnings and sustained a median MEQ loss of –97 percent, while the remaining 23 firms (14 percent) had positive cumulative earnings but nevertheless suffered a median market equity loss of –12 percent.

The results in Table 18-1 suggest that most distressed firms maintain public trading status, at least for a protracted period. Of those financially distressed firms that did not remain public (a total of 539 firms, including distressed firms that were acquired, underwent Chapter 11 or Chapter 7 bankruptcy, or were delisted/went private), the majority were acquired (290 firms, or 54 percent), 17 percent and 2 percent underwent Chapter 11 and Chapter 7 bankruptcy, respectively, and 27 percent were delisted/went private.

18.2.3 Perspective III: Severe Distress, GDP Growth, and Aggregate Profits

Our third perspective is on relationships among severe financial distress, macroeconomic growth, and aggregate corporate profits. Changes in macroeconomic growth affect the profitability of almost all firms, to a greater or lesser extent. In a robust economy, markets expand and profits increase dramatically, so fewer firms are prone to financial distress. In a recession, markets contract and profits are squeezed, so many firms become either moderately or severely distressed. We calculated the relative frequencies of bankruptcies and liquidations (as a measure of severe financial distress) among publicly traded U.S. nonfinancial firms over time, and compared these relative frequencies to contemporaneous U.S. gross domestic product (GDP) growth and changes in aggregate corporate profits.

To generate the relative frequencies, we initially identified 662 publicly traded U.S. nonfinancial firms that had entered Chapter 11 or Chapter 7 bankruptcy over the years 1980 to 2000. Approximately three-quarters of these were bankruptcies (469 firms), and one-quarter were liquidations (193 firms). Next, we calculated the *relative* frequency of bankruptcies and liquidations for each year by tallying the number of bankruptcies and liquidations in that year and dividing the total by the number of publicly traded U.S. nonfinancial firms at year-end.

The relative frequencies are displayed in Figure 18-2. The figure also shows annual values of U.S. GDP growth and the percentage change in the aggregate profits of U.S. nonfinancial firms. On average, the relative frequency of bankruptcies and liquidations was

FIGURE 18-2 Percent Change in Aggregate U.S. Nonfinancial Corporate Profits, Bankruptcy and Liquidation Rate, and U.S. GDP Growth Rate

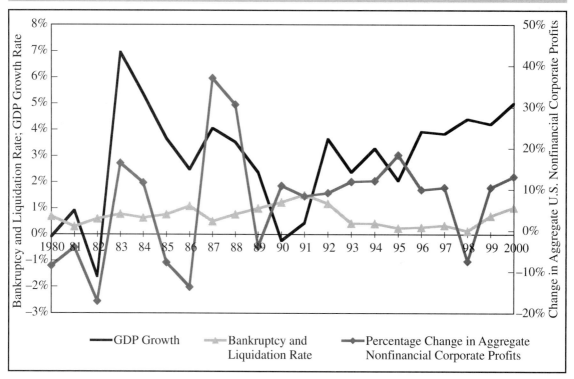

Annually, 1980–2000
Source: Standard & Poor's *Research Insight* database; U.S. Commerce Dept.

fairly low at 0.7 percent. This value is much smaller than the average relative frequency of mergers and acquisitions, 4.1 percent, reported in Table 16-2, though this statistic covers a longer period (1960 to 2000). Consistent with the results in Table 18-1, these results suggest that distressed firms are more likely to be acquired than to enter into bankruptcy.

The relative frequency of bankruptcies and liquidations appears to be inversely related to contemporaneous economic growth, as we expect. The relative frequency peaked in 1991, coincident with the 1990 to 1991 recession. However, the correlation between this relative frequency and GDP growth is modest at only –0.18. The correlation between the bankruptcy/liquidation rate and changes in aggregate corporate profits is even smaller in magnitude, –0.05. Apparently the relationship between the relative frequency of bankruptcies and economic growth is complex, perhaps exhibiting lead or lag relationships, or reflecting other factors (Ramsey and Rothman 1996).

18.2.4 Perspective IV: The Price Path to Bankruptcy

Our fourth perspective on severe financial distress is provided in Figure 18-3. This figure shows statistics on changes in the MEQs of bankrupt firms for the 12 months leading up to their bankruptcy filing date, based on 662 publicly traded U.S. nonfi-

FIGURE 18-3   Monthly Median and Quartile Market Equity Values of Bankrupt Firms as Percentages of Their Respective Market Equity Values 12 Months before Bankruptcy Filing Month

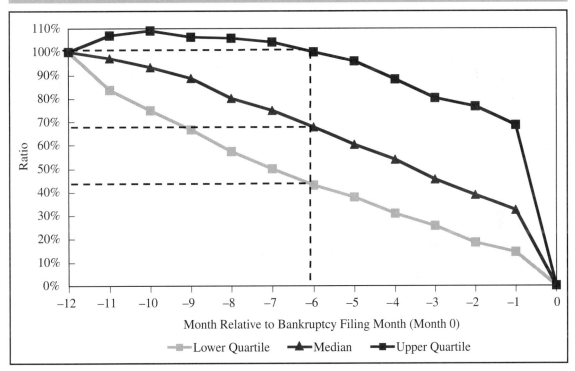

662 Publicly Traded U.S. Nonfinancial Firms, 1980–2000
Source: Standard & Poor's *Research Insight* and CRSP databases.

nancial firms that filed for bankruptcy over the years 1980 to 2000. At the median, bankrupt firms lose about 6 percent of their month –12 MEQ each month through month –1, and 32 percent of value is lost in the filing month. These results indicate that the market fairly well anticipates the typical bankrupt firm's demise. However, the progression of value loss varies substantially across firms. As highlighted in the figure, the median firm lost approximately one-third of its month –12 MEQ by month –6; however, the upper-quartile firm lost none of its month –12 MEQ by month –6, while the lower quartile firm lost 57 percent. Moreover, the upper quartile of bankrupt firms retained at least 77 percent of their month –12 MEQ at month –1. This final result indicates that a substantial proportion of bankruptcy filings are sudden shocks to the market.

18.2.5   Perspective V: Selected Bankruptcies: 1995–2000

Finally, Table 18-2 provides a (nonexhaustive) list of 36 of the largest publicly traded U.S. nonfinancial firms to file for bankruptcy over the years 1995 to 2000. For each firm, the table shows the date of the filing, the company's name, its principal line of business, and its total assets at the time of the filing. Clearly, bankrupt firms span a broad range of industries and firm sizes.

			Assets
Date	**Company**	**Business**	**($ million)**
10/05/00	Owens Corning	Building and computer materials	6,494
12/29/00	LTV Corp.	Steel production	6,101
02/02/00	Integrated Health Services	Healthcare	5,393
06/01/99	Loewen Group International	Funeral services	4,674
06/09/00	Safety-Kleen	Chemical waste	4,367
12/6/00	Armstrong World	Floor coverings	4,164
04/04/00	CHS Electronics	Computer products	3,572
01/18/00	Mariner Post-Acute	Healthcare	3,037
06/07/99	Harnischfeger Ind.	Surface mining equipment	2,876
10/14/99	Sun Healthcare Group	Medical services	2,468
06/22/00	Genesis Health Ventures	Healthcare	2,430
12/29/99	Fruit of the Loom, Inc.	Underwear, T-shirts	2,289
04/20/99	TransAmerican Energy	Natural gas	2,131
11/14/00	ICG Communications	Communications services	2,020
10/5/98	Boston Chicken, Inc.	Retail food chain	2,005
03/11/99	MedPartners	Pharmaceuticals	1,862
11/14/00	Pillowtex Corp.	Home furnishings	1,683
03/2799	Service Merchandise	Retail merchandise	1,627
08/27/96	FoxMeyer Health	Distributor pharmaceutical	1,577
06/16/00	Heilig-Meyers	Home furnishings retailer	1,456
10/12/95	Petrie Stores	Women's retail	1,274
5/12/95	Rockefeller Center	Properties	1,250
12/27/96	Marvel Entertainment	Publishes comic books	1,213
9/18/95	Caldor Corporation	Discount retailers	1,136
6/24/98	Grand Union*	Supermarket chain	1,061
09/05/97	Levitz Furniture	Retail furniture stores	934
11/3/95	Edison Brothers	Specialty retailer	894
6/23/95	Bradlees, Inc.	Specialty retailer	885
9/28/98	Acme Metals, Inc.	Steel products	829
1/16/98	Pegasus Gold, Inc.	Silver and gold mining	754
09/24/96	Best Products	Discount retail chain	717
01/05/96	Anacomp, Inc.	Micrographic products	659
06/25/96	Morrison Knudsen*	Construction	628
01/27/97	Mid-America Waste Systems	Nonhazardous solid waste	515
05/29/96	Kenetech Corp.	Wind power	401
06/03/96	Sizzler International	Family restaurants	277

TABLE 18-2 title: **TABLE 18-2 Selected Bankruptcies among Publicly Traded U.S. Nonfinancial Firms, 1995–2000**

*Prepack.

Sources: Standard & Poor's *Research Insight* database, CRSP database, SEC website (EDGAR).

18.3 DEBT RESTRUCTURING

The immediate problem with most firms in severe financial distress is that they cannot adequately service their debt. If they are otherwise viable for the long-term, a distressed firm may attempt a private debt restructuring or *workout* with its creditors to restructure its debt obligations. However, this can be a very difficult task, especially if the firm has public debt outstanding.

18.3.1   Public Debt, the Holdout Problem, Exchange Offers, and Coercion

One of the most difficult problems in a debt restructuring is resolving the *holdout problem.* The problem is that all debt claimants must agree on the reassignment of debt claims, but one or more of the claimants is likely to have an incentive to hold out for a better deal, which stymies the resolution. John (1993) explains the problem and its resolution via *coercion*:

> Achieving an agreement among creditors outside of the formal bankruptcy process will depend upon what type of debt is restructured, e.g., private debt or public debt. The restructuring of public debt is governed by the Trust Indenture Act of 1939, which requires unanimous consent of every bondholder to change the maturity, principal or coupon rate of interest in the bond indenture. Such stringent voting rules preclude a debt restructuring in which the core terms of widely held public debt can be changed. Consequently, almost all restructurings of public debt take the form of an exchange offer . . .
>
> In an exchange offer, the bondholders are given the option to exchange their old bonds for a package of new securities (often including some form of equity). The idea here is to swap the existing "hard" contract for a "softer" mix. Since participation is optional, individual bondholders may choose to "hold out" in the expectation that their bonds would be more valuable (in the post-exchange, less-distressed firm) than the new package of securities. Since all bondholders have similar incentives (assuming that they do not collude), the exchange offer is likely to fail. The terms of the new packet of securities are often set to coerce participation. Coercive techniques are used by corporations to implement successful exchange offers. Exchange offers are often accompanied by modification of the covenants of the original bonds through a technique known as consent solicitations or exit covenants. In these cases, the tendering bondholders are also asked to vote to change or eliminate the existing debt covenants. The acceptance of the exchanged debt is made conditional on approval of the consent solicitation by the required majority. In these cases, the consent solicitation is so designed that the benefits of nonparticipation are exceeded by the loss from holding onto the old bonds stripped of covenants . . . (p. 65)[1]

A Case in Point: Massey Ferguson's Debt Restructuring

Baldwin and Mason (1983) examined the actual resolution of claims in the 1980 to 1981 debt restructuring of Massey Ferguson Ltd, a large manufacturer of agricultural equipment that reached the point of financial collapse in 1980 after sustaining massive losses. The authors addressed the question of whether Massey avoided deadweight costs of financial distress through the negotiated restructuring of debt claims with its creditors. The authors point out that Chapter 11 reorganization was probably not feasible in the Massey case because the firm had manufacturing operations in more than 31

---

[1]John's discussion emphasizes the problem of a distressed firm in dealing with covenants in its debt contracts. In a series of papers, Beniesh and Press (1993, 1995a, 1995b) examined technical violations of debt covenants among severely distressed firms.

Junkyard Dogs

The article below discusses the recent spate of defaults on high-yield or *junk* corporate bonds.

The rate of junk bond defaults rose to 5.4 percent in the second quarter from 4.82 percent a year earlier and will soar to 8.4 percent next June as credit quality drops, threatening the survival of many companies, credit rating agency Moody's Investors Service warned on Friday. Top junk bond experts, however, called Moody's overly pessimistic, and one said junk bonds offer investors legitimate prospects for solid total returns in the next year. The second-quarter default rate was the second highest since 1991 as calculated by Moody's, which is considered conservative in its assessments. Moody's said the default rate, which rose last year, will surge as more financial problems hit low-rated companies that sold junk bonds in 1997 and 1998, when investor risk tolerance was "extremely high."

David Hamilton, the Moody's analyst who wrote the report, said some Wall Street commentators labeled last year's surge a one-time event. Indeed, the rate dipped early this year. "Moody's has maintained that the brief lull in defaults at the beginning of the year represented a Trojan Horse, and that it would not take long for (companies) to surprise the market and again start defaulting," he wrote. "This prediction is proving to be prescient." Junk bonds carry ratings of Ba1 or lower from Moody's and are considered to carry high ownership risk.

OVERLY PESSIMISTIC?

Edward Altman, the Max L. Heine professor of finance at NYU's Stern School of Business and an expert on junk bonds, said Moody's projections are overly pessimistic. "I would expect the rate to be in the vicinity of 5 to 6 percent for cal-

endar year 2000, and perhaps go even slightly higher by the middle of 2001," he said. "I find 8.4 percent on the high side. That's huge." And Gregory Peters, head of high yield strategy at Salomon Smith Barney, said, "It's our opinion that we will look at the default rate running in the 4.5 to 5 percent range."

Altman last week issued his own report showing a 5.22 percent trailing 12-month default rate. He said banks are tightening credit standards, making it more difficult for companies with marginal credit quality to refinance short-term debt as it comes due.

How much banks tighten, he said, is significant to the 17 percent of junk bonds that are "distressed"—yielding at least 10 percentage points more than comparable U.S. Treasuries. He said a "fair proportion" of these will default. Still, he said if the default rate is in fact cresting, now could be a good time for investors to buy junk bonds. Junk bonds are showing signs of recovery, having posted total returns above 2 percent since June 1, according to Merrill Lynch & Co. Altman noted that in 1991 the default rate topped out at 10.3 percent and junk bond investors enjoyed 43 percent total returns. "I'm expecting the rate to peak in less than a year, if it hasn't already," he said. "When that happens, there will be a lot of money to be made in the high-yield bond market for those companies that do not default."

$9.6 BILLION DEFAULTED

Moody's said 37 companies it rates defaulted on $9.6 billion of debt in the second quarter. That compares to 23 companies defaulting on $7.4 billion in the first quarter, when the annualized default rate was 5.66 percent, Moody's said. The amount that went into default in the second quarter surpassed the $8.7 billion in new junk bonds sold during the period, according to Thomson Financial Securities Data. No industry dominated second quarter defaults, Moody's said, and 72 percent of defaulting companies, accounting for $8.3 billion of debt, were based in the United States. Key to Moody's report is the concept of "aging." Moody's said companies are most likely to default on bonds 3.5 years after they sell them. Peters said that in fact companies are defaulting faster. "Issuers are defaulting sooner, often in their first two years," he said. "We're paying now for the excesses of 1997 and 1998, when money was easier to get. It is unreasonable to expect the default rate will keep rising as bonds mature." In an interview, Hamilton said many of the dicier credits that most benefited from this excess have already defaulted. "The survivors are now entering the point where, historically speaking, the risk of default is highest," he said.

Source: "Moody's: Junk Bond Default Rate Soaring," *Reuters*, New York, July 14, 2000. © 2000 Reuters. Reprinted by permission.

countries, and Massey's debt was owned by local lenders and denominated in local currencies. Liquidation was somewhat more feasible, and several creditors pursued this avenue of relief. Ultimately, though, 250 creditors hammered out a refinancing package after two weeks of negotiations. Evidence suggests that some deadweight costs of bankruptcy were avoided by a cooperative settlement, including a 26 percent rise in Massey's stock price over the two-week negotiation period.

18.3.2 Investment Incentives under Financial Distress/Debt Restructuring

As we discussed in Chapters 3, 5, and 6, financial distress can exacerbate the distortion of a firm's investment incentives that occurs when a firm has debt in its capital structure. Several research papers have addressed this issue as it applies to firms in severe financial distress.

Bergman and Callen (1991) modeled the strategic behavior of management (acting in shareholders' interest) and creditors in debt renegotiations. Under conditions in which firm value at debt maturity barely suffices to repay the promised amount, "management will optimally use its discretion over the investment decisions of the firm to wrest concessions from the firm's creditors by threatening to sap firm value through suboptimal investment policies . . . [S]uch opportunistic behavior becomes optimal even if the firms is solvent, and shareholders stand to lose from carrying out their threats. As long as the potential loss is 'small enough,' threats will be communicated and creditors will accede to 'reasonable' demands. We suggest that, in many instances, this type of exchange underlies debt renegotiations between owners and creditors" (p. 138).

Mooradian (1994) argued that asymmetric information and conflicts of interest combine to force distressed but efficient firms (i.e., viable firms that should continue) to liquidate and distressed, inefficient firms (i.e., nonviable firms that should be liquidated) to continue. This can occur if inefficient firms can *mimic* efficient firms in debt restructurings such that in the resulting pooling equilibrium, efficient and inefficient firms are equally likely to continue or liquidate. Thus, "one of two investment inefficiencies occurs: inefficient firms continue when they should be liquidated or efficient firms are liquidated when they should continue" (p. 1404).

They then show that Chapter 11 is a useful mechanism for screening inefficient firms out of debt renegotiation. Inefficient firms voluntarily choose Chapter 11 because negotiations therein generally result in some value retained by shareholders. "This separation induces voluntary filing for bankruptcy by inefficient firms and consequently enables efficient firms to continue when they would otherwise be liquidated" (p. 1403). Thus, although inefficient firms continue in Chapter 11 reorganizations (and thus this investment inefficiency is not resolved), at least efficient firms avoid liquidation via private debt renegotiation.

Bernardo and Talley (1996) analyzed problems with commonplace *exit-exchange offers*. In such exchanges, creditors receive either (a) a package of new securities (including debt, equity, or cash) in exchange for their preexisting debt, or (b) new debt with lower face value but higher priority. One problem with exit-exchange offers is that each creditor must decide *simultaneously* on whether (a) to consent to restructure their claim, and (b) to accept the new debt or debt package offered by the firm. The authors argued that managers and shareholders might, in their self-interest, select inefficient investment projects strategically to enhance their bargaining positions vis-à-vis creditors (e.g., shareholders might choose projects that distort the terms and success rates of the exchange offer).

The authors also recognized several transactional frictions that can impede efficient restructuring, including the situation "in which debtholders are numerous, so that it is prohibitively costly for them to coordinate their bargaining strategy amongst themselves. Collective action problems can force individual bondholders within such atomistic credit structures to behave strategically against one another. For example, when faced with a debt-for-debt exit-exchange offer, it may be optimal for a typical bondholder to exchange her debt for more senior debt with lower face value, in a unilateral effort to win priority over fellow debtholders. This unilateral strategic concern can lead to equilibrium behavior in which all debtholders choose to tender, even though they will be made collectively worse off because all their new debt will have the same relative priority, but lower face value" (pp. 872–873).

18.3.3 Vulture Investors

Investors who specialize in the debt or equity of distressed firms became prominent in the 1980s, and have been given the ungracious name of *vulture investors* (see Rosenberg 2000). They generally purchase substantial blocks of the firm's equity or debt with the intent of influencing management or even gaining control of the company.

Hotchkiss and Mooradian (1997) examined 288 firms that defaulted on public debt between 1980 and 1993, and found that vulture investors were involved in 172, or 60 percent, of the cases. In most of these cases, vultures purchased debt claims that involved over one-third of the firm's outstanding debt, sufficient to give them influence. They found that vulture investors often play a key role in the governance, restructuring, or reorganization of these firms: "The improvement in post-restructuring operating performance relative to the pre-default level is greater when the vulture investor becomes CEO or chairman or gains control of the target firm. We also find positive abnormal returns for the target's common stock and bonds in the two days surrounding the announcement of a vulture purchase of public debt or equity. Our evidence suggests that vulture investors add value by disciplining managers of distressed firms" (p. 401).

Let Us Prey

Day after day, company after company files for protection under the bankruptcy laws—the amount of assets is greater now than at any time since 1991, and is expected to keep growing. A sorry situation for corporate America but an opportunity for vulture investors. These players seek tasty morsels amid the carnage; that is, buying distressed debt securities they hope will pay off big when a company is reorganized, either in bankruptcy court or to forestall Chapter 11.

While there's no accurate beak count, more vultures than ever are plying this trade, from grizzled veterans like Carl Icahn to canny hotshots like David Matlin. And it's a more sophisticated, dangerous game than ever. To illustrate how dangerous, check out these two tales of toppled telecommunications ventures:

- When ICO Global Communications (otc: IGJA—news—people) filed for Chapter 11 in 1999, the future looked bleak for the mobile-phone satellite system. Enter telecom guru Craig McCaw, who last May orchestrated a $1.2 billion bailout of ICO and folded it into Teledesic, his own satellite company. Vulture investors profited outrageously. They had purchased their securities at 20 cents on the dollar and got back 50 cents six months later.

- Iridium (otc: IRIDQ—news—people), an ICO competitor with $5 billion in debt, had filed for bankruptcy just two weeks before ICO did. McCaw got involved this time, too, but he didn't have the same acquisitive appetite for Iridium as he did for ICO. ICO had the advantage that its satellites had not been launched, allowing McCaw to refashion them for Teledesic's purposes. Iridium's fleet was already aloft.

He merely lent Iridium $2.5 million to tide it over, so-called debtor-in-possession financing, in which the most recent lender goes to the head of the line in the reorganization. Some vultures pounced on the news of McCaw's arrival. They picked up Iridium bonds for 30 cents on the dollar. But McCaw chose not to rescue Iridium, and the bonds were wiped out.

In the last recession there were great companies with bad balance sheets. In this economic slowdown you see a lot of bad companies with bad balance sheets.

"This isn't the kind of merchandise that was available in the early 1990s," says Lorraine Spurge, chief executive of Los Angeles-based financial advisory firm Spurge Ink.

If you're an individual investor without the resources and savvy of an Icahn, should you invest? Only if you understand you're at the whim of, among a host of other things, the big players like Icahn who control the reorganization process. Even the smaller-time vultures, with $50 million to $100 million under management, have to focus on a smaller number of opportunities, says Jeffrey Altman, senior vice president of Franklin Mutual Advisors, which has $2 billion invested in distressed securities.

Should you have some mad money and insist on playing, however, we have a list of pros' picks you might try, in hopes you won't be Iridiumed. They're either in Chapter 11 or are otherwise hurting, but offer at least the prospect of a big payday . . .

What about mutual funds? A few, like Third Avenue Value (TAVFX) and Fidelity Capital & Income (FAGIX), have been known to dabble in defaulted bonds, but only have tiny portions of their portfolios there. (Altman's distressed investments are only about 10 percent of Franklin's total.) Most of the players, like Oaktree Capital Management, cater to pension fund and endowment clients. There are also a raft of hedge funds scoping for prey, like Angelo, Gordon, with its $1.4 billion earmarked for distressed investments. These take wealthy individuals as clients. Other players include funds of funds, such as the portfolio being

(continued)

assembled by Edward Bowman for clients of PNC Bank.

Leon Black, the onetime Drexel banker who made his name and fortune in distressed securities, is rumored to be reentering the market, raising a new $3.5 billion fund. Wilbur Ross, best known as an investment banker in the early-1990s, has gotten into the vulture investing business and is raising money a second time for U.S. and Asia deals. Entirely new players, like LBO funds, are sniffing, too.

But the money flowing in is still just a small fraction of the distressed debt out there to look at: $650 billion, face value, of distressed debts. (An IOU is defined as distressed if it's trading at more than 1,000 basis points over Treasurys.) This sickly paper is selling at a combined market value of $400 billion. That's twice the value of the bad debt up for grabs in the 1990 vulture-fest . . .

The buzzards' bounty should increase because of the huge amount of junk issued in the 1990s that is due to mature soon: $28 billion this year, $53 billion in 2002, and $66 billion in 2003. Problems paying off the principal or refinancing the debt could produce delicious disasters that vultures can exploit.

Source: "Let Us Prey," by P. Berman, L. Goldman *Forbes Magazine*, Apr. 2, 2001. © 2001 Forbes Magazine. Reprinted by permission.

18.3.4   Exchanging Equity for Debt

Several academic papers have focused on agreements between a distressed firm and its creditors to exchange equity for debt as a means of reducing the firm's leverage and thereby alleviating distress.

James (1995) examined 102 cases of debt restructurings over the years 1981 to 1990. In 31 percent of the cases, banks took equity in exchange for debt. James also examined the conditions under which a bank would take equity: "I show that the role banks play in debt restructurings depends on the financial condition of the firm, the existence of public debt in the firm's capital structure and the ability of public debt to be restructured. Empirically, I find that for firms with public debt outstanding, banks never make concessions unless public debtholders also restructure their claims. When banks do take equity, on average they obtain a substantial proportion of the firm's stock, and they maintain their position for over two years" (p. 1209).

James (1996) argued that "bank participation in a restructuring can play an important role in resolving information and holdout problems that impede a public debt exchange offer . . . Bank concessions and public debt reductions may, however, be related, even in the absence of information and holdout problems. In particular, since secured bank lenders are unlikely to make concessions unless their claims are impaired, banks are expected to make concessions only when firms are in severe financial distress. These firms are likely to need the greatest debt reduction to avoid bankruptcy. As a result, even in the absence of holdout and information problems, bank concessions may occur in conjunction with concessions by public bondholders. I refer to this explanation as the 'share the pain' hypothesis'" (pp. 711–712).

To test these arguments, James examined 68 exchange offers involving financially distressed firms over the years 1980 to 1990: "I find that the structure of exchange offers and the likelihood of an offer's success are significantly related to whether the bank participates in the restructuring transaction. Exchange offers made in conjunction with bank concessions are characterized by significantly greater reductions in public debt outstanding and significantly less senior debt offered to bondholders. Overall, the results suggest that the structure of a firm's public and private claims significantly affects the firm's ability to modify its capital structure in financial distress" (p. 711).

Lie, Lie, and McConnell (2001) examined 126 debt-reducing exchange-offer announcements over the years 1980 to 1994. They found that an average announcement-period abnormal return of –2.2 percent, and addressed two questions: "Why do firms undertake debt-reducing exchange offers? And, what is the information conveyed by such offers? The answers are interrelated: Debt-reducing exchange offers are undertaken by financially weak firms in an effort to stave off further financial distress and, thereby, preserve value for shareholders. A successfully completed exchange offer significantly reduces the likelihood that a firm will enter Chapter 11. Announcements of debt-reducing exchange offers apparently contain two pieces of information: (1) the firm is financially weaker than would have been apparent from other publicly available information, and (2) management is attempting to preserve value for shareholders" (p. 179).

Brown, James, and Mooradian (1993) developed an asymmetric information-based model of the optimal security that a distressed firm should offer in a restructuring exchange. They assume that private (or *inside*) lenders are well informed about the firm's prospects, while public (or *outside*) lenders, as well as shareholders, are at an informational disadvantage (Chapter 15). Their model predicts that "in public debt exchange offers, firms with unfavorable private information will offer equity claims to convince bondholders that the firm's prospects are poor. In contrast, offering equity to well-informed private lenders conveys favorable private information to outsiders" (p. 93). The authors tested their model by via an event study of the market's reaction to exchange offers in distressed restructurings: "Consistent with our analysis, we find positive average abnormal returns around restructurings that offer equity to private lenders and senior debt to public debtholders, and we find significant negative average abnormal returns when private lenders are offered senior debt and public lenders are offered equity" (p. 93).

18.3.5 Determinants of Success in Private Debt Restructuring Negotiations

Under what circumstances would a distressed firm be successful in a private debt restructuring? Gilson, John, and Lang (1990) provide some evidence: "[We investigated] the incentives of financially distressed firms to restructure their debt privately rather than through formal bankruptcy. In a sample of 169 financially distressed companies, about half successfully restructure their debt outside of Chapter 11. Firms more likely to restructure their debt privately have more intangible assets, owe more of their debt to banks, and owe fewer lenders. Analysis of stock returns suggests that the market is also able to discriminate ex ante between the two sets of firms, and that stockholders are systematically better off when debt is restructured privately" (p. 315).

Asquith, Gertner, and Scharfstein (1994) examined the restructuring decisions of 102 firms that had issued speculative-grade or "junk" bonds and subsequently became distressed. Their sample consisted of distressed junk-bond issuers that tried to avoid bankruptcy through public and private debt restructurings, asset sales, mergers, or capital expenditure reductions: "Our main finding is that a firm's debt structure affects the way financially distressed firms restructure. The combination of secured private debt and numerous public debt issues seems to impede out-of-court restructurings and increases the probability of a Chapter 11 filing . . . " (p. 625).

18.4 WHOLESALE RESPONSES TO FINANCIAL DISTRESS: ACQUISITION, TAKEOVER, OR BUYOUT

In this section, we briefly reprise our discussion in Chapter 16 about the roles of acquisitions, takeovers, and buyouts as means of dealing with a distressed firm.

18.4.1 Acquisition or Takeover of a Distressed Firm Can Create Value

The evidence in Figure 18-1, Table 18-1, and in Shrieves and Stevens (1979) and Clark and Ofek (1994) all suggest that target-firm financial distress is a major factor in a substantial proportion of acquisitions. Being acquired by a stronger firm in its industry can create value for a distressed firm's shareholders for at least four reasons. *First*, the combination may result in valuable economies of scale. *Second*, the combination may enhance product-market power. *Third*, the acquiring firm may be able to enhance the troubled firm's operations through superior management techniques. *Fourth*, the acquiring firm may be able to contribute badly needed capital to the troubled firm, which may have been lacking both internally generated cash and effective access to external capital markets.

Hostile takeovers also are often triggered by financial distress: prior to takeover, target firms generally substantially underperform other firms in their industry, and the motive for the takeover is often to correct managerial failure. Martin and McConnell (1991) examined a sample of takeovers to test the hypothesis that takeovers serve to discipline the managements of target firms that are performing poorly. They documented evidence consistent with this hypothesis: (a) Prior to the takeover, target firms tend to substantially underperform other firms in their industry, and (b) the turnover rate for target management increases following completion of the takeover. Also, diversified firms that perform poorly and lose value are often targets for a *bustup takeover* (Mitchell and Lehn 1990; Berger and Ofek 1996).

18.4.2 LBOs and Financial Distress

The classic circumstance that warrants a leveraged buyout (LBO, especially a management buyout, or MBO) is one in which a firm is struggling because its management lacks incentives to pursue value-enhancing activities. A LBO can alleviate this problem by both increasing managerial equity ownership and imposing the discipline of debt. However, Opler and Titman (1993) found that "firms with high expected costs of financial distress (e.g., those with high research and development expenditures) are less likely to do LBOs" (p. 1985).

18.5 BANKRUPTCY, REORGANIZATION, AND EMERGENCE

The term *bankruptcy* is derived from *banca rotta*, the Italian for "broken bench." In ancient Rome, when a businessman failed to pay his debts, it was the custom to destroy his trading bench. The U.S. Bankruptcy Code provides two types of bankruptcy filings for corporations. The first is a filing under *Chapter 11* of the code. In a Chapter 11 filing, the goal of the court and the parties involved is to determine whether and how the firm can be *reorganized*, with respect to both its operations and its financial structure, and reemerge as a going concern.

The second is a filing under *Chapter 7* of the code. In a Chapter 7 filing, the court supervises the *liquidation* of the firm's assets and the distribution of proceeds to claimants, after which the firm ceases to exist. Almost exclusively, a firm that ultimately chooses to liquidate under Chapter 7 initially filed under Chapter 11 and within these proceedings it is determined that the best course of action is to liquidate, at which point the case is generally refiled under Chapter 7.[2] In the remainder of this section, we discuss research on Chapter 11 proceedings. In the next section, we discuss Chapter 7 liquidations.

18.5.1 The Design of Chapter 11 Proceedings

A distressed firm may *voluntarily* file a bankruptcy petition, seeking protection from its creditors. Alternatively, creditors can file a petition that forces the firm into *involuntary bankruptcy*. In either case, the ultimate intent of a Chapter 11 filing is to determine whether and how the distressed firm can reemerge as a going concern. (In some cases, the ultimate result is that the firm is liquidated via an auction. This is done either within Chapter 11 or by converting the case to Chapter 7.)

To preserve the value of the enterprise, it is generally important for the focal firm to continue operating throughout the proceedings. Therefore, one of the first questions that must be addressed is, Who will operate the firm during the proceedings? Generally, the firm's current management is allowed to run the firm during the proceedings, though under restrictive terms. This arrangement is called *debtor-in-possession*. In unusual cases, a trustee is appointed to oversee the firm's assets and operations.

The main negotiations in reorganization revolve around decisions regarding (a) the structure of the firm's assets and operations after it reemerges from the proceedings, and (b) the postproceedings structure of the firm's debt and equity claims. Regarding (a), the objective is to determine a viable structure for the firm's assets and operations—that is, a structure that allows the firm to operate on a profitable basis. This often involves selling some of the firm's assets. Regarding (b), the objective is to reconfigure the firm's debt and equity claims in a way that both respects the priority status of these claims and results in a viable capital structure.

The Absolute Priority Rule

Regarding both structure issues, the absolute priority rule (APR) is a governing factor. Claimants with higher priority must be paid in full before other claimants receive anything. The order of priority is administrative claims; statutory priority claims such as tax claims, rent claims, consumer deposits, and unpaid wages and benefits; secured creditors' claims, unsecured creditors' claims; and finally, equity claims.

In practice, this priority structure is often violated, at least with respect to the creditors' versus shareholders' claims. In some cases, shareholders emerge with an equity claim despite the fact that creditors have been *impaired*—that is, they have not been paid in full, and instead have accepted compromised debt contracts or cash in lieu of their original claims. In other cases, creditors accept equity claims, and may emerge as the dominant shareholders. In still other cases, the firm's original equity securities are extinguished and replaced with new equity securities that are held by other parties, including prior creditors.

---

[2]For example, troubled retailer Service Merchandise Co., Inc., filed voluntary petitions for reorganization under Chapter 11 in March 1999. However, by early 2002 it failed to meet goals for its reorganization plan, and on January 4, 2002, announced that it would convert to Chapter 7 liquidation.

Ames and Washington Group Attempt to Reorganize

AMES DEPARTMENT STORES

Ames Department Stores, Inc. (AMESQ) and the statutory Creditors Committee in its Chapter 11 case announced today that they are working diligently toward the development of a consensual plan of reorganization that will enable Ames to emerge from bankruptcy this year.

The joint announcement followed the January 10 meeting of the Company and the Committee, during which the Committee expressed satisfaction and confidence with the progress Ames has made to date operating under Chapter 11, its ability to emerge from bankruptcy and with the excellent working relationship that has developed between the Company and the Committee.

Over the last several months Ames has taken a variety of actions to address its problem areas and to assure its success as a reorganized entity. Foremost among these has been its decisive action in closing 151 store locations as well as one distribution center. The closing of unprofitable stores together with the contemplated conversion to equity of all of Ames' obligations to unsecured creditors will contribute significantly to Ames' restored profitability. As part of its restructuring, the Company also anticipates that all existing equity will be cancelled.

Ames also announced the receipt of a proposal from GE Capital to provide exit financing in connection with the plan of reorganization. As currently contemplated, a junior lien will be provided to the vendors that provide trade credit to the Company after it emerges from reorganization.

The Company has informed the Committee that it is in compliance with all financial covenants under its DIP lending agreements.

Joseph R. Ettore, Ames' Chairman and Chief Executive Officer, told the Committee:

"Ames has had a successful holiday season in all respects including sales, gross margins, and earnings. The Chapter 11 process that started 5 months ago has enabled Ames to close under-performing stores and streamline operations. It will also permit the Company to reduce debt and create an attractive balance sheet so that Ames can excel as a major regional discounter. We are very pleased by the strong support that some vendors have already started to provide and look forward to a strong working relationship with them in the future."

Ames Department Stores, Inc. is a regional, full-line discount retailer with annual sales over $3 billion. With stores in the Northeast, Mid-Atlantic and Mid-West, Ames offers value-conscious shoppers quality, name-brand products across a broad range of merchandise categories . . .

Cautionary Statement Regarding Forward-looking Information

Statements, other than those based on historical facts which address activities, events, or developments that the Company expects or anticipates may occur in the future are forward-looking statements which are based upon a number of assumptions concerning further conditions that may ultimately prove to be inaccurate. Actual events and results may materially differ from anticipated results described in any forward-looking statements. The Company's ability to achieve such results is subject to certain risks and uncertainties. Consequently, these cautionary statements qualify all of the forward-looking statements and there can be no assurance that the results or developments anticipated by the Company will be realized or that they will have the expected effects on the Company or its business or operations.

WASHINGTON GROUP INTERNATIONAL

Washington Group International, Inc. announced that its Plan of Reorganization was confirmed today by the U.S. Bankruptcy Court for the District of Nevada in Reno, clearing the way for the company to complete its financial restructuring.

Confirmation of the Plan constitutes Court approval of the company's proposed debt-for-equity exchange, agreed to last week by the steering committees of the company's secured lenders and unsecured creditors.

The Plan also provides for the settlement of outstanding litigation between Washington Group and Raytheon Company.

The company's secured lenders will receive 80 percent of the primary equity in the newly reorganized company and $20 million in cash. The company's unsecured creditors will receive 20 percent of the primary equity in the newly reorganized company and the right to purchase, through warrants, up to an additional 25 percent of the new common stock of the reorganized company over four years following the effective date of the company's Plan of Reorganization.

Under the plan, existing Washington Group common stock (WNGXQ) will be cancelled as of the plan's effective date. New shares of common stock are expected to be issued to the company's secured lenders and unsecured creditors in 45 to 60 days.

Stephen G. Hanks, Washington Group President and Chief Executive Officer, welcomed the Court's decision.

"With confirmation, we now have the financial platform to ensure that we can continue to provide the superior engineering and construction services for which we are known," said Hanks. "I am extremely proud of our employees and their performance during our financial restructuring. During the year 2001, we have booked almost $3 billion in new work, maintained our leadership positions in the fastest growing markets in our industry, and set safety records on dozens of projects. Our disciplined management of cash flow and our balance sheet has left us free of term debt. Throughout our financial situation, we have maintained our clients and our employees. It is almost a miracle that the company could go through this process and still retain its position in the fastest growing market segments in the industry."

Washington Group filed for protection under Chapter 11 of the federal bankruptcy code on May 14, 2001. The company said that its secured lenders voted overwhelmingly in favor of the reorganization plan.

Washington Group International, Inc., is a leading international engineering and construction firm with more than 30,000 employees at work in 43 states and more than 35 countries. The company offers a full life-cycle of services as a preferred provider of premier science, engineering, construction, program management, and development in 14 major markets.

This news release contains forward-looking statements within the meaning of the Private Securities Litigation Reform Act of 1995, which are identified by the use of forward-looking terminology such as may, will, could, should, expect, anticipate, intend, plan, estimate, or continue or the negative thereof or other variations thereof. These include, among others, statements with respect to the terms of the plan of reorganization and the structure of the reorganized company. Forward-looking statements are necessarily based on various assumptions and estimates and are inherently subject to various risks and uncertainties, including risks and uncertainties relating to the possible invalidity of the underlying assumptions and estimates, the involvement of Washington Group's creditors and equity holders in the Chapter 11 proceeding, bankruptcy court approvals incident to Washington Group's operations in Chapter 11 and the ultimate reorganization of Washington Group, and possible changes or developments in social, economic, business industry, market, legal, and regulatory circumstances and conditions and other actions taken or omitted to be taken by

(continued)

third parties, including the corporation's customers, suppliers, business partners, and competitors and legislative, regulatory, judicial, and other governmental authorities and officials.

Source: "Ames and Creditors Committee Work Toward Plan of Reorganization; Committee Expresses Satisfaction and Confidence with Ames' Progress," Jan. 14, 2002. Copyright © 2002 Business Wire. Reprinted by permission.
"Washington Group's Plan of Reorganization Approved," Nov. 20, 2001. Copyright © 2001 Business Wire. Reprinted by permission.

All decisions in reorganization are matters of (court-supervised) negotiation, so the fate of the various claimants often depends of the relative quality of their legal representation, as in any court case. For this reason, a rich informal lexicon has developed regarding reorganizations. For example, a *cramdown* refers to the confirmation of a plan of reorganization over the objections of one or more classes of creditors. Given the circumstances, an important question arises regarding the *efficiency* of court-supervised reorganization. Next, we discuss research on this issue.

18.5.2   The Efficacy of Chapter 11 Proceedings: Theory and Evidence

Several research papers have addressed the efficiency of Chapter 11 proceedings, as we discuss next.

Theory on the Efficacy of Bankruptcy Law

Berkovitch, Israel, and Zender (1998) developed a theoretical model of optimal bankruptcy proceedings that focuses on the bargaining process. They view the law as a "commitment device to ensure actions that are ex ante optimal . . . " (p. 441). They show that the court has two mechanisms, both in the form of restrictions, to implement an optimal bankruptcy outcome. These are "direct restrictions on the bargaining game between the claimants, and the use of a 'restricted auction.' In both cases the restrictions prevent the strategic use of bankruptcy by firms not in financial distress, provide for truthful revelation of information so that distress results in an ex post efficient allocation of resources, and establish a bias toward the manager in reorganizations that provides correct ex ante decision making incentives" (p. 441).

Easterbrook (1990) argued that formal bankruptcy proceedings serve two functions: "(1) to deliver the penalty for failure by forcing a wrapping up when a business cannot pay its debts and (2) to reduce the social costs of failure" (p. 411). He took issue with legal scholars (e.g., Roe 1983, Baird 1986, and Jackson 1986) who have argued that the optimal bankruptcy law involves liquidating auctions exclusively, because an auction mechanism allocates the firm's resources to their highest-value uses, and avoids the manipulations that are possible in Chapter 11. Of course, reorganizations generally do not involve auctions: "Instead judges determine a value and parcel out interests on the assumption that this valuation is correct. Errors inevitable in this process lead many persons to conclude that bankruptcy is inefficient. [We argue] that the conclusion does not follow. The costs of error in valuation may be less than the cost of conducting an auction. Legal rules endure because they are efficient or because they transfer wealth. Transfers are an implausible explanation of the current bankruptcy regime, leaving efficiency as the prevailing explanation" (p. 411).

In their theory of workouts, Gertner and Scharfstein (1991) questioned the efficacy of reorganization law: "We present a model of a financially distressed firm with outstanding bank debt and public debt. Coordination problems among public debtholders introduce investment inefficiencies in the workout process. In most cases these inefficiencies are not mitigated by the ability of firms to buy back their public debt with cash and other securities—the only feasible way that firms can restructure their public debt" (p. 1189). They showed theoretically that reorganization law increases investment, but that such increases may or may not enhance the firm's efficiency, depending on details of the distressed firm's financial structure.

Evidence on Deviations from the APR

Several empirical studies provide evidence indicating that violations of the APR are common. Eberhart, Moore, and Roenfeldt (1990) examined the pricing of bankrupt firms' securities and investigated the occurrence of deviations from the APR. They focused on firms that filed after the 1978 Bankruptcy Reform Act. In general, the Act made it easier for firms to file a bankruptcy and to reorganize: "Claims ultimately awarded to shareholders of firms in reorganization were examined for a sample of 30 filings under the 1978 Bankruptcy Reform Act. We measured the amount paid to shareholders in excess of that which they would have received under the absolute priority rule and found that this amount represents, on average, 7.6 percent of the total awarded to all claimants. Evidence is also reported that common share values reflect a significant proportion of value ultimately received in violation of absolute priority, suggesting that deviations from the rule were expected by the equity markets" (p. 1457)."

Weiss (1990) examined both the direct costs of bankruptcy and violations of the APR for 37 NYSE and AMEX firms that filed for bankruptcy over the period 1979 to 1986. He found "direct costs average 3.1 percent of the book value of debt plus the market value of equity, and priority of claims is violated in 29 cases. The breakdown in priority of claims occurs primarily among the unsecured creditors and between the unsecured creditors and equity holders. Secured creditors' contracts are generally upheld" (p. 285).

Eberhart and Sweeney's (1992) empirical analysis focused on the extent to which absolute priority rule violations affected payoffs to junior bondholders, who generally held public debt. They found that: "on average, bondholders benefit, albeit slightly, from absolute priority rule (APR) violations. This paper also examines the degree to which the bond market, in the bankruptcy-filing month, anticipates departures from the APR and other influences on the payoff to bondholders. In other words, we investigate the informational efficiency of the market for bankrupt bonds. Overall, despite the complex and lengthy nature of bankruptcy proceedings, the results support efficiency" (p. 943).

Eberhart and Senbet (1993) provided a theoretical analysis that shows that "departures from the APR are effective in controlling the risk-shifting incentive of financially distressed firms . . . APR violations . . . are most effective when the more traditional methods are least effective: as the probability of a conversion or call approaches zero with a worsening of the firm's financial condition, a deviation from the APR becomes the dominant force in reducing risk-shifting. Thus, an APR violation complements the traditional methods of controlling the risk incentive by serving as an 'insurance' policy against their failure when the firm is financially distressed" (p. 102).

Claimholder Incentive Conflicts in Reorganization

Brown (1989) investigated the issue of incentive conflicts in reorganizations, and the role of the bankruptcy code in resolving them: "When a firm is in financial distress, in most cases a set of mutually advantageous reorganization plans exist. [T]he bankruptcy code, by providing rules governing the negotiation process, yields a unique solution to the reorganization process. In addition, the structure imposed by the code mitigates the holdout problem created by the individual claimant's divergent incentives" (p. 109). The holdout problem in this case involves bondholders, who gain by not participating because, as other bondholders tender, their claim becomes less risky.

Is Managerial Self-Interest Manifest in Severe Financial Distress?

Loderer and Sheehan (1989) examined levels of, and changes in, insiders' stockholdings in firms that eventually go bankrupt against a control sample of nonbankrupt firms, using data for the years 1971 to 1985. They found no evidence that insiders of bankrupt firms "bail out" of their firms' stocks prior to bankruptcy, despite substantial and protracted wealth losses. The authors suggest that "this could happen either because corporate insiders of failing firms are reluctant to trade on the basis of their private information or because they are unable to predict, with better accuracy than the market, changes in firm value" (p. 1060).

Effects of Financial Distress on Organizational Efficiency

Wruck (1990) delineated several issues associated with financial distress and bankruptcy, focusing on the effects of financial distress on a firm's organizational structure and efficiency: "Imperfect information and conflicts of interest among the firm's claimholders influence the outcome of financial distress . . . The evidence demonstrates that financial distress has benefits as well as costs, and that financial and ownership structure affect the net costs" (p. 419).

Here we cite one each of the costs and benefits of financial distress that Wruck outlined. Regarding costs, "In pursuing their own interests, claimants have incentives to present biased and inaccurate data as though it were unbiased and accurate. Shareholders have incentives to claim the firm is insolvent only on a flow basis . . . because it increases the likelihood that they will retain their equity stake and therefore preserve the option value of their claim. Creditors have incentives to claim the firm is insolvent on a stock basis . . . because it increases the likelihood that they will be awarded the equity. Managers have an incentive to side with the party less likely to fire them. Resolving these conflicts consumes resources and in the extreme can destroy huge amounts of value" (pp. 423–424).[3]

Regarding benefits, "When liquidation or reorganization is the firm's highest-valued alternative, default creates value by providing an event that triggers change. Financial distress gives creditors the right to demand restructuring because their contract with the firm has been breached. They can push the firm to liquidate or reorganize. Leverage can, therefore, lead to value maximization by triggering liquidation . . . The value of a firm likely to liquidate too soon or linger too long is reduced" (p. 431).

---

[3]A firm is insolvent on a flow basis if cash flow going forward is only *temporarily* lower than the level of its obligations. Being insolvent on both a flow basis and a stock basis means that the firm's cash flow going forward is *permanenetly* lower than the level of its obligations.

Fire Sales in Bankruptcy?

Pulvino (1999) addressed the question of whether asset sales in bankruptcy occur at *fire sale* prices. He focused on sales of commercial aircraft to determine whether proceeds are greater under Chapter 11 reorganization than under Chapter 7 liquidation, and whether prices obtained under either procedure differ from those obtained in comparable sales by nondistressed airlines. "Results indicate that prices obtained under both bankruptcy regimes are substantially lower than prices obtained by nondistressed airlines. Furthermore, there is no evidence that prices obtained by firms reorganizing under Chapter 11 are greater than those obtained by firms liquidating under Chapter 7. An analysis of aircraft sales indicates that Chapter 11 is also ineffective in limiting the number of aircraft sold at discounted prices" (p. 151).

A Case in Point: Eastern Airlines

Weiss and Wruck (1998) analyzed the woeful case of Eastern Airlines, which became distressed in the late 1980s: "Eastern Airlines' bankruptcy illustrates the devastating effect on firm value of court-sponsored asset stripping, i.e., the use of creditors' collateral to invest in high-variance negative net present value projects. During its bankruptcy, Eastern's value dropped over 50 percent. A substantial portion of this value decline occurred because an overprotective court insulated Eastern from market forces and allowed value-destroying operations to continue long after it was clear that Eastern should have been shut down. The failure of Eastern's Chapter 11 demonstrates the importance of having a bankruptcy process that protects a distressed firm's assets, not simply from a run by creditors, but also from overly optimistic managers and misguided judges" (p. 55).

Financial Recontracting in Private Debt Renegotiation versus Chapter 11

Franks and Torous (1994) examined 82 firms that either entered bankruptcy through Chapter 11 (37 firms) or informally completed a distressed exchange of publicly traded debt (45 firms) over the years 1983 to 1988. The median time that the Chapter 11 firms took to reorganize was 27 months, while the distressed exchanges completed a workout in a median of 17 months. They also found that "recovery rates for creditors, on average, are higher in distressed exchanges than in Chapter 11 reorganizations, as are equity deviations from absolute priority. The difference in deviations potentially provides valuable information on the higher costs of formal reorganization. Also, cash is used more extensively to redeem creditor's claims in Chapter 11 than in distressed exchanges. The greater use of cash can be attributed to provisions of the Bankruptcy Code that permit conservation of cash and facilitate asset sales" (p. 349).

Gilson (1997) provided evidence that restructuring costs for a severely distressed firm are generally much lower if bankruptcy, rather than a private workout, is chosen: "This study provides evidence that transactions costs discourage debt reductions by financially distressed firms when they restructure their debt out of court. As a result, these firms remain highly leveraged and one-in-three subsequently experience financial distress. Transactions costs are significantly smaller, hence leverage falls by more and there is less recurrence of financial distress, when firms recontract in Chapter 11. Chapter 11 therefore gives financially distressed firms more flexibility to choose optimal capital structures" (p. 161).

Prepackaged Bankruptcies

In the late 1980s and early 1990s, the caseload of bankruptcies increased dramatically. This situation led to the emergence of the *prepackaged bankruptcy*. In a *prepack*, the claimants have already worked out the terms of the reorganization, and basically file just to make the agreement official. Ideally, a prepack avoids the holdout problem of a formal workout and also minimizes the time spent in Chapter 11 proceedings.

Tashjian, Lease, and McConnell (1996) examined the outcomes of a sample of prepacks: "We provide comprehensive data on the attributes and outcomes of the restructuring process for a sample of 49 financially distressed firms that restructured by means of a prepackaged bankruptcy. Our findings complement previous research on out-of-court restructurings and traditional Chapter 11 filings. By most measures, including the time spent in reorganization, the direct fees as a percent of pre-distress assets, the recovery rates by creditors, and the incidence of violations of absolute priority of claimholders, we find that prepacks lie between out-of-court restructurings and traditional Chapter 11 bankruptcies" (p. 135).

Choosing from among a Workout, Chapter 11, or a Prepackaged Bankruptcy

Chatterjee, Dhillon, and Ramirez (1996) analyzed the restructuring decision by examining the characteristics of samples of firms that chose to resolve their insolvency via a workout, Chapter 11 proceedings, or a prepackaged bankruptcy. "We provide evidence that the restructuring decision depends on the degree of the firm's leverage, the severity of its liquidity crisis, the extent of creditor's coordination, and the magnitude of its economic distress . . . We find that economically distressed firms file for Chapter 11, while economically viable firms prefer workouts. Further, prepackaged bankruptcies are used by firms that are economically viable but face immediate liquidity problems" (p. 5).

The Resolution of Bankruptcy via Auction

Bhattacharyya and Singh (1999) examined the resolution of bankruptcy via auction, which involves soliciting (generally cash) bids for either the entire firm or for particular outstanding claims. Supporters of the auction method argue that it separates the reorganization and liquidation decisions from the issue of settling outstanding claims. The latter issue is settled more readily if claimants face a pile of cash, rather than a firm with disputed value. This method has the additional attraction of allocating the firm's assets to their most productive use—presumably in the hands of the highest bidder.

However, the authors argue that prescribing an auction, without specifying the procedure in detail, "does not eliminate incentive conflicts between senior and junior claimants. Instead, some of the incentive conflicts that arise in the reorganization setting show up in the choice of sale procedures themselves. We show that senior and junior claimants have conflicting preferences over common auction procedures. Consequently, the right to design a sale procedure itself has value over and above the rights to any cash flows arising out of the sale . . . In addition, the residual right to design the method of sale has to be allocated to some party in order to ameliorate incentive conflicts" (p. 271). For instance, senior claimants have an incentive to underinvest in the search for bidders, and junior claimants always overinvest. This is an important issue, because practitioners often spend a good deal of time, effort, and expense in designing methods for selling corporate assets (e.g., the case of Conrail).

A Case in Point: Winstar Communication's Chapter 11 Sale

New York–based Winstar Communications, Inc., went public on the Nasdaq market under the name Robern Apparel, Inc., in April 1991, with total assets (TA) of approximately $12 million. The firm changed its name to Robern Industries, and then to Winstar Communications, as it evolved into a communications company in the 1990s. By 2001, Winstar had TA of $5 billion, and was a major competitive local exchange carrier (CLEC) operating in the United States and several other countries, providing wireless and wireline data and voice telecommunications services. Winstar's network reached into 5,400 buildings worldwide, collectively housing 150,000 businesses.

However, in the 10 years of its existence, the firm never had a profitable year. Indeed, annual losses increased each year, reaching $765 million in 2000. In early April 2001, Winstar announced that it would layoff 2,000 workers (half of its employees), and on April 16, 2001, the firm announced that it missed $75 million in interest payments on senior debt. Lucent Technologies declared that Winstar also defaulted on $400 million in financing that it extended to Winstar, which would trigger cross-defaults under other agreements, including its bank facility. Despite deep-pocketed backers including Microsoft and Compaq Computer, Winstar voluntarily filed for Chapter 11 on April 18, 2001, listing assets of $4.98 billion and debts of $5 billion. The company was delisted from Nasdaq on April 26.

Winstar started an accelerated sale of itself on November 21, but on December 17, U.S. District Judge Joseph J. Farnan Jr. denied Winstar's request to sell the company because no buyer approved by Farnan could be found. At that point, Winstar asked the court to approve converting the bankruptcy case from a Chapter 11 reorganization to a Chapter 7 liquidation. At the last minute, however, Winstar found a buyer. On December 20, IDT Corp. (NYSE: ticker IDT) announced that it would purchase substantially all the operating assets of Winstar. The purchase price was $42.5 million and was to be paid $30 million in cash and $12.5 million in IDT class B common stock.

18.5.3   Emerging from Chapter 11: Postbankruptcy Structure and Performance

Several authors have conducted empirical research on postbankruptcy structure or performance.

Postbankruptcy Structure

Alderson and Betker (1995) examined the relation between a bankrupt firm's liquidation costs and its post-bankruptcy capital structure. They found that "firms with high liquidation costs emerge from Chapter 11 with relatively low debt ratios. The debt of these firms is more likely to be public and unsecured, and to have less restrictive covenant terms; these firms are also more likely to raise new equity capital. Assets with high liquidation costs thus lead firms to choose capital structures that make financial distress less likely" (p. 45).

Gilson (1990) studied the effects of bankruptcy on a firm's stakeholders. "In 111 publicly traded firms that either file for bankruptcy or privately restructure their debt between 1979 and 1985, bank lenders frequently become major stockholders or appoint new directors. On average, only 46 percent of incumbent directors remain when bankruptcy or debt restructuring ends. Directors who resign hold significantly fewer seats on other boards following their departure. Common-stock ownership becomes more concentrated with large blockholders and less with corporate insiders. Few firms are acquired. Collectively, these results suggest that corporate default leads to significant changes in the ownership of firms' residual claims and in the allocation of rights to manage corporate resources" (p. 355).

Postbankruptcy Performance

Hotchkiss (1995) examined the postbankruptcy performance of 197 publicly traded firms that emerged from Chapter 11 bankruptcy over the period 1979 to 1988. They found: "Over 40 percent of the sample firms continue to experience operating losses in the three years following bankruptcy; 32 percent reenter bankruptcy or privately restructure their debt. The continued involvement of prebankruptcy management in the restructuring process is strongly associated with poor post-bankruptcy performance. The substantial number of firms emerging from Chapter 11 that are not viable or need further restructuring provides little evidence that the process effectively rehabilitates distressed firms and is consistent with the view that there are economically important biases toward continuation of unprofitable firms" (p. 3).

Indro, Leach, and Lee (1999) examined 171 Chapter 11 cases over the years 1980 to 1991 for sources of gains to shareholders from bankruptcy resolution. They found that "winners are relatively smaller firms with higher proportions of convertible debt, tend to file for bankruptcy for strategic reasons, have low share-ownership concentration, and suffer comparatively larger pre-filing stock price declines. Among winners, shareholder returns are greater for firms that have higher levels of private debt and research and development (R&D) expenditures, and operate in more concentrated industries. In addition, . . . an ex ante trading strategy of purchasing bankrupt stocks with a greater than 50 percent probability of being a winner on the day after bankruptcy filing and holding the stocks for a year, on an average, can generate average compounded . . . holding-period returns of +71 percent . . . " (p. 21).

18.6   THE LIQUIDATION ALTERNATIVE

In a corporate liquidation, the firm's assets are sold, proceeds are used to retire debt, and remaining cash, if any, is distributed to the firm's stockholders as a *liquidating dividend*. A firm's liquidation may be either voluntary or involuntary. Liquidations of either type are fairly rare, suggesting that other resolutions, including private workout, being acquired or bought out, or a Chapter 11 filing, are generally preferred. However, in some cases liquidation may be the value-maximizing alternative. A firm may generate more value for its creditors and shareholders by liquidating than by continuing to operate.

Several authors have conducted empirical studies of liquidating firms, all of which are based on small samples due to the dearth of cases. Below we provide authors' summaries of five such studies.

Pulvino (1998): "[R]esults presented in this paper have implications for the debate over bankruptcy law reform. While some authors argue that insolvent firms should be forced into immediate cash liquidation via Chapter 7 of the U.S. bankruptcy code (e.g., Baird 1986), opponents object to this solution on the grounds that it may fail to maximize proceeds to liquidating firms' claimholders (e.g., Aghion, Hart, and Moore 1992).

They argue that problems associated with raising capital and lack of competition for distressed firms' assets will cause liquidating firms to sell assets at discounts to fundamental value . . . assets will be transferred to well-financed industry outsiders who, because of the industry-specific nature of assets, are less-productive users. Results presented in this paper imply that immediate cash liquidation of distressed firms' assets via Chapter 7 of the U.S. bankruptcy code could result in suboptimal outcomes; claimholders may get only a fraction of the value of their assets and assets may be distributed to financially unconstrained buyers rather than high-value users" (p. 941).

Titman (1984): "A firm's liquidation can impose costs on its customers, workers, and suppliers. An agency relationship between these individuals and the firm exists in that the liquidation decision controlled by the firm (as the agent) affects other individuals (the customers, workers, and suppliers as principals). The analysis in this paper suggests that capital structure can control the incentive/conflict problem of this relationship by serving as a pre-positioning or bonding mechanism. Appropriate selection of capital structure assures that incentives are aligned so that the firm implements the ex-ante value-maximizing liquidation policy" (p. 137).

Kim and Schatzberg (1987): "This paper examines possible motives for and consequences of voluntary corporate liquidations. Specifically, the procedural and tax differences between voluntary liquidations and other control-changing transaction devices are analyzed. An empirical investigation of successful liquidations shows that the announcement of liquidation reduces the risk of liquidating shares, that the shareholders receive substantial gains from successful liquidations, and that the average gains to the acquiring shareholders are not significantly different from zero. These findings suggest that the liquidating firms' assets have been underutilized before liquidation and that voluntary liquidations lead to higher-valued reallocations of corporate resources" (p. 311).

Skanz and Marchesini (1987): "The purpose of this paper is to examine the shareholder wealth effect of complete divestiture or voluntary liquidation. For a sample of 37 firms, the formal announcement of the intention to liquidate generates significant positive risk-adjusted shareholder returns. The announcement-month average excess return is +21.4 percent" (p. 65).

"Many reasons have been advanced to explain the motivations behind corporate divestitures. In the case of complete voluntary liquidation, the fundamental fact is that the sum of the firm's parts is worth more than the whole, i.e., the firm is worth more as a liquidating concern than as a going concern. Several factors may contribute to this phenomenon. First, the assets (or divisions) may be worth more in the hands of more competent managers. Second, any diseconomies associated with excessive diversification can be eliminated by piecemeal sale through liquidation. Third, and most important, the special tax treatment afforded liquidations provides a source of value over and above the firm's value as a going concern" (p. 74).

The authors explained the *special tax treatment* in liquidations as follows: "The most frequently cited reason for liquidating related to favorable tax effects from Section 337 or '12-month' liquidation, the method employed by most firms in the study. Except for depreciation recapture, the corporation avoids taxes on any accounting gains from the sale of assets—including inventory when sold to a single buyer . . . Nevertheless, the buyer has a basis in the asset equal to the fair market value (purchase price). As a result, the seller is able to sell tax shields without an unfavorable tax consequence" (pp. 67–68).

Mehran, Nogler, and Schwartz (1998): "To investigate CEOs' incentives to liquidate their firms, we examine the effects of insider ownership and compensation in stock options on 30 voluntary liquidation decisions by industrial firms in the period 1975 to 1986. We find that liquidation decisions are influenced by CEO incentive plans and increased shareholder value. Firms with more outside board members, smaller market-to-book ratios, and attempts by outsiders to gain control are more likely to be liquidated. Although few top executives of liquidating firms subsequently take comparable jobs, at least 41 percent of CEOs who downsize are made better off by liquidation" (p. 319).

18.7 Summary of Learning Objectives

A firm becomes severely distressed when it is unable to service its debt obligations. Such firms must (a) negotiate a private restructuring of their debt contracts, (b) have their debt retired or assumed by an acquirer; or (c) default and file for bankruptcy. If bankruptcy is the alternative, the firm is either reorganized or liquidated.

We began this chapter with several statistical perspectives on severe financial distress. Severe or protracted financial distress is not uncommon among publicly traded U.S. firms. However, most survive as publicly traded firms, though perhaps half must at least restructure their debt. On average, 0.7 percent of all publicly traded U.S. nonfinancial firms file for bankruptcy annually, while perhaps three times as many distressed firms are acquired. The annual bankruptcy rate is weakly negatively related to contemporaneous GDP growth. The market generally anticipates a failed firm's probable demise many months before the firm files for bankruptcy, but in perhaps one-fourth of the cases a bankruptcy filing is a sudden surprise.

Next, we discussed private debt restructuring. A distressed firm may negotiate to exchange new debt (which is less onerous) for existing debt, or to exchange equity for debt. The *holdout problem* is often an important obstacle to successful debt restructuring negotiations. This problem is often resolved with a combination of exchange offers and coercion. Severe financial distress can distort a firm's investment incentives before, during, and after debt restructuring negotiations. *Vulture investors* specialize in investing in the debt or equity of distressed firms. They take major positions in the firm's securities so that they can influence the firm's governance, restructuring, or reorganization.

We also briefly discussed acquisition, takeover, and buyout transactions as responses to severe financial distress. Our estimates indicate that approximately one-third of all firms that are acquired are distressed firms. As a resolution to distress, being acquired can be a value-creating solution for at least four reasons: (a) gaining economies of scale, (b) enhancing product-market power, (c) enhancing operations via superior management, and (d) combining investment opportunities with available capital. Many takeovers have been undertaken to correct the target management's failure. A leveraged buyout (i.e., a MBO) gives a firm's management the dual incentives of increased equity ownership and the discipline of debt, which can, and often does, lead to improved performance.

We discussed bankruptcy, the reorganization process, and emergence from bankruptcy. Banktuptcy filings generally occur under Chapter 11 (reorganization), but can be refiled as Chapter 7 cases for liquidation. Reorganization is the general result of negotiations under Chapter 11. Scholars have debated the efficiency of bankruptcy laws, citing problems such as routine violations of the *absolute priority rule* (APR). On the other hand, Chapter 11 can overcome some of the serious negotiating problems among the various parties. Firms emerging from Chapter 11 reorganization generally remain distressed, but that is probably because they tend to be the weakest among all firms that are in financial distress, which is in turn because distressed firms that are more economically viable generally choose a private workout.

Finally, we discuss liquidation as an alternative to reorganization. Liquidations may be either voluntary or involuntary. Liquidations are fairly rare, but on occasion they may be the value-maximizing alternative for a distressed firm. Liquidations impose substantial costs on the distressed firm's stakeholders. On the other hand, liquidation is tax-advantaged.

Review Questions and Problems

1. Discuss the evidence presented in Section 18.2 on the rates of severe financial distress among U.S. firms and the fates of severely distressed firms.
2. Explain the *holdout problem*, and how it can be resolved via exchange offers and coercion.
3. Explain how a distressed firm's investment decisions influence the terms of a debt renegotiation.
4. Explain the pooling equilibrium that can develop among severely distressed firms, and how the availability of Chapter 11 proceedings can separate otherwise pooled firms into those that restructure debt privately and those that file Chapter 11.
5. Discuss exit-exchange offers.
6. How do *vulture investors* operate?
7. Discuss the circumstances under which a distressed firm can successfully exchange equity for debt.
8. Discuss factors that determine the success of private debt restructuring negotiations.
9. List four reasons why being acquired can create value for a distressed firm's shareholders.
10. Discuss the design and efficacy of the U.S. bankruptcy law.
11. Define the absolute priority rule (APR). Why are deviations from it observed?
12. Discuss the evidence on the effects of bankruptcy on a firm's stakeholders.
13. Discuss evidence on the postreorganization financial structure and performance of bankrupt firms.
14. Why do some distressed firms liquidate?
15. Why are voluntary liquidation announcements so well received by the market?
16. Discuss the special tax treatment of liquidations.
17. Discuss the incentives of a distressed firm's CEO to liquidate.

Creative Thinking Issues

1. Argue why changes in the bankruptcy rate among U.S. firms are likely to lead, to be contemporaneous with, or to lag changes in GDP growth over time.
2. Empirical evidence suggests a hierarchy of managerial preferences for alternatives under severe distress, with trying to survive as a public firm without default or restructuring at the top, followed by negotiating a private workout, being acquired

or bought out, Chapter 11 reorganization, and finally Chapter 7 liquidation. Do you think such a hierarchy of preferences exists? Is this the correct ordering of such a hierarchy?

3. Are U.S. bankruptcy proceedings efficient? Form an opinion after reading Roe (1983), Baird (1986), Jackson (1986), Easterbrook (1990), Gertner and Scharfstein (1992), Aghion, Hart, and Moore (1992), Berkovitch, Israel, and Zender (1998), and Eberhart and Weiss (1998).

Projects and Analyses

1. Select a firm that has recently filed for bankruptcy under Chapter 11. Chart the history of its earnings, equity (market and book), and leverage for several years leading up to the filing. Identify the root cause of the firm's failure. If the firm has completed its reorganization, discuss the firm's postbankruptcy status and performance.

2. Analyze changes over time in the earnings, liquidity, total assets, debt, and equity of a sample of firms that have gone bankrupt in recent years. If possible, gather and analyze data for all years from the firm's IPO to its failure. What patterns appear? (See Table 18-2 for a list of bankruptcies.)

PART

V

Organizational Architecture, Risk Management, and Security Design

Part Five consists of the final chapter of the text, Chapter 19. In this chapter, we provide a second comprehensive perspective on the firm (complementing Chapter 8). We do this by introducing the concept of a firm's *organizational architecture*. In addition, we introduce two new topics: *risk management* using derivatives, and *optimal security design*.

CHAPTER

Organizational Architecture, Risk Management, and Security Design

19

19.1 INTRODUCTION

In this, the final chapter of the text, we have two goals. *First*, we provide a second comprehensive perspective on the firm (i.e., to complement Chapter 8) by introducing the concept of *organizational architecture*, which has two constructs—*business architecture* and *financial architecture*. *Second*, we introduce the topics of *risk management* and *optimal security design*. The former includes, but is not limited to, the use of *derivatives* to hedge risk. The latter deals with the intricacies of designing securities to mitigate contracting problems. The two goals are related, because much of management's effort in designing an efficacious organizational architecture involves managing risk and designing securities.

The typical firm has become more complex over time. In tandem, managers must take great care to ensure that all of the components of the firm's financial architecture (i.e., all financial contracts) are (a) consistent with all components of the firm's business architecture, and (b) compatible with each other. In other words, a firm's management must approach its business operations and financial contracting from an *integrated* perspective. Advances in security design and the emergence of derivative-based hedging instruments help managers cope with this increased complexity.

The chapter is organized as follows. In Section 19.2, we introduce our concept of organizational architecture and its two constructs, business architecture and financial architecture. In Section 19.3, we discuss the components of a firm's business architecture. In Sections 19.4 to 19.7, we provide separate discussions of each of the components of a firm's financial architecture, with emphasis on the use of derivatives in Section 19.7. In Section 19.8, we briefly discuss several theoretical articles on optimal security design, and then discuss numerous examples of recent innovations in the design of corporate securities. Finally, Section 19.9 summarizes the chapter's learning objectives, as usual.

19.2 ORGANIZATIONAL ARCHITECTURE

Our concept of a firm's organizational architecture is captured in Figure 19-1. It consists of two constructs: business architecture, shown on the left of the figure; and financial architecture, displayed on the right. Both constructs include several components, and each component includes several elements.[1]

---

[1]In their concept of organizational architecture, Brickley, Smith, and Zimmerman (2001) emphasize (a) the assignment of corporate decision rights, (b) the structure of performance evaluation systems for managers, and (c) methods of rewarding or penalizing managers according to their performance. See also Nadler, Shaw, and Gerstein (1992).

FIGURE 19-1   A model of Organizational Architecture

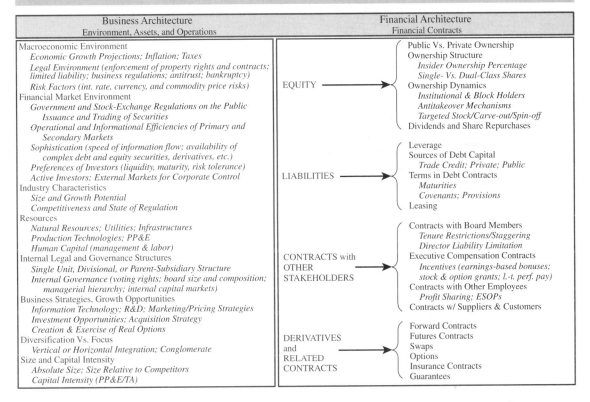

19.2.1   Business Architecture

A firm's business architecture includes all aspects of its environment, assets, and operations that collectively describe the circumstances under which, and the manner in which, it conducts its business, with the exception of its financial contracts. The firm's financial contracts collectively form the firm's financial architecture.

We list eight components of a firm's business architecture (a) macroeconomic environment, (b) financial market environment, (c) industry characteristics, (d) resources, (e) internal legal and governance structures, (f) business strategies and growth opportunities, (g) diversification versus focus, and (h) size and capital intensity. Each component includes several elements, as indicated. We discuss each of these components and elements in Section 19.3.

19.2.2   Financial Architecture

A firm's financial contracts collectively form its financial architecture. A typical firm's financial architecture includes four components (a) equity, (b) liabilities, (c) contracts with other stakeholders, and (d) derivatives and related contracts. Each of these components includes several elements, as indicated. We devote separate sections of the chapter to each of these components.

19.2.3 The Importance of Adopting an Integrated Approach to Constructing a Firm's Organizational Architecture

It is important for a firm's management to recognize that their business and financial architectures are intricately intertwined. In previous chapters, we discussed a number of such relationships. For example, in Chapters 1 and 6 we discussed the collateral hypothesis, which posits that a firm's debt capacity is limited by the value of its collateralizable assets. In Chapter 7, we discussed the possible role of leverage in a firm's competitive strategy. Taxes, which are a function of profits, may influence a firm's leverage (Chapter 6) and leasing policy (Chapter 15). Suppose a firm needs certain equipment as part of the *resources* component of its business architecture. Will the firm finance the acquisition of this equipment using internal funds, by issuing debt or equity, or by entering into a lease contract? As we discuss in Section 19.7, research suggests that a firm's use of derivatives depends on other elements of the firm's organizational architecture, such as taxes, investment opportunities, leverage, and executive compensation.

Conceivably, arguments can be made to relate any of the components/elements of a firm's business or financial architectures to any other component/element. Regarding the components and elements of the firm's business architecture, the direction of causality (i.e., in terms of which component/element drives another component/element) generally runs from a higher-level component/element in the list in Figure 19-1 to a lower level component/element. Regarding overall organizational architecture, the direction of causality generally runs from components/elements (individually and collectively) in the firm's business architecture to components/elements in the firm's financial architecture. Nevertheless, all elements of a firm's organizational architecture must be melded, because they all contribute to the firm's risk and profitability, and ultimately to the firm's ability to create value for its stockholders.

19.3 BUSINESS ARCHITECTURE

In this section, we discuss each of the eight components of a firm's business architecture listed on the left side of Figure 19-1, as well as the elements within each component.

19.3.1 Macroeconomic Environment

The macroeconomic component of a firm's business architecture includes three elements: (a) *economic growth projections, inflation, and taxes*, (b) *legal environment*, and (c) *macroeconomic risk factors*.

Economic Growth Projections, Inflation, and Taxes
Both short-term and long-term expectations of macroeconomic growth, inflation, and taxes influence a firm's expected profitability, its capital expenditure plans, and the risk of financial distress.

In Chapter 8, we examined three distinct subperiods in recent U.S. economic history: 1960 to 1973; 1974 to 1982; and 1983 to 2000. The first subperiod was characterized by high real gross domestic product (GDP) growth, low interest rates and inflation, relatively high taxes, high productivity growth, and moderate real returns on stocks. The second subperiod was characterized by low real GDP growth, high interest rates and inflation, lower taxes, weak productivity growth, and low real returns on stocks. The final subperiod was characterized by a return to high real GDP growth, lower interest rates and inflation, lower taxes, fairly high productivity growth, and exceptionally high real returns on stocks. In Chapter 18, we found that the relative frequency of bankruptcies among publicly traded U.S. nonfinancial firms over the period 1980 to 2000 was (slightly) negatively correlated with both contemporaneous GDP growth and changes in aggregate corporate profits, as expected.

Taxes, both corporate and personal, on both ordinary income and capital gains, can affect a firm's capital structure decision (Chapter 6), and dividend and stock repurchase policies (Chapter 14). Taxes also can affect the efficacy of transactions such as leasing (Chapter 15), acquisitions (Chapter 16), the issuance of targeted stock and spin-offs (Chapter 17), and liquidation (Chapter 18). In Section 19.7, we explain how taxes can also affect a firm's hedging decisions.

Legal Environment

Numerous aspects of the legal environment are important to firms. The most fundamental aspects of the law pertain to (a) the protection of property rights, (b) the enforcement of legal contracts, and (c) the limited liability afforded stock holders as owners of a corporation.

Government regulations on the conduct of business are also important. Although several U.S. industries have been *deregulated* in recent decades (transportation, communications, and utilities), firms in all industries are regulated to some extent. The federal government regulates international trade, labor contracts, and the quality of consumer products. Mergers and acquisitions (M&As) are subject to review regarding their compliance with antitrust legislation. Restrictions on M&A activity affect the structure and competitiveness of an industry, as well as an individual firm's opportunities to grow through acquisitions. Finally, bankruptcy law, including filings under either Chapter 11 (reorganization) or Chapter 7 (liquidation) of the U.S. Bankruptcy Code, provide for the resolution of a firm's financial claims in the event of default.

Macroeconomic Risk Factors

Macroeconomic risk factors, most notably interest rate risk, currency risk, and commodity price volatility, can affect both a firm's business and financial architectures. In Chapter 15, we discussed the emergence of interest rate volatility in the late 1970s and early 1980s, which revolutionized the U.S. corporate bond market. Firms' decided en masse to shorten debt maturities and to issue floating-rate securities. Interest rate derivatives also emerged at this time to help firms hedge interest rate risk.

The floating of major currencies in the 1970s, coupled with the accelerated globalization of business in the 1980s and 1990s, resulted in an increase in firms' exposure to currency risk. Markets for currency derivatives have expanded tremendously over the past 20 years in response to firms' demands for instruments to hedge currency risk. Markets for derivatives that allow firms to hedge commodity price risk have also expanded in recent years.

19.3.2 Financial Market Environment

Five elements of the financial market environment are part and parcel of a firm's business architecture (a) *government and stock-exchange regulations on the issuance and trading of securities*, (b) *the operational and informational efficiencies of the financial markets*, (c) *the technological sophistication of financial markets*, (d) *preferences of investors*, and (e) *activist investors and the external markets for corporate control.*

Government and Stock-Exchange Regulations on the Issuance and Trading of Equity

The U.S. Securities and Exchange Commission (SEC), state governments, and securities exchanges regulate the public issuance and trading of corporate securities in the United States. Regulations include mandatory due diligence, disclosure, registration, and restrictions on insider trading.

For the initial and continued listing of a stock, stock exchanges impose requirements such as minimum number of stockholders, minimum price per share, and minimum trading volume. These requirements may affect a firm's financial decisions, such as (a) whether to offer its equity to the public or maintain private ownership, (b) on which exchange its stock should be listed, and (c) the number and proportion of shares to place in the public market.

Operational and Informational Efficiencies of Financial Markets

The *operational efficiency* of a securities market relates to both primary and secondary markets. Regarding the primary market, operational efficiency refers to the extent to which a firm can issue securities quickly, at a fair price, and with low flotation costs. Our analyses in earlier chapters show that substantial economies of scale are present in the public issuance of corporate securities. For both stock and bond issues, underwriter spreads are strongly inversely related to issue size. Regarding the secondary market, operational efficiency refers to the *liquidity* that the market provides investors as they seek to trade. The market for a security is liquid to the extent that investors can trade quickly, at a fair price, and with low transaction costs.

The *informational efficiency* of a financial market refers to the various aspects of market efficiency (i.e., the extent to which market prices accurately and quickly reflect value-relevant information) that we discussed in Chapter 9.

Both of these aspects of efficiency can affect a firm's effective access to the capital markets for the purpose of raising external debt or equity capital. Small firms and firms in which information asymmetry is substantial often have difficulty establishing and maintaining liquid and efficient markets for their securities.

Technological Sophistication of Financial Markets

In part, the technological sophistication of financial markets refers to *speed of information flow*. Both the operational and informational efficiencies of a securities market are directly related to the speed at which accurate, value-relevant information is communicated to both issuers and investors, and impounded into security prices.

Technological sophistication also refers to the availability of complex securities and transactions. To the extent that sophisticated contracting devices are available to a firm, it can develop a more efficient financial architecture, mitigating contracting problems of the types we have discussed throughout the text. For instance, in Chapter 15 we discussed the rich array of debt funding sources and contract terms, both private and public, that are available to U.S. firms, depending on their circumstances. Banks and finance companies offer debt capital through private debt contracts. Other financial institutions, such as insurance companies and pension funds, also purchase private and semiprivate debt contracts (as well as publicly issued notes and bonds).

The public debt markets provide an alternative means by which firms can raise debt capital through the public issuance of notes and bonds. In Chapter 17, we discussed sophisticated equity securities such as targeted stock and the dual-class equity structure, and sophisticated transactions including equity carve-outs and spin-offs. This discussion directly relates to the topic of *optimal security design*, which we pursue in Section 19.8.

Financial System Architecture

Boot and Thakor (1997) developed a theory of *financial system architecture*. They focused on the structural design of the markets and institutions that make up our financial system, rather than on the design of an individual firm's financial architecture (as will be our bent later in this chapter). Nevertheless, their concepts are related because an individual firm can develop its own financial architecture only to the extent that an accommodative *financial system* exists.

The authors addressed the question of the configuration of an efficient financial system: "In particular, we examine why bank lending and capital market financing coexist and the factors—such as regulation and the stage of economic development—that determine which dominates" (p. 694). Their answer is that they coexist because each has a relative advantage in resolving firms' financial contracting problems: "Banks arise . . . to resolve asset-substitution moral hazard. The financial market arises to permit noncolluding agents to compete, and this facilitates the transmission of valuable information about market conditions with a concomitant impact on firms' real decisions. We find that borrowers who pose relatively onerous asset-substitution moral hazard prefer bank financing, and borrowers who pose less serious moral hazards go directly to the capital market. Moreover, increased financial market sophistication diminishes banks' market share" (pp. 726–727).

Preferences of Investors

Investors' preferences also play a key role in shaping a firm's financial architecture. For instance, investors' desires for *liquidity* affect a firm's dividend policy (and by extension, the firm's ability to fund growth internally). In addition, investors' planned *investment horizons* may affect the maturities of corporate debt issues, and investors' *risk tolerance* may affect both a firm's capital investment program and its leverage by affecting both the firm's willingness to take risk and its cost of capital.

Activist Stockholders and the External Markets for Corporate Control

In Chapter 8, we discussed the prevalence and roles of activist stockholders, and in Chapter 16 we discussed the external markets for corporate control. Activist stockholders have the prerogative of launching proxy contests to attempt to remove and replace a firm's board members, or to initiate proposals for reforming the firm's governance. The external markets for corporate control affect a firm's organizational architecture in several respects. For instance, a small firm may guide the development of both its business and financial architectures with the ultimate (value-maximizing) objective of being an attractive acquisition target for a larger firm in the industry. The threat of a takeover may prompt a firm's management to take actions that are in the interest of stockholders, rather than their own interests. Alternatively, to thwart a takeover attempt, a firm may (a) increase its leverage, (b) repurchase shares, (c) alter its ownership structure, (d) adopt antitakeover devices, or (e) arrange a buyout.

19.3.3   Industry Characteristics

In Chapter 7, we discussed several aspects of a firm's industry that can affect elements of its business and financial architectures. These aspects include (a) *the size and growth potential of the industry*, and (b) *the competitiveness of the industry*. We discussed the possible effects of an industry's size, growth potential, and competition on a firm's business strategy, leverage, and executive compensation policies.

Regarding (a), note initially that firms in high-growth industries are likely to have substantial growth opportunities. The Myers (1977) theory of the underinvestment (or debt overhang) problem posits that risky debt can be problematic for a firm with substantial growth opportunities, but that short-term debt may be less problematic. Having internal capital (i.e., financial slack) may be an even better solution, though this suggests that a high-growth firm would optimally refrain from paying dividends. Regarding (b), we have discussed how information asymmetry can affect financing decisions (e.g., Myers and Majluf 1984). The information asymmetry problem is likely to be more severe in highly competitive industries.

The regulatory status of a firm's industry also affects its business and financial architectures. Firms in a regulated industry are likely to have fewer profitable growth opportunities, but also are likely to be less risky, so they are likely to have higher optimal leverage (based on the Traditional Trade-off Theory). Regulated firms are also less prone to principal-agent conflicts and information asymmetry problems, so having diffusely owned equity is less problematic. On the other hand, industry deregulation can be a traumatic experience for a firm, as it must adjust to competition by developing its business strategy, and altering its ownership structure, dividend policy, and leverage.

As a part of its strategy for competing within an industry, a firm may adopt a high-leverage strategy both to signal its intent to compete aggressively and as a means of deterring entry. Alternatively, the firm may adopt a more conservative, low-leverage strategy that may allow it to squeeze out more highly levered firms in the industry (the Long Purse Hypothesis).

19.3.4   Resources

The third component of a firm's business architecture, resources, includes three elements (a) *natural resources, utilities, and infrastructure*; (b) *production technologies and property, plant, and equipment (PP&E)*; and (c) *human capital, both managerial and labor*. The importance of each of these resources depends on the firm's industry and the products or services that it produces.

Natural Resources, Utilities, and Infrastructures

For manufacturing firms, the availability of natural resources is a critical determinant of a plant's location and efficiency. The cost of natural resources is an important determinant of the profitability, and indeed the overall viability, of a production effort. Firms also need reliable, low-cost electric, gas, water, and waste-disposal utilities, as well as efficient transportation infrastructures such as roads and airports.

Production Technologies and PP&E

A firm can gain a critical competitive advantage in its industry by obtaining and employing advanced, cost-effective production technologies and equipment. As we noted above, equipment can often be leased. For many firms, PP&E represents the single largest expense, but it can often be financed with mortgage debt.

Human Capital

Human resources are vital for every firm, and increasingly so in the high technology, information-intensive economy of the United States. A person's capability and willingness to perform a task depends on his or her education, work ethic, and compensation incentives. The cost of labor services depends in large part on the general income levels of the region, but also on other factors such as whether workers are unionized. Recruiting and training both rank-and-file employees and managers can be very expensive and risky, as employees may leave the firm before the firm's investment in their training is fully amortized. Contracting devices can be used to retain, motivate, and reward key employees.

19.3.5   Internal Legal and Governance Structures

An important aspect of a firm's internal legal structure is the decision whether to operate as a single unit, to have multiple divisions, or to adopt a parent-subsidiary structure. Internal governance structures include stockholders' voting rights, the firm's board of directors, management hierarchy, and the operation of an internal capital market.

Single Unit, Division, or Parent–Subsidiary Structure

By a firm's legal structure, we refer to its status as a single unit, a multidivisional organization, or a parent-subsidiary structure. Merton and Bodie (1992) provided the following valid reasons for companies to establish subsidiaries: "[a] to better control risk exposure of either the parent to the subsidiary or the subsidiary to the parent, [b] to enhance the company's ability to evaluate individual performance and to create different compensation systems for a diverse set of its businesses, [c] to conform with regulatory requirements specific to a particular business environment" (p. 100).

On the other hand, conglomerate parent-subsidiary structures are often inefficient, as we discussed in Chapter 17. Many of the conglomerates of the 1960s and 1970s, which may have developed because of relatively ineffective external capital markets, have been busted up via takeover or have voluntarily broken up via issuances of target stock or equity carve-outs, often followed by a spin-off.

Internal Governance

In Chapter 8, we discussed the firm's internal governance structures. These structures include (a) the voting rights of stockholders, (b) the firm's board of directors, (c) the firm's managerial hierarchy, and (d) the firm's internal capital market.

The firm's stockholders generally have the right to vote on major issues such as the election of board members, M&A decisions, and the sale of major assets such as a division. As we noted earlier, activist stockholders occasionally attempt to garner sufficient proxy votes to effect a change in corporate governance, such as the termination of staggered boards.

A firm's board provides oversight of the firm's senior management. Board members also serve as consultants. The optimal board probably includes both insiders and outsiders. Insiders have an advantage in terms of knowing the firm's business and strategies, but they might not dare to challenge the CEO regarding dubious plans and decisions. Outside directors bring an independent voice and a broader set of experiences to the board. A board may also be more effective if it is smaller.

A firm's managerial hierarchy can range from steep to flat. In a steep hierarchy, top management wields the bulk of the decision-making power within the organization; in a flat hierarchical structure, lower-level managers have much more autonomy and decision-making power.

A firm's *internal capital market* (discussed in Chapter 13) refers to competition among division managers for allocations of the firm's limited internal capital to projects proposed by the division managers. The efficiency of an internal capital market has been debated in the literature. It provides some advantages, including increased monitoring incentives and better asset redeployability. However, an internal capital market also entails problems, such as incentive problems and the cross-subsidization problem.

19.3.6   Business Strategies and Growth Opportunities

In Chapter 8, we argued that a firm's business strategy has three essential elements: (a) targeting specific product and service markets, (b) establishing goals in terms of market share and profits, and (c) developing an effective competitive strategy against rivals.

Growth opportunities can be very valuable *real options*, but they can also entail financing problems. We again point to Myers's underinvestment problem, wherein a levered firm with valuable growth opportunities may fail to pursue them if a substantial portion of the benefits accrues to the firm's creditors. To avoid this problem, the firm should limit or shorten the maturity of its debt or maintain financial slack so that internal equity funds can be used to finance projects.

Moreover, the information asymmetry problem is likely to be more severe for a firm that has profitable investment opportunities, at least to the extent that these opportunities are created as a result of strategic planning. Information asymmetry increases the cost of external financing, so firms with strategic growth opportunities may be forced to rely more heavily on internal equity to finance them. Again, it is useful to maintain financial slack under such circumstances.

19.3.7   The Scope of the Firm: Diversification versus Focus

In Chapters 16 and 17, we discussed the issue of firm diversification versus focus. At one extreme is the conglomerate, which has interests in many disparate industries. At the other extreme, we have the focused firm, which is committed to a narrow product market in a single industry. Another important dimension is the extent to which the firm is vertically integrated. Vertical integration can be used to secure either a firm's supply of raw materials or its customers. These aspects of a firm's business structure can affect its financial architecture. For instance, to the extent that a firm can reduce its risk via vertical integration, it may increase its debt capacity. On the other hand, a diversified firm may be able to increase share value by divesting (e.g., issuing targeted stock or conducting an equity carve-out).

19.3.8   Firm Size and Capital Intensity

Both the absolute size of a firm and its size relative to industry competitors can profoundly affect a firm's financial architecture, as we have discussed at many points in previous chapters. For instance, we found that large firms tend to have higher (book) leverage, and are more likely to raise short-term and long-term debt capital in the public debt markets (commercial paper and corporate bonds) versus the private debt markets (bank loans).

Regarding relative size, we recall Williams's (1995) arguments, discussed in Chapter 7, that an industry is generally characterized by a few large firms that are highly profitable, capital intensive, and more highly levered, and many smaller firms that are marginally profitable, labor intensive, and less levered. Size has its advantages, in terms of economies of scale and market power. However, if a large firm's senior management does not have an effective organizational architecture, bureaucratic inefficiencies may dominate economies of scale and the overall firm may be inefficient.

Regarding capital intensity, we discussed the *Collateral Hypothesis*. According to this hypothesis, a firm's debt capacity is limited to the value of its collateralizable assets, which basically consist of the firm's PP&E. This criterion relates to the Traditional Trade-off Theory of optimal capital structure in that collateralizable assets are more likely to maintain their value in bankruptcy or liquidation if the firm itself fails. The probability that creditors will incur losses in the event that the firm fails is lower if the firm has collateralizable assets. On the other hand, the collateral value of PP&E is limited if it is illiquid, which in turn depends in part on whether the assets could be sold at their fair value in the event that the firm's industry is depressed.

19.4   FINANCIAL ARCHITECTURE: EQUITY

The first component of a firm's financial architecture is the firm's equity. We divide this component into four elements: (a) the public versus private ownership decision, (b) ownership structure, (c) ownership dynamics, and (d) dividend and stock-repurchase policies. In this section, we briefly review discussions in previous chapters of each of these aspects of a firm's equity.

19.4.1   Public versus Private Ownership

In Chapters 3, 4, and 12, we discussed the fundamental trade-offs involved in the separation of ownership and control, and specific trade-offs involved in keeping a firm private and closely held versus going public and allowing ownership to become diffuse. On the one hand, stockholders can reduce the risk of their private portfolios by diversifying their equity investments across firms. In addition, secondary markets for public equity naturally develop, which increase the liquidity of equity shares. On the other hand, a consequence of diffuse ownership is that none of the stockholders of a given firm have sufficient proportional stake in the firm to warrant their effort to manage— or even to monitor—the decisions made by hired managers. Hence, the firm will incur agency costs of managerial discretion unless contracting devices are brought to bear to mitigate management's incentives to pursue self-serving activities, such as shirking, empire building, and avoiding more profitable but riskier projects.

The decision whether to go public may also hinge on information asymmetry problems. For instance, public equity is problematic if a substantial portion of the firm's value depends on strategic information that the firm's insiders must keep confidential. The signal of insiders' ownership may alleviate this problem, but at the cost of lessening the diversification and liquidity benefits of diffuse ownership.

19.4.2   Ownership Structure and Dynamics

In several chapters throughout the text, we focused on the importance of the ownership structure of a public firm's equity. For instance, theory espoused in Chapters 3 and 4 emphasized the importance of management's holding equity to mitigate costs associated with both stockholder–management principal–agent problems and information asymmetry. We also discussed the role of blockholders (either individual or institutional investors) as monitors of a firm's management.

In very few firms is equity ownership static. In Chapter 16, we discussed several means by which the ownership of an entire firm can change hands in a single transaction. These means include a merger, acquisition, takeover, or buyout. In Chapter 17, we discussed the roles of a dual-class equity structure, targeted stock, equity carve-outs, spin-offs, and levered recaps to resolve problems associated with financial distress.

19.4.3   Dividends and Stock Repurchases

In Chapter 14, we discussed several contracting problems associated with a firm's dividend policy, all of which illustrate the interaction of this element of a firm's financial architecture with other elements. *First*, dividend income is subject to ordinary income taxes, and dividend payments are not a deductible expense. Thus, a policy of paying dividends may increase a firm's cost of equity capital and attract a clientele of investors who prefer the firm's dividend policy.

Second, a firm's management has a private incentive to retain free cash flow rather than paying it out as dividends. In this case it is incumbent upon the firm's board of directors to force the disgorgement of free cash. *Third*, the management of a levered firm, acting in the interest of its stockholders, has an incentive to increase dividends as a means of expropriating wealth from the firm's creditors. *Fourth*, the underinvestment problem suggests that a levered firm may pay dividends rather than pursue a profitable investment project if much of the benefit of the project accrues to the firm's creditors.

Stock repurchase activity among publicly traded U.S. nonfinancial firms has increased tremendously over the past 20 years, so much so that in each of the years 1997 to 2000 the aggregate volume of stock repurchases exceeded aggregate dividends for such firms. In Chapter 14, we discussed the following motives for a firm to repurchase its shares: (a) The firm's shares are undervalued, (b) repurchases force the disgorgement of free cash flow, (c) reducing the firm's outstanding equity can result in an expropriation of wealth from the firm's creditors, and (d) repurchases can serve as a takeover defense.

19.5   FINANCIAL ARCHITECTURE: LIABILITIES

We organize the liabilities component of a firm's financial architecture into four elements: leverage, sources, terms, and leases.

19.5.1   Leverage

We covered basic theories of leverage and optimal capital structure in Chapter 6. A firm's optimal leverage, if such exists, depends on a number of aspects of the firm's industry, assets, and operations. The Traditional Trade-off Theory posits that each firm has a unique optimal debt-to-equity ratio depending on the trade-off between the tax benefits of debt (i.e., the deductibility of interest) and the present value of expected future costs of financial distress and bankruptcy, both of which increase, but at different rates, with leverage.

Agency theory provides additional insights into the leverage decision. Leverage can increase stockholder value by disciplining a firm's management—forcing it to disgorge cash that may otherwise have been used to pursue inefficient investments. However, agency costs of debt detract from such benefits; management, acting in the interest of stockholders, has an incentive to take actions that expropriate wealth from bondholders (e.g., increasing the firm's risk, issuing additional debt, selling assets, paying dividends, and repurchasing shares.)

Information asymmetry theory also weighs in on the leverage issue. The foremost theory of this genre is the Pecking-Order Hypothesis. Under conditions of information asymmetry, external financing is more costly than internal financing, and external equity is more costly than external debt. According to this hypothesis, a firm should maintain sufficient financial slack to avoid the need for external financing. If external financing is required, debt financing is less costly than equity financing.

Finally, as noted earlier, leverage also can be used as a tool in industry competition. A firm may adopt an aggressive competitive strategy that includes high leverage, or may maintain low leverage so as to be able to outlast highly levered competitors when industry profits wane.

19.5.2   Sources of Debt Capital

A firm's decision with respect to debt funding source, particularly as between private sources such as banks and finance companies versus issuing debt publicly, depends in part on the extent to which the firm is beset by principal-agent conflicts and information asymmetry problems. Early in Chapter 15, we discussed the prevalence of firms' use of trade credit to finance their inventories. One rationale given for the widespread use of trade credit is that the seller may be in a better position than a financial institution to evaluate, monitor, and control the buyer's credit risk.

We also reviewed theories that espouse the important role of banks in resolving both principal-agent conflicts and information asymmetry problems associated with debt financing. Banks (and finance companies) are better than the public debt markets in terms of (a) receiving and keeping confidential strategic information, and (b) monitoring a firm's management, and thus mitigating stockholder–management agency problems. Indeed, banks often double as business consultants. For these reasons, banks are often referred to as *inside lenders*, as opposed to lenders in the credit markets, who are referred to as *outside lenders* because they do not normally perform such functions. Moreover, monitoring by a bank may facilitate some firms' ability to issue public debt. We also cited arguments that a loan commitment from a bank can give the borrower protection against a rival, who may otherwise be able to *squeeze* the firm financially. On the other hand, for large firms for which principal-agent conflicts and asymmetric information problems are not severe, the economies of scale associated with the public debt markets generally dominate, so such firms generally issue debt securities publicly.

19.5.3 Terms in Debt Contracts

The terms included in a corporate debt contract, particularly publicly issued notes and bonds, can serve to mitigate both principal-agent conflicts and asymmetric information problems. Traditional terms that can be established or adjusted for this purpose include (a) the maturity of the debt, (b) covenants that restrict management's activities, (c) alternative retirement provisions such as convertibility, callability, or a sinking fund. In addition, innovations in debt contract terms that we discuss later in the chapter, and the establishment of specialized debt markets (e.g., shelf registration, Rule 144A private placements, and the Eurobond market) have enhanced opportunities for more firms to issue debt in the public (or quasi-public) debt markets. We discuss more exotic terms in corporate bond contracts within the context of optimal security design in Section 19.8.

19.5.4 Leasing

U.S. nonfinancial firms make extensive use of leasing, particularly as an alternative means of financing equipment. Leasing provides a clear example of the links between a firm's business architecture and its financial architecture. In Chapter 15, we discussed research on motives for leasing. The leading theory is that if the lessor's tax rate is higher than lessee's tax rate, a lease creates a tax arbitrage. By leasing, a firm with a low marginal tax rate transfers the tax shield associated with the leased equipment to a lessor who has a high marginal tax rate. However, the availability and overall advantage of a lease depends on the nature of the equipment—particularly, its liquidity in a secondary market.

19.6 FINANCIAL ARCHITECTURE: CONTRACTS WITH OTHER STAKEHOLDERS

A firm's overall organizational architecture can be efficiently designed only if management incorporates all of the contracts in which the firm engages. This must include contracts with extended stakeholders, including board members, executives, other employees, suppliers, and customers.

19.6.1 Contracts with Board Members

Regarding contracts with board members, the major issues addressed in the literature involve tenure restrictions and the issue of staggering the election of board members. In addition, it may be important to provide board members with incentive contracts similar to those provided to the firm's executives. Director liability is also an issue, as we discussed in Chapter 8.

19.6.2 Executive Compensation Contracts

As we learned in Chapter 8, executive compensation contracts often are complex. They are generally laden with various incentive devices, ostensibly to mitigate agency costs of managerial discretion. The compensation of a firm's CEO generally contains several components, including some or all of the following: base salary, earnings-based bonus, long-term incentive pay, and grants of stock or stock options.

19.6.3   Contracts with Other Employees

In recent years, an increasing number of U.S. firms have established incentives, such as profit-sharing bonuses or stock options, for their junior managers or even for rank-and-file employees. Employee stock ownership plans, or *ESOPs*, are another example of the growing complexity of compensation contracting with a firm's rank-and-file employees. ESOPs became popular in the 1980s, and can provide substantial tax advantages for both the employer and the employees. Moreover, they may provide a powerful incentive for employees to work hard (rather than to shirk) either to make the firm's profit goals or to increase the firm's stock price, as the case may be. Profit-sharing plans and ESOPs represent an explicit recognition on the part of a firm's management that its employees are important stakeholders.

However, an alternative view of both profit sharing and ESOPs is that, with them, employees must shoulder more of the firm's risk. Moreover, ESOPs may serve senior management's private interests by placing more of the firm's shares in the hands of relatively passive (or pro-management) stockholders.

19.6.4   Contracts with Suppliers and Customers

In Chapter 7, we discussed the nature of contracts with suppliers and customers. We mentioned that contracts with suppliers and customers could reduce a firm's risk (or shift it to external parties), provide some protection against rivals, and perhaps increase the firm's debt capacity. Regarding the last point, in Chapter 15 we documented evidence on the extensive use of trade credit, which provides some of these benefits.

19.7   FINANCIAL ARCHITECTURE: DERIVATIVES AND RELATED CONTRACTS

In this section, we discuss firms' motives for (a) hedges with derivatives, (b) the purchase of insurance, and (c) the issuance of guarantees. We have not yet discussed derivatives, so we initially define the basic derivatives contracts, including forward contracts, futures contracts, options, and swaps. Then we review several articles that focus on firms' hedging motives. We follow with discussions of firms' uses of insurance contracts and guarantees.

As you read this material, consider alternative roles for derivatives, insurance contracts, and guarantees within a firm's overall organizational architecture. For instance, a firm might fix all of the other components and elements in its architecture save these contracts, and then use these contracts as *fine-tuning devices* to optimize the overall architecture. However, it may be better to fully integrate derivatives, insurance contracts, and guarantees into the design of the firm's architecture from the beginning. This is because decisions regarding individual elements of the firm's business or financial architecture may be affected by whether the firm can, for instance, employ a derivative to hedge a particular risk.

19.7.1 Basic Classes of Derivatives and Their Use in Hedging

In this subsection, we briefly describe the basic classes of derivatives, which include forward contracts, futures contracts, swaps, and options, and illustrate their use in corporate hedging.[2]

Forward and Futures Contracts

A forward contract is a private, tailored, bilateral agreement between two parties in which one party agrees to purchase, and the other to sell, a specified number of units of a specified asset at a given future date and at a specified price. Forward contracts are common on foreign currency, and commodities such as gold and oil.

The price written into a forward contract is generally the *fair price*, in the sense that both parties are willing to make the commitment without the need for either party to make an up-front cash payment to the other party as an inducement. If the focal asset trades in an active spot market (or futures market), it is relatively easy to determine this fair price.

A futures contract is similar to a forward contract, in that they both involve a promise to buy/sell an asset from/to another party at a given future date and price. However, futures differ from forward contracts in two important respects. *First*, futures trade as standardized contracts on exchanges such as the Chicago Board of Trade. The exchange provides full intermediation of each trade in the sense that, for a given trade agreed upon by two parties on the floor of the exchange, the exchange assumes the short position against one party's long position, and a long position against the other party's short position. This is done to eliminate both parties' concerns about the other party's default.

Second, futures trading features *daily resettlement in cash* and *marking-to-market*. At the end of each trading day, an official settlement price (similar to the closing price for a stock) is declared by the exchange, and the price of each contract is *remarked* to this new price. Simultaneously, depending on whether the new settlement price is higher or lower than the settlement price of the previous trading day, parties with short positions must pay parties with long positions, or vice versa, a cash amount proportional to this daily price change.

Swaps

A swap contract is a bilateral agreement to exchange periodic cash flows, one variable and the other fixed, over a specified period of time. Consider the following example of an *interest rate swap*. Counterparty A agrees to pay counterparty B $50,000 at the end of each of the next 10 years. In exchange, counterparty B will simultaneously pay to counterparty A an amount equal to the product of $1 million times the then-going annual yield on 1-year U.S. Treasury bills (T-bills). If the T-bill rate is 5 percent, the exchange is neutral, because counterparty B will also be paying $50,000 (= $0.05 \times \$1$ million). However, if and when the yield on 1-year T-bills is greater than 5 percent, net cash will flow from counterparty B to counterparty A, while the reverse will be true if and when the yield is less than 5 percent. Figure 19-2 provides another numerical example of a simple interest rate swap.

---

[2]For more extensive analysis of derivatives, consult one of the many textbooks devoted to the subject, such as Hull (2001).

FIGURE 19-2 An Illustration of Net Payments in an Interest Rate Swap

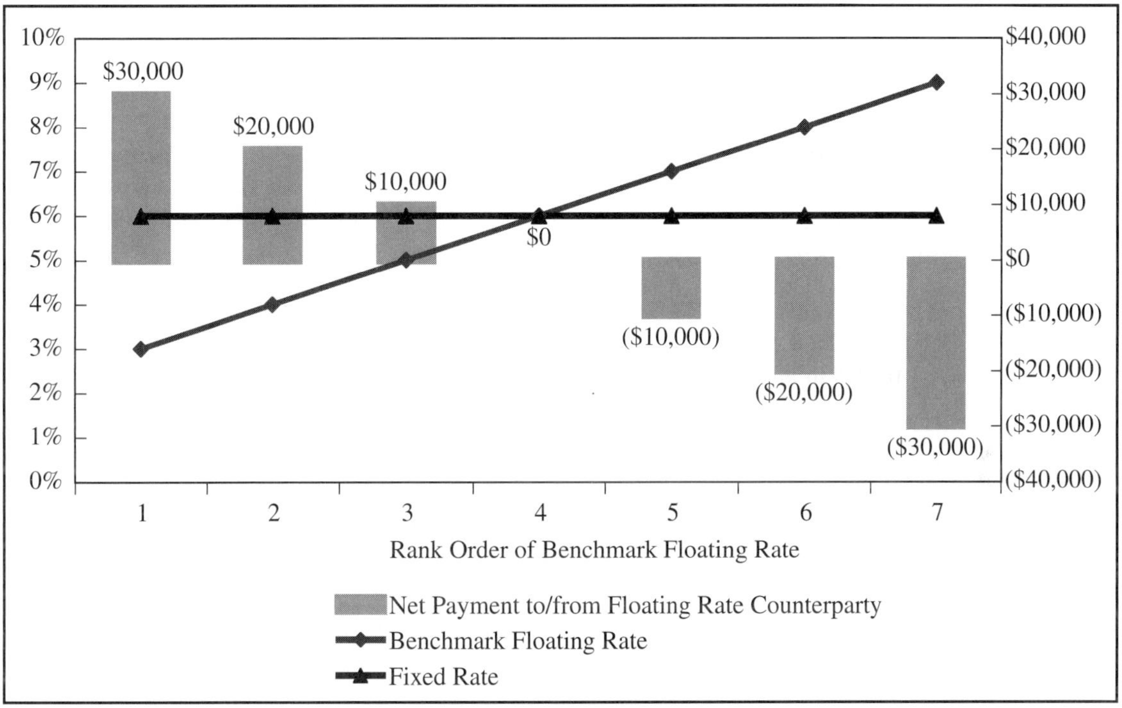

(Notional Amount is $1 million.)

A swap contract is in essence a portfolio, or series, of forward contracts. This can be seen most clearly by reference to a *currency swap*. In a currency swap, counterparty A contracts with counterparty B to swap periodic cash flows (generally interest and principal payments on a common amount of debt) over several years. The cash exchanged is in two different currencies, and the exchange rate is fixed in advance.

Options

We introduced options in Chapter 2, so we will not repeat that discussion here. However, it is important to reemphasize the pervasiveness of options in corporate contracting. *First*, the equity of a levered firm can be viewed as a call option on the firm's assets. *Second*, both the call and conversion provisions in bond contracts are types of call options. *Third*, warrants that are sometimes included when stocks or bonds are issued (i.e., as *units*) are call options. *Fourth*, executives are often awarded stock options as part of their compensation, and these are call options as well. As we discussed in previous chapters, all of these applications of call options serve to mitigate agency costs or asymmetric information problems (and perhaps serve other purposes as well).

Put options are also useful in mitigating these problems, and are particularly useful as devices to hedge risk. Next, we illustrate the use of put options, as well as forward or futures contracts, to hedge revenue risk for a gold mining company. Later in this section, we discuss corporate insurance. An insurance contract is essentially a put option on the insured asset.

An Illustration of Hedging with Derivatives

Figure 19-3 provides an illustration of the use of derivatives to hedge risk. Here we consider the case of a gold mining firm. The firm is contemplating the risk of new mining operations that will yield a quantity of gold in, say, six months. The cost of mining the gold is $C = \$225/oz$. At the current *spot price* of gold, $S_0 = \$245/oz.$, the operations are profitable. However, when the mined gold is delivered to market at time T (i.e., in six months), the spot price at that time, S_T, may be higher or lower than the current spot price, which constitutes a significant risk for the firm.

If the firm decides to forgo a hedge, its profit per ounce of production depends, in a linear fashion, on the realized market price of gold six months from now. The upward-sloped black line in the figure shows the relationship between the firm's per-ounce profit and the realized price of gold.

Instead, the firm can use forward or futures contracts to hedge its risk. Suppose the forward/futures price of gold for delivery in six months is $F_{0,T} = \$250$ oz. To hedge, the firm takes a short (or *delivering*) position in the appropriate number of gold forward/futures contracts. This locks in the price that the firm will receive for the gold that it will deliver in six months, and thus renders the firm's per-ounce profit constant

FIGURE 19-3 Profit or Loss per Ounce for a Gold Manufacturer Three Cases: Unhedged, Hedged via a Forward/Futures Contract, Hedged via a Put Option

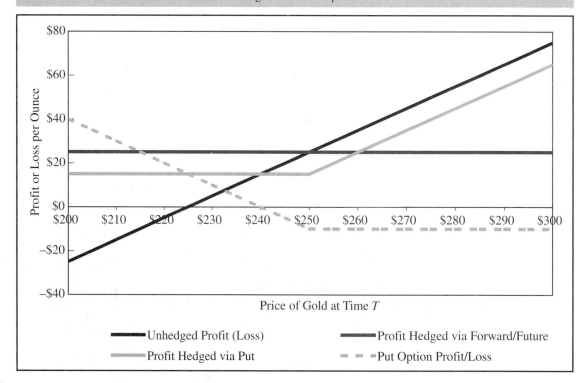

at \$25 oz (= $F_{0,T} - C$ = \$250 – \$225), regardless of the realized market price of gold at the delivery date. This situation is depicted with the horizontal black line in the figure.

Alternatively, the firm can employ a *contingent hedge* using put options. Suppose a put option on gold (per ounce) is available that has an exercise price of X = \$250, expires in six months, and is trading at a price, or *premium*, of \$10/oz. The firm can purchase a sufficient number of put options to hedge its entire production quantity. If the realized price of gold in six months is greater than \$250/oz., the put option will expire worthless, and the firm will have realized a loss on the put contracts that is equal to the premium paid for them, \$10/oz.

On the other hand, if S_T is less than \$250, the put option will pay off at a rate of (\$250 – S_T) per ounce. The per-ounce profit on these put options, as a function of S_T, is depicted with the dashed grey line segments in the figure. Therefore, by hedging with put options, the firm can reshape the relationship between their per-ounce profit and the delivery-date spot price of gold. The dark-grey line segments in the figure depict this modified relationship.

Note that in both hedging cases, the firm sacrifices profit that would be realized at higher values of S_T (i.e., had the firm not hedged), but avoids losses that would be realized at lower values of S_T. In effect, the firm shifts some or all of its price risk to another party, who accepts this risk at some price. In the case of the futures hedge, the price of risk is reflected in the futures price, $F_{0,T}$. In the case of the put hedge, the price of risk is reflected in the option premium. This price may be cheap compared to the expected cost of closing the mine and laying off employees if the price of gold falls. Finally, note that the firm could engage a *partial hedge*, rather than the full hedge depicted, by taking a smaller position in the chosen derivative that is sufficient to cover only a portion of the gold that it plans to deliver.

19.7.2   Theory and Evidence on Corporate Motives for Hedging

In a perfect market where stockholders are well diversified, there is no rationale for hedging or insurance. Moreover, if we admit one market imperfection, that hedging and insurance entail transaction costs, such transactions are wasteful. Why do firms use hedging instruments or purchase insurance? Many authors have provided alternative theories on corporate motives for these activities. Below we summarize theoretical arguments and empirical evidence presented in several papers. Not surprisingly, they focus on real-world factors that we have discussed previously—principal-agent conflicts, the asymmetric information problem, transaction costs, and taxes.

Measuring and Hedging Exchange Rate Exposure

How can we determine whether a firm is *exposed* to exchange rate risk? Is a firm's exchange rate risk related to the relative level of its foreign business? Is a firm's tendency to use currency derivatives related to its exchange rate risk? Several studies have addressed these questions empirically.

Jorian's (1990) study addressed the first two questions. *First*, he developed a measure of a firm's exchange rate risk using the following modified market-model regression:

$$R_{i,t} = \beta_{0,i} + \beta_{1,i}R_{S,t} + \beta_{2,i}R_{M,t} + \varepsilon_{i,t}, \tag{19.1}$$

where $R_{i,t}$ is the firm i's monthly stock return, $R_{S,t}$ is the contemporaneous percentage change in a given exchange rate, and $R_{M,t}$ is the return on the market portfolio. The estimated value of the coefficient $\beta_{1,i}$, denoted as $\hat{\beta}_{1,i}$ is his measure of a firm's exchange rate risk.

Second, he established the following cross-sectional regression to determine whether a firm's exchange rate risk is related to its foreign business:

$$\hat{\beta}_{1,i} = \gamma_0 + \gamma_1 FS/TS_i + u_i, \tag{19.2}$$

where FS/TS_i is the ratio of firm i's foreign sales to its total sales.

The author estimated Equations 19.1 and 19.2 using data on 287 publicly traded U.S. firms that varied (cross-sectionally) in terms of their relative foreign sales (FS/TS_i) over the period 1981 to 1987. For the exchange rate variable in Equation 19.1, he used a trade-weighted measure of the value of the dollar derived from the weights in the Multilateral Exchange Rate Model computed by the International Monetary Fund (IMF).

Jorian summarizes his empirical results as follows: "Evidence is presented that the relationship between stock returns and exchange rates differs systematically across multinationals . . . The comovement between stock returns and the value of the dollar is found to be positively related to the percentage of foreign operations of U.S. multinationals" (p. 331).

Allayannis and Mozundar (2000) addressed the third question. They examined the use of foreign currency derivatives by S&P 500 nonfinancial firms. They identified S&P 500 nonfinancial firms as of 1995, and examined whether they had foreign sales, and whether they used currency derivatives, over the period 1993 to 1995. They found that 71 percent of the firms had foreign sales, and 75 percent of these firms used currency derivatives. Moreover, they found that hedgers reduce the volatility of net cash flow via hedging, and also reduce the sensitivity of their investments to internal cash flow, results that are consistent with the Froot, Scharfstein, and Stein (1993) model we will discuss later. (see also Allayannis and Ofek 2001).

Tax Rate Convexity as an Incentive to Hedge

Smith and Stulz (1985) and Graham and Smith (1999) argue that firms that face a progressive, or *convex*, tax rate structure have an incentive to hedge, because it can reduce the firm's expected tax liability. This effect is illustrated in Figure 19-4. The figure shows a firm's possible tax liability under circumstances in which it does or does not hedge.

The firm in this illustration has the opportunity to hedge a specific risk that would affect its earnings in the coming year. If the firm does not hedge, its earnings will be either $1 million or $3 million, each with a probability of 0.5, depending on the outcome of the risk factor. If the firm does hedge, its earnings will be $2 million with certainty. The firm faces marginal tax rates of 25 percent on the first $1 million of earnings, 30 percent on the next $1 million of earnings, and 50 percent on all income greater than $2 million. Thus, if the firm has earnings of $1 million, $2 million, or $3 million, it must pay taxes of $0.25 million, $0.55 million, or $1.05 million, respectively.

If the firm does not hedge, its expected tax liability is $0.65 million (= 0.5 × 0.25 + 0.5 × 1.05). If the firm does hedge, its tax liability is $0.55 million, with certainty.

FIGURE 19-4   The Effect of Hedging on a Firm's Expected Tax Liability Given Tax Rate Convexity.

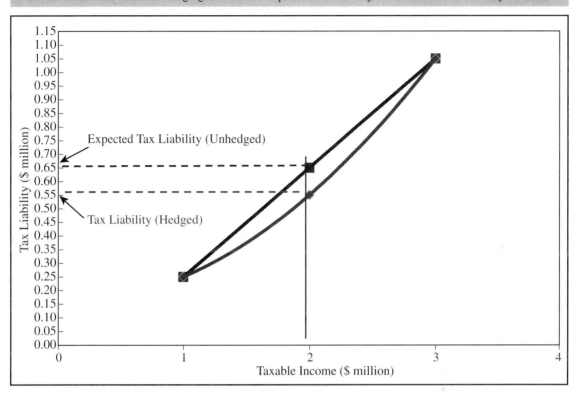

Therefore, the firm can reduce its expected tax liability by hedging. In general, if a firm faces a convex tax rate structure and a risk factor affects income to the extent that marginal income tax rates are crossed depending on the outcome of the risk, the firm can reduce its expected income tax liability by hedging.

Nance, Smith, and Smithson (1993) examined this tax motive for hedging by comparing the characteristics of 104 firms that used hedging instruments (forwards, futures, swaps, or options) to 65 firms that did not use hedging instruments. They summarize their empirical results as follows: "The data suggest that firms which hedge face more convex tax functions, have less coverage of fixed claims, are larger, have more growth options in their investment opportunity set, and employ fewer hedging substitutes" (p. 267).

Hedging Mitigates the Underinvestment Problem

Bessembinder (1991) argued that hedging can help to resolve the underinvestment problem: "Corporate risk hedging with forward contracts increases value by reducing incentives to underinvest. This occurs because the hedge decreases the sensitivity of senior claim value to incremental investment, allowing equity holders to capture a larger portion of the incremental benefit from new investment. Hedging also allows the firm to credibly commit to meet obligations in states where it otherwise could not, which improves contract terms the firm can negotiate with customers, creditors, and managers. These benefits cannot be duplicated by individual hedging, and each result holds independent of agents' risk preferences" (p. 519).

Gay and Nam (1998) also empirically examined the issue of whether derivatives can reduce the underinvestment problem. They examined a total of 486 publicly traded, U.S. nonfinancial firms in 1995, of which 325 were derivatives users. They examined the importance of internally generated cash flow, cash stocks, and investment opportunities on a firm's use of derivatives: "We find evidence of a positive relation between a firm's derivatives use and its growth opportunities . . . For firms with enhanced investment opportunities, derivatives use is greater when they also have relatively low cash stocks. Firms whose investment expenditures are positively correlated with internal cash flows tend to have smaller derivatives positions, which suggests potential natural hedges. Our findings support the argument that firms' derivatives use may partly be driven by the need to avoid potential underinvestment problems" (p. 53).

Mitigating the Risk-Shifting (or Asset Substitution) Problem via Hedging

Campbell and Kracaw (1987) provided a theoretical analysis of the dual issues of the risk shifting (or asset substitution) incentive of a levered firm and hedging. As we discussed in Chapters 3, 6, and 15, debt can entail deadweight costs if creditors know that the borrower has both the incentive and opportunity to increase the firm's risk to expropriate wealth from the creditors. The authors argue that a credible commitment to hedge can reduce these deadweight costs by reducing risk.

Growth Opportunities and Hedging

Geczy, Minton, and Schrand (1997) conducted an analysis of 372 firms among the 1990 Fortune 500 list of nonfinancial firms that had reported their use of currency derivatives pursuant to recent disclosure rules imposed by the Financial Accounting Standard Board. The firms in their sample had "potential exposure to foreign currency risk from foreign operations, foreign-denominated debt, or a high concentration of foreign competitors in their industries. Approximately 41 percent of these firms use currency swaps, forwards, futures, options, or combinations of these instruments" (p. 1323).

They summarize their findings as follows: "We examine the use of currency derivatives in order to differentiate among existing theories of hedging behavior. Firms with greater growth opportunities and tighter financial constraints are more likely to use currency derivatives. This result suggests that firms might use derivatives to reduce cash flow variation that might otherwise preclude firms from investing in valuable growth opportunities. Firms with extensive foreign exchange-rate exposure and economies of scale in hedging activities are also more likely to use currency derivatives. Finally, the source of foreign exchange-rate exposure is an important factor in the choice among types of currency derivatives" (p. 1323).

Hedging to Reduce External Funding Needs and Increase Debt Capacity

Several papers have focused on the avoidance of external financing and increasing debt capacity as motives for hedging. Froot, Scharfstein, and Stein (1993) argued that if a firm hedges certain risks, it will reduce the probability that it will have to engage in costly external financing (and the probability that the firm will forego profitable investments because they lack cheaper internal funds), and in this sense hedging creases value through explicit and implicit cost savings. Stulz (1996) and Leland (1998) argued that hedging with derivatives, by reducing the firm's cash flow volatility, can increase the firm's debt capacity (see also Smith and Stulz 1985).

Haushalter's (2000) empirical analysis provides supportive evidence. He studied 100 oil and gas producers from 1992 to 1994, finding that the extent to which these firms hedge is related to financing costs: "In particular, companies with greater financial leverage manage price risks more extensively . . . hedging is related to economies of scale in hedging costs and to the basis risk associated with hedging instruments. Larger companies and companies whose production is located primarily in regions where prices have a high correlation with the prices on which exchange-traded derivatives are based are more likely to manage risks" (p. 107).

Howton and Perfect (1998) compared derivatives use by 451 nonfinancial, nonutility firms in the Fortune 500 or S&P 500 indexes (FSP firms) against 461 firms that were randomly selected, using annual report data for 1994. They found that over 61 percent of the FSP firms, and 36 percent of the randomly selected firms, used derivatives. They also found that "in both samples, swaps are the most often used interest-rate contract, and forwards and futures the most often used currency contract . . . For the FSP sample, our examination of the determinants of derivatives use produces results that are generally consistent with previous studies. Derivatives use is directly related to financial distress and external financing costs, tax considerations, and currency-risk exposure, and inversely related to hedging substitutes" (pp. 111, 119–120).

However, Tufano (1998) makes the counterargument that hedging can exacerbate agency costs, especially the "potential cost of corporate risk management strategies that are based on cash-flow hedging. Cash-flow hedging strategies allow firms to avoid the deadweight costs of external financing by setting their internal cash flows equal to their investment needs. In the presence of agency conflicts between managers and stockholders, these hedging strategies can be used to reduce stockholder wealth, insofar as they remove the valuable discipline that obtaining new external financing imposes on managers" (p. 67).

Management's Risk Aversion and Corporate Hedging

Smith and Stulz (1985) argued that managerial risk aversion is a motive for hedging. The argument is that a risk-averse manager has a private incentive to invest in less risky projects, even though higher risk projects that are more valuable may exist. If some of the risk of a high-risk project can be hedged, management may accept it, and the partially hedged project may yet benefit stockholders.

Tufano (1996) examined gold mining firms for their tendencies and motives to hedge gold price risk during the period 1990 to 1993. He found that over 85 percent of the firms in the industry used devices to manage gold price risk. He documents evidence indicating that the tendency of a manager to hedge is related to the manager's risk aversion, rather than other motives cited in the literature: "I find little empirical support for the predictive power of theories that view risk management as a means to maximize stockholder value. However, firms whose managers hold more options manage less gold price risk, and firms whose managers hold more stock manage more gold price risk, suggesting that managerial risk aversion may affect corporate risk management policy. Further, risk management is negatively associated with the tenure of firms' CFOs, perhaps reflecting managerial interests, skills, or preferences" (p. 1097).

Cases in Point

In their paper, Lewent and Kearney (1990), employed at Merck & Co., Inc. (a major pharmaceutical company), discussed the risk management practices at the firm during the late 1980s. Merck had substantial international sales, so its exposure to exchange rate risk was substantial. The authors discuss how Merck identified, measured, and hedged currency risk. Merck's hedging analytics include five steps: (a) forecasting changes in a given exchange rate, (b) assessing the impact of exchange rate movements on the firm's strategic plan, (c) developing a rationale for hedging the risk, (d) selecting the appropriate hedging instrument, and (e) using simulations to develop a cost-effective hedging program.

Regarding (e), their analysis led them to prefer *options* over other instruments to hedge exchange rate risk: "With its significant presence worldwide, Merck has exposures in approximately 40 currencies . . . Forward foreign exchange contracts, foreign currency debt, and currency swaps all effectively fix the value of the amount hedged regardless of currency movements. With the use of options, by contrast, the hedging firm retains the opportunity to benefit from natural positions—albeit at a cost equal to the premium paid for the option . . . Given the possibility of exchange rate movements in either direction, we were unwilling to forgo the potential gains if the dollar weakened; so options were strictly preferred. We also concluded, moreover, that a certain level of option premiums could be justified as the cost of an insurance policy designed to preserve our ability to carry through with our strategic plan" (pp. 20, 26–27).

Brown (2001) investigated the foreign exchange risk management program of a leading manufacturer of durable equipment with sales in more than 50 countries, to which he applies the pseudonym HDG Inc. His paper is based on a three-month field study at the firm, where he gained access to transactions-level data and internal documents. He summarizes his close analysis of the firm's risk management program in a question-and-answer form, as given below.

First, how is the risk management program structured? I show that HDG has a foreign exchange hedging program that is systematic, extensive, and an integral part of foreign operations. The primary mechanism for this interaction is the use of *hedge rates* for budgeting, pricing, and *ex post* evaluation of foreign operations and managers.

Second, what are the motivating factors that determine why the firm manages foreign exchange risk? Many common explanations for risk management (such as minimizing expected taxes, avoiding costs of financial distress, managerial risk aversion, and coordination of cashflows and investment) do not mesh with the evidence from HDG nor are they espoused by management. The official hedging policy provides little guidance in trying to answer this question. However, other documents, discussions with management, and statistical tests support alternative reasons for risk management at HDG. These include smoothing earnings (perhaps to lessen informational asymmetries), facilitating internal contracting via the hedge rate, and obtaining competitive pricing advantages in the product market.

Third, how does the firm structure the derivative portfolios used for foreign exchange risk management? Primarily because of accounting treatment and competitive pricing concerns, HDG has a strong preference for using options to structure its hedges. In fact, for some illiquid currencies for which options are less viable, HDG would rather not hedge at all than use forwards. The transaction-level data allow for the examination of cross-sectional and time-series variation in hedge ratios as well as statistical analysis of factors that impact hedging behavior. The results from statistical tests indicate that exchange rate volatility and exposure volatility are important determinants of optimal hedging policies. In addition, it appears managerial views and recent hedging history are also key factors. (pp. 443–444)

Chacko, Tufano, and Verter (2001) examined a case of a novel use of call options. They studied a firm that justified its novel use of derivatives as a cash-flow hedging strategy. Cephalon Inc., a biotech firm, bought a large block of call options on its own stock. If the FDA approved the firm's new drug, the firm would have large cash needs, which the options were designed to meet. The case appears to support the hedging rationale articulated by Froot, Scharfstein and Stein (1993), that is, that hedging can alleviate the deadweight costs of external financing.

However, the authors also present a list of issues, regarding risk management theory and practice, which were raised as a result of their analysis of this case:

- Risk management choices are made in a rich corporate context. Here, accounting rules (and managers' interpretation of their impact on firm value) have a critical effect on the firm's risk management choices. In this case, the rationale for risk management seems as much motivated by managing earnings as by managing cash flows.
- Risk management is usually motivated by the presence of deadweight costs, either of financing or financial distress. However, if managing risk itself also entails deadweight costs, then firms must compare *relative* deadweight costs.
- Academic models of risk management require managers to measure the size of these deadweight costs, but provide little guidance about how to calculate these costs. We found little reliable data that a manager could use to benchmark the costs of external financing. As an empirical matter, in this case, deadweight costs of financing may be quite small or possibly even negative.
- Risk management decisions seem motivated as much by fluctuations in the cost and availability of financing as by fluctuations in either operating cash flows or desired investment.
- While firms can hedge market-wide risks, they are often unable to protect against purely idiosyncratic business risks except by using insurance. This clinical study documents a firm using the capital markets to manage a combination of an idiosyncratic risk and financing uncertainty.
- Finally, even in this clinical study, where management was quite clear in its explanation of its objectives, one cannot reject an alternative explanation that the transaction simply allowed the firm to bet on the success of its drug. (pp. 450–451)

19.7.3   Corporate Motives for Purchasing Insurance

As we noted above, an insurance contract is essentially a put option, purchased by the insured from an insurer to protect the value of an asset. Corporate insurance is an obvious and common example of firms' attempts to manage risk.

A Preliminary Note: Hedging versus Insurance

Hedging with derivatives and the purchase of insurance are closely related. As we discussed, a firm can hedge a risk by purchasing a put option, and mechanically, insurance *is* a put option. However, Smith and Stulz (1985) point out a crucial difference between hedging (in their discussion, via forward or futures contracts) and the purchase of insurance: "[F]or corporations, the determinants of the demand for insurance differ crucially from the determinants of hedging policies. For a corporation, the purchase of insurance provides real services due to the expertise of insurance companies in evaluating some types of risks and administering claims settlement procedures . . . while forward or future contracts provide no apparent real services" (p. 391). The intermediary role of an insurance company can be important in terms of both monitoring assets that are insured and mitigating asymmetric information problems by taking confidential possession of inside information.

In two papers, Mayers and Smith (1982, 1987) provide interesting perspectives on corporations' use of insurance from the viewpoint of modern corporate finance theory. In their 1982 paper, they argued that firms purchase insurance to mitigate agency costs: "The corporate form provides an effective hedge since stockholders can eliminate insurable risk through diversification. Thus, the purchase of insurance by firms at actuarially unfair rates would represent a negative net present value project, reducing stockholder wealth . . . Our analysis treats insurance purchases by corporations as just another part of the firm's financing decision . . . [We] demonstrate how the inclusion of insurance among the corporation's set of contracts can control particular incentive conflicts. We suggest that insurance firms have a comparative advantage over outside stockholders, bondholders, customers, etc., in monitoring certain aspects of the firm's real activities, so that a firm which purchases insurance will engage in a different set of activities than a firm which does not" (pp. 281–282).

In Mayers and Smith (1987), the authors extend their argument that insurance can be used to mitigate agency costs: "A casualty loss generates option-like characteristics in assets because their value depends on further discretionary investment. With risky debt in the capital structure of the firm, the stockholders can have incentives to forego the discretionary investment, even though it has a positive net present value. Thus, there is a potential incentive conflict between the bondholders, who want the investment to be made, and the stockholders, who do not. A state-preference model is used to examine this problem. The analysis shows how this problem modifies the firm's choice of investment decisions. Two mechanisms for controlling this underinvestment problem are examined: 1. restrictions on the amount of debt in the firm's capital structure, and 2. the inclusion of a covenant in the bond contract requiring insurance coverage. As is shown, full coverage generally is not required. The maximum deductible depends on the amount of debt in the firm's capital structure and the feasible set of net casualty losses" (p. 45).

A Case in Point

Doherty and Smith (1993) analyzed the insurance strategy of British Petroleum (BP), one of the largest industrial companies in the world. Their analysis points up the issue for any firm of whether, and under what circumstances, it should purchase insurance versus *self-insuring*.

The authors initially note the standard insurance practices among large industrial firms: "For large public companies, conventional practice is to buy insurance to hedge against large potential losses while self-insuring against smaller ones. The underlying logic of this strategy . . . is essentially this: . . . small losses—the kind that stem from localized fires, employee injuries, vehicle crashes, and so forth—occur with such regularity that their total cost is predictable. To the extent such losses are predictable in the aggregate, buying insurance amounts simply to exchanging known dollars of premium for roughly equivalent and relatively known dollars of loss settlements . . . Larger losses, by contrast, are rare and much less predictable. Because such losses are borne by the company's owners (mainly by its stockholders but also, if the losses are large enough, by its bondholders), they should be hedged with insurance" (p. 4).

However, the authors document that BP takes the opposite tack. BP insures against most smaller losses, and self-insures larger losses. The rationale is as follows: "the primary source of demand for insurance by widely held public companies is not, as standard insurance textbooks assume, to transfer risk from the corporation's owners, but rather to take advantage of insurance companies' efficiencies in providing risk-assessment, monitoring, and loss-settlement services. [However] . . . the capacity of insurance markets to underwrite very large (or highly specialized) exposures is quite limited. Given BP's size, when losses become large enough to be of concern, they exceed the capacity of the industry. In essence, BP has a comparative advantage relative to the insurance industry in bearing large losses" (p. 4).

19.7.4 Guarantees

Firms use guarantees in a variety of circumstances. Both manufacturers and retailers generally provide guarantees on their products. A parent may guarantee the debt that is being issued by one of its subsidiaries.

Functionally, a guarantee is equivalent to writing a put option—buyers realize at least a minimum value for a product, asset, or security, or it can be returned in exchange for cash. In Chapter 4, we discussed the role of product guarantees in mitigating contracting problems associated with information asymmetry. In Chapter 15, we discussed the guarantee implicit in trade credit. If the buyer is unsatisfied with the purchased goods, it can return them before payment is due.

Merton and Bodie (1992) provide an extensive discussion of financial guarantees. In part of their discussion, they focus on parent guarantees of a subsidiary's obligations: "Such guarantees are often quite important to the subsidiary firm. In some cases, suppliers or customers might not even be willing to do business with the subsidiary if they doubt that the parent company would honor the subsidiary's commitments . . . In managing guarantees of its subsidiaries, a parent company may find it efficient to use management methods that would not be feasible for an external guarantor. Unlike an external party, the parent's management can have access to virtually all of the proprietary business information available to the subsidiary's management without jeopardizing the competitive position of the subsidiary. Such access greatly reduces problems of asymmetric information between the guarantor and the guarantee . . . It is therefore likely that moral-hazard and other principal–agent problems are less severe here than they would be with an outside guarantor" (p. 100).

19.8 SECURITY DESIGN

In this section, we review a number of articles that have focused on the issue of the optimal design of corporate securities. The first subsection reviews articles that are more theoretical in nature; the second reviews articles that discuss specific examples of designed corporate securities.

19.8.1 The Optimal Design of Securities: Theory

Allen and Gale (1994) take perhaps the broadest view of security design by examining the role of basic corporate securities (i.e., debt and equity) as *risk-sharing* devices. They ascribe to financial markets the role of *distributors of risk* throughout the economy. Financial markets develop continuously to provide ever-more sophisticated means of performing this task.

We can relate their work directly to our concept of organizational architecture. For instance, early *innovations* include the development of the corporate form of business, whereby the limited liability provision itself establishes risk sharing among the firm's owners, creditors, other stakeholders, and society at large. Moreover, a firm's debt and equity claims involve an asymmetric sharing of the firm's risk, with the bulk of the risk borne by stockholders, who can reduce this risk via diversification, so long as equity markets exist.

Allen and Gale (1988) pointed out that the general objective of security design for a public firm should be to maximize the issuer's proceeds. Their model shows that "the firm's income stream should be split so that in every state all payoffs are allocated to the security held by the group that values it most" (p. 229). In their model, *transaction costs* are critical to optimal security design.

In Harris and Raviv's (1989) model, the focus is on the assignment of both (priority versus residual) cash flows and voting rights, where the latter concerns the issue of *corporate control*, which is critical in their model: "We postulate that a conflict of interest exists between contestants for control and outside investors. The conflict arises because private benefits of control give contestants an incentive to acquire control even when this reduces firm value. Security design is a tool for resolving these conflicts and maximizing firm value. Our main result is that a single voting security is optimal" (p. 255). The voting security is, of course, (levered) equity; riskless debt should be *nonvoting*.

Like Allen and Gale, Zender (1991) focuses on the problem of allocating cash flows and control rights. However, his emphasis is on the investment incentive problem under conditions of asymmetric information, given that only one party can make investment decisions. Under these circumstances, the optimal securities are equity with control rights and debt with no control rights: "the debtholder's cash flows are fixed in order to provide the equityholder with efficient incentives for investment . . . [T]he optimal financial instruments completely resolve incentive problems induced by asymmetric information, and allow agents to maximize the surplus extracted from production when limited wealth makes cooperation a necessity" (pp. 1645, 1661).

Boot and Thakor (1993) also stress the importance of security design as a means of mitigating the information asymmetry problem: "We explain why an issuer may wish to raise external capital by selling multiple financial claims that partition its total asset cash flows, rather than a single claim. We show that, in an asymmetric information environment, the issuer's expected revenue is enhanced by such cash flow partitioning because it makes informed trade more profitable. This approach seems capable of shedding light on corporate incentives to issue debt and equity . . . " (p. 1349). Their argument is that "splitting a security into two components—one 'informationally insensitive' and the other more 'informationally sensitive' than the composite security—makes informed trading more profitable. The reason is that informed traders with constrained wealth endowments earn a higher return on their investment in information by allocating their wealth to the information-sensitive security. The consequent stimulation of informed trading moves the equilibrium price of the intrinsically more valuable security closer to its fundamental value, and increases the higher-valued issuer's total expected revenue" (pp. 1349–1350).

19.8.2 Examples of Security Design

Security design is not a new idea. For example, the *convertible bond* has existed for decades; its longevity attests to its successful design. In Chapter 15, we discussed how a convertible bond is superior to a nonconvertible (or straight) bond in mitigating contracting problems related to both stockholder–creditor principal–agent conflicts and information asymmetry.

Since the 1970s, a number of new features of corporate bonds have emerged as a result of security design innovation. The process of designing securities to fit circumstances (i.e., to mitigate contracting problems) has come to be known as *financial engineering*. Basically, financial engineering involves the creation of new financial securities, markets, or strategies that help issuers, investors, or both to (a) reduce costs, (b) manage risk, or (c) pursue profit opportunities. (Many of the products developed via financial engineering involve derivatives.)

In this subsection, we provide brief descriptions of several of these new corporate bond features, as well as other contracting innovations. We also provide the likely rationale for the development of each.

Floating-Rate Notes

Floating-rate notes provide coupon interest at a rate that varies with a specific short-term interest rate. In 1979, Gulf Oil Company became the first nonfinancial firm to issue a floating-rate bond, a $250 million, 30-year, callable bond that garnered the AAA rating. The coupon rates on early *floaters* were generally pegged to the rate on short-term U.S. Treasury securities. However, preference has shifted over time to the three-month London Interbank Offered Rate (LIBOR) as the pegging rate.

Floating-rate notes were developed primarily in response to investors' concerns about the price risk of long-term fixed-coupon bonds in the face of volatile interest rates. Because a floating-rate bond essentially always pays the going short-term interest rate (possibly subject to a *cap* or *floor*), its price is much more stable than the price of a fixed-coupon bond with respect to a change in interest rates.

Some floating-rate notes are callable, and others are noncallable. However, even if a floater is callable, the yield premium required for the call provision is likely to be lower than that required on a fixed-coupon bond. This is so because, barring a substantial change in the issuer's default risk, the price of the bond should always be close to its par value. This is a distinct advantage for the issuing firm, because it can enjoy the flexibility of the early retirement (call) provision without having to pay the price for it in terms of higher coupon interest.

A firm's choice of fixed or floating coupon may depend in part on the correlation of the firm's earnings and the rate of inflation (which in turn affects short-term interest rates). For a company whose earnings before interest and taxes (EBIT) is highly *positively* correlated with inflation, floating-rate debt will tend to reduce earnings volatility. However, if the firm's EBIT is *negatively* correlated with inflation, floating-rate debt will tend to exacerbate earnings volatility, and perhaps even increase the probability of default.

Low-Coupon, Zero-Coupon, and Deferred-Coupon Bonds

PepsiCo issued the first zero-coupon bond in 1982. *Zeros* were popular in the 1980s, and spawned variants such as (a) *original-issue discount* (OID) bonds, whose coupon rate is less than their required yield, so they sell at a discount when issued, (b) *deferred-coupon* bonds, which pay no coupon interest for a number of years, and only thereafter pay coupon interest, and (c) *payment-in-kind* bonds, or PIKs, which actually pay coupon interest in the form of additional bonds instead of cash. However, most of these innovations have fallen out of favor in recent years for several reasons. For instance, zeros were issued in part to take advantage of a tax loop hole (i.e., on capital gains versus coupon income) that has since been eliminated.

Nevertheless, they may be useful in special circumstances. For example, one advantage of low-coupon debt is that the issuing firm has minimal (or no) cash flow until maturity. Therefore, such a bond would be useful for a firm that is not expected to realize substantial payoffs on its investments for a number of years. Moreover, tax law allows the issuing firm to amortize the interest expense over the life of the bond, so the firm enjoys the tax advantage of the debt on an annual basis but defers the actual cash payments to the distant future. However, as our analysis of the relationship between debt maturity and risk in Chapter 10 shows, such bonds are likely to be very risky.

Opler (1993) explained the usefulness of postponable interest in the form of PIK bonds, which are often associated with a leveraged buyout (LBO): "Leveraged buyouts are sometimes funded with payment-in-kind (PIK) debt which gives the issuer the right to meet interest payments by issuing additional debt. At first glance, the advantages of this type of financing may not be clear, especially because issuing this debt is likely to signal that the buyout's managers anticipate cash flow problems. However, one important advantage of PIK debt is that it can significantly reduce financial distress costs. Without PIK debt, a firm in financial distress will have to renegotiate the allocation of rights to cash flow using a workout or Chapter 11; with PIK debt, the firm does an "automatic workout" by giving debtholders greater claims to cash flow in the form of new debt claims. Thus, PIK debt avoids the costs of negotiating some type of debt for equity swap which typically occurs in a workout" (p. 82).

High-Yield ("Junk") Bonds

The high-yield, or *junk*, bond market is the market for corporate bonds that have speculative-grade ratings. The new-issue market for high-yield bonds was the brainchild of Michael Milken and the now-defunct firm of Drexel Burnham Lambert. Beginning in the late 1970s, Drexel began underwriting bonds issued by smaller, financially weaker firms whose credit rating would fall well into the *speculative-grade* category.

Prior to this time, such firms were effectively barred from the public debt markets, and were forced to issue privately placed debt. This is not to say that high-risk corporate bonds did not exist up to this point. Indeed, over time many firms that had originally issued bonds with investment-grade ratings subsequently experienced financial distress, and their bond ratings fell into the speculative-grade categories. Such bonds are referred to as *fallen angels.* However, Drexel initiated the public placement of *new issue* speculative-grade bonds.

Drexel's success in developing this market is probably due in large part to the fact that the heretofore sole sources of debt financing for smaller, high-risk firms were commercial banks and insurance companies, which imposed serious constraints and high interest rates on these companies. Such firms were eager to take advantage of a new source of debt funds that would involve fewer constraints and lower costs.

The new-issue high-yield bond market faltered temporarily in the early 1990s with the demise of Drexel and the 1990–1991 recession. However, the market recovered steadily throughout the 1990s, and appears to be a mainstay, at least for some types of high-risk firms. We provided evidence to this effect in Figure 10-1 and Table 15-2.

Mandatory Convertibles

Traditional convertible bonds are convertible at the bondholder's option (though the issuer can, in effect, force conversion by calling the bonds). In contrast, in a new type of convertible security, the date of conversion is mandated in advance. The generic name for this security is *mandatory convertible.* However, individual investment banks that devise and underwrite them give them *brand names.* Examples include Morgan Stanley's PERCS (Preferred Equity-Redemption Cumulative Stock), Merrill Lynch's PRIDES (Preferred Redeemable Increased Dividend Securities), and Salomon Brothers' DECS (Debt Exchangeable for Common Stock, or Dividend Enhanced Convertible Securities).

Arzac (1997) describes the securities as follows: "Mandatory convertibles . . . are equity-linked securities that pay a higher dividend than the common stock for a number of years, and then convert into common stock at a prespecified date and have limited appreciation potential" (p. 54). He provides the following example of a mandatory convertible, a PERCS issued by Citicorp: "In October 1992, Citicorp issued $1 billion of PERCS at $14.75, which was also the price of its common stock at the time. The PERCS paid an annual dividend of $1.217 (or 8.25 percent of the issue price) while Citicorp's common was paying no dividend. In addition, the PERCS were required to be converted into common stock on November 30, 1995, with the value of the common stock issued per PERCS not to exceed $20.28" (p. 55).

Mandatory convertibles have been quite successful since their inception in 1988. Arzac reported that "mandatory convertibles . . . accounted for a quarter of the $20 billion convertible market in 1996" (p. 54). He argues that they are useful in mitigating the information asymmetry problem: "In general, convertible securities reduce the costs of 'information asymmetry' that can make equity offerings especially expensive for some smaller, high-growth companies (or any firm with little additional debt capacity where management is convinced its shares are undervalued). Mandatory convertibles play a similar role for larger, often highly leveraged or financially troubled, companies that are seeking equity capital, but want to avoid unnecessary dilution. Much as convertibles accomplish for smaller growth firms, mandatory convertibles enable large issuers with growth (or recovery) prospects that may not be fully reflected in their current stock prices to 'signal' their confidence" (p. 55).

Reset Notes and Rating Sensitive Notes

Two closely related innovations in the high-yield corporate debt market are *reset notes* and *rating sensitive notes*. Both types of notes offer a variable coupon rate. For the reset note, the coupon rate is reset periodically (usually annually) such that, in the estimation of the original underwriter(s), the new coupon rate would be sufficient to render the note's market price equal to its par value. Thus, if after issuance the issuer's financial position deteriorated, the coupon rate on the note would be increased; if its financial position improved, the coupon rate would fall.

The coupon rate on a rating sensitive note is changed if and when the firm's credit rating, measured by S&P or Moody's ratings, changes, according to a predefined schedule. For instance, a firm may issue a rating sensitive note that has an original rating of B and a coupon rate of 14 percent. If the firm's credit rating improves to BB, the coupon rate would be reduced to 13 percent, but if the firm's credit rating falls to CCC, the coupon rate would automatically increase to 15.5 percent.

These notes were clearly devised to reduce the price risk associated with high-yield corporate notes. From a theoretical perspective, the coupon-adjustment feature could also help to alleviate deadweight agency costs of debt, as the firm clearly has less incentive to take actions that would reduce the value of the notes.

Strip Financing

Strip financing is defined as a situation in which investors hold a firm's debt *and* equity securities. Strip financing may be partial (in which case only some investors hold both debt and equity) or complete (where all investors hold both debt and equity). Opler (1993) explains the usefulness of strip financing as follows: "By aligning the incentives of bondholders and equityholders, complete strip financing essentially eliminates any need for restructuring financial claims in financial distress. Even when it is partial, strip financing will also decrease the costs of renegotiation because of a greater confluence of interests among negotiating parties . . . " (p. 81).

Gold-Denominated Depositary Shares

Chidambaran, Fernando, and Spindt (2001) focused on a good example of security design—Freeport McMoRan's *gold-denominated depositary shares*. The authors explain the circumstances that led to the firm's decision to issue these securities.

"In 1993 and early 1994, Freeport McMoRan Copper and Gold Inc. (ticker tymbol FCX) faced a substantial challenge in financing the expansion of its Grasberg gold and copper mine in Irian Jaya, Indonesia. The mine, high in the mountains, was the world's largest gold reserve and one of the largest copper reserves. FCX needed to invest heavily to expand mine capacity and achieve the economies of scale required to become more competitive. Despite a heavy debt burden and a stock that was trading below the value of its assets, FCX successfully raised $359 million at a favorable financing cost through two series of gold-linked depositary shares backed by preferred stock. These claims enjoyed an enhanced credit quality because the link to gold prices credibly reduced default risk" (p. 488).

Asset-Backed Commercial Paper

In Chapter 15, we documented evidence that commercial paper has increased in importance over the past 20 years, representing 3.3 percent of the aggregate liabilities of U.S. nonfinancial firms in 2000, up from 1.4 percent in 1980. Part of this success is due to innovations in the commercial paper market, including the development of *asset-backed commercial paper*, or ABCP. ABCP is commercial paper issued by a special purpose corporation (SPC), and is backed by the receivables of several firms, who receive the proceeds of the issuance, less fees paid to the SPC. ABCP can give riskier firms indirect access to the low-cost commercial paper market.

Stone and Zissu (1997) explain the advantages of ABCP programs as follows: "ABCP programs can be viewed as "synthetic" revolving bank credit facilities in the sense that they can provide the same flow of funds as revolving credits by using a vehicle constructed specifically to refinance pools of receivables. The benefits of ABCP relative to bank lines of credit may take the form of either lower interest rates, less restrictive financial covenants, or both . . . " (p. 72).

Leveraged Loan Syndication

Bank loans have also indirectly gone public though the recent development of the *leveraged loan syndication market*. Barnish, Miller, and Rushmore (1997) explain "the bank loan market has recently come to operate more like a capital market in which one or more underwriters structure and price loans for syndication to groups of investors. This market-driven evolution has been most dramatic in the leveraged lending segment . . . where wide margins have attracted a large and growing field of underwriters, intermediaries, and investors" (p. 79).

The authors argue that enhanced liquidity is the key to the success of the leveraged syndicated loan market. It has given risky borrowers greater access to debt capital at lower interest costs.

Strategic Use of the Put Provision

As we previously discussed, the put provision in a bond contract allows the *bondholder* to present the bond for payment of principal prior to the bond's stated maturity. Firms have added this provision for at least two reasons. *First*, because the put provision is valuable to the bondholder, the interest cost on the bond is lower than it would otherwise be. *Second*, the manager of an issuing firm may include a special type of put provision known as the *event-triggered* put provision, which can be exercised by the bondholders if and when the issuing firm is threatened with a takeover. Thus, the event-triggered put provision is an *antitakeover* device that management uses to thwart a takeover, and perhaps also to protect their jobs.

It would seem that the put provision would provide the ultimate protection for bondholders against the firm's attempt to expropriate bondholder value. However, the limitations of the put provision in this respect can be illustrated by referring to the risk-shifting agency problem. Suppose that, after issuing a putable bond, the firm shifts to a high-risk operating or marketing strategy that will lead either to great success or utter bankruptcy. In the former case, the put provision will not be needed: in the latter case the put provision will be virtually worthless, because in bankruptcy the bondholders' claim is the same with or without the put provision. Our examination of public, Rule 144A, and private placement issues of corporate notes and bonds revealed no issues that contained a put provision.

The Clawback Provision (or Equity Call Provision)

One of the most recent innovations in the high-yield public corporate bond market is the *clawback bond*, named because of a unique provision included in the bond contract, the *clawback provision*.[3] The clawback provision gives the issuer an option to redeem a specified fraction of the bond issue (usually about one-third) within a specified period (usually three years) at a predetermined price (usually at or slightly above par value), *but only by using funds from a subsequent equity offering*. For this reason, the clawback provision is also known as an *equity call provision*.

Goyal, Gollapudi and Ogden (1998) conducted an empirical analysis of clawback bonds. They found that nearly one-third of all speculative-grade corporate bonds issued in the United States in recent years have included the clawback provision. The authors argue that the clawback provision serves to mitigate deadweight losses that would otherwise occur when equity is offered subsequent to a debt offering.

The emergence of the clawback bond is also associated with another important innovation—the public issuance of bonds by young, privately held firms. In the case of the private issuers of clawback bonds, the clawback provision can be exercised using funds from the firm's initial public offering, and as such these bonds are referred to as *IPO clawbacks*. Firms with privately held equity issued 80 percent (68 of 85) of all clawback bonds issued between March 1992 and June 1994.

The Make-Whole Call Provision

In the early 1990s, a new type of call provision emerged in corporate bond contracts, called the *make-whole call provision*. By the late 1990s, this type of call provision became the standard, included in approximately two-thirds of the callable bonds issued by U.S. nonfinancial firms.

Like the traditional call provision, the make-whole call provision allows a firm to retire its bonds prior to their stated maturity. However, the make-whole call requires the firm to pay a call price that is set at the time of the call and that is sufficient to provide bondholders an ex post return over the life of the bond to date that is equal to the return they would have received on a noncallable Treasury bond that had (approximately) the same original maturity as the called bond. In this sense, bondholders are *made whole* upon a call, hence the name.

The Eurobond Market

Eurobonds are bonds sold outside the country in whose currency they are denominated. Investors generally hold Eurobonds in *bearer form*, rather than on a registered basis. Otherwise, Eurobonds are similar to domestic corporate bonds. The Eurobond market is almost entirely free of official regulation by any agency comparable to the SEC. Instead, the market is *self-regulated* by the Association of International Bond Dealers. Borrowers in the Eurobond market are generally large, well-known firms with high credit ratings. Major Eurobond issuers in 2000 included Enron Corporation, IBM Corporation, LTV Steel Corporation, Polo Ralph Lauren Corporation, and Staples Inc., among many others.

Researchers have shown that such firms may be able to borrow at lower cost in the Eurobond markets than in their own domestic market, in part because the market

---

[3] The term *clawback* was adapted from British law, where the term means *retrieval* or *recovery*. For instance, a British tax law may allow the government to recover funds from certain individuals who have received government benefits in advance but who, *ex post*, do not qualify for the benefits.

allows the firm to search the world for the location and currency in which borrowing costs may be low. Another advantage of the Eurobond market is the swiftness with which the firm can issue debt, generally in a few days, in contrast to the lengthy delays associated with the regulated U.S. public corporate bond market.

Project Finance

Finally, we briefly discuss *project finance*, which has become an important means by which huge infrastructure projects are privately financed. Brealey, Cooper, and Habib (1996) discussed the history of project finance:

> Throughout most of the history of the industrialized world, much of the funding for large-scale public works such as the building of roads and canals has come from private sources of capital. It was only toward the end of the 19th century that public financing of large "infrastructure" projects began to dominate private finance, and this trend continued throughout most of the 20th century. Since the early 1980s, however, private-sector financing of large infrastructure investments has experienced a dramatic revival. And, in recent years, such private funding has increasingly taken the form of project finance. The principal features of such project financings have been the following:
>
> - A project is established as a separate company, which operates under a concession obtained from the host government.
> - A major proportion of the equity of the project company is provided by the project manager or sponsor, thereby tying the provision of finance to the management of the project.
> - The project company enters into comprehensive contractual arrangements with suppliers and customers.
> - The project company operates with a high ratio of debt to equity, with lenders having only limited recourse to the government or to the equity-holders in the event of default. (p. 25)

The authors then argue that the structure and contracting features of project finance are means by which principal-agent conflicts problems among the various stakeholders in the project can be mitigated. These stakeholders include the government, contractors, suppliers, other investors, project sponsors, lenders, and the final customers that will be served by the project's construction. The most important common aspect of the multilateral contractual arrangements involved in project finance is that each contract is designed to allocate a particular major risk to the party that is best able to appraise and control that risk.

19.9   Summary of Learning Objectives

In this chapter we attempted to synthesize much of the material presented in previous chapters by developing a model of a firm's *organizational architecture*. The model facilitates an *integrated* approach to the development of a firm. A firm's organizational architecture includes two major constructs: *business architecture* and *financial architecture*. A firm's business architecture includes all aspects of its environment, assets, and operations that collectively describe the circumstances under which, and the manner in which, it conducts its business, with the exception of its financial contracts. The firm's financial contracts collectively form the firm's financial architecture.

Both business and financial architectures include a number of components, and each component includes several elements. An efficient organizational architecture is built by recognizing the importance of each component and element, as well as the fact that they must work in harmony with other components and elements in the overall architecture.

One of the components of a firm's financial architecture—derivatives and related contracts—constitutes a new topic in the textbook. Firms use derivatives (including forward contracts, futures contracts, swaps, and options) to hedge various types of risk (interest rate risk, currency risk, and commodity price risk). Firms also use derivative-like contracts, including insurance and guarantees, to manage risk.

We also discussed the related topic of security design. A firm should design the securities that it issues so as to maximize stockholder wealth. Securities should be sold to the investor group that values them most highly. As a fundamental issue, theoretical research has shown that equity (which encompasses control rights and a residual claim on the firm's cash flows) and debt (which does not encompass control rights but has a priority claim on cash flows) are optimal generic securities.

Finally, we discussed a number of recent trends and innovations in the corporate bond market. Recent innovations include (a) the floating-rate note, (b) low-coupon, zero-coupon, and deferred-coupon (PIK) bonds, (c) high-yield (or *junk*) bonds, (d) mandatory convertibles, (e) the reset note and rating-sensitive note, (f) strip financing, (g) gold-denominated depository shares, (h) asset-backed commercial paper, (i) leveraged loan syndication, (j) the put provision in a debt contract, (k) the clawback bond, (l) the make-whole call provision, (m) the Eurobond market, and (n) project finance.

Review Questions and Problems

1. List and briefly discuss the elements in each of the following eight components of a firm's business architecture.
   a. Macroeconomic environment
   b. Financial market environment
   c. Industry characteristics
   d. Resources
   e. Internal legal and governance structures
   f. Business strategies and growth opportunities
   g. Diversification versus focus
   h. Size and capital intensity
2. List and briefly discuss the elements in each of the following four components of a firm's financial architecture.
   a. Equity
   b. Liabilities
   c. Contracts with other stakeholders
   d. Derivatives and related contracts
3. Explain why it is important to adopt an integrated approach to the development of a firm's organizational architecture. Include illustrative examples.
4. Define each of the following derivatives, and briefly explain how they can be used to hedge risk.
   a. A forward contract
   b. A futures contract
   c. A swap
   d. An option (put or call)

5. Briefly explain how hedging can mitigate each of the following real-world problems.
   a. Taxes
   b. The cost of external financing
   c. Debt capacity constraints
   d. The negative effects of management risk aversion
   e. The underinvestment problem
   f. The asset substitution problem
6. Explain how you would determine whether a given firm is exposed to currency risk.
7. Suppose firm XYZ's expected income for this year would place it in a marginal tax bracket of 24 percent without hedging. However, one source of hedgeable risk would either raise or lower the firm's taxable income by $88 million, with equal probability. If taxable income is higher by this amount, the firm faces a 45 percent marginal tax rate on this amount, but if taxable income is lower it faces a 15 percent marginal tax rate on this amount. If a costless hedge were available for this risk, how much would the firm expect to save in taxes by hedging?
8. Why do firms purchase insurance?
9. Under what circumstances would a firm self-insure?
10. Discuss why a parent would guarantee the products or debt of a subsidiary.
11. Discuss the importance of security design within the context of a firm's organizational architecture.
12. Describe and briefly discuss each of the following innovations in security design.
    a. The floating-rate note
    b. Low-coupon, zero-coupon, and deferred-coupon (PIK) bonds
    c. High-yield (or *junk*) bonds
    d. Mandatory convertibles
    e. The reset note and rating-sensitive note
    f. Strip financing
    g. Gold-denominated depository shares
    h. Asset-backed commercial paper
    i. Leveraged loan syndication
    j. The put provision in a debt contract
    k. The clawback bond
    l. The make-whole call provision
    m. The Eurobond market
    n. Project finance (i.e., for infrastructure)

Creative Thinking Issues

1. Can you think of any additional components or elements that should be added to a firm's organizational architecture, beyond those shown in Figure 19-1?
2. In our organizational architecture model, we argue that the direction of causality generally runs from components and elements of a firm's business architecture to components and elements of its financial architecture. Can you think of some instances in which there are *feedback effects*—that is, where financial architecture affects, say, the firm's assets and operations? For each such instance, give your opinion about whether this represents a problem with the firm's financial architecture.

Projects and Analyses

1. Choose any one of the components or elements in our model of a firm's organizational architecture and develop an outline of relationships of this component/element to other components or elements.
2. Choose two firms in any particular industry (e.g., one large and one small), and sketch the details of each firm's organizational architecture. How are they similar? How do they differ? Why do they differ?

Solutions to Selected
End-of-Chapter Review
Questions and Problems

Chapter 1

1. a. Merger or acquisition: 79.6%
   b. Bankruptcy or liquidation: 13.4%
   c. Buyout: 7.0%
7. For General Electric:
   a. PP&E/TA: 9.2%
   b. D/TA: 46.1%
   c. D/TA_{mkt}: 23.4%
   d. MEQ/BEQ: 9.4
   e. MEQ/[NI(3 years)/3]: 43.6

Chapter 2

4. WACC = 11.8%
5. $r_E = 16.17\%$
6. $r_p = 16.0\%$; $\sigma_p = 22.1\%$
7. $\sigma_p = 24.1\%$
8. $r_C = 7.0\%$; $\sigma_C = 12.0\%$
9. $r_{Msft} = 11.25\% > 10\%$; do not recommend
10. $P = 23.29$
11. If $X = 250$, then $D = 215.96$ and
    $E_L = 284.04$; $r_D = 15.8\%$ and $r_{LE} = 32.0\%$
    If $X = 400$, then $D = 321.87$ and $E_L = 178.13$; $r_D = 18.1\%$ and $r_{LE} = 37.5\%$

Chapter 3

14. a. $E_L = 178$; D(original) = 322
    b. $\Delta E_L = +31.4$; ΔD(original) = −31.4
15. a. $E_L = 178$; D(original) = 322
    b. $\Delta E_L = +7$; $\Delta D = -7$
16. a. $E_L = 178$; $D = 322$
    b. $\Delta E_L = -23.7$; $\Delta D = +23.7$
17. a. $E_L = 178$; $D = 322$
    b. Yes: Stockholder's net gain is +52.

Chapter 4

6. (1) Specifications in the loan contract, (2) ability of the lender to monitor, and (3) effectiveness of the legal system
8. (1) Float, (2) turnover, and (3) bid-ask spread

9. a. Willingness to invest in his or her own project.
   b. (1) Entrepreneur is investing a portion of his or her personal wealth into the project, and (2) entrepreneur loses benefits of personal diversification.
18. Adverse selection and incentive problems emerge.

Chapter 5

15. (a) The default clause, (b) periodic payments, (c) collateral, (d) monitoring provisions, (e) contingent renewal (bank line of credit), etc.

Chapter 6

4. $34 million.
5. *Stages:* (1) negative net cash flow and earnings, and a falling market equity value; (2) management's attempts to reduce costs; (3) late payments to stakeholders and possibly more drastic actions; (4) end stage: bankruptcy.
6. For $\alpha = 0.005$, $D^* = \$34$ million.
7. For $\alpha = 0.01$, $D^* = 17$ million.

Chapter 7

10. a. Business Services; Chemicals and Allied Products; Electronic and Other Electric Equipment
    b. Chemicals and Allied Products; Business Services; Communications
13. (a) Take advantage of profitable investment opportunities; (b) engage in self-serving empire building
16. For Business Services in composite: (PP&E/TA) = 13.8%; D/TA = 19.7%; ROE = 35.3%; MEQ/BEQ = 7.9

17. For IBM:
    ROE = (NI/Sales) × (Sales/TA)
    × (TA/BEQ)
    = (8.1/88.4) × (88.4/87.5) × (87.5/20.3)
    = (0.092) × (1.01) × (4.31) = 0.399 = 39.9%
18. For Chemicals and Allied Products:
    ROE = (NI/Sales) × (Sales/TA) ×
    (TA/BEQ)
    = (31.3/223.1) × (223.1/211.7) × (211.7/88.0)
    = (0.140) × (1.054) × (2.406) = 0.356 = 35.6%
19. For IBM:
    ROE = 8.1/20.3 = 0.399 = 39.9%;
    MEQ/BEQ = 149.1/20.4 = 7.3

Chapter 8

14. *Broadly:* Advantages of diffuse ownership versus net deadweight costs of principal-agent conflicts and information asymmetry
    Narrowly: Tobin's Q
15. Better management talent, first mover advantages, economies of scale, internal financing of expansion
18. *Negative relationship:* underinvestment hypothesis, greater information asymmetry for a growth firm
    Positive relationship: Positive relationship between realized profitability and ability to finance with debt
21. *Pro:* Align management's and shareholders' interests.
    Con: Capital investment decisions may be distorted.
26. a. 12%
    b. 12.85%
27. Earnings are smoothed, and stock returns reflect non–cash flow factors (e.g., a shock to the discount rate).

Chapter 9

3. *Weak form:* Prices reflect past price patterns (thus technical analysis is worthless).
   Semistrong form: Prices reflect all publicly available information (and thus prices respond immediately and unbiasedly to news).
   Strong form: Prices reflect all information, both public and private (thus no one can profit on private information).
5. Abnormal return = –14.957%
7. $r_{E,Msft}$ = 17.67%

10. a. E_{IBM} = $61.42
    b. Overpriced
11. a. E_{GE} = $28.13
    b. Overpriced
12. a. E_{Merck} = $75.66
    b. Overpriced
13. $PVPFIO_{Merck}$ = $82.325

Chapter 10

2. (a) Use of the proceeds of the bond offering, (b) future operations (e.g., an asset sale), (c) future debt financing, (d) freedom to pay dividends to shareholders
8. *First,* the issuing firm selects an underwriter.
   Second, the issuer decides the amount of the offering.
   Third, the firm decides on the terms, covenants, provisions that will be included in the contract.
   Fourth, the issue is registered with the SEC.
   Fifth, the bond is rated.
   Sixth, the underwriter generates a tentative price for the issue.
   Seventh, the issue is marketed and sold to public investors.
13. For the Cellular Communications bond:
    a. Numerical rating estimate: 16.5
    b. Large firm size appears to mitigate against a higher numerical rating score.
14. a. Yield spread = 14.66% – 8.45% = 6.21%
    b. Expected return premium = 10.49% – 8.45% = 2.04%
15. a. y= 11.24%
    b. σ_D= 15.7%
    c. r_D = 8.57%
16. Yield spread matrix value: 129 basis points
    Actual spread = 806 basis points – 696 basis points = 110 basis points
    Reason for difference: perhaps the "+" modifier
17. a. From Table 10-10, conversion provision may represent approximately 41% of value, so nonconvertible portion represents 59%, or $59 per bond.
    b. $22.50 per bond
    c. $81.50 per bond

Chapter 11

1. *Stage 1:* Concept development, basic business plan, prototypes, explore market potential. [Personal loans; common stock]

Stage 2: Detailed business plan, assemble management team, test prototype, finalize product/service lines. [Notes with warrants; conv. pref. stock; partnership interest; common stock]

Stage 3: Secure initial PP&E, initial products sold. [Guaranteed bonds; notes with warrants; conv. pref. stock; partnership interest; common stock]

Stage 4: Secure additional PP&E, develop marketing strategy, expand production capacity, working capital needs emerge. [Guaranteed bonds; conv. bonds; conv. pref. stock; common stock]

Stage 5: Expand production capacity, working capital needs grow. [Secured debt; conv. bonds; conv. pref. stock; common stock]

Stage 6: Marketing strategy refined. [Subordinated debt; conv. bonds; conv. pref. stock]

Stage 7: Marketing and R&D. [Subordinated debt; conv. bonds; conv. pref. stock]

Stage 8: Recap, buyout, sell to acquirer, go public.

7. At 40%, value of VC's interest is $64 million (choice).
   At 60%, value of VC's interest is $54 million.

Chapter 12

1. *Benefits:* Reduce personal portfolio risk, reduce firm's cost of equity, reduce debt, stock option plans, issue more equity in the future.
   Costs: Underpricing, issuance costs, loss of control, agency costs, information asymmetry, performance pressures, distractions.

2. Employing an underwriter; choice of listing market; projecting the firm's initial assets, operational, ownership, governance, management, and capital structures; price discovery; selecting offering method

4. a. $16 million
   b. Gain = ($16 million + $4 million) – $15.15 million = $4.85 million

Chapter 13

2. (1) Rules for determining project profitability.
   (2) Method for choosing from among alternative profitable projects under rationing.

6. Senior management can monitor a manager over time to determine *ex post* the extent to which he or she engages in inefficient empire building; senior management can order an *ex ante* audit of a proposal, or threaten to do so.

10. Private placement, stock and stock option grants, ESOPs, DRIPs.

16. Underwriter spread, adverse selection costs, warrants

17. Offering size, firm size, listing market, competitive bidding versus negotiation, rights versus general offering, shelf versus traditional registration, units

Chapter 14

2. $NPV = \$17.07$ million $- \$15$ million $= \$2.07$ million, so Yes, and $ENTEQ'_0 = \$1.07$ million.

3. 1995: $INV = -\$1,175$ million

6. Board votes to declare a dividend on declaration date—type, amount payable, and record dates specified. Earlier ex-day must then be determined.

7. $DIV_t = \$1.15$ or $DIV_t = \$1.50$

8. Dividend: Net $= \$2$ million $\times (1 - 0.28) = \$1.44$ million
   Repurchase: Net $= \$2$ million $\times (1 - 0.14) - \$2$ million $\times (0.015) = \$1.69$ million

9. Dividend: Net $= \$2$ million $\times (1 - 0.28) - \$2$ million $\times 0.15 = \$1.14$ million
   Repurchase: Net $= \$2$ million $\times (1 - 0.14) - \$2$ million $\times 0.015 - \$2$ million $\times 0.15 = \$1.39$ million

10. $1.78125 per share

17. *First,* the firm's assets are reduced.
    Second, the firm's equity base is reduced.
    Third, if the firm has debt outstanding, leverage increases.
    Fourth, the market price of the firm's stock may rise.
    Fifth, repurchases may enhance liquidity via the firm adding to demand for shares.
    Sixth, repurchases may reduce liquidity by reducing the number of floating shares, or because the firm becomes an informed trader.

Chapter 15

6. a. Miscellaneous liabilities: 29.0%; Corporate bonds: 26.1%.
   b. Commercial paper, corporate bonds, other loans and advances

c. Trade credit, taxes payable, bank loans, commercial mortgages, industrial development bonds (IDBs), miscellaneous liabilities

8. Private placement: 10.33%; public issue: 9.78%

17. *Theory 1:* The seller/financier may be in a better position than a financial institution to both evaluate and monitor or control the buyer/borrower's credit risk.

    Theory 2: The buyer has a problem accessing the capital markets directly, whereas the seller does not.

    Theory 3: The seller's trade credit terms serve to indirectly price-discriminate among customers with varying but unobservable creditworthiness.

    Theory 4: The buyer has access to the purchased products for a brief period before actually paying for them; with a return guarantee, trade credit is a powerful signal of quality.

23. Substitute for debt; tax arbitrage; financial contracting costs

Chapter 16

3. Operating synergy, financial synergy and diversification, bankruptcy avoidance, financial slack, hubris, self-interest of the bidder's management

4. Failure of the target firm's management, busting up an inefficient diversified firm, hubris, industry shocks

5. To increase managerial incentives, to avert a takeover, to realize tax reduction benefits

8. One determinant: Cash or stock, depends on concerns of the bidding firm's management about loss of control.

Chapter 17

6. Loss of tax benefits of debt and depreciation, transaction costs, agency costs, negative liquidity effects.

Chapter 18

1. From Table 18–1 (a five-year perspective, 1995 to 2000): One-third of firms still public are distressed. Of firms that did not survive: 848 firms were acquired (a third of these

were distressed), 95 firms went bankrupt with reorganization (almost all distressed), 12 firms went bankrupt with liquidation (almost all distressed), and 169 firms were bought out, delisted, and so on (vast majority distressed).

9. *First*, valuable economies of scale may result.

   Second, product-market power may be enhanced.

   Third, acquirer may have superior management.

   Fourth, acquirer may contribute badly needed capital to the troubled firm.

Chapter 19

1. a. Economic growth projections, inflation, taxes; legal environment (enforcing property rights and contracts; limited liability; business regulations; antitrust laws; bankruptcy); risk factors (interest rate, currency and commodity price risks)

   b. Government and stock-exchange regulations on the public issuance and trading of securities; operational and informational efficiencies of primary and secondary markets; sophistication (speed of information flow; available complex debt and equity securities, derivatives, etc.); preferences of investors (liquidity, maturity, risk tolerance); active investors; external markets for corporate control

2. a. Public versus private ownership; insider ownership percentage; single- versus dual-class shares; ownership dynamics; institutional and block holders; anti-takeover mechanisms; targeted stocks, carve-outs, spin-offs; dividends and share repurchases

   b. Leverage; sources of debt capital (trade credit, private versus public); terms in debt contracts (covenants, provisions); leasing

5. a. Hedging can reduce taxes if the firm faces a convex tax rate schedule.

7. Savings = $5.28 million

12. k. The clawback provision allows the firm to retire a portion of the debt before maturity, but only by using proceeds from an equity offering (usually an IPO).

Index